Organizational Behavior and the Practice of Management

Third Edition

David R. Hampton
San Diego State University

Charles E. Summer
University of Washington

Ross A. Webber
University of Pennsylvania

Scott, Foresman and Company

Glenview, Illinois
Dallas, Texas
Oakland, New Jersey
Palo Alto, California
Tucker, Georgia
London, England

To Dorothy, Carol, and Mary Lou

Library of Congress Cataloging in Publication Data

Hampton, David R.   comp.
    Organizational behavior and the practice of
management.

    Includes bibliographies and index.
    1.   Organizational behavior—Addresses, essays,
lectures.   2.   Psychology, Industrial—Addresses,
essays, lectures.   3.   Management—Addresses, essays,
lectures.   I.   Summer, Charles Edgar.   II.   Webber,
Ross A.   III.   Title.
HD58.7.H35   1978   658.4   77-24496
ISBN 0-673-15119-0

Acknowledgments

The authors and publisher gratefully acknowledge the following sources for permission to reprint the following material. Permission
to reprint additional articles and illustrations is acknowledged within the text.
Exhibit 2.3, page 71: From Bavelas, Alex, "Communication Patterns in Task-Oriented Groups," in *Journal of the Acoustical Society
of America*, Vol. 22 (1950). Pages 218–24: "Team Spirit vs. the Individual Achiever," by Alvin F. Zander, from *Psychology Today* 8
(November 1974), pp. 64–65 and 67–68. Copyright © 1974, Ziff-Davis Publishing Company. Reprinted by permission of *Psychology
Today* and Alvin F. Zander. Exhibit 3.4, page 122: From Vardaman, G. T., and Halterman, C. C., *Managerial Control Through
Communication.* Copyright © 1968 John Wiley and Sons, Inc. Exhibit 5.1, page 250: From Webber, R. A. "The Relation of Group
Performance to the Age of Members in Homogeneous Groups," in *Academy of Management Journal*, Vol. 17, No. 3 (September
1974). Exhibit 5.2, page 253: From Cummings, L. L.; Huber, G. P.; and Arendt, E., "Effects of Size and Spatial Arrangements on Group
Decision Making," in *Academy of Management Journal*, Vol. 17, No. 3 (September 1974). Exhibit 5.3, page 256: Reprinted by
permission of *Psychology Today* Magazine, Copyright © 1971 Ziff-Davis Publishing Company. Exhibit I, page 308: Adapted from
Haire, M.; Ghiselli, E.; Porter L. *Managerial Thinking.* Copyright © 1966 John Wiley and Sons, Inc. Exhibit 8.4, pages 470–71:
Reproduced with permission from *Management: Basic Elements of Managing Organizations* by R. A. Webber (Homewood, IL:
Richard D. Irwin, Inc., 1975 ©), pp. 349–50. Exhibit 9.2, page 548: "From *Introduction to Modern Behaviorism*, Second Edition, by
Howard Rachlin. W. H. Freeman and Company. Copyright © 1976." Exhibit 9.4, pages 552–54: Reprinted by permission of the
publisher from "Behavior Modification on the Bottom Line," by W. Clay Hamner and Ellen Hamner, *Organizational Dynamics*,
Spring 1976, © 1976 by AMACOM, a division of American Management Associations. Figure 1, page 562: From March, J. G., and
Simon, H. A., *Organizations.* Copyright © 1958 John Wiley and Sons, Inc. Exhibit 10.1, page 597: Reprinted with permission of
Macmillan Publishing Co., Inc. from *Handbook of Leadership* by R. M. Stogdill. Copyright © 1974 by The Free Press, a Division of
Macmillan Publishing Co., Inc. Table 1, page 729: From Walton, Richard E., "Third Party Roles in Interdepartmental Conflict," in
Industrial Relations, Vol. 7, No. 1, October 1967, copyright by Regents of the University of California. Exhibit 12.2 page 782:
Reprinted by special permission from *The Journal of Applied Behavioral Science*, "Confrontation as a Training Design in Complex
Organizations," By Golembiewski and Blumberg. Volume 3, Number 4, p. 534. Copyright 1967 NTL Institute for Applied Behavioral
Science.

Preface

Most people who read this book are headed for or have already begun careers—and, potentially, managerial careers—in organizations. Our purpose in this third edition of *Organizational Behavior and the Practice of Management* is to help them in two ways. First, we want to help them understand the territory of organizations—individual, interpersonal, and group behavior, and the interplay of human, technological, and structural factors. Second, we want to demonstrate how this understanding can be used to practice management.

Part One of the book, Individual and Group Behavior, concentrates on illuminating and explaining individual, interpersonal, and group behavior in organizations. Motivation theory and research guide our examination of individual behavior. Communication and influence theory and research guide our study of interpersonal processes. Interaction theory and research guide our study of groups. Many other theories and varieties of research, as you will see, also play a part in making the behavior of people at work understandable and in suggesting techniques for motivating, communicating, influencing, and group decision-making.

Part Two, Organizational Behavior, and Part Three, Managerial Behavior, concentrate on management, making use of what has been learned in Part One. Part Two consists of two chapters that explore how managers can design the structure of organizations and of jobs within that structure, and two chapters that explore planning or setting objectives for organizations and individuals and controlling work-related behavior. As you will see, the techniques for organizing, planning, and controlling that will be discussed synthesize many ideas and much research. Techniques such as matrix organization structures, job enrichment, management by objectives, and behavior modification, for example, all illustrate the use of behavioral science theory in the practice of management.

Part Three, Managerial Behavior, shifts the emphasis from the design and use of structural and administrative managerial techniques to the development of techniques for interpersonal and intergroup competence. Its topics include leadership, conflict management, and organization development. Here, we will see how behavioral science research and theory can inform and strengthen this side of the practice of management.

We have revised *Organizational Behavior and the Practice of Management* to take advantage of new developments in research and theory. New features of the third edition include:

Group Decision-Making. The chapter on group decision-making has been substantially expanded and updated, incorporating discussion of such topics as groupthink and the nominal group technique.

Job Design. A new chapter reports on job enrichment and the design of autonomous work groups.

Objectives. A new chapter discusses the development of organizational and individual objectives and the use of management by objectives.

Control. A new chapter discusses alternative approaches to control, including policies and procedures, performance measurement and feedback, and operant conditioning.

Leadership. A new chapter updates theory and research on leadership, including path-goal theory and the Vroom-Yetton decision model.

Though the third edition has been extensively revised and updated, it continues the distinctive treatment of concepts and research findings in organizational behavior as a foundation for the practice of management that has earned previous editions their reputation in the field. That reputation has also been based on the comprehensiveness and quality of the text and selected readings. The book has been tested for readability and, despite its comprehensiveness and rigor, it has compared favorably with many other texts. In preparing this third edition we have sought to preserve these characteristics.

We should like to express our gratitude to all those who have helped us to meet our objective. Many authors and publishers have kindly permitted us to reprint selections of their work in this volume. It would be fitting if our use of their works will draw deserved attention to the whole book or articles from which we have borrowed parts.

A number of users of preceding editions and other reviewers have generously shared their thoughts with us. Graham Baxter (University of Pittsburgh), Douglas T. Hall (Northwestern University), Raymond E. Hill (University of Michigan), Ronald J. Hunaday (Bowling Green State University), James M. Hund (Emory University), Edward J. Morrison (University of Colorado), and Rosemary Pledger and Walter E. Natemeyer (University of Houston at Clear Lake City), are among those who have helped. We thank them. We also express our thanks to Bob Johnson and Bruce Borland of Scott, Foresman and Company for their careful planning and organizing and their outstanding editorial assistance.

David R. Hampton
Charles E. Summer
Ross A. Webber

Contents

Part One
Individual and Group Behavior   3

Chapter Three   Communication   114

Chapter Four   Group Dynamics   182

Chapter Seven   Work Design   376

Chapter Eight Objectives for Organizations and Individuals 456

Chapter Nine Controlling Organizational Behavior 524

Part Three
Managerial Behavior   593

Chapter Ten   Leadership   594

Organizational Behavior and the Practice of Management

Third Edition

Part One
Individual and Group Behavior

INDIVIDUAL MOTIVATION

POWER AND INFLUENCE

COMMUNICATIONS

GROUP DYNAMICS

GROUP DECISION-MAKING

Chapter One

Individual Motivation

In 1822 the English philosopher Jeremy Bentham wrote, "Nature has placed mankind under the governance of two sovereign masters, *pain* and *pleasure*" (see Burtt, 1939, p. 791). The same thought had been expressed long before and has echoed long after Bentham. It can be found in Plato's *Protagoras*, and in modern terms as a central assumption of motivation theory.

Human beings, like other animals, seek to approach those states which are pleasurable and to avoid those which are painful. Historically, most of the research which has explored these ideas has concentrated on animals. Many of us remember from our psychology courses that animals do indeed try to obtain food when hungry, and to avoid electrical shocks and other unpleasant stimuli. Fortunately, however, knowledge of motivation is not restricted to knowledge of rodent motivation. There has been increased concentration on human motivation, and, of particular interest to us, human motivation and behavior in organizations. After all, ever since the United States rejected Thomas Jefferson's attractive but simplistic vision of a nation of independent yeomen, and chose Alexander Hamilton's dream of a wealthy, complex, and interdependent society, most of us have had to work in an organization. So the pleasures and pains of organizational life are of personal concern to us.

A few basic facts will guide our exploration of individual behavior in organizations. First, behavior on the job is a function of what the person brings to the situation and what the situation brings to the person. When people come to work in organizations they do not come "empty handed," as it were. They bring a supply of energy or potential to perform. They bring various needs or motives which predispose them to release their energy or behave in particular ways—ways which seem to them likely to satisfy their needs.

What the person brings to the situation is but one blade of the scissors. The other blade is what the situation brings to the person. It is only as the blades come together that the pattern of behavior is cut. The characteristics of the organizational or work situation provide cues which can arouse particular tendencies to behave. Circumstances can signal to the individual that particular job-oriented behaviors may lead to satisfaction of needs. The commission system can notify salespeople that selling more means more income. Not surprisingly in our society, the prospect of more income may mean increased status, esteem, and other pleasures.

In this chapter we take a close look at the needs people bring with them into organizations. We discuss how motives develop. We also discuss how motives dispose people to behave in particular ways, and how managers can profit by matching task requirements and behavioral predispositions. Our central interest is how individual predispositions and situational characteristics come together to produce particular ways of behaving on the job. Finally, we preview the subject of how managers can behave skillfully to increase the probability that subordinates will perform effectively—a subject we return to later in the book.

NEEDS THEORY: THE HIERARCHY OF NEEDS

The early needs theorists, such as Murray (1938), suggested lists of needs that may be of academic interest, but that hold out little promise of providing any readily usable tool for understanding the everyday task performances of people at work. But such a tool was forthcoming. It was the hierarchy of needs concept developed by Abraham Maslow (1943) and popularized by numerous management writers, the foremost being Douglas McGregor (1960).

Maslow's hierarchy of needs is simplicity itself. The central idea is that human needs—physiological, safety, love, esteem, and self-actualization—are arranged in a hierarchy of prepotency. Physiological needs are at the bottom of the hierarchy, and self-actualization needs at the top. Though people are in a state of want all of the time, according to the theory, what they want is a function of the pattern of need satisfactions in the hierarchy. They can start out with lofty aspirations relative to love, esteem, and self-actualization, but be driven to more basic needs if those more basic needs become unsatisfied.

A tragic episode in American history provides an illustration. In the early 1800s, a band of pioneers led by a man named Donner crossed the western plains with ox-drawn covered wagons, and climbed into the Sierra Nevada. For most of the party, the trip ended there. Marooned by enormous snow drifts and slowly freezing on the wind-swept slopes, they were unable to move forward or back. As they exhausted their supply of food, the party gradually deteriorated.

Some years ago, a diary kept by a member of the party was published (Croy, 1955), in which the writer described his compatriots at the beginning of the journey as "salt of the earth"—God-fearing and individualistic, but cooperative and concerned for each other's welfare. During the protracted ordeal in the mountains, they withdrew upon themselves: concern shifted from the larger group to the immediate family; then to the individual; finally, as in McKinlay Kantor's (1955) description of a Civil War prison camp, the strong began to prey on the weak for personal survival, and the ultimate horror emerged—cannibalism.

To the party, food eventually came to be all important and all motivating. If one is without food long enough, one becomes a sort of human piranha— thinking, dreaming, and hunting food without any other concern.* Such a food-seeking monster is not interested in building monuments, wearing fine clothes, or worshipping God. The satisfaction of the physiological drives is essential to the maintenance of life; thus Maslow described them as prepotent for the motivation of behavior.

Happily, the hierarchical model suggests that, as physical needs are met (at least at a minimum level), new needs emerge to motivate behavior. We have seen that humans are "wanting creatures," striving to satisfy many different needs in an order of potency as follows: (1) physiological, (2) safety, (3) love,

---

* For a classic example of this kind of behavior, see Hamsun (1967). For a contemporary example, see Read (1974).

(4) esteem, and (5) self-actualization. Therefore, just as unmet basic needs drove the Donner party down the hierarchy, satisfied basic needs open up higher level wants.

This dynamic quality of the needs hierarchy has important consequences for the motivation of people at work. As lower-level needs are relatively satisfied, they become less directly motivating for behavior. One is motivated mainly by the next level of unsatisfied need. Thus gratified needs, in a sense, disappear. They are not motivating. Since all managers attempt to influence human behavior, they must consider what needs are relatively unsatisfied, and hence can serve as levers for motivation. If workers are no longer starving or profoundly insecure, offering them work whose only rewards are seen to be food and safety will not arouse the motive power of unmet needs.

The question arises, then, of the relationship between work and such higher needs as love, esteem, and self-actualization. Historically, the primary source of satisfaction for love, or social needs, has been the family. But American families in the twentieth century have changed. We have fewer children than our grandparents did. More fundamentally, the consanguine family unit has become a conjugal family unit. Infrequently do grandparents, children, uncles, aunts, cousins, and grandchildren live together, as they used to. Often the separate generations do not even live in the same neighborhood, city, or state. This means that the family unit is smaller.

Inside this smaller unit, encouraged by the availability of bicycles, motor scooters, motorcycles, and "personal" cars, family members tend to turn to outside associates for recreation and for satisfaction of the needs for membership, affection, affiliation, and so on. Moreover, in our modern society, maintaining a family to supply love and social satisfaction requires a job and at least a modicum of economic stability. Thus the job has come to serve as the primary source of social satisfaction.

Employers of the nineteenth and early twentieth century saw no need for social satisfaction on the job. In office and shop their posted policies frequently included dictums forbidding "socializing," "idle gossip," or "conspiratorial meetings." When Frederick Taylor and scientific management came along, managers were advised to treat people strictly as individuals and to offer individual piece-rate incentive pay which would encourage employees to produce to their maximum ability. Managers in the 1920s were aware, and in the famous Hawthorne plant studies at Western Electric academic researchers corroborated, that many workers (if not most) limited their personal effort in order to maintain their membership in an informal social structure (Homans, 1950; Roethlisberger and Dickson, 1939). At some point, for virtually everyone except the individualistic "rate-busters," the desire for communication, support, and friendship with associates on the job and during work hours became more important than the little bit of extra money that might be earned.

In addition to the two ways that the job aids in the satisfaction of the affiliation need (that is, maintenance of a family and of social relations with fellow workers), Freud (see Strachey, 1962) suggested a third socializing contribution of the job. A job forces people to set aside their own concerns and confront the world. A job imposes discipline. It requires interpersonal communication that assists individuals to learn about the norms of society around them—and to maintain a sense of reality, identity, and stability by continually testing their own views against societal norms. Not that these norms are always right, but the job and the contact with the world that the job requires enables people to live more easily in that world and to find desired social satisfactions.

Research on the mental health and attitudes of long-term unemployed males (Ginzberg, 1943) support Freud's suggestions. These studies indicate very directly the relevance of the job to a person's sense of membership in society. Even though welfare and a variety of governmental programs remove their fears and anxieties about the satisfaction of physiological and security needs, the unemployed feel out of place. They are not members of society; they are not fulfilling the requirements of the head of a household. In many cases they become withdrawn and depressed, unable even to take satisfaction in their families. They are simply not confronting the world in ways that the culture values.

When social needs are relatively satisfied, however, the desire for esteem tends to move into consciousness. And one's job plays a prominent part in determining one's self-esteem and the esteem received from others. Kenneth Clark (1965) has described the loss of self-esteem which is part of the under-employment experience of many black Americans (as well as others). Having a job is no guarantee of deriving feelings of pride and dignity from it. Elliot Liebow relates a memorable discussion with Tally of *Tally's Corner* which illustrates the point:

> "You know that boy came in last night? That Black Moozlem? That's what I ought to be doing. I ought to be in his place."
> "What do you mean?"
> "Dressed nice, going to [night] school, got a good job."
> "He's no better off than you, Tally. You make more than he does."
> "It's not the money. [Pause] It's position, I guess. He's got position. When he finish school he gonna be a supervisor. People respect him. . . . Thinking about people with position and education gives me a feeling right here [pressing his fingers into the pit of his stomach]."
> "You're educated, too. You have a skill, a trade. You're a cement finisher. You can make a building, pour a sidewalk."
> "That's different. Look, can anybody do what you're doing? Can anybody just come up and do your job? Well, in one week I can teach you cement finishing. You won't be as good as me 'cause you won't have the experience but you'll be a cement finisher. That's what I mean. Anybody can do what I'm doing and that's what gives me this feeling. [Long pause] Suppose I like this girl. I go over to her house and I meet her father. He starts talking about what he done today. He talks about operating on somebody and sewing them up and about surgery. I know he's a doctor 'cause of the way he talks. Then she starts talking about what she did. Maybe she's a boss or a supervisor. Maybe she's a lawyer and her father says to me, 'And what do you do, Mr. Jackson?' [Pause] You remember at the courthouse, Lonny's trial? You and the lawyer was talking in the hall? You remember? I just stood there listening. I didn't say a word. You know why? 'Cause I didn't even know what you was talking about. That's happened to me a lot."
> "Hell, you're nothing special. That happens to everybody. Nobody knows every-

thing. One man is a doctor, so he talks about surgery. Another man is a teacher, so he talks about books. But doctors and teachers don't know anything about concrete. You're a cement finisher and that's your specialty."

"Maybe so, but when was the last time you saw anybody standing around talking about concrete?"*

The organization with which one is affiliated is also a possible source of self-esteem. In reply to the question "What do you do?" Americans often respond with "I'm associated with IBM," or "I'm with General Electric." Fifty years ago the replies would have been "I'm a machinist," or "I'm an accountant." The earlier responses were a legacy of the traditional societies of Europe, where a person's craft has always been a major determinant of self-esteem, status, or prestige. However, craft in these societies is generally determined by birth or family, which are the true determinants of status or prestige. The United States has always been a much less rigid society in terms of social class; for example, attitudes toward status distinctions vary with geography and socioeconomic background—the criteria for social esteem in the Northeast among the middle class is quite different from those in the Southwest among the working class. But being associated with a particular company of wide repute is a reliable source of status. Thus, in the United States, the corporation as a source of feelings of esteem and prestige has begun to obliterate the older tradition of status differentiation on the basis of vocation or craft.

Within the corporation, elaborated hierarchies of positions and their attendant status symbols and perquisites also reflect the desire for status differentiation. Management ignores at its peril the necessity to correlate pay, title, authority, and symbols of status. A large regional insurance office is a case in point. The two or three huge rooms stretch out like an airplane hangar, aisle after aisle. With clerks, secretaries, representatives, claims people, supervisors, and department heads all seated at seemingly identical desks row after row, the scene resembles a Franz Kafka novel in its mechanistic oppressiveness. Not surprisingly, the management has difficulty with superior-subordinate relations, and particularly with supervisory morale. Giving out important-sounding job titles—or even more money—would be inadequate to satisfy the desire for status on the job. One of the principal causes of dissatisfaction is the lack of physical manifestation of status differences, including individual offices to give quiet and privacy.

Finally, as Maslow (1943) puts it: "Even if all these needs are satisfied, we may still often (if not always) expect that a new discontent and restlessness will soon develop, unless the individual is doing what he is fitted for. A musician must make music, an artist must paint, a poet must write if he is to be ultimately happy. What a man *can* be, he *must* be. This need we may call self-actualization" (p. 382).

While Maslow's hierarchy-of-needs theory has proved very stimulating and useful to students of management (chiefly, it has made them carefully consider the relationship of the job to motivation), it has met with criticism. Some critics (Cofer and Appleby, 1964) have raised questions about the ade-

---

* Copyright © 1967 by Little, Brown and Company (Inc.). From *Tally's Corner: A Study of Negro Streetcorner Men* by Elliot Liebow, by permission of Little, Brown and Co.

quacy of Maslow's research. Maslow had selected examples and data "from among personal acquaintances and friends and from among public and historical figures" (1954, p. 200). In addition, McClelland (1955) has expressed doubts about both the universality of the needs hierarchy and the adequacy of the concept of self-actualization. He suggests that many of the needs are not biological and universal, but are socially acquired and vary from culture to culture. What would be regarded as fulfilling or actualizing one's potential varies from society to society, and from beholder to beholder within one society.

NEEDS THEORY: A TWO-FACTOR THEORY OF MOTIVATION

In terms of both the attention it has attracted in the field of industrial psychology and the extent to which business organizations have made use of it, the "motivation-hygiene" theory developed by Herzberg (1968) must be included in any discussion of individual motivation at work. One thing Herzberg discovered that a person will work for, based on what it means in one's life—i.e., which of one's needs it satisfies—Herzberg calls "hygiene factors." They meet the lower order physiological and safety needs described by Maslow, and thus provide the necessary hygiene for the person to survive, exist, and be ready to go on to higher order need fulfillment through higher order accomplishments. A person who likes to ski (a higher order accomplishment) would have no hope unless he or she is healthy. Therefore, one will be motivated to work, eat well, take exercise, and do a host of other things simply to *avoid* being in such an unhealthy physical state that one cannot hope to pursue a more positive accomplishment. In this sense, the hygiene factor is always seen to mean the need to *avoid loss* of security or physical needs. Security needs are met in many organizations by such things as pension plans and health insurance. People do indeed value these things. But they value them as a means of *avoiding dissatisfaction.*

There are people in the U.S.A. today who laugh at the idea of a steady job, or the idea of a pension plan which ties the employee to the corporation. Why is this true? Because something seems to be missing here. One may not want to work at a dull job for forty years just to have security in later years of life! What is missing is the second factor—the *motivating* factor. Whereas the hygiene need means avoiding dissatisfaction through loss of lower order needs, the motivating factor means positively pursuing higher order needs. The skier does not brush his or her teeth and take exercise because all he or she wants from life are good teeth and muscles. Were this true, he or she would be completely happy staying in a room for the 8-hour day, accompanied by good teeth and well-toned muscles. Employees do not gain full satisfaction by working from 9 to 5 every day only to have food when they are over retirement age.

What we are saying here is that there are two classes of needs to which all people in work situations respond. It is the pursuit of higher order needs—to be responsible, to feel inside that "I've done something worthwhile," to grow in ability and skill to cope with life—which motivates a person to be interested in competent, skillful work. Hygiene factors may attract a person to join an organization and to put in the hours, but they do not cause an intrinsic interest in the work itself.

Many managerial techniques to be discussed later in this book rely on this kind of reasoning. Job enrichment and work group design (Chapter 7) are particularly dependent on building motivating factors into jobs. Organization Development (Chapter 12) is a method that often involves people in higher need accomplishment. A number of theories of leadership (Chapter 10) would require the leader to provide support to subordinates so that they might satisfy needs for social friendship, accomplishment, and self-esteem, rather than simply threaten subordinates with loss of their pay and pension plans. In very crude terms, motivating factors provide the "carrot" of self-esteem, while hygiene factors protect one from the "stick" of punishments (loss of pay, loss of job, etc.).

SOCIALLY ACQUIRED MOTIVES

McClelland, Atkinson (1964), and others have contributed a quarter of a century of careful research on socially acquired motives. As a way of introducing the study of certain such motives, we would like to ask you to perform an easy and brief exercise.

Take a quick (10 to 15 seconds) look at the picture on the next page. Now, allowing yourself no more than five minutes, make up and write an imaginative story about what the picture suggests. Don't merely describe the picture, but relax and let your imagination fly. No one but you will see the story anyway.

To make sure you have a story plot, the following questions can serve as guides for your creative writing:

1. What is happening? Who are the people?
2. What has led up to this situation? That is, what has happened in the past?
3. What is being thought? What is wanted? By whom?
4. What will happen? What will be done?

Remember, only 10 to 15 seconds for looking at the picture, and no more than five minutes for writing your story.

This picture is one of a group of six pictures which make up the *Test of Imagination* (1968), a Thematic Apperception Test. Each of the pictures is ambiguous. People who look at them and then compose imaginative stories project their own needs into the story content. The story you wrote thus can tell something about your own motives (though we have no reason to think we have adequately sampled your own fantasies to describe your motives definitively). Under normal and adequate test conditions, each person would be asked to write six stories, each in response to a different picture. A total score would then be obtained.

Psychologists have developed reasonably reliable and valid means for analyzing and scoring the content of stories for this test and similar ones. The stories can be scored for three particularly important motives: the need for

Reprinted with permission of the Tests and Scoring Division, McBer and Company, 137 Newbury Street, Boston, Massachusetts 02116.

achievement, the need for affiliation, and the need for power. They are important, as we shall see, because they dispose people to behave in ways which critically affect the performance of many jobs and tasks.

The Achievement Motive

David McClelland, one of the psychologists who has contributed most to the study of the achievement motive, has discussed responses written by business executives to the particular picture you saw. Here is one of the stories and McClelland's (1962) analysis:

> The man is an engineer at a drafting board. The picture is of his family. He has a problem and is concentrating on it. It is merely an everyday occurrence—a problem which requires thought. How can he get that bridge to take the stress of possible high winds? He wants to arrive at a good solution of the problem by himself. He will discuss the problem with a few other engineers and make a decision which will be a correct one—he has the earmarks of competence (p. 101).

This author's thoughts are almost entirely on a specific task problem and how to solve it. He describes a problem, wants to solve it, thinks about how to solve it, thinks about obstacles, and thinks about people who might help. According to established protocols for scoring stories (Atkinson, 1958), each idea about a particular motive theme yields one point. This story would receive most of its points for n (need for) Achievement.

McClelland (1962, pp. 104–105) goes on to sketch the characteristics of people with high n Achievement:

1. They like situations in which they take personal responsibility for finding solutions to problems.
2. They tend to set moderate achievement goals and to take "calculated risks."
3. They want concrete feedback on how well they are doing.

The Affiliation Motive

"People who need people," as Barbra Streisand sings it, "are the luckiest people." Lucky or not, people certainly do vary in their needs for socializing. People with high n Affiliation tend to think often about the quality of their personal relationships. They might savor the good times they have had with some people and be concerned about shortcomings in their relations with others. It is to these topics, rather than to defining and solving task problems, that their minds run when they are daydreaming or not required to concentrate on anything in particular.

To illustrate, here is another story from McClelland (1962):

> The engineer is at work on Saturday when it is quiet and he has taken time to do a little daydreaming. He is the father of the two children in the picture—the husband of the woman shown. He has a happy home life and is dreaming about some

pleasant outing they have had. He is also looking forward to a repeat of the incident which is now giving him pleasure to think about. He plans on the following day, Sunday, to use the afternoon to take his family for a short trip (p. 101).

McClelland explains that such a story emphasizes affiliative themes, since the author's thoughts are about relations with other people. This is the theme most people emphasize when they write stories about this picture.

Schachter (1959), a psychologist, has completed many ingenious experiments and field studies which have contributed much to understanding the affiliation motive. He has demonstrated the tendency of people to seek out others to gain confirmation for their own beliefs or to relieve the stress of uncertainties. In one experiment, he led the subjects to believe that they would experience some pain as part of the experiment. He told the subjects they would have to wait for that stage of the experiment. Then he asked if they would prefer to wait alone or with other subjects. Most people in such a miserable predicament wanted company.

In another study, Festinger et al. (1956) observed a group ("cult" might be a better term) who believed the world would end but that they would be spared the disaster and removed to another planet by beings from that planet. When the zero hour arrived and passed and nothing happened, what did the group do? Disband? No, the members discussed their views and interpretations more vigorously than ever and intensified their efforts to interest outsiders in joining their group. The disappointment seemed to stimulate compensatory behavior to build a strengthened basis for the group's beliefs.

Though there is not nearly as much research on affiliative motivation as on achievement motivation, there is enough to suggest that there is a common goal in such behavior—social interaction with others. But such behavior has multiple origins. In some instances affiliative behavior is linked with anxiety reduction, as in the experiment which caused the subjects to anticipate pain. In others, affiliative behavior contributes more to securing social approval of one's views, as in the end-of-the-world cult.

Whatever the origins of the need for affiliation, the patterns of behavior it tends to produce are similar. Persons with a high need for affiliation seek the company of others and take steps to be liked by them. They try to project a favorable image in interpersonal relations. They smooth out disagreeable tensions in meetings. They help and support others and want to be liked in return.

The Power Motive

The kind of story about the man at the work table with the family picture which would seem rich in the preoccupation with power might go something like this:

The man is an engineer. He is thinking of how he will present his plan at the design committee meeting. He wants to sell the idea and he knows he must persuade them to his view. He believes he will carry the day and refute any criticisms. He wants badly to get the new project manager job which will be opening up. He thinks if he can win this coming battle he will be in a strong position to move up the ladder. Then he will be able to get people moving in the right direction at long last.

As you can see, there is no notice of satisfaction in solving the technical problem (achievement), and no notice of the family (affiliation); there is only power —control and influence. Individuals high in n Power spend more time thinking about how to obtain and exercise power and authority than do those low in n Power. The former need to win arguments, to persuade others, to prevail. They feel uncomfortable without some sense of power.

One of the problems with the subject of power is its negative emotional connotations. We are accustomed to think of it as being at least a bit nasty. To manipulate, to be "Machiavellian," suggests something distasteful to most people. But possession of a strong power drive is not necessarily undesirable, the equivalent of a character defect. As McClelland (1970) has taken pains to point out, power really has two faces. The first is the one which arouses negative reaction. This face of power is the one concerned with dominance-submission, with having one's way, with having a strong impact in controlling others.

The other face of power is positive. It reflects the process by which persuasive and inspirational behavior on the part of a leader can evoke feelings of power and ability in subordinates. The active leader who helps a group form goals and who helps them in attaining their goals plays a part, not in subordinating and dominating people, but in aiding their expression of their strength and competence in reaching their goals. A selection by McClelland following this chapter develops the concepts of power more fully.

Given that individuals do differ in the relative potency of their needs for achievement, affiliation, and power, and that it is possible through tests or just sampling a person's conversation to get some idea of his or her motive pattern, one question remains: How do such needs develop? How do individuals come to exhibit differing configurations of n Achievement, n Affiliation, and n Power?

DEVELOPMENT OF SOCIAL MOTIVES

Social motives are learned. They are not learned or acquired consciously in the way one learns the alphabet or addition. Rather, the acquisition of motives is accidental, a byproduct of behaving, of trying actively to cope with one's environment. It may be, for example, that while one is learning the alphabet or addition one tastes something of the pleasure of achievement.

That taste can be rewarding, and as behavioral psychologists have long known, rewards following an act reinforce the act, or in other words, increase the probability of its recurrence. Where the active, problem-solving behavior of the child operates on the environment to elicit satisfying results, more than the answer to the problem gets learned; the mode of behavior associated with success is reinforced as well. McClelland (1962) describes an experiment which illustrates some of the conditions which nurture behaviors associated with the need for achievement:

> A group of boys were blindfolded and asked to stack irregularly shaped blocks on top of each other with their left hands, at home in front of their parents. Separately, the mothers and fathers were asked how high they thought their sons could stack the blocks. Both parents of a boy with high n Achievement estimated that their boy should do better; they expected more of him than did the parents of a boy with low n Achievement. They also encouraged him more and gave him more affection and reward while he was actually doing the task. Finally, the fathers of boys with high n Achievement directed the behavior of their sons much less when they were actually stacking the blocks; that is, they told them less often to move their hands this way or that, to try harder, to stop jiggling the table, and so forth, than did the fathers of boys with low n Achievement (p. 110).

Apparently, under conditions which encourage independence and moderate risk-taking, people can acquire the taste for challenges of manageable proportions—challenges which are likely to yield neither failure nor too easy success, but maximal feelings of achievement.

Similarly, a strong need for affiliation or power probably would be the product of a history of rewards being associated with sociable or dominant behavior. It takes a particular history to produce the view that "one learns from experience that being close and friendly with people is more important than career success" (Moment and Zaleznik, 1963). What has been learned by one who holds such a view is that, as one copes in the world, the most valuable rewards come through good social or interpersonal relations. It is easy to see how the affectionate and supportive fathers in the blockstacking experiment might have nurtured the affiliation motive. We can speculate, though, that the psychic rewards available to the boys high in n Achievement may have been contingent upon successful performance of ambitious goals.

To stick with the same example and with a mood of speculative interpretation, we can imagine that the more dominant and directive fathers behave the same way outside the experiment. Conceivably, their children, having a different model to emulate, may try more often to exercise power and direction over their playmates and, depending upon how successfully such modes operate on the environment, acquire or not acquire a need to relate to others in a dominating way. In any event, our purpose is only to suggest, not develop fully, some picture of how socially acquired needs are molded. In essence, they are one outcome of the whole of an individual's problem-solving or developmental history.

As White (1959) suggests, one of the mainsprings of human motivation is an interest in getting to know what the world is like and in learning to get what one wants from it. He calls this a competence motive, which probably underlies the development of the other motives already discussed. Teachers hope that this drive (for competence) exists in their students as a desire to master an academic discipline, and in general expand themselves intellectually. Obviously, the competence motive may also take other directions. The reward of self-esteem may be derived from competence in a wide variety of vocational and avocational activities. A selection by White following this chapter expands on the competence motive.

This competence motive can be seen as active even in very young infants, in the fun of random fingering of objects, poking around, and touching whatever is in reach. Later, it is exploring, tinkering, taking things apart, putting them together, and the like. Whether an adult's sense of competence is strong or weak depends on the balance of successes and failures he or she has experienced in his or her various encounters with the world. Whether one's needs for achievement, affiliation, and power are strong or weak depend upon their past associations with problem-solving performances and rewards. Lawrence and Lorsch (1969) summarize the process succinctly:

> As the individual system strives to master problems, certain behaviors turn out to be consistently rewarding; that is, they provide solutions to the problems the individual faces. Consequently, the next time the individual needs to solve a problem he tries the same pattern of behavior again. Over time, as some of these patterns are consistently rewarding, the individual learns to rely on them. Thus, we say that a person is highly motivated to compete against a standard of excellence (need for achievement), or has a higher need for warm friendly relations (need for affiliation), etc. As a result of this learning process, different individuals develop the different patterns of these motives already described (pp. 68–69).

But there is at least one significant additional force at work in the learning process: anxiety. Learning not only takes place when acts are followed by positive states or rewards, but also when acts are followed by a reduction of negative states of unpleasant tension. There are states which are gratifying to avoid as well as states which are gratifying to approach. As Sullivan (1950) observes:

> The first of all learning is called out to avoid recurrence of the extremely unpleasant tension of anxiety, which is, and always continues to be, the very antithesis of everything good and desirable. . . . The child soon learns to discriminate *increasing* from *decreasing* anxiety and to alter activity in the direction of the latter. The child learns to chart a course by the anxiety gradient (p. 95).

In part, then, the reduction of anxiety associated with successful problem-solving behavior contributes to the strengthening of such behavior. If competing against a standard of excellence pays off by relieving anxiety, the need for achievement is strengthened. If warm, friendly relations with others are associated with success, the need for affiliation is strengthened. If persuasiveness and dominance are associated with success, the need for power is strengthened.

MOTIVES AND BEHAVIOR

Different motives tend to express themselves in different behavior. When a need or motive is strong in a person, its effect is to predispose the person to behavior which has become associated with the satisfaction of that need. For example, having a high n Achievement predisposes the individual to engage in setting goals, trying to improve performance to reach the goals, and realistically seeking and using feedback on performance; n Achievement has no emphasis on people.

The needs for affiliation and power are rather different. They both orient the individual towards interpersonal behavior. For n Affiliation, interpersonal relations, when they are good, are their own reward. For n Power, interpersonal relations provide the path to exercising influence over others.

These bits of information may be interesting, but we might ask why practical hard-headed managers should want to know them. How can they behave more skillfully if they understand that socially acquired motives such as n Achievement, n Affiliation, and n Power mean readiness or predisposition to behave in particular ways? There are a great many things they can do. We explore a few here and expand our study of practical administrative implications in Chapters 8, 9, and 10.

Suppose, for example, we could learn what sorts of behavior patterns are instrumental in the effective performance of particular tasks. With this knowledge we could then consider what motives predispose people to such behavior. We could seek out such people and hire them for the task. To illustrate, consider the behavioral manifestations of n Achievement in relation to two jobs: that of a sales representative and of a manager.

Where are the opportunities in a society for taking personal responsibility for problem-solving, for taking calculated risks, and for obtaining concrete feedback on performance? Generally, business offers such opportunities on a large scale. One might expect, then, that people high in n Achievement might gravitate towards business. This is exactly what McClelland (1962) found: "... in three countries representing different levels and types of economic development, managers or executives scored considerably higher on the average in achievement thinking than did professionals or specialists of comparable education and background" (p. 102). And within business itself, there tends to be a concentration of people high in n Achievement where these opportunities are most clearly present: sales jobs. Successful sales representatives, in particular, tend to be high in n Achievement.

On the other hand, there is the old saw that the best sales rep may not make the best sales manager. Why? Because management involves planning, organizing, and leading people. And, as McClelland (1970) points out, "it is fairly clear that a high need to Achieve does not equip a man to deal effectively with managing human relationships" (p. 30).

Perhaps other motives better predispose individuals to effective managerial behavior: n Affiliation and n Power differ from n Achievement in that they are interpersonally oriented needs. The power motive impels people to strive for a position where they can exercise influence; it may also aid them in being effective in that position. As J. Sterling Livingston (1971) puts it:

> Power seekers can be counted on to strive hard to reach positions where they can exercise authority over large numbers of people. Individual performers who lack this drive are not likely to act in ways that will enable them to advance far up the managerial ladder. They usually scorn company politics and devote their energies to other types of activities that are more satisfying to them. But, to prevail in the competitive struggle to attain and hold high-level positions in management, a person's desire for prestige and high income must be reinforced by the satisfac-

tion he gets or expects to get from exercising the power and authority of a high office.

The competitive battle to advance within an organization, as Levinson (1969) points out, is much like playing 'King of the Hill.' Unless a person enjoys playing that game, he is likely to tire of it and give up the struggle for control of the top of the hill. The power game is a part of management, and it is played best by those who enjoy it most (p. 87).

Thus far, we have written about each motive as a pure case. This has facilitated exposition, but it may be misleading. To illustrate, here is a third story from McClelland (1962) about the picture we showed you earlier:

A successful industrial designer is at his "work bench" toying with a new idea. He is "talking it out" with his family in the picture. Someone in the family dropped a comment about a shortcoming in a household gadget, and the designer has just "seen" a commercial use of the idea. He has picked up ideas from his family before—he is "telling" his family what a good idea it is, and "confidentially" he is going to take them on a big vacation because "their" idea was so good. The idea will be successful, and family pride and mutual admiration will be strengthened (p. 101).

In this case the author expresses a strong interest in interpersonal relations. However, he adds the innovation of a product. The introduction of this idea evidences some concern for achievement. He does not think only about people, but also about task accomplishment.

Thus, that a given individual might be high in one motive does not mean that he or she would necessarily score low in any other motive. For example, to score high in *n* Power is not necessarily to lack concern for people or achievement. It all depends on the mix and the situation. As Litwin and Stringer (1968) suggest: "A man with a strong *n* Power, little concern for warm, affiliative relationships, and strong authoritarian values would certainly tend toward autocratic and dictatorial action. On the other hand, a man with a strong *n* Power, considerable sensitivity to others' feelings, and a desire to give service to others would probably make an excellent Peace Corps worker or missionary" (pp. 19–20).

As Livingston has argued and as Litwin and Stringer's example suggests, some degree of *n* Power might be a critical attribute of managers or Peace Corps workers if their effectiveness required sustained effort to influence others. Similarly, some degree of *n* Affiliation would seem indispensable where task performance depended upon maintaining cordial interpersonal relations. It is difficult to conceive of any managerial position not requiring some degree of power and affiliation behavior. But what mixture is optimal can only be determined by analysis of the specific tasks to be performed.

The potential payoff is, of course, what was suggested: selecting and placing people whose motive patterns predispose them to behave in ways which contribute to task performance—managerial tasks or other tasks. Research by Lawrence and Lorsch (1969) provides a straightforward illustration of how sensitivity to motive patterns may contribute to organizational effectiveness.

In two cases, the researchers looked at not only the motive patterns of people in the organization but at the tasks they performed as well. Earlier research had led Lawrence and Lorsch to expect that a motivational analysis of both tasks and individuals could lead to improved placement. They said:

> We have found it useful to identify the behaviors which are required to perform a particular set of tasks effectively and then to determine what individual characteristics are most often associated with this behavior. For example, in attempting to achieve more effective performance on the part of "integrators" in an organization, it was learned, from an analysis of the task and an examination of personality characteristics of more and less effective performers in this job, that a relatively high need for affiliation, along with moderately high achievement, was associated with effectiveness. These jobs provided a high expectation of meeting these needs, and people with this need pattern found these jobs interesting and performed more effectively (pp. 70–71).

With this much background, examine the following two selling tasks described by Lawrence and Lorsch (pp. 71–77) and see if you are able to identify the motive patterns associated with successful performance.

Case One: Selling Hospital Equipment

The medical division of a large, diversified manufacturing company produced and sold expensive ($5000 to $200,000) electromechanical devices and systems to hospitals. The equipment was used in hospital operating rooms. To carry out the sales task, the division was organized into three regions. Each region comprised ten or so district offices. Each district office was staffed with six to eight sales reps and sixteen to twenty servicemen. The latter group both installed and serviced equipment.

When the researchers studied what the selling task involved, they observed three distinguishable phases. The first of these, which could vary from one to fifteen years, was a period in which sales reps needed to develop good relations with hospital administrators and doctors. The reps needed to foster their trust and confidence. The second phase was a shorter period, six months to three years, of more concentrated selling. The sales rep needed to create an opportunity to demonstrate and sell equipment. The third phase began with the installation of the equipment and continued with its servicing for many years, as many as twenty-five.

In terms of the existing measures of sales performance, there were some clear-cut differences between district offices. The researchers were able to make a comparison between four outstandingly successful district offices and four offices with average sales performance. What was compared were the motivation patterns of the sales reps. They were given Thematic Apperception Tests (TAT), and the tests were scored for *n* Achievement, *n* Affiliation, and *n* Power, the purpose being to see if there were any differences between the motives of the reps in the outstanding offices and those in the average offices. What do you think the results were?

If you are like the researchers, you would have looked for a difference in achievement motivation to be the answer. After all, as we said earlier, successful salespeople tend to be high in n Achievement. In fact, while reps in both average and outstanding offices scored high in n Achievement, those in average offices had the higher scores. The sales reps in the outstanding offices, however, scored higher in n Affiliation. Remember, there seemed to be little opportunity for immediate, frequent, and tangible feedback on how well the sales reps were doing in this particular sales task. Those high in n Achievement would not very readily get what they require. On the other hand, those who enjoy and need good companionable relationships, those who find such relationships intrinsically satisfying. and who require less performance feedback and fewer signposts of achievement would seem better matched to performing the job successfully. They would seem better attuned to the behavior the task required. And that, indeed, proved to be the case.

Case Two: Selling Clothing to Retailers

In this case, the company was a medium-sized manufacturer of women's sportswear. Of its thirty salespeople, all paid on a commission basis, management observed performance differences; some were turning in unsatisfactory results. Top management retained consultants to investigate the sources of below-average performance.

The consultants studied the nature of the sales task. Though the orthodox view in the company seemed to be that the salesperson's job was to write orders, the consultants found the task to be more complex. The salespeople had to help the retail store personnel in the selection and merchandising of goods. They had to help build the retail store's sales volume by showing store personnel how to display and move their merchandise. The task was more helping to operate the retail stores successfully through selling the manufacturer's products than it was simply taking orders.

Because the consultants suspected that testing procedures would be unwelcome and disruptive in this organization, they sought to assess the motive patterns of both outstanding and below-average salespeople by interviewing them. They queried them to see how they conceived of the sales task. The person's picture of the task, the consultants reasoned, would provide them with a basis for inferring motive patterns. What differences in motive patterns did they find?

The outstanding salespeople did conceive of their task as one of helping build the retailers' volume. This effort yielded satisfaction for them. By taking some risks in guiding store personnel in merchandise selection, they were able to obtain feedback in terms of sales-volume increases as a means of gauging their own performance and, of course, increasing their own commissions. The consultants interpreted this as evidence that the outstanding salespeople were high in n Achievement. Their less effective colleagues derived their main satisfaction from the commission check. They did not express satisfaction in the business-building process itself. The pattern of their remarks about their work persuaded the consultants that the less successful salespeople were lower in *n* Achievement. And although the consultants did not mention *n* Power, we might speculate that the need to influence the customer may play a part in successful performance of this task.

It would appear that *n* Achievement contributes primarily to entrepreneurial behavior rather than simply to any sort of selling behavior. So to the extent that any job (managerial or otherwise) contains entrepreneurial components, *n* Achievement, as a quality of people performing the job, may lead to greater effectiveness. Wainer and Rubin (1969) conducted a study based upon this line of thought. They measured the motive patterns of the heads of fifty-one small, technically based companies in the Boston area. They assumed that all of these jobs were entrepreneurial in nature and that high *n* Achievement would directly influence the entrepreneurs' skills and the performance of their companies. They did find that *n* Achievement levels were high among the leaders of the best-performing companies.

However, when all of the data were considered, the results were too complicated to assume any simple linear relationship between the leader's *n* Achievement and company performance; *n* Affiliation and *n* Power were combined in various ways with *n* Achievement in the leaders of the best-performing companies.

> In summary, the *highest performing companies* in this sample were led by entrepreneurs who exhibited a high *n* Achievement and a moderate *n* Power. Those entrepreneurs who had a high *n* Achievement coupled with a high *n* Power performed less well than their high *n* Achievement counterparts who exhibited only a moderate level of *n* Power. Within the moderate *n* Achievement group, higher performing companies were led by entrepreneurs who had high *n* Affiliation (*ibid.*, pp. 182–83).

Wainer and Rubin speculate that a high *n* Power could produce autocratic or authoritarian leadership behavior. Such a pattern would interfere with making effective use of talented employees in research and development activities. Therefore, high *n* Power could cancel out high *n* Achievement and make for less effective companies.

On the other hand, high *n* Affiliation could serve, indirectly, to compensate for moderate *n* Achievement. As Wainer and Rubin suggest: "It may be that for those individuals who have only a moderate level of *n* Achievement, a high level of *n* Affiliation enables them to form close interpersonal relationships with their colleagues. In this way, the moderate *n* Achievement individual may be able to acquire the assistance he needs from his colleagues, some of whom may well have a higher level of *n* Achievement than he himself has" (p. 184).

EXPECTANCY THEORY

At the beginning of this chapter, we suggested that patterns of behavior in organizations are determined by two things. One is the needs that a person brings to the job situation. These are internal to the personality. The other is the situation "outside" the person, including the opportunities available for satisfying needs.

Expectancy theory takes into account both of these factors in trying to explain how and why people might go through life exhibiting a series of actions which fit their own personalities (their needs, abilities, aspirations) and which are at the same time attuned to the exigencies of the situation they find themselves in at any one moment.

In addition, expectancy theory holds that a human being is both emotional (seeking satisfaction of needs) and reasonable (thinking through what alternative actions will satisfy needs) at the same time. We in effect try to predict, "If I do this particular thing, it will lead to that particular payoff for me."

In order to illustrate how the human mind works under these conditions, we will trace through actions of a hypothetical college student, Alan Halvorson, who is trying to decide what to do on a given evening in early October.

As he sits in his dormitory room, Alan faces a number of *action possibilities*. He may study for an examination in accounting which he knows he has the next day (action A1 in Exhibit 1.1). Or he may go to a local tavern or discotheque with a group of friends (action A2). Or he may take the person he has been dating to see a movie (action A3). Each of these alternatives may produce its own set of payoffs for Alan. Which one he ultimately chooses will be the one which will provide, at least in Alan's eyes, the greatest payoffs.

Using the diagram in Exhibit 1.1, let us take one alternative, that of studying for the accounting examination, and see how Alan's mind evaluates its worth. Alan has needs for a variety of *basic payoffs*; for example, the need for security, the need for support from others, the need for independence, and the need to accomplish or achieve some level of task performance. To calculate payoffs, Alan's mind goes through an analysis like this: Some of the payoffs are *basic payoffs*. By studying the night before he feels a sense of achievement and self-development (BP4). If he studies with a group of friends, he might also achieve gratification of social and friendship needs (BP1).

Other payoffs are *instrumental payoffs*. They are not "built into" the action in the sense of directly paying off in basic needs. One such payoff (IP1) is a good grade on the examination, which may lead to the security of a well-paid job after graduation (BP2). This same good grade (IP1) may also gain the support of others—more specifically, the support of the professor in writing a reference letter (BP3).

The arrows on the diagram represent causation or *prediction* in the mind of the actor: "If I study, I will get a good grade. If I get a good grade I may well get a good salary after I graduate." These predictions are called *expectancies*. They are estimated in the form of probabilities: If I study tonight there is a good chance (80%) that I will get a good grade (80% × IP1) and a certainty that I will enjoy socializing with friends at the same time (BP1 × 100%). As in the payoff matrix, the *expectancy* of payoff for any one outcome is the value of the outcome *times* the probability of it occurring.

The total motivational force for studying the night before (A1), as com-

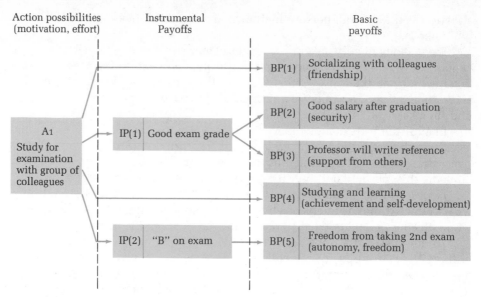

Action possibilities
(motivation, effort)

Instrumental
Payoffs

Basic
payoffs

A1
Study for
examination
with group of
colleagues

IP(1) Good exam grade

IP(2) "B" on exam

BP(1) Socializing with colleagues
(friendship)

BP(2) Good salary after graduation
(security)

BP(3) Professor will write reference
(support from others)

BP(4) Studying and learning
(achievement and self-development)

BP(5) Freedom from taking 2nd exam
(autonomy, freedom)

Exhibit 1.1 The Expectancy Model of Motivation

pared to going to a movie (A2) or going to a discotheque (A3), is then the sum of the expectancies of all payoffs associated with that action.

From this same example, we can begin to get some notion of why expectancy theory is important in leadership behavior of professors, or supervisors at the workplace. Referring again to Exhibit 1.1, let us assume that Alan, like many of us, has some need for autonomy (BP5). Professor Jackson has specified (in the jargon of leadership theory, he has "initiated structural rules") that anyone who receives a grade of "B" or better on this examination will be exempt from taking a second examination in November. This level of performance (IP2) is thus an instrumental payoff to another reward, the freedom from further controls (BP5).

As we shall see, the path-goal theory of leadership holds that supervisors and professors must, if subordinates are to know the "ground rules," help people to see various instrumental payoffs, and be consistent in applying rewards. They must help subordinates see "paths" to instrumental and basic payoffs, both of which are one's personal goals.

What would happen if Professor Jackson *later* said to the class, "I have decided that it would be good learning if everyone in the class takes the November examination, regardless of what grade you made on the last examination"? Do you see that this kind of lack of clarity, or inconsistency, actually "messes up" a person's ability to "see," "predict," or "expect" things from the environment out there? Such leadership behavior can cause "future shock" and extreme uncertainty in predicting probabilities. It was precisely this kind of behavior that officials in a prisoner of war camp applied to prisoners during the Korean war which caused the prisoners to "unfreeze" from their previous beliefs. Later, it was clarification of rewards and punishments, and restoring of the basic need for security through clear and consistent application of instrumental rewards, that "brainwashed" prisoners into new forms of attitudes and behavior. Expectancy theory is, then, a powerful way of understanding and controlling individual behavior.

Of course, everyone knows that human beings do not drop everything else and become mathematicians to figure out this complex can of worms for every action taken! If you were to take seriously this rational analysis on all actions every day, deciding on when to study, when to go out on a date, or when to go sailing, you would be, to put it colloquially, a raving maniac by the end of the first week. This does not mean that expectancy motivation analysis is of no value. What actually happens is that an individual makes quick subjective estimates of all of the payoffs that may accrue. He or she does not know *all* of the instrumental or basic payoffs, nor does he or she know all of the weights (valences) or probabilities involved.

BEHAVIORISM: POSITIVE REINFORCEMENT

So far in this chapter, we have looked at a variety of theories which explain human motivations. In each, the researchers looked deeply into the human mind to explain certain emotional feelings (the need for security, for example) or certain thought processes (expectancy reasoning, for example). We now must call attention to a final way of looking at individual human behavior: the behavioristic viewpoint.

Behaviorists like B. F. Skinner (1953, 1976), a principal proponent of this view, do *not* look deeply into the human mind for motives or thought. Rather, they concentrate on observing *behavior* as it is *learned* by human beings as they repeat behaviors that have pleasant consequences and avoid behaviors that have unpleasant consequences. This learning process was first observed in lower order species. For example, psychologists would *positively reinforce* a pigeon which pecks a red disc by rewarding it with grain. The pigeon learns to repeat this behavior because it satisfies a need. Or, the psychologist might *negatively reinforce* the pecking behavior by simply omitting the grain reward, in which case, over time, the former pattern of behavior would be extinguished. It would fade away or disappear. The same would occur if the psychologist punished the red-disc pecking behavior by applying electric shocks, except that the behavior would disappear more quickly.

Reinforcement rewards may be continuous (after each occurrence) or intermittent (after a number of occurrences). And there are ways to vary the intermittent reinforcements (after a fixed number of occurrences, after a variable number of occurrences, at a fixed time interval, etc.). Each of these patterns of reinforcement has *different* effects on how fast learning takes place and how "permanent" the newly learned behavior becomes. Continuous reinforcement, for example, is faster than most, and behavior learned in this way is not very resistant to fading away.

Space does not permit a thorough explanation of the behavioristic viewpoint in this chapter. Chapter 9, which deals with controlling organizational behavior, will cover the theory in more detail and give a number of examples of its application in business settings.

MOTIVATION AND MANAGEMENT

The manager is employed to contribute to realizing organizational effectiveness. An important part of this challenge is to enlist the efforts of subordinates to this same end. Argyris (1957) suggests that conventional management wisdom, in emphasizing such practices as task specialization and chain of command, does not provide the best guidance in coping with this task. Argyris describes the growth or development of human personality, and advances the idea that organizational arrangements are often incongruent with the fulfillment of human needs. The ways in which workers respond actively to this incongruence often lead managers to employ further directive leadership and more controls, which turn out to be counterproductive. More recently, Argyris has suggested that one way workers adjust to organizational pressures, seemingly successfully, is through apathy. This would hardly seem to lead to optimum organizational effectiveness, however.

The theories we have been considering lead to a more knowledgeable approach to motivation. Generally, if managers can make task performance a path to need satisfaction, they raise the probability that employee effort will be committed to organizational purpose (assuming, of course, that the tasks are themselves well fitted to organizational objectives). Consider a few of the possibilities which come into view when managers become sensitive to the particular patterns of needs possessed by subordinates. The more pronounced individuals' needs to be liked and approved by others, the more susceptible they are to efforts to control their behavior by making approval contingent on producing the desired behavior. Just as one might better motivate people high in *n* Achievement by offering the opportunity for setting goals, taking calculated risks, and obtaining feedback in their job, one might better motivate someone high in *n* Affiliation by offering the potential reward of social approval or increased friendly interpersonal contact. For the individual high in *n* Power, increased opportunity to influence others, obtained by winning promotions, for example, might be particularly attractive and rewarding. Similarly, for the individual with prepotent needs for esteem or security, influence can be increased by designing jobs and personnel policies which provide satisfaction of those needs in return for satisfactory performance.

Tailoring influence to subordinates' needs presupposes some basis for recognizing the pattern of those needs. The manager cannot go about administering and interpreting tests, so how is he or she to know what motives are stronger than others in specific individuals? The question is perhaps not so difficult to answer as one might think. Although motives are invisible, their presence can be inferred from behavior. What people do the manager can see.

What they want she or he can infer from what they say and do. In essence, the manager can see in characteristic, established ways of behaving the expression of underlying motives. For example, if she or he reasons back from the visible signs of setting challenging goals, taking personal responsibility for results, taking moderate risk, and so on, the manager has a basis for believing *n* Achievement is probably at work.

Once managers recognize that they depend upon the volition of subordinates, and that their problem—and challenge—is to attune their leadership behavior and organizational goals, controls, rewards, and structures to human nature, they sharpen their awareness of their opportunities and constraints, and can learn to provide stimuli more likely to become transformed, upon perception by subordinates, into personal motivation, behavior, and valued organizational consequences. More specifically, they can motivate by carefully forming the climate that characterizes the work situation.

SUMMARY

Everyone has a history of behaving and of experiencing pleasures and pains. This history makes each person more likely to behave in some ways and less likely to behave in others. "Being likely to behave in some way" is what we mean when we say that someone has a need or a strong need of a particular type. A need amounts to a propensity to act in a certain way.

We have discussed several of these needs. Maslow's hierarchy of needs, for example, includes physiological needs, and needs for safety, love, esteem, and self-actualization. He suggested that these are arranged in an order of "prepotency," in which successive needs come into operation only as more basic ones are satisfied. Since satisfied needs do not motivate behavior, one implication for management is that jobs must appeal to unmet needs if they are to motivate employees.

Beyond this theory of motivation are other theories. Socially acquired needs for achievement, power, and affiliation, as well as the general need for competence, also identify patterns of behavior important to management. The behavior associated with each need can be instrumental in successful job performance. We saw, for example, that the need for achievement is associated with success at one type of sales task and that the need for affiliation is associated with success at another.

But motivation and successful performance depend upon more than needs. They depend upon the situation and how it interacts with the individual. There must be cues in the situation which encourage the belief or expectancy that effort will result in performance and performance will be rewarded. The more clearly managers understand what kind of behavior will lead to improved performance, the more carefully they can consider who is likely to behave that way and what administrative and organizational conditions will help stimulate that behavior.

Finally, we looked briefly at a view of human behavior which says that people *learn* to behave in certain ways through trial and error. In this process, people tend to repeat behaviors which have yielded rewards in the past, and to eliminate or "let die" behaviors that (1) have yielded no results, or (2) have resulted in unpleasant consequences. This view of behavior will be discussed more thoroughly in Chapter 9.

REFERENCES

Argyris, C. *Personality and Organization.* Harper & Row, 1957.

Atkinson, J. W. *An Introduction to Motivation.* Van Nostrand, 1964.

———, ed. *Motives in Fantasy, Action, and Society.* Van Nostrand, 1958.

Bentham, Jeremy. "An Introduction to the Principles of Morals and Legislation," in *The English Philosophers from Bacon to Mill* ed. E. A. Burtt. Random House, 1939.

Campbell, J. P., M. D. Dunnette, E. E. Lawler III, and K. E. Weick, Jr. *Managerial Behavior, Performance, and Effectiveness.* McGraw-Hill, 1970.

Clark, K. B. *Dark Ghetto: Dilemmas of Social Power.* Harper & Row, 1965.

Cofer, C. N., and M. H. Appleby. *Motivation: Theory and Research.* Wiley, 1964.

Croy, H. *Wheels West.* Hastings House, 1955.

Festinger, L. *A Theory of Cognitive Dissonance.* Stanford University Press, 1957.

———, H. Riecken, and S. Schachter. *When Prophecy Fails.* University of Minnesota Press, 1956.

Ginzberg, E., et al. *The Unemployed.* Harper & Row, 1943.

Hamsun, K. *Hunger* (1899). Farrar, Strauss, & Giroux, 1967.

Herzberg, F. "One More Time: How Do You Motivate Employees?" *Harvard Business Review,* Vol. 46, No. 2 (January 1968).

Homans, G. *The Human Group.* Harcourt Brace Jovanovich, 1950.

Kantor, M. *Andersonville.* World, 1955.

Lawrence, P. R., and J. W. Lorsch. *Developing Organizations: Diagnosis and Action.* Addison-Wesley, 1969.

Levinson, H. "On Becoming a Middle-Aged Manager." *Harvard Business Review,* Vol. 47, No. 4 (July–August 1969), pp. 51–60.

Liebow, E. *Tally's Corner.* Little, Brown, 1967.

Litwin, G. H., and R. A. Stringer, Jr. *Motivation and Organizational Climate.* Graduate School of Business Administration, Harvard University, 1968.

Livingston, J. S. "Myth of the Well-Educated Manager." *Harvard Business Review,* Vol. 49, No. 1 (January–February 1971), pp. 79–89.

Maslow, A. H. "A Theory of Human Motivation." *Psychological Review,* Vol. 50, No. 4 (July 1943), pp. 370–96.

———. *Motivation and Personality.* Harper & Row, 1954.

McClelland, D. C. "Comments on Professor Maslow's Paper." In *Nebraska Symposium on Motivation, III,* ed. M. R. Jones. University of Nebraska Press, 1955.

———. "Business Drive and National Achievement." *Harvard Business Review,* Vol. 40, No. 4 (July–August 1962), pp. 99–112.

————. "The Two Faces of Power." *Journal of International Affairs*, Vol. 24, No. 1 (1970), pp. 29–47.

McGregor, D. *The Human Side of Enterprise.* McGraw-Hill. 1960.

Moment, D., and A. Zaleznik. *Role of Development and Interpersonal Competence.* Division of Research, Graduate School of Business Administration, Harvard University, 1963.

Murray, H. A. *Explorations in Personality.* Oxford University Press, 1938.

Nord, W. "Improving Attendance Through Rewards." *Personnel Administration,* November 1970, pp. 37–41.

Read, P. P. *Alive: The Story of the Andes Survivors.* Lippincott, 1974.

Roethlisberger, F. J., and W. J. Dickinson. *Management and the Worker.* Harvard University Press, 1939.

Schachter, S. *The Psychology of Affiliation.* Stanford University Press, 1959.

Skinner, B. F. *Science and Human Behavior.* Free Press, 1953.

————. *About Behaviorism.* Knopf, 1976.

Strachey, J. (tr. and ed.). *Civilization and Its Discontents,* by Sigmund Freud. Norton, 1962.

Sullivan, H. S. "Tensions, Interpersonal and International," in H. Cantril (ed.), *Tensions That Cause Wars.* University of Illinois Press, 1950.

Test of Imagination. Behavioral Science Center of the Sterling Institute, Boston, Massachusetts, 1968.

Wainer, H. A., and I. M. Rubin. "Motivation of Research and Development Entrepreneurs: Determinants of Company Success, Part I." *Journal of Applied Psychology,* Vol. 53, No. 3 (June 1969), pp. 178–84.

White, R. W. "Motivation Reconsidered: The Concept of Competence." *Psychological Review,* Vol. 66 (September 1959), pp. 297–334.

Readings

The Two Faces of Power

David C. McClelland

In the chapter text, we saw that McClelland's theory of achievement not only explains that some people are motivated by achievement while others are not, but also explains how this motive is learned by a human being in the process of learning and growth. McClelland recognized that there is sometimes a thin line between an action which is motivated by sheer need for personal achievement and desire for power over other human beings. In this article, he clarifies two types of power, one socially (ethically) desirable and the other socially undesirable (or harmful). He ends with some safeguards that might be used to harness the constructive use of power while discouraging its destructive use.

For over twenty years I have been studying a particular human motive — the need to Achieve, the need to do something better than it has been done before. As my investigation advanced, it became clear that the need to Achieve, technically n Achievement, was one of the keys to economic growth, because men who are concerned with doing things better have become active entrepreneurs and have created the growing business firms which are the foundation stones of a developing economy.[1] Some of these heroic entrepreneurs might be regarded as leaders in the restricted sense that their activities established the economic base for the rise of a new type of civilization, but they were seldom leaders of men. The reason for this is simple: n Achievement is a one man game which need never involve other people. Boys who are high in n Achievement like to build things or to make things with their hands, presumably because they can tell easily and directly whether they have done a good job. A boy who is trying to build as tall a tower as possible out of blocks can measure very precisely how well he has done. He is in no way dependent on someone else to tell him how good his performance is. So in the pure case, the man with high n Achievement is not dependent on the judgment of others; he is concerned with improving his own performance. As an ideal type, he is most easily conceived of as a salesman or an owner-manager of a small business, in a position to watch carefully whether or not his performance is improving.

While studying such men and their role in economic development, I ran head on into problems of leadership, power, and social influence which n Achievement clearly did not prepare a man to cope with. As a one-man firm grows larger, it obviously requires some division of function and some organizational structure. Organizational structure involves relationships among people, and sooner or later someone in the organization, if it is to survive, must pay attention to getting people to work together, or to dividing up the tasks to be performed, or to supervising the work of others. Yet it is fairly clear that a high need to Achieve does not equip a man to deal effectively with managing human relationships. For instance, a salesman with high n Achievement

Copyright by the Trustees of Columbia University in the City of New York. Permission to reprint from the *Journal of International Affairs*, Volume 24, Number 1, pp. 29–47, 1970, is gratefully acknowledged to the Editors of the *Journal*.

does not necessarily make a good sales manager. As a manager, his task is not to sell, but to inspire others to sell, which involves a different set of personal goals and different strategies for reaching them. I shall not forget the moment when I learned that the president of one of the most successful *achievement*-oriented firms we had been studying scored exactly zero in n Achievement! Up to that point I had fallen into the easy assumption that a man with a high need to Achieve does better work, gets promoted faster, and ultimately ends up as president of a company. How then was it possible for a man to be head of an obviously achieving company and yet score so low in n Achievement? At the time I was tempted to dismiss the finding as a statistical error, but there is now little doubt that it was a dramatic way of calling attention to the fact that stimulating achievement motivation in others requires a different motive and a different set of skills than wanting achievement satisfaction for oneself. For some time now, research on achievement motivation has shifted in focus from the individual with high n Achievement to the climate which encourages him and rewards him for doing well.[2] For no matter how high a person's need to Achieve may be, he cannot succeed, if he has no opportunities, if the organization keeps him from taking initiative, or does not reward him if he does. As a simple illustration of this point, we found in our research in India that it did no good to raise achievement motivation through training if the trained individual was not in charge of his business.[3] That is to say, even though he might be "all fired up" and prepared to be more active and entrepreneurial, he could not in fact do much if he was working for someone else, someone who had the final say as to whether any of the things he wanted to do would in fact be attempted. In short, the man with high n Achievement seldom can act alone, even though he might like to. He is caught up in an organizational context in which he is managed, controlled, or directed by others. And thus to understand better what happens to him, we must shift our attention to those who are managing him, to those who are concerned about organizational relationships—to the leaders of men.

Since managers are primarily concerned with influencing others, it seems obvious that they should be characterized by a high need for Power, and that by studying the power motive we can learn something about the way effective managerial leaders work. If A gets B to do something, A is at one and the same time a leader (i.e., he is leading B), and a power-wielder (i.e., he is exercising some kind of influence or power over B). Thus, leadership and power appear as two closely related concepts, and if we want to understand better effective leadership, we may begin by studying the power motive in thought and action. What arouses thoughts of being powerful? What kinds of strategies does the man employ who thinks constantly about gaining power? Are some of these strategies more effective than others in influencing people? In pursuing such a line of inquiry in this area, we are adopting an approach which worked well in another. Studying the achievement motive led to a better understanding of business entrepreneurship. Analogously, studying the power motive may help us understand managerial, societal, or even political leadership better.

There is one striking difference between the two motivation systems which is apparent from the outset. In general, in American society at least, individuals are proud of having a high need to Achieve, but dislike being told they have a high need for Power. It is a fine thing to be concerned about doing things well (n Achievement) or making friends (n Affiliation), but it is reprehensible to be concerned about having influence over others (n Power). The vocabulary behavioral scientists use to describe power relations is strongly negative in tone. If one opens *The Authoritarian Personality*,[4] one of the major works dealing with people who are concerned with power, one finds these people depicted as harsh, sadistic, fascist, Machiavellian, prejudiced, and neurotic. Ultimately, many claim, the concern for power leads to Nazi-type dictatorships, to the slaughter of innocent Jews, to political terror, police states, brainwashing, and the exploitation of helpless masses who have lost their freedom. Even less political terms for power than these have a distinctively negative flavor—dominance-submission, competition, zero sum game (if I win, you lose). It is small wonder that people do not particularly like being told they have a high need for Power.

The negative reactions to the exercise of power became vividly apparent to me in the course of our recent research efforts to develop achievement motivation.[5] Out of our extensive research on the achievement motive, we conceived of possible ways to increase it through short intensive courses. At first people were interested and curious. It seemed like an excellent idea to develop a fine motive like n Achievement, particularly among under-achievers in school or relatively inactive businessmen in underdeveloped countries. But most people were also skeptical. Could it be done? It turned out that many remained interested only as long as they were really skeptical about our ability to change motivation. As soon as it became apparent that we could indeed change people in a relatively short period of time, many observers began to worry. Was it ethical to change people's personalities? Were we not brainwashing them? What magical power were we employing to change an underlying personality disposition presumably established in childhood and laboriously stabilized over the years? Once these questions were raised, we became aware of the fundamental dilemma confronting anyone who becomes involved in any branch of the "influence game." He may think that he is exercising leadership—i.e., influencing people for their own good—but if he succeeds, he is likely to be accused of manipulating people. We thought that our influence attempts were benign. In fact, we were a little proud of ourselves. After all, we were giving people a chance to be more "successful" in business and at school. Yet we soon found ourselves attacked as potentially dangerous "brainwashers."

To some extent, ordinary psychotherapy avoids these accusations because the power of the therapist seems to be relatively weak. Therapy does not work very well or very quickly, and when it does, the therapist can say that the patient did most of the work himself.

But consider the following anecdote. Johnny was a bright but lazy sixth-grade student in math. His parents were concerned because he was not motivated to work harder, preferring to spend his evenings watching television, and they were delighted when psychologists explained that they had some new techniques for developing motivation to which they would like to expose Johnny. Soon after the motivation training regime began, they noticed a dramatic change in Johnny's behavior. He never watched television, but spent all of his time studying, and was soon way ahead of his class in advanced mathematics. At this point, his parents began to worry. What had the psychologists done to produce such a dramatic change in their son's behavior? They had wanted him changed, but not *that* much. They reacted very negatively to the power that the psychologists seemed to have exercised over him.

This experience was enough to make us yearn for the position of the detached-scientist or consulting-expert so vividly described by John Gardner in *The Anti-Leadership Vaccine*[6] as the preferred role for more and more young people today. For the "scientist" ordinarily does not directly intervene—does not exercise power—in human or social affairs. He observes the interventions of others, reports, analyzes and advises, but never takes responsibility himself. Our research had led us to intervene actively in Johnny's life, and even that small, relatively benign exercise of influence had led to some pretty negative responses from the "public." My own view is that young people avoid sociopolitical leadership roles not so much because their professors brainwash them into believing that it is better to be a professional, but because in our society in our time, and perhaps in all societies at all times, the exercise of power is viewed very negatively. People are suspicious of a man who wants power, even if he does so for sincere and altruistic reasons. He is often socially conditioned to be suspicious of himself. He does not want to be in a position where he might be thought to be seeking power and influence in order to exploit others, and as a result he shuns public responsibility.

Yet surely this negative face of power is only part of the story. Power must have a positive face too. After all, people cannot help influencing one another. Organizations cannot function without some kind of authority relationships. Surely it is necessary and desirable for some people to concern themselves with management, with working out influence relationships that make it possible to achieve the goals of the group. A man who is consciously concerned with the development of proper channels of influence is surely better able to contribute to group goals than a man who neglects or represses power problems and lets the working relationships of men grow up unsupervised by men. Our problem, then, is to try to discern and understand two faces of power. When is power bad and when is it good? Why is it often perceived as dangerous? Which aspects of power are viewed favorably, and which unfavorably? When is it proper, and when improper, to exercise influence? And finally, are there different kinds of power motivation?

It will not be possible to answer all of these questions definitively, but the findings of recent research on the power motive as it functions in human beings will help us understand the two faces of power somewhat better. Let us begin with the curious fact that turned up in the course of what are technically "arousal" studies. When an experimenter becomes interested in a new motive, he ordinarily begins to study it by trying to arouse it in a variety of ways in order to see how it influences what a person thinks about. Then these alterations in thought content are worked into a code or a scoring system which captures the extent to which the thinking of the subject is concerned about achievement or power or whatever motive state has been aroused. For instance, Veroff,[7] when he began his study of the power motive, asked student candidates for office to write imaginative stories while they were waiting for the election returns to be counted. He contrasted these stories with those written by other students who were not candidates for office. That is, he assumed that the students waiting to hear if they had been elected were in a state of aroused power motivation and that their stories would reflect this fact in contrast to the stories of students not in such a state. From the differences in story content he derived a coding system for n Power (need for Power) based on the greater concern for having influence over others revealed in the stories of student candidates for election. Later arousal studies by Uleman[8] and Winter[9] further defined the essence of n Power as a concern for having a *strong impact on others.* That is, when power motivation was aroused in a variety of ways, students thought more often about people having strong impact on others. This was true not only for student candidates for office awaiting election returns, but also for student experimenters who were about to demonstrate their power over subjects by employing a winning strategy in a competitive game that they had been taught beforehand.[10]

What surprised us greatly was the discovery that drinking alcohol also stimulated similar power thoughts in men. This discovery was one of those happy accidents which sometimes occurs in scientific laboratories when two studies thought to be unrelated are proceeding side by side. When we began studying the effects of social drinking on fantasy, we had no idea that alcohol would increase power fantasies. Yet we immediately found that it increased sex and aggression fantasies, and one day it occurred to us that certain types of exploitative sex and certainly aggression were instances of "having impact" on others and therefore could be considered part of an n Power scoring definition. We later found that drinking alcohol in small amounts increased the frequency of *socialized* power thoughts while in larger amounts it promoted thinking in terms of *personalized* power. We began to notice that these two types of power concern had different consequences in action. For instance, Winter found that some college students with high *n* Power scores tended to drink more heavily while others held more offices in student organizations. These were not, however, the same people. That is, a student with high *n* Power either drank more heavily or he was a club officer, though he was usually not both, possibly because heavy drinking would prevent him from being elected to a responsible office. In other words, Winter identified alternative manifestations of the power drive — either heavy drinking or holding office. Later we found that the orientation of the power thoughts of these two types of people was quite different. Men whose power thoughts centered on having impact for the sake of others tended to hold office, whereas those whose thoughts centered on personal dominance tended to drink heavily, or to "act out" in college by attempting more sexual conquests or driving powerful cars fast, for example.

Other studies have further illuminated this picture, and while it is still not altogether clear, its main outlines can be readily sketched.[11] There are two faces of power. One is turned toward seeking to win out over active adversaries. Life tends to be seen as a "zero-sum game" in which "if I win, you lose" or "I lose, if you win." The imagery is that of the "law of the jungle" in which the strongest survive by destroying their adversaries. The thoughts of this face of power are aroused by drinking alcohol or, more socially, by putting a person in a personal dominance situation in which he is threatened. At the level of action, a personal power concern is associated with heavy drinking, gambling, having more aggressive impulses, and collecting "prestige supplies" like a convertible or a Playboy Club Key. People with this personalized power concern are more apt to speed, have accidents, and get into physical fights. If these primitive and personalized power-seeking characteristics were possessed by political officeholders, especially in the sphere of international relations, the consequences would be ominous.

The other face of the power motive is more socialized. It is aroused by the possibility of winning an election. At the fantasy level it expresses itself in thoughts of exercising power for the benefit of others and by feelings of greater ambivalence about holding power — doubts of personal strength, the realization that most victories must be carefully planned in advance, and that every victory means a loss for someone. In terms of activities, people concerned with the more socialized aspect of power join more organizations and are more apt to become officers in them. They also are more apt to join in organized informal sports, even as adults.

We have made some progress in distinguishing two aspects of the power motive, but what exactly is the difference between the way the two are exercised? Again a clue came from a very unexpected source. It is traditional in the literature of social psychology and political science to describe a leader as someone who is able to evoke feelings of obedience or loyal submission in his followers. A leader is sometimes said to have charisma if, when he makes a speech, for example, the members of his audience are swept off their feet and feel that they must submit to his overwhelming authority and power. In the extreme case they are like iron filings that have been polarized by a powerful magnet. The leader is recognized as supernatural or superhuman; his followers feel submissive, loyal, devoted, and obedient to his will. Certainly this is the most common description of what happened at mass meetings addressed by Hitler or Lenin. As great demagogues they established their power over the masses which followed loyally and obediently.

Winter wished to find out exactly, by experiment, what kinds of thoughts the members of an audience had when exposed to a charismatic leader.[12] He wanted to find out if the common analysis of what was going on in the minds of the audience was in fact accurate. So he exposed groups of business school students to a film of John F. Kennedy's Inaugural Address as President of the United States sometime after he had been assassinated. There was no doubt that this film was a highly moving and effective presentation of a charismatic leader for such an audience at that time. After the film was over he asked them to write imaginative stories as usual, and contrasted the themes of their stories with those written by a comparable group of students after they had seen a film explaining some aspects of modern architecture. Contrary to expectation, he did not find that the students exposed to the Kennedy film thought more afterwards about submission, following, obedience, or loyalty. Instead the frequency of power themes in their stories increased. They were apparently strengthened and uplifted by the experience. They felt more powerful, rather than less powerful and submissive. This suggests that the traditional way of explaining the influence which a leader has on his followers has not been entirely correct. He does not force them to submit and follow him by the sheer overwhelming magic of his personality and persuasive powers. This is in fact to interpret effective leadership in terms of the kind of personalized power syndrome described above, and leadership has been discredited in this country precisely because social scientists have often used this personal power image to explain how the leader gets his effects. In fact, he is influential by strengthening and inspiriting his audience. Max Weber, the source of much of the sociological treatment of charisma, recognized that charismatic leaders obtained their effects through *begeisterung*, a word which means "inspiration" rather than its usual translation as "enthusiasm."[13] The leader arouses confidence in his followers. The followers feel better able to accomplish whatever goals he and they share. There has been much discussion of whether the leader's ideas about what will inspire his followers come from God, from himself, or from some intuitive sense of what the people need and want. But whatever the source of the leader's ideas, he cannot inspire his people unless he expresses vivid goals and aims which in some sense they want. Of course, the more he is meeting their needs, the less "persuasive" he has to be, but in no case does it make much sense to speak as if his role is to force submission. Rather it is to strengthen and uplift, to make people feel like origins, not pawns of the socio-political system.[14] His message is not so much: "Do as I say because I am strong and know best. You are children with no wills of your own and must follow me because I know better," but rather "Here are the goals which are true and right and which we share. Here is how we can reach them. You are strong and capable. You can accomplish these goals." His role is to clarify which goals the group should achieve and then to create confidence in its members that they can achieve them. John Gardner described these two aspects of the socialized leadership role very well when he said that leaders "can conceive and articulate goals that lift people out of their petty preoccupations, carry them above the conflicts that tear a society apart, and unite them in the pursuit of objectives worthy of their best efforts."[15]

Clearly the more socialized type of power motivation cannot and does not express itself through leadership which is characterized by the primitive methods of trying to win out over adversaries or exert personal dominance. In their thinking about the power motive, social scientists have been too impressed by the dominance hierarchies established by brute force among lower animals. Lasswell and other political scientists have described all concern with power as a defense, an attempt to compensate for a feeling of weakness. At best this describes the personalized face of the power motive, not its socialized face—and even at that, we can only say that the personalized power drive *perceives* the world in defensive terms, not that it originates as a defense. Personal dominance may be effective in very small groups, but if a human leader wants to be effective in influencing large groups, he must rely on much more subtle and socialized forms of influence. He necessarily gets more interested in formulating the goals toward which groups of people can move. And if he is to move the group toward achieving them, he must help define the goals clearly and persuasively, and then be able to strengthen the will of the individual members of the group to work for those goals.[16]

Some further light on the two faces of power was shed by our experience in trying to exert social leadership by offering achievement motivation development courses for business leaders in small cities in India. As noted above, when we began to succeed in these efforts, some observers began to wonder whether we were coarsely interfering in people's lives, perhaps spreading some new brand of American imperialism by foisting achievement values on a people that had gotten along very well without them. Their reaction was not unlike the one just described in which an outsider seeing a leader sway an audience concludes that he must have some mysterious magical power over the audience. Did we have a similar kind of *power over* the Indian businessmen who came for motivation training? Were we psychological Machiavellians?

Certainly we never thought we were. Nor, we are certain, did the businessmen perceive us as very powerful agents. How then did we manage to influence them? The course of events was very much like the process of social leadership described by John Gardner. First, we set before the participants certain goals which we felt would be desired by them—namely, to be better businessmen, to improve economic welfare in their community, to make a contribution in this way to the development of their country as a whole, to provide a pilot project that the rest of the underdeveloped world might copy, and to advance the cause of science. These goals ranged all the way from the specific and personal—improving one's business—to improving the community, the nation, and the world. While a selfish appeal to personal power generally has not been as effective as an appeal which demonstrates that increased personal power leads to important social goals, the goals which we presented certainly were objectives that interested the businessmen we contacted. Second, we provided them with the means of achieving these goals, namely, the courses in achievement motivation development which we explained were designed to make them personally better able to move quickly and efficiently towards these objectives. We offered new types of training in goal setting, planning, and risk taking which research had shown would help men become more effective entrepreneurs. No one was pressured to undergo this training or pursue these goals. If there was any pressure exerted, it was clearly in the eyes of the outside observer noting the effects of our "intervention"; it was not in the minds of the participants at the time. Third, the major goal of all of our educational exercises was to make the participants feel strong, like origins rather than pawns. Thus we insisted that the initial decision to take part in the training sessions must be their own, and that they not come out of a sense of obligation or a desire to conform. In fact, we depicted the training as a difficult process, so that a high degree of personal involvement would be necessary to complete it. During the training, we never set goals for the participants, but let them set their own. We made no psychological analyses of their test behavior which we either kept for our private diagnosis or presented to them as evidence of our superior psychological knowledge. Rather we taught them to analyze their own test records and to make their own decisions as to what a test score meant. After the course they set up their own association to work together for common community goals. We did not provide them with technical information about various types of new businesses they might enter, but let them search for it themselves. We had no fixed order of presenting course materials, but constantly asked the participants to criticize the material as it was presented and to direct the staff as to what new types of presentations were desired. Thus, in our ceaseless efforts to make the participants feel strong, competent, and effective, we behaved throughout the entire experiment like effective socialized leaders. We expressed in many ways our faith in their ability to act as origins and solve their own problems. In the end many of them justified our faith. They became more active, as we expected them to, and once again validated the ubiquitous psychological findings that what you expect other people to do they will in fact tend to do.[17] Furthermore, we have good evidence that we succeeded only with those businessmen whose sense of personal efficacy was increased. This demonstrated the ultimate paradox of social leadership and social power: to be an effective leader, one must turn all of his so-called followers into leaders. There is little wonder that the situation is a little confusing not only to the would-be leader, but also to the social scientist observing the leadership phenomenon.

Now let us put together these bits and pieces of evidence about the nature of power, and see what kind of a picture they make. The negative or personal face of power is characterized by the dominance-submission mode: if I win, you lose. It is *primitive* in the sense that the strategies employed are adopted early in life, before the child is sufficiently socialized to learn more subtle techniques of influence. In fantasy it expresses itself in thoughts of conquering opponents. In real life it leads to fairly simple direct means of feeling powerful—drinking heavily, acquiring "prestige supplies," and being aggressive. It does not lead to effective social leadership for the simple reason that a person whose power drive is fixated at this level tends to treat other people as pawns rather than as origins. And people who feel that they are pawns tend to be passive and useless to the leader who is getting his childish satisfaction from dominating them. Slaves are the poorest, most inefficient form of labor ever devised by man. If a leader wants to have far-reaching influence, he must make his followers feel powerful and able to accomplish things on their own.

The positive or socialized face of power is characterized by a concern for group goals, for finding those goals that will move men, for helping the group to formulate them, for taking some initiative in providing members of the group with the means of achieving such goals, and for giving group members the feeling of strength and competence they need to work hard for such goals. In fantasy it leads to a concern with exercising influence *for* others, with planning, and with the ambivalent bitter-sweet meaning of many so-called "victories." In real life, it leads to an interest in informal sports, politics, and holding office. It functions in a way that makes members of a group feel like origins rather than pawns. Even the most dictatorial leader has not succeeded if he has not instilled in at least some of his followers a sense of power and the strength to pursue the goals he has set. This is often hard for outside observers to believe, because they do not experience the situation as it is experienced by the group members. One of the characteristics of the outsider, who notices only the success or failure of an influence attempt, is that he tends to convert what is a positive face of power into its negative version. He believes that the leader must have "dominated" because he was so effective, whereas in fact direct domination could never have produced so large an effect.[18]

There is, however, a certain realistic basis for the frequent misperception of the nature of leadership. In real life the actual leader balances on a knife edge between expressing personal dominance and exercising the more socialized type of leadership. He may show first one face of power, then the other. The reason for this lies in the simple fact that even if he is a socialized leader, he must take initiative in helping the group he leads to form its goals. How much initiative he should take, how persuasive he should attempt to be, and at what point his clear enthusiasm for certain goals becomes personal authoritarian insistence that those goals are the right ones whatever the members of the group may think, are all questions calculated to frustrate the well-intentioned leader. If he takes no initiative, he is no leader. If he takes too much, he becomes a dictator, particularly if he tries to curtail the process by which members of the group participate in shaping group goals. There is a particular danger for the man who has demonstrated his competence in shaping group goals and in inspiring group members to pursue them. In time both he and they may assume that he knows best, and he may almost imperceptibly change from a democratic to an authoritarian leader. There are, of course, safeguards against slipping from the more socialized to the less socialized expressions of power. One is psychological: the leader must thoroughly learn the lesson that his role is not to dominate and treat people like pawns, but to give strength to others and to make them feel like origins of ideas and of the courses of their lives. If they are to be truly strong, he must continually consult them and be aware of their wishes and desires. *A firm faith in people as origins prevents the development of the kind of cynicism that so often characterizes authoritarian leaders.* A second safeguard is social: democracy provides a system whereby the group can expel the leader from office if it feels that he is no longer properly representing its interests.

Despite these safeguards, Americans remain unusually suspicious of the leadership role for fear that it will become a vehicle of the personal use and abuse of power. Students do not aspire to leadership roles because they are sensitive to the negative face of power and suspicious of their own motives. Furthermore, they know that if they are in a position of leadership, they will be under constant surveillance by all sorts of groups which are ready to accuse them of the personal abuse of power. Americans probably have less respect for authority than any other people in the world. The reasons are not hard to find. Many Americans originally came here to avoid tyranny in other countries. We have come to hate and fear authority in many of its forms because of its excesses elsewhere. As a nation, we are strongly committed to an ideology of personal freedom and non-interference by government. We cherish our free press as the guardian of our freedom because it can ferret out tendencies toward the misuse or abuse of personal power before they become dangerous to the public. In government, as in other organizations, we have developed elaborate systems of checks and balances of divisions of power which make it difficult for any one person or group to abuse power. In government, power is divided three ways—among the executive, the legislative, and the judicial branches. In business it is divided among management, labor, and owners. And in the university, among trustees, administration, and students. Many of these organizations also have a system for rotating leadership to make sure that no one acquires enough power over time to be able to misuse it. A Martian observer might conclude that as a nation we are excessively, almost obsessively worried about the abuse of power.

It is incredible that any leadership at all can be exercised under such conditions. Consider the situation from the point of view of a would-be leader. He knows that if he takes too much initiative, or perhaps even if he does not, he is very likely to be severely attacked by some sub-group as a malicious, power hungry status-seeker. If he is in any way a public figure, he may be viciously attacked for any mis-step or chancy episode in his past life. Even though the majority of the people are satisfied with his leadership, a small vociferous minority can make his life unpleasant and at times unbearable. Furthermore, he knows that he will not be the only leader trying to formulate group goals. If he is a Congressman, he has to work not only with his fellow Congressmen, but also with representatives of independent sources of power in the executive branch and the governmental bureaucracy. If he is a college president, he has to cope with the relatively independent power of his trustees, the faculty and the student body. If he is a business manager, he must share power with labor leaders. In addition, he knows that his tenure of office is likely to be short. Since it is doubtful that he will ever be able to exert true leadership, there seems little purpose in preparing for it. Logically, then, he should spend his time preparing for what he will do before and after his short tenure in office.

Under these conditions why would any promising young man aspire to be a leader? He begins by doubting his motives and ends by concluding that even if he believes his motives to be altruistic, the game is scarcely worth the candle. In other words, the anti-leadership vaccine, which John Gardner speaks of, is partly supplied by the negative face that power wears in our society and the extraordinary lengths to which we have gone to protect ourselves against misused power. It is much safer to pursue a career as a professional adviser, assured some continuity of service and some freedom from public attack—because, after all, one is not responsible for decisions—and some certainty that one's motives are *good*, and that power conflicts have to be settled by someone else.

How can immunity against the anti-leadership vaccine be strengthened? Some immunity surely needs to be built up if our society is not to flounder because of a lack of socialized leadership. Personally, I would not concoct a remedy which is one part changes in the system, one part rehabilitation of the positive face of power, and one part adult education. Let me explain each ingredient in turn. I feel least confident in speaking about the first one, because I am neither a political scientist, a management expert, nor a revolutionary. Yet as a psychologist, I do feel that America's concern about the possible misuse of power verges at times on a neurotic obsession. To control the abuses of power, is it really necessary to divide authority so extensively and to give such free license to anyone to attack a leader in any way he likes? Doesn't this make the leadership role so difficult and unrewarding that it ends up appealing only to cynics? Who in his right mind would want the job of college president under most operating conditions today? A president has great responsibility—for raising money, for setting goals of the institution that faculty, students, and trustees can share, for student discipline, and for appointment of a distinguished faculty. Yet often he has only a very shaky authority with which to execute these responsibilities. The authority which he has he must share with the faculty (many of whom he cannot remove no matter how violently they disagree with the goals set for the university), with the trustees, and with students who speak with one voice one year and quite a different one two years later. I am not now trying to defend an ineffective college president. I am simply trying to point out that our social system makes his role an extraordinarily difficult one. Other democratic nations, Britain, for example, have not found it necessary to go to such extremes to protect their liberty against possible encroachment by power-hungry leaders. Some structural reform of the American system definitely seems called for. It is beyond the scope of this paper to say what it might be. The possibilities range all the way from a less structured system in which all organizations are conceived as temporary,[19] to a system in which leaders are given more authority or offered greater protection from irresponsible attack. Surely the problem deserves serious attention. If we want better leaders, we will have to find ways of making the conditions under which they work less frustrating.

The second ingredient in my remedy for the anti-leadership vaccine is rehabilitation of the positive face of power. This paper has been an effort in that direction. Its major thesis is that many people, including both social scientists and potential leaders, have consistently misunderstood or misperceived the way in which effective social leadership takes place. They have confused it regularly, we have pointed out, with the more primitive exercise of personal power. The error is perpetuated by people who speak of leaders as "making decisions." Such a statement only serves to obscure the true process by which decisions should be taken. It suggests that the leader is making a decision arbitrarily without consulting anyone, exercising his power or authority for his own ends. It is really more proper to think of an effective leader as an educator. The relationship between leading and educating is much more obvious in Latin than it is in English. In fact the word *educate* comes from the Latin *educare* meaning *to lead out.* An effective leader is an educator. One leads people by helping to set their goals, by communicating them widely throughout the group, by taking initiative in formulating means of achieving the goals, and finally, by inspiring the members of the group to feel strong enough to work hard for those goals. Such an image of the exercise of power and influence in a leadership role should not frighten anybody and should convince more people that power exercised in this way is not only not dangerous but of the greatest possible use to society.

My experience in training businessmen in India has led me to propose the third ingredient in my formula for producing better leaders—namely, psychological education for adults. What impressed me greatly was the apparent ease with which adults can be changed by the methods we used. The dominant view in American psychology today is still that basic personality structure is laid down very early in life and is very hard to change later on. Whether the psychologist is a Freudian or a learning theorist, he believes that early experiences are critical and shape everything a person can learn, feel, and want throughout his entire life span. As a consequence, many educators have come to be rather pessimistic about what can be done for the poor, the black, or the dispossessed who have undergone damaging experiences early in life. Such traumatized individuals, they argue, have developed non-adaptive personality structures that are difficult, if not impossible, to change later in life. Yet our experience with the effectiveness of short term training courses in achievement motivation for adult businessmen in India and elsewhere does not support this view. I have seen men change, many of them quite dramatically, after only a five-day exposure to our specialized techniques of psychological instruction. They changed the way they thought, the way they talked, and the way they spent their time. The message is clear: adults can be changed, often with a relatively short exposure to specialized techniques of psychological education. The implication for the present discussion is obvious. If it is true, as John Gardner argues, that many young men have learned from their professors that the professional role is preferable to the leadership role, then psychological education offers society a method of changing their views and self-conceptions when they are faced with leadership opportunities. The type of psychological education needed will of course differ somewhat from the more simple emphasis on achievement motivation. More emphasis will have to be given to the means of managing motivation in others. More explanations will have to be given of the positive face of leadership as an educational enterprise, and will have to provide participants with a better idea of how to be effective leaders. These alterations are quite feasible; in fact they have been tried.

Repeatedly we have discovered that leaders are not so much born as made. We have worked in places where most people feel there is not much leadership potential—specifically, among the poor and dispossessed. Yet we have found over and over again that even among people who have never thought of themselves as leaders or attempted to have influence in any way, real leadership performance can be elicited by specialized techniques of psychological education. We need not be as pessimistic as is usual about possibilities for change in adults. *Real leaders* have been developed in such disadvantaged locations as the Delmarva peninsula of the United States, the black business community of Washington, D.C., and the relatively stagnant small cities of India. Thus I can end on an optimistic note. Even if the leadership role today is becoming more and more difficult, and even if people are tending to avoid it for a variety of reasons, advances in scientific psychological techniques have come at least partly to the rescue by

providing society with new techniques for developing the socialized and effective
leaders that will be needed for the prosperity and peace of the world of tomorrow.

NOTES AND REFERENCES

1. David C. McClelland. *The Achieving Society* (Van Nostrand, 1961).
2. George H. Litwin and Robert A. Stringer. *Motivation and Organizational Climate*
   (Harvard University, Graduate School of Business Administration, Division of
   Research, 1968).
3. David McClelland and D. G. Winter. *Motivating Economic Achievement* (The
   Free Press, 1969).
4. Theodor W. Adorno, E. Frenkel-Brunswick, D. J. Levinson, and R. N. Sanford.
   The Authoritarian Personality (Harper & Row, 1950).
5. McClelland and Winter, *op. cit.*
6. John W. Gardner. *The Anti-Leadership Vaccine* (1965 Annual Report, The
   Carnegie Corporation of New York).
7. Joseph Veroff. "Development and Validation of a Projective Measure of Power
   Motivation." *Journal of Abnormal and Social Psychology,* No. 54, 1957, 1–8.
8. J. Uleman. *A New TAT Measure of the Need for Power* (Unpublished Doctoral
   Dissertation, Harvard University, 1965).
9. D. G. Winter. *Power Motivation in Thought and Action* (Unpublished Doctoral
   Dissertation, Harvard University, 1967).
10. Uleman, *op. cit.*
11. David C. McClelland et al. *Alcohol, Power and Inhibition* (Van Nostrand, 1969).
12. Winter, *op. cit.*
13. For a fuller discussion of what Weber and other social scientists have meant by
    charisma, see Samuel N. Eisenstadt, *Charisma, Institution Building, and Social
    Transformation: Max Weber and Modern Sociology* (The University of Chicago
    Press, 1968); also Robert C. Tucker, "The Theory of Charismatic Leadership."
    Daedalus, No. 97, 1968, 731–56.
14. Richard deCharms. *Personal Causation* (Academic Press, 1968).
15. Gardner, *op. cit.*
16. To be sure, if he is a gang leader, he may display actions like physical
    aggression which are characteristic of the personalized power drive. But to the
    extent that he is the leader of a large group, he is effective because he is presenting,
    by personal example, objectives for the gang which they find attractive, rather
    than because he can keep many people in line by threatening them.
17. Robert Rosenthal and Lenore Jacobson. *Pygmalion in the Classroom* (Holt,
    Rinehart and Winston, 1968).
18. Why is a successful influence attempt so often perceived as an instance of
    personal domination by the leader? One answer lies in the simplifying nature of
    social perception. The observer notices that a big change in the behavior of a
    group of people has occurred. He also can single out one or two people as
    leaders in some way involved in the change. He does not know how the leaders
    operated to bring about the change since he was not that intimately involved
    in the process. As a result, he tends to perceive the process as an instance of the
    application of personal power, as founded on a simple dominance-submission

relationship. The more effective the leader is, the more personal power tends to be attributed to him, regardless of how he has actually achieved his effects.

19. Warren G. Bennis and Philip E. Slater. *The Temporary Society* (Harper & Row, 1968).

Motivation Reconsidered: The Concept of Competence
Robert W. White

This reading is somewhat difficult, but worthwhile if one studies it for maximum understanding. White does not disagree with other theories in this chapter, but he says that they leave out two very important things. First, by viewing behavior in short time periods when a person takes one action and receives some result, they fail to explain the long, endless, coping that people do in between crises, and in between what looks like goal-directed (or drive-reduction) behavior. Second, the other theories in this chapter fail to give a sense of the very complex and endless learning or growth process. Only if one has some notion of these two things will he or she have a more complete understanding of human behavior.

When parallel trends can be observed in realms as far apart as animal behavior and psychoanalytic ego psychology, there is reason to suppose that we are witnessing a significant evolution of ideas. In these two realms, as in psychology as a whole, there is evidence of deepening discontent with theories of motivation based upon drives. Despite great differences in the language and concepts used to express this discontent, the theme is everywhere the same: Something important is left out when we make drives the operating forces in animal and human behavior.

The chief theories against which the discontent is directed are those of Hull and of Freud. In their respective realms, drive-reduction theory and psychoanalytic instinct theory, which are basically very much alike, have acquired a considerable air of orthodoxy. Both views have an appealing simplicity, and both have been argued long enough so that their main outlines are generally known. In decided contrast is the position of those who are not satisfied with drives and instincts. They are numerous, and they have developed many pointed criticisms, but what they have to say has not thus far lent itself to a clear and inclusive conceptualization. Apparently there is an enduring difficulty in making these contributions fall into shape.

In this paper I shall attempt a conceptualization which gathers up some of the important things left out by drive theory. To give the concept a name I have chosen the word *competence*, which is intended in a broad biological sense rather than in its narrow everyday meaning. As used here, competence will refer to an organism's capacity to interact effectively with its environment. In organisms capable of but little learning, this capacity might be considered an innate attribute, but in the mammals and especially man, with their highly plastic nervous systems, fitness to interact with the environment is slowly attained through prolonged feats of learning. In view of the directedness and persistence of the behavior that leads to these feats of learning, I consider it necessary to treat competence as having a motivational aspect, and my central argument will be that the motivation needed to attain competence cannot be wholly derived from sources of energy currently conceptualized as drives or instincts. We need a different kind of motivational idea to account fully for the fact that man and the higher mammals develop a competence in dealing with the environment which they certainly do not have at birth and certainly do not arrive at simply through maturation. Such an idea, I believe, is essential for any biologically sound view of human nature.[1]

EFFECTANCE

The new freedom produced by two decades of research on animal drives is of great help in this undertaking. We are no longer obliged to look for a source of energy external to the nervous system, for a consummatory climax, or for a fixed connection between reinforcement and tension-reduction. Effectance motivation cannot, of course, be conceived as having a source in tissues external to the nervous system. It is in no sense a deficit motive. We must assume it to be neurogenic, its "energies" being simply those of the living cells that make up the nervous system. External stimuli play an important part, but in terms of "energy" this part is secondary, as one can see most clearly when environmental stimulation is actively sought. Putting it picturesquely, we might say that the effectance urge represents what the neuromuscular system wants to do when it is otherwise unoccupied or is gently stimulated by the environment. Obviously there are no consummatory acts; satisfaction would appear to lie in the arousal and maintaining of activity rather than in its slow decline toward bored passivity. The motive need not be conceived as intense and powerful in the sense that hunger, pain, or fear can be powerful when aroused to high pitch. There are plenty of instances in which children refuse to leave their absorbed play in order to eat or to visit the toilet. Strongly aroused drives, pain, and anxiety, however, can be conceived as overriding the effectance urge and capturing the energies of the neuromuscular system. But effectance motivation is persistent in the sense that it regularly occupies the spare waking time between episodes of homeostatic crisis.

In speculating upon this subject we must bear in mind the continuous nature of behavior. This is easier said than done; habitually we break things down in order to understand them, and such units as the reflex arc, the stimulus-response sequence, and the single transaction with the environment seem like inevitable steps toward clarity. Yet when we apply such an analysis to playful exploration we lose the most essential aspect of the behavior. It is constantly circling from stimulus to perception to action to effect to stimulus to perception, and so on around; or, more properly, these processes are all in continuous action and continuous change. Dealing with the environment means carrying on a continuing transaction which gradually changes one's relation to the environment. Because there is no consummatory climax, satisfaction has to be seen as lying in a considerable series of transactions, in a trend of behavior rather than a goal that is achieved. It is difficult to make the word "satisfaction" have this connotation, and we shall do well to replace it by "feeling of efficacy" when attempting to indicate the subjective and affective side of effectance.

It is useful to recall the findings about novelty: the singular effectiveness of novelty

---

[1] For an elaboration of these points, omitted here, the reader is referred to pp. 297–321 of the original.

in engaging interest and for a time supporting persistent behavior. We also need to consider the selective continuance of transactions in which the animal or child has a more or less pronounced effect upon the environment—in which something happens as a consequence of his activity. Interest is not aroused and sustained when the stimulus field is so familiar that it gives rise at most to reflex acts or automatized habits. It is not sustained when actions produce no effects or changes in the stimulus field. Our conception must therefore be that effectance motivation is aroused by stimulus conditions which offer, as Hebb (1949) puts it, difference-in-sameness. This leads to variability and novelty of response, and interest is best sustained when the resulting action affects the stimulus so as to produce further difference-in-sameness. Interest wanes when action begins to have less effect; effectance motivation subsides when a situation has been explored to the point that it no longer presents new possibilities.

We have to conceive further that the arousal of playful and exploratory interest means the appearance of organization involving both the cognitive and active aspects of behavior. Change in the stimulus field is not an end in itself, so to speak; it happens when one is passively moved about, and it may happen as a consequence of random movements without becoming focalized and instigating exploration. Similarly, action which has effects is not an end in itself, for if one unintentionally kicks away a branch while walking, or knocks something off a table, these effects by no means necessarily become involved in playful investigation. Schachtel's (1954) emphasis on focal attention becomes helpful at this point. The playful and exploratory behavior shown by Laurent is not random or casual. It involves focal *attention* to some object—the fixing of some aspect of the stimulus field so that it stays relatively constant—and it also involves the focalizing of *action* upon this object. As Diamond (1939) has expressed it, response under these conditions is "relevant to the stimulus," and it is change in the *focalized* stimulus that so strongly affects the level of interest. Dealing with the environment means directing focal attention to some part of it and organizing actions to have some effect on this part.

In our present state of relative ignorance about the workings of the nervous system it is impossible to form a satisfactory idea of the neural basis of effectance motivation, but it should at least be clear that the concept does not refer to any and every kind of neural action. It refers to a particular kind of activity, as inferred from particular kinds of behavior. We can say that it does not include reflexes and other kinds of automatic response. It does not include well-learned, automatized patterns, even those that are complex and highly organized. It does not include behavior in the service of effectively aroused drives. It does not even include activity that is highly random and discontinuous, though such behavior may be its most direct forerunner. The urge toward competence is inferred specifically from behavior that shows a lasting focalization and that has the characteristics of exploration and experimentation, a kind of variation within the focus. When this particular sort of activity is aroused in the nervous system, effectance motivation is being aroused, for it is characteristic of this particular sort of activity that it is selective, directed, and persistent, and that instrumental acts will be learned for the sole reward of engaging in it.

Some objection may be felt to my introducing the word *competence* in connection with behavior that is so often playful. Certainly the playing child is doing things for fun, not because of a desire to improve his competence in dealing with the stern hard world. In order to forestall misunderstanding, it should be pointed out that the usage here is parallel to what we do when we connect sex with its biological goal of reproduction. The sex drive aims for pleasure and gratification, and reproduction is a consequence that is presumably unforeseen by animals and by man at primitive levels of understanding. Effectance motivation similarly aims for the feeling of efficacy, not for the vitally important learnings that come as its consequence. If we consider the part played by competence motivation in adult human life we can observe the same parallel. Sex may now be completely and purposefully divorced from reproduction but nevertheless pursued for the pleasure it can yield. Similarly, effectance motivation may lead to continuing exploratory interests or active adventures when in fact there is no longer any gain in actual competence or any need for it in terms of survival. In both cases the motive is capable of yielding surplus satisfaction well beyond what is necessary to get the biological work done.

In infants and young children it seems to me sensible to conceive of effectance motivation as undifferentiated. Later in life it becomes profitable to distinguish various motives such as cognizance, construction, mastery, and achievement. It is my view that all such motives have a root in effectance motivation. They are differentiated from it through life experiences which emphasize one or another aspect of the cycle of transaction with environment. Of course, the motives of later childhood and of adult life are no longer simple and can almost never be referred to a single root. They can acquire loadings of anxiety, defense, and compensation, they can become fused with unconscious fantasies of a sexual, aggressive, or omnipotent character, and they can gain force because of their service in producing realistic results in the way of income and career. It is not my intention to cast effectance in the star part in adult motivation. The acquisition of motives is a complicated affair in which simple and sovereign theories grow daily more obsolete. Yet it may be that the satisfaction of effectance contributes significantly to those feelings of interest which often sustain us so well in day-to-day actions, particularly when the things we are doing have continuing elements of novelty.

THE BIOLOGICAL SIGNIFICANCE OF COMPETENCE

The conviction was expressed at the beginning of this paper that some such concept as competence, interpreted motivationally, was essential for any biologically sound view of human nature. This necessity emerges when we consider the nature of living systems, particularly when we take a longitudinal view. What an organism does at a given moment does not always give the right clue as to what it does over a period of time. Discussing this problem, Angyal (1941) has proposed that we should look for the general pattern followed by the total organismic process over the course of time. Obviously this makes it necessary to take account of growth. Angyal defines life as "a process of self-expansion"; the living system "expands at the expense of its surroundings," assimilating parts of the environment and transforming them into functioning parts of itself. Organisms differ from other things in nature in that they are "self-governing entities" which are to some extent "autonomous." Internal processes govern them as well as external "heteronomous" forces. In the course of life there is a relative increase in the preponderance of internal over external forces. The living system expands, assimilates more of the environment, transforms its surroundings so as to bring them under greater control. "We may say," Angyal writes, "that the general dynamic trend of the organism is toward an increase of autonomy. . . . The human being has a characteristic tendency toward self-determination, that is, a tendency to resist external influences and to subordinate the heteronomous forces of the physical and social environment to its own sphere of influence." The trend toward increased autonomy is characteristic so long as growth of any kind is going on, though in the end the living system is bound to succumb to the pressure of heteronomous forces.

Of all living creatures, it is man who takes the longest strides toward autonomy. This is not because of any unusual tendency toward bodily expansion at the expense of the environment. It is rather that man, with his mobile hands and abundantly developed brain, attains an extremely high level of competence in his transactions with his surroundings. The building of houses, roads and bridges, the making of tools and instruments, the domestication of plants and animals, all qualify as planful changes made in the environment so that it comes more or less under control and serves our purposes rather than intruding upon them. We meet the fluctuations of outdoor temperature, for example, not only with our bodily homeostatic mechanisms, which alone would be painfully unequal to the task, but also with clothing, buildings, controlled fires, and such complicated devices as self-regulating central heating and air conditioning. Man as a species has developed a tremendous power of bringing the environment into his service, and each individual member of the species must attain what is really quite an impressive level of competence if he is to take part in the life around him.

We are so accustomed to these human accomplishments that it is hard to realize how long an apprenticeship they require. At the outset the human infant is a slow learner in comparison with other animal forms. Hebb (1949) speaks of "the astonishing inefficiency of man's first learning, as far as immediate results are concerned," an inefficiency which he attributes to the large size of the association areas in the brain and the long time needed to bring them under sensory control. The human lack of precocity in learning shows itself even in comparison with one of the next of kin: as Hebb points out, "the human baby takes six months, the chimpanzee four months, before making a clear distinction between friend and enemy." Later in life the slow start will pay dividends. Once the fundamental perceptual elements, simple associations, and conceptual sequences have been established, later learning can proceed with ever increasing swiftness and complexity. In Hebb's words, "learning at maturity concerns patterns and events whose parts at least are familiar and which already have a number of other associations."

This general principle of cumulative learning, starting from slowly acquired rudiments and proceeding thence with increasing efficiency, can be illustrated by such processes as manipulation and locomotion, which may culminate in the acrobat devising new stunts or the dancer working out a new ballet. It is especially vivid in the case of language, where the early mastery of words and pronunciation seems such a far cry from spontaneous adult speech. A strong argument has been made by Hebb (1949) that the learning of visual forms proceeds over a similar course from slowly learned elements to rapidly combined patterns. Circles and squares, for example, cannot be discriminated at a glance without a slow apprenticeship involving eye movements, successive fixations, and recognition of angles. Hebb proposes that the recognition of visual patterns without eye movement "is possible only as the result of an intensive and prolonged visual training that goes on from the moment of birth, during every moment that the eyes are open, with an increase in skill evident over a period of 12 to 16 years at least."

On the motor side there is likewise a lot to be cumulatively learned. The playing, investigating child slowly finds out the relationships between what he does and what he experiences. He finds out, for instance, how hard he must push what in order to produce what effect. Here the S-R formula is particularly misleading. It would come nearer the truth to say that the child is busy learning R-S connections—the effects that are likely to follow upon his own behavior. But even in this reversed form the notion of bonds or connections would still misrepresent the situation, for it is only a rare specimen of behavior that can properly be conceived as determined by fixed neural channels and a fixed motor response. As Hebb has pointed out, discussing the phenomenon of "motor equivalence" named by Lashley (1942), a rat which has been trained to press a lever will press it with the left forepaw, the right forepaw, by climbing upon it, or by biting it; a monkey will open the lid of a food box with either hand, with a foot, or even with a stick; and we might add that a good baseball player can catch a fly ball while running in almost any direction and while in almost any posture, including leaping in the air and plunging forward to the ground. All of these feats are possible because of a history of learnings in which the main lesson has been the effects of actions upon the stimulus fields that represent the environment. What has been learned is not a fixed connection but a flexible relationship between stimulus fields and the effects that can be produced in them by various kinds of action.

One additional example, drawn this time from Piaget (1952), is particularly worth mentioning because of its importance in theories of development. Piaget points out that a great deal of mental development depends upon the idea that the world is made up of objects having substance and permanence. Without such an "object concept" it would be impossible to build up the ideas of space and causality and to arrive at the fundamental distinction between self and external world. Observation shows that the object concept, "far from being innate or readymade in experience, is constructed little by little." Up to 7 and 8 months the Piaget children searched for vanished objects only in the sense of trying to continue the actions, such as sucking or grasping, in which the objects had played a part. When an object was really out of sight or touch, even if only because it was covered by a cloth, the infants undertook no further exploration. Only gradually, after some study of the displacement of objects by moving, swinging, and dropping them, does the child begin to make an active search for a vanished object, and only still more gradually does he learn, at 12 months or more, to make allowance for the object's sequential displacements and thus to seek it where it has gone rather than where it was last in sight. Thus it is only through cumulative learning that the child arrives at the idea of permanent substantial objects.

The infant's play is indeed serious business. If he did not while away his time pulling strings, shaking rattles, examining wooden parrots, dropping pieces of bread and celluloid swans, when would he learn to discriminate visual patterns, to catch and throw, and to build up his concept of the object? When would he acquire the many other foundation stones necessary for cumulative learning? The more closely we analyze the behavior of the human infant, the more clearly do we realize that infancy is not simply a time when the nervous system matures and the muscles grow stronger. It is a time of active and continuous learning, during which the basis is laid for all those processes, cognitive and motor, whereby the child becomes able to establish effective transactions with his environment and move toward a greater degree of autonomy. Helpless as he may seem until he begins to toddle, he has by that time already made substantial gains in the achievement of competence.

Under primitive conditions survival must depend quite heavily upon achieved competence. We should expect to find things so arranged as to favor and maximize this achievement. Particularly in the case of man, where so little is provided innately and so much has to be learned through experience, we should expect to find highly advantageous arrangements for securing a steady cumulative learning about the properties of the environment and the extent of possible transactions. Under these circumstances we might expect to find a very powerful drive operating to insure progress toward competence, just as the vital goals of nutrition and reproduction are secured by powerful drives, and it might therefore seem paradoxical that the interests of competence should be so much entrusted to times of play and leisurely exploration. There is good reason to suppose, however, that a strong drive would be precisely the wrong arrangement to secure a flexible, knowledgeable power of transaction with the environment. Strong drives cause us to learn certain lessons well, but they do not create maximum familiarity with our surroundings.

This point was demonstrated half a century ago in some experiments by Yerkes and Dodson (1908). They showed that maximum motivation did not lead to the most rapid solving of problems, especially if the problems were complex. For each problem there was an optimum level of motivation, neither the highest nor the lowest, and the optimum was lower for more complex tasks. The same problem has been discussed more recently by Tolman (1948) in his paper on cognitive maps. A cognitive map can be narrow or broad, depending upon the range of cues picked up in the course of learning. Tolman suggests that one of the conditions which tend to narrow the range of cues is a high level of motivation. In everyday terms, a man hurrying to an important business conference is likely to perceive only the cues that help him to get there faster, whereas a man taking a stroll after lunch is likely to pick up a substantial amount of casual information about his environment. The latent learning experiments with animals, and experiments such as those of Johnson (1953) in which drive level has been systematically varied in a situation permitting incidental learning, give strong support to this general idea. In a recent contribution, Bruner, Matter, and Papanek (1955) make a strong case for the concept of breadth of learning and provide additional evidence that it is favored by moderate and hampered by strong motivation. The latter "has the effect of speeding up learning at the cost of narrowing it." Attention is concentrated upon the task at hand and little that is extraneous to this task is learned for future use.

These facts enable us to see the biological appropriateness of an arrangement which uses periods of less intense motivation for the development of competence. This is not to say that the narrower but efficient learnings that go with the reduction of strong drives make no contribution to general effectiveness. They are certainly an important element in capacity to deal with the environment, but a much greater effectiveness results from having this capacity fed also from learnings that take place in quieter times. It is then that the infant can attend to matters of lesser urgency, exploring the properties of things he does not fear and does not need to eat, learning to gauge the force of his string-pulling when the only penalty for failure is silence on the part of the attached rattles, and generally accumulating for himself a broad knowledge and a broad skill in dealing with his surroundings.

REFERENCES

Angyal, A. *Foundations for a Science of Personality.* Commonwealth Fund, 1941.

Bruner, J. S., J. Matter, and M. L. Papanek. "Breadth of Learning as a Function of Drive Level and Mechanization." *Psychological Review*, Vol. 62 (1955), 1–10.

Diamond, S. "A Neglected Aspect of Motivation." *Sociometry*, Vol. 2 (1939), 77–85.

Hebb, D. O. *The Organization of Behavior.* Wiley, 1949.

Johnson, E. E. "The Role of Motivational Strength in Latent Learning." *Journal of Comparative Physiology and Psychology*, Vol. 45 (1953), 526–30.

Lashley, K. S. "The Problem of Cerebral Organization in Vision." In *Visual Mechanisms*, ed. H. Kluver, pp. 301–22. Jacques Cattell, 1942.

Piaget, J. *The Origins of Intelligence in Children*, tr. M. Cook. International University Press, 1952.

Schachtel, E. G. "The Development of Focal Attention and the Emergence of Reality." *Psychiatry*, Vol. 17 (1954), 309–24.

Tolman, E. C. "Cognitive Maps of Rats and Men." *Psychological Review*, Vol. 55 (1948), 189–208.

Yerkes, R. M., and J. D. Dodson. "The Relation of Strength of Stimulus to Rapidity of Habit-Formation." *Journal of Comparative Neurology*, Vol. 18 (1908), 459–82.

Expectancy Theory

John P. Campbell, Marvin D. Dunnette, Edward E. Lawler III, and
Karl E. Weick, Jr.

*This reading will give a more complete explanation of expectancy theory than that
presented in the chapter text. The authors give the term "first level outcome" to
what was called "instrumental payoffs" in the text, and "second level outcomes"
for what the text called "basic payoffs." In addition, these authors clearly see the
instrumental (first-level) payoffs as they look in a work organization. That is, when
a person is "thinking through what he will do," instrumental payoffs are the various
incentives — pay, promotion, time off — provided by management. If the person carries
through the action and is successful, these same payoffs are then "rewards." The
authors also clarify one point the text did not: The basic payoffs differ in their value
to a person. Borrowing a term from physics, the weight of one basic payoff compared
to another is called its valence.*

EARLY COGNITIVE THEORIES

Concomitant with the development of drive x habit theory, Lewin (1938) and Tolman
(1932) developed and investigated cognitive, or expectancy, theories of motivation.
Even though Lewin was concerned with human subjects and Tolman worked largely
with animals, much of their respective theorizing contained common elements. Basic
to the cognitive view of motivation is the notion that individuals have cognitive *expectancies* concerning the outcomes that are likely to occur as the result of what they
do, and that individuals have preferences among outcomes. That is, an individual has
an "idea" about possible consequences of his acts, and he makes conscious choices
among consequences according to their probability of occurrence and their value to
him.

Thus, for the cognitive theorist, it is the anticipation of reward that energizes behavior and the perceived value of various outcomes that gives behavior its direction.
Tolman spoke of a *belief-value* matrix that specifies for each individual the value he
places on particular outcomes and his belief that they can be attained.

Atkinson (1964) has compared drive theory and expectancy theory. Although he
points out some differences, he emphasizes that both theories are actually quite similar
and contain many of the same concepts. Both include the notion of a reward or favorable outcome that is desired, and both postulate a learned connection contained within
the organism. For expectancy theory this learned connection is a behavior-outcome
expectancy, and for drive theory it is an S-R habit strength.

However, the theories differ in two ways which are important for research on
motivation in an organizational setting. For example, they differ in what they state is
activated by the anticipation of reward. Expectancy theory sees the anticipation of a
reward as functioning selectively on actions expected to lead to it. Drive theory views
the magnitude of the anticipated goals as a source of general excitement — a nonselec-
tive influence on performance.

Expectancy theory is also much looser in specifying how expectancy-outcome
connections are built up. Drive theory postulates that S-R habit strengths are built up

through repeated associations of stimulus and response; that is, the reward or outcome must actually have followed the response to a particular stimulus in order for the *S-R* connection to operate in future choice behavior. Such a process is sufficient but not necessary for forming expectancy-outcome relationships. An individual may form expectancies vicariously (someone may tell him that complimenting the boss's wife leads to a promotion, for example) or by other symbolic means. This last point is crucial since the symbolic (cognitive) manipulation of various *S-R* situations seems quite descriptive of a great deal of human behavior.

These two differences make the cognitive or expectancy point of view much more useful for studying human motivation in an organizational setting. In fact, it is the one which has been given the most attention by theorists concerned with behavior in organizations.

INSTRUMENTALITY-VALENCE THEORY

Building on expectancy theory and its later amplifications by Atkinson (1958), W. Edwards (1954), Peak (1955), and Rotter (1955), Vroom (1964) has presented a process theory of work motivation that he calls *instrumentality theory.* His basic classes of variables are expectancies, valences, choices, outcomes, and instrumentalities.

Expectancy is defined as a belief concerning the likelihood that a particular act will be followed by a particular outcome. Presumably, the degree of belief can vary between 0 (complete lack of belief that it will follow) and 1 (complete certainty that it will). Note that it is the perception of the individual that is important, not the objective reality. This same concept has been referred to as *subjective probability* by others (e.g., W. Edwards, 1954).

Valence refers to the strength of an individual's preference for a particular outcome. An individual may have either a positive or a negative preference for an outcome; presumably, outcomes gain their valence as a function of the degree to which they are seen to be related to the needs of the individual. However, this last point is not dealt with concretely in Vroom's formulation. As an example of these two concepts, one might consider an increase in pay to be a possible outcome of a particular act. The theory would then deal with the valence of a wage increase for an individual and his expectancy that particular behaviors will be followed by a wage increase outcome. Again, valence refers to the perceived or expected value of an outcome, not its real or eventual value.

According to Vroom, outcomes take on a valence value because of their *instrumentality* for achieving other outcomes. Thus he is really postulating two classes of outcomes. In the organizational setting, the first class of outcomes might include such things as money, promotion, recognition, etc. Supposedly, these outcomes are directly linked to behavior. However, as Vroom implicitly suggests, wage increases or promotion may have no value by themselves. They are valuable in terms of their instrumental role in securing second level outcomes such as food, clothing, shelter, entertainment, and status, which are not obtained as the direct result of a particular action.

According to Vroom, instrumentality, like correlation, varies between +1.0 and −1.0. Thus a first level outcome may be seen as always leading to some desired second level outcome (+1.0) or as never leading to the second level outcome (−1.0). In Vroom's theory the formal definition of valence for a first level outcome is the sum of the products between its instrumentalities for all possible second level outcomes and their respective valences.

To sum up, Vroom's formulation postulates that the motivational force, or effort, an individual exerts is a function of (1) his expectancy that certain outcomes will result from his behavior (e.g., a raise in pay for increased effort) and (2) the valence, for him, of those outcomes. The valence of an outcome is in turn a function of its instrumentality for obtaining other outcomes and the valence of these other outcomes.

51

Campbell et al.:
Expectancy Theory

A HYBRID EXPECTANCY MODEL

Since his formulation first appeared, a number of investigators have attempted to extend Vroom's model to make it more explicit and more inclusive in terms of relevant variables (Graen, 1967; L. W. Porter & Lawler, 1968). Although we shall not discuss the contributions of these writers in detail, we would like to incorporate a number of their ideas in our own composite picture of an expanded expectancy model. However, any imperfections in what follows should be ascribed to us and not to them.

One major addition to Vroom's model is the necessity for a more concrete specification of the task or performance goals toward which work behavior is directed. Graen (1967) refers to this class of variables as *work roles*, but we prefer to retain the notion of *task goals*. Task goals may be specified externally by the organization or the work group, or internally by the individual's own value system. Examples of task goals include such things as production quotas, time limits for projects, quality standards, showing a certain amount of loyalty to the organization, exhibiting the right set of attitudes, etc.

We would also like to make more explicit a distinction between first and second level outcomes. First level outcomes are outcomes contingent on achieving the task goal or set of task goals. A potential first level outcome is synonymous with the term "incentive," and an outcome which is actually realized is synonymous with the term "reward." The distinction is temporal. Like task goals, first level outcomes may be external or internal. Some examples of external first level outcomes granted by the organization are job security, pay, promotions, recognition, and increased autonomy. An individual may also set up his own internal incentives or reward himself with internally mediated outcomes such as ego satisfaction.

As pointed out in the discussion of Vroom's model, first level outcomes may or may not be associated with a plethora of second level outcomes; that is, the externally or internally mediated rewards are instrumental in varying degrees for obtaining second level outcomes such as food, housing, material goods, community status, and freedom from anxiety.

The concepts of valence for first and second level outcomes and the instrumentality of first for second level outcomes are defined as before, but the notion of expectancy decomposes into two different variables. First, individuals may have expectancies concerning whether or not they will actually accomplish the task goal if they expend effort (expectancy I); that is, an individual makes a subjective probability estimate concerning his chances for reaching a particular goal, given a particular situation. For example, a manufacturing manager may think the odds of his getting a new product into production by the first of the year are about 3 to 1 (i.e., expectancy I = 0.75). Perhaps the primary determiner of expectancy I is how the individual perceives his own job skills in the context of what is specified as his task goals and the various difficulties and external constraints standing in the way of accomplishing them. Certainly, then, an employee's perceptions of his own talents determine to a large degree the direction and intensity of his job behavior. This first kind of expectancy should be more salient for more complex and higher level tasks such as those involved in managing.

Second, individuals possess expectancies concerning whether or not achievement of specified task goals will actually be followed by the first level outcome (expectancy II). In other words, they form subjective probability estimates of the degree to which rewards are *contingent* on achieving task goals. The individual must ask himself what the probability is that his achievement of the goal will be rewarded by the organization. For example, the manufacturing manager may be virtually certain (expectancy II = 1.0) that if he does get the new product into production by the first of the year, he will receive a promotion and a substantial salary increase. Or, and this may be the more usual case, he may see no relationship at all between meeting the objective and getting a promotion and salary increase.

None of the authors cited so far have explicitly labeled these two kinds of expectancies. Indeed, in a laboratory or other experimental setting the distinction may not be necessary since the task may be so easy that accomplishing the goal is always a certainty (i.e., expectancy I is 1.0 for everybody) or the contingency of reward on behavior may be certain and easily verified by the subject (i.e., expectancy II is 1.0 for everybody). Vroom (1964) defines expectancy as an action-outcome relationship which is represented by an individual's subjective probability estimate that a particular set of behaviors will be followed by a particular outcome. Since Vroom presents no concrete definitions for the terms "action" and "outcome," his notion of expectancy could include both expectancy I and expectancy II as defined above. Thus effort expenditure could be regarded as an action, and goal performance as an outcome; or performance could be considered behavior, and money an outcome. Vroom uses both kinds of examples to illustrate the expectancy variable and makes no conceptual distinction between them. However, in the organizational setting, the distinction seems quite necessary. Rewards may or may not be contingent on goal accomplishment, and the individual may or may not believe he has the wherewithal to reach the goal. A schematic representation of this hybrid model is shown in Figure 1.

We have purposely been rather vague concerning the exact form of the relationships between these different classes of variables. This schematic model is in no way meant to be a formal theory. To propose explicit multiplicative combinations or other configural or higher order functions is going a bit too far beyond our present measurement capability. Rather, we shall sum up the relationships contained in our expanded model as follows:

1. The valence of a first level outcome (incentive or reward) is a function of the instrumentality of that outcome for obtaining second level outcomes (need satisfactions) and the valences of the relevant second level outcomes.

2. The decision by an individual to work on a particular task and expend a certain amount of effort in that direction is a function of (*a*) his personal probability estimate that he can accomplish the task (expectancy I), (*b*) his personal probability estimate that his accomplishment of the task goal will be followed by certain first level outcomes or rewards (expectancy II), and (*c*) the valence of the first level outcomes.

3. The distinction between external and internal goals and rewards leads to a number of potential conflict situations for the individual. For example, an individual might estimate his chances for accomplishing a particular task as virtually certain (i.e., expectancy I = 1.0). However, the internal rewards which are virtually certain to follow (i.e., expectancy II = 1.0) may have a very low or even negative valence (e.g., feelings of extreme boredom or distaste). If external rewards, such as a lot of money, have a very high valence, a serious stress situation could result from outcomes which have conflicting valences. It would be to an organization's advantage to ensure positive

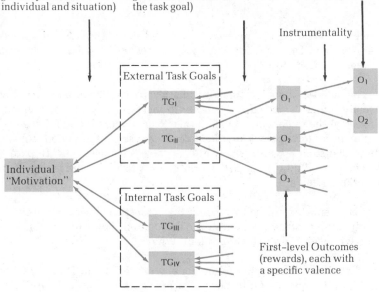

Expectancy I
(perceived probability of
goal accomplishment,
given a particular
individual and situation)

Expectancy II
(perceived probability of
receiving first-level outcome,
given achievement of
the task goal)

Second-level Outcomes
(needs), each with
a specific valence

Instrumentality

External Task Goals

Internal Task Goals

Individual
"Motivation"

First-level Outcomes
(rewards), each with
a specific valence

Figure 1 A Schematic Representation of a Hybrid
Expectancy Model of Work Motivation

valences for both internal and external rewards. Other conflict situations could be
produced by high positive valences for outcomes and low estimates of type I expectancies (i.e., the individual does not think he can actually do the job).

REFERENCES

Atkinson, J. S., Ed. *Motives in Fantasy, Action and Society.* Van Nostrand, 1958.
————. *An Introduction to Motivation.* Van Nostrand, 1964.
Edwards, W. "The Theory of Decision Making." *Psychological Bulletin,* Vol. 51
    (1954), 380–417.
Graen, G. B. *Work Motivation: The Behavioral Effects of Job Content and Job Context
    Factors in an Employment Situation.* Unpub. Ph.D. dissertation, University of
    Minnesota, 1967.
Lewin, K. *The Conceptual Representation and the Measurement of Psychological
    Forces.* Duke University Press, 1938.
Peak, H. "Attitude and Motivation." In *Nebraska Symposium on Motivation,* ed.
    M. R. Jones, pp. 149–88. University of Nebraska Press, 1955.
Porter, L. W., and E. E. Lawler III. *Managerial Attitudes and Performance.* Dorsey-
    Irwin, 1968.
Rotter, J. B. "The Role of the Psychological Situation in Determining the Direction of
    Human Behavior." In *Nebraska Symposium on Motivation, op. cit.,* 1955.
Tolman, E. C. *Purposive Behavior in Animals and Men.* Century (by permission of
    the University of California Press, 1932).
Vroom, V. H. *Work and Motivation.* Wiley, 1964.

Questions for Discussion

1.   In much of West Africa, managers have had great difficulty in attracting and holding employees in factory work. They work a few weeks, collect their money, and go back to their villages. Why?

2.   The graduated personal federal income tax (rising above 90 percent at upper levels) severely limits the executive's ability to increase his or her take-home pay by salary increases at the top organizational levels. Recently, the Internal Revenue Service has been attempting to tax stock dividends and bonuses at the same income tax rate. Do you think that such taxes adversely affect business management? In particular, do you think such taxes limit the business world's ability to attract and motivate ambitious and hard-working people?

3.   In spite of repeated efforts to organize them, most engineers and professors have refused to join unions. Many might even agree that strong collective action would help them as a body, but they do not want to join. Why?

4.   Harry Levinson reported the following observation in "Is There an Obsolescent Executive in Your Company — Or in Your Chair?" (*Think*, Jan.–Feb. 1968): "Some years ago I taught at a widely known university which offered two advanced graduate programs for executives. One group of men was between 30 and 38 years old, and the other between 45 and 55. The older group seemed less willing to learn and less able to look at alternative courses of action. They seemed to have more at stake in already fixed positions which they did not want to examine." Why might this be so?

5.   In many organizations there is little or no consistent relationship between pay, promotion, and performance. Discuss the motivational implications of this condition. What theory of motivation helps explain these implications?

6.   Discuss the needs or motives that would predispose an individual to perform effectively each of the following tasks: union business agent or union steward, college textbook sales representative, high school student counselor, insurance sales rep, mass-production line foreman.

7.   Often, the basis for selecting a sales manager out of the sales staff is performance as a sales rep. Why might picking a highly effective and highly achievement-oriented sales rep for the job of sales manager be a mistake?

8.   According to Herzberg's motivator-hygiene theory, and drawing on your knowledge of human needs, why might the same routine, lower-level job be positively motivating in underdeveloped countries, like Ethiopia, yet nonmotivating in developed countries?

Cases for Discussion

The Community of Scholars

When I was working on my MBA degree I became involved with a group of fellow students in publishing a student evaluation of professors. This was done as a project of the Business Students Association. We informally solicited opinions from students on all faculty members. There was no standard questionnaire, no systematic sampling; we just asked people at coffee, in classes, and around the campus. We got together and pooled our inputs.

Next we decided to organize the information in three categories: quality of instruction, grading, and workload. We gave grades for quality of instruction: A for excellent, B for good, C for average, and D for poor. We gave numbers for grading and workload. For grading 1 meant stringent, 4 meant liberal, 2 and 3 meant degrees in between. For workload 1 meant heavy, 4 meant light, 2 and 3 meant degrees in between.

We dropped the bomb in the middle of the spring quarter. That is, we printed the evaluation and mailed a copy to each student, administrator, and faculty member. The reaction we got was unbelievable. Here are excerpts from a few letters, written in reaction by professors and administrators, all of which were critical of our action:

"Since you 'solicit and encourage input from the administration, faculty members . . .' let me provide you with some. As you know, I have encouraged your organization to work on some means of reporting to us on your classroom experiences.

"I feel, however, that your initial attempt will impede rather than assist your efforts in providing significant feedback. The evaluation seems to be more a product of haste than care."

"In reply to the gross distortions contained in the recent BSA release, entitled 'Faculty Evaluation,' first, let me assure you that I am very much in favor of faculty evaluations so long as they are conducted professionally, scientifically, and under officially recognized and qualified supervision. Furthermore, the University has provided that faculty evaluations be regularly made so there is no real need for an additional evaluation, unless someone has a personal reason for developing his own. The Evaluation stated it was evaluating courses but ended in evaluating faculty. Why?"

"I have had some discussions with the officers of the BSA concerning the Faculty Evaluation that was published by the Association and distributed to the faculty at the beginning of the week, and have come to the conclusion that this was not the result of a scientific evaluation of the faculty's teaching abilities. My view concerning this Evaluation as it now stands is that it has no validity whatsoever, and it is my hope that the faculty will totally disregard the ratings."

I had conversations with several professors (who did not know I was involved in the evaluation) and noted the following reactions:

"Students should never have been allowed to do this."

"I think this thing is just the last straw. The legislature is against us, the public, the governor, and the trustees are giving us a very bad time, and now the students have turned on us. It just touched a sore spot and while we can't react to all our other adversaries we can react to this one."

"One of our political animals, Professor Blank, was partly to blame for this. He spent a lot of time with the BSA students who prepared the Evaluation, before they did it. It would be altogether out of character, I think, for him to spend his time in this way out of an innocent desire to encourage student participation."

"I think the ratings were about 90 percent accurate. I can't think of a single instance where anybody was any more than one grade off."

"The Dean's comment about achieving scientific validity was crass hypocrisy. Does he mean scientific validity equal to that we achieve when we grade students? But I am not going to tell him—I haven't got tenure."

"I was surprised to see myself as being somewhat liberal in grading and really surprised, not happily, to see myself as giving a light workload. I'll have to do something about that."

Questions

1.   What accounts for the intense reactions of faculty and administrators?

2.   What concepts in the chapter might explain some of the reactions?

Adamson Advertising

Adamson Advertising Agency is a middle-size agency in a large southern city. I worked there as an artist for six years.

When I started at Adamson, the departments were organized along functional lines. All the creative types were in one major creative group. It was divided into such departments as art, copy, television and radio production, and newspaper and magazine production. The other major groups were marketing and account executives.

An account executive was assigned to manage each account. He was to direct a team drawn from creative and marketing personnel and provide service for the client. For several reasons this arrangement was not working well.

We kept adding and losing accounts rapidly. The creative and other employees were supposed to approach the client only after checking with the account executive, but they were making independent contacts. Sometimes the account executive was the last to hear about changes.

To cope with all of these problems, top management reorganized the agency. The old functional departments were broken up into new organizational units built around each client. This strengthened the position of the account executive, and he was able to control his team better.

Employees were physically regrouped according to the new organization. This meant that artists no longer sat with other artists exclusively. More likely the artist sat with a copywriter, a market research man, a television production man, and so on.

I noticed after several months that another change had occurred. Formerly a man had been evaluated mostly on his skill as a professional. Now, what seemed more important was his ability to satisfy the client. Meeting a deadline was valued more than the niceties of art work. I suppose that this was good for the business, but it had serious effects on those people whose job satisfaction came mostly from being good artists, writers, or whatever.

In fact, the creative personnel grumbled a great deal, and several of them quit within a year, saying that the job just was not what it used to be.

Question

How might motivational concepts discussed in this chapter explain the reaction of the creative employees who grumbled and quit?

Chapter Two

Power and Influence

The Bases of Power

Influence Processes
Influence Through Fear
Influence Through Tradition
Influence by Blind Faith
Influence Through Rational Agreement
Influence Through Joint Determination

Exercising Influence

A graduating business student is seeking a position in the communications industry. He is fortunate to have been granted an interview with the president of a major television network, a young, dynamic personality who has made it to the top while still in his thirties. While the student is describing his study of organizational management and situational leadership, the president interrupts him with a forceful, "That's all nonsense! The only thing that counts with a manager is whether he can impose his will on the other guy."

The television executive may be focusing too narrowly on "imposing," but certainly a central aspect of a manager's job is to *influence* others to do certain things. Power and influence are basic facts of organizational life. Unfortunately, in spite of (or perhaps because of) the widespread use of the terms "influence," "power," and "authority," no consistent and universally accepted definitions exist. We shall use them as follows: *influence* is the process by which one person follows another's advice, suggestion, or order; *power* is a personal or positional attribute which is the base of an influencer's influence; and *authority* is only one of several power bases — one which is granted to influencer-managers by higher organizational officials (Peabody, 1964).

THE BASES OF POWER

Thus, when someone is influenced by another, we infer that the influencer possesses power. Influence implies power, and power is necessary for influence. But power is not just the brute force of coercing a reluctant follower. It takes many forms (French and Raven, 1959):

Coercive power is based on a follower's perception that an influencer has the ability to inflict punishment — and that the punishment will be unpleasant or will frustrate some need.

Reward power is based on a follower's perception that an influencer has the capacity to administer some reward, and that the reward will be pleasant or will satisfy some need.

Legitimate power is based upon a follower's internalized values which convince him or her that an influencer has the legitimate right to influence — and that he or she is bound to accept. This base of power is at the core of a traditional influence system where leadership positions are endowed with formal authority.

Referent power is based on a follower's desire to identify with a charismatic leader, who is followed out of blind faith. The identification can be maintained so long as the follower behaves as the leader directs.

Expert power is based on a follower's perception that the leader has special knowledge or expertise which can be useful in satisfying some need of the follower.

Representative power is based on followers democratically delegating power to the leader for the purpose of representing their interests and making decisions in their behalf.

You will note that in each of these definitions of the various bases of power the role of the follower is crucial. If you are holding a loaded gun to my head, and if you communicate a willingness to fire, the chances are that I will do as you ask. The odds are stacked in your favor. However, history certainly demonstrates that many people in similar situations have chosen *not* to obey. The implication is clear: The influence process depends upon both an influencer's power and a follower's expectations. Followers evaluate an influencer's power and decide whether or not to obey. Perhaps they don't have much choice, and perhaps the decision is not always consciously considered, but they still have the power to decide whether or not to go along. This point should be kept in mind as we examine the various influence processes.

INFLUENCE PROCESSES

Exhibit 2.1 relates followers' needs, power bases, influence processes, and style of leadership. It suggests six fundamental means by which influence can occur: through appeal to fear, tradition, blind faith, rational faith, rational agreement, and joint determination. Each of these influence processes, in turn, is associated with a particular style of leadership.

Exhibit 2.1 Power, Influence, and Needs

Follower's Need Hierarchy	Influence Process	Leader's Power Basis	Leadership Style
competence, achievement			
	joint-determination	representative	participative
power, autonomy			
	rational agreement	expert	persuasive
esteem, prestige	rational faith		
	blind faith	referent	
social, affiliation			authoritarian
	tradition	reward	
safety, security			
	fear	coercive	autocratic
physiological			

Influence Through Fear

Across the span of human history, and in most societies even today, fear is one of the most common influence systems. Fear of being hurt physically or psychologically has long characterized families, tribes, armies, and kingdoms.

In business organizations, fear often takes the form of anxiety about losing a job. In the early nineteenth century, during the fledgling industrial revolution, managers were advised to pay only subsistence wages, to provide only enough to allow workers to obtain minimum food and shelter. Paying subsistence wages enabled managers to maximize their use of fear because employees were always on the knife-edge of starvation. Because they had not been able to put any money aside, they would begin to starve immediately upon dismissal. Employers could appeal very immediately to insecurity and the needs for physiological necessities.

Under influence by fear, it makes no difference whether subordinates understand the reasons for directives or agree with them. Agreement or disagreement is simply irrelevant. All that the influencer cares about is whether subordinates understand what they are supposed to do. Coercion will lay less heavily on subordinates if they understand and agree with the directive, but understanding and agreement do not fundamentally alter the situation.

A prominent British government minister recently made a speech in which she bemoaned the apparent decline of fear as a motivator in British industry. She felt that somehow people just do not work hard enough because they do not fear loss of their jobs. Perhaps social legislation, full employment, and governmental guarantees against starvation have reduced the ability of the British employer to utilize fear. Fear as a motivator at work also declines during full employment when other jobs are available. Much the same thing is probably also true in the United States. Of course, the elimination of job-loss fear has been a major goal of government and labor unions for many years. Nonetheless, managers from time to time may wistfully wish for the simplicity of using influence by fear.

The use of fear as a managerial tool can be inverted in many modern organizations. A history of IBM (Rogers, 1969) maintains that Thomas Watson Sr. made a conscious effort to eliminate the use of fear in management's relations with blue-collar and clerical workers, while encouraging fear of ridicule and dismissal as a primary motivator of managerial personnel. Because of their high pay and organizational prestige, middle managers may be particularly subject to fear. In addition, they have no union to represent their interests, and usually no due-process appeal procedures.

A study of the advertising business (Bensman, 1967) suggests that sensitivity to the use of fear depends upon an employee's age and career stage. Little fear exists at lower professional levels because pay is relatively poor and because interorganizational mobility is accepted practice. Being dismissed is not a serious blot on a young account executive's record. But managers and professionals aged 30 to 45, the period of greatest earnings and living expenses, become anxious and receptive to motivation through fear. They are locked in because it is unlikely that they can move to new positions with equal pay, and because their life-style depends on substantial income. In time, however, many manage to save enough so that the power of fear declines. If an executive lasts in advertising until age 45 or so, she or he has probably accumulated enough capital to be able to work elsewhere for less money. In the past, some dismissed or disillusioned older advertising executives went into teaching. The modest pay, along with their substantial savings, enabled them to maintain their homes in suburbia without too much sacrifice. Such financial and job mobility is of course affected by general economic conditions and job opportunities.

Perhaps the most dramatic reversal in the use of fear occurred in the United States Army. The "new" army attempted to improve life for enlistees in preparation for the conversion to an all-volunteer army. The use of threats and punishment by officers was discouraged. In Vietnam in the late 1960s and early 1970s, however, enlisted men in substantial numbers turned to fear as a control mechanism to keep their superiors in line. Threats of violence and actual "fraggings" (tossing a fragmentation grenade into an officer's quarters) all but completely reversed the balance of power and fear in the field. An army judge (Linden, 1972) argued that once an officer is intimidated by even the threat of fragging, he is useless to the military because he can no longer carry out orders. Through intimidation and scare stories, fragging became so influential that virtually all officers had to take into account the possibility of retaliation before giving an order to those under their command.

In spite of its attractiveness to some leaders, however, fear as an influence device has one great handicap: It is expensive. A leader must monitor followers closely to see that they are doing what they are told, and that they are not departing from their instructions. If noncompliance is detected, the leader must punish it in order to maintain the followers' fear. This process of policing and punishing can be exceedingly expensive. Hitler's Minister of Economics, Albert Speer, observes in his memoirs (1970) that he made a mistake in using slave labor in some Nazi manufacturing plants. Of course he did — he was imprisoned for twenty years on the charge — but his conclusion also has economic grounds.

A study of a slave-labor bomb manufacturing plant (Kogan, 1947) demonstrated what Speer meant by showing the sabotage that can be accomplished by resistant workers, even under conditions most oriented around fear. The laborers hindered production by withholding the simplest personal judgments and persistently asking for detailed instructions on what to do next. In addition, they were able to sabotage production by improperly fitting the bomb fuses. The sabotage was evident only when the weapon was dropped; duds were numerous. Their insubordination was impossible for the guards to detect unless they stood directly over the workers. Therefore, in order to influence the slaves to behave as desired, it became necessary to increase the probability of their being caught — and this required more guards. The plant soon had almost as many guards as slaves. It would have been more sensible to eliminate the slaves and assign the guards to the work!

Most applications of fear suffer from this expense of monitoring performance and applying sanctions. It is essential that the influencer maintain the follower's conviction that transgressions will be detected and punished (Horai and Tedeschi, 1969). Crime syndicate loan sharks must convey to their clients the mixed message of absolute honesty and commitment to the contract — in both directions. The potential "deadbeat" must know with certainty that retribution will be swift. And in law enforcement it appears that a high probability of detection and a certainty of modest punishment is a greater deterrence to crime than low probability of detection and uncertain severe punishment. The problem is that detection and conviction can be more expensive than punishment (Campbell and Church, 1969).

In addition, fear seems to be self-limiting. Under prolonged stress of fear, people tend to lose their sensitivity to it. Inaction, indifference, or even acceptance of death may be the response to unlikely rewards and likely punishment over a period of time.

Influence Through Tradition

Tradition has probably been the most common influence mechanism in human history. One obeys the king because he is the king, or because he is a representative of God, or, as in ancient Egypt, because he *is* God. St. Paul expressed the basis for such influence in Romans 13:1, "Let everyone submit himself to the ruling authorities, for there exists no authority not ordained by God." Response is quasi-automatic, almost unconscious, the kind of habitual obedience that is the intent of close-order drill learned during the first weeks in military training (Timasheff, 1938). Perhaps there is even some implicit recognition of the power of authority, but the response becomes institutionalized and inculcated into the class structure and ideology of the society (Bendix, 1956). One responds out of respect for one's betters or because there is some natural social order that is customary. Many Nazis performed horrible deeds, not because they were insane, but because their culture had trained them to respond without question to an authoritarian directive (Arendt, 1963; Harrower, 1976).

Responding to traditional authority is not simply habit, of course. In the United States Marines, it draws on the follower's internalized sense of responsibility to all who fought at Montezuma, Tripoli, Tarawa, or Vietnam; the young private is part of them, and he would feel guilty if he did not do his duty. Thus, the great advantage of a tradition-based influence system is that it offers positive motivation instead of the negative orientation of fear. It says, in effect, "respect authority, be obedient, and do what you're told—and if you do, you will be rewarded with acceptance into the community." Such acceptance means security and affiliation.

The submergence of self into the group for short periods of time during games, while singing in a choir, marching in a protest demonstration, even at times in military drill, is attractive to many people. A deeply traditional, ascriptive society may extend this to all existence. It can offer the greatest degree of certainty that is possible in human society, because it specifies who has authority, defines each person's obligations, and relieves most people of much onerous decision-making. In effect, a tradition-based system can perpetuate childhood. As Fromm (1941) pointed out, and as Vroom (1964) later documented, many people find such a state most attractive. For such people, the influence mechanism is not even perceived as imposed; it is absorbed and integrated into their personality so thoroughly that they feel that they are exercising free choice. Influence and control is highest when it is least apparent.

Tradition as the basis for obedience was commonly assumed in nineteenth-century management practice, when a firm's management structure was closely allied with the class structure of the society (Fayol, 1949). It was assumed that "lowers" should respond to "uppers." At first, those higher-up were assigned certain obligations for the well-being of people lower down, but this ethic was gradually dropped in favor of Social Darwinism, in which success was rewarded with lesser responsibility. Yet the assumption remained: Inferiors should respond to their betters; the manager should create *esprit de corps*, but fundamentally subordinates should respond because that is their obligation. Under this influence system, as with fear, it makes no difference whether followers understand the reasons for a directive or agree with it, and they certainly have not participated in its formulation.

Although we Americans like to think of ourselves as egalitarian, we do have many superior-subordinate relationships which attempt to program obedience: parent-child, teacher-student, employer-employee—all have in common some traditional feeling that within certain limits the subordinate will respond to the superior's suggestions. The Russian leader Nicolai Lenin observed at the beginning of Communist rule in Russia that the Russian economy was built upon fear, and that this had grave defects. What Russia needed in 1919, according to Lenin, was "Soviet-Americanism"; what Lenin meant was that American workers tended to do what they were told and worked consistently without being policed because they expected to (Brodersen, 1966). In 1938 the president of a large American corporation observed that the average workers expected to do what they were told, within certain limits (Barnard, 1938). Within this "zone of indifference" they were willing to do as they were directed. Those limits have probably narrowed in the last forty years; we are less willing than we once were to automatically respond to authority and do what we are told. A decline in respect for authority in general in American society may be reflected in a decline in response to authority figures.

Lenin thought that the United States was characterized by a high degree of respect for authority. Actually, this country has probably demonstrated *less* respect for authority than most nations. As far back as the early colonies, and as illustrated by Alexis de Tocqueville (1837) in the early 1800s, foreign observers have commented on the anti-authoritarian climate in America. Children were disrespectful to parents, buildings were torn down not long after completion, and a secular religion of progress ruled the land. Common explanations for this situation include (1) our youth as a nation and our intention to forge a new history rather than just continuing the English past; (2) our distrust of central government; (3) the shortage of labor which provided individual opportunity; and (4) the availability of land. In the early United States, a son did not have to live indefinitely with a stern father, waiting to take over the farm. The boy could leave, and did—for a job in the city or his own piece of land. The myth of the frontier and the man with the gun had enough reality to help shape attitudes toward authority in the developing nation.

Thus, prevailing attitudes toward authority and responsiveness to tradition are cultural phenomena. Two further examples clearly indicate this:

In 1959 a survey of German and American mothers (*Newsweek*, Sept. 13, 1968) asked them to rank ten favorable attributes of their children in order of desirability. The list included such characteristics as sociability, creativity, obedience, popularity, and so on. German mothers ranked obedience first. U.S. mothers ranked obedience last—desirable, but not as desirable as social compatibility, respect for others' rights, and self-confidence, among others. (Some observers have suggested that, since 1959, we got what we asked for.) A current survey might rank obedience higher, in reaction to perceived over-permissiveness, but its low ranking in 1959 seems consistent with America's past attitudes toward authority.

Uri Bronfenbrenner (1970) offers insights into the United States as compared with the Soviet Union. He probed teen-agers' willingness to engage in antisocial or antiauthoritarian behavior, such as cheating on examinations, breaking street lights, stealing public property, etc., under three conditions:

When teachers or parents were to be told of the act.
When only their friends were to be told.
When no one but themselves was to know.

Soviet girls indicated virtually no willingness to engage in antiauthoritarian acts under *any* circumstances. In the United States, young girls were much less willing to engage in such behavior than were boys. Soviet boys were willing to perform these acts if no one was to know, much less if teachers or parents were to be told, and *least* if friends were to know. The Soviet culture, reinforced by fear or tradition, holds such behavior in low regard. Such is apparently not the case in the United States. American boys were *most willing* to engage in antisocial behavior when their friends were to know—*even more willing than if no one else were to know.* Apparently such public behavior brings admiration and prestige because of its bravado.

Note that in the traditional system the follower responds to the leader's *position.* In the army the officer is identified by his uniform and his insignia. One obeys the order, regardless of the characteristics of the person giving the order, because the position is respected. Whether the officer is tall or short, fat or thin, black or white, is irrelevant; the follower responds to the position. This impersonality of influence and its associated stability and predictability constitute the great advantages of tradition as a means of influence.

Influence by Blind Faith

Influence through blind faith is a kind of Alexander or Napoleon syndrome. One responds to the great leader who has "charisma" (Weber, 1964). In the past, charisma was considered a gift of God, a gift of grace, or magical powers that were given to a few favored persons. Only fools would not respond to the charismatic leader. But what is a charismatic leader today? Have we not moved away from the ignorance and superstition of earlier blind followers? Or have we just shifted the source of authority from magic to psychology (Bryne, 1971)?

People tend to respond to the leader who has characteristics they admire, to the person who is a "super model" of what they themselves would like to be.

Perhaps most fundamentally, they respond out of strong emotional attachment or even love for the leader in whom they have blind faith. The relationship is personal rather than general because charisma is not simply an attribute of the leader, but of the fit between the leader's characteristics and the followers' needs. Lawrence of Arabia possessed charisma for the Arabs in World War I, but his dramatic, stylistic behavior offered no appeal to postwar Britons who did not support him in his bid for political office. In contrast, Winston Churchill's brand of charisma was not felt widely until Great Britain faced extinction in 1940; then his personal attributes matched people's concerns. These attributes became less relevant with the end of the European war in 1945, and Churchill was voted out of office.

Seventy years ago management literature asserted that one was born either a manager or a follower. Either one had natural leadership abilities, or one did not. There is less belief in this argument now, because charismatic, natural leaders seem all too rare. They do exist in business, of course, but we cannot depend on an abundant supply of them. Business and government simply require more managers than there are charismatic people. It is now believed that people can develop into effective managers through education and experience. Indeed, in highly structured bureaucracies, personal charisma might even be a handicap in getting ahead. Nonetheless, business still seems to want managers with attributes of "natural leadership" and "command presence"; witness one finding that starting salaries for men over six feet tall were $1000 per year *more* than for men under that magic height!

Some great leaders combine different influence techniques. General Patton was not above using fear, if necessary. A believer in tradition, he wore the uniform and the emblems of a traditional position; but he was also a charismatic leader who generated faith among his men. Such charismatic leaders tend to be individualistic. They demonstrate unique styles and affectations (Patton's ivory-handled revolvers, John Kennedy's refusal to wear an overcoat or hat, Robert Kennedy's tousled hair) as a method of distinguishing themselves. The readings by Machiavelli, Korda, and McMurry at the end of this chapter describe some means of expanding personal power.

The basic difference between traditional and blind-faith influence systems is impersonality as opposed to personality. Classical management theory rests upon the traditional model—a hierarchical structure in which authority resides in *positions,* and interpersonal communications follow the chain of command. The assumed organization shape is the pyramid. In contrast, the implied shape in the charismatic organization is more ambiguous (see Exhibit 2.2).

Charismatic leaders influence people through personality, not position. Therefore, they endeavor to bring themselves in direct contact with many people throughout the organization. They bypass the chain of command because they want to tie people to themselves, not to their "lieutenants." Franklin Roosevelt was often criticized as being a poor manager because his assignment of duties was sloppy, and he evidenced little respect for the structure of

Tradition–based Organization

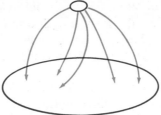

Blind–faith–based Organization

Exhibit 2.2 Authority Structure and Type of Influence

government. He would personally contact people throughout the system and give them projects unknown to their peers or superiors. He cultivated individual, personalized relationships, not organizational, impersonal positions (Schlesinger, 1959). General Robert Johnson of Johnson & Johnson demonstrated quite similar behavior. He would descend on his plants unannounced, bypass the resident manager in charge, and move directly to individuals at various levels whom he cultivated personally. Such behavior can be upsetting to organizationally minded people, but it can create a sense of identification with the top and a willingness to sacrifice which can be very powerful. It may also be more effective in generating change than fear or tradition-based systems.

Fear, tradition, and blind faith as authoritarian leadership. Influence through fear, tradition, and blind faith—drawing on coercive, reward, legitimate, or referent power—are all essentially authoritarian situations. The leader tells followers to do something; followers respond either because they fear being punished, because they want the reward, because they feel a responsibility to obey, or because they love the leader and believe in his or her abilities. But in all four instances it is essentially one-way authoritarian communication, in which followers respond without questioning whether specific directives are appropriate to the task. They neither understand the reasons for the order, nor is their agreement relevant.

Influence through faith is more limited than the other authoritarian forms, however. The charismatic leader's power is partially dependent on performance. If a series of failures should occur, the leader's charisma and referent power will fade.

We have implied that the follower's response to the authoritarian leader's power is generally rational, in that it reflects the follower's belief that obedience serves his or her interest in avoiding pain, sustaining life, remaining a member, and so on. Another view maintains that fear, tradition, and blind faith all draw upon a nonrational power phenomenon (Timasheff, 1938). Many people are characterized by a predisposition to submission. Whether this is instinctual or learned behavior is not clear. Is it derived from the ancient experience of the species, going back to the primeval dominance of the tyrant ape (Morris, 1966), or does it reflect contemporary child-rearing patterns (Erikson, 1950)? The essential argument, however, is that most people have an automatic, unconscious, and hynotic-like response to dominators *just because they are dominant.* Certain rituals, symbols, tones of voice, etc., reinforce the dominator by inhibiting the follower's rational judgment which might interfere with automatic response. Support for this view is found in the disturbing research by Milgram (1974) where most people were willing to apply electrical shocks to others just because an apparent scientist requested it.

Influence by Rational Faith

If we could count the number of influence incidents in modern organizations, especially among managers and professionals, we would probably find the most common influence process to be rational faith. Followers respond because, on the basis of evidence that the leader has knowledge and ability, they believe he or she knows what he or she is talking about. This is similar to your relationship with a doctor. You can make a fairly rational judgment that she is qualified, from the diplomas, license, and certificates on the office walls. It is even possible to learn about the quality of her medical school and residency hospital. You can ask friends about their experiences with her. In general, then, you can decide that she knows what she is talking about and that she has your interests at heart (Albanese, 1973). Nonetheless, however rational your decision about the person, your response to her specific suggestions is based pretty much on faith. You probably cannot even read her handwriting on the prescription form, much less know precisely how the medicine will help you. In most cases you simply accept it.

For a business example of this process, consider the following incident:

> A young staff specialist is hired to provide expertise to a number of production managers. Initially, the only influence process available to the specialist is persuasion—gaining the rational agreement of the managers. To be effective he prepares elaborate, clear presentations (even rehearsing with a colleague to anticipate any questions). By data, logic, and argument, he attempts to gain the agreement of his superiors. After a year of this kind of relationship, he goes one day to talk with one of the managers. An hour has been reserved for the presentation. He arrives and begins his pitch. After a couple of minutes, however, the busy manager interrupts: "I'm just too busy to go over this. We'll *do whatever you want to do.*"

The manager is presumably being rational, but he is also acting on faith. The rationality is based on his prior experience with the specialist; the staff man's track record is good. His past advice has helped the production department, so the manager decides that he is competent and concerned. Nonetheless, in accepting the latest proposal without detailed examination, the manager is acting on faith that it is as good as earlier ones.

This process of influence by acceptance of the person is widespread because it is time saving, and because it recognizes that authority based on knowledge must be reconciled with authority based on position. The person with certain knowledge impresses the person with position; the latter accepts the former's influence. Specialists derive great satisfaction from this situation, because it appeals to their needs for esteem, competence, power, and achievement—a potent combination. Of course, danger threatens line managers in this relationship. They may unwittingly abdicate their effective authority and control to the specialist because they do not have time to question the specialist's ideas, or even because they lose their ability to do so.

Influence Through Rational Agreement

Another type of influence is operating when one obeys because one understands the reasons why an action is necessary and agrees that it is the proper thing to do. The leader has been persuasive, able to explain rationally why an activity must be performed. Obviously, this process consumes more time than any of the influence means discussed so far. The explanations imply substantial discussion and even two-way conversations, in contrast to the one-way broadcasts characterizing fear, tradition, and faith.

In trying to convince or persuade the follower, a leader is paying a compliment to the follower. In effect the leader is saying, "I think you have the ability and the knowledge to understand what I am asking, and I respect you enough to take the time to explain." Thus, the follower may feel that she or he is being treated in a somewhat more adult manner. The follower's needs for esteem and competence are at least appealed to.

Much of the time, charismatic leaders will draw on referent and expert power to persuade followers rather than ordering them. As a result, the followers tend to feel that they share in the leader's power rather than being dominated by it. Success reinforces the leader's power, and people respond out of rational and blind faith. Winston Churchill motivated his people because he persuasively articulated the challenge facing the nation and successfully built on their faith in and respect for him.

Because influence based on expert power is such a common phenomena in modern organizations (perhaps *the* most common influence process), let us examine expert power from two perspectives: as persuasiveness and as access to information.

Expert power and persuasion.   Most of us don't possess Churchill's personality, but persuasion may be the only option for potential influencers who have no other power but expertise. Armed with knowledge alone, they attempt to convince others to follow their advice. Research suggests that persuasion will be more effective under the following conditions (Zimbardo and Ebbesen, 1969; Miller and Burgoon, 1973; Applbaum and Anatol, 1974):

1. If the influencer has high credibility based on perceived expertise and trustworthiness. (For many years there has been a belief in the "sleeper effect" under which the audience would in time forget the credibility of a distrusted persuader and eventually come to believe the message after initial rejection. This has recently been quite strongly disproven for most people [Capon and Hulbert, 1973; Gillig and Greenwald, 1974].)

2. If the influencer initially expresses some views that are also held by the audience or potential followers.

3. If the information is perceived as privileged for a few when large numbers want to hear it (Fromkin and Brock, 1971).

4. If the influencer's personal appearance and characteristics please or at least don't offend the audience.

5. If the followers have recently responded on a smaller but similar matter (Freedman and Fraser, 1966; Pliner et al., 1974).

6. Up to an indefinite limit, the more extreme the change asked for by the influencer, the more actual change he or she is likely to get.

7. If one side of the argument is presented, when the audience is generally friendly or when the influencer's position is the only one that will be presented.

8. If both sides of the argument are presented, when the audience starts out disagreeing or when it is probable that they will hear the other side from someone else.

9. When opposite views are presented one after another, the one presented last will probably be more effective.

10. There will probably be more opinion change in the desired direction if the influencer explicitly states his or her conclusions than if the influencer lets the audience draw their own. If the audience is quite intelligent, however, their implicit conclusion-drawing is likely to be better.

11. Appeal to fear will frequently work if the influencer advances explicit and possible recommendations for action. But, if the influencer has none to offer, the appeal to fear may be rejected.

12. Audience participation through group discussion and decision-making helps to overcome resistance. Having members of the audience state the espoused views is likely to increase adoption of the new views (Widgery and Miller, 1973).

13. The support of just one or two others can overcome the majority's initial resistance if the minority is consistent in expressing certainty.

There are no consistent findings on whether emotional or rational appeals are more effective. It depends on the kind of audience and their state at the time. In general, however, people are more easily persuaded when their self-esteem is low.

If the persuader accumulates success, his or her influence may shift from rational agreement to rational faith. The widespread existence of this influence style, even at high management levels, is well illustrated by the words of President Harry Truman (Rossiter, 1956):

> And people talk about the powers of a President, all the powers that a Chief Executive has, and what he can do. Let me tell you something—from experience!
>
> The President may have a great many powers given to him in the Constitution and may have certain powers under certain laws which are given to him by the Congress of the United States; but the principal power that the President has is to

bring people in and try to persuade them to do what they ought to do without persuasion. That's what I spend most of my time doing. That's what the powers of the President amount to.

Expert power and access to information. Based upon his analysis of the German Socialist Party, many years ago, Michels (1915) formulated his famous "Iron Law of Oligarchy." Part of his argument was that hierarchies become strong and organizations autocratic because it is impossible to keep everyone informed no matter how much the members may desire democracy. Only a few can monitor the necessary information flows and know enough about what is going on to participate in organizational decisions. These few who occupy critical communication points accumulate expert power and emerge as leaders who make decisions that affect others.

Support for Michels' observation is reported by more recent behavioral research on the effect of communication networks on speed and accuracy in solving problems. In the initial work on communication nets, Bavelas (1950) calculated an "index of relative centrality." The larger the number in the nets (see Exhibit 2.3), the more central the position is in the communication flow and the more likely the incumbent is to accumulate power and exercise influence in the group. His research indicated that the network with the least centralized structure (the circle) made the most errors on a relatively simple task; errors decreased as the structure became more centralized (the "Y" and wheel). As centralization increased, so too did agreement on who was the leader (the one with the highest centrality index). Finally, those persons most satisfied were the most central.

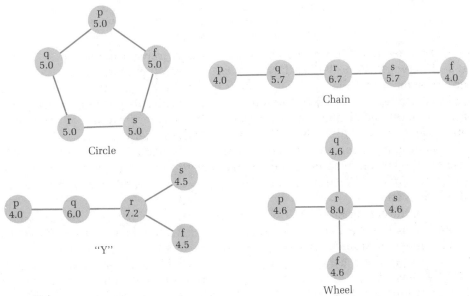

Exhibit 2.3 Communication Nets

In a group structured as a wheel, the person at the hub can communicate with all of the people at the spokes. The latter, however, can communicate only with the hub. Regardless of personality, whether he or she is a big politico on campus or just a beautiful body, after repeated problems the person at the hub emerges as the decision maker or leader. A "natural leader" at one of the spoke positions may attempt to lead, but among all groups tested the "spoke"-person came to recognize that the hub must be the decision maker. Why? Because the person at the hub can get all the necessary information easier than anyone else. In a simple problem, such as identifying which color marble is common to all five participants, the hub collects the colors from all others, compares, decides, and simply announces the answer. Since he or she occupies a critical communication link, he or she accumulates expert power and emerges as leader-manager.

Later network research (Guetzkow and Simon, 1955) added an "all-channel" group, in which everyone can communicate with everyone else, as indicated in Exhibit 2.4. Yet, in a series of trials, most of the all-channel people

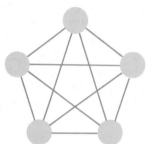

Exhibit 2.4   All–Channel Communication Network

find it impractical to operate on this basis, so they transform themselves into a wheel network. Voluntarily, they restrict their communication links. In most groups some individual emerges as the occupant of the critical communication point at the hub. The others communicate only with this individual. The process is facilitated if one individual is clearly a leader in terms of analytical ability and articulateness. Nonetheless, even where the members of the group are balanced as to personality and prestige, the all-channel net tends to convert itself to the wheel. In short, differentiated expert power emerges because of the difficulty and inefficiency of transmitting all information to every member of the organization.

As in the earlier research, the more central a person is in the net, the more satisfied he or she is likely to be. Centrality means that he or she receives and sends more communications and is better able to solve the problems. Centrality is satisfying because you know more about what is going on. Such centrality rapidly develops in the wheel net; there is little room for spontaneity. A hierarchy emerges, in which the central person sends and receives information from all, thus conforming to the formal demands of the system. Thus on simple, repetitive problems, centrality assists development of problem-solving procedures that complete the tasks faster, with fewer errors, and with fewer communications (Glanzer and Glanzer, 1961).

The advantage of centralization depends upon the nature of the task, however. For example, if mottled-colored agates are substituted for the solid color marbles, the groups have troubles. Finding the common marble is just about impossible for the wheel. The hub-person in the wheel is overwhelmed because the perception and communication problems are just too great. He or she collects all the marble descriptions—but no two are alike! Their differentiated expert power quickly evaporates in this situation. The all-channel nets also have difficulty, but *some* are able to find a solution because of their feedback advantages. By remaining all-channel and by not restricting their communications, as they did with simple problems, everyone can listen in so that freer exchange of perceptions is possible. Under such a system, power is equally distributed.

Influence Through Joint Determination

Near the end of the sad riot at Columbia University in 1968, the police bodily dragged students out of the administration building which they had been occupying. Amid the kicking, screaming, and swearing, one young female student in the grip of an officer exclaimed, "God, how exciting; that's the first time I've ever felt part of anything in my life!" Her words are testimony to the power and satisfaction that people find in collective action, where they perceive that they have participated in determining the group's actions.

Since the imaginative and influential research of Lewin (1948), most students of organizational behavior have come to accept that a person's participation in setting a goal increases the likelihood that he or she will act to insure that the goal is met. Presumably, when the follower has participated in determining what is to be done, understanding and agreement that a certain course of action is necessary and proper follows. In this participation, some quite high-level needs on the part of the followers are involved. They exercise some power and have an opportunity to express themselves and their abilities. Ideally, there is voluntary implementation through this participation and determination.

If practicing managers are less enthusiastic about participation (Haire et al., 1966), it is partly because of the difficulty of applying such an influence mechanism and of creating the sense of virtual ownership that motivates the employee to participate and contribute. In addition, even more than rational agreement, this influence style can be very time consuming. The leader also runs a grave risk of abdicating authority by turning over control of the followers to the followers themselves. We shall discuss participative influence and leadership at greater length in Chapters 8 and 10.

Influence does not run unidirectionally from leader to follower; it flows both ways. Even in the classic case of operant conditioning, influence flows both ways. If a scientist places a pigeon in a box with a feeding mechanism, the hungry bird will peck in various places in the box. When he accidentally pecks a red button, the scientist reinforces the behavior by giving the pigeon a piece of corn. When the pigeon pecks the red button again, he once more receives corn, and so on. Soon the pigeon will peck the button repeatedly. The scientist is controlling the pigeon, but the pigeon is also controlling the scientist! All the bird has to do is peck a button and the scientist gives him food. What is cause, and what is effect?

Thus, influence is reciprocal. To control, one must be controlled to some extent. That is, the *influencer* must be influenced. Fear-dispensing dictators *must* punish insubordination or they will lose their credibility—others' belief that they will respond to (be controlled by) the offense. Similarly, a tradition-based system will collapse unless it provides its loyal, obedient supporters with warmth and security. Charismatic leaders expecting blind faith must respond to certain follower demands. Basically, they must give of themselves. They must allow their followers to see them, meet them, hear them, even talk to them (Fidel Castro's leadership of Cuba is a classic example of this kind of behavior). Every influence mechanism and every leader thus implies two-way influence and some mutual control. A former Assistant Secretary of State has written of his awareness of the two sides of control during his first days in office (Frankel, 1969):

> The taste of power, or whatever it was that I tasted the first day, went to my head too, but not quite as I had been warned it would. I had come into the office with projects and plans, and I was caught in an irresistible movement of paper, meetings, ceremonies, crises, trivialities. There were uncleared paragraphs and cleared ones, and people waiting for me to tell them what my plans were, and people doing things that had nothing to do with my plans. I had moved into the middle of a flow of business that I hadn't started and wouldn't be able to stop. There were people in place to handle this flow, and established machinery in operation to help me deal with it. The entire system was at my disposal. In a word, I had power. And power had me.

This mutuality has an important implication: influence is expandable. It is not a fixed pie that can only be divided; it is not a zero-sum game requiring one person to lose influence when another person gains. Both may gain influence as they mutually benefit from a relationship. Even more important, some research (Patchen, 1962; Franklin, 1975) suggests that influence downward may be enhanced, rather than reduced, by influence upward. For example in Exhibit 2.5, B's influence on C seems to be a function of C's perception of both C's influence on B *and* B's influence on A. Ries (1970) indicates that *both* managers and workers in more effective organizations perceived themselves as having greater influence. In other words, the more total influence everyone has in the system, the greater total system effectiveness.

Exhibit 2.5 Reciprocal Influence Pattern

SUMMARY

Influence is a central aspect of the managerial role. For influence to occur, managers must possess power. However, power, as we have seen, can rest upon one or more bases: coercion (force), control over rewards, legitimacy (tradition), referent (identification), expertise, and representation. Each of these bases appeals to one or more of potential followers' needs. The processes by which influence can occur are through appeal to fear, tradition, blind faith, rational faith, rational agreement, and joint-determination.

The use of expert power is of special importance for managers and staff professionals in modern organizations. Coercion or force is both expensive and of questionable morality; control over rewards is increasingly ineffective when employees have welfare, unemployment, social security, and other supportive institutions to fall back on; legitimate power, too, is increasingly ineffective in modern society, where all traditional authority is subject to doubt. Expert power, then, seems to be the major source of most managerial influence; its effective use depends upon knowledge or expertise, persuasiveness, and access to important information.

REFERENCES

Albanese, R. "Criteria for Evaluating Authority Patterns." *Academy of Management Journal*, Vol. 16, No. 1 (March 1973), pp. 102–11.

Applbaum, R. L., and K. W. Anatol. *Strategies for Persuasive Communication.* Merrill, 1974.

Arendt, H. *Eichmann in Jerusalem.* Viking, 1963.

Barnard, C. I. *The Functions of the Executive.* Harvard University Press, 1938.

Bavelas, A. "Communication Patterns in Task-Oriented Groups." *Journal of the Acoustical Society of America*, Vol. 22 (1950), pp. 725–30.

Bendix, R. *Work and Authority in Modern Industry.* Wiley, 1956.

Bensman, J. *Dollars and Sense.* Macmillan, 1967.

Brodersen, A. *The Soviet Worker.* Random House, 1966.

Bronfenbrenner, U. *Two Worlds of Childhood.* Russell Sage Foundation, 1970.

Bryne, D. *The Attraction Paradigm.* Academic Press, 1971.

Campbell, B. A., and R. M. Church (eds.). *Punishment and Aversive Behavior.* Appleton-Century-Crofts, 1969.

Capon, N., and J. Hulbert. "The Sleeper Effect: An Awakening." *The Public Opinion Quarterly*, Vol. 37, No. 3 (1973), pp. 339–58.

Erikson, E. H. *Childhood and Society.* W. W. Norton, 1950.

Fayol, H. *General and Industrial Management.* Pitman, 1949.

Frankel, C. *High on Foggy Bottom.* Harper & Row, 1969.

Franklin, J. L. "Down the Organization: Influence Processes Across Levels of Hierarchy." *Administrative Science Quarterly*, Vol. 20, No. 2 (June 1975), pp. 153–64.

Freedman, J. L., and S. C. Fraser. "Compliance Without Pressure: The Foot-in-the-Door Technique." *Journal of Personality and Social Psychology*, Vol. 4 (1966), pp. 195–202.

French, J. R. P., and B. H. Raven. "The Bases of Social Power." In *Studies in Social Power*, ed. by D. Cartwright. University of Michigan Press, 1959.

Fromkin, H. L., and T. C. Brock. "A Commodity Theory Analysis of Persuasion." *Representative Research in Social Psychology,* Vol. 2 (1971), pp. 653–54.

Fromm, E. *Escape from Freedom.* Holt, Rinehart, and Winston, 1941.

Gillig, P. M., and A. G. Greenwald. "Is It Time to Lay the Sleeper Effect to Rest?" *Journal of Personality and Social Psychology,* Vol. 29, No. 1 (1974), pp. 132–39.

Glanzer, M., and R. Glanzer. "Techniques for the Study of Group Structure and Behavior: II—Empirical Studies of the Effects of Structure in Small Groups." *Psychological Bulletin,* 1961, pp. 1–27.

Guetzkow, H., and H. Simon. "The Impact of Certain Communication Nets Upon Organization and Performance in Task-Oriented Groups." *Management Science,* Vol. 1, Nos. 3, 4 (April–July 1955), pp. 233–50.

Haire, M., E. Ghiselli, and L. Porter. *Managerial Thinking.* Wiley, 1966.

Harrower, M. "Were Hitler's Henchmen Mad?" *Psychology Today,* Vol. 10, No. 2 (July 1976), pp. 76 ff.

Horai, J., and J. T. Tedeschi. "Effects of Credibility and Magnitude and Punishment on Compliance to Threats." *Journal of Personality and Social Psychology,* Vol. 12 (1969), pp. 164–69.

Ivancevich, J. M. "An Analysis of Control, Bases of Control, and Satisfaction in an Organizational Setting." *Academy of Management Journal,* December 1970, pp. 427–36.

Kogan, E. *Der SS Staat.* Bermann-Fischer, 1947. (Cited in Bendix, op. cit.)

Lewin, K. *Resolving Social Conflicts: Selected Papers on Group Dynamics.* Harper & Row, 1948.

Linden, E. "The Demoralization of an Army." *Saturday Review* (January 8, 1973), p. 12.

Michels, R. *Political Parties.* Dover Publications, 1959 (originally published in 1915).

Milgram, S. *Obedience to Authority.* Harper & Row, 1974.

Miller, G. R., and M. Burgoon. *New Techniques of Persuasion.* Harper & Row, 1973.

Morris, D. *The Naked Ape.* McGraw-Hill, 1966.

Patchen, M. "Supervisory Methods and Group Performance Norms." *Administrative Science Quarterly,* December 1962, pp. 275–93.

Peabody, R. L. *Organizational Authority.* Atherton, 1964.

Pliner, P., H. Hart, J. Koh, and D. Saari. "Compliance Without Pressure: Some Further Data on the Foot-in-the-Door Technique." *Journal of Experimental Social Psychology,* Vol. 10 (1974), pp. 17–22.

Ries, V. "Influence Structure in Yugoslav Enterprise." *Industrial Relations,* Vol. 9 (1970), pp. 148–66.

Rogers, W. H. *Think: A History of IBM and the Watsons.* Stein & Day, 1969.

Rossiter, C. *The American Presidency.* Harcourt Brace Jovanovich, 1956.

Schlesinger, A. M., Jr. *The Coming of the New Deal.* Houghton Mifflin, 1959.

Speer, A. *Inside the Third Reich.* Macmillan, 1970.

Student, K. R. "Supervisory Influence and Work-Group Performance." *Journal of Applied Psychology,* Vol. 52 (1968), pp. 188–94.

Timasheff, N. S. "The Power Phenomenon." *American Sociological Review,* Vol. 3 (August 1938), pp. 499–509.

de Tocqueville, A. C. *Democracy in America.* Knopf, 1945 (originally published 1837).

Vroom, V. *Work and Motivation*. Wiley, 1964.

Weber, M. *The Theory of Social and Economic Organization*. Free Press, 1964.

Widgery, R. N., and G. R. Miller. "Attitude Change Following Counterattitudinal Advocacy: Support for the Aversive Consequences Interpretation of Dissonance Theory." *The Journal of Communication*, Vol. 23 (September 1973), pp. 306–14.

Zimbardo, P. G., and E. B. Ebbeson. *Influencing Attitudes and Changing Behavior*. Addison-Wesley, 1969.

Authority: Its Nature and Motives
Herbert A. Simon, Donald W. Smithburg, and Victor A. Thompson

From a psychological standpoint the exercise of authority involves a relationship between two or more persons. On the one side we have a person who makes proposals for the action of others. On the other side we have a person who accepts the proposals— who "obeys" them. Now a person may accept another's proposals under three different sets of circumstances:

1. He may examine the merits of the proposal, and, on the basis of its merits become convinced that he should carry it out. We shall exclude such instances of acceptance from our notion of authority, although some writers on administration have called this the "authority of ideas."
2. He may carry out the proposal without being fully, or even partially, convinced of its merits. In fact he may not examine the merits of the proposal at all.
3. He may carry out the proposal even though he is convinced it is wrong—wrong either in terms of personal values or of organizational values or both.

We will treat both the second and third cases as instances of the acceptance of authority. Of course in any actual instance all three of the "pure types" of acceptance listed above may be combined in various proportions. In actual practice authority is almost always liberally admixed with persuasion.

Because the person who accepts proposals may do so for a variety of motives, there will be seen in any organization a number of different types of authority relationships, corresponding to these different motives for acceptance.

People accept the proposals of persons in whom they have great confidence. In any organization there are some individuals who, because of past performance, general reputation, or other factors, have great influence or authority. Their proposals will often be accepted without analysis as to their wisdom. Even when the suggestions of such a person are not accepted, they will be rejected reluctantly and only because a stronger authority contradicts them.

The authority of confidence may be limited to a special area of competence in which a person has acquired a reputation.

The willingness to accept authority on the basis of confidence, both within and outside organizations, goes even one step further. Not only is the layman generally unable to judge the quality of the advice he is getting from the specialist, but he often is in no position to judge the competence of the specialist, except on the basis of certain superficial and formal criteria that give the specialist his *status*.

There are at least two kinds of status, which may be called *functional status* and *hierarchical status*. It is with functional status that we are concerned at the moment.

A person has functional status in a particular area of knowledge when his decisions and recommendations in that area are accepted as more or less authoritative.

In the established professions, status is generally conferred on the basis of standards developed by the profession itself. The M.D. degree is conferred on the young doctor by the medical profession (acting through an "accredited" medical school). Law and engineering degrees and the certificate of the public accountant are awarded in much the same way. In other cases, job experience in a particular field confers functional status in that field. A person with long experience in a professional position in the Interstate Commerce Commission may acquire status as a transportation economist.

Confidence can be a powerful support for hierarchical as well as for nonhierarchical authority. A subordinate will much more readily obey a command of a superior if he has confidence in the intelligence and judgment of that superior or if he believes that the superior has knowledge of the situation not available to himself.

In particular, where a problem requiring decision affects the work of several units in an organization, the superior who has hierarchical authority in the formal organization plan over all the units involved is often accepted as the person best located — because he has the "whole picture" — to make the decision. Hence, the coordinating functions that are commonly performed by those in hierarchical authority are based, in part at least, upon the authority of confidence — upon the belief of subordinates that the superior is the best informed about the situation as a whole.

The most generally recognized weapon of the superior is the sanction — the ability of the superior to attach pleasant or unpleasant consequences to the actions of the subordinate.

The relationship of the authority of sanctions with the organizational hierarchy can be viewed from a more general standpoint. When a person joins an organization he is accepting a system of relationships that restricts his individuality or his freedom of action. He is willing to do so because he feels that, in spite of the organizational restraints, being a member of the organization is preferable to other alternatives available to him. To continue as a member of the organization, he must continue, to some extent, to abide by the complex of procedures which constitutes the organization. Although, increasingly, the power to discharge an employee is not lodged in any specific superior (because of merit systems, central personnel offices, labor unions, etc.), nevertheless, this power resides somewhere in the organization, being, in fact, one of its working procedures. The sanctions discussed in this section are increasingly *organization* sanctions, brought into play through the working procedures of the organization, and not the special prerogatives or powers of *individual superiors*.

For the most part the authority of sanction rests on the behavior responses that are induced by the *possibility* that a sanction may be applied. An organization member is seldom presented with an ultimatum "to do so and so or suffer the consequences." Rather, he anticipates the consequences of continual insubordination or failure to please the person or persons who have the ability to apply sanctions to him, and this anticipation acts as a constant motivation without expressed threats from any person.

There is another reason why employees accept the proposals of other organization members — a reason less rationalistic but probably more important than the desire to avoid the organization sanctions discussed above. People accept "legitimate" authority because they feel that they *ought* to go along with the "rules of the game."

Throughout their development to maturity and after, people are educated in the beliefs, values, or mores of society. They learn what they ought to do and what they ought not to do. One of the values with which they are indoctrinated is that a person should play according to the rules of the game. This ethic is acquired very early. When a child enters a ball game in the sand lot he does not expect the game to be altered at various points to suit his convenience. Rather he expects to adjust his behavior to the rules of the game. Although there may be disputes as to what the rule is on some point, once this is established, the proposition that he should abide by the rule is unquestioned.

Likewise, when people enter organizations most of them feel that they ought to abide by the rules of the game—the working procedures of the organization. These working procedures define how the work will be done; how working problems will be solved when they arise; how conflicts will be settled. They prescribe that on such and such matters the individual will accept the suggestions of this or that person or organization; secure the advice of such and such unit; clear his work with so and so; work on matters that come to him in such and such a way; etc.

The working procedures of an organization prescribe that the individual member will accept the proposals of other members in matters assigned to them. This acceptance is one of the rules of the game which he feels he should abide by. Thus, individuals in organizations also accept the authority of other persons because they think they *ought* to accept it.

The working relationships in an organization designated by the term "hierarchy" constitute a particular organization procedure for handling the authority of legitimacy. Acceptance of the working procedures of an organization by a member includes acceptance of the obligation to go along with the proposals of an hierarchical superior, at least within a limit of toleration—the "area of acceptance." Thus, whether the other reasons for obedience are operating or not (confidence, identification, or sanctions), organization members will feel that they ought to obey their superiors. Legitimacy is one of the most important sources of the authority of the hierarchical superior.

The feeling that hierarchical authority is legitimate is immensely strengthened by previous social conditioning. Hierarchical behavior is an institutionalized behavior that all organization members bring to the organization with them. Like the players in the Oberammergau Passion Play who begin to learn their roles in early childhood, "inferiors" obey "superiors" because they have been taught to do so from infancy, beginning with the parent-child relationship and running through almost constant experience with social and organizational hierarchies until death brings graduation from this particular social schooling. Hierarchical behavior involves an inferior-superior role-taking of persons well versed in their roles. "Inferiors" feel that they ought to obey "superiors"; "superiors" feel that they ought to be obeyed.

Our society is extremely hierarchical. Success is generally interpreted in terms of hierarchical preferment. Social position and financial rewards are closely related to hierarchical preferment, as also are education and even perhaps romantic attainment. Advancement up a hierarchy is generally considered a sign of moral worth, of good character, of good stewardship, of social responsibility, and of the possession of superior intellectual qualities.

Hierarchy receives a tremendous emphasis in nearly all organizations. This is so because hierarchy is a procedure that requires no training, no indoctrination, no special inducements. It rests almost entirely on "pre-entry" training—a training so thorough that few other organization procedures can ever compete with it. Furthermore, hierarchy is a great simplification.

Leaders' Control and Members' Compliance

Amitai Etzioni

A CLASSIFICATION OF POWER

Power is an actor's ability to induce or influence another actor to carry out his directives or any other norms he supports.[1] Goldhamer and Shils state that "a person may be said to have power to the extent that he influences the behavior of others in accordance with his own intentions."[2] Of course, "his own intentions" might be to influence a person to follow others' "intentions" or those of a collectivity. In organizations, enforcing the collectivity norms is likely to be a condition determining the power-holder's access to the means of power.

Power positions are positions whose incumbents regularly have access to means of power. Statements about power positions imply a particular group (or groups) who are subject to this power. For instance, to state that prison guards have a power position implies the subordination of inmates. In the following analysis we focus on power relations in organizations between those higher and those lower in rank. We refer to those in power positions, who are higher in rank, as *elites* or as organizational *representatives*. We refer to those in subject positions, who are lower in rank, as *lower participants*.

Power differs according to the means employed to make the subjects comply. These means may be physical, material, or symbolic.[3]

Coercive power rests on the application, or the threat of application, of physical sanctions such as infliction of pain, deformity, or death; generation of frustration through restriction of movement; or controlling through force the satisfaction of needs such as those for food, sex, comfort, and the like.

Remunerative power is based on control over material resources and rewards through allocation of salaries and wages, commissions and contributions, "fringe benefits," services, and commodities.

Normative power rests on the allocation and manipulation of symbolic rewards and deprivations through employment of leaders, manipulation of mass media, allocation of esteem and prestige symbols, administration of ritual, and influence over the distribution of "acceptance" and "positive response." (A more eloquent name for this power would be persuasive, or manipulative, or suggestive power. But all these terms have negative value connotations which we wish to avoid.)

There are two kinds of normative power. One is based on the manipulation of esteem, prestige, and ritualistic symbols (such as a flag or a benediction); the other, on allocation and manipulation of acceptance and positive response.[4] Although both powers are found both in vertical and in horizontal relationships, the first is more frequent in vertical relations, between actors who have different ranks, whereas the second is more common in horizontal relations, among actors equal in rank—in particular, in the power of an "informal" or primary group over its members. Lacking better terms, we refer to the first kind as *pure normative power* and to the second as *social power*.[5] Social power could be treated as a distinct kind of power. But since powers are here classed according to the means of control employed, and since both social and pure normative powers rest on the same set of means—manipulation of symbolic rewards— we treat these two powers as belonging to the same category.

From the viewpoint of the organization, pure normative power is more useful, since it can be exercised directly down the hierarchy. Social power becomes organizational power only when the organization can influence the group's powers, as when a teacher uses the class climate to control a deviant child or a union steward agitates the members to use their informal power to bring a deviant into line.

Organizations can be ordered according to their power structure, taking into account which power is predominant, how strongly it is stressed compared with other organizations in which the same power is predominant, and which power constitutes the secondary source of control.

NEUTRALIZATION OF POWER

Most organizations employ all three kinds of power, but the degree to which they rely on each differs from organization to organization. Most organizations tend to emphasize only one means of power, relying less on the other two.[6] Evidence to this effect is presented below in the analysis of the compliance structures of various organizations. The major reason for power specialization seems to be that when two kinds of power are emphasized at the same time, over the same subject group, they tend to neutralize each other.

Applying force, for instance, usually creates such a high degree of alienation that it becomes impossible to apply normative power successfully. This is one of the reasons that rehabilitation is rarely achieved in traditional prisons, that custodial measures are considered as blocking therapy in mental hospitals, and that teachers in progressive schools tend to oppose corporal punishment.

Similarly, the application of remunerative powers makes appeal to "idealistic" (pure normative) motives less fruitful. In a study of the motives that lead to purchase of war bonds, Merton pointed out that in one particularly effective drive (the campaign of Kate Smith), all "secular" topics were omitted and the appeal was centered on patriotic, "sacred" themes. Merton asked a sample of 978 people: "Do you think that it is a good idea to give things to people who buy bonds?"

Fifty percent were definitely opposed in principle to premiums, bonuses, and other such inducements, and many of the remainder thought it a good idea only for "other people" who might not buy otherwise.[7]

By omitting this [secular] argument, the authors of her scripts were able to avoid the strain and incompatibility between the two main lines of motivation: unselfish, sacrificing love of country and economic motives of sound investment.[8]

It is possible to make an argument for the opposite position. It might be claimed that the larger the number of personal needs whose satisfaction the organization controls, the more power it has over the participants. For example, labor unions that cater to and have control over the social as well as the economic needs of their members have more power over those members than do unions that focus only on economic needs. There may be some tension between the two modes of control, some ambivalence and uneasy feeling among members about the combinations, but undoubtedly the total control is larger. Similarly, it is obvious that the church has more power over the priest than over the average parishioner. The parishioner is exposed to normative power, whereas the priest is controlled by both normative and remunerative powers.

The issue is complicated by the fact that the *amount* of each kind of power applied must be taken into account. If a labor union with social powers has economic power which is much greater than that of another union, this fact may explain why the first union has greater power in sum, despite some "waste" due to neutralization. A further complication follows from the fact that neutralization may also occur through application of the "wrong" power in terms of the cultural definition of what is appropriate to the particular organization and activity. For example, application of economic power in religious organizations may be less effective than in industries, not because two kinds of power are mixed, but because it is considered illegitimate to use economic pressures to attain religious goals. Finally, some organizations manage to apply two kinds of power abundantly and without much waste through neutralization, because they segregate the application of one power from that of the other. The examination below of combat armies and labor unions supplies an illustration of this point.

We have discussed some of the factors related to the tendency of organizations to specialize their power application. In conclusion, it seems that although there can be little doubt that such a tendency exists, its scope and a satisfactory explanation for it have yet to be established.

THREE KINDS OF INVOLVEMENT: A COMPARATIVE DIMENSION

Involvement, Commitment, and Alienation

Organizations must continually recruit means if they are to realize their goals. One of the most important of these means is the positive orientation of the participants to the organizational power. *Involvement*[9] refers to the cathectic-evaluative orientation of an actor to an object, characterized in terms of intensity and direction.

The intensity of involvement ranges from high to low. The direction is either positive or negative. We refer to positive involvement as *commitment*[10] and to negative involvement as *alienation*.[11] (The advantage of having a third term, *involvement*, is that it enables us to refer to the continuum in a neutral way.[12]) Actors can accordingly be placed on an involvement continuum which ranges from a highly intense negative zone through mild negative and mild positive zones to a highly positive zone.[13]

Three Kinds of Involvement

We have found it helpful to name three zones of the involvement continuum, as follows: *alienative*, for the high alienation zone; *moral*, for the high commitment zone; and *calculative*, for the two mild zones. This classification of involvement can be applied to the orientations of actors in all social units and to all kinds of objects. Hence the definitions and illustrations presented below are not limited to organizations but are applicable to orientations in general.

Alienative Involvement. Alienative involvement designates an intense negative orientation; it is predominant in relations among hostile foreigners. Similar orientations exist among merchants in "adventure" capitalism, where trade is built on isolated acts of exchange, each side trying to maximize immediate profit.[14] Such an orientation seems to dominate the approach of prostitutes to transient clients.[15] Some slaves seem to have held similar attitudes to their masters and to their work. Inmates in prisons, prisoners of war, people in concentration camps, enlisted men in basic training, all tend to be alienated from their respective organizations.[16]

Calculative Involvement. Calculative involvement designates either a negative or a positive orientation of low intensity. Calculative orientations are predominant in relationships of merchants who have continuous business contacts. Attitudes of (and toward) permanent customers are often predominantly calculative, as are relationships among entrepreneurs in modern (rational) capitalism. Inmates in prisons who have established contact with prison authorities, such as "rats" and "peddlers," often have predominantly calculative attitudes toward those in power.[17]

Moral Involvement.[18] Moral involvement designates a positive orientation of high intensity. The involvement of the parishioner in his church, the devoted member in his party, and the loyal follower in his leader are all "moral."

There are two kinds of moral involvement, pure and social. They differ in the same way pure normative power differs from social power. Both are intensive modes of commitment, but they differ in their foci of orientation and in the structural conditions under which they develop. Pure moral commitments are based on internalization of norms and identification with authority (like Riesman's inner-directed "mode of conformity"); social commitment rests on sensitivity to pressures of primary groups and their members (Riesman's "other-directed"). Pure moral involvement tends to develop in vertical relationships, such as those between teachers and students, priests and parishioners, leaders and followers. Social involvement tends to develop in horizontal relationships like those in various types of primary groups. Both pure moral and social orientations might be found in the same relationships, but, as a rule, one orientation predominates.

Actors are means to each other in alienative and in calculative relations; but they are ends to each other in "social" relationships. In pure moral relationships the means-orientation tends to predominate; hence, for example, the willingness of devoted members of totalitarian parties or religious orders to use each other. But unlike the means-orientation of calculative relationships, the means-orientation here is expected to be geared to needs of the collectivity in serving its goals, and not to those of an individual.

NOTES AND REFERENCES

1. T. Parsons. *The Social System* (New York: The Free Press of Glencoe, Inc., 1951), p. 121.
2. H. Goldhamer, & E. A. Shils. "Types of Power and Status" *American Journal of Sociology* (1939), **45**:171.
3. We suggest that this typology is exhaustive, although the only way we can demonstrate this is by pointing out that every type of power we have encountered so far can be classified as belonging to one of the categories or to a combination of them.
4. T. Parsons. *The Social System* (New York: The Free Press of Glencoe, Inc., 1951), p. 108.
5. This distinction draws on the difference between social and normative integration, referred to by T. Parsons, R. F. Bales, & E. A. Shils, *Working Papers in the Theory of Action* (New York: The Free Press of Glencoe, Inc., 1953), p. 182, as the distinction between the "integrative" and the "latent pattern maintenance" phases. In volume in progress, Shils distinguishes between social and ideological primary groups (private communication). J. S. Coleman, "Multidimensional Scale Analysis," *American Journal of Sociology* (1957), **63**:255, has pointed to the difference between group-oriented and idea-oriented attachments.

6. In more technical language, one can say that the three continua of power constitute a three-dimensional property space. If we collapse each dimension into high, medium, and low segments, there are 27 possible combinations or cells. Our hypothesis reads that most organizations fall into cells which are high on one dimension and low or medium on the others; this excludes 18 cells (not counting three types of dual structures discussed below).

7. R. K. Merton. *Mass Persuasion: The Social Psychology of a War Bond Drive* (New York: Harper & Row, Publishers, 1946), p. 47.

8. *Ibid.*, p. 45.

9. *Involvement* has been used in a similar manner by Nancy C. Morse, *Satisfactions in the White-Collar Job* (Survey Research Center, University of Michigan, 1953), pp. 76–96. The term is used in a somewhat different way by students of voting, who refer by it to the psychological investment in the outcome of an election rather than in the party, which would be parallel to Morse's usage and ours. See, for example, A. Campbell, G. Gurin, and W. E. Miller, *The Voter Decides* (New York: Harper & Row, Publishers, 1954), pp. 33–40.

10. Mishler defined *commitment* in a similar though more psychological way: "An individual is committed to an organization to the extent that central tensions are integrated through organizationally relevant instrumental acts." Cited by C. Argyris, *Personality and Organization* (New York: Harper & Row, Publishers, 1957), p. 202.

11. We draw deliberately on the associations this term has acquired from its usage by Marx and others. For a good analysis of the idea of alienation in Marxism, and of its more recent development, see D. Bell, "The 'Rediscovery' of Alienation," *Journal of Philosophy*, 56 (1959), pp. 933–52. And D. Bell, *The End of Ideology* (New York: The Free Press of Glencoe, Inc., 1960), pp. 335–68. See also D. G. Dean, "Alienation and Political Apathy," *Social Forces*, 38 (1960), pp. 185–89.

12. An example of empirical indicators which can be used to translate the involvement continuum into directly observable terms is offered by E. A. Shils, and M. Janowits, "Cohesion and Disintegration in the Wehrmacht in World War II," *Public Opinion Quarterly*, 12 (2), (1948), pp. 282–83. They classify "modes of social disintegration" in the armed forces as follows: desertion; active surrender; passive surrender; routine resistance; "last-ditch" resistance. In the terms used here, these measures indicate varying degrees of involvement, from highest alienation (desertion) to highest commitment (last-ditch resistance).

Nettler (1958) has developed a 17-item unidimensional scale which measures alienation from society. It seems that a similar scale could be constructed for measuring alienation from or commitment to organizational power without undue difficulties. A. Kornhauser, H. L. Sheppard, and A. J. Mayer, *When Labor Votes* (New York: University Books, 1956), pp. 147–48, have developed a 6-item scale, measuring the orientation of union members to their organization, which supplies another illustration of the wide use and measurability of these concepts, which are central to our analysis.

13. Several sociologists have pointed out that the relationship between intensity and direction of involvement is a curvilinear one: the more positive or negative the orientation, the more intensely it is held. L. Guttman, "The Cornell Technique for Scale and Intensity Analysis," *Education and Psychology Measurement J* (1947), pp. 247–79.

14. H. H. Gerth, and C. W. Mills. *From Max Weber: Essays in Sociology* (New York: Oxford University Press, 1946), p. 67.

15. K. Davis, "The Sociology of Prostitution," *American Sociological Review*, 2 (1937), pp. 748–49.

16. For a description of this orientation in prisons see D. Clemmer, *The Prison Community* (New York: Holt, Rinehart & Winston, Inc., 1958), pp. 152 ff. Attitudes toward the police, particularly on the part of members of the lower class, are often strictly alienative. See for example, E. Banfield, *The Moral Basis of a Backward Society* (New York: The Free Press of Glencoe, Inc., 1958).

17. G. M. Sykes. *The Society of Captives* (Princeton: Princeton University Press, 1958), pp. 87–95.

18. The term moral is used here and in the rest of the volume to refer to an orientation of the actor; it does not involve a value-position of the observer. See T. Parsons, and E. A. Shils, *et al. Toward a General Theory of Action* (Cambridge, Mass.: Harvard University Press, 1952), pp. 170 ff.

A Theory of Authority

Chester I. Barnard

Now a most significant fact of general observation relative to authority is the extent to which it is ineffective in specific instances. It is so ineffective that the violation of authority is accepted as a matter of course and its implications are not considered. It is true that we are sometimes appalled at the extent of major criminal activities; but we pass over very lightly the universal violations, particularly of sumptuary laws, which are as "valid" as any others. Even clauses of constitutions and statutes carrying them "into effect," such as the Eighteenth Amendment, are violated in wholesale degrees.

Violation of law is not, however, peculiar to our own country. I observed recently in a totalitarian state under a dictator, where personal liberty is supposed to be at a minimum and arbitrary authority at a maximum, many violations of positive law or edict, some of them open and on a wide scale; and I was reliably informed of others.

Nor is this condition peculiar to the authority of the state. It is likewise true of the authority of churches. The Ten Commandments and the prescriptions and prohibitions of religious authority are repeatedly violated by those who profess to acknowledge their formal authority.

These observations do not mean that all citizens are lawless and defy authority; nor that all Christians are godless or their conduct unaffected by the tenets of their faith. It is obvious that to a large extent citizens are governed; and that the conduct of Christians is substantially qualified by the prescriptions of their churches. What is implied is merely that which specific laws will be obeyed or disobeyed by the individual citizen are decided by him under the specific conditions pertinent. This is what we mean when we refer to individual responsibility. It implies that which prescriptions of the church will be disobeyed by the individual are determined by him at a given time and place. This is what we mean by moral responsibility. . . .

We may leave the secondary stages of this analysis for later consideration. What we derive from it is an approximate definition of authority for our purpose: Authority is the character of a communication (order) in a formal organization by virtue of which it is accepted by a contributor to or "member" of the organization as governing the action he contributes; that is, as governing or determining what he does or is not to do so far as the organization is concerned. . . .

If a directive communication is accepted by one to whom it is addressed, its authority for him is confirmed or established. It is admitted as the basis of action. Disobedience of such a communication is a denial of its authority for him. Therefore, under this definition the decision as to whether an order has authority or not lies with the persons to whom it is addressed, and does not reside in "persons of authority" or those who issue these orders. . . .

Our definition of authority no doubt will appear to many, whose eyes are fixed only on enduring organizations, to be a platform of chaos. And so it is—exactly so in the preponderance of attempted organizations. They fail because they can maintain no authority, that is, they cannot secure sufficient contributions of personal efforts to be effective or cannot induce them on terms that are efficient. In the last analysis the authority fails because the individuals in sufficient numbers regard the burden involved in accepting necessary orders as changing the balance of advantage against their interest, and they withdraw or withhold the indispensable contributions.

We must not rest our definition, however, on general opinion. The necessity of the assent of the individual to establish authority *for him* is inescapable. A person can and will accept a communication as authoritative only when four conditions simultaneously obtain: (a) he can and does understand the communication; (b) *at the time of his decision* he believes that it is not inconsistent with the purpose of the organization; (c) *at the time of his decision,* he believes it to be compatible with his personal interest as a whole; and (d) he is able mentally and physically to comply with it.

(a) A communication that cannot be understood *can* have no authority. An order issued, for example, in a language not intelligible to the recipient is no order at all—no one would so regard it. Now, many orders are exceedingly difficult to understand. They are often necessarily stated in general terms, and the persons who issued them could not themselves apply them under many conditions. Until interpreted they have no meaning. The recipient either must disregard them or merely do anything in the hope that that is compliance.

Hence, a considerable part of administrative work consists in the interpretation and reinterpretation of orders in their application to concrete circumstances that were not or could not be taken into account initially.

(b) A communication believed by the recipient to be incompatible with the purpose of the organization, as he understands it, could not be accepted. Action would be frustrated by cross purposes. The most common practical example is that involved in conflicts of orders. They are not rare. An intelligent person will deny the authority of that one which contradicts the purpose of the effort as *he* understands it. In extreme cases many individuals would be virtually paralyzed by conflicting orders. They would be literally unable to comply—for example, an employee of a water system ordered to blow up an essential pump, or soldiers ordered to shoot their own comrades. I suppose all experienced executives know that when it is necessary to issue orders that will appear to the recipients to be contrary to the main purpose, especially as exemplified in prior habitual practice, it is usually necessary and always advisable, if practicable, to explain or demonstrate why the appearance of conflict is an illusion. Otherwise the orders are likely not to be executed, or to be executed inadequately.

(c) If a communication is believed to involve a burden that destroys the net advantage of connection with the organization, there no longer would remain a net inducement to the individual to contribute to it. The existence of a net inducement is the only reason for accepting *any* order as having authority. Hence, if such an order is received it must be disobeyed (evaded in the more usual cases) as utterly inconsistent with personal motives that are the basis of accepting any orders at all. Cases of voluntary resignation from all sorts of organizations are common for this sole reason. Malingering and intentional lack of dependability are the more usual methods.

(d) If a person is unable to comply with an order, obviously it must be disobeyed, or, better, disregarded. To order a man who cannot swim to swim a river is a sufficient case. Such extreme cases are not frequent; but they occur. The more usual case is to order a man to do things only a little beyond his capacity; but a little impossible is still impossible.

Naturally the reader will ask: How is it possible to secure such important and enduring cooperation as we observe if in principle and in fact the determination of authority lies with the subordinate individual? It is possible because the decisions of individuals occur under the following conditions: (a) orders that are deliberately issued in enduring organizations usually comply with the four conditions mentioned above; (b) there exists a "zone of indifference" in each individual within which orders are acceptable without conscious questioning of their authority; (c) the interests of the persons who contribute to an organization as a group result in the exercise of an influence on the subject, or on the attitude of the individual, that maintains a certain stability of this zone of indifference.

(a) There is no principle of executive conduct better established in good organizations than that orders will not be issued that cannot or will not be obeyed. Executives and most persons of experience who have thought about it know that to do so destroys authority, discipline, and morale. For reasons to be stated shortly, this principle cannot ordinarily be formally admitted, or at least cannot be professed. When it appears necessary to issue orders which are initially or apparently unacceptable, either careful preliminary education, or persuasive efforts, or the prior offering of effective inducements will be made, so that the issue will not be raised, the denial of authority will not occur, and orders will be obeyed. It is generally recognized that those who least understand this fact—newly appointed minor or "first line" executives—are often guilty of "disorganizing" their groups for this reason, as do experienced executives who lose self-control or become unbalanced by a delusion of power or for some other reason. Inexperienced persons take literally the current notions of authority and are then said "not to know how to use authority" or "to abuse authority." Their superiors often profess the same beliefs about authority in the abstract, but their successful practice is easily observed to be inconsistent with their professions.

(b) The phrase "zone of indifference" may be explained as follows: If all the orders for actions reasonably practicable be arranged in the order of their acceptability to the person affected, it may be conceived that there are a number which are clearly unacceptable, that is, which certainly will not be obeyed; there is another group somewhat more or less on the neutral line, that is, either barely acceptable or barely unacceptable; and a third group unquestionably acceptable. This last group lies within the "zone of indifference." The person affected will accept orders lying within this zone and is relatively indifferent as to what the order is so far as the question of authority is concerned. Such an order lies within the range that in a general way was anticipated at time of undertaking the connection with the organization. For example, if a soldier enlists, whether voluntarily or not, in an army in which the men are ordinarily moved about within a certain broad region, it is a matter of indifference whether the order be to go to A or B, C or D, and so on; and goings to A, B, C, D, etc., are in the zone of indifference.

The zone of indifference will be wider or narrower depending upon the degree to which the inducements exceed the burdens and sacrifices which determine the individual's adhesion to the organization. It follows that the range of orders that will be accepted will be very limited among those who are barely induced to contribute to the system.

(c) Since the efficiency of organization is affected by the degree to which individuals assent to orders, denying the authority of an organization communication is a threat to the interests of all individuals who derive a net advantage from their connection with the organization, unless the orders are unacceptable to them also. Accordingly, at any given time there is among most of the contributors an active personal interest in the maintenance of the authority of all orders which to them are within the zone of indifference. The maintenance of this interest is largely a function of informal organization. Its expression goes under the names of "public opinion," "organization opinion," "feeling in the ranks," "group attitude," etc. Thus the common sense of the community informally arrived at affects the attitude of individuals, and makes them, as individuals, loath to question authority that is within or near the zone of indifference. The formal statement of this common sense is the fiction* that authority comes down from above, from the general to the particular. This fiction merely establishes a presumption among individuals in favor of the acceptability of orders from superiors, enabling them to avoid making issues of such orders without incurring a sense of personal subserviency or a loss of personal or individual status with their fellows.

Thus the contributors are willing to maintain the authority of communications because, where care is taken to see that only acceptable communications in general are issued, most of them fall within the zone of personal indifference; and because communal sense influences the motives of most contributors most of the time. . . .

* The word "fiction" is used because from the standpoint of logical construction it merely explains overt acts. Either as a superior officer or as a subordinate, however, I know nothing that I actually regard as more "real" than "authority."

From The Prince: Of the Things for Which Men, and Especially Princes, Are Praised or Blamed
Niccolo Machiavelli

It now remains to be seen what are the methods and rules for a prince as regards his subjects and friends. And as I know that many have written of this, I fear that my writing about it may be deemed presumptuous, differing as I do, especially in this matter, from the opinions of others. But my intention being to write something of use to those who understand, it appears to me more proper to go to the real truth of the matter than

From *The Prince* by Niccolo Machiavelli, translated by Luigi Ricci and published by Oxford University Press. Reprinted by permission of the publisher.

to its imagination; and many have imagined republics and principalities which have never been seen or known to exist in reality; for how we live is so far removed from how we ought to be done, will rather learn to bring about his own ruin than his preservation. A man who wishes to make a profession of goodness in everything must necessarily come to grief among so many who are not good. Therefore it is necessary for a prince, who wishes to maintain himself, to learn how not to do good, and to use this knowledge and not use it, according to the necessity of the case.

OF CRUELTY AND CLEMENCY, AND WHETHER IT IS BETTER TO BE LOVED OR FEARED

Proceeding to the other qualities before named, I say that every prince must desire to be considered merciful and not cruel. He must, however, take care not to misuse this mercifulness. Cesare Borgia was considered cruel, but his cruelty had brought order to the Romagna, united it, and reduced it to peace and fealty. If this is considered well, it will be seen that he was really much more merciful than the Florentine people, who, to avoid the name of cruelty, allowed Pistoia to be destroyed. A prince, therefore, must not mind incurring the charge of cruelty for the purpose of keeping his subjects united and faithful; for, with a very few examples, he will be more merciful than those who, from excess of tenderness, allow disorders to arise, from whence spring bloodshed and rapine; for these as a rule injure the whole community, while the executions carried out by the prince injure only individuals. And of all princes, it is impossible for a new prince to escape the reputation of cruelty, new states being always full of dangers. . . .

Nevertheless, he must be cautious in believing, and acting, and must not be afraid of his own shadow, and must proceed in a temperate manner with prudence and humanity, so that too much confidence does not render him incautious, and too much diffidence does not render him intolerant.

From this arises the question whether it is better to be loved more than feared, or feared more than loved. The reply is, that one ought to be both feared and loved, but as it is difficult for the two to go together, it is much safer to be feared than loved, if one of the two has to be wanting. For it may be said of men in general that they are ungrateful, voluble, dissemblers, anxious to avoid danger, and covetous of gain; as long as you benefit them, they are entirely yours; they offer you their blood, their goods, their life, and their children, as I have before said, when the necessity is remote, but when it approaches, they revolt. And the prince who has relied solely on their words, without making other preparations, is ruined; for the friendship which is gained by purchase and not through grandeur and nobility of spirit is bought but not secured, and at a pinch is not to be expended in your service. And men have less scruple in offending one who makes himself loved than one who makes himself feared; for love is held by a chain of obligation which, men being selfish, is broken whenever it serves their purpose; but fear is maintained by a dread of punishment which never fails.

Still, a prince should make himself feared in such a way that if he does not gain love, he at any rate avoids hatred; for fear and the absence of hatred may well go together, and will be always attained by one who abstains from interfering with the property of his citizens and subjects or with their women. And when he is obliged to take the life of any one, let him do so when there is a proper justification and manifest reason for it; but above all he must abstain from taking the property of others, for men forget more easily the death of their father than the loss of their patrimony. Then also pretexts for seizing property are never wanting, and one who begins to live by rapine will always find some reason for taking the goods of others, whereas causes for taking life are rarer and more fleeting.

But when the prince is with his army and has a large number of soldiers under his control, then it is extremely necessary that he should not mind being thought cruel; for without this reputation he could not keep an army united or disposed to any duty. Among the noteworthy actions of Hannibal is numbered this, that although he had an enormous army, composed of men of all nations and fighting in foreign countries, there never arose any dissension either among them or against the prince, either in good fortune or in bad. This could not be due to anything but his inhuman cruelty, which together with his infinite other virtues, made him always venerated and terrible in the sight of his soldiers, and without it his other virtues would not have sufficed to produce that effect. Thoughtless writers admire on the one hand his actions, and on the other blame the principal cause of them.

And that it is true that his other virtues would not have sufficed may be seen from the case of Scipio (famous not only in regard to his own times, but all times of which memory remains), whose armies rebelled against him in Spain, which arose from nothing but his excessive kindness, which allowed more license to the soldiers than was consonant with military discipline. He was reproached with this in the senate by Fabios Maximus, who called him a corrupter of the Roman militia. Locri having been destroyed by one of Scipio's officers was not revenged by him, nor was the insolence of that officer punished, simply by reason of his easy nature; so much so, that someone wishing to excuse him in the senate, said that there were many men who knew rather how not to err, than how to correct the errors of others. This disposition would in time have tarnished the fame and glory of Scipio had he persevered in it under the empire, but living under the rule of the senate this harmful quality was not only concealed but became a glory to him.

I conclude, therefore, with regard to being feared and loved, that men love at their own free will, but fear at the will of the prince, and that a wise prince must rely on what is in his power and not on what is in the power of others, and he must only contrive to avoid incurring hatred, as has been explained.

The Psychology of Power
Michael Korda

"Action makes more fortunes than caution"—that is a piece of advice worth remembering whenever you are tempted to do nothing. The consequences of acting are always more interesting than those of *failing* to act, and you cannot play the power game without moving your pieces (and risking them). At some point, a knowledge of the anatomy of power must lead to practical decisions.

The variety of plays that people use to attain the goal of power is endless, and more a matter of temperament than study, but certain moves are basic, in the sense that all

From *Power! How to Get It, How to Use It*, by Michael Korda. Copyright © 1975 by Michael Korda and Paul Gitlin, Trustee for the Benefit of Christopher Korda. Reprinted by permission of Random House, Inc., and Weidenfeld & Nicolson Ltd.

others are merely variations of them. In fact, the number of basic moves available to the player is comparatively limited, the crucial division being between "games of weakness" and "games of strength." Games of weakness are much underestimated, particularly by men, since they seem to lack *machismo*. This is a pity, because they are extremely effective.

Games of weakness can be seen quite clearly when people who have considerable power are asked to get their subordinates a raise. People whose whole life and soul are wrapped up in the ability to make tough decisions, for whom "eyeball-to-eyeball" confrontations and "showdowns" are virtually a lifestyle, can be reduced to whimpering helplessness by a secretary who wants to be raised from $140 a week to $150. Suddenly they are powerless, brought low by the specter of taking action on behalf of someone else's needs, however small. A person who has just negotiated singlehandedly a $425,000 deal and who would do anything short of physical violence at the board of directors' meeting to get a raise for himself will plead incapacity, weariness, overwork, and, above all, powerlessness to avoid going to bat for someone else's $10 a week—his hands raised palms upward, elbows cocked, shoulders slumped, the Gallic gesture of resignation that signifies impotent sympathy, the instinctive body language of the weakness game.

When it comes to raises, the *smaller the amount involved, the more difficult it is to put through.* Raising an executive from $45,000 to $50,000 is easy enough, and it may even be felt that not giving him the $5,000 at the end of the year would be either an insult or a warning of imminent dismissal. Raising a secretary from $140 a week to $150, on the contrary, is sure to involve a bitter struggle, and require emotional appeals, blackmail, and a personal commitment. Executive salaries, however large, are seen as reflections of the corporation, and are thus *collective* decisions, while smaller salary increases are by their very nature *personal* requests, requiring the executive involved to lay his own prestige on the line. The smaller the sum of money, the more personal it is going to appear, which explains why the best way to get a big raise is already to be making a lot of money.

Denying power can be fruitful in many other ways. Any competent negotiator knows it is better to curse the management, flaunt his weakness, blame everything on the computer or the board of directors, and by joining his opponent, thus implying that they are both victims of the same rapacious organization, negotiate a lower price for whatever is at stake.

The important thing to note is that he has turned humiliation into a productive and profitable *system*. If we can inspire pity, instill in the other person the belief that we are all victims of the same system, we may get what we want for the price we all intended to pay in the first place. Pride and a public show of authority are things we simply can't afford, hence the difficulty, in modern life, of finding anyone who will admit to being responsible for an unpleasant decision.

The humiliation factor is an effective weapon in the hands of the person who knows how to use it and who doesn't suffer from the nagging itch to show his power. Take women's liberation. Faced with the demands of women for equality in the office, men first reacted by counterattacking with anger—the big stick, so to speak. When that failed, as it did in many places, they swiftly adopted a different gameplan: the fellow-victim pose. With more effective results. The trick is to counter any complaint with one's own sufferings. "I'd love to talk about it, Sue, but not this week; if you could see my calendar, you wouldn't believe it. . . ." "I know, I know, I think you should have more money too, but, hell, things are tough for everyone, I'm going to be here until eight tonight going over these reports, I haven't had time to answer yesterday's phone calls yet, and as far as money goes, I haven't had a raise in two years. . . ." "Look, this just isn't the time, I have troubles with the Board, if I try to get more money now, it just won't work, so be patient, okay?"

My friend Harry, for instance, who is as strong as an ox and whose nature is, to put it mildly, combative, has adopted hypochondria as his protective cloak. From a bad cold, he can clinch three good deals, turn down four requests for capital, and shame his secretary into staying until 7 P.M. typing letters. Ask him for a raise and he inquires if you have any nose spray on you, frowning with the pain of terminal sinusitis.

There's no winning against this kind of self-abasement. Unless you're willing to counter every suggestion of ill health with something even more drastic and grave of your own, you are lost. An English author who felt he wasn't getting enough attention from his American publisher announced by telephone, on arrival in the lobby of the building, that he suffered from a fear of elevators. Since it was difficult to hold a meeting by the cigar and news counter, his editor came down to meet him, and together they walked up 15 flights of stairs. This reduced the editor to such trembling exhaustion that he was more than willing to give way on every point of contention, and in fact conceded most of them while gasping for breath somewhere between the fifth and fifteenth floors.

Shamelessness is the key to winning weakness games. If you have committed yourself to doing something you cannot do (or simply don't want to do), soul-wracking sobs and hand wringing should be brought into play. The trick is to make the other person feel guilty, the master stroke being to make *him* apologize to *you* because you've gone back on your word. If, for example, you have negotiated a contract in good faith and decided that it would be a mistake to go through with it, the honest thing would be to proceed with it and take the consequences; the courageous thing would be to refuse to sign it on the grounds that you had made a mistake; the intelligent move, however, is to say that the executive committee has refused to allow it to go through, and to persuade your opposite number that you have risked everything on his behalf and failed. This enables you to repudiate the contract and acquire a reputation for candor as well.

Perhaps because of the general brutalization of our age, we often expect power to be wielded with as much savagery and contempt as possible, as if toughness were synonymous with success. This may explain the popularity of professional football among businessmen and politicians, who like to feel that their work, while sedentary and basically manipulative, calls for the same kind of physical courage and toughness that football players are supposed to need.

In extreme cases (of which there are many) people will even provoke a dispute in order to prove how tough they are. Many business executives are secretly delighted to catch errors in their subordinates' work, or go to great trouble to create "showdown" situations so that they can win them. Setting unrealistic goals for one's subordinates and then losing one's temper when they fail to meet them is a common way of demonstrating power. Another way is to find what an executive's opinion is on something before a meeting, tempt him into exposing it in public, then force him to do the opposite of what he wants to do. Many people don't feel comfortable unless they encounter opposition—if they ask someone to do something and it's done without protest, they feel they've asked for too little. Faced with this kind of power tactic, the proper response is to cushion one's answers and present several alternative solutions to any problem.

Thus, if you are asked, "When can we ship out the first hundred thousand units of this item?" the proper answer is *not* "June 21st." This will merely provoke the power player into telling you, "I want them shipped by June 15th or heads will roll," and you are trapped. The intelligent response to this question is "When are they needed?" This places your opponent in the position of having to fix a date. It is always better to respond to a question with another question, and very important to avoid being the first to mention a specific date or sum of money. Whenever a person who has more power than you asks a question like "How much do you think this property is worth?" you may be sure that he has already decided what *he* thinks it's worth. The only answer that will satisfy him is his own, so it is best to treat all such questions as if they were rhetorical.

A great many people are absolutely committed to "the tough style." They simply cannot bring themselves to show the slightest weakness, and, given the choice, would rather be tough than right. They are never happy unless they can force other people to do things by threats, bullying, and invective, even when the people they're fighting are perfectly happy to do what they've been told.

What is seldom noticed is that the people who *don't* talk tough very often get ahead of those who do. Aggression is so much a part of our national lifestyle that it's hard for most people to recognize ambition unless it's accompanied by brutality. Nothing gives a person greater freedom and more opportunities than being disregarded as a serious contender for power. A great deal can be gained by simply learning to smile, an exercise that is not all that easy for many people to perform. The person who wants to use power must learn to control his facial muscles, his temper, and himself, and avoid taking "tough stands" where they aren't necessary. Flexibility and cheerfulness are better weapons than brute force, and if used properly have the advantage of making your rivals forget that you're a competitor for power.

Of course you can't expect a smile to do the whole job for you. You have to understand something about hierarchies, too. People who believe in hierarchy move upward, if they move at all, by steps. Theirs is essentially a linear and static view of power, as if life were a ladder, to be climbed one rung at a time. You can't get to the top without touching every rung, which means that the rungs themselves become, in a sense, more important than the people on them, the extreme examples of such a power system being the army and the Civil Service.

An army division, for example, requires a major general to command it. His duties and functions are defined by the regulations, and provided he can maintain the discipline and efficiency of his unit in peacetime, and give it at least a minimal fighting spirit in wartime, no more is expected of him. He cannot turn his division into a corps. His post exists and must be filled, whether by a gifted and ambitious soldier in the style of Patton or by a nonentity—indeed the nonentity may do the better job in some circumstances. In any event, a divisional commander (and there are many civilian jobs that resemble this position) can only move vertically, and must abandon his division to gain promotion—he can aspire to become a corps commander, for instance, or to be chosen for some staff post that carries with it the rank of lieutenant general, but there is no way for him to win an extra star by expanding his division.

In civilian life certain departmental executives exist in similar situations. They can rise only by leaving their present job and taking on a bigger, more important one, rising step by step, either continuously (i.e., within the same company) or discontinuously, by changing jobs and rising upward in different companies with each change.

Both methods are identical in one important respect: upward progress can only be made one step at a time, and each step taken means abandoning the one below it, just as you have to take your foot off rung A of a ladder to place it on rung B. This kind of promotion requires a great deal of time, and the competition for each rung is severe. Worse, you have to abandon what you have in order to reach for what you want, thus increasing your risk of falling off and landing back in the heap at the foot of the ladder. And you are planning your career in terms of an existing and rigid structure, which means that you're playing according to someone else's rules.

Very different is the position of those who can *expand* their jobs, gradually enveloping enough people and functions so that they have to be promoted to regularize their acquisitions, made, as it were, by reaching out arms like an amoeba, then filling in the spaces.

Note the difference between the "expander's" pattern of power and that of the "ladderer." The expander never gives up his original job or any of the ones he acquires; instead of moving upward, he expands outward, flowing like lava. He *adds* to his jobs and titles and responsibilities, trusting that he will pick up enough people on the way to make it possible for him to delegate the more onerous parts of his workload. The trick is to learn how to delegate without giving up responsibility, *until one is finally responsible for everything without having to do anything.*

The really fierce power games tend to be played by "expanders" rather than "ladderers," since the "expander" can spread out rapidly, amalgamating and absorbing whole departments, destroying old titles and creating new ones to describe his expanded functions. By contrast, the "ladderer" can only go up one rung at a time and must wait for the person above him to move. Let us assume that the "creative director" of an advertising agency, a "ladderer," wishes to rise quickly in his company. He is already a department head, so he would have to displace the first vice president to move one step up the ladder.

Unless the first vice president is completely incompetent, this is likely to prove difficult, if not impossible, and would require the creative director to persuade the other department heads to join in a conspiracy, with obvious risks. Of course, the creative director may lobby vociferously for a vice presidency of his own, but this will not change his status one bit: he is still standing on the rung below the one he covets, with three other people beside him. If he gets a vice presidency, the other department heads will demand the same title for themselves, which results in its immediate debasement and reduces its power significance to zero. This process, a kind of Gresham's Law of titles, has been so complete in some companies that many vice presidents refuse to use the title on their cards and writing paper, or insist on adding a second, descriptive title to the one they already have, as in "Vice President and Manager of Business Systems," or "Creative Vice President." Other corporations further complicate matters by creating two kinds of vice presidents (sometimes referred to in one cosmetics company as the sheep and the goats), one a meaningless give-away to placate people who haven't received the raise they expected, the other more or less genuine, in that the recipient is a corporate officer and is authorized to sign contracts and go to jail on behalf of his employer. Hence the importance of knowing just what kind of vice president you are dealing with, the rule of thumb being that a vice president without a corner office or a sofa more than five feet long is the corporate equivalent of a Kentucky Colonel—i.e., the holder of an honorary title without power.

If our creative director gets his vice presidency, he will be swiftly followed by the other department heads. Those on the rung will simply have swollen a bit, thus making life on the rung a little more crowded and uncomfortable than it was before. Until the man above him either falls off the ladder or moves his Gucci loafers up to the rung above him and becomes president, the creative director—whatever his title—is stuck.

The "expander" has no such problem. He does not think in terms of rungs, he simply overflows, taking over bits and pieces of other people's departments, projects so boring or difficult that nobody else wants them, above all tasks that require liaison and communication between departments. Soon he will have created a complex and almost invisible system of alternative management, probably more effective than the real one represented by the first vice president, since it is closer to actual operational problems, while at the same time spreading out so widely that it will quickly be necessary to "do something for him," as the management phrase goes. A good "expander" will swallow up so many of his superior's functions that eventually nothing is left but the title, which can be discarded together with its incumbent, when he has been reduced to powerlessness.

Expanding represents the surest power game of all. The promotion ladder only exists as long as people believe in it, and are willing to trudge up it. The moment somebody begins to spread out like a tide, it floats away.

More important still is the control of information. Almost everybody is dependent on the supply of information, yet "information input" is usually regarded as a clerical task, not much better than menial labor. Hours are spent in discussing major questions of policy, but the information on which these decisions have to be made is sought after in the most casual way. An executive planning a promotional campaign that may cost a hundred thousand dollars is perfectly capable of turning to a person whose salary is under $200 a week and saying, "Listen, check the production people to see when the product is coming off the lines, and make sure sales and shipping get the stuff into these cities so it's there before the ads run, okay?" For the next two hours he may debate with his subordinates the merits of print vs. television, the right color for displays, whether the model in the ads should be sexy or motherly, whatever else is on his and their minds, but the only important thing has been delegated to someone who may well be a secretary.

By the same token, information always comes from below, and the more important it is, the farther down one has to go to collect it. If the same executive wants to find out how much money was spent on a comparable campaign a year earlier, he will ask his secretary to find out, and she will ask the advertising manager's secretary, such routine matters being beneath his attention, and together they will go back to the files and add up whatever figures they can find. Because they are not privy to high policy, there may be hidden items they know nothing about, with the result that their meticulously collected figures will be entirely misleading. Nevertheless, six well-paid executives will base their assumptions on these figures unquestioningly.

Those who play the information game know not only how to obtain and control information but also how to make it practically incomprehensible. Their object is to render the information at their disposal as mysterious and inaccessible as possible, compiling it in such complex forms that only they can explain what (if anything) it means.

The advent of the computer has made their task much easier, not only because most computerized information is printed in odd ways on forms that fold like an accordion and tend to slip off the desk onto the floor in a hopeless jumble, but also because any information produced by the computer needs interpretation. Whatever the question, the computer is likely to provide several responses, none of them in quite the form that will answer the question easily, and all of them leaving out the essential knowledge of just what facts were fed into the computer in the first place. The person who controls the computer is thus in a singular position of power, and all the more so since he is in charge of an extremely expensive piece of machinery. Once a corporation has invested several million dollars in a computer system, it is obliged to pay some attention to the information the computer produces.

Gradually the person who controls information can use his monopoly to good effect in any discussion. Faced with disagreement, he can say, "You're speaking from opinion; I'm speaking from facts!" This device (your *opinion* vs. my *fact*) is remarkably effective. In the first place, nobody can get at the "facts" once all the information has been channeled to one person. In the second place, the "facts" are now reported in a form that only one person can understand. Even if you can persuade the executive who controls the information to show you the figures, you will have to ask him to explain what they mean, which automatically increases his power over you. Finally, any protracted argument about these "facts" would mean challenging them, which implies an exhaustive study of the information system itself. Nobody in his right mind cares to do that, and the possessor of "facts" is therefore in a fairly invulnerable position.

Controlling information has another advantage as a game of power. It tends to make the person who controls it seem indispensable—and the indispensability game, though risky in the long run, is an excellent secondary move in acquiring and holding power.

All struggles between management and personnel are contained in the problem of indispensability. The employee must consider himself indispensable, even if he or she doubts it, while the management must hold the opposite view. Many people spend their working lives attempting to make themselves indispensable, a search for absolute security that seldom pays dividends. First of all, the management point of view is basically correct: nobody *is* indispensable; however important you are, replacing you is at worst a question of inconvenience, expense, and time. People who attempt to prove their indispensability are obliged to expand at a geometric rate—they can never have enough tasks, titles, duties, and responsibilities to establish their indispensability to their own satisfaction, just as nobody who requires love to feel secure can have enough love. To expand in order to get more power, or more money, or more prestige, is a feasible ambition. To expand until you are *secure* is impossible. In every corporation, the people who think themselves indispensable, and are generally regarded as such by their colleagues, eventually get fired. The reason is simple, but seldom accepted: no corporation can afford to believe that its existence is dependent on the health, sanity, and good will of a relatively small number of people, especially if it's true.

One of my dearest friends set out to make himself indispensable to his company, and almost did so. Not only were his projects enormously profitable, but he gradually extended a kind of moral control over the entire office. Important files were locked away in his drawers, totemic pieces of furniture were removed from their places in the middle of the night and carried to his office; he had the lock to the lavatory on his side of the office changed, so that nobody could go to the bathroom without coming to him for the key. Constantly fatigued, harassed, and complaining, he involved himself in every problem, from the company picnic to the typography of the annual report. What is more, he had mastered the most important strategy of indispensability, which is to create an outside legend: a good part of his time was spent in giving interviews, going to parties, and appearing on television, and since any management prefers to believe what they hear and see from the outside rather than what they can observe for themselves, his claim to indispensability went unchallenged.

As one of his colleagues says, "For three years we lived with this legend. All the power gravitated toward this guy, and if you objected or argued, he would explain how tired he was—he had this thing of taking off his glasses and massaging the bridge of his nose to show that he was exhausted—then he'd tell you that he wasn't sure how much longer he could go on carrying all these burdens people were heaping on him. 'How much more can flesh and blood bear?' he would ask, but if you tried to do the smallest thing without asking him, he would quietly undo whatever you'd done, and make you do it his way. You couldn't win. If you got in at eight in the morning, he'd tell you that he'd been in on Sunday for hours; if you came in on Sunday, he'd tell you that he'd been up to four in the morning trying to make sense of other people's work. He made a practice of making at least one change in *everything*, however minor, so he could always tell you that he hoped you wouldn't mind if he added 'the finishing touch.'

"Then one day he walked out to take another job, and it was like the end of the world. It wasn't just that nobody could be sure what was in the files, or what it meant, we couldn't even *find* them. Everything was so centralized that when he took away his little pocket address book, we couldn't find the telephone numbers of our customers—we hardly even knew who they *were*. We'd been happy to let him take over. It simply meant less work for us, and, better than that, no responsibility. But within a couple of weeks it was as if he'd never been there. Life went on; it was a lot better in fact. We didn't go bankrupt, and we didn't go to pieces. But I realized one thing: *nobody is indispensable.*"

The more you try to prove how much you're needed, the more you are likely to attract the attention of people who wonder whether your job is necessary in the first place.

Someone who tries to make himself indispensable is like a swimmer clinging to a piece of flotsam in a raging storm when it might be safer to let go and swim. The world is full of people who will work a 14-hour day to hold a job that could easily be done in 7 hours, exhausting themselves and irritating everyone above and below them in the useless struggle to prove that life couldn't go on without them. It's better by far to make it clear that a great many other people could probably do your job as well, but that for the moment you are the one doing it.

The ability to say no can be pyramided into a position of unique influence and authority. It is perfectly represented by Ms. Mildred Pearlman, a New York City civil servant in charge of reclassifying the city's 3,600 job titles: "You start by saying no to all requests," Ms. Pearlman told the *New York Times;* "then if you have to go to yes, okay. But if you start with yes you can't go to no."

Power and money await anyone who can manage to say no all the time. Almost everybody likes to be thanked and loved, no matter how powerful he or she is, and saying yes is therefore a constant temptation for most people. The true "no-sayers" like Mildred Pearlman are incorruptible and invaluable, nor do they mind looking ridiculous. Their mode of operation is simple: they say no to everything until overruled, secure in the knowledge that they are likely to be right at least 60 percent of the time and forgiven for the other 40 percent.

A talented "no-player" can rise very fast, since most executives are happy to find someone who will say no for them. How much easier it is to listen to an impassioned plea for a new project, or a $5,000 raise, or an expensive marketing survey, or a new Xerox machine, and say, "Yes, you're right, it makes good sense and I'm for it. Just clear it with X first on the budget side, and we'll go right ahead. . . ." X's job, of course, is to listen in stony silence and say no, immune to pleas, threats, and common sense.

The most important thing for those who want to play the "no-game" is to be consistent—the moment you start saying yes to some things, making value judgments, acceding to certain requests because they're reasonable, you've become simply another decision maker.

Closely allied to "no-saying" and indispensability is the use of *responsibility* as a power game. When responsibility players look worried, they're worried about what *you* are doing, not about what *they* are doing. People who play the responsibility game almost always appear more worried than the people who are actually in charge. Just as there's a place for someone who can say no, there's also a place for a person who can manage to look worried even when things are going well. Constant pessimism can be irritating to those in charge, but events will almost surely justify pessimism sooner or later, so the pessimist, if he is patient, will eventually gain a reputation for good judgment.

If negativism and pessimism are means to power, humor usually is not. People who like power take themselves seriously, and distrust humor in all but its most savage forms. Besides, people who have a great deal of power get accustomed to hearing other people laughing at their jokes, so even if they *do* have a sense of humor, it tends to atrophy from a surfeit of unwarranted appreciation. Many powerful people see jokes, in any case, not so much as a humorous diversion but as a means of dominating the conversation. Thus, if six people are engaged in a discussion, a person trying to emphasize his position of power may say, "Listen, before we go any further, I've got a funny story to tell you," and proceed to tell it at great length, not to amuse, but to prove he can interrupt the discussion on a whim. An excellent clue to power personality can be found in the use of such phrases as "You're going to love this," or "I'm going to tell you something you'll find hilarious," or "Listen to this, you'll *die!*" Jokes and "funny" stories that begin with a command are almost always weapons of power, and are not to be confused with good fellowship or humor.

Precedence is of course a gold mine of power games, the basic technique being to call people into your own office, rather than going to theirs, which implies giving up your power spot and entering theirs. This is simple enough, but ignores the complexities of territorialism. Many powerful people, particularly the aggressive ones, *prefer* to go to other people's offices, since they are then invading the other person's turf. Thus a man who wants to establish his precedence over another may go into the other person's office, sit down, and put his feet on the desk, thus infringing on the intimate territory of his inferior. These small signs of conquest are numerous, and include using objects as ashtrays when that's obviously not what they were intended for, giving orders to somebody else's secretary, spilling coffee, and even lying down on someone else's carpet to do back exercises when the other person is seated at his or her desk. The important thing in such games is to simultaneously establish territorial rights and appear more casual than your opponent, giving the impression that you believe *his* office belongs to you by making yourself at home there. Generally speaking, people playing the power game will call subordinates into their own power spot to give orders and go into their subordinates' offices to issue warnings, threats, and denunciations. A special situation (though doubtless familiar to many) is to call a meeting in your own office and make sure there aren't enough chairs, thus obliging people either to carry their own down the hall or sit on the floor.

The theatrical side of power is often overlooked, perhaps because most people in business want to be thought calm and conventional in their behavior, and rational in their decisions. However, the element of theater exists, and not just in the kind of tantrum that is usually associated with Broadway rehearsals and dressing-room feuds. Since office life is often dull, the ability to produce drama is a helpful element in acquiring and maintaining power, in much the same fashion as the later Roman emperors were obliged to provide both bread *and* circuses to keep the mob quiet and busy. A dull executive, who lacks the talent for dramatizing his own career and the work of people around him, is bound to lose popular support. Astute power players know just how to create and publicize epic crises in order to get the credit for solving them, and how to predict catastrophe just before announcing good news in order to make the good news sound even better. In fact, if this game is played properly, even *bad* news can be made to sound like a triumph—it's simply necessary to make the predictions so terrible that anything short of bankruptcy will come as a relief.

A command of such games eventually gives a person a certain mythic quality as a "miracle worker" or, in the currently popular phrase, "a troubleshooter." Nobody is likely to notice that the "trouble" was either imaginary or self-created in the first place. If you have a good reason to believe that the monthly figures for your department are going to be down $200,000 from last year's, the correct thing to do is not to waste time inventing excuses but to go into action with the news that catastrophe has struck, that the figures will be down at least $400,000, that "heads are going to roll." It should be noted that the first step is to imply that it is *other* people's heads which are at issue. The best way to do this is to call your staff into your office and stage a scene appropriate to *Othello*, accusing everyone of betraying you and threatening dire reprisals.

Once you have established that you are not at fault, you can move to the next position, which is to take responsibility for disaster in a noble and self-sacrificing manner. Your superiors will have heard of your attack on your subordinates, and having indirectly established that they are at fault, you can now quietly announce that things look bad for the month and that you're willing to be made the scapegoat. It is okay to offer your resignation if you think there's a good chance it won't be accepted, which is usually the case. By now, you will have prepared those above you for the worst, reinforcing their fears by sending out calamitous memoranda, and by staying in the office until everyone else has gone home. It is also useful to see as much as you can of the higher management executives. The more you involve them, the more *your* problem becomes "our" problem and the responsibility for it is spread above you as well as below you. When, at the proper moment, you announce that the loss is "only" $200,000, it will be thought that you have worked a miracle, and with a little bit of effort you can extract as much credit as you would have from an *increase* in the figures.

What you have done is to make a prosaic failure into a full-scale drama, with yourself as the hero. Since everybody is happy to watch a drama unfolding and even happier to be able to play supporting roles in it, the figures themselves will soon seem unimportant and meaningless, and any judgment that is being made on your career from above will be based on the exciting quality of your performance.

Creating artificial catastrophes is a game that can be played at every level, and is particularly useful in making other people feel guilty and in warding off unwelcome requests. You can usually keep your subordinates in their places by making their mistakes into major dramas. I have heard an executive say, "This is the worst day of my life," sitting slumped at his desk in an attitude of despair, only to discover that he has been struck down by a misplaced file. Nobody respects a person who suffers silently or, worse yet, boringly. The trick is to suffer in style.

Power and the Ambitious Executive

Robert N. McMurry

The most important and unyielding necessity of organizational life is not better communications, human relations, or employee participation, but power. I define *power* as the capacity to modify the conduct of other employees in a desired manner, together with the capacity to avoid having one's own behavior modified in undesired ways by other employees. Executives must have power because, unfortunately, many employees resent discipline; to these employees, work is something to be avoided. In their value systems "happiness" is the ultimate goal. For the organization to be made productive, such persons must be subjected to discipline.

Without power there can be no authority; without authority, there can be no discipline; without discipline, there can be difficulty in maintaining order, system, and productivity. An executive without power is, therefore, all too often a figurehead—or worse, headless. The higher an executive is in his management hierarchy, the greater his need for power. This is because power tends to weaken as it is disseminated downward.

GAINING AND KEEPING POWER

If the executive owns the business, that fact may ensure his power. If he does not, and sometimes even when he does, his power must be acquired and held by means which are essentially political. Of critical importance, since most of his power is derived or delegated, his power must be dependable. Nothing is more devastating to an executive than to lose support and backing in moments of crisis. It is for this reason that the development of continuing power is the most immediate and nagging concern of many professional managers.

How can chief executives and other managers who possess little or no equity in a business consolidate enough power to protect their jobs and enforce their dictates when necessary? The eight recommendations which follow are the fruit of 30 years of observation of a great number of executives managing a variety of enterprises.

A number of these conclusions conflict with the findings of other writers. The most that can be said in defense of my recommendations is that they did not spring from an ivory tower. They are based on strategies and tactics employed by demonstrably successful executives who lacked financial control of their enterprises. The executives were working pragmatists. Their prime criterion of a desirable course of action was: Will it work? While the strategies presented here are not infallible, they have proven their worth more often than not in the hard and competitive world of business.

1. The executive should take all the steps he can to ensure that he is personally compatible with superiors.

In the case of the chief executive, this means compatibility with the owners and/or their representatives, such as bankers, lawyers, and family members; in the case of other managers, senior executives and owners are the key groups. The point is that though a manager may have all the skills, experience, and personal attributes his position requires, if his values and goals are not reasonably consonant with those of the persons who hold power and he is not acceptable to them personally, his tenure will probably be brief.

To protect against subsequent disillusionment and conflict, the prospective manager should, before he joins the company, endeavor to become acquainted with his prospective superior or superiors informally. This could be done at dinner with them, on the golf course, or on a trip. At such a meeting he can learn his superior's values, standards, prejudices, and expectations. If any significant evidence of incompatibility emerges, he should call off negotiations—incompatibility tends to worsen rather than improve with continued contact.

If at all possible, the manager's wife should meet the superior, also under informal conditions, since compatibility with her can play an important part in the new man's acceptance. Likewise, if it can be arranged for the manager's wife to meet the chief's wife, early in the course of negotiations, that should be done. Compatibility between these two can be very advantageous; incompatibility can be fatal.

2. Whether he comes to the company from outside or is being promoted from within, the executive should obtain an employment contract.

While many owners and senior executives protest that they never make such agreements and that it is against their policy to do so, the prospective manager must insist that every policy is subject to change and that he will not accept the position without one. A failure to win out at this most critical juncture can be fatal to him. The reason is not so much that failure strips him of any vestige of job security and power but that it indicates to those in command that he is somewhat docile and submissive and probably can be pushed about at their whim.

This is particularly true where the executive's primary assignment is to salvage and rehabilitate a sick or failing operation or to initiate and pioneer a new and radically different field of activity that no one in the business knows much about. The compensation may be alluring, the status attractively elevated, and the challenge exciting. But the risks have to be great. If worse comes to worst and the executive is removed, he will have a tidy sum to carry him over the six months or longer that he needs to find a new job.

3. On taking a major assignment, the executive should obtain from his superiors a clear, concise, and unambiguous statement in writing of his duties, responsibilities, reporting relationships, and scope of authority.

Such a document is absolutely essential if the manager is not later to make the humiliating and frustrating discovery that the parameters of his job have been changed, often with no notice to him. He may have been led to believe at the outset that he had certain responsibilities and commensurate authority to carry them out. Later he may learn that he has no such authority and that some of the people who were to report to him in effect do not do so. He may discover that figuratively he has been castrated; all of his authority has been taken from him, leaving him powerless. If, when he protests, he cannot substantiate his charges with a written commitment, he is likely to be told, "You have misunderstood our original agreement."

4. The executive should take exceptional care to find subordinates who combine technical competence with reliability, dependability, and loyalty.

As many a top executive has learned to his sorrow, he is constantly vulnerable to sabotage by his underlings. This is especially the case where he comes in from outside and "does not know where the bodies are buried." It is for this reason that he should be so careful in the choice of his immediate subordinates.

In theory, each superior, regardless of his level in the management hierarchy, should have a strong, competent number-two man who is ready and willing to step into his place should he be promoted, retire, leave the company, or for any reason be unable to continue to function. Some executives do just this. But in practice the policy can be hazardous, at least in terms of the senior man's job security.

An aggressive, ambitious, upwardly mobile number-two man is dangerous to any chief, weak or strong. For one thing, the number-two man is often very difficult to control. He has his own personal array of goals and objectives which may or may not be consistent with those of his superior and/or the company. Since he is usually inner directed and a man of strong convictions, it is often difficult to divert him from the course which he has set for himself and which he sincerely believes to be best for him (and secondarily for the company). The risk is considerably lessened if the chief has only one strong subordinate, for then it is easier to watch and constrain him.

Moreover, since the strong subordinate tends to be an individualist, he is more apt to find himself in conflict with his peers. He has a compulsive need to achieve *his* goals regardless of the needs or expectations of the others or of the welfare of the enterprise as a whole. Not only may his influence be seriously divisive, but he tends to fragment the enterprise, to induce a centrifugal effect in it. This is why such businesses as advertising and consulting are so notoriously prone to fragmentation; they attract too many entrepreneurs.

Strong, decisive, qualified men are rarely willing to remain for more than a brief time in a secondary role. Their impatience is accentuated if, for any reason, they do not respect their superior or feel frustrated in their careers. Sometimes they conclude that their greatest opportunity lies not in seeking advancement by moving to another company but by undermining and eventually supplanting their present superior.

In consequence, the politically astute top executive seeks subordinates who not only have the requisite technical skills but who are also to some degree passive, dependent, and submissive. Their "loyalty" is often a euphemism for docility. They tend to be security-conscious and prone to form a dependent relationship with their chief. If the chief has held his position for many years, this building of a submissive group has usually taken place slowly by a process of trial and error. But when he comes in from outside or takes over as the result of a merger, he is often prone (and is usually well advised) to bring his own associates with him or to give preferment to men whom he knows and has worked with previously.

5. A useful defensive tactic for the executive is to select a compliant board of directors.

Of course, the chief executive is the one most immediately concerned with this ploy, but second- and third-level managers, too, may have a vital interest in this matter. In recent years, changes in directors' responsibilities have made it somewhat more difficult to stack the board in the old-fashioned sense. But its membership and operation can still be influenced in a significant way.

Inside directors tend usually to be more malleable than outside directors. Few will be courageous enough to cross swords with the chief executive. While board members by law are the stockholders' representatives and thus are the holders of ultimate power in the business, in practice this is often little more than a polite fiction. In many instances they have largely abdicated their management or even corporate supervisory responsibilities.

Sometimes the directors are too busy to interfere in operations. Not infrequently they have little equity in the business and, hence, are disinterested in it. Sometimes they have been chosen principally because they are "big names" who add status and respectability to the company but can devote little time to its affairs. Much as some observers and authorities dislike such tendencies, they are the realities. The top-management group that knows how to use and exploit power will make sure that it, too, enjoys the blessings of a compliant board.

6. In business, as in diplomacy, the most important stratagem of power is for the executive to establish alliances.

The more alliances the executive can build, the better. He can establish several kinds of relationships:

With his superiors—He can make personal contact with and sell himself to the owner of the business or, where the ownership is widely diversified, to the more influential stockholders. One chief executive I know has luncheon once each month with the widow of the founder of his company. As long as she is convinced that he is a "wonderful man," he has both power and tenure.

Where banks, insurance companies, or mutual funds have a controlling voice in the company, the executive can seek to ingratiate himself with their key executives. If certain of his directors are unusually dominant, he does everything he can to win their favor and support. This does not necessarily mean that he is obsequious and sycophantic in his relationships with them. On the contrary, he may regularly stand up to them and confront them directly.

The key to success in a relationship of this nature is the ascertainment of the other person's expectations. If the man or woman whose support he hopes to win likes tigers, he is a tiger; if the person prefers a mouse, he restrains his more aggressive impulses. Above all, he studies each person's prejudices and values and is careful never to offend them.

With his peers—The adroit manager also builds allegiances with others at his own level. While these people may not be direct sources of power to him, they can often be valuable as supplementary means of support and intelligence. Included among his contacts should be prominent industry figures. Since government intervention in business is increasing daily, acquaintance with senators, congressmen, and major department heads in government can also be helpful. (The owners of a company doing business with the Defense Department will think twice before sacking an executive who is on intimate terms with the Secretary or his deputy.)

One good means of ensuring support from peers is to identify common goals and objectives toward which all can strive. An even more powerful step is to find a common enemy—an antibusiness government official, let us say, or a hostile labor leader. Often influential rivals for power or even disgruntled subordinates can be neutralized by being taken into groups having common goals or enemies.

With subordinates—I have already mentioned the importance of selecting dependent subordinates in whose selfish interest it is to support their chief. Such persons may also be useful as sources of internal intelligence. The information they provide is not always completely accurate or reliable, but it can be cross-checked against data from a variety of other sources.

7. The executive should recognize the power of the purse.

He knows that the best control he can exercise over his subordinates is fiscal. Hence he seeks as quickly as possible to position himself where he approves all budgets. Nothing is as effective in coping with a recalcitrant staff as the power to cut off financial support for their projects. On the other hand, nothing so often promotes gratitude and cooperation as fiscal support of subordinates' favorite projects.

8. The executive should understand the critical importance of clear and credible channels of communication upward from all levels of his personnel and downward from him to them.

Without such channels the executive is an isolate who does not know what is transpiring in his enterprise. His commands will be heard only partially by his subordinates; they will be infrequently understood and rarely acted on. He should recognize that many of his staff have strong motives to keep the truth from him and to block or distort his downward communications.*

To overcome deficiencies of communication, the executive must learn not to depend too much on his hierarchy of assistants (many of whom are not communication centers at all, but barriers to it). Where possible, he will address his people directly, conducting periodic "State of the Company" reports to them and encouraging direct feedback from them by soliciting anonymous questions and expressions of dissatisfaction. He must supplement his formal channels of upward and downward communication by all available means, such as work councils, opinion polls, interviews with natural leaders, and community surveys.

PERSONAL STYLE

The place of a chief or other top executive in a business in which he has little or no equity is somewhat analogous to that of a diplomat working in an unfriendly, if not openly hostile, country. He may have much overt status and prestige, but he has little real power. He needs to accomplish certain goals, but he has little true leverage to apply to those people whom he seeks to influence. In view of this, he sometimes finds it necessary to use indirect, oblique, Machiavellian stratagems to gain his ends.

Observation of many politically astute executives in action indicates that most of them utilize supplementary ploys in coping with and influencing owners, associates, employees, and other groups. They know that an executive-politician must:

Use caution in taking counsel—He may take the views of others into account, but he knows the decisions must be his. Advice is useful, but unless its limits are recognized, it can easily become pressure.

Avoid too close superior-subordinate relationships—While he must be friendly with his subordinates, he is never intimate with them. His personal feelings must never be a basis for action concerning them. His door may be "open"—but not too far.

Maintain maneuverability—He never commits himself completely and irrevocably. If conditions change, he can gracefully adapt himself to the altered circumstances and change course without loss of face.

Use passive resistance when necessary—When under pressure to take action which he regards as inadvisable, he can stall. To resist such demands openly is likely to pre-

---

* For a fuller explanation of this point, see my article "Clear Communications for Chief Executives," HBR March–April, 1965, p. 131.

cipitate a crisis. Therefore he initiates action, but in such a manner that the undesired program suffers from endless delays and ultimately dies on the vine.

Not hesitate to be ruthless when expedient—No one really expects the boss to be a "nice guy" at all times. If he is, he will be considered to be a softy or a patsy and no longer deserving of respect. (A surprisingly large segment of the population has a strong need to be submissive. Hence these people are more comfortable under a ruthless superior. This can be clearly seen in the rank and file of many labor organizations.)

Limit what is to be communicated—Many things should not be revealed. For instance, bad news may create costly anxieties or uncertainties among the troops; again, premature announcements of staff changes may give rise to schisms in the organization.

Recognize that there are seldom any secrets in an organization—He must be aware that anything revealed "in confidence" will probably be the property of everyone in the establishment the next morning.

Learn never to place too much dependence on a subordinate unless it is clearly to the latter's personal advantage to be loyal—Although some people are compulsively conscientious, most are not. Most give lip service to the company or the boss, but when the crunch comes, their loyalty is exclusively to themselves and their interests.

Be willing to compromise on small matters—He does this in order to obtain power for further movement. Nothing is more often fatal to executive power than stubbornness in small matters.

Be skilled in self-dramatization and be a persuasive personal salesman—He is essentially an actor, capable of influencing his audiences emotionally as well as rationally. He first ascertains his audience's wants and values. He then proceeds to confirm them, thus absolutely ensuring his hearer's acceptance of his message.

Radiate self-confidence—He must give the impression that he knows what he is doing and is completely in command of the situation, even though he may not be sure at all.

Give outward evidence of status, power, and material success—Most people measure a leader by the degree of pomp and circumstance with which he surrounds himself. (This is why the king lives in a palace and the Pope in the Vatican.) Too much modesty and democracy in his way of life may easily be mistaken for a lack of power and influence. For example, most subordinates take vicarious pride in being able to say, "That's my boss who lives in the mansion on the hill and drives a Rolls Royce."

Avoid bureaucratic rigidity in interpreting company rules—To win and hold the allegiance of his subordinates, an executive must be willing to "bend the rules" from time to time and make exceptions, even when they are not wholly justified.

Remember to give praise as well as censure—Frequently, because he is under pressure from his superiors, he takes out his frustrations on his subordinates by criticizing them, sometimes unreasonably. He must remember that, if their loyalty is to be won and held, they merit equal amounts of praise and reassurance.

Be open-minded and receptive to opinions which differ from his—If he makes people feel that anyone who disagrees with him is, ipso facto, wrong, his power will suffer. Listening to dissent is the principal means by which he can experience corrective contact with reality and receive warning that the course he is following will lead to trouble. Also, openness to disagreement helps him to use his power fairly—or, more accurately, use it in a manner that will be perceived as fair by subordinates.

CONCLUSION

The position of a top executive who has little or no equity in the business is often a perilous one, with little inherent security. If things go well, his tenure is usually ensured; if they go badly, all too often he is made the scapegoat. Since many of the factors that affect his performance are beyond his control, he is constantly subject to the threat of disaster. His only hope for survival under these conditions is to gain and retain power by tactics that are in a large measure political and means that are, in part at least, Machiavellian.

Such strategies are not always noble and high-minded. But neither are they naive. From the selfish standpoint of the beleaguered and harassed executive, they have one primary merit: they enhance his chances of survival.

Questions for Discussion

1.   What are the major reasons why a follower follows?

2.   Do you think appeals to fear, tradition, and blind faith are declining as influence processes in American society? Why or why not?

3.   Why is fear so attractive to managers as an influence technique? What are the managerial drawbacks of the use of fear?

4.   What is the relation between tradition as an influence process and a culture's respect for authority?

5.   If you drop an empty cigarette package on a street in Bern, Switzerland, some citizen is likely to tell you to pick it up. If you drive down a Zurich street in the wrong direction in the middle of the night, someone will probably record your license plate number and report you to the police. In general, the Swiss observe their laws strictly. What does the influence model suggest about this?

6.   A successful company president responded to a discussion of influence by observing, "I never met a man I couldn't motivate by either money or sex." What do you think of his views?

7.   Describe and analyze two examples of influence in which you were involved or which you observed.

8.   Describe a person who has "charisma" *for you*. What attributes do you admire? How does she or he behave?

9.   Why is it important to understand the follower to understand the influencer?

10.   Discuss how influence extends upward as well as downward in organizations — and how the two directions are interdependent.

11.   Describe the influence processes which characterize most hierarchical, bureaucratic organizations. What effects might these have on behavior?

Cases for Discussion

An Attempt to Consolidate Cooperatives in Ecuador

A credit cooperative is known to most persons in the United States as a credit union or a savings and loan cooperative. Members place their savings in the cooperative, as they would in a bank, but loans are available only to members at, they hope, a lower rate of interest. Yearly, all profits are returned to the members, divided on the basis of the amount of savings they have in the cooperative.

A cooperative is normally governed by a five-member board elected from the membership. These members include a president, vice president, treasurer, and the heads of the credit and supervisory committees. The credit committee approves all loans and the supervisory committee insures that the cooperative is being operated according to its bylaws. Professional managers can be hired by the cooperative, but this is feasible only when the cooperative is large.

Credit cooperatives have been formed in many underdeveloped areas because of the lack of credit at reasonable interest rates for the small merchant and farmer. Credit cooperatives provide it. At the same time, they mobilize capital in the community by teaching the members the importance of regular saving.

Credit cooperatives were started in Ecuador for these purposes. Ecuador is a small country, larger only than Uruguay in South America, with a population of about five million. It is an extremely poor country, relying on the export of bananas for most of its income. It has a geographic handicap for future economic development because the Andes mountains run completely through the center of the country. The ruggedness of these mountains makes trade and communication between areas very difficult, and may partially explain why the coastal region of Ecuador has had a better record of cooperative development than has had the mountain region.

As a young American member of the Peace Corps, I was assigned to work with the credit cooperatives in Cuenca, the third largest city in Ecuador, with a population of about 80,000. Cuenca is situated in the mountain region, eight hours from the coast and fifteen hours from the capital city, Quito. Thus, it is not surprising that the cooperatives in Cuenca have been doing so poorly that most people in the city had never even heard of them.

There were three formally organized cooperatives in Cuenca. After an initial period of growth, two of them were stagnating. The third cooperative had failed completely, although it had not been disbanded.

The best of the three cooperatives was called "La Merced," after the patron saint of the neighborhood in which the cooperative was formed. The president, Sr. Caldera, and the treasurer, Sr. Marchan, were knowledgeable in the mechanics of operating a cooperative, but were not aggressive in promoting the concept. As a result, the cooperative had only 100 members and $100 in capital. Most of its members were women, small businessmen, and merchants, which hampered the economic growth of the cooperative. If the cooperative was to give its intended service, the membership had to be expanded. Unfortunately, the cooperative had not attracted many new members in the past six months.

The other functioning cooperative in Cuenca was headed by Sr. Mendosa. Sr. Mendosa exhibited tremendous pride in being the founder and president of an organization of this kind. He ran the entire show and he took great pride in doing so. He was not only the president, but the treasurer; he approved all the loans (which, by the way, was illegal). He did not delegate any authority and he resented criticism of his operation by anyone. He restricted membership to only his friends and spoke of his role as one of looking out for their welfare, but of course their voice in the cooperative was insignificant.

The third cooperative was made up of local carpenters. It failed because the membership did not seem to understand what a credit cooperative was or how it was to operate. The cooperative was never officially disbanded, and only a complete transfusion could save it, but even this was doubtful, since it had a reputation of failure.

After having worked with these cooperatives for a few months, I felt that Cuenca should have more people involved in credit unions than just the 200 then participating. I thought the idea of a single large cooperative for the entire city was desirable and feasible. Instead of independently improving the three existing cooperatives, I thought it would be more sensible to merge them into one. This would result in a nucleus of trained personnel to manage the cooperative and a base of 200 members from which to convince others that the cooperative was a success.

Greatly excited because I thought I could make a substantial contribution to the economic life of the city, I set up appointments with the presidents of the three cooperatives.

I approached each of the cooperatives with my idea. Sr. Mendosa strongly rejected the plan and dismissed me, saying that the other cooperatives should be dissolved, with their members joining his organization. The other two cooperatives in turn rejected Mendosa's position, but they did agree to discuss consolidation of their two groups.

When the meeting was held, the purpose of the merger was explained and how it was to be accomplished was carefully detailed. Each cooperative would officially withdraw from the National Federation and a new one would immediately be established so that there would be no loss in services for the present members. With the larger amount of members and capital, the new cooperative would be able to make larger loans to its members with greater regularity. All old officers of the two cooperatives would resign and a new directorship would be elected by the new, combined membership.

At this point the idea began to run into difficulties. The president of "La Merced," Sr. Caldera, did not like the idea of disbanding his cooperative, because the name would be changed. He felt that the name had religious significance and should be retained. The president of the carpenters, Sr. Maldonado, on the other hand, did not want to retain the name of "La Merced" because it would seem as if they were being forced to capitulate to the other cooperative—and besides he did not like the religious association. The subsequent argument forced a polarization of those present, each backing the position of their own cooperative; each side became more adamant in their position as time went by.

When the discussion turned to the election of officials, fear was expressed that if one cooperative outnumbered the other, their directors might be completely re-elected, leaving the other cooperative without representation. This problem was partially bypassed when it was suggested that the president should be elected from one cooperative, a vice president from the other, etc. This, however, met with resistance on the point of which cooperative was to elect the president. Each cooperative wanted to retain its own president, and neither president wanted to accept the second position in favor of the other. The mistrust by members of one cooperative toward the members of the other gradually became obvious.

The meeting was finally adjourned with no progress toward consolidation but with heightened suspicion and animosity between the two cooperatives. Later, when I met with individuals in each cooperative, I could see that they did not want to discuss the matter further. Future plans were dropped and the idea died.

Questions

1. Discuss why the North American failed to influence the Latin Americans.

2. How might he have proceeded differently?

Cynthia Wyeth and the Gibralter Bank

Cynthia Wyeth joined the Gibralter Bank after earning her MBA at Walton University. She was somewhat older than the other students because she had worked as a secretary in another bank after earning her B.A. six years before. Cynthia started as a junior analyst in the International Department because of her special interest in Spanish in which she had majored in college.

Her MBA program initially had been difficult for Cynthia because of its mathematical emphasis, but Cynthia discovered that she had a much greater flair for quantitative methods than she would have thought possible back in high school and college when humanities seemed more appropriate for females. In addition, she was very active in extracurricular activities at Walton serving as Vice-President of the MBA Association and a member of the joint faculty-student curriculum committee. Given that female MBA candidates were still rare at Walton at the time, Cynthia was a very visible person. She ranked quite high in the class upon graduation and received several attractive job offers.

Cynthia joined the Gibralter Bank because it was a prestigious institution, which she well knew because her father had been Executive Vice-President of one of Gibralter's major rivals. In fact, as a child, Cynthia had known Gibralter's President as an old family friend called "Uncle Ned." Mr. Frederick Adams was now retired (but still a board member of Gibralter). Cynthia's first positions had been as junior and senior analyst which were partly interesting and partly boring: she enjoyed the banking content, but resented the repetitive telephone quotes and expected clerical work. She did, however, establish an enviable reputation for reliability and competence.

Cynthia was then promoted to Assistant Administrative Manager in the International Department where she did a marvelous job improving clerical services and reducing secretarial turnover. Subsequently, she was promoted to Department Administrative Manager and named Assistant Vice-President. With her very firm, benevolent style, she was equally successful. With time, however, Cynthia became a little dissatisfied. Although her pay and hierarchical status were good, she felt that she was not really learning *banking*. Accordingly, she spoke to the Executive Vice-President about a promotion to Regional Executive or Country Manager. The EXVP said he would look into it, but months went by and nothing happened. Rather casually, Cynthia mentioned her feelings to Uncle Ned at a social gathering. Two weeks later, Cynthia was offered the position as Employment Manager for the whole bank. The position carried a Vice-Presidency and a nice increase. When she talked about it to the International Department Executive Vice-President, he countered with an offer of a transfer to the position of Country Manager in charge of Central America. The area is the smallest in terms of business, but the position carries full authority for loans and investments, substantial autonomy, and great opportunity to travel to deal with clients.

Cynthia is wondering which position to accept. Her main concern seems to be which job would carry more authority and which would be easier in which to establish her influence and power.

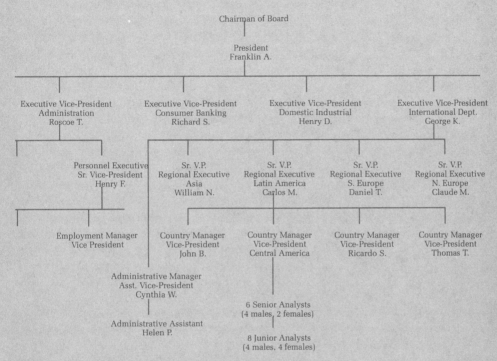

Exhibit I Partial Organization Chart of Gibralter Bank

Questions

1. What problems do you think Cynthia would have establishing her influence and power as Employment Manager?

2. What problems do you think Cynthia would have in establishing her influence and power as Country Manager?

3. What problems might she encounter with clients as an executive in the International Department?

4. What recommendations would you make to Cynthia? What position and how should she establish her influence?

Everything a manager does—from motivating and influencing others, to controlling and modifying their behavior—revolves around communications. Put simply, communicating is what managers do; it consumes some 50 to 90 percent of their time (Horne and Lupton, 1965; Mintzberg, 1973). Exhibit 3.1 summarizes typical interpersonal communications of a sample of managers in various positions (Webber, 1966).

A standard definition of communication doesn't exist. To some, it refers solely to the message conveyed; to others, it occurs when one mind affects another; to still others, it is the fabric that holds human groups together (Nwanko, 1973; Dance, 1970). Thayer (1968, pp. 26–27) writes that communication has occurred when an individual ". . . took-something-into-account, whether that something was something someone did or said or did not do or say, whether it was some observable event, some internal condition, the meaning of something being read or looked at, some feeling intermingled with some past memory—literally anything that could be taken-into-account by human beings in general and that individual in particular." Such communication can be official or unofficial, formal or informal. It can take place by word of mouth, memoranda, through meetings, or over the telephone.

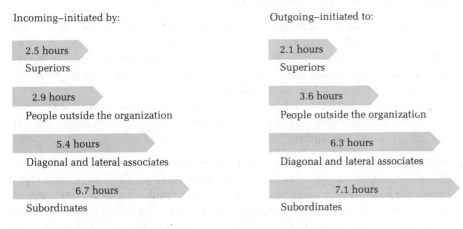

Incoming–initiated by:

2.5 hours
Superiors

2.9 hours
People outside the organization

5.4 hours
Diagonal and lateral associates

6.7 hours
Subordinates

Outgoing–initiated to:

2.1 hours
Superiors

3.6 hours
People outside the organization

6.3 hours
Diagonal and lateral associates

7.1 hours
Subordinates

Exhibit 3.1   Typical Managerial Communications (Webber 1966)
Distribution of Communications–Mean Hours Per Week

We can distinguish between three kinds of communications: instrumental, consummatory, and incidental (Zajonc, 1966):

- *Instrumental communication* is goal-directed; the sender seeks to achieve definite effects in the receiver. Such communication is *transmitted*.
- *Consummatory communication* arises as a consequence of an emotion or motivational state of the sender—joy, anger, fear, and so forth. It is the spontaneous expression of this state of mind and is thus *emitted*.
- *Incidental communication* imparts information to another without the sender having any intention or knowledge of doing so.

This chapter will emphasize instrumental communication. Even here, however, in goal-directed, intentionally transmitted communication, problems can occur in the process of communicating. These problems result mainly because people see things differently, say things differently, and hear things differently. First, we will examine a general model of communication, and then explore potential barriers to effective communication.

A GENERAL MODEL OF COMMUNICATION

Exhibit 3.2 summarizes the general model of communication (Shannon and Weaver, 1949). It consists of six basic stages:

1. Thinking: the genesis and framing of the idea or message in the sender's mind.
2. Encoding: putting the thought into some form for possible communication. Ideation and encoding are closely related. On many matters we think in terms of language, but on others we experience feelings that we may encode in facial expressions, body movements, art, or music, as well as words. Thus, we can communicate in three ways:

   - by actual physical touch (a tap on the shoulder, a pat on the back, a slap on the cheek, a handshake).
   - by visible movements of some portions of our bodies (a pointing finger, an eye winking, a head nod, a smile, a grimace or scowl, perhaps even our posture, leg-crossing and arm-folding).
   - by symbols which stand for something we experience initially (audible symbols such as crying, speaking, and music, and visible symbols such as pictures, sculpture, and writing).

   "The medium is the message" goes the popular phrase from Marshall McLuhan. While exaggerated, the point has validity: The way a message is transmitted may carry more meaning than the sender's words. Research on face-to-face communications suggests that only a small portion of the information communicated is contained in words (perhaps 7 percent). Most of the message is transmitted by facial expression and physical posture (55 percent) and vocal intonation and inflection (38 percent) (Mehrabian, 1970). Judgments from visual cues are more accurate than judgments from

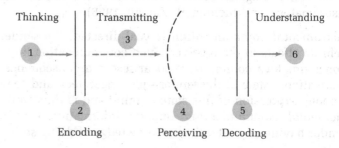

Exhibit 3.2 General Communication Model

vocal cues (Burns and Beier, 1973). The aphorism that "actions speak louder than words" recognizes the symbolic component of behavior as communication. For example, Hall (1966) reports that when a government researcher was conducting interviews with managers about their views on equal employment opportunity, the people who kept her waiting and who never seemed to have as much time as planned were suggesting that they were not pleased with the program—a point doubly made by the managers who remained sitting behind their desks during the entire visit.

3. Transmitting the signal: this is the actual broadcasting of the message via some medium. If the sender encodes into language, the message may be transmitted orally (in person, over the phone, or through other electronic means) or in writing (in long hand, typed, printed, and so on).

4. Perceiving: the receiver must perceive the incoming communication with one or more senses—sight, hearing, feeling, taste, smell.

5. Decoding: the receiver puts the incoming communication into some form that will make it understandable.

6. Understanding: the receiver understands the message as it was intended to be understood by the sender.

In summary, the following steps occur in a communication: The sender develops and encodes a message in a form that can be transmitted; the message is sent in the form of gestures, speech, written words, drawn diagrams, pictures, or other symbols. Hopefully, the message is perceived, decoded, and understood by the receiver. But, as we will see, there are many possibilities for communication to be blocked or distorted.

BARRIERS TO UNDERSTANDING

The communications model described above is fairly simple, but in actuality there are many opportunities for blocking or distorting communication, including distorted perceptions, distrust of the source, defensive behavior, erroneous translation, distortions from the past, and lack of congruence. We will now examine each of these potential barriers in some detail.

Distorted Perceptions

A college professor's lecture hall might be uncomfortably warm on the first day of fall semester. Many students' thoughts may be on the recent past of cool surf, cool beer, and cool companions. One academic experiment suggests that at any given instant in a college lecture hall, 20 percent of both men and women are thinking about sex, 60 percent are off on some mental trip of their own, and the remaining 20 percent are concentrating on the professor (Cameron, 1968). Most of us simply fail to absorb and utilize much of the information which reaches us.

Misunderstanding may be further confounded by selective inattention. It may be that receivers "hear" the sender saying something which is not intended and which in fact may not be communicated. As an unfortunate example, paranoid personalities typically complain that others are rejecting and persecuting them; they tend only to hear hostility and aggression, whether or not it is present. What is involved in many of our examples of faulty communication is perceptual distortion resulting from the ways in which we "see" things. "I believe in what I can see and touch" has long been the slogan of practical people who consider themselves pragmatic and realistic. But what we see, like all of our perceptions, is not necessarily reality. The major points of perceptual distortion result from expectations, needs, fears, and organizing schema.

Perception is affected by a person's needs, motivations, and experience. Hungry people look for food and seek signs of it, ignoring items of lesser importance (McClelland and Atkinson, 1948). They may even perceive nonedible objects as food because they have a heightened awareness of stimuli that will satisfy needs and depressed awareness of irrelevant ones. Relevant stimuli reach awareness more readily than neutral ones. Similarly, words that have a sexual as well as nonsexual connotation (e.g., "screw") tend to be more quickly identified in unclear carbon copies when they have been recently experienced in the sexual rather than the mechanical context (Wiener, 1955). The importance of all this for the sender is obvious; the potential receiver's *interest in the message* is most important for understanding—even more important than anything the communicator can do about style, language, or delivery (Higham, 1957).

In addition to selectively perceiving, we tend to organize and complete fragmented and partial perceptions. Even the simplest perception is organized by the perceiver; the perceived characteristics of any part are a function of the whole to which it appears to belong. Apparently, one of the chief functions of the mind is "filling up gaps" (Bartlett, 1951). That is, we constantly try to connect new material into an old pattern in order to make it meaningful. We seem to prefer the simple and the regular to the complex and irregular, to organize what is received into tidy bundles. This is one reason why it is so difficult to communicate a new idea, for it has to be fitted into the existing structure of the mind. In the blooming confusion that is life, with its multiple stimuli, such organization and simplification is essential, but dangerous.

For example, we tend to perceive people as stereotypes, and this categorization is an important determinant of how their subsequent behavior will be interpreted. Jews, blacks, and other minorities have long been convenient scapegoats for those in fear of society's complexities. The world appears simpler if one assigns people to distinct categories and then ignores the individual. If a middle-aged parent doesn't bother to learn how clean, industrious, and patriotic is *this* particular long-haired, bearded student, his or her hippie stereotype is not disturbed and the parent can maintain the illusion that he or she understands university turmoil.

Research on the authoritarian personality indicates that some people are especially predisposed to categorize in this manner—those with a low tolerance for ambiguity (Adorno et al., 1950; Ilando, 1973). One test of this characteristic consists of flashing a series of small dots on a screen. Initially, everyone agrees that the dots form a dog. Then the configuration is slowly modified so the figure changes. People with low tolerance for ambiguity tend to lag in perceiving and recognizing a new shape; they hold on to the perception of the dog. In contrast, subjects with higher tolerance for ambiguity can relinquish the familiar shape, tolerate a period during which they don't know the shape, and recognize sooner the emerging form of a cat.

Research on prejudice in relation to American Jews found that, when examining photographs of people, those low in ambiguity tolerance tended to categorize more of them as Jewish than did subjects with greater tolerance (Scodel and Austrin, 1954). Recent classroom experiments, where normally neatly dressed and clean-shaven students donned wigs, false beards, and hippie garb for a few days, show the distortion is still with us. They were refused credit more than before their masquerade, and received more traffic tickets and general police harassment, although their own behavior had not changed. Unfortunately, many college students return the bias by perceiving police personnel as stereotypes (Brooks and Friedrich, 1970). And of course women in organizations are frequently subject to stereotyping by even the best-intentioned male managers. They are seen as too passive, dependent, emotional, unreliable and family-oriented (Rosen and Jerdee, 1974). Contrary to the popular cliché, however, it appears that men evaluate the performance of attractive females higher than the equal performance of less attractive women (Landy and Sigall, 1974).

The power of selective perception is illustrated by the popular television program "All in the Family." Some viewers write to applaud Archie Bunker for his "realistic" (racist?) views while others applaud the show for making fun of bigotry (Vidmar and Rokeach, 1974). The show may reinforce rather than reduce racial and ethnic prejudice.

Distrusted Source

Another interference to a professor's lecture might exist because he or she is "conservative" and "establishment." The professor might be "tuned out" by some students who don't want to hear what he or she has to say. It is all biased or irrelevant—so they may think, and so perceive the communication. Consider that the largest number of telephone calls that a major television network ever received due to a televised event occurred during a World Series game when José Feliciano sang the national anthem. Thousands of viewers were apparently offended by his long hair, his guitar, and his distinctive personal styling of the song. They refused to see and hear the deep-felt emotion and love of country that the blind singer was attempting to communicate to them.

An even more unfortunate tale of similar miscommunication comes out of the United States' ill-fated involvement in the Cuban invasion of 1961. The planners were receiving communications about the internal conditions in

Cuba from three sources: (a) Cuban refugees disenchanted with Castro, (b) CIA operatives and paid informers inside Cuba, and (c) neutral parties having diplomatic relations with Havana. The first two indicated that Castro's popularity was declining, that the people were demoralized, and that a landing would spark spontaneous support from the island's inhabitants. The third parties disputed these observations. Evaluating the sources, government officials believed the reports which they wanted to believe. Because the contradictory messages came mainly from persons representing socialist governments whose veracity was suspect, their messages were dismissed (Schlesinger, 1965). We all tend to evaluate the sender and judge his or her communication accordingly. This is rational except when receivers are unaware of how their biases distort their perceptions (Hovard and Weiss, 1951).

Sometimes receivers have both expectations and hopes about communications. If a communication is expected to be bad—and is—one's hope that it might be good is dashed. However, if the communication is even only slightly better than expected, hope may dominate and the message may be distorted in an overly favorable way (Harvey and Clapp, 1965). Thus:

A negative message from a low credibility source will be responded to positively if it is perceived to be less negative than expected.

A negative message from a low credibility source will be responded to negatively if it is perceived to be negative as expected.

A negative message from a low credibility source will be responded to most negatively if it is perceived to be more negative than expected (Smith, 1973).

The receivers' skepticism about messages from senders thought to have biased attitudes results in the paradox that unintended communications carry greater weight than intended transmissions. The classic theater provides numerous examples of misdelivered letters and overheard conversations that change the course of the drama. Such fortuitous occurrences may be poor writing but they reflect an established fact that information overheard unintentionally (or when receivers perceive that the message was not intended for them) is more likely to be believed than similar instrumental communication. For example, overhearing people (especially peers) talking about the dangers of smoking pot seems to have a greater impact on young people than formal lectures designed to warn, frighten, and dissuade (Allyn and Festinger, 1961; Hannemann, 1973). An audience is just more likely to reject an open attack on their beliefs than something overheard incidentally (Festinger and Maccoby, 1964; Walster and Festinger, 1962). Since receivers don't believe the communication is intended for them, their defenses are not aroused.

Clearly, we evaluate every incoming communication by evaluating the source. Such evaluative attitudes by the receiver sometimes get back to the sender—particularly if the sender is a subordinate. In this case, superiors may be so anxious about protecting and enhancing their positions that they are

unwilling to accept communications about the negative effects of their behavior. They will shift such conversation away from negative content toward
the loyalty of the *bearer* of the message (symbolically, they endeavor to slay
the bearer of bad tidings—as sometimes actually occurred in antiquity). Such
bosses are likely to get their way. They will hear nothing from their employees until they resign. The Turks have a proverb that says, "The man who
tells the truth should have one foot in the stirrup." Not surprisingly, good news
is communicated more fully and spontaneously than bad news (Tesser et al.,
1973).

Defensive Behavior

Perceptual distortions are manifest in "defensive behavior" which is common
when an individual perceives or anticipates threat. Its arousal is more likely
among people of extremely high or low self-esteem and it prevents a listener
from concentrating upon the message. As shown in Exhibit 3.3 there are six
categories of defensive and supportive climates which retard or facilitate
communication (Gibb, 1966; Berger, 1973):

Exhibit 3.3   Communication Climates

Defensive Climate		*Supportive Climate*
evaluation	Speech or other behavior which appears to "judge" the other person increases defensiveness.	description
control	Speech which is used to control the listener evokes resistance.	problem orientation
strategy	When the sender is perceived as engaged in a stratagem involving ambiguous motivations, receivers become defensive because they don't want to be manipulated.	spontaneity
neutrality	When neutrality in speech appears to listeners to indicate a lack of concern for their welfare, they become defensive.	empathy
superiority	When people communicate to another that they feel superior in position, power, wealth, intellectual ability, physical characteristics, or in other ways, they arouse defensiveness.	equality
certainty	Those who are dogmatic, who seem to know the answers, to require no data, tend to put others on guard.	provisionalism

Being able to listen without evaluation and premature criticism is particularly appropriate for organizational superiors. Shortly after the death of

Winston Churchill, Lord Avon (the late Anthony Eden) discussed what he considered Churchill's outstanding leadership characteristic. He said that the indefatigable former Prime Minister always seemed to be available, he was ready to listen, he never cut off a suggestion with a curt dismissal, but encouraged elaboration. To be sure, the great man was often formidable and abusive to subordinates who made mistakes in policy implementation; and he could be dictatorial in ordering the conduct of his own policy. But, he was invariably receptive to new ideas. It was not a threatening experience to broach a new matter to Churchill. The next day he might assert that the proposal was unacceptable, but the initial presentation was respected. Consequently, he was approached—and some of the unsolicited ideas were good.

Perhaps similar behavior characterizes effective business executives. In spite of the importance of initiating communications, high executives may depend even more upon others to bring information to them. One study suggests that higher-rated executives spend more time talking with people *who come to them* than do lower-rated executives (Webber, 1966). As a result, the latter spend more time initiating conversations.

This same research also suggests that effective executives conduct more of their numerous discussions in intimate, two-person talks than in group meetings or via correspondence. They seem to throw out invitations for individuals to come see them personally rather than waiting for the next scheduled meeting. Such a style may facilitate the frank expression of opinions and ideas; there is less psychological cost in admitting ignorance and asking questions.

Erroneous Translation

An old adage says, "There are only three races: men, women and children, and none of them speak the same language." Unfortunately there are many more languages than three, perhaps as many as there are individuals in the world. Thus, even if sender and receiver ostensibly know the same language, erroneous decoding may occur. The problem is twofold: First, each individual's "language" is a reflection of her or his experience, and second, words are ambiguous. Let us consider both briefly.

Originators of a message can encode it only within the framework of their own experience and knowledge. Similarly, receivers can decode only within their own experience. Exhibit 3.4 illustrates this: If the circles do not meet, there are no common experiences or empathetic psychological sets; communication is impossible (Vardaman and Halterman, 1965; Alpert and Anderson, 1973).

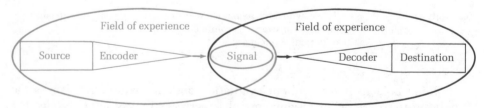

Exhibit 3.4 Commonness of Experience Necessary for Communication

In addition to the problem of experience gaps, words are troublesome. Words themselves do not have meanings (Hayakawa, 1964). The words "police" or "pig" are not the things they name. Only people have meanings which they attach to words. A pioneer semanticist was once being interviewed by a magazine reporter. The scholar said that, "Language is a very tricky thing; words don't mean what you think." The reporter asked, "What do you mean?" "Well, it's like this," went the reply, "when a young lady says you are 'going too far,' what she really means is that you are 'coming too close.'" Today young women are unlikely to use such an old-fashioned phrase, but certain words which they use can create common misunderstanding. Junior high school girls refer to certain classmates as "whores," which, while frightening to the parents involved, seems to mean that the teenagers in question flirt with other boys while going steady. The so-called generation gap may be wider in vocabulary than in actual beliefs or behavior.

Such words as "police," "pig," "law and order," "school busing," "boy," "lady," and even "democracy," have different meanings and different impacts on certain whites, blacks, males, and females. Senders may believe that they have encoded in the proper language, but the receiver's understanding may be different than intended. Russell Baker (1972) offers a humorous illustration of miscommunication between parents and children:

> The parent in Chicago looks across the table at the big new person who worries him. "What are you going to do?" he asks.
>
> "I may go to Boston to see about getting some guys to get up a camper trip to Winnipeg," comes the answer.
>
> To the parent the answer sounds insane. To 'do' in his old vocabulary means to put down roots, to make something, to act — this for the purpose of building, maintaining and sitting fast by hearth-and-home, where the Depression can't touch him and war is far away.
>
> To the big new people, however, it often means 'to be in motion.' When a parent says, "What are you going to do?" he is asking, "How are you going to go about settling down?" What the big new people often hear is "Where are you off to next?" Not surprisingly, conversation collapses, sometimes in shrieks.*

The problem of mismatching vocabularies is particularly common in organizations where staff specialists tend to utilize arcane terminology such as "stochastic variables," when the line manager wants to know the odds.

If you were to speak with different people who had heard Feliciano sing the *Star-Spangled Banner*, observed the high school girls' behavior, or been in on the Cuban planning, you would probably hear very different words which would make it difficult for you, the outsider, to know what really happened. Because of selective perception and different meanings attributed to words, individual experiences are never the same. Many problems in communication arise when we forget this. When an admiring or irate observer talks about an event, she or he is talking about an inference, an event that occurred *inside,*

*© 1972 by The New York Times Company. Reprinted by permission.

not about reality. Reality and communication may only be approximated if many observers tend to agree on their inferences (Boulding, 1961; Korzybaki, 1962).

Distortions from the Past

There is another form of psychological interference that also interferes with understanding. This is interference from the past that causes rigidities of interpretation and response. These rigidities stem from anxiety-producing early experiences which are carried over into new situations where they are inappropriate (Sullivan, 1955). We are "time-binding" in this respect; we tend to transfer and repeat (Zaleznik and Moment, 1964). Transference is the re-experience of past relationships in the present with full effective force. We all perceive and decode communications through a mechanism laden with yesterdays. Frequently, influential events and people from our individual histories are transferred to the present as if they were still before us. Thus, the stress that many males feel while working under a female superior may run much deeper than the sexist attitudes that the women's liberation movement complains of; it may reflect the burden of mother and son experiences from which many men never escape.

The repetition compulsion is expressed through repeating experiences which have been painful, apparently in an effort to master the original experience—frequently with no success. Perception and interpretation of incoming communications will sometimes be distorted to suit these rigidities.

Lack of Congruence

"I didn't mean it," "You always hurt the one you love," and other similar comments reflect the fact that we often communicate more than we intend to — and that, in fact, unintended communications may be directly contradictory to our intentions. Often these are factors about ourselves that we are not entirely aware of. These communication ambiguities create what Bennis (1961) terms an "arc of distortion." For example, in Exhibit 3.5, we see that A is really communicating at least two things to B, the intended as well as the selectively unintended. This makes it difficult for B to determine how to respond. Receivers usually attempt to discover at which level the sender would like to communicate on, and then reciprocate at that level.

Inconsistency between message content and style of transmission is a common contributor to the arc of distortion. In the reading by Zaleznik and Moment which follows this chapter (1964), a young research scientist enters the laboratory director's office with a letter from another organization offering a post. After some miscommunication between the two, the director heatedly exclaims, "I'm not disturbed. If you think it is best for you to go somewhere else, that is OK with me. We can get another plasma physicist any day, just as good as you. They are standing in line to get in here."

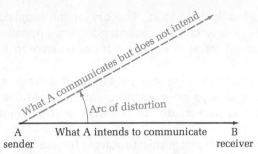

Exhibit 3.5   The Arc of Distortion

Obviously, the words and manner of communication are at odds. The real message seems to be that the director is offended that one of his people might leave him, and afraid that others might lower their opinion of him because he can't hold on to his employees. Unfortunately, the director may not really understand his own feelings, and this hinders communication. Understanding of self and understanding of others is closely related — and both are necessary for real communication.

Individuals can be considered to have three levels of reality: experience, awareness, and intention. Exhibit 3.6 illustrates that experience is the deepest reality; it is our existential being, what we *really* feel or think — guilt, fear, love, and so on. Awareness is what we *think* we are, what we admit to our conscious level. The most superficial level is what we *intend* to communicate, the words that we broadcast. Rogers' general law of interpersonal relationships (1961) suggests that communication between two people will be most effective and understanding most complete when each is congruent. That is, if what A intends to broadcast, what A is aware of, and what A truly experiences are all the same, and if the same is also true of B, then B will be able to understand and reciprocate A's communication.

For example, infants are fantastic communicators, within a limited range of messages. If they feel hunger, fear, or joy, the feeling floods their conscious-

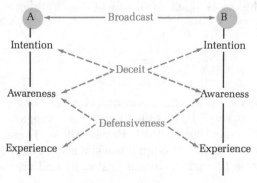

Exhibit 3.6   The Levels of Reality and Gaps
in Communication

ness and is automatically broadcast. The cry or the gurgle is understood by adults who find the young child's congruence very appealing. Unfortunately (or perhaps fortunately), most of us lose our congruence to some degree as we mature.

Emotionally maladjusted people provide sad examples of personal incongruence. Because of gaps between their internal realities, communication within themselves has broken down. Because of this, communication with others is damaged.

To some extent we all share this problem, for we all have our gaps. The gap between what is admitted to awareness and what is really felt is called *defensiveness.* It is what is repressed to the unconscious. The gap between awareness and what is intended is called *deceit.* This suggests the sender's effort to communicate something different from or less than what he or she is aware of.

Much psychotherapy rests upon the assumption that if counselors are congruent, this will gradually draw out their patients and move them toward congruence because of the climate of security, understanding, and liking. Gradually the relationship becomes mutually satisfying.

As we've implied, communication is most effective when the pertinent aspects of oneself are admitted to consciousness and are announced. Concealment, deceit, denial, and defensiveness hinder true understanding, and therefore true communication. Look back at the harsh words of the laboratory director to his ambitious subordinate. The manager's lack of congruence and his efforts to deny anger and hurt feelings undermine his communications with his young researcher.

Full disclosure, however, can be threatening. Do I dare communicate my congruence? Do I dare announce my experience? Will I be rejected if my fear (or my love) is known? Do I have the courage to enter into a relationship that may change me? If a person can answer these questions affirmatively, he or she is probably a self-actualizing person. The self-actualizing or fully functioning person *is* congruent; he or she is able to be open without feeling excessive anxiety, and hence is open to others and to authentic communication (Maslow, 1954).

TRANSACTIONAL ANALYSIS

Transactional Analysis (T.A.) offers another view of congruent communications. Like Rogers' theory discussed above, T.A. suggests three levels or "states" in all individuals (Berne, 1961; Harris, 1969). These are the "Child," the "Parent," and the "Adult." Though these states are common to all, the content of each is unique to each individual, shaped and colored by their own experience.

The Child is imbued with those feelings and emotions we internalized as infants, when words were not yet available to codify and label what was taking place. Infants perceive the world around them but can only store information on the basis of emotions they have felt, this being the infant's only understanding. Our creativity, curiosity, desire to explore, and urge to touch, feel, and experience, all reside in our Child.

The Parent within us represents the unquestioned or imposed external events perceived by us when we were children from the actions of our parents. This state represents the "do's and don'ts" as administered by parents, rules, laws, and maxims, which have been recorded as absolute truths.

The third state, the Adult, is the final one in the evolution of a personality. Its inception occurs when we have the ability to find out for ourselves how life is different from the "taught concepts" of our Parent and the "felt concepts" of our Child. Our Adult constrains the excesses of both our Parent and our Child. Its primary function is checking out old data, validating it or invalidating it, and refiling it for future use. It is the aim of T.A. to develop and strengthen the Adult, to free the Adult from the trouble-making influences and demands of the Parent and the Child.

Strengthening the Adult against the persistent demands of the other two enables an individual to have freedom of choice, freedom to change, freedom to respond to new stimuli in new ways, and—most relevant to our concerns —facilitates communication. As the reading by Harris at the end of this chapter indicates, communication between two people is most efficient and effective when they interact consistently "Adult" to "Adult." This means without invoking archaic "rules," past judgments, or ancient emotions, but sticking to the current facts and feelings in a reasoned and controlled manner. Many examples of T.A. in action are found in the reading by Bessey and Wendlinger.

ORGANIZATIONAL DISTORTIONS OF COMMUNICATIONS

Since organizations consist of many people, much communication must be passed from one person to another. However, the receiver of a message who in turn sends it on to the next person tends to distort the message in systematic ways (especially when by word-of-mouth) (Campbell, 1958; Bass, 1965; Taschdjian, 1974):

> *Condensation:* What is repeated tends to be shorter, simpler, and less detailed than what was received. Often only the salient points are passed on and in a condensed, coded form. Hence, contrast is enhanced within messages as some items are emphasized and some ignored. In particular, the beginning and end of a message tend to be expanded at the expense of the middle.
>
> *Closure:* Receivers tend to fill in gaps when a message is ambiguous. This is particularly dramatic when the receiver must articulate these gaps when relaying a message. If one person hears that someone from the home office may come next week, the message may be passed on as a fact that the vice-

president is coming; the next relayer may add that Vice-President Jones is coming to chew people out for being over budget.

Expectation: People tend to hear what they expect to hear. This is perpetuated in relaying messages because the first receiver tends to report what he or she expected to hear from the sender in the first place. This bias then becomes the message for the second receiver to interpret through his or her own bias. It should be readily apparent how communications can become fantastically corrupted as they move along a lengthy chain of command.

Association: Guilt by association is a wide-spread source of distortion. If bad news or past errors have come from a certain person or department, similar current communications tend to be associated with them, sometimes without reason.

In addition, communications tend to be manipulated in the interest of the communicator or relayer. That is, people communicate (or withhold communication) in order to achieve some goal, to satisfy some personal need, or to improve their immediate situation. They tend to communicate with those who will help them achieve their aims and not with those who will retard their accomplishment. We tend to direct our communications toward those who can make us feel more secure and gratify our needs, and away from those who threaten us or make us feel anxious. Thus, studies consistently demonstrate that most of us prefer to speak with higher status people with power to help us (Athanassiades, 1973).

Subordinates may be reluctant to ask superiors for help when they need it because this might be interpreted as an admission of their inadequacy. And superiors tend to delete from their communications to subordinates any references to their own mistakes or errors of judgment (Jackson, 1959).

These controlled communications particularly characterize a subordinate's upward initiation of communications. Most of us tend to minimize actual disagreement—a situation immortalized in the phrases "organizational man," and "yes men." A survey in three large industrial organizations found that information communicated up the hierarchy is screened or filtered, particularly when the information might reflect upon the competence, security, or progress of the subordinates (Read, 1962). And those who are most ambitious are the most inaccurate communicators: A negative correlation exists between a person's ambition and the accuracy with which he or she communicates upward in the hierarchy. Where people don't trust each other, the primary goal of upward communications becomes reducing the sender's anxiety rather than accurate transmission of ideas (Mellinger, 1956). In general, a manager's willingness to expose the truth about himself or herself varies with the relative status of the other person—less exposure to superiors, more to subordinates (Hall, 1973; Brenner and Sigband, 1973).

THE MANAGER'S SITUATION

Congruency and full disclosure suggest ways for improving interpersonal understanding especially relevant to parents, spouses, and counselors. In these situations, congruity aids disclosure and understanding. Indeed, the spontaneity and sincerity that are associated with this model have become extremely attractive to many groups, especially the young, and something of a fad through sensitivity training and encounter groups. "Letting it all hang out" has its attractions.

A manager, however, has a different problem than the parent, husband or wife, or therapist. Understanding through communicating is usually only a *means* for the manager; as we have emphasized, the *end* is influence. One communication adviser concludes, "If we can free ourselves from our need to influence and direct others to our way of thinking, we can then begin to listen to others with understanding" (Deunk, 1967). This is probably true, but managers and leaders can never completely give up the need to influence others. It is at the core of their roles and often of their personalities. Tension between communication and influence is deep at the core of management.

Influencing people and events is more important for managers (and politicians) than understanding through communication. If this sounds harsh, you should recognize that communication and influence are not necessarily in conflict or mutually contradictory. It is just that a certain degree of concealment or deceit may be essential. No person of responsibility can reveal everything that underlies a communication. To do so might hinder his or her effectiveness and unnecessarily frighten and hurt people.

Note that a need for modest deceit is not peculiar to people of power. It affects everyone. As children we learn from our parents not to be quite so congruent; not to tell old Aunt Belle that she has bad breath and an ugly nose, and that we hate it when she tries to kiss us. We are told to bear it in silence so as not to hurt her feelings. Similarly, most parents control their impulse to tell their children to get lost because they can't stand them, nor does a husband tell his wife of his attraction to his cute secretary. Parents and spouses know that their feelings will pass, so useless hurt is avoided by deceit. Indeed, in the case of the child and Aunt Belle, society labels it not deceit but "courtesy," "manners," or "concern." As the old French diplomat Clemenceau put it, "Etiquette is nothing but hot air, but that is what our automobiles ride on and look how it smooths out the bumps!"

There is no perfect resolution to this tension between communication, influence, and concern:

Congruence probably leads to better communication and understanding.

But: (1) personal defensiveness is difficult to overcome even with sensitivity training or psychological counseling;

(2) some deceit may be essential to express concern for others; and

(3) managers as managers tend to be more concerned with influencing behavior than in perfect understanding.

Yet: the more a sender departs from congruence, the more difficult it probably will be to communicate understanding.

Lively controversy continues regarding how much openness is desirable or possible in organizational relationships. By virtue of their achievement-oriented personalities and time-pressured positions, most managers tend to be quite task-oriented. This leads them to discourage nontask communications, and the organizational culture frequently is critical of demonstration of emotion. Their attention is focused on the task, but such intellectual preoccupation tends to restrict the exercise of the faculty of observation. Consequently, they are frequently insensitive to others' behavior—especially their nonverbal behavior. Lamb and Turner (1969) argue that it would indeed be desirable if managers could be more spontaneous and less intellectually disciplined about their behavior, but they recognize the essential difficulty:

> Those who argue cultishly for a more 'natural' life are wrong in thinking that Valhalla will be obtained only by rejecting the preoccupation of contemporary life and attaining some relaxed and mystical state. Clearly none of this concerns the manager. He has got to continue to apply intellectual disciplines and they will become increasingly more demanding with the increased complexity and specialization of work procedures. They cannot help but be increasingly applied, also, to dealings with people. The big question is, however, can some way be found to exercise enhanced observation without loss of intellectual control? (p. 7).

To test empirically whether there is any relationship between open communications and company performance, Willets (1967) examined interper-personal relations among top executives in 20 small manufacturing concerns. He found it necessary to differentiate between three kinds of communications:

> Open communication of *task-oriented* ideas between executives was correlated significantly with higher company performance.

> Open communication *about feelings* in a rational, nonemotional way was correlated with higher company performance.

> Spontaneous, emotional communications *of* feelings was not associated with higher performance (and there may be a negative association).

Thus, it seems logical that a team of managers should be able to work together more effectively if they communicate fully regarding their tasks, what material to order, what equipment to repair, and so on. It also appears that the team will be more effective if managers discuss their feelings in a calm, rational, and dispassionate way. Losing tempers and showing fear and anxiety, however, seem to be both effect and cause of poorer performance. In short, the culture of the executive suite allows rational, logical discussion of problems, but discourages demonstrating emotion; it frowns on letting-it-all-hang-out in a spontaneous, congruent way. To behave in this way may seriously jeopardize a manager's career, for he or she may be perceived as "just not executive material."

SUMMARY

Communication is the vehicle for exercising influence, but the objectives of influence sometimes compete with effective understanding. The steps in the communication process include: thinking, encoding, transmitting, perceiving, decoding, and understanding. Potential barriers exist at all steps in this model:

Sender broadcasts before adequate thought or clarification and without examining his or her assumptions.

Transmission is noisy, unreliable, improper, or inconsistent with the message, situation, or people involved.

Receiver evaluates the sender and distorts his or her perception of the message because of the existing situation or past experiences. Receivers may: (a) hear what they expect, or (b) want to hear, (c) ignore conflicting information, (d) ignore nonverbal cues.

Receivers decode the message incorrectly because their vocabularies are different than the sender's; they do not agree on the meanings (especially symbolic) of words and actions.

Organizational communications are selectively filtered and distorted to further personal interests and protect individuals.

Congruence between the communicator's experience, awareness, and intention would seem to promote better understanding. Yet, most managers face a dilemma because their primary intention is less *understanding* than it is *influencing* others' behavior. Communicating, for managers, is a means rather than an end.

REFERENCES

Adorno, T. W.; E. Frankel-Brunswik; D. J. Levinson; and R. N. Sanford. *The Authoritarian Personality: Studies in Prejudice.* Harper and Row, 1950.

Allyn, J., and L. Festinger. "The Effectiveness of Unanticipated Persuasive Communications." *Journal of Abnormal Social Psychology*, Vol. 62 (1961), pp. 35–40.

Alpert, M. I., and W. T. Anderson, Jr. "Optimal Heterophily and Communication Effectiveness: Some Empirical Findings." *The Journal of Communications*, Vol. 23 (September 1973), pp. 328–43.

Athanassiades, J. C. "The Distortion of Upward Communications in Hierarchical Organizations." *Academy of Management Journal*, Vol. 16, No. 2 (1973), pp. 207–26.

Baker, R. "Observer." *The New York Times Magazine* (February 3, 1972).

Bartlett, F. C. *The Mind at Work and Play.* Allen and Unwin (London), 1951.

Bass, B. *Organizational Psychology.* Allyn and Bacon, 1965.

Bennis, W. G. "Interpersonal Communication." From Bennis et al. (eds.), *The Planning of Change.* Holt, Rinehart, and Winston, 1961.

Berger, C. R. "Attributional Communication, Situational Involvement, Self-esteem and Interpersonal Attraction," *The Journal of Communication*, Vol. 23 (September 1973), pp. 284–305.

Berne, E. *Transactional Analysis in Psychotherapy.* Grove Press, 1961.

Boulding, K. E. *The Image: Knowledge in Life and Society.* University of Michigan Press, 1961.

Brenner, M. H., and N. B. Sigband. "Organizational Communication – An Analysis of Empirical Data." *Academy of Management Journal*, Vol. 16, No. 2 (1973), pp. 323–26.

Brooks, W. D., and G. W. Friedrich. "Police Image: An Exploratory Study," *The Journal of Communications*, Vol. 20 (1970), pp. 370–74.

Burns, K. L., and E. G. Beier. "Significance of Vocal and Visual Channels in the Decoding of Emotional Meaning." *The Journal of Communication*, Vol. 23 (1973), pp. 118–30.

Cameron, P. Talk to the American Psychological Association, August 30, 1968.

Campbell, D. T. "Systematic Error on the Part of Human Links in Communication Systems." *Information and Control*, Vol. 1 (1958), pp. 334–69.

Dance, F. E. X. "The Concept of Communication," *Journal of Communication*, Vol. 20 (1970), pp. 201–10.

Deunk, N. H. "Active Listening: A Forgotten Key to Effective Communication." *Hospital Administration*, Spring 1967, pp. 34–35.

Festinger, L., and N. Maccoby. "On Resistance to Persuasive Communications." *Journal of Abnormal Social Psychology*, Vol. 68 (1964), pp. 359–66.

Frenkel-Brunswik, E. "Intolerance of Ambiguity as an Educational and Perceptual Personality Variable." *Journal of Personality*, Vol. 18 (1949), pp. 108–43.

Gibb, J. R. "Defensive Communication." *The Journal of Communication*, March 1966, pp. 141–48.

Hall, J. "Communication Revisited." *California Management Review*, Vol. 15, No. 3 (1973), pp. 56–67.

Hall, E. T. *The Hidden Dimension*. Doubleday, 1966.

Hannemann, G. J. "Communicating Drug Abuse Information Among College Students." *The Public Opinion Quarterly*, Vol. 37, No. 2 (1973), pp. 171–91.

Harris, T. A. *I'm OK – You're OK*. Harper and Row, 1969.

Harvey, O. J., and W. F. Clapp. "Hope, Expectancy and Reactions to the Unexpected." *Journal of Personality and Social Psychology*, Vol. 2 (July 1965), pp. 45–52.

Hayakawa, S. I. *Language in Thought and Action*. Harcourt, Brace & World, 1964.

Higham, T. M. "Basic Psychological Factors in Communication." *Occupational Psychology*, January 1957, pp. 1–10.

Horne, J. H., and T. Lupton. "The Work Activities of Middle Managers." *Journal of Management Studies*, Vol. 1 (1965) pp. 14–33.

Hovland, C. I., and W. Weiss. "The Influence of Source Credibility on Communication Effectiveness." *Public Opinion Quarterly*, Vol. 15 (1951–1952), pp. 635–50.

Ilardo, J. A. "Ambiguity Tolerance and Disordered Communication." *The Journal of Communication*. Vol. 23 (December 1973), pp. 371–91.

Jackson, J. M. "The Organization and Its Communication Problems." *Advanced Management*, (February 1959), pp. 17–20.

Korzybaki, A. *Science and Sanity: An Introduction to Non-Aristotelian Systems and General Semantics*, 4th Ed. Institute of General Semantics, 1962.

Lamb, W., and D. Turner. *Management Behavior*. International Universities Press, 1969.

Landy, D., and S. Sigall. "Beauty Is Talent: Task Evaluation as a Function of the Performer's Physical Attractiveness." *Journal of Personality and Social Psychology*, Vol. 29, No. 3 (1974), pp. 299–304.

Maslow, A. *Motivation and Personality*. Harper & Row, 1954.

McClelland, D. C., and J. W. Atkinson. "The Projective Expression of Needs." *Journal of Psychology*, Vol. 25 (1948), pp. 205–22.

Mehrabian, Albert. Cited in *The Denver Post*, August 25, 1970.

Mellinger, G. D. "Interpersonal Trust as a Factor in Communications." *Journal of Abnormal and Social Psychology*, Vol. 52 (1956), pp. 120–29.

Mintzberg, H. *The Nature of Managerial Work*. Harper & Row, 1973.

Nwankwo, R. L. "Communication as Symbolic Interaction." *The Journal of Communication*, Vol. 23 (1973), pp. 195–215.

Read, W. H. "Upward Communication in Industrial Hierarchies." *Human Relations*, Vol. 52 (1962), pp. 3–15.

Rogers, C. R. *On Becoming a Person*. Houghton-Mifflin, 1961.

Rogers, C. R., and F. J. Roethlisberger. "Barriers and Gateways to Communication." *Harvard Business Review*, Vol. 30, No. 4 (July–August 1952), pp. 46–52.

Rosen, B., and T. H. Jerdee. "Sex Stereotyping in the Executive Suite." *Harvard Business Review*, Vol. 52 (March–April 1974), pp. 45–58.

Schlesinger, A. M., Jr. *A Thousand Days*. Houghton-Mifflin, 1965.

Scodel, A., and H. Austrin. "The Perception of Jewish Photographs by Non-Jews and Jews." *Journal of Abnormal Social Psychology*, Vol. 19 (1954), pp. 329–34.

Shannon, C. E., and W. Weaver. *The Mathematical Theory of Communication*, University of Illinois Press, 1949.

Smith, D. D. "Mass Communications and International Image Change." *Journal of Conflict Resolution*, Vol. 17, No. 1 (1973), pp. 115–29.

Sullivan, H. S. *Conceptions of Modern Psychiatry*. William Alanson White Psychiatric Foundation, 1940; Tavistock Publications, 1955.

Taschdjian, E. "The Entropy of Complex Dynamic Systems." *Behavioral Science*, Vol. 19 (1974), p. 93.

Tesser, A., S. Rosen, and E. Waranch. "Communicator Mood and the Reluctance to Transmit Undesirable Messages (The Mum Effect)." *The Journal of Communications*, Vol. 23 (September 1973), pp. 266–83.

Thayer, L. *Communication and Communication Systems*. Irwin, 1968, pp. 26–27.

Vardaman, G. T., and Halterman, C. C. *Managerial Control Through Communication*. Wiley, 1968.

Vidmar, E., and M. Rokeach. "Bunker's Bigotry: A Study in Selective Perception and Exposure." *Journal of Communication*, Vol. 24, No. 1 (1974), pp. 36–48.

Walster, E., and L. Festinger. "The Effectiveness of Overheard Persuasive Communications." *Journal of Abnormal and Social Psychology*, Vol. 65 (1962), pp. 395–402.

Webber, R. A. "Managerial Behavior, Personality, and Organizational Structure." Unpublished Ph.D. Dissertation, Columbia University, 1966.

Webber, R. A. *Time and Management*. Van Nostrand Reinhold, 1972.

Wiener, M. "Word Frequency or Motivation in Perceptual Defense." *Journal of Abnormal Social Psychology*, Vol. 31 (1955), pp. 214–18.

Willits, R. D. "Company Performance and Interpersonal Relations." *Industrial Management Review*, Vol. 8, No. 2 (Spring 1967), pp. 91–107.

Zajonc, R. R. *Social Psychology: An Experimental Approach*. Brooks/Cole, 1966.

Zaleznik, A., and D. Moment. *The Dynamics of Interpersonal Behavior*. John Wiley & Sons, 1964.

Readings

Analyzing Interpersonal Communication: The Case of Mr. Hart and Bing

The case is presented in two versions, A and B. Version A presents Mr. Hart's point of view, and version B presents Bing's point of view.

The shop situation reported in this case occurred in a work group of four men and three women who were engaged in testing and inspecting panels for electronic equipment. The employees were paid on a piecework incentive basis. The personnel organization of the company included a counselor whose duty it was to become acquainted with the workers and talk over any problems they wished to discuss with him. The following statements of the views of two men consist of excerpts from five interviews that the counselor had with each of them within a period of about two weeks.

VERSION A (MR. HART)

Say, I think you should be in on this. My dear little friend Bing is heading himself into a showdown with me. Recently it was brought to my attention by the Quality Control checker that Bing has been taking double and triple set-up time for panels which he is actually inspecting at one time. In effect, that's cheatin', and I've called him down on it several times before. A few days ago it was brought to my attention again, and so this time I really let him have it in no uncertain terms. He's been getting away with this for too long and I'm gonna put an end to it once and for all. I know he didn't like my calling him on it because a few hours later he had the union representative breathin' down my back. But you know what talkin' to those people is like; they'll sometimes defend an employee, even though they think he's takin' advantage of the company. Well, anyway, I let them both know I'll not tolerate the practice any longer, and I let Bing know that if he continues to do this kind of thing, I'm gonna take official action with my boss to have the guy fired or penalized somehow. This kind of thing has to be curbed. Actually, I'm inclined to think the guy's mentally deficient, because talking to him has actually no meaning to him whatsoever. I've tried just about every approach to jar some sense into that guy's head, and I've just about given it up as a bad deal. I just can't seem to make any kind of an impression upon him. It's an unpleasant situation for everyone concerned, but I'm at a loss to know what more I can do about it.

I don't know what it is about the guy, but I think he's harboring some deep feelings against me. For what, I don't know, 'cause I've tried to handle that bird with kid gloves. But his whole attitude around here on the job is one of indifference, and he certainly isn't a good influence on the rest of my group. Frankly, I think he purposely tries to agitate them against me at times, too. It seems to me he may be suffering from illusions of grandeur, 'cause all he does all day long is sit over there and croon his fool head off.

Thinks he's a Frank Sinatra! No kidding! I understand he takes singin' lessons and he's working with some of the local bands in the city. All of which is OK by me; but when his outside interests start interfering with his efficiency on the job, then I've gotta start paying closer attention to the situation. For this reason I've been keepin' my eye on that bird and if he steps out of line any more, he and I are gonna part ways.

I feel quite safe in saying that I've done all I can rightfully be expected to do by way of trying to show him what's expected of him. You know there's an old saying, "You can't make a purse out of a sow's ear." The guy is simply unscrupulous. He feels no obligation to do a real day's work. Yet I know the guy can do a good job, because for a long time he did. But in recent months, he's slipped for some reason and his whole attitude on the job has changed. Why, it's even getting to the point now where I think he's inducing other employees to "goof off" a few minutes before the lunch whistle and go down to the washrooms and clean up on company time. I've called him on it several times, but words just don't seem to make any lasting impression on him. Well, if he keeps it up much longer, he's gonna find himself on the way out. He's asked me for a transfer, so I know he wants to go. But I didn't give him an answer when he asked me, 'cause I was steamin' mad at the time, and I may have told him to go somewhere else.

I think it would be good for you to talk with him frequently. It'll give him a chance to think the matter through a little more carefully. There may be something that's troubling him in his personal life, although I've made every effort to find out if there was such a thing, and I've been unsuccessful. Maybe you'll have better luck.

VERSION B (Bing)

According to the system 'round here, as I understand it, I am allowed so much "set-up" time to get these panels from the racks, carry them over here to the bench and place them in this jig here, which holds them in position while I inspect them. For convenience's sake and also to save time, I sometimes manage to carry two or three over at the same time and inspect them all at the same time. This is a perfectly legal thing to do. We've always been doing it. Mr. Hart, the supervisor, has other ideas about it, though; he claims it's cheating the company. He came over to the bench a day or two ago and let me know just how he felt about the matter. Boy, did we go at it! It wasn't so much the fact that he called me down on it, but more the way in which he did it. He's a sarcastic bastard. I've never seen anyone like him. He's not content just to say in a manlike way what's on his mind, but he prefers to do it in a way that makes you want to crawl inside a crack in the floor. What a guy! I don't mind being called down by a supervisor, but I like to be treated like a man, and not humiliated like a school teacher does a naughty kid. He's been pullin' this stuff ever since he's been a supervisor. I knew him when he was just one of us, but since he's been promoted he's lost his friendly way and seems to be havin' some difficulty in knowin' how to manage us employees. In fact, I've noticed that he's been more this way with us fellows since he's gotten married. I dunno whether there's any connection there, but I do know he's a changed man over what he used to be like when he was a worker on the bench with us several years ago.

When he pulled this kind of stuff on me the other day, I got so damn mad I called in the union representative. I knew that the thing I was doing was permitted by the contract, but I was just intent on making some trouble for Mr. Hart, just because he persists in this sarcastic way of handling me. I'm about fed up with the whole damn situation.

I'm tryin' every means I can to get myself transferred out of his group. If I don't succeed and I'm forced to stay on here, I'm going to screw him every way I can. He's not gonna pull this kind of kid stuff any longer on me. When the union representative questioned him on the case, he finally had to back down, 'cause according to the contract an employee can use any timesaving method or device in order to speed up the process as long as the quality standards of the job are met. During the discussion with me and the union representative, Mr. Hart charged that it was a dishonest practice and threatened to "take it up the line" unless the union would curb me on this practice. But this was just an idle threat, 'cause the most he can do is get me transferred out of here, which is actually what I want anyway.

You see, he knows that I do professional singing on the outside. He hears me singin' here on the job, and he hears the people talkin' about my career in music. I guess he figures I can be so cocky because I have another means of earning some money. Actually, the employees here enjoy havin' me sing while we work, but he thinks I'm disturbing them and causing them to "goof off" from their work. It's funny, but for some reason I think he's partial to the three female employees in our group. He's the same with all us guys as he is to me, but with the girls he acts more decent. I don't know what his object is. Occasionally, I leave the job a few minutes early and go down to the washroom to wash up before lunch. Sometimes several others in the group will accompany me, and so Mr. Hart automatically thinks I'm the leader and usually bawls me out for the whole thing.

So, you can see, I'm a marked man around here. He keeps watchin' me like a hawk. Naturally this makes me very uncomfortable. That's why I'm sure a transfer would be the best thing. I've asked him for it, but he didn't give me any satisfaction at the time. While I remain here I'm gonna keep my nose clean, but whenever I get the chance I'm gonna slip it to him, but good.

The Administrator's Skill: Communication
Fritz J. Roethlisberger

What is taking place when two people engaged in a common task interact? What do the actors involved perceive is taking place, what is a useful way for the executive to think about these interpersonal proceedings in which he is engaged, and what skills can he practice which will make him more effective as an administrator of people?

I want to discuss these questions in terms of a specific, down-to-earth case in an industrial plant—a case of misunderstanding between two people, a worker and a foreman. (It is not important that they happen to be foreman and worker: to all intents and purposes they might as well be superintendent and foreman or, for that matter, controller and accountant.)

A CASE OF MISUNDERSTANDING

In a department of a large industrial organization there were seven workers (four men and three women) engaged in testing and inspecting panels of electronic equipment. In this department one of the workers, Bing, was having trouble with his immediate supervisor, Hart, who had formerly been a worker in the department.

Had we been observers in this department we would have seen Bing carrying two or three panels at a time from the racks where they were stored to the bench where he inspected them together. For this activity we would have seen him charging double or triple setup time. We would have heard him occasionally singing at work. Also we would have seen him usually leaving his work position a few minutes early to go to lunch, and noticed that other employees sometimes accompanied him. And had we been present at one specific occasion, we would have heard Hart telling Bing that he disapproved of these activities and that he wanted Bing to stop doing them.

VIEWS OF MISUNDERSTANDING

Let me start with the simplest but the toughest question first: "What is going on here?" I think most of us would agree that what seems to be going on is some misunderstanding between Hart and Bing. But no sooner do we try to represent to ourselves the nature of this misunderstanding than a flood of different theories appear. Let me discuss briefly five very common ways of representing this misunderstanding: (1) as a difference of opinion resolvable by common sense, by simply referring to the facts; (2) as a clash of personalities; (3) as a conflict of social roles; (4) as a struggle for power; and (5) as a breakdown in communication. There are, of course, other theories too—for example, those of the interactionists, the field theory of Kurt Lewin, and even the widely held views of Adam Smith or Karl Marx. But for our purposes here the five I have mentioned will suffice.

Common Sense

For the advocates of common sense—the first theory, though most of them would not call it that—the situation resolves itself quickly:

Either Hart is right or Bing is right. Since both parties cannot be right, it follows that if Hart is right, then Bing is wrong; or if Bing is right, then Hart is wrong. Either Bing should or should not be singing on the job, carrying two or three panels at a time and charging double or triple setup time, and so on.

"Let us get these facts settled first," say the common-sense advocates. "Once ascertained, the problem is easily settled. Once we know who is doing what he should not be doing, then all we have to do is to get this person to do what he should be doing. It's as simple as that."

But is it? Let us look again at our case. Let us note that there are no differences of opinion between Hart and Bing about some matters. For example both would agree that Bing is taking double or triple setup time when he carries his panels two or three at a time to his bench for inspection. Both would agree that Bing sings on the job and occasionally leaves his work place a bit early for lunch.

Where they differ is in the way each *perceives* these activities. Hart perceives Bing's activities as "cheating," "suffering from illusions of grandeur," "thinking he is Frank Sinatra," "interfering with Bing's efficiency as well as the efficiency of other workers," "disturbing the other workers," "inducing them to goof off," and "influencing them against [Hart]." To Bing, on the other hand, these activities are "perfectly legal," "something we've always been doing," "something that is not disturbing the other workers," and so forth.

Among these many different conflicting claims and different perceptions, what are the facts? Many of these evaluations refer to personal and social standards of conduct for which the company has no explicit rules. Even in the case of taking double and triple setup time, there are probably no clear rules, because when the industrial engineer set the standards for the job, he did not envisage the possibility of a worker doing what Bing is now doing and which, according to Bing, is a time-saving device.

But we can waste effort on this question. For, even if it were clear that Hart is not exploring the situation, that he is not getting these important facts or rules which would settle who is right and who is wrong, it would still be true that, so far as Hart is concerned, he *knows* who is right and who is wrong. And because he *knows*, he has no reason to question the assumptions he is making about Bing's behavior.

Now this is very likely to happen in the case of advocates of the common-sense theory. Significantly, Hart himself is a good advocate of it. Does this have anything to do with the fact that he is not being very successful in getting Bing to do what he should be doing? Let us postpone this question for future consideration.

Clash of Personalities

For the second school of thought, what is going on between Hart and Bing can be viewed essentially as a clash of personalities—an interaction between two particular personality structures. According to this view, what is going on cannot be known in detail until much more information about these different personality structures is secured. Hence we can only speculate that what is going on may be something of this order:

Neither Hart nor Bing feels too sure of himself, and each seems to be suffering from feelings of inadequacy or inferiority. Being unable to recognize, admit, or accept these feelings, however, each one perceives the behavior of the other as a personal attack upon himself. When a person feels he is being attacked, he feels strongly the need to defend himself. This, then, is essentially what is taking place between Hart and Bing. Because of his feelings of inferiority, each one is defending himself against what he perceives to be an attack upon himself as a person. In psychology, the feelings of each man are conceived as being rooted somehow in his "personality."

That this theory is pointing to some very important phenomena can hardly be questioned. Certainly I will not argue its validity. I am only concerned with what it is telling us and what follows from it. As I understand it, this theory says that neither Hart nor Bing is aware of his own feelings of inadequacy and defense mechanisms. These are the important facts that each is ignoring. From this it follows that there is little hope of correcting the misunderstanding without helping Bing and Hart to become aware of these feelings and of their need to defend against them. Short of this, the solution lies in transferring Bing to a supervisor whose personality will be more compatible with Bing's, and in giving Hart a worker whose personality will be more compatible with Hart's.

Conflict of Social Roles

Let us look at the third explanation. Instead of viewing the misunderstanding as an interaction between two individual personality units, it can also be viewed as an interaction between two social roles:

With the promotion of Hart to the position of a supervisor of a group in which he had been formerly a worker, a system of reciprocal expectancies has been disturbed. Bing is expecting Hart to behave toward him in the same way Hart did when Hart was a worker; but by telling Bing to stop "crooning his fool head off," for example, Hart is not behaving in accordance with the role of a friend. Similarly, Hart, as the newly appointed supervisor, is expecting that Bing should do what he tells Bing to do, but by singing Bing is not behaving in accordance with the customary role of the worker.

According to this theory, as any recent textbook on sociology will explain, when two actors in a relationship reach differing definitions of the situation, misunderstanding is likely to arise. Presumably this is what is happening between Hart and Bing. The role-expectation pattern has been disturbed. Bing views his singing as variant but permissive; Hart views it as deviant. From these differing definitions of what each other's role should be misunderstanding results. According to this view, it will take time for their new relationship to work out. In time Bing will learn what to expect from Hart now that Hart is his supervisor. Also in time Hart will define better his role *vis-à-vis* Bing.

Struggle for Power

The fourth way of representing what is going on between Hart and Bing would be in terms of such abstractions as "authority" and "power":

When Bing refuses to stop singing on the job when Hart tells him to, Bing is being disobedient to the commands or orders of a holder of power. When this occurs, Hart, who according to this theory is a "power holder," has the right to exercise or apply sanctions, such as dismissal or transfer. But the threat to exercise these sanctions does not seem to be too effective in getting Bing to stop, because Bing is a member of the union, which also has power and the right to apply sanctions. By going to his union representative, Bing can bring this power structure into play.

In other words, what is going on in the case is not merely an interaction between two individual or social personalities; it is also a struggle between two kinds of institutionalized power. It is an issue between the management and the union which may even precipitate a strike. Management will charge that it cannot have workers in the plant who are disobedient to the orders of their foremen. The union will charge that Bing is merely introducing a labor-saving device which the foreman has not enough sense to recognize. To avoid things getting to this stage, the struggle-for-power theory would recommend that if Hart and Bing between them cannot settle their differences, they should refer them to the grievance machinery set up for this purpose by union and management.

According to this theory, Hart got into trouble not because he had authority but because when he tried to exercise it and was unsuccessful, he lost it. Authority ceases to exist when it cannot be exercised successfully.[1]

Breakdown in Communication

The fifth way of stating what is going on would be to say that Hart and Bing think they are talking about the same things when in fact they are not:

Hart assumes he understands what Bing is doing and saying; Bing assumes he understands what Hart is doing and saying. In fact, neither assumption holds. From this "uncritical assumption of understanding," misunderstanding arises.

Thus, when Hart tells Bing to stop "crooning his fool head off," Bing assumes that Hart is talking about Bing's singing when Hart may in fact be talking about his difficulties in maintaining his position as formal leader of the group. Hart assumes that Bing is singing deliberately to flaunt his authority, whereas in Bing's mind singing may be a way of relating himself to people and of maintaining his conceptions of himself.[2]

According to this theory, Hart and Bing are not on the same wave length, and as a result communication bypassing occurs. Each is behaving in accordance with the reality as he perceives it to be, but neither is aware of the assumptions that underlie his perceptions. Their misunderstandings arise as a result.

This theory strikes a new note that I should like to explore further.

ROOTS OF MISUNDERSTANDING

So far our theories have explained well why there is misunderstanding and conflict; they have not shown so clearly how any new behavior patterns on the part of Hart or Bing or both can emerge or be encouraged to emerge from the present ones. In them we have found no responsible actor, no learner, and no practitioner of a skill.

Could it be that what is going on between Hart and Bing results also in part from the fact that nobody is taking any responsibility for what is going on? May we not assume that people can learn through experience how to determine their relationships with each other as well as be determined by them? Let us therefore look at these interpersonal proceedings from the point of view of a person who is responsibly involved in them and who may be capable of learning something from them.

From now on I shall be chiefly concerned with Hart, not because I think Hart is any more or less guilty than Bing of creating misunderstanding, but because I wish to develop a useful way of thinking for persons in a position of responsibility like Hart. This way of thinking, I hope, will not be in conflict with our other theories. It will merely spell out what a supervisor must learn if he is to take into account the significant processes which these other theories say have been going on.

So, instead of viewing Hart in his dealings with Bing as a supervisor expressing his personality, playing a social role, or exercising power, let us view him as a practitioner of a skill of communication. Let us see what skills, if any, he is using. And if we find, as I fear we may, that he has not been too skillful, let us see if he can learn to become a more skillful practitioner, and how this can be done.

Hart's Trouble

When we ask ourselves what Hart is doing to facilitate misunderstanding, we meet again a number of different theories. Although I am not sure that these theories are pointing to different things, each uses a slightly different terminology, so I shall state them separately:

1. *Hart is making value judgments*—According to one view, the biggest block to personal communication arises from the fact that Hart is making value judgments of Bing from Hart's point of view. Hart's tendency to evaluate is what gets him into trouble. Not only is he evaluating Bing, but he is trying to get Bing to accept his evaluation as the only and proper one. It is the orientation that angers Bing and makes him feel misunderstood.[3]

2. *Hart is not listening*—According to another and not too different view, Hart gets into trouble because he is not listening to Bing's feelings. Because he is not paying attention to Bing's feelings, he is not responding to them as such. Instead, we find him

responding to the effect of Bing's feelings upon his own. Not only is he ignoring Bing's feelings, but also he is ignoring the effect of what he is saying upon them. This kind of behavior also leads to Bing's feelings of being misunderstood.[4]

3. *Hart is assuming things that may not be so* — Still another point of view says that Hart is getting into trouble because he is making assumptions about Bing's behavior that may not be so. Hart is confusing what he sees with what he assumes and feels.

When Hart sees Bing leaving early for lunch, for example, he assumes that Bing is doing this deliberately, intentionally, and personally to discredit him and to test his authority. Because of this assumption he feels angry and his feelings of anger reinforce his assumption. Now if Bing's going to lunch a few minutes early is such an attempt to discredit him, then Hart's anger and his attempt to retaliate make sense. But if he starts with this assumption and makes no attempt to check it, then his anger makes less sense. Hart may be assuming something that is not so.

Again, Hart shows he may be making assumptions that are not so by the way he talks in trying to get Bing to stop singing at work or to stop inspecting panels two or three at a time. When he uses phrases like "crooning your fool head off" and "cheating the company," is he not assuming that Bing should feel about these activities in the same way that he himself does? And if Bing does not feel this way, then obviously, in Hart's view, Bing must be a "fool," "defective," or a "sow's ear." To Hart, Bing *is* a sow's ear. And how does one feel toward a sow's ear? Toward such an entity one must feel (by definition) helpless and hopeless. Note that Hart's assumptions, perceptions, and feelings are of a piece; each reinforces the other to make one total evaluation.

In short, all of Hart's evaluations are suspect because he confuses what he sees with what he assumes and feels. As a result, there is no way for Hart to take another look at the situation. How can Hart check his evaluations when he is not aware that he is making them? By treating inferences as facts, there is no way for him to explore the assumptions, feelings, and perceptions that underlie his evaluations.[5] For Hart, Bing *is* the way he perceives Bing to be. There is no way for him to say that "because of the assumptions I make and because of the way I feel, I perceive Bing in this way."

4. *Hart is making his false assumptions come true* — A fourth theory emphasizes still another point. This theory says that the very kind of misevaluations which our last theory says Hart is guilty of must provoke *ipso facto* the very kind of behavior on the part of Bing of which Hart disapproves.[6] In other words, Hart is getting into trouble because, by his behavior, he is making his assumptive world come true.

Let us examine this theory first by looking at the effect of Hart's behavior on Bing. Very clearly Bing does not like it. Bing tells us that when Hart behaves in the way Hart does, he feels misunderstood, humiliated, and treated like a child. These feelings give grounds to his perception of Hart as "a sarcastic bastard," "a school teacher" pulling "kid stuff" on him. These perceptions in turn will tend to make Bing behave in the way that will coincide more and more with Hart's original untested assumptions about Bing's behavior. Feeling like a "marked man," Bing will behave more and more like a "sow's ear." Although he will try to "keep his nose clean," he will "slip it to [Hart], but good" whenever he gets the chance.

That this kind of misevaluation on the part of Hart will tend to produce this kind of behavior on the part of Bing is, according to this view, a fact of common experience. To explain it one does not have to assume any peculiar personality structure on the part of Bing — an undue sensitivity to criticism, defensiveness, or feeling of inferiority. All one has to assume is an individual personality with a need to maintain its individuality. Therefore, any attempts on the part of Hart which will be perceived by Bing as an attempt to deny his individual differences will be resisted. What Hart says about Bing is, from Bing's point of view, exactly what he is *not*. Bing *is* what he is from his own frame of reference and from the point of view of his own feelings, background, and situation. Bing *is* what he assumes, feels, and perceives himself to be. And this is just what Hart's behavior is denying.

In spite of the different terminology and emphasis of these theories, they all seem to point to certain uniformities in the interpersonal proceedings of Hart and Bing which should be taken into account regardless of the actors' particular personalities or social roles. For the misunderstandings that arise, Hart and Bing are not to blame; the trouble resides in the process of interpersonal communication itself.

Problem of Involvement

So far it would seem as if we had made Hart the villain in the piece. But let us remember that although Hart has been intellectually and emotionally involved in what has been going on, he has not been aware of this involvement. All of our theories have implied this. Hart's ego has been involved; his actual group memberships have been involved; his reference groups have been involved; his feelings, assumptions, and perceptions have been involved — but Hart is not aware of it. If any new behavior on the part of Hart is to emerge — and *all* our theories would agree to this — Hart must in some sense become aware of and recognize this involvement. Without such an awareness there can be no reevaluation or no change in perception. And without such a change no learning can take place.

How can this change be accomplished? Some theories would seem to imply that misunderstanding will be minimized only when Hart *logically understands* the nature of his involvement with Bing. Hart will learn to evaluate Bing more properly only when he understands better the personality structures of himself and Bing and the social system of which they are a part. Only by the logical understanding and critical probing of his and Bing's feelings of inadequacy and defense mechanisms can he make a proper evaluation and bring about any real change in his behavior.

But there is another view. It holds that logical understanding is not of the first importance. Rather, misunderstanding will be minimized when Hart learns to *recognize and accept* responsibility for his involvement. Better understanding will be achieved when Hart learns to recognize and accept his own and Bing's individual differences, when he learns to recognize and accept Bing's feelings as being different from his own, and when as a result he can allow Bing to express his feelings and differences and listen to them.[7]

Let me explore this second theory further, for it suggests that Hart might possibly learn to do a better job without having to become a professional social scientist or be psychoanalyzed. Moreover, it coincides with some facts of common experience.

How Can Hart Be Helped?

Some administrators have achieved the insights of the second theory through the school of "hard knocks" rather than through the help of books or by being psychoanalyzed. So should there not be simple skills which Hart can be taught, which he can learn and practice, and which would help him to recognize and accept his involvement and deal with it better?

Now it may be that Hart, because of certain personal deficiencies, is not able to recognize or accept his own feelings—let alone Bing's. That this holds for some supervisors goes without question. But does it apply to all? I do not think so, nor do I think it applies to Hart. Is it not possible that some supervisors may not be able to do these things because they have never learned how to do them?

The fact is, if our analysis up to this point is sound, that Hart does not get into trouble because he feels hopeless and helpless in the face of a worker who sings on the job, leaves early for lunch, and so on, and who refuses to stop doing these things when Hart tells him to. Any one of us who has had to deal with a worker behaving like Bing will recognize and remember feelings of inadequacy like Hart's only too well. We do not need to have very peculiar or special personality structures to have such feelings. Rather, Hart's trouble is that he assumes, and no doubt has been told too often, that he should *not* have feelings of inadequacy. It resides in the fact that he has not developed or been given a method or skill for dealing with them. As a result, these feelings are denied and appear in the form of an attribute of Bing—"a sow's ear."

In other words, I am suggesting that Hart gets into trouble partly because no one has assured him that it is normal and natural—in fact, inevitable—that he should have some feelings of inadequacy; that he cannot and *should* not try to escape from them. No one has helped him to develop a method of dealing with his own feelings and the feelings of Bing. No one has listened to him or helped him to learn to listen to others. No one has helped him to recognize the effect of his behavior on others. No one has helped him to become aware of his assumptions and feelings and how they affect the evaluations he makes.

Instead, too many training courses have told Hart what an ideal supervisor should be and how an ideal supervisor should behave. Both explicit and implicit in most of the instruction he receives is the assumption that an ideal supervisor should not become emotionally involved in his dealings with people. He should remain aloof, be objective, and deny or get rid of his feelings. But this goes against the facts of his immediate experience; it goes against everything upon which, according to our theories, his growth and development depend. Indeed, to "behave responsibly" and be "mature" in the way he is instructed to, without becoming emotionally committed, would be, to use the *New Yorker's* phrase, "the trick of the week!"

Is it any wonder, therefore, that Hart remains immature—socially, intellectually, and emotionally? He gets no understanding of how these frustrations and misunderstandings must inevitably arise from his dealings with others; he gets no help on how to deal with them when they do arise. He probably has had many training courses which told him how to recognize and deal with workers who are sow's ears. He probably has had no training course which helped him to see how his assumptions and feelings would tend to produce sow's ears by the bushel. He has not been helped to see how this surplus of sow's ears in modern industry might be diminished through the conscious practice of a skill. Thus he has not even been allowed to become intellectually involved and intrigued in the most important problem of his job. Yet there *are* training courses designed for just such a purpose, and they have worked successfully.[8]

CONCLUSION

Am I indulging in wishful thinking when I believe that there are some simple skills of communication that can be taught, learned, and practiced which might help to diminish misunderstanding? To me it is this possibility which the recent findings of general semantics and human relations are suggesting. They suggest that although man is determined by the complex relationships of which he is a part, nevertheless he is also in some small part a determiner of these relationships. Once he learns what he cannot do, he is ready to learn what little he can do. And what a tremendous difference to himself and to others the little that he can do—listening with understanding, for example—can make!

Once he can accept his limitations and the limitations of others, he can begin to learn to behave more skillfully with regard to the milieu in which he finds himself. He can begin to learn that misunderstanding can be diminished—not banished—by the slow, patient, laborious practice of a skill.

But we can expect too much from this possibility, so let me conclude by sounding two notes of caution:

1. Although these skills of communication of which I am speaking deal in part with words, they are not in themselves words, nor is the territory to which they apply made up of words. It follows, then, that no verbal statement about these skills, however accurate, can act as a substitute for them. They are not truly articulate and never can be. Although transmissible to other persons, they are but slowly so and, even then, only with practice.

2. Let us remember that these interpersonal proceedings between Hart and Bing, or A and B whoever they may be, are extremely complex. So far as I know, there exists no single body of concepts which as yet describes systematically and completely all the important processes that our separate theories have said are taking place and how they relate to each other. Let us therefore accept gracefully and not contentiously that these interpersonal proceedings, unlike the atom, have not been as yet "cracked" by social science. Only then can we as students of human behavior live up to our responsibility for making our knowledge fruitful in practice.

NOTES AND REFERENCES

1. For an elaboration of this view see Robert Bierstedt, "An Analysis of Social Power," in *The American Sociological Review* (December 1950), p. 730.

2. For an analysis of this theory see Wendell Johnson, "The Fateful Process of Mr. A Talking to Mr. B," *Harvard Business Review* (January–February 1953), p. 49.

3. See Carl R. Rogers and F. J. Roethlisberger, "Barriers and Gateways to Communication," in *Harvard Business Review* (July–August 1952), pp. 46–50.

4. Ibid., pp. 50–52.

5. For a fuller explanation see Irving Lee, *How to Talk with People* (New York: Harper & Brothers, 1953).

6. For example, see Hadley Cantril, The *"Why" of Man's Experience* (New York: The Macmillan Company, 1950).

7. For a fuller explanation see Carl R. Rogers, *Client-Centered Therapy* (Boston: Houghton Mifflin, 1953).

8. See Kenneth R. Andrews, "Executive Training by the Case Method," and F. J. Roethlisberger, "Training Supervisors in Human Relations," *Harvard Business Review* (September 1951), pp. 58 and 47.

The Case of Blackman and Dodds

Abraham Zaleznik and David Moment

This case is an interchange between the director of a research laboratory and one of his subordinates. The director, whom we shall call Dr. Blackman, was a man in his late forties, with considerable stature as a researcher and research administrator. Many ambitious and able young researchers wanted to work in his laboratory. Dr. Dodds, his subordinate, was a promising young researcher who had recently been assigned to the laboratory as a staff scientist. He requested a meeting with Dr. Blackman at which the following interchange took place. (Dr. Dodds entered the office and showed his superior, Dr. Blackman, a letter. This letter was from Professor Wilkin of another research institution, offering Dr. Dodds a position; Dr. Blackman read the letter over.)

DODDS: What do you think of that?

BLACKMAN: I knew it was coming. He asked me if it would be all right if he sent it. I told him to go ahead, if he wanted to.

DODDS: I didn't expect it, particularly after what you said to me the last time. (*Pause.*) I'm really quite happy here. I don't want you to get the idea that I am thinking of leaving. But I thought I should go and visit—I think he expects it—and I wanted to let you know that just because I was thinking of going down, that didn't mean I was thinking of leaving here, unless of course, he offers me something extraordinary.

BLACKMAN: Why are you telling me all this?

DODDS: Because I didn't want you hearing from somebody else that I was thinking of leaving here because I was going for a visit to another institution. I really have no intention of leaving here you know, unless he offers me something really extraordinary that I can't afford to turn down. I think I'll tell him that, that I am willing to look at his laboratory, but unless there is something unusual there for me, I have no intention of leaving here.

BLACKMAN: It's up to you.

DODDS: What do you think?

BLACKMAN: Well, what? About what? You've got to make up your mind.

DODDS: I don't consider too seriously this job. He is not offering anything really extraordinary. But I am interested in what he had to say, and I would like to look around his lab.

BLACKMAN: Sooner or later you are going to have to make up your mind where you want to work.

DODDS: [*Sharply.*] That depends on the offers, doesn't it?

BLACKMAN: No, not really; a good man always gets offers. You got a good offer and you move, and as soon as you have moved, you get other good offers. It would throw you into confusion to consider all the good offers you will receive. Isn't there a factor of how stable you want to be?

DODDS: But I'm not shopping around. I already told you that. He sent me this letter; I didn't ask him to. All I said was I think I should visit him, and to you that's shopping around!

Abridged from "The Case of Blackman and Dodd" from *The Dynamics of Interpersonal Behavior* by Abraham Zaleznik and David Moment. Copyright © 1964 John Wiley & Sons, Inc. Reprinted by permission of John Wiley & Sons, Inc.

BLACKMAN: Well, you may choose to set aside your commitment here if he offers you something better. All I am saying is that you will still be left with the question of you've got to stay some place, and where is that going to be?

DODDS: You really don't think that I could find a better job than the one you have offered me here?

BLACKMAN: I don't know. I'm not thinking about that.

DODDS: How would it look if I were to leave?

BLACKMAN: To me, if you wanted to go, I'd say fine, if that's what you want. But frankly I think there would be a few raised eyebrows if you were to leave now.

DODDS: But I'm not shopping around. I want you to understand that.

BLACKMAN: You've got the problem of all young men who are sought after. You've got to decide what you will accept and what you won't accept.

DODDS: Look, I came in here, and I want to be honest with you, but you go and make me feel all guilty, and I don't like that.

BLACKMAN: You are being honest as can be.

DODDS: I didn't come in here to fight. I don't want to disturb you.

BLACKMAN: I'm not disturbed. If you think it is best for you to go somewhere else, that's okay with me. We can get another plasma physicist any day, just as good as you. They are standing in line to get in here. What bothers me is how restless you want to appear to me and Wilkin. For one thing, you've got everything analyzed out in terms of what you want: tenure, appointment, and space. Things like that.

DODDS: That's obvious. I can't understand you. You really think that no one will ever be able to make me an offer that will make me want to leave this place.

BLACKMAN: All I am saying is that it looks funny. You asked me how it would look, and I'm telling you it would look funny so soon after you getting fixed up here.

DODDS: Well, I was just trying to be honest, and. . . .

BLACKMAN: [Interrupting.] All the jobs you get offered at this stage in your career are the same. They are all the same. One may give you a little more salary, but it will have a lousy lab. Another may offer you tenure and a higher title, but you would be dead in ten years if you went there. What you should be looking for is an opportunity to do work and to develop in an environment. Your colleagues, the really important ones, don't give a damn whether you are a Junior or Associate research worker. Don't get me wrong. I don't want to hold you back. If you feel it's best for you to go, I wouldn't want to hold you here under any circumstances. I just want to give you some advice.

DODDS: But I don't see what this has to do with me. All I said was I would consider his offer if it was so good I couldn't afford to turn it down. Do you think I should turn it down even if it is a better job?

BLACKMAN: All I'm saying is maybe it's too fast.

DODDS: What of it? Are you telling me that a young person coming up shouldn't take the best job offered to him?

BLACKMAN: What should they take?

DODDS: Young people should take the best jobs they can get, and go where they want.

BLACKMAN: Yes, but not too fast.

DODDS: How fast?

BLACKMAN: I don't know. Enough time to settle in and do a job of work.

DODDS: One, two, three years?

BLACKMAN: It depends.

DODDS: When should I be thinking of leaving this laboratory, then? When do you think would be the best time for me to go?

BLACKMAN: I can't answer that. It's up to you to decide.

DODDS: If I were to leave this year what would it look like?

BLACKMAN: I think it would look like Dodds had a lot of opportunism and self-interest. You know what I mean? Like he was restless. It would not look good.

DODDS: I don't understand you. I came in here to be honest with you, and you make me feel guilty. All I wanted was to show you this letter, and let you know what I was going to do. What should I have told you?

BLACKMAN: That you had read the letter, and felt that under the circumstances it was necessary for you to pay a visit to Wilkin, but that you were happy here, and wanted to stay at least until you had got a job of work done.

DODDS: I can't get over it. You think there isn't a place in the world I'd rather be than here in this lab. . . .

In our haste to delineate important features of interpersonal dynamics illustrated in this interchange we should not miss the innocent and poignant qualities of the talk between Dr. Dodds and Dr. Blackman. Each man was speaking for himself—a person with a unique history. Yet each was speaking universally. Dr. Dodds inadvertently represented every bright, young, and ambitious person who tastes daily both the sweet excitement of work and bitter anxiety for the future. The anxiety portrayed in the interview overcame the sense of aliveness available from the pleasures of work. Dr. Dodds presented, therefore, all his insecurities and doubts about himself as a professional worker and as a subordinate.

We could infer that Dr. Dodds was stimulating his environment to provide feedback important to his growing self-esteem. His innocent denial of any intent to seek reassurance, love, or status was contradicted by the assertion that he could leave the laboratory anytime he chose to, and that he was free of the enmeshing obligations intrinsic to work in organizations.

Dr. Dodds appeared to be acting out a denial of dependency and obligation while asserting a degree of independence and noncommitment not really his own. This denial probably echoed his past experience. How was the young researcher recreating a conflict externally and in reality that had long persisted internally and in fantasy? We are unable to answer this question from the case alone, but it remains a valid one. We can see that Dr. Dodds *evoked* the conflicts in such a way as to express simultaneously his strivings for independence and his uncertain sense of self-esteem.

The speculation on the continuity between a single event and a personal history raises for exploration two concepts important for understanding interpersonal dynamics. The first is the concept of *transference reactions;* the second is the *tendency to repeat.* Both processes enable the individual to connect the relationship between past and present in interpersonal relations.

Another affective quality apparent in the interview, one raised explicitly by Dr. Dodds, is the sense of guilt. "Look, I came in here, and I want to be honest with you, but you go and make me feel all guilty and I don't like that." Assuming that Dr. Dodds accurately represented the feeling as guilt, he did not indicate guilt over what. It is difficult to pursue this question without first establishing where the guilt resided and its origin. Dr. Dodds established the guilt as residing within himself, but he projected its genesis to something that his superior had done. He did not consider that it might have been generated from within himself and that *perhaps* it had existed before the conversation.

Projection, or the tendency to externalize feelings, ideas, and wishes, is one of the ego's methods of coping with anxiety. It is possible that the activation of the environment to produce guilt within one's self and the occasion for projection is a manifestation of an unconscious sense of guilt and attendant anxiety. But this is an interesting speculation not supported by the data at hand.

Other indications of defense appear in the form of denial. Dr. Dodds replied to the suggestion that he was receiving advice, "But I don't see what this has to do with me." The sequence of interaction following this statement connotes a shift into logicizing or intellectualizing the issue. Dr. Dodds assumed the position of questioner to assert the force of the rational issue of "Are you telling me that a young person coming up shouldn't take the best job offered to him?" It is with this interchange that we can conveniently shift our attention to the person in the superordinate position, Dr. Blackman.

The logical conundrum posed by Dr. Dodds' question "How fast?" an individual should move to a new job and a new setting illuminates some of the dilemmas facing the older person in a position of authority. The authority figure can respond to his own anger and mounting aggression when he feels himself being used or tested. Such anger and aggression are evident early in the interaction when Dr. Blackman, in response to the innocent question, "What do you think?" replied sharply, "Well, what? About what? You've got to make up your mind." Or, his response can establish the locus of responsibility in the subordinate by a comment such as: "It's up to you." He can respond as a kindly father would and offer advice: "You've got the problem of all young men who are sought after; you've got to decide what you will accept and what you won't accept." Or, he can speak with the organizational and professional responsibilities as his referent as illustrated by Dr. Blackman's comment, "I knew it (the letter) was coming. He asked me if it would be all right if he sent it. I told him to go ahead if he wanted to."

However, to maintain that the authority figure can choose a response does not do justice to the individual. The choice the superior has is in fact constrained by his own personal history, and more immediately by how much affect is aroused, by the nature of his own authority problems (transference reactions), and by the structure of his defenses. Yet the issue of choice is a real one, despite the constraints of history, since each of the response possibilities creates new consequences. The subordinate who cannot tolerate being "fathered" because his dependency doubts are too real to be acknowledged will react angrily to such attempts, no matter how well intended they are. Perhaps every possible response will be to no avail, at least temporarily, because of the latent historical implications of events. Stated more clearly, the subordinate may present such live intrapersonal issues, for instance, dependency and doubt, as to render the authority figure almost helpless. The possibility of helplessness in a superior-subordinate relationship has to be reckoned with and may in the end be the most singular of all the dilemmas of exercising authority. Issues and situations exist in which all that can be done is to avoid making matters worse. This experience is common in parent-child relationships during adolescence; remnants of such relationship appear in the interview. The balance between dependence and independence is precarious during adolescence and does not become secure until long afterward. It is related to the stabilization of identity discussed by Erikson[1] and White.[2] The interpersonal setting in organizations is one area in which this battle is fought.

During the interview helplessness was apparent when Dr. Blackman offered the most frank answer at his command in response to Dr. Dodds' question, "What should I have told you?" Dr. Blackman replied, "That you had read the letter, and felt that under the circumstances it was necessary for you to pay a visit to Wilkin, but that you were happy here, and wanted to stay at least until you had got a job of work done." This statement represents what Dr. Blackman *wished* to hear. In a real sense, he could say little beyond this suppressed wish. Dr. Dodds' next comment indicated that he had not heard Dr. Blackman: "I can't get over it. You think there isn't a place in the world I'd rather be than here in this lab. . . ."

The response toward the inductions of helplessness, "the point of no return" in interpersonal relations, is yet a matter of choice, subject to all the constraints alluded to above. Helplessness often produces rage; frequently a subordinate unconsciously seeks to produce a sense of helplessness in a superior, at least at the latent level. Sometimes individuals in subordinate positions, faced with their own ambiguous identities and tenuous senses of self-esteem, are on the brink of helplessness themselves; they are overcome, if only momentarily, with the gaping knowledge that their dependency wishes run counter to the demands of responsibility and cannot in reality be gratified, even if disguised. This taste of helplessness seems to dissolve only when a similar sense of helplessness can be evoked in the authority figure. . . .

The repetition compulsion is strongest around those experiences that have been the most painful for the individual. The tendency to repeat is the attempt to master and solve the original painful experience, but usually without success. The interview between Dr. Dodds and Dr. Blackman suggests repetition in that the subordinate *created the reality* of a new job possibility as though to suggest that he accepted and rejected *actively* in contrast to being accepted or rejected *passively*. The repetition compulsion frequently occurs around expressing actively the painful experiences one endured passively.

The tendency to repeat, as a psychological phenomenon, has deep implications for interpersonal relations. The choice of persons with whom to interact, the modes of behavior, the experienced emotion during interpersonal encounters would have some relationship to the dilemmas of the past which the individual sought to solve through repetition. . . .

REFERENCES

1. Erik Ericson, *Problem of Ego Identity*, p. 101.
2. R. W. White, *Lives in Progress*, pp. 333–39.

Analyzing the Transaction

Thomas A. Harris

. . . The transaction consists of a stimulus by one person and a response by another, which response in turn becomes a new stimulus for the other person to respond to. The purpose of the analysis is to discover which part of each person — Parent, Adult, or Child — is originating each stimulus and response.

There are many clues to help identify stimulus and response as Parent, Adult, or Child. These include not only the words used but also the tone of voice, body gestures, and facial expressions. The more skillful we become in picking up these clues, the more data we acquire in Transactional Analysis. We do not have to dig deep into anecdotal material in the past to discover what is recorded in Parent, Adult, and Child. We reveal ourselves today.

The following is a list of physical and verbal clues for each state.

PARENT CLUES — Physical: Furrowed brow, pursed lips, the pointing index finger, head-wagging, the "horrified look," foot-tapping, hands on hips, arms folded across chest, wringing hands, tongue-clucking, sighing, patting another on the head. These are typical Parent gestures. However, there may be other Parent gestures peculiar to one's own Parent. For instance, if your father had a habit of clearing his throat and looking skyward each time he was to make a pronouncement about your bad behavior, this mannerism undoubtedly would be apparent as your own prelude to a Parent statement, even though this might not be generally seen as Parent in most people. Also, there are cultural differences. For instance, in the United States people exhale as they sigh, whereas in Sweden they inhale as they sigh.

PARENT CLUES — Verbal: I am going to put a stop to this *once and for all*; I can't for the life of me . . . ; Now always remember . . . ; ("always" and "never" are *almost always* Parent words, which reveal the limitations of an archaic system closed to new data); How many times have I told you? If I were you . . .

Many evaluative words, whether critical or supportive, *may* identify the Parent inasmuch as they make a judgment about another, based not on Adult evaluation but on *automatic,* archaic responses. Examples of these kinds of words are: stupid, naughty, ridiculous, disgusting, shocking, asinine, lazy, nonsense, absurd, poor thing, poor dear, no! no!, sonny, honey (as from a solicitous saleslady), How dare you?, cute, there there, Now what?, Not again! It is important to keep in mind that these words are *clues,* and are not conclusive. The Adult may decide after serious deliberation that, on the basis of an Adult ethical system, certain things *are* stupid, ridiculous, disgusting, and shocking. Two words, "should" and "ought," frequently are giveaways to the Parent state, but, . . . "should" and "ought" can also be Adult words. It is the automatic, archaic, *unthinking* use of these words which signals the activation of the Parent. The use of these words, together with body gestures and the context of the transaction, help us identify the Parent.

CHILD CLUES — Physical: Since the Child's earliest responses to the external world were nonverbal, the most readily apparent Child clues are seen in physical expressions. Any of the following signal the involvement of the Child in a transaction: tears; the quivering lip; pouting; temper tantrums; the high-pitched, whining voice; rolling eyes; shrugging shoulders; downcast eyes; teasing; delight; laughter; hand-raising for permission to speak; nail-biting; nose-thumbing; squirming; and giggling.

CHILD CLUES — Verbal: Many words, in addition to baby talk, identify the Child: I wish, I want, I dunno, I gonna, I don't care, I guess, when I grow up, bigger, biggest, better, best (many superlatives originate in the Child as "playing pieces" in the "Mine Is Better" game). In the same spirit as "Look, Ma, no hands," they are stated to impress the Parent and to overcome the NOT OK.

There is another grouping of words which are spoken continually by little children. However, these words are not clues to the Child, but rather to the Adult operating in the little person. These words are why, what, where, who, when, and how.

ADULT CLUES—Physical: What does the Adult look like? If we turn off the video on the Parent and Child tapes, what will come through on the face? Will it be blank? Benign? Dull? Insipid? Ernst[1] contends that the blank face does not mean an Adult face. He observes that listening with the Adult is identified by continual movement—of the face, the eyes, the body—with an eyeblink every three to five seconds. Nonmovement signifies nonlistening. The Adult face is straightforward, says Ernst. If the head is tilted, the person is listening with an angle in mind. The Adult also allows the curious, excited Child to show its face.

ADULT CLUES—Verbal: As stated before, the basic vocabulary of the Adult consists of why, what, where, when, who, and how. Other words are: how much, in what way, comparative, true, false, probable, possible, unknown, objective, I think, I see, it is my opinion, etc. These words all indicate Adult data processing. In the phrase "it is my opinion," the opinion may be derived from the Parent, but the statement is Adult in that it is identified as an opinion and not as fact. "It is my opinion that high school students should vote" is not the same as the statement "High school students should vote."

With these clues to assist us, we can begin to identify Parent, Adult, and Child in transactions involving ourselves and others.

Any social situation abounds with examples of every conceivable type of transaction. On a fall day some years ago I was riding a Greyhound bus to Berkeley and made a note of a number of transactions. The first was a Parent-Parent exchange (Figure 1) between two cheerless ladies, seated side by side, across from me. They were developing a rather extensive philosophy around the point of whether or not the bus would get to Berkeley on time. With great knowing, sympathetic nods of the head they produced a long exchange which began with the following transactions:

Lady 1: (Looks at her watch, winds it, mumbles, catches the eye of the lady next to her, sighs wearily.)

Lady 2: (Sighs back, shifts uncomfortably, looks at *her* watch.)

Lady 1: Looks like we're going to be late again.

Lady 2: Never fails.

Lady 1: You ever see a bus on time—ever?

Lady 2: Never have.

Lady 1: Just like I was saying to Herbert this morning—you just don't get service any more like you used to.

Lady 2: You're absolutely right. It's a sign of the times.

Lady 1: It costs you, though. You can count on that!

These transactions are Parent-Parent in that they proceed without the benefit of reality data and are the same kind of judgmental exchange these ladies, as children, overheard between their mommies and aunties over the vicissitudes of riding streetcars. Lady 1 and Lady 2 enjoyed recounting the "awfuls" more than they would have enjoyed getting the facts. This is because of the good feeling that comes from blaming and finding fault. When we blame and find fault, we replay the early blaming and fault-finding which is recorded in the Parent, and this makes us feel OK, because the Parent

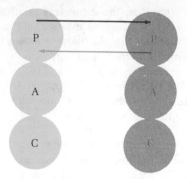

Figure 1 Parent-Parent Transaction

is OK, and we are coming on Parent. Finding someone to agree with you, and play the game, produces a feeling well-nigh omnipotent.

Lady 1 made the first move. Lady 2 could have stopped the game had she responded, at any point, with an Adult statement to any of Lady 1's statements:

Lady 1: (Looks at her watch, winds it, mumbles, catches the eye of the lady next to her, sighs wearily.)
ADULT RESPONSE POSSIBILITIES:
    1. Nonacknowledgment of sigh, by looking away.
    2. A simple smile.
    3. (If Lady 1 were sufficiently distressed): Are you all right?

Lady 1: Looks like we're going to be late again.
ADULT RESPONSE POSSIBILITIES:
    1. What time is it now?
    2. This bus is usually on time.
    3. Have you been late before?
    4. I'll ask.

Lady 1: You ever see a bus on time—ever?
ADULT RESPONSE POSSIBILITIES:
    1. Yes.
    2. I don't usually ride the bus.
    3. I've never thought about it.

Lady 1: Just like I was saying to Herbert this morning—you just don't get service any more like you used to.
ADULT RESPONSE POSSIBILITIES:
    1. I can't agree with that.
    2. What kind of service do you mean?
    3. The standard of living is as high as ever, the way I see it.
    4. I can't complain.

These alternative responses would have been Adult, but not complementary. Someone who is enjoying a game of "Ain't It Awful" does not welcome the intrusion of facts. If the neighbor girls enjoy an every-morning session of "Husbands Are Stupid," they will not welcome the new girl who announces brightly that her husband is a jewel.

This brings us to the first rule of communication in Transactional Analysis. When stimulus and response on the P-A-C transactional diagram make parallel lines, the transaction is complementary and can go on indefinitely. It does not matter which way the vectors go (Parent-Parent, Adult-Adult, Child-Child, Parent-Child, Child-Adult) if they are parallel. Lady 1 and Lady 2 did not make sense in terms of the facts, but their dialogue was complementary and continued for about ten minutes.

The "enjoyable misery" of the two lady passengers came to an end when the man in front of them asked the driver if they would be in Berkeley on time. The driver said, "Yes—at 11:15." This, too, was a complementary transaction between the man and the driver, Adult-Adult (Figure 2). It was a direct answer to a direct request for information. There was no Parent component (How are our chances of getting to Berkeley on time for a change?) and no Child component (I don't know why I always manage to get on the slowest bus). It was a dispassionate exchange. This kind of transaction gets the facts.

Behind the two women were two other people, whose activity illustrates another type of transaction, Child-Child. One was a fuzzy-faced, surly-looking boy with unkempt hair, who was wearing dusty, black trousers matched by a black-leather jacket. The other adolescent was dressed similarly and wore a look of forced dissipation. Both were engrossed in reading the same paperbacked book, *Secrets of the Torture Cult.* Had two priests been poring over the same book one might have assumed they were looking for Adult data about this strange subject; but from observing these two adolescent boys one was more likely to assume that this was a Child-Child transaction, involving somewhat the same cruel pleasure two five-year-old boys might find in discovering how to pull the wings off flies. Let us assume the adolescents acted on their new knowledge and found a way to torture someone as outlined in their text. There would be no Adult input (no understanding of consequences) and no Parent input ("It's horrible to do something like that"). Even if the transaction turned out badly for them (the arrival of the police—or of a mother in the case of the five-year-olds pulling wings off flies), the two persons involved in the transaction itself would have been in agreement. Therefore, it is complementary, Child-Child (Figure 3).

Additional Illustrations of Complementary Transactions

Parent-Parent Transactions (See Figure 1):

STIMULUS: Her duty is home with the children.
RESPONSE: She obviously has no sense of duty.

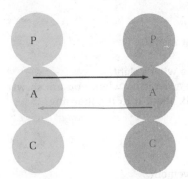 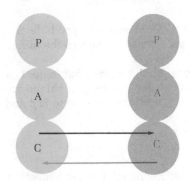

Figure 2   Adult-Adult Transaction   **Figure 3**   Child-Child Transaction

STIMULUS: It is disgusting the way taxes keep going up to feed all these no-goods at the public trough.
RESPONSE: Where will it all end?

STIMULUS: Kids nowadays are lazy.
RESPONSE: It's a sign of the times.

STIMULUS: I'm going to get to the bottom of this once and for all.
RESPONSE: You should! You have to nip this kind of thing in the bud.

STIMULUS: Illegitimate, you know.
RESPONSE: Oh, *that* explains it.

STIMULUS: John fired? How *dare* they do such a thing?
RESPONSE: There, there, honey. I don't know why he worked for that stupid company in the first place.

STIMULUS: She married him for his money.
RESPONSE: Well, that's *all* she got.

STIMULUS: You can never trust one of those people.
RESPONSE: Exactly! Their kind are all alike.

Adult-Adult Transactions (See Figure 2):

STIMULUS: What time is it?
RESPONSE: I have 4:30.

STIMULUS: That is a good-looking suit.
RESPONSE: Thank you.

STIMULUS: This new ink dries very quickly.
RESPONSE: Is it more expensive than the other kind?

STIMULUS: Please pass the butter.
RESPONSE: There you are.

STIMULUS: What smells so good, dear?
RESPONSE: Cinnamon rolls in the oven . . . almost ready!

STIMULUS: I don't know what to do. I can't decide what's right.
RESPONSE: I don't think you should try to make a decision when you are so weary. Why don't you go to bed and we'll talk about it in the morning?

STIMULUS: Look's like rain.
RESPONSE: That's the forecast.

STIMULUS: Public relations is a function of management.
RESPONSE: You mean it can't be arranged through an agency?

STIMULUS: The *Lurline* sails at 1 o'clock Friday.
RESPONSE: What time do we have to be there?

STIMULUS: John has seemed worried lately.
RESPONSE: Why don't we have him over for dinner?

STIMULUS: I am tired.
RESPONSE: Let's go to bed.

STIMULUS: I see where federal taxes are going up again next year.
RESPONSE: Well, that's not good news. But if we're going to keep spending we've got
to get the money somewhere.

Child-Child Transactions (See Figure 3):

It becomes readily apparent that there are very few game-free complementary
Child-Child transactions. This is because the Child is a get-stroke rather than a give-
stroke creature. People have transactions to get stroking. Bertrand Russell said: "One
can't think hard from a mere sense of duty. I need little successes from time to time to
keep . . . a source of energy."[2] Without Adult involvement in the transaction, no stroking accrues to anyone, and the relationship becomes uncomplementary, or dies of
boredom.

A clear social example of this phenomenon is the hippie movement. The flower
children extolled a life of Child-Child transactions. Yet the dreadful truth began to become apparent: It's no fun to do *your* thing if everybody else is only interested in doing
his thing. In cutting off the Establishment they cut off the Parent (disapproval) and the
Adult ("banal" reality); but, having cut off the disapproval, they found they had also
cut off the source of praise. (A couple of four-year-olds may decide to run away from
home, but give up the idea when they think it would be nice to have an ice-cream cone,
and that takes mommies.) The flower children looked to each other for strokes but these
became more and more impersonal and meaningless: Boy to girl: "Of course I love you.
I love everybody!" Life thus began to settle down into more and more primitive means
of stroking, such as fantasy stroking (withdrawal with drugs) and continual sexual activity. Sex can be solely a Child-Child activity inasmuch as the sexual urge is a genetic
recording in the Child, as are all primary biological urges. The most pleasurable sex
is more, however, in that there is an Adult component of considerateness, gentleness,
and responsibility for the feelings of another. Not all hippies are devoid of these values,
just as not all hippies are devoid of a Parent and Adult. Many, however, live on a self-
seeking basis and, in a sense, use each other for sensory stimulation.

Happy hippie relationships, or childhood friendships which are full of fun, will
be found to contain not wholly Child-Child transactions but Adult data-processing and
Parent values as well. For example, two little girls playing:

GIRL 1 (CHILD): I'll be the mamma and you be the little girl.
GIRL 2 (CHILD): I always have to be the little girl.
GIRL 1 (ADULT): Well, let's take turns; you be the mamma first, and then next time I'll
be the mamma.

This exchange is not Child-Child because of the Adult input (problem solving)
apparent in the last statement.

Also, many of the transactions of small children are Adult-Adult, although they may seem "childish" because of data deficiency:

LITTLE GIRL: Emergency, Emergency! Buzzy [the cat] lost a tooth.
SISTER: Does the good fairy bring money to cats?

Both stimulus and response are Adult—valid statements on the basis of the data at hand. Good data processing; wrong data!

Complementary Child-Child transactions can more readily be observed in what persons *do* together than in what they say to each other—as is true of very small children. A couple holding on to each other for dear life and screaming at the top of their lungs in the middle of a roller coaster ride are having a Child-Child transaction. Tagliavini and Tassinari singing the Act III duet from *Mefistofele* could be said to be having an intense Child-Child transaction. Grandma and Grandpa walking barefoot on the beach could be said to be having a Child-Child transaction. Yet the Adult made the arrangements for these happy experiences. It took money to ride the roller coaster. Tagliavini and Tassinari trained for years in order to experience the ecstasy of singing. Grandma and Grandpa share the joys of togetherness made possible by a lifetime of give-and-take. A relationship between people cannot last very long without the Adult. Thus we may say that complementary Child-Child transactions exist with the permission and supervision of the Adult. When the Adult is not around, the Child gets snarled up in crossed transactions, which will be described later in this chapter.

PARENT-CHILD TRANSACTIONS

Another type of complementary transaction is one between Parent and Child (Figure 4). The husband (Child) is sick, has a fever, and wants attention. The wife (Parent) knows how ill he feels and is willing to mother him. This can go on in a satisfactory way indefinitely as long as the wife is willing to be mothering. Some marriages are of this nature. If a husband wants to play "little boy" and his wife is willing to be parental, take the responsibility for everything, and look after him, this *can be* a satisfying marriage so long as neither wishes to change roles. If one or the other tires of the arrangement, the parallel relationship is disturbed, and trouble begins.

In Figure 5 we diagram a complementary transaction between George F. Babbitt (Parent) and Mrs. Babbitt (Child):

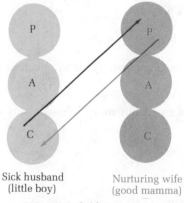

Sick husband
(little boy)

Nurturing wife
(good mamma)

Figure 4   Child-Parent Transaction

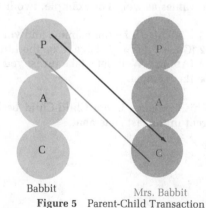

Babbit

Mrs. Babbit

Figure 5   Parent-Child Transaction

BABBITT (looking at the newspaper): "Lot's of news. Terrible big tornado in the South. Hard luck, all right. But this, say, this is corking! Beginning of the end for those fellows! New York Assembly has passed some bills that ought to completely outlaw the socialists! And there's an elevator-runners' strike in New York and a lot of college boys are taking their places. That's the stuff! And a mass-meeting in Birmingham's demanded that this Mick agitator, this fellow DeValera, be deported. Dead right, by golly! All these agitators paid with German gold anyway. And we got no business interfering with the Irish or any other foreign government. Keep our hands strictly off. And there's another well-authenticated rumor from Russia that Lenin is dead. That's fine. It's beyond me why we don't just step in there and kick those Bolshevik cusses out."

MRS. BABBITT: "That's so."[3]

CHILD-ADULT TRANSACTIONS

Another type of complementary transaction is one between Child and Adult (Figure 6). A person in the grip of NOT OK feelings may reach out to another person for realistic reassurances. A husband may fear an upcoming business encounter, which a promotion depends on. Even though he is qualified in every respect, he has an overload of Child data coming into his computer: I'm not going to make it! So he says to his wife, "I'm not going to make it," hoping for her recount of the reality reasons why he can make it if he doesn't let his NOT OK Child ruin his chances. He knows she has a good Adult and "borrows it" when his own is impaired. Her response is different from a Parent response, which might be reassuring even if reality data were not present or which might simply deny the Child feelings: "Of course you'll make it; don't be stupid!"

ADULT-PARENT TRANSACTIONS

Another type of complementary transaction is Adult-Parent (Figure 7) and is represented by a man who wants to quit smoking. He has adequate Adult data as to why this is important to his health. Despite this, he asks his wife to play the Parent, to destroy his cigarettes when she finds them, to "come on strong" if he lights one. This transaction has very good game possibilities. As soon as he turns the responsibility over to

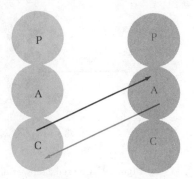

Figure 6   Child-Adult Transaction

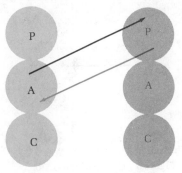

Figure 7   Adult-Parent Transaction

his wife's Parent, the husband can be a naughty little boy and play "If It Weren't for You I Could" or "Try and Catch Me."

UNCOMPLEMENTARY, OR CROSSED, TRANSACTIONS

The kind of transaction that causes trouble is the *crossed transaction* (Figure 8). Berne's classical example is the transaction between husband and wife where husband asks: "Dear, where are my cuff links?" (An Adult stimulus, seeking information). A complementary response by wife would be, "In your top left dresser drawer," or "I haven't seen them but I'll help you look." However, if Dear has had a rough day and has saved up a quantity of "hurts" and "mads" and she bellows, "Where you left them!" the result is a crossed transaction. The stimulus was Adult but the wife turned the response over to the Parent.

This brings us to the second rule of communication in Transactional Analysis. When stimulus and response cross on the P-A-C transactional diagram, communication stops. The husband and wife can't talk about cuff links anymore; they first have to settle why he never puts anything away. Had her response been Child ("Why do you always have to yell at me?") (Figure 9), the same impasse would have developed. These crossed transactions can set off a whole series of noisy exchanges which end with a bang somewhere in the purple outer reaches of "So's your old man!" Repetitious patterns of this type of exchange are what constitute games such as "It's All You," "If It Weren't for You I Could," "Uproar," and "Now I've Got You, You S.O.B.,".…

The origin of the non-Adult responses is in the NOT OK position of the Child. A person dominated by the NOT OK "reads into" comments that which is not there: "Where did you get the steaks?" "What's wrong with them?"; "I *love* your new hairdo!" "You never did like it long"; "I hear you're moving." "We can't really afford it but this neighborhood is getting run down"; "Pass the potatoes, dear." "And you call *me* fat." As one of my patients said, "My husband says I could read something into a cookbook."

Additional Illustrations of Crossed Transactions

PATIENT (A): I would like to work in a hospital like this.
NURSE (P): You can't cope with your own problems. (Figure 10)

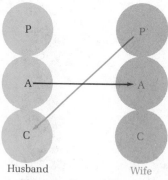

Husband   Wife

Figure 8 Crossed Transaction

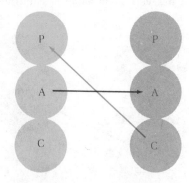

Figure 9 Crossed Transaction

MOTHER (P):   Go pick up your room.
DAUGHTER (P):   You can't tell me what to do. You're not the boss around here. Dad's
the boss! (Figure 11)

THERAPIST (A):   What is your principal hang-up in life?
PATIENT (C):   Red tape, red tape (pounding table), damn it, *red tape!* (Figure 12)

SON (A):   I have to finish a report tonight that's due tomorrow.
FATHER (P):   Why do you always leave things to the last minute? (Figure 13)

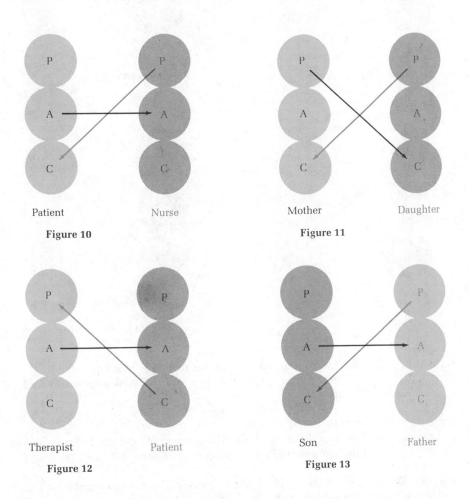

Patient   Nurse
Figure 10

Mother   Daughter
Figure 11

Therapist   Patient
Figure 12

Son   Father
Figure 13

MAN (A), standing with friend: We were trying to get this gas cap unlocked and
dropped the key behind the bumper. Could you help us get it out?
SERVICE STATION ATTENDANT (P):   Who did it? (Figure 14)

LITTLE GIRL (A):   Dirty shirts are warm.
MOTHER (P):   Go take a bath. (Figure 15)

ADOLESCENT GIRL (P):   Well, frankly, my Father likes Palm Springs best.
FRIEND (P):   Our family tries to avoid the tourist places. (Figure 16)

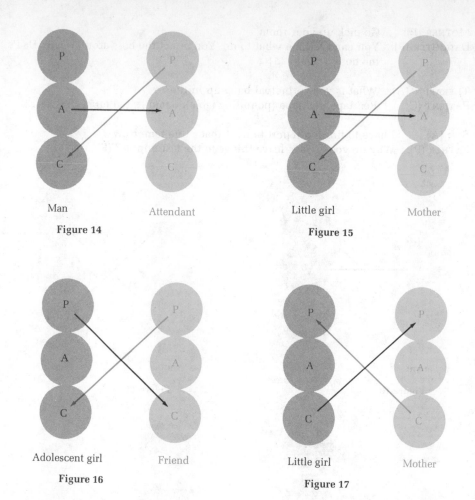

Man   Attendant

Figure 14

Little girl   Mother

Figure 15

Adolescent girl   Friend

Figure 16

Little girl   Mother

Figure 17

LITTLE GIRL (C):   I hate soup. I'm not going to eat it. You cook icky.
MOTHER (C):   I'm just going to leave and then you can cook your own icky food. (Figure 17)

LITTLE BOY (C):   My Daddy has a million dollars.
LITTLE GIRL (C):   That's nothing. My Daddy has "finnegan" dollars. ("Finnegan" was this four-year-old's way of saying "infinity.") (Figure 18)

BABBITT'S DAUGHTER, VERONA (A): "I know, but—oh, I want to contribute—I wish I were working in a settlement house. I wonder if I could get one of the department stores to let me put in a welfare-department with a nice rest-room and chintzes and wicker chairs and so on and so forth. Or I could—"

BABBITT (P): "Now you look here! The first thing you got to understand is that all this uplift and flipflop and settlement work and recreation is nothing in God's world but the entering wedge for socialism. The sooner a man learns he isn't going to be coddled, and he needn't expect a lot of free grub, and, uh, all these free classes and flipflop and doodads for his kids unless he earns 'em, why, the sooner he'll get on the job and produce—produce—produce! That's what the country needs, and not all this fancy stuff that just enfeebles the will-power of the working man and

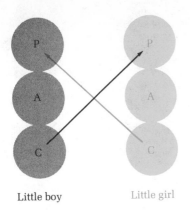

Little boy   Little girl

Figure 18

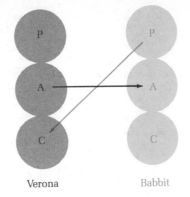

Verona   Babbit

Figure 19

gives his kids a lot of notions above their class. And you — if you'd tend to business instead of fooling and fussing — All the time! When I was a young man I made up my mind what I wanted to do, and stuck to it through thick and thin, and that's why I'm where I am today." (Figure 19).[4]

Parent responses, like Babbitt's, still stem from the NOT OK in the Child. He felt that his children did not appreciate him, that they did not comprehend how hard he had struggled; he still felt NOT OK around those who had more than he did. If he had let his Child come on straight, he might have wept. So he took the safer course and turned the transaction over to the Parent, wherein resided self-righteousness, correctness, and "all the answers."

The person whose NOT OK Child is always activated cannot get on with transactions which will advance his dealing with reality because he is continually concerned with unfinished business having to do with a past reality. He can't accept a compliment gracefully because he doesn't think he deserves it, and there must be a barb in it somewhere. He is involved in a continuous attempt to maintain the integrity of the position that was established in the situation of childhood. The person who always comes on Child is really saying, "Look at me, I'm not OK." The person who is always coming on Parent is really saying, "Look at you, you're not OK (and that makes me feel better)." Both maneuvers are an expression of the NOT OK position and each contributes to the prolongation of despair.

The NOT OK position is not solely expressed in the response. It also can be found in the stimulus. Husband says to wife, "Where did you hide the can opener?" The main stimulus is Adult in that it seeks objective information. But there is a secondary communication in the word *hide.* (Your housekeeping is a mystery to me. We'd go broke if I were as disorganized as you. If I could once, just once, find something where it belongs!) This is Parent. It is a thinly veiled criticism. This stimulates a *duplex transaction* (Figure 20).

The progress of this transaction depends on which stimulus the wife wishes to respond to. If she wants to keep things amiable and feels OK enough not to have been threatened she may respond, "I hid it next to the tablespoons, darling." This is complementary in that she gives him the information he desires and also acknowledges good-naturedly his "aside" about her housekeeping. If her Adult computes that it is

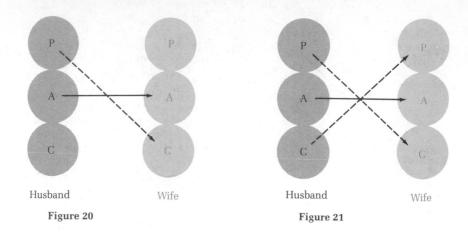

Husband   Wife   Husband   Wife

Figure 20   **Figure 21**

important to her marriage to do something about her husband's gentle suggestion, she may take the hint and become more organized. With her Adult handling the transaction, she can.

However, if her NOT OK Child is hooked, her primary response will be to the word *hide*, and she may respond along the lines of, "So what's the matter with you—you blind or something?" And there endeth the quest for the can opener while they wrangle over each other's merits and demerits in the area of organization, blindness, stupidity, etc. His beer is still unopened, and a game of "Uproar" is well along.

Some transactions of this nature can involve stimulus and response at all levels: A man comes home and writes "I love you" in the dust on the coffee table. The Adult is in command of the situation, although both his Parent and Child are involved (Figure 21). The Parent says, "Why don't you ever clean this place up?" The Child says, "Please don't get mad at me if I criticize you." The Adult takes charge, however, on the basis that to be loving is important to my marriage, so I won't let my Parent or my Child come on straight. If I tell her I love her she won't get mad at me, but perhaps she'll get the idea that it is important, after all, for a man in my position to have a home that looks nice.

This can turn into a complementary transaction if the wife is OK enough to take a little constructive criticism. The outcome would be happy if she shined up the house, met her husband at the door with a tall, cool drink, and told him what a sweet, sentimental, imaginative husband he is: Other husbands just moan and groan—but look what a jewel I've got! This approach is bound to succeed. However, if she can't do this, her Parent will probably retort, "When was the last time you cleaned the garage" or her Child will send her out on the town to run up the charge accounts. This transaction illustrates that even though the Parent and Child are involved, the outcome can be amiable and advance a good marriage *if* the Adult is in charge.

The Adult has a choice as to how it will respond to a stimulus in a complementary way that will protect both the relationship and the individuals in the relationship. This sometimes takes some very rapid (intuitive) computing:

The scene is a cocktail party. The transaction is initiated by a man who (Child) pinches woman's bottom. She responds (Adult): "My mother always told me to turn the other cheek." Why is this response identified as Adult?

She could have responded Parent; "You dirty old man!" or even slapped him.

Had she responded Child, she may have cried, become embarrassed, angry, shaky, or seductive.

Her response was Adult, however, in that she got a lot of information across in her one response.

1. I had a mother *who always told me* — so you watch out!
2. *Turn the other cheek* — I know the Bible, too, so you see I'm not that kind of girl.
3. The humor of the play on words told him, "My Child is getting a laugh, and you're OK, and I can take a joke."
4. Transaction completed!

The person who always comes out "smelling like a rose" does not do so accidentally. He has a high-speed Adult. As handy as this is in social situations, as above, it is not as critical there as in the home. You can walk away from a cocktail party. Walking away from home is something else.

The question arises: How can the Adult work better and faster? When someone knocks on the front door of life, who is going to get there first — the Parent, the Adult, or the Child?

HOW TO STAY IN THE ADULT

The Adult develops later than the Parent and Child and seems to have a difficult time catching up throughout life. The Parent and Child occupy primary circuits, which tend to come on automatically in response to stimuli. The first way, therefore, to build the strength of the Adult is to become sensitive to Parent and Child signals. Aroused feelings are a clue that the Child has been hooked. To know one's own Child, to be sensitive to one's own NOT OK feelings, is the first requirement for Adult data processing. Being aware that, "That is my NOT OK Child" makes it possible to keep from externalizing the feelings in actions. Processing this data takes a moment. Counting to ten is a useful way to delay the automatic response in order that the Adult maintain control of the transaction. "When in doubt, leave it out" is a good practice for curtailing archaic, or destructive, Child reactions. Aristotle claimed that the real show of power is in restraint. The strength of the Adult shows first also in restraint — in restraining the automatic, archaic responses of Parent and Child, while waiting for the Adult to compute appropriate responses.

Parent signals can be monitored in the same way. It is helpful to program into the computer certain Adult questions to apply to Parent data: Is it true? Does it apply? Is it appropriate? Where did I get that idea? What is the evidence?

The more one knows of the content of Parent and Child, the more easily one can separate Parent and Child from the Adult. In England psychotherapy is called "sorting yourself out." This is precisely the process required for developing the Adult. The more sensitive one is to one's own Parent and Child, the more separated, autonomous, and strong becomes the Adult.

One way to practice identifying the Parent and Child is to monitor the internal dialogue. This is relatively simple, inasmuch as there are no external demands for response, and one has time to examine the data. When one feels badly, gloomy, regretful, depressed, one can ask the question, "Why is my Parent beating on my Child?" Internal, accusatory dialogues are commonplace. Bertrand Russell wrote about Alfred North Whitehead: "Like other men who lead extremely disciplined lives, he was liable to distressing soliloquies and when he thought he was alone, he would mutter abuse of himself for his supposed shortcomings."[5]

When one is able to say, "That is my Parent," or "That is my Child," one says it with the Adult, so by the very process of questioning one has shifted to the Adult. One is able to feel immediate relief in a stressful situation simply by asking, "Who's coming on?"

As one becomes sensitive to one's own Child, one begins to become sensitive to the Child in others. No man loves the man he fears. We fear the Parent in others; their Child we can love. One helpful practice in a difficult transaction is to *see* the little boy, or the little girl, in another person, and talk to that little boy or girl, not in a condescending way but in a loving, protective way. When in doubt, stroke. When one is responding to another's Child, one is not afraid of the other's Parent.

An example of "talking to the little boy" appears in Adele Rogers St. Johns, *Tell No Man*, wherein Hank Gavin says:

I—I had a sort of sight of her *through* what she was now. I'd had this happen a couple of times on big deals with men, heads of companies—I got a sight of them as though I were seeing *through*—and it was sometimes a kind of strange, wistful, desperate fellow—like the kid he'd been when he went fishing with angleworms. That may sound far out, but it had happened a couple of times, and—and I'd made the pitch to—to *that* fellow and it worked.[6]

That fellow was the Child.

Another way to strengthen the Adult is to take the time to make some big decisions about basic values, which will make a lot of smaller decisions unnecessary. These big decisions can always be re-examined, but the time it takes to make them does not have to be spent on every incident in which basic values apply. These big decisions form an ethical basis for the moment-to-moment questions of what to do.

Conscious effort is required to make these big decisions. You can't teach navigation in the middle of a storm. Likewise, you can't build a system of values in the split second between your son's statement "Johnny punched me in the nose," and your response. You can't carry through a constructive transaction with the Adult in charge if basic values and priorities have received no thought beforehand.

If you own a cruiser, you become an expert navigator because you have acquainted yourself with the consequences of being a poor one. You don't wait until the storm hits to figure out how to work the radio. If you have a marriage, you become an expert partner because you have acquainted yourself with the consequences of being a poor one. You work out a value system to underlie your marriage, which then serves you when the going gets rough. Then the Adult is prepared to take over transactions with a question such as, "What's important here?"

The Adult, functioning as a probability estimator, can work out a system of values that encompasses not only the marriage relationship but all relationships. Unlike the Child, it can estimate consequences and postpone gratifications. It can establish new values based on a more thorough examination of the historical, philosophical, and religious foundations for values. Unlike the Parent, it is concerned more with the preservation of the individual than with the preservation of the institution. The Adult can consciously commit itself to the position that to be loving is important. The Adult can see more than a parental mandate in the idea "it is more blessed to give than to receive."

The kind of giving which is Adult is reflected upon by Erich Fromm:

> The most widespread misunderstanding is that which assumes that giving is "giving up" something, being deprived of, sacrificing. People whose main orientation is a nonproductive one feel giving as an impoverishment . . . just because it is painful to give, one *should* [Parent] give; the virtue of giving, to them, lies in the very act of acceptance of sacrifice. . . .
>
> For the productive character [Adult] giving has an entirely different meaning. Giving is the highest expression of potency. In the very act of giving I experience my strength, my wealth, my power. This experience of heightened vitality and potency fills me with joy. I experience myself as overflowing, spending, alive, hence as joyous. Giving is more joyous than receiving, not because it is a deprivation, but because in the act of giving lies the expression of my aliveness [OK].[7]

This kind of giving can be a chosen way of life. This choice can underlie all decisions as the Adult asks: What is important here? Am I being loving? Once such value decisions are made one can constructively intercept "Where did you hide the can opener?" and proceed with a day-to-day strengthening of the I'M OK — YOU'RE OK position.

In summary, a strong Adult is built in the following ways:

1. Learn to recognize your Child, its vulnerabilities, its fears, its principal methods of expressing these feelings.
2. Learn to recognize your Parent, its admonitions, injunctions, fixed positions, and principal ways of expressing these admonitions, injunctions, and positions.
3. Be sensitive to the Child in others, talk to that Child, stroke that Child, protect that Child, and appreciate its need for creative expression as well as the NOT OK burden it carries about.
4. Count to ten, if necessary, in order to give the Adult time to process the data coming into the computer, to sort out Parent and Child from reality.
5. When in doubt, leave it out. You can't be attacked for what you didn't say.
6. Work out a system of values. You can't make decisions without an ethical framework. . . .

REFERENCES

1. F. Ernst, lecture on "Listening" delivered at the Institute for Transactional Analysis, Sacramento, California, Oct. 18, 1967.
2. B. Russell, *The Autobiography of Bertrand Russell* (Boston: Little, Brown, 1967).
3. Sinclair Lewis, "Babbitt," *Major American Writers*, eds. H. M. Jones and E. E. Leisy (New York: Harcourt Brace Jovanovich, 1945), p. 1736.
4. Lewis, *Babbitt.*
5. Russell, *The Autobiography of Bertrand Russell.*
6. A. Rogers St. Johns, *Tell No Man* (New York: Doubleday, 1966).
7. E. Fromm, *The Art of Loving* (New York: Harper, 1956).

TA Applied to Supervision

William C. Bessey and Robert M. Wendlinger

*The principles of Transactional Analysis, outlined in the previous selection by
Harris, are here applied to supervision. Specifically, the selection is concerned with
"what the supervisor can do to encourage employees to move from the Child ego
state to the Adult ego state when this is necessary—in other words, to grow." The
selection begins by analyzing the supervisor's Parent, Adult, and Child ego states,
determining that supervisors must put their Adults in control (as "the executive of
the personality," according to the authors). This is not to say that the supervisor's
Parent and Child ego states have no place at work. Berne, in Games People Play,
describes the "excluding Adult" as "devoid of the charm, spontaneity, and fun
which are characteristic of the healthy child, and . . . unable to take sides with
the conviction or indignation which is found in healthy parents." Thus, as Bessey
and Wendlinger put it, "The supervisor should be in the Adult ego state a good
share of the working day but can use both the Nurturing Parent and Child ego states
at the appropriate times. The question ever before the supervisor, however, is: When
are the appropriate times?"*

THE SUPERVISOR'S ADULT AS EXECUTIVE OF THE PERSONALITY

James and Jongeward help to resolve this question of appropriate time in their concept
of the Adult as executive:

> Each person has the potential to put his Adult in executive control of his ego states.
> If freed from negative or irrelevant influence from his Parent and Child, he is
> emancipated to make his own autonomous decisions.
>   . . . He evaluates before acting and takes full responsibility for his thoughts,
> feelings, and behavior. He assumes the task of determining which of the possible
> responses in his ego states are appropriate, using that which is OK from his Parent
> and his Child. [1]
>   The Adult ego state as executive does not mean that the person is always acting
> from the Adult. It means that the Adult allows appropriate expression of all ego
> states because each has its contribution to make to a total personality. [2]

The supervisor's Adult decides the issue and keeps control of the Parent and Child
ego states at appropriate times. The feeling of, say, compassion may have its source in
the Parent ego state but it is controlled by the Adult and is displayed with Adult control.
   Stated another way, the Adult as executive can be regarded as *empathetic* rather
than *sympathetic*. The sympathetic supervisor will feel sorry for the subordinate and
want to help, perhaps by doing something *for* him or her (Parent-Child). The empathetic supervisor has the same feelings, but his Adult as executive tells him that the
way to help is to encourage a subordinate to approach a problem from his or her own
Adult and not the Child (Adult-Adult).
   A supervisor whose Adult is in control can move a subordinate away from the
Child ego state into the Adult, i.e., help the subordinate to grow. Many transactions

From D. Jongeward, *Everybody Wins*, 1973, Addison-Wesley, Reading, Massachusetts.

between supervisors and employees present a golden opportunity to encourage employee growth and development. To illustrate what can happen, here are three ways that a stimulus about the subject of expense control might be handled.

Illustration

Jim: Here's an idea I have for avoiding another hassle with the Expense Control Department. (A)

Supervisor: Good! Let's take a look at it. (A)

This was an Adult to Adult transaction with no difficulties.
Here is the same problem presented from another ego state.

Illustration

Jim: What should I do about that problem with Expense Control? (C)

Supervisor: That's OK. I'll take care of it. (P)

Now we have a Child-Parent transaction. It is complementary, i.e., the employee got the Parent response he expected, so at least there is communication. But the supervisor has kept the employee in his Child, himself in Parent, and made some additional work for himself as well.

The supervisor, with his Adult in control, can encourage his subordinate also to come on Adult instead of Child. While the employee may *intend* the transaction to be Child-Parent, the supervisor does not permit his own Parent ego state to be "hooked."

Illustration

1. Jim: What should I do about that problem with Expense Control? (C)
2. Supervisor: Yeah, that's a dandy. What do you think you'll do? (A)
3. Jim: I don't know. (Pause) Can *you* talk to them? (C)
4. Supervisor: It's *your* expenses they're shooting at, isn't it? (A)
5. Jim: Yes, but what will I say? I didn't know what the procedures were! (C)
6. Supervisor: It's a problem. (A)
7. Jim: (Silence)
8. Supervisor: Are you a little leery of the Expense boss? (P)
9. Jim: Yes, as a matter of fact. (A)
10. Supervisor: He's a stickler. (A)
11. Jim: Well, OK. I'll bone up on the expense manual and at least tell them how I can do it from now on. (A)

In this transaction, the supervisor resists Jim's efforts to put him in the Parent role (1, 3, 5) and responds as Adult (2, 4, 6). As a result, the transaction becomes crossed briefly, and communication temporarily stops (7). Jim is in a difficult spot as he does not want communication to stop with the supervisor (after 7). So there is "built-in" pressure on him to move to his Adult and deal with the problem. With a little nurturing (8) and consistent Adult on the part of the supervisor (10), Jim moves gradually to the Adult ego state (9, 11).

THE KEY TO GROWTH

The subordinate's Child ego state is the most vulnerable part of his or her personality. It contains all the not-OK feelings that the subordinate has. And when the supervisor is presented as Critical Parent, the not-OK part of the subordinate's Child is sure to be activated, or hooked.

> *Employee:* I don't think it was fair that I didn't get that promotion.
> *Supervisor:* Well, we gave it a lot of thought. If you're not happy with the way we do things around here, maybe you'd better look around for something else.
> *Employee:* (Silence)

In TA terms, the supervisor's Critical Parent has assumed control of the situation, i.e., "You do what I want and don't ask any questions." The supervisor who consistently comes on Critical Parent to enforce unreasonable standards of performance, or who uses threats "to get things done," may accomplish goals temporarily. But the Adapted Child in the subordinate will rebel, in silence, through lower productivity, or in departure from the organization.

The most damaging aspects of the Critical Parent stimulus in organizations are that (a) the not-OK part in the subordinate's Child is hooked, and (b) the subordinate — as in the above example — cannot deal with Adult reality while under the influence of not-OK feelings.

THE KEY APPLIED TO SUPERVISION

The difficulty in dealing with Adult reality while under the influence of not-OK feelings is recognized in many texts on supervision, which recommend that the supervisor-employee relationship focus on *behavior* and not on the *person*. Imagine, for example, the following situation:

> You've turned in a report to your boss, who says to you, "This is a lousy report." Not good to hear and not good supervision. But suppose the supervisor had said instead, "You are incompetent." Most people would agree that this last is much worse. Why? The first statement is directed at the *report*; you can very well improve it. The second would be directed at *you*; you are incompetent; and there is nothing you can do to correct it. A real "spinal cord shriveller," in Berne's terms.

The guideline is commonly stated as *Focus on Behavior, Not the Person*. Focus on the lengthy, disorganized report, not on John Smith. Your targets then become tardiness, errors, and late assignments — not May, Sue, or Bill. This principle of avoiding criticism of the person is one of the ABC's of supervision.

In a counseling session, a supervisor might say to an employee:

> "You *act* like you disapprove of so-and-so."
> "You *give the impression* you don't care."
> "You *say* things that get people sore at you."

All of these statements focus on what the person *does*, not what he or she *feels*. . . .

Illustration

169

Bessey, Wendlinger:
TA Applied to
Supervision

In a supervisory situation, how does the principle work? Let's say you are a bank operations officer and one of your tellers is good on all counts except that, when busy, he is impatient and testy with customers. You've talked with the teller about this several times, but you've had more complaints this week.

1. *Supervisor:* We've had two more complaints this week. What can you do to improve your customer relations?
2. *Teller:* Who were they?
3. *Supervisor:* (Relates the specific incidents.)
4. *Teller:* Oh, those two. They both were in at the busiest times. That woman wanted me to spend all day telling her about banking!
5. *Supervisor:* I know what a strain people can be, but she said that you cut her dead! What happened?
6. *Teller:* I just said, "I can't talk when I'm counting money."
7. *Supervisor:* That sounds pretty blunt.
8. *Teller:* You want me to balance, don't you?
9. *Supervisor:* Yes. *And* be polite. You know the bank practice. Another complaint in 90 days will mean a formal reprimand in your file.

In this example the teller stays in the Child ego state, but the supervisor stays in the Adult ego state with some nurturing (5). The focus is on behavior throughout:

1. What can you *do?*
2. The teller is not *rude,* but *behaved* in a rude way.
7. That *sounds* blunt, not "you *are* blunt."
9. The teller needs *to be* polite, not *feel* polite or like the customers.

The supervisor accepted the teller's feelings of irritation (that's the teller's business) but was clear on what such behavior would lead to. The supervisor addressed the employee's Adult and encouraged the teller to think about the consequences of the unacceptable behavior.

Make It Their Problem

An actual incident will illustrate the approach we feel will best facilitate growth of the Adult ego state.

Some years ago, one of the co-authors participated in an exceptional role-playing session. The class was called *Manager Coaching* [3] and the participants were the ten division heads and the executive vice president of an electronics firm. In this particular session the class was role-playing an appraisal interview between a division head and one of the plant managers. Their roles were explained to the participants in the following way.

Division Head — John Taylor

You've been very busy this last year and you feel you've been losing touch with one of your plant managers, Guy Parks. He's a good man but there have been a few signs that he's unhappy or over his head or letting up or *something* — you're not sure. You hope to use this time to draw him out and see what's on his mind and, to use your expression, "get on the same side of the table" with him.

Plant Manager—Guy Parks (This role was explained to the class members but not to the executive playing John Taylor.)

You have this meeting scheduled with the boss and you're not looking forward to it. He'll want to know what you've been doing and thinking and all about the problems of the plant. He really doesn't understand the plant methods any more. Things have changed. He says he wants to "get on your side of the table," but if you do tell him your thoughts and ideas, he never does anything about them anyhow. You plan to be polite but brief (if you can) and get back to the plant.

The division head, John, studied his role, thought out his approach, and told the class what he hoped to accomplish in the interview. (Guy was out of the room.)

The interview went pretty much as expected—John setting the stage, patiently trying to draw Guy out and establish some genuine communication, with Guy keeping a polite reserve. As it continued, John began to show the strain—Guy's lack of response in front of that particular group put a great deal of pressure on John. The last part of the interview proceeded like this:

John: I hope that we can discuss some of these things, Guy. I'd like to see us on the same side of the table.
Guy: Plant II is in good shape, John.
John: Do we need to discuss the long-term goals?
Guy: If you'd like.

Then note John's reply:

John: *Guy, you act like you don't want to cooperate in this interview.*
Guy: Well, uh, no, John, I don't mean . . .
John: That's the impression you give.
Guy: Oh, no, I think we *ought* to get together on these things.

Guy then began to talk freely and the class broke up the interview by giving John a round of applause.

What happened here? What took place in that brief moment that visibly changed John's whole demeanor and set Guy busily to work "cooperating"? By saying, "You act like you don't want to cooperate," John shifted the problem from himself to Guy, where it really belonged. He presented the subordinate with his own behavior and asked, "How about this?" Because John focussed on behavior and not on the person, he activated Guy's Adult rather than intimidating his Child, as he might easily have done.

He also conveyed another equally important message to Guy: "You're OK—you have the brains and can carry the load."

The application of this approach can cover a broad range of behavior. . . .

What the supervisor does in [such] instances is consistently provide Adult input to the subordinate. This is difficult to do. If the supervisor's Adult ego state is not in control, he or she might respond from the Critical Parent. Or, having failed to solve the problem immediately, the supervisor's own not-OK Child might become defensive and would be hooked.

Some employees will resist any attempt to "make it their problem" and will actually prefer a supervisor to come on either Nurturing or Critical Parent. This is because of the basic psychological position—You're OK, I'm not-OK, etc.—that the employee has taken about himself and others, and the kinds of feelings that are collected to reinforce his basic position. An employee who has strong not-OK feelings, for example, may collect feelings of fear, depression, anger, etc., from transactions with his or her supervisor. . . .

One way that a subordinate can collect favorite feelings, or "trading stamps," from a supervisor is to play games. These are fairly extended transactions, socially acceptable on the surface, but carrying an ulterior or psychological message underneath, and resulting in a "payoff," i.e., the player's favorite feeling, at the end.

In the game of *Kick Me*, for example, a subordinate may provoke a put-down from the supervisor:

Employee: I had too much work to do yesterday and just don't have that report
             ready.
Supervisor: This is the second time you've been late on this project. I'm going to
             have to give it to someone else.

The employee has initiated a socially acceptable transaction, apparently Adult to Adult. But the underlying or psychological message is quite different:

Employee: I'm a bad boy, kick me.
Supervisor: Yes, you are a bad boy and here's your kick.

The employee wins by losing, having collected the favorite feeling of rejection, which reinforces this particular not-OK position.

The effective supervisor, with the Adult in control, and aware of the games that office people play, will be able to recognize such provocations and invitations and turn them aside. . . .

THE NEED FOR AUTHENTICITY

The supervisor, when attempting to "make it the other person's problem," need not exclude his or her own Child and Parent ego states from all transactions.

There may be times when it is appropriate for a supervisor to act as a firm Parent:

"If you don't wear the safety glasses, you'll be suspended for one week. It's your choice." (That is, it's your problem.)

Here is a statement once used by a supervisor during an argument over emergency overtime:

"You mean you *won't* do it, or you don't *want* to do it?"

If there is a consistent pattern, however, the reasons for undue rebellion on the subordinates' part need close examination.

The supervisor need not hesitate to release Child feelings, provided these feelings are genuine and he or she is not playing a role or attempting to manipulate approval from the other. Sometimes an honest outburst by a supervisor can lead to productive results. . . .

Illustration

Here is a supervisor dealing with an overly sensitive subordinate in an authentic manner:

Supervisor: John, sometimes it's like walking on eggs talking to you! I never know when I'm going to set you off.

John: (Alarmed and defending himself) That's really *your* problem, isn't it?

Supervisor: How do you feel about it, John? Do you like having this kind of situation?

John: (Sarcastically) I wasn't aware that I was so touchy.

Supervisor: It's the impression you give—almost every day.

This kind of session is risky. John may have strong not-OK feelings in his Child which are easily triggered. It takes Adult nerve on the supervisor's part to initiate a confrontation. But it can lead to significant growth for both parties and a lasting bond between them if the encounter is *authentic*.

According to James and Jongeward:

The authentic person experiences the reality of himself by knowing himself, being himself, and becoming a credible, responsive person. He actualizes his own unprecedented uniqueness and appreciates the uniqueness of others. He does not dedicate his life to a concept of what he imagines he should be . . . he does not use his energy putting on a performance, maintaining pretence, and manipulating others into his games . . . he can reveal himself instead of projecting images that please, provoke, or entice others. [4]

Not all transactions will be highly charged with emotion, requiring the supervisor to muster up the courage to initiate the session and then struggle to keep the Adult in control. The supervisor can accept the subordinate's Child, encourage an open discussion of the employee's feelings, and then candidly explore the consequences of the subordinate's *behavior*.

This will change the level of awareness that employees have about their actions and give them a chance to think things over with their Adults.

A supervisor can say, for example:

"What do you think about the assignment? Are you a little leery of it?" (The supervisor accepts the possibility of the Child's fear.)

"Do you *like* having me on your back? I guess it's a real bother. How can you get me off?"

"I know you like to work on your own. How can we do it?"

"If you reject these improvement goals, you put me in a position where I *have* to get into it."

IS IT A PROBLEM?

When an employee's behavior in the Child ego state is not important to the requirements of the job, the supervisor has little reason to "make it his problem." Who cares if the night watchman is a grouch? The effective supervisor accepts the behavior along with a hundred other individual characteristics he or she may see during the day. The supervisor is patient with it and may even enjoy it. The painfully shy unit assembler, the boastful college recruit, the "entertainer" at coffee breaks, the technician with the "far out" philosophy are all OK fellow human beings.

Is It Really the Subordinate's Problem?

The effective supervisor will also be certain that the problem is really the subordinate's problem, and not his or her own. This is part of his being authentic. It is "his problem" only when the Child ego state is dominating the *employee* at an inappropriate time. If the *supervisor's* Child ego state is causing the problem, he or she can do little to help the employee.

Illustration

One department head tried to practice the "make it their problem" approach on his staff and supervisors to no avail. The problem, as he perceived it, involved tardiness and casual supervisory practices. At the same time, he was checking in at the office after 9 A.M., taking an afternoon off for golf when the spirit moved him, and playing favorites with the office women. His attempt to change the work habits of his staff was not an authentic I'm OK — You're OK transaction and he failed in his approach.

A supervisor needs to have the Adult ego state in control in order to draw the employee into the Adult.

The Need for Authenticity in "Making It Their Problem"

Some people feel it necessary to their careers or well-being to always take the offensive. Some political leaders confide that they never apologize or admit they're wrong. They simply change the subject or accuse *others* of something. They become experts at the "put down," i.e., discounting others, and at avoiding a defensive position. This approach is not recommended here.

In applying an understanding of ego states and related techniques, a genuine interest in, and respect for, the other person is vital. The subordinate is presented with the problem because *it is truly the subordinate's problem* and cannot be solved by anyone else. The supervisor helps the subordinate to more rewarding behavior, and the superior-subordinate relationship then becomes an authentic I'm OK — You're OK transaction. The supervisor is relieved of a problem and, at the same time, may set into motion a genuine growth process on the part of the employee. . . .

FOOTNOTES AND REFERENCES

1. M. James and D. Jongeward, *Born to Win: Transactional Analysis with Gestalt Experiments* (Reading, Mass.: Addison Wesley, 1971), p. 235.
2. *Ibid.*, p. 249.
3. From the program "Improving the Coaching Practices of Managers." (New York, New York: Mahler Associates, 1961).
4. James and Jongeward, *op. cit.*, pp. 1–2.

Questions for Discussion

1. Add a "feedback loop" to the general model of communication described in this chapter. How would such a loop affect the communication process?

2. Describe and analyze **a** faulty communication exchange in which you were involved or which you observed. What went wrong? How might the exchange have been handled differently?

3. An old song title goes, "Your lips tell me no, no, but your eyes tell me yes, yes." Describe a communication situation demonstrating inconsistency between verbal and nonverbal communication, or between message content and style of transmission.

4. An older, traditional professor (but not one to be taken lightly) has observed that today young people constitute the most inarticulate generation in decades. Much of their conversation is punctuated with "you know," "right?" profanity, and unfinished sentences, all of which reflect an inability to communicate. What do you think about this phenomenon?

5. Describe examples of instrumental, consummatory, and incidental communication.

6. The world is a busy and confusing place, initiating multiple stimuli for everyone. People simplify incoming stimuli and communications in order to handle this voluminous confusion. How do they do it?

7. Describe the behavior of a person, or a situation, demonstrating "defensive behavior" in communication.

8. Describe the behavior of a person, or a situation, demonstrating "supportive climate" in communication.

9. How do communication difficulties contribute to the development of hierarchies? What communication difficulties do hierarchies contribute to?

10. In a popular book published some years ago, Vance Packard wrote about *The Status Seekers*. The motivation to seek status is apparently widespread in organizations. How is communication manipulated to protect or promote status?

Cases for Discussion

Frank Perriman's Appointment

Indefatigable Mutual Insurance is a large national company with over 10,000 employees in the 50 states and Canada. Its basic organization has been as shown in Exhibit 1. Each regional vice-president had access to the president, but most actual communications between the field and home office were with the functional vice-presidents who set policy and monitored performance in their respective functional areas. The two senior vice-presidents have acted as staff to the president in their areas of expertise: one in actuarial and statistical matters, the other in investments and finance. In general, Indefatigable Insurance has been a highly centralized, regionally dispersed organization.

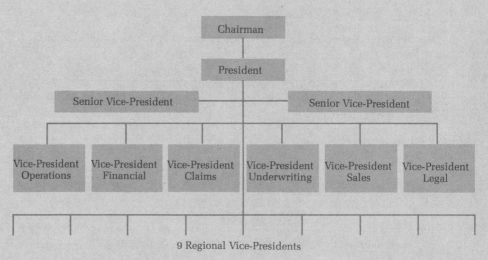

Exhibit 1   Indefatigable Mutual Insurance: Organization Chart

Frank Perriman has had exceptional and striking success at Indefatigable. After experience primarily in sales, Frank was appointed regional vice-president of the Middle Division at age 35 — the youngest such appointment in the company's history. One annual report contained an individual picture of Frank (the only regional V.P. so

Reprinted with permission from *Management: Basic Elements of Managing Organizations* by Ross A. Webber (Homewood, Il: Richard D. Irwin, Inc., © 1975), pp. 252–53.

honored) with a caption describing him as an example of what could happen to young men at Indefatigable. In general, however, most company executives were fairly old.

After eight years as regional vice-president, in June Frank was promoted to senior vice-president (thus making three senior V.P.'s) and transferred to the home office. The president sent the notifications shown in Exhibits 2 and 3.

Exhibit 2   Indefatigable Mutual Insurance: Organization Bulletin

> HOME OFFICE ADMINISTRATION
> June 29
>
> ORGANIZATION BULLETIN—General #349
>
> Effective August 1, Mr. Frank Perriman, Vice President and Division Manager, Middle Division, will transfer to the President's staff at the home office.
>
> Mr. Perriman will be responsible to the President for achieving Division performance in accordance with Company policies and objectives.
>
> Mr. Perriman will assist Regional Managers in obtaining well-coordinated efforts by all departments and will establish and use measurements of results for each Division.
>
> Regional Vice-Presidents will report to and be responsible to Mr. Perriman.
>
> Thomas Achison
> President

Exhibit 3   Indefatigable Mutual Insurance: Organization Bulletin

> HOME OFFICE ADMINISTRATION
> July 14
>
> ORGANIZATION BULLETIN—General #351
>
> Effective July 14, the Board of Directors made the following election:
>
> Mr. Frank Perriman—Senior Vice-President.
>
> Thomas Achison
> President

Questions

1.   What do the Bulletins communicate to you? What do you think they communicate to the organization? Discuss.

2.   What problems do you think Perriman will confront? Analyze.

3. How have the Bulletins contributed to these problems? Analyze.

4. What recommendations would you have for Perriman? For the President? Why?

Communications About "Elizabeth Sternberg"

The case "Elizabeth Sternberg" appeared recently in a management textbook written by a male professor at a prominent university and published by a large publishing firm. Shortly after the book was published, the publishing company forwarded to the author a copy of a critical letter from a female professor at another prominent university. The author of the text then wrote a reply to the critic. The text of the case and letters follows:

The Case of Elizabeth Sternberg

Elizabeth had always admired her parents. Of course, she argued with them from time to time, but she loved to be home, to cook and sew, and to help with her younger brothers and sisters. To her parents, Liz was a model child. She never did especially well in school, but never received an F either. School social life was more important than studies to Elizabeth. Yet she was a little shy, more a group follower than a leader. Although she dated frequently, most of the boys seemed too immature for her.

Liz never planned to go to college. Her real dream was to get married and have children. At 17, however, this seemed a way off, and after high school graduation she expected to look for a job—but not for about six months. The summer and autumn went very slowly. Many of her friends left the neighborhood; some of the boys joined the military, some traveled, others went off to college. Liz missed the excitement of the crowded halls and active conversation of high school. Finally, in November she took a clerical job in the regional office of a large insurance company.

From the beginning, Liz fitted right in. She did what she was told, was polite and willing. She thought the work was fine, but she really enjoyed the beautiful new office, so clean and neat, and even more she liked the girl friends she made, the fun of chatting and planning bridal and baby showers. Liz found herself taking a more active role in planning these affairs than she had ever done in school.

It was her social sensitivity that prompted Liz to drop a note into the suggestion box. The office had been arranged in long straight rows and columns, all rather forbidding looking. Liz suggested that the setup be modified to several semicircles. This would facilitate communicating with the group leader located in the middle and be-

Reprinted with permission from *Management: Basic Elements of Managing Organizations* by R. A. Webber (Homewood, Il: Richard D. Irwin, Inc., © 1975), pp. 139–40.

tween cooperating desks. It would also create a sense of belonging (and perhaps promote gossip). Management subsequently introduced the arrangement, and everyone was pleased.

As time passed, Liz Sternberg's Prince Charming never appeared, so she continued working. She perfected her typing, shorthand, and telephone style so much that she received several merit raises. She was even assigned a position as office claims agent and became the first female to handle routine policy-holder claims over the telephone. She was flattered by the promotion, but the job did make it more difficult to keep up with her friends in the office. Nonetheless, she enjoyed talking with policy-holders, who also liked to deal with her. Everyone thought she did an outstanding job.

Shortly after Liz's 25th birthday last year her mother passed away. At first, Liz wanted to quit her job to take care of the family, but her father said it wasn't necessary and she had her own life to live. It has been a rough twelve months for Liz.

Last week, the regional vice president called Liz into his office, praised her, and offered her a promotion to assistant office manager in charge of hiring and training all clerical employees. The position included a private office and a salary that exceeded her father's. Liz was in a terrible quandry. She just couldn't see herself as a manager giving orders to girls like she had been herself a few years before. And she did not want to be thought of as a career woman.

This morning Elizabeth Sternberg quit her job and went home.

Text of letter to the author

Dear Dr. Jones:

I recently received an examination copy of your new management text. My initial reaction to the book was positive, to the point where I was seriously considering it for adoption. However, upon more careful examination, my enthusiasm was severely dampened by its prejudicial treatment of women. Insofar as this is a significant reason for my not adopting the book, and for discouraging my colleagues from adopting it, I thought you'd be interested in my comments.

There are almost 30 case studies in the book. Only two refer to women. In one, "City Community College," the organization (i.e., the nursing school) is the focus and the people are mentioned only incidentally. The other, "Elizabeth Sternberg," focuses on a woman who is depicted as being gossipy, unmotivated, socially-oriented, wanting a marriage, not a job. Right now, 20 percent of our M.B.A. students are women. In most major business schools, 15 to 20 percent of the students are women. This case can only hurt them in their fight to achieve professional recognition from their male classmates by providing reinforcement of just that stereotype which they are desperately trying to overcome. Use of your text as a text would be doing them a great disservice.

The point being made in "Elizabeth Sternberg" (i.e., that not all people want to self-actualize on the job) is valid—for men as well as women. Why not have the case be "Elliot Sternberg," about an assembly-line worker who doesn't want to assume more responsibility? Several studies here and in England have shown that many automobile assembly-line workers don't want anything but short hours and money.

In future editions, it would be constructive to have a female manager or two included in some of the cases. There are women in executive positions—such as Katherine

Graham, Julia Walsh (first woman on the American Stock Exchange), or Catherine Cleary. Reference to successful women managers would be of great help to women — and men — M.B.A. students.

I hope the above comments will be of assistance.

Sincerely,

Sylvia French
Assistant Professor of Organizational Behavior
Famous University

Text of Letter from Author to Critic

Dear Professor French:

I was disturbed and a bit angered by your letter regarding the supposed "sexist bias" in my new management text. Frankly, your criticism is unfair and ill-founded.

You completely ignore the long and flattering biography of "Ruth Shuman" that begins Part 5. You ignore the central position of Vice-President "Judith Greene" in Trustworthy Company case, and that a major issue in that case is response to ambitious, capable MBA females. Ms. Greene has visited with my classes when discussing this case. You ignore that Regina Neal, Director in the case of Northside Child Health-Care Center, is a female M.D. You ignore that the administrators in the case of Open or Closed in the Operating Room are females. You dismiss that fact that all the strong characters in City Community College are women and the weak ones are men and that the case illustrates the fallacy of placing a male in charge just because he is a male. You ignore the unflattering portrayal of Howard Andresen and his response to women's interest. You ignore that this is one of the very first management books to systematically include references to "him and her," "she and he," "his and hers." An experienced female editor worked with me on this and we were very conscious of these points.

As to Elizabeth Sternberg. It is true she appears to be an old-fashioned "girl," but that case came from an experienced female manager and she felt that there are many Elizabeths and that women managers must learn how to deal with them. My female MBA students respond very positively to that case, and it is an excellent vehicle for bringing out the sexist views of male students who think all females are or should be like Elizabeth. It also can be used to show how Elizabeth could have handled that job by "feminizing" it as Caroline Bird suggests.

Finally, your letter is disturbing because of the stereotype you assign me to. The rights, aspirations, and career problems of women are a major portion of my advanced course. I am actively engaged in research on male and female relations in task groups. I have already published research which is sharply critical on how males treat females who are in the minority in task situations. I will shortly publish research which is the first I am aware of where I have constituted groups with females in the majority and males in the minority.

For all these reasons, I believe you should re-examine the book. It really is one of the most responsive books around on the issues that you (and I) are concerned about. I am confident that you will realize that we are allies, not adversaries.

Very truly yours,

Walker Jones
Professor of Management

Question

Analyze these letters in terms of the barriers to communication discussed in the chapter.

Chapter Four

Group Dynamics

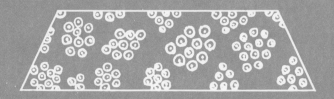

One of the pioneering researchers in the field of organizational behavior, an Australian named Elton Mayo, took issue with the then prevalent idea that motivating people to work was simply a matter of arranging economic or other incentives. As he put it (Mayo, 1945), "Economic theory in its human aspect is woefully inadequate; indeed it is absurd. Humanity is not adequately described as a horde of individuals, each activated by self-interest . . ." (p. 59). A substantial portion of human behavior is understandable, Mayo maintained, not by looking at individuals and their motives or at organizations and their management practices or even at the interplay of these factors, but by focusing on *groups* of people.

Entire fields within the behavioral sciences — social psychology and the sociology of groups — have been concerned with the study of people in groups, and several thousand studies of group behavior have demonstrated that Mayo was right. For example, the reading by Alvin Zander included at the end of this chapter discusses a series of studies that show how group performance can be influenced by a group's collective desire for success or fear of failure, independent of the level of achievement motivation of individual members. Since group dynamics can better account for some attitudes and behavior than can individual characteristics, managers cannot ignore the nature and role of groups of people at work.

To help you sharpen your appreciation of groups as a factor in organizations and to learn how to adapt management practices to the structure and dynamics of groups, this chapter will explore the anatomy and physiology of groups (that is, the basic "parts" of a group and how they interact in real "living" groups). We will also consider what individuals receive from their membership in groups, how technology and management practices shape groups, and how the informal organization develops and functions.

THE ANATOMY OF GROUPS

If this were a class in a medical school, we could dissect cadavers and identify parts of the human body. Each would have a heart, liver, stomach, and so on. We could also find certain standard parts and interrelationships among those parts inside each body. Changes in the condition of the stomach could affect the liver; changes in the condition of the liver could affect the heart, and so on.

But what about the inside of a group? If we could take groups apart, would we find that certain "parts" and interrelationships between them are common to all groups? The answer is yes. We would find three interrelated elements within every group: interaction, activity, and sentiment (Exhibit 4.1).

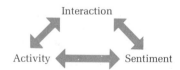

Interaction

Activity ⟷ Sentiment

Exhibit 4.1 The Elements of Groups

Interaction refers to behavior between people. When we look at the behavior of two or more people we can observe who does what and who responds and how they respond. The interaction may not involve speech. Two tennis players or two dancers may interact without talking. Whenever the acts of two or more persons face-to-face are mutually related, it is possible to recognize and speak of interaction.

The pattern of interactions can vary greatly from group to group. Consider, for example, the various classes you attend. One class might primarily involve lectures in which the instructor initiates and virtually monopolizes the interaction. This is a one-way or nearly one-way interaction pattern. In another class involving primarily discussion, perhaps interactions are more evenly distributed among several persons. This is a more nearly balanced pattern. Whatever the particulars, the pattern of interaction itself can be recognized and described, quite apart from what is said or done.

Activities, simply enough, are the things people do. They walk, talk, sit, eat, write, sleep, type, play In different classrooms you may note differences in the pattern of activities between teacher and the class. Such differences in activities may be measured and taken as indications of performance. Student participation in class discussions may, for example, be defined as desirable, assessed, and rewarded. In business and other organizations, productivity is often the measure of activity which is of central importance.

The term *sentiment* includes those emotional and mental processes that are inside people and can't be seen, but whose presence is inferred from people's activities and interactions. A smile suggests one sort of feeling, a menacing fist another. Within groups, the attitudes, feelings, opinions, and beliefs which are shared are of special interest.

The range of sentiments which a group can share is virtually limitless, but certain ones are especially common and important. These sentiments, usually called *norms,* are the shared ideas and beliefs about what conduct is good and what conduct is bad. Whether the group defines high productivity as good or as bad, for example, is especially important to managers.

THE PHYSIOLOGY OF GROUPS

If our interest were limited to compiling a "parts list" of groups, we could consider our work done. But we need to see how the parts are interrelated, how they affect one another in real live groups.

Consider the following comparison of two groups of prisoners of war; look for the universal parts — interaction, activity, and sentiment — within each group, and for the ways differences in one part are associated with differences in the others within the same group. Focus on the structure and dynamics of each group as a way of understanding the behavior of the members within it.

During and after the Korean War in the early 1950s, widespread concern was voiced about the behavior of U.S. Army prisoners of war in North Korea. Since there were few escapes, many deaths from disease, and numerous instances of apparent collaboration, many Americans in this country were distressed. POW behavior was interpreted to indicate that America's youth were decadent, soft, ignorant of their mission, and unpatriotic (Kinkead, 1959). The implication: Unless U.S. moral fiber stiffens, all will be lost to Communism.

Many of the prisoners were taken after the Chinese attacked across the Yalu River and the Americans retreated in one of the few routs in U.S. Army history. Disorganized, separated from their units, wandering in a strange land, the soldiers were captured by the Chinese and marched to prison camps. On the march the Chinese continually reminded them that they were the Americans' friends and that the prisoners were lucky to have been captured by the Chinese. If they had been taken by the North Koreans, the Chinese maintained, the Americans would have been killed because as capitalist imperialists they had attacked the homeland of the North Koreans.

During the march there were few contrasts between conditions for the prisoners and for their guards. The Chinese captors shared their limited food and medicine and, by and large, had things about as bad as the prisoners.

At the prison camps, officers were separated from enlisted men. In some instances lower ranking men were intentionally placed in charge of noncommissioned officers. Groups were systematically broken up and people transferred between barracks in order to forestall the development of a military or informal organization.

With some notorious exceptions, the Chinese used relatively little physical torture, and even their so-called brainwashing techniques were relatively simple. After a man was interrogated, however, he was not sent back to his old unit. He would reappear elsewhere in the camp, perhaps with new clothes. This meant that the prisoners in the barracks did not know what kind of experience they were facing or what kind of questions they were going to be asked. It was difficult for them to prepare themselves psychologically for the experience. Finally, there was some suspicion over how their former buddy had behaved.

Under these conditions, there was low morale, much illness and a high death rate, few escapes, and compromising answers in the interviews.

Prisoners of the Nazis

In the Nazi camps sharp disparities existed between the condition of American Army prisoners and German guards. The prisoners received worse food, clothing, and shelter.

The Nazis dealt with the prisoners through a military structure by recognizing rank, requiring American officers to police and maintain the internal organization.

During interrogations, prisoners were brought in individually, questioned, and returned to the unit. If any torture had been applied, the theory was that the unfortunate sufferer would serve as an example to frighten the others and induce them to talk when they were brought in.

Under these conditions, there was a relatively low death rate from illness, almost no instances of collaboration, and many escapes.

An Interpretation

First-hand observers were impressed by the different attitudes characterizing newly liberated American prisoners in Korea, compared with American prisoners freed in Germany. Cheering, jubilation, and happiness characterized the latter; quiet, sullenness, and anxiety the former. Subsequent investigation indicated the aforementioned differences in the conditions, treatment, and organization of the prisoners in Nazi Germany and Communist Korea. Though it is true that the American soldiers in Korea were neither as clear about the issues nor as convinced of their country's correctness as their counterparts in World War II were, Edgar Schein (1956), a psychologist who studied the POWs from Korea, suggests that the structure and process of the groups within the camps were more immediate causes of the prisoners' demoralization.

The major problems in the Communist prisoner of war camps resulted from inadequate military or social structure; neither support nor discipline was given to the individual. In the German camps, on the other hand, there was a structure which enabled a prisoner to prepare himself and to gain some strength from his buddies prior to interrogation. He also had to come back to his friends, which would be difficult and dangerous if he compromised himself to the Nazis. In the Chinese camps the prisoner did not have adequate preparation for the interviews, and he did not have to go back to face his barracks mates. Consequently, when asked questions that sounded rather unimportant and innocuous, or when told that his friend had provided information, the soldier tended to respond more than he should.

Escapes were rare in Korea, according to Schein, because escape is a group activity; trust is essential. The men simply could not get organized. Because of frequent transfers, they did not have time to develop the cooperative efforts necessary for escape. In addition, of course, they were Occidentals in an Oriental country, and this made escape much more difficult than it had been for American prisoners in Germany. So, in the Communist prisoner of war camps, morale was low, the will to survive declined, and the death rate was greater than physical differences between the Chinese and Nazi camps would explain.

Put in terms of group dynamics, there were important differences in interaction, activity, and sentiment between the Nazi and the Chinese camps. In the Nazi camps interaction among POWs was facilitated. The abundant interaction led to activities such as escape attempts and resistance to the enemy. In turn, these activities and interactions fostered sentiments of loyalty, pride, and purpose.

In the Chinese camps interaction was fragmented, sporadic, and inadequate. The captors, by preventing interaction, made it difficult or impossible for sentiments of trust, loyalty, and group identity to develop and survive. In turn, the lack of shared sentiments and of opportunities for interaction resulted in fewer activities to resist the enemy and fewer activities to support individual prisoners.

Groups are systems, and that implies that their parts are interrelated and interdependent. A change in one part of the anatomy of a group, as we have just seen, can mean changes in other parts because the parts are linked together in physiological interdependence and operate as a functioning whole.

In a selected reading for this chapter, Robert J. Naughton, a former prisoner of war in Vietnam, compares his experience as an isolated captive in South Vietnam with his experience as a member of a group of POWs in North Vietnam.

WHAT THE GROUP OFFERS THE INDIVIDUAL

The experiences of POWs in Germany, Korea, and Vietnam imply that the group serves three functions for the individual: (1) the satisfaction of complex social needs, (2) emotional support in identifying oneself and dealing with the world, and (3) assistance in meeting goals. The Korean memoirs of General William Dean (1954) well describe some of these functions. General Dean won the Congressional Medal of Honor for his heroism in Korea. Nonetheless, he points out that he talked to his captors more than he should have. After prolonged solitary confinement and existence on poor rations slipped under a door, Dean had an overwhelming compulsion to talk when taken to the Chinese interrogator. He responded positively to his interrogator even though he knew the man was his enemy.

Satisfaction of Social Needs

Most fundamentally, people join groups because of a need for affiliation. The basis of affiliation ranges from simple enjoyment of other human beings to more complex desires for group affirmation of an individual's self-conception. Thus, affiliation can either be a means to an end or an end in itself. For General Dean, desires for companionship flowed automatically from the human relationship—even between the prisoner and his keeper. Similarly, veteran soldiers comment on the tendency of new recruits to stick together for friendship and support when under stress—even though they know it increases rather than decreases the danger.

Research indicates that employees who have no opportunity for social contact find their work unsatisfying. This lack of satisfaction may reflect itself in low production, high turnover, and absenteeism. In the earliest of his classic research efforts, Mayo (1946) observed that employees in a textile plant who worked in isolated jobs were highly dissatisfied and consistently failed to meet production standards. When the company permitted these workers to take rest periods as a group, production and satisfaction increased. Similarly, other observers have suggested that maids in hospitals feel uncomfortable when they work only in the company of doctors and nurses (Burling et al., 1956). Some hospitals have discovered that, when three or four maids are grouped together as a team, turnover is reduced and a more effective job is done. And Roy (1960), in one of this chapter's selected readings, vividly describes the enjoyment and assistance derived from informal games, banter, and horseplay on the job.

Identification and Emotional Support

Our prisoner of war examples do not mean that compromise and collaboration are inevitable just because people crave affection; the process is more subtle. As General Dean points out, he simply was not sure what was right and what was wrong. Isolated from human companionship and communication, he lost touch with the essential basis and support for ethical behavior—social corroboration of individual conscience. Even the development of that conscience is heavily influenced by social contact, because self-identification is greatly affected by others. This is clear in teenagers, for example, who try to be everything their friends expect. Choices of styles in music, clothes, and hair all reflect teenagers' efforts to define themselves in terms of their companions. Self-image derives from social image.

In a wartime prison camp, a strong group could assist the individual to define the basis of ethical behavior. So also in the shop and office, the group can guide the individual in knowing what is desirable and undesirable behavior. How much time should be taken for a coffee break? Is it all right to talk to fellow employees while the boss is in the room? Must all copy be shown to the advertising manager? Even where there are established rules, a question remains: Is everyone expected to live by the letter of the law? Most employees do not want to violate the generally accepted rules of the game; at the same time, they do not want to conform to restrictive rules that everyone else ignores. They want to know the right thing to do. The group fills an important function by providing its members with a kind of guide to correct behavior—not correctness in terms of written policies but in terms of what is actually acceptable.

Research in military units indicates that the group can give support, perhaps even courage, to the individual in a dangerous situation. Young Joe Marm, a second lieutenant on duty in South Vietnam in the autumn of 1965, grabbed up two side arms and a pile of grenades, ran up a hill alone, and attacked and destroyed a machine gun nest, killing eight Viet Cong. Upon being recommended for the Congressional Medal of Honor, Marm was asked why he made the attack. His reply was simple: "What would the fellows have thought of me if I had been afraid to do it?" (*New York Times*, Nov. 17, 1966). Similarly, in studies of soldiers in World War II, there is evidence that those men closely tied to cohesive groups were more responsible in carrying out their duties, more confident of being able to perform well as soldiers, less fearful in battle, and less likely to capitulate or surrender under stress (Shils, 1950). These studies also indicated that the soldier's willingness to show bravery and make sacrifices was correlated not with loyalty to country or understanding of the war issues but with loyalty to the immediate group. In other words, soldiers who performed heroic acts were motivated largely by the desire not to let their buddies down.

Of course, some people have stronger self-identification and conscience than others. They could stand against a group or initiate action on their own. Nonetheless, the group can assist most individuals, if not all, in being true to themselves. Support of the group in maintaining morale and identity was critical in the Korean prisoner of war situation; its absence helped to explain why there was so much distrust, sickness, and death among the prisoners. As the poet John Donne said, *"No man is an island entire of itself."*

Assistance in Meeting Objectives

Groups do more than just satisfy social, psychological, and metaphysical needs. The group can assist in solving very specific problems and protect individuals from their mistakes. A new sales clerk may not be sure about how to handle a complicated problem of returning merchandise. A lab technician may be hesitant about asking his or her boss to repeat instructions, yet may be afraid that the experiment will be ruined without additional information. In each case the employee turns to fellow workers for assistance; most prefer this source of help. Blau (1955) has illustrated how federal agents consistently prefer getting assistance from fellow employees as opposed to going to their manager. Indeed, this ability to provide assistance is a source of substantial prestige for the giver.

So far, we have emphasized what the group can do for the individual; in addition, a group as a unit develops goals. The behavior of groups in pursuit of these goals is of primary concern to the manager. Before we consider this, however, let us investigate the development of groups on the job.

HOW THE ORGANIZATION SHAPES THE GROUP

Groups do not exist in vacuums. The technologies they work with (be they computers or punch-presses) and the management practices they work under predetermine the environment in which groups develop and function. That is, by selecting equipment and defining work methods, by planning, organizing, leading, and controlling, managers, in effect, design the scenery, set the stage, and write the script. Employees, then, are actors whose formal roles have built-in activity and interaction requirements. As we saw in the case of American POWs in China and Germany, the striking differences in the behavior and feelings of the two groups seemed especially to have been influenced by the way their captors controlled interaction. Lacking the coercion and drama, of course, the same shaping of activities and interaction patterns can be observed in all organizations (Exhibit 4.2). The specific impact of technology and management practices will be discussed in the following sections.

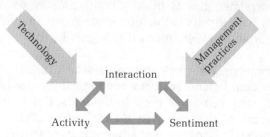

Exhibit 4.2 Determinants of Group Dynamics

Technology

Leonard Sayles' study (1958) of over 300 work groups in several industries showed that technology heavily influenced their formation and their behavior patterns. By positioning people in the work system, technology not only prescribes their activities and predisposes their interactions, it also confronts each group with particular working conditions and problems and endows the group with greater or lesser bargaining power. One of Sayles' colleagues, James Kuhn (1961), demonstrated these effects of technology on work groups in two industries—electrical equipment and rubber tires. Kuhn found that work groups in the electrical equipment industry did not engage in wildcat strikes and other disruptive tactics as often as work groups in the rubber tire industry. The explanation for this difference in conflict was found in technological differences between the two manufacturing tasks. Tire manufacture presented work groups with more noxious conditions and, inadvertently, positioned groups so that only a few disgruntled employees could force all work to stop by stopping their own work. In the electrical equipment industry, the technology confronted groups with fewer problems and gave them less power.

Other studies have revealed how technological changes in work processes can inadvertently destroy the foundation of cooperative and effective groups. For example, a change in coal-mining methods replaced small work teams with factory-like individualized work positions (Trist and Bamforth, 1951). Though the new technology seemed superior, its damage to work groups resulted in a net loss of work effectiveness and human satisfaction. The feelings of loyalty and the mutual help provided members of the former work teams had been eradicated by technological change.

Management Practices

The way planning, organizing, leading, and controlling are carried out also shapes the patterns of interaction, activity, and sentiment of groups. Like technology, management practices determine who is more likely to interact and share activities with whom. A managerial decision to group employees into departments on the basis of function, for example, sets the stage for interaction among employees performing similar tasks. Organizing by product or client, on the other hand, groups employees performing different functions, but for the same product.

An advertising agency, for example, first organized its creative branch into departments on the basis of functions such as copy, art, and production. This meant that artists sat together, shared ideas, admired and criticized one another's work, and so on. Copywriters did the same in their group. When the agency reorganized, however, into a client-centered structure, these groups were destroyed and new groups were formed for each client. These groups consisted of a mixture of artists, copywriters, and other specialists. Their capacity to provide technical expertise and the highly valued approval of fellow specialists to one another was substantially less than had been provided by the original functional groups. On the other hand, their capacity to provide a coordinated effort focused on client requirements exceeded that of the original groups.

Whether the related management practices of leading, planning, and controlling are imposed upon groups or shared with them also can make a big difference in group interaction, activity, and sentiment. The effects of a shift from imposed to shared management have been the subject of a thousand studies, and behavioral science-oriented management theory has stressed the benefits of the latter (Miles, 1975). To cite but one illustration: A supervisor in the painting operation of a toy manufacturing company met with the eight or so toy painters to discuss their several discontents about the engineered and managerially controlled production arrangement in which they worked (Strauss, 1955). They were bothered by fumes, heat, and the monotony of a mechanically paced conveyor belt. As these several problems were reviewed, the painters proposed several specific changes, one of which would result in their collectively deciding upon their own pace of work and controlling it by a regulating dial. With some misgivings, the supervisor adopted each recommendation. The results: improved productivity and morale within the group.

Though managers, through technology, structure, and administrative practices, do shape work groups, they often do so inadvertently. Production systems usually reflect a mentality that can be summed up in the phrase "technological imperative"—it is the physical equipment and its layout that is considered; people are merely plugged in as necessary to operate the machines. Whatever grouping (or isolation) of employees that results is accidental. Administrative practices may also be imposed, according to a "managerial imperative." for a purpose such as control. Again, the human and social effects may be accidental. In any event, since choices of technology and management practices do cause changes in group dynamics, we need to look more closely at how these changes develop.

THE DEVELOPMENT OF INFORMAL ORGANIZATION

In carrying out their assigned job duties, employees interact with others. But the process does not stop here. Unplanned sentiments inevitably emerge. People dislike or like (and rarely are neutral about) the people with whom they work. In turn, these sentiments encourage them to elaborate their communications and activities with others in a variety of unplanned and informal patterns (Homans, 1950). The process can be illustrated as shown in Exhibit 4.3.

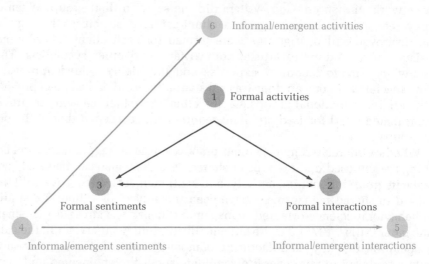

Exhibit 4.3   Emergent Informal Group Dynamics

Thus, when management brings people together in the office or plant where it expects them to communicate and work together, inevitable elaboration occurs. It does not always follow the numerical order in the figure, but as Strauss and Sayles (1966) suggest:

> Employees form friendship groups based on their contact and common interest—and these groups arise out of the life of the organization. Once these groups have been established, however, they develop a life of their own that is almost completely separate from the work process from which it arose. This is a dynamic, self-generating process. Brought together by the formal organization, employees interact with one another. Increasing interaction builds favorable sentiments toward fellow group members. In turn, these sentiments become the foundation for an increased variety of activities, many not specified by the job description: special lunch arrangements, trading of job duties, fights with those outside the group, gambling on paycheck numbers. And these increased opportunities for interaction build stronger bonds of identification. Then the group becomes something more than a mere collection of people. It develops a customary way of doing things—a set of stable characteristics that are hard to change. It becomes an organization in itself (p. 89).

Most people have need for affiliation and membership. Yet once they have established mutual relationships, many individuals want to be better than their companions. Everyone wants to be equal, but as George Orwell put it in *Animal Farm*, "some want to be more equal than others." With affiliation, a new need emerges—desire for social esteem, prestige, or status—that is, some differentiation of social position from associates and peers.

Prestige or status are frequently defined as a set of unwritten rules about the kind of conduct that people are expected to show in one's presence: what degree of respect or disrespect, familiarity or unfamiliarity, reserve or frankness. Notwithstanding the barbs of contemporary social critics, prestige-seeking is not solely a twentieth-century American phenomenon. People have apparently always created social structure, differentiating the power and glory among themselves. "Like it or not," Gellerman (1963) tells us, "people have evidently been sorting themselves out into chiefs and Indians, nobles and peasants, executives and hourly workers from time immemorial, and they show no signs of stopping" (p. 151). The classless society is yet to appear, and as the Yugoslav Milovan Djilas (1957) courageously showed us, the Communist states also develop class distinctions.

Even within the small informal group, subtle status differences begin to emerge. The type of membership and status within a work group that a person enjoys depends upon factors that she or he brings to the organization, and factors derived from the job.

External factors. What a person brings to the workplace influences status on the job. This pertains to who and what a person is, not what she or he does. When one of the authors worked in a large chemical manufacturing company, a fellow engineer was the second largest stockholder in this large company. Stock ownership was widely dispersed and his inherited ownership was less than 1%, but it still constituted a large fortune. In the formal organization, however, he was only an engineer with no real indication that his stock ownership was going to help him directly in his hierarchical career. Nonetheless, he obviously had status in the plant regardless of what he did—especially since he prominently displayed on his desk Christmas cards received from the chairman of the board.

Among the off-the-job qualities that confer status are education, age, seniority, sex, and ethnic background. In the past, women and blacks had been accorded low status.

Fairly recent evidence suggests that this legacy still affects the interaction of groups consisting of white, male Americans and minority group members or white females. White, male Americans still tend to assume leadership in task teams, and minority group members as well as white females tend to follow (Webber, 1974; Aries, 1976).

Other ethnic groups had also been arranged according to a status hierarchy, with Anglo-Saxons usually at the top, and people of southern European background near the bottom. However, the relative positions on this status ladder varied from one community to another. For example, to be a "regular" at one plant required Irish extraction, regardless of other personal characteristics. At other plants, one might have found it helpful to be Polish, and so on (Zaleznik et al., 1958).

Personality also plays a role, although research findings in this area are not clear. Among informal student groups there is evidence that higher status is associated with physical size, appearance and dress, self-confidence and self-assurance, sociability or friendliness, and intelligence—although the leaders must not exceed their followers by a very large margin in any of these characteristics (Stogdill, 1948). The importance of these factors in determining status changes from time to time and with cultures. We have asked many classes of American students for factors determining informal group status. Age is seldom mentioned, and if it is, only as the last item. In most of history and in most societies, age has been the major determinant of formal and informal status—as witness Japanese industry (Takezawa, 1966).

Internal factors. The job also influences the status system. In fact, when management creates an organization, it consciously creates a status system based primarily on pay and authority. Titles, job descriptions, evaluation programs, pay systems, and work-measurement practices all influence the informal social structure.

- *Job title*—Obviously a superintendent is more important than a general supervisor, and a general supervisor outranks a supervisor. Engineers outrank technicians; secretaries are above stenographers. In almost every organization, although organizations are certainly not consistent on this, job titles are subtly graded according to levels of status, and the status of each individual depends in part on the job he or she holds.
- *Pay*—This is one of the most important determinants of status. Higher pay means higher status, and even a difference of a few cents per hour may have a significant effect on a job's status. How one is paid also helps to determine status. Being a salaried employee on a monthly payroll may be less convenient, but it carries much more prestige than getting a weekly or daily wage.
- *Work schedules*—The freedom to choose one's hours, or being excused from punching the time clock, is a mark of distinction. Working a day schedule is usually thought of as a higher-status job than a shift schedule.
- *Mobility*—Generally, a job which allows a person to move around freely, interacting and communicating with many different people, is thought of as having higher prestige than a position that allows no autonomy or discretion over one's movements. This mobility is also related to autonomy or freedom from close management supervision. Again, this is a status factor generally giving higher prestige in the informal social structure.
- *Symbols of office*—There is a vast range of physical factors which are desirable in themselves but which also serve as symbols for higher status. These include such things as in which company lunchroom you can eat. Can you leave the building for morning coffee? Do you have a reserved parking space? What kind of clothing do you wear in the office? In your office, what kind of furnishings do you have? telephone? desk? carpeting? and so on.

What we are suggesting is that people on the job structure themselves in various relationships, integrating on-job and off-job status factors. An informal social structure will be created; employees will look up to certain people and consider certain jobs attractive; they may even plan their careers around movement through these positions. The highest status positions will tend to be occupied especially by people high in both external and internal status factors. This informal status system may approximate the formal structure of the company, but it will probably deviate in a number of ways, as we shall illustrate later in this chapter.

Group Cohesion

The success of informal groups in achieving their objectives depends to an important extent upon the internal strength or cohesion of the group. Part of the difficulty in the Chinese prisoner of war camps was inadequate group cohesion. That is, stable values and standards of behavior never developed; group members could not work together in mutual dependency. Cohesion is both cause and consequence: it aids the pursuit of group objectives, and, at the same time, it can be strengthened by the sharing of concerted effort. But the sources of cohesion are many and varied, as the following summary suggests.

Homogeneity.   One of the most cohesive work groups we ever observed was composed entirely of an ethnic or national group called the "West of Englanders." All of the six to seven people in the group had come from the southwest—Land's End—section of England many years before, and they maintained their sense of identification—perhaps because they were very much an ethnic minority among Italians and Poles. These production workers (including a supervisor) held a stable set of values and assistance expectations; they controlled production (at a fairly high level) and were remarkably successful in getting management to respond to them.

In contrast, groups whose members have different interests and backgrounds are often less effective in promoting their interests. When, for example, people with sharp differences in rates of pay and job duties work near each other, the resulting group is seldom cohesive. The group may often be characterized by conflicting cliques, which hinder common action.

Even when doing similar work, competition among members of a group will often hinder cohesion—unless the group can agree to regulate the competition. At a large automobile dealer's, the bottom three of twenty-five salespeople are fired each month, regardless of their sales. Under these circumstances, the salespeople would hardly become a cohesive group. On the other hand, where expulsion depends upon absolute rather than relative performance, a basically homogeneous group with good cohesion will assist poor performers in improving their output.

Stable membership contributes to higher cohesion. With time, the members come to know each other, they learn the values and expectations of the group, and they learn how to behave. This was one of the problems in the prisoner of war camps referred to earlier. Where the barracks groups were systematically broken up, no cohesive groups could develop. "A tightly knit group," Lasswell and Kaplan (1950) maintain, "significantly means both a group difficult to enter and one whose members closely identify with one another. The less permeable the group, the more value attaches to membership and, in turn, the more intense the adherence to group perspective" (p. 35).

Communication.   To be a group, people must be able to talk with one another. Only in this way can their similarities and common interests be developed, their values and standards established, and joint action initiated. Groups in which the members can communicate easily with one another are more likely to be cohesive. Internal group unity can be thwarted in such areas as noisy steel mills, long assembly lines, or even quiet offices, where "gossiping" is frowned upon and there is no privacy for conversation.

Isolation.   Physical isolation from other groups tends to build cohesiveness. Familiar to the student is the contrast between the school spirit of a college isolated in the country and the nonchalance characterizing students in large, urban universities in New York, Los Angeles, Chicago, Washington, D.C., or Philadelphia. Miners have demonstrated, in countless lengthy strikes, that isolated workers will stick together more stubbornly than workers who are socially integrated with the rest of the community.

Even simple physical boundaries on a group may be essential for cohesion. If a group can't identify its members and clearly differentiate itself, cohesion will be low. This is another of the problems in long assembly lines: it is difficult to distinguish logical groups. A large insurance company has a one-story office building which resembles nothing so much as an airplane hangar—or a setting from a Kafka novel. Several hundred clerical and supervisory personnel work together in one large area with no physical boundaries between people. It is difficult for cohesive groups to emerge.

Size.   This insurance office also illustrates that too many people hinder development of cohesive groups. Larger groups hinder communication, lower homogeneity, and encourage breaking up into small cliques. Small departments, therefore, tend to be more closely knit than large ones. Loyalty, as in the military, is a product of frequent, face-to-face contacts. It is simply easier to have close relationships with all members of a small group than with all members of a large one.

Outside pressure.   We have already mentioned how members of groups tend to herd together under stress. Continuous outside pressure from management may produce high cohesion. Under organizational stress, lateral and peer communications tend to increase while vertical communications decrease. Personal differences are minimized when threatened by a common danger—or a tough supervisor. And this closeness may remain after the threat is relieved. Perhaps the most closely knit army veterans of World War II are those of the 11th Armored Division, which was so badly mauled by the Germans in the Battle of the Bulge. They still publish a newsletter, meet frequently, hold annual conventions, and maintain high camaraderie, in spite of great differences among the members in economic and social achievement since the war.

A tough management policy toward personnel may well encourage development of strong informal groups as a protective and retaliatory device. On the other hand, the more sophisticated and manipulative manager who, like the Korean War captors, systematically promotes internal competition, transfers people, and prevents communication will hinder the development of group cohesion.

Status of the group. Our earlier discussion of individual needs suggests that people often prefer to identify with high-status groups. This means that people are more likely to feel loyalty toward a high-status group than toward a low-status group. The factors conferring status upon a group as a whole are very much the same as those giving status to the individual within the informal organization. They include special skills, monopoly control over certain functions, responsibility and autonomy, opportunities for promotion out of the area, physical location and working conditions, influence of the supervisor in organization affairs, and so on.

Although it is true that high-status groups tend to have higher cohesion, it is not clear whether status *per se* is the cause of high cohesion—or whether the factors conferring status (such as seniority, ease in communication, autonomy, and freedom from close supervision) simply allow cohesion to develop.

ATTITUDE AND BEHAVIOR EXPECTATIONS

On several occasions in 1976, when the alarm bell rang at London's Battersea Fire Station, the station's 15 firemen leaped into action, slid down the brass pole, and raced aboard the fire engine (*Los Angeles Times*, July 8, 1976). The driver started the engine. Then the station's newly appointed commander, David Callingham, climbed on. The driver turned off the engine, and all the firemen got off and returned to their earlier activities. Another station responded to the alarm.

The men were not striking, one of them explained, but were simply refusing to take the engine out with Callingham aboard. The group objected to Callingham's alleged "bloody-minded and officious" conduct in ordering too many practice drills, too many fire engine scrubdowns, and too many cups of tea for himself. The group had its own expectations about how much discipline and spit-and-polish was reasonable. Callingham violated their limits and so was subjected to the group's own discipline, which resulted in his embarrassment and the need for fire department hearings to review the case. Every group develops its own attitudes and standards of behavior and, like the firemen, may seek to impose those attitudes and standards upon members and outsiders.

Group expectations grow out of needs to maintain the group, remove sources of stress, and promote cooperation. They are functional for the group, even if dysfunctional to certain individuals and to the larger organization. For example, Stanford University pioneered in coed dormitories where males and females could live in an intersexual setting. Surprisingly, perhaps, many students maintained that there was less sexual intimacy than under the old system. What reportedly happened is that an "incest taboo" developed. Residents tended to form platonic friendships, as traditional sexual roles broke down under the close living. "It's like a brother-sister relationship with sexual overtones" is how one coed put it (*Daily Pennsylvanian*, Nov. 18, 1969). The "taboo" makes for easier living because it promotes naturalness and lessens intrasex competition. Without such rules, dorm life would be too stressful.

To a greater or lesser extent, all informal groups are characterized by such attitudinal norms and behavioral expectations. Of special importance in work groups are attitudes toward assistance and effort. As mentioned, one of the reasons for the development of informal groups is mutual assistance. Accordingly, most work groups value and expect cooperation and helpfulness among regular members of the group—hints on how to machine parts, assistance on difficult jobs, warning against management inspection, assistance in camouflaging mistakes, and a whole host of informal practices. In order to maintain standing in a group and receive its benefits, this aid must be given.

If the basic attitude of the group toward the company is positive, informal expectations can greatly assist management. If the group is fundamentally interested in getting the job done, the workers will fill in the gaps and work out the ambiguities in management assignments. They will be willing to shift with the varying demands of the job in order to assist hard-pressed colleagues without specific management direction. Even under the best conditions, however, a strong informal group will oppose some of management's desires. And when basic attitudes toward management are adverse, the group's behavioral expectations may be directed against management's desires in a variety of amazing ways—ways that managers and workers develop to compensate for inadequacies in the formal system of rewards.

Output and Effort Standards

Limitation of output has long been a prominent antimanagement behavior pattern. A wide variety of studies, starting with the Hawthorne research of the late 1920s, has demonstrated how informal groups limit their output (Roethlisberger and Dickson, 1939). Indeed, much earlier, Frederick W. Taylor (Dale, 1970) devoted much of his life to attempting to stamp out the widespread "soldiering," which he thought endangered the very existence of the United States.

The term "soldiering" connoted antimanagement motivation, but this need not be the case. Any group of individuals tends to develop some conception of a "fair day's work." In the absence of piece rates, in particular, a group tends to develop agreement on how much should be done. To be sure, not everyone concurs, but among both students and crate handlers, there is a tendency to define what should be done so that there is relative equality of effort. The definition of output is not always harmful to management; the level of effort decided upon by the group may be higher than some individuals would otherwise demonstrate. In addition, the group's standard of performance may facilitate management's prediction of output, thus simplifying scheduling and costing.

Group Discipline

Like all societies, informal groups at work develop common values and behavioral expectations — management is dangerous, don't fink on your buddies, don't goof off, but don't work too hard. Whether the members of the group act or don't act upon these norms and standards depends upon whether the individual wants to be a member of the group and whether the group can enforce its desires. The more eager an individual is to be a member of a group, the more he or she will conform to its norms of behavior, and the easier it will be to enforce group rules. As Festinger (1950) put it: "If a person wants to stay in a group, he will be susceptible to influences coming from the group, and he will be willing to conform to the rules which the group sets up" (p. 91).

Withdrawal of the group's contribution to the individual is the primary method of enforcement. The group strongly influences the behavior of its members by providing them with support, reinforcement, security, encouragement, protection, rationale, rationalization, etc., for their "proper" behavior, and by punishing them for deviations through the use of ridicule, hostility, threat of expulsion, etc. When an individual is genuinely attached to a group and is in close and continuous contact with it, his or her behavior and beliefs are extremely resistant to change by forces outside the group. In such circumstances the group can exercise firm control.

In addition, among some informal social groups there are indications that popularity is associated with respect for the group's norms. One study (Argyle, 1957) concludes, "Deviates are rejected while conformers become popular" (p. 155). The closer individuals conform to the accepted norms of the group, the better liked they will be; the better liked they are, the closer they conform; the less they conform, the more disliked they will be. To the extent that these judgments (based upon observations of teenagers) are general, people like to be liked, so they tend to engage in actions that will maintain or increase the esteem received from those around them.

SUMMARY

There are three basic elements common to all groups — interaction, activity, and sentiment. All of the elements are interrelated and interdependent. A change in one will produce changes in the others.

Groups can offer their members social satisfaction, emotional support, and assistance in meeting objectives. Whether they do so or not depends greatly upon how the technology and management practices of the organization shape the pattern of group interaction, activity, and sentiment. Arrangements and practices that foster interaction tend to encourage the development of group activities and shared group sentiments.

But whatever interactions, activities, and sentiments are directly required by the formal system of management, groups develop informal patterns of their own. These include informal status systems and some degree of cohesiveness. Groups also develop their own attitudes and behavior expectations which customarily prescribe output and effort standards.

In short, there is a rich fabric of emergent group dynamics in organizations. Managers must understand how groups develop and operate lest they premise their actions on the mistaken assumption that people at work are isolated individuals who can be managed effectively, without considering the social context in which they work.

REFERENCES

Argyle, M. *The Scientific Study of Social Behavior.* Methuen, 1957.

Aries, E. "Interaction Patterns and Themes of Male, Female, and Mixed Groups." *Small Group Behavior,* Vol. 7, No. 1 (1976), pp. 7–18.

Blau, P. *The Dynamics of Bureaucracy.* University of Chicago Press, 1955.

Burling, T., E. Lentz, and R. Wilson. *The Give and Take in Hospitals.* Putnam, 1956.

Dean, W. F. *General Dean's Story* (as told to W. L. Worden). Viking Press, 1954.

Djilas, M. *The New Class.* Praeger, 1957.

Festinger, L., S. Schachter, and K. Back. *Social Pressure in Informal Groups.* Harper and Row, 1950.

Gellerman, S. *Motivation and Productivity.* American Management Association, 1963.

Homans, G. C. *The Human Group.* Harcourt Brace Jovanovich, 1950.

———. "Fundamental Processes of Social Exchange," from Chapter 1 in *Sociology,* ed. N. Smelser. Wiley (1967), pp. 27–28.

Kinkead, E. *In Every War But One.* Norton, 1959.

Kover, A. J. "Reorganization in an Advertising Agency: A Case Study of a Decrease in Integration." *Human Organization,* Vol. 22, No. 4 (Winter 1963–1964), pp. 252–59.

Kuhn, J. W. *Bargaining in Grievance Settlement.* Columbia University Press, 1961.

Lasswell, H. D., and A. Kaplan. *Power and Society: A Framework for Political Inquiry.* Yale University Press, 1950.

Mayo, E. *The Human Problems of an Industrial Civilization.* Graduate School of Business Administration, Harvard University, 1946.

———. *The Social Problem of an Industrial Civilization.* Graduate School of Business Administration, Harvard University, 1947.

Miles, R. E. *Theories of Management: Implications for Organizational Behavior and Development.* McGraw-Hill, 1975.

Roethlisberger, F. J., and W. Dickson. *Management and the Worker.* Harvard University Press, 1939.

Roy, D. "Banana Time—Job Satisfaction and Informal Interaction." *Human Organization,* Vol. 18 (1960), pp. 158–68.

Sayles, L. R. *Behavior of Industrial Work Groups.* Wiley, 1958.

Schein, E. "The Chinese Indoctrination Program for Prisoners of War." *Psychiatry,* Vol. 19 (1956), pp. 149–72.

Shils, E. A. "Primary Groups in the American Army." In *Continuities in Social Research: Studies in the Scope and Method of the American Soldier,* ed. R. K. Merton and P. F. Lazarsfeld. Free Press (1950), pp. 16–39.

Stogdill, R. "Personal Factors Associated with Leadership: A Survey of the Literature." *Journal of Psychology,* Vol. 25 (1948), pp. 35–71.

Strauss, G. "Group Dynamics and Intergroup Relations." In *Money and Motivation,* W. F. Whyte. Harper and Brothers (1955), pp. 90–96.

Takezawa, S. "Socio-Cultural Aspects of Management in Japan." *International Labour Review,* Vol. 94, No. 2, August 1966.

Taylor, F. W. Lectures given at Harvard University 1909–1914, cited by E. Dale in *Readings in Management,* 2nd ed. McGraw-Hill, 1970.

Trist, E. L., and K. W. Bamforth. "Some Social and Psychological Consequences of the Longwall Method of Coal-getting." *Human Relations,* Vol. 4, No. 1 (February 1951), pp. 3–38.

Webber, R. A. "Majority and Minority Perceptions in Cross-Cultural Teams." *Human Relations,* Vol. 27, No. 9 (1974), pp. 873–89.

Zaleznik, A., C. R. Christensen, and F. J. Roethlisberger. *The Motivation, Productivity and Satisfaction of Workers: A Prediction Study.* Graduate School of Business Administration, Harvard University, 1958.

Readings

Banana Time: Job Satisfaction and Informal Interaction

Donald F. Roy

This paper undertakes description and exploratory analysis of the social interaction which took place within a small work group of factory machine operatives during a two-month period of participant observation. The factual and ideational materials which it presents lie at an intersection of two lines of research interest and should, in their dual bearing, contribute to both. Since the operatives were engaged in work which involved the repetition of very simple operations over an extra-long workday, six days a week, they were faced with the problem of dealing with a formidable "beast of monotony." Revelation of how the group utilized its resources to combat the "beast" should merit the attention of those who are seeking solution to the practical problem of job satisfaction, or employee morale. It should also provide insights for those who are trying to penetrate the mysteries of the small group.

Convergence of these two lines of interest is, of course, no new thing. Among the host of writers and researchers who have suggested connections between "group" and "joy in work" are Walker and Guest, observers of social interaction on the automobile assembly line.[1] They quote assembly-line workers as saying, "We have a lot of fun and talk all the time,"[2] and, "If it weren't for the talking and fooling, you'd go nuts."[3]

My account of how one group of machine operators kept from "going nuts" in a situation of monotonous work activity attempts to lay bare the tissues of interaction which made up the content of their adjustment. The talking, fun, and fooling which provided solution to the elemental problem of "psychological survival" will be described according to their embodiment in intra-group relations. In addition, an unusual opportunity for close observation of behavior involved in the maintenance of group equilibrium was afforded by the fortuitous introduction of a "natural experiment." My unwitting injection of explosive materials into the stream of interaction resulted in sudden, but temporary, loss of group interaction.

My fellow operatives and I spent our long days of simple repetitive work in relative isolation from other employees of the factory. Our line of machines was sealed off from other work areas of the plant by the four walls of the clicking room. The one door of this room was usually closed. Even when it was kept open, during periods of hot weather, the consequences were not social; it opened on an uninhabited storage room of the shipping department. Not even the sound of work activity going on elsewhere in the factory carried to this isolated work place. There were occasional contacts with "outside" employees, usually on matters connected with the work; but, with the exception of the daily calls of one fellow who came to pick up finished materials for the next step in processing, such visits were sporadic and infrequent.

Moreover, face-to-face contact with members of the managerial hierarchy were few and far between. No one bearing the title of foreman ever came around. The only

Reproduced by permission of the Society for Applied Anthropology from *Human Organization*, Vol. 18, No. 4, 1960.

company official who showed himself more than once during the two month observation period was the plant superintendent. Evidently overloaded with supervisory duties and production problems which kept him busy elsewhere, he managed to pay his respects every week or two. His visits were in the nature of short, businesslike, but friendly exchanges. Otherwise he confined his observable communications with the group to occasional utilization of a public address system. During the two-month period, the company president and the chief chemist paid one friendly call apiece. One man, who may or may not have been of managerial status, was seen on various occasions lurking about in a manner which excited suspicion. Although no observable consequences accrued from the peculiar visitations of this silent fellow, it was assumed that he was some sort of efficiency expert, and he was referred to as "The Snooper."

As far as our work group was concerned, this was truly a situation of laissez-faire management. There was no interference from staff experts, no hounding by time-study engineers or personnel men hot on the scent of efficiency or good human relations. Nor were there any signs of industrial democracy in the form of safety, recreational, or production committees. There was an international union, and there was a highly publicized union-management cooperation program; but actual interactional processes of cooperation were carried on somewhere beyond my range of observation and without participation of members of my work group. Furthermore, these union-management get-togethers had no determinable connection with the problem of "toughing out" a twelve-hour day at monotonous work.

Our work group was thus not only abandoned to its own resources for creating job satisfaction, but left without that basic reservoir of ill-will toward management which can sometimes be counted on to stimulate the development of interesting activities to occupy hand and brain. Lacking was the challenge of intergroup conflict, that perennial source of creative experience to fill the otherwise empty hours of meaningless work routine.[4]

The clicking machines were housed in a room approximately thirty by twenty-four feet. They were four in number, set in a row, and so arranged along one wall that the busy operator could, merely by raising his head from his work, freshen his reveries with a glance through one of three large barred windows. To the rear of one of the end machines sat a long cutting table; here the operators cut up rolls of plastic materials into small sheets manageable for further processing at the clickers. Behind the machine at the opposite end of the line sat another table which was intermittently the work station of a female employee who performed sundry scissors operations of a more intricate nature on raincoat parts. Boxed in on all sides by shelves and stocks of materials, this latter locus of work appeared a cell within a cell.

The clickers were of the genus punching machines; of mechanical construction similar to that of the better-known punch presses, their leading features were hammer and block. The hammer, or punching head, was approximately eight inches by twelve inches at its flat striking surface. The descent upon the block was initially forced by the operator, who exerted pressure on a handle attached to the side of the hammer head. A few inches of travel downward established electrical connection for a sharp, power-driven blow. The hammer also traveled, by manual guidance, in a horizontal plane to and from, and in an arc around, the central column of the machine. Thus the operator, up to the point of establishing electrical connections for the sudden and irrevocable downward thrust, had flexibility in maneuvering his instrument over the larger surface of the block. The latter, approximately twenty-four inches wide, eighteen inches deep, and ten inches thick, was made, like a butcher's block, of inlaid hardwood; it was set in the machine at a convenient waist height. On it the operator placed his materials, one sheet at a time if leather, stacks of sheets if plastic, to be cut with steel dies of assorted sizes and shapes. The particular die in use would be moved, by hand, from spot to spot over the materials each time a cut was made; less frequently, materials would be shifted on the block as the operator saw need for such adjustment.

Introduction to the new job, with its relatively simple machine skills and work routines, was accomplished with what proved to be, in my experience, an all-time minimum of job training. The clicking machine assigned to me was situated at one end of the row. Here the superintendent and one of the operators gave a few brief demonstrations, accompanied by bits of advice which included a warning to keep hands clear of the descending hammer. After a short practice period, at the end of which the superintendent expressed satisfaction with progress and potentialities, I was left to develop my learning curve with no other supervision than that afforded by members of the work group. Further advice and assistance did come, from time to time, from my fellow operatives, sometimes upon request, sometimes unsolicited.

THE WORK GROUP

Absorbed at first in three related goals of improving my clicking skill, increasing my rate of output, and keeping my left hand unclicked, I paid little attention to my fellow operatives save to observe that they were friendly, middle-aged, foreign-born, full of advice, and very talkative. Their names, according to the way they addressed each other, were George, Ike, and Sammy.[5] George, a stocky fellow in his late fifties, operated the machine at the opposite end of the line; he, I later discovered, had emigrated in early youth from a country in Southeastern Europe. Ike, stationed at George's left, was tall, slender, in his early fifties, and Jewish; he had come from Eastern Europe in his youth. Sammy, number three man in the line, and my neighbor, was heavy set, in his late fifties, and Jewish; he had escaped from a country in Eastern Europe just before Hitler's legions had moved in. All three men had been downwardly mobile as to occupation in recent years. George and Sammy had been proprietors of small businesses; the former had been "wiped out" when his uninsured establishment burned down; the latter had been entrepreneuring on a small scale before he left all behind him to flee the Germans. According to his account, Ike had left a highly skilled trade which he had practiced for years in Chicago.

I discovered also that the clicker line represented a ranking system in descending order from George to myself. George not only had top seniority for the group, but functioned as a sort of lead man. His superior status was marked in the fact that he received five cents more per hour than the other clickermen, put in the longest workday, made daily contact, outside the workroom, with the superintendent on work matters which concerned the entire line, and communicated to the rest of us the directives which he received. The narrow margin of superordination was seen in the fact that directives were always relayed in the superintendent's name; they were on the order of, "You'd better let that go now, and get on the green. Joe says they're running low on the fifth floor," or, "Joe says he wants two boxes of the 3-die today." The narrow margin was also seen in the fact that the superintendent would communicate directly with his operatives over the public address system; and, on occasion, Ike or Sammy would leave the workroom to confer with him for decisions or advice in regard to work orders.

Ike was next to George in seniority, then Sammy. I was, of course, low man on the totem pole. Other indices to status differentiation lay in informal interaction, to be described later.

With one exception, job status tended to be matched by length of workday. George worked a thirteen-hour day, from 7 A.M. to 8:30 P.M. Ike worked eleven hours, from

7 A.M. to 6:30 P.M.; occasionally he worked until 7 or 7:30 for an eleven and a half- or a twelve-hour day. Sammy put in a nine-hour day, from 8 A.M. to 5:30 P.M. My twelve hours spanned from 8 A.M. to 8:30 P.M. We had a half hour for lunch, from 12 to 12:30.

The female who worked at the secluded table behind George's machine put in a regular plant-wide eight-hour shift from 8 to 4:30. Two women held this job during the period of my employment; Mable was succeeded by Baby. Both were Negroes, and in their late twenties.

A fifth clicker operator, an Arabian *emigré* called Boo, worked a night shift by himself. He usually arrived about 7 P.M. to take over Ike's machine.

THE WORK

It was evident to me, before my first workday drew to a weary close, that my clicking career was going to be a grim process of fighting the clock, the particular timepiece in this situation being an old-fashioned alarm clock which ticked away on a shelf near George's machine. I had struggled through many dreary rounds with the minutes and hours during the various phases of my industrial experience, but never had I been confronted with such a dismal combination of working conditions as the extra-long workday, the infinitesimal cerebral excitation, and the extreme limitation of physical movement. The contrast with a recent stint in the California oil fields was striking. This was no eight-hour day of racing hither and yon over desert and foothills with a rollicking crew of "roustabouts" on a variety of repair missions at oil wells, pipe lines, and storage tanks. Here there were no afternoon dallyings to search the sands for horned toads, tarantulas, and rattlesnakes, or to climb old wooden derricks for raven's nests, with an eye out, of course, for the tell-tale streak of dust in the distance which gave ample warning of the approach of the boss. This was standing all day in one spot beside three old codgers in a dingy room looking out through barred windows at the bare walls of a brick warehouse, leg movements largely restricted to the shifting of body weight from one foot to the other, hand and arm movements confined, for the most part, to a simple repetitive sequence of place the die, —— punch the clicker, —— place the die, —— punch the clicker, and intellectual activity reduced to computing the hours to quitting time. It is true that from time to time a fresh stack of sheets would have to be substituted for the clicked-out old one; but the stack would have been prepared by someone else, and the exchange would be only a minute or two in the making. Now and then a box of finished work would have to be moved back out of the way, and an empty box brought up; but the moving back and the bringing up involved only a step or two. And there was the half hour for lunch, and occasional trips to the lavatory or the drinking fountain to break up the day into digestible parts. But after each momentary respite, hammer and die were moving again: click, —— move die, —— click, —— move die.

Before the end of the first day, Monotony was joined by his twin brother, Fatigue. I got tired. My legs ached, and my feet hurt. Early in the afternoon I discovered a tall stool and moved it up to my machine to "take the load off my feet." But the superintendent dropped in to see how I was "doing" and promptly informed me that "we don't sit down on this job." My reverie toyed with the idea of quitting the job and looking for other work.

The next day was the same: the monotony of the work, the tired legs and sore feet and thoughts of quitting.

THE GAME OF WORK

In discussing the factory operative's struggle to "cling to the remnants of joy in work," Henri de Man makes the general observations that "it is psychologically impossible to deprive any kind of work of all its positive emotional elements," that the worker will find *some* meaning in any activity assigned to him, a "certain scope for initiative which can satisfy after a fashion the instinct for play and the creative impulse," that "even in the Taylor system there is found luxury of self-determination."[6] De Man cites the case of one worker who wrapped 13,000 incandescent bulbs a day; she found her outlet for creative impulse, her self-determination, her meaning in work by varying her wrapping movements a little from time to time.[7]

So did I search for *some* meaning in my continuous mincing of plastic sheets into small ovals, fingers, and trapezoids. The richness of possibility for creative expression previously discovered in my experience with the "Taylor system"[8] did not reveal itself here. There was no piecework, so no piecework game. There was no conflict with management, so no war game. But, like the light bulb wrapper, I did find a "certain scope for initiative," and out of this slight freedom to vary activity, I developed a game of work.

The game developed was quite simple, so elementary in fact, that its playing was reminiscent of rainy-day preoccupations in childhood, when attention could be centered by the hour on colored bits of things of assorted sizes and shapes. But this adult activity was not mere pottering and piddling; what it lacked in the earlier imaginative content, it made up for in clean-cut structure. Fundamentally involved were: a) variation in color of the materials cut, b) variation in shape of the dies used, and c) a process called "scraping the block." The basic procedure which ordered the particular combination of components employed could be stated in the form: "As soon as I do so many of these, I'll get to do those." If, for example, production scheduled for the day featured small, rectangular strips in three colors, the game might go: "As soon as I finish a thousand of the green ones, I'll click some brown ones." And, with success in attaining the objective of working with brown materials, a new goal of "I'll get to do the white ones" might be set. Or the new goal might involve switching dies.

Scraping the block made the game more interesting by adding to the number of possible variations in its playing; and what was perhaps more important, provided the only substantial reward, save for going to the lavatory or getting a drink of water, on days when work with one die and one color of material was scheduled. As a physical operation, scraping the block was fairly simple; it involved application of a coarse file to the upper surface of the block to remove roughness and unevenness resulting from the wear and tear of die penetration. But, as part of the intellectual and emotional content of the game of work, it could be in itself a source of variation in activity. The upper left-hand corner of the block could be chewed up in the clicking of 1000 white trapezoid pieces, then scraped. Next, the upper right-hand corner, and so on until the entire block had been worked over. Then, on the next round of scraping by quadrants, there was the possibility of a change of color or die to green trapezoid or white oval pieces.

Thus the game of work might be described as a continuous sequence of short-range production goals with achievement rewards in the form of activity change. The superiority of this relatively complex and self-determined system over the technically simple and outside-controlled job satisfaction injections experienced by Milner at the beginner's table in a shop of the feather industry should be immediately apparent: "Twice a day our work was completely changed to break the monotony. First Jennie would give us feathers of a brilliant green, then bright orange or a light blue or black. The "ohs" and "ahs" that came from the girls at each change was proof enough that this was an effective way of breaking the monotony of the tedious work."[9]

But a hasty conclusion that I was having lots of fun playing my clicking game should be avoided. These games were not as interesting in the experiencing as they might seem to be from the telling. Emotional tone of the activity was low, and intellectual currents weak. Such rewards as scraping the block or "getting to do the blue ones" were not very exciting, and the stretches of repetitive movement involved in achieving them were long enough to permit lapses into obsessive reverie. Henri de Man speaks of "clinging to the remnants of joy in work," and this situation represented just that. How tenacious the clinging was, how long I could have "stuck it out" with my remnants, was never determined. Before the first week was out this adjustment to the work situation was complicated by other developments. The game of work continued, but in a different context. Its influence became decidedly subordinated to, if not completely overshadowed by, another source of job satisfaction.

INFORMAL SOCIAL ACTIVITY OF THE WORK GROUP: TIMES AND THEMES

The change came about when I began to take serious note of the social activity going on around me; my attentiveness to this activity came with growing involvement in it. What I heard at first, before I started to listen, was a stream of disconnected bits of communication which did not make much sense. Foreign accents were strong and referents were not joined to coherent contexts of meaning. It was just "jabbering." What I saw at first, before I began to observe, was occasional flurries of horseplay so simple and unvarying in pattern and so childish in quality that they made no strong bid for attention. For example, Ike would regularly switch off the power at Sammy's machine whenever Sammy made a trip to the lavatory or the drinking fountain. Correlatively, Sammy invariably fell victim to the plot by making an attempt to operate his clicking hammer after returning to the shop. And, as the simple pattern went, this blind stumbling into the trap was always followed by indignation and reproach from Sammy, smirking satisfaction from Ike, and mild paternal scolding from George. My interest in this procedure was at first confined to wondering when Ike would weary of his tedious joke or when Sammy would learn to check his power switch before trying the hammer.

But, as I began to pay closer attention, as I began to develop familiarity with the communication system, the disconnected became connected, the nonsense made sense, the obscure became clear, and the silly actually funny. And, as the content of the interaction took on more and more meaning, the interaction began to reveal structure. There were "times" and "themes," and roles to serve their enaction. The interaction had subtleties, and I began to savor and appreciate them. I started to record what hitherto had seemed unimportant.

Times

This emerging awareness of structure and meaning included recognition that the long day's grind was broken by interruptions of a kind other than the formally instituted or idiosyncratically developed disjunctions in work routine previously described. These additional interruptions appeared in daily repetition in an ordered series of informal interactions. They were, in part, but only in part and in very rough comparison, similar to those common fractures of the production process known as the coffee break, the coke break, and the cigarette break. Their distinction lay in frequency of occurrence and in brevity. As phases of the daily series, they occurred almost hourly, and so short were they in duration that they disrupted work activity only slightly. Their significance lay not so much in their function as rest pauses, although it cannot be denied that physical refreshment was involved. Nor did their chief importance lie in the accentuation of progress points in the passage of time, although they could perform that function far more strikingly than the hour hand on the dull face of George's alarm clock. If the daily series of interruptions be likened to a clock, then the comparison might best be made with a special kind of cuckoo clock, one with a cuckoo which can provide variation in its announcements and can create such an interest in them that the intervening minutes become filled with intellectual content. The major significance of the interactional interruptions lay in such a carryover of interest. The physical interplay which momentarily halted work activity would initiate verbal exchanges and thought processes to occupy group members until the next interruption. The group interactions thus not only marked off the time; they gave it content and hurried it along.

Most of the breaks in the daily series were designated as "times" in the parlance of the clicker operators, and they featured the consumption of food or drink of one sort or another. There was coffee time, peach time, banana time, fish time, coke time, and, of course, lunch time. Other interruptions, which formed part of the series but were not verbally recognized as times, were window time, pickup time, and the staggered quitting times of Sammy and Ike. These latter unnamed times did not involve the partaking of refreshments.

My attention was first drawn to this times business during my first week of employment when I was encouraged to join in the sharing of two peaches. It was Sammy who provided the peaches; he drew them from his lunch box after making the announcement, "Peach time!" On this first occasion I refused the proffered fruit, but thereafter regularly consumed my half peach. Sammy continued to provide the peaches and to make the "Peach time!" announcement, although there were days when Ike would remind him that it was peach time, urging him to hurry up with the mid-morning snack. Ike invariably complained about the quality of the fruit, and his complaints fed the fires of continued banter between peach donor and critical recipient. I did find the fruit a bit on the scrubby side but felt, before I achieved insight into the function of peach time, that Ike was showing poor manners by looking a gift horse in the mouth. I wondered why Sammy continued to share his peaches with such an ingrate.

Banana time followed peach time by approximately an hour. Sammy again provided the refreshments, namely, one banana. There was, however, no four-way sharing of Sammy's banana. Ike would gulp it down by himself after surreptitiously extracting it from Sammy's lunch box, kept on a shelf behind Sammy's work station. Each morning, after making the snatch, Ike would call out, "Banana time!" and proceed to down his prize while Sammy made futile protests and denunciations. George would join in with mild remonstrances, sometimes scolding Sammy for making so much fuss. The banana was one which Sammy brought for his own consumption at lunch time; he never did get to eat his banana, but kept bringing one for his lunch. At first this daily theft startled and amazed me. Then I grew to look forward to the daily seizure and the verbal interaction which followed.

Window time came next. It followed banana time as a regular consequence of Ike's castigation by the indignant Sammy. After "taking" repeated references to himself as a person badly lacking in morality and character, Ike would "finally" retaliate by opening the window which faced Sammy's machine, to let the "cold air" blow in on Sammy. The slandering which would, in its echolalic repetition, wear down Ike's patience and forbearance usually took the form of the invidious comparison: "George is a good daddy! Ike is a bad man! A very bad man!" Opening the window would take a little time to accomplish and would involve a great deal of verbal interplay between Ike and

Sammy, both before and after the event. Ike would threaten, make feints toward the window, then finally open it. Sammy would protest, argue, and make claims that the air blowing in on him would give him a cold; he would eventually have to leave his machine to close the window. Sometimes the weather was slightly chilly, and the draft from the window unpleasant; but cool or hot, windy or still, window time arrived each day. (I assume that it was originally a cold season development.) George's part in this interplay, in spite of the "good daddy" laudations, was to encourage Ike in his window work. He would stress the tonic values of fresh air and chide Sammy for his unappreciativeness.

Following window time came lunch time, a formally designated half-hour for the midday repast and rest break. At this time, informal interaction would feature exchanges between Ike and George. The former would start eating his lunch a few minutes before noon, and the latter, in his role as straw boss, would censure him for malobservance of the rules. Ike's off-beat luncheon usually involved a previous tampering with George's alarm clock. Ike would set the clock ahead a few minutes in order to maintain his eating schedule without detection, and George would discover these small daylight saving changes.

The first "time" interruption of the day I did not share. It occurred soon after I arrived on the job, at eight o'clock. George and Ike would share a small pot of coffee brewed on George's hot plate.

Pickup time, fish time, and coke time came in the afternoon. I name it pickup time to represent the official visit of the man who made daily calls to cart away boxes of clicked materials. The arrival of the pickup man, a Negro, was always a noisy one, like the arrival of a daily passenger train in an isolated small town. Interaction attained a quick peak of intensity to crowd into a few minutes all communications, necessary and otherwise. Exchanges invariably included loud depreciations by the pickup man of the amount of work accomplished in the clicking department during the preceding twenty-four hours. Such scoffing would be on the order of "Is that all you've got done? What do you boys do all day?" These devaluations would be countered with allusions to the "soft job" enjoyed by the pickup man. During the course of the exchanges news items would be dropped, some of serious import, such as reports of accomplished or impending layoffs in the various plants of the company, or of gains or losses in orders for company products. Most of the news items, however, involved bits of information on plant employees told in a light vein. Information relayed by the clicker operators was usually told about each other, mainly in the form of summaries of the most recent kidding sequences. Some of this material was repetitive, carried over from day to day. Sammy would be the butt of most of this newscasting, although he would make occasional counter-reports on Ike and George. An invariable part of the interactional content of pickup time was Ike's introduction of the pickup man to George. "Meet Mr. Papeatis!" Ike would say in mock solemnity and dignity. Each day the pickup man "met" Mr. Papeatis, to the obvious irritation of the latter. Another pickup time invariably would bring Baby (or Mable) into the interaction. George would always issue the loud warning to the pickup man: "Now I want you to stay away from Baby! She's Henry's girl!" Henry was a burly Negro with a booming bass voice who made infrequent trips to the clicking room with lift-truck loads of materials. He was reputedly quite a ladies' man among the colored population of the factory. George's warning to "Stay away from Baby!" was issued to every Negro who entered the shop. Baby's only part in this was to laugh at the horseplay.

About mid-afternoon came fish time. George and Ike would stop work for a few minutes to consume some sort of pickled fish which Ike provided. Neither Sammy nor

I partook of this nourishment, nor were we invited. For this omission I was grateful; the fish, brought in a newspaper and with head and tail intact, produced a reverse effect on my appetite. George and Ike seemed to share a great liking for fish. Each Friday night, as a regular ritual, they would enjoy a fish dinner together at a nearby restaurant. On these nights Ike would work until 8:30 and leave the plant with George.

Coke time came late in the afternoon, and was an occasion for total participation. The four of us took turns in buying the drinks and in making the trip for them to a fourth floor vending machine. Through George's manipulation of the situation, it eventually became my daily chore to go after the cokes; the straw boss had noted that I made a much faster trip to the fourth floor and back than Sammy or Ike.

Sammy left the plant at 5:30, and Ike ordinarily retired from the scene an hour and a half later. These quitting times were not marked by any distinctive interaction save the one regular exchange between Sammy and George over the former's "early washup." Sammy's tendency was to crowd his washing up toward five o'clock, and it was George's concern to keep it from further creeping advance. After Ike's departure came Boo's arrival. Boo's was a striking personality productive of a change in topics of conversation to fill in the last hour of the long workday.

Themes

To put flesh, so to speak, on this interactional frame of "times," my work group had developed various "themes" of verbal interplay which had become standardized in their repetition. These topics of conversation ranged in quality from an extreme of nonsensical chatter to another extreme of serious discourse. Unlike the times, these themes flowed one into the other in no particular sequence of predictability. Serious conversation could suddenly melt into horseplay, and vice versa. In the middle of a serious discussion on the high cost of living, Ike might drop a weight behind the easily startled Sammy, who hit him over the head with a dusty paper sack. Interaction would immediately drop to a low comedy exchange of slaps, threats, guffaws, and disapprobations which would invariably include a ten-minute echolalia of "Ike is a bad man, a very bad man! George is a good daddy, a very fine man!" Or, on the other hand, a stream of such invidious comparisons as followed a surreptitious switching-off of Sammy's machine by the playful Ike might merge suddenly into a discussion of the pros and cons of saving for one's funeral.

"Kidding themes" were usually started by George or Ike, and Sammy was usually the butt of the joke. Sometimes Ike would have to "take it," seldom George. One favorite kidding theme involved Sammy's alleged receipt of $100 a month from his son. The points stressed were that Sammy did not have to work long hours, or did not have to work at all, because he had a son to support him. George would always point out that he sent money to his daughter; she did not send money to him. Sammy received occasional calls from his wife, and his claim that these calls were requests to shop for groceries on the way home were greeted with feigned disbelief. Sammy was ribbed for being closely watched, bossed, and henpecked by his wife, and the expression "Are you a man or mouse?" became an echolalic utterance, used both in and out of the original context.

Ike, who shared his machine and the work scheduled for it with Boo, the night operator, came in for constant invidious comparison on the subject of output. The socially isolated Boo, who chose work rather than sleep on his lonely night shift, kept up a high level of performance, and George never tired of pointing this out to Ike. It so happened that Boo, an Arabian Moslem from Palestine, had no use for Jews in general; and Ike, who was Jewish, had no use for Boo in particular. Whenever George would extol Boo's previous night's production, Ike would try to turn the conversation into a general discussion on the need for educating the Arabs. George, never permitting the development of serious discussion on this topic, would repeat a smirking warning, "You watch out for Boo! He's got a long knife!"

The "poom poom" theme was one that caused no sting. It would come up several times a day to be enjoyed as unbarbed fun by the three older clicker operators. Ike was usually the one to raise the question, "How many times you go poom poom last night?" The person questioned usually replied with claims of being "too old for poom poom." If this theme did develop a goat, it was I. When it was pointed out that I was a younger man, this provided further grist for the poom poom mill. I soon grew weary of this poom poom business, so dear to the hearts of the three old satyrs, and, knowing where the conversation would inevitably lead, winced whenever Ike brought up the subject. . . .

Serious themes included the relating of major misfortunes suffered in the past by group members. George referred again and again to the loss, by fire, of his business establishment. Ike's chief complaints centered around a chronically ill wife who had undergone various operations and periods of hospital care. Ike spoke with discouragement of the expenses attendant upon hiring a housekeeper for himself and his children; he referred with disappointment and disgust to a teen-age son, an inept lad who "couldn't even fix his own lunch. He couldn't even make himself a sandwich!" Sammy's reminiscences centered on the loss of a flourishing business when he had to flee Europe ahead of Nazi invasion.

But all serious topics were not tales of woe. One favorite serious theme which was optimistic in tone could be called either "Danelly's future" or "getting Danelly a better job." It was known that I had been attending "college," the magic door to opportunity, although my specific course of study remained somewhat obscure. Suggestions poured forth on good lines of work to get into, and these suggestions were backed with accounts of friends, and friends of friends, who had made good via the academic route. My answer to the expected question, "Why are you working here?" always stressed the "lots of overtime" feature, and this explanation seemed to suffice for short-range goals.

There was one theme of especially solemn import, the "professor theme." This theme might also be termed "George's daughter's marriage theme"; for the recent marriage of George's only child was inextricably bound up with George's connection with higher learning. The daughter had married the son of a professor who instructed in one of the local colleges. This professor theme was not in the strictest sense a conversation piece; when the subject came up, George did all the talking. The two Jewish operatives remained silent as they listened with deep respect, if not actual awe, to George's accounts of the Big Wedding which, including the wedding pictures, entailed an expense of $1000. It was monologue, but there was listening, there was communication, the sacred communication of a temple, when George told of going for Sunday afternoon walks on the Midway with the professor, or of joining the professor for a Sunday dinner. Whenever he spoke of the professor, his daughter, the wedding, or even of the new son-in-law, who remained for the most part in the background, a sort of incidental like the wedding cake, George was complete master of the interaction. His manner, in speaking to the rank-and-file of clicker operators, was indeed that of master deigning to notice his underlings. I came to the conclusion that it was the professor connection, not the straw-boss-ship or the extra nickel an hour, which provided the fount of George's superior status in the group.

If the professor theme may be regarded as the cream of verbal interaction, the "chatter themes" should be classed as the dregs. The chatter themes were hardly themes at all; perhaps they should be labelled "verbal states," or "oral autisms." Some were of doubtful status as communication; they were like the howl or cry of an animal responding to its own physiological state. They were exclamations, ejaculations, snatches of song or doggerel, talkings-to-oneself, mutterings. Their classification as themes would rest on their repetitive character. They were echolalic utterances, repeated over and over. An already mentioned example would be Sammy's repetition of "George is a good daddy, a very fine man! Ike is a bad man, a very bad man!" Also, Sammy's repetition of "Don't bother me! Can't you see I'm busy? I'm a very busy man!" for ten minutes after Ike had dropped a weight behind him would fit the classification. Ike would shout "Mamariba!" at intervals between repetition of bits of verse, such as:

> Mama on the bed,
> Papa on the floor,
> Baby in the crib
> Says giver some more!

Sometimes the three operators would pick up one of these simple chatterings in a sort of chorus. "Are you man or mouse? I ask you, are you man or mouse?" was a favorite of this type.

So initial discouragement with the meagerness of social interaction I now recognized as due to lack of observation. The interaction was there, in constant flow. It captured attention and held interest to make the long day pass. The twelve hours of "click, ———— move die, ———— click, ———— move die" became as easy to endure as eight hours of varied activity in the oil fields or eight hours of playing the piece-work game in a machine shop. The "beast of boredom" was gentled to the harmlessness of a kitten.

BLACK FRIDAY: DISINTEGRATION OF THE GROUP

But all this was before "Black Friday." Events of that dark day shattered the edifice of interaction, its framework of times and mosaic of themes, and reduced the work situation to a state of social atomization and machine-tending drudgery. The explosive element was introduced deliberately, but without prevision of its consequences.

On Black Friday, Sammy was not present; he was on vacation. There was no peach time that morning, of course, and no banana time. But George and Ike held their coffee time, as usual, and a steady flow of themes was filling the morning quite adequately. It seemed like a normal day in the making, at least one which was going to meet the somewhat reduced expectations created by Sammy's absence.

Suddenly I was possessed of an inspiration for modification of the professor theme. When the idea struck, I was working at Sammy's machine, clicking out leather parts for billfolds. It was not difficult to get the attention of close neighbor Ike to suggest *sotto voce*, "Why don't you tell him you saw the professor teaching in a barber college on Madison Street? . . . Make it near Halsted Street."

Ike thought this one over for a few minutes, and caught the vision of its possibilities. After an interval of steady application to his clicking, he informed the unsuspecting George of his near West Side discovery; he had seen the professor busy at his instructing in a barber college in the lower reaches of Hobohemia.

George reacted to this announcement with stony silence. The burden of questioning Ike for further details on his discovery fell upon me. Ike had not elaborated his story very much before we realized that the show was not going over. George kept getting redder in the face, and more tight-lipped; he slammed into his clicking with increased vigor. I made one last weak attempt to keep the play on the road by remarking that barber colleges paid pretty well. George turned to hiss at me, "You'll have to go to Kankakee with Ike!" I dropped the subject. Ike whispered to me, "George is sore!"

George was indeed sore. He didn't say another word the rest of the morning. There was no conversation at lunchtime, nor was there any after lunch. A pall of silence had fallen over the clicker room. Fish time fell a casualty. George did not touch the coke I brought for him. A very long, very dreary afternoon dragged on. Finally, after Ike left for home, George broke the silence to reveal his feelings to me: "Ike acts like a five-year-old, not a man! He doesn't even have the respect of the niggers. But he's got to act like a man around here! He's always fooling around! I'm going to stop that! I'm going to show him his place! . . . Jews will ruin you, if you let them. I don't care if he sings, but the first time he mentions my name, I'm going to shut him up! It's always 'Meet Mr. Papeatis! George is a good daddy!' And all that. He's paid to work! If he doesn't work, I'm going to tell Joe!"

Then came a succession of dismal workdays devoid of times and barren of themes. Ike did not sing, nor did he recite bawdy verse. The shop songbird was caught in the grip of icy winter. What meager communication there was took a sequence of patterns which proved interesting only in retrospect.

For three days, George would not speak to Ike. Ike made several weak attempts to break the wall of silence which George had put between them, but George did not respond; it was as if he did not hear. George would speak to me, on infrequent occasions, and so would Ike. They did not speak to each other.

On the third day George advised me of his new communication policy, designed for dealing with Ike, and for Sammy, too, when the latter returned to work. Interaction was now on a "strictly business" basis, with emphasis to be placed on raising the level of shop output. The effect of this new policy on production remained indeterminate. Before the fourth day had ended, George got carried away by his narrowed interests to the point of making sarcastic remarks about the poor work performances of the absent Sammy. Although addressed to me, these caustic depreciations were obviously for the benefit of Ike. Later in the day Ike spoke to me, for George's benefit, of Sammy's outstanding ability to turn out billfold parts. For the next four days, the prevailing silence of the shop was occasionally broken by either harsh criticism or fulsome praise of Sammy's outstanding workmanship. I did not risk replying to either impeachment or panegyric for fear of involvement in further situational deteriorations.

Twelve-hour days were creeping again at snail's pace. The strictly business communications were of no help, and the sporadic bursts of distaste or enthusiasm for Sammy's clicking ability helped very little. With the return of boredom, came a return of fatigue. My legs tired as the afternoons dragged on, and I became engaged in conscious efforts to rest one by shifting my weight to the other. I would pause in my work to stare through the barred windows at the grimy brick wall across the alley; and, turning my head, I would notice that Ike was staring at the wall too. George would do very little work after Ike left the shop at night. He would sit in a chair and complain of weariness and sore feet.

In desperation, I fell back on my game of work, my blues and greens and whites, my ovals and trapezoids, and my scraping the block. I came to surpass Boo, the energetic night worker, in volume of output. George referred to me as a "day Boo" (day-shift Boo) and suggested that I "keep" Sammy's machine. I managed to avoid this promotion, and consequent estrangement with Sammy, by pleading attachment to my own machine.

When Sammy returned to work, discovery of the cleavage between George and Ike left him stunned. "They were the best of friends!" he said to me in bewilderment.

George now offered Sammy direct, savage criticisms of his work. For several days the good-natured Sammy endured these verbal aggressions without losing his temper; but when George shouted at him "You work like a preacher!" Sammy became very angry, indeed. I had a few anxious moments when I thought that the two old friends were going to come to blows.

Then, thirteen days after Black Friday, came an abrupt change in the pattern of interaction. George and Ike spoke to each other again, in friendly conversation: I noticed Ike talking to George after lunch. The two had newspapers of fish at George's cabinet. Ike was excited; he said, "I'll pull up a chair!" The two ate for ten minutes. . . . It seems that they went up to the 22nd Street Exchange together during lunch period to cash pay checks.

That afternoon Ike and Sammy started to play again, and Ike burst once more into song. Old themes reappeared as suddenly as the desert flowers in spring. At first, George managed to maintain some show of the dignity of superordination. When Ike started to sing snatches of "You Are My Sunshine," George suggested that he get "more production." Then Ike backed up George in pressuring Sammy for more production. Sammy turned this exhortation into low comedy by calling Ike a "slave driver" and by shouting over and over again, "Don't bother me! I'm a busy man!" On one occasion, as if almost overcome with joy and excitement, Sammy cried out, "Don't bother me! I'll tell Rothman! [the company president] I'll tell the union! Don't mention my name! I hate you!"

I knew that George was definitely back into the spirit of the thing when he called to Sammy, "Are you man or mouse?" He kept up the "man or mouse" chatter for some time.

George was for a time reluctant to accept fruit when it was offered to him, and he did not make a final capitulation to coke time until five days after renewal of the fun and fooling. Strictly speaking, there never was a return to banana time, peach time, or window time. However, the sharing and snitching of fruit did go on once more, and the window in front of Sammy's machine played a more prominent part than ever in the renaissance of horseplay in the clicker room. In fact, the "rush to the window" became an integral part of increasingly complex themes and repeated sequences of interaction. This window rushing became especially bound up with new developments which featured what may be termed the "anal gesture."[10] Introduced by Ike, and given backing by an enthusiastic, very playful George, the anal gesture became a key component of fun and fooling during the remaining weeks of my stay in the shop: Ike broke wind, and put his head in his hand on the block as Sammy grabbed a rod and made a mock rush to open the window. He beat Ike on the head, and George threw some water on him, playfully. In came the Negro head of the Leather Department; he remarked jokingly that we should take out the machines and make a playroom out of the shop.

Of course, George's demand for greater production was metamorphized into horseplay. His shout of "Production please!" became a chatter theme to accompany the varied antics of Ike and Sammy.

The professor theme was dropped completely. George never again mentioned his Sunday walks on the Midway with the professor.

CONCLUSIONS

Speculative assessment of the possible significance of my observations on informal interaction in the clicking room may be set forth in a series of general statements.

First, in regard to possible practical application to problems of industrial management, these observations seem to support the generally accepted notion that one key source of job satisfaction lies in the informal interaction shared by members of a work group. In the clicking-room situation the spontaneous development of a pattern combination of horseplay, serious conversation, and frequent sharing of food and drink reduced the monotony of simple, repetitive operations to the point where a regular schedule of long work days became livable. This kind of group interplay may be termed "consumatory" in the sense indicated by Dewey, when he makes a basic distinction between "instrumental" and "consumatory" communication.[11] The enjoyment of communication "for its own sake" as "mere sociabilities," as "free, aimless social intercourse," brings job satisfaction, at least job endurance, to work situations largely bereft of creative experience.

In regard to another managerial concern, employee productivity, any appraisal of the influence of group interaction upon clicking-room output could be no more than roughly impressionistic. I obtained no evidence to warrant a claim that banana time, or any of its accompaniments in consumatory interaction, boosted production. To the contrary, my diary recordings express an occasional perplexity in the form of "How does this company manage to stay in business?" However, I did not obtain sufficient evidence to indicate that, under the prevailing conditions of laissez-faire management, the output of our group would have been more impressive if the playful cavorting of three middle-aged gentlemen about the barred windows had never been. As far as achievement of managerial goals is concerned, the most that could be suggested is that leavening the deadly boredom of individualized work routines with a concurrent flow of group festivities had a negative effect on turnover. I left the group, with sad reluctance, under the pressure of strong urgings to accept a research fellowship which would involve no factory toil. My fellow clickers stayed with their machines to carry on their labors in the spirit of banana time.

Theoretical Considerations

Secondly, possible contribution to ongoing sociological inquiry into the behavior of small groups, in general, and factory work groups, in particular, may lie in one or more of the following ideational products of my clicking-room experience:

1. In their day-long confinement together in a small room spatially and socially isolated from other work areas of the factory the Clicking Department employees found themselves ecologically situated for development of a "natural" group. Such a development did take place; from worker intercommunications did emerge the full-blown sociocultural system of consumatory interactions which I came to share, observe, and record in the process of my socialization.

2. These interactions had a content which could be abstracted from the total existential flow of observable doings and sayings for labelling and objective consideration. That is, they represented a distinctive subculture, with its recurring patterns of reciprocal influencings which I have described as times and themes.

3. From these interactions may also be abstracted a social structure of statuses and roles. This structure may be discerned in the carrying out of the various informal activities which provide the content of the subculture of the group. The times and themes were performed with a system of roles which formed a sort of pecking hierarchy. Horseplay had its initiators and its victims, its amplifiers and its chorus; kidding had its attackers and attacked, its least attacked and its most attacked, its ready accep-

tors of attack and its strong resistors to attack. The fun went on with the participation of all, but within the controlling frame of status, a matter of who can say or do what to whom and get away with it.

4. In both the cultural content and the social structure of clicker group interaction could be seen the permeation of influences which flowed from the various multiple group memberships of the participants. Past and present "other-group" experiences or anticipated "outside" social connections provided significant materials for the building of themes and for the establishment and maintenance of status and role relationships. The impact of reference group affiliations on clicking-room interaction was notably revealed in the sacred, status-conferring expression of the professor theme. This impact was brought into very sharp focus in developments which followed my attempt to degrade the topic, and correlatively, to demote George.

5. Stability of the clicking-room social system was never threatened by immediate outside pressures. Ours was not an instrumental group, subject to disintegration in a losing struggle against environmental obstacles or oppositions. It was not striving for corporate goals; nor was it faced with the enmity of other groups. It was strictly a consumatory group, devoted to the maintenance of patterns of self-entertainment. Under existing conditions, disruption of unity could come only from within.

Potentials for breakdown were endemic in the interpersonal interactions involved in conducting the group's activities. Patterns of fun and fooling had developed within a matrix of frustration. Tensions born of long hours of relatively meaningless work were released in the mock aggressions of horseplay. In the recurrent attack, defense, and counterattack there continually lurked the possibility that words or gestures harmless in conscious intent might cross the subtle boundary of accepted, playful aggression to be perceived as real assault. While such an occurrence might incur displeasure no more lasting than necessary for the quick clarification or creation of kidding norms, it might also spark a charge of hostility sufficient to disorganize the group.

A contributory potential for breakdown from within lay in the dissimilar "other group" experiences of the operators. These other-group affiliations and identifications could provide differences in tastes and sensitivities, including appreciation of humor, differences which could make maintenance of consensus in regard to kidding norms a hazardous process of trial and error adjustments.

6. The risk involved in this trial and error determination of consensus on fun and fooling in a touchy situation of frustration — mock aggression — was made evident when I attempted to introduce alterations in the professor theme. The group disintetrated, *instanter*. That is, there was an abrupt cessation of the interactions which constituted our groupness. Although both George and I were solidly linked in other-group affiliations with the higher learning, there was not enough agreement in our attitudes toward university professors to prevent the interactional development which shattered our factory play group. George perceived my offered alterations as a real attack, and he responded with strong hostility directed against Ike, the perceived assailant, and Sammy, a fellow traveler.

My innovations, if accepted, would have lowered the tone of the sacred professor theme, if not to "Stay Away From Baby" ribaldry, then at least to the verbal slapstick level of "finding Danelly an apartment." Such a downgrading of George's reference group would, in turn, have downgraded George. His status in the shop group hinged largely upon his claimed relations with the professor.

7. Integration of our group was fully restored after a series of changes in the patterning and quality in clicking-room interaction. It might be said that reintegration took place *in* these changes, that the series was a progressive one of step-by-step im-

provement in relations, that re-equilibration was in process during the three weeks that passed between initial communication collapse and complete return to "normal" interaction.

The cycle of loss and recovery of equilibrium may be crudely charted according to the following sequence of phases: (a) the stony silence of "not speaking"; (b) the confining of communication to formal matters connected with work routines; (c) the return of informal give-and-take in the form of harshly sarcastic kidding, mainly on the subject of work performance, addressed to a neutral go-between for the "benefit" of the object of aggression; (d) highly emotional direct attack, and counter-attack, in the form of criticism and defense of work performance; (e) a sudden rapprochement expressed in serious, dignified, but friendly conversation; (f) return to informal interaction in the form of mutually enjoyed mock aggression; (g) return to informal interaction in the form of regular patterns of sharing food and drink.

The group had disintegrated when George withdrew from participation; and, since the rest of us were at all times ready for rapprochement, reintegration was dependent upon his "return." Therefore, each change of phase in interaction on the road to recovery could be said to represent an increment of return on George's part. Or, conversely, each phase could represent an increment of reacceptance of punished deviants. Perhaps more generally applicable to description of a variety of reunion situations would be conceptualization of the phase changes as increments of reassociation without an atomistic differentiation of the "movements" of individuals.

8. To point out that George played a key role in this particular case of re-equilibration is not to suggest that the homeostatic controls of a social system may be located in a type of role or in a patterning of role relationships. Such controls could be but partially described in terms of human interaction; they would be functional to the total configuration of conditions within the field of influence. The automatic controls of a mechanical system operate as such only under certain achieved and controlled conditions. The human body recovers from disease when conditions for such homeostasis are "right." The clicking-room group regained equilibrium under certain undetermined conditions. One of a number of other possible outcomes could have developed had conditions not been favorable for recovery.

For purposes of illustration, and from reflection on the case, I would consider the following as possibly necessary conditions for reintegration of our group: (a) Continued monotony of work operations; (b) Continued lack of a comparatively adequate substitute for the fun and fooling release from work tensions; (c) Inability of the operatives to escape from the work situation or from each other, within the work situation. George could not fire Ike or Sammy to remove them from his presence, and it would have been difficult for the three middle-aged men to find other jobs if they were to quit the shop. Shop space was small, and the machines close together. Like a submarine crew, they had to "live together"; (d) Lack of conflicting definitions of the situation after Ike's perception of George's reaction to the "barber college" attack. George's anger and his punishment of the offenders were perceived as justified; (e) Lack of introduction of new issues or causes which might have carried justification for new attacks and counter-attacks, thus leading interaction into a spiral of conflict and crystallization of conflict norms. For instance, had George reported his offenders to the superintendent for their poor work performance; had he, in his anger, committed some offense which would have led to reporting of a grievance to local union officials; had he made his anti-Semitic remarks in the presence of Ike or Sammy, or had I relayed these remarks to them; had I tried to "take over" Sammy's machine, as George had urged; then the interactional outcome might have been permanent disintegration of the group.

9. Whether or not the particular patterning of interactional change previously noted is somehow typical of a "re-equilibration process" is not a major question here.

My purpose in discriminating the seven changes is primarily to suggest that re-equilibration, when it does occur, may be described in observable phases and that the emergence of each succeeding phase should be dependent upon the configuration of conditions of the preceding one. Alternative eventual outcomes may change in their probabilities, as the phases succeed each other, just as prognosis for recovery in sickness may change as the disease situation changes.

10. Finally, discrimination of phase changes in social process may have practical as well as scientific value. Trained and skillful administrators might follow the practice in medicine of introducing aids to re-equilibration when diagnosis shows that they are needed.

NOTES AND REFERENCES

1. Charles R. Walker and Robert H. Guest. *The Man on the Assembly Line* Harvard University Press, Cambridge, 1952.
2. *Ibid.*, p. 77.
3. *Ibid.*, p. 68.
4. Donald F. Roy. "Work Satisfaction and Social Reward in Quota Achievement: An Analysis of Piecework Incentive." *American Sociological Review*, XVIII (October 1953), pp. 507–14.
5. All names used are fictitious.
6. Henri de Man. *The Psychology of Socialism*. Henry Holt and Company, New York, 1927. pp. 80–81.
7. *Ibid.*, p. 81.
8. Roy, *op. cit.*
9. Lucille Milner. *Education of An American Liberal*. Horizon Press, New York, 1954, p. 97.
10. I have been puzzled to note widespread appreciation of this gesture in the "consumatory" communication of the working men of this nation. For the present I leave it to clinical psychologists to account for the nature and pervasiveness of this social bond.
11. John Dewey. *Experience and Nature*. Open Court Publishing Co., Chicago, 1925, pp. 202–06.

Team Spirit vs. the Individual Achiever

Alvin F. Zander

Most people would agree these days that organizations run on individual achievement. With few exceptions, it seems, we consider teamwork and pride in one's group to be either old-fashioned notions or sources of restraint on individual effort. Even in athletics, the traditional bastion of esprit de corps, individual aspiration appears to be gaining the upper hand as superstars leave their championship teams for monetarily greener pastures. Selfless commitment to a group goal, we assume, is an outmoded value, obsolete in business firms where the only thing members have in common is their employer.

Most psychological research reflects this emphasis on the individual. "Need for Achievement" (often called N-Ach, or Ms for *motive for success*) has been one of the most studied variables in our field. David McClelland, a pioneer in this area, has even attempted to show that the rise of great civilizations depended on the citizens having high aspirations for individual achievement. Psychologists have seen no need for comparable research on a "need for group achievement." But a great deal of recent research, both in large organizations and in group dynamics laboratories, shows that teamwork and team spirit never die, and are often more important than individual achievement.

In many organizations, I have seen people work harder for small work teams than for themselves. The success of these organizations, moreover, whether they be businesses, Government agencies or factories, often depends upon this teamwork.

A couple of years ago, for example, I had the opportunity to study assembly-line groups in a slipper factory. Each line was composed of six to eight women who sat behind each other and sewed different parts to slippers moving by on a belt. At the end of the line the completed products fell into a box and were counted on a meter. The management set each group's daily production goal and told them how they did, but did not base their salary on how many they completed or whether they met the goal. Yet when I asked them a series of questions to determine whether they placed more importance on their own or their group's success, they overwhelmingly felt the group to be more important.

TEAMWORK IN BREWERIES AND BUSINESS

I found a similar situation in a Swedish brewery, where I asked the members of work groups the same kinds of questions. These men worked in groups of six to 10 on a wide variety of tasks that ranged from driving trucks to research and plant management. Most rated their concern for their group's achievement as high as for their own, while expressing much less concern for the success of the company as a whole. I also found that in United Fund organizations, the executive board members felt more pride in their local organization's success than in their personal efforts. And in spite of the individual athletes who make headlines when they strike off for themselves, team spirit is the rule rather than the exception in sports. In fact, both amateurs and professionals generally feel that a team can't become a winner without it.

SELF-CENTERED STRIVER

Because most leaders and administrators ignore or underestimate the importance of teamwork and group spirit, there has been little research on work groups. While desire for group success appears to be a promising source of energy for a social group, we know surprisingly little about what makes its members want to succeed or what creates a sense of group pride. Most textbooks on management and administration assume that the organization man is a self-centered striver. Even when such a person works hard for the company, many managers and psychologists presume his interest lies primarily in taking care of himself. Rarely has anyone seriously considered that members value group success so strongly that this desire increases their effort.

The first laboratory experiments my students and I conducted on this problem established clearly that groups with stronger team spirit perform better than those with less. As we progressed, we began to see similarities in the ways our groups performed and the ways that the Achievement Motivation theory of John W. Atkinson and N. T. Feather predicted individuals would perform. So we developed a model to explain team spirit, patterned after Atkinson and Feather's model to explain individual striving. Our group model then guided our subsequent research strategy.

Atkinson and Feather propose that when a person has an opportunity to choose a goal and to decide how hard he will work for it, the final decision depends on two conflicting tendencies: his need for achievement and his fear of failure. They believe these tendencies form enduring dispositions, which can be measured by analyzing the stories their subjects make up about a set of pictures from the Thematic Apperception Test. Basically, the two opposing tendencies work like this: People with strong motives for success (high Ms) tend to choose goals that are challenging—neither so easy as to make success certain, since then it wouldn't be much of an achievement, nor so difficult as to make failure certain. People with strong motives to avoid failure (high Maf), on the other hand, tend to choose goals at the extremes of difficult—either too easy, so they will be assured of success, or too difficult, so they can say, in effect, "I made a noble effort, but I never really had a chance anyway." All decisions about goals, then, represent a compromise between the individual's two motives and his evaluation of how rewarding it would be to succeed.

Groups, we suggest, operate in a similar manner. When members have a strong desire for their group to succeed (high Dgs) they tend to choose "realistic" goals and work hard for them. When they have a strong desire to avoid failure (high Dgaf) they tend to choose either very easy or very hard goals, and may not work as much. Like their individual counterparts, groups with low Dgs tend not to perform as well as groups with high Dgs. Similarly, groups with strong desire to avoid failure perform more poorly than groups with low Dgaf. To say that a *person* has a strong desire for group success simply means that he will feel satisfied if his group accomplishes its goal; likewise, a strong fear of failure means that he will feel embarrassed if his group does not succeed.

The main difference between group achievement motivation and individual achievement motivation lies in our assumption that the desire for group success is not a permanent trait of individuals, but rather a motive that develops in particular situations. Since group achievement motivation has strong effects that are separate from the effects of individual achievement motivation, many of our laboratory experiments have aimed at discovering what particular circumstances nourish its development.

In one experiment, we attempted to induce a strong sense of unity in some of our subject groups (high-school boys) by telling them that their abilities and temperaments were well matched, that they were a team, and by asking them to choose a group name. In other groups we tried to develop a weaker sense of unity by addressing them as individuals, and telling them they did not match up well. When we asked the boys to set performance goals for themselves on a "Communications Coding Test," members of the strong group consistently set more realistic and challenging intermediate goals than members of weak groups, who tended to choose very easy or very difficult goals. Thus a sense of unity is one factor that prompts a group's wish for success and improves its actual performance.

LEADERS, GOALS AND DOMINOS

In another experiment we asked groups of boys to make certain patterns with dominos as quickly as they could. In each group we designated one boy as a leader who had to put his piece in the proper place before the other members could add theirs. When we asked them to specify goals, we found that the boys with more important, central positions chose realistic goals more regularly than those in less important, peripheral positions.

We found a similar situation in local United Fund organizations. Board members who held central positions in their groups expressed more concern for the success of their agency than did members in more peripheral positions. A second important factor that increases team spirit and desire for success, then, is having increased responsibility for one's group's outcome.

In order to test the effects of the desire to avoid failure, we designed a somewhat different experiment. We tried to arouse Dgs in some groups by giving them poker chips when they met their goals and Dgaf in other groups by taking chips away from an initial pile of 30 when they failed. We explained that we would count their total chips at the end of the test as the group score. The Dgs groups generally chose more reasonable goals than the Dgaf groups. Working conditions that emphasize the negative consequences of failure, we may infer, actually reduce performance.

One of the surest ways a group can develop a strong fear of failure is for it to have failed often in the past. Some of our earliest experiments showed that repeated failure leads group members to see themselves and others as less helpful, to feel less responsible for their group's outcome, and to say that it was less important for them to belong to the group. All of these effects tend to decrease Dgs and maintain a vicious cycle of failure. Groups that set their own goals can sometimes climb out of this cycle by reducing their goal to a level they can reach, although they often resist such an admission of defeat. But groups that do not exercise effective control over their own goals do not even have this way out.

WHICH FUNDS WORKED, AND WHY

We recently examined in detail a real-life example of repeated failures among United Fund organizations. Half of the 46 groups we studied had failed to reach their fund-raising goals for the past four years in a row. The others had been successful in all of the previous four years. Officers in the failing Funds did not lower their goals, presumably because of community pressure to aim at meeting their needs fully. We discovered that the board members of these Funds felt differently about their organizations than members of successful Funds.

Members of the failing groups worked longer hours, enjoyed their work less, had less pride in their organization and in their personal efforts, blamed volunteers to a greater degree, and thought success was less important. In setting goals, they preferred to beat their previous year's performance rather than to meet their set goal, and would have chosen to eliminate goal-setting altogether, if possible. Failure clearly laid the groundwork for future failure: so long as they could not meet their quota, motivation dropped and efficiency decreased, contributing to another poor performance, another cycle of failure, and more difficult goals. Successful Funds, on the other hand, set challenging goals, harder than any they had yet attained, but not impossible. Success bred stronger motivation and increased efficiency, which in turn led to further success and an upward spiral of performance.

FORCING GROUP FAILURES

Research on other organizations often shows that managers tend to set unrealistically high goals for their workers. If the same process we've found in our laboratory and the United Fund operates in corporations and public agencies, these managers may be forcing their workers into failure. Regardless of the goal a manager sets, a group will develop aspirations of its own. By setting the official goal too high, an ambitious manager may actually induce the groups he or she supervises to set their own aspirations below the level they are capable of attaining.

The simplest and perhaps most effective road out of this bind is to include workers in the goal-setting process, which will moderate management's hopes. It is then very important to combat, as much as possible, the negative consequences that usually follow from revising goals downward to reachable levels.

Management must also provide accurate and continual feedback to groups about their performance. We have found that without feedback, many groups naturally overestimate their output and consequently set goals much higher than they can reach. This tendency alone can sometimes initiate a cycle of failure.

As we concluded our series of experiments on the conditions that facilitate Dgs or Dgaf, we still faced one major question: How could we be sure these group-oriented motives act independently of motives for individual achievement and fear of failure? Some of our colleagues had already suggested that we may have simply created conditions that tapped individual motives and thereby raised or lowered performance. To settle this issue, we designed a couple of fairly complex experiments.

In the first, we formed 16 groups of high-school boys, each with one high on motive to succeed, one high on motive to avoid failure, and one who scored intermediate on both measures. As in an earlier experiment, we asked them to arrange dominos in various specific patterns, with one central person always placing his domino before the other two could place theirs. Half of the time the high-Ms person occupied the central position, while the high-Maf person took it the other half. We reasoned that if the two behaved differently in the peripheral position, but similarly in the central position, then the group situation must be responsible for inducing the high-Maf person to act like a high-Ms person when he occupied the central role. This was precisely what happened.

The high achievers acted as expected in both positions; they chose realistic but challenging goals. The high fear of failure boys acted as expected when they occupied peripheral roles, choosing goals either too high or too low. But they acted like high achievers when they moved into central positions. This shows clearly that in appropriate circumstances, group responsibility and spirit can overcome the effects of personal motives.

POKER CHIPS AND GROUP SUCCESS

In the second experiment, John Forward tried to create conditions that would bring individual and group motives into conflict. We reasoned here that if group motives have independent effects, our subjects would feel tension when the two motives conflicted. We repeated an earlier experiment in which we set up a reward condition (we gave poker chips for success) and a cost condition (we took chips away for failures), with subjects we had selected for either high Ms or high Maf. As we expected, the high Ms subjects reported more tension in the cost condition, where achieving personal success and avoiding group failure would call for different goals; while the high-Maf subjects reported more tension in the reward condition, where avoiding personal failure conflicted with achieving group success.

These experiments show that when a person works in a group, his behavior and attitudes result from two different sets of motives: those that form part of his enduring personality, and those that arise in a particular circumstance. These motives may match and amplify each other, or they may come into conflict. But our evidence suggests that when they do collide, a strong sense of group involvement can overcome personal fear of failure or lack of achievement motivation.

Since group motives develop in some circumstances and not in others, people in positions to influence the structure of organizations can do much to nourish them. The most important step would be to shift control downward wherever possible, giving those who do the work more real say about how much they do and how they do it. This in effect places each member in a more central position, transferring more responsibility for the group's success or failure on his shoulders.

Each group should be able to evaluate its own performance, and on the basis of its past efforts and the organization's present needs, have a strong voice in setting current goals. Then members will react to the results of the group's work not as another piece of interesting information, but as a source of satisfaction or dissatisfaction, which cannot help but influence their future performance. Satisfaction feeds the desire for more, and the successful group usually chooses to raise its goals progressively upward.

OPEN CHANNELS, CLOSE RAPPORT

It is also essential to keep channels of communication open among group members, perhaps with regular meetings or discussions. Good communication not only aids evaluation and goal-setting, but helps the members recognize themselves as a group and see that others have strong commitments to it.

I once studied a mirror factory in which the workers, who were strongly group motivated, were quite satisfied nevertheless with their production goals being set by the number of orders the company received. The sense of teamwork I observed seemed to be promoted mainly by the workers' involvement in other group and company decisions. In particular, groups held regular meetings to discuss ways of cutting costs and improving production.

Unlike assembly lines or annual fund-raising organizations, many groups have no set of tasks to repeat, and many do not produce a single product the group as a whole has responsibility for. It is more difficult to develop group pride in such conditions; good communication among members and frequent, reliable feedback become essential.

While we did not test the hypothesis directly in our experiments, we came to suspect that the presence of other strong motives may weaken Dgs. Organizational structures that emphasize and reward individual achievement tend to splinter rather than unify groups. Similarly, when a group exists mainly to determine how many dollars each member will take home in his pay envelope, as in group incentive plans, group pride may not develop at all.

MAN DOESN'T LIVE BY N-ACH ALONE

In spite of the theories of psychologists, administrators and educators, our society does not run on individual achievement motivation alone. I fear that our beliefs that it does have led us to assume that people who can't cut the mustard on their own initiative can't cut it at all. We have designed our schools, businesses, and public agencies primarily for individual achievers, and lost the valuable contributions others could make in different circumstances. And by operating our elementary schools on the "succeed on your own or not at all" motto, we may be depriving many of our children of the success experiences they need to develop individual initiative and to overcome fear of failure. By creating conditions that nourish group desire for success and then by rewarding group accomplishments, I believe many of our institutions could become more flexible and more involving for a larger part of our population.

Motivational Factors of American Prisoners of War in Vietnam

Commander Robert J. Naughton, U.S. Navy

This essay reports a naval officer's experiences as a prisoner of war in Vietnam. Though neither a trained social scientist nor a professional writer, the author provides a revealing description of his thoughts, feelings, and actions, and those of his fellow prisoners. Typically, POWs first were kept in solitary confinement. Later, they were moved into communal cells which they shared with a number of other prisoners. The author notes how this change in the social conditions of confinement was associated with changes in the sentiments and activities of the prisoners. Our purpose in including this selection is to provide a clear-cut look at the relationship between the individual alone and the individual as a group member, not to focus on what prison conditions were like, per se, nor to express agreement or disagreement with any of the author's views.

INTRODUCTION

January 1973 witnessed the end of the longest continual armed conflict in the 200-year history of the United States. Sixty days after the signing of the Paris agreement, the longest recorded incarceration of American prisoners of war (POW's) ended for more than 500 men, over 450 of whom had been held in the Democratic Republic of Vietnam (DRV). Several of these men had endured more than 8 years as prisoners of the DRV, while one POW held by the Vietcong was detained over 9 years.

The POW's received a warm and tumultuous welcome from the people of the United States. This served to create a unanimity among Americans which had been lacking during the long years of the Vietnam conflict. The Nation's public display of pride and relief was a genuine show of interest and concern for "their" POW's.

The Vietnam POW's, however, were not the first prisoners of war who had received publicity. Those American men who had been held prisoners in all recent wars have

"Motivational Factors of American Prisoners of War Held by the Democratic Republic of Vietnam" by Commander Robert J. Naughton from *Naval War College Review*, Vol. XXVII, No. 4, January–February 1975, pp. 2–14. Reprinted by permission of *Naval War College Review* and the author.

been the subject of public examination, and their return to the United States has provided a great deal of human interest news copy.

The post-Korean period was the most lucid example of such investigation. Eugene Kinkead's widely read book, *In Every War But One*, based on psychological factors that influenced the prisoners, emphasized the poor conduct of American POW's in Korea. Similar works combined with the conclusions reached in the *Secretary of Defense Advisory Committee POW Report* prompted the issuance of the Executive Order Code of Conduct. The perceived necessity for an executive order delineating the expected standard of conduct for POW's was a *de facto* condemnation of Korean POW's. For the many U.S. servicemen who served honorably as POW's in Korea, it is unfortunate that the books defending their conduct, such as *March to Calumny*, received less notoriety than those which condemned, but the intent here is not to debate the guilt stigma of Korean POW's nor to exonerate the innocent. Instead, it will be enough to note that such writings do exist.

Now there exists another group of subjects, the Vietnam prisoners, whose experiences might substantiate, repudiate, or expand upon the findings of the studies of prisoners held in previous wars. A military examination of the Code of Conduct's influence on Vietnam's POW's and its further applications, a psychological investigation into the personality effects of from 6 to 9 years of foreign detention, and the sociological problems involved in living 5 years with the same man under adverse stress conditions should be of intense interest for research. Indeed, the findings would be of value not only to military leaders and behavioral scientists but to any human beings who have more than a casual curiosity toward their fellow man.

No amount of descriptive words can completely peel back the skin of the POW and reveal his inner self. But perhaps an acquaintance with the confined environment in which a POW must survive and some insight into the methods by which a man copes with this situation will help the reader better understand his actions.

A prisoner's world is subject to a variety of influences, both internal and external, influences that can cause a man's perceptions to expand and contract as the situation changes. Hence, conscious acts, willful choices, and resistance motivations have shifting roots within a prisoner. For example, the rationale of a new captive differs from that of a man hardened by years of prison life; a consuming injury can alter one's outlook, and resistance with group support is not the same as standing alone. The expansion of individual experiences to general behavioral axioms by which motives are assigned to all POW's is inherently dangerous, but some factors of resistance behavior are universal. Such general propositions observed to be true are examined in this paper.

CAPTURE AND INTERROGATION

Consider, if you will, a pilot in the relative safety of a smooth flying jet aircraft with the comforts of a CVA "ready room" fresh in his mind. Suddenly he finds himself huddling in a flooded rice paddy—still shaken by the combined effects of his aircraft being hit, abrupt ejection, and an unwanted parachute descent to earth—"skivvie-clad" and tightly bound amidst a crowd of angry, club-waving Vietnamese peasants, screaming in a language unintelligible to him. He is now a prisoner of war!

When such events occur in staccato fashion within 15 to 20 minutes, they represent an abrupt, disconcerting change. The most dominant emotion is a sense of *bewildering fear* at the alien surroundings and *uncertainty* of one's ultimate fate. Things held dear—

friends, home. and family—take on greater importance when they are no longer accessible. Embodied in this sense of loss is the uncertainty of time. How long? Ever?

Throughout captivity, this or some other form of fear is a prisoner's constant companion, always capable of influencing his behavior. It is more accurate to say that in the years ahead the POW will learn to control his fear rather than conquer it.

Behavior at such a time is patterned largely by instinct—one acts as a programmed individual and military man. Such programming is attributable to information bits acquired through age, culture experiences, and training. That one's actions are instinctive means that resistance efforts draw on learning and values formulated earlier in life. For example, past survival school training and the ingrained knowledge that the Code of Conduct is the order of the day embody the spirit of resistance and give a man an instinctive *modus operandi* from the outset of captivity.

The POW soon comes to realize that this patterned, instinctive reaction to events is his only guide on what to do next. *He is alone*, a helpless object vulnerable to the enemy's wrath. One manifestation of the subconscious loneliness is the relief one feels when an American aircraft passes overhead. This nostalgia and sense of kinship with other pilots was experienced by U.S. POW's in Hanoi during every bombing raid from May 1967 to April 1968, a brief respite from the gnawing loneliness inside each prisoner of war.

The impact of this loneliness is further intensified as the POW comes to realize that his programmed, instinctive reactions will not cover every situation. He understands that at some point he must consciously deal with the question of how to relieve the constant pain of the binding ropes—without giving the inquisitors any information.

Resolving the dilemma of resistance and survival is exacerbated by the strict rules that prevail in the captor-captive relationship. It is unlikely that an American prisoner has previously been involved in a contest in which the stakes have been so high and the regulations so invariable. A man's life in the United States is a series of second chances, getting a break, or receiving a helping hand. But in a Hanoi interrogation cell, such relief does not occur. Here there is no chance that someone will enter the sweat-stained room with bumpy walls designed to muffle screams and say, "We will let you go this time, but don't do it again."

Some would attribute the captive's resistance to loyalty or devotion to duty; and, in later periods of POW life, devotion to duty and patriotism may be an accurate description of resistance motivation. However, in the early days of captivity, *pride* is a more correct motivational assessment. Pride is a driving desire to prove yourself to yourself and to those whose opinion you respect, and so strong is this desire for self-respect that many have endured torture to the point of crippling pain. The combination of pride and obligation seems to motivate men, time and time again, to resist to the limit of their endurance—despite the knowledge that the prisoner will probably be forced to conform in the long run.

It is important to note that physical well-being as well as mental resolve influence a prisoner's conduct. Strong physiological needs are always present for a POW. Some men crave water even before their parachutes deliver them to earth, and several sweltering days without washing, plus involuntary immersion in rice paddy water with a human excrement additive, produce an almost maniacal desire for a bath. For many men, maimed in the course of capture, physiological priorities center on injuries and a struggle to stay alive. Still, men with twisted legs, shattered arms, crushed faces, and flame-charred bodies do resist from the outset rather than seek aid by compromising their principles. But such action is beyond the ordinary and cannot be expected from all. It is a strong motivation that induces a physically disabled man to select the arduous course of action because of what he knows is expected of him.

It has been stated that initial behavior is instinctive. Instinct is used here in the classical sense[1] in that the newness of the environment dictates "trial and error" or "best guess" behavior based on innate feelings. However, as the years of prison transform new captives into oldtimers, and the bitter lessons are learned, a man is better able to determine proper courses of action. His actions are still instinctive in the sense that behavior is limited by the goals perceived as attainable.[2] This prison maturity replaces earlier guesswork, thereby enabling a POW to recognize the frequent fluctuations in the captor's attitude and take advantage of these changes for his own benefit.

LIVING ALONE

The new captive is first thrust into another completely new and unnatural environment, that of living in solitary confinement. Few people have ever lived for any length of time without any form of human companionship. Both U.S. penal institutions and the 1949 Geneva Conventions on Prisoner of War Treatment set 30 days of solitary as maximum punishment. A poll of U.S. POW's captured in the DRV before 1969 reveals that 90 percent of the men endured solitary living conditions for periods ranging from a few days to more than 4 years, and an equal percentage had been subjected to physical torture. Men of varied personalities are affected by "solo" living in different ways. The combination of emotional stresses and physical hardships prompts hallucinations within some new prisoners. Some memories of the first days in Hanoi are confused and dotted with haunting recollections of irrational outbursts and disturbing dreams.

The physical condition of the cells within what became known as the "Hanoi Hilton" contributes to the depressive state of a new POW. An 8-foot by 8-foot concrete room, bare board bunks, a heavy, iron-braced door with a shuttered peephole, and a small barred window looking onto a wall crowned with broken bottles comprise the appointments of his new home. The daily schedule is quickly learned, and the two meals do not fill the endless hours of a prisoner's day. To a "solo" prisoner, the daily fare of two meals has more value as a relief from boredom than as nourishment. Even the sporadic bathing schedule provides a welcome respite from the oppressing heat of one's cell if little else. A POW's bath entails dipping cold water from a tank resembling a horse trough and spreading it over one's body by means of a cup.

The sound of the turnkey opening doors usually announces the time to eat or bathe, but the rattle of keys at an unscheduled time often means he will be called to a quiz.* Quizzes usually mean being called upon to do something against one's will, and there is a feeling of relief when the jingle of keys fades into the distance or when another's door is opened.

It ought not to be surprising that in this isolated existence a POW seeks some contact with familiarity wherever he can find it. Something so innocuous as smoking a cigarette provides a feeling of security in that the act of smoking is a familiar experience, and, to one who has tried a Vietnamese cigarette, it is obvious that an ulterior motive is required to enjoy it.

The pleasure derived from such familiar associations indicates the POW's desire to conquer his alien environment and to gain control of his emotions. Since knowledge

---

* The term "quiz" was coined by POW's to denote prisoner meetings with some Vietnamese representative of the camp organization. Quizzes could entail interrogation, propaganda, discipline, torture, or indoctrination.

is the armor by which we arm ourselves against adversity, a prisoner constantly strives to learn about his surroundings. Thus, the physical camp layout, the guard change schedule, and the turnkey's idiosyncrasies are all objects of study. A person knows he operates better in familiar surroundings or when he possesses the "home court" advantage. The POW subconsciously realizes that action under extreme emotional stress provides a poor basis for rational behavior. He is motivated to establish a better platform from which to act.

A universal activity of solo POW's is to peer through cracks, under doors, or through the bars in the hope of seeing another POW. Despite Vietnamese efforts to avoid even sight contact between Americans, a fleeting glimpse is occasionally available as a Yank shuffles from his cell to a quiz or to pick up his chow. Eventually the day comes when an "old head" is able to communicate with the "new" man. By means of a few well chosen words, spoken or written, the new man is given the tap code used for clandestine communication among POW's, advice on prison pitfalls, words of encouragement, and the senior officer's policy of resistance, called BACK-US.* This information is passed at great risk to the transmitter, for the camp maintains strict regulations against communication enforced by guards roaming the halls of the Hanoi Hilton who report even suspected violations to camp officers. To be caught means severe torture, as many prisoners would learn during the communication purges.

A man named Ho Chi Minh once said, "Communication is the lifeblood of resistance." The impact of communicating is precisely that for the POW. For some POW's, covert communication is their sole contact with others over a period of months and years. Any device capable of making noise may be used to transmit information from the highest priority to idle chatter to pass the time and combat loneliness.

A man in solitary with only rats for roommates also spends a great deal of time involved in introspection. His attitude is a poignant mixture of feeling sorry for himself and as one with a duty to perform. Thoughts center on assessing one's situation, prospects, and the dilemma of how to exist, a dilemma which prevails for years. Reflections on the war are subject to the constant Vietnamese propaganda which the camp authorities provide through a crude wooden encased radio speaker in the window. Fortunately for the POW, the broadcasts are very naive and intended for someone with no more than a seventh grade education or the right psychological set.

The POW's attempt to evaluate his situation prompts a circular reasoning that meanders through the present, past, back to the present, and ultimately to the future. When one accurately assesses the war, as he knew it prior to being shot down, certain questions begin cropping up: Who really cares about POW's? How often does anybody think of one who is a POW? What reasons are there to expect the war to end in 1, 2, 3 . . . years?

The biggest question a POW poses to himself is, "How would I live my life if I were to live it over again?" To answer such a question, a man recalls many events and decisions of his past life and how alternate decisions might have altered his present circumstances. A mental playback of the events leading to his capture provides hours of speculative thought as to what went wrong. Pondering the decisions made earlier in life raises a fantasy of foregone occupations. The life of a schoolteacher, a business-

---

* BACK-US was an acronym which contained the essence of the senior officer's resistance policy in the Little Vegas area of the Hanoi Hilton in 1967. Each letter represented the following:

B—don't Bow when in front of cameras.
A—stay off the Air, i.e., don't read on camp radio.
C—you are not a Criminal.
K—don't Kiss the Vietnamese goodby by making good statements when we leave.
US—Unity before Self.

man, or an airline pilot now seems to have greater appeal; and when one dwells on his past, thoughts linger on pleasant memories reconstructed in fine detail. Ultimately the question, "Why was that particular event enjoyable or important?" causes one to evaluate himself and ask, "What is important? What do I value?"

The surfacing of values, the examining of past goals, and the facing of the reality of a prisoner of war situation lead most POW's to consider the dilemma of the present, the guilt felt by each man who has been forced to act against his will during initial interrogations. Before talking to other POW's, each man perceives himself to be the only one who has given information. But every man knows he cannot endure the Vietnamese rope torture indefinitely without giving some information. The natural outcome of this thought process is to form a workable plan for the future, namely, a motivational force to resist, to honorably survive the trials that lie ahead.

The early solitary period of captivity is marked by a high frequency of quizzes, intended largely to determine what type of prisoner a new man might become. Thus, there is ample opportunity for the prisoner to employ his newly devised plan of intended action. One is always, on these occasions, taken from his cell to a designated room to be quizzed alone, with only his convictions for support. One might say the general POW attitude at quiz, knowing one can be forced to comply is never to give "something for nothing." It is a point of pride that no information is given as long as the prisoner is capable of resistance.

Each prisoner formed his own judgment of tactics employed by the interrogators during quizzes, but several generalities seem to be widely held. The Vietnamese interrogator needed to feel that he was in control. Therefore, a direct challenge to his authority could not go unanswered. It was not necessary for the POW to yield control of himself to the interrogator but merely to convey the impression of such. For example, there were many instances when an uncooperative POW was told by the interrogator, "You know I can force you to answer, don't you?" When the POW acknowledged, "Yes, you most likely can," the question or demand was often dropped.

It is also generally agreed that the interrogator had some preconceived answers to the questions he asked concerning military matters and covert POW activities. If the POW perceived these desired answers to be erroneous, he responded to reinforce this error. However, when the Vietnamese had a correct answer in mind, an attempt to create doubt in the interrogator's mind was usually a better tactic than a flat denial of fact. Of course, these deceptive methods were not perfect, and, when unsuccessful, the POW ended up in ropes, on his knees holding up the wall, sitting on the stool, or in some other form of punishment.

Perhaps the peak experience of this phase of a POW's life occurs when he makes a truly maximum effort to physically resist torture.*[3] It may be the first time in his life that he musters every ounce of physical strength, mental courage, and determination. The feeling of being totally consumed by this effort is truly unique; and even when this maximum effort, with nothing held back, proves to be not enough, one at least feels pure and satisfied for having done his absolute best. Such an experience usually leaves a POW broken and physically disabled, but is nonetheless of great psychological value to him.

* Maslow referred to the peak experience as ". . . a self-validating self-justifying moment which carries its own intrinsic value with it."

LIVING IN GROUPS

Life in an 8 by 8-foot cell with one, two, or three other men is nearly as unique as living alone. However, the absence of loneliness makes it considerably easier to cope with the difficulties associated with small group living. The axiom "misery loves company" holds true. Close conditions, where four men eat, sleep, and perform hygienic functions in the same room, require some adjustment and concession by all concerned. Individual physical traits of snoring or body odor, combined with personality idiosyncrasies of vulgar speech, braggadocio, and loquaciousness, can cause strained relations among roommates. However, with few exceptions, U.S. officers interned in North Vietnam came to appreciate the need for compromise and self-sacrifice for the good of the group.

Accommodation becomes a way of life, and various means are employed to make existence tolerable. One such means is to routinize the events of the day and to rigidly maintain that routine. Planning such common events as exercising, sweeping the floor, cleaning the cell, telling stories, and the time of communication with other cells serves a twofold purpose. It gives an element of order to life and permits some control of one's action. Otherwise a prisoner must perform the most common daily acts of eating, bathing, rising, and going to bed at a time designated by the prison guards, and the schedule is subject to frequent unannounced changes. The value of order and self-control is best appreciated in the light of the prisoner uncertainties and required compliances.

Routine also permits a POW the opportunity to vary his activity from time to time in order to relieve boredom. An example would be to not exercise on the Fourth of July or to let another empty the "honey bucket" because it is the duty man's birthday. Thus, to deviate from the routine becomes a form of celebration.

Another practice that may seem humorous is the method by which some POW groups parceled out food. The best method of handling the potential trouble of unequal food portions is to raffle off the meals and to rely on the "luck of the draw" method for distribution. Such procedures ultimately become a source of entertainment as home-made dice are cast to determine which bowl of soup each man receives.

An important element of harmony is a sense of humor in the *illegitimae non carborundum* sense. The ability to laugh in the face of adversity is a valuable asset. It is difficult to express how great it feels to laugh after months of crying. The man who finally has a roommate following months of solitary living is ready to laugh at anything, and the slightest provocation prompts uncontrollable hysterics. There can always be found an element of "sick prison humor" in the most dire situations. One could find a bit of humorous irony in being tortured to write a statement that he is being treated well. Since the situation appears humorous even today, perhaps the sickness still prevails.

Living together in a small prison cell means constant association and interaction for 24 hours a day, not the mere 8 hours a day at work or at home that most people equate with "knowing a person." In that respect, when a POW has the same roommate for 2, 3, 4, and 5 years, it is safe to conclude they know each other better than they know their wives.

The exchange of ideas that takes place among men in a common predicament and the knowledge they gain from each other can greatly broaden one's perspectives. There is no need to hide one's feelings on a subject for image purposes because one has no image. Roommates know each other in their true colors; and within the sanctity of one's small cell, the familiarity among POW's prompts an open expression of opinions on many subjects that are not usually discussed at cocktail parties or in rap sessions.

This atmosphere of frankness and the commonality of the situation make resistance behavior, its methods, limits, and consequences, a popular subject for examination. Decisions on the subject usually represent a consensus view rather than the dictates of the senior member of the group. The ultimate authority rests with the senior man, but "having one's say" removes the resentment associated with an authoritarian environment and more firmly commits members of the group to a program they have helped to formulate. However, perhaps because a man's proud belief that his above-the-norm capability demands higher standards, group decisions tend to require less stringent courses of action than those individually formed.

Even small group membership enables a man to project his thinking beyond concerns for his own survival. Resistance may now be viewed as a contribution to the war effort as well as individual responsibility. The adverse effects of his compliance with the enemy become more vivid when shared and discussed with roommates in the same predicament. Thus, as a man lives in closer union with his fellow POW's, his motives are more likely to become less selfish.

Consensus decisions, common problems, and close quarters generate unity and *esprit* among members of the small group, a necessity if a group is to be effective. An indication that POW's possess these qualities and care for one another is evidenced by the prevalent atmosphere of gloom when a cellmate is at quiz. Genuine concern promulgates itself through unselfish acts of sharing, cheering up each other, or communicating at great risk with a solo man purely for his psychological needs.

Communication provides a sense of group accomplishment for it demands group effort. This function often requires two men to visually clear the area by watching for approaching guards while the other two men "communicate." Each message successfully passed produces a euphoric satisfaction within the group. This reaction may appear overstated, but to a group whose purpose is primarily negative, that is, not doing something, to accomplish anything in a positive manner is significant.

To dispel the notion that U.S. POW's held in the DRV were a group of superhumans, it seems appropriate to make some subjective observations of isolated individual behavior within the context of living together. Before October of 1969, when the treatment of POW's improved, torture abounded, solitary confinement was common, and very few men engaged in correspondence with the outside world. During this period the most significant improvement in POW treatment was that torture stopped. The POW's were then assembled in large numbers, and this change in confinement prompted a change of attitude in some POW's. In this sanctuary from physical abuse, some men discovered a boldness within themselves and felt compelled to exhibit ultimate resistance.

This could be called the "irons theory" in that POW's challenged the camp authorities to put them in leg irons and handcuffs again. Its advocates considered minor camp restrictions to be harassment that should be resisted, forgetting that for years prisoners were humiliated by the requirement to bow in the presence of a Vietnamese. Now in the atmosphere of relaxed camp discipline, the "iron men" found it personally elevating to curse and ridicule a guard in a language that guards could barely understand, if at all. It may not be surprising that these hard-line beliefs did not surface until prisoners lived in large communities where the visibility of toughness had a larger audience. It is worth noting that these men were not those of senior rank with whom the final authority and responsibility rested. In fact, this antagonistic behavior conflicted with the "live and let live" policy issued by the senior officers during periods of relative calm.

There might have been an element of sincerity involved, or these men might have been motivated by the belief that prisoners should push for as much as they could get. The possibility also exists that an element of "one-upmanship" or a desire to atone for less stiff resistance in the early years of captivity might have been present. Whatever the motivation of these men, it was obvious that a strong desire for self-esteem existed among them.

Other men also followed rules for personal conduct that was not a group characteristic—POW's motivated to conduct themselves in a manner they believed would best represent the United States to the North Vietnamese because they felt the POW's were the only Americans with whom most North Vietnamese had contact. Although prison guards were by no means the elite of North Vietnamese society, they would eventually return to their villages and answer the inevitable question: "What were those Americans who bombed our country really like?" In other words, was the Vietnamese minister of propaganda really telling the truth that U.S. pilots were bloodthirsty, arrogant, insensitive criminals?

These POW's believed that an attitude of aloofness, support of the U.S. Government, and resisting propaganda efforts in a professional manner were what would ultimately gain respect for a POW as a man. Puerile actions such as belittling the DRV and its citizens merely supported the Communist claims that American POW's were the "blackest criminals in the DRV."

By November of 1970, most of the U.S. POW's were concentrated in one camp as a result of the U.S. commando raid on the Son Tay POW camp. Communal living, with 20 to 50 men in a single cell, marked the final experience for the veteran POW who endured the gamut of living conditions within the DRV.

It was rather exciting to meet men whose names and background had been memorized but whose faces were heretofore unseen. New friendships were born; common acquaintances and experiences were discovered; and time was passed listening to new stories and biographies. It was a time of high emotion compared to an earlier drab existence, but as one man candidly remarked, "It is a bit depressing to hear so many tell their stories and not hear one happy ending."

The organization of the POW's within this larger camp was immediately structured in military fashion. Each cell had a senior ranking officer (SRO) with a staff of flight leaders. Every man was assigned to a flight with the flights alternating the menial housekeeping tasks of cleaning, distributing food, washing dishes, and clearing for communications.

Never did the Vietnamese permit contact between prisoners in different cells, and the senior officers were located in a rather remote section of the camp. The establishment and protection of communication channels became vital to the organization. Those responsible for the transmission of information within the camp deserve a great deal of credit for a job well done. To some men the communication process occupied so much of their time that it became a way of life, a truly professional operation.

Through their efforts, a close link was established between the leaders and the rest of the POW's, and a rather elaborate set of goals was promulgated to all POW's from the senior officer and his staff.

These goals were embodied in what was known as the "plums." The plums covered many areas of duty in detail and identified our common goal. The compendium of those plums follows: to support the Code of Conduct by doing and saying nothing harmful to the U.S. interests, to actively resist propaganda efforts of the Vietnamese, and to work together in order to go home with honor. These concepts were not new to the U.S. captives and had been implied by individual SRO's previously. However, the assurance that everyone would be presenting a united front to the enemy greatly increased the group's cohesiveness.

The organization of POW's was essentially involved with the Vietnamese in a struggle for control. The Vietnamese appeared to have an innate fear of an organized group of Americans, and, therefore, they rejected the terms of the Geneva Conventions of 1949. Americans held in North Vietnam were never granted POW status but were continually referred to as "criminals" by the Vietnamese. By attributing any good treatment to their own benevolence rather than to the just right of prisoners, a sense of authority was maintained in the minds of the Vietnamese.

When security precautions dictated the POW's be concentrated in one camp, the camp authorities (as they always referred to themselves, thereby implying control) were especially wary. The Vietnamese never recognized military rank among POW's and attempted to exert internal control by placing a junior officer in charge, thus reducing the structure and organization established by the POW's in that room. This rather puerile effort was eroded through universal resistance, and internal control remained with the SRO ostensibly as well as in fact.

The idea of control is further typified by the manner in which the Vietnamese resisted any suggestion for camp improvement if it came from a POW, whether or not the suggestion would be mutually beneficial. Thus, the POW's indirectly approached their captors to gain improved conditions rather than directly confronting them in a forthright manner.

The rescinding of the early regulation that a POW bow before any Vietnamese indicated tacit admission by the Vietnamese that control of another's body did not constitute control of his will. With this admission, quizzes and attempts at political indoctrination, humorously naive and ineffective as they might have been, ceased altogether and propaganda efforts lessened toward resisting POW's.

There is a distinct difference between propaganda for the purpose of indoctrinating prisoners and propaganda released to the world in order to sway public opinion. Indoctrination efforts caused little concern to the POW's and were often a source of entertainment or a source for tidbits of news from the outside world. However, the propaganda directed toward world opinions could not be predicted and therefore was a primary target of a POW's resistance efforts. The Hanoi parade of POW's in 1966, the circulation of grotesque pictures of pilots taken immediately after capture, the coercing of POW's by torture to meet with foreign visitors to Hanoi, the torturing of POW's to write good-treatment statements, or the circulation of deceptive photographs suggesting universal good treatment of prisoners were examples of such propaganda. The POW's realized the harmful public effects these tactics could have, both on the U.S. war effort and on its allies, and were motivated to resist participation in these events to the same degree that they resisted providing the DRV military information. Thus, when torture for such devious reasons ceased in the later years, the POW felt some sense of relief. No longer was one forced to do these things against his will. An understanding of this perceived exploitation and the reasons for torture explains the bitterness of some returnees against the DRV.

Returning to the notion of control within the camp, it should be noted that the prisoners had their own ideas of control and influence. When it was felt that the mail situation was intolerable, a letter writing moratorium was enacted for a period of 9 months in order to create the impression that POW's were no longer allowed to correspond with their families. This would dispel any possible misconception that the treatment of POW's was good, and it was hoped subsequent pressure on the DRV would prompt the Vietnamese to distribute more mail.

On another occasion, prisoners were forbidden to hold religious services, to form a choir, or to have any POW speak in front of the group. This restriction against religious services was met with a unified POW demonstration in which 350 POW's throughout the camp started to yell and sing in unison. The reaction of the Vietnamese was greater than had been anticipated—they actually thought a revolt was in progress. Several senior POW officers were taken out of the camp, and the camp discipline was tightened. For several days the atmosphere within the camp was tense, but eventually the right to hold church services was won. Similar struggles for camp control, however, continued until the POW's were released.

Even though a man is dedicated to group goals, he remains very much an individual. Manifestations of this individuality come in many forms such as the power need of those who controlled the communications[4] or those who were prestige motivated and thus voluntarily filled the thankless roles of education officer, entertainment officer, cigarette control officer, doctor, or chaplain when their rank did not warrant a role of leadership.[5]

A few within the group could not resign themselves to accept camp improvement for fear such acceptance would compromise resistance. Therefore, if a prisoner accepted any form of improved treatment, such as writing a Christmas card home or the use of a pencil and paper, he would not be performing his duty.

Perhaps reluctance to accept camp improvements in the DRV prisons could be explained by Maslow's metagrumble theory[6] where such qualms could be present only in a truly self-actualizing man as he strove for perfection and thus rejected any compromise. A more likely explanation would be that the POW's possessed a basic distrust of the Vietnamese and their motives—an attitude not without foundation. The North Vietnamese made propaganda a way of life and used religious services, medical treatment, and POW mail as bribes or exploitation. Small wonder that a popular expression among POW's was, "Beware of Gooks bearing gifts."*

To a degree, attitudes within the formal POW organization—a source for POW motivation—changed during the final years. Motivation continued to become more altruistic or patriotic than egoistic within the POW organization, situationally enhanced by large group living. The managing and protection of a united organization provided an atmosphere that enabled thinking to be more long range and altruistic. A certain security was felt and a better opportunity was provided to perform as honorable men, as outlined in the organizational objectives. Could it be that the decision to support and participate in the activities of the large POW group was derived from agreement with its goals, or was it a desire to gain the personal protection afforded by group membership? There did exist the moral obligation to fulfill one's contract as a military officer. Perhaps a man was motivated by pure love of his country, or was it a hatred of a philosophy so alien and detrimental to his survival? Was the POW's philosophy pragmatic or idealistic?

It appeared that the POW was duty motivated and tended to be more altruistic as he became more actively a part of the larger POW organization. The ego-centered pride motivation of initial captive days expanded to include consideration of other POW's and ideals. However, embodied within that duty were as many factors as there are caveats in the label of patriotism.

It has been stated before that POW's resisted making statements harmful to the United States and its allies. But that is not to say the POW's agreed 100 percent with all aspects of the war in Vietnam and the way in which it was conducted. The group of U.S. POW's in North Vietnam represented both liberal and conservative political philosophies, but there was universal agreement that the POW camp was not the place from which to air those views to the world. A POW had an obligation—yes, duty—to

---

* Editor's note: "Gook" was the derogatory term used for the North Vietnamese by American servicemen. It is also a more general racist epithet which many American service personnel applied to orientals of various nations.

conduct himself in the manner expected of a POW as embodied in the spirit of the Code of Conduct.

It was also the duty of a POW to remain a POW until released through government channels. Such reasoning supports a finding that a near universal rejection of the early releases by the DRV of a few officer POW's* from 1968 to 1972 was a cohesive factor. The criticism of those accepting parole ranged from vocal condemnation to charitable doubt, but there was no one who defended the acceptance of early release as honorable behavior for an officer. The determination to avoid such stigma was a binding influence among resisting prisoners.

One last observation is important. POW's in general felt that they had invested a long time serving as POW's in the war. Most of these men did not want their position undercut through the U.S. Government conceding defeat or its inability to win. Hence, the men clung to their position of resistance to the last day. Some might call this irrational or just plain stubborn. But many POW's have said, after having spent more than 6 years in prison, they were willing to spend another year if it meant the difference between walking out of Vietnam or crawling out. They meant it!

The comparison of POW communal life to standard group behavior theories is enormous. No doubt many aspects of prisoner existence will fill books of the future. Since these men will be collectively evaluated, as were the Korean POW's, it does seem appropriate to conduct an examination of the Vietnam POW organizational effectiveness. An appropriate criteria by which to measure the effectiveness of any group is contained in the Field Theory of Lewin, The Interaction Process Analysis of Bales, and The Human Group Theory.[7] These men have designated many factors that influence an organization's productivity, but some are more germane to this discussion than others.

A common factor for a successful group in the theories of Bales and Homan is the requirement of positive interaction. The interaction among people who had lived in confined quarters had been present whether desired or not. A characteristic of American POW's in the DRV had been their willingness to promulgate to all fellow captives personally tragic or triumphant prison experiences. Accounts of torture sessions, quizzes, or personal thoughts were related regardless of whether a man's participation had been a point of pride or shame. Such revelations had helped others to learn vicariously and represented nearly perfect interaction. Events that occurred throughout the camp were transmitted to everyone. Sometimes listening to a POW sweep the hall or the camp courtyard with the tapcode rhythm was slightly reminiscent of listening to the evening news events of the day.

Another standard of groups is contained in the writings of Lewin[8] who held cohesion to be the key element of a successful group and tied it directly to the productivity of the body. The satisfactions, the degree of closeness, the amount of pride, the ability to meet crises, and the willingness to be frank and honest in expressing ideas among members of the group were some criteria needed for cohesiveness. Lewin's concept of cohesiveness, lacking among Korean POW's, provided an apt description of the Vietnam war POW's. The common goals, united actions, and other instances previously cited support this contention.

---

* Of the POW's who were released early, only one man went home with the permission of the senior American officer in camp. No stigma was attached to this seaman's release by any POW. His resistance had been exemplary from capture to release.

The most comprehensive set of standards for a successful group was stated by Shepherd.[9] He listed five features by which to measure group effectiveness:

- Objectives: Is its purpose the same as that of its members?
- Role Differentiation: Does each member know what is required of him?
- Values and Norms: Is that which is desired and that which is expected clear?
- Membership: Is the membership clear-cut and heterogeneous?
- Communication: No one withholds relevant information.

All of these features as they apply to the U.S. prisoner organization in Vietnam have been examined within this paper. It is left to the reader to pass judgment on the organized group's effectiveness.

For my part, I would like to stress again that the high standards of behavior the U.S. POW's demanded of themselves were largely due to the personal integrity of these men. From one who has spent considerable time in their midst, I have nothing but the highest regard for them as military officers. America is fortunate to have been represented by such a select group under the most trying of circumstances.

NOTES

1. Abraham H. Maslow, *Motivation and Personality* (New York: Harper & Row, 1970), p. 88.
2. *Ibid.*, p. 31.
3. Abraham H. Maslow, *Toward a Psychology of Being* (Princeton, N.J.: Van Nostrand, 1968), p. 79.
4. David A. Kolb, et al., *Organizational Psychology* (Englewood Cliffs, N.J.: Prentice-Hall, 1971), p. 125.
5. Clovis R. Shepherd, *Small Groups* (San Francisco: Chandler, 1964), p. 25.
6. Abraham H. Maslow, *Eupsychian Management, a Journal* (Homewood, Ill.: Irwin and Dorsey, 1965), p. 238.
7. Shepherd, pp. 23–41.
8. *Ibid.*, p. 26.
9. *Ibid.*, p. 122.

Questions for Discussion

1.   Perhaps the most group-oriented phase of life is the early teen years. For example, the decision to smoke or not is more strongly influenced by peers than by parents (even if the parents do not smoke). Discuss what groups do for the young teenager.

2.   For the past 200 years, European observers have commented on the group orientation of Americans. In comparison with people in more tradition-directed countries, Americans seem more "other-directed" (in David Reisman's phrase). For example, a study of parents faced with a decision about rules for their children indicated that German parents would directly apply family or church teachings. In contrast, American parents were much more likely to consult friends and neighbors with children of similar ages. Discuss why you think Americans apparently have been and are so group-oriented.

3.   Describe and analyze the status system in any group of which you are a member or which you have observed: family, fraternity, club, team, job, etc.

4.   Describe and analyze the cohesiveness of the group you selected. What factors strengthen its cohesion; what factors hinder it?

5.   Describe a situation where you were (or someone you observed was) subjected to group pressures to conform. How did the group enforce discipline? Did it work? Why?

6.   Years ago, managers and others tended to criticize work groups for "irrationally" foregoing opportunities to make more money on incentive jobs by restricting production. How might such output restriction actually be "rational"?

7.   Describe the way technology and/or management practices shape groups in any organization in which you have been an employee, student, or member.

8.   Compare the experiences of POWs in China, Germany, and Vietnam in terms of interaction, activity, and sentiment.

Cases for Discussion

The Dying Fraternity

Omega Alpha Sigma is a mess—at least physically if not socially. The living room of its ramshackle house has never really recovered from last fall's post homecoming game bash when a keg of beer leaked all over the floor (and nearly drowned two brothers sleeping there). The upstairs is just as bad, with leaking pipes, dirty bathrooms, and bedrooms looking like a Portnoy's mother's nightmare. In fact, a high point (or low point depending on one's perspective) was achieved when Whitney Framingham's parents arrived uninvited and unannounced one Saturday afternoon to find Whit in bed with a coed in a room strewn with dirty clothes. His mother screamed, his father cursed, and both abruptly departed with threats of discontinuing the monthly checks. Whit was not sure what upset them more, his bed companion or the messy room, but the money did stop. He is getting by for the rest of his senior year, however, through loans from his more fortunate brothers whose parents have not made uninvited visits.

We are all that way—helpful and respectful of each other's rights; no one butts in. I have never been to any brother's home, and I'm not sure where most even come from, but we are all close when at school. Tennis, squash, and soccer are the principal non-party activities of the fraternity. The key players on all three varsity teams are in ΩΑΣ, and the school is nationally ranked in all three sports. Scholastic concerns are a poor third.

In addition, there is Crazy Max. Max is not his real name, but he is crazy. He was a student two years ago. Apparently, he has never really recovered from a bad acid trip, never attended class since, and never gone home. He lives in the house on free room and board and handouts while trying to hide from the green devils he sees every-where.

The acceptance of Max has an ironic contrast in the only rule the fraternity seems to have: no hard drugs, or even pot, to be used in the building. The fine of $50 is never imposed, but the rule is more observed than not.

Omega Alpha Sigma is near extinction. Fraternity membership in general at this university has been shrinking—down from 75 to 25 percent of the male students in less than ten years. The university administration has been lukewarm toward them for some time. Several fraternity houses on which the school held mortgages have been torn down and the land used for dormitory apartments. ΩΑΣ has enrolled no pledges this year. In spite of the president's begging, the brothers have neither appointed a pledge chairman nor organized any effort to obtain new members. The budget is in balance only because four brothers' girlfriends have moved in, contributing funds and cooking skills.

In an effort to bring the chapter back to the straight and narrow, the middle-aged chairman of the national council visited the house one night earlier this year. He lighted the white candles; we all repeated the mystic oath and sang the secret song. He left feeling encouraged, but somehow we are not seeking new members nor fixing up the building as we solemnly promised that we would.

Question

Discuss the state of this organization—e.g., its purpose, structure, and cohesion.

Demilitarized Zone

Battalion Landing Team 1/3, U.S. Marines, had been formed in Da Nang in February. The 1st Battalion of the 3rd Marine Regiment had been pulled in from Khe Sanh to provide a nucleus to which were added a battery of 105 mm howitzers, a battery of 4.2 in. mortars, and a platoon each of tanks, antitanks, amphibian tractors, plus various other small service and support elements. All of these units were veterans of long months (years in some cases) of combat; all were under strength and sorely in need of equipment repair and replacement. It was at this juncture that I, a young first lieutenant, was ordered to the 105 battery after having served 10 months with the "grunts" (infantry) as an artillery forward observer and fire support coordinator. Somewhat "salty" as a result of my combat experience, I was looking forward to the brief rest the BLT refitting would bring.

We sailed out to Okinawa. Here, no mortar or rocket attacks, no firefights, mud, or cold chow. Here, instead, barracks, hot water, plenty of money which had been piling up "on the books," and a happy horde of bar girls to help you invest it. Work, certainly —rebuild and replace worn-out gear, join new troopers fresh from the U.S. and train them—but play hard too, play with the hedonistic fatalism of a Roman gladiator. Marine, you're going back to "Nam" soon, back to combat.

Even given these distractions, I think we developed an effective team. My three senior noncommissioned officers were Gunnery Sergeant Laplace, operations chief; Sergeant Von Polske, assistant operations chief; and Staff Sergeant Rivera, communications chief.

Laplace was a young man, at 28 just a few years older than I. He was brilliant, and during his eight-year career had amassed a greater knowledge of fire direction and gunnery than I have encountered before or since. A fantastic promotion record accompanied this knowledge. He had "broken me in" as a Fire Direction Officer and I had the professional admiration for him that you have for a good teacher. I relied heavily on his technical knowledge in the FDC and delegated much of this activity to him.

Von Polske, on the other hand, was old for his rank (mid 30's), having been "busted" several times. He was a brown little bear of a man with a black handlebar mustache; roguish humor masked a violent temper. Yet he was to display an impressive cool in battle and, at times, astounding bravery which exerted a very strong influence on the troopers.

Rivera, too, was in his mid 30s, very professional and a calm, likeable sort. A Puerto Rican, he was a "loner" and tended to stay with his men and their radio equipment, thus earning a reputation as an empire builder. But I appreciated his competence, so I left him alone. Later, I felt I owed him a debt for unhesitatingly following me forward under fire in the nightmare of our first battle.

In April we somehow crammed all that gear we never knew we rated aboard a Navy ship. A brief sniff of Taiwan, a cancelled exercise in the Philippines, and we left Subic Bay as Special Landing Force Alpha, the amphibious strike force for I Corps, the five northernmost provinces of the Republic.

Late that month, we were taken by helicopter into the now-infamous Que Son Valley on Operation Union. The battery, now half filled out with green troopers (many of our vets had rotated home from Okinawa), had been attacked and surrounded in a landing zone by a battalion of main-force Viet Cong. Casualties had been miraculously light, but a close call gets to you after it's over.

Now, only a day or two out of Operation Union, we are to take part in the first Allied invasion of the DMZ, assaulting the beach just south of the Ben Hai River. The rifle companies are helo-lifted inland, and sweep north to the river. The battery goes ashore in amphibian tractors and sets up among the sand dunes just in from the beach. North Vietnamese shore batteries throw a few rounds at the shipping, but our landing goes otherwise unopposed. It is strange, quiet, eerie. We dig in, but you can't really, not in beach sand—it's like digging in a bowl of salt.

Suddenly the "grunts" knock heads with heavy NVA forces, and we begin to receive requests for fire. In my Fire Direction Center (FDC) we acknowledge the requests, hurriedly compute the firing data, and send it down to the guns. The 105's bark. A lull comes, a short moment to relax.

Then we hear a faint boom, somewhere off to the north. For an eternal second we stare at each other in disbelief. Boom! Boom! Then realization: "Incoming! Incoming!" Kick your Marines in the ass to get them into their flak jackets and helmets and the unnecessary ones out of the FDC and into those pitiful sand trenches amid banshee screams of arriving shells. Eeeeyow, wham! Shrapnel whistles. Terror, stone cold terror. You've been under mortars before, but they don't howl at you on the way in—the screaming strikes you with paralytic fear. Incredibly, you move, act, function (thank God for ingrained training), compute data to return fire.

After 24 hours of intermittent dueling we are ordered south, out of the DMZ and we hope out of range. Our "grunts" have fought their way to the river and are now sweeping south.

Our new position is among the ruins of what was once apparently a small French plantation house. Ironically, it's a pretty spot. But something has died here recently— we can smell it. My FDC is established in a corner formed by two parts of standing wall; the troops sandbag the rest of it, then turn to digging foxholes for themselves. It is late afternoon and quiet. We speak in low voices. We are like a dog in a corner, licking its wounds. Weary, I roll up in my poncho to sleep.

I am startled awake in the darkness. Standing near me and apparently unaware of my presence, several men are arguing violently. I recognize the voices of Gunnery Sergeant Laplace, Sergeant Von Polske, and Staff Sergeant Rivera.

Laplace: "What the hell you use for brains, Rivera? You saw how many of your radios got knocked out back up the beach. I have got to have comm with Dong Ha, or else they don't know where we are!"

Rivera: "I'm the Comm Chief in this battery, and if anybody talks to Dong Ha it'll be me, not you!"

Laplace: "It's my FDC! I run it and all the comm gear in it! If I tell you to put another radio in my FDC, you damn well . . ."

Von Polske, breaking in: "Shut up, Frenchy. Listen, you motherless Puerto Rican idiot, I been watchin' you hoard your precious damn radios over there with your damn communicators. You act like an old damn lady, Rivera. I'm gonna break you (cocking his fist) . . ."

Me, by this time on my feet and in among the three men: "Shut up, all three of you. Von Polske, go get in your foxhole. Rivera, get back over to Comm where you belong and send back a radio set on Dong Ha's frequency. Laplace, get back in the FDC and put that radio up when it gets there."

A few days later, Von Polske asked for a transfer out of the battery. I was never able to regain Rivera's confidence or full cooperation. Laplace seemed to come around, but I was never totally sure of him after having overheard his part in the argument. What had previously seemed to me to be a smooth working relationship had broken down, never to be fully regained.

Question

Analyze the relation between the formal and informal status systems in this unit. What did the lieutenant do?

Group Decision-Making

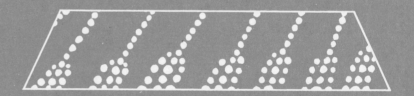

Chapter 4 stressed the determinants of group behavior and the informal development of group dynamics. We saw that the interactional characteristics of many groups are often the accidental or inadvertent consequences of technology, structure, and administration and that these interaction patterns lead to an informal elaboration of activities and sentiments quite beyond anything envisioned by management.

But it is also true that managers often deliberately create and convene groups—as committees—for the purpose of solving problems or making decisions. One study, for example, surveyed 150 companies, 73 percent of which indicated that they used committees regularly (Dale, 1952). Another study of a large sample of companies having over 10,000 employees reported that 94 percent of such companies used committees (Tillman, 1960). If anything, committees are probably even more commonly used than these data indicate. They are virtually universal in sizable business firms, government departments, hospitals, universities, armies, and other organizations.

But if committees are much used, they are not much loved. Managers commonly deride committees for taking too much time, evading individual responsibility, and producing too much conformity and compromise (Ofner, 1959). The old aphorism, "A camel is a horse that was designed by a committee," reflects the contempt managers often feel for committees.

In this chapter, we will examine the evidence comparing individual and group or committee decision-making. We will also discuss factors affecting group performance, problems of group decision, and means of improving the decision-making ability of groups. First, however, we will compare an idealized version of the decision process with the reality of managerial decision-making in organizations.

DECISION-MAKING: IDEAL AND REAL

The conditions for ideally rational decision-making may be summarized as follows: (1) an individual is confronted with a number of different, specified alternative courses of action; (2) to each of these alternatives is attached a set of consequences; and (3) the individual possesses criteria that permit all sets of consequences to be ranked according to preference so that the alternative that has the preferred consequences may be selected (Miller and Starr, 1960). Given these conditions, the process of decision-making includes the following steps:

1. Diagnose—identify and clarify the problem's nature and causes. Give the requirements for a satisfactory solution and indicate limits within which the solution must function.
2. Find alternative solutions—alternatives range from doing nothing to finding a way around the difficulty, removing the difficulty, or even modifying the objective.

3. Analyze and compare alternatives—compare alternatives as to advantages and disadvantages. Ensure that the alternatives from which a choice is to be made are really the ones that should be under consideration.

The rational model of decision-making assumes that the decision maker (1) is aware of the problem, (2) is aware that a decision must be made, (3) has a set of alternatives, and (4) possesses a criterion for making the decision. But these are significant assumptions. Problems seldom pop up with identifying flags. Frequently, managers just do not know that they have problems; the problems are not "felt." If managers are pressed for time and operating satisfactorily, they simply do not use present time to search for future problems (Moore and Anderson, 1954). Few managers systematically search for or consider alternatives unless their present course is creating stress. But creative problem solving must be preceded by continuous saturation, search, and scanning.

The ideal model of rational decision-making also assumes that the decision maker is aware of all possible alternatives and that he or she decides after examining all of them. Obviously this is impossible because time is limited. Managers cannot determine all or even most possibilities; they must pursue a focusing strategy. So they draw up a partial list based on their own experience, that of associates, articles, and advertisements, and hopefully some creative thought. Frequently, managers fail to postpone evaluation until all alternatives are listed; they evaluate as they develop alternatives. The search for alternatives may cease as soon as a satisfactory one is found, even though all possibilities have not been exhausted and a better solution might remain unexamined. Of necessity, time limits search and leads managers to seek satisfactory rather than optimal answers (March and Simon, 1960). All of this makes sense, but it limits rationality.

In the broad sense, managers tend to place action ahead of diagnosis and to reward speed. Many managers frequently shortcut the decision-making process by combining causal determination with problem definition. For example, in a case we have discussed with numerous executive groups, a vice president has constructed a new assembly line to which he has assigned a rather passive and reluctant engineer as foreman. The new unit is not producing at the desired rate. When considering this situation, time and again managers start with the conclusion that the foreman's weakness is the problem. Such premature judgment dangerously distorts further thought about the matter. The foreman is not the *problem*; the problem is a growing backlog of orders and customer cancellations stemming from lagging production. The weak foreman may be the *cause* of inadequate production, but he is not the problem. This is an important distinction. Defining the foreman as the problem tends to focus subsequent thought on how to change or dismiss him. Seeing him as a cause will at least allow thinking to explore what other causative factors may be involved (such as faulty selection of operators, inadequate training, and equipment bugs).

A further illustration of this distortion can be drawn from the Bay of Pigs invasion in 1961. In their deliberations about Cuba, government officials defined the problem as Castro. Therefore, solutions were oriented around how to get rid of him—since he seemed immune to exhortations to change his ways. But Fidel was not the problem. He was a cause, but only one of several having historical roots well before he appeared. The problem was the threat of Cuba's geography and personnel. How might the land be used against American interests (a point that became all too evident later in the missile crisis) and how could Cuban agents foment terror and revolution in Latin America (as Che Guevara attempted to do)? These were the problems, not Castro. If Cuba could have been isolated from the rest of the world, its land denied to others, and its agents confined, Castro's presence would have been irrelevant to the United States. The proper solution is unknown, of course, but defining Fidel as the problem was misleading and dangerous. Time pressure encourages decision makers to confuse problems, causes, and solutions.

In contrast to the perfectly rational model of decision-making, Alexis and Wilson (1967) summarize the actual process as follows:

1. Problem-solving of necessity entails the use of *strategies* (plans or patterns) of search behavior when the slightest degree of complexity prevails. The greater the *cognitive strain* imposed by problem constraints such as time, information retention, and recall activities, the simpler are the search rules. The problem solver may minimize cognitive strain in part by choices of strategies.
2. Problem-solving behavior is *adaptive*. Individuals start with a tentative solution, search for information, modify the initial solution, and continue such processes until there is some balance between expected and realized behaviors.
3. In even the most restricted problem-solving situation, the problem solver's personality and aversion or preference for risk enter into the choice of strategies, use of information, and ultimate solution.

Decision makers may move more slowly as they gain in experience, wisdom, and assurance. When some executives were requested to name the contemporary figure that they most admired and why, the two people mentioned most frequently were Dwight Eisenhower and Harry Truman. The reasons given were similar for both: courage and decisiveness. Some people have criticized President Eisenhower as not being decisive, but few question President Truman in this regard. If anything, he made decisions too easily without sufficient diagnosis, but he never shrank from a decision and he rarely worried about past ones. He said that he always went to sleep shortly after his head touched his pillow (Truman, 1955). Obviously, these executives admired this ability. It was an attribute they wished they had in their own jobs. In his own memoirs, however, Truman's Secretary of State Dean Acheson (1969) observed that Truman gradually slowed down his decision-making, overcame his tendency to jump immediately into action, and expanded the period of diagnosis. Yet he still retained the ability to reach a decision by a deadline. Acheson advanced some sarcastic observations on a tendency of later presidents not to decide, but to struggle "to keep their options open." For Acheson, this was merely indecision.

More systematic research with scientists indicates that more creative people work slowly and cautiously while they are analyzing the problem and gathering basic data. Once they obtain data and approach synthesis and decision, they work rapidly. Less creative people spend less time analyzing the problem but more time in attempting to synthesize their material (Bem et al., 1965).

But the final and perhaps most sizable difference between a simplistic ideal formulation of rational decision-making and the complex reality of the decision process in modern organizations lies in who makes decisions. In theory the manager seems to be an isolated analyst. In reality managers and others interact — in pairs and in larger groups — to make decisions. These interactions produce important differences between individual and group decision-making. An understanding of decision-making in organizations, therefore, requires investigating these differences.

COMPARING INDIVIDUAL AND GROUP
DECISION-MAKING PERFORMANCE

As we have indicated, managers gripe about committees, but they spend massive amounts of time in committee meetings. Indeed, if you plan to have a managerial career, you can look forward to spending thousands of hours participating in committees attempting to make decisions. The evidence comparing the speed and accuracy, creativity, and risk-taking tendencies of individual and group or committee decision-making, therefore, should help you recognize the conditions under which either method is likely to work better.

Speed and Accuracy

Numerous studies have compared the performance of individuals and groups in solving structured problems, i.e., problems for which some known preferred solution exists. The weight of evidence indicates that groups make more accurate decisions, but are often slower than individuals (Shaw, 1932; Lorge et al., 1958; Taylor and Faust, 1952; Hall, 1971; Webber, 1972).

Several factors account for the comparative accuracy of groups. Blau and Scott (1963) maintain that groups are superior to individuals on certain types of problem-solving because social interactions (1) provide an error-correcting mechanism, (2) furnish social support to group members, and (3) foster competition among members for respect. And Argyle (1957) observes: "The collective judgment of a group is superior to the judgment of most of the individuals. Two distinct processes are involved—firstly, discussion leads to the improvement of individual judgments, and secondly, the combination of individual judgments is advantageous." Maier (1967) cites the following as additional group assets: (1) because they combine the knowledge of several persons, groups have more knowledge than one member; and (2) groups produce more alternative methods of approaching a problem.

Creativity

Several experiments using unstructured tasks, i.e., tasks where many innovative solutions might be possible, have also revealed differences between individuals and groups. Most of these studies compared the number of ideas listed by individuals working alone and by groups working together. All subjects were requested to "brainstorm" (Osborn, 1957)—list all ideas in a freewheeling way—without any criticism or evaluation. When the scores of sets of four individuals who worked alone were combined, averaged, and compared with the scores of sets of four-person groups, the results show that individuals typically were more successful than groups (Taylor, Berry, and Block, 1958; Dunnette, Campbell, and Jaastad, 1963). Specifically:

1. Individuals produced more ideas.
2. Individuals produced more unique ideas.
3. Individuals produced better ideas.

The comparative inferiority of groups to individuals at tasks requiring creativity appears to result from the inhibitions group members feel at indiscriminately voicing ideas that pop into their heads. People fear they will look foolish or stupid and censor themselves. This occurs despite instructions in how brainstorming is to be done without criticism or evaluation.

Thus, at this point we can observe that the comparative superiority of individuals or groups is contingent upon the task to be performed. Groups are apparently better at solving structured problems. Individuals working alone, whose results can later be combined, are apparently better at generating ideas to solve unstructured problems.

Risk-Taking

A substantial number of studies have sought to determine whether individuals or groups make riskier decisions (Clark, 1971; Dion, Baron, and Miller, 1970). The surprising but still controversial finding is that groups may be more willing to take risks than individuals. Many people, especially business managers, argue that group decision-making inhibits daring and risk-taking, and promotes a conservative course when a choice must be made between more or less risky actions. The apparent ability of groups to err less frequently is cited as evidence of their conservatism. Nonetheless, laboratory experiments indicate the opposite effect: group decisions following discussion tend to be riskier than individual decisions (Bem et al., 1965). Perhaps individuals can better hide their responsibility in the group (Wallach et al., 1964), or perhaps resonance from other group members overcomes uncertainty and builds courage (ibid., 1962) — or facilitates self-delusion — but in the experimental setting with ad hoc groups created by the researcher, the risk-orientation of groups is quite consistent.

What actually occurs does not seem to be that groups invariably promote risky decisions. Rather, they reinforce the prevailing cultural or climatic attitude (Marquis, 1968). If the initial individual attitudes are on the conservative side of a neutral point, subsequent group discussion moves the decision toward more decisive conservatism. Similarly, if the average attitude is slightly toward risk-taking, group discussion tends to produce a "risk-shift." This shift is particularly pronounced because most people tend to think that they are personally less conservative and more risk-oriented than "average" others. Consequently, they may be quite surprised to discover that those others are not as conservative as expected. This leads to a shift of personal positions in the direction of greater risk.

Obviously, one must be cautious about extrapolating from laboratory research to real life — especially on the subject of risk. Some researchers (Lewin and Weber, 1966) have argued that ad hoc groups of college students temporarily together in an afternoon class are very different from teams of executives who have a past and will have a future of working together, and have established status relationships which influence their deliberation. Such "traditional" or real-life groups may handle risk very differently.

FACTORS AFFECTING GROUP PERFORMANCE

Not all groups perform alike. How well groups solve problems or make decisions is influenced by both the characteristics of the group members and by the group's structural characteristics, such as its size and spatial arrangement. In this section we will consider these aspects of group performance.

Member Characteristics

Undoubtedly, personality affects the task performance of groups, but research here is quite rare because most group study is concerned with the relation between individual personality and individual behavior rather than group behavior (McGrath and Altman, 1966). The general findings on personality and task performance are mixed.

Homogeneity of attitudes is thought to be desirable (Schutz, 1958). In Schutz's research, it did not seem to matter whether any or all group members subscribed to a *particular* attitude. Performance of group tasks was equally effective as long as members of the same group shared the *same* attitude. However, group task performance was likely to be less effective when the group was composed of individuals who were mixed in their attitudes.

In contrast, other research (Hoffman, 1959; Hoffman and Maier, 1961) suggests that groups with heterogeneous personality types are more successful in solving problems than groups containing individuals similar in personality.

In three-person groups, Ghiselli and Lodahl (1958) found that the most effective groups were composed of one highly dominant individual with two others of average or low dominance scores. Similarly, another study (Haythorne, 1953) of two-person groups indicated the most effective combination for cooperative task assignments was a highly dominant individual paired with a submissive individual.

Sociability or extroversion seems also to be related to performance. In one study (Gurnee, 1937), group errors were greater when the groups were composed of "nonsocial, solitary and independent individuals."

Most of the studies referred to above must be interpreted cautiously, because the tasks involved were mainly simple and repetitive, rather than the complex problems that characterize much managerial decision-making. A combined laboratory and field experiment (Bither, 1971) utilized a management game to simulate more realistic problem complexity and its relationship to members' personalities. Bither concludes (pp. 59–61):

> The results of this research suggest that the greater the degree to which individuals in a task group involved in complex decision making possess skills that enable them to deal effectively with other group members, the greater will be the success of the group. This in no way implies that groups homogeneous in need patterns will be more successful than heterogeneous groups. Neither does it imply that individuals who like one another will be more successful in a group than any other mixture of individuals. Thus the common remark, "I don't have to like him—I just have to work with him" may contain a good deal of truth in terms of successful group operations.
>
> A second implication of this research is that the degree to which individuals in the group possess needs for dominance will have a powerful effect upon the structure of the group. In addition, a limited amount of evidence is presented which suggests that the personality need-dispositions of the most dominant individual in the group may have great influence upon the success of the group. Although the evidence is limited, it appears that if the dominant individual has a high need for social recognition and a low need for autonomy, the group is more likely to be successful. Finally, the degree to which the dominant individual possesses skills in social intelligence is likely to influence the success of the group positively.
>
> These findings do not suggest that personality is a substitute for ability. They do indicate that, when ability is either unknown or relatively equal among possible

candidates for complex group task assignments, a consideration of the mix of personalities to be assigned to the group is likely to pay off in terms of increased group effectiveness.

The data of this study suggest that a low score on the personality characteristic of need for autonomy and high scores on two other characteristics—the need for social recognition and the trait of social intelligence—may be important characteristics for the dominant individual to possess if his membership group is to attain high achievement on complex decision tasks.*

Age and position level also seem to affect group performance on exercises (see Exhibit 5.1). Various groups participated in Webber's research (1974): among others, they included high-level general executives averaging 47 years of age, 40-year-old middle managers, 32-year-old managers, and graduate and

Exhibit 5.1 How Age/Position Level Is Related To Individual and Group Performance (Webber, 1974)

Subjects	Mean Score (no. correct)	Mean Time (min)	Mean Group Effectiveness (group score minus mean of indivs. in group)	Mean Group Excellence (group score minus best indiv. score in group)
Executives (mean age 47)				
40 indiv.	13.4	4.0		
8 groups	15.8	9.0	+1.8	−1.4
Middle managers (mean age 40)				
55 indiv.	13.3	4.2		
11 groups	15.1	6.2	+1.7	−2.9
Young managers (mean age 32)				
90 indiv.	13.2	4.2		
18 groups	15.3	5.3	+2.3	−3.1
M.B.A. students (mean age 25)				
90 indiv.	14.3	4.7		
18 groups	16.3	6.0	+3.7	0
B.S. students (mean age 20)				
40 indiv.	11.5	5.5		
8 groups	17.5	6.0	+3.5	+1.5

* From *Personality as a Factor in Management Team Decision Making* by S. W. Bither. Reprinted by permission of S. W. Bither.

undergraduate business students about 25 and 20 years old respectively. The findings are instructive. There were no significant differences in task performance among the different categories of people when they worked as individuals. *Yet, lower level young persons were more effective in utilizing group decision-making than older, higher level managers.* The difference between group performance and average individual performance decreased with increasing age and level of the group members; younger groups improved more over their individual performances. In fact, college students constituted the *only groups* that had higher group scores than their best individual. Among all the others, the best individual was better than the group.

So younger people seem to be more effective in utilizing groups for decision-making than older and higher level managers. Time and age seem to weaken the ability to work jointly with others — or perhaps the younger students came through an educational system that placed greater emphasis on group activity. The reasons might also include less sensitivity to status, more personal flexibility, greater willingness to express opinions, and more "team spirit." Nonetheless, all age groups offered advantages and disadvantages compared to most individuals — more correct answers, fewer errors, but slower progress.

Structural Characteristics

Two structural characteristics of groups — size and spatial arrangement — are also of particular interest to managers. Though more research has focused on the former than on the latter, both size and spatial arrangement have been examined for their effects upon group decision-making.

Several studies investigated the effects of group size upon various aspects of group performance, member attitudes, and group interaction. Certain effects have been observed and confirmed frequently enough to suggest a few generalizations. These include:

1. Middle-sized groups, i.e., groups of approximately five to eleven members, tend to make more accurate decisions than groups outside that range (Manners, 1975; Ziller, 1957; Thomas and Fink, 1963).
2. Small groups, i.e., groups of approximately two to five members, tend to be able to achieve consensus more effectively than larger groups (Manners, 1975; Hare, 1952).
3. Larger groups generate more ideas, but as size increases the number of ideas relative to the number of members decreases, due to the interference of a variety of social obstacles (Collins and Guetzkow, 1964; Gibb 1951). These social obstacles include the formation of subgroups, some of which develop goals inconsistent with those of the larger group, and feelings of greater inhibition about speaking in front of large groups (Davis, 1969).

4. Groups of four or five persons appear to foster greater member satisfaction than larger or smaller groups (Slater, 1958; Hackman and Vidmar, 1970). Groups of only two or three can make members anxious over their high personal visibility and responsibility. Groups larger than five present more of the frustrating social obstacles mentioned above.

Of course, managers face considerations apart from these findings when forming and convening committees. Often, for example, the number of committee members will be determined by the number of departments or interest groups that must be represented in the decision process. Nevertheless, it becomes apparent that group size will affect the quality of the decision process, the likelihood that consensus can be achieved, and the satisfaction that committee members will have with the group's decision. Where managers can exercise discretion in fixing the size of a decision-making group, the choice can be guided by the relative importance of these results. For example, if the degree of consensus is of primary importance, it is useful to choose a smaller group of two to five; on the other hand, if the quality of the group's decision is of primary importance, it should be more useful to choose a middle-sized group of five to eleven (Cummings, Huber, and Arendt, 1974; Manners, 1975).

Most of the research on the spatial arrangement of groups has focused on the effects of alternative seating arrangements, on the interaction of members, and on the emergence of leadership. In general, the evidence suggests that the way people are seated in small face-to-face discussion groups strongly influences who talks to whom and who leads whom. People are more likely to talk with persons across from them rather than adjacent to them (Steinzor, 1950). People who emerge as leaders tend to occupy the position which is the greatest mean distance from other persons in the group (Steinzor, 1950). In juries and other groups, for example, people who emerge as informal leaders occupy positions at or next to the ends of tables significantly more often than people who occupy intermediate positions along the sides (Strodtbeck and Hook, 1961; Howells and Becker, 1962).

Very little research has asked whether these effects of spatial arrangements on emergent interaction and leadership make any difference in how well a group makes its decisions. One study, however, did compare groups having equidistant seating patterns with groups in which one seat was a greater distance from the others, which were equidistant from one another (Cummings, Huber, and Arendt, 1974). The purpose was to compare a neutral spatial arrangement with one which predisposed the emergence of a leadership position (but did not designate a leader). This was done for groups of three, four, and five members (see Exhibit 5.2).

All the groups were presented with the popular "lost on the moon" experiential exercise, in which the groups must decide on the rank-order-of-importance of various items of equipment possessed by astronauts who have

Spatial arrangements	Size		
	3 Members	4 Members	5 Members
Leadership-centered	A • C • • B	A • B • C• • D	A • B • • E C • • D
Neutral	A • C • • B	A • • B C • • D	• E A • • D B • • C

Exhibit 5.2 Leadership-centered and Neutral Spatial
Arrangements for Groups of Different Sizes
(Cummings et al., 1974)

become stranded a considerable distance from their space ship on the moon (Hall, 1971). The results:

1. Neutrally structured groups produced better quality decisions.
2. Neutrally structured groups produced solutions more quickly.
3. Members of neutrally structured groups achieved greater consensus.

Thus, it would appear that an important way to strengthen group decision-making (at least in groups of three to five persons) is to arrange conditions to avoid predisposing the emergence of a leader. Equidistant member-positions are associated with better performance and more satisfied members. In larger groups, however, because more distractions become possible, it seems more likely that leadership could be more helpful in regulating interaction and aiding in focusing on the task.

PROBLEMS IN GROUP DECISION-MAKING

If group decision-making is as good as much of the evidence indicates, then one could reasonably ask, "Why do managers gripe so much about it?" The answer is probably because group decision-making doesn't work as well in the office as it does in the laboratory or seminar. In real organizational group decision situations, two tendencies in particular damage group decision processes: individual dominance and groupthink.

Individual Dominance

Because of personality, organizational position, or personal status, one individual may be excessively dominant (Smelser, 1961). For example, in groups containing managers and their superiors, the presence of a senior manager tends to inhibit problem diagnosis and discussion. Lower status members are sometimes reluctant to participate. This speeds the decision-making process, of course, because the leader can push right along to the selection state. Nonetheless, the advantage of group participation in problem analysis is lost. Awareness of this phenomenon may explain why Alfred Sloan (1964), when he headed General Motors, established committees with himself as chairman but did not attend early group meetings. It appears that by his absence, he wanted to facilitate open and candid discussion during the analytical stage of the problem-solving process. Only when progress toward a solution was deemed desirable and possible did he participate.

A high-status person such as a certified expert may continue to dominate a group after its attention has shifted to a problem outside her or his area of expertise (Doyle, 1971). An experience in the classroom dramatically demonstrated this distortion. Five-person teams were participating in a vocabulary-type exercise. Since one team was short one member, a psychology professor was drafted to complete the team. On the first set of words, the students deferred to the professor's judgment — even when some were skeptical. They deferred because he was of higher status and possessed impressive academic credentials. By chance, however, he also happened to have a rather poor vocabulary. The group did badly. When the students became aware of his inadequacies, they rejected him as leader (and even as a valuable team member).

Under the pressures of hierarchical or status differences, some group members may conform merely for social approval; conformity and agreement may set in so early that all opinions are not considered; and group members may become so dependent on other persons for knowledge and information that they cannot make contributions on their own. All these developments hinder group performance.

Groupthink

The term group cohesiveness refers to the attractiveness a group has for its members. Some groups have more team spirit, greater closeness among the members, and strong feelings of unity. Such groups are said to be more cohesive than those whose members are indifferent toward belonging.

Cohesiveness can improve group performance. The desire to be together, as Davis (1969) observes, can simply increase the time that group resources are available to be applied to the task at hand (p. 79). Cohesive groups can provide acceptance and support to individual members, thereby reducing anxieties that may otherwise weaken their performance (Seashore, 1954). They can also produce the cooperation so necessary for success in many tasks.

But like many a good thing, cohesiveness is capable of producing undesirable side effects. When group cohesiveness is strong it can sometimes make the members' desire for uniformity and consensus stronger than their desire for accuracy and correctness (Back, 1951; Schachter et al., 1951; and Berkowitz, 1954). When this happens the decision-making process can do a better job of producing unanimity than high quality decisions. This excessive like-mindedness has been termed *groupthink* (Janis, 1972).

Groupthink, as Janis defines it, "refers to a deterioration of mental efficiency, reality testing, and moral judgment that results from in-group pressures" (p. 9). Three preconditions increase the likelihood that groupthink will develop (p. 197):

1. The group is cohesive.
2. The group becomes insulated from qualified outsiders.
3. The leader promotes his or her favored solution.

Once it does develop, the groupthink syndrome exhibits most of the following symptoms (pp. 197–98):

1. an illusion of invulnerability, shared by most or all the members, which creates excessive optimism and encourages taking extreme risks;
2. collective efforts to rationalize in order to discount warnings which might lead the members to reconsider their assumptions before they recommit themselves to their past policy decisions;
3. an unquestioned belief in the group's inherent morality, inclining the members to ignore the ethical or moral consequences of their decisions;
4. stereotyped views of enemy leaders as too evil to warrant genuine attempts to negotiate, or as too weak and stupid to counter whatever risky attempts are made to defeat their purposes;
5. direct pressure on any member who expresses strong arguments against any of the group's stereotypes, illusions, or commitments, making clear that this type of dissent is contrary to what is expected of all loyal members;
6. self-censorship of deviations from the apparent group consensus, reflecting each member's inclination to minimize to himself the importance of his doubts and counterarguments;
7. a shared illusion of unanimity concerning judgments conforming to the majority view (partly resulting from self-censorship of deviations, augmented by the false assumption that silence means consent);
8. the emergence of self-appointed mindguards—members who protect the group from adverse information that might shatter their shared complacency about the effectiveness and morality of their decisions.*

It is apparent that each of these symptoms damages realistic thinking. The combination can be altogether devastating.

IMPROVING GROUP DECISIONS

Fortunately, the damage to group decision processes inflicted by individual dominance and groupthink are not inevitable. Research evidence demonstrates, for example, that ad hoc groups instructed in the few simple steps described in Exhibit 5.3 can make better decisions than uninstructed groups (Hall, 1971). Even groups of mental patients so instructed make better decisions on the "lost on the moon" exercise than uninstructed business execu-

* Reprinted from *Victims of Groupthink* by Irving L. Janis. Copyright © 1972 by Houghton Mifflin Company. Used by permission of the publisher.

Exhibit 5.3 Group-Decision Instructions

Consensus is a decision process for making full use of available resources and for resolving conflicts creatively. Consensus is difficult to reach, so not every ranking will meet with everyone's *complete* approval. Complete unanimity is not the goal — it is rarely achieved. But each individual should be able to accept the group rankings on the basis of logic and feasibility. When all group members feel this way, you have reached consensus as defined here, and the judgment may be entered as a group decision. This means, in effect, that a single person can block the group if he thinks it necessary; at the same time, he should use this option in the best sense of reciprocity. Here are some guidelines to use in achieving consensus:

1. Avoid arguing for your own rankings. Present your position as lucidly and logically as possible, but listen to the other members' reactions and consider them carefully before you press your point.

2. Do not assume that someone must win and someone must lose when discussion reaches a stalemate. Instead, look for the next-most-acceptable alternative for all parties.

3. Do not change your mind simply to avoid conflict and to reach agreement and harmony. When agreement seems to come too quickly and easily, be suspicious. Explore the reasons and be sure everyone accepts the solution for basically similar or complementary reasons. Yield only to positions that have objective and logically sound foundations.

4. Avoid conflict-reducing techniques such as majority vote, averages, coin-flips and bargaining. When a dissenting member finally agrees, don't feel that he must be rewarded by having his own way on some later point.

5. Differences of opinion are natural and expected. Seek them out and try to involve everyone in the decision process. Disagreements can help the group's decision because with a wide range of information and opinions, there is a greater chance that the group will hit upon more adequate solutions.

Source: J. Hall, "Decisions." *Psychology Today,* November 1971.

tives (Hall, 1971). Clearly, useful procedures for interacting groups are learnable.

The preconditions and symptoms associated with groupthink also imply several changes in group interaction and leadership behavior. For example, leaders can refrain from pushing the group to adopt their pet solutions. Outside experts can be invited in. Leaders can support and protect the expression of dissent. They can even assign a member the role of critical evaluator or devil's advocate to challenge all proposals. In a selected reading for this chapter, Janis elaborates upon these and additional methods of preventing and counteracting groupthink.

Another method for improving group decisions comes from the findings discussed earlier that the pooled results of individuals working alone on the same problem yield more and better solutions than those produced by face-to-face groups. It follows that committees might be required to engage in idea generation or other phases of decision-making without interaction, or with carefully regulated and balanced interaction. Eliminated or reduced interaction may prevent the adverse effects of individual dominance, groupthink, or other factors such as personality clashes. The two best-known "pseudo-group" decision-making processes are the Delphi technique and the nominal group technique (Delbecq, Van de Ven, and Gustafson, 1975).

The Delphi Technique

The Delphi technique (Dalkey, 1969) represents one of the most promising efforts to eliminate factors other than knowledge from group problem-solving. It (1) keeps group membership anonymous, and/or (2) lists members but keeps specific communications anonymous, and (3) allows only written communication. Each member takes a position. The central thrust of those positions is communicated to all members. On the second round, members can modify their positions or not—but they must give specific written reasons for departing from the central range of the other first-round responses. This iterative process is continued for several rounds. Dalkey reports that such a process leads to better decisions than face-to-face groups.

Breinholt and Webber (1972) replicated the Hall study described earlier, using his "lost on the moon" exercise, but they included Delphi groups. Hall's results indicated that face-to-face groups instructed on how to derive a group consensus performed better than the uninstructed groups. The Delphi groups progressed to better performance than either of Hall's categories and better than Breinholt and Webber's uninstructed groups. Eliminating personality and status from group deliberations via a Delphi-like technique does seem promising. Nonetheless, it should be pointed out that the very best group performance in the research occurred with an uninstructed group where apparently a very knowledgeable member was able to dominate.

The Nominal Group Technique

Unlike the Delphi technique, where the participants usually remain anonymous, never meet face-to-face, and communicate only in writing, nominal group participants know each other or become acquainted because they meet face-to-face and talk to one another. The interaction of nominal group participants, however, is carefully controlled by the following procedure (which is explained and illustrated more thoroughly in one of the selected readings at the end of this chapter):

1. Seven to ten participants sit around a table in view of one another.
2. After the problem for decision and the nominal group instructions are given, the participants silently list their ideas on a pad of paper.

3. After five or ten minutes a recorder obtains one idea from each member in turn and writes that idea on a flip chart. No discussion takes place during this step.
4. Step three is repeated until all ideas are listed on the flip chart.
5. Each idea is discussed. Participants seek clarification and express support or nonsupport.
6. Each participant then secretly records a rank-ordering of ideas.
7. The decision is the idea that emerges in first place as a result of averaging the ranking of all participants (Delbecq, Van de Ven, and Gustafson, 1975).

One advantage to this method is that it does tend to counter the disproportionate influence exercised by persons who are especially assertive, articulate, and persuasive, but who may not have very many or very good ideas. The good ideas of less assertive, articulate, or persuasive persons may be more influential than they would be in free-wheeling interacting groups. On the other hand, the effects of status and rank differences may not be eliminated because everyone can see how a high status person reacts to various ideas. Even with secret voting some persons may be influenced by the source rather than the quality of an idea.

Research evidence, however, tends to show that nominal groups are superior to interacting groups, particularly in the earlier phases of decision-making which include fact finding and idea generation (Van de Ven and Delbecq, 1971). This is not invariably the case though; one study suggested that nominal groups were not superior to interacting groups where the participants are pervasively aware of the problem about which ideas are being generated and are not inhibited by dominant persons from communicating their ideas (Green, 1975). Other evidence indicates that the balanced interaction of nominal groups may be superior to Delphi groups in generating ideas and fostering involvement in the tasks (Van de Ven and Delbecq, 1974; Van de Ven, 1974).

In general, the research on both Delphi and nominal group techniques suggests that they can help improve the quality of group decisions because they mitigate the problems of interacting groups—individual dominance and groupthink. A skillful chairperson, therefore, may adapt these techniques to particular decision-making situations. The challenge is to both utilize the added power for effective decisions that exists in groups and to contain the forces that so often pollute group decision-making.

SUMMARY

Decision theory tends to depict decision makers as isolated, rational individuals who become fully informed about problems and weigh alternatives dispassionately. Decision-making reality involves a far less computer-like process. Information is incomplete, problems are imperfectly formulated, and social interaction as much as rational calculation may influence the result.

Much of the social interaction of managerial decision-making takes place in committees and other groups; however, there are important differences between individual and group decision-making. The evidence indicates, for example, that groups make more accurate decisions when solving structured problems, but they are slower than individuals. On the other hand, individuals working alone, but whose output can later be combined, tend to produce more and better ideas than the same number of persons interacting as a group. But when it comes to risk-taking, groups tend to move farther in the direction of either increased or reduced risk. Individuals are inclined, on the average, to change their decisions less radically in either direction.

Both the characteristics of group members and the structure of the group — its size and spatial arrangement — affect decision quality and the ease of consensus. Within limits, increased size can improve quality, but it can also make reaching consensus more difficult. Unequal seating arrangements and differences in seating position can predispose interaction and leadership emergence.

Finally, though group decision processes can work effectively, they often do not because of individual dominance and groupthink. The first of these replaces group decisions with individual decisions through the greater status and rank of one person. The second prevents high quality thinking and dissident ideas because of an excessive desire for consensus to preserve the warm and cozy atmosphere of a cohesive group. Fortunately, however, groups can employ procedures like the Delphi and nominal group techniques to combat these obstacles to effective group decision-making.

REFERENCES

Acheson, D. *Present at the Creation: My Years in the State Department.* W. W. Norton, 1969.

Alexis, M., and C. Z. Wilson. *Organizational Decision-Making.* Prentice-Hall, 1967.

Argyle, M. *The Scientific Study of Social Behavior.* Methuen, 1957.

Back, K. W. "Influence Through Social Communication." *Journal of Abnormal Social Psychology,* Vol. 46 (1951), pp. 9–23.

Bem, D. J., M. A. Wallach, and N. Kogan. "Group Decision Making Under Risk of Aversive Consequences." *Journal of Personality and Social Psychology,* Vol. 1 (1955), pp. 453–60.

Berkowitz, L. "Group Standards, Cohesiveness, and Productivity." *Human Relations,* Vol. 7 (1954), pp. 505–19.

Bither, S. W. "Personality as a Factor in Management Team Decision Making." Center for Research of the College of Business Administration, Pennsylvania State University, 1971.

Blau, P., and W. E. Scott. *Formal Organizations.* Chandler, 1963.

Breinholt, R., and R. A. Webber. "Comparing Delphi Groups, Uninstructed and Instructed Face-to-Face Groups." 1972.

Clark, R. D. III. "Group Induced Shift Toward Risk: A Critical Appraisal." *Psychological Bulletin,* Vol. 76 (1971), pp. 251–71.

Collins, B. E., and H. Guetzkow. *A Social Psychology of Group Processes for Decision Making.* Wiley, 1964.

Cummings, L. L., G. P. Huber, and E. Arendt. "Effects of Size and Spatial Arrangements on Group Decision Making." *Journal of the Academy of Management*, Vol. 17, No. 3 (September 1974).

Dale, E. *Planning and Developing the Company Organization Structure.* American Management Association, 1952.

Dalkey, N. C. "The Delphi Method: An Experimental Study of Group Opinion." Rand Corporation Memorandum RM 5888-PR, June 1969.

Davis, J. H. *Group Performance.* Addison-Wesley, 1969.

Dion, K. L., R. S. Baron, and N. Miller. "Why Do Groups Make Riskier Decisions Than Individuals?" in L. Berkowitz (ed.), *Advances in Experimental Social Psychology*, Vol. 5, Academic Press (1970), pp. 305–77.

Doyle, W. "Effects of Achieved Status of Leader on Productivity of Groups." *Administrative Science Quarterly*, Vol. 16, No. 1 (March 1971), pp. 40–50.

Dunnette, M. D., J. D. Campbell, and K. Jaastad. "The Effect of Group Participation on Brainstorming Effectiveness for Two Industrial Samples." *Journal of Applied Psychology*, Vol. 47 (1963), pp. 30–37.

Ghiselli, E. E., and T. M. Lodahl. "Patterns of Managerial Traits and Group Effectiveness." *Journal of Abnormal and Social Psychology*, Vol. 57 (1958), pp. 61–66.

Gibb, J. R. "The Effects of Group Size and of Threat Reduction Upon Creativity in a Problem-Solving Situation." *American Psychologist*, Vol. 6 (1951), p. 324.

Green, Thad B. "An Empirical Analysis of Nominal and Interacting Groups." *Academy of Management Journal*, Vol. 18, No. 1 (1975), pp. 63–73.

Gurnee, H. "A Comparison of Collective and Individual Judgments of Facts." *Journal of Experiment Psychology*, Vol. 21 (1937).

Gustafson, D. H., et al. "A Comparative Study of Differences in Subjective Likelihood Estimates Made by Individuals, Interacting Groups, Delphi Groups, and Nominal Groups." *Organizational Behavior and Human Performance*, Vol. 9 (1973), pp. 280–91.

Hackman, R. and N. Vidmar. "Effects of Size and Task Type on Group Performance and Member Reactions." *Sociometry*, Vol. 33 (1970), pp. 37–54.

Hall, J. "Decisions." *Psychology Today* (November 1971), pp. 51 ff.

Hare, A. P. "Interaction and Consensus in Different Sized Groups." *American Sociological Review*, Vol. 17 (1972), pp. 261–67.

Haythorn, W. "The Influence of Individual Members on the Characteristics of Small Groups." *Journal of Abnormal and Social Psychology*, Vol. 48 (1953), pp. 276–84.

Hoffman, L. R. "Homogeneity of Member Personality and its Effect on Group Problem Solving." *Journal of Abnormal and Social Psychology*, Vol. 58 (1959), pp. 27–32.

———, and N. R. Maier. "Quality and Acceptance of Problem Solutions by Members of Homogeneous and Heterogeneous Groups." *Journal of Abnormal and Social Psychology*, Vol. 62 (1961), pp. 401–7.

Howells, L. T., and S. W. Becker. "Seating Arrangements and Leadership Emergence." *Journal of Abnormal and Social Psychology*, Vol. 64 (1962), pp. 148–50.

Janis, I. L. *Victims of Groupthink.* Houghton Mifflin, 1972.

Lewin, A. Y., and W. F. Weber. "Risk Taking in Ad Hoc and Traditional Groups." Paper presented to Institute of Management Science, September 8, 1966.

Lorge, I., D. Fox, J. Davitz, and M. Brenner. "A Survey of Studies Contrasting the Quality of Group Performance and Individual Performance, 1920–1957." *Psychological Bulletin*, Vol. 55 (1958).

Maier, N. R. F. "Assets and Liabilities in Group Problem Solving: The Need for an Integrative Function." *Psychological Review*, Vol. 74 (1967), pp. 239–48.

Manners, G. E., Jr. "Another Look at Group Size, Group Problem Solving, and Member Consensus." *Academy of Management Journal*, Vol. 18, No. 4 (December 1975), pp. 715–24.

March, J. G., and H. A. Simon. *Organizations*. Wiley, 1960.

Marquis, D. G. "Individual and Group Decisions Involving Risk." *Industrial Management Review*, Vol. 9, No. 3 (Spring 1968), pp. 69–75.

McGrath, J. E., and I. Altman. *Small Group Research*. Holt, Rinehart and Winston, 1966.

Miller, D. W., and M. K. Starr. *Executive Decision and Operations Research*. Prentice-Hall, 1960.

Moore, O. K., and S. B. Anderson. "Search Behavior in Individual and Group Problem Solving." *American Sociological Review*, Vol. 19 (1954).

Ofner, J. "Are Committees Worthwhile?" *Commerce Magazine*, Vol. 56, No. 2 (March 1959), pp. 64–65.

Osborn, A. F. *Applied Imagination*. Scribners, 1957.

Schachter, S., et al. "An Experimental Study of Cohesiveness and Productivity." *Human Relations*, Vol. 4 (1951), pp. 229–38.

Schutz, W. C. *FIRO: A Three Dimensional Theory of Inter-Personal Behavior*. Holt, Rinehart and Winston, 1958.

Seashore, S. E. *Group Cohesiveness in the Industrial Work Group*. University of Michigan, Institute for Social Research, 1954.

Shaw, M. E. "A Comparison of Individuals and Small Groups in the Rational Solution of Complex Problems." *American Journal of Psychology*, Vol. 44 (1932).

Slater, P. E. "Contrasting Correlates of Group Size." *Sociometry*, Vol. 21 (1958), pp. 129–39.

Sloan, A. P., Jr. *My Years with General Motors*. Doubleday, 1964.

Smelser, W. T. "Dominance as a Factor in Achievement and Perception in Cooperative Problem-Solving Interactions." *Journal of Abnormal and Social Psychology*, Vol. 62 (1961), pp. 535–42.

Steinzor, B. "The Spatial Factor in Face-to-Face Discussion Groups." *Journal of Abnormal and Social Psychology*, Vol. 45 (1950), pp. 552–55.

Strodtbeck, F. L., and H. L. Hook. "The Social Dimensions of a Twelve Man Jury." *Sociometry*, Vol. 24 (1961), pp. 397–415.

Taylor, D., P. C. Berry, and C. H. Block. "Does Group Participation When Using Brainstorming Facilitate or Inhibit Creative Thinking?" *Administrative Science Quarterly*, Vol. 23 (1958), pp. 23–47.

———, and W. L. Faust. "Twenty Questions: Efficiency in Problem Solving as a Function of Size of Group." *Journal of Experimental Psychology*, Vol. 44 (1952), pp. 360–68.

Thomas, E. J., and C. F. Fink. "Effects of Group Size." *Psychological Bulletin*, Vol. 60 (1963), pp. 371–84.

Tillman, R., Jr. "Problems in Review: Committees on Trial," *Harvard Business Review* (May–June 1960).

Van de Ven, A. H. *Group Decision-Making Effectiveness*. Kent State University Center for Business and Economic Research Press, 1974.

———, and A. F. Delbecq. "The Effectiveness of Nominal, Delphi, and Interacting Group Decision Making Processes." *Academy of Management Journal*, Vol. 17, No. 4 (1974), pp. 605–21.

Van de Ven, A. H., and A. F. Delbecq. "Nominal Versus Interacting Group Processes for Committee Decision-Making Effectiveness." *Academy of Management Journal,* Vol. 14, No. 2 (1971), pp. 203–12.

Wallach, M. A., N. Kogan, and D. J. Bem. "Group Influence on Individual Risk Taking." *Journal of Abnormal and Social Psychology,* Vol. 65 (1962), pp. 75–86.

———, ———, and ———. "Diffusion of Responsibility and Level of Risk Taking In Groups." *Journal of Abnormal and Social Psychology,* Vol. 68 (1964), pp. 263–74.

Webber, R. A. "The Relation of Group Performance to the Age of Members in Homogeneous Groups." *Academy of Management Journal,* Vol. 17, No. 3 (September 1974), pp. 570–74.

Ziller, R. C. "Group Size: A Determinant of the Quality and Stability of Group Decisions." *Sociometry,* Vol. 20 (1957), pp. 165–73.

Readings

Committee Management

Alan C. Filley

The committee is one of the most maligned, most frequently employed forms of organization structure. Despite the criticisms, committees are a fact of organization life. For example, a recent survey of 1200 respondents revealed that 94 percent of firms with more than 10,000 employees and 64 percent with less than 250 employees reported having formal committees.[1] And, a survey of organization practices in 620 Ohio manufacturing firms showed a similar positive relationship between committee use and plant size.[2] These studies clearly indicate that committees are one of management's important organizational tools.

My thesis is that committee effectiveness can be increased by applying social science findings to answer such questions as:

- What functions do committees serve?
- What size should committees be?
- What is the appropriate style of leadership for committee chairmen?
- What mix of member characteristics makes for effective committee performance?

COMMITTEE PURPOSES AND FUNCTIONS

Committees are set up to pursue economy and efficiency within the enterprise. They do not create direct salable value, nor do they supervise operative employees who create such value.

The functions of the committee have been described by business executives as the exchange of views and information, recommending action, generating ideas, and making major decisions,[3] of which the first may well be the most common. After observing seventy-five conferences (which were also referred to as "committees"), Kriesberg concluded that most were concerned either with communicating information or with aiding an executive's decision process.[4] Executives said they called conferences to "sell" ideas rather than for group decision-making itself. As long as the executive does not manipulate the group covertly, but benefits by its ideas and screening processes, this activity is probably quite legitimate, for members are allowed to influence and to participate, to some extent, in executive decision-making.

Some committees also make specific operating decisions which commit individuals and organization units to prescribed goals and policies. Such is often the province of the general management committee composed of major executive officers. According to one survey, 30.3 percent of the respondents reported that their firms had such a committee and that the committees averaged 8.6 members and met 27 times per year.[5]

Several of the characteristics of committee organization have been the subject of authoritative opinion, or surveys of current practice, and lend themselves to evaluation through inferences from small-group research. Current practice and authoritative opinion are reviewed here, followed by more rigorous studies in which criteria of effectiveness are present. The specific focus is on committee size, membership, and chairmen.

COMMITTEE SIZE

Current Practice and Opinion

The typical committee should be, and is, relatively small. Recommended sizes range from three to nine members, and surveys of actual practice seldom miss these prescriptions by much. Of the 1658 committees recorded in the Harvard Business Review survey, the average membership was eight. When asked for their preference, the 79 percent who answered suggested an ideal committee size that averaged 4.6 members. Similarly, Kriesberg reported that, for the 75 conferences analyzed, there were typically five or six conferees in the meetings studied.[6]

Committees in the federal government tend to be larger than those in business. In the House of Representatives, Appropriations is the largest standing committee, with fifty members, and the Committee on Un-American Activities is smallest, with nine. Senate committees average thirteen members; the largest, also Appropriations, has twenty-three.[7] The problem of large committee size is overcome by the use of subcommittees and closed executive committee meetings. The larger committees seem to be more collections of subgroups than truly integrated operating units. In such cases, it would be interesting to know the size of the subcommittees.

Inferences from Small-Group Research

The extent to which a number is "ideal" may be measured in part in terms of the effects that size has on socio-emotional relations among group members and thus the extent to which the group operates as an integrated whole, rather than as fragmented subunits. Another criterion is how size affects the quality of the group's decision and the time required to reach it. Several small experimental group studies have evaluated the effect of size on group process.

Variables related to changes in group size include the individual's capacity to "attend" to differing numbers of objects, the effect of group size on interpersonal relations and communication, its impact on problem-solving functions, and the "feelings" that group members have about proper group size and the nature of group performance. To be sure, the effects of these variables are interrelated.

Attention to the group. Each member in a committee attends both to the group as a whole and to each individual as a member of the group. There seem to be limits on a person's ability to perform both of these processes — limits which vary with the size of the group and the time available. For example, summarizing a study by Taves,[8] Hare[9] reports that "Experiments on estimating the number of dots in a visual field with very short-time exposures indicate individual subjects can report the exact number up to and including seven with great confidence and practically no error, but above that number confidence and accuracy drop."

Perhaps for similar reasons, when two observers assessed leadership characteristics in problem-solving groups of college students, the raters reached maximum agreement in groups of six, rather than in two, four, eight, or twelve.[10]

The apparent limits on one's ability to attend both to the group and the individuals within it led Hare to conclude: "The coincidence of these findings suggests that the ability of the observing individual to perceive, keep track of, and judge each member separately in a social interaction situation may not extend much beyond the size of six or seven. If this is true, one would expect members of groups larger than that size to tend to think of other members in terms of subgroups, or 'classes' of some kind, and to deal with members of subgroups other than their own by more stereotyped methods of response."[11]

Interpersonal relations and communication. Given a meeting lasting a fixed length of time, the opportunity for each individual to communicate is reduced, and the type of communication becomes differential among group members. Bales et al.[12] have shown that in groups of from three to eight members the proportion of infrequent contributors increases at a greater rate than that theoretically predicted from decreased opportunity to communicate. Similarly, in groups of from four to twelve, as reported by Stephen and Mishler,[13] size was related positively to the difference between participation initiated by the most active and the next most active person.

Increasing the group size seems to limit the extent to which individuals want to communicate, as well. For example, Gibb[14] studied idea productivity in forty-eight groups in eight size categories from 1 to 96. His results indicated that as group size increases a steadily increasing proportion of group members report feelings of threat and less willingness to initiate contributions. Similarly, Slater's[15] study of 24 groups of from two to seven men each working on a human relations problem indicated that members of the larger groups felt them to be disorderly and time-consuming, and complained that other members became too pushy, aggressive, and competitive.

Functions and conflict. An increase in group size seems to distort the pattern of communication and create stress in some group members, yet a decrease in group size also has dysfunctional effects. In the Slater study check-list responses by members rating smaller groups of 2, 3, or 4 were complimentary, rather than critical, as they had been for larger groups. Yet observer impressions were that small groups engaged in superficial discussion and avoided controversial subjects. Inferences from post hoc analysis suggested that small group members are too tense, passive, tactful, and constrained to work together in a satisfying manner. They are afraid of alienating others. Similar results have been reported in other studies regarding the inhibitions created by small group size, particularly in groups of two.[16]

Groups of three have the problem of an overpowerful majority, since two members can form a coalition against the unsupported third member. Four-member groups provide mutual support when two members oppose the other two, but such groups have higher rates of disagreement and antagonism than odd-numbered groups.[17]

The data reported above are not altogether consistent regarding the reasons for dysfunctional consequences of small groups. The "trying-too-hard-for-agreement" of the Slater study seems at odds with the conflict situations posed in the groups of three and four, yet both agree that for some reason tension is present.

Groups of five. While it is always dangerous to generalize about "ideal" numbers (or types, for that matter), there does appear to be logical and empirical support for groups of five members as a suitable size, if the necessary skills are possessed by the five members. In the Slater study, for example, none of the subjects felt that a group of five was too small or too large to carry out the assigned task, though they objected to the other sizes (two, three, four, six, and seven). Slater concluded:

> Size five emerged clearly . . . as the size group which from the subjects' viewpoint was most effective in dealing with an intellectual task involving the collection and exchange of information about a situation, the coordination, analysis, and evaluation of this information, and a group decision regarding the appropriate administrative action to be taken in the situation. . . .
>
> These findings suggest that maximal group satisfaction is achieved when the group is large enough so that the members feel able to express positive and negative feelings freely, and to make aggressive efforts toward problem solving even at the risk of antagonizing each other, yet small enough so that some regard will be shown for the feelings and needs of others; large enough so that the loss of a member could be tolerated, but small enough so that such a loss could not be altogether ignored.[18]

From this and other studies,[19] it appears that, excluding productivity measures, generally the optimum size of problem-solving groups is five. Considering group performance in terms of quality, speed, efficiency and productivity, the effect of size is less clear. Where problems are complex, relatively larger groups have been shown to produce better quality decisions. For example, in one study, groups of 12 or 13 produced higher quality decisions than groups of 6, 7, or 8.[20] Others have shown no differences among groups in the smaller size categories (2 to 7). Relatively smaller groups are often faster and more productive. For example, Hare found that groups of five take less time to make decisions than groups of 12.[21]

Several studies have also shown that larger groups are able to solve a greater variety of problems because of the variety of skills likely to increase with group size.[22] However, there is a point beyond which committee size should not increase because of diminishing returns. As group size increases coordination of the group tends to become difficult, and thus it becomes harder for members to reach consensus and to develop a spirit of teamwork and cohesiveness.

In general, it would appear that with respect to performance, a task which requires interaction, consensus and modification of opinion requires a relatively small group. On the other hand, where the task is one with clear criteria of correct performance, the addition of more members may increase group performance.

THE CHAIRMAN

Current Practice and Opinion

Most people probably serve on some type of committee in the process of participating in church, school, political, or social organizations and while in that capacity have observed the effect of the chairman on group progress. Where the chairman starts the meeting, for example, by saying, "Well, we all know each other here, so we'll dispense with any formality," the group flounders, until someone else takes a forceful, directive role.

If the committee is to be successful, it must have a chairman who understands group process. He must know the objectives of the committee and understand the problem at hand. He should be able to vary decision strategies according to the nature of the task and the feelings of the group members. He needs the acceptance of the group members and their confidence in his personal integrity. And he needs the skill to resist needless debate and to defer discussion upon issues which are not pertinent or where the committee lacks the facts upon which to act.

Surveys of executive opinion support these impressions of the chairman's role. The Harvard Business Review survey stated that "The great majority [of the suggestions from survey respondents] lead to this conclusion: the problem is not so much committees in management as it is the management of committees." This comment by a partner in a large management consulting firm was cited as typical: "Properly used, committees can be most helpful to a company. Most of the criticism I have run into, while probably justified, deals with the way in which committees are run (or committee meetings are run) and not with the principle of working with committees."[23]

A chairman too loose in his control of committee processes is by no means the only difficulty encountered. Indeed, the chronic problem in the federal government has been the domination of committee processes by the chairman. This results from the way in which the chairman is typically selected: he is traditionally the member of the majority party having the longest uninterrupted service on the committee. The dangers in such domination have been described as follows:

> If there is a piece of legislation that he does not like, he kills it by declining to schedule a hearing on it. He usually appoints no standing subcommittees and he arranges the special subcommittees in such a way that his personal preferences are taken into account. Often there is no regular agenda at the meetings of his committee — when and if it meets . . . they proceed with an atmosphere of apathy, with junior members, especially, feeling frustrated and left out, like first graders at a seventh grade party.[24]

Inferences from Small Group Research

The exact nature of the chairman's role is further clarified when we turn to more rigorous studies on group leadership.

We shall confine our discussion here to leader roles and functions, using three approaches. First, we shall discuss the nature of task leadership in the group and the apparent reasons for this role. Then we shall view more specifically the different roles which the leader or leaders of the group may play. Finally, we shall consider the extent to which these more specific roles may be combined in a single individual.

Leader control. Studies of leadership in task-oriented, decision-making groups show a functional need for and, indeed, a member preference for directive influence by the chairman. The nature of this direction is illustrated in a study by Schlesinger, Jackson, and Butman.[25] The problem was to examine the influence process among leaders and members of small problem-solving groups when the designated leaders varied on the rated degree of control exerted. One hundred six members of twenty-three management committees participated in the study. As part of an initial investigation, committee members described in a questionnaire the amount of control and regulation which each member exercised when in the role of chairman. Each committee was then given a simulated but realistic problem for 1.5 hours, under controlled conditions and in the presence of three observers.

The questionnaire data showed that individuals seen as high in control were rated as more skillful chairmen and as more valuable contributors to the committee's work.

The study also demonstrated that leadership derives from group acceptance rather than from the unique acts of the chairman. "When the participants do not perceive the designated leader as satisfactorily performing the controlling functions, the participants increase their own attempts to influence their fellow members."[26] The acceptance of the leader was based upon task (good ideas) and chairmanship skills and had little to do with his personal popularity as a group member.

The importance of chairman control in committee action has been similarly demonstrated in several other studies.[27] In his study of 72 management conferences, for example, Berkowitz[28] found that a high degree of "leadership sharing" was related inversely to participant satisfaction and to a measure of output. The norms of these groups sanctioned a "take-charge" chairman. When the chairman failed to meet these expectations, he was rejected and both group satisfaction and group output suffered. These studies do not necessarily suggest that committees less concerned with task goals also prefer a directive chairman. Where the committees are composed of more socially oriented members, the preference for leader control may be less strong.[29]

Leadership roles. A second approach to understanding the leadership of committees is to investigate leadership roles in small groups. Pervading the research literature is a basic distinction between group activities directed to one or the other of two types of roles performed by leaders. They are defined by Benne and Sheats[30] as task roles, and as group-building and maintenance roles. Task roles are related to the direct accomplishment of group purpose, such as seeking information, initiating, evaluating, and seeking or giving opinion. The latter roles are concerned with group integration and solidarity through encouraging, harmonizing, compromising, and reducing conflict.

Several empirical investigations of leadership have demonstrated that both roles are usually performed within effective groups.[31] However, these roles are not always performed by the same person. Frequently one member is seen as the "task leader" and another as the "social leader" of the group.

Combined task and social roles. Can or should these roles be combined in a single leader? The prototypes of the formal and the informal leader which we inherit from classical management lore tend to lead to the conclusion that such a combination is somehow impossible or perhaps undesirable. The research literature occasionally supports this point of view as well.

There is much to be said for a combination of roles. Several studies have shown that outstanding leaders are those who possess both task and social orientations.[32] The study by Borgotta, Couch, and Bales illustrates the point. These researchers assigned leaders high on both characteristics to problem-solving groups. The eleven leaders whom they called "great men" were selected from 126 in an experiment on the basis of high task ability, individual assertiveness, and social acceptability. These men also retained their ratings as "great men" throughout a series of different problem-solving sessions. When led by "great men" the groups achieved a higher rate of suggestion and agreement, a lower rate of "showing tension," and higher rates of showing solidarity and tension release than comparable groups without "great men."

When viewed collectively two conclusions emerge from the above studies. Consistent with existing opinion, the leader who is somewhat assertive and who takes charge and controls group proceedings is performing a valid and necessary role. However, such task leadership is a necessary but not a sufficient condition for effective committee performance. Someone in the group must perform the role of group-builder and maintainer of social relations among the members. Ideally both roles should probably be performed by the designated chairman. When he does not have the necessary skills to perform both roles, he should be the task leader and someone else should perform the social leadership role. Effective committee performance requires both roles to be performed, by a single person or by complementary performance of two or more members.

COMMITTEE MEMBERSHIP

The atmosphere of committee operations described in the classic literature is one where all members seem to be cooperating in the achievement of committee purpose. It is unclear, however, if cooperation is necessarily the best method of solving problems, or if competition among members or groups of members might not achieve more satisfactory results. Cooperation also seems to imply a sharing or homogeneity of values. To answer the question we must consider two related problems: the effects of cooperation or competition on committee effectiveness, and the effects of homogeneous or heterogeneous values on committee effectiveness.

Cooperation or Competition

A number of studies have contrasted the impact of competition and cooperation on group satisfaction and productivity. In some cases the group is given a cooperative or competitive "treatment" through direction or incentive when it is established. In others, competition and cooperation are inferred from measures of groups in which members are operating primarily for personal interest, in contrast with groups in which members are more concerned with group needs. These studies show rather consistently that "group members who have been motivated to cooperate show more positive responses to each other, are more favorable in their perceptions, are more involved in the task, and have greater satisfaction with the task."[33]

The best known study regarding the effects of cooperation and competition was conducted by Deutsch[34] in ten experimental groups of college students, each containing five persons. Each group met for one three-hour period a week for six weeks, working on puzzles and human relations problems. Subjects completed a weekly and post-experimental questionnaire. Observers also recorded interactions and completed overall rating scales at the end of each problem.

In some groups, a cooperative atmosphere was established by instructing members that the group as a whole would be evaluated in comparison with four similar groups, and that each person's course grade would depend upon the performance of the group itself. In others, a competitive relationship was established by telling the members that each would receive a different grade, depending upon his relative contribution to the group's problem solutions.

The results, as summarized by Hare, show that:

Compared with the competitively organized groups, the cooperative groups had the following characteristics:

(1) Stronger individual motivation to complete the group task and stronger feelings of obligation toward other members.

(2) Greater division of labor both in content and frequency of interaction among members and greater coordination of effort.

(3) More effective inter-member communication. More ideas were verbalized, members were more attentive to one another, and more accepting of and affected by each other's ideas. Members also rated themselves as having fewer difficulties in communicating and understanding others.

(4) More friendliness was expressed in the discussion and members rated themselves higher on strength of desire to win the respect of one another. Members were also more satisfied with the group and its products.

(5) More group productivity. Puzzles were solved faster and the recommendations produced for the human-relations problems were longer and qualitatively better. However, there were no significant differences in the average individual productivity as a result of the two types of group experience nor were there any clear differences in the amounts of individual learning which occurred during the discussions.[35]

Similar evidence was found in the study of 72 decision-making conferences by Fouriezos, Hutt, and Guetzkow.[36] Based on observer ratings of self-oriented need behavior, correlational evidence showed that such self-centered behavior was positively related to participant ratings of high group conflict and negatively related to participant satisfaction, group solidarity, and task productivity.

In general, the findings of these and other studies suggest that groups in which members share in goal attainment, rather than compete privately or otherwise seek personal needs, will be more satisfied and productive.[37]

Homogeneity or Heterogeneity

The effects of member composition in the committee should also be considered from the standpoint of the homogeneity or heterogeneity of its membership. Homogeneous groups are those in which members are similar in personality, value orientation, attitudes to supervision, or predisposition to accept or reject fellow members. Heterogeneity is induced in the group by creating negative expectations regarding potential contributions by fellow members, by introducing differing personality types into the group, or by creating subgroups which differ in their basis of attraction to the group.

Here the evidence is much less clear. Some homogeneous groups become satisfied and quite unproductive, while others become satisfied and quite productive. Similarly, heterogeneity may be shown to lead to both productive and unproductive conditions. While the answer to this paradox may be related to the different definitions of homogeneity or heterogeneity in the studies, it appears to have greater relevance to the task and interpersonal requirements of the group task.

In some studies, homogeneity clearly leads to more effective group performance. The work of Schutz[38] is illustrative. In his earlier writing, Schutz distinguished between two types of interpersonal relationships: power orientation and personal orientation. The first emphasizes authority symbols. The power-oriented person follows rules and adjusts to external systems of authority. People with personal orientations emphasize interpersonal considerations. They assume that the way a person achieves his goal is by working within a framework of close personal relations, that is, by being a "good guy," by liking others, by getting people to like him. In his later work, Schutz[39] distinguished among three types of needs: *inclusion*, or the need to establish and maintain a satisfactory relation with people with respect to interaction and association; *control*, or the need to establish and maintain a satisfactory relation with people with respect to control and power; and *affection*, or the need to establish and maintain a satisfactory relation with others with respect to love and affection.

Using attitude scales, Schutz established four groups in which people were compatible with respect to high needs for personal relations with others, four whose members were compatible with respect to low personal orientation, and four which contained subgroups differing in these needs. Each of the twelve groups met twelve times over a period of six weeks and participated in a series of different tasks.

The results showed that groups which are compatible, either on a basis of personalness or counterpersonalness, were significantly more productive than groups which had incompatible subgroups. There was no significant difference between the productivity of the two types of compatible groups. As might be expected, the difference in productivity between compatible and incompatible groups was greatest for tasks which required the most interaction and agreement under conditions of high-time pressure.

A similar positive relationship between homogeneity and productivity is reported for groups in which compatibility is established on the basis of prejudice or degree of conservatism, managerial personality traits, congeniality induced by directions from the researcher, or status congruence.[40] In Adams' study, technical performance first increased, then decreased, as status congruence became greater. Group social performance increased continuously with greater homogeneity, however.

The relationship posited above does not always hold, however. In some studies, heterogeneous groups were more productive than homogeneous. For example, Hoffman[41] constructed heterogeneous and homogeneous groups, based on personality profiles, and had them work on two different types of problems. On the first, which required consideration of a wide range of alternatives of a rather specific nature, heterogeneous groups produced significantly superior solutions. On the second problem, which required primarily group consensus and had no objectively "good" solution, the difference between group types was not significant. Ziller[42] also found heterogeneity to be associated with the ability of Air Force crews to judge the number of dots on a card.

Collins and Guetzkow[43] explain these contradictory findings by suggesting that increasing heterogeneity has at least two effects on group interaction: it increases the difficulty of building interpersonal relations, and it increases the problem-solving potential of the group, since errors are eliminated, more alternatives are generated, and wider criticism is possible. Thus, heterogeneity would seem to be valuable where the needs for task facilitation are greater than the need for strong interpersonal relations.

Considering our original question, it appears that, from the standpoint of cooperation versus competition in committees, the cooperative committee is to be preferred. If we look at the effects of homogeneous or heterogeneous committee membership, the deciding factor seems to be the nature of the task and the degree of interpersonal conflict which the committee can tolerate.

SUMMARY AND CONCLUSIONS

Research findings regarding committee size, leadership, and membership have been reviewed. Evidence has been cited showing that the ideal size is five, when the five members possess the necessary skills to solve the problems facing the committee.

Viewed from the standpoint of the committee members' ability to attend to both the group and its members, or from the standpoint of balanced interpersonal needs, it seems safe to suggest that this number has normative value in planning committee operations. For technical problems additional members may be added to ensure the provision of necessary skills.

A second area of investigation concerned the functional separation of the leadership role and the influence of the role on other members. The research reviewed supports the notion that the committee chairman should be directive in his leadership, but a more specific definition of leadership roles makes questionable whether the chairman can or should perform as both the task and the social leader of the group. The evidence regarding the latter indicates that combined task and social leadership is an ideal which is seldom attained, but should be sought.

The final question concerned whether committee membership would be most effective when cooperative or competitive. When evaluated from the standpoint of research on cooperative versus competitive groups, it is clear that cooperative membership is more desirable. Committee operation can probably be enhanced by selecting members whose self-centered needs are of a less intense variety and by directions to the group which strengthen motivations of a cooperative nature. When the proposition is evaluated from the standpoint of heterogeneity or homogeneity of group membership, the conclusion is less clear. Apparently, heterogeneity in a group can produce both ideas and a screening process for evaluating their quality, but the advantage of this process depends upon the negative effects of heterogeneous attitudes upon interpersonal cooperation.

REFERENCES

1. Rollie Tillman, Jr. "Problems in Review: Committees on Trial." *Harvard Business Review,* 38 (May–June 1960), pp. 6–12; 162–72. Firms with 1001 to 10,000 reported 93 percent use; 250 to 1000 reported 82 percent use.
2. J. H. Healey. *Executive Coordination and Control.* Monograph No. 78 (Columbus: Bureau of Business Research, The Ohio State University, 1956), p. 185.
3. "Committees." *Management Review,* 46 (October 1957), pp. 4–10; 75–78.
4. M. Kriesberg. "Executives Evaluate Administrative Conferences." *Advanced Management,* 15 (March 1950), pp. 15–17.
5. Tillman, op. cit., p. 12.
6. Kriesberg, op. cit., p. 15.
7. "The Committee System—Congress at Work." *Congressional Digest,* 34 (February 1955), pp. 47–49; 64.
8. E. H. Taves. "Two Mechanisms for the Perception of Visual Numerousness." *Archives of Psychology,* 37 (1941), p. 265.
9. A. Paul Hare. *Handbook of Small Group Research.* (New York: The Free Press of Glencoe, 1962), p. 227.
10. B. M. Bass, and F. M. Norton. "Group Size and Leaderless Discussions." *Journal of Applied Psychology,* 35 (1951), pp. 397–400.
11. Hare, op. cit., p. 228.
12. R. F. Bales, F. L. Strodtbeck, T. M. Mills, and M. E. Roseborough. "Channels of Communication in Small Groups." *American Sociological Review,* 16 (1951), pp. 461–68.
13. F. F. Stephen, and E. G. Mishler. "The Distribution of Participation in Small

Groups: An Exponential Approximation." *American Sociological Review*, 17 (1952), pp. 598–608.

14. J. R. Gibb. "The Effects of Group Size and of Threat Reduction upon Creativity in a Problem-Solving Situation." *American Psychologist*, 6 (1951), p. 324. (Abstract)

15. P. Slater. "Contrasting Correlates of Group Size." *Sociometry*, 21 (1958), pp. 129–39.

16. R. F. Bales, and E. F. Borgotta. "Size of Group as a Factor in the Interaction Profile." In *Small Groups: Studies in Social Interaction*, A. P. Hare, E. F. Borgotta, and R. F. Bales, eds. (New York: Knopf, 1965, rev. ed.), pp. 495–512.

17. Ibid., p. 512.

18. Slater, op. cit., pp. 137–38.

19. R. F. Bales. "In Conference." *Harvard Business Review*, 32 (March–April 1954), pp. 44–50; Also A. P. Hare. "A Study of Interaction and Consensus in Different Sized Groups." *American Sociological Review*, 17 (1952), pp. 261–67.

20. D. Fox, I. Lorge, P. Weltz, and K. Herrold. "Comparison of Decisions Written by Large and Small Groups." *American Psychologist*, 8 (1953), p. 351. (Abstract)

21. A. Paul Hare. "Interaction and Consensus in Different Sized Groups." *American Sociological Review*, 17 (1952), pp. 261–67.

22. G. B. Watson. "Do Groups Think More Efficiently Than Individuals?" *Journal of Abnormal and Social Psychology*, 23 (1928), pp. 328–36; Also D. J. Taylor and W. L. Faust. "Twenty Questions: Efficiency in Problem Solving as a Function of Size of Group." *Journal of Experimental Psychology*, 44 (1952), pp. 360–68.

23. Tillman, op. cit., p. 168.

24. S. L. Udall. "Defense of the Seniority System." *New York Times Magazine* (January 13, 1957), p. 17.

25. L. Schlesinger, J. M. Jackson, and J. Butman. "Leader-Member Interaction in Management Committees." *Journal of Abnormal and Social Psychology*, 61, No. 3 (1960), pp. 360–64.

26. Ibid., p. 363.

27. L. Berkowitz. "Sharing Leadership in Small Decision-Making Groups." *Journal of Abnormal and Social Psychology*, 48 (1953), pp. 231–38; Also N. T. Fouriezos, M. L. Hutt, and H. Guetzkow. "Measurement of Self-Oriented Needs in Discussion Groups." *Journal of Abnormal and Social Psychology*, 45 (1950), pp. 682–90; Also H. P. Shelley. "Status Consensus, Leadership, and Satisfaction with the Group." *Journal of Social Psychology*, 51 (1960), pp. 157–64.

28. Berkowitz. Ibid., p. 237.

29. R. C. Anderson. "Learning in Discussions: A Resume of the Authoritarian-Democratic Studies." *Harvard Education Review*, 29 (1959), pp. 201–14.

30. K. D. Benne, and P. Sheats. "Functional Roles of Group Members." *Journal of Social Issues*, 4 (Spring 1948), pp. 41–49.

31. R. F. Bales. *Interaction Process Analysis* (Cambridge: Addison-Wesley, 1951); also R. M. Stogdill and A. E. Coons (eds.), *Leader Behavior: Its Description and Measurement*, Monograph No. 88 (Columbus: Bureau of Business Research, The Ohio State University, 1957); also A. W. Halpin. "The Leadership Behavior and Combat Performance of Airplane Commanders." *Journal of Abnormal and Social Psychology*, 49 (1954), pp. 19–22.

32. E. G. Borgotta, A. S. Couch, and R. F. Bales. "Some Findings Relevant to the Great Man Theory of Leadership." *American Sociological Review*, 19 (1954), pp. 755–759; Also E. A. Fleishman, and E. G. Harris. "Patterns of Leadership Behavior Related to Employee Grievances and Turnover." *Personnel Psychology*, 15, No. 1 (1962), pp. 43–56; Also Stogdill and Coons, Ibid.; Also H. Oaklander and E. A. Fleishman. "Patterns of Leadership Related to Organizational Stress in Hospital Settings." *Administrative Science Quarterly*, 8 (March 1964), pp. 520–32.

33. Hare. *Handbook of Small Group Research, op. cit.*, p. 254.

34. M. Deutsch. "The Effects of Cooperation and Competition upon Group Process." In *Group Dynamics, Research and Theory*, D. Cartwright and A. Zander, eds., (New York: Harper and Row, 1953).

35. Hare. *Handbook of Small Group Research, op. cit.*, p. 263.

36. Fouriezos, Hutt, and Guetzkow. *op. cit.*

37. C. Stendler, D. Damrin and A. Haines. "Studies in Cooperation and Competition: I. The Effects of Working for Group and Individual Rewards on the Social Climate of Children's Groups." *Journal of Genetic Psychology*, 79 (1951), pp. 173–97; Also A. Mintz. "Nonadaptive Group Behavior." *Journal of Abnormal and Social Psychology*, 46 (1951), pp. 150–59; Also M. M. Grossack. "Some Effects of Cooperation and Competition upon Small Group Behavior." *Journal of Abnormal and Social Psychology*, 49 (1954), pp. 341–48; Also E. Gottheil. "Changes in Social Perceptions Contingent upon Competing or Cooperating." *Sociometry*, 18 (1955), pp. 132–37; Also A. Zander and D. Wolfe. "Administrative Rewards and Coordination Among Committee Members." *Administrative Science Quarterly*, 9 (June 1964), pp. 50–69.

38. W. C. Schutz. "What Makes Groups Productive?" *Human Relations*, 8 (1955), pp. 429–65.

39. W. C. Schutz. *FIRO: A Three-Dimensional Theory of Interpersonal Behavior.* (New York: Holt, Rinehart and Winston, 1958).

40. I. Altman and E. McGinnies. "Interpersonal Perception and Communication in Discussion Groups of Varied Attitudinal Composition." *Journal of Abnormal and Social Psychology*, 60 (May 1960), pp. 390–93; Also W. A. Haythorn, E. H. Couch, D. Haefner, P. Langham and L. Carter. "The Behavior of Authoritarian and Equalitarian Personalities in Groups." *Human Relations*, 9 (1956), pp. 57–74; Also E. E. Ghiselli and T. M. Lodahl. "Patterns of Managerial Traits and Group Effectiveness." *Journal of Abnormal and Social Psychology*, 57 (1958), pp. 61–66; Also R. V. Exline. "Group Climate as a Factor in the Relevance and Accuracy of Social Perception." *Journal of Abnormal and Social Psychology*, 55 (1957), pp. 382–88; Also S. Adams. "Status Congruency as a Variable in Small Group Performance." *Social Forces*, 32 (1953), pp. 16–22.

41. L. R. Hoffman. "Homogeneity of Member Personality and Its Effect on Group Problem-Solving. *Journal of Abnormal and Social Psychology*, 58 (1959), pp. 27–32.

42. R. C. Ziller. "Scales of Judgment: A Determinant of Accuracy of Group Decisions." *Human Relations*, 8 (1955), pp. 153–64.

43. B. E. Collins and H. Guetzkow. *A Social Psychology of Group Process for Decision-Making.* (New York: John Wiley and Sons, 1965), p. 101.

Preventing Groupthink

Irving L. Janis

A PRETZEL-SHAPED QUESTION

One obvious way to prevent groupthink is simply to make one person responsible for every important decision, eliminating all the problems of group dynamics from the outset. But clearly this solution would be self-defeating. Only the most authoritarian of leaders fails to recognize the peril in relying solely on his own deliberations.

For constructive thinking to go on, a group must have a fairly high degree of like-mindedness about basic values and mutual respect. The members must forgo trying to score points in a power struggle or to obtain ego gratification by deflating rivals. These basic conditions are not likely to be created until the policy-making group becomes at least moderately cohesive. But then the quality of the group's deliberations may deteriorate as a result of the concurrence-seeking tendency that gives rise to the symptoms of groupthink. Consequently, the problem of preventing costly miscalculations and lapses from rational thinking in decision-making bodies is complicated: How can policy-makers benefit from the cohesiveness of their group without suffering serious losses from groupthink? This sort of intricate psychological issue has been called a pretzel-shaped question and it may require pretzel-shaped answers.

THEREFORE, WHAT?

The difficulties of making inferential leaps from generalizations about the conditions that foster groupthink to concrete proposals for preventive action are essentially the same for our pretzel-shaped problem as for any other complicated social problem, such as environmental pollution. Kenneth Hare has pointed out that although life scientists have accumulated considerable knowledge about the causes and consequences of air pollution and other forms of environmental contamination, the scientists with the greatest expertise do not have the competence single-handedly to propose public policies for preventing eco-catastrophes:

> the greatest hazard in our path is inherent in Lyndon Johnson's acid query, "Therefore, what?" which he is said to have thrown at a group of professors who had just briefed him on the Middle Eastern situation. The political interest in the environment demands proposals for *action*. . . . At present, we are not equipped to make such proposals.

The same must be said even more emphatically about the problem of counteracting the psychological pollution of groupthink, for much less is known about the causes and consequences of concurrence-seeking behavior than is known about environmental contaminants. Yet, as Hare points out, the researchers who have the deepest understanding of the problems are not acting in a socially responsible way if they attempt to withdraw completely from the arena of practical reform. Hare argues that "no important social problem is ever simple and none ever lies fully within the competence of a single academic discipline." He recommends that instead of evading the issue by repeating that "this is an interdisciplinary problem," everyone who knows something relevant should participate in developing a new discipline that will tackle the social and technical engineering problems. So great is the need for synthesis and multivariate analysis of theoretical and applied problems in all disciplines, according to Hare, that a marked change is to be expected in the trend of basic sciences. Whereas the past century has been the era in which each subdiscipline dissected reality in fine detail, Hare foresees that in the next century scientists will try to understand how complex systems work and how they can be changed.

If we are to overhaul the machinery of policy-making in complex governmental, industrial, and welfare organizations, we must certainly apply Hare's advice and stop complaining about the interdisciplinary complexities of the problems and start creating a new discipline that synthesizes whatever is relevant from them all. What is urgently needed is a new type of intervention research, in which experienced executives familiar with the policy-making system from the inside and a variety of specialists familiar with various decision-making processes from the outside collaborate to develop viable improvements. If this type of enterprise materializes, one line of intervention research might be devoted to testing plausible recommendations, inferred from tentative generalizations about the conditions under which groupthink flourishes, for improving the quality of executive decision-making.

My answer to the acid-test question "Therefore, what?" is heavily influenced by many prior social psychological experiments and detailed observations bearing on group dynamics, including my own studies of task-oriented groups. In this field of research, we become sensitized to the vagaries of human response to seemingly straightforward treatments for improving the quality of group products—vagaries that often force the investigator to conclude that the remedy is worse than the disease. Furthermore, even if free from undesirable side effects, the new treatments are undoubtedly a long way from providing a complete cure. In most cohesive groups, concurrence-seeking tendencies are probably much too powerful to be subdued by administrative changes of the type to be proposed. At best, those changes might somewhat decrease the strength of concurrence-seeking tendencies, thereby reducing the frequency of error. But is it worthwhile, then, for an organization to expend effort, time, and money to try to introduce and assess improvements with such limited potentialities? The answer depends partly on how much damage can be expected from collective miscalculations by an organization's policy-making group. When there is no known antibiotic to cure a virulent respiratory disease, it is still worthwhile during an epidemic to find out whether some elementary precautions, such as staying away from crowded places, will lower significantly the chances of being infected. The prescriptions I am proposing are perhaps like those elementary precautions; they may sometimes help to keep us out of danger while the search for an effective cure continues. It is with considerable ambivalence, therefore, that I offer my suggestions for preventing groupthink.

THREE PRESCRIPTIONS AND THEIR UNDESIRABLE SIDE EFFECTS

The three suggestions for preventing groupthink . . . have major drawbacks. One reason for dwelling on the drawbacks is to underline the fact that these prescriptive hypotheses, as well as others to be discussed shortly, must be validated before they can be applied with any confidence. In my opinion, despite potential drawbacks, they warrant the trouble and expense of being tested as potentially useful means for partially counteracting groupthink whenever a small number of executives in any organization meet with their chief executive to work out new policies. Certain of the anti-groupthink procedures might also help to counteract initial biases of the members, prevent pluralistic ignorance, and eliminate other sources of error that can arise independently of groupthink.

1. *The leader of a policy-forming group should assign the role of critical evaluator to each member, encouraging the group to give high priority to airing objections and doubts. This practice needs to be reinforced by the leader's acceptance of criticism of his own judgments in order to discourage the members from soft-pedaling their disagreements.*

If the proposed practice is wholeheartedly approved and reinforced by the chief executive and the other top executives in the organization's hierarchy, it might help to counteract the spontaneous group pressures that give rise to a premature consensus. This will not happen, however, unless the leader conveys to the members by his own actions that the task of critical appraisal is to be given precedence over maintaining traditional forms of deference. It is difficult for the members of an amiable executive group to adopt such a norm, but without this basic change in orientation, no other recommendation for improving the quality of group decision-making is likely to be successful because each can easily be subverted by a group intent on pleasing the leader. The leader must demonstrate that he can be influenced by those who disagree with him. He will fail to reinforce the new norm if he shows his displeasure by terminating a discussion when it is not moving in the direction he wants or if his facial expressions and other nonverbal communications belie his words.

The proposed leadership practice has some potential disadvantages that must be taken into account. Prolonged debates within the group can sometimes be costly when a rapidly growing international crisis requires an immediate policy solution in order to avert catastrophe. Open criticism can also lead to damaged feelings when the members resolutely live up to their role as critical evaluators and take each other's proposals over the bumps. Feelings of rejection, depression, and anger might be evoked so often when this role assignment is put into practice that it could have a corrosive effect on morale and working relations within the group. The critical-evaluator role assignment might have to be supplemented by an in-service training program to give executives special skills for avoiding the pitfalls of uninhibited debate. Further, a judicious chairman would be needed, one whose talents as a mediator enable him to head off disruptive quarrels and demoralizing stalemates.

The effectiveness of a group of critical evaluators will depend on the background and personality of the members. A policy-making group of bristling curmudgeons might waste their time on endless reiterations of clashing points of view. Seldom, if ever, do we find in a policy-making committee the ideal type of genuinely reasonable people who can be counted on to function as constructive discussants, to take account of their colleagues' points of view, and to make judicious but principled compromises when the time comes for consensus. Nevertheless, many policy-making groups are probably made up of people who are capable of functioning more effectively in the desired direction if norms that foster critical evaluation are adopted.

2. *The leaders in an organization's hierarchy, when assigning a policy-planning mission to a group, should be impartial instead of stating preferences and expectations at the outset. This practice requires each leader to limit his briefings to unbiased statements about the scope of the problem and the limitations of available resources, without advocating specific proposals he would like to see adopted. This allows the conferees the opportunity to develop an atmosphere of open inquiry and to explore impartially a wide range of policy alternatives.*

The expected benefit of this leadership practice is that it avoids setting a group norm that will evoke conformity with the leader's views. Among the hazards, however, is a potential cleavage between the leader and the members, which could become a disruptive power struggle if the chief executive regards the emerging consensus among the members as anathema to him. Having lost the opportunity at the outset to steer the group, an inflexible chief might fight with the others, reject their consensus, or disband the group entirely. Even if no rift develops, the chief may feel so frustrated that he becomes more directive than ever. Perhaps the proposed nondirective leadership practice will work only when the chief can be genuinely openminded in all stages of decision-making and values the judgment of the group sufficiently to abstain from using his power when the others reach a consensus that displeases him.

3. *The organization should routinely follow the administrative practice of setting up several independent policy-planning and evaluation groups to work on the same policy question, each carrying out its deliberations under a different leader.*

This practice—which many specialists in administrative sciences advocate for other reasons—would prevent insulation of an executive in-group from challenging information and independent judgments by well-qualified outsiders. Many executives object to it, however, on the grounds that the more people consulted, the greater is the risk of a security leak. This risk would have to be tolerated, or the security problem would have to be solved by adopting measures that could be applied to a larger number of participants without being inordinately costly in time, money, efficiency, and morale. Another drawback is that the more organizational units involved in policy formation, the greater is the opportunity for intraorganizational politics to play a determining role. Harold Wilensky has emphasized this drawback in *Organizational Intelligence:*

> President Eisenhower . . . made the National Security Council "the climax of a ponderous system of boards, staffs and interdepartmental committees through which national security policy was supposed to rise to the top" [Schlesinger wrote in *A Thousand Days*]. As a result, the NSC was converted into a forum for intramural negotiations; what Dean Acheson called "agreement by exhaustion" blurred policy discord. An ironic feature of such a system is that men of good will are moved to obfuscate their positions and overstate agreements with their rivals, on behalf of an ultimate consensus. . . . When they cannot cope with issues by glittering generalities representing the lowest common denominator of agreement, such supercommittees avoid controversial issues entirely, delay decisions, refer issues to other committees, or engage in logrolling, as when the Navy trades off support for more Air Force wings in return for Air Force support for more Navy carriers. Sharp questions, cogent arguments, minority positions, a clear calculation of gains and costs are lost to view.

Furthermore, when many different planning and evaluation groups deliberate, none of them feels responsible for making a careful assessment of the policy's drawbacks. These are the circumstances that encourage a "let George do it" attitude and the even more pervasive presumption that "George must have already done it." Warren Weaver speaks of an organization whose top administrators take great pride in the series of scheduled steps that each new proposal has to go through before reaching them, without realizing that they are allowing responsibility to be so diffuse that no one actually takes on the task of making a careful evaluation: "By the time the proposal reaches the higher levels of responsibility, the number of examinations and successive interim approvals is so impressive that there is an almost overwhelming temptation to assume that the real decision has already been made."

To minimize the risks, guidelines might be formulated that specify the responsibilities of each group and define the role of each participant, emphasizing that primary loyalty is expected to the organization as a whole rather than to a local unit. Further, it may be possible to select statesmenlike executives capable of surmounting the chronic rivalries that plague every large bureaucracy — men who can be counted on to assess objectively the potential gains and losses for each policy alternative without always giving priority to the special interests of their own unit in its power struggles within the organization. The ultimate success of a multiple-group procedure probably depends on whether these and other safeguards can be introduced. Otherwise the multiple-group antidote to groupthink could spawn a virulent form of politicking that is a worse disease than the one it is supposed to prevent.

MORE PRESCRIPTIONS TO OFFSET INSULATION

Additional prescriptive hypotheses based on inferences from the generalizations . . . concerning the conditions under which groupthink is least likely to occur might help prevent groupthink. The costs and potential losses are essentially the same as those just described for the first three prescriptions; the reader will undoubtedly think of additional ones. Suffice it to say that all the recommendations pose obvious risks: The proposed procedures may lower group cohesiveness and correspondingly lower the morale of the participants, as consensus continues to elude them. They may also prove to be prohibitively costly in taking up the precious time of already overburdened executives. Nevertheless, these prescriptions seem to hold the promise of somewhat reducing the chances of groupthink at a moderate cost, if they are implemented flexibly by sensible executives who do not suffer fools gladly and who do not gladly allow themselves to be made into fools. Like the first three, the additional prescriptions offer only a partial cure.

The next three prescriptions take account of the need to offset the potentially adverse effects of insulation of the policy-making group; they would be especially applicable when the multiple-group structure cannot be implemented.

4. *Throughout the period when the feasibility and effectiveness of policy alternatives are being surveyed, the policy-making group should from time to time divide into two or more subgroups to meet separately, under different chairmen, and then come together to hammer out their differences.*

The formation of subgroups might reduce the chances that the entire group will develop a concurrence-seeking norm and increase the chances that illusory assumptions will be critically examined before a consensus is reached. Subgrouping was one of the procedures used by the Executive Committee during the Cuban missile crisis, and it appears to have contributed to the effectiveness of that group's critical appraisals.

5. *Each member of the policy-making group should discuss periodically the group's deliberations with trusted associates in his own unit of the organization and report back their reactions.*

Here I am assuming that each policy-maker's circle of associates can be trusted to adhere to the security regulations that govern the policy-makers. I also assume that each circle will include men with somewhat different types of expertise, outlooks, and values, so that they can be expected to make independent criticisms and perhaps offer some fresh solutions. In order for the home-office meetings to be effective, each policy-maker would have to conduct them in a nondirective style that encourages free discussion, taking on the role of information-seeker rather than of proselytizing boss. When reporting back to the group, each policy-maker would have to take on the role of information-transmitter and try to describe accurately all varieties of reactions, not specially singling out those that support his own views.

Consider what would have happened at the Bay of Pigs planning sessions if, instead of restricting discussion to the small group of advisers dominated by the two CIA leaders who had evolved the plan, Secretary Rusk had conducted a genuine evaluation meeting with trusted associates in the State Department, Secretary McNamara had done the same in the Defense Department, and each of the others had done likewise in his home office. Chances are that the members of the planning group would have been rudely shaken out of their complacency as they encountered strong negative reactions like the horror that Chester Bowles is reported to have experienced at the one planning session he attended. When Bowles submitted his criticisms in a memorandum and spoke privately to Rusk, his objections were quickly brushed aside; Rusk did not permit the memorandum to be shown to the President or to anyone else. Wouldn't a member of a policy-making group be much less likely to protect the group from such outside influence, to take on the functions of a mindguard, if he were to encounter strong objections to a preferred policy alternative from more than one colleague, especially when he knew that the policy-making group was expecting him to report back on what was actually said at the meetings in his home office?

6. One or more outside experts or qualified colleagues within the organization who are not core members of the policy-making group should be invited to each meeting on a staggered basis and should be encouraged to challenge the views of the core members.

In order to counteract a false sense of complacency about risky decisions, the visitors would have to be trustworthy associates carefully selected because of their capacity to grasp new ideas quickly, perspicacity in spotting hidden catches, sensitivity to moral issues, and verbal skill in transmitting criticism. Such outsiders were, in fact, deliberately brought into the Executive Committee's meetings during the Cuban missile crisis, and they were urged to express their objections openly. This atmosphere was quite different from the one that prevailed throughout the Bay of Pigs planning sessions, where, with rare exceptions, the discussants at every meeting were always the same men.

Additional safeguards might be needed to ensure that the objective of inviting well-qualified visitors is not neutralized or subverted. First, visitors who are likely to raise debate-worthy objections should be invited long before a consensus has been reached, not after most of the core members have made up their minds, as was the case when Senator Fulbright was invited to participate in the Bay of Pigs deliberations. Second, each visitor should be asked to speak out about his qualms and not brood silently, as Bowles felt constrained to do when he attended a Bay of Pigs planning session. Third, after the visitor speaks his piece, the chairman should call for open discussion of his objections instead of moving on to other business, as President Kennedy did after Senator Fulbright gave his rousing speech at the final planning session about the undesirable political and moral consequences of the Bay of Pigs invasion plan.

These prescriptions are designed to help offset leadership practices that bias the group's deliberations and that establish concurrence-seeking as an informal group norm.

7. At every meeting devoted to evaluating policy alternatives, at least one member should be assigned the role of devil's advocate.

Whenever assigning the role of critical evaluator to every member of the group is not feasible, assigning the devil's advocate role to one or two members may be of some limited value. In recent years, however, use of a devil's advocate has become popular among high-level executives, and many go through the motions without any apparent effect. For example, President Johnson and other leading members of his Tuesday Lunch Group claimed that they had devil's advocates in their midst each time they decided to intensify the air war against North Vietnam. But those devils were not very devilish. James C. Thomson has informed us, on the basis of his observations during several years of service on the White House staff, that the devil's advocates in Johnson's inner circle quickly became domesticated and were allowed by the President to speak their piece only as long as they remained within the bounds of what he and other leading members of the group considered acceptable dissent. George Reedy, who was President Johnson's press secretary for a time, adds that within Johnson's councils "[the official devil's advocate's] objections and cautions are discounted before they are delivered. They are actually welcomed because they prove for the record that decision was preceded by controversy." Alexander George also comments that, paradoxically, the institutionalized devil's advocate, instead of stirring up much-needed turbulence among the members of a policy-making group, may create the "comforting feeling that they have considered all sides of the issue and that the policy chosen has weathered challenges from within the decision-making circle." He goes on to say that after the President has fostered the ritualized use of devil's advocates, the top-level officials may learn nothing more than how to enact their policy-making in such a way as to meet the informed public's expectation about how important decisions should be made and "to project a favorable image into the 'instant histories' that will be written shortly thereafter."

The problem, then, is how to avoid tokenism on the part of the chief executive, how to inject a genuine effort that will not belie the instant historians' reassuring picture of healthy controversy. If the leader genuinely wants the group to examine opposing arguments, he will have to give the devil's advocate an unambiguous assignment to present his arguments as cleverly and convincingly as he can, like a good lawyer, challenging the testimony of those advocating the majority position. This does not mean that the leader has to transform the meetings with his policy advisers into a kind of formal debate or that the devil's advocate should be strident, rude, or insolent in pressing for an alternative point of view. The most effective performers in the role are likely to be those who can be truly devilish by raising new issues in a conventional, low-key style, asking questions such as, "Haven't we perhaps overlooked . . . ?" "Shouldn't we give some thought to . . . ?" The chief executive must make it clear by what he says and does that the listeners are expected to pay close attention to all the devilish arguments and to take them up one by one for serious discussion. The group might adopt essentially the same supplementary procedures suggested for dealing with the points raised by outsiders who introduce fresh notes into the group's deliberations.

During the Cuban missile crisis, President Kennedy gave his brother, the Attorney General, the unambiguous mission of paying devil's advocate, with seemingly excellent results in breaking up a premature consensus. But the vehemence with which Robert

Kennedy plunged into the role may have cost him a considerable amount of popularity among his colleagues on the Executive Committee, and had he not been the President's brother, this might have damaged his government career. Perhaps rotating the role among the most talented role-players in the group would help solve this problem and hamper the build-up of subtle pressures that induce domestication of the role. With one fresh contender after another on hand to challenge the consensus of the majority, the devil could get his due at the meetings and not afterward.

8. Whenever the policy issue involves relations with a rival nation or organization, a sizable bloc of time (perhaps an entire session) should be spent surveying all warning signals from the rivals and constructing alternative scenarios of the rivals' intentions.

To counteract the members' shared illusions of invulnerability and their tendency to ignore warning signals that interfere with complacency, the leader may have to exert special efforts to induce himself and his colleagues to pay sufficient attention to potential risks to make realistic contingency plans. Even when men have a role assignment requiring them to be vigilant, they are likely to disregard intelligence reports and warnings about a potential danger if there is a preexisting consensus among members of their reference group that the particular threat is improbable. Thomas Schelling speaks of the "poverty of expectations" that prevented the military commanders at Pearl Harbor from considering that the warning signals they were receiving during 1941 might point to an oncoming Japanese attack. "Unlike movies," he points out, "real life provides no musical background to tip us off to the climax."

When participants in a policy-planning group are being briefed about their rival's latest moves, audio-visual aids that provide the equivalent of melodramatic background music might overcome their poverty of expectations, especially when their complacency is grounded in unanimous agreement that the warning signals point only to minor threats that can be safely ignored.

Setting aside a block of time for thorough consideration of the potential risks probably has to be made an institutionalized requirement; otherwise any bearer of ill tidings is likely to meet the fate of Cassandra, whose accurate prophecies of catastrophe were never taken seriously. Briefings by intelligence specialists might be supplemented by films or illustrated talks prepared by a skilled scenario writer who deliberately takes on the role of *Cassandra's advocate*, calling attention as vividly as possible to alarming interpretations of the evidence at hand that might otherwise be overlooked.

I am not proposing that Hollywood-like productions become standard fare in high government counsels, which could bring us closer to the day when the Pentagon will routinely commission horror films for use along with other forms of scare propaganda to persuade congressional committees to increase their appropriations to the armed forces. What I have in mind is an occasional presentation of multiple scenarios as a stimulant to the imagination of the members of a policy-making group, which could arouse a state of constructive vigilance in an inert group that has been reposing in tranquil overconfidence. Perhaps the model for the presentation of multiple scenarios should be the great Japanese film *Rashomon*, directed by Akira Kurosawa. This film presents four entirely different scenarios successively, each explaining the same events (a sexual assault and a murder) in a different way, attributing entirely different motivations to the principals, yet accounting equally well for the known facts.

Of course if the most ominous interpretation of an enemy's activities is presented convincingly, a group of government policy-makers might overreact to relatively innocuous events and become all too ready to launch a preemptive first strike. In the series of Rashomon-like alternative scenarios there should always be at least one that plausibly attributes benign intentions to the enemy; this might help prevent such overreactions. To ensure careful weighing of the evidence, additional safeguards against precipitous judgment might be needed. For example, after bringing in outside experts to brief the policy-making group, the leader might assign several members the task of evaluating all warning messages and information about risks that need to be taken into account for contingency planning. In carrying out this task, the participants might find it useful to assume that there is some truth and also some exaggeration in every unwelcome message, before they begin any discussion that moves in the direction of either acting on it or dismissing it as irrelevant.

Psychodramatic role-play exercises might also be used to overcome the influence of stereotypes and to facilitate understanding of the rivals' warnings, enabling the group to predict more accurately the probable responses to one or another course of action. For example, after intelligence experts have given a factual briefing on, say, the Chinese Communists' ambiguous threats during a new international crisis in the Far East, the members of a foreign policy planning group who are most familiar with the beliefs and values of the Chinese leaders might try out a psychodramatic procedure in which they assume the role of their opposite numbers in Peking. The psychodrama might be enacted as a meeting during which the Chinese leaders talk over their options for dealing with the crisis and the countermoves they might make if the United States takes a hard line versus an ameliorative stance. Had this type of role-play exercise been conducted by Truman's advisers in the fall of 1950, they might have taken much more seriously the repeated warnings from Communist China and become reluctant to approve General MacArthur's catastrophic policy of pursuing the North Korean army to the Manchurian border.

The same type of role-playing might be useful in overcoming complacency in a group that collectively judges a series of warnings to be inapplicable and sees no reason to prepare contingency plans for dealing with the potential danger. Suppose that a role-play exercise had been carried out by the group of United States Navy commanders in Hawaii on December 2, 1941, the day that Admiral Kimmel, after being informed by the chief of naval intelligence that no one in the Navy knew where the Japanese aircraft carriers were, jokingly asked if they could be heading straight for Hawaii. If the exercise of playing the role of Japan's supreme military command had been carried out seriously, isn't it likely that at least a few of the high-ranking naval officers responsible for the defense of Hawaii would have argued against the prevailing view that the war warnings they had been receiving during the past week did not warrant the expense of a full alert at Pearl Harbor or a 360-degree air patrol around the Hawaiian Islands?

9. After reaching a preliminary consensus about what seems to be the best policy alternative, the policy-making group should hold a "second chance" meeting at which every member is expected to express as vividly as he can all his residual doubts and to rethink the entire issue before making a definitive choice.

In order to prevent a premature consensus based on unwarranted expectations of invulnerability, stereotypes about the enemy, and other unexamined assumptions shared by members of the group, the second-chance session should be held just before the group takes a definitive vote or commits itself in any other way. At this special meeting, every member should be encouraged to become the devil's advocate and Cassandra's advocate, challenging his own favorite arguments and playing up all the risks. Everyone should deliberately set himself the task of presenting to the group any objections he can think of that have not yet been adequately discussed. In order to stimulate a freewheeling, open discussion in which residual doubts are frankly expressed, the members might be asked to read in advance an eloquent document presenting opposing arguments prepared by opponents of the chosen policy. In giving out such an assignment on occasions when a consensus has been reached rapidly, the leader might take as his model the statement made by Alfred P. Sloan, a former chairman of General Motors who reportedly announced at a meeting of his fellow policymakers:

> Gentlemen, I take it we are all in complete agreement on the decision here. . . . Then I propose we postpone further discussion of this matter until our next meeting to give ourselves time to develop disagreement and perhaps gain some understanding of what the decision is all about.

To encourage members to reveal vague forebodings, it might not be a bad idea for the second-chance meeting to take place in a relaxed atmosphere far from the executive suite, perhaps over drinks (as sometimes happens spontaneously anyhow). According to a report by Herodotus dating from about 45 B.C., whenever the ancient Persians made a decision following sober deliberations, they would always reconsider the matter under the influence of wine. Tacitus claimed that during Roman times the Germans too had a custom of arriving at each decision twice, once sober, once drunk. Some moderate, institutionalized form of allowing second thoughts to be freely expressed before the group commits itself might be remarkably effective for breaking down a false sense of unanimity and related illusions, without endangering anyone's reputation or liver.

Guidelines for Conducting NGT Meetings

Andre L. Delbecq, Andrew H. Van de Ven, and David H. Gustafson

In order to illustrate the NGT [Nominal Group Technique] process, it will be useful to set up an imaginary meeting situation. We will use the case of twenty participants from various large organizations, attending a training conference on group techniques. Our illustration will be a demonstration NGT meeting, the purpose of which is to allow participants to develop questions concerning how to conduct such meetings in back-home settings.

There is a secondary benefit in selecting this particular case illustration. The illustrated meeting format has been shown to be an effective training device which readers may wish to use as a means to introduce other individuals to NGT.

Reprinted from *Group Techniques for Program Planning,* by Andre L. Delbecq, Andrew H. Van de Ven, and David H. Gustafson, pp. 40–66. Copyright ©1975 Scott, Foresman and Company.

The leader should see that a number of preliminary steps are taken care of before the actual NGT meeting gets underway. These include: selecting and preparing the meeting room, providing the necessary supplies, and presenting the opening statement.

The Meeting Room

The major activities of an NGT meeting take place in small groups. The leader must therefore choose a meeting room large enough to accommodate the participants in groups of from five to nine members at individual tables. It is also important that the tables be spaced far enough apart so that the noise and activity at one table does not interfere with other tables.

Although a variety of seating arrangements are serviceable, the focus of an NGT meeting is on the *list* of ideas placed on a flip chart rather than on individual participants. Therefore, it is helpful to seat participants at a rectangular table arranged as an open "U" with a flip chart at the open end of the table (Figure 1). Having a serviceable writing area is also helpful, as the meeting begins with a period of independent written activity.

Supplies

The following supplies should be provided at NGT meetings:

1) Flip chart for each table.
2) Roll of masking tape.
3) Pack of 3 × 5 cards for each table.
4) Felt pens for each table.
5) Paper and pencil for each participant.

The use of the various items will become apparent as we proceed with the description of the meeting. At the moment, however, a word about flip charts is worthwhile.

NGT meetings rely heavily on writing ideas in front of each small group. Therefore, a flip chart or some similar device is imperative. Alternatives to flip charts, which are sometimes unavailable, are: sheets of newsprint, poster board, a roll of butcher paper which may be cut into sheets, or large blackboards (since all items need to be retained in front of each group for voting, the small blackboard is generally undesirable).

Welcoming Statement

When individuals come together to engage in group tasks, perceptions of why the group was formed will affect performance. For example, members who perceive that their group was formed on the basis of congeniality will proceed in a congenial but less effective problem-solving manner than will group members who perceive they were gathered together because of their analytic abilities and problem-solving skills. It is important, therefore, that the NGT leader clarify the member roles and group objectives for the meeting. Appropriate role definitions will help reduce status barriers among members, encourage free communication, and decrease the tendency for high-status individuals to be unduly verbal.

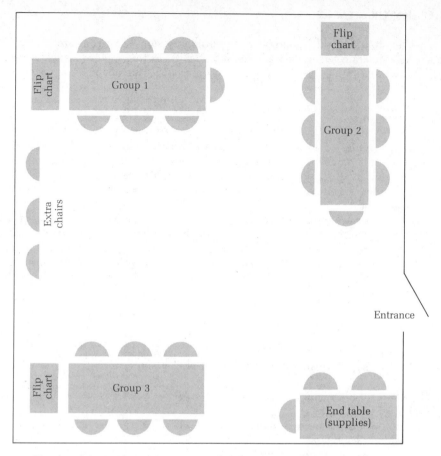

Figure 1   Meeting Room Arrangement for Three NGT Tables

Thus, the leader's welcoming statement should include:

1) A cordial and warm welcome.
2) A sense of importance concerning the group's task.
3) Clarification of the importance of each member's contribution.
4) An indication of the use or purpose of the meeting's output.

We can exemplify such an introduction by going back to our illustration meeting of twenty participants from large organizations gathered to learn about the NGT technique. The leader of the meeting might begin as follows:

"I want to express my appreciation to each of you for attending this workshop on NGT. I am aware that there are many other training opportunities as well as informal activities going on at our convention at the present time. I appreciate the sacrifice you have made to take advantage of this workshop. I welcome each of you warmly to this session.

"Our objective is an important one. At the conclusion of this meeting, we should be able to anticipate and answer many of the questions and difficulties which administrators face when trying to utilize the NGT process. Obviously, unless we are prepared to meet these challenges, our ability to successfully implement this useful technique will be very limited.

"In our meeting it is important that *each* of us fully participate. Indeed, success will depend on our equal and full participation. Each of us is here as an important group resource. There are no status differences between us in this particular meeting. Our success depends on every member fully sharing the insight from his or her own administrative, professional, or technical perspective. I appreciate, therefore, the willingness of every one of you to fully share your ideas and work intensely during the next ninety minutes we are together.

"The ideas which you generate in this workshop will become the basis for follow-up training, skill development, and discussion."

THE NGT PROCESS

For purposes of illustration, we will now focus on a single table of six or seven group members, with a leader who also serves as a recorder. As we will discuss later in the chapter, it is possible to have one leader to provide process directions to several tables, in which case it would be necessary to have a trained recorder at individual tables.

Step 1: Silent Generation of Ideas in Writing

The first step in an NGT meeting is to have the group members write key ideas silently and independently. The benefits of this step are:

1) Adequate time for thinking and reflection.
2) Social facilitation (that is, the constructive tension created by observing other group members working hard).
3) Avoidance of interruptions.
4) Avoidance of undue focusing on a particular idea or train of thought.
5) Sufficient time for search and recall.
6) Avoidance of competition, status pressures, and conformity pressures.
7) The benefit of remaining problem-centered.
8) Avoidance of choosing between ideas prematurely.

In order to facilitate these benefits, the leader proceeds to instruct the group in the first step of the process by:

1) Presenting the nominal question to the group in written form.
2) Verbally reading the question.
3) Directing the group to write ideas in brief phrases or statements.
4) Asking the group to work silently and independently.
5) Modeling good group behavior.

To proceed with our meeting example, the leader would carry on as follows:

"Would each of you please look carefully at the question at the top of the worksheet which I am going to hand out."

The leader passes a set of worksheets to each table. Worksheets are simply lined tablet paper with the nominal question written at the top.

"You will notice that the question which is the focus of our meeting is the following: What barriers do you anticipate in trying to use the NGT technique back home?

"I would like each of you to take five minutes to list your ideas in response to this question, in a brief phrase or a few words, on the worksheet in front of you. Please work independently of other members in identifying barriers which *you* anticipate in trying to use NGT back home. During this period of independent thinking I ask that you not talk to other members, interrupt their thinking, or look at their worksheets. Since this is the opportunity for each of us to prepare his or her contributions to the meeting, I would appreciate intense effort during the next five minutes. At the end of five minutes, I will call time and suggest how we can proceed to share our ideas. Are there any questions? Let's proceed then with our individual effort for the next five minutes."

The leader turns to his own worksheet and begins to write.

Step 1 guidelines. There are four key guidelines for serving as leader in Step 1:

1) Resist nonprocess clarifications.
2) Have the question in writing.
3) Model good group behavior by writing in silence.
4) Sanction individuals who disrupt the silent independent activity.

It is important to note that . . . the leader should avoid providing answers to the question for the group. Experimental evidence clearly shows that a leader who engages in detailed clarification of group tasks tends to lead the group toward his or her interpretation of the task. In this case, the more the leader "clarifies" the question by providing exemplary answers, the more the group focuses on the leader's frame of reference.

For example, if the leader in our case illustration was asked: "By barriers, do you mean lack of necessary skills?" and answered by saying: "Sure, that might be a barrier. For example, perhaps the person trying to use the technique back home did not have prior experience with the technique," he or she will have led the group to focus on leadership skills as a barrier. In fact, for the particular group of administrators present, other barriers such as status impediments, group compositions, etc., might be far more important.

The appropriate answer the leader should give is: "Any barrier which comes to your mind should be written on your worksheet."

If a member of the group still asks for greater clarification of the question, a useful technique is for the leader to answer: "Think of the question as an inkblot. I want you to look at the words on the worksheet and write those ideas which come to *your* mind when you read the question." Such a response is obviously dependent on having the question in writing in front of the group members.

As alternatives to worksheets, the leader can write the stimulus question on a flip chart in front of the group. In any case, having the question in writing clearly aids group concentration on the appropriate question and decreases need for clarification.

The NGT leader is normally not an outsider to the meeting, but rather a working participant. As such, he or she should provide a model of appropriate group behavior during the silent generation phase. A leader who is working hard at the task provides an example of good group behavior. A leader who distracts the group by engaging in other tasks, talking to people, or wandering around the room increases the tendency for other members to deviate from silent, independent reflection and writing.

If individuals in the group begin to whisper to each other, leave their places, sigh, or otherwise disrupt the silent writing period, it is important that the leader quickly and impersonally sanction the distracting behavior. The simplest and most effective method is to look away from the violating parties and speak to the entire group saying, "I hope that we won't interrupt those who are still at work by talking or moving about. There are still two minutes remaining in our work period, and I ask that we continue to think and write our ideas down in silence for the remainder of this short period."

Step 2: Round-Robin Recording of Ideas

The second step of NGT is to record the ideas of group members on a flip chart visible to the entire group. Round-robin recording means going around the table and asking for one idea from one member at a time. The leader writes the idea of a group member on the flip chart and then proceeds to ask for one idea from the next group member in turn. Figure 2 presents a typical list of ideas generated by a group in response to the question used in our case illustration. The benefits of round-robin recording are:

1) Equal participation in the presentation of ideas.
2) Increase in problem-mindedness.
3) Depersonalization—the separation of ideas from personalities.
4) Increase in the ability to deal with a larger number of ideas.
5) Tolerance of conflicting ideas.
6) Encouragement of hitchhiking.[1]
7) Provision of a written record and guide.

Figure 2   List of Items Generated in Response to Question: "What barriers do you anticipate in trying to use the NGT technique back home?"

1.	Leader dominance
2.	Lack of ability to write a good nominal question
3.	Uncertainty about who should be invited
4.	Resistance to a structured group process
5.	Lack of skill in conducting this type of meeting
6.	Length of time the process takes
7.	Avoiding redundancy in the listing process
8.	Avoiding dominance in discussion of items
9.	Unequal writing skill among group members
10.	Shyness in exposing one's own items
11.	Size of the group may be too large to use technique
12.	How to get critical individuals to attend
13.	Resistance of high-status people to open discussion
14.	Lack sufficient self-confidence to run unfamiliar meeting
15.	Inadequate leader legitimacy
16.	Inadequate physical facilities
17.	Insufficient motivation to work seriously
18.	Artificial redundancy in a long list

There is general agreement among scholars that the sharing of all ideas and equalization of participation increases group creativity. The rather mechanical format of going to each member in turn to elicit ideas establishes an important behavior pattern. By the second or third round of idea giving, each member is an achieved participant in the group. A precedent for further participation has been accomplished without competition with high-status members, more aggressive personalities, or more emotional members.

A major concern in group meetings is problem-centeredness. Earlier we documented the importance of a group identifying all the elements of a problem and avoiding premature problem definition. By listing the entire array of ideas *before* discussion and voting, the group ensures that significant ideas will not get lost or forgotten. Lists also facilitate hitchhiking and allow for the consideration of conflicting ideas without pressure.

The fact that a list is *written* is of particular importance. A written idea is more objective and less personal than a verbal statement. If the idea is in writing, individuals are better able to separate it from the personality or position of the individual contributing it. Also, groups are able to deal with a larger number of ideas in writing. As a rough rule of thumb, individuals remember 40 percent of what they can hear, but 70 percent of what they can both see and hear. The written list also becomes the group's secretary, providing minutes and a working draft for later refinement.

Going from member to member eliciting only one idea at a time has its benefits as well. It is not unusual for as much as a third of an individual's ideas relative to a problem to remain unspoken. Embarrassment, conservatism, fear of self-disclosure, etc., contribute much to the often spoken of "hidden agenda." In pilot studies, individual group members were asked to present their entire list to the group at one time. The effects were to: (1) have members hide a substantial number of ideas; and (2) decrease the depersonalization of ideas since it was easy to identify a cluster of ideas with an individual. Round-robin listing minimizes both negative features. First, individuals are given models for self-disclosure. The example of early risk-takers encourages other group members to present more controversial ideas. Second, as the list progresses in length, it is more and more difficult and less rewarding to try to remember who presented what idea. Instead, the list becomes a depersonalized group product.

Finally, the written list is an important early group reward. Members are impressed with the array of ideas generated by the group, the amount of overlap of ideas providing areas of agreement and consensus, the differentiated contributions of individual group members, and the immediate richness of resources for further analysis. At the same time, the group is protected against premature focus on selected ideas or problem simplification.

Inasmuch as round-robin listing is at the heart of the NGT feedback process, careful attention to this step is warranted.

Step 2 guidelines.   Leader requirements for this step include:

1) Clear verbal statement of the step:
   a. the objective is to map the group's thinking.
   b. ideas should be presented in brief words or phrases.
   c. ideas will be taken serially.

    d. duplicate items should be omitted.

    e. variations on themes are desirable.

2) Effective mechanical recording.

3) Direct sanction of inappropriate group behavior.

To return to our illustration, the leader would begin Step 2 with the following statement:

"During the last five minutes, each of us has used our worksheets to list important barriers to utilizing the NGT technique back home. Now I would like to have each of you share your ideas with the other members of the group.

"This is an important step because our list of ideas will constitute a guide for further discussion, help us understand the richness of ideas we have to work with, and stimulate additional ideas.

"In order to accomplish this goal as quickly and efficiently as possible, I am going to go around the table and ask individuals, one at a time, to give me one idea from their worksheet, summarized in a brief phrase or a few words. After the entire list is on the board, we will have the opportunity to discuss, clarify, and dispute the ideas.

"If someone else in the group lists an idea which you also had on your worksheet, you need not repeat the idea. If, however, in *your* judgment the idea on your worksheet contains a different emphasis or variation, we would welcome the idea. Variations on a theme are important and will help us be creative.

[Turning to the first person] "Mr. Smith, would you give me one idea from your list?"

The leader then proceeds to list the ideas on the flip chart, numbering each idea as it is written on the chart. Usually after the second time around the table, one member of the group will say: "I don't have any further ideas." The leader should respond: "Fine, Joe, you can pass. However, feel free to take another turn if some other idea occurs to you." Thus, the individuals who pass will feel free to reenter the listing exercise when their turn comes up on subsequent rounds. The leader should take a turn each round also, listing one idea from his or her worksheet just like the members.

Recording guidelines.   Serving as recorder is a natural skill for some individuals, but a skill others must develop. There are several important hints for effective recording:

1) Record ideas as rapidly as possible.

2) Record ideas in the words used by the group member.

3) Provide assistance in abbreviating only in special situations.

4) Make the entire list visible to the group by tearing off completed sheets from the flip chart and taping them to the wall.

A group's patience is short during the listing of ideas. It is important, therefore, for the leader to complete the step as quickly as possible. Rapid writing (not easy for most of us to master consistent with legibility) is a goal to attain.

It is also important to put the ideas up on the flip chart in the words used by the group member. For example, if the member presents an idea as "what are the physical requirements" these are the words that should appear on the chart. Writing "facilities needed" or some other leader's expression is a violation of etiquette, but more important, decreases the member's role and unduly enlarges the leader's role.

There are situations where individuals seem incapable of presenting their ideas in brief statements. A member might say: "The need for adequate physical facilities limits the effectiveness of the technique to special situations and physical locations." Recorders will soon wear out their felt pens and patience dealing with such lengthy statements. It is appropriate to ask members: "Could you think of a slightly shorter way of placing the idea on the flip chart?" The burden of abbreviation can thus be sent back to the member. A stubborn member who seems determined to speak in epistles rather than phrases can be disciplined by saying: "Would you think about that idea for a few minutes and I will come back to you and ask for a few words or short phrase we can place on the chart." Then the leader can continue, and return to the wordy group member after two or three others have given their ideas. In rare situations (usually research situations with individuals of very limited education) it is appropriate for the recorder to help a member summarize or abbreviate ideas. This, however, should be avoided where possible. The advantages of using the words of the group member are: (1) an increased perception of equality and member importance; (2) greater ego identification with the task; and (3) a lack of feeling that the leader-recorder is manipulating the group.

Members of NGT groups will sometimes engage in one of several disruptive behaviors during the round-robin listing phase. These include: trying to discuss ideas rather than list them; arguing with ideas as they are presented; asking the leader to rule on duplications; and engaging in side conversations. All of these behaviors should be sanctioned when they occur. A member who says: "I'm not quite sure of this idea. Perhaps we should talk about it before we put it on the list," should be encouraged to simply list the idea with an indication that adequate discussion time for all ideas will follow.

The decision as to whether an item is the same as or different from an earlier idea should not be debated. Place responsibility back on the group member by saying, "If you feel your idea is slightly different, let's put it up on the chart."

The goal of Step 2, then, is a rapid, accurate list of ideas in brief words or phrases, recorded in writing on a flip chart in front of the entire group. This list becomes the guide for further discussion and a depersonalized mapping of the group's ideation.

Step 3: Serial Discussion for Clarification

The third step of NGT is to discuss each idea in turn.[2] The benefits of this step are:

1) Avoidance of focusing unduly on any particular idea or subset of ideas.
2) Opportunity for clarification and elimination of misunderstanding.
3) Opportunity to provide the logic behind arguments and disagreements.
4) Recording of differences of opinion without undue argumentation.

Serial discussion means taking each idea listed on the flip chart in order, and allowing a short period of time for the discussion of each idea. The leader points to Item 1, reads it out loud, and asks the group if there are any questions, statements of clarification, or statements of agreement or disagreement which members would like to make about it. The leader allows for discussion, and then moves the group on to Item 2, Item 3, etc.

The dynamics of the resulting communication concerning each idea are important to understand. First, the central object of the discussion is to clarify, not to win arguments. In its simplest form, clarification helps other members understand the meaning of the brief words or phrases on the chart. (It is hardly necessary to belabor the point that written communication is often subject to misunderstanding.) After a brief explanation of what is meant by a specific set of words, most members will reliably record their judgments about the item even if the phrase or words used on the flip chart are awkward.

Clarification is not restricted, however, to comments concerning what the words expressing an item "mean." In the brief discussion, members of the group can convey the logic or analysis behind the item, and the relative importance they place on the item. Likewise, individuals can express their agreement or disagreement with either the expressed logic or the felt relative importance.

Unfortunately, expressions of disagreement in groups can become the signals for lobbying, aggressive interaction, or disruptive argumentation. Most individuals are intuitively aware that prominence and aggression in interaction are highly associated with influence over meeting outcomes in conventional discussion settings. Thus, in other types of meetings, an aggressive or high-status group member can often dominate the group's formal outcome even though other members still disagree with his or her logic.

The purpose of serial discussion is to enhance clarification but minimize influence based on verbal prominence or status. To accomplish these dual objectives, the leader should "pace" the discussion, i.e., he or she should not allow discussion to: (1) unduly focus on any particular idea; or (2) degenerate into argumentation. Suppose, for example, Member X feels that Item 7 is very important, and Member Y feels that Item 7 is specious. The role of the leader is to allow both points of view to be aired, but then to move the group on to a discussion of Item 8, since the purpose of serial discussion is to disclose thinking and analysis, not to resolve differences of opinion. Differences of opinion will be accurately recorded in the voting procedure.

Likewise, if the group spends most of its time discussing the first six items, and very little time discussing later items, those later items may suffer from lack of adequate clarification. The leader should attempt, therefore, to balance discussion across all items, making sure that no item suffers from inadequate clarification due to time constraints.

Step 3 guidelines.   The main responsibilities of the leader, therefore, relative to serial discussion are:

1) To verbally define the role of the step as clarification.
2) To pace the group in order to avoid undue argumentation or neglect of some items at the expense of others.

In our training-meeting illustration, the leader would begin by saying:

"Now that we have listed our ideas on the flip chart, I want to take time to go back and briefly discuss each idea.

"The purpose of this discussion is to clarify the meaning of each item on our flip chart. It is also our opportunity to express our understanding of the logic behind the idea, and the relative importance of the item. We should feel free to express varying points of view or to disagree.

"We will, however, want to pace ourselves so that each of the items on the chart receives the opportunity for some attention, so I may sometimes ask the group to move on to further items.

"Finally, let me point out that the author of the item need not feel obliged to clarify or explain an item. Any member of the group can play that role.

[Going to the flip chart, the leader points to Item 1.] "Are there any questions or comments group members would like to make about Item 1?"

Generally, groups will spend a little time on each item without much leader intervention once the serial discussion has progressed for a few minutes. It will be quite natural for the group to be a little wordier and discuss early items longer than later items. For example, if the group generates eighteen items, the first six or seven will be discussed longer than the later items. This will not affect final voting so long as the later items are discussed long enough for adequate clarification. People will also become more time conscious as the discussion progresses and more disciplined in avoiding lengthy, nonfunctional discussion.

Where an argument occurs, a leader can intervene by saying: "I think we understand both points of view at this point. Perhaps, however, we should move on to the next item in the interest of time."

Since personal satisfaction is related to the opportunity to discuss items, the leader should not overpace or drive the group through the item list. Groups generally will pace themselves if the leader clearly indicates the available time for this step of the meeting.

Finally, we should note that individuals should not be asked to clarify their own items. Imagine a situation when a subordinate technician listed an item such as: "Inadequate supervisory clarification." Several administrators are present, including his own supervisor. If a group member turns to the author of the item and says: "Joe, what do you mean by that statement?" it could put Joe on the spot. A skillful leader should always intervene and say: "Let's not ask individuals to explain items unless they choose to. Mary, what do the words mean to you?" Although most of the time individuals will volunteer to clarify their own items, the precedent should be established that clarification is a group task, not necessarily the unilateral responsibility of the author of the item.

Step 4: Preliminary Vote on Item Importance

The average NGT meeting will generate over twelve items in each group during its idea-generation phase. Through serial discussion, group members will come to understand the meaning of the item, the logic behind the item, and arguments for and against the importance of individual items. In some manner, however, the group must aggregate the judgments of individual members in order to determine the relative importance of individual items.

Management Science has devoted great effort to determining appropriate mechanisms for aggregating group judgments. It has been shown that the following method increases judgmental accuracy (the ability of a group to arrive at a decision which reflects true group preferences):[3]

1) Having individual members of the group make independent judgments.
2) Expressing these individual judgments mathematically by rank-ordering and/or rating items.

3) Using the mean (x) value of independent judgments as the group's decision.

4) Feeding back the results of individual judgments, talking over these results, and revoting.

The above technique has been used effectively as a voting procedure in NGT. A word about several alternative conventional means for reaching a group decision — consensus, majority rule, and independent listing — will help the reader understand the value of this simple mathematical voting procedure recommended in NGT.

Imagine a group with a list of eighteen items. Thirty minutes remain before the meeting is to adjourn. The group must choose those ideas of greatest merit before concluding the meeting.

Member X feels that Item 13 is very important and speaks forcefully to this point. Member Y feels that Item 13 is not important and also speaks forcefully to this position. The reconciliation of the diverse points of view is complex. Consensus must be achieved through discussion in such a way that the two individuals involved are not offended, too much time is not used, and the cohesion of the group is not disrupted. In the press of time, Member X will be under pressure to modify his or her position and reduce the importance of Item 13 in order to accommodate Member Y. Member Y will conversely be under pressure to change his or her judgment. Thus, consensus may lead to regression toward the mean; in order to maintain group cohesion, individuals may distort their independent judgments to accommodate each other.[4]

Majority rule also distorts judgments. First, the minority position counts for zero. The minority position may be less than 100 percent correct, but counting the position as zero distorts judgment. Further, majority rule may also lead to political maneuvering in order to achieve quorums, bringing into play dynamics separate from judgmental estimates.

Finally, show of hands, open discussion, or other forms of public voting are greatly subject to social pressure. If two high-status members of a six-person group and a third member who is a friend of Member X vote for a particular item, the social pressures are heavy upon Member X to also vote for the item.

Let us look at another alternative voting process, independent listing. In this process, each member of the group writes on a separate sheet of paper the five items that he considers most important. In the case of a flip chart with eighteen items, when the independent listing of each member's priority items is completed, the voting results might be as follows:

ITEM	VOTES
1	2
2	1
3	5
7	5
9	5
10	2
11	1
13	5

Independent listing avoids status, personality, and conformity pressures, and allows each member's vote to influence the group. However, it can be modified to obtain still further information. The listing in the above figure would seem to indicate that items 3, 7, 9, and 13 were the most important. Yet such a process does not yield any measure of degree of importance. Rank-ordering can provide greater information. Imagine that the members were asked to assign a value of 5 to the most important item, and a value of 1 to the least important item. Now the results of the voting are again tallied:

ITEM	VOTES
1	3-2
2	1
3	5-5-4-5-4
7	1-2-1-3-1
9	4-3-2-4-2
10	3-2
11	2
13	1-2-5-5-1

Now it is clear that items 3, 7, 9, and 13, which seemed to be equal in importance when single listing was used, are really very different in importance when ranked.

To summarize, we can increase judgmental accuracy by having group members make individual judgments and express these judgments mathematically. With this brief introduction, we can proceed with a description of a simple voting process often used in NGT meetings.

Step 4 guidelines. The simplest and most often used voting procedure in NGT is a rank-ordering which entails the following leadership steps:

1) Ask the group to select from the entire list of ideas on the flip chart a specific number of "priority" or most important items:
   a. have group members place each priority item on a separate 3 × 5 card.
   b. after members have their set of priority cards, have them rank-order the cards, one at a time.
2) Collect the cards and shuffle them, and record the vote on a flip chart in front of the group.

After a good deal of experimentation, the above steps have been routinized into a simple format. However, they rely heavily on very clear instructions from the leader, so the following guidelines should be read carefully.

The leader begins the voting procedure with a statement as follows:

"We have now completed our discussion of the entire list of ideas, have clarified the meaning of each idea, and have discussed the areas of agreement and disagreement. At this time, I would like to have the judgment of each group member concerning the most important ideas on the list.

"To accomplish this step I wonder if each of you would take five 3 × 5 index cards.

[The leader hands a set of index cards to participants at the table.]

"I would like you to select the five most important items from our list of eighteen items. This will require careful thought and effort on your part.

"As you look at the flip chart sheets and find an item which you feel is very important, please record the item on an index card.

[The leader goes to the flip chart and draws an index card.]

"Please place the number of the item in the upper left-hand corner of the card. For example, if you feel Item 13 is very important, you would write 13 in the upper left-hand corner.

[The leader writes 13 in the upper left-hand corner of the card he has drawn on the flip chart.]

"Then write the identifying words or phrase on the card.

[The leader writes the phrase for Item 13 on the card.]

"Do this for each of the five most important items from our list of eighteen items. When you have completed this task, you should have five cards, each with a separate phrase written on the card, and with identifying numbers using the numbering system from our list of ideas on the flip chart.

"*Do not* rank-order the cards yet. Spend the next few minutes carefully selecting the five cards. We will all rank-order the cards together.

"Are there any questions?"

The leader then proceeds to select five priority cards.

A question comes immediately to mind. Why five cards? As a rule of thumb, individuals are able to accurately rank or rate about seven ($\pm$ 2) items. That is, group members can select five to nine priority items with some reliability of judgment. We have arbitrarily selected five for our example. Where lists are shorter (around twelve) selecting five priority items is recommended. Where lists are longer (around twenty) selecting eight priority items is desirable. For research purposes, major budgetary meetings, technical meetings, etc., increasing the number of priority items beyond five is desirable.

People easily become confused and use their own numbering system (1 through 5) rather than number the cards in accordance with the numbers on the flip chart, or else write all their ballots on a single card. Using the visual example of an index card drawn on a flip chart helps eliminate confusion.

Some members of the group will complete their selection much quicker than others. When the leader notes that several members have finished voting but others have not, a useful intervention is to say:

"Some of us have not yet completed our selection of the five most important items. If you have already finished, please take time to recheck to be sure you have made the best selection. Also, let's not disturb those group members who are still making decisions."

In some situations, it is helpful to give the group criteria for choosing the five most important items. This is particularly true where the group composition is somewhat heterogeneous. Examples of criteria are: the five items we should act upon during the next planning period; the five items to which we should allocate our funding; the five items of greatest immediate importance, etc.

After each member of the group has selected five items and written them on separate cards, the leader proceeds as follows:

"Please spread out your cards in front of you so you can see all five at once. Looking at your set of five cards, decide which one card is the most important. Which card is more important than the other four cards?

[The leader gives the group an opportunity to study their cards.]

"Please write a number 5 in the lower right-hand corner of the card and underline the number three times.

"Turn that card over and look at the remaining four cards. Of the remaining four cards, which is the least important? Write a number 1 in the lower right-hand corner and underline that number three times."

The leader then proceeds to have the group choose the most important of the remaining three cards (number rank 4), the least important of the remaining two cards (number rank 2) and to have the group write number 3 on the last card. Figure 3 illustrates a sample index card. The group is given time to reexamine their rank-ordering before passing the cards to the leader. When all the cards are in, the leader shuffles them to preserve anonymity, so that no individual member's voting pattern can be identified.

The procedure of ranking one card at a time is to slow the group members into making careful iterative decisions, rather than hasty decisions. The technique of going from most important to least important is optional but helps maintain interest.

The leader then makes a ballot sheet on a flip chart, numbering the left-hand side of the sheet in accordance with the number of items (e.g., eighteen) from the round-

Figure 3   Index Card Illustrating Rank-Order Voting Process.

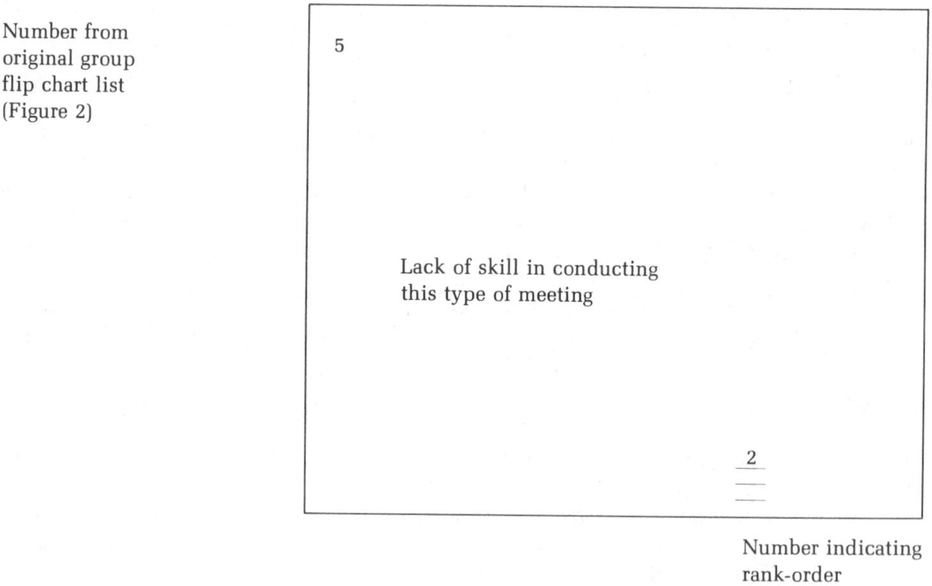

Number from
original group
flip chart list
(Figure 2)

5

Lack of skill in conducting
this type of meeting

2

Number indicating
rank-order

robin listing. He or she then asks one group member to read the item number and the rank number from the stack of voting cards. For example, the index card illustrated in Figure 3 would be read 5 – 2, meaning Item 5 was ranked 2. With one group member reading and the leader recording, the preliminary vote is tallied as in Figure 4.

Figure 4 Voting Tally Sheet on a Flip Chart with Recorded Votes.

299

Delbecq et al.:
Conducting
NGT Meetings

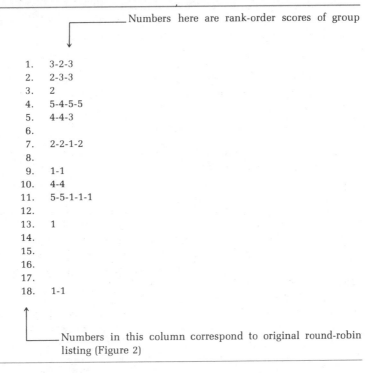

Numbers here are rank-order scores of group

1. 3-2-3
2. 2-3-3
3. 2
4. 5-4-5-5
5. 4-4-3
6.
7. 2-2-1-2
8.
9. 1-1
10. 4-4
11. 5-5-1-1-1
12.
13. 1
14.
15.
16.
17.
18. 1-1

Numbers in this column correspond to original round-robin listing (Figure 2)

The reason for underlining the rank number can now be explained. In large groups, individuals will sometimes become confused and write their rank number next to the item number at the top of the card. Unless the rank number is underlined, the person tallying the votes can become confused.

In many situations an NGT meeting will end with Step 4. In other instances where increased judgmental accuracy is desired, two additional steps can be added. These are: discussion of the preliminary vote, and revoting.

Step 5: Discussion of the Preliminary Vote

A brief step which can be added to increase judgmental accuracy is a discussion of the preliminary vote as recorded on the flip chart tally (Figure 4). The purpose of the discussion is to:

1) Examine inconsistent voting patterns.
2) Provide for the opportunity to rediscuss items which are perceived as receiving too many or too few votes.

If, for example, an item receives a vote of $(5-5-3-1-1)$ there are several possible explanations. Some members of the group may have *information* different from other members. Some members may *understand* the meaning of the item differently from other members. Or, it may simply be that the vote represents a very disperse set of *judgments*. In important situations, it may be worth discussing an item with such split votes, however, to make sure that the differences aren't artificially caused by unequal information, misinformation, or misunderstanding.

It is possible that an item receiving a vote of (5 – 5) might be discussed by the two members who feel the item is the most important, although no other group members selected it as one of their priority items.

Although discussion prior to revoting seldom results in radical changes, where the judgments of the group are concerned with critical or technical matters, the additional clarification can result in a more accurate final vote.

Step 5 guidelines.   The role of the leader in Step 5 is to:

1) Define the task of this discussion as clarification, not social pressure.
2) Ensure that the discussion is brief, so as not to distort perceptions of items not discussed.

Studies of voting show that a three-step process — voting, discussion, revoting — provides a more accurate indication of preferences than voting alone. However, the evidence is somewhat contradictory. Without getting into the scientific debate, we would offer the following speculation: groups who do not talk over votes sometimes make errors due to misinformation, misunderstanding, or unequal information. A brief discussion of the first vote assures that this does not occur. On the other hand, lengthy discussion of earlier judgments can distort group judgment by focusing too much attention on the items discussed as against the total array of items. Thus, in some studies, discussion decreases accuracy. In striking a balance between costs and benefits of discussion and revoting, the way the leader introduces Step 5 and the amount of time devoted to the step are important. With respect to the latter, the discussion of the vote should be short so as not to distort judgments. With respect to role definitions, the following statements at the beginning and end of the discussion are appropriate:

> [At the beginning . . .] "It may be worthwhile to briefly examine the voting pattern in front of us to see if there are any inconsistencies, surprises, or differences members wish to comment on.
>
> "The purpose of this discussion is not to pressure any member to change his or her vote. On the other hand, if we gain additional clarification, some members may wish to modify their original vote."

> [At the end . . .] "Once again, the purpose of this discussion has not been to pressure you to change your original vote. Indeed, you should think carefully before doing so. However, if you honestly have a new perspective as a result of the discussion, you should change your vote."

Step 6: Final Vote

Step 6 is the final NGT step. This vote combines individual judgments into a group decision. The final vote:

1) Determines the outcome of the meeting.
2) Provides a sense of closure and accomplishment.
3) Documents the group judgment.

It is possible to follow the same voting procedure as outlined in the discussion of Step 4, the preliminary vote. It is also possible to use more refined voting techniques, such as rating. Moving to a more refined voting procedure depends upon the degree of judgmental accuracy desired, the topic under investigation, and the degree of information possessed by the group. Greater refinement beyond rank-ordering can become specious if individuals are not really able to make fine distinctions. However, as a general rule, the mean (x) of a group's ratings of items on a $0-10$ scale or a continuous scale increases the degree of judgmental accuracy where group members are qualified to make more refined distinctions.

Figures 5 and 6 provide voting forms which are quick and useful ways to obtain mathematical ratings. The group members are first asked to choose (7 ± 2) items as

Figure 5 A Rating Form for NGT Final Voting.

No. from flip chart	Item Description	Most Important
		100
_____	_____	90
		80
_____	_____	70
		60
_____	_____	50
		40
_____	_____	30
		20
_____	_____	10
		0
		Least Important

Instructions

1. Choose the five most important items from the flip chart, and list them in rank-order above.

2. Identify the item by using the number and description from the flip chart.

3. Draw a line from the item to the scale (0–100) at the right, indicating the relative importance of each item.

Figure 6   A Rating Form for NGT Final Voting

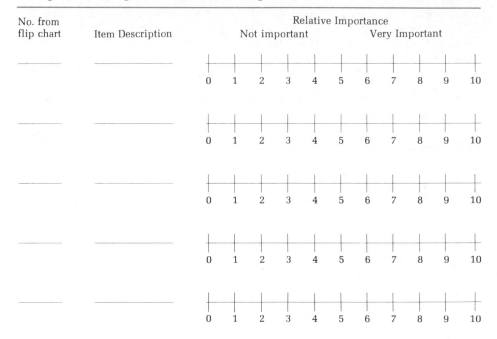

No. from flip chart	Item Description	Relative Importance

Instructions

1. Choose the five most important items from the flip chart, and list them in rank-order above.

2. Identify the items by using the number and description from the flip chart.

3. Rate each item in terms of its importance on the 0–10 scale, with 0 being unimportant, and 10 being very important.

most important. Then, making use of the rating forms in Figures 5 and 6, members rate the relative importance of the selected priority items.

In summary, if one desires an understanding of the magnitude of differences between priorities, a *rating* of priorities is recommended. . . . On the other hand, if the topic is very general, a simple *reranking* of priorities as in Step 4 may be sufficient. . . .

NOTES AND REFERENCES

1. Hitchhiking as used here refers to the fact that ideas listed on the flip chart by one member may stimulate another member to think of an idea he had not written on his worksheet during the silent period. In this case, he is free to add the new idea to his worksheet and report it for listing on the flip chart when his turn arrives.

2. Interaction has a positive impact on evaluation. The benefit of discussion seems to relate primarily to the opportunity for increased clarification, information giving, and the sharing of analysis and logic behind judgments. This opportunity for clarification accounts for the tendency of group judgment to be superior to isolated

individual judgment. [See Chapter 2 of Delbecq, Van de Ven, and Gustafson, *Group Techniques for Program Planning* (Scott, Foresman, 1975).]

3. Mathematical evidence in support of these propositions is provided in G. Huber and A. L. Delbecq, "Guidelines for Combining the Judgments of Individual Group Members in Decision Conferences." *Academy of Management Journal,* Vol. 15, No. 2 (June 1972).

4. For a discussion of effective consensus methods and some disadvantages of voting see A. C. Filley, *Interpersonal Conflict Resolution* (Scott, Foresman, 1975).

Questions for Discussion

1.   How do we all depart from being "ideally rational" in our decision-making?

2.   Under what circumstances would you prefer individual decisions to group decisions?

3.   Under what circumstances would you prefer group decisions to individual decisions?

4.   What factors seem to affect group performance in decision-making?

5.   What advantages *might* the Delphi and nominal group decision-making techniques have over face-to-face group communication and decision-making?

6.   Why might groups be willing to reach more risky decisions than individuals?

7.   How and at what stage of decision-making is the group sometimes helpful to the individual decision-maker? When does the group tend to interfere?

8.   Describe any actual group decision-making experience which you judge to have been contaminated by individual dominance.

9.   Describe any actual group decision-making experience which you judge to have been contaminated by groupthink.

Cases for Discussion

Watergate and Groupthink

What follows is a collection of observations and opinions regarding the Watergate burglary and coverup:

Of course, no book has ever been produced on any Presidency as revealing and as damaging as the Nixon transcripts covering the period in the spring of 1973 when he was scurrying around to find his way out of the Watergate maze (Safire, 1975, p. 12).

. . . if one didn't know what the letters identifying the speakers in those transcripts meant, one would have difficulty determining which man was the President of the United States. "H" (Haldeman) comes over as stronger and far more decisive, "E" (Ehrlichman) as the shrewdest and craftiest, while "P" (President) is the vaguest, most confused and disorganized (*The Washington Post*, 1974, p. 17).

What emerges overwhelmingly, is Nixon's ability, at least on the surface, to think well of himself, to believe he is always acting fairly, and to deny to himself almost any of his nasty, aggressive feelings (Mazlish, 1972, p. 110).

The White House staff . . . seems to have been chosen more for its zeal to protect the boss than for ability to serve him with information and argument (Ways, 1973, p. 200).

When Nixon introduced his first cabinet on national TV he said, "This is not a group of yes-men." Walter Hickel [Secretary of the Interior] was fired 15 months later for turning thumbs down on the Cambodia invasion (Mankiewicz, 1973, p. 178).

Having chosen to seal himself off from regular contact with his Cabinet officers and any others who might offer dissenting views, [Nixon] was now utterly dependent on the small circle of men he had designated to stand between him and the outside world (Rather, 1974, p. 285).

. . . one disclosure that surprised some of the highest ranking officials in the administration was the inner relationship of the President, H. R. (Bob) Haldeman and John D. Ehrlichman . . . their readiness to correct, or disagree with the President and his frequent deference to their judgment . . . (*The Washington Post*, 1974, p. 138).

[Haldeman] made certain that every memorandum that went to the President . . . had concurring or objecting views from any other staffer or department the memo-writer's idea affected (Safire, 1975, p. 280).

Haldeman's real source of power was his ability to determine who would see the President, and what memorandum would be placed before his eyes. . . . He was able to brag, "Even Mitchell comes through me" (Lurie, 1973, pp. 66–67).

. . . the second meeting ended with Liddy's plan still dangling. None of us was quite comfortable with it. . . . We knew the daily pressures from the White House for political intelligence, and I think we had a sense that this was how the game was played (Magruder, 1974, p. 180).

. . . it was agreed that Liddy should go ahead with the wiretapping of Larry O'Brien's office at the Watergate. . . . I think Mitchell came close to rejecting the Liddy plan. . . . It was another of what I called his throwaway decisions, made under pressure to please the White House (Magruder, 1974, p. 198).

It was impossible not to get caught up in the "enemies" mentality. We believed in the President and what he was doing, and yet we were surrounded by critics and demonstrators. . . . Some of our opponents used illegal means, and we became inured to the belief that we, too, must use tough, even illegal means to achieve our ends (Magruder, 1974, p. 197).

As Magruder, Mitchell, Dean, and later, Mardian and La Rue met to "plan" the cover-up there was: No sense of "embarrassment or shame," but a certain self-righteousness to our deliberations. . . . We were not covering up a burglary, we were safeguarding world peace (Magruder, 1974, p. 229).

If anything, the Nixon men were afflicted by an illusion of vulnerability . . . (Safire, 1975, p. 273).

. . . powerful men in the White House came to think of themselves as inhabitants of a beleaguered and distressed city, surrounded by enemies whose strength and malice they exaggerated (Ways, 1973, p. 199).

In testimony before the Senate Watergate Committee, John Mitchell maintained that he had deliberately withheld information about the burglary and cover-up in order to guarantee the President's re-election (*The New York Times*, 1973, p. 38).

Janis has an insight here, better described as the "Am I crazy?" syndrome. When you are in a meeting in the Roosevelt Room across from the Oval Room in the White House, and men of power and experience around you accept certain givens—like media hostility or the impossibility of reconciliation with liberal Republicans—you ask yourself, less out of fear of being turned down than out of fear of being an ass, whether you can continue to have any of your opinions respected if you challenge assumptions that the group agreed upon long ago (Safire, 1975, p. 274).

The "fatal flaw" of the Nixon Administration, [former Attorney General Elliot

Richardson] observed, has been the proclivity of the White House to perceive critics and opposition as "enemies," and the willingness to "adopt tactics used against an enemy" in handling such criticism (Weissman, 1974, p. 14).

When I objected to the torrent of interviews given by the President . . . I was ostracized for three months (Safire, 1975, p. 274).

So each time we join a group for the comfort of group security, we must sacrifice some of our individuality. We must abdicate some small part of our conscience to the conscience of the group. We must be team players.

It is this, I think, that explains why Nazis could slaughter Jews, why jailers can torture prisoners, why we did what we did at My Lai. It explains, too, why Bart Porter followed orders to commit perjury. He was a team player (Hoppe, 1973).

Nixon's sundry rationales changed as his perimeter of defense tightened . . . first . . . deny knowledge of any wrongdoing, then . . . admit knowing others were involved but simultaneously maintain their innocence. . . . Finally, . . . in his May 1973 brief to the public . . . Nixon used the phrase "national security" 24 times (Myerson, 1973, p. 26).

Question

Assess the foregoing information as evidence for or against the proposition that groupthink influenced Watergate-related White House decisions.

References

Hoppe, A. *San Francisco Chronicle,* June 11, 1973.

Janis, I. L. *Victims of GROUPTHINK: A Psychological Study of Foreign-Policy Decisions and Fiascoes.* Houghton Mifflin, 1972.

Lurie, L. *The Impeachment of Richard Nixon.* Berkeley Medallion Books, 1973.

Magruder, J. S. *An American Life: One Man's Road to Watergate.* Atheneum, 1974.

Mankiewicz, F. *Perfectly Clear.* Quadrangle/The New York Times Book Co., 1973.

Mazlish, B. *In Search of Nixon: A Psychohistorical Inquiry.* Basic Books, 1972.

Myerson, M. *Crime in the Suites.* International Publishers, 1973.

The New York Times. *The Watergate Hearings: Break-In and Cover-Up.* Bantam Books, 1973.

Rather, D. and G. P. Gates. *The Palace Guard.* Harper & Row, 1974.

Safire, W. *Before the Fall: An Inside View of the Pre-Watergate White House.* Doubleday, 1975.

The Washington Post. *The Fall of a President.* Dell, 1974.

Ways, M. "Watergate as a Case Study in Management." *Fortune,* Vol. 88, No. 5 (November 1973), pp. 109 ff.

Weissman, S., ed. *Big Brother and the Holding Company: The World Behind Watergate.* Ramparts Press, 1974.

Managerial Attitudes Toward Group Influence and Decision-Making

As part of a larger survey of managerial attitudes,* thousands of managers in many nations and organizations have responded to the following questions:

a) "In a work situation, if the subordinates cannot influence me, then I lose some influence on them" (check one).

_____	_____	_____	_____	_____
strongly agree	agree	undecided	disagree	strongly disagree

b) "Group goal setting offers advantages that cannot be obtained by individual goal setting."

_____	_____	_____	_____	_____
strongly agree	agree	undecided	disagree	strongly disagree

Haire, Ghiselli, and Porter suggest that agreement with these statements indicates a "democratic" belief in the desirability of subordinate participation in managerial decision making. Disagreement indicates an "autocratic" attitude.

We have given the same questionnaire to many additional managers, with results supplementing those of the original international study. On the axis shown in Exhibit 1, you will find a summary of some samples.

Exhibit 1   Managerial Attitudes

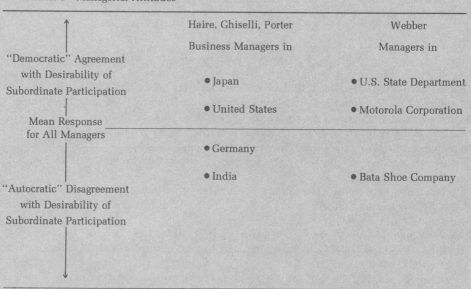

	Haire, Ghiselli, Porter Business Managers in	Webber Managers in
"Democratic" Agreement with Desirability of Subordinate Participation	• Japan	• U.S. State Department
	• United States	• Motorola Corporation
Mean Response for All Managers		
	• Germany	
	• India	• Bata Shoe Company
"Autocratic" Disagreement with Desirability of Subordinate Participation		

* M. Haire, E. Ghiselli, and L. Porter, *Managerial Thinking*. Wiley, 1966.

Our sample of managers in the Motorola Corporation agrees with Haire, Ghiselli, and Porter's larger sample of U.S. business managers; thus the questionnaire tends to be verified. The U.S. State Department sample includes several hundred Foreign Service officers in the lower and middle ranks. The Bata Shoe Company is a large multinational firm headquartered in Canada, but manufacturing and selling in many nations. The executives sampled were the company heads in various nations—the majority of which were relatively poor and still in the early stages of development.

The State Department agreement with the desirability of subordinate decision making is markedly different from all U.S. business managers questioned (including some not summarized on the diagram).

Question

Discuss why these managers might hold these attitudes toward group decision making and subordinate participation—particularly Bata and the State Department as compared with Motorola.

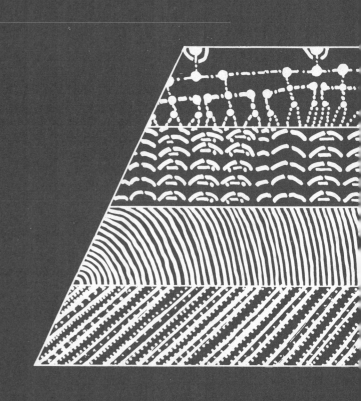

Part Two

Organizational Behavior

ORGANIZATION DESIGN

WORK DESIGN

OBJECTIVES FOR ORGANIZATIONS
AND INDIVIDUALS

CONTROLLING ORGANIZATIONAL BEHAVIOR

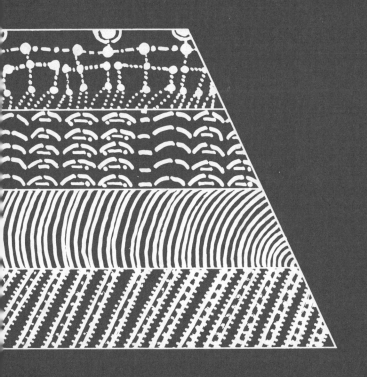

Organization Design

Of the major factors that determine how people behave in organizations, this chapter takes up two powerful ones—the network of tasks tied to the organization's goal, and the authority and decision-making (coordinating) structure which exists in some form in all organizations. These factors are of equal importance with the factors already discussed if we are to gain a comprehensive understanding of the way people behave in complex organizations.

It hardly seems necessary to say that the work of sales managers for Procter & Gamble is bound to influence their actions in certain ways. And these influences will be different from those which affect a factory employee for General Motors or a research chemist for the Food and Drug Administration. Likewise, mechanical engineering students at Purdue are bound to have somewhat different motivations than law students at Michigan, medical students at Indiana, or forestry students at Oregon. Thus it is the purpose of this chapter to show how the *network* of tasks and the *coordinating structure* of the organization act as important influencers on organizational behavior.

TECHNOLOGY AND BEHAVIOR

The job is one important influence on behavior, but there is another and more complex factor that must also be considered. It is *technology*, or the entire network of jobs taken together, along with the organization goal. This is a somewhat elusive concept, but in essence is quite simple. Let us take an example from sports in order to illustrate it.

Football is a game invented at some point but which has evolved over the years. It requires a ball of a certain shape. Nobody can play American football with a round object. It requires goal posts of certain measurements, placed geographically. Nobody can play football with a tennis net strung over the fifty-yard line. It is played by a team facing another team. Nobody could play football with two men using swords and face masks in a gymnasium. The goal is to run the ball over the goal line or to kick it between goal posts. Nobody could play football if he decided that the team should go fishing.

Up to this point, we should recognize that the technology of football requires a conscious objective (organization goal), that this objective in turn requires specifically and rationally designed capital equipment (ball, goals), and specifically trained manpower (the team). All three must exist as a total entity. Not only that, but they are related in a special way. The manpower and the equipment are means to an end. Teams and balls are means to scoring across the goal line. They are interdependent.

As the game has developed, there have come to be certain specialized tasks which make scoring easier. The team has a better chance of succeeding at what it sets out to do if one man is assigned to the position of guard, another to the position of center, and another to the position of quarterback. The job of each man must not only be performed in a certain way (the center passes the ball between his legs, he does not throw it over his shoulder), but many of the jobs must be performed in a certain time sequence (the guards must block on the scrimmage line before the passer can successfully throw the ball).

Two more elements of technology now emerge. First, there is a specialization of tasks. This particular *pattern of specialization* (guards, tackles, quarterbacks), rather than some other pattern, is related to final success as a means to a larger end. Second, there is a *pattern of interrelationships* that govern the quality of one job and the timing of it in relation to others. In other organizations, these are sometimes called rules or procedures.

The total taken together, along with the capital equipment and manpower, is the technology of football. It is a rationally integrated system of a final goal with a network of subparts and procedures to connect the parts. If any part is missing, or operates in a way not in accord with the logical design of the system, either there is no football game at all, or both the *team* and each *individual* player in his own job are less successful. This is to say that if technology is not present, the members of a team cannot "win." Furthermore, if both teams have sloppy technology, society (the public) cannot "win" either. Technology thus becomes a requirement of achievement for both people working in organizations and for people who depend on them.

Technology, Achievement, and Competence: A Simple Example

Imagine a college student who has the physical skill and mental desire for sports. Furthermore, his physical and mental characteristics tell him that football is the place that offers most satisfaction (tennis and basketball do not seem to fit as well). Suppose that he tries out and begins to play at a university with a good team, and that his position is quarterback. Everyone else is well trained. They are good at their own specializations, they work hard to know the interrelationships—the rules, the plays, the procedures. Our quarterback's achievement can come from three sources. One has to do with his own job or doing his own thing. Second, he is enabled to be a quarterback only because others are doing their own things. The third has to do with the organization's goal. He feels good when the team wins. The first of these sources of achievement is *personal accomplishment* and the other two are *organizational accomplishment.*

Now, imagine our man in another situation. He goes to a school offering only club football and is asked to play with a group of men with good physical characteristics but who have played little football. They are not "specialists" simply because no real technology exists. There is the usual snapping of the ball from the center, but the line is uncertain as to which way to run, how to block, or when to execute various plays. There may still be the social satisfaction of playing with friendly people, but there is very much less chance that our man can feel a sense of *personal* achievement in his own *individual* task. He may have been the greatest quarterback in the nation, but he cannot be as competent or achieve as much in his own eyes as in the previous situation. Nor can he ever feel the achievement that comes with winning games *as a team*. In short, the technology of football, though it may constrain his freedom to do as he pleases on the field, is an absolute requirement if he is to use his own abilities to feel competent and to feel high levels of achievement in this part of his life.

Notice that the technology of football is separate and distinct from the technology of basketball or tennis. They require different specializations for participants, different rules and procedures to govern the *interrelationships* of the players, and different capital equipment. But they cannot escape having technologies. And the performance of a basketball guard — his sense of personal competence and achievement — is bound to be affected by (1) the existence of a technology, and (2) every participant's reasonable compliance with it. The same can be said for the violinist in a symphony orchestra, the loader of an oceangoing ship at a dock, and the research chemist working in a large pharmaceutical company.

Technology and Other Values in Life

Before showing how the above analysis applies in complex organizations, there is an important question which should be answered. Do, in fact, many people place their jobs and careers foremost in their lives, relative to such other satisfactions as they gain from leisure, recreation, giving and receiving affection in the family, or engaging in social activities?

People do differ in this respect. Some are more career-oriented than others. The level and nature of jobs also differ in the extent to which they provide a sense of achievement (the studies reported later deal mostly with managers at all levels). Nevertheless, we can predict a considerable increase in the *probability* that all persons in an organization, from top to bottom, will feel competence and achievement in their work lives if organizations are technologically structured for success in each employee's own job, and success of the organization as a whole.

From Maslow's theory of needs we might also predict that, since career achievement and competence are primarily a matter of self-esteem and esteem of others, it is unlikely that people can take advantage of opportunities for achievement in well-designed technological organizations unless they have also been successful in satisfying their basic physical needs, safety needs, and social needs. Very hungry workers (whether their hunger is for food, safety, or affection) are not likely to be able to think about, or be interested in, the work they are doing. Nor are they likely to feel a need for the technical coordination they must follow with others at work.

Finally, it should be pointed out that career interests are not an absolute matter for most persons. Few people are compulsive career slaves, on the one hand, or compulsive love and affection slaves, on the other. Life is a complex of trade-offs. Well-designed technologies simply offer a chance or avenue for achievement, competence, and self-esteem. And when an individual looks for places to act out these needs, he or she often pays a price in giving his or her time in one direction rather than another.

In the past fifteen years, a considerable amount of research has been undertaken to identify the different kinds of technology which are required in order to achieve different kinds of organizational goals. All of this research points to the facts that:

- The goal of one organization differs significantly from the goal of another organization. The crucial difference lies in whether the goal is relatively stable, known, and constant over time, or whether it is relatively unstable, chaotic, or changing.
- The subgoals and specializations in one organization (the means to the larger end) differ from those of another organization. The crucial difference lies in whether the *parts* of the organization are fairly close to one another in work and attitudes (relatively homogeneous), or relatively far apart (heterogeneous) in work and attitudes. From a total organization point of view, this factor is also a measure of simplicity versus complexity.

For example, take the goal of producing bread. It is a relatively stable goal. Though tastes change to a degree, and the organization must be somewhat flexible in producing raisin bread versus wholewheat bread, the external environment is fairly stable. Bread is bread. The organization does not have to worry about some competitor who will upset its entire technology (machines, job specializations, procedures) because people suddenly start eating plastic capsules. Furthermore, the three major functions which are subgoals of a baking company — product development, manufacturing, and sales — are, in the total spectrum of industry, relatively simple. The chemistry of bread baking is not too complex for a chemist, the production methods are not too complicated, and the selling is easier and more comprehensible than marketing jet airliners.

On the other end of the scale of stability-complexity, take the goal of producing electronic computers. It is relatively unstable, because competitors are very rapidly developing numerous important changes in the product. Not only this, but the diversity and complexity of the three basic functions are present in a much higher degree than in the case of bread: The people who do research and development have the whole field of electronics and mathematics to contend with, the people who produce the computers have a welter of technical processes and methods to contend with, and the people who do the selling have to know the customer's product (e.g., banking) and its subfunctions (bookkeeping, check clearing, figuring of interest rates, etc.).

Stability of the final goal and diversity of the jobs necessary to attain it are important to the *human* side of enterprise. It determines (1) how specialized or different the people are in the various parts of the organization, (2) how difficult it is for them to coordinate the total technology, (3) what kinds of coordinating system they use, and (4) the attitudes of all those coordinated toward the coordinators and the system or coordinating process itself. This last point is especially important. For example, we shall see that when people pursue highly stable but simple goals (bread) there is a good chance that they feel satisfied when they have a line executive who possesses the knowledge of bread science, manufacture, and sales, and who conveys an "order" to them specifying what next week's or next year's production quotas will be. They would resent unnecessary "coordinators" being appointed to muddle up the system. On the other hand, when people pursue a highly unstable goal, or a goal requiring complex and diverse specialized jobs (computers), regarding which no one person could know all of the complex facts, they feel satisfied doing much of the coordinating themselves, or with the help of coordinators who serve as information centers. They would resent having a boss who could not possibly know all of the facts (even if he or she is president) pronouncing what the scientific characteristics of next year's product should be, whether a certain kind of machine could be used in the factory, and whether the customer will use it in preference to a competitor's product.

The following sections discuss how the organizational goal, differing as it does in stability and diversity, determines the character of the four other aspects mentioned above: the degree of diversity among various parts of the organization, the difficulty of coordinating the parts, the kinds of coordinating mechanisms used, and the attitudes of people toward the coordinating system.

Specialization and Diversity

Few organizational goals can be pursued without specialization of function. In the most noteworthy research on this subject to date, Lawrence and Lorsch (1967) found that container companies, producing packaging for other industries (a relatively stable and less complex goal), and plastics companies, producing a range of products (a relatively unstable and complex goal), both had to have three main specializing functions or parts—a product-development department staffed with scientists and engineers, a manufacturing department staffed with plant personnel, and a sales department staffed with marketing personnel.

Two crucial questions arise about these specialized parts. How do people with different specialties differ in their attitudes? Does the technology of producing containers cause people in a container company to be more different or less different from one another than the people in the plastics company with its different technology? In another sense, the second question asks how homogeneous or heterogeneous the people are in one organization compared to another.

The article by Lorsch and Lawrence accompanying this chapter describes how the different specialists in two of the plastics companies did indeed have different orientations, outlooks, and attitudes. Additional evidence from their original research is presented here (Lawrence and Lorsch, 1967).

The most obvious way people differed was in their orientations toward work goals and work objectives. Because their jobs dealt with sales, the people in marketing were naturally interested in and paid attention to customers, sales appeals, competitive practices, and the like. People in production were quite naturally preoccupied with such things as machinery, technical processes, and labor turnover in the plants.

Of more concern to us here is the attitude different specialists had toward interpersonal affairs at work. In the jargon of behavioral science research, were they *task-oriented* or *people-oriented*? In the production area, where engineers and plant managers dealt with rather certain and predictable actions in day-to-day operations, the people holding these jobs preferred interactions which were aimed at getting the job done, did not feel concerned about engaging in social relationships, and in case of difficulty with another person would simply feel "well, let's just get on with the job."

According to the researchers, the reason why production people had this attitude was that production procedures and goals were there to coordinate their work with other persons within the production department. And such a coordinating mechanism was effective because the production technology was relatively stable—the product was known, the amount and quality to be produced were known, and the various departments which had to process the materials were known.

This kind of motivation is similar to that which is felt when one stops at a traffic light and sees another car immediately behind. The traffic light is, of course, a predictable and orderly procedure which connects the actions of motorists. First, one does not necessarily feel any interest in social relationships with the other driver. The technology (traffic lights, sequence of cars stopping or moving on red or green) helps drivers do their own jobs (drive where they are going) and coordinates drivers for the good of the organization (all cars stopped or moving are part of an organization to move traffic). Furthermore, if the driver behind shouts or blows his or her horn impatiently, it is easy to shrug one's shoulders, get on with the driving, and let the other driver fume. Or, if another driver should come up to one's car and start engaging in friendly conversation when the light is red, one might wonder whether interpersonal communication is really necessary at that point.

Now let us look at an uncertain task and an uncertain goal. Driving over an interstate highway in Colorado in November, a person drives into an unexpected snowstorm. With no snow tires, he or she is stuck at the foot of a mountain pass with other motorists. Not only is a great deal of technical interchange desired with those who have the goal of crossing the mountain range to Salt Lake City, but some exchange of friendly chatter would not seem out of place. Certainly any motorist who came from the other direction would be involved in considerable interchange.

This last illustration of a group of people with an unstable environment and goal, and no coordinating device, is not unlike what the researchers found in the sales specializations of the companies they studied. The sales and marketing people who were dealing with a relatively *uncertain* task and who were accustomed to being concerned about (note the attitude) maintaining social relationships with customers, also cared more about fostering positive social relationships with *coworkers inside the marketing department.*

Another attitude which differs between specializations is highlighted in this research: A person filling a position in one specialty tends to have a different orientation toward *time* than people in another specialty. Sales personnel had the attitude that they had to solve problems and take action immediately (tomorrow's success or failure depended on it), and production specialists were similar. However, scientific personnel felt that their workday could be spent quite comfortably without solving an immediate problem. A crude synonym for this attitude might be "patience" versus "impatience" about actions or decisions.

Of the six plastics companies studied in depth, specialists in each of the three functions exhibited the same types of attitudes. Regardless of which company or organization one belongs to, the special technology in one part of the organization, and its degree of certainty or stability, will tend to shape one's attitudes toward goals, interpersonal relations, and time.

One of the important points highlighted in the research was that the most successful companies of the six studied had *pronounced* differences in departmental attitudes. Often, we read that "provincialism" or "bias" toward one's own work is bad for the organization. But here we see it as necessary to success. This is not too surprising. If a football team is to win, the tackle had better keep his mind on being a good tackle and not try to act like a quarterback.

Turning now to companies with different technologies, the plastics companies were compared with the container companies, in which no significant new products had been introduced for the past twenty years, and whose customers wanted proven containers that were produced regularly on high-speed automatic lines. As one executive said, "We and our competitors all use the same machines produced by the same company. The product has got to be virtually the same as your competitors, and there is not any price competition. All we have to know is how many cases does the customer want and when?" (ibid., p. 92). The production technology was therefore certain, and the market goals were even more certain. Since the product development people had less turbulent goals than those in plastics, they were more like the drivers at the traffic light than the drivers on the mountain pass. In short, although the researchers found that the differences in attitude between specialists were the same in both plastics and container technologies, the differences were *less* in the stable container technology than in the more turbulent plastics technology. Sales people still preferred interpersonal or social activities, and production people were still more task-oriented. But the two groups were more alike — homogeneous — in a container company than in a plastics company.

This diversity has far-reaching consequences for other human aspects of a company, as we shall see. It affects how people coordinate with each other in different companies — by themselves, in committees or task groups, relying on formal hierarchy to do the coordinating, or something in between (the use of special coordinating departments such as product managers, project managers, or the like). It also has an effect on how comfortable people feel with whatever mode of coordination is used.

Difficulties in Coordination

One of the great difficulties in the industrialized world, both from the standpoint of organizational success in reaching a goal and from the standpoint of human satisfaction (freedom from conflict), is that differences in specialization mean that people of widely different specialties cannot talk to each other and understand one another. Specialization is thus double-edged — we cannot do without it for organization success, and for each person achieving something in his or her own domain, but it potentially causes stress and conflict. Thorsten Veblen, a well known social critic of earlier in this century, said that people in one field often have a *trained incapacity* to deal with total problems in the real world. The very training for which they spend so much money and to which they devote so much effort, and which is so prized by other people (the organization), incapacitates them to solve a problem if it has factors in it from outside their field.

It is not surprising, therefore, that research scientists who develop products in the plastics industry, and who must develop products that the customer will buy, would have difficulty knowing and understanding customers, competitive prices, or sales appeals. Since they differ considerably in attitude from the people in the sales department, they are also not likely to find much common ground for engaging in direct and time-consuming interchange with marketing people. Nor is it surprising that, in the container companies, the coordination problem would be easier, since (1) each of the three functions — product development, sales, production — was more known and stable, and (2) the people in each function were less different from their co-workers in another function. Let us see what effect this difference in degree of cooperation has on the way people coordinate their actions, and on how they feel toward the "system."

STRUCTURE AND BEHAVIOR

Given the fact that people in different parts of an organization are cognitively different, and given the difficulties in technical and interpersonal relations that this creates, how have organizations evolved ways of coordinating potentially conflicting subtechnologies and people?

Formally Structured Coordination Systems

One way, particularly suitable for organizations with relatively stable goals and relatively homogeneous parts, is a formally structured organization. By structured we mean rationally worked out job descriptions for operating positions and people, policies and procedures for coordinating diverse jobs, and managerial positions and people specializing in effectuating the coordination itself.

The traffic system is an example. The requirements for a driver's license involve certain actions an *individual* driver is expected to carry out, including parking, entering a main thoroughfare, and the use of certain hand or light signals. This is the job description of the driver, and spells out this specialization. It is partly determined by how the automobile is constructed, and partly by requirements for *cooperation* among drivers operating automobiles. It sequentially spells out how one driver is related to others—it creates a coordinated organization.

The football team is another example. The guard has his specified actions as an *individual* specialist, but the *plays* connect each player's actions to the team. The quarterback is a coordinating specialist who relates the operating work of guards, ends, and other players. The man in this position decides (note the *decision-making* responsibility) which play to use.

In an industrial setting, the pilot who flies a commercial scheduled airliner from one airport to another has the technical operating responsibility of flying the airplane. The copilot and flight engineer have other technical operating duties to perform, as do the stewardesses in the cabin. Somewhere both the timing and the altitude of the flight in relation to other flights must be worked out in advance. This is done by someone (equivalent to a *staff* manager) in the Civil Aeronautics Board offices, who works out the traffic procedures between and around airports. To take care of detailed and unexpected events, someone must make ad hoc decisions and adjustments. This is the work of an air traffic controller in the airport tower, whose technical work is that of a *line* manager.

Note that when some people are specialists in operating work and others are specialists in coordinating work, there is a separation of planning and decision-making from operating. This does not mean that pilots have no decisions to make, but that they are subject to coordinating decisions made by those who specialize in coordinating.

In the selection by Woodward accompanying this chapter, the separation of coordinating from operating was found to be most pronounced in firms that operated in stable technologies—what she called continuous process technologies, such as in chemical or oil refining companies. We will look at some of her findings in the selection, from the full text of her initial studies (1965), and from her more recent studies (1970).

Woodward studied one hundred manufacturing companies in a certain geographic area of England, to determine among other things whether all companies use formal organization structure as a means of managing. She found that some companies depend heavily on this kind of managerial coordination and others do not. This was an important finding at the time, since many management textbooks seemed to suggest that formal procedures and clear job descriptions, with line managers and staff managers doing most of the decision-making, were the proper ways to manage *all* enterprises.

She found that as companies move up the scale of diversity and complexity, and particularly when they deal with a stable and known product goal such as that of producing oil and chemical products for a mass market, there was indeed more and more separation of coordinating from operating. Furthermore, there was a separation within the coordinating function between those who *plan* production (coaches who develop the plays for a football game, or officials who work out traffic patterns for use around airports), and those who *supervise* production (quarterbacks who decide which play to use and call it to the players, or air traffic controllers who decide when an airplane is to enter the traffic pattern and call it to the pilot).

The size of the company made little difference in how many managerial positions there were. It was the stability of production and external environment that was the crucial determining factor. Some firms produced custom made products, such as men's suits to order. They were most unstable of all, because the goal was always changing on the basis of customer needs, and entire production schedules and procedures had to be changed frequently. Others, which produced automobile parts in large batches or in mass production for a certain time period (such as a year's supply before a model change), were more stable in their goal and the system needed to achieve it. The most stable of all were the chemical and gasoline companies, which produced a steady flow of gasoline in standard units. A gallon this year is the same as a gallon next year. And quantities are produced for finished product inventories.

In the companies with custom-made products, the average number of levels in the managerial hierarchy was three, but it was four for large-batch product companies, and six for process industries such as chemicals. The ratio of managers to employees ranged among custom-product companies from 1:24 to 1:49; in large-batch industries from 1:14 to 1:18; and in process industries from 1:7 to 1:8. This increase in the number of managers may be in part a result of empire building or the proliferation of bureaucratic positions, as Parkinson's Law suggests. But it is also heavily influenced by the nature of the goal being pursued, and the complexity or change required in the entire interconnected network of operating specializations. Otherwise, there is no explanation of why bureaucrats in less stable companies did not build as many levels of management as those in more stable companies!

The same relationship between stability of goal and use of formal structures was found by Lawrence and Lorsch *within* a company. In six companies in the plastics industry, the manufacturing departments had the most formalized structure. They had more levels in their managerial hierarchy, a higher ratio of supervisors to subordinates, and more frequent reviews of managerial performance.

At the other end of the formality spectrum, the research departments had fewer levels in the management hierarchy, more subordinates reporting to each supervisor, fewer managers for the same number of operators, and less reliance on formal job descriptions and procedures. The sales department, the goals of which were more stable than research but more changing and chaotic than production, fell between the two on these dimensions.

Effect of Structured Coordination on Behavior and Motivation

Structure — procedures, job descriptions, and coordinating direction — can have either positive or negative effects on people's feelings and emotions. We have already referred to the fact that people in *all* coordinating systems have a greater chance of achievement if the system fits the goal. If the goal calls for formal organization, those with high needs for achievement do not seem to mind. They may even welcome it. A football player cannot achieve much with his talents if he tried (or if someone tries to make him) to utilize the rules of golf, a game in which there is no synchronization between players in action.

In addition to achievement, we should recognize that, regardless of which human need one is using a job and career for, this can be done more easily if others do their part correctly. One might be using a job for money to buy housing and food, for security in an industrial world, or for status and prestige rather than for achievement. If the goal of the organization, and therefore its technology, calls for formal organization, the person cannot be successful in achieving any of these human needs without the formal organization.

Though we shall see presently that people do resent hierarchies for various reasons, research evidence shows that many people go about behaving in formal or structured organizations with ease and apparent satisfaction. We have already seen, for example, that production people in organizations tend to prefer contacts with others who are also task-oriented.

Woodward found that in companies which had very clear formal jobs and procedures "most of those interviewed seemed to resent authority less when exercised over them by the process than by a superior." This is not too surprising. We resent a traffic light much less than we would resent hundreds of cars with no rules of the road, or a policeman who had no rules to go by other than what he sees and decides himself. This is another way of saying that structural systems in one sense actually permit more delegation, and they do not require so much of one person meddling into another's work affairs. This same study showed that in three engineering companies which moved from custom-type goals to more stable large-batch goals, production managers spent more time coordinating procedures with their bosses (in one company, this portion of the manager's day increased from 34 percent to 47 percent), but *less* time talking to their subordinates (in one company this portion of the manager's time decreased from 33 percent to 16 percent). Because of this, people at successively lower levels simply felt less pressure from above, and were able to pursue their tasks without interference or changes directed from above.

Those familiar with Porter's famous "parable of the spindle" will recognize this phenomenon. He did research in a restaurant about conflict between the waitress who was giving "orders" to the cook, and the cook who had to give her the right item of food at the right time if she were to do her job correctly. In the particular restaurant, as no doubt in many others, there was frustration on the part of both people. With no rules and procedures, each was dependent on the whims of the other. In short, there was not much *stability* of expectation for the waitress or the cook. However, the friction was reduced considerably when a simple spindle was installed, with a procedure whereby the waitress clipped orders to the wheel in a certain order and the cook filled the orders in the same sequence. Each person was thereby freed *by the structure of technology* (a formally related network of jobs) to pursue his or her work.

The studies by Lawrence and Lorsch (1967) throw additional and important light on this kind of situation. They studied two container companies, both of which, you will recall, were pursuing a goal that was relatively stable. This in turn caused the *parts* of the company to be less diverse. One company was a high performer, with decision-making concentrated at higher levels, and more clarity in procedures, rules, and job descriptions. The researchers found that, because its structure fit the requirements of the goal, the company was successful, and the morale and feelings of managers inside the company were better (they *felt* successful). "While a few managers indicated that they were unhappy because of their own lack of involvement, the vast majority saw the situation as necessary and conducive to their effectively performing their jobs. When conflicts arose, they knew that they would get them resolved by the top managers, who had both the knowledge of the environment and the influence required."

Here is a verbatim comment from a salesman in the more structured container company: "On new customers the sales vice president tells me whether we can do the business. However, the real person is the chief executive, because he wants to be updated immediately on everything, and does get himself involved in everything. He runs this place completely. And he gets fancy if something happens that he wasn't aware of and wasn't involved in. . . .

"I thought at first when I came here this was meddling. However, now, as I think about it, at least you have a guy who is going to give you decisions. If I want answers quickly, I'll go directly to him, keeping the other people tied in as I go . . ." (p. 118).

Dynamic Coordination Systems

A second way of coordinating is dynamic, carried out more by ad hoc, give-and-take communication than by operating according to stable and known procedures, or referring coordinating problems to higher line managers. Because of the information needed to deal with changing customer requirements, new scientific discoveries, new production methods, and the like, the coordination procedures used by Lawrence and Lorsch's plastics executives were much more temporary in nature than the more stable coordination procedures of, say, the container companies. Whereas the latter produces items which remain the same month in and month out, plastics managers may have to react to changes relatively frequently.

Consequently, the plastics companies tended to coordinate with a wide variety of task forces, committees, and informal groups. The people who coordinated the three parts (production, research, and sales) were those who had knowledge of the detailed and up-to-date information necessary to make decisions. Those who made up the task forces and committees were not always the top people in their departments' authority hierarchies. It happened that because production was the most stable of the three, the top people in production tended to have the necessary knowledge and thus represented their department in decision-making groups. But the opposite tended to be true in research. The individual scientists toward the bottom of the hierarchy were the only ones with the knowledge necessary to join a task force. In sales, it was a variety of middle-level sales managers who were most familiar with customers, advertising, or other marketing functions.

One of the characteristics of dynamic systems is that a wide variety of people engage in problem solving that is less structured along departmental lines, and less structured along vertical hierarchical lines. People seem to be less conscious of clear-cut job descriptions, and all those involved in coordination become somewhat involved in the functions of others. That is not to say that there is no formal organization. Individuals still maintain the orientations of their primary specialty, and line managers still have their say in affairs. However, it is they who have created the task forces and committees, who rely on them for coordination, and who appoint a different kind of coordinator — product manager, project manager, and similar positions. The people in these positions — serving as information centers for the specialist representatives, setting goals and targets, and occasionally "translating" one specialized department's needs for others — may write summary reports for top management, and try to get consensus among the operating departments.

Effect of Dynamic Coordination on Behavior and Motivation

If people in a dynamic system can achieve a reasonable degree of frankness and openness as they solve problems, and if they feel disposed to invest large amounts of emotional energy in problem solving and confrontation (two matters to be discussed later), such a system offers a number of positive motivations. One, the fact that one can perform one's job regardless of what satisfactions are being sought, is similar to the motivation discussed in connection with well-designed structured systems. Relatively free interaction is the necessary way to proceed, in view of the fact that there are few stable goals and procedures on which to rely.

Another motivation — achievement and feelings of competence and involvement — is in some respects more likely in such a system than in more structured organizations. This can be explained by reference to Maslow's need hierarchy and McClelland's social motives, discussed in Chapter 1. There is opportunity for more influence on the total organization, and for involvement in a greater spectrum of the firm's decisions. Such involvement comes quite close to the motivating factors described by Herzberg (1968).

It is also reasonable to assume that such systems offer greater opportunity for human interaction, and thus for satisfaction of social needs on the job.

That such an approach can work is evidenced by the following statement by a manager in one of the Lawrence and Lorsch's plastics companies (1967): "Our problems get thrashed out in our committees. We work them over until everybody agrees this is the best effort you can make. We may decide this isn't good enough. Then we decide to ask for more plant, more people, etc. We all have to be realistic and take a modification sometimes and say this is the best we can do.

"In recent meetings we have had a thrashing around about manpower needs. At first we didn't have much agreement, but we kept thrashing around and finally agreed on what was the best we could do" (p. 74).

NEGATIVE MOTIVATIONS OF INAPPROPRIATE STRUCTURES

The principal argument in this chapter is that the structure of an organization — the individual jobs themselves, and the total network of jobs tied together — has a higher probability of producing positive work motivation if it is designed so that it fits the *kind of goal* being pursued by the *particular organization*. The reason is simple: Whatever the diverse personal motives of individuals in the company, they are more likely to pull in the right direction if the "right" structure is designed.

We can highlight this argument by looking at two kinds of situations which produce *negative* motivation. If we define "morale" as simply the positive or negative attitudes people have toward the organization they work in, negative morale can just as easily be caused by faults in the structure as positive morale can be caused by the structure which fits the goal. Many of the world's woes are caused by systems that are either overstructured or understructured.

Overstructured Systems

Suppose you drive to work each day on a four-lane superhighway between two small towns in western Nebraska. There is not an automobile in sight. There is hardly *ever* another automobile. Yet at each of five intersections between your home and your job there is a stoplight. After about a month, never having seen another car pull out into the highway, you lose some respect for the system, and run a red light. However, you find that there is a policeman stationed at each stoplight, and when you run the light he hauls you into court and the judge fines you fifty dollars. Regardless of how you feel about rules and authority in the beginning, if you are required to travel on that highway Monday through Friday in order to get to work, you might come to view the procedures and supervision with hostility.

This kind of situation has been depicted in much of the research done in industrial sociology and social psychology. The Argyris (1957) theory shows how managers may apply rules and regulations above and beyond what is required to get the job done. Employees, seeing this happen, may retaliate by forming negative attitudes toward the company and the coordinators. The selection by Thompson (1961) accompanying this chapter shows what can happen when an excessively formal organization of officials, lacking the knowledge necessary to coordinate a complex and changing situation, nevertheless insist on the rights of office instead of concentrating on the work to be done, the *necessary* technology, and the nature of the goal. These are "bureaucrats" in the bad sense of the word. Nobody wins. Those using their jobs only for security are frustrated anyway. Those seeking achievement find much less chance to do a good job.

One significant piece of research on this state of affairs is the study of firms in the English and Scottish electronics industries by Burns and Stalker (1961), abstracted in a selection accompanying this chapter. Essentially, they found that people in organizations, especially managers, have four competing forces acting upon them which determine what decisions they make. They are workers with careers and jobs, they are members of groups that have sectional interests (which may lead to playing politics), they are individuals with rank and prestige (which may lead to defending prerogatives), and they are people with outside interests—home, sports, leisure, and so on.

In the stable electronics companies, which had been manufacturing simple electric switches or fuse boxes, the formal organization had been appropriate. People in various departments had their routines, they were not too far apart in attitudes and orientations, and they were willing to refer decisions up the line to a boss who knew most of the facts involved and who could make realistic decisions. However, when these companies tried to enter more complex markets, involving consumer products such as television and radio or parts for electronic computers, most of them failed because they would not give up the old structured approach and adopt a more dynamic approach.

Unstable and fast-changing goals and technologies are bound to cause anxiety, stress, and strain. This stress is likely to show up in excessive politics, defense of prerogatives, or simply devoting more energy to outside life than to career and work life. Unlike some earlier research (Argyris, 1957), Burns and Stalker did not find that all such frustrations lead to strife and organizational failure. Instead, some of the firms took the unstable conditions in stride. The anxiety and frustration which quite naturally accompany chaotic conditions outside a company were turned to productive work and goal accomplishment, rather than to bureaucratic politics and false authority.

To the extent that all organizations have some tendency toward rigidity when changing times upset established procedure, management must give serious attention to certain kinds of remedies. One is the provision for integrator positions to operate with task forces of different specialists; another is the designation of people who "know the facts," regardless of where they are in the hierarchy, to serve on task forces. A third is decentralization, wherein the whole company is split into task forces. Organization development, or the breaking down of established formal structures and reformulating new and appropriate ones, is discussed in Chapter 12.

Understructured Systems

Suppose you drive to work each day on a four-lane highway connecting a suburb with a freeway. There are five intersections between your home and the freeway. Each is equipped only with four-way stop signs rather than traffic lights. There are hundreds of cars pulling out from these intersections each day during the rush hour. Since there is no stoplight, there are frequent traffic jams as drivers make a stop or go decision from their own points of view. There even may be prolonged arguments, aimed at protection of status and prestige when some drivers get mad because others ignored them. After you have driven this route for a while, you begin to lose respect, not only for the system, but for many of your fellow "co-operators." If you must drive on that highway Monday through Friday week in and week out under these conditions, it would not be long before you might view a traffic light as a blessing, and a supervisor (policeman) as a desirable person to have around. Regardless of how much you like or dislike authority at the beginning, you would come to be more concerned about the task to be done and moved by the desire to get on with it.

Understructured organizations can be as devastating to human sensibilities (and to organization goals) as overstructured ones. This should be cause for concern by those who think that all organizations should use the greatest possible amount of human interaction and communication. Anyone who has heard derisive remarks about "too much committee management" will recognize the limitations of dynamic coordination systems.

Both Woodward, in her study of 100 diverse firms, and Burns and Stalker, in their study of electronic firms in England and Scotland, found that it takes large amounts of energy and commitment to engage in the dynamic, unstructured relationships necessary in the organic type of organization. Indeed, part of the reason (in addition to status and politics) why Burns' electronics managers did not enter into the amorphous relationships needed for swiftly moving events was that they were unwilling to commit the necessary time and energy to something totally unknown.

A very important series of incidents is reported by Lawrence and Lorsch (1967) to support this view. The researchers singled out two companies in the container industry with relatively stable goals and technologies, and two companies in the plastics industry with relatively diverse and changing technologies and goals. Each pair of companies contained one company that was very successful in its own industry and one company that was low in performance. In addition, the high-performance company in each industry seemed to have a system for coordinating which was appropriate to its technology. The high-performance plastics company had a dynamic system of coordinating and the high-performance container company had a more structured system of coordinating. Particularly, the latter coordinated by formal referral of coordination problems up to the line executives who had the requisite knowledge to solve them. This is roughly equivalent to centralized decision-making, since a smaller group of executives toward the top made many of the coordinating decisions. On the other hand, the plastics company's more dynamic system involved a wider spread of people from various levels giving inputs to coordinating decisions through committees, task forces, and integrators. This is roughly equivalent to a decentralized or participative form of coordination.

At first, using only the data they obtained in plastics companies, the researchers hypothesized that the high-performance company had good coordination and good goal achievement because of (1) improved motivation, energy, and goal commitment as a result of participative decision-making; and (2) better technical and economic decisions because a wider range of knowledge was brought to bear on the technical problems of running the business.

But later they found that they could not use this hypothesis to explain why the high-performance container company was equally successful, because decision-making was *not* spread downward in this manner. In fact, it was centralized at the top of the line hierarchy. They therefore concluded that it was the fact that decisions were made at a place on the decentralized-centralized continuum *appropriate to the tasks to be done* which caused the firms to prosper and be successful. It was the latter factor which made for effective system performance and good morale among those who worked in each company. The resolution of conflict was accomplished best with each company acting in its own appropriate way.

An interesting violation of this principle occurred in the low-performance container company: There had been a systematic attempt to get middle managers involved in making decisions about scheduling and other customer service issues. While this apparently gave them more feeling of having influence over these decisions than managers in the high performing (container) organization, it also left them with a feeling of frustration because they were not able to achieve any clear resolution. As one production manager said:

> Presently there are thousands of guys involved in the scheduling process around here. It just doesn't work with so many cooks in the stew. . . . What happens now is that when an order comes in it is my decision to take care of it and to schedule it into the first available production space and then give some other orders a later production date. This date usually goes back to the sales office, and they aren't happy, and they will start for the regional manager or the [integrating department] in headquarters to try to get this date improved. Consequently, the [integrating] guys are always dabbling with us about the schedule. This really gets frantic sometimes. On the other hand, there has to be a bit of this in the situation we are in. Hell, I don't know all the facts out here in an outlying plant. . . . It is just an order, and we don't know what's behind it or how important it is to the company. This, I think, also accounts for a lot of meddling in the scheduling.

What was happening in this company was that people down the line were being asked, either in the name of participative management or to satisfy the needs of overly dependent top executives, to make decisions that they did not and could not make because they did not have the necessary information.

This phenomenon also affected the sales department of the low-performance container company. One salesman complained that his regional sales manager had been turned into a production scheduler, and was so swamped with petty problems (i.e., problems away from his main job) that he could hardly keep his mind on the customers.

Finally, because the participative committees did not work for either the good of the company or the people, the decisions made at lower levels were frequently reversed at higher levels. The researchers concluded: "The managers at the middle levels were frustrated by their inability to handle these conflicts as they had been led to believe they should, and the problems intensified and festered as they were passed upward" (p. 117).

Whether higher level managers realized they were asking for participation but were not able to allow it is not clear. They probably believed that "good human relations means decentralized decision-making." In any event, people who are told that they can (and should) make more decisions, but are then not allowed to do so, might well conclude that they have been dishonestly manipulated by the system.

SUMMARY AND CONCLUSIONS

The vast majority of people in the world engage in some form of work or task. They may do so to satisfy any or all of the human needs discussed in Chapter 1. To the extent that people are able to work effectively together to achieve organizational goals, there is more chance for individuals in an industrial society to achieve their own goals, be they for security, status and prestige, personal achievement, or simply doing their own thing.

This is not to say that work is without strife. We see strife of various kinds in all organizations. Part of this strife can be caused by the psychological makeup a person brings to the organization. Recall that, in organizations that are an early part of life (including family, childhood groups, university classes, and so on), some people have learned to be comfortable with authority (dependent), some have learned to be discomfited by authority (counterdependent), and others have learned to accept a mix of authority and freedom (interdependent). Having acknowledged this, and the fact that people at either extreme (dependent-counterdependent) will have difficulty living in any organization, our purpose here is to show how the organization itself can make life better or worse for people. If there is a fit of the goal, the technology, and the coordinating system, chances are that the system will affect *all* participants' attitudes and satisfactions in a positive way. On the other hand, if there is *not* a fit of the goal, the technology, and the coordinating system, it affects all participants' attitudes and satisfactions in a negative way.

We have seen that there are different ways of structuring organizations. Sometimes they are structured so that there are detailed specifications for different tasks, and of the relationships of those tasks. Other times there is much less formal specification of tasks, and more reliance on people working things out informally, among themselves.

At this point, one important condition for organization design should be explained. By the logic presented in this chapter, the manager does not start with the characteristics of people, and design a structure to fit them. Only in an organization with absolute congruence of individual objectives with the goals of the organization itself would this be possible. If the organization has output goals other than simply the friendly cooperation of internal participants, the structure must be designed to fit those goals.

REFERENCES

Argyris, C. *Personality and Organization.* Harper & Row, 1957.

Burns, T., and G. M. Stalker. *The Management of Innovation.* London: Tavistock, 1961.

Herzberg, F. "One More Time: How Do You Motivate Employees?" *Harvard Business Review,* Vol. 46, No. 1 (January–February 1968).

House, R. J., and L. A. Wigdor. "Herzberg's Dual-Factor Theory of Job Satisfaction and Motivation: A Review of the Evidence and a Criticism." *Personnel Psychology,* Vol. 20, No. 4, Winter 1967.

Lawrence, P. R., and J. W. Lorsch. *Organization and Environment.* Harvard University Graduate School of Business Administration, 1967.

Lorsch, J. W., and P. R. Lawrence. "Organizing for Product Innovation." *Harvard Business Review,* Vol. 43, No. 1 (January–February 1965).

McGregor, D. *The Human Side of Enterprise.* McGraw-Hill, 1960.

Thompson, V. A. *Modern Organization.* Knopf, 1961.

Woodward, J. *Management and Technology.* London: Her Majesty's Stationery Office, 1958.

———. *Industrial Organization: Theory and Practice.* Oxford University Press, 1965.

———. *Industrial Organization: Behavior and Control.* Oxford University Press, 1970.

Readings

Organizing for Product Innovation
Jay W. Lorsch, Paul R. Lawrence

In this article we shall report the results of a pilot study on the problem of obtaining collaboration and coordination between research, sales, and production specialists involved in product innovation in two organizations producing basic plastic products. In presenting the findings we shall emphasize these points:

(1) The research, sales, and production specialists working on different tasks connected with product innovation develop different viewpoints and methods of operation and tend to work best in different kinds of organizational structures. This specialization and the differences associated with it are important for the effective operation of the separate sales, research, and production units, but they also contribute to the disagreements and differences of opinion between these departments which inevitably occur around the product-innovation process.

(2) Successful product innovation depends not only on this specialization but also on the development of methods of coordination which enable executives with diverse points of view to resolve their disagreements and achieve a unity of effort.

(3) One method of obtaining effective coordination is to establish a separate organizational unit which has as its primary task coordinating the activities of sales, production, and research. Such a unit is most effective when its members have a balanced point of view which enables them to work effectively with each of the specialist groups. By this we mean that the coordinators do not consistently favor the viewpoints of salesmen or researchers or production men but understand the interest of *all three* groups and can work back and forth effectively among them.

(4) A second method of improving collaboration is to use teams or committees in which the members have learned to fight constructively with each other, confronting their differences and resolving them rather than avoiding them. The members must have authority to make decisions — and they must not be too high up in the organization. Effective coordination seems to result when they are at a sufficiently low level in the company structure to have detailed technical and/or market knowledge bearing on the conflicts they try to resolve.

- How can we get our research people to be more responsive to the needs of the market?
- What can we do to get our salesmen more involved in selling new products and seeking new applications?
- Why are our production people so conservative when it comes to introducing new products?
- How can we get sales, research, and production people to pull in the same direction on product development?

Questions such as these have become of increasing concern to executives in companies operating in the many industries characterized by rapid technological and market change, in which new and improved products are the key to corporate success. Several years ago we were all concerned with obtaining effective research organizations. It was generally believed that if a climate could be developed in which talented scientists and engineers could work creatively, we would be assured of a constant flow of product improvements and new products. As companies have become successful in developing more effective research organizations, however, it has become increasingly apparent that creative, innovative researchers are not enough by themselves. What is needed, as the questions above indicate, is an organization which provides collaboration between scientific innovators and sales and production specialists, so that:

- The skills of the innovators can be directed at market needs and technological problems.
- Sales and production specialists can be actively involved in the commercialization of ideas developed in the laboratory.
- And, as a result, ideas can be transferred smoothly from laboratory prototype to commercial reality.

HOW COMPANIES INNOVATE

We can begin our discussion of the problems of organizing for innovation by briefly examining the essential functions of any organization. Basically, an organization, whether it be the product division of a diversified chemical company or a corner drug store, provides a means by which more than one person can work together to perform a task that one individual could not perform alone. This means each individual or unit of the larger organization will be performing some specialized portion of the organization's task.

The first function of an organization, then, is to divide the total task into specialized pieces. The organization's second function is to provide a means by which units working on different parts of the total task may coordinate their activities to come out with a unified effort. While these processes of specialization and coordination are essential in any organization, they are particularly crucial for companies competing in developing new products.

Perhaps the best way to understand the specialization and coordination required in the innovation process is to describe the steps involved in developing products in the two plastics companies we studied. These were prominent companies in their industry, chosen to show similarities and contrasts in their organizatonal approach to product innovation. To protect their identity, we shall refer to them as the "Rhody" and "Crown" companies. It should be stressed that the two companies sold their products for industrial applications and there was, therefore, a constant demand not only for major new products but also for a flow of modifications in properties and processes that could improve the performance of old products and yield new applications for them. In our description of the innovation process we will be referring to the steps required for both types of innovation.

REQUIRED COLLABORATION

As we have already indicated, there are three major groups of specialists in each organization. Sales, production, and research specialists are each coping with a different sector of the organization's environment, and each should have a different portion of the total skills and knowledge required to discover a product idea and convert it into a tangible product:

- The sales department in dealing with the market environment should be in a position to extract information about market trends and customer needs.
- The research department in dealing with the scientific environment should be able to provide data about the technical and scientific feasibility of any new product development.
- The production department should have a store of knowledge about the limits of plant processes from the production environment.

Information from the sales department about customer needs and from production about processing limits has to be passed on to the research unit so that this information can be assimilated with the scientific feasibility of developing or modifying a product. Within the limits set by the needs of the customer and the capacities of the production process, the research units are then required to come up with a new development. If they succeed, it is then necessary to transfer information back to the sales department about product characteristics and to the production department about process specifications. With this information sales should be in a position to make and implement market plans, and production should have the data for planning and executing its task of manufacturing the product.

In short, product innovation requires close coordination between research and sales, on the one hand, and between research and production, on the other. This coordination is necessary not only to provide the two-way flow of technical information described earlier, but also to develop mutual trust and confidence between the members of the units which are required to collaborate in product development. Sales personnel must have confidence in research's knowledge of science, while research scientists must have confidence in sales' appraisal of the market. Similarly, there must be mutual confidence between research and production about production's ability to operate the process efficiently according to specifications and about research's capacity to develop a process that can be operated efficiently.

Product innovation, then, requires close collaboration between the sales and research units and the production and research units if the specialists involved are effectively to bring their separate skills to bear on a successful product development. However, the complexity and uncertainty of the factors which must be dealt with (at least in companies developing a multiplicity of new products) make it necessary for this coordination to take place at the *lower* levels of the organization. Executives in both Rhody and Crown indicate that it is difficult for managers at the upper levels of the organization to keep in touch with the multitude of rapidly changing factors which must be considered in the day-to-day process of developing many new products. Only the specialists on the firing line have the detailed knowledge of markets and technologies to make the frequent day-to-day decisions which the innovation process requires.

So far we have presented only a description of what *should* happen in both organizations if innovation is to be successfully accomplished. But our interests are in investigating not only what should happen but also, and more importantly, what *actually* happens in each organization as a result of the processes of specialization and coordination required for product innovation. We want to find out in what ways the groups of specialists working on diverse tasks in the two companies are different in their ways of thinking, in the ground rules they work by, and in terms of the organizational structures in which they work.

When we undertook our study, we decided to find out first how groups of specialists actually were differentiated. We expected the differences to be related to the problems of obtaining coordination between units. Our findings about departmental differences are classified in terms of four main dimensions: (a) degree of departmental structure, (b) members' orientation toward time, (c) members' orientation toward others, and (d) members' orientation toward the environment.

Each of the differences between departments is seen to be a function of the characteristics of the environmental sector (market, science, or plant) with which a unit is coping in performing its task. Groups, such as production units, which have a very certain environment (as measured by the certainty of information at a given time, the rate of change in the environment, and the time range of the task) are highly structured. Because they are working with a highly stable environment, they tend to develop explicit routines and highly programmed ways of operating, adopt a directive interpersonal style, and also find a short-range time orientation useful for the performance of their task.

On the other hand, units, such as research, which are coping with less certain environments tend to be less structured, are characterized by a more permissive interpersonal orientation, and have a longer time orientation. These characteristics are consistent with an uncertain, nonroutine task, since effective performance of such a task requires opportunity for open consultation among colleagues in seeking solutions to problems and freedom to consider and attempt different courses of action.

Principal Patterns

How do the differences in orientation and structure characterize the departments in Rhody and Crown? Exhibit 1 summarizes our findings on this question. The data presented here are representative of the *general* pattern which exists in both organizations; some minor variations between the two organizations are not depicted. We see that:

Members of each department tend primarily to be oriented toward the sector of the environment with which their task involves them. Research people tend to be more oriented toward discovering new scientific knowledge, while sales people are more concerned with customer problems and market conditions, and production personnel indicate a primary concern with production costs and processing problems.

Exhibit 1 Patterns of Specialization

	Departmental Structure	*Orientation Toward Time*	*Orientation Toward Others*	*Orientation Toward Environment*
Research	Low	Long	Permissive	Science
Sales	Medium	Short	Permissive	Market
Production	High	Short	Directive	Plant

In time orientation, the research scientists tend to be more concerned with long-range matters which will not have an impact on company profits for several years in the future. Sales and production specialists are primarily concerned with the more immediate problems which affect the company's performance within the current year.

The interpersonal orientations of the members of the units in both companies are also different. Research and sales personnel tend to prefer more permissive interpersonal relationships, while production specialists indicate a preference for a more directive manner of working with their colleagues.

As for the degree of departmental structure, the research units have the lowest amount and the production units have the highest. The sales units, which seem to be performing a task of medium certainty, have a structure which falls between the extremes represented by research and production.

What we find in both companies, then, are units which are quite different from each other both in terms of members' orientations and the structure in which the members work. These differences in ways of thinking about the job and in ground rules and operating procedures mean that each of these groups tends to view the task of innovation somewhat differently.

Impact on Ability

While we next want to examine the influence of these differences on the process of obtaining coordination, we should first emphasize a point which too often has been overlooked: The differences have a *positive* effect on the ability of each individual unit to perform its particular task. The common orientations and ground rules within a unit and a departmental structure which facilitate task performance direct the efforts of people in the unit to their segment of the organizational task and enhance their ability to carry out their mission. Because the units are performing different tasks, we have to expect that they will develop different departmental structures and that their members will be oriented differently. If attempts were made to standardize the structures of all units and to have all members of the organization oriented in the same direction, we would lose the benefits of specialization.

The two companies in our study recognize this fact to differing degrees. At Rhody the differences along the four dimensions tend to be greater than at Crown. Each department at Rhody not only has a structure conducive to the performance of its task, but also tends to be more highly concerned with a single task dimension or with a particular period of time than does the same unit at Crown. While in both organizations the specialization of units enables them to address their separate tasks, the units at Rhody, by virtue of their higher degree of specialization, often seem to be better able to perform their individual tasks.

ORGANIZATIONAL PARADOX

While specialized orientations and structures facilitate a unit's task performance, we would expect the patterns to be closely related to the problems of coordination in both firms. Because members of a given department hold common attitudes about what is important in their work and about dealing with each other, they are able to work effectively with each other. But to the extent that the ground rules and orientations held by members of one department are different from those held by members of another, we would expect the departments to have increased difficulty achieving the high degree of coordination required for effective innovation.

The data we collected through a questionnaire about the effectiveness of coordination between departments at Rhody and Crown confirm this expectation. When two units are similar in departmental structure and in the orientations of their members, we find that they have few problems in obtaining effective collaboration *with each other*. But when units tend to be on opposite poles along the four dimensions, we find that there are more problems in integrating their efforts. Within each organization there is clear evidence that the greater the differences in orientation and structure between any pair of units, the greater the problems of obtaining effective coordination.

Although this relationship holds within each company, we find an interesting paradox when the two organizations are compared. As already indicated, there is a higher degree of specialization and differentiation at Rhody than at Crown. Pairs of units which are required to collaborate at Rhody tend to be less similar than the comparable pairs of units at Crown. Since units at Crown are more similar, this *should* mean that Crown encounters fewer problems of coordination. However, this does not turn out to be the case. Rhody appears to be achieving better integration than Crown, even though it also has a higher degree of differentiation. In short, within each organization there is a relationship between the effectiveness of coordination and the degree of differentiation, but the organization which has the highest degree of specialization also has the most effective collaboration.

The significance of this paradox grows if we recall that specialization is a two-sided coin. Specialization is useful because it is necessary for the performance of individual departments; on the other hand, it can have negative consequences in that it is at the root of the problems of achieving the coordination required for innovation. At Rhody we have a situation in which one organization is able to have its cake (in the form of specialization) and to eat it too (in the form of coordination).

CONTRASTING METHODS

Does the explanation reside in the methods used by the two organizations to facilitate coordination between units? We believe it does.

Attempts at devising methods to improve coordination between the specialized departments involved in product innovation are certainly not novel. New-product departments, or coordinating departments with other appellations, have been established in many organizations with the primary function of coordinating the activities of research, sales, and production specialists in the development of new products. Similarly, many firms have appointed liaison individuals who are responsible for linking two or more groups of functional specialists. Another frequent device has been to develop short-term project teams with representatives from the several functional departments to work on a new product. Finally, many companies have relied on permanent cross-functional coordinating teams to deal with the continuing problems of innovation around a given group of products.

Both Rhody and Crown have developed the same types of devices:

(1) In each company there is a coordinating department which has the primary task of coordinating or integrating the innovation activities of the research, production, and sales units.

(2) Each company is making use of permanent cross-functional coordinating committees which have representatives from each of the basic departments and the coordinating department. The primary function of these committees is to serve as a setting in which coordination can take place.

Since both organizations are utilizing the same devices to achieve coordination, it is pertinent to ask whether there are differences in the functioning and effectiveness of these devices. The answer provided by our investigation is an emphatic *yes*.

We now turn to an examination of these differences, looking first at the coordinating departments, then at the committees.

COORDINATING DEPARTMENTS

In addition to seeking teamwork among research, production, and sales, the coordinating departments at Rhody and Crown perform certain other tasks. At Crown the department is also involved in market planning and the coordination of sales efforts. At Rhody the coordinating department is also involved in technical service and market-development activities. As might be expected, both departments have developed orientations and structural characteristics somewhat different from those of the other units in the companies.

Key to Coordination

While various similarities exist between the two coordinating groups, there is also, as our measurements reveal, a major distinction:

At Rhody the coordinating department falls in a middle position on each of the four dimensions we have considered. That is, if we compare the department's degree of structure and its members' orientations with those of the sales, production, and research departments, it always has an intermediate value, never an extreme one. For instance, members of the coordinating department have a balanced orientation along the time dimension. They are equally concerned with the short-range problems of sales and production and the long-range matters with which research wrestles. Similarly, coordinating personnel have a balanced concern with production, scientific, and market environments. The degree of departmental structure and the interpersonal orientation of coordinating members also fall between the extremes of the other departments.

At Crown the coordinating department is in the middle along the structure and interpersonal dimensions but tends to be highly oriented toward short-range time concerns and toward the market environment. Personnel indicate a high concern with immediate sales problems, and less concern with longer-range matters or with research or production environments. On both the time and the environment dimensions, therefore, the coordinating department is not intermediate between the departments it is supposed to be linking.

The foregoing difference appears to be related to differences in the effectiveness of the two units. Our questionnaires and interviews indicate that the coordinating department at Rhody is generally perceived by members of that organization to be doing an effective job of linking the basic departments. On the other hand, the coordinating department at Crown is not perceived to be as effective as most members of the Crown organization think it should be.

Observations by Executives

The reactions of executives in the two companies pretty well explain for us why the intermediate position of the Rhody coordinating department is associated with effective coordination, while the imbalance in certain orientations of the Crown unit inhibits its performance. The following are a few typical comments from Rhody managers:

"The most important thing is that we have the coordinating department with its contacts with the customers and its technically trained people who are in contact with research. They are the kingpins. They have a good feel for research's ability, and they know the needs of the market. They will work back and forth with research and the other units."

"Generally speaking, the feeling of close cooperation between the coordinating unit and sales is echoed in the field. The top salesmen all get along well with the coordinating guys. You take a good coordinating fellow and a good salesman and that makes a powerful team. In our business the boys upstairs in the coordinating unit are top notch. They know what the lab can do, and they know the salesman's problems."

But at Crown the comments of executives have a different tone:

"My biggest criticism of our situation is that the coordinating department isn't a good enough mechanism to link the research activities to the customer. We need a better marketing strategy on certain products and some long-term plans. The lack of planning in the coordinating department is deplorable. One of our troubles is that the coordinating people are so tied up in day-to-day detail that they can't look to the future. They are still concerned with 1964 materials when they should be concerned with 1965 markets."

"Our problem is we can't clearly define the technical problems the customer is having. Theoretically the coordinating men should be able to handle this for research because they know the customer best. But they are so involved in present business that it takes all their time. They have a budget they have to live up to, and the best way to make money is to sell existing products. They know that selling existing products is more profitable than selling new products, so they keep on selling existing products to live up to the expectations of the budget."

In other words, we have a marked difference in reaction. What managers at Rhody are stressing is that the coordinating unit in their organization is effective because it has a familiarity with the problems, orientations, and ways of operating of the basic units it connects. At Crown the primary complaints about that organization's less-effective coordinating unit are that its members tend to be too oriented toward immediate sales matters.

The situation in these two organizations seems to indicate that for a coordinating department to be effective in linking the several specialized departments, it must be intermediate between any two along each of the several dimensions of orientation and structure. When a coordinating department is in this position, its members have more in common with members of the other units. Coordinating personnel tend to think and act in ways which are more understandable and agreeable to members of the other departments—and this facilitates collaboration. If members of the coordinating department have orientations and ground rules which are more suited to one specialized unit, as is the situation at Crown, their ways of thinking will necessarily be different from the other departments—and this situation will impair their effectiveness as co-ordinators.

CROSS-FUNCTIONAL GROUPS

Even in an organization like Rhody, where the coordinating unit is doing an effective job of facilitating cooperation between the specialized units, certain disagreements between the various specialist units seem to be inevitable. Management's problem is to provide a setting in which attempts at resolving these disagreements can be made effectively. Both organizations in this study have turned to permanent cross-functional coordinating committees as devices for providing a setting in which to work at achieving coordination between units.

In investigating the functioning of these committees in the two organizations, we again want to obtain an assessment of their effectiveness as well as some understanding of the factors which might be related to their performance. If we listen to some of the comments made by members of both organizations, the differences between the devices in the two companies become apparent.

At the Rhody company, managers make comments such as these about the cross-functional teams:

"Our problems get thrashed out in committee. We work them over until everybody agrees this is the best effort you can make. We may decide this isn't good enough; then we may decide to ask for more people, more plant, and so forth. We all sometimes have to take a modification and be realistic and say this is the best we can do."

"I may want us to do some work on a particular new product. The coordinating guy may say, 'Let's get the customer to change his process instead.' A research guy may say we need both. It is the way we do it that becomes argumentative and rightfully so. These things take several meetings to work out, but we are never really stalemated. We have decided in our committee that we won't stalemate. There is more than one way to our ends. If I don't agree with the others, then I abdicate my position—sometimes gracefully and sometimes not.

"We had a disagreement about releasing confidential information to a customer and had quite a discussion about it. This was only the second time we had gotten so formal as to have a vote. I was outvoted three to one, but that afternoon I was the one who had to call the customer and give him the information as we had decided."

"Since we have had these committees, we are working more closely with other groups. It is really working out. In the past, production was reluctant to give us information, and they wanted to keep the prerogative of making process changes. Since this committee has been operating, there has been a greater exchange of information. . . ."

At Crown the executives speak differently about their experiences with cross-functional committees:

"Unfortunately, the committees are not decision-making groups as much as I would like. Generally there is a reporting session. We don't have time going over all these things to make some of the decisions which need to be made. I would like to see more hashing out of the problems and making of decisions. Of course we do make decisions every day between us."

"If I want something very badly and I am confronted by a roadblock, I go to top management to get the decision made. If the research managers are willing to go ahead, there is no problem. If there is a conflict, then I would go to their boss."

"I think these meetings only intensify the arguments. I haven't learned much that I didn't know already before I got to the meeting. It used to be that we had some knock-'em down, drag-out fights, but then we would get things settled. But this doesn't take place anymore, so there isn't any place for us to resolve our difficulties."

These and similar comments indicate that members of the Rhody organization find the cross-functional committees an important aid in achieving collaboration, while members of the Crown organization do not. They also indicate, as do our observations of meetings of these committees in both organizations, that there are at least two important differences between the functioning of these committees in the two organizations. Before going into these contrasts, however, we must first point to an important distinction in the organizational structures of the two companies.

The Crown organization tends to have a higher degree of structure (tighter spans of control, more specific rules and procedures, and so forth) in *all* its parts than does the Rhody organization. One important aspect of this difference is that the level at which decisions about product innovation are supposed to be made is much lower in the organizational hierarchy at Rhody than at Crown.

Decision Authority

The significance of this distinction becomes apparent if we turn to look at the teams at Rhody. In this organization team members are in most cases first-line supervisors who (being right down at the working level) have the detailed market and technical knowledge required to make decisions. They are the only persons who attend the meetings, and they usually have the formal authority to make decisions.

Our observation of meetings at Rhody, along with comments made by company executives, indicate that there are ground rules or norms operating in cross-functional committees which sanction the open confrontation of disagreement between members. Members of the committees tend to recognize their differences and seek ways of resolving them within the constraints of the situation with which they are dealing. This working through of disagreements often takes a great deal of emotional and intellectual effort, but members of the committees at Rhody tend to persevere until some resolution is reached. After decisions are made, the members of the committees are highly committed to them. As we learned from one executive, even though a member is not in initial agreement with the decision taken, he is expected to—and he does—carry out the actions worked out in the meetings.

In contrast with the situation at Rhody, we find at Crown (as we would expect from the greater degree of structure throughout this company) that members of the committees are at a higher level than their counterparts at Rhody, but even these managers often do not have the authority to make decisions. Furthermore, because they are at a higher level, they usually do not have either the technical or market knowledge required to make the detailed decisions necessary to develop products.

As a consequence of this situation, members of the Crown committees often bring both their superiors and their subordinates to the meetings with them—the superiors in order to provide someone who has the authority to make decisions, the subordinates so that someone is present who has the detailed technical and market knowledge to draw on for decisions. Bringing in all these participants results in meetings two or three times as large as those at Rhody.

Resolving Conflict

Our observations of meetings at Crown and the comments of executives indicate that there are other shortcomings in the Crown committees. The norms of behavior in these groups sanction withdrawal from disagreement and conflict. Whenever there is a disagreement, the members tend to avoid discussing the matter, hoping it will magically go away. If this doesn't place the problem out of sight, they find another avenue of avoidance by passing it on to their superiors. As a consequence, many decisions which should be made at Crown seem to get dropped. They are not picked up again until they have festered for so long that somebody *has* to deal with them—and it is often too late by that time.

There will always be disagreements between members of departments which have highly different orientations and concerns. The problem facing members of coordinating committees is to learn to fight together constructively so that they can resolve these differences. At Rhody members of the cross-functional teams have developed this ability. They work at resolving conflict at their own level. They do not withdraw from disputes, nor do they try to smooth over their differences or arrive at some easy compromise. Rather, they seem willing to argue the issues involved until some understanding is reached about the optimal solution in a given situation.

In essence, the committees at Rhody have developed the ability to confront their differences openly and search persistently for solutions which will provide effective collaboration. At Crown, on the other hand, the committees avoid fights and forfeit the opportunity to achieve the coordination required for innovation.

CONCLUSION

The foregoing comparisons seem to provide an answer to the paradox of the Rhody organization achieving both greater specialization and more effective coordination than the Crown company does. The effective coordinating unit and cross-functional coordinating committees allow members at Rhody to concentrate on their specialties and still achieve a unity of effort. Sales, research, and production specialists are each able to address their separate departmental tasks and work in a climate which is conducive to good performance. At the same time, the men in the coordinating department, who have a balanced orientation toward the concerns of the three departments of specialists, help the three units to achieve a unity of effort. The cross-functional committees also provide a means by which the specialist groups and the coordinators can work through their differences and arrive at the best common approach.

At Crown, in spite of the fact that the specialist departments are more similar in orientation and structure than are the units at Rhody, there is more difficulty in obtaining unity of effort between them. Since the coordinators are overly concerned with short-term matters and sales problems, they do not effectively perform their function of linking the three groups of specialists. The cross-functional committees do not contribute much to coordination between these departments, either. They do not provide a setting in which problems can be solved, since authority to make decisions often resides in the higher levels of the organization and since norms have developed within the committees which encourage members to avoid conflict and pass it on to their superiors.

But what about the results the two companies have achieved in the market place? We have been asserting that both a high degree of specialization and effective coordination are important in achieving product innovation in this situation, but we have not presented any evidence that Rhody, with its greater specialization and more effective coordination, is in fact doing a better job of product innovation than is Crown. The following figures do show that the Rhody organization *is* achieving a higher level of innovation than Crown: At Rhody, new products developed in the last five years have accounted for 59% of sales. At Crown, the figure is only 20%, or just about one-third of Rhody's.

Part of this difference may have been due to some variation in market and technical factors confronting the two organizations. However, since these two organizations have been operating in the same industry and have been confronted by similar market conditions and technical problems, and because of the different levels of coordination and specialization achieved in each company, it seems safe to conclude that there is indeed a relationship between innovation performance and the internal organizational factors we have been discussing.

MANAGEMENT CHALLENGE

While this discussion has been based on an examination of two organizations in the plastics industry, there is no question that the requirements for specialization and coordination are just as urgent in other industries confronted with the need for product innovation. It seems safe to generalize that, whatever the field or function, managers interested in improving their record with new products must recognize two essential organizational ingredients of success:

1. Specialists who are clearly oriented toward their individual tasks and who work in organizational structures which are conducive to task performance.

2. Effective means of coordination which permit specialists with diverse knowledge and orientations to work together. (There will be disagreements and conflicts among these specialists, but the organization must provide a means to resolve the conflicts in such a way that the full energy of research, sales, and production people can be brought to bear on innovation.)

Our discussion has focused on two devices to achieve this coordination — *coordinating departments* whose members have a balanced point of view enabling them to work effectively among the several specialist groups, and *cross-functional coordinating committees* in which members have learned to confront their differences and fight over them constructively so they can reach an optimal resolution. But other means of coordination are also available. The challenge confronting managers responsible for organizing for innovations is to work at developing means of coordination which permit effective specialization *and* effective coordination. This is the combination that is needed to produce the constant flow of innovations necessary for corporate growth in changing markets.

Management and Technology
Joan Woodward

*The Human Relations Research staff of the South East Essex Technical College
studied one hundred manufacturing firms in a certain area of England from 1955 to
1957. The objective of the research was to find out how these firms were organized
and what caused them to organize in certain ways. The following extracts from the
report of the researchers show what they found.*

The 100 firms in the survey were organized and run in widely different ways. In only
about half did the principles and concepts of management theory appear to have had
much influence on organizational development.

In 35 firms there was an essentially 'line' or 'military' type of organization; two
firms were organized functionally, almost exactly as recommended by Frederick Taylor
fifty years ago [*Shop Management*, 1910]. The rest followed in varying degrees a line-
staff pattern of organization; that is, they employed a number of functional specialists
as 'staff' to advise those in the direct line of authority.

The number of distinct levels of management between board and operators varied
from two to twelve; while the span of control of the chief executive[1] ranged from two
to nineteen, and that of the first line supervisor—i.e., the first level of authority that
spent more than 50% of the time on supervisory duties—from seven to ninety. (An
individual's span of control is the number of people directly responsible to him.)

Did any common thread underlie these differences? One possible explanation was
that they reflected the different personalities of the senior managers, another that they
arose from the historical background of the firms. While such factors undoubtedly
influenced the situation, they did not adequately explain it; they were not always associated with differences in organizational patterns or in the quality of human relations.

A new approach lay in recognizing that firms differed not only in size, kind of
industry and organizational structure, but also in objectives. While the firms were all
manufacturing goods for sale, their detailed objectives depended on the nature of the
product and the type of customer. Thus some firms were in more competitive industries
than others, some were making perishable goods that could not be stored, some produced for stock, and others to orders; in fact, marketing conditions were different in
every firm. The underlying purpose varied too. For example, one firm had originally
undertaken manufacture to demonstrate that the products of its mines could be effective substitutes for other more commonly used materials.

These differences in objectives controlled and limited the techniques of production
that could be employed. A firm whose objective was to build prototypes of electronic
equipment, for example, could not employ the technical methods of mass-production
engineering. The criterion of the appropriateness of an organizational structure must
be the extent to which it furthers the objectives of the firm, not, as management teaching
sometimes suggests, the degree to which it conforms to a prescribed pattern. There can
be no one best way of organizing a business.

From *Problems of Progress in Industry No. 3: Management and Technology* by Joan
Woodward. Reprinted with the permission of the Controller of Her Britannic Majesty's
Stationery Office.

[1] The chief executive was in some cases the Chairman, in others the Managing Director, and
in others the General or Works Manager. In every case he represented the highest level of
authority operating fulltime on the spot.

This is perhaps not sufficiently recognized; management theorists have tried to develop a 'science' of administration relevant to all types of production. One result is that new techniques such as operational research and the various tools of automation have been regarded as aids to management and to industrial efficiency rather than as developments which may change the very nature of management.

The firms were grouped according to their technical methods. Ten different categories emerged. (See Exhibit 1.)

Exhibit 1 Production Systems in South Essex Industry

	I Production of simple units to customers' orders (5 firms)
Group I Small Batch and Unit Production (Types I through V)	II Production of technically complex units (10 firms)
	III Fabrication of large equipment in stages (2 firms)
	IV Production of small batches (7 firms)
	V Production of components in large batches subsequently assembled diversely (3 firms)
Group II Large Batch and Mass Production (Types V through VIII)	VI Production of large batches, assembly line type (25 firms)
	VII Mass production (6 firms)
	VIII Process production combined with the preparation of a product for sale by large-batch or mass-production methods (9 firms)
Group III Process Production (Types VIII through X)	IX Process production of chemicals in batches (13 firms)
	X Continuous flow production of liquids, gases, and solid shapes (12 firms)
	(8 firms unclassified because too mixed or changing)

Firms in the same industry did not necessarily fall into the same group. For example, two tailoring firms of approximately equal size had very different production systems; one made bespoke suits, the other mass-produced men's clothing.

MEASUREMENT OF TECHNICAL COMPLEXITY

The ten production groups listed in Exhibit 1 form a scale of technical complexity. (This term is used here to mean the extent to which the production process is controllable and its results predictable.) For example, targets can be set more easily in a chemical plant than in even the most up-to-date mass-production engineering shops, and the factors limiting production are known more definitely so that continual productivity drives are not needed.

The analysis of the research revealed that firms using similar technical methods had similar organizational structures. It appeared that different technologies imposed different kinds of demands on individuals and organizations, and that these demands had to be met through an appropriate form of organization. There were still a number of differences between firms—related to such factors as history, background, and personalities—but these were not as significant as the differences between one production group and another and their influence seemed to be limited by technical considerations. For example, there were differences between managers in their readiness to delegate authority; but in general they delegated more in process than in mass-production firms.

ORGANIZATION AND TECHNICAL COMPLEXITY

Organization also appeared to change as technology advanced. Some figures showed a direct and progressive relationship with advancing technology (used in this report to mean 'system of techniques'). Others reached their peak in mass production and then decreased, so that in these respects unit and process production resembled each other more than the intermediate stage. Exhibits 2 and 3 show these two trends. (Details are given for the three main groups of production systems. See Exhibit 1.)

The number of levels of authority in the management hierarchy increased with technical complexity. (See Exhibit 2.)

The span of control of the first-line supervisor on the other hand reached its peak in mass production and then decreased. (See Exhibit 3.)

The ratio of managers and supervisory staff to total personnel in the different production systems is shown in some detail in Exhibit 4 as an indication of likely changes in the demand for managers as process production becomes more widespread. There were over three times as many managers for the same number of personnel in process firms as in unit-production firms. Mass-production firms lay between the two groups, with half as many managers as in process production for the same number of personnel.

The following characteristics followed the pattern shown in Exhibit 2—a direct and progressive relationship with technical complexity.

1. *Labour costs* decreased as technology advanced. Wages accounted for an average of 36 percent of total costs in unit production, 34 percent in mass production and 14 percent in process production.

Exhibit 2 The Number of Levels of Authority in Management Hierarchy

Number of Levels of Authority	System of Production		
	Unit Production	Mass Production	Process Production
	Number of Firms		
8 or more		1	5
7		2	5
6		3	7 (median)
5		7	6
4	3	16 (median)	2
3	18 (median)	2	
2	3		

The median is the number of levels in the middle firm in the range—for instance, the sixteenth of the 31 mass-production firms.

2. *The ratios of indirect to direct labour* and of administrative and clerical staff to hourly paid workers increased with technical advance.

3. *The proportion of graduates* among the supervisory staff engaged on production increased too. Unit-production firms employed more professionally qualified staff altogether than other firms, but mainly on research or development activities. In unit-production and mass-production firms it was the complexity of the product that determined the proportion of professionally qualified staff, while in process industry it was the complexity of the process.

Exhibit 3   Span of Control of First Line Supervision

Number of Persons Controlled	*System of Production*		
	Unit Production	Mass Production	Process Production
	Number of Firms		
Unclassified	1	1	
81–90		3	
71–80		1	
61–70		5	
51–60	1	4	
41–50	3	9 (median)	
31–40	4	5	2
21–30	8 (median)	2	5
11–20	6	1	12 (median)
10 or less	1		6

Exhibit 4   The Ratio of Managers and Supervisory Staff to Other Personnel

System of Production	*Size of Firm*		
	400–500 Employees	850–1000 Employees	3000–4600 Employees
Unit	1:22	1:37	1:25
Mass	1:14	1:15	1:18
Process	1:8	1:7	1:7

4. *The span of control of the chief executive* widened considerably with technical advance.

The following organizational characteristics formed the pattern shown in Exhibit 3. The production groups at the extremes of the technical scale resembled each other, but both differed considerably from the groups in the middle.

1. *Organization was more flexible* at both ends of the scale, duties and responsibilities being less clearly defined.

2. The amount of *written, as opposed to verbal, communication* increased up to

the stage of assembly-line production. In process-production firms, however, most of the communications were again verbal.

3. *Specialization between the functions of management* was found more frequently in large-batch and mass production than in unit or process production. In most unit-production firms there were few specialists; managers responsible for production were expected to have technical skills, although these were more often based on length of experience and on 'know-how' than on scientific knowledge. When unit production was based on mass-produced components more specialists were employed however. Large-batch and mass-production firms generally conformed to the traditional line-and-staff pattern, the managerial and supervisory group breaking down into two sub-groups with separate, and sometimes conflicting, ideas and objectives. In process-production firms the line-and-staff pattern broke down in practice, though it sometimes existed on paper. Firms tended either to move towards functional organization of the kind advocated by Taylor, or to do without specialists and incorporate scientific and technical knowledge in the direct executive hierarchy. As a result, technical competence in line supervision was again important, although now the demand was for scientific knowledge rather than technical 'know-how.'

4. Although production control became increasingly important as technology advanced, *the administration of production*—what Taylor called 'the brainwork of production'—was most widely separated from the actual supervision of production operations in large-batch and mass-production firms, where the newer techniques of production planning and control, methods engineering and work study were most developed. The two functions became increasingly reintegrated beyond this point.

THE EFFECT OF TECHNOLOGY UPON HUMAN RELATIONS

The attitudes and behaviour of management and supervisory staff and the tone of industrial relations in the firms also seemed to be closely related to their technology. In firms at the extremes of the scale, relationships were on the whole better than in the middle ranges. Pressure on people at all levels of the industrial hierarchy seemed to build up as technology advanced, became heaviest in assembly-line production and then relaxed, so reducing personal conflicts. Some factors—the relaxation of pressure, the smaller working groups, the increasing ratio of supervisors to operators, and the reduced need for labour economy—were conducive to industrial peace in process production. Thus, although some managements handled their labour problems more skillfully than others, these problems were much more difficult for firms in the middle ranges than those in unit or process production. The production system seemed more important in determining the quality of human relations than did the numbers employed.

SIZE AND TECHNOLOGY

No significant relationship was revealed between the size of the firm and the system of production. (See Exhibit 5.) There were small, medium, and large firms in each of the main production groups.

Exhibit 5 Production Systems Analysed by Number Employed

Production System	Number Employed:			Total Number of Firms
	101–250	251–1000	Over 1000	
Unit	7	13	4	24
Mass	14	12	5	31
Process	12	9	4	25
Totals	33	34	13	80

' There were firms which employed relatively few people and yet had all the other characteristics of a large company, including a well-defined and developed management structure, considerable financial resources, and a highly paid staff with considerable status in the local industrial community. This was particularly true of the smaller process-production firms. Some of these employed less than 500 people but had more of the characteristics of large-scale industry than unit- or mass-production firms with two or three times as many employees. As indicated already the ratio of management staff to the total number employed was found to increase as technology advanced. It appeared also that the size of the management group was a more reliable measure of the 'bigness' of a firm than its total personnel.

Moreover, although no relationship was found between organization and size in the general classification of firms, some evidence of such a relationship emerged when each of the production groups was considered separately. For example, in the large-batch and mass-production group the number of levels of authority and the span of control of both the chief executive and the first line supervisor both tended to increase with size.

STRUCTURE AND SUCCESS

Again, no relationship between conformity with the 'rules' of management and business success appeared in the preliminary analysis of the research data. The twenty firms graded as outstandingly successful seemed to have little in common.

When, however, firms were grouped on a basis of their production systems, the outstandingly successful ones had at least one feature in common. Many of their organizational characteristics approximated to the median of their production group. For example, in successful unit-production firms the span of control of the first line supervisor ranged from 22 to 28, the median for the group as a whole being 23; in successful mass-production firms it ranged from 45 to 50, the median for the group being 49; and in successful process-production firms it ranged from 11 to 15, the median for the group being 13. (See Exhibit 3.) Conversely the firms graded as below average in most cases diverged widely from the median.

The research workers also found that when the 31 large-batch and mass-production firms were examined separately there was a relationship between conformity with the 'rules' of management and business success. The medians approximated to the pattern of organization advocated by writers on management subjects. Within this limited range of production systems, therefore, observance of these 'rules' does appear to increase administrative efficiency. This is quite understandable because management theory is mainly based on the experience of practitioners in the field, much of which has been in large-batch and mass-production firms. Outside these systems, however, it appears that new 'rules' are needed and it should be recognized that an alternative kind of organizational structure might be more appropriate.

THE ORGANIZATIONAL DEMANDS OF PRODUCTION SYSTEMS

What are the demands made by different technical methods? Is it possible to trace a relationship between a system of production and its associated organization pattern? To find answers to such questions as these, twenty of the firms included in the survey were picked out at intervals along the scale of technical complexity and studied in more detail. They included six unit or small-batch production firms, six large-batch or mass-production firms, five process-production firms, and three in which process production was combined with preparation of the product for sale by large-batch or mass-production techniques.

In each firm the research workers studied:

(1) The manufacturing process itself, analysing the subsidiary tasks necessary to the achievement of primary objectives.

(2) The number and nature of the decisions that had to be taken at each level of the management hierarchy.

(3) The kind of cooperation required between the various members of the management team.

(4) The kind of control which had to be exercised by senior executives.

The research workers then made an analysis of what they term the 'situational demands' in each firm. This means the demands on the organization of the technical situation, the system of techniques imposed by the firm's objectives. They also considered what organizational and operational expedients were likely to be effective in meeting the demands and how far the firms' existing organizational structures did in fact meet them.

The conclusions which follow derive both from these follow-up studies and from the case studies.

CO-ORDINATION

Unit production appeared to demand co-ordination between functions on a day-to-day operational basis. In several firms product development was indistinguishable from production itself. In bespoke tailoring, for example, the cutter developed and produced at the same time, adjusting designs during manufacture to suit individual requirements.

Mass-production firms had elaborate and extensive research and development programmes, but staff responsible for research were not involved in day-to-day production problems or marketing activities. Any policy decisions taken as a result of their work were long-term and far-reaching and often involved considerable expenditure; thus they were taken only at the highest level of management. In some cases the functions were physically separated, research and development being undertaken on a separate site. In others, firms did no research or development at all; they relied for new ideas on outside research bodies or on more informal sources. But although day-to-day integration of functions did not appear to be necessary, and could be dangerously disruptive, cooperation in exchanging information was essential. Product-development staff relied upon information from marketing about the way customers were thinking and from production about manufacturing facilities for the new products. (All this refers only to research relating to the product and not to the development of production methods. Methods research is an integral part of the production function and obviously must be closely integrated with other production activities.)

In *process production* too, functions were in many cases independent of each other, though not as clearly as in mass production, because of the close relationship between product development and process development. More fundamental research on new products was almost entirely self-contained. It was not controlled by existing production facilities or by customers' requirements; indeed, in many cases a market had yet to be found. When development reached the pilot-plant stage, however, closer integration was required between research and production; in some cases this was needed on the job itself; in others co-operation in exchanging information was sufficient.

But while more coordination of the three basic tasks was normally required in unit production than in mass or process production, it was occasionally required in the two latter. For instance, in process production, development staff were required to work closely with marketing personnel when creating a market for a new product. In both process and mass production, development staff had to co-operate with production personnel when bringing a new product into large-scale manufacture.

SITUATIONAL DEMANDS

This discussion clarifies the action of "situational demands." For example, each technical situation requires a different kind of cooperation between the members of a management team. Consequently the system of communication through which co-operation is brought about must also differ from one situation to another. Communications systems cannot be good or bad in themselves; they are good only if they link people together in such a way as to further the objectives of the firm. Thus unit production requires a communication system which brings people together on a day-to-day operational basis; but in mass and process production such a system might well reduce efficiency.

MANAGEMENT DECISIONS

The number and nature of the decisions that had to be made also depended on the technical demands of the manufacturing process.

In *unit production:*

(a) More decisions had to be made here than in other kinds of production, all of them relatively short-term and almost equal in importance. In many a firm a policy decision had to be made each time an order was accepted, but it committed the firm only for the period in which that article was produced. For large equipment such as television transmitters, the period could be as long as several years; even so it was shorter than that of many decisions in mass and process production.

(b) There was little distinction between policy decisions and problem-solving decisions, a problem-solving decision almost inevitably developing into a policy decision.

(c) A large proportion of the decisions made affected all the basic functions of manufacture. For example, when a raw material supply failed, the decision to use a substitute involved not only those concerned with production activities but also the development and marketing personnel; sometimes it was even necessary to reopen negotiations with the customer, too.

In *mass production,* decisions were more varied both in character and importance:

(a) Policy decisions about objectives, and the activities essential to achieving these objectives, were fewer but usually of greater importance than in unit production because they committed the firm further into the future and had to be based on a wider variety of background facts.

(b) Problem-solving decisions did not develop into policy decisions as often as they did in unit-production firms.

(c) As the basic functions of manufacture were more independent of each other, policy decisions sometimes affected one function only and could often be taken by the senior executive responsible for that function. The planning of a territorial sales organization, for example, normally involved decisions by the marketing personnel only. (One exception to this was found, however, in a firm where the area sales managers were linked with production units located in various parts of the country. Thus, any change made in the organization of the sales force affected the schedules of the production units and was therefore based on a joint decision of the two senior executives responsible for marketing and production respectively.)

(d) Decisions were also more predictable—not their exact content, of course, but at least the kind of decisions likely to occur.

In *process production:*

(a) Policy decisions were fewer than in mass or unit production but committed the firms concerned further into the future. One firm was planning to erect a new plant which, it was estimated, would take three years to build and twenty years to give an adequate return on the investment. Production facilities, once determined, would be extremely inflexible, as in most other chemical plants. Success would depend, therefore, on an assured market for the product during the next twenty years. Even in process industry not all policy decisions were as long-term as this; nevertheless, many were too important to be the responsibility of one individual. The organizational framework had to allow for joint decisions by senior management and more of the decisions were made at board level than in other systems.

(b) Problem-solving decisions, on the other hand, had to be made as near as possible to the point at which the crisis occurred; they were normally associated with operational difficulties and were of great urgency. Policy decisions were even more distinct from problem-solving decisions than in mass production.

(c) Making decisions became an increasingly rational process. The imponderables became progressively fewer and the consequences of a particular course of action could be foreseen more exactly; management hunches were required less and less. This is probably the most important single factor linking technology with organization, and it has far-reaching implications.

THE EFFECT ON HUMAN RELATIONS

Technical complexity has been defined as the extent to which control can be exercised over the physical limitations of production. At the beginning of the technical scale, it seemed, physical limitations were so difficult to control that little attempt was made to do so; consequently people were subjected to relatively little pressure. No one, for example, tried to hustle the engineers engaged on the development of a complicated piece of equipment; on the contrary, it was traditional that they were unlikely to work well 'with a gun at their backs.'

In large-batch and mass production, continuous efforts to push back the limitations of production put considerable pressure on employees. Targets were set progressively higher, incentives of many different kinds were offered, and production tended to proceed by drives. But in the last resort the pace was still set by the amount of effort the operators were prepared to put into the job.

At the top of the scale the exercise of control was so mechanical and exact that pressure on people was again at a minimum. Productivity was related only indirectly to human effort; on the whole, people were hard-pressed only when things went wrong. Moreover, the plant itself constituted a framework of discipline and control. Any demands on the operators were in fact made by the process rather than by supervision. Most of those interviewed seemed to resent authority less when exercised over them by the process than by a superior.

As technology advances the entire concept of authority in industry may have to change. In process firms the relationship between superior and subordinate was much more like that between a travel agent and his clients than that between a foreman and operators in mass production. The process foreman's job was to arrange things within limits, set by the plant, which both he and the operators understood and accepted. This common understanding and appreciation of the demands of the job is much the same as that found in unit production.

There is, for example, a different attitude to time-keeping. In the mass-production firms visited, the foremen had to work hard to prevent their operators from slipping off to wash their hands or to gather at the clock before finishing time; but in the process firms operators would arrive early for the night-shift of their own free will in order to allow the men they were relieving to get away for a quick drink at the local before closing time. The process workers were aware that the plant could not be left unattended and they themselves made the necessary arrangements.

There appear to be considerable differences between production systems in the extent to which the 'situational demands' create conditions conducive to human happiness. Managers and supervisors get more satisfaction from their jobs at the advanced levels of technology; from the operator's point of view, too, it would appear that the relaxation of pressure and the higher quality of relationships between supervisor and subordinates will more than compensate for any increased monotony and boredom arising from monitoring occupations.

Bureaucracy and Bureaupathology

Victor A. Thompson

SOME CHARACTERISTICS OF MODERN ORGANIZATIONS

Modern organization has evolved from earlier forms by incorporating advancing specialization. In an earlier period organizations could depend much more on the "line of command." The superior could tell others what to do because he could master the knowledge and techniques necessary to do so intelligently. As science and technology developed, the superior lost to experts the *ability* to command in one field after another, but he retained the *right* as part of his role.

A great structure of specialized competencies has grown up around the chain of command. Organizations have grown in size because they must be able fully to employ the new specialists and the specialized equipment associated with them if the organizations are to meet their competition. As more specialists appear and the organization continues to grow in size, it becomes necessary to group employees into units, and the units into larger units. Some of the larger of these units in government have been called "bureaus," and so the kind of organization resulting from this process has been called "bureaucracy." (These units were called "bureaus" from the French word for writing table or desk.)

BUREAUPATHIC BEHAVIOR

Dependence upon specialization imparts to modern organizations certain qualities. Among these are routinization, strong attachment to subgoals, impersonality, categorization, resistance to change, etc. The individual must adjust to these qualities because they cannot be eliminated from bureaucratic organization. In our society there are many people who have been unable to make this adjustment and who therefore find modern organization a constant source of frustration. They suffer from the social disease of "bureausis." In the last part of this article we shall try to diagnose this disease.

Personal behavior patterns are frequently encountered which exaggerate the characteristic qualities of bureaucratic organization. Within bureaucracy we often find excessive aloofness, ritualistic attachment to routines and procedures, and resistance to change; and associated with these behavior patterns is a petty insistence upon rights of authority and status. From the standpoint of organizational goal accomplishment, these personal behavior patterns are pathological because they do not advance organizational goals. They reflect the personal needs of individuals. To the extent that criticism of modern bureaucracy is not "bureaucratic," it is directed at these self-serving personal behavior patterns. Responsible criticism of bureaucratic pathology does not constitute a nostalgic longing to go back to a simpler era, but is an attempt to find the causes of pathological behavior with the hope of eliminating it. When people use the term "bureaucratic" in a critical sense, they are frequently referring to these personally oriented behavior patterns. Because the term is also used in a descriptive, noncritical sense, as Weber used it and as it has been used throughout this book, we shall avoid this critical use of the term and use in its stead a word which clearly denotes the pathological. We shall call these behaviors "bureaupathic."

The appropriation of major aspects of bureaucratic organization as means for the satisfaction of personal needs is pathological. It is a form of behavior which is functional for less than the system as a whole, including in this connection the clientele as part of the system. It involves a shifting in the costs[1] of the system by those with more authority to those with less, be they subordinates or clientele. It is a kind of behavior possible to those in the organization who have the best opportunity to use the organization to satisfy personal needs, namely, those in authority positions. It can only be exercised "downward." It cannot be exercised by clientele over authoritative officials, and it cannot be exercised by subordinates over superiors. It is, in short, a phenomenon of the system of authority, both hierarchical and nonhierarchical.[2]

This pathological behavior starts with a need on the part of the person in an authority position to control those subordinate to himself. To "control" means to have subordinate behavior correspond as closely as possible with one set of preconceived standards. While the need to control arises in large part from personal insecurity in the superior, it has conceptual sources as well, which we shall briefly state.

In the United States, we have still the ghost of the absolute king in the guise of the theory of sovereignty. Sovereignty theory supports the monistic conception of bureaucratic organization, with its associated institution of hierarchy. The superior has the right, by delegation ultimately from the absolute sovereign, to obtain a unique outcome; and he has the duty, or the responsibility to his superior, to obtain it. In profit organizations, it is held that there is only one outcome which will satisfy profit maximization under the specific conditions of the market. It is also held that the duty to seek this outcome is an overriding one because only in this way can the welfare of all be best promoted, even though in individual instances it may not seem so. In the monocratic society of Russia, only one outcome can be tolerated because only one is consistent with the laws of history; only one is possible. (Why it is necessary to seek bureaucratic control in the face of this historical determination has never been satisfactorily explained so far as we know.)

Although these conceptual sources for the need to control exist, they are hardly compelling. Much more important in explaining the authoritative need to control is personal insecurity.[3] Here we may well recap these sources of personal insecurity and anxiety in modern bureaucratic organization.

Hierarchical structure with its monopoly of "success" is a potent source of anxiety. The person in a superordinate position has a near final control over the satisfaction of subordinates' needs, their personal goals.[4] While at the bottom of the hierarchy the standards which must be met are frequently made explicit and objectively measurable, managerial personnel have generally resisted a like invasion of their own superordinate rights.[5] As we have said before, the objectivity of performance standards decreases as one mounts the hierarchy until at some point they become largely subjective. At the same time, we would expect an increasing concentration of success-hungry people in the upper reaches of the hierarchy. Strong status needs and strong doubts as to what will please the person who can satisfy those needs can only result in anxiety and, for many, in "automaton conformity"[6] to the wishes of the boss. Hierarchical anxiety is much like Calvinism in that it generates painful doubt as to who is chosen. Like Calvinism, these doubts can be reduced, not only by automaton conformity but by excessive activity and the appearance of extreme busyness.[7]

Anxiety is also associated with insecurity of function. To occupy a position not fully accepted by significant others in the organization tends to make one isolated, a minority in a hostile world. This kind of insecurity may result from a new specialty not yet fully accredited and accepted; or it may result from the authoritative assignment of jurisdiction (the delegation of nonhierarchical authority) in defiance of the needs of specialization.

Finally, the source of insecurity which is becoming the most significant in modern organizations is the growing gap between the rights of authority (to review, to veto, to affirm) and the specialized ability or skill required to solve most organizational problems. The intellectual, problem-solving, content of executive positions is being increasingly diverted to specialists, leaving hierarchical rights (and duties) as the principal components of executive posts.[8] Persons in hierarchical positions are therefore increasingly dependent upon subordinate and nonsubordinate specialists for the achievement of organizational (or unit) goals. The superior tends to be caught between the two horns of a dilemma. He must satisfy the nonexplicit and nonoperational demands of a superior through the agency of specialized subordinates and nonsubordinates whose skills he only dimly understands.[9] And yet, to be counted a success he must accept this dilemma and live with its increasing viciousness throughout his life. He must live with increasing insecurity and anxiety.[10] Although a particular person may have great maturity and general psychological security, an insecure superior at any point in the hierarchy above him can, and probably will, generate pressures which must inevitably be passed down the line, creating insecurity and tensions all the way to the bottom.[11] Given a person's hierarchical relationship with his superior, he is always subject to blame for outcomes which he could control only remotely, if at all.

THE BUREAUPATHIC REACTION

Insecurity gives rise to personal (nonorganizational) needs which may be generalized in the need for control. This need often results in behavior which appears irrational from the standpoint of the organization's goals because it does not advance them; it advances only personal goals and satisfies only personal needs. In so doing, it creates conditions which do not eliminate the need for control but rather enhance it.[12]

Alvin W. Gouldner studied the succession to the position of plant manager by a man from outside the plant.[13] This man was obligated to upper management and felt dutybound to realize its efficiency and production values. He started out, therefore, with heavy pressure from above. Coming from outside, he did not understand the informal system prevailing in the plant and was unable to use it. As his insecurity and anxiety mounted, he turned more and more to the formal system of rules, defined competencies, impersonality, and close supervision. He met resistance and felt his position between the horns of the dilemma, between those above and those below, increasingly insecure. He reacted with increased aloofness and formality. He exaggerated the characteristics of bureaucratic organization. He became bureaupathic.

The example illustrates the circularity in the bureaupathic reaction. Since the manager's behavior was so strongly influenced by his personal needs to reduce his own anxiety, the employees' responses deviated more and more from organizational needs, thereby increasing the manager's anxiety and completing the circle. The mechanisms underlying this process are not difficult to understand. Control standards encourage minimal participation.[14] They encourage employees to meet the standards and no more. Furthermore, meeting the control devices tends to become the aim of the subordinates because that is how they manage their own insecurities and avoid sanctions. For example, if agents are rated on the number of violations they uncover, cases of compliance are not likely to give them great joy.[15] Strict control from above encourages employees to "go by the book," to avoid innovations and chances of errors which put black marks on the record. It encourages the accumulation of records to prove compliance, resulting in *paperasserie*, as the French call it.[16] It encourages decision by precedent, and unwillingness to exercise initiative or take a chance. It encourages employees to wait for orders and do only what they are told. It is not hard to understand, therefore, why the superior may come to feel that he must apply more control. If he is also subject to strict bureaupathic control from above, this situation is likely to contribute to ulcers, if not, indeed, to complete breakdown.

An exaggerated dependence upon regulations and quantitative standards is likely to stem from a supervisor's personal insecurity in the parentlike role of the boss. It has been observed that women supervisors are more likely to insist upon strict compliance with all organizational rules and regulations than are men. The bureaupathic tendency of women has been attributed to their greater insecurity in the superordinate role because the general role of women in our society is somewhat subordinate.[17] A battery of regulations makes it unnecessary for the superior to give the detailed face-to-face order very often. Everybody, including the supervisor, is simply carrying out instructions imposed from above. If they are unpleasant instructions, it is not the supervisor's fault. For much the same reason, an insecure superior will probably appreciate a large number of quantitative control standards because his ratings of his subordinates then appear to be inevitable results of the performances of the subordinates, not merely the personal judgments of the superior. The anger and aggressions of the subordinates can then be displaced to the impersonal "system," and the superior can continue to get their indispensable co-operation upon which his own "success" depends.[18] Furthermore, disparities of power are hidden by the rules, and if punishment is meted out, it comes from the rules, not from the superior. In all of these ways, the rules and regulations make the parentlike role less uncomfortable for insecure people.[19]

Only the observable and measurable aspects of behavior can be controlled. These aspects are often the most trivial and unimportant from the standpoint of the long-range success of the organization. Where the need to control exists, therefore, it often manifests itself in procedures, reports, and clearances governing trivia, while at the same time very important matters are left to discretion because controlling them is not feasible. The need to control is sufficiently widespread to have given sometimes a petty and ludicrous quality to modern organization. We venture to predict that if one looks hard enough in any modern organization, he will find instructions just as ridiculous as those of the military on how to wash a dog, pick a flower, or use a fork.[20] Since the controls can successfully be applied only to the observable and measurable aspects of a job, and since the employee must concentrate on satisfying the control standards in order to reduce his own personal insecurities, his emphasis shifts from the more important, qualitative aspects of the job to the less important, quantitative aspects. In an employment office, for example, the goal shifted from good placement, in the beginning, to the highest possible number of people put to work. Interviewers felt constrained to use whatever sanctions they have to induce a client to take a job, whether he wanted it and was suited to it or not.[21]

EXAGGERATED ALOOFNESS

Organizational relationships are by nature less warm and personal than the relations of friendship. It is only when this impersonality is exaggerated to cold aloofness and apparent disinterest that we can with any fairness call it pathological. As with other kinds of bureaupathic behavior, exaggerated aloofness can usually be attributed to personal insecurity.

A cold aloofness protects an insecure superior from commitments to his subordinates which he fears will be inconsistent with demands upon him from above. It makes it easier for him to mete out punishment or to perform other aspects of his hierarchical role, such as rating his subordinates. It protects him from the aggressions of his subordinates by maintaining a psychic distance between him and them. In extreme cases it can come close to a complete breakdown of communication between the superior and his subordinates.

The same considerations apply to relations between officials and clients. A certain impersonality is necessary both to protect the goals of the organization and to secure objective and therefore effective service to the client. This impersonality may be exaggerated into a cold disinterest by an insecure official. When officials are caught between demands or "rights" of clients and tight administrative controls from above, dissociation from the clients and disinterest in their problems may seem to be the only way out of the dilemma. Client hostility, generated by what appears to be official emphasis on the wrong goals, creates tension. Inconsiderate treatment of the clients may become a device for reducing tensions and maintaining the cohesion of the officials. Blau has shown how such a situation leads to backstage demeaning of clients which, by putting psychic distance between the officials and the clients, protects the officials. Officials then tend to seek satisfactions from the abstract values of the enterprise rather than from the concrete values of personal service to a client.[22]

Within the organization, technically unnecessary interdependence creates insecurity of function. As we have seen in previous chapters, authority is sometimes delegated for political rather than technical reasons, to meet personal rather than organizational needs. Because the resulting relationship is not accepted and is constantly under attack, the person with the delegated authority lives in insecurity. Here, also, patterns of cold and imperious aloofness are often observed, and abstract values rather than personal service become goals. Officials exercising such disputed, delegated authority frequently demean their clients as narrow-minded, if not stupid. Procedures to govern the relationship are elaborated and, because they stabilize the relationship, such procedures acquire an exaggerated value for these officials.

RESISTANCE TO CHANGE

Bureaucratic organizations have to administer change carefully. Perhaps most people resist change just for the sake of change. The burden of proof is on the side of those advocating change. However, resistance to change may also be exaggerated by insecure officials; it may become bureaupathic. In an organizational context dominated by the need to control, innovation is dangerous because, by definition, it is not controlled behavior. It creates risks of errors and therefore of sanctions. To encourage innovation, an insecure superior would have to extend the initiative to subordinates and thereby lose control. Furthermore, in an insecure, competitive group situation, innovation threatens the security of all members of the group and for this reason tends to be suppressed by informal group action, as well as by the insecure superior. Innovation is facilitated by a secure, noncompetitive group administrative effort dominated by a professional outlook. Since this kind of situation is thought to be rare in modern bureaucracy, some people might regard excessive resistance to change as an inherent feature of bureaucratic organization, rather than as a form of bureaupathology. We feel, however, that excessive bureaucratic inertia is much less widespread than is supposed.[23] In an era of ever more rapid change, it seems unlikely that man has evolved a kind of organization which is particularly resistive to innovation. The traditionalistic organization was the kind most resistive, and in many places it had to be blasted off the scene by revolutionary action. The bureaucratic form replaced it, partly because it was able to accommodate to a changing world.

There is another source of resistance to change which is not bureaupathic and which is therefore subject to rational corrective procedures. The communication pattern determines who gets feed-back information. A particular official may never get intimate knowledge of the results of his own actions. Consequently, he may feel no need for a change which others who do have this knowledge think should be made. Bringing the "offending" official into direct communication with respondents might cure in a hurry this particular case of resistance to change.

INSISTENCE ON THE RIGHTS OF OFFICE

The bureaupathic official usually exaggerates the official, non-technical aspects of relationships and suppresses the technical and the informal. He stresses rights, not abilities. Since his behavior stems from insecurity, he may be expected to insist on petty rights and prerogatives, on protocol, on procedure—in short, on those things least likely to affect directly the goal accomplishment of the organization. For example, a rather functionless reviewing officer will often insist violently on his right of review and scream like an injured animal if he is by-passed. He will often insist on petty changes, such as minor changes in the wording of a document. If he has a counterpart at a higher organizational level, he will probably insist on exclusive contact with that higher clearance point. By controlling this particular communication channel he protects his authority and influence, even perhaps enhancing them somewhat by being the sole interpreter of the higher-clearance-point's requirements.[24] In like fashion and for the same reasons, an insecure superior can be expected to exert his right to the monopoly of outgoing and incoming communication. Everything must go through "formal channels." In this way he can hide his weakness and suppress information which might reveal his insecurity. He also hopes to maintain his influence and authority by suppressing the influence of external specialists, the "staff." One of the great difficulties of modern organization arises from the inescapable fact that specialist communication must break through such blockades.

Insistence upon the full rights of the superordinate role is what is meant by "close supervision." It seems to be related to doubts about the loyalty or ability of subordinates, combined with pressure from above.[25] Close supervision can be regarded as bureaupathic under conditions where the right to act and the ability to do so have become separated because of the advance of specialization. However, where the position has a great deal of technical content so that subordinates are technically dependent upon their supervisor, as in a railroad maintenance section, close supervision may be tolerated and even demanded by subordinates. It may be a necessary means to the organization's goal. The right to supervise closely gets further legitimation from the technical ability to do so.[26]

BUREAUPATHOLOGY AND ORGANIZATION STRUCTURE

Institutions are staffed by persons, and so personality is always an element in institutional behavior. It will account for differences of degree and minor variations in form. For the major outlines of institutional behavior, however, we must seek the causes in the institutions themselves. Bureaupathic behavior is caused by the structures and conditions within our bureaucratic organizations. To say this is not to deny the reinforcing impact of personality. Some people are undoubtedly more inclined than others to be aloof, to get enmeshed in details, to be officious, to be excessively cautious, to be insensitive to others, to be insecure. What we do deny is that there is a bureaupathic personality type, or that observed cases of bureaupathic behavior will always, or even usually, be associated with one type of person.[27] Any person, regardless of personality type, may behave in some or all of the ways we have just described under the appropriate conditions, and these conditions occur very frequently in the modern bureaucratic organization.

It has been argued that a kind of rigidity grows out of prolonged role enactment, and that bureaucrats, over a period of time, become insensitive to the needs of clients.[28] We have shown that a certain impersonal treatment is inherent in bureaucratic structure. The charge of insensitivity may therefore be a bureaucratic reaction. One must not forget that clients are notoriously insensitive to the needs of bureaucrats. The question is, when does bureaucratic insensitivity become pathological? In many bureaucratic organizations, relations with clients are warm and cordial, as for example, between the postman and the householder.

Although prolonged role enactment undoubtedly has a profound effect on a person,[29] what is the "bureaucratic role"? People move around quite freely in bureaucracies. They perform various roles. We do not think it makes sense to speak of the "bureaucratic role." We have emphasized specialist roles and hierarchical roles. In the hierarchy, people go from position to position as they advance. Specialists often move from organization to organization. The truly prolonged role is the entrepreneurial professional role, such as the physician. It seems doubtful that physicians, as a group, are "insensitive to the needs of clients."

Although there is no "bureaucratic role," there is bureaucratic structure. It is obvious that some people are able to achieve personal goals within this structure more easily and comfortably than others. These people have been called bureaucratic types; but they are not necessarily bureaupathic. In fact, it may be that the person who moves most easily within the bureaucratic structure is the one who can hide his insecurity, his "inner rumblings," as Whyte puts it. His insecurity may express itself internally as ulcers but not externally as bureaupathic behavior.

Bureaupathic behavior is one result of the growing insecurity of authority in modern organizations. This insecurity exists because nonhierarchical authority is so frequently delegated without regard to the ability to exercise it, such is the practice of politics.[30] More important, however, is the fact that the culturally defined institution of hierarchy, with its rather extreme claim of rights, is increasingly uncomfortable with advancing specialization. Hierarchical rights change slowly; specialization, the result of technology, changes with increasing speed. The situation is unstable. The legitimacy of organizational authority is in danger. Bureaupathic behavior is one result of this situation.

BUREAUPATHOLOGY AND ROUTINIZATION

The bureaupathic response to insecurity is facilitated by the routinization of organizational problem solving. When the development of appropriate routines is the dominant imperative, when technical problems must be solved, the emphasis must be on abilities rather than rights.[31] Charismatic patterns predominate. These facts are illustrated by wartime experience.

When World War II broke out, a large regulatory structure had to be quickly created. People with many types of skill, from many walks of life, and with many different statuses were quickly assembled in Washington. A whole host of brand new problems was given to them. In those early days, emphasis was on technical problem solving. Anyone who could come up with an idea on how to proceed "got ahead." Bureaupathic patterns were almost nonexistent. The emphasis was on what one could do, not on rights and prerogatives. People became quite scrambled up, with permanently low-status people temporarily elevated to high-status positions. Very young people found themselves in high positions.

Gradually technical problems were mastered and reduced to procedures and programs. Bureaupathic patterns became more pronounced. There were constant re-organizations, a growing volume of reports, increasing insistence upon clearance protocol, authority impressed for its own sake, not as a problem-solving device. Hierarchical dominance was pressed through a great variety of rituals — "control" boards, frequent staff meetings, calls to the "front office," progress reports, increasing insistence upon formal channels, etc.[32] These manifestations of authority were ritualistic because they were not related to winning the war, but to the "need for control." The organization product was not affected by them, because it was secured through an elaborate routine, of which no one comprehended more than a small part. Bureaupathic behavior occupied much more of the time of officials. They became kings' messengers after the kings were gone.[33]

NOTES AND REFERENCES

1. The obligation to accept another's decision may have a number of negative aspects, or *costs*. First is the dislike of subordination itself. Furthermore, the decision may not accord with one's moral beliefs, or it may conflict with one's self-interest. It may not appeal to one's reason and is likely in any case to require some change in habits. Therefore, the possible costs involved in being a subordinate or a regulated client are subordination costs, moral costs, self-interest costs, rationality costs, and inertial costs. See Herbert A. Simon, Donald W. Smithburg, and Victor A. Thompson: *Public Administration* (New York: Alfred A. Knopf; 1959), ch. xxi.

2. Writers on bureaucracy like Merton, Selznick, Gouldner and others use essentially the same concept of "bureaucratic," although, except by Gouldner, the distinction between the descriptive and critical sense of the term is never made clear. In general, they start with a need of some authority figure for control, followed by behavior which creates conditions exaggerating the need for control, etc., in a vicious circle. On this point see James G. March and Herbert A. Simon: *Organizations* (New York: John Wiley & Sons, Inc.; 1958) 36–46; and Chris Argyris: "The Individual and Organization: Some Problems of Mutual Adjustment." *Admin. Sci. Q.*, Vol. II (1957), 1–22, and "Understanding Human Behavior in Organizations: One Viewpoint," in Mason Haire, ed.: *Modern Organization Theory* (New York: John Wiley & Sons, Inc.; 1959).

3. Although the conceptual basis for the need to control is more thoroughly worked out in Russia, it has been observed that the attempt by Russian top management to concentrate power and control in its own hands results from insecurity generated by pressure from above. See Reinhard Bendix: *Work and Authority in Industry* (New York: John Wiley & Sons, Inc.; 1956), ch. vi.

4. For a theory of individual accommodation to the organization based on hierarchically generated anxiety, see Robert V. Presthus: "Toward a Theory of Organizational Behavior." *Admin. Sci. Q.*, Vol. III, No. I (June 1958), 48 ff.

See also Peter Blau: *The Dynamics of Bureaucracy* (Chicago: University of Chicago Press; 1955), 173.

5. This resistance was apparently the basis of the managerial opposition to Taylorism and Scientific Management generally. See Bendix: *op. cit., 274–81.*

6. See Erich Fromm: *Escape From Freedom* (New York: Holt, Rinehart and Winston, Inc.; 1941), 185. See also Clara Thompson: *Psychoanalysis: Evolution and Development* (New York: Thomas Nelson & Sons; 1950), 208. See also Fromm: *Man for Himself: An Inquiry into the Psychology of Ethics* (New York: Holt, Rinehart and Winston, Inc.; 1947), 72. Of 75 middle-management people questioned by Harold Leavitt, most thought that conformance to the wishes of the boss was the principal criterion for evaluating subordinates. Harold J. Leavitt: *Managerial Psychology* (Chicago: University of Chicago Press; 1958), 288.

7. See Rollo May: *The Meaning of Anxiety* (New York: The Ronald Press Company; 1950), p. 172.

8. For a discussion of this process in industrial management, see Bendix: *op. cit.,* pp. 226 ff. His discussion is based on a work by Ernest Dale: *Planning and Developing the Company Organization Structure* (New York: American Management Association, Inc.; 1952), Research Report No. 20. Advancing specialization in the problem-solving aspect of organizations is further reflected in these figures from Bendix: *op. cit., 211 ff.* Between 1899 and 1947 the proportion of administrative to production workers in American industry increased from 7.7 percent to 21.6 percent. From 1910 to 1940 the work force in America increased by 49 percent. Entrepreneurs increased by 17 percent; manual workers, by 49 percent; and salaried employees, by 127 percent. Bendix sees bureaucratization in industry as the continuing subdivision of the functions of the early owner-manager.

9. Of course, the extent of the dilemma varies with position in the hierarchy and with the extent to which complex specialties are required by the particular organization. The ongoing process of specialization will move the dilemma down the hierarchy and to more and more organizations.

10. Middle-management executives interviewed by William H. Whyte referred to their lives as "treadmills" or "rat races," thereby expressing the tensions generated by this dilemma. *The Organization Man* (Garden City, New York: Doubleday & Company, Inc., 1953), 176.

11. William Caudill has shown that tensions starting at the very top of a mental hospital were easily communicated all the way down to the patients, creating symptoms in them that were generated entirely within the hospital. *The Psychiatric Hospital as a Small Society* (Cambridge: Harvard University Press, 1958).

12. March and Simon (op. cit.) criticize some of the sociological treatments of bureaupathic behavior because they feel that these theories do not explain why functional learning on the part of authority figures does not take place. It will be recalled that these theories posit a need for control, followed by behaviors which create conditions which exaggerate the need for control. If this behavior is conceived as organization problem solving, there is indeed a problem of functional learning involved. However, bureaupathic behavior is functional in personal rather than organizational terms. It must be admitted that most of these sociological treatments do not clearly distinguish between personal and organizational goals—between bureaupathic and bureaucratic behavior. The "dysfunctional learning" involved is failure to learn that employees cannot very effectively be treated according to the machine model. However, this learning

can be considered dysfunctional only by applying the machine model to management. If management operated like a rational machine, it would learn that employees are not machines. The basic methodological flaw of the "management" approach is that it assumes that persons described by the term "management" behave according to sociopsychological laws different from those governing the behavior of others—that the manager is an independent variable in the organization.

13. The following discussion of succession is taken from his *Patterns of Industrial Bureaucracy* (Glencoe, Illinois: The Free Press; 1954), Part Two.

14. Ibid., 174–6.

15. See Blau: *op. cit.*, 192.

16. Walter Rice Sharp: *The French Civil Service: Bureaucracy in Transition* (New York: The Macmillan Co.; 1931), 446–50.

17. See Arnold W. Green and Eleanor Melnick: "What Has Happened to the Feminist Movement." Alvin W. Gouldner, ed.: *Studies in Leadership: Leadership and Democratic Action* (New York: Harper & Brothers; 1950), 277–302.

18. See Blau: *op. cit.*, 175–6.

19. Gouldner: *Patterns of Industrial Bureaucracy*, ch. ix. On the relationship between ritualistic compliance with regulations and personal insecurity, see Rose Laub Coser: "Authority and Decision Making in a Hospital: A Comparative Analysis." *Am. Sociol. Rev.* (February 1958). See also Reinhard Bendix: *Higher Civil Servants in American Society* (Boulder, Colorado: University of Colorado Press; 1949), 14–19, 112–22.

20. There is another source of extreme, detailed controls in modern organizations, one which can be dealt with rationally. Units are frequently established whose goals are defined *entirely* in terms of writing instructions. Since they have nothing assigned to them except to write instructions, in time they can be expected to "cover" everything—even as a monkey, if given enough time on the typewriter, would eventually type out the complete works of Shakespeare. Involved in this situation is goal factoring, not bureaupathic behavior.

21. Blau: *op. cit.*, 96.

22. Ibid., 91–5. See also Erving Goffman: *The Presentation of Self in Everyday Life* (Garden City, New York: Doubleday & Company, Inc.; 1959), 177.

23. In a state employment office and a federal enforcement agency, Blau found little evidence of resistance to change. The cases he did find were based upon the fear of a superior and fear of the loss of security in relations with subordinates or clients. (Op. cit., 184–9.) He found that new employees and less competent employees were more resistive to change than others. (Ibid., 197.) He found also that ritualistic compliance with rules and regulations stemmed from personal insecurity in important relationships at work. (Ibid., 188.) Secure officials welcomed change because it made their work interesting by providing new challenges.

24. See Victor A. Thompson: *The Regulatory Process in OPA Rationing* (New York: King's Crown Press; 1950), 298–303.

25. In addition to other references cited throughout this chapter, see Walter L. Dorn: "The Prussian Bureaucracy in the 18th Century." *Polit. Sci. Rev.*, Vol. XLVI (September 1931). See also Alexander Barmine: *One Who Survived* (New York: G. P. Putnam's Sons; 1945); and "The Stewardship of Sewell Avery." *Fortune*, Vol. XXXIII (May 1946).

26. See D. Katy, N. Maccoby, G. Gurin, and L. G. Floor: *Productivity, Supervision and Morale among Railroad Workers* (Ann Arbor: Survey Research Center, University of Michigan; 1951). See also A. W. Halpin: "The Leadership Behavior and Combat Performance of Airplane Commanders." *J. Abnorm. and Soc. Psychol.*, Vol. XLIX (1954), 19–22.

27. For example, attempts have been made to show that "compulsive neurotics" predominate in bureaucracy. See Otto Sperling: "Psychoanalytic Aspects of Bureaucracy." *Psychoan. Q.*, Vol. XIX (1950), 88–100.

28. Theodore R. Sarbin: "Role Theory," in Gardner Lindzey, ed.: *Handbook of Social Psychology* (Reading, Massachusetts: Addison-Wesley Publishing Company, Inc.; 1954), Vol. I, 223–58. Sarbin points out that this proposition is only an hypothesis, and one would have to find these qualities of rigidity and impersonality in nonoccupational behavior as well in order to demonstrate it. We might point out that one would also have to show that these qualities were not present at the beginning of the period of "prolonged role enactment." Sarbin relies somewhat on Robert K. Merton's well-known essay, "Bureaucratic Structure and Personality," in *Social Theory and Social Structure*, rev. ed. (Glencoe, Illinois: The Free Press; 1957). However, Merton does not seem to be talking about the interaction of self and role. Generally, he is explaining "bureaucratic" behavior by reference to bureaucratic structure (graded careers, seniority, *esprit de corps*, the appropriateness of secondary, i.e., impersonal, relations, etc.). He also suggests that the ideal patterns of bureaucratic behavior become exaggerated by being affectively backed, as we have argued. However, he does not explain the origin of this affect ("sentiments") to our satisfaction. We have argued that it comes from personal insecurity in an authority position. Merton does not distinguish between the descriptive and critical uses of the term "bureaucratic."

29. See Willard Waller: *The Sociology of Teaching* (New York: John Wiley & Sons, Inc.; 1932).

30. In organizational terms, politics means those activities concerned with the delegation of authority on bases other than a generally recognized ability to exercise it. It involves some kind of exchange between the person desiring the authority and the authority figure who has it to give. It is made possible by the fact that authority may be delegated. Since the specialist content of executive positions is increasingly attentuated as one mounts the hierarchy, so that ability criteria become less and less relevant, placement in these positions becomes more and more a political phenomenon, a matter of "office politics"; the incumbents are "political types." See Harold Lasswell: *Politics: Who Gets What, When, How* (New York: McGraw-Hill Book Co.; 1936).

31. Studies of decision-making groups in business and government show that the groups prefer strict and formal performances by the conference leader when the subject matter is trivial but not when the subject is important. L. Berkowitz: "Sharing Leadership in Small, Decision-Making Groups." *J. Abnorm. and Soc. Psychol.*, Vol. XLVIII (1953), 231–8.

32. See Victor A. Thompson: op. cit., Part Two.

33. The technical problem military organizations must solve is winning a war. In peacetime, with no technical problem to solve, bureaupathic patterns are more pronounced. Arthur K. Davis says they live and survive in peacetime on ritual. "Bureaucratic Patterns in the Navy Officer Corps." *Social Forces*, Vol. XXVII (1948), 143–53. He hypothesizes that "the effectiveness of military leaders tends to vary inversely with their exposure to a conventionally routinized military career." This study is reproduced in Merton, *et al.*, eds.: *Reader in Bureaucracy* (Glencoe, Illinois: The Free Press; 1952), 380 ff.

Management of Innovation

Tom Burns, G. M. Stalker

THE PRELIMINARY STUDY

At this time, the rayon mill [described later] was growing and commercially prosperous. But two sets of circumstances which the study revealed did not seem easy to square with first-hand knowledge of other firms and with the conceptions of management available in the literature. Partly because of the lead given from the head office in London, the functions of each manager and worker were clearly specified; they were expected to follow, and did follow, the instructions which issued in a steady flow from the general manager and down through the hierarchy. Yet the system, lubricated by a certain paternalism, worked smoothly and economically, and there was no evidence that any individual felt aggrieved or belittled.

The other feature of interest lay in the comparative impotence of the Research and Development Laboratory. It was formally responsible for solving problems and curing faults in the process other than those which could be tended by people on the spot, for improving the existing process and products, and for introducing new products or methods. But its activities were regarded with much suspicion and some hostility by many production managers and supervisors; its studies were repetitive and often inconclusive; it was very largely occupied with finding answers to enquiries from the London office which arrived almost daily, and large arrears of which, at that time, had accumulated.

Very soon an opportunity presented itself of carrying out a similar study of the organization of an engineering concern with very large development interests. The wholly different conditions in which management acted, and the different codes of conduct and beliefs which individual managers brought to their jobs, were abundantly clear at the very beginning. As in the first concern, the study began with a series of interviews with managers and foremen, the principal purpose of which was to obtain descriptions of the jobs performed by individuals and the way in which they fitted in with others. After the first few such interviews a pattern appeared in them which was entirely unanticipated. The usual procedure was that after listening to the researchers, explaining his presence in the factory and his present purpose the informant would say, 'Well, to make all this clear, I'd better start from the beginning.' He would then proceed to give an account of his career in the firm, and of the activities and duties characteristic of the positions he had filled. This account was commonly lucid, well-organized, and informative, but would stop short at a point some months earlier. The question about his present functions, and whom they affected would then be framed again, rather more pointedly. There would be a pause. He would then explain, equally lucidly, what he would be doing when the present emergency had passed or the current reorganization or new development had matured, and his part of the concern could settle down to work as it was now planned.

Later, it became evident that ranks in the hierarchy of management as well as functions were ill-defined, and that this was so because of the deliberate policy of the head of the concern. At this time, the most obvious consequence of this state of affairs was

From *The Management of Innovation*, by Tom Burns and G. M. Stalker, published by Tavistock Publications, Ltd., 1961. Reprinted by permission of Associated Book Publishers Ltd.

a pervasive sense of insecurity which was openly discussed by some managers and was also evident in individual conduct and in the formation of cliques and cabals.[1] Yet there was also the striking fact of the concern's commercial and technical success. Was there a causal connexion between the insecurity and stress displayed by individuals and the concern's effectiveness? An American study,[2] published about this time, suggested that there might be. Yet many of the actions arising from anxiety about career prospects and status were so clearly dissociated from the concern's tasks, even running counter to their accomplishment, and so much energy was consumed in internal politics, that it still seemed more plausible to regard insecurity, and the conduct to which it gave rise, as defects of the management system rather than its mainspring. Possibly, though, these defects were an inevitable concomitant of industrial change in the present state of our knowledge of organization.

This, at all events, was the view of the head of the concern. An organization chart was inapplicable, he believed, to the structure of management in the concern — it was 'probably a dangerous way of thinking about the way any industrial concern worked.' The first requirement of the management system was that it should make the fullest use of the capacities of its members; any man's job, therefore, should be as little defined as possible, so as to allow it to expand or contract in accordance with his special abilities. Any anxieties and frictions that might be generated were an inevitable circumstance of life as it is, and one could not 'manage them out of the organization' — not, at least, without neglecting or damaging some more vital interest.

Further study suggested, however, that 'initiative' no less than 'insecurity' and 'stress' might be dependent on the way in which management organized itself to carry out its task. The adaptation of *relationships* between individuals, rather than of individuals themselves, towards the requirements of the technical and commercial tasks of the firm became the focal point of the broader study which was then initiated, with the financial backing of the Department of Scientific and Industrial Research and in partnership with G. M. Stalker.

THE SCOTTISH STUDY

The Scottish Council (Development and Industry) is a voluntary body supported financially by industrial firms, local government bodies, and trade unions, and works in close touch with the Scottish Home Department and the Board of Trade. It has actively encouraged the growth in Scotland of industries using newer techniques. The declared purpose of the electronics scheme is to enable firms to acquire new technical resources and exploit them in commercial fields reasonably familiar to them. It is to this end that the firms are helped to build up laboratory teams on the basis of suitable contracts provided by defence ministries.

For our part, we hoped to be able to observe how management systems changed in accordance with changes in the technical and commercial tasks of the firm, especially the substantial changes in the rate of technical advance which new interests in electronics development and application would mean.

The major consideration for most firms entering the scheme was fear of shrinking markets or of keener competition in a static market; only one or two seemed prompted by an expansionist urge and the attraction of enterprise in new fields. A second distinction revealed itself between firms which negotiated a development contract before engaging a laboratory team, and those which began by investing in people who might be expected to produce ideas for development. Following roughly the same lines of division, a third distinction was visible between firms which confined the activities of their laboratory teams to work on defence contracts or on improving products developed elsewhere (to the extent of refusing to invest their own capital in development), and those prepared to exploit the team as a technical resource.

No firm attempted to match its technical growth with a comparable expansion of sales activities; in particular, no attempts were made at organized and thorough exploration of user needs for products which firms thought it possible to develop, or even for those which they had developed.

Most of the Scottish firms failed to realize their expectations. In half the cases, laboratory groups were disbanded or disrupted by the resignation of their leaders. Others were converted into test departments, 'trouble-shooting' teams, or production departments. Common to all predicaments was, first, the determined effort from the outset to keep the laboratory group as separate as possible from the rest of the organization; second, the appearance of conflicts for power, and over the privileged status of laboratory engineers; and third, the conversion of management problems into terms of personalities—to treat difficulties as really caused by the ignorance, stupidity or obstructiveness of the other side. These failures were interpreted by us as an inability to adapt the management system to the form appropriate to conditions of more rapid technical and commercial change.

There seemed to be two divergent systems of management practice. Neither was fully and consistently applied in any firm, although there was a clear division between those managements which adhered generally to the one, and those which followed the other. Neither system was openly and consciously employed as an instrument of policy, although many beliefs and empirical methods associated with one or the other were expressed. One system, to which we gave the name 'mechanistic,' appeared to be appropriate to an enterprise operating under relatively stable conditions. The other, 'organic,' appeared to be required for conditions of change. In terms of 'ideal types' their principal characteristics are briefly these:

In mechanistic systems the problems and tasks facing the concern as a whole are broken down into specialisms. Each individual pursues his task as something distinct from the real tasks of the concern as a whole, as if it were the subject of a sub-contract. 'Somebody at the top' is responsible for seeing to its relevance. The technical methods, duties, and powers attached to each functional role are precisely defined. Interaction within management tends to be vertical, i.e., between superior and subordinate. Operations and working behaviour are governed by instructions and decisions issued by superiors. This command hierarchy is maintained by the implicit assumption that all knowledge about the situation of the firm and its tasks is, or should be, available only to the head of the firm. Management, often visualized as the complex hierarchy familiar in organization charts, operates a simple control system, with information flowing up through a succession of filters, and decisions and instructions flowing downwards through a succession of amplifiers.

Organic systems are adapted to unstable conditions, when problems and requirements for action arise which cannot be broken down and distributed among specialist roles within a clearly defined hierarchy. Individuals have to perform their special tasks in the light of their knowledge of the tasks of the firm as a whole. Jobs lose much of their formal definition in terms of methods, duties, and powers, which have to be redefined continually by interaction with others participating in a task. Interaction runs laterally as much as vertically. Communication between people of different ranks tends to resemble lateral consultation rather than vertical command. Omniscience can no longer be imputed to the head of the concern.

The central problem of the Scottish study appeared to be why the working organization of a concern did not change its system from 'mechanistic' to 'organic' as its circumstances changed with entry into new commercial and technical fields. The answer which suggested itself was that every single person in a firm not only is (a) a member of a working organization, but also (b) a member of a group with sectional interests in conflict with those of other groups, and (c) one individual among many to whom the rank they occupy and the prestige attaching to them are matters of deep concern. Looked at in another way, any firm contains not only a working organization but a political system and a status structure. In the case of the firms we studied, the existing political system and status structure were threatened by the advent of a new laboratory group. Especially, the technical information available to the newcomers, which was a valuable business resource, was used or regarded as an instrument for political control; and laboratory engineers claimed, or were regarded as claiming, élite status within the organization.

Neither political or status preoccupations operated overtly, or even consciously; they gave rise to intricate manoeuvres and counter-moves, all of them expressed through decisions, or discussions about decisions, concerning the internal structure and the policies of the firm. Since political and status conflicts only came into the open in terms of the working organization, that organization became adjusted to serving the ends of the political and status system of the concern rather than its own.

The individual manager became absorbed in conflicts over power and status because they presented him with interests and problems more immediately important to him and more easily comprehended than those raised by the new organizational milieu and its unlimited liabilities. For increases in the rate of technical and commercial change meant more problems, more unfamiliar information, a wider range of work relationships, and heavier mental and emotional commitments. Many found it impossible to accept such conditions for their occupational lives. To keep their commitments limited meant either gaining more control over their personal situation or claiming exemption because of special conditions attached to their status. These purposes involved manoeuvres which persistently ran counter to the development of an organic system, and raised issues which could only be resolved by a reversion to a mechanistic system.

The Scottish study developed eventually into two complementary accounts of the ways in which the adaptation of management systems to conditions of change was impeded or thwarted. In one set of terms, the failure to adapt was attributed to the strength of former political and status structures. In other terms, the failure was seen as the consequence of an implicit resistance among individual members of concerns to the growth of commitments in their occupational existence at the expense of the rest of their lives.

THE ENGLISH STUDY

During the winter of 1955–6, the authors read papers dealing with some of the general findings of the Scottish study at a number of meetings. One of these was attended by senior officials of the Ministry of Supply. In later conversations with Burns, they suggested that major firms in the electronics industry in England might like to have an opportunity of hearing about the Scottish study and of discussing its implications for their own concerns. This suggestion led to a meeting in November 1957 at the Ministry of Supply, which was attended by managing directors and other senior members of eleven English firms, and by government officials.

While this discussion made it clear that the problems discussed in the summary report of the Scottish study were not unfamiliar, the ways in which the problems revealed themselves in different firms, and the responses and actions which they had evoked, were varied and idiosyncratic. Burns was therefore invited to make a brief study of each firm. Each of these studies concentrated on two topics: the management difficulties which seemed peculiar to firms engaged in rapid technical progress, and the particular problem of getting laboratory groups on the one hand (research—development—design) to work effectively with production and sales groups on the other.

The survey of English firms was completed in the first half of 1958 and the findings reported to the eight firms which had participated, out of eleven invited to do so. A general report was also distributed, and discussed at a one-day conference of the heads of firms and of government officials held at the Department of Scientific and Industrial Research in July 1958.

The eight English firms which eventually took part in the survey were not only much larger but much more committed to electronics development and manufacture than were the firms of the Scottish study, which were in the earliest stages of their careers in electronics. The situations available for study were more complicated; they were also more intimately related to the commercial and industrial destinies of the firms and to the lives of the people in them.

There was, for example, much more variety in the kind of group within the firm affected by an acceleration in the rate of technical change, and in the responses to change made by different firms. In firms which operated consciously on organic lines, changes from any direction were regarded as what they manifestly were—circumstances which affected every part of the firm and everybody's job, in some way. Organizational changes, additional tasks, and growth in any particular direction tended to be seen as the concerted response of the firm to a new situation; although debate and conflict were present, they were manifestly present and could be treated as part of the new situation to be reckoned with. In firms which operated according to mechanistic principles, the response to change was usually to create a new group, or to reconstitute the existing structure, or to expand an existing group which would be largely responsible for meeting the new situation, and so 'not disrupt the existing organization.'

This latter response, which in the Scottish firms characteristically led to the segregation of the new development team from the rest of management, was now visible in the way some firms dealt with big changes in market conditions. A Head Office sales department, or a new sales forecasting and market study group, might be created. Management might be reconstructed on product division lines, so as to extend the control of sales over the activities of the firm. Engineers might be recruited from development laboratories, or directorships offered to men of outstanding reputation from other firms. More significantly still, a new technical departure might be made the province of a newly created laboratory group independent of the laboratory concerned with the obsolescent techniques. In such cases, the confinement to a prescribed section of its organization of the total response of the firm to change meant that for the rest of the firm the challenge of the new situation became instead a threat offered by the 'new men' to the power, standing and career prospects they had hitherto enjoyed. This was especially the case with development engineers. Previously the element in every firm which had been identified with expansion and innovating change, they now saw their leading role passing—in part—to sales. The development-production conflicts typical of the Scottish study were overshadowed in the English firms by sales-development conflicts, by the resistance of the professional innovators to an innovating change.

Political conflict appeared to be clearly related to the particularism which was fostered by the separating out of the tasks of the firm according to specialist functions. Given a mechanistic system, changes of all kinds, including expansion, continually threw up new institutions within the firm which were intended to carry the whole of a new defined task and which themselves engendered political problems.

The conceptions of mechanistic and organic management have also proved useful in analysing the arrangements made inside firms for passing work through from the earliest stages of development to final manufacture. The tendency to regard the whole process as an articulated series of separate specialist functions made for the creation of 'hand over' frontiers between departments and for language barriers; it also went with a predilection for tethering functionaries to their posts. The need for communications beyond the formal transmission of instructions and drawings led to the appointment of liaison specialists—interpreters whose job was to move across the linguistic and functional frontiers and to act as intermediaries between the people 'getting on with the job.' Organic systems recognized the supreme importance of common languages and of each functionary's being able to seek out and interpret for himself the information he needed. The fewer distinguishable stages, the fewer interpreters and intermediaries, the more effectively were designs passed through the system.

Many of the insights generated by the English study were suggested in the first place by the distinctive response made by different concerns to a major change in market conditions as against techniques, as was the case with the firms in the Scottish study. The decline in government work and the increased emphasis on selling in the so-called 'commercial market' affected all concerns in the same way, although to a different extent. The first observable distinction was between the firms which saw that a sales function had been discharged by the laboratory engineer working on government development contracts, and that a similar role was equally necessary with commercial users, and those which overlooked this sales function in connexion with defence ministries and regarded market exploration and development as the province of salesmen. There were a number of aspects of this difference. Some concerns had always been wary of committing themselves too heavily to government work; others had allowed themselves to become educated into commercial unfitness by too complete a dependence on defence contracts. In general, it could be said that the first kind of firm tended to regard the market as a source of design ideas which the firm then attempted to realize, the second kind as a sink into which should be poured applications of techniques developed within the firm. Successful manufacturers of domestic radio and television receivers offered the most striking demonstration of the first principle. So much so, that in these firms not only the management system but the way in which individuals' jobs were defined, and the code of conduct prevailing in the concern, seemed to be generated by constant preoccupation with the market on the part of every member of management.

The differences between the two kinds of management system seemed to resolve themselves into differences in the kind of relationships which prevail between members of the organization, whether of the same or of different rank, and thus into the kinds of behaviour which members of an organization treat as appropriate in their dealings with each other. It was possible to distinguish various modes of behaviour used by individuals according to a single dimension of conduct: the bounds set to what—in the way either of requests, instructions, or of considerations and information—the individual would regard as feasible, acceptable, worth taking into account, and so forth. The observable way in which people in a concern dealt with each other—the code of conduct—could therefore be regarded as the most important element in a concern's organization, given the structure of the management hierarchy and the skills and other resources at its disposal. It expresses the framework of beliefs which decision-making invokes. In a realistic, operational sense, it *is* the organization.

In so far as differences in the obligations and rights attaching to different status within the concern are disputed, and in so far as the allocation of control over resources becomes a matter of political conflict, the style of conduct employed by the contending parties shows differences. That is to say, each side has differing beliefs about what considerations should enter into decisions, and about what are the feasible limits of the demands for action which may be made of themselves and which they may make on others. Conflicts thus wear the aspect of ideological disputes, whether these are conducted in overt terms or are implicit. The head of the concern enters at this point as a key figure who, in manifest or latent ways, denotes the code of conduct which should obtain.

TECHNICAL PROGRESS AND THE OCCUPATIONAL SELF

Organic systems are those which are best adapted to conditions of change. By common consent, such conditions are at present affecting a widening sector of industrial and occupational life. The code of conduct characteristic of organic systems – those better fitted to survive and grow in changing conditions – comprehends more eventualities than that necessary in concerns under stable conditions. More information and considerations enter into decisions, the limits of feasible action are set more widely.

The extension of the boundaries of feasible action and pertinent consideration makes for a fuller implication of the individual in his occupational role. As the pace of change, especially technical change, accelerates, and as the organic systems better equipped to survive under these conditions also expand, the occupational activities of the individual assume greater and greater importance within his life. This is in keeping with the commonly observed tendency for occupational status to assume an increasingly dominant influence over the location of individuals in British society. But it also denotes a greater subjection of the intellectual, emotional, and moral content of the individual's life to the ends presented by the working organizations of the society in which he exists.

Developing a system of organized industrial activity capable of surviving under the competitive pressures of technical progress, therefore, is paid for by the increased constraint on the individual's existence. In Freudian terms, men's conduct becomes increasingly 'alienated,' 'work for a system they do not control, which operates as an independent power to which individuals must submit.'[3] Such submission is all the more absolute when it is made voluntarily, even enthusiastically.

In the next chapter of this book it is suggested that a social technology, as exhibited in the institutional forms of modern society, has been developed *pari passu* with modern technology in the material sense. Modern organizational forms, governmental and industrial, represent the application of rational thought to social institutions in the same way that technology is the product of the rational manipulation of nature. In the same way, too, it congeals the processes of human affairs – 'fixing' them so that they become susceptible to control by large-scale organizations. The reverse aspect of this tendency is the increasing subjection of the individual to the psychological and material domination of the social order, a domination increasingly objective and universal as civilization advances technically.

REFERENCES

1. Burns, Tom. "The Reference of Conduct in Small Groups; Cliques and Cabals in Occupational Milieux." *Human Relations,* 8 (1955), 467–86.
2. Argyris, C. *Executive Leadership.* New York: Harper, 1953.
3. Marcuse, H. *Eros and Civilization.* London: Routledge, 1956.

Questions for Discussion

1. In studying English literature, one finds that some scholars refer to the eighteenth century as "The Age of Reason" (people were governed by reason and rationality) and to the nineteenth century as "The Age of Romanticism" (people were governed by emotions). Assume that the world really is as Chapter 6 posited: that people in organizations will be satisfied if the network of jobs fits the goal. Would you say these people are reasonable, emotional, or both?

2. How does the following argument (posed in Chapter 1) relate to the argument in Chapter 6 (which holds that people will be satisfied if working in an organization where technology, authority, and leadership fit the organization's goal)?

"Behavior on the job is a function of what the person brings to the situation and what the situation brings to the person. When people come to work in organizations they do not come 'empty handed,' as it were. They bring a supply of energy or potential to perform. They bring various needs or motives which predispose them to release their energy or behave in particular ways—ways which seem to them likely to satisfy their needs."

(Hint: you may also want to read the paragraph in the beginning of Chapter 1 which follows the one quoted above.)

3. Is it possible that a worker may have a *task* (one individual at a workplace) which is negatively motivating, and at the same time be involved in a *technology* (many individuals in an interrelated network of tasks) which is positively motivating? Relate this answer to a term used in the military—*esprit de corps*. Is it possible for a nurse in a hospital or the manager of a branch bank to have this *esprit de corps*?

4. In fundamental terms, why does "the establishment" or "the system" exist? Do people want it to exist? (Hint: first clearly state what you mean by "establishment" or "system.")

5. According to the argument in Chapter 6, people join an organization and work in it for a variety of reasons. From the reasoning in Chapter 6, what is the *principal* reason why a person might find the system or the establishment unacceptable?

6. Why might people resent the rules, job descriptions, and procedures in an organization structure, in terms of:

    a) what they bring to the situation (see also Chapter 1)?

    b) what the situation brings to them in the way of "bad" technology (see Chapter 6 and your answer to Question 5)?

    c) what the boss brings to the situation that might create bad technology (see the Thompson reading)?

Cases for Discussion

Autotronic Corporation of America

I am president of Autotronic Corporation of America, which produces a range of equipment for sports-car owners. Our largest selling item is a tachometer which measures the revolutions per minute (rpm) of the engine. We have found that the best way to get these to the consumer is by having salesmen call on two types of customers: large, chain discount stores; and repair garages run by independent owners (not repair departments of automobile agencies). Most of the latter use tachometers made by Datsun, Mazda, Porsche, or other makes if the agency sells these cars.

We're having continuous trouble getting the plant personnel and the sales personnel to work together. Here is a typical instance which I call "provincialism." The sales manager and his salesmen go out and meet these garage owners. They know them personally, and go to a great deal of effort to give them what they want. They spend great amounts of time discussing sports cars, races, gadgets, and the like with managers and purchasing agents or discount chains. Because the salesman is a sports-car enthusiast and the customers are usually the same, they get along well.

Not long ago one of the discount-chain purchasing managers phoned the sales manager. He said they had, through error, computed their inventories of our TX-4 instrument and were out of stock with the summer season coming on. He wanted 650 instruments within a week. He told our sales manager it was really important to him.

Our sales manager went out to the factory personally. He got the production manager and said, "Mike, I've come this time with a must. We've got to have 650 TX-4's in 3 days."

The production manager told him he'd like to comply but that he only had 200 in stock. "Furthermore," he said, "we're working on a large run of model TX-13 for Sears. I could probably squeeze in a run of 400 TX-4's, but that would mean shutting down the production line, and taking a day to reset all of the tooling and machinery. We have scheduled production of the TX-4 about four weeks from now, when our machines will be set for another model close to that specification. The cost of setup time won't be great then. It will be now with that extra day. As you know, the financial V.P. holds us accountable for costs. If the plant cost for each instrument goes up, it reflects on us."

In a long conversation, each man simply tried to convince the other. They kept repeating their own arguments. In the end, the production manager just said he wouldn't do it.

The sales manager later told me he wouldn't go to see the financial V.P. because every time he's been there in the past the man stressed cost cutting. He said he'd rather try to appease the customer than try to convince the financial V.P.

I've told them they're acting like prima donnas and that they've got to learn how to solve these kinds of questions for themselves.

Questions

1. What is going on in this situation and why is it going on?

2. Is the situation good or bad for the company, or for the individuals involved?

Roosevelt Hospital

Roosevelt Hospital is a large, privately endowed hospital in Louisville, Kentucky. The hospital cares for patients who pay for services as well as patients who do not have funds. The latter were referred to as "charity" patients; now, hospital personnel usually refer to them as "limited resource" patients. Money for such patients is provided by the city of Louisville, by the state and federal governments, and by endowment funds. Recently, the city of Louisville requested all hospitals receiving such funds to provide statistics on cost per patient per day for such items as room and board, pharmaceuticals, and doctors' fees. Because the hospital director knows that the city will channel funds to hospitals that do not show excessive costs, he has instituted certain control reports, such as a report on the total cost of drugs for one patient that exceeds $1000.

Two months ago, Dr. Gillam, a staff physician, decided to try experimentally a drug for a limited resource patient who had chronic arthritis. The drug, Milozene, was reported in medical journals as "a tentative help for severe arthritic conditions. It has passed all federal tests for safety, but we have not established that it actually results in patient improvement. That will not be known until clinical experiments have occurred over two to three more years."

The cost of Milozene is $150 per ounce. Gillam estimated that 30 ounces of the drug would be needed for extended treatment. When the $4500 requisition reached Dr. Jackson, the hospital pharmacologist who acts as purchasing agent, the latter called Dr. Gillam to inquire why it was being purchased. Dr. Gillam explained and the pharmacologist ordered and paid for the requisitioned amount.

Dr. Prichard, the hospital director, asked Dr. Gillam, Mr. Travis, the financial director, and Dr. Jackson to come to his office for a general discussion of hospital costs, and said he had noticed a large number of high-cost requisitions made by Dr. Gillam.

Dr. Prichard: "Jane, of course I'm not questioning your judgment on treating patients. I just thought we'd understand better our cost situation if we took the Milozene requisition as a case in point. As you know, we're under public pressure to lower costs, and under city pressure in terms of further support."

Dr. Gillam: "Well, I did have the patient's interest in mind. I've used most of what is known in the way of medications. The patient responded somewhat. I know Milozene is an 'iffy' proposition, and that it may or may not help. In addition, I knew for sure I could include this in medical research. It is valuable research either way — if Milozene is found not to be an effective drug, that's as important to know as that it is effective. What I'm saying is that there's a payoff for our $4500, regardless of what the results are for the patient. We won't know for another year."

Dr. Prichard: "But don't you remember the decision of our board two years ago about the place of research in the hospital? It was agreed that we are primarily a health-care hospital, and not a research hospital. We leave that to the universities and the university hospitals. I'm surprised that you didn't consider that, and that Dr. Jackson didn't raise it at the time he saw the requisition."

Dr. Gillam: "In view of the possible benefit to the patient, I view it as health care."

Dr. Jackson: "Well, Jane gave me those reasons at the time we talked. I ordered the Milozene not on my own judgment, but hers. It really isn't my job to treat patients. I'm here to check the specifications of items wanted by the staff and to make sure we get those exact specifications from manufacturers."

Mr. Travis: "As members of the Board of Trustees, Dr. Prichard and I have been troubled deeply about such costs. Both city and federal agencies have strongly intimated that charity and poverty funds may be channeled to Louisville General Hospital rather than to us, unless we can show we produce maximum care for the community for dollars invested. As of now, our costs exceed General by $13 per day per patient. We're $4 higher in doctor fees, $2 higher in rooms and meals, and $7 higher in drugs. I frankly believe Dr. Gillam made this decision on the basis of research, and that it was the wrong decision."

Dr. Gillam: "I said I had the patient's health in mind. If Dr. Prichard will give us some policy to follow, I'm more than glad to go along with it. I simply don't want to worry about decisions like this."

Dr. Prichard: "Of course we don't want to intrude on the prerogatives of the individual doctor."

Mr. Travis: "But don't you think we might work out some guidelines, or some procedures whereby the doctor gets a ruling on such matters from someone higher up? Or maybe we could simply have someone check with the doctors to help them clarify their own courses of action."

Dr. Prichard: "I don't see how we could ever operate other than on the individual doctor's judgment. Maybe everyone should just bear in mind that we want good patient care and wise use of our precious dollars."

Dr. Jackson: "Well, I'd be glad to follow any procedure you may work out."

Dr. Prichard: "I thank you all for coming in. And I'm sure it was worth our time. Let's just think about what's been said, and from time to time talk among ourselves when these things come up."

The meeting broke up with usual good-natured comments about one another's family, the current political situation, and like matters. Each then returned to work. Later, Dr. Gillam commented: "Prichard is a gentleman and we all like him. Actually, he does conduct the most ineffective meetings in his office. If I'd thought about it carefully, I wouldn't have ordered the Milozene. But I simply cannot be a good doctor and researcher and be an economist-financier, too. I'm not interested in those things, know nothing about them, and cannot in the future worry during the day about such decisions. I'm bothered about the state of affairs in Louisville. I blame Roosevelt's rather bad reputation in part on Prichard. Some of us are also troubled because all of the best young doctors seem to be going to Louisville General. One of them told me he looks at Roosevelt as a good hospital, but one that is a little tired and messy to work in."

Questions

1. How is the environment of Roosevelt Hospital affecting its goals?

2. How are the various technical specialties influenced by these goals?

3. How are the motivations of people affected by the technology (goals plus tasks)?

4. What causes the problems the staff has in coordinating with one another?

5. Does the hospital seem overstructured or understructured?

Work Design

In Chapter 6, we saw that managers must visualize a firm as a total entity, as one complete system operating within a larger environment. The task of managers from this viewpoint is to shape the organization structure to forces operating outside the firm. We have called this task *organization design.* Some writers call it the "macro-design approach," because it deals with design of large systems of work (e.g., the firm) operating in still larger systems (society). Such a way of thinking is part of the manager's set of useful intellectual tools for managing an effective enterprise.

But there is another viewpoint which has received much attention in recent years, both in the world of social science and the world of practical affairs. This approach is called *work design.* Whereas organization design operates from the vantage point of the highest levels in an organization, looking downward, work design requires a viewpoint at the bottom of the organization, looking upward. This has been called the "micro-design approach" because the analyst deals with smaller systems of work (one individual job, or a group task) operating within a larger system (the firm).

The purposes of this chapter are (1) to provide an understanding of why work design at this level is important in modern society; (2) to describe in some detail three different techniques for work design: job enlargement, job enrichment, and the creation of autonomous work groups; (3) to analyze the differing human motivations connected with each of these techniques; and finally, (4) to point out certain difficulties a manager must consider if he or she attempts to apply work design in a specific situation.

THE IMPORTANCE OF WORK DESIGN IN MODERN ORGANIZATIONS

In the past few years work design has received much attention by psychologists, the managements of certain corporations, and even the governments of many industrially developed countries. What has caused this concern? What are corporations doing in the way of work design? Why is so much attention being given by governments to foster new practices in work design?

Effects of Programmed Jobs on Human Beings

A wealth of research and common sense supports the fact that large organizations in today's industrial world do indeed involve people in specialized tasks and that, if the world wants advanced technology, one of the prices it pays is less satisfaction for people at work, especially at lower levels of the organization. The work of Douglas McGregor (1960) points to the futility of the "carrot and stick" form of compensation, under which salary and pay are used, in effect, to say "here is a specialized and meaningless job for which we will offer you money rewards. If you will spend eight hours a day doing something that does not offer intrinsic satisfaction, you may earn pensions for your old age and money to spend on holidays and weekends." Argyris (1957) argued that people in such jobs have a way of reacting to such frustrations. They may become aggressive toward the organization, or simply apathetic and disinterested. This sets in motion a chain reaction – an escalation of conflict between workers and managers. The managers look at such workers and think "people just don't seem to want to work. What is needed are more job studies, higher pay, and more rules." According to Argyris, this not only misses the cause of the problem, but actually compounds it. It offers more rules and technical planning handed down from above. Sooner or later, as workers and managers make successive counter-moves, nobody really wins. The organization becomes a conflict arena in which labor battles management, or it becomes an apathetic place where people care little for satisfying work or for accomplishment of organization goals.

In addition to the fact that traditional production-line work sometimes seems futile in stimulating productivity, and the fact that it breeds conflict between managers and workers, there is evidence that such work patterns affect the physical health of human beings. Work satisfaction has been found to influence how long a person lives and whether one is prone to heart disease and peptic ulcers (*Work in America*, 1972, pp. 66–67). In terms of mental health, a study of workers on assembly lines (Kornhauser, 1964) showed that about 40 percent had some symptoms of mental health problems, the single most important cause being low job satisfaction. Two characteristics of such jobs stood out in this study as important contributors to dissatisfaction: dull, repetitive work, with little variety; and work which is *programmed* in detail by someone else. The latter is reflected in the *feeling* by the person that he or she has little control or influence over his or her work life. We shall see that these two characteristics, which in turn breed a third feeling in the worker – that "I am not responsible for what goes on" – are the three central characteristics which current work design experiments hope to attack. Such experiments are intended to increase the variety of tasks performed by a human being; to provide a means for more self-control by individuals and groups; and, by doing these things, to create a situation in which workers can feel more involved and responsible for events in the workplace.

Effects of Programmed Jobs on Productivity

A second reason why social scientists and practicing managers have devoted attention to work design is that traditional assembly-line organization, with its paced, repetitive jobs, can cause lower productivity for the organization. Since organizations produce the nation's goods and services, this could well mean a lower standard of living for all people.

For a number of years, some psychologists, influenced by early research of the Survey Research Center at the University of Michigan, believed that satisfied workers produced more output, or output with less cost in hours of labor. A more valid view is today expressed by a leading psychologist (Lawler, 1974): "If this were true (i.e., that satisfaction causes employees to produce more), there would be no problem finding new work designs that would increase job satisfaction without harming organizational effectiveness. Unfortunately, my own research and that of many other psychologists shows that satisfaction does not cause employees to work harder. In fact, it has a very low relationship to performance and is probably best thought of as a consequence of performance (rather than a cause). Despite this, there is evidence that increasing the job satisfaction of employees can increase the effectiveness of organizations. Why is this so? Satisfied employees are absent less, late less, and less likely to quit. Absenteeism, turnover, and tardiness are very expensive—more costly than most realize. Thus . . . organization changes that increase job satisfaction can increase the economic effectiveness of organizations even though they do not increase motivation" (p. 21).

Some indication of the costs referred to here can be seen in the problem faced by the Scania Division of Saab, the Swedish automobile company which has engaged in extensive work redesign. Employee turnover in the Division was about 45 percent each year, meaning that one of every two workers quit during the year. In the auto assembly plant of Scania, the turnover rate was about 70 percent each year. Time lost from absences was about 20 percent of all work hours in the plant during the year (*Organizational Dynamics*, 1973, p. 55).

Effects of Changing Cultural Attitudes Toward Work

At the same time that technology of production is becoming more and more specialized and repetitive, thus rendering jobs *less* demanding in education and skills, young people entering the workforce have *more* education and a greater variety of skills. The Saab automobile company's demand for talent (based on production-line technology) was one thing but the supply of workers was another. A survey taken in 1969 showed that only 4 percent of the students graduating from high school in Sweden indicated willingness to take a rank-and-file factory job. The Saab/Scania Division became heavily dependent on imported foreign workers, with 58 percent of the factory workers coming from less affluent nations (*Organizational Dynamics*, 1973, p. 55).

This same phenomenon has been noted in Norway, Switzerland, and the United States. The message for management here is, "To protect your supply of workers, something must be changed."

Automation and Work Design

A final reason for increased attention to work design is a curious one, and may sound contradictory at first. It is that the automated assembly line itself may well force managers to design jobs with more "autonomy" or participation in them (Taylor, 1971). The reasoning is as follows. Automated production processes, such as large continuous-flow oil refineries and chemical plants, literally operate by themselves, *as long as everything proceeds according to the program designed into the system, and the machines, by engineering experts.* The "worker" does not work on the product in the sense that, say, a cabinetmaker works on wood. Rather, the worker stands near the machinery, recording information, and perhaps even reading books or engaging in other hobbies until something goes wrong with the process. At this point, the worker gets a signal. He or she must *then* take some initiative. However, the worker must consider not only the machine at the workplace, but also what is happening in other parts of the process which are related to the particular machine. This requires *feedback*, or information about what is going on in the system. It also requires some creativity and thought. It may well require the operator to deal with another person who is supplying his or her machine with input materials (since this must be adjusted by another operator) or with still another person whose machine is getting its input charge from our worker's machine. This is "vertical integration," to use an economist's term. It means that the operator's job must deliberately be designed to provide information about what is going on "out there," what place his or her job occupies in the total system, and to allow the independent thought (autonomy) necessary to correct unusual events when something goes wrong with the programmed and supposedly repetitive process. We shall see that feedback, autonomy, and self-control are three hallmarks of job enrichment and autonomous work group designs.

Major Organizations Involved in Work Design

Given the kind of pressures discussed above, a number of leading private corporations in the United States and abroad have over the past 20 years engaged in one kind of work redesign or another. A selected sample of these projects was reported in a study requested by the U.S. Secretary of Health, Education, and Welfare. Compiled by a special research task force, the resulting study (*Work in America*, 1972) has caused a great deal of interest in both government and business circles. The appendix to this study, describing 34 work design projects in the United States, Norway, Yugoslavia, England, and Holland, follows this chapter. In addition, even more detailed descriptions of the projects at American Telephone and Telegraph Corporation (Ford, 1973) and the Scania Division of Saab Automobile Company in Sweden (*Organizational Dynamics*, 1973) also follow this chapter.

Another indication of the extent to which corporations use work design techniques can be found in a study by Alan Wilkinson (1970), an executive in Imperial Chemicals, Ltd., the large British subsidiary of duPont. He located 35 projects being carried out in 25 companies in Norway, Denmark, Sweden, the Netherlands, and the United Kingdom. Twenty of these had been in operation long enough for him to make some judgments about how they fared. We shall see presently that, as with many activities in life, some were successful, some were unsuccessful, and some were about neutral on the success scale.

The Kibbutz as an Example of Work Design

No summary of design projects would be complete without mention of the *kibbutz* organizations in Israel (Fine, 1973). Fostered by the Israeli Government, these are semiautonomous organizations in relation to society (their external environment). They have some characteristics of private corporations and other characteristics of miniature governments. For instance, they exist to produce goods and services. They are also similar to producers' cooperatives in the United States, where grain farmers, orange growers, and owners of apple orchards join together to finance and share common grain elevators, common storage warehouses, or common marketing and advertising facilities. "Today about 240 kibbutzim with approximately 90,000 members in units averaging 250–300 persons are scattered over Israel. They produce about 33 percent of the agricultural and 8 percent of the industrial products of the country" (Fine, 1973, p. 241).

The aim of the kibbutz is to *integrate* into one unit the ecological resources (land, ecology), the production system (work and workflow, and sales to outsiders) and the internal social unit (human beings with needs for meaning in their work, and involvement with ecology and production). Weekly meetings of the "general assembly" are held in which at least in principle there is no time limit or agenda limit imposed on anyone, and in which most decisions are made without formal votes. In case of real disagreements, votes are taken about how to execute decisions about goals of the organization. The assembly also acts in a legislative function, making policy decisions and setting goals regarding all aspects of kibbutz life; discusses and sets budgetary resource allocations; and sets precedents. In a judicial sense, it interprets previous decisions when important disagreements arise over their meaning.

A similarity to U.S. corporations is that the general assembly elects each year a secretariat of eight to ten members, each the head of one of the specialized committees that make staff-type studies and recommendations: the economic secretary, treasurer, works manager, social committee chairman, education committee chairman, and cultural committee chairman. The general secretary of the secretariat presides at meetings of this "executive committee," which coordinates the work of all committees and meets in advance of the general assembly to work out conflicts beforehand and to try to synthesize diverse interests. It can only recommend "matters of principle" (goals and major policies), but has the power of decision on matters relating to the administration of these policies (i.e., to make the more detailed decisions necessary to carry out goals and major policies). The secretariat also appoints and works with branch managers in each specialized segment of the society.

The one big difference between the kibbutz and a corporation is that the former strives for absolute economic equality and social equality of members. The kibbutz has responsibility for satisfying the needs of all members, and remuneration and rewards are based on each individual's needs (as assessed by the secretariat and its committees). There is no pay or privilege based on a person's relative contribution to the production of goods and services (Fine, 1973, p. 242).

Since World War II, there has been a trend for *kibbutzim* to establish manufacturing plants and to diversify into both agricultural goods and manufactured goods. Factories average today about 40 workers; nine employ between 100 and 500 workers. Though productivity in the *kibbutzim* seems to compare favorably with productivity in the same type of factory organized in a different way (for example, owned by the General Federation of Labor), there are signs that this form of organization has some difficulty in organizing to achieve efficient production in large, specialized, and capital-intensive industries. As the kibbutz has grown, or federated with others to achieve economies of scale, a more elaborate and formal representative system (rather than the face-to-face committees of the assembly and secretariat) has evolved. The reading "Worker Participation in Israel" explores in more detail the traditional kibbutz organization.

The Interest of Government in Work Design

Interest of the United States government in work design has already been mentioned. Concerned about the quality of work life in organizations, and about the effect this can have in turn on cultural attitudes in general, the Secretary of Health, Education, and Welfare commissioned a task force which published *Work in America* (1972). The task force covered a number of problems in work life, such as education, training, and the rate of unemployment in the nation. But it stated that work design was *the* central problem of work in America. Shortly thereafter, the United States Senate considered S 3916, a bill designed "to provide research for solutions to the problem of alienation among American workers and technical assistance to companies, unions and state and local governments which seek to find ways to deal with this problem." Senators Kennedy, Javits, Nelson, and Stevenson sponsored the bill. Hearings were held before the Subcommittee on Employment, Manpower, and Poverty of the Senate Labor and Public Welfare Committee (United States Senate, 1972). These hearings revealed that a wide range of labor leaders, business leaders, and workers consider work design to be a matter of utmost importance in the national society.

As we examine various design experiments which have been carried out to date, we shall see that the governments of Norway, Sweden, and Israel have devoted considerable attention to this subject. Even more recently, the Federal Republic of Germany invited Lisl Klein, a researcher from Britain's Tavistock Institute, to "review the present situation in relation to the design of jobs and the organization of work." Klein's report (1976) summarizes developments in Norway, Sweden, the United Kingdom, Holland, and other countries.

THREE APPROACHES TO WORK DESIGN

From the experience of systems such as the *kibbutz*, which have evolved slowly since early in this century, and from research in the social sciences dating roughly from 1951, social scientists have been able to identify three broad approaches to job design, each of which has been advocated as an alternative to the production-line form of repetitive work which is programmed by staff experts, rather than by workers themselves. These are job enlargement, job enrichment, and creation of autonomous work groups. These have certain similarities, but differ in important respects. It is the purpose of the following sections to summarize what these approaches are, and to illustrate them with examples from real world organizations.

Job Enlargement

An earlier (and simpler) approach to job redesign was developed during the 1950s. As the term implies, it essentially consists of making a job "larger" by increasing the number of tasks to be performed. Another term for this is "horizontal job loading" (moving several interrelated tasks into one job) (Herzberg, 1968). We can understand this technique better by describing how a traditional assembly line might be converted to a line with enlarged jobs.

Briefly, the assembly line pattern of jobs is created by breaking down the total product (say, an automobile) into specialized "stations." Each station is composed of a particular kind of machinery and tools necessary to do the job, and a worker with specialist skills for doing the job. The worker's actions are planned for a minimum of time, effort, and fatigue.

Stations are connected to each other by a *workflow plan* (sometimes called a procedure, a program, a production schedule, or an input-output system). The whole network of stations and connections is designed by manufacturing process engineers, specialists themselves on the plant staff.

An example of this design can be seen in Exhibit 7.1. When the Saab Company in Sweden decided to build a new automobile engine plant in the early 1970s, headquarter's engineers considered the production line design as one alternative for the automobile engine assembly department. They knew that the input to the assembly department came from four separate assembly lines in four other departments: cylinder blocks, cylinder heads, connecting rods, and crankshafts. When the four parts arrived at the engine assembly department, the engineers estimated that the assembling of an engine could be broken into seven steps, each performed at a separate station. The engine could be placed on a conveyor belt which moves it from station to station. Once the line was in motion, the pace, or timing of the flow in the line—the speed of the conveyor belt—would determine the actions and behavior of all machines and workers on the line.

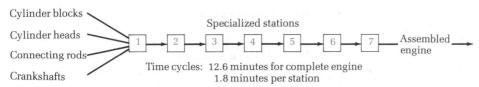

Exhibit 7.1   Design of Automobile Engine Assembly in
Saab/Scania: First Alternative

From *Saab Automobile Engine Department*, Charles E. Summer.
Copyright, 1978.

Precise planning by the engineers at Saab estimated that it would take the average engine 12.6 minutes to flow down the line and be ready for transporting out to the department which attaches the engine to the chassis. The average length of time an individual worker faced a particular engine (the *time cycle of work*) would thus be 1.8 minutes. (At General Motors' assembly plant in Lordstown, Ohio, the average time cycle has been *36 seconds*—a worker faced a new automobile part 800 times in each 8-hour shift) (*Organizational Dynamics*, 1973).

It is not hard to see why Scania Division was experiencing the difficulties mentioned earlier in the various manufacturing facilities operated by the Company. When management faced the problem of building a new engine plant for the Saab automobile, one alternative they came up with is a classic example of job enlargement. Instead of having seven specialists work on different stages of assembling an engine, why not let one person simply follow an engine (or move it on an individualized transport cart) to the various machines or to various locations where heavy tools were stored? Thus, one person might do all of the work on one engine (see Exhibit 7.2).

What about the time cycle of work? The average time a worker would spend on each engine was estimated at 30 minutes, up from 1.8 minutes in the production line.

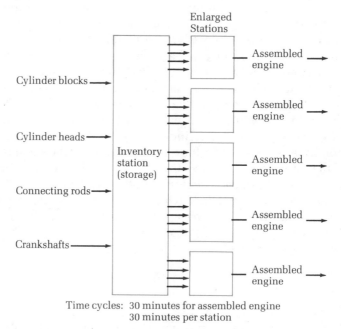

Time cycles: 30 minutes for assembled engine
30 minutes per station

Exhibit 7.2 Design of Automobile Engine Assembly in Saab/Scania: Second Alternative

From *Saab Automobile Engine Department*, Charles E. Summer. Copyright, 1978.

As you can see, job enlargement is a relatively simple process, which can be applied in a variety of situations. An automobile repair garage (or the service department of an automobile dealership) might be organized so that mechanics are specialized at different work stations: one for brakes, one for cylinder blocks, one for tires, and one for electrical problems. If the agency is large, one person may work 40 minutes per automobile in replacing brake liners, then turn to the next brake lining job. Another may spend 20 minutes per car replacing spark plugs, then turn to more spark plugs. Management can, if it wishes, horizontally enlarge the job by resplitting the pie. The same mechanic may perform a variety of functions. We shall see that this would also enable the individual to participate, via job enrichment, in the diagnosing of automobile problems in collaboration with the customer who owns the automobile.

Motivational effects of job enlargement. Four potential motivational effects of job enlargement stand out: a lack of *boredom* (because of an increase in the variety and novelty of work); a feeling that work is more *meaningful* (more valuable to the company, more important to society); a feeling of personal *competence* (because one is using more of one's abilities, because one is learning more); and a feeling of *responsibility* for the task (because one can see the whole task, or a greater part of it, rather than just a 36-second operation) (Donaldson, 1975).

One can easily see that a worker who assembles an entire engine, for example, might feel that his or her work is more interesting, that it is more valuable for the company and society, that he or she is a more skilled and competent person, and that he or she is personally responsible for whether or not the engine works.

However, an important caution should be raised here, one which is specifically related to job enlargement (limitations and contingencies of work redesign in general will be treated in a later section). The danger with job enlargement is that, as Herzberg (1968) puts it, it may simply enlarge the meaninglessness of a job. Is a worker more motivated if he or she solders wire in an engine in addition to tightening a bolt? Herzberg likens this to adding zero to zero.

As we shall see, this problem is not encountered with job enrichment or the creation of autonomous work groups.

Moving from Enlargement to Enrichment

One interesting work design which has received much attention is that tried by American Telephone and Telegraph Company. It is referred to by Ford (1973) in the reading following this chapter as "expanding the module of work." This article shows that work design can be applied to a white-collar clerical operation as well as to manufacturing processes.

In the next section, we shall see that job enrichment moves one step further than enlargement by including planning and control functions, as well as increased operating functions, in one job. At this point, we will describe how AT&T enlarged jobs in the module of work. Later, we shall see that job enlargement is curiously related to job enrichment. It would be impossible for AT&T to

Original Design: 14 Operating and 7 Control Stations

Yellow pages
copy from
customer

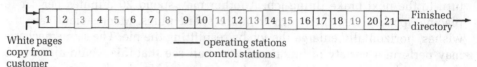

White pages
copy from
customer

———— operating stations
———— control stations

Second Design: Job Enrichment – 7 Combined Stations
and 7 Operating Stations

Yellow pages
copy from
customer

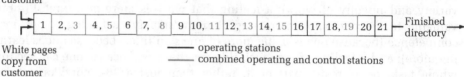

White pages
copy from
customer

———— operating stations
———— combined operating and control stations

Third Design: One Position Produces Complete "Thin" Directory

Yellow pages
copy from
customer

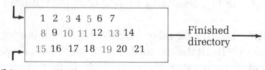

White pages
copy from
customer

Fourth Design: "Thick" Directory Split by Alphabet

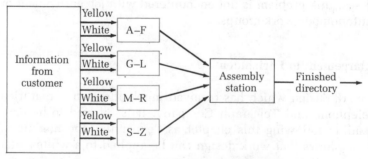

Exhibit 7.3   Job Design Alternatives for Publishing Telephone
Directories at Indiana Bell Telephone Co.

allow an employee to plan and control his or her own work without first including in the job a long enough time cycle that planning can take place.

The particular jobs to be enlarged consisted of those required to produce
telephone directories in the state of Indiana. Under traditional production-
line methods, the company had a standard procedure (workflow) which con-

nected 21 separate operations (see Exhibit 7.3). Stations included manuscript reception from the customer, manuscript verification for accuracy, keypunching a card made for that particular entry in the phone book, verification of accuracy of keypunch, ad copy reception (for yellow pages) from customer, verification of accuracy of advertisement, and so on.

Turnover rates were high. Twenty-eight people holding these clerical jobs left in one year prior to redesign of work. The Indiana Bell "supervisory family" (as Ford calls it) decided to try to make the work more appealing. They further decided to eliminate each of the verification steps, which had been instituted because the telephone company is so vulnerable to customer complaints, and even governmental retaliation, if customers' complaints about quality become significant. They experimented to see if each person might do error-free work, without anyone else acting in a quality control capacity. Elimination of verification steps brought down the number of operations required to produce a telephone directory from 21 to 14.

For smaller telephone directories, such as the one for Napanee, Indiana, management designed a process whereby each operator is responsible for the entire publication process (Exhibit 7.3).

Job Enrichment

In a sense, job enrichment is similar to job enlargement in that it involves "expanding the module of work" (Ford, 1973). However, there are two crucial differences. One involves the kind of tasks that are included in the enriched job; the other follows from the first, and involves differences in the motivational effects resulting from enriched jobs.

Job enrichment involves including a *planning* task, a *control* task, or both, in a job which previously only involved operating tasks. It is, therefore, "vertical job loading" (Herzberg, 1968), in that the planning and control of work (which was done by someone "higher up" on the organizational chart) is now done by the operators themselves. In this approach to work design, mechanics in automobile service departments—in addition to being assigned a larger module of work—would be assigned the job of talking with customers when they come into the shop, which had been done by the manager of the service department. The mechanic would ascertain, with the customer, what is wrong with the car and what repairs are needed. To go one step further, mechanics might plan their own work for the entire day, rather than being assigned certain tasks by the manager.

Herzberg (1968) reports on one enrichment program in the department responsible for handling correspondence with stockholders of a large corporation. When stockholders write to the corporation, for any reason, covering a great variety of subjects and questions, this department has responsibility for doing research to get the right answer. Under the old system, the total work was split between correspondents and a supervisor. The correspondents answered routine problems, such as information on company products and finances, by doing research in catalogs, annual reports, and the like. However, if any request appeared which was out of the ordinary, they turned this over to the supervisor (for example, the president's travel plans or speech-making schedule). Planning and control standards were also built into the job of the supervisor, who kept records of how many letters were coming in, decided how many should be completed in a certain time period, and conveyed this to the correspondents. The supervisor also designed standard form letters, which could be sent to stockholders who were asking standard (repetitive) questions. Because stockholder relations can be a rather delicate subject for corporations, all finished letters were passed over the supervisor's desk. The supervisor was thought to be more experienced in the nuances of good stockholder relations.

After the job enrichment design was instituted, all of this changed. For one thing, correspondents were told to consult, on their own initiative, various people throughout the company who were expert resource people on a given unusual request. For example, one might decide to consult someone in the controller's department, or the plant safety section, or the president's secretary (for information on the travel plans or speaking schedule). Only in the case of new correspondents, who had not gained enough experience and learning, were letters passed over the supervisor's desk for quality checking. The supervisor stopped setting standards. Correspondents were assigned responsibility for *quality* — the duty of composing whatever personalized answers they thought necessary, without using the standard form letters previously designated by higher authority. The *number* of letters to be typed was left up to correspondents. The supervisor only made general statements about the workload, rather than mentioning the actual quantity of letters in the waiting pool or the number which should be answered in a certain time period.

Job enrichment differs from job enlargement on another characteristic. The *information feedback flows* received from those who give inputs into the job, or transmitted to those who depend on the output of the job, are changed. Notice that flow of information from all parts of the company into the correspondent section formerly went through a supervisor. He or she then made judgments and passed information on to the correspondents. By changing from form letters (which was a flow of information from the supervisor who designed the letter to the stockholder) to personalized letters (which was a flow of information from the correspondent as an individual directly to the stockholder) another information flow was changed. In terms of motivation of individual human beings, we shall see that such a change in feedback loops has a subtle, but powerful, effect.

Another example will help clarify the change in information flows, or, as some systems analysts say, in "feedback loops." In the fertilizer plant of Monsanto Chemical Company, management faced the problem of a bottleneck in the position of bagger, where fertilizer is placed in bags at the end of the production process. The problem became acute enough that management asked all baggers to attend a seminar which would diagnose why the slowup occurred. The employees themselves were asked to make changes in the way their jobs were performed (note the planning function), and what the production goal for each bagging operation should be (note the transfer of standard-setting from higher management to operators) (*Work in America*, 1972, Appendix 1).

The information feedback loops before the change meant that managers set production goals, operators executed the bagging, and managers monitored the actual output produced and fed-back the information to an individual operator as to "how you are doing." After restructuring, the feedback loop was within one human brain. The operators had helped set output standards in the first place, now they also monitored their performance output. They in essence "talked to themselves," saying, "I am over standard," or "I am under standard."

In the example of the auto mechanic in the agency service shop, the enriched job now includes a flow of information directly from the customer to the mechanic and from the mechanic to the customer, rather than from all motorists to the shop supervisor, who then passed information on to the mechanic.

This aspect of job enrichment is stressed by Ford (1973) in the attached reading. In defining modules of work in the American Telephone and Telegraph Company, the designers try not only to build into the job a meaningful task module, but they also attempt to attach each job, and therefore each job holder, to either a customer outside the business or to another department or section within the company which depends on the work of the particular employee (see Exhibit 7.2). In this way, employees are assured of enough information, directly from the people who find their work useful, to plan or control their own work themselves.

Motivational effects of job enrichment.   Another difference in job enlargement and job enrichment is that they produce different motivational effects. Most experts on work motivation agree that the effects of the latter are more powerful than job enlargement, and include an additional and crucial motivation.

The four motivational effects mentioned in connection with job enlargement—lack of boredom, more meaningful work, feelings of competence, and responsibility for the task—operate more powerfully with job enrichment. The stockholder correspondents feel that, because planning and control activities in addition to operating activities are part of their jobs, the work is more useful and important to the company and to society. For the same reason, they have taken on activities that require more creativity and skills, thus promoting even more strongly the feeling of competence. Since they are in direct contact with the outside world which uses their work, the feeling of responsibility to the customer and to the client is more powerful than if other people in the company are the ones who deal with customers and clients.

The additional, and crucial, motivation under enrichment design is called by most psychologists "autonomy" or "self-control." By engaging in the planning and control of work, as contrasted with only doing the work, there is a considerably greater feeling that one is in control of one's own destiny, rather than under the control of another person who designed the production line, or the form letters which must be typed, or the standards which must be met. This is not possible without arrangement of direct communication feedback loops. It is impossible to make decisions which *control* one's activities unless one has the information needed to make wise decisions. Nor can there be *learning* and *development.* The stockholder correspondent, whose brain was never connected to all of the research resource departments in other parts of the company, never learned enough to answer difficult problems wisely. It was the supervisor whose brain *was* connected to information of this kind, who had information stored in the form of experience, and who could as a result exercise judgment and wisdom. The correspondent had been, in effect, an "underdeveloped person," dependent upon the supervisor, rather than a developed and competent person, independently going about the task. There is a famous Biblical passage which states, "You shall know the truth and the truth shall make you free." Freedom in this sense is based on knowledge gained from direct feedback flows.

Autonomous Work Group Designs

For many authorities on work design, the most important development of all has been the design of autonomous work groups, as contrasted with the design of one individual job for one individual human being. Scholars know this best as the design of "socio-technical systems," a term used by the Tavistock Institute of Human Relations in London. Starting with their studies of coal mining in England (Trist and Bamforth, 1951), the approach of this Institute has gradually spread. In India, Calico Mills, a private corporation producing textiles, hired Tavistock to try to improve production in the weaving department (Rice, 1958). Later the Norwegian government, the Norwegian Confederation of Employers, and the Trade Union Congress of Norway jointly formed a relation with Tavistock, resulting in a large number of experiments under the epithet "Industrial Democracy" (Karlsen, 1972). The work of this Institute has also profoundly influenced the many experiments which have been made in Sweden, where a survey by the Swedish Employers Confederation shows some five hundred firms doing something with attributes of the autonomous group approach (Klein, 1976).

Since the socio-technical or autonomous group approach to work design is more complex than either job enlargement or job enrichment, it is best to start with some examples of what actually happens in this kind of design of work. Later, we shall examine the unique characteristics or "theory" of what autonomous group design is, and how managers and consultants go about executing this design.

In the original study of coal mining in England, Trist and Bamforth (1951) found that the cycle necessary to mine coal was 24 hours long. It was performed in three shifts in the modern, mechanized line. Forty to fifty men had been split into approximately as many specialized tasks in order to do three things, each of which had to be performed in sequence. First there was preparation of the wall (work face) in the mine by blasting, cleaning, and splitting of rock. Second there was the mining of the coal, including loading it on cars, and moving it. Third, someone had to advance the roof supports, and move haulage tracks and conveyor equipment. The forty or so specialists (for example, one was a carpenter who built roof supports, another was a carpenter who dismantled roof supports) had to work in sequence throughout the twenty-four hour cycle, since nobody's work could be done until someone else had done his or her work correctly. Scheduling of work was, of course, a nightmare for managers. They had to be sure that the proper number and classification of workers was present at the precise time during the cycle that he or she was needed. Production engineers call this "balancing the line."

The mine operated in three eight-hour shifts. Each shift had its own piece-rate pay system. Management had invested in large machines which could help produce much more coal than miners with pick axes could ever produce. They had also invested in complex conveyor machinery which was much more efficient than having each miner, or a specialist transporter, carry out the coal.

The new machinery had been introduced with the expectation that productivity would be increased. But to everyone's astonishment, the production of this mine was actually less than some mines in Durham that were using old-fashioned methods!

The consultants from Tavistock were hired to find out what the trouble was. They studied the more "backward" mines in Durham. Here is what they found.

In the modern mine, when workers were split up into extreme specialties and operated on three shifts, individual workers could not "see" the whole cycle. They could only see the relatively minor part of the whole that they themselves performed. "Seeing," in this case, is a means of information gathering or feedback. Without this, one could not possibly detect the results of one's own action on others who were *dependent* on the task being performed. It would be impossible for a person to exercise any self-control without such information. Further, as each specialty got smaller, workers lost some of their interest in, or feeling of responsibility for, the whole task of mining coal. Worse still, each shift literally never saw the next shift working. And each shift was paid on the basis of how much work *it* did, not on the basis of how much coal was mined. Consequently, lacking interest in the total cycle and having interest in one's own rate of output, it would be very easy to quickly build a support roof—which might not make it easy for the miner in the next shift to get at the coal. Or, it would be easy to get paid for quickly preparing a mine face—leaving the miner on the next shift with some extra mess to clean up before he or she could do that work.

The consultants then looked at the "old-fashioned" mines in Durham. There, the workers, along with the pit manager, had rather naturally and off-handedly worked out a system for dividing work within and across shifts. They had not used the rationality and specialization of the modern coal mining engineers. Rather, they had used a combination of production rationality *plus* social rationality. This combined thinking had produced a certain work design. What happened was that all 40 miners who worked a particular coal face (workers from all three shifts) had themselves worked out a system of job rotation, both within each shift and between shifts. Each individual not only could perform a variety of jobs, but moving from job to job also provided both an expanded time cycle (job enlargement) and information and knowledge of the performance of the whole cycle (job enrichment). This latter, so necessary in self-control and autonomy, is indispensible for the development of an interest in and a feeling of responsibility for the completion of a whole task.

Returning now to Scania's automobile engine plant, notice the following things which management engineered into this design. First, they gave the groups of five to twelve workers the choice of two degrees of job enlargement. A group may choose whether some employees follow the engine around the bay and assemble an entire engine, with a 30-minute/work-time cycle. This has already been described (see Exhibit 7.1). Or, employees may decide to assemble one-third of a whole engine, which has a time cycle of 10 minutes (*Organizational Dynamics*, 1973, p. 56). This is shown in Exhibit 7.4. Volvo,

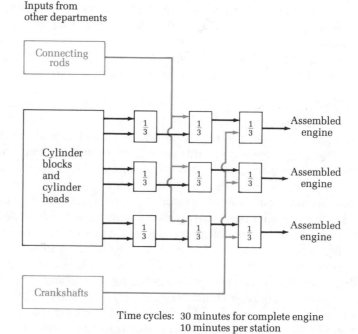

Time cycles: 30 minutes for complete engine
10 minutes per station

Exhibit 7.4   Design of Automobile Engine Assembly in Saab/Scania: Third Alternative

From *Saab Automobile Engine Department*, Charles E. Summer. Copyright, 1978.

a competitor of Saab, has accomplished the same thing in its production of automobile bodies. There the term "multiple balances" is used to describe this increase in time cycle. In the department where the body travels down an overhead conveyor, the group of workers follows the same body for seven or eight stations down the line for a total period of twenty minutes. This is seven or eight times the length of the average job cycle used under the older, specialized/automatic-paced line (*Organizational Dynamics*, 1973, p. 58).

The second aspect of Saab/Scania's work redesign system involves delegating to the teams the authority to decide their own work *pace* and the number and duration of work breaks, *provided that* 470 engines are produced in each ten-day period. Apparently this objective was set "loose enough" to allow for a good deal of flexibility and choice on the part of groups.

Saab/Scania has also developed autonomous work groups in the production of truck chassis. One can see in the attached reading that these groups of people with related jobs decide among themselves how they will do their jobs, within production standards and quality standards developed by higher management. They have enlarged jobs, in the sense of including the simpler maintenance jobs on machinery (not on the chassis); and enriched jobs in the sense of performing quality control in their own area, rather than having it performed by a separate quality control department in the plant. Both of these characteristics of an enriched job — the inclusion of allied service-type functions and control-type functions along with the operating function — are hallmarks of the most successful applications of job enrichment and autonomous group designs. As we saw in the research on coal mining in England, groups may also decide to rotate jobs if they wish.

Motivational effects of autonomous group designs. At this point, we can stand back from the individual case histories of autonomous group design, and pull together the central theory of motivation suggested by the above experiments.

The general argument of this section is as follows. Autonomous group design takes advantage of the "enlargement" effect found in job enlargement. It also produces the "enrichment" effect found in job enrichment. However, there is a subtle but important difference in the reactions of people operating under group design compared to individual job design. Part of this difference is caused by the fact that, in modern technology, an important *technical* limitation of job enrichment can be overcome by creating groups rather than dealing with individuals. The other part is caused by the fact that certain *social* limitations of job design can be overcome by using work group design.

Work group design makes use of those motivations associated with both the enlargement and the enrichment of any task. The effects of adding *variety* (the "enlargement effect") to the job by extending the time cycle in turn produces four somewhat different motivations for group members. There is a relief from boredom: the kind of boredom that results from repeating the same small task *ad infinitum*. This is not a positive reinforcement for the individual. It is only relief from a negative reinforcement. The positive reinforcement comes into play when the group senses meaningfulness, or involvement, in the task. By being able to see the larger and more holistic product actually produced, members are enabled to see that their efforts have more usefulness to society.

Variety also increases the group's feeling of competence. Instead of using a minute part of one's personal abilities, a larger number of abilities are called into play in the group. Finally, variety increases group feeling of responsibility for the task. All concerned can more likely "see" the contribution being made if there is a "whole task" to be performed rather than part of a task.

The effects of adding a control and planning function to the group assignment (the enrichment effect) supplies quite another motivation, the feeling of group freedom and autonomy. Receiving *direct feedback* from the relevant user of the group's efforts not only means that the group is more competent as a planning and controlling group but also that the group is more in control of its own destiny during the work day.

So far the motivational effects of autonomous work group design sound almost the same as those derived from individual job enrichment. This is true to a certain extent. There are, however, two distinctions to be made between human reactions to these two alternatives for work design. The first has to do with the fact that the *same* motivations can be achieved under group design to a greater *degree*. The second has to do with a deprivation of social needs (a negative reaction of human beings) which is sometimes produced by individual job enrichment but is not produced by a work group strategy. We shall consider each of these separately.

A stronger degree of meaningfulness, competence, and responsibility can be built into group designs than into individual designs for a simple reason: Modern technology is by nature a very complex thing. It takes $1\frac{1}{2}$ million parts to produce a Boeing 747. It takes 1200 parts to produce a Saab truck engine. Nobody is going to eliminate the many specializations required. The more complicated the technology, the more impossible it is to train one person to build the whole product. To suggest, for example, that one person be trained in all the knowledge and skills to produce a truck engine from raw aluminum and steel would be nonsense. A good production worker might find that he or she needs the help of an engineer to calculate compression ratios in the cylinders. On the other hand, a good engineer might need the help of a skilled machine operator to produce the cylinder so that it does not leak oil around the rings.

The point is that more significant *parts* or chunks of the task can be created by using a group of people than by using one individual. If the segment of work is not too large, all people in the group can become skilled in the delimited part of the whole. Or, a particular individual in the group may specialize in more complicated tasks. This is frequently done by including in the group a "resource" person, who can be called upon for expertise in a certain operation.

A second motivational difference between job enrichment and autonomous group design occurs because these two strategies produce different social need satisfactions for human beings. Researchers have noticed that in some experiments of *individual job enrichment*, the individual actually experiences a negative motivation. Recalling the need for face-to-face social contacts with fellow workers (Chapter 1), we can understand why. If the individual worker's task is made *too* independent, so that one performs a whole job at his or her workplace, not personally and directly dependent on others who supply the materials and not personally and directly in contact with those who use one's output, two things can happen. The social meaningfulness of the job (internalized knowledge that one's output is *useful* to someone else) disappears, even though the *personal* meaningfulness may still be present (i.e., the pride in doing a whole piece of work). This is precisely the reason why some people enjoy team sports like basketball and football, rather than an individual sport like pole vaulting. It is undoubtedly one of the reasons why psychologists have found that the mere *presence of others* can profoundly influence the productivity and behavior of an individual, as compared to the situation in which the individual performs exactly the same behavior *alone*

(Zajonc, 1966). Psychologists have called this "social facilitation." It is the difference in performance, and motivation to perform, that may occur when a concert pianist or professional golfer practices alone versus when the individual plays before a large audience. Another social psychologist discovered that frequent interaction by a human being with other human beings is more likely to promote favorable attitudes between workers than it is to promote negative attitudes, particularly if this interaction occurs in both directions — such as one person supplying a product to another, and the other person supplying feedback to the first (Homans, 1950).

This phenomenon is precisely what happened in one of the earlier experiments in autonomous group design (Rice, 1958). In the Calico textile weaving mills in India, the consultants had intended to design autonomous work groups for weaving textiles. They started with a paced production line along which workers tended looms, each performing a different specialty. The specialties were necessary because customer demands meant that the line had to be changed occasionally between three grades of cloth: medium weave, coarse weave, and fine weave. These shifts in turn meant that a complicated pattern of different work, and different timing, had to be performed on each grade. This was like shifting gears in an automobile, when a host of other events in the system must change actions. If one gear is shifted, the other gears move at differing speeds, the crankshaft moves differently, the oil pump vanes turn differently to supply oil, the wheels move faster, the fan belt turns the generator faster, and on and on. Such an interdependent system must work like clockwork. And clockwork requires trained engineers to plan the exact "balance" of the production line at each station, including the *flows between* stations.

To break up this specialized clockwork, the consultants had to incorporate the "enlargement effect." They did this by breaking the plant into smaller modules, each of which produced only one grade of cloth (fine weave, medium weave, coarse weave). This stopped the endless complexity of differing time cycles, and changeovers of individual jobs required by each grade. In the new one-product production line they combined a number of jobs or stations. Each weaver now had two looms to tend and was able to produce a whole product. But this went too far. The workers who worked in this fashion felt isolated and alienated from the social process in the plant. They were so independent that they felt alone! For this reason, a design was finally worked out which placed small *groups* of workers in charge of forty looms. They then performed *interdependent* tasks. They had the opportunity to participate with others in both weaving and socializing.

LIMITATIONS AND CONTINGENCIES IN WORK DESIGN

So far, this chapter has presented what seems to be a strong case for the redesign of jobs using techniques of job enlargement, job enrichment, and the creation of autonomous work groups. Work redesign is appealing in more than one respect. It seems to be a factual matter—to have an experimental and scientific basis. It seems to promote two important values in society: satisfaction of human beings and productivity of goods and services. The productivity matter, though not covered in detail in the chapter text, can be inferred from the appendix to *Work in America*, which follows this chapter. Experiments reported in that source invariably show improved satisfaction of workers, and in most instances show some kind of gain in productivity.

Yet work redesign must not be taken as a utopian technique to cure all of the ills of the modern industrial system. It is easy to be in favor of brotherly love and a high standard of living for everyone, without recognizing some of the tough conflicts managers must face when trying to institute new designs.

It is the purpose of this section to review three important limitations a manager will face when trying to engineer work design principles into practice. First there is the matter of individual differences. Some psychologists fall into the trap of treating everyone alike. It is likely that since each human being is a different personality, all people may not embrace management's (or social scientists') efforts with open arms. Second, there are some costs to work design which every organization must face, particularly the cost that has been described by engineers as the "learning curve." Finally, it is possible that managers or social scientists can become so enthusiastic about the work design concept that they overemphasize enrichment and participation to the exclusion of other factors at work in the job situation. Each of these will be discussed in more detail.

Individual Differences: The Achievement Motive

As in many instances when so called "pure" behavioral sciences are applied to the world of practical affairs, the application of work design inevitably runs squarely into the problem of individual differences. By "individual differences" psychologists mean a fairly simple phenomenon. There is no such thing as an "average" human being. People differ in many dimensions. The importance of work life means one thing to one person and another thing to another. Edward Lawler, a psychologist specializing in job enrichment, puts it this way:

> One of the most commonly suggested cures for worker alienation and job dissatisfaction is job enrichment. It has been suggested that if we enrich people's jobs, the result will be lower absenteeism, lower turnover, less tardiness, higher productivity, higher job satisfaction, and less alienation. We now have a considerable amount of research data on the effect of job enrichment. It does, indeed, show that the average person is both happier and more effective working on an enriched job than he or she is working on the traditional, standardized, specialized, repetitive, routine job. However, as I remarked before, not everyone is average.
>
> There are many people (at this point, we are not sure how many) who are happier working on repetitive, monotonous, boring jobs. In a recent study, for example, I found a number of telephone operators who did not react favorably to enriched

jobs. The older employees, in particular, tended to prefer the more repetitive jobs because they had adjusted to them and knew how to do them well. In addition, the new design threatened to disrupt some of the comfortable interpersonal relationships they had established. Thus, any job enrichment effort that enriches the jobs of everyone in a work area or of everyone doing a particular type of work is bound to make some people less happy and less productive. Admittedly, as a rule, performance and satisfaction go up, but can we afford to engage in work redesign practices that make the work experiences of some people more negative? I don't think we can, when there is an alternative available, and in this case there often is an alternative (1974, pp. 21–22).*

One of the first research studies which uncovered the problem of individual differences was performed by Turner and Lawrence (1965) of the Harvard Business School. During the course of trying to isolate detailed characteristics of a job which lead to worker satisfaction, they discovered that workers in factories located in small towns reacted differently to enlarged or enriched jobs than did workers in factories in larger cities. More specifically, the small town workers seemed to gain significant satisfaction from enlarged and enriched jobs. City workers, on the other hand, did not show feelings of satisfaction when placed in this type of job. It was left to another team of researchers, Hulin and Blood (1967, 1968), to explain what was happening in this situation. Whether or not an individual enjoys an enriched job depends partly on his or her *values, beliefs,* and *attitudes* toward work to begin with. That is, one comes to a job with certain norms formed by a host of experiences one has gone through *before* coming to work. According to this line of reasoning, merely what happens to a person in the short space of time he or she is involved on a particular job is not going to do very much to change these norms, especially compared to the years it takes to form them in the first place. Family, high school, college, friendship groups, other people who are viewed as models for behavior—all coincide to form one's attitudes toward work.

Though cultural norms of the whole society do go through swings from one generation to another, from the "work ethic" to the "leisure ethic" to the "alienation ethic," there is a wealth of evidence that at any one point in time people differ very significantly as to whether they value work, productivity from work, or work career development. We know from Chapter 1 that McClelland discovered a wide variety of levels of achievement motivation in individuals within the United States.

This difficulty in applying work design should be a signal to the manager. Considerable caution must be exercised in trying to install such systems across the board, for all individuals. Hulin and Blood (1968) have also discovered that for people who do not hold the work ethic as a central value, placing them in work designs discussed in this chapter not only may produce no effect. It may

---

* Reprinted by permission of the publisher from *Organizational Dynamics,* Summer, 1974, ©1974 by AMACOM, a division of American Management Associations.

even produce *negative* attitudes toward the enriched activities. These findings are supported by other researchers (Hackman and Lawler, 1971).

Short-Run vs. Long-Run Productivity

When the stockholder correspondents' jobs, described earlier in this chapter, were enlarged, Herzberg (1968) found that at first the quality and accuracy of letters written by the correspondents dropped noticeably. Further, the speed of response to inquiries from stockholders declined. It was only after two months that quality and output increased. This is a phenomenon which has been found in many experiments with work redesign.

For example, when the consultants worked diligently over a period of months with the first group in the Calico Mills weaving factory, productivity improved steadily. It was during this time that workers *learned* to operate under the new system. The consultants were teachers in a very real sense. The time the consultants and workers spent together represented what engineers have for a long time called the "learning curve." This phrase refers to a graph with productivity on the vertical axis and time on the horizontal axis. Assuming a person has never before done a particular job (say, carpentry), productivity would initially be very low. As skills increase, the productivity line begins to climb toward the right of the graph, signifying the "learning" of knowledge about, and skill in performance of, carpentry.

When the system of work groups was extended from the first weaving shed to *other* sheds, where people on the production line had already learned a set of skills for producing cloth by a different method, "[productivity] dropped steeply through a period of five weeks. At the same time the figures for damage [to the cloth being woven] rose steadily" (Rice, 1958, p. 7).

Time and again in the history of work design, the learning curve has been observed to take its toll of productivity. It has varied in severity of impact from case to case depending on the complexity of the skill to be learned. It is obvious that the length of time required to become a skilled cabinetmaker is longer than that required to build board fences.

Overemphasis on Job Structure and Participation

The original experiments in autonomous work group design were carried out by trained sociologists who also had an acute sense of the total work system, including insight about many variables which affect *both* human behavior *and* the economic performance of the enterprise. They gave equal amount of interest and attention to such matters as pay scales, rational allocation of authority from higher management, and equity of pay between the "chosen work groups" versus the "masses in the plant not touched by this new system." They even noted in India, for example, that the people working in the mill came from small villages, where they had learned to want close, family-type interactions. This, they explained, was one reason why the autonomous group system worked well in this particular situation.

It is perhaps worth noting that Rice, the researcher from Tavistock Institute who went to India to participate in that project, worked as a consultant to the Calico Mills and therefore felt a keen sense of responsibility for improving productivity as well as social relations. During the 1960s, however, when most efforts in work design shifted to Norway, it was planned at the very highest levels. The Confederation of Employers, the Trade Union Congress of Norway, and the Institute for Industrial Social Research all banded together in a grand scheme under the epithet "Industrial Democracy."

At this high level of planning two things took place which somewhat altered the course of subsequent investigations. First, social relations began to be emphasized to a greater extent than technical matters in the studies and in the reports issued on such studies. Other factors in the situation, such as selection of employees on the basis of skill required, or the need of employees for monetary rewards, began to receive less attention in the reports.

The *relationship* between the experts doing job design and the organizations using their services also changed. Many professional researchers from universities deliberately designated their function as "action researchers" as contrasted with "consultants." Whereas Rice in India felt that, "my primary professional responsibility was to give such assistance as I could to the solution of problems causing concern to the client," (1958, p. 7) the researchers in Norway assumed a different set of values and a different relationship with the public. Their general objective was to discover "under what conditions can more rights and responsibilities be achieved for the individual in the work place?" (Klein, 1976, p. 30). Rice (1958) meticulously reported the changes necessary in the pay system, productivity system, and authority system of the plant, giving as much space and weight to these factors as to the social system. He felt that the socio-technical system would not work in society unless all of these were balanced. But a significant portion of the reports which flowed from Norway, Sweden, and the United States (e.g., *Work in America*) seem to focus so heavily on the social system that the other matters originally thought equally important were given less weight, ignored, or not reported as thoroughly in final published reports.

Whether this is due to a conscious value choice on the part of researchers, or to their unintentionally ignoring certain other factors, is difficult to know in most instances. For example, the researchers compiling *Work in America* for the Department of Health, Education, and Welfare made a quite serious statistical error in reporting what scientific research has discovered about what workers in the United States really want out of their jobs. Original research on this question was done by the University of Michigan Survey Research Center. Questionnaires were filled out by a large sample of people in diverse careers, in which they were asked to rank 25 aspects of work in order of personal importance to them. Results were tabulated for each career category (for example, managers, skilled workers, professionals, factory workers). Lower-level factory workers listed more pay and job security higher than interesting work. The Michigan group reported these occupational data to the task force working on *Work in America*. However, when the report was written, *all* categories were lumped together into one category: "worker." This new listing "proved" that interesting work was listed first, pay was listed fifth, and job security seventh (Fine, 1974).

Many labor leaders in Europe and the United States have made this same point: That pay is very important to workers and that job enrichment projects are no substitute for this vital need in their lives. This position is also taken by certain research psychologists (Lawler, 1974) in the United States.

These problems need not mean that work design as presented in this chapter is useless, or that it is based on erroneous principles. What they do mean is that the wise manager will consider the applicability of job design principles to the specific situation in the particular company, government agency, or other organization. Whether or not the principles will work in a given organization is contingent upon a look at the real motivations of the specific people involved, on how the pay scales fit with jobs, and on what kinds of jobs are under consideration.

REFERENCES

Argyris, Chris. *Personality and Organization.* Harper & Row, 1957.

Blood, M. R., and C. L. Hulin. "Alienation, Environmental Characteristics and Worker Pressures." *Journal of Applied Psychology,* Vol. 51, 1967.

Donaldson, Lex. "Job Enrichment: A Multidimensional Approach." *Human Relations,* Vol. 28, No. 7, September 1975.

Fine, K. S. "Job Enrichment: A Reevaluation." *Sloan Management Review,* Vol. 15, No. 2, Winter 1974.

———. "Worker Participation in Israel." In *Workers' Control,* edited by Gary Hunnius, G. D. Garson, and John Case. Vintage Books/Random House, 1973. The author's summary credits also Menachem Rozner, "Principal Types and Problems of Direct Democracy in the Kibbutz," a monograph published by the Social Research Center on the Kibbutz at Givat Haviva, 1965, and certain unpublished research on kibbutz industrialization being performed by the Social Research Center in conjunction with the Institute for Social Relations at the University of Michigan.

Ford, Robert N. "Job Enrichment Lessons from AT&T." *Harvard Business Review,* Vol. 51, No. 1, January–February 1973.

Hackman, J. R., and E. E. Lawler III. "Employee Reactions to Job Characteristics." *Journal of Applied Psychology,* Vol. 55, 1971.

Herzberg, Frederick. "One More Time: How Do You Motivate Employees?" *Harvard Business Review,* January–February 1968.

Homans, George. *The Human Group.* Harcourt Brace Jovanovich, 1950.

Hulin, C. L., and M. R. Blood. "Job Enlargement, Individual Differences and Worker Response." *Psychological Bulletin,* Vol. 69, 1968.

Karlsen, J. I. *A Monograph on the Norwegian Industrial Democracy Project.* Oslo, Work Research Institutes. Doc. No. 15, 1972.

Klein, Lisl. *New Forms of Work Organization.* Cambridge University Press, 1976.

Kornhauser, Arthur. *Mental Health of the Industrial Worker.* John Wiley & Sons, 1964.

Lawler, E. E. III. "For a More Effective Organization, Match the Job to the Man." *Organizational Dynamics,* Vol. 3, No. 1, Summer 1974.

McGregor, Douglas. *The Human Side of Enterprise.* McGraw-Hill, 1960.

Organizational Dynamics. "Job Re-Design on the Assembly Line: Farewell to the Blue-Collar Blues?" Vol. 2, No. 2, Autumn, 1973.

Rice, A. K. *Productivity and Social Organization, The Ahmedabad Experiment.* London, Tavistock Institute, 1958.

Taylor, James C. "Some Effects of Technology in Organizational Change." *Human Relations,* Vol. 24, 1971.

Trist, E. L., and K. W. Bamforth. "Some Social and Psychological Consequences of the Longwall Method of Coal Getting." *Human Relations,* Vol. 4, 1951.

Turner, A. N., and P. R. Lawrence. *Industrial Jobs and the Worker.* Harvard University, Graduate School of Business, 1965.

United States Senate, Committee on Labor and Public Welfare, Subcommittee on Employment, Manpower and Poverty. *Hearings: S3916.* July 25 and 26, 1972.

Wilkinson, A. *A Survey of Some Western European Experiments in Motivation.* London, Institute of Work Study Practitioners, 1970.

Work in America. Report of a special task force to the Secretary of Health, Education and Welfare. Massachusetts Institute of Technology Press, 1972.

Zajonc, R. B. *Social Psychology, an Experimental Approach.* Brooke-Cole, 1966.

Further Readings

Agervold, M. "Swedish Experiments in Democracy." In *The Quality of Working Life.* A. B. Cherns and L. E. Davis (eds). The Free Press, 1975.

Anshen, Melvin. "Managerial Decisions." In *Automation and Technological Change.* Edited by J. T. Dunlop. The American Assembly, Columbia University, 1962.

Argyris, Chris. *Interpersonal Competence and Organizational Effectiveness.* Irwin-Dorsey, 1962.

Bavelas, Alex, and George Strauss. "Group Dynamics and Intergroup Relations." In *Organizations and Human Behavior.* Prentice-Hall, Inc., 1967.

Bell, Daniel. *Work and Its Discontents.* Beacon Press, 1956.

Biggane, James F. and Paul A. Stewart. *Job Enlargement, A Case Study.* Bureau of Labor and Management, College of Business, State University of Iowa Research Series, No. 25, 1963.

Boguslaw, Robert. *The New Utopians.* Prentice-Hall, 1965.

Butera, F. "Contribution to the Analysis of Structural Variables Affecting Emerging Patterns of Job Design: The Olivetti Case." In *The Quality of Working Life.* A. B. Cherns and L. E. Davis (eds.). The Free Press, 1975.

Davis, Louis E. "The Coming Crisis for Production Management: Technology and Organization." *International Journal of Production Research,* Vol. 9, 1971.

————, and James C. Taylor. *Design of Jobs.* Penguin Books, 1972.

Emery, F. E. *Characteristics of Socio-Technical Systems.* Tavistock Institute, 1959.

————. "The Democratization of the Workplace." *Manpower and Applied Psychology,* Vol. 1, 1967.

————. (ed.) *Systems Thinking.* Penguin Books, 1969.

————, and E. Thorsrud. *Form and Content in Industrial Democracy.* Tavistock Institute, 1969.

Engelstad, P. H. "Socio-Technical Approach to Problems of Process Control." In *Papermaking Systems and Their Control.* F. Bolam (ed.). British Paper and Board Makers Association, 1970.

Ford, R. N. *Motivation Through the Work Itself*. American Management Association, 1969.

Goldman, Robert B. *Work Values: Six Americans in a Swedish Plant*. Worker Exchange Program, New York State School of Industrial and Labor Relations, Cornell University, 1975.

Guest, R. H. *Organizational Change: The Effect of Successful Leadership*. Dorsey Press, 1962.

Hackman, J. R., G. Oldham, R. Janson, and K. Purdy. "A New Strategy for Job Enrichment." *California Management Review*, Vol. 17, Summer, 1975.

Herbst, P. G. *Autonomous Work Group Functioning*. Tavistock Institute, 1962.

———. *Socio-Technical Design*. Tavistock Institute, 1974.

Hunnios, Garry, G. D. Garson, and John Case. *Workers' Control, A Reader on Labor and Social Change*. Vintage Books, 1973.

Industrial Democracy. Swedish Trade Union Confederation. Program Developed by the 1971 Conference, Stockholm, 1972.

Jenkins, David. "Democracy in the Factory." *The Atlantic*, April, 1973.

———. *Job Power, Blue and White Collar Democracy*. Doubleday and Company, 1973; Penguin Books, 1974.

Johansson, S. B. "On the Need of New Concepts for Production Management." 2nd International Conference on Production Research. Copenhagen, Technical University of Denmark, August, 1973.

Katz, D., and R. L. Kahn. *The Social Psychology of Organizations*. John Wiley, 1966.

Kimberly, John. "Politics for Innovation in the Service Sector." O.E.C.D. Directorate for Scientific Affairs, 1973.

King, D. "Vocational Training in View of Technical Change." E.P.A. Project No. 418, March, 1960.

Klein, Lisl. *Multiproducts, Ltd*. London, Her Majesty's Stationery Office, 1964.

Levitan, Sar and W. B. Johnston. "Job Re-Design, Reform, Enrichment: Exploring the Limitations." *Monthly Labor Review*, Vol. 96, July, 1973.

Lewin, Kurt. *Field Theory in Social Science*. Harper & Row, 1951.

Mann, F. C. and L. R. Hoffman. *Automation and the Worker*. Henry Holt, 1960.

Marrow, A. J., D. G. Bowers, and S. F. Seashore. *Management by Participation*. Harper & Row, 1967.

Morse, John J. "A Contingency Look at Job Design." *California Management Review*, Vol. 16, No. 1, Fall, 1973.

Paul, W. J., K. B. Robertson, and Frederick Herzberg. "Job Enrichment Pays Off." *Harvard Business Review*, Vol. 47, No. 2, March–April 1969.

Reif, W., and F. Luthans. "Does Job Enrichment Really Pay Off?" *California Management Review*, Vol. 15, Fall, 1972.

Rice, A. K. *The Enterprise and Its Environment: A System Theory of Management and Organization*. London, Tavistock Institute, 1963.

Roson, Jerome M. (ed.) *The Worker and the Job: Coping With Change*. Prentice-Hall, 1974.

Rush, H. M. F. *Job Design for Motivation*. The Conference Board, 1971.

Schein, E. H. "Management Development as a Process of Influence." *Industrial Management Review*, Vol. 2, 1961.

Siroja, David, and J. M. Greenwood. "Understand Your Overseas Work Force." *Harvard Business Review*, January–February, 1971.

Touraine, Alain. "An Historical Theory in the Evolution of Industrial Skills." In *Modern Technology and Civilization*. McGraw-Hill, 1962.

Trist, E. L., G. W. Higgin, H. Murray, and A. B. Pollock. *Organizational Choice*. London, Tavistock Institute, 1963.

U. S. Department of Labor. *Survey of Working Conditions, November 1970.* Prepared by Survey Research Center, University of Michigan. Government Printing Office, 1972.

Van Beek, H. G. "The Influence of Assembly Line Organization on Output, Quality and Morale." *Occupational Psychology,* Vol. 38.

Walker, C. R. *Toward the Automatic Factory.* Yale University Press, 1957.

Walton, Richard. "The Diffusion of New Work Structures." *Organizational Dynamics,* Vol. 3, No. 3, Winter 1975.

————. "How to Counter Alienation in the Plant." *Harvard Business Review,* Vol. 50, No. 6, November–December 1972.

————. *Work Place Alienation and the Need for Major Innovation.* Graduate School of Business Administration, Harvard University, 1972.

Weinberg, Arthur S. "A Worker Exchange Program at Saab-Scania." Final Report, New York State School of Industrial and Labor Relations, Worker Exchange Program, 1975.

White, L. A. *The Evolution of Culture.* McGraw-Hill, 1959.

Williams, L. K., and B. C. Williams. "The Impact of Numerically Controlled Equipment on Factory Organization." *California Management Review,* Vol. 7, No. 2.

Wilson, N. A. B. *On the Quality of Working Life.* London, Department of Employment, Research and Planning Division, Manpower Paper #7, Her Majesty's Stationery Office, 1973.

Winpisinger, William. "Job Enrichment: A Union View." *Monthly Labor Review,* Vol. 96, April 1973.

Zaltman, Gerald, Robert Duncan, and Jenny Holbek. *Innovations and Organizations.* John Wiley and Sons, 1973.

Readings

Work in America: Case Studies

	Establishment(s) or Employee Groups	Year Initiated	No. Employees Affected	Problem
General Foods	Pet Food Plant Topeka, Kans. All plant employees.	1971	70	In designing this new plant management sought to solve problems of frequent shutdowns, costly recycling and low morale that plagued an existing plant making the same product.
AT&T	Long Lines Plant, N.Y. Private Line Telephone District. Framemen.	1966	35–40	There was low productivity, high errors, schedule slippage and no worker's pride.
AT&T	Shareholder Correspondents, Treasury Department.	1965	95–120	High turnover, absenteeism, low morale, low productivity.
Bell System	17 groups of workers in diverse occupations, including toll operators, installers, clerks, equipment engineers.	1967	about 1,200	Are the methods and results of the AT&T Shareholder Correspondents Study transferable to other employee groups?
Polaroid Corp.	Production-line employees.	1959	2,000+	Top management wanted to increase the meaningfulness of work.

Reprinted from "*Work in America:* Appendix 1—Case Studies" by V. Macaluso, W. McCreedy, D. Bond, S. King, and P. Forkel, by permission of the MIT Press, Cambridge, Massachusetts.

Technique Used	Human Results	Economic Results	Reference(s)
Workers were organized into relatively autonomous work groups with each group responsible for a production process. Pay is based on the total number of jobs an employee can do.	Job attitudes a few months after the plant opened indicated "positive assessments" by both team members and leaders. Increased democracy in the plant may have led to more civic activity.	The plant is operated by 70 workers, rather than the 110 originally estimated by industrial engineers. Also, there were "improved yields, minimized waste and avoidance of shutdowns."	Walton, Richard E. —*Workplace Alienation and the Need for Major Innovation*, May 1972 (unpublished)
The framemen's work was expanded to include taking full responsibility for the job and negotiating with the "customer."	Grievances were practically eliminated (from rate of one per week). Morale was higher in the year's experiment.	There was no significant change in absenteeism or tardiness. However, at the end there was a slight increase in productivity with fewer workers and less overtime.	Ford, R. N., *Motivation Through The Work Itself*, AMA, 1969, pp. 211–256
Workers were given less supervision and more job freedom. The authors of letters to complainants were allowed to sign without review by supervisors.	There was more pride in group achievement. Higher job satisfaction was measured.	After a year's trial absenteeism decreased from 2% to 1.4%. Turnover practically eliminated.	Ford, R. N., *op. cit.* at pp. 20–44 Foulks, F. K., *Creating More Meaningful Work*, AMA, 1969, pp. 97–120
Same as AT&T Shareholder Correspondents Study.	After a year's experience, where measured, attitudes improved and grievances dropped.	Turnover decreased by 9.3% in the experimental group and increased 13.1% in the control group. Overtime hours decreased about 50%.	Ford, R. N., *op. cit.* at pp. 45–79
Factory operators were rotated between their factory jobs and more desirable non-factory jobs.	For some there was challenge and reward while learning, then frustration until they were permanently transferred.	Turnover and absenteeism decreased. Recruitment was easier for factory jobs, since they were no longer dead-end.	Foulks, F. K., *op. cit.* at pp. 35–55

	Establishment(s) or Employee Groups	Year Initiated	No. Employees Affected	Problem
Texas Instruments, Inc.	Small group of women—electronic instrument assemblers.	1967	600	Top management wanted better utilization of human resources.
Hunsfos Pulp & Paper Mill Kristiansand, Norway	Chemical pulp department of paper-mill.	1964	32	Segregation of jobs, lack of overlapping skills and permanent shifts increasingly hindered work as the process became more complex.
Nobø Fabrikker A/S Trandheim, Norway	New unit making electrical panels for metal manufacturing plant.	1965	10 to 40	Management wished to improve simple repetitive jobs.
H. P. Hood & Sons Boston, Mass.	Unspecified number of company plants and occupations.	Over 20 years ago.	Not specified.	There was no specific problem. The goal was to improve operations and to involve employees more in the affairs of the company.
Rade Koncar Zagreb, Yugoslavia	Plant manufacturing heavy electrical equipment. All employees.	1945	1946—890; 1966—7,946	National need for rapid industrialization and a desire to transfer management to the worker-producer.

Technique Used	Human Results	Economic Results	Reference(s)
The group was asked to set its own production goal and given more information concerning costs and terms of the government contract on which it was working.	A survey revealed that employees were deriving more satisfaction from their work and had fewer complaints about so-called maintenance items.	During the experiment, assembly time per unit decreased from 138 to 32 hours. Absenteeism, turnover, leaving time, complaints and trips to health center decreased.	Foulks, F. K., *op. cit.* at pp. 56–96
The group of 32 workers was given greater responsibility for the operation of the department as a whole and was encouraged to increase its control of the process.	Workers showed greater job interest through their suggestions.	In the four-year experiment, the average quality bonus increased about 24%.	P. H. Engelstad, Socio-Technical Approach to Problems of Process Control, *Papermaking Systems And Their Control*, 1970
Production groups and subgroups were established and put on group bonus rates. A "contact person" (with department head) was substituted for the supervisor and was chosen by election.	. . . general satisfaction among the workers . . . and absenteeism . . . much lower than for the factory as a whole.	In the one-year experiment, production rates increased 22% and hourly earnings increased 11%.	Ødegaard, L. A., Summary of Third Field Experiment, Industrial Democracy Project, Phase B (unpub.)
On numerous occasions workers teamed with supervisors to simplify work, often using films of actual operations. Workers with two or more years of seniority are secure against layoff.	The program manager reported, "the employees do not resist the approach, an attitude which may have been fostered by a cash award system for suggestions."	Not explicitly stated.	Foulks, F. K., *op. cit.* at pp. 169–176
Under worker's self-management, all workers are members of working units, and have the right and obligation to manage their units, make decisions, establish economic policy, and to submit suggestions, criticisms, questions, etc. "to authoritative management," who is obligated to consider them.	Not explicitly stated.	From a small company in 1945, Rade Koncar has taken a leading role in equipment for power plants, including nuclear, and transformer plants.	Mladen, K.; *Self-Management in the Enterprise*, Medunarodna Stampa Interpress, 1967

	Establishment(s) or Employee Groups	Year Initiated	No. Employees Affected	Problem
Sisak Ironworks Yugoslavia	Iron and Steel Industry in Sisak, Caprag.	1961	About 6,000	Low productivity of labor.
I.C.I.	Imperial Chemical Industries— Gloucester, Great Britain Factory floor workers.	1968	19,500	Low morale. "Five walkouts in a week."
P. P. G. Industries	P. P. G. Industries Lexington, N.C. Twist frame operators.	1969	675	Loss of efficiency in twist frame machines because frame cleaning was dirty work; repetitive and routine.
Monsanto	Electronics Division West Caldwell, N.J. Foremen.	Not specified.	Not specified.	High employee turnover among new hires.
Monsanto Chemical	Textile Division Pensacola, Fla. Chemical operators.	1968	50	Rising production costs beset the automated control room for chemical reaction and conversion.
Weyerhauser	Weyerhauser Co. Tacoma, Wash. Paper production employees.	1968	300 (pilot project)	Low productivity.

Technique Used	Human Results	Economic Results	Reference(s)
Self-management bodies were established in each department in which the workers decided on production norms and pay rates (including incentives).	Not specified.	In eight years, product improved. Production was expanded and modernized.	The Economic Resources of the Production Departments and Distribution According to the Results of Labor in the Sisak Ironworks; Beograd, 1970
Weekly staff assignments provide job rotation. Small groups (8) input "own ideas" into work process.	". . . it's their (the workers) factory, not just a place where they come to work," a supervisor reported.	Since the experiment there has been a 20% reduction in labor, 20% increase in production, 25% increase in pay, and a 30% cut in supervision.	Smith, Dan, *In Place of Strife at ICI*, HR 13, Info Service, Steel House, London, Sept. 1970, pp. 420–426
The frame cleaner job was eliminated. Since cleaning takes 15% of the time on each job, the machine operators took over the cleaning function.	Personnel and production managers report that "morale is high."	Productivity increased by 12% over the previous two years.	Rush, Harold M. F., *Job Design for Motivation*, Report from the Conference Board, 1971, pp. 67–70
The foremen were given responsibility for interviewing, indoctrinating, and giving skills training to new hires.	Not specified.	Turnover, which had been high among unskilled jobs, averaged 6% annually in the five years of the program.	Rush, Harold M. F., *op. cit.* at pp. 75–76
Four employee "task forces" (one from each shift) restructured certain jobs and eliminated some dirty jobs through automation. Operators now manage their own restructured jobs.	Employee suggestions increased 300%.	Waste loss dropped to zero, operators monitor 50% more instruments and half of the old supervisors not needed.	Rush, Harold M. F., *op. cit.* at pp. 70–73
An "I Am" plan (short for "I Am Manager of My Job") was implemented, based on the assumption that all people want to be responsible, to succeed, and can best manage their own jobs.	The project manager said, "they became a fraternity . . . and were enthusiastic about the challenge of their new jobs."	"Increased productivity" according to an executive.	Rush, Harold M. F., *op. cit.* at pp. 55–60

	Establishment(s) or Employee Groups	Year Initiated	No. Employees Affected	Problem
Araphoe	Araphoe Chemical Boulder, Colo. Chemists.	1968	125	Low productivity and morale.
Syntex	Syntex Corporation Mexico City, Mexico; Research Center Palo Alto, Calif. Salesmen.	1966	Not specified.	The innovativeness of scientists was not being utilized.
American Velvet Co.	All employees of manufacturer of velvet. Stonington, Conn.	Not specified.	400	None specified.
Monsanto	Agriculture Division Muscatine, Iowa Machine operators.	1967	150	There was a production "bottleneck" in the bagging section.
Oldsmobile	Oldsmobile Division, GM Lansing, Mich. Engineering and assembly employees.	1970	Two plants	High absenteeism and turnover.

Technique Used	Human Results	Economic Results	Reference(s)
Each chemist was made directly responsible for an entire project.	Not specified.	Productivity increased and deadlines on customer orders were met more promptly.	Rush, Harold M. F., *op. cit.* at pp. 33–39
Team work groups were formed "where employee set own standards and quotas."	A vice president reports, "less skepticism, more volunteering, more introspection, an instantaneous feedback, managers more concerned with career paths – career planning of employees, rank-and-file employees appear more committed and involved."	Volume sales in the two experimental groups increased by 116% and 20% over the control groups.	Rush, Harold M. F., *Behavioral Science, Concepts and Management Application,* 1970, pp. 130–138
Workers plan and organize own work and have profit-sharing plan.	"Consultation, participation, and involvement are a way of life at the top of the company and at the production level as well."	Not specified.	Foulks, F. K., *op. cit.* at pp. 176–184
Seminars were held with employees who analyzed their own jobs and made changes. Production goals were set by baggers.	Not specified.	Production increased 75% in the four months after the change.	Rush, Harold M. F., *Job Design for Motivation,* Report from the Conference Board, 1971, pp. 73–74
A volunteer hourly employee task force held meetings with foremen and other employees, conducted surveys, and made broad recommendations to improve employee relations.	"The results included more positive employee relations."	Absenteeism decreased 6% in engineering and 6.5% in assembly – while rising 11% in the rest of Oldsmobile. There were "improved product quality . . . and reduced costs."	GM Publication, *Oldsmobile's Action on Absenteeism and Turnover,* Nov. 1971

	Establishment(s) or Employee Groups	Year Initiated	No. Employees Affected	Problem
Norsk	Norsk Hydro Oslo, Norway Production workers.	1966	About 50	Competition was becoming tougher and profits were declining.
Texas Instruments	Texas Instruments, Inc. Dallas, Tex. Maintenance personnel.	1967	120	100% quarterly turnover and failure to get buildings clean.
Corning Glass Works Medfield, Mass.	Instrument assembly workers.	1965	6	Not specified.
Donnelly Mirrors, Inc. Holland, Mich.	Auto mirror mfg. All employees.	Long-term project	460	To "come to grips with the problems of productivity."
Monsanto-Textiles Co. Pensacola, Fla.	Production workers of nylon tire yarn.	1971	6,000	Not specified.

Technique Used	Human Results	Economic Results	Reference(s)
Autonomous work groups were established without first hands (supervisors). A group bonus plan was installed based on productivity.	The percentage of workers expressing overall job satisfaction increased from 58 to 100.	Production costs per ton decreased 30% over the first six months of the project, but other factors were also involved. Absenteeism was 4% in the experimental factory vs. 7% for the control factory.	Bregard, A., Gulowsen J., et al. *Norsk Hydro, Experiment in the Fertilizer Factories*, Work Research Institute, Jan. 1968
Workers were organized into 19 member cleaning teams. Each member voice in planning, problem-solving, goal-setting, and scheduling.	Not specified.	Quarterly turnover dropped from 100% to 9.8%. Personnel requirements dropped from 120 to 71. Cost savings averaged $103,000 annually between 1967–1969. Building cleanliness ratings increased from 65% to 85%.	Rush, Harold M. F., *Job Design for Motivation*, Report from the Conference Board, 1971, pp. 39–49
Assembly line techniques were abandoned. Workers were allowed to assemble entire electrical hot plates with the freedom to schedule their work as a group so as to meet weekly objectives.	"I feel like a human being. You know what you have to do and you push to do it," says an employee.	In the six months after the change, rejects dropped from 23% to 1% and absenteeism from 8% to 1%.	*U.S. News and World Report,* July 17, 1972, p. 50
Workers determine their annual salaries. They receive productivity bonuses and must find ways to assure that the bonuses are paid through higher production, elimination of needless jobs, etc.	Not specified.	Wages, costs, and profits all have increased during the past few years, even as the company has lowered its prices.	*U.S. News and World Report, op. cit.* at p. 51
Four-day classroom sessions were held to involve production workers in problem-solving. Also, employees set production goals and rotated jobs.	"For the employee the program means 'humanized' working conditions," the plant manager reported.	"The cost of the program more than pays for itself in higher productivity through fewer idle machines and lower repair costs—a possible gain of 100,000 pounds of yarn a year," says the plant manager.	*U.S. News and World Report, op. cit.* at p. 52

	Establishment(s) or Employee Groups	Year Initiated	No. Employees Affected	Problem
Alcan Aluminum Corp. Oswego, N.Y.	Rolling mill operators.	1965	Not specified.	High rates of absenteeism and tardiness.
Micro-Wax Dept. — Shell Stanlow Refinery, Ellesmere Port; Cheshire, England	Chemical operators.	1963	Not specified.	Low productivity, low morale, and possibility of "shutdown."
Philips Electrical Industries — Holland	Assembly workers.	1960	240–300	Not specified.
Ferado Company United Kingdom	Production workers making brake linings.	Not specified.	Not specified.	Not specified.
Netherlands PTT	Clerical workers — data collection.	Not specified.	100	Jobs were routine. Workers and supervisors were both "notably uninterested" in their work.

Technique Used	Human Results	Economic Results	Reference(s)
Time clocks were removed and production jobs designed to give workers unusual freedom and decision-making responsibilities. Salaries were guaranteed during absences or layoffs.	"Monotony is relieved," says the plant manager.	Absenteeism decreased to about 2.5% compared to an industry average of about 10%. Productivity increased.	"The Honor System," *Wall Street Journal,* May 22, 1970 "Alcan Hails in Dumping Time Clock," *The Plain Dealer,* Sept. 29, 1969
Operators formed group teams that provided both more flexibility within shift teams and rotation in jobs. Time clocks were also removed.	"It is well known that absence and sickness may be symptomatic of alienation . . . from the work situation. Thus . . . [these] statistics are partly an indication of morale," said that plant manager.	"Output" in three sections increased by 35%, 40%, and 100% over 1965. Absence and sickness decreased from 4.3% in 1963 to 3.3% in 1969.	Burden, Derek, *A Participative Approach to Management,* Shell U.K., April 15, 1970
Independent work groups were formed and made responsible for job allocations, material and quality control, and providing delegates for management talks.	The members of semi-autonomous groups derived more satisfaction from their work compared with workers in the old situation.	By 1967, waste and repairs decreased by 4% and there was an unspecified savings of lower managerial personnel.	Davis & Trist— *Work in America,* Approaches to Improving Quality of Working Life, June 1972, p. 18
Groups of six men were trained to use all machines involved in the process and allowed to move from one machine to the other. Each group sees the batch of marketable products they have made.	Job satisfaction in the plant has been found to increase.	There is less turnover, and original delivery times have been cut by seven-eighths.	Wilson, N. A. B., *On the Quality of Working Life,* A Personal Report to the NATO Committee on Challenges of Modern Society, p. 40
Jobs were enlarged to comprise a whole collaborative process (e.g., listing, punching, control punching, corrections, etc.) instead of a single stage of this process.	88% of the workers in the experimental group said the work had become more interesting.	There was a 15% increase in output per man-hour.	Wilson, N. A. B., *op. cit.* at p. 36

	Establishment(s) or Employee Groups	Year Initiated	No. Employees Affected	Problem
Kaiser Aluminum Corporation Ravenswood, W.Va.	Maintenance workers in reduction plant.	1971	60	Productivity was low. There were walkouts and slowdowns.
Bankers Trust Company New York	Production typists in stock transfer operations.	1969	200	Production was low and quality poor. Absenteeism and turnover were high and employee attitudes were poor . . . Jobs were routine, repetitive and devoid of intrinsic interest . . . Too much overseeing.
Operations Division, Bureau of Traffic — Ohio Dept. of Highways	Six field construction crews.	Not specified.	Not specified.	Low productivity and poor quality of performance.

Technique Used	Human Results	Economic Results	Reference(s)
Time clocks were removed and supervision virtually eliminated. Workers now decide what maintenance jobs are to be done and in what priority and keep their own time cards.	"Morale has improved along with pride in workmanship," said the maintenance chief.	Tardiness is now "non-existent." Maintenance costs are down 5.5%. Maintenance work is done with more "quality."	Thompson, Donald B., "Enrichment in Action Convinces Skeptics," *Industry Week*, Feb. 14, 1971
Typists were given the opportunity (1) to change their own computer output tapes, (2) to handle typing for a specific group of customers, (3) to check their own work, and (4) to schedule their own work. Training was given in these areas.	A quantitative survey disclosed improved attitudes and greater satisfaction.	Absenteeism and tardiness were reduced while production and quality increased. Job enrichment programs were extended.	Detteback, William W., Assistant Vice Pres. Bankers Trust, and Kraft, Philip, Partner; Roy W. Walters Associates, "Organization Change Through Job Enrichment," *Training and Development Journal*, August 1971
Three experimental groups were established, each with a different degree of self-determination of work schedules. Crews were unaware that they were participating in an experiment.	Data showed that as participation increased, so did morale.	There was no significant change in productivity.	Powell, Reed M., and Schlacter, John L., "Participative Management: A Panacea?," *Academy of Management Journal*, June 1971, pp. 165–173

Worker Participation in Israel

Keitha Sapsin Fine

In the following abstract, the author describes the traditional kibbutz organization as it evolved in the production of agricultural products. As pointed out at the end of the reading, many kibbutzim have added manufacturing industries to their traditional economies. The plant organization is considerably different from the original agricultural organizations. However, the classic pattern described in the reading is more relevant to our present chapter, which concentrates on design of autonomous work groups.

INDUSTRIALIZATION OF THE KIBBUTZIM

Social Organization of the Kibbutzim

It is common knowledge that collective agricultural settlements pioneered the colonization and development of Palestine.[1] Today 240 kibbutzim with approximately 90,000 members in units averaging 250–300 persons are scattered over Israel. They produce about 33 percent of the agricultural and 8 percent of the industrial products of the country, and have supplied many of the outstanding leaders of the modern state.

Members of the original movement, fleeing hostile European countries and stimulated by the challenge of settlement, carried the seeds of Socialism and Zionism to Palestine prior to the First World War. There, they established many settlements, similar in socioeconomic organization and values, although often differing in religious and political affiliations. During the 1920s the various kibbutzim cohered into several federations for purposes of religious and political unity, to undertake activities more effectively performed at a central level (for example, allocation of new manpower), and in order to present a common front in bargaining for needed financing with the Jewish National Fund, from which settlements still lease some land, the Jewish Agency and the Histadrut. The federations still perform similar functions today, and in addition, individual kibbutzim now also belong to giant purchasing and marketing cooperatives.

The principles of direct democracy which underlie the social organization and administration of the kibbutzim are their outstanding characteristics and strength. These principles—voluntarism, cooperativism, and egalitarianism—aim at the "complete identification of the individual with the society."[2] Individuals internalize the collective goals embodied in the principles and feel no conflict between private desires and the needs of society.[3] This process is facilitated by the psychology of "total inclusion" induced by the framework of the kibbutz, by overlapping among institutional areas, and by the "functional interdependence" (i.e., "the overlapping of the ecological unit with the social unit and the economic productive unit") created by the close linkages between kibbutz institutions and life patterns.[4] Integration is also the aim of the educational process and all decision-making mechanisms. The most important mechanism for social control is nonformalized public opinion—which replaces hierarchy elsewhere.

Practically, identification is actualized in a process of direct decision making in the

From "Worker Participation in Israel" by Keitha Sapsin Fine, from *Worker's Control* edited by Gerry Hunnius, G. David Garson, and John Case. Reprinted by permission of Keitha Sapsin Fine.

weekly meetings of the general assembly of the kibbutz. These meetings are the central forum for communications among all members—they serve to integrate and balance the various interests of the social groups and departments in the kibbutz. Free discussion takes place with no time limit; votes are rarely formal. The unitary ideal is reflected in the absence of a separation between executive, legislative, and judicial powers. In its executive functions, the general assembly takes decisions by majority vote in the case of disagreements, and ratifies departmental proposals. As a legislature it makes policy decisions on aspects of kibbutz life, discusses and votes on budgets, and sets precedents on problems. As a judiciary it makes final decisions on individual cases, and interprets previous decisions and codes.

The general assembly annually elects a secretariat of eight to ten members who are heads of the committees which deal with various aspects of kibbutz life; these include the economic secretary, the treasurer, the works manager, and the heads of the social, education, and cultural committees. The secretariat is chaired by a general secretary whose duty is to coordinate all the activities. It meets in advance of the general meeting to work out any conflicts beforehand and synthesize interests. It has the power of decision on some questions of administration, but never on matters of principle, on which it can only prepare proposals. The secretariat also initially appoints and works with the branch managers for each sector of the economy.

The social conditions which support all these mechanisms are the relatively small scale of the unit (that is, size commensurate with direct access to decision making); a high degree of social awareness on the part of the membership; absolute equality among members—which carries the assumptions of no individual economic rewards or privileges and the responsibility of the kibbutz for satisfying the needs of its members; a number of persons able to carry out multitudinous functions within the society; and, of course, a wholly voluntary commitment to and participation in the society. A major goal of kibbutz life has always been to satisfy the needs of members for self-realization, and thus the creative expansion of job opportunities, based on an assumption of the positive relationship between work and satisfaction, is a continual problem. A major means of dealing with this has been by way of job rotation, primarily used for disagreeable work or where the potential for self-actualizing activity is low, and in managerial roles to prevent the solidification of a Weberian type bureaucracy.[5]

It is generally agreed that in the past these conditions for direct democracy were met by the social and economical organizational structures of the kibbutz. They in turn were made possible by the very strong network of cooperatives surrounding the kibbutz, which acted as a "buffer zone" between the kibbutz and the greater society, allowing it to preserve its autonomy, yet also easing adaptation to the requirements of modernization by permitting a continuous process of change to occur in an absence of open conflict between the kibbutzim and the larger society. The problem currently is to understand if and how recent changes—heterogeneity of population, the emergence of several generations, growth, complexity, technology, and industrialization—have affected the ideals and organization of the kibbutzim. Specifically, one must ask key questions at two levels: first, whether the requirements of modernization—such as technological specialization—are antithetical to the preservation of kibbutz values and to decision making by direct democracy; and second, whether the development of the entire society has so altered conditions externally supportive to a kibbutz way of life that efforts by the kibbutzim to change their organizational structures to meet new social conditions, yet preserve their basic values, will founder on causes outside their control.

It has been suggested that features of both the social system of the kibbutz and its members are supportive of a transfer of work from agriculture to industry within the framework of collectivism.[6] Some such aspects of the value system of the kibbutz are its ideological flexibility which encourages a response to changes in objective circumstances by reinterpretation of norms; its future planning orientation which provides for constant change; and the continued emphasis on production and productive work as a service to the kibbutz with a concomitant opposition to specialization and professionalization. Important characteristics of the social and economic structures are the absence of rewards attached to a work position, the general network of social relationships, few role distinctions, and the norm of rotation in managerial functions. Attributes of individuals which encourage a belief in modernization without a loss of collectivism include their previous experience in transforming themselves from urban immigrants to a new class of agricultural laborers; the generally high level of technology, efficiency, and planning they introduced into agriculture; their own high educational levels and the desire for more training; the dispersion of managerial ability because of the democratic principles on which the kibbutz is organized; individual initiative; and achievement need as a reward in the absence of other kinds of incentives.

THE GENERAL ECONOMY OF THE KIBBUTZ

The chief economic strength of the kibbutzim has remained agricultural. In the early 1960s kibbutzim provided 18.7 percent of Israel's agricultural labor force, and cultivated one third the arable land and one third of its irrigated area.[7] They lead in the cultivation of noncitrus fruits and farm 18 percent of the fruit plantations. They produce 26.8 percent of the eggs, 40.6 percent of the poultry meat, and about 30 percent of the beef in the country. Although they also cultivate 40 percent of the nation's field crops and 12 percent of the vegetables, there has been a decided shift toward the moshavim in these sectors. Overall, by 1964 kibbutz agricultural production had increased to seven times its 1949 level compared to six times for the country as a whole, leveling off at about 31 percent between 1960 and 1964. Kibbutz agricultural productivity is almost uniformly higher than that of the general economy or the moshavim; between 1949 and 1960 it increased at an average annual rate of about 10 percent. By the same token, available data on agricultural worker output also indicates a higher degree of efficiency and rapid growth in labor productivity—not unexpectedly, since the kibbutzim have always strived to become self-supporting units, when possible voluntary savings are high and have always been reinvested.

Despite their almost uniformly higher rates of productivity, however, the kibbutz economies ran at a pronounced deficit until the late thirties, and again between 1954 and 1960; only since 1961 have small surpluses been recorded. This situation can be explained by a combination of factors external and internal to the kibbutz that affect its profitability. These include: higher production costs induced by early overdiversification, remote locations, poor soil, drought, and higher labor costs because the institutional setup requires a higher number of labor days per member than, for example, in the moshav; periods of adverse agricultural prices, the chronic manpower shortage; high interest rates in the absence of large savings; high educational expenses; and the steep annual rise (5 percent to 6.5 percent) in the standard of living between 1955 and 1964.[8] In addition, ideological beliefs concerning the concept of leisure, the refusal to "weed out" less profitable units which would be obliterated by competition in a capitalist system, and opposition to the use of hired labor have compelled the kibbutzim to become capital- rather than labor-intensive economies.[9] The reversal toward small surpluses in the early sixties was the result of financial and planning help from the government, more sophisticated—if more profit oriented—economic analyses by the kibbutzim, a stabilized population, returns from earlier conversions to fruit and cattle, and perhaps more important for our purposes, the benefits from and continued development of generally profitable nonagricultural enterprises.

As we examine the development and organization of kibbutz industry below, we should keep in mind that the gap noted between rates of productivity and profitability in agriculture on the basis of efficiency/effectiveness (cost/benefit) criteria does not hold in the research available on kibbutz industries, particularly when they are compared with their counterparts in the private sector.[10] This suggests that explanations which rely on the institutional setup (the organization) or on the ideology of the kibbutzim to explain adverse profitability are at best incomplete and at worst erroneous. As we shall see it is also misleading to analyze the shift since the thirties from a labor to capital-intensive economy as a negative one on the grounds that the reluctance to employ hired labor has been a financial drain on the kibbutzim.

INDUSTRIALIZATION

Unlike the ideological foundation underpinning an agricultural way of life, industrialization of the kibbutzim was primarily stimulated by the pragmatic needs of communities some distance from urban and service centers. During the thirties land and water shortages, fluctuations in labor needs due to the seasonal nature of agriculture, and the necessity for kibbutz members to seek outside employment in order to supplement the community's income acted as a further inducement to industrialize.[11] But for the most part, the early endeavors were considered adjuncts to the agricultural way of life, not substitutes for it. It was really not until World War II, when British needs provided the major impetus toward industrialization, that the kibbutzim seriously began to look toward manufacturing as a labor activity worthy of development. After independence the government's deliberate emphasis on agriculture depressed the trend until after the mid-fifties when farm products came into surplus and the entire society began a large scale industrial push.[12]

Both economic and noneconomic reasons underlie the rapid industrialization of the kibbutzim from this time on: the desire for a stable source of income and a better standard of living (nothing in kibbutz ideology ever dictated a life of eternal poverty and hardship); a generalized commitment to diversify, partly in order to provide new kinds of jobs for and thus retain younger members; an aging population no longer able to undertake heavy agricultural work; an increasingly efficient and mechanized agricultural sector which required less labor; the need to help absorb the new influx of immigrants; and because by producing goods needed by the collective a kibbutz could reduce its dependence on the market economy.

Those kibbutzim that have industrialized are generally the older and best established. The hundred or so founded since statehood are generally the smallest and weakest communities and are heavily subsidized. Ideologically, it is interesting that the most industrialized kibbutzim are affiliated with the Left but non-Communist Hakibbutz Ha'artzi Federation (the strongest), which controls the Socialist and second most important Israeli party, Mapam; and with Hakibbutz Hameuhad, a militant Socialist group which controls the Ahdut Ha'avodah party, rather than with the Ihud which is connected to the ruling Mapai party.

Since the mid-fifties, the numbers of kibbutz industries, those employed in them, and production as a proportion of their annual income (now one fourth to one third) and the national figures have all increased steadily.[13] In 1956 kibbutz plants represented

1.5 percent of the total number and employed 2.4 percent of the industrial labor force; in 1964 the numbers of plants had fallen to 1.2 percent of the national total but the percentage of the national workforce they employed had risen to 3.4 percent. In 1963 approximately 150 separate industries represented 5 percent of the total Israeli gross industrial production, or about £1200 million. Most plants today employ about 40 workers; nine employ between 100 and 500. Although the largest number of enterprises remain small, these figures indicate their size is increasing.

NOTES AND REFERENCES

1. Technically, there are three types of agricultural cooperatives in Israel: the wholly collective kibbutzim; the moshavim, or cooperative small landholders' settlements; and the moshav shitufi, a combination of the other two.
2. Menachem Rozner, "Principal Types and Problems of Direct Democracy in the Kibbutz," monograph published by the Social Research Center on the Kibbutz at Givat Haviva, 1965, p. 1. The most recent, but largely unpublished to date, research on kibbutz industrialization and its effects is ongoing by the Social Research Center in conjunction with the Institute for Social Relations at the University of Michigan. Sources cited were made available by the author.
3. Rozner, *op. cit.*, p. 10.
4. *Ibid.*, p. 27.
5. *Ibid.*, pp. 14–5. Since the forties there have not been enough professionals to permit job rotation in these roles. The rotation of office holders in kibbutz social organizations is one to two years; two to three years in economic organizations and three to five years in public service jobs outside the kibbutz. In addition, in any one year nearly fifty percent of the membership serve on kibbutz committees.
6. Menachem Rozner, "Social Aspects of Industrialization in the Kibbutz" (Givat Haviva; Social Research Center on the Kibbutz, 1969), p. 285. Available from: Givat Haviva Educational Foundation, 150 Fifth Avenue, New York, New York 10011.
7. Eliyahu Kanovsky, *The Economy of the Israeli Kibbutz* (Cambridge: Harvard University Press, 1965), p. 129. Altogether the labor economy works seventy percent of the 1,200,000 acres under cultivation. Statistics that follow are from this source.
8. *Ibid.*, pp. 87–125. The chronic manpower shortage is one of the most severe problems faced by kibbutzim today. The decline of the kibbutz movement as a whole has been largely due to the fact that a majority of immigrants since 1948 came from Middle Eastern cultures with strong traditions in support of a patriarchal family as the center of religious, social, and economic life. This life style was incompatible with the ideology of the kibbutzim. Therefore, new immigrants who chose an agricultural way of life gravitated to the noncollective moshavim, which have outstripped the kibbutzim in growth. In addition, the advent of statehood exacerbated defections. In the Hakibbutz Ha'artzi Federation (the strongest), defections averaged 5.6 percent yearly between 1949 and 1959, versus a preindependence rate of 2 percent to 2.5 percent which was more than replaced by immigration (*ibid.*, p. 137). In addition, about 10 percent of the kibbutz membership has always worked outside the kibbutzim in "public duties," mainly in the Federations, the Histadrut, the government or other services. Boris Stern, *The Kibbutz That Was* (Washington, D.C., Public Affairs Press, 1965), p. 105. Finally, the rural to urban population shift common to all developing countries and a "generation gap" took their

toll on growth, as did rampant ideological controversies throughout the movement in the early 1950s. Since 1960 the total kibbutz population seems to have stabilized around 80,000 or 3.6 percent of the Jewish population. Perhaps eventual settlement of new lands retained as a result of the 1967 acquisitions will present the opportunity for a rebirth of the movement, although this does seem both unlikely and politically undesirable.

9. Opposition to the use of hired labor has clearly also curtailed development and obviated the chance for economies of scale. Its use, particularly as kibbutzim have industrialized, has been extremely controversial and is an issue to which we shall return.

10. Melman, *op. cit.*

11. Industrialization was clearly more related to the wish to reduce kibbutzim dependence on the Jewish Agency and later on the overall society than to the desire to reduce the number of members working in public sector jobs.

12. Between 1958 and 1964 national income from agriculture declined from 13.6 percent to 9.9 percent while income from manufacturing rose to 25.4 percent (Kanovsky, *op. cit.*, pp. 39–40). Stern also notes that in the same period, a comparison of the growth of manufacturing in twenty veteran kibbutzim — with that in the whole economy showed that the latter increased by 21 percent and the kibbutz activity, including handwork and workshop operations, increased 79 percent.

13. The following data are based on Kanovsky, *op. cit.*, pp. 60–4.

Job Enrichment Lessons from AT&T
Robert N. Ford

There is a mounting problem in the land, the concern of employed persons with their work life. Blue-collar workers are increasingly expressing unhappiness over the monotony of the production line. White-collar workers want to barter less of their life for bread. More professional groups are unionizing to fight back at somebody.

The annual reports of many companies frequently proclaim, "Our employees are our most important resource." Is this a statement of conviction or is it mere rhetoric? If it represents conviction, then I think it is only fair to conclude that many business organizations are unwittingly squandering their resources.

The enormous economic gains that sprang from the thinking of the scientific management school of the early 1900's — the time-and-motion study analysts, the creators of production lines — may have ended insofar as they depend on utilizing

Author's note: I wish to acknowledge the collaboration of Malcolm B. Gillette of AT&T and Bruce H. Duffany of Drake-Beam & Associates in the formulation of the job enrichment strategy discussed in this article.

human beings more efficiently. Without discarding these older insights, we need to consider more recent evidence showing that the tasks themselves can be changed to give workers a feeling of accomplishment.

The growing pressure for a four-day workweek is not necessarily evidence that people do not care about their work; they may be rejecting their work in the form that confronts them. To ask employees to repeat one small task all day, at higher and higher rates of speed, is no way to reduce the pressure for a shorter workweek, nor is it any longer a key to rising productivity in America. Work need not be so frequently a betrayal of one's education and ability.

From 1965 to 1968 a group of researchers at AT&T conducted 19 formal field experiments in job enrichment. The success of these studies has led to many company projects since then. From this work and the studies of others (many of them discussed previously in HBR — see the ruled insert on page 99), we have learned that the "life-saving" portion of many jobs can be expanded. Conversely, the boring and unchallenging aspects can be reduced — not to say eliminated.

Furthermore, the "nesting" of related, already enriched jobs — a new concept — may constitute another big step toward better utilization of "our most important resource."

First in this article I shall break down the job enrichment strategy into three steps. Then I shall demonstrate what we at AT&T have been doing for seven years in organizing the work beyond enrichment of individual jobs. In the course of my discussion, I shall use no illustrations that were not clearly successful from the viewpoint of both employees and the company.

While obviously the functions described in the illustrations differ superficially from those in most other companies, they are still similar enough to production and service tasks in other organizations to permit meaningful comparison. It is important to examine the nature of the work itself, rather than the external aspects of the functions.

Moreover, in considering ways to enrich jobs, I am not talking about those elements that serve only to "maintain" employees: wages, fringe benefits, clean restrooms, a pleasant atmosphere, and so on. Any organization must meet the market in these respects or its employees will go elsewhere.

No, employees are saying more than "treat me well." They are also saying "use me well." The former is the maintenance side of the coin; the latter is the work motivation side.

ANATOMY OF ENRICHMENT

In talking about job enrichment, it is necessary to go beyond such high-level concepts as "self-actualization," "need for achievement," and "psychological growth." It is necessary to specify the steps to be taken. The strategy can be broken down into these aspects — improving work through systematic changes in (a) the module of work, (b) control of the module, and (c) the feedback signaling whether something has been accomplished. I shall discuss each of these aspects in turn.

Work Module

Through changing the work modules, Indiana Bell Telephone Company scored a striking success in job enrichment within the space of two years. In Indianapolis, 33 employees, most of them at the lowest clerical wage level, compiled all telephone directories for the state. The processing from clerk to clerk was laid out in 21 steps, many of which were merely for verification. The steps included manuscript reception, manuscript verification, keypunch, keypunch verification, ad copy reception, ad copy verification, and so on—a production line as real as any in Detroit. Each book is issued yearly to the customers named in it, and the printing schedule calls for the appearance of about one different directory per week.

In 1968, the year previous to the start of our study, 28 new hires were required to keep the clerical force at the 33-employee level. Obviously, such turnover had bad consequences. From every operating angle, management was dissatisfied.

In a workshop, the supervisors concluded that the lengthy verification routine, calling for confirmation of one's work by other clerks, was not solving the basic problem, which was employee indifference toward the tasks. Traditional "solutions" were ineffective. They included retraining, supervisor complaints to the employees, and "communicating" with them on the importance to customers of error-free listing of their names and places of business in the directories. As any employee smart enough to be hired knows, an incorrect listing will remain monumentally wrong for a whole year.

The supervisors came up with many ideas for enriching the job. The first step was to identify the most competent employees, and then ask them, one by one, if they felt they could do error-free work, so that having others check the work would be pointless. Would they check their own work if no one else did it?

Yes, they said they could do error-free work. With this simple step the module dropped from 21 slices of clerical work to 14.

Next the supervisory family decided to take a really big step. In the case of the thinner books, they asked certain employees whether they would like to "own" their own books and perform all 14 remaining steps with no verification unless they themselves arranged it with other clerks—as good stenographers do when in doubt about a difficult piece of paperwork. Now the module included every step (except keytape, a minor one).

Then the supervisors turned their attention to a thick book, the Indianapolis directory, which requires many hands and heads. They simply assigned letters of the alphabet to individuals and let them complete all 14 steps for each block of letters.

In the past, new entries to all directories had moved from clerk to clerk; now all paperwork connected with an entry belonging to a clerk stayed with that clerk. For example, the clerk prepared the daily addenda and issued them to the information or directory assistance operators. The system became so efficient that most of the clerks who handled the smaller directories had charge of more than one.

Delimiting the module. In an interview one of the clerks said, "It's a book of my own." That is the way they felt about the books. Although not all modules are physically so distinct, the idea for a good module is usually there. Ideally, it is a slice of work that gives an employee a "thing of my own." At AT&T I have heard good modules described with pride in various ways:

- "A piece of turf" (especially a geographic responsibility).
- "My real estate" (by engineers responsible for a group of central offices).
- "Our cradle-to-grave modem line" (a vastly improved Western Electric switching-device production line).
- "Our mission impossible team" (a framemen's team, Long Lines Department).

The trouble with so much work processing is that no one is clearly responsible for a total unit that fails. In Indianapolis, by contrast, when a name in a directory is misspelled or omitted, the clerk knows where the responsibility lies.

Delimiting the module is not usually difficult when the tasks are in production, or at least physically defined. It is more difficult in service tasks, such as handling a telephone call. But modules make sense here, too, if the employee has been prepared for the work so that nobody else need be involved—in other words, when it is not necessary to say to the caller, "Let me connect you with my supervisor about that, please" or "May I give you our billing department, please?"

It is not always true that any one employee can handle a complete service. But our studies show that we consistently erred in forming the module; we tended to "underwhelm" employees. Eventually we learned that the worker can do more, especially as his or her experience builds. We do not have even one example from our business where job enrichment resulted in a *smaller* slice of work.

In defining modules that give each employee a natural area of responsibility, we try to accumulate horizontal slices of work until we have created (or recreated) one of these three entities for him or her:

1. A customer (usually someone outside the business).
2. A client (usually someone inside the business, helping the employee serve the customer).
3. A task (in the manufacturing end of the business, for example, where, ideally, individual employees produce complete items).

Any one of these three can make a meaningful slice of work. (In actuality, they are not separated; obviously, an employee can be working on a task for a *customer*.) Modules more difficult to differentiate are those in which the "wholeness" of the job is less clear—that is, control is not complete. They include cases where—

. . . the employee is merely one of many engaged in providing the ultimate service or item;

. . . the employee's customer is really the boss (or, worse yet, the boss's boss) who tells him what to do;

. . . the job is to help someone who tells the employee what is to be done.

While jobs like these are harder to enrich, it is worth trying.

Control of the module

As an employee gains experience, the supervisor should continue to turn over responsibility until the employee is handling the work completely. The reader may infer that supervisors are treating employees unequally. But it is not so; ultimately, they may all have the complete job if they can handle it. In the directory-compilation case cited— which was a typical assembly-line procedure, although the capital investment was low —the supervisors found that they could safely permit the employee to say when sales of advertisements in the yellow pages must stop if the ads were to reach the printer on time.

Employees of South Central Bell Telephone Company, who set their own cutoff dates for the New Orleans, Monroeville, and Shreveport phone books, consistently gave themselves less time than management had previously allowed. As a result, the sale of space in the yellow pages one year continued for three additional weeks, producing more than $100,000 in extra revenue.

But that was only one element in the total module and its control. The directory clerks talked *directly* to salesmen, to the printer, to supervisors in other departments about production problems, to service representatives, and to each other as the books moved through the production stages.

There are obvious risks on the supervisors' side as they give their jobs away, piece by piece, to selected employees. We have been through it enough to advise, "Don't worry." Be assured that supervisors who try it will say, as many in the Bell System have said, "Now, at last, I feel like a manager. Before I was merely chief clerk around here."

In other studies we have made, control has been handed by the supervisor to a person when the employee is given the authority to perform such tasks as these:

- Set credit ratings for customers.
- Ask for, and determine the size of, a deposit.
- Cut off service for nonpayment.
- Make his or her own budget, subject to negotiation.
- Perform work other than that on the order sheet after negotiating it with the customer.
- Reject a run or supply of material because of poor quality.
- Make free use of small tools or supplies within a budget negotiated with the supervisor.
- Talk to anyone at any organizational level when the employee's work is concerned.
- Call directly and negotiate for outside repairmen or suppliers (within the budget) to remedy a condition handicapping the employee's performance.

Feedback

Definition of the module and control of it are futile unless the results of the employee's effort are discernible. Moreover, knowledge of the results should go directly to where it will nurture motivation — that is, to the employee. People have a great capacity for mid-flight correction when they know where they stand.

One control responsibility given to excellent employees in AT&T studies is self-monitoring; it lets them record their own "qualities and quantities." For example, one employee who had only a grade-school education was taught to keep a quality control chart in which the two identical parts of a dry-reed switch were not to vary more than .005 from an ideal dimension. She found that for some reason too many switches were failing.

She proved that the trouble occurred when one reed that was off by .005 met another reed that was off by .005. The sum, .010, was too much in the combined component and it failed. On her own initiative, she recommended and saw to it that the machine dies were changed when the reeds being stamped out started to vary by .003 from the ideal. A total variance of .006 would not be too much, she reasoned. Thus the feedback she got showed her she was doing well at her job.

This example shows all three factors at work — the module, its control, and feedback. She and two men, a die maker and a machine operator, had the complete responsibility for producing each day more than 100,000 of these tiny parts, which are not unlike two paper matches, but much smaller. How can one make a life out of this? Well, they did. The six stamping machines and expensive photometric test equipment were "theirs." A forklift truck had been dedicated to them (no waiting for someone else to bring or remove supplies). They ordered rolls of wire for stamping machines when they estimated they would need it. They would ship a roll back when they had difficulty controlling it.

Compared with workers at a plant organized along traditional lines, with batches of the reeds moving from shop to shop, these three employees were producing at a fourfold rate. Such a minigroup, where each person plays a complementary part, is radically different psychologically from the traditional group of workers, where each is doing what the others do.

(In the future, when now undreamed-of computer capacities have been reached, management must improve its techniques of feeding performance results directly to the employee responsible. And preferably it should be done *before* the boss knows about it.)

IMPROVING THE SYSTEM

When a certain job in the Bell System is being enriched, we ask the supervisory family, "Who or what is the customer/client/task in this job?" Also, "How often can the module be improved?" And then, "How often can control or feedback be improved? Can we improve all three at once?"

These are good questions to ask in general. My comments at this stage of our knowledge must be impressionistic.

The modules of most jobs can be improved, we have concluded. Responsibilities or tasks that exist elsewhere in the shop or in some other shop or department need to be combined with the job under review. This horizontal loading is necessary until the base of the job is right. However, I have not yet seen a job whose base was too broad.

At levels higher than entrance grade, and especially in management positions, many responsibilities can be moved to lower grade levels, usually to the advantage of every job involved. This vertical loading is especially important in mature organizations.

In the Indianapolis directory office, 21 piece-meal tasks were combined into a single, meaningful, natural task. There are counterparts in other industries, such as the assembly of an entire dashboard of an automobile by two workers.

We have evidence that two jobs — such as the telephone installer's job and the telephone repairman's job — often can make one excellent "combinationman"'s job. But there are some jobs in which the work module is already a good one. One of these is the service representative, the highly trained clerk to whom a customer speaks when he wants to have a telephone installed, moved, or disconnected, or when he questions his telephone bill. This is sometimes a high-turnover job, and when a service representative quits because of work or task dissatisfaction, there goes $3,450 in training. In fact, much of the impetus for job enrichment came through efforts to reduce these costs.

In this instance the slice of work was well enough conceived; nevertheless, we obtained excellent results from the procedures of job enrichment. Improvements in the turnover situation were as great as 50%. Why? Because we could improve the control and feedback.

It should be recognized that moving the work module to a lower level is not the same as moving the control down. If the supervisor decides that a customer's account is too long overdue and tells the service representative what to do, then both the module and the control rest with the supervisor. When, under job enrichment procedures, the service representative makes the decision that a customer must be contacted, but checks it first with the supervisor, control remains in the supervisor's hands. Under full job enrichment, however, the service representative has control.

Exhibit I shows in schematic form the steps to be taken when improving a job. To increase control, responsibility must be obtained from higher levels; I have yet to see an instance where control is moved upward to enrich a job. It must be acknowledged, however, that not every employee is ready to handle more control. That is especially true of new employees.

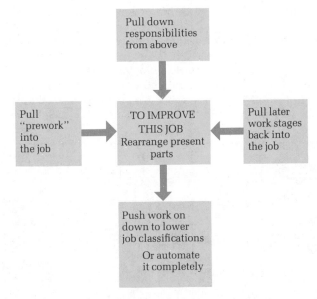

Exhibit I   Steps in Improving a Job

Moreover, changing the control of a job is more threatening to supervisors than is changing the module. In rejecting a job enrichment proposal, one department head said to us, "When you have this thing proved 100%, let me know and we'll try it."

As far as feedback is concerned, it is usually improvable, but not until the module and control of it are in top condition. If the supervisory family cannot come up with good ways for telling the employee how he or she is doing, the problem lies almost surely in a bad module. That is, the employee's work is submerged in a total unit and he or she has no distinct customer/client/task.

When the module is right, you get feedback "for free"; it comes directly from the customer/client/task. During the learning period, however, the supervisor or teacher should provide the feedback.

When supervisors use the performance of all employees as a goad to individual employees, they thwart the internalization of motivation that job enrichment strives for. An exception is the small group of mutually supporting, complementary workers, but even in this case each individual needs knowledge of his or her own results.

These generalizations cannot be said to be based on an unbiased sample of all jobs in all locations. Usually, the study or project locations were not in deep trouble, nor were they the best operating units. The units in deep trouble cannot stand still long enough to figure out what is wrong, and the top performers need no help. Therefore, the hard-nosed, scientifically trained manager can rightfully say that the jury is still out as to whether job enrichment can help in all work situations. But it has helped repeatedly and consistently on many jobs in the Bell System.

JOB 'NESTING'

Having established to its satisfaction that job enrichment works, management at AT&T is studying ways to go beyond the enriching of individual jobs. A technique that offers great promise is that of "nesting" several jobs to improve morale and upgrade performance.

By way of illustration I shall describe how a family of supervisors of service representatives in a unit of Southwestern Bell Telephone Company improved its service indexes, productivity, collection of overdue bills, and virtually every other index of performance. In two years they moved their Ferguson District (adjacent to St. Louis) from near the bottom to near the top in results among all districts in the St Louis area.

Before the job enrichment effort started, the service representatives' office was laid out as it appears in *Exhibit II*. The exhibit shows their desks in the standard, in-line arrangement fronted by the desks of their supervisors, who exercised close control of the employees.

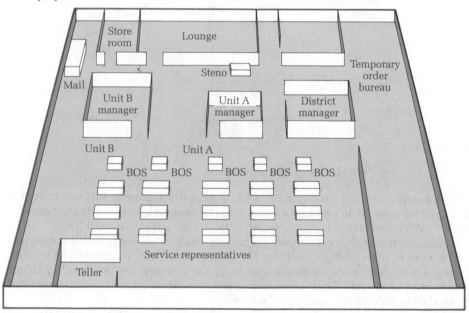

BOS – Business office supervisor

Exhibit II   Ferguson District Service Representatives Office Layout
Before Job Enrichment

As part of the total job enrichment effort, each service rep group was given a geographical locality of its own, with a set of customers to take care of, rather than just "the next customer who calls in" from anywhere in the district. Some service reps – most of them more experienced – were detached to form a unit handling only the businesses in the district.

Then the service representatives and their business office supervisors (BOS) were moved to form a "wagon train" layout. As *Exhibit III* shows, they were gathered into a more-or-less circular shape and were no longer directly facing the desks of the business office supervisors and unit managers. (The office of the district manager was further removed too.)

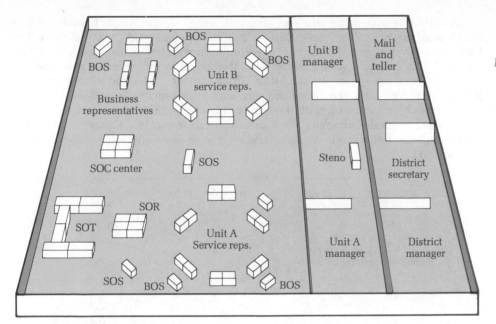

BOS – Business office supervisor

SOS – Service order supervisor
SOC – Service order control
SOR – Service order reviewers
SOT – Service order typists

Exhibit III   Service Representatives Office Layout After
Job Enrichment Program Was Implemented

Now all was going well with the service representatives' job, but another function in the room was in trouble. This was the entry-level job of service order typist. These typists transmit the orders to the telephone installers and the billing and other departments. They and the service order reviewers—a higher-classification job—had been located previously in a separate room that was soundproofed and air-conditioned because the TWX machines they used were noisy and hot. When its equipment was converted to the silent, computer-operated cathode ray tubes (CRTs), the unit was moved to a corner of the service reps' room (see *Exhibit III*).

But six of the eight typists quit in a matter of months after the move. Meanwhile, the percentage of service orders typed "on time" fell below 50%, then below 40%.

The reasons given by the six typists who quit were varied, but all appeared to be rationalizations. The managers who looked at the situation, and at the $25,000 investment in the layout, could see that the feeling of physical isolation and the feeling of having no "thing" of their own were doubtless the real prime factors. As the arrangement existed, any service order typist could be called on to type an order for any service representative. On its face, this seems logical; but we have learned that an employee who belongs to everybody belongs to nobody.

An instantly acceptable idea was broached: assign certain typists to each service rep team serving a locality. "And while we're at it," someone said, "why not move the CRTs right into the group? Let's have a wagon train with the women and kids in the middle." This was done (over the protest of the budget control officer, I should add).

The new layout appears in *Exhibit IV*. Three persons are located in the station in the middle of each unit. The distinction between service order typist and service order reviewer has been abolished, with the former upgraded to the scale of the latter. (Lack of space has precluded arranging the business customer unit in the same wagon-train fashion. But that unit's service order review and typing desks are close to the representatives' desks.)

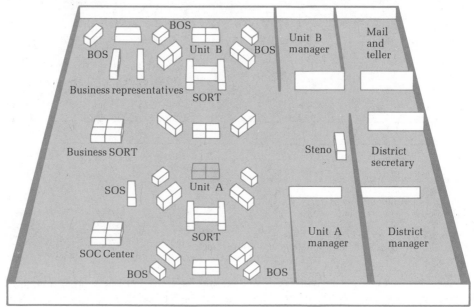

SORT: Service order review and typing

Exhibit IV Office Layout After Service Order
Typists Were Nested

Before the changes were started, processing a service request involved ten steps — and sometimes as many persons — not counting implementation of the order in the Plant Department. Now the procedure is thought of in terms of people, and only three touch a service order on its way through the office. (See *Exhibit V*.) At this writing, the Ferguson managers hope to eliminate even the service order completion clerk as a specialized position.

Has the new arrangement worked? Just before the typists moved into the wagon train, they were issuing only 27% of the orders on time. Within 30 days after the switch to assigned responsibility, 90% of the orders were going out on time. Half a year later, in one particular month, the figure even reached 100%.

These results were obtained with a 21% jump in work load — comparing a typical quarter after "nesting" with one before — being performed with a net drop of 22 worker-

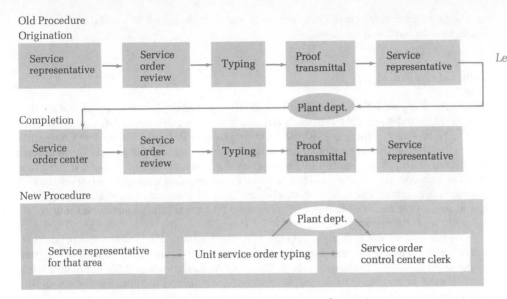

Exhibit V Old and New Processing Procedures in Request-for-Service Department

weeks during the quarter. On a yearly basis it is entirely reasonable to expect the elimination of 88 weeks of unnecessary work (conservatively, $1\frac{1}{2}$ full-time employees). Unneeded messenger service has been dispensed with, and one of two service order supervisor positions has been eliminated. The entire cost has been recovered already.

The service order accuracy measurement, so important in computerization, has already attained the stringent objectives set by the employees themselves, which exceeded the level supervisors would have set. Why are there fewer errors? Because now employees can lean across the area and talk to each other about a service order with a problem or handwriting that is unclear. During the course of a year this will probably eliminate the hand preparation of a thousand "query" slips, with a thousand written replies, in this one district.

And what of the human situation? When on-time order issuance was at its ebb, a supervisor suggested having a picnic for the service representatives and the typists. They did, but not a single typist showed up. Later, when the on-time order rate had climbed over 90%, I remarked, "Now's the time for another picnic." To which the supervisor replied facetiously, "Now we don't need a picnic!"

The turnover among typists for job reasons has virtually ceased. Some are asking now for the job of service representative, which is more demanding, more skilled, and better paid. Now, when the CRTs or the computer is shut down for some reason, or if the service order typist runs out of work, supervisors report that typists voluntarily help the service reps with filing and other matters. They are soaking up information about the higher-rated jobs. These occurrences did not happen when the typists were 100 feet away; then they just sat doing nothing when the work flow ceased. (Because of this two-way flow of information, incidentally, training time for the job of service representative may drop as much as 50%.)

As the state general manager remarked when the results were first reported, "This is a fantastic performance. It's not enough to enrich just one job in a situation. We must learn how to put them together.''

Different Configuration

While the Ferguson District supervisory family was making a minigroup out of the service reps and their CRT typists, a strikingly different minigroup was in formation in the Northern Virginia Area of the Chesapeake and Potomac Telephone Company. There the family hit on the idea of funneling to selected order typists only those orders connected with a given central office, such as the Lewinsville frame. Soon the typists and the framemen—those who actually make the changes as a result of service orders—became acquainted. The typists even visited "their" framerooms. Now some questions could be quickly resolved that previously called for formal interdepartmental interrogations through supervisors.

At the end of the first eight months of 1972, these 9 CRT typists were producing service order pages at a rate one third higher than the 51 service order typists in the comparison group. The absence rate in the experimental unit was 0.6% compared with 2.5% for the others, and the errors per 100 orders amounted to 2.9 as against 4.6 in the comparison group.

The flow of service orders is from (a) service rep to (b) service order typist to (c) the frameroom. The Ferguson District enjoyed success when it linked (a) and (b), while productivity for the Lewinsville frame improved when (b) and (c) were linked. Obviously, the next step is to link (a), (b), and (c). We are now selecting trial locations to test this larger nesting approach.

LESSONS LEARNED

In summary fashion, at the end of seven years of effort to improve the work itself, it is fair to say that:

• Enriching existing jobs pays off. To give an extreme example, consider the fact that Illinois Bell Telephone Company's directory compilation effort reduced the work force from 120 persons to 74. Enriching the job started a series of moves; it was not the only ingredient, but it was the precipitating one.

• Job enrichment requires a big change in managerial style. It calls for increasing modules, moving control downward, and dreaming up new feedback ideas. There is nothing easy about a successful job enrichment effort.

• The nesting or configuring of related tasks—we call it "work organization"—may be the next big step forward after the enrichment of single jobs in the proper utilization of human beings.

It seems to produce a multiplier effect rather than merely a simple sum. In the Ferguson District case the job modules were not changed; the service representatives were not asked to type their own orders on the cathode ray tubes, nor were the typists asked to take over the duties of the service representatives. The results came from enriching other aspects (control and feedback) and, more important, from laying out the work area differently to facilitate interaction among responsible people.

• While continuing job enrichment efforts, it is important not to neglect "maintenance" factors. In extending our work with job nesting, for example, we plan to experiment with "office landscaping," so called. The furniture, dividers, planters, and acoustical treatment, all must add to the feeling of work dedication. By this I mean we will dedicate site, equipment, and jobs to the employees, with the expectation that they will find it easier to dedicate themselves to customer/client/task. Especially in new installations, this total work environmental approach seems a good idea for experimentation. We will not be doing it merely to offset pain or boredom in work. The aim is to facilitate work.

• A "pool" of employees with one job (typing pool, reproduction pool, calculating pool, and so on) is at the opposite extreme from the team or "minigroup" which I have described. A minigroup is a set of mutually supporting employees, each of whom has a meaningful module or part in meeting the needs of customer/client/task. What is "meaningful" is, like a love affair, in the eye of the beholder; at this stage, we have difficulty in describing it further.

A minigroup can have several service representatives or typists; one of each is not basic to the idea. The purpose is to set up a group of employees so that a natural, mutual dependence can grow in providing a service or finishing a task. It marks the end of processing from person to person or group to group, in separate locations or departments and with many different supervisors.

The minigroup concept, however, still leaves room for specialists. In certain Scandinavian auto plants, for example, one or two specialists fabricate the entire assembly of the exhaust pollution control system or the electrical system. Eventually, a group of workers may turn out a whole engine. In the United States, Chrysler has given similar trial efforts a high priority. The idea is to fix authority at the lowest level possible.

• Experience to date indicates that unions welcome the kind of effort described in our studies. Trouble can be expected, of course, if the economics of increases in productivity are not shared equitably. In the majority of cases, the economics can be handled even under existing contracts, since they usually permit establishment of new jobs and appropriate wage grades between dates of contract negotiation.

An employee who takes the entire responsibility for preparing a whole telephone directory, for example, ought to be paid more, although a new clerical rating must be established. Job enrichment is not in lieu of cash; good jobs and good maintenance are two sides of the same coin.

• New technology, such as the cathode ray tube, should enable us to break free of old work arrangements. When the Ferguson District service order typists were using the TWX machines, nesting their jobs was impractical because the equipment would have driven everybody to distraction. Installation of the high-technology CRTs gave the planners the opportunity to move together those employees whose modules of work were naturally related. This opportunity was at first overlooked.

Everyone accepts the obvious notion that new technology can and must eliminate dumb-dumb jobs. However, it probably creates more, rather than fewer, fragments of work. Managers should observe the new module and the work organization of the modules. This effort calls for new knowledge and skills, such as laying out work so attractively that the average employee will stay longer and work more effectively than under the previous arrangement.

Moreover, technology tends to make human beings adjuncts of machines. As we move toward computerized production of all listings in the white pages of the phone books, for example, the risk of an employee's losing "his" or "her" own directories is very great indeed. (Two AT&T companies, South Central Bell and Pacific Northwest Bell, are at this stage, and we must be certain the planned changes do not undermine jobs.) Making sure that machines remain the adjunct of human beings is a frontier problem which few managers have yet grappled with.

• Managers in mature organizations are likely to have difficulty convincing another department to make pilot runs of any new kind of work organization, especially one that will cause the department to lose people, budget, or size. Individual job enrichment does not often get into interdepartmental tangles, but the nesting of jobs will almost surely create problems of autonomy. This will call for real leadership.

• When the work is right, employee attitudes are right. That is the job enrichment strategy—get the work right.

Job Redesign on the Assembly Line: Farewell to Blue-Collar Blues?

William F. Dowling

The authors of the much-quoted, much-praised, and much-criticized HEW report *Work in America* wound up their study with a rhetorical bang: "Albert Camus wrote that 'without work life goes rotten. But when work is soulless, life stifles and dies.' Our analysis of work in America leads to much the same conclusion: Because work is central to the lives of so many Americans, either the absence of work or employment in meaningless work is creating an increasingly intolerable situation."

Most who argue that the rhetoric in the report is exaggerated and the thesis overstated would exempt the assembly line, particularly the auto assembly line, from their dissent. The auto assembly line epitomizes the conditions that contribute to employee dissatisfaction: fractionation of work into meaningless activities, with each activity repeated several hundred times each workday, and with the employees having little or no control over work pace or any other aspect of working conditions.

Two generations of social scientists have documented the discontent of auto workers with their jobs. Yet the basic production process hasn't changed since Ford's first Highland Park assembly plant in 1913. We read a lot about the accelerating pace of technology: Here's a technology that's stood still for 60 years despite the discontent.

The social explanations are easy. The automakers—when they thought about the problem at all—dismissed it. The economic advantages of the assembly line seemingly outweighed any possible social costs—including the high wages, part of which might properly be considered discontentment pay. In short, the cash register rang more clearly than the gripes.

Recently, the situation has changed. The advent of an adversary youth culture in the United States, the rising educational levels, with a concomitant increase in employee expectations of the job, the expansion of job opportunities for all but the least skilled and the most disaffected, have raised the level of discontent. One of the big three automakers, for example, now has an annual turnover rate of close to 40 percent. G.M.'s famous Lordstown Vega plant, the latest triumph of production engineering—with the average time per job activity pared to 36 seconds and workers facing a new Vega component 800 times in each eight-hour shift—has been plagued with strikes, official and wildcat, slowdowns, and sabotage. At times, the line has shut down during the second half of the day to remedy the defects that emerged from the line during the first half.

Reprinted by permission of the publisher from *Organizational Dynamics*, Autumn 1973, © 1973 by AMACOM, a division of American Management Associations.

IS JOB REDESIGN THE ANSWER?

Much has been written about the two automobile plants in Sweden, Volvo and Saab-Scania, that have practiced job redesign of the assembly line on a large scale. The results, variously reported, have appeared in the world press. Also receiving wide press coverage have been the efforts of Philips N.V. in The Netherlands to redesign jobs on the lines assembling black-and-white and color TV sets. So much for instant history!

We visited the three companies during a recent trip to Europe and shall attempt to evaluate and compare them. But first a caveat: We eschew chic terms, such as job enrichment, autonomy, job rotation, and employee participation, in favor of the drabber job redesign for several reasons. First, the other terms have taken on emotional connotations; they've become the rallying ground for true believers who view them as a partial answer or panacea to the problem of employee alienation in an industrial society. The term job redesign, by contrast, has no glamor and no followers. Second, most efforts at job redesign, certainly the three we're going to write about, include elements of job enrichment, autonomy, job rotation, and employee participation in varying degrees at different times, but none of the competing terms affords a sufficiently large umbrella to cover what's happened and what's planned in the three organizations. Last, true believers passionately define their faiths differently; using any of the other terms as central would involve us in tiresome and trivial questions of definition. Hence, our choice of job redesign. It's comprehensive, and noncontroversial. . . .

JOB REDESIGN AT PHILIPS

First Generation, 1960–1965

We start with Philips because, of our three companies, Philips is the pioneer; its experience with job redesign goes back to 1960. We use the term first generation, second generation, and so on to mark the stages of the Philips program because this is Philips' terminology — obviously appropriated from computer lingo.

In the first experiment, concern was more with the deficiencies of long assembly lines than it was with improving job satisfaction. Breaking up the existing line of 104 workers into five shorter assembly lines, installing buffer stocks of components between groups, and placing inspectors at the end of each group instead of the whole assembly line reduced waiting times by 55 percent, improved feedback, and improved the balance of the system — various short chains being stronger than one long chain because the line can never travel faster than the worker with the longest average time per operation.

Almost incidentally, morale also improved: Only 29 percent of the workers on the assembly line responded positively to the survey question "I like doing my job," versus a 51 percent positive response from the test line. Furthermore, when the test line was restructured with half the number of workers, so that each one performed twice the original cycle and workplaces alternated with empty seats, production flowed more smoothly and quality improved. Dr. H. G. Van Beek, a psychologist on the original study team, drew a dual lesson from the experiment: "From the point of view of production, the long line is very vulnerable; from the point of view of morale — in the sense of job satisfaction — downright bad."

Subsequent experiments in several plants involved rotating workers between different jobs on the assembly line, enriching jobs by having employees set their own pace within overall production standards, and enlarging them by making employees responsible for inspecting their own work. Most of the gains from the experiments Philips entered under the heading of "social profit." In other words, morale and job satisfaction improved but bread-and-butter items such as productivity and scrap showed little improvement.

Second Generation, 1965–1968

The key feature of the second phase, a program that involved a few thousand employees scattered over 30 different locations, was the abolition of foremen. With supervisors' enlarged span of control, the men on the assembly line acquired autonomy and more control over their jobs. Even an authoritarian supervisor would find that he was spread too thin to exercise the same amount of control as the previous foreman had.

Once again, the bulk of the profits were social. The bill for waste and repairs dropped slightly, and, of course, Philips pocketed the money that had been paid to the foremen. Otherwise, the gains to Philips were nonmonetary.

Third Phase, 1968

This phase, one that is ongoing, has focused on giving various groups of seven or eight employees total responsibility for assembling either black-and-white TV sets or color selectors for color TV sets, a task equivalent in complexity to assembling a black-and-white set from scratch.

We want to emphasize the word *total*: The group responsible for assembling the black-and-white sets, for example, not only performs the entire assembling task but also deals directly with staff groups such as procurement, quality, and stores, with no supervisor or foreman to act as intermediary or expediter. If something is needed from another department or something goes wrong that requires the services of another department, it's the group's responsibility to deal with the department.

"This third phase has had its problems," concedes Den Hertog, staff psychologist. "Typically, it's taken about six months for the groups to shake down—adjust to the increased pressures and responsibilities." Establishing effective relationships with unfamiliar higher-status employees in staff departments has proved the biggest single problem. On the other hand, anyone in an experimental group can opt out at any time —an option that has yet to be taken up. Of course, it may be the satisfaction of being a member of a select group, even physically separated from other work groups by a wall of green shrubbery, that accounts for no employee's having made a switch. Hertog, however, believes that the increase in intrinsic job satisfactions has more than compensated for any pains of adjustments and accounts for the lack of turnover.

What about results? What's the measurable impact of the program? There have been additional costs, such as increased training costs; more important, small, autonomous groups require new and smaller machines to perform traditional assembly line tasks. On the other hand, there have been measurable benefits. Overall, production costs in manhours have dropped 10 percent, while waiting times have decreased and quality levels have increased by smaller but still significant amounts.

To restructure work and redesign jobs in ways that increase employee job satisfaction at no net cost to the company over the long run is all that Philips, as a matter of policy, requires of such programs. Short-term deficits caused by purchases of new equipment are something it's prepared to live with.

Where is Philips going from here? Obviously, the potential for effective job redesign is large. With 90,000 workers in 60 plants, Philips has barely scratched the surface. Part of the answer would seem to lie in the future strength of the movement for employee participation and power equalization that is particularly strong in Norway and Sweden and is gaining adherents in The Netherlands.

At Philips the primary response has been the establishment of worker consultation in some 20 different departments. Worker consultation is just what it sounds like: Employees meet with first- and second-level supervision to discuss problems of joint interest. Worker consultation exists at different levels in different departments, stresses Hertog, who attributes the difference to the level of maturity of the group itself: "In some groups we're still at the flower pot phase, talking about what should be done to improve meals in the cafeteria, while at other extremes we have departments where we have left the selection of a new supervisor for the group up to the workers."

It's significant that those groups who have considered the question of job redesign consistently have criticized Philips for not doing more of it. The expansion of job redesign, in part, would seem to depend on the expansion of work consultation and the pressures exerted by the workers themselves to get job redesign extended.

JOB REDESIGN AT SAAB-SCANIA

To claim that Saab-Scania has abolished the auto assembly line would misrepresent the facts. Saab-Scania, or to speak more precisely, the Scania Division, has instituted small-group assembly of auto engines—not the whole car—in its new engine plant. Even so, this effort is limited to 50 employees in a plant with a workforce of approximately 300, most of whom monitor automatic transfer machines that perform various machining tasks. (See Figure 1.) There's only one manual loading operation in the entire machining process.

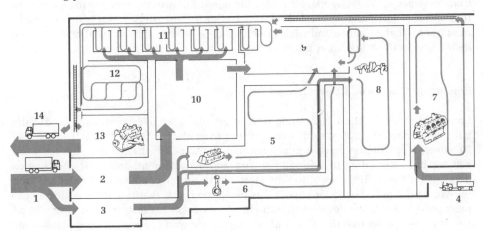

1. Goods reception	8. Machining crankshafts
2. Arrival inspection purchased factory parts	9. Pre-assembly
3. Raw material store	10. Parts store
4. Engine blocks (material) from own foundry	11. Group assembly
5. Machining cylinder heads	12. Engine testing
6. Machining connecting rods	13. Ready stock
7. Machining engine blocks	14. Engines to Trollhättan and Uusikaupunki

Figure 1 Diagram of Engine Plant, Saab-Scania

More important, the humanization of the auto assembly line is the most dramatic single instance in a series starting in 1969 that Palle Berggen, the head of the industrial engineering department, characterized as "one phase in the development of enhanced industrial democracy."

We won't quarrel with his description, although we think he succumbed to the rhetoric of public relations. Scania, in its actions from 1969 on, has responded to some problems for which the best word is horrendous. Employee turnover was running around 45 percent annually, and in the auto assembly plant, 70 percent. Absenteeism was also extraordinary—close to 20 percent. Under such conditions, the maintenance of an even flow of production, something crucial in an integrated work system like Scania's, presented insuperable problems. Also, it was increasingly difficult to fill jobs on the shop floor at all. A survey taken in 1969 indicates what Scania was up against: Only four out of 100 students graduating from high school in Sweden indicated their willingness to take a rank-and-file factory job. In consequence, Scania became heavily dependent on foreign workers—58 percent of the current workforce are non-Swedes. This in turn created problems, both expected and otherwise—among the former problems of training and communications, among the latter, an epidemic of wildcat strikes, previously unknown in Sweden, that largely resulted from the manipulation by extreme left elements of foreign workers ignorant of the tradition among Swedish employees of almost total reliance upon the strong trade union organization to protect their interests.

Any response to these conditions *had* to have as its number one objective the maintenance of productivity. To assert anything else is window dressing—unconvincing as well as unnecessary. No one can fault an industrial organization for undertaking a program whose primary goal is the maintenance of productivity.

This is not to deny that one byproduct of the program has been "enhanced industrial democracy." What happened is that the pursuit of productivity led to an examination of the conditions that created job satisfactions; these, in turn, suggested the series of actions "that enhance industrial democracy"—a term subject to almost as many definitions as there are interpreters.

Production Groups and Development Groups

Employee representation is nothing new at Scania. Like every company in Sweden with more than 50 employees, it's had an employee-elected Works Council since 1949. However, these bodies have no decision-making function; their role is limited to receiving and responding to information from top management, and their effectiveness depends on the willingness of top management to seriously consider suggestions from the Works Council. David Jenkins, in his recent book *Job Power*, tells of asking a company president if he had ever been influenced by worker suggestions. His reply: "Well, yes. We were going to build a new plant and we showed the workers the plans at one of the meetings. They objected very much to the fact that the plant would have no windows. So we changed the plans and had some windows put in. It doesn't cost much more and, actually, the building looks better. And the workers feel better."

The production and development groups initiated in the truck chassis assembly plant in 1969, by contrast, have real decision-making power. Production groups of five to 12 workers with related job duties decide among themselves how they will do their jobs, within the quality and production standards defined by higher management; they can rotate job assignments—do a smaller or larger part of the overall task. At the same time, the jobs of all members of the production group were enlarged by making them jointly responsible for simple service and maintenance activities, housekeeping, and quality control in their work area, duties formerly performed by staff personnel.

Development groups, a parallel innovation, consist of foremen, industrial engineers, and two representatives of one or more production groups whose function is to consider ideas for improving work methods and working conditions. Representatives of the production groups are rotated in a way that guarantees that every member of a production group will serve each year on a development group.

Employee reception of the production group has been mixed but largely positive. The results appear to be favorable, although Scania has done little or nothing to measure them quantitatively. However, impressions have been sufficiently favorable so that within four years production and development groups have expanded to include 2,200 out of the 3,600 employees in the main plant at Södertälje, and within the year they will be extended throughout the company.

Work Design in the Engine Plant

The four machine lines for the components in the engine factory — the cylinder block, the cylinder head, the connecting rod, and the crankshaft — mainly consist of transfer machines manned or monitored by individual operations. Group assembly is restricted to the seven final assembly stations, each of which contains a team of fitters that assemble an entire engine.

Team members divide the work among themselves; they may decide to do one-third of the assembly on each engine — a ten-minute chore — or follow the engine around the bay and assemble the entire engine — a 30-minute undertaking. In fact, only a minority prefer to do the total assembly job. (Using traditional assembly line methods, each operation would have taken 1.8 minutes.) The team also decides its own work pace, and the number and duration of work breaks within the overall requirement of assembling 470 engines in each ten-day period, a specification that allows them a good deal of flexibility in their pacing. Incidentally, over half the employees in the engine plant are women, while the assembly teams are over 80 percent female. We personally saw four assembly teams with only a single man in the lot.

Benefits and Costs

Kaj Holmelius, who is responsible for planning and coordination of the production engineering staff, ticked off the principal credits and debits, along with a few gray areas in which it would be premature to estimate results. On the plus side, he cited the following:

(1) Group assembly has increased the flexibility of the plant, making it easier to adjust to heavy absenteeism.

(2) The group assembly concept is responsible for a lower balancing loss due to a longer station time.

(3) Less money is invested in assembly tools. Even allowing for the fact that you have to buy six or seven times as many tools, the simpler tools make for a smaller overall cost.

(4) Quality has definitely improved, although by how much it's hard to estimate.

(5) Productivity is higher than it would have been with the conventional assembly line — although once more, there is no proof. Lower production speed per engine, because it's not economical to use some very expensive automatic tools, is outweighed by higher quality and reduced turnover.

(6) Employee attitudes have improved, although there have been no elaborate surveys taken. To Holmelius the best indication of job satisfaction is that it's impossible to fill all the requests to transfer from other parts of the plant to the assembly teams.

On the negative side, in addition to the reduced production speed, group assembly takes up considerably more space than the conventional assembly line.

In the neutral corner is the impact on absenteeism and turnover. Absenteeism is actually higher in the engine plant—18 percent versus 15 percent for overall plant operations at Södertälje. However, Holmelius attributes the difference to the fact that the engine plant employs a heavier percentage of women. As for turnover, with the plant in operation for a little more than a year, it's too early to tell. Because of an economic slowdown, turnover generally is down from the 45 percent crisis level of 1969 to 20 percent, and it's Holmelius' belief that turnover in the assembly teams will prove significantly lower than average.

WHAT'S THE FUTURE OF GROUP ASSEMBLY?

It's easier to point out the directions in which Scania does *not* plan to extend group assembly. An experiment with having employees assemble an entire truck diesel engine —a six-hour undertaking involving 1,500 parts—was abandoned at the employees' request; they couldn't keep track of all the parts. Similarly, group assembly wouldn't work with the body of the trucks—truck bodies are too complex, and group assembly would require twice the space currently needed. The moot question at the moment is car assembly. So far, group assembly has been applied only to assembling doors. We suspect that in any decision, economic calculations will predominate, including, of course, the inherently fuzzy calculation about the economic value of job satisfaction.

JOB REDESIGN AT VOLVO

Job redesign at Volvo began, almost accidentally, in the upholstery shop of the car assembly plant during the mid-1960s, but a companywide effort had to wait until 1969, when Volvo faced the same problems that plagued Scania—wildcat strikes, absenteeism, and turnover that were getting out of hand and an increasing dependence on foreign workers. Turnover was over 40 percent annually; absenteeism was running 20 to 25 percent, and close to 45 percent of the employees of the car assembly plant were non-Swedes. One other event in 1971 made a difference: Volvo acquired a young, hard-driving new managing director, Pehr Gyllenhammar, who developed a keen interest in the new methods of work organization.

Ingvar Barrby, head of the upholstery department, started job redesign by persuading production management to experiment with job rotation along the lines he had read about in Norway. The overwhelmingly female workforce complained frequently about the inequity of the various jobs involved in assembling car seats; some jobs were easier than others, while still others were more comfortable and less strenuous, and so on. To equalize the tasks, Barrby divided the job into 13 different operations and rotated the employees among tasks that were relatively arduous and those that were relatively comfortable. Jealousy and bickering among employees disappeared: First, jobs were no longer inequitable; second, employees perceived that they had exaggerated the differences between jobs anyway—the grass-is-greener syndrome. More important, turnover that had been running 35 percent quickly fell to 15 percent, a gain that has been maintained over the years.

Job Alternation and "Multiple Balances"

Volvo uses these phrases instead of the more commonly used job rotation and job enrichment, but the concepts are the same. In job alternation or job rotation, the employee changes jobs once or several times daily, depending on the nature of the work in his group. Take Line IV A, for example, whose function is to do the external and internal sealing and insulation of car bodies. Because internal sealing is such uncomfortable work — employees work in cramped positions inside the car body — the work is alternated every other hour. The remaining jobs are rotated daily.

"Multiple balances" is our old friend, job enrichment, under another name. One example involves the overhead line where the group follows the same body for seven or eight stations along the line for a total period of 20 minutes — seven or eight times the length of the average job cycle.

Not all employees have had their jobs rotated or enriched — only 1,500 out of 7,000 in the car assembly at Torslanda are affected by the program. Because participation is strictly voluntary, the figures at first glance seem to indicate a massive show of disinterest on the part of Volvo employees. Not so. True, some employees prefer their jobs the way they are. The bigger problem is that Volvo has, to date, lacked the technical resources to closely scrutinize many jobs to determine whether and how they can be enlarged or enriched, or it has scrutinized them and determined that it isn't economically feasible to enlarge or enrich them. A company spokesman gave the job of coating under the car body to prevent rust as an example of a thoroughly unpleasant job that so far has defied redesign.

Production Teams at Volvo Lundbyverken

In the truck assembly plant at Lundbyverken, Volvo has carried job redesign several steps further, with production teams who, in form and function, roughly duplicate the production groups previously described at Scania. The production team, a group of five to 12 men with a common work assignment, elects its own chargehand, schedules its own output within the standards set by higher management, distributes work among its members, and is responsible for its own quality control. In these teams, group piecework replaces individual piecework and everyone earns the same amount, with the exception of the chargehand. Currently, there are 23 production teams involving 100 out of the plant's 1,200 employees. Plans call for the gradual extension of the production team approach to cover most, if not all, of the factory workforce.

The Box Score at Volvo

Have the various forms of job redesign, job rotation, job enrichment, and production teams paid off for Volvo? If so, what forms have the payoffs taken? Anything we can measure or monetize? Or are we reduced to subjective impressions and interesting although iffy conjectures about the relationship between factors such as increased job satisfaction and reduced turnover?

The two plants deserve separate consideration: Absenteeism and turnover traditionally have been lower at the truck assembly plant than at the car assembly plant. The jobs are inherently more complex and interesting—even before job enrichment, some individual jobs took up to half an hour. The workers, in turn, are more highly skilled and tend to regard themselves as apart from and above the rank-and-file auto worker. They see themselves more as junior engineers. Within this context, it's still true that the introduction of production teams has led to further improvement: less labor turnover, less absenteeism, an improvement in quality, and fewer final adjustments.

At the auto assembly plant the picture isn't clear. Turnover is down from 40 to 25 percent. However, an economic slowdown undoubtedly accounts for some of the decline, while other actions unrelated to job redesign may account for part of the remainder. When Volvo surveyed its employees to probe for the causes of turnover and absenteeism, most of the causes revealed were external—problems with housing, child care, long distances traveling to the plant, and so on. Volvo responded with a series of actions to alleviate these causes, such as extending the bus fleet, together with the community, to transport employees, loaning money to employees to purchase apartments at very favorable rates of interest, putting pressure on the community to expand day care centers, and so on. Such measures presumably contributed to the decline of turnover. Nevertheless, Gyllenhammar is convinced that "we can see a correlation between increased motivation, increased satisfaction on the job, and a decrease in the turnover of labor." Absenteeism is a sadly different picture: It's double what it was five years ago, a condition that Gyllenhammar attributes to legislation enabling workers to stay off the job at practically no cost to themselves.

As for output in that part of the auto assembly plant covered by job enrichment or job enlargement, there was no measurable improvement. Quality, on balance, has improved, and the feeling is that improved quality and decreased turnover had more than covered the costs of installing the program.

The Future of Job Redesign at Volvo

Despite the relatively ambiguous success of Volvo's job redesign efforts, whatever Volvo has done in the past is a pale prologue to its future plans. In about nine months, Volvo's new auto assembly plant at Kalmar will go on stream. And, for once, that overworked term "revolutionary" would seem justified.

Physically, the plant is remarkable. Gyllenhammar describes it as "shaped like a star and on each point of the star you have a work group finishing a big share of the whole automobile—for example, the electrical system or the safety system or the interior." Assembly work takes place along the outer walls, while component parts are stored in the center of the building. Architecturally, the building has been designed to preserve the atmosphere of a small workshop in a large factory, with each work team having its own entrance, dressing room, rest room, and so on. Each team is even physically shielded from a view of the other teams.

Each work team, of 15 to 25 men, will distribute the work among themselves and determine their own work rhythm, subject to the requirement of meeting production standards. If the team decides to drive hard in the morning and loaf in the afternoon, the decision is theirs to make. As with production teams in the truck assembly plant, the team will choose its own boss, and deselect him if he turns out poorly.

The new plant will cost about 10 percent more—some 10 million Swedish kroner —than a comparable conventional auto assembly plant. Time alone will tell whether the extra investment will be justified by the decreased turnover, improved quality, and even reduced absenteeism that its designers confidently expect at the new facility. In announcing the plan for the new factory, Gyllenhammar's economic objectives were modest enough, his social objectives more ambitious. "A way must be found to create a workplace that meets the needs of the modern working man for a sense of purpose and satisfaction in his daily work. A way must be found of attaining this goal without an adverse effect on productivity." With luck, he may achieve both.

Questions for Discussion

1. In what important ways does the problem of "macro organization design" differ from the problem of "micro organization design"? (The first of these design problems was discussed in Chapter 6.)

2. Explain why automation of the physical production machinery at a given job location necessitates redesign of individual jobs and work groups.

3. One of the principal differences in the kibbutz form of work group design and the work designs now being used by business corporations in the United States is in the manner the *rewards* (monetary wages and salaries) are allocated. In the kibbutz, a person's pay is determined by his/her need, not by how much work he or she performs or how much he or she contributes to production. The opposite is true in most U.S. corporations. What advantages do you see in the kibbutz arrangement? What disadvantages?

4. What do you believe are the two most important reasons why the governments of the U.S., Germany, Norway, and Sweden have studied and supported projects to redesign jobs?

5. Recall the example of the large automotive repair agency which might enlarge jobs by having one mechanic work on *both* brakes *and* spark plugs. This would contrast with another design for large agencies where one mechanic works in the brake department and another in the ignition department. What advantages might the company derive from job enrichment or enlargement? What disadvantages?

6. Compare the motivational effects of job enrichment on the "average" human being with the motivational effects of job enlargement. Are they similar or dissimilar?

7. Illustrate (using the stockholder correspondent design by Herzberg) *why* job enrichment might result in greater feelings of responsibility by the worker—responsibility to those outside the organization who are dependent on the organization for goods and services.

8. Illustrate this same feeling of responsibility—i.e., in Question 7—in the case of the coal mining workers in the Tavistock study.

9. Why is the autonomous work group design sometimes more feasible in high technology industries (which require large numbers of people, a great variety of job specializations, and large numbers of physical parts to be incorporated in the final product)?

10. Whether or not job redesign increases the satisfaction of human beings at work depends in part on forces *outside* the firm, in the broader cultural context of the organization. Can you think of some examples when job redesign was carried out *without* increasing the satisfaction of the workers involved? Cite the reasons *why* this happened.

Cases for Discussion

Saab Automobile Engine Assembly Department

This case will give some background information on the work group design movement since the 1950s, describe the Saab Company and its Scania Division, show what was done in the engine assembly department to design work groups, and give reactions of some United States production workers (from Ford, General Motors, and Chrysler Corporations in Detroit) to the Saab system of work design.

Background of the Work Group Design Movement

The movement known as "work group design" can be traced to a study by the Tavistock Institute in the early 1950s of ways to increase productivity in British coal mines (1). Briefly, the research group studied a modern mine in which management had invested in large machines and conveyor equipment and organized work in three shifts. Over the twenty-four hours, industrial engineers had planned forty specialist jobs and assigned these to forty workers. These forty workers together performed the three "big" functions in mining: preparing the coal face (blasting jobs, splitting jobs, cleaning jobs), mining the coal (including loading jobs and hauling jobs), and advancing the coal face (dismantling roof supports was one carpenter job, reconstructing supports another, moving haulage tracks another, moving conveyor equipment another). Each of these specialists had to perform in sequence over the twenty-four hour period, since each job depended on correct quality and timing of *every other* job. Scheduling was a nightmare for managers. If a bottleneck occurred in one job, all others must stop and wait.

To the astonishment of managers, this mine's productivity per shift (or per day) was *less than* that of an old fashioned mine in Durham, where the workers and managers together had worked out a system of job rotation, and where workers had some choice as to what they did next. This is similar to a group of boys and girls who gather on a vacant lot to play baseball and discuss, "Who's going to play first base, who's going to pitch?"

Researchers have pointed out that the reason Durham's mine produced better was that workers not only had greater job variety (less boredom), but they could "see" what was going on in other jobs and adjust their own jobs accordingly. With feedback telling them how other jobs before theirs, or after theirs, were going, they *could* adjust flexibly on the spot to bottlenecks. Not only could they, but they *did*—they were motivated to do so by several things. They could see and understand the total operation. They could be committed to, or involved in, something bigger and more important than just one carpenter job which builds a scaffold. Over time, as they learned more and more jobs they felt more competent, and the self adjustment to bottlenecks gave them more feeling of autonomy and self-control. The intellectual ability to help schedule, plus the motivational inclination to do so, relieved managers of the enormously complex job of keeping track of all events, working out solutions, and conveying orders to the forty specialists. Another and similar redesign of work was carried out by Tavistock in the Calico Textile Mills in India in the 1950s.

In the 1960s both the government and labor unions in Norway supported numerous similar projects which they called "industrial democracy" (because workers have more knowledge and self-control) (2). Several hundred such projects have been carried out in Sweden with support from government, labor, and management. In 1971, a report commissioned by the federal government of the U.S.A. labeled job redesign as the single most important way to overcome worker alienation (3). In 1975, the Government of West Germany commissioned a study to inform government officials about the possible benefits of such designs (4). In 1976 the Government of France took a similar step.

If one studies the Kibbutz movement in Israel, a number of similarities to work group design and worker motivation can be seen. Today, 240 Kibbutzim produce about 33% of the agricultural and 8% of the industrial products of the country (5).

The movement is not without its critics. Serious researchers have pointed out that there may be negative effects on productivity, on the motivation of workers, or both. It is safe to say that at this point in time no proof has been given that group design in itself increases both productivity and morale of workers in all situations.

The Saab-Scania Company (6)

As Sweden's third largest company, Saab-Scania employs 35,000 people. The Scania Division employs 15,000 people in seven plants. One of these plants is the Gasoline Engine Plant, employing 350 people. The plant is divided into four departments. One produces cylinder blocks, one produces cylinder heads, one (the pre-assembly department) imports connecting rods and crankshafts from England and assembles these to the blocks and heads. The fourth (engine assembly department) receives the blocks and heads and attaches flywheels, carburetors, distributors, spark plugs, and camshaft chains to them for production of a complete engine. It is this department we are concerned with here. It employs fifty people. The department has a capacity for producing 110,000 engines a year. The production standard set for the department by management varies. Currently, the plan is for each of five production teams to produce 480 engines each 10 days, or one engine each 30 minutes, using the new organization design.

Possible Design: The Production Line

The mass production assembly line form of organization was investigated by the Company, but not used in this new plant which was opened in 1972. For comparison purposes, if such had been used, there would have been seven stations along the conveyor line upon which the unfinished engine travelled. Each would be specialized: carburetor, spark plugs, flywheel, camshaft chain, etc. Each would have been attached to the engine by a worker who worked only on the particular part. Engineers estimate that under this system each operation would have taken about 1.8 minutes.*

Group Design

Instead, company management, reacting to the fact that they have a difficult time employing younger people (only four out of a hundred high school graduates are willing

* See Exhibit 7.1.

to take assembly line jobs, 58% of the workforce is foreign labor); to the fact that turnover has been as high as 75% a year in the assembly plant; and to absenteeism rates of 20%, opted to re-design assembly jobs.

One way the new system was designed was to employ job rotation—a combination of job enlargement, job enrichment, and job rotation. Under the plan, a worker may elect to assemble the whole engine, following it down the conveyor line in a 30-minute period. Or, one may elect to assemble one-third of an engine, following it over two or three stations in 10 minutes (job enlargement). Few people have taken the first option. Each group may decide who does what work (including job rotation), when and how long each person may take breaks, and who will do the maintenance work (clean machines and floor) or quality control inspection. These forms of self control are similar to job enrichment. Management does require that each person or group produce on the average one engine every 30 minutes, or 470 engines in a 10-day period.†

Another way this has been done at various times is to assign a certain number of engines per hour to a group of three to four workers.‡ For example, taking the output standard of one engine each 30 minutes, the company currently has five production teams—three with four members and two with three members. The three-member groups turn out six engines an hour while the four-member groups turn out eight engines an hour, for a total hourly production of 36 engines in the whole department, and therefore the whole plant. It was this system to which U.S. workers responded in their visit to Sweden (see below). Some indication of how this compares to U.S. assembly lines can be seen from the fact that, at about the same time, the Pontiac plant in Detroit turned out 240 engines an hour, and the Cadillac plant turned out 88 per hour.

Visit of American Workers from Detroit: Second Week (7)

In late 1974, six assembly line workers from Detroit spent four weeks working in the Engine Assembly Department under auspices of Cornell University's New York State School of Labor Relations, with funds supplied by the Ford Foundation. The rest of this case describes some of their reactions. A researcher, Mr. Robert Goldman, accompanied them to interview them and report their reactions.

During the second week, Joe Rodriguez, a 36-year old Mexican-American who works in Ford's engine plant, came to the researcher's room "deeply troubled." "He had found that people in group assembly work harder than anyone in Detroit on the assembly line, and it bothered him." What particularly upset him and Bill Cox (a 33-year old shop steward and machinist from Chrysler) was that an hour before closing that night, all group workers received scrapers and got to work on the floor. Joe said that in America auto workers "don't do janitors' work," and that machines operated by janitors do the scraping in Detroit. Bill Cox said that if anyone had taken his picture (scraping the floor) and sent it back to the States (where union rules also prevent production line workers from doing janitors' jobs) he might be "in trouble."

Cox was also bothered by the pace and amount of work done, and the fact that most people in the Scania plant on assembly lines, "Wouldn't touch that group assembly" because of the heavy work load. He had heard this from sufficient numbers of workers to make the statement. He continued:

"If you went over to America and took an American assembly-line worker off the most boring job there, brought him over here and let him work in group assembly and

† See Exhibit 7.2.
‡ See Exhibit 7.4.

tell him, 'now you've got your choice; which way would you have it? The boring job where you work at a normal pace or the job that isn't boring because they change around from job to job, but you have to work at a faster pace to get your production, which would you have?' I'm willing to bet that the American would take the boring job."

On this subject, Rodriguez said: "As immigrants who need work, these foreign workers [the largest number are Finnish; there are also Italians and Spanish] accept what is presented to them. They really don't question it. They just work hard. I believe that the [Finnish] worker in order to show that he/she is equal to the task, to hold up one's pride, will bust his ———. If I've got to bust my ——— to be meaningful, forget it; I'd rather be monotonous." Rodriguez said he had talked to one group of Italian, Finnish and Swedish workers who said that hard work one day gave them a chance to work less the next.

The researcher who accompanied the workers talked with two workers that seemed to confirm Cox' and Rodriguez' opinions. A young Finnish worker said she had heard from several people in the assembly department that the work is too strenuous, and she herself did not want to work there. Sonja Martinsson, a Swedish worker in group assembly was "delighted" with her assignment. She switched from a job in a bank to blue collar work because the money is better. The work provides variety, is never boring, and gives her a chance to cooperate with others. The togetherness feeling was her main source of satisfaction. When the researcher asked her how younger workers, who feel alienated and do not see much meaning to work, react to the system, she pointed out that not many people under 30 have applied and been accepted for the department. "You have to have a certain attitude toward work. You are taught in a special way in your home, the old way, as we say here. Which means you have responsibility . . . I don't think the younger people value work . . . they just have another point of view." When asked about the difference in Finns and Swedes, she said, "I think Finnish people are more willing to work hard . . . I'm not so sure the Swedish people are doing that."

Ruth Russell, 31, a worker in the Cadillac engine plant, "shared Sonja's enthusiasm for group work precisely because the workers in the department had the 'old' attitude toward work." She agreed that the new crop of workers "does not enjoy or appreciate working that way."

The researcher concluded that what emerged from the second week assessments made by the American workers, "Was that group assembly at Saab-Scania seems to have limited appeal; that it does not appear to meet the needs of young people; and that it attracts the most work oriented, responsible and highly motivated individuals. In short, it is a work design that demands a high measure of commitment and expenditure of effort. These observations may have something to say to managers who have become so wrapped up in their commitment to and rhetoric about work reform that they may have lost sight of some fundamental worker needs and perceptions. They may need to review their programs and revisit with the workers."

American Worker Reactions: Third Week

At the end of the third week, all six Americans met with Arthur Weinberg, project coordinator, and Robert Goldman, reporter. The question was posed: "If you had to make a choice now, from the point of view of group assembly only, between Detroit and [the Scania engine assembly department], what would it be?"

Lynette Stewart, a 21-year old black woman studying toward a nursing degree and a full time shift worker on the Cadillac assembly line, said she preferred Detroit. She had found ways "to create a challenge for myself in my job by making up stock faster than necessary and so getting time to do some studying at work."

Ruth Russell, a 31-year old wife and mother, "clearly preferred Saab-Scania because my job at Cadillac, putting head bolts on engines, was so annoying." The foreman's hovering presence "bugged" her, the noise, the monotony, the dirt in the plant made work unpleasant if not miserable. She found a sense of values among her hard working group assembly colleagues to which she could "relate easily."

Bill Cox chose Saab-Scania if he could work at a normal pace, but he did not think the difference was too great even at a normal pace. While there is a little more variety in group assembly work, he said, in the end it "also gets boring. It would be just a different kind of boredom."

Herman Lommerse, a 53-year old person who has worked in Cadillac, Chevrolet and Chrysler plants, does not find life too bad or bothersome at Cadillac. He chose Detroit—"for reasons similar to Lynette's. I do not like being dependent on other group members. One person might have been drunk on the weekend, and on Monday the others would have to make up for him by harder work. In Detroit, I do my job and I'm done with it."

Bill Gardner, a 41-year old black man who has done such jobs as nickle plating and other assembly jobs for Pontiac, and who carries a heavy course load at night in the University of Michigan, said he "could not work here and enjoy it. At Pontiac we worked out a lot of problems over a long time that makes me feel it is a better working condition, and a better psychological place to work." He thought that group assembly was ideal for a small jobbing place but not for American mass production.

Joe Rodriguez had trouble with the question. "If pressed" he would have to say that at a normal pace that he determines for himself, and with all the conveniences of living he has in Detroit, he would choose Sweden. But he felt that the question was not answerable because it was based too much on the job alone. If he took everything else in his working and living style into account, he would have to choose the United States.

Reactions to the Scania Truck Chassis Assembly Plant

At one point the six workers were shown through the Scania truck chassis assembly plant. It was a mass production assembly line operation, but workers had larger jobs than on an equivalent line in the U.S. The reporter says of this visit: "The lighting was excellent, the temperature comfortable, the plant clean, and the line moved smoothly. Here, our workers felt, was the pride of Saab-Scania—a plant far more impressive than the gasoline engine plant."

References

1. Trist, E. L., and K. W. Bamforth. "Some Social and Psychological Consequences of the Longwall Method of Coal Getting." *Human Relations*, Vol. 4, 1951.
2. Karlsen, J. I. *A Monograph on the Norwegian Industrial Democracy Project.* Oslo, Work Research Institutes, Doc. No. 15, 1972.
3. *Work in America.* Report of a special task force to the Secretary of Health, Education and Welfare. Massachusetts Institute of Technology Press, 1972.
4. Klein, Lisl. *New Forms of Work Organization.* Cambridge University Press, 1976.

5. Fine, K. S. "Worker Participation in Israel." In *Workers' Control*, edited by Gary Hunnius, G. D. Garson and John Case. Vintage Books/Random House, 1973. The author's summary credits also Menachem Rozner, "Principal Types and Problems of Direct Democracy in the Kibbutz," a monograph published by the Social Research Center on the Kibbutz at Givat Haviva, 1965, and certain unpublished research on kibbutz industrialization being performed by the Social Research Center in conjunction with the Institute for Social Relations at the University of Michigan.

6. Statistics in this section have been drawn from "Job Re-Design on the Assembly Line: Farewell to the Blue Collar Blues?" *Organizational Dynamics*, Vol. 2, No. 2, Autumn 1973; and Goldman, Robert S., *Work Values: Six Americans in a Swedish Plant*, a report on a project carried out by the New York State School of Industrial and Labor Relations, Cornell University, March, 1975.

7. All data in this section comes from Goldman, Robert S., *op. cit.* Quotations are from Robert Goldman, the interviewer and reporter who accompanied the workers, unless specifically attributed to one of the workers themselves.

Questions

1. What advantages did Saab-Scania management seek from the new work group design in this specific company?

2. What advantages do behavioral scientists (as contrasted with Saab-Scania management) see in this form of design for all organizations "in general"? That is, what theoretical (as opposed to specific instances) advantages are predicted from work group design?

3. What problems, or disadvantages, can be inferred from the reactions of United States workers, or other facts in the case? (Note: Some of these are economic, and some behavioral/motivational. Explain these in some depth).

4. If you were President of Saab-Scania Division, you would face a dilemma. Some of the factors (in Questions 1 and 2 above) predict that the new design should be maintained in the Assembly Department and extended to other Departments. Others predict that the design should be modified or discontinued in the Assembly Department or that it should be extended to other departments with caution. What would your *judgment* be? 1) Would you maintain the status quo organization in the Assembly Department, modify it, or discontinue it (consider the short run, and the long run)? 2) Would you try to extend this form of organization from automobile engines to the truck engine department?

Western State University

This case has to do with the job duties of professors who teach the undergraduate required course in Organizational Behavior in the School of Business of Western State

University, a university of 21,000 students in a state west of the Mississippi River. One thousand two hundred students are enrolled in the junior-senior years of the undergraduate program leading to the BBA degree. Each year, a total of six hundred students take Organizational Behavior 401, a course required of all seniors.

University business schools differ in the organization structure for dealing with two activities which must be performed in required courses. They differ in (1) who determines what subject matter shall be taught (i.e., the syllabus topics), and (2) who determines what textbooks and reading materials shall be required of students.

Under alternative structure (1), professors teach the course (they perform the operating work), while the department head, with advice of faculty, determines one or both of these two things (i.e., he or she performs the planning work).

Under structure (2), professors who teach the course act as a committee which decides, hopefully by consensus, the answers to the two planning questions.

Under alternative structure (3), the school does not attempt to arrive at any standardization between courses. At Western State, the broad objective of the course is stated in the catalog, "To achieve an understanding of human motivations in work organizations." Each professor is free to choose what topics to cover on the syllabus, and what text materials to use, within this objective.

From one viewpoint, structure (1) is "centralized" both in terms of a standard plan and in terms of who decides. Structure (2) is centralized in terms of standard plans, but decentralized in terms of dynamics (participative committee) to decide upon the common procedure. Structure (3) is decentralized to the individual professor level in both respects. Structure (2) seems closest to what some behavioral scientists mean by the "autonomous work group" (note that it is the *group* that is autonomous). Structure (3) is decentralized in that the *individual* professor is autonomous in two senses: There are no standard plans (syllabus and textbooks) and no person or group which decides for all sections.

From another viewpoint, if a school moves from structure (1) to (3) it would be enriching individual tasks. Conversely, if it moves from (3) to (1) it would be assigning planning work formerly done by professors to others, thus moving away from enrichment.

Total enrollment in OB 401 is split into fifteen sections of forty students. Six professors teach the course. Three professors teach three sections per year and three professors teach two sections.

The traditional structure at Western has been that each professor not only teaches his/her sections, but also plans all facets of the course. Up until recently, Professor Ball and two other professors (accounting for seven sections) used a text which covers individual motivations, small group motivations, and large organization motivations. Professor Hamilton and one other professor (five sections) believe the course should cover only large organizations. They used a sociology text plus two paperbacks. One Professor (Barrett) believes in the case method, addressed to studying individual and small groups, plus some experience exercises.

Eighteen months ago the Dean received a letter signed by thirteen students, objecting to the fact that different materials and different subjects were covered by the six professors teaching the course. Two of these students were in Ball's 3 sections, three from Hamilton's 3 sections, two from Barrett's 2 sections and six from other sections. Here are the key points made in the letter:

- "A number of us are taking OB 403 as an elective. About 20% of Professor Ball's syllabus overlaps with that course. Subjects like leadership of small groups and individual motivation are covered in both courses, causing a waste of student time and money." (The Dean later did a survey that showed that 28% of students in OB 401 also take OB 403.)

- "Professor Hamilton's sections seem to leave out some subjects that are important in our careers, such as conflict in small groups. This also results in inclusion of different and less interesting subjects."
- "Professor Barrett's sections, though interesting, do not seem to include much of the literature in the behavioral sciences. He is an effective teacher, but we know from other students, and from what is done at other universities, that we should be getting this material."

As the Dean thought about this problem he knew that the Department of Organization Theory and Behavior (of which these teachers are a part) was ranked the fifth best in the nation by a national business magazine. This magazine had polled professors in given fields (such as Organizational Behavior and Accounting) asking them to rank which departments in the nation were best in their fields. He attributed the ranking to the fact that the School had allowed professors great freedom to teach, thus "creating a great motivation and energy on the professors' parts." He also felt that, "The Dean can hardly be expert in OB, accounting, economics, and all other subjects to make a decision about what to teach."

"The more I study this problem the more difficult it becomes. I looked at the student ratings for this course. We rate on a five point scale: outstanding, excellent, good, fair and poor. The School's average experience is that 30% of the students in a required course will rank a professor outstanding, 28% excellent, 25% good, 14% fair, and 3% poor. Here are the rankings for the OB 401 sections:

	Outstanding	Excellent	Good	Fair	Poor
Ball, *3 sections*	80%	15%	5%	0%	0%
Hamilton, *3 sections*	58	30	5	5	2
Barrett, *2 sections*	55	28	10	5	2
Others, *5 sections*	54	32	9	4	1

"After much soul-searching, and a real feeling of responsibility for needs of students, needs of the faculty, and excellence of instruction over the years, I decided that the teachers should meet in committee and decide on a common text and subject coverage. The need for justice to students was the most important point. Other factors are important but carry less weight."

One year after the common materials had been agreed upon and instituted in the classroom, the casewriter interviewed the professors.

Professor Ball commented: "I can honestly say that those eight two-hour committee meetings have decreased the quality of work in my course. I cannot get as interested in some of the sociology materials we now have to teach, though I was a party to the agreement. My student ratings have decreased from 80% outstanding and 15% excellent to 68% outstanding and 11% excellent, because I must include subjects I know are less interesting to students. Of course, I will do the best I can with the new syllabus if the Dean and others think we must have it."

Professor Hamilton: "I cannot display as much enthusiasm in teaching matters of individual motivation and small group conflict as I can in matters of organization design and management by objectives. Somehow, the former are not my interests. I'm still trying, because we owe it to students to do as good a job as possible. Also, the meetings themselves took valuable time that I usually give to planning my course."

Professor Barrett echoed Hamilton's remark about enthusiasm. "The case method and experience exercises not only turn me on, but they turn the majority of students on. I know that the other subjects are good, but a teacher cannot be all things to everyone. I can't show students as much enthusiasm. I am a bit frustrated by the question, however. I enjoyed the committee meetings, and believe that we can now share the responsibility as a group, rather than being 'loners,' each going one's own way."

As of this time, eighteen months after the whole question was raised, the Dean feels "uneasy about the common syllabus situation. I've reviewed the teacher evaluations. I see that student opinion of both course materials and teacher effectiveness have decreased. I intend to review the whole situation next year and see if my position is the same then as when I made the original decision."

Questions

1. In one sense the job of the work group (all 401 teachers) at Western was enriched by the Dean's decision. What evidence is there in the case that this *increased* a teacher's satisfaction with his/her work? What basic motivation was satisfied that increased satisfaction?

2. What evidence is there that the "autonomous work group" *decreased* a teacher's satisfaction with his/her work? What basic motivation was removed that had this effect?

3. The text referred to the problem of individual differences—what has this got to do with the Dean's problem?

4. If you were the Dean, would you want the group to continue meeting each year to up-date the syllabus? What factors do you consider in making this decision?

Chapter Eight

Objectives for Organizations and Individuals

Perhaps this is the most important chapter in the book. Organizations exist to accomplish purposes and objectives. Everything else—motivation, power and influence, group behavior, organization and job design, controls and rewards, leadership, conflict management, organization development—are studied in order to implement organizational purposes and objectives.

But what objectives? What should an organization's objectives be? What characteristics should an objective have? How can objectives for the organization be split into contributing subsidiary objectives for departments? What about the problem of having multiple objectives, some of which are not mutually compatible? Finally, how should managers proceed to set objectives so that they will be reasonably well chosen and reasonably likely to be implemented?

The purpose of this chapter is to explore these fundamental questions. We will explore the need for defining an organization's basic strategy and purpose, and for translating this definition into networks of concrete objectives. We will examine evidence on the relationship of objectives and objective-setting methods to motivation and performance. Finally, we will look at management by objectives, its advantages and the difficulties experienced in its application.

STRATEGY AND PURPOSE

The starting point in the task of managing an organization is definition of the organization's basic purpose. This definition is the critical first act of strategic planning. All other planning, and all organizing, leading, and controlling that is done, should implement the organization's basic puspose. Only if that purpose is identified, however, can plans, policies, procedures, organization structures, leadership behavior, controls, rewards, and a thousand decisions be tested for their contribution to the central purpose for which the organization exists.

The definition of an organization's basic purpose is not satisfied by stating what business, industry, or field the organization is in. Observing that an automobile manufacturer's purpose is to make and sell cars is not enough. Observing that a bank is a bank, a prison is a prison, or a hospital is a hospital is similarly useless. Such statements suggest no direction, no distinctive strategy, no particular character.

What *is* required is a more specific statement of precisely what *kind* of automobile manufacturer, bank, prison, or hospital this is, and where it is headed. What is its distinctive competence? Who are its customers, patients, inmates, or whatever? Exactly what do we provide them with? The answers to these questions provide a sense of the character or personality of an organization and its basic direction and purpose.

Defining the Basic Purpose

Henry Ford's idea of an inexpensive car for the masses provided the distinguishing, broad, and central purpose of Ford Motor Company. It may produce the Continental and Marquis too, but its main emphasis over the long run has been lower-priced models. On the other hand, Alfred P. Sloan, Jr.'s idea of "a car for every purse and purpose" was the strategy that guided General Motors.

Sometimes the choice of a strategy is more a matter of finding an opportunity unexploited by the giants. California's Union Bank, for example, operates in the shadow of Bank of America with its more than 1,000 branches. Twenty-five years ago when B. of A. and other large California banks were engaged in a race to establish large numbers of consumer-oriented branches all over the state, Union Bank made a decision that this was not the sole way in which growth could occur. Furthermore, it was a way in which Union Bank would inevitably be defeated by its larger competitors. Union Bank had a single Los Angeles office in the 1950s, but it was a bank which already had developed a distinctive competence and served a distinctive part of the community. It was a business-oriented bank that had been successful in lending money at higher-than-average interest rates to companies which were often worse-than-average credit risks. Union had more frequent loan losses, but because its rates were higher Union's "bottom line" reflected higher-than-average profitability.

Union decided that its growth would be sought, not in the race to add consumer branches, but in establishing comparatively few "regional head offices" in urban areas to serve business clients. It became a major factor in financing real estate developers, professional athletic teams, and other assorted businesses that grew over the last few decades. It did not dissipate its energies in trying to do what the other banks did. Instead, it looked outside to find new business clients who often had difficulty in borrowing from other banks, and it worked inside to develop skills at analyzing businesses less on the basis of traditional financial records and more on the basis of understanding the client's operations and prospects.

The same problem of defining the organization's mission confronts managers of nonbusiness organizations. Some prisons, for example, may exist to accomplish the limited purpose of holding prisoners for trial. This is the common function of a county jail. Other prisons may undertake missions of rehabilitation and training. Some hospitals have a teaching mission as well as the job of providing patient care.

The Price of Purposelessness

It is important that managers define basic purposes for their organizations because the failure to do so may lead to meandering and undistinguished organizational performance at best, and pointless exhaustion of resources at worst. Dumb luck may allow success for a time, but without the guidance provided by a sharply defined purpose, managers have no basis for testing decisions to see that they implement long-term and fundamental purposes. Management without purpose degenerates into expediency and opportunism, as distinguished from building enduring institutions (Selznick, 1957).

Even though expediency and opportunism are terms that have strong negative connotations, it could be argued that management actually requires and organizations can benefit from the quick adaptiveness that these terms also imply. This is a valid point. The problem is that when managers are not guided by clear organizational purposes and a sense of organizational character, their quick expedients and attempts to seize the baubles of apparent opportunities are often perversely destructive. Even successful organizations with known basic purposes are susceptible to momentary forgetfulness. For example, the exceptionally successful Mallinckrodt Chemical Works strayed from its range of competence once to invest $1.5 million in commercial paper. Its choice? The Penn Central Transportation Company, which promptly went bankrupt. In retrospect, Mallinckrodt's Chairman reasserted the corporation's basic purpose: "I'm damn sure no one at Mallinckrodt will ever again run the risk of picking up an extra percent or two investing in commercial paper. We decided our job is making our money from the manufacturing of our products, not playing the money market" (*Business Week*, March 23, 1974, p. 62). There is also the example of the associates of President Nixon, whose basic job of securing his reelection was progressing nicely, but who decided to diversify their activities by going into the burglary business (Ways, 1973).

Finally, though it is undoubtedly a good thing for students of management to make sure they understand the organizational value of clear purposes, realism demands that we confess that it is rare indeed to find an organization whose purposes are lucid. As Peter Drucker observes, "Few companies have any clear idea of what their mission is and that is one of the . . . major causes of their worst mistakes" (*Business Week*, February 9, 1974, p. 55). Managers are often so driven by immediate tasks and problems that they are inclined never to formulate their organization's deep central purposes, to forget them once formulated, or to fail to modify them as circumstances change. A fairly typical day for a manager might well include such events as: news of a schedule slippage, threatened resignation of a key employee, a complaint alleging discrimination, news of a parts shortage, a luncheon for a retiring employee, a meeting to discuss means of pollution abatement to comply with recent legislation, plus a dozen other conversations about various problems. Just how much thinking about basic purposes is achieved by the average manager in such circumstances appears, understandably, to be rather limited. It may be that the empathy and compassion expressed by Oliver Wendell Holmes, Jr. in another context is appropriate, "Detached reflection cannot be demanded in the presence of an uplifted knife."

Nonetheless, what often distinguishes the more effective managers from their run-of-the-mill colleagues is precisely the amount and quality of detached reflection about organizational purposes and missions they do accomplish. In fact, the uplifted knives of frequent crises are as much a consequence of the lack of defined organizational purpose as they are its cause. Analyses of the perennial troubles of Chrysler Corporation (Vanderwicken, 1975b) and of the disastrous fiscal condition of New York City (Clines, 1976), for example, point toward the failure to establish basic purposes and strategies as the critical weakness. Chrysler has never targeted a specific segment of the domestic-make auto market. New York City (which is, financially, equivalent to the eighth largest industrial corporation) has never even created an inventory of all the programs its agencies pursue, much less a basic strategy and purpose to provide a way of evaluating proposed programs and putting priorities on existing ones. In both examples, the failure to meet the challenge of establishing basic strategy and purpose contributes to the organization's comparatively poor reputation for management.

The selected reading by Philip Selznick which accompanies this chapter will explain that it is only when the organization has defined its basic purpose and character that it can proceed to set objectives which are logically related to building and realizing that character. Another selected reading by McCaskey cautions against attempting to specify detailed objectives for all organizations at all times.

FROM PURPOSE TO OBJECTIVE

Statements of basic strategy and purpose, if they are formulated, can set the direction for an organization. But, if they are to become truly useful in managing organizations, they must be translated into what philosophers and scientists call operational definitions. They must, in other words, be expressed as specific, concrete, measurable activities and desired results. Thus translated, purposes become what managers call *objectives.*

Objectives, as distinguished from pontifications, philosophies, or vague hopes, are concrete commitments that have the following characteristics:

1. They are specific.
2. They are reality-oriented.
3. Their achievement can be verified.
4. They specify the time they will be achieved.

The examples of organizational objectives shown in Exhibit 8.1 illustrate these characteristics. They are specific, point toward real or concrete accomplishments, and their achievement is verifiable at a specified time. In all but one case, the last one, the result sought by the objective is quantifiable. For the law school, the result sought is not quantifiable, but it is no less verifiable: 1978 will reveal whether or not the objective of accreditation was realized.

Assuming that each listed organizational objective is congruent with the organizational purpose it is meant to implement, the organization has defined, operationally, where it is headed. It has also established a framework that can help guide decision-making and other conduct within the organization toward the objective. But since organizations have many special-purpose

1. Increase our share of the domestic-make automobile market 5 percent by 1980.

2. Reduce short-term construction loans to 20 percent of total loans by 1978.

3. Earn 20 percent on investment (after taxes) in the next fiscal year.

4. Publish 120 new and revised textbooks in 1979.

5. Reduce 1980 overtime use by the city's waste collectors by 25 percent below 1979 overtime use.

6. Reduce by 50 percent (by 1978) the number of complaints refused by the District Attorney for reasons of failures by this Police Department to complete reports properly, show probable cause, or conduct proper search and seizure.

7. Achieve full accreditation of this law school by the California Committee of Bar Examiners by 1978.

departments and individuals with diverse responsibilities, it will be necessary to refine or factor basic organizational objectives into contributing objectives for departments and individuals.

THE HIERARCHY OF OBJECTIVES

The process of translating a basic organizational objective into contributing subsidiary objectives for departments within the organization is accomplished by a process variously described as means-ends analysis or building a hierarchy of objectives (March and Simon, 1958). Exhibit 8.2 depicts how corporate and various departmental objectives (which can be looked upon as means that contribute to a single end—the corporate objective) form a hierarchy. Suppose, for example, the corporate objective is to increase its market share for a particular product by 10 percent in 1981. As Exhibit 8.2 shows, this objective would then be used to derive an objective for the manufacturing department of producing 51,275 units; an objective for the sales department of selling 46,325 units; and an objective for the engineering department of reducing the product's weight by 18 pounds.

Though each departmental objective is an end for that department, it is also a means to accomplish the organizational objective. The organizational objective sets a framework within which the hierarchy of contributing subsidiary objectives can be set. The process can also be carried a step or two further within departments, with the establishment of objectives for sections within the department and for individual employees within the sections.

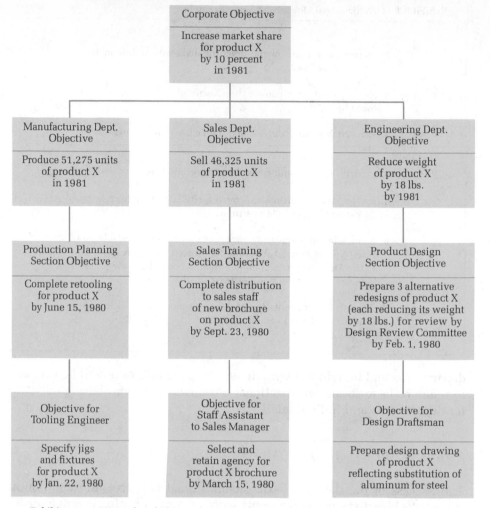

Exhibit 8.2 A Hierarchy of Objectives

Exhibit 8.2 also shows what such objectives for sections and individuals might look like.

As the corporate objective is taken down and organization structure by this kind of means-end analysis, each lower level objective has a shorter time span and is more precisely specified than the higher level objective it serves. But as Exhibit 8.2 implies, a chart of objectives might be drawn for a whole organization, revealing what departments, sections, and individuals are responsible for what results at any given time.

MULTIPLE OBJECTIVES

The foregoing discussion of the hierarchy of objectives was simplified by our unstated assumption that our sample organization had only one corporate objective—to increase the market share for product X by 10 percent in 1981.

In reality, we can think of no organization that pursues a single objective. They all pursue several simultaneously.

The Variety of Objectives

Peter Drucker (1974) suggests that business organizations require objectives in every area where performance is necessary to survival; for business organizations, these include:

1. Marketing
2. Innovation
3. Human Organization
4. Financial Resources
5. Physical Resources
6. Productivity
7. Social Responsibility
8. Profit Requirements (p. 100).

Each area requires more than a single specific, concrete objective. Marketing, for example, requires objectives for old products and services, for new ones, for methods of distribution, for promotion, for service, and so on. Market-share objectives are also particularly important. In the domestic-make U.S. auto market, for example, a single percentage point in market-share can mean hundreds of millions of dollars of revenues. General Motors traditionally holds about half of this market, Ford about one quarter, and Chrysler about 13 percent. Greater market-share tends to mean greater profitability because the larger volume means important economies of scale in both production and sales (Shoeffler, Buzzell, and Heany, 1974). Assembling and advertising one car is cheaper for GM than for its competitors because GM makes so many of them.

Innovation objectives may be less easy to define and measure than market standing, but in most competitive fields innovations in products and services are essential to survival. For example, Lubrizol Corporation, an extremely successful manufacturer of chemical additives for lubricants, has over 700 products, hardly any of which are over six years old (Vanderwicken, 1975a). Various other pharmaceutical, chemical, and electronics companies are similarly dependent upon maintaining a flow of new products.

Objectives are also necessary for the management of human, financial, and physical resources. The development of skilled and experienced employees and managers cannot prudently be left to chance. Neither can the availability of necessary money and materials. Needs for all of these resources have to be defined so that detailed plans to obtain them can be developed.

Productivity objectives are paramount in many departments and for many individual jobs. Production and sales quotas are typical productivity goals. Because they can often reflect key variables quantitatively and their achievement can thus be easily measured, they are likely to assume great importance.

Social responsibility objectives, on the other hand, have proven to be less susceptible to quantification and verification. The *qualities* sometimes valued by social responsibility objectives—clean air, impartial employment practices, clean water—have often been neglected because of emphasis on the *quantities* reflected in productivity goals.

Profitability is the business objective that is mentioned most often. For top-level executives, profitability tends to be of paramount concern since they are most likely to be evaluated by that standard (Merrill, 1974; Dent, 1959; and England, 1967). But at lower levels in the organization structure, managers must decide many issues without clear evidence of the impact of their decision on corporate profits. Such managers often guide their decisions by subsidiary objectives such as productivity and costs.

Conflict Among Objectives

As we have seen, each organizational objective is the apex of a particular hierarchy of subobjectives. Since there are multiple organizational objectives, there will be several hierarchies of objectives descending into the departments. Any given manager will thus face the requirement of satisfying a whole battery of objectives. Exhibit 8.3, for example, even though it is only a partial list, suggests the variety of objectives the manager of a manufacturing department is supposed to meet in 1981.

The most important consequence of having so many and such diverse objectives is that conflicts develop among them. Managers' time, talent,

Exhibit 8.3 A Partial List of Objectives for 1981 for the Manager of a Manufacturing Department

- Produce 51,275 units of Product X.

- Reduce average setup time for milling operations by 10 percent.

- Complete training of 23 lathe operators.

- Increase productivity of deburring operation by 15 percent.

- Reduce rejects in final inspection by 10 percent.

- Decrease overtime usage by 27 percent.

- Reduce the number of Stage 2 grievances by 40 percent.

- Increase the number of minority group employees by at least 10 percent.

- Reduce the amount of liquid waste pollutants entering the Kenesha River from cellulose steeping facilities by 75 percent.

energy, and other resources are limited. The demands posed by the objective of producing 51,275 units of product X may be at odds, for example, with the objective of training 23 lathe operators. Machine-time may be so limited that training can only be done by sacrificing productivity. Or, the equipment changes needed to reduce pollutants may also require some sacrifice of productivity.

Of course, objectives may have been established in the first place with some recognition of potential difficulties stemming from conflicts, as well as from equipment breakdowns, strikes, and other problems. Nevertheless, not all conflicts are foreseen and sometimes managers are forced to decide to let one objective suffer in order to fulfill another. The difficulties arise in determining whether one objective is more important, in deciding which actions can be deferred, and in creatively envisioning courses of action that may synthesize seemingly conflicting requirements. As we have indicated, coping with those difficulties is helped in part by providing a framework of purpose and strategy. It is also helped by an explicit and systematic effort to set objectives throughout the organization.

OBJECTIVES, MOTIVATION, AND PERFORMANCE

A major assumption that underlies management's interest in setting objectives or goals for every corner of the organization (in addition to the idea that it can clarify and reduce conflicts among objectives) is the idea that having objectives will improve performance. Other related assumptions include the idea that objectives which are specific and reasonably challenging are more likely to lift performance. It is also widely believed that, for best results, goals should be set participatively, not simply imposed by superiors. Our purpose in this section will be to assess the evidence for each of these assumptions.

First, however, we should consider how objectives and objective-setting could be connected with motivation and performance in the first place. The expectancy theory of motivation (see Chapter 1) provides a useful approach (Steers and Porter, 1974). Simply put, the theory holds that the strength or force of motivation to perform is the combined result of a person's belief that the performance will lead to a reward *and* the value he or she places on the reward. Objectives and objective-setting practices play a part in determining the motivation to perform because they affect *the definition of performance* and, thereby, beliefs and expectations about the likelihood that effort can lead to performance, and performance to reward. They also affect beliefs about the value of the reward. When sales representatives set a goal of increasing sales by 10 percent and calculate that this result will mean an increased commission of $325 per month, they have acquired information that may strongly affect the strength of their motivation to perform and, indeed, their actual performance.

Locke, a principal researcher on the effects of goals or objectives on performance, proposes that goals or intentions are the most immediate and direct motivational determinants of task performance (Locke, Cartledge, and Knerr, 1970). Changes in job contents, pay and promotion systems, and other conditions affect performance only through their influence on the individual's goals and intentions. According to this view of motivation and performance, therefore, managers must indeed understand the role of objectives if they are to be able to learn how to exert influence over motivation and performance most effectively.

Fortunately, a substantial number of studies have been conducted on the effects of objectives on motivation and performance (Steers and Porter, 1974; Latham and Yukl, 1975). They shed a considerable amount of light on what kinds of goals and what goal-setting methods tend to improve performance.

How Specific Should Objectives Be?

The evidence, from both field and laboratory studies, indicates strongly that having goals is itself effective in lifting performance. Individuals who have task goals tend to perform better than individuals who do not have such goals (Lawrence and Smith, 1955; Blumenfeld and Leidy, 1969; Roman, Latham, and Kinne, 1973; Wexley and Nemeroff, 1975). Individuals who have specific task goals tend to perform better than individuals who have only broad definitions of their responsibilities, even if the latter are urged to "do your best" (Mace, 1935; Fryer, 1964; Bryan and Locke, 1967; French, Kay, and Meyer, 1966; Raia, 1965; and Stedry and Kay, 1966). The implication is clear that managers should concentrate on achieving the clearest possible specification of performance objectives for subordinates, rather than rely on exhorting them to do well with vaguely defined objectives.

How Difficult Should Objectives Be?

A number of studies support the proposition that the more difficult the objective, the higher the performance—so long as the objective is accepted (Locke, 1968; Stedry and Kay, 1966; Zander and Newcomb, 1967; Blumenfeld and Leidy, 1969; and Dachler and Mobley, 1973). Objectives that are challenging can arouse the need for achievement (Stringer, 1966). As we explained in Chapter 1, achievement-oriented behavior includes setting or accepting realistic but moderately risky goals and taking personal responsibility for solving problems and accomplishing results.

If the goal is too easy, it is less likely to engage the urge to achieve. If it is too difficult it leads to the belief that trying will not succeed. Only if the difficult goal is accepted and becomes the individual's level of aspiration does it tend to lift performance. Only if the goal appears reachable (even though there is some risk of failure) and only if the reward for reaching it seems worthwhile is the goal likely to be accepted.

One laboratory study of the effects of goal difficulty on performance (Stedry, 1960) has particularly important implications for objective-setting by participative methods. In the experiment, which involved solving mathematical problems, some subjects were asked to set their own goals before the experimenter assigned goals. Others were assigned goals first and later asked to set their own goals. The sequence affected goal acceptance. If people had set their own goals first, they tended to reject the goals the experimenter sought to assign. Assigned goals, it appears, should be mentioned to people, perhaps only as proposals or suggestions, but before inviting people to propose their own goals. This sequence promotes goal acceptance.

Finally, it should be noted that nearly all of the research on how the difficulty of a goal affects performance looks at only one goal. But we know that people must meet several objectives. What happens when some of these goals are more difficult than others? One study (Stedry and Kay, 1966) did vary the level of difficulty of two goals—output and rework costs. When one goal began to appear impossible, people focused on the other. When both goals were perceived as possible, but one as more difficult than the other, the more difficult one was associated with a greater variability of performance. This result may mean that other factors were at work, such as beliefs that one goal was more or less important (Steers and Porter, 1974).

Is Participation in Setting Objectives Important?

Whereas classic management theory assumed that objectives were to be set by managers and passed down the chain of command to subordinates, the behavioral approach to management (McGregor, 1960; Likert, 1961) ardently believes that a participative objective-setting procedure is necessary to improve motivation and performance. As McGregor put it, "Genuine commitment is seldom achieved when objectives are externally imposed. Passive acceptance is the most that can be expected; indifference or resistance are the more likely consequences. Some degree of *mutual* involvement in the determination of objectives is a necessary aspect of managerial planning" (p. 868).

What is the evidence on whether participation in setting objectives makes any difference in motivation and performance?

The best description of the evidence on this question is that it is mixed. Research results permit no easy conclusion that participation increases motivation or improves performance. The idea that people who participate in setting the objectives will be more likely to accept them seems most reasonable. A number of studies that have tried to test this relationship, however, to see if it raises motivation, effort, and performance, have not found any consistent evidence that participation does yield such results (French, Kay, and Meyer, 1966; Duttagupta, 1975; Carroll and Tosi, 1970). On the other hand, other studies have found evidence that greater participation in setting objectives was associated with enhanced motivation to perform (Latham and Yukl, 1975; Lawler and Hackman, 1969; Tomekovic, 1962).

Upon reviewing earlier research on this issue, Campbell et al. (1970) conclude that prolonged discussions between supervisors and subordinates to set goals and explore means of arriving at them may not be more motivating, but *they may help subordinates develop a much clearer idea of what they are supposed to do.* "Given two individuals with an equal desire to expend effort, the individual with the greater specific knowledge concerning the nature of the organization's goals and their priorities should perform at a higher level" (pp. 377–78). In other words, goal-setting can have both cognitive and motivational effects, but a participative approach to planning may conceivably have more impact upon cognition than upon motivation.

Additional Considerations

Sophisticated and well-intentioned managers might proceed, on the basis of this evidence, to establish specific and reasonably difficult objectives throughout their organization. They might also invite subordinates to participate in setting these objectives on grounds that it might motivate them, but at least the participative process could develop useful information. Unfortunately, such a carefully considered approach could still yield disappointing results.

Several factors might influence the outcome of participation. Participation might not have much impact on people who are highly authoritarian or who have low needs for independence (Vroom, 1960). It might also have little motivational impact on people who have strong needs for achievement (Steers, 1975). Such people may find all the talk superfluous, since they set challenging goals for themselves anyway. Supervisors who are seen as threatening by subordinates might arouse so much anxiety that participative objective-setting could detract from performance (French, Kay, and Meyer, 1966). A climate of mistrust and a history of failure could also weaken the stimulus that specific, difficult goals set by participation might otherwise have.

MANAGEMENT BY OBJECTIVES

The title of this textbook, *Organizational Behavior and the Practice of Management,* reflects the interdependence of science and technology. Organizational behavior has become a common term for the use of behavioral science to understand human behavior in organizations. The practice of management refers to the technologies or methods used by managers. Our intention, as set forth in the first edition and reiterated in each succeeding edition, has always been to help channel the developing knowledge of organizational behavior into the training of future managers. We attempt to do this by discussing theories and research findings (such as those concerning objectives and objectives-setting)

and using them to evaluate alternative management practices or technologies —
such as management by objectives.

Historically, science and technology have always been interdependent.
Sometimes, perhaps more often than most people recognize, the technological
creations of practical-minded people come first and scientific understanding
and use come later. The steam engine and the telescope, for example, are often
cited as illustrations of how technology gives to science, rather than science
to technology (Walker, 1962; Singer, 1956). This sequence of technology first
and science later appears also to have occurred with the development of what
is called management by objectives, or MBO for short.

MBO is an approach to managing — particularly to the processes of planning, leading, and controlling — which makes goals or objectives the heart of
the practice of management. MBO has been used by a few organizations,
General Electric, for example, for a quarter of a century, and has been written
about extensively for approximately as long (The General Electric Company,
1954; Drucker, 1954). The use of MBO in various corporations, government,
and other organizations provided much of the data for the behavioral science
researchers whose field studies of the effects of goals and participative goal-
setting were discussed in the preceding section. In this way the technology of
MBO taught science some useful things about the relationship of objectives,
motivation, and performance.

How MBO Works

Though MBO and MBO-like programs exhibit variations from organization to
organization, MBO contains at least the following key steps:

1. Supervisors provide subordinates with a framework reflecting their own
   purposes and objectives.
2. Subordinates propose objectives for themselves.
3. Supervisors and subordinates discuss, sometimes modify, and eventually
   agree upon a set of objectives for the subordinate.
4. Subordinates review their own progress and describe it periodically (as
   agreed) to their supervisors.
5. The sequence is repeated as necessary.

Exhibit 8.4 provides an illustration of a detailed list of objectives (many of
which quantify results) set through MBO for a sales representative. This
chapter's selected reading by Douglas McGregor exemplifies skillful use of
the MBO process. McGregor's example, which reports the objective-setting
process as experienced by an administrative vice-president and a personnel
manager, also shows that MBO can work for staff departments and can be applied where results cannot be quantified.

Exhibit 8.4   Specific Goals for Technical Sales Representative

Background

This territory covers the states of Indiana and Illinois and includes approximately 420 accounts which have been active in the past three years. 1975 total volume will be about $4.8 million, with some 40 percent coming from four major accounts. Approximately 310 accounts will have made one or more purchases from us by the end of the year. Principal volume chemicals in this territory are DMT, RDP, and sulfuric acid, going primarily to the plastic industry.

1976 Sales Goal

The territory should be able to produce a twelve-month volume of approximately $5.4 million next year; this is our sales target.

1976 Specific Goals for Marshall Greenbaum

1. To obtain a broader base of customers for DMT and RDP for the purpose of spreading our competitive risk in the plastics industry.

    This objective will have been met when initial DMT and RDP orders are booked from five accounts in the territory not sold in 1975.
2. To improve our franchise with the "big four" customers in this area, so that continuing competitive efforts do not diminish our share of the total business of these important customers.

    This objective will have been met when useful Technical Service Laboratory projects have been initiated for two of these customers.
3. To improve my personal business relationships with those prospects in the area included in the group of approximately 75 companies which purchased nothing from us in the past three years.

    This objective will have been met when I have been able to perform some gratuitous service for, or to arrange cordial social contacts with, fifteen executives in at least ten of these companies who have a voice in purchasing decisions.
4. To improve the frequency with which I am able to make in-person contact with the bulk of our customers, specifically those not included in the territory's big four.

    This objective will have been met if I have developed and am following a suitably revised basic travel plan by July 1.
5. To develop additional increments of volume with old, and also prospective new, customers in the medium-size company category.

    This objective will have been accomplished if:
    a. 1976 total volume goals are met, and
    b. such customers account for an additional 5 percent of total dollar income, i.e., 65 percent of sales.
6. To improve the ratio of the more profitable "growth" chemicals sales to basic chemicals sales in this territory.

    This objective will have been met when the percentage of total sales dollars accounted for by "growth" chemicals has been increased from 65 to 70 percent.
7. To hold down direct costs of selling which are under my control with the end of contributing to optimum territorial profit.

    This objective will have been met if the year-end average of monthly expenses reported does not exceed the median range of those for territories of comparable type, volume, and geographical size.

Exhibit 8.4 (*continued*)

471

*Management
by Objectives*

8. To determine whether it is desirable to acquire additional resellers in the southern part of Illinois, in view of the steady growth in numbers of new, smaller end-user prospects for some of our specialty products.

   This objective will have been met if, by April 1, I am able to obtain a clear-cut policy on the appointment of resellers, together with an adequate understanding of the economics supporting this policy.

9. To gain a comprehensive knowledge of the natural gas industry which, while not the territory's dominant industry potential in terms of pounds, represents the highest profit potential, by industry, in the territory.

   This objective will have been met when I am able to contribute one or more basic new ideas to them developed either personally or with the Technical Service Laboratory.

10. To master a thorough knowledge of all uses for RDP, the product for which there is the third largest number of individual customers in this territory.

    This objective will have been met if, by October 1, I have completed an intensive program of indoctrination at the Technical Service Laboratory of not less than three full days' duration.

Source: From Ross A. Webber, *Management* Richard D. Irwin, 1975, pp. 349–50.

Benefits of MBO

Since MBO synthesizes in practice many of the advantages revealed by our earlier analysis of objectives and objective-setting, it would seem likely that it would arouse motivation and enhance performance. Most of the early MBO enthusiasts intuitively believed this and observed various applications of MBO and related goal-setting practices that persuaded them that MBO would indeed improve motivation and performance (Schleh, 1961; Odiorne, 1965; Humble, 1967; Hughes, 1965; Wikstrom, 1968; and McGregor, 1957). In other instances, systematic research on applications of MBO have confirmed its ability to improve motivation and/or performance (Kay, Meyer, and French, 1965; Ivancevich, 1974; and Raia, 1974).

Even though their own study of MBO in the Black and Decker Corporation did not provide conclusive evidence that MBO lifted motivation and productivity, Carroll and Tosi (1973) did identify the following benefits of MBO:

1. It directs work activities toward organizational goals.
2. It forces and aids in planning.
3. It provides clear standards for control.
4. It provides improved motivation among managers.
5. It makes for better use of human resources.
6. It reduces role conflict and ambiguity.
7. It provides more objective appraisal criteria.
8. It better identifies problems.
9. It improves the development of personnel.

In general, MBO appears to so well reflect what behavioral scientists have learned about objectives, motivation, and performance, that it could have been no better designed even if it had been consciously created after the behavioral science research.

MBO IN PRACTICE

The benefits of MBO are not always realized, however. A study of the use of MBO in the *Fortune* 500 (an annual listing of the nation's 500 largest corporations) indicates that, although nearly half of them report some use of MBO, fewer than 10 percent say they have successful MBO programs (Schuster and Kindall, 1974). "Somewhere between the concept of MBO and its implementation," writes one thoughtful observer, "something has seriously gone wrong" (Levinson, 1970, p. 125).

Actually, the situation for MBO resembles the situation for group decision-making as discussed in Chapter 5. In the case of group decision-making, there was impressive evidence that groups could make decisions in many ways more effectively than individuals. In practice, however, group decision processes are often flawed by individual dominance and groupthink. In the case of MBO, the potential advantages of establishing objectives in MBO fashion are impressive and those advantages have been realized in some successful applications. But those successful applications may be exceptional. The MBO process is often flawed by several troubles. These include:

1. Burdensome procedures.
2. Lack of management support.
3. Focus on the measurable as distinguished from the important.
4. Overemphasis on results as distinguished from the processes and methods by which results are achieved.
5. Authoritarian administration with illusory participation of subordinates.
6. An individualistic approach that neglects cooperation among people and departments.

Burdensome Procedures

MBO requires that managers spend a considerable amount of time in separate discussions with each participating subordinate. There are sessions for setting and communicating objectives and for discussing progress. Objectives are also expressed in writing and their thoughtful preparation also takes time. Since managers typically feel they have inadequate amounts of time to accomplish their work anyway, they sometimes protest that MBO makes demands upon their time they can ill-afford to meet, especially where subordinates already understand what is expected of them (Carroll and Tosi, 1973).

Another complaint is that MBO sometimes degenerates into a paperwork ritual that is unsupported by and reflects no serious commitment on the part of higher level management (Ivancevich, 1972; Ivancevich, 1974; Ivancevich, Donnelly, and Lyon, 1970). This is fairly likely to be the case if top managers adopt MBO merely to imitate what everybody else is doing and then delegate the program's administration to the personnel department. It is perhaps even more likely if personnel (often a weak staff department) itself initiates and administers MBO. In any event, when managers have no real commitment to the program the interest of subordinates understandably pales.

Adverse Effects of Quantification

Another difficulty in applying MBO arises from the zeal for quantifying objectives. Not all valuable results and performances lend themselves to quantification. For example, it may be difficult to measure customer service precisely, but it may nonetheless be extremely important to improve customer service. The tendency in MBO is to find some quantity that appears to represent the desired objective of customer service, say, number of visits per customer, and fix upon some increase of that quantity as a measure of the objective's achievement.

Sometimes, the choice of what to measure is trivial but harmless. At other times the measured quantity drives the employee to engage in activities that are contrary to the true objective unfaithfully represented by the measurement or contrary to some other objective. The employee might, for example, cut short visits with customers to be able to visit more of them (Levinson, 1970). The result: an increase in customer visits, many of which will be too short to learn of customer problems and too short to build much goodwill.

Overemphasis on Results

A related effect flows from the tendency to overemphasize results, occasionally at the expense of the processes by which the results are achieved. To understand this problem, it is helpful to recall that MBO began as a reaction to appraisal systems and a management focus that seemed inordinately concerned with judging employee performance by various personal traits or characteristics, such as loyalty, punctuality, cooperativeness, ability, and compliance with various procedures and regulations. Critics such as Drucker (1954) and McGregor (1957) urged that this emphasis was misplaced and that appraisal, and management, ought to assess performance by results—results that implemented established objectives.

The problem is that substituting emphasis on results for emphasis on process may not only intensify motivation for achieving results, but can also encourage an "ends justify the means" mentality. Achievement-oriented managers and employees hell-bent on meeting short-term goals may damage fundamental processes and ways of functioning that, in the long-run, are more important than short-term triumphs. Sales can be increased and quotas met and surpassed by overstocking customers, but the deception can contaminate and destroy the long-term relationship.

Participative Technique—Authoritarian Philosophy

Another fairly common complaint about the practice of MBO recalls the old idea that a tool can only be as good as the person who uses it. MBO is a set of techniques, to be sure, but it is a set of techniques that reflects a philosophy. Tenets of that philosophy include the assumptions that most people are responsible and competent, that they come to work with some desire to achieve and to participate in directing their activities, and that both they and the employing organization can benefit from jointly trying to establish objectives and self-control practices acceptable to both. When MBO is applied without this philosophy, but merely as a participative tool in an authoritarian hand, then the subordinate's participation becomes a sham. Subordinates are the first to see this and withdraw their energy. They often feel hostile and resentful, and engage in passive resistance. The authoritarian manager is the last to understand what has happened and concludes that MBO is no damn good, or that people are no damn good (McGregor, 1960), or both.

Excessive Emphasis on Individuals

Finally, it is sometimes observed that MBO, as practiced, focuses on the objectives of individuals, when organizational results are really the product of the contributions of many people representing different departments. Ideally, in the MBO stage of setting objectives each supervisor reviews the objectives of each subordinate to assure that they are compatible with those of adjacent subordinates within the supervisor's domain. In this way coordination and cooperation are to be assured, as well as individual accountability.

The fallacy is that it is the rule rather than the exception that in the complex, interdependent relationships common within modern organizations, people are responsible for results that are partly determined by other people in other departments, or who are otherwise not in any subordinate relation to the person responsible for the results. Pretending that all of this interdependence, with its implied need for cooperation and shared accountability, can be split into individual objectives may be unrealistic. Worse, it leads to no affirmative attention to and support for group rather than individual objective-setting and performance-monitoring. The selected reading by Douglas Sherwin illustrates both the problem and a constructive approach to its solution at Phillips Products Co., Inc.

SUMMARY

Defining the basic strategy and purpose of an organization is a critical and difficult management responsibility. It is critical because clarity of purpose provides direction. It is difficult because short-run problems and opportunities compete aggressively for time and energy.

Once established, however, the basic purpose must be translated into specific, concrete objectives with times set for completion. For each of the many organizational objectives that may be set, a hierarchy of subsidiary contributing objectives must be set for successively lower levels in the organization. Thus, many objectives will in effect be requiring that managers serve many masters simultaneously.

Research evidence attests to the usefulness of specific and reasonably difficult objectives in improving motivation and performance. The findings on the effects of participation are mixed.

Management by objectives (MBO) is a practice that synthesizes many of the implications of the research on objectives. It can improve motivation and performance as well as generally sharpen the processes of planning and controlling. But it is often imperfectly implemented, producing complaints of burdensome requirements, disguised authoritarianism, and inadequate stress on cooperation among interdependent persons and groups.

REFERENCES

Blumenfeld, W. E., and T. E. Leidy. "Effectiveness of Goal Setting as a Management Device: Research Note." *Psychological Reports,* Vol. 24 (1969), p. 24.

Bryan, J. F., and E. A. Locke. "Goal Setting as a Means of Increasing Motivation." *Journal of Applied Psychology,* Vol. 51 (1967), pp. 274–77.

Campbell, J. P., M. D. Dunnette, E. E. Lawler, III, and K. E. Weick, Jr. *Managerial Behavior, Performance, and Effectiveness.* McGraw-Hill, 1970.

Carroll, S. J., and H. L. Tosi, Jr. *Management by Objectives: Applications and Research.* Macmillan, 1973.

Carroll, S. J., and H. L. Tosi. "Goal Characteristics and Personality Factors in a Management by Objectives Program." *Administrative Science Quarterly,* Vol. 15 (1970), pp. 295–305.

Clines, F. X. "Sanitation Department to Test Profit-Motivation System." *New York Times,* Apr. 29, 1976.

Dachler, H. P., and W. H. Mobley. "Construct Validation of an Instrumentality-Expectancy-Task-Goal Model of Work Motivation." *Journal of Applied Psychology,* Vol. 58 (1973), pp. 397–418.

Dent, J. K. "Organizational Correlates of the Goals of Business Management." *Personnel Psychology,* Vol. 12 (Autumn 1959), pp. 365–94.

Drucker, P. *Management: Tasks, Responsibilities, Practices.* Harper & Row, 1974.

―――. *The Practice of Management.* Harper & Row, 1954.

Duttagupta, D. *An Empirical Evaluation of Management by Objectives.* Master's thesis, Baruch College, New York, 1975.

England, G. W. "Organizational Goals and Expected Behavior of American Managers." *Academy of Management Journal,* Vol. 10 (June 1967), pp. 107–17.

French, J. R., E. Kay, and H. H. Meyer. "Participation and the Appraisal System." *Human Relations,* Vol. 19 (1966), pp. 3–19.

Fryer, F. W. *An Evaluation of Level of Aspiration as a Training Procedure.* Prentice-Hall, 1964.

General Electric Company. *Professional Management in General Electric: Book 3.* The General Electric Company, 1954.

Hughes, C. L. *Goal Setting: Key to Individual and Organizational Effectiveness.* American Management Association, 1965.

Humble, J. W. *Management by Objectives in Action.* McGraw-Hill, 1970.

Ivancevich, J. M. "A Longitudinal Assessment of Management by Objectives." *Administrative Science Quarterly,* Vol. 17 (1972), pp. 126–38.

———. "Changes in Performance in a Management by Objectives Program." *Administrative Science Quarterly,* Vol. 19 (1974), pp. 563–74.

———., J. H. Donnelly, and H. H. Lyon. "A Study of the Impact of Management by Objectives on Perceived Need Satisfaction." *Personnel Psychology,* Vol. 23 (1970), pp. 139–51.

Latham, G. P., and G. A. Yukl. "A Review of Research on the Application of Goal Setting in Organizations." *Academy of Management Journal,* Vol. 18 (1975), pp. 824–45.

———. "Assigned versus Participative Goal Setting with Educated and Uneducated Woods Workers." *Journal of Applied Psychology,* Vol. 60 (1975), pp. 299–302.

Lawler, E. E., III, and J. R. Hackman. "Impact of Employee Participation in the Development of Pay Incentive Plans: A Field Experiment." *Journal of Applied Psychology,* Vol. 53 (1969), pp. 467–71.

Lawrence, L. C., and P. C. Smith. "Group Decisions and Employee Participation." *Journal of Applied Psychology,* Vol. 39 (1955), pp. 334–37.

Levinson, H. "Management by Whose Objectives?" *Harvard Business Review,* Vol. 48, No. 4 (1970), pp. 125–34.

Likert, R. *New Patterns of Management.* McGraw-Hill, 1961.

Locke, E. A. "Toward a Theory of Task Motivation and Incentives." *Organizational Behavior and Human Performance,* Vol. 3 (1968), pp. 157–89.

———., N. Cartledge, and C. S. Knerr. "Studies of the Relationship Between Satisfaction, Goal-Setting and Performance." *Organizational Behavior and Human Performance,* Vol. 5 (1970), pp. 427–36.

Mace, A. C. *Incentives: Some Experimental Studies* (Rep. 72). London: Industrial Health Research Board, 1935.

McGregor, D. "An Uneasy Look at Performance Appraisal." *Harvard Business Review,* Vol. 35 (1957), pp. 89–94.

———. *The Human Side of Enterprise.* McGraw-Hill, 1960.

March, J., and H. Simon. *Organizations.* Wiley, 1958.

Merrill, D. E. "How Do You Measure the Effectiveness of a Business." *Organizational Dynamics,* Vol. 2, No. 2 (Autumn 1973), pp. 42–53.

Odiorne, G. *Management by Objectives.* Pitman, 1965.

Raia, A. P. "Goal Setting and Self Control." *Journal of Management Studies,* Vol. 2 (1965), pp. 34–53.

———. *Managing by Objectives.* Scott, Foresman, 1974.

Ronan, W. W., G. P. Latham, and S. B. Kinne. "Effects of Goal Setting and Supervision on Worker Behavior in an Industrial Situation." *Journal of Applied Psychology,* Vol. 58 (1973), pp. 302–307.

Schleh, E. C. *Management by Results.* McGraw-Hill, 1961.

Selznick, P. *Leadership in Administration.* Harper & Row, 1957.

Shoeffler, S., R. D. Buzzell, and D. F. Heany. "Impact of Strategic Planning on Profit Performance." *Harvard Business Review,* Vol. 52, No. 5 (March–April 1974), pp. 137–45.

Shuster, F. E., and A. F. Kindall. "Management by Objectives: Where We Stand—A Survey of the *Fortune* 500." *Human Resource Management,* Vol. 13, No. 1 (Spring 1974), pp. 8–11.

Singer, C., et al. *A History of Technology.* Oxford University Press, 1956.

Stedry, A. C. *Budget Control and Cost Behavior.* Prentice-Hall, 1960.

————., and E. Kay. "The Effects of Goal Difficulty on Performance." *Behavioral Science*, Vol. 11 (1966), pp. 459–70.

Steers, R. M. "Task-Goal Attributes, n Achievement, and Supervisory Performance." *Organizational Behavior and Human Performance*, Vol. 13 (1975), pp. 392–403.

————., and L. W. Porter. "The Role of Task-Goal Attributes in Employee Performance." *Psychological Bulletin*, Vol. 81 (1974), pp. 434–52.

Stringer, R. A. "Achievement Motivation and Management Control." *Personnel Administration*, Vol. 29, No. 6 (1966), pp. 3 ff.

Tomekovic, T. "Level of Knowledge of Requirements as a Motivational Factor in the Work Situation." *Human Relations*, Vol. 15 (1962), pp. 197–216.

Vanderwicken, P. "Lubrizol Ignores the Management Manuals." *Fortune* (February 1975a), pp. 132 ff.

————. "What's Really Wrong at Chrysler." *Fortune* (May 1975b), pp. 176 ff.

Vroom, V. *Some Personality Determinants of the Effects of Participation.* Prentice-Hall, 1960.

Walker, C. R. *Modern Technology and Civilization.* McGraw-Hill, 1962.

Ways, Max. "Watergate as a Case Study in Management." *Fortune* (November 1973), pp. 109 ff.

Wexley, K. N., and W. F. Nemeroff. "Effects of Positive Reinforcement and Goal Setting as Methods of Management Development." *Journal of Applied Psychology*, Vol. 60 (1975), pp. 446–50.

Wikstrom, W. S. *Managing by and with Objectives.* National Industrial Conference Board, 1968.

Zander, A., and T. Newcomb, Jr. "Group Levels of Aspiration in United Fund Campaigns." *Journal of Personality and Social Psychology*, Vol. 6 (1967), pp. 157–62.

Readings

Leadership in Administration
Philip Selznick

*In this essay, Philip Selznick discusses the critical management challenge of
defining the distinctive character and competence of an organization. He refers to
meeting this challenge as the exercise of institutional leadership, which he
distinguishes from administration — the process of designing suitable organization
structures and making other arrangements to assure efficient operations. Selznick's
use of the term "leadership" is an unusual, even unique, use of the term in
management literature. However, it is akin to the activity of defining strategy and
purpose discussed in this chapter and it calls for orders of understanding and
skill that are, regrettably, most uncommon.*

The main task of this essay has been to explore the meaning of institutional leadership, in the hope of contributing to our understanding of large-scale organization. We
have not offered recipes for the solution of immediate problems. Rather, we have
sought to encourage reflection and self-knowledge, to provide some new guides to
the diagnosis of administrative troubles, and to suggest that the posture of statesmanship may well be appropriate for many executives who now have a narrower view and
a more limited aspiration.

This final chapter summarizes the main ideas developed above, with some added
notes on responsibility and creativity in leadership.

BEYOND EFFICIENCY

It is easy to agree to the abstract proposition that the function of the executive is to
find a happy joinder of means and ends. It is harder to take that idea seriously. There
is a strong tendency not only in administrative life but in all social action to divorce
means and ends by overemphasizing one or the other. The cult of efficiency in administrative theory and practice is a modern way of overstressing means and neglecting ends.
This it does in two ways. First, by fixing attention on maintaining a smooth-running
machine, it slights the more basic and more difficult problem of defining and safeguarding the ends of an enterprise. Second, the cult of efficiency tends to stress techniques of organization that are essentially neutral, and therefore available for any goals,
rather than methods peculiarly adapted to a distinctive type of organization or stage
of development.

Efficiency as an operating ideal presumes that goals are settled and that the main
resources and methods for achieving them are available. The problem is then one of
joining available means to known ends. This order of decision-making we have called
routine, distinguishing it from the realm of *critical* decision. The latter, because it

involves choices that affect the basic character of the enterprise, is the true province of leadership as distinct from administrative management. Such choices are of course often made unconsciously, without awareness of their larger significance, but then the enterprise evolves more or less blindly. Leadership provides guidance to minimize this blindness.

In many situations, including those most important to the ultimate well-being of the enterprise, goals may not have been defined. Moreover, even when they are defined, the necessary means may have still to be created. Creating the means is, furthermore, not a narrow technical matter; it involves molding the social character of the organization. Leadership goes beyond efficiency (1) when it sets the basic mission of the organization and (2) when it creates a social organism capable of fulfilling that mission. A company's decision to add a new product may be routine if the new is but an extension of the old. It is a critical decision, however, when it calls for a re-examination of the firm's mission and role, e.g., whether to remain primarily a producer of a raw commodity or to become a manufacturer of consumer goods. The latter choice will inevitably affect the outlook of management, the structure and control of the company, and the balance of forces in the industry.

Not only the setting of goals by top leadership but many other kinds of decisions at all administrative levels can be part of critical experience. Anything may enter the area of critical experience providing it affects the ability of the organization to uphold its distinctive aims and values. If an atmosphere congenial to creative research is required, the methods of assigning work, policing diligence, or judging output must be governed by that aim. This often produces tension between those executives most sensitive to the special needs of the enterprise and those who seek to apply more general and more neutral techniques of efficiency.

In going beyond efficiency, leadership also transcends "human engineering," at least as that is usually understood. Efficiency may require improved techniques of communication and supervision, but these techniques are largely indifferent to the aims they serve. The human relations specialist like his predecessor, the efficiency expert, is characteristically unmoved by program, by the content of what is to be done. His inspiration does not derive from the aim of creating a particular kind of auto firm or hospital or school. Rather his imagination is stirred by the processes of group interaction and the vision of a harmonious team, whatever its end may be.

This does not mean that communication and other forms of human interaction are unimportant to leadership. They do become vitally important when they are given content, when they serve the aim of fashioning a distinctive way of thinking or acting and thus help establish the human foundations for achieving a particular set of goals. Indeed, the *attainment* of efficiency, in the sense of transforming a basically inefficient organization into one that runs according to modern standards, may itself be a leadership goal. But here the task is a creative one, a matter of reshaping fundamental perspectives and relationships. It should not be confused with the routine administrative management of an organization already fully committed to the premises of rational accounting and discipline.

BEYOND ORGANIZATION

The design and maintenance of organizations is often a straightforward engineering proposition. When the goals of the organization are clear-cut, and when most choices can be made on the basis of known and objective technical criteria, the engineer rather than the leader is called for. His work may include human engineering in order to smooth personal relations, improve morale, or reduce absenteeism. But his problem remains one of adapting known quantities through known techniques to predetermined ends.

From the engineering perspective, the organization is made up of standardized building blocks. These elements, and the ways of putting them together, are the stock-in-trade of the organization engineer. His ultimate ideal is complete rationality, and this assumes that each member of the organization, and each constituent unit, can be made to adhere faithfully to an assigned, engineered role. Furthermore, the role assigned does not stem so much from the peculiar nature of *this* enterprise; rather, the roles are increasingly generalized and similar to parallel roles in other organizations. Only thus can the organization engineer take advantage of the growth of general knowledge concerning the conditions of efficient administrative management.

The limits of organization engineering become apparent when we must create a structure *uniquely adapted to the mission and role of the enterprise.* This adaptation goes beyond a tailored combination of uniform elements; it is an adaptation in depth, affecting the nature of the parts themselves. This is really a very familiar process, brought home to us most clearly when we recognize that certain firms or agencies are stamped by distinctive ways of making decisions or by peculiar commitments to aims, methods, or clienteles. In this way the organization as a technical instrument takes on values. As a vehicle of group integrity it becomes in some degree an end in itself. This process of becoming infused with value is part of what we mean by institutionalization. As this occurs, *organization management* becomes *institutional leadership.* The latter's main responsibility is not so much technical administrative management as the maintenance of institutional integrity.

The integrity of an enterprise goes beyond efficiency, beyond organization forms and procedures, even beyond group cohesion. Integrity combines organization and policy. It is the unity that emerges when a particular orientation becomes so firmly a part of group life that it colors and directs a wide variety of attitudes, decisions, and forms of organization, and does so at many levels of experience. The building of integrity is part of what we have called the "institutional embodiment of purpose" and its protection is a major function of leadership.

The protection of integrity is more than an aesthetic or expressive exercise, more than an attempt to preserve a comforting, familiar environment. It is a practical concern of the first importance because the defense of integrity is also a defense of the organization's *distinctive competence.* As institutionalization progresses the enterprise takes on a special character, and this means that it becomes peculiarly competent (or incompetent) to do a particular kind of work. This is especially important when much depends on the creation of an appropriate atmosphere, as in the case of efforts to hold tight transportation schedules or maintain high standards of quality. A considerable part of high-level salesmanship is an effort to show the firm's distinctive capability to produce a certain product or perform a special service. This is important in government too, where competing agencies having similar formal assignments work hard to develop and display their distinctive competencies.

The terms "institution," "organization character," and "distinctive competence" all refer to the same basic process—the transformation of an engineered, technical arrangement of building blocks into a social organism. This transition goes on unconsciously and inevitably wherever leeway for evolution and adaptation is allowed by the system of technical controls; and at least some such leeway exists in all but the most narrowly circumscribed organizations. Leadership has the job of guiding the transition from organization to institution so that the ultimate result effectively embodies desired aims and standards.

Occasionally we encounter a self-conscious attempt to create an institution. The history of the *New York Times*, for example, suggests such an effort. Ideals of objectivity and public instruction have deeply affected many aspects of the organization, including the nature of the staff, the pace of work, the relations to advertisers, and its role among other newspapers. Of course, it is relatively easy to see a newspaper as an institution because it so apparently touches familiar ideals. Whether it truly embodies those ideals is a question that appeals to all as relevant and sensible. But we have argued that the formation of institutions is a far more widespread phenomenon and is a process that must be understood if the critical experience of leadership is to be grasped.

Institutional analysis asks the question: What is the bearing of an existing or proposed procedure on the distinctive role and character of the enterprise? Very often, of course, organization practices are institutionally neutral, just as many body functions are independent of the personality structure. But the question must be put. Thus recent efforts to establish statistical and administrative control units for the judiciary look to improvements in the division of labor among judges, and to similar matters, for the achievement of a more "orderly flow of litigation." The proponents of greater efficiency reaffirm their adherence to the principle of judicial independence, and they believe this principle is not affected by improved administrative controls; they seek to "serve, not supervise." In this case it seems altogether likely that a wide measure of reform in judicial administration is possible without seriously undermining the judge's traditional image of his own role and sense of independence. Nevertheless, the experience of other institutions suggests that the managerial trend can have far-reaching effects, and the question of whether a set of proposed administrative reforms endangers the maintenance of desired values is always legitimate and necessary.

The lesson is this: Those who deal with the more obvious ideals—such as education, science, creativity, or freedom—should more fully recognize the dependence of these ideals on congenial though often mundane administrative arrangements. On the other hand, those who deal with more restricted values, such as the maintenance of a particular industrial competence, should be aware that these values too involve ideals of excellence, ideals that must be built into the social structure of the enterprise and become part of its basic character. In either case, a too ready acceptance of neutral techniques of efficiency, whatever their other merits, will contribute little to this institutional development and may even retard it.

The study of institutions is in some ways comparable to the clinical study of personality. It requires a genetic and developmental approach, an emphasis on historical origins and growth stages. There is a need to see the enterprise as a whole and to see how it is transformed as new ways of dealing with a changing environment evolve. As in the case of personality, effective diagnosis depends upon locating the special problems that go along with a particular character-structure; and we can understand character better when we see it as the product of self-preserving efforts to deal with inner impulses and external demands. In both personality and institutions "self-preservation" means more than bare organic or material survival. Self-preservation has to do with the maintenance of basic identity, with the integrity of a personal or institutional "self."

In approaching these problems, there is necessarily a close connection between clinical diagnosis of particular cases and the development of sound general knowledge. Our problem is to discover the characteristic ways in which *types* of institutions respond to *types* of circumstances. The significant classifications may well depart from common-sense distinctions among enterprises according to whether they perform economic, political, religious, or military functions. We may find that more general characteristics, such as professionalized managerial control, competence to make full use of creative talents, or dependence on volunteer personnel, are more helpful in classifying organizations and in understanding the types of problems they face and the solutions that may be available. Students of personality have had similar objectives and have made greater, although still very crude, efforts to get away from common-sense rubrics. Yet, despite theoretical difficulties, real progress has been made, and clinical success in diagnosis and therapy lends confidence to the larger scientific quest.

RESPONSIBLE LEADERSHIP

As the organization becomes an institution new problems are set for the men who run it. Among these is the need for institutional responsibility, which accounts for much of what we mean by statesmanship.

From a personal standpoint, responsible leadership is a blend of commitment, understanding, and determination. These elements bring together the selfhood of the leader and the identity of the institution. This is partly a matter of self-*conception*, for whatever his special background, and however important it may have been in the decision that gave him his office, the responsible leader in a mature institution must transcend his specialism. Self-*knowledge* becomes an understanding not only of the leader's own weaknesses and potentialities but of those qualities in the enterprise itself. And the assumption of command is a self-*summoning* process, yielding the will to know and the will to act in accordance with the requirements of institutional survival and fulfillment.

From a policy standpoint, and that is our primary concern, most of the characteristics of the responsible leader can be summarized under two headings: the avoidance of opportunism and the avoidance of utopianism.

Opportunism is the pursuit of immediate, short-run advantages in a way inadequately controlled by considerations of principle and ultimate consequence. To take advantage of opportunities is to show that one is alive, but institutions no less than persons must look to the long-run effects of present advantage. In speaking of the "long-run" we have in mind not time as such but how change affects personal or institutional identity. Such effects are not usually immediately apparent, and therefore we emphasize the lapse of time. But changes in character or identity may occur quite rapidly.

Leadership is irresponsible when it fails to set goals and therefore lets the institution drift. The absence of controlling aims forces decisions to be made in response to immediate pressures. Of course, many large enterprises do drift, yet they survive. The penalties are not always swift, and very often bare survival is possible even though the fullest potentialities of the enterprise are not realized and significant changes in identity do occur.

The setting of institutional *goals* cannot be divorced from the enunciation of governing *principles*. Goal-setting, if it is institutionally meaningful, is framed in the language of character or identity, that is, it tells us what we should "do" in order to become what we want to "be." A decision to produce a new product or enter a new market, though it may set goals, is nevertheless irresponsible if it is not based on an understanding of the company's past and potential character. If the new venture, on analysis, requires a change in distinctive competence, then *that* becomes the new goal. Such a goal is bound up with principles because attaining and conserving a distinctive competence depends on an understanding of what standards are required and how to maintain them. If a grain processing firm moves into the chemical industry, it must learn how to build into its new division the competence to keep pace with rapid technological changes on pain of falling behind in the struggle against obsolescent products and techniques. Because the technique of attaining this is seldom based on explicitly formulated principles, it would be prudent to staff the new division, *especially* at the top, with men drawn from the chemical industry rather than with men drawn from the parent firm and representing its tradition and orientations.

When an enterprise is permitted to drift, making short-run, partial adaptations, the greatest danger lies in uncontrolled effects on organization character. If ultimately there is a complete change, with a new character emerging, those who formed and sustained the organization at the beginning may find that they no longer fit the organization. There is also the likelihood that character will not really be transformed: it will be *attenuated and confused*. Attenuation means that the sought-for distinctive competence becomes vague and abstract, unable to influence deeply the work of staff and operating divisions. This occurs when the formulation of institutional goals is an afterthought, a way of rationalizing activities actually resulting from opportunistic lines of decision. A confused organization character is marked by an unordered and disharmonious mixture of capabilities. The practical result is that the organization cannot perform any task effectively, and this weakens its ability to survive in the face of strong competition.

In addition to sheer drift stemming from the failure to set institutional goals, opportunism also reflects an excessive response to outside pressures. To be sure, leaders must take account of the environment, adapting to its limitations as well as to its opportunities, but we must beware of institutional surrender made in the name of organizational survival. There is a difference between a university president who *takes account* of a state legislature or strong pressure groups and one who permits these forces to determine university policy. The leader's job is to *test* the environment to find out which demands can become truly effective threats, to *change* the environment by finding allies and other sources of external support, and to *gird* his organization by creating the means and the will to withstand attacks.

Here, too, we come back to the problem of maintaining institutional integrity. The ultimate cost of opportunistic adaptation goes beyond capitulation on specific issues. A more serious result is that outside elements may enter the organization and dominate parts of it. When this happens the organization is no longer truly independent, no longer making specific compromises as necessity dictates while retaining its unity and distinctive identity. Rather, it has given over a piece of itself to alien forces, making it possible for them to exercise broader influence on policy. The transformation of compromise or even defeat into partial organizational surrender can sometimes be a conscious measure of last resort, but it also occurs without full awareness on the part of the participants. In our study of the Tennessee Valley Authority, referred to above, just such a phenomenon was observed. A political compromise with local and national agricultural interests was implemented by permitting part of the TVA as an organization to be controlled by those forces, with extensive and unanticipated effects on the role and character of the agency. The avoidance of opportunism is not the avoidance of all compromise; it is the avoidance of compromise that undermines institutional integrity.

Opportunism also displays itself in a narrow self-centeredness, in an effort to exploit other groups for immediate, short-run advantages. If a firm offers a product or service to other firms, expectations of dependability are created, especially in the matter of continuing supply. If supplies are abruptly discontinued, activities that depended upon them will suffer. Hence a firm's reputation for dependability and concern for others becomes a matter of great importance wherever continuing relationships are envisioned. To act as if only a set of impersonal transactions were involved, with no responsibility beyond the strict terms of a contract, creates anxiety in the buyer, threatens to damage *his* reputation for dependability, and in the end weakens both parties.

The responsible leader recognizes the need for stable relations with the community of which his organization is a part, although he must test the environment to see how real that requirement is. A large and enduring enterprise will probably have to contribute to the maintenance of community stability, at least within its own field of action. In industry, this may take the form of participation in trade associations and other devices for self-regulation. The marginal firm, on the other hand, can afford to be irresponsible in dealing with the community because it is less dependent on stable relations with other firms or with a special clientele or labor force. Such firms have also less need of responsibility to themselves as institutions, for they have fewer hostages to fortune. Generally, responsibility to the enterprise and to the community go hand in hand, each increasing as the transition from organization to institution becomes more complete.

If opportunism goes too far in accepting the dictates of a "reality principle," utopianism hopes to avoid hard choices by a flight to abstractions. This too results in irresponsibility, in escape from the true functions of leadership.

In Chapter Three we outlined some of the sources of utopianism. One of these is the *overgeneralization of purpose.* Thus "to make a profit" is widely accepted as a statement of business purpose, but this is too general to permit responsible decision-making. Here again, the more marginal the business, that is, the greater its reliance upon quick returns, easy liquidation, and highly flexible tactics, the less need there is for an institutionally responsible and more specific formulation of purpose. Indeed, the very generality of the purpose is congenial to the opportunism of these groups. But when institutional continuity and identity are at stake, a definition of mission is required that will take account of the organization's distinctive character, including present and prospective capabilities, as well as the requirements of playing a desired role in a particular industrial or commercial context.

Utopian wishful-thinking enters when men who purport to be institutional leaders attempt to rely on overgeneralized purposes to guide their decisions. But when guides are unrealistic, yet decisions must be made, more realistic *but uncontrolled* criteria will somehow fill the gap. Immediate exigencies will dominate the actual choices that are made. In this way, the polarities of utopianism and opportunism involve each other.

Another manifestation of utopianism is the hope that the solution of technical problems will solve institutional problems. We have discussed the "retreat to technology" as a way of avoiding responsibility for the multiple ends that must be satisfied if the institution as a whole is to be successful. To be "just a soldier," "just an engineer," or even "just a businessman" is inconsistent with the demands of statesmanship. It is utopian and irresponsible to suppose that a narrow technical logic can be relied on by men who make decisions that, though they originate in technical problems, have larger consequences for the ultimate evolution of the enterprise and its position in the world.

This brand of utopianism is associated with adventurism, a willingness to commit the organization as a whole on the basis of a partial assessment of the situation derived from a particular technological perspective, such as that of the propagandist in foreign affairs or the engineer or designer in industry. Here again the utopian as technologist becomes the victim of opportunism.

Responsible leadership steers a course between utopianism and opportunism. Its responsibility consists in accepting the obligation of giving direction instead of merely ministering to organizational equilibrium; in adapting aspiration to the character of the organization, bearing in mind that what the organization has been will affect what it can be and do; and in transcending bare organizational survival by seeing that specialized decisions do not weaken or confuse the distinctive identity of the enterprise.

CREATIVE LEADERSHIP

To the essentially conservative posture of the responsible leader we must add a concern for change and reconstruction. This creative role has two aspects. First, there is what we have called the "institutional embodiment of purpose." Second, creativity is exercised by strategic and tactical planning, that is, analyzing the environment to determine how best to use the existing resources and capabilities of the organization. This essay has not treated the problem of externally oriented strategies. On the other hand, what can be done to establish policy internally depends upon the changing relation between the organization and its environment.

The inbuilding of purpose is a challenge to creativity because it involves transforming men and groups from neutral, technical units into participants who have a peculiar stamp, sensitivity, and commitment. This is ultimately an educational process. It has been well said that the effective leader must know the meaning and master the techniques of the educator. As in the larger community, education is more than narrow technical training; though it does not shrink from indoctrination, it also teaches men to think for themselves. The leader as educator requires an ability to interpret the role and character of the enterprise, to perceive and develop models for thought and behavior, and to find modes of communication that will inculcate general rather than merely partial perspectives.

The main practical import of this effort is that *policy will gain spontaneous and reasoned support*. Desired ends and means are sustained and furthered, not through continuous command, but as a free expression of truly accepted principles. This presumes that at least the core participants combine loyalty to the enterprise with a sensitive awareness of the principles by which it is guided. Loyalty by itself is not enough, just as blind patriotism is insufficient. There must also be an ability to sense when a course of action threatens institutional integrity.

To be sure, this ideal of rational, free-willed consent is virtually impossible to achieve in organizations that have narrow, practical aims and whose main problem is the disciplined harnessing of human energy to achieve those aims. But such organizations, just because of this narrowness, are but meagerly institutionalized and have correspondingly little need for executive statesmanship. The creativity we speak of here is particularly necessary — and peculiarly possible — where, as discussed earlier, the transition from organization to institution is in process or has occurred.

To create an institution we rely on many techniques for infusing day-to-day behavior with long-run meaning and purpose. One of the most important of these techniques is the elaboration of socially integrating myths. These are efforts to state, in the language of uplift and idealism, what is distinctive about the aims and methods of the enterprise. Successful institutions are usually able to fill in the formula, "What we are proud of around here is. . . ." Sometimes, a fairly explicit institutional philosophy is worked out; more often, a sense of mission is communicated in more indirect but no less significant ways. The assignment of high prestige to certain activities will itself help to create a myth, especially if buttressed by occasional explicit statements. The specific ways of projecting a myth are as various as communication itself. For creative leadership, it is not the communication of a myth that counts; rather, creativity depends on having the will and the insight to see the necessity of the myth, to discover a successful formulation, and above all to create the organizational conditions that will sustain the ideals expressed.

Successful myths are never merely cynical or manipulative, even though they may be put forward self-consciously to further the chances of stability or survival. If a state university develops a concept of "service to the community" as its central ideal, as against more remote academic aspirations, this may have its origins in a sense of insecurity, but it will not be innocent in application. To be effective, the projected myth cannot be restricted to holiday speeches or to testimony before legislative committees. It will inevitably color many aspects of university policy, affecting standards of admission, orientations of research, and the scope of the curriculum. The compulsion to embody the myth in practice has a dual source, reflecting inner needs and outer demands. Externally, those who can enforce demands upon the institution will not be content with empty verbal statements. They will expect conformity and the myth itself will provide a powerful lever to that end.

The executive acts out the myth for reasons of self-expression, but also for quite practical administrative reasons. He requires *some* integrating aid to the making of many diverse day-to-day decisions, and the myth helps to fulfill that need. Sharp discrepancies between theory and practice threaten his own authority in the eyes of subordinates; conformity to the myth will lessen "trouble" with outside groups. Not least important, he can hope that the myth will contribute to a unified sense of mission and thereby to the harmony of the whole. If the administrator is primarily dedicated to maintaining a smooth-running machine, and only weakly committed to substantive aims, these advantages will seem particularly appealing.

In the end, however, whatever their source, myths are institution builders. Making the myth effective willy-nilly entrenches particular objectives and capabilities, although these may not be the ones that initially inspired the sponsors of the enterprise. Myth-making may have roots in a sensed need to improve efficiency and morale; but its main office is to help create an integrated social organism.

The art of the creative leader is the art of institution-building, the reworking of human and technological materials to fashion an organism that embodies new and enduring values. The opportunity to do this depends on a considerable sensitivity to the politics of internal change. This is more than a struggle for power among contending groups and leaders. It is equally a matter of avoiding recalcitrance and releasing energies. Thus winning consent to new directions depends on how secure the participants feel. When many routine problems of technical and human organization remain to be solved, when the minimum conditions for holding the organization together are only precariously met, it is difficult to expend energy on long-range planning and even harder to risk experimental programs. When the organization is in good shape from an engineering standpoint it is easier to put ideals into practice. Old activities can be abandoned without excessive strain if, for example, the costs of relatively inefficient but morale-saving transfer and termination can be absorbed. Security is bartered for consent. Since this bargain is seldom sensed as truly urgent, a default of leadership is the more common experience.

On the same theme, security can be granted, thereby releasing energies for creative change, by examining established procedures to distinguish those important to a sense of security from those essential to the aims of the enterprise. Change should focus on the latter; stability can be assured to practices that do not really matter so far as objectives are concerned but which do satisfy the need to be free from threatening change. Many useless industrial conflicts have been fought to protect prerogative and deny security, with but little effect on the ultimate competence of the firm.

If one of the great functions of administration is the exertion of cohesive force in the direction of institutional security, another great function is the creation of conditions that will make possible in the future what is excluded in the present. This requires a strategy of change that looks to the attainment of new capabilities more nearly fulfilling the truly felt needs and aspirations of the institution. The executive becomes a statesman as he makes the transition from administrative management to institutional leadership.

A Contingency Approach to Planning: Planning with Goals and Planning Without Goals

Michael B. McCaskey

Most descriptions of organization and individual planning assume that setting goals is basic to any planning worthy of the name (2, 7, 27). In some important planning situations, however, it is difficult or impossible to set goals, and conventional descriptions

The author would like to thank Marvis Oehm, David Berlew, Richard Goodman, Harold Kassarjian, William McKelvey, John Morse, and Stephen Rhinesmith for their comments on earlier drafts of this paper.

of planning do not seem to apply. In fact, many managers realize that some of their most important planning takes place without ever explicitly considering specific goals.

This paper seeks to open up discussion on the subject and foster research by challenging conventional descriptions of planning. Planning can be improved by acknowledging that there is more than one way to plan and by using a contingency approach to specify what type of planning is appropriate when.

A frustrating classroom experience started me thinking about the possibility of planning without goals. Recently I conducted an expectations sharing exercise with a class to set mutual expectations about the goals and processes of the course (13, 14). Recognizing the powerful impact expectations can have on behavior, the exercise involves students and the instructor in making their expectations clear and well-matched. Members draw up a psychological contract on what they want to learn and how they want to learn it. Although this exercise usually expedites the learning process, this time it was a frustrating failure. Afterwards, it became clear that I had run the exercise in a way that was implicitly tied to planning toward specific goals. In addition, this particular group of MBA students seemed highly individualistic and wary of becoming a cohesive group; therefore, they seemed to need a different kind of planning process.

Planning processes might be thought of as ranging along a continuum from more to less definition of desired outcomes. Toward one end is conventional planning with specific, objective goals. Because this first type of planning is so familiar, it will be described only briefly. Toward the other end of the continuum is a more intuitive type of planning for which there exists only scattered bits of evidence in the literature (9). A good portion of this paper is devoted to trying to build a conceptualization of the second type of planning. The two processes are not mutually exclusive and, as hopefully will be made clear later, both types have strengths and weaknesses. Each has its time and its place, and a skillful manager undoubtedly uses both, depending on the situation.

PLANNING WITH SPECIFIC GOALS

In one of the most comprehensive and thoughtful books on goal-directed planning, Steiner describes the planning process as follows:

> Planning is a process that begins with objectives; defines strategies, policies, and detailed plans to achieve them; which establishes an organization to implement decisions; and includes a review of performance and feedback to introduce a new planning cycle (27, p. 7).

In this mode, plans should be formally prepared and should be "to the fullest possible extent objective, factual, logical and realistic" (27, p. 20). Such an approach is so often used and so highly touted because it can bring very powerful results. Management by objectives, PERT diagrams, PPBS, and behavioral objectives are a few examples of this type of planning.

Planning with goals is a rational, analytical approach which assumes goals can be stated and accepts a narrowing of focus in order to efficiently use energy. It should be noted that this description of a rational, analytical approach differs from Baybrooke and Lindblom's description of the rational/comprehensive approach as an exhaustive treatment of all the potentially relevant issues (5, 16). Here, instead of performing an exhaustive examination of issues, if people are committed to the goals, there can be a forceful converging of efforts to meet deadlines and to achieve goals. People given such plans spend less time exploring alternative futures because they know what they need to accomplish. After plans have been made, people can take the goals as a given, which provides a measure of stability and can supply a sense of purpose. This helps individuals structure their life space, decide what activities should be carried out, and how time should be spent.

On the other hand, the first type of planning imposes some limits on flexibility. Narrowing focus to accomplish goals reduces the chances that planners will explore alternative futures once movement toward goals has begun. Exploration takes place mainly in the planning phase, and the action phase implements what has been decided in formulating the plan. Based on feedback about performance or changing conditions, planners may revise and slightly modify their plans in successive planning cycles. Planners might also be inventive within the perceived path to the goal or in revising the goal in a manner proximate to the original goal. But, given man's limited cognitive abilities and energies (18), less time is available for finding new possibilities outside those connected to the goal or goal path. A planning with goals process is not intrinsically rigid, but it is by its nature less open-ended than the second type of planning. In certain situations (specified in a later section of this paper) some closure is desirable, but a narrowing in how the field of choices is perceived should be recognized as a characteristic feature of planning with goals. Planners using this process, therefore, are less likely to discover a wholly new goal or opportunity.

DIRECTIONAL PLANNING

In the second type of planning, the planner or planners identify a domain and direction. *Domain* is the area in which the organization or individual will work. The *direction* is the actor's tendencies, the favored styles of perceiving and doing. Instead of specifying concrete, measurable goals, the planners work more from who they are and what they like to do. This type of planning might be called planning without goals, but I prefer a label like "Planning from Thrust" or "Directional Planning" which points to the positive characteristics of the process. Whereas planning with goals moves toward external desired ends, the second type of planning identifies a preferred style of acting for the organization or individual and an arena for activity. The emphasis switches from carefully formulating what goal out there is to be accomplished to consideration of the agent's thrust.

Domain refers to what aspects of the environment are to be of concern and what the organization's own criteria for assessing performance will be (21). Domain refers to the problem of the individual or organization delimiting a particular space in which he has, or wishes to develop, special competence. The choice or creation of a domain marks the boundaries for commitment and action on the part of an individual or organization.

The first type of planning is goal-directed, the second is direction-moving. The distinctive difference between the two is similar to Angyal's contrast between the terms *teleological* and *directional* (1). Translating to our present concern, in planning with goals a planner describes a certain goal, a "telos," that he wants to reach. He often develops a goal path, specifying the steps to be taken which are fitted to a time-table, to achieve his goal. It is the goal which helps define the plans, and in this sense the planning with goals process is teleological.

In planning from thrust the planner uses a very different mode. He identifies an intrinsic pattern of movement that, in itself, is worth pursuing for the individual or organization. Planning here is directional, and the direction is determined intrinsically without reference to external goals. A device sometimes used to identify direction for an individual is to consider events and activities in the recent past which have been most deeply satisfying to him. From those events the individual tries to identify a pattern which describes a direction for himself. Whether or not this technique is used, the important point is that direction is not determined by goals. After the direction has been identified, goals might be named as a secondary process. This is substantially different from the first type of planning, however. As Angyal expresses it, "It is not the goal which defines the direction, but, on the contrary, the intrinsic pattern of a direction which defines what object may become a goal" (1, p. 55). Objects which lie along the path in which the direction is moving may become goals. But even when goals are chosen, one goal might easily be substituted for another as long as it lies on the general path of the direction. When using directional planning, activities are not as focused and the process does not have the closure that the first type of planning does.

A chief characteristic of planning from thrust is that, as the individual or organization interacts with the environment, the domain and direction change as a result. We are so accustomed to setting goals before acting (or at least saying that we do) that we overlook the ways in which we can discover goals by acting (17). Having once acted, planners obtain new information about what they want to do and what market opportunities and constraints there are. Planning from thrust generally undergoes several cycles of acting and planning, each cycle adding to the successive formulation of plans. Note that this planning approach differs markedly from the first approach, which attempts to define goals *before* acting. Here acting is seen as one method aiding the discovery and formulation of goals.

Organization theorists (29) have emphasized the need for organizations to adapt flexibly to or to buffer increasingly turbulent environmental conditions. However, how the organization tries to impact the domain, to make that part of the environment more stable or more favorable for the organization, is often underestimated. For example, improving the tires and the suspension system of the automobile added to its flexibility in traveling over rough terrain. Just as important, though, the environment was made more stable by smoothing out the roads on which the machine traveled (26). Organizations, by advertising, lobbying, public relations work, merging with competitors, and by buying suppliers or retail outlets, are trying to smooth the environment and impact their domains toward more favorable conditions.

At the same time, agents for economic and political units in the environment are bargaining, pulling and tugging, to define the organization's domain and direction to suit their needs. By citing several case studies on the start-up of mental health programs, Sarason argues that the creation of a new domain usually takes place within the context of existing old domains (23). The existing organizations and individuals resist the new one or try to define the new organization's domain in ways that suit their own domain. For example, local mental health professionals, through licensing and through their influence with legislators and funding agencies, can block or at least shape the development of new centers having anything to do with mental health services. The organization adjusts to the environment; and the environment, partly in response to efforts by the organization, perhaps can be perceived as adjusting to the organization. By the interaction of the environment and the organization, the domain and the direction are more knowledgeably defined.

In many situations the press of ongoing business precludes an organization's waiting until plans are precisely defined. Decisions must be made, budgets drawn up, and resources allocated. As decisions are made, some possibilities are diminished, others enhanced. The individual or the organization begins to understand more accurately where it can influence the environment to align it with the domain and direction chosen, and where the choice of domain and direction must be revised to meet the demands (power blocks, economic realities, other limitations) of the environment. Having acted, people find they are more likely to be rewarded for certain behaviors than for other behaviors. In some sense, then, a person or an organization only creates or discovers its identity by acting.

This continuous interaction makes domain and direction planning dynamic since it is revised as new opportunities or constraints arise. This type of planning, therefore, needs heavy feedback loops from the domain side and from the planners' side.

Kotter and Lawrence's research (15) on the effectiveness of six mayors of moderately large U.S. cities illustrates the importance of feedback loops for domain and direction planning. One of the patterns distinguishing the three effective mayors (judged to have increased the "net health" of their cities) from the three ineffective mayors was the process by which the mayors formulated policy.

The effective mayors spent one or two years interacting on an informal basis with people in the various groups and organizations in their city. They sought these people out and, based on their exchanges, were able to formulate a direction and an agenda which included the most important problems and opportunities facing the city. The effective mayors maintained close contact with their constituencies and made incremental changes in their plans as situations changed over the years.

The ineffective mayors, on the other hand, made less use of such feedback loops. One formulated his plans according to what a previous, successful mayor had done and found it hard to modify these plans. The second mayor immediately articulated his goals for the city based on his previously successful business operations and his view of the world. The third ineffective mayor was essentially planless and made large, erratic changes in his plans in response to the crisis of the day. None of the ineffective mayors aggressively sought out information from groups and organizations in the city about their problems. None of the ineffective mayors actively engaged with the environment in the process of developing plans for their city, nor did they use feedback to revise their plans.

This pattern is very similar to one Schrage uncovered in his research on successful R & D entrepreneurs (25). The successful entrepreneurs *actively* sought information from their environment—including financial institutions, competitors, suppliers, customers, and their own employees. The unsuccessful entrepreneurs, by way of contrast, worked from their idea of what different parts of their environment *should* be doing, rather than seeking out information on what they actually were doing.

While the second type of planning is more flexible, it entails higher energy costs. More information must be processed, and coding is less certain. Organization members explore possibilities, some of which will eventually be rejected and defined as outside the domain of the organization, and planning towards specific goals provides security and order, a stability which provides individuals with a sense of purpose. Planning *without* specifying goals entails greater stress for people since there can be more ambiguity about basic purposes and personal roles (10). This point must not be passed over lightly. Thrust planning and the ambiguity it involves can be very wearing on people.

The high stress costs involved in using the second type of planning make it difficult to live with over a long period of time. Most people, if given a choice, move their lives and organizational procedures toward more routine. They prefer to consider questions of identity and purpose more or less settled, as is the case in planning toward goals. Even in a company that was exciting because many things were not settled, the drive in a business context was to use resources more efficiently. In 1964, Joseph Wilson, then President of the Xerox Corporation, made the following statement about the company's future orientation to planning:

> Xerox was an organization four years ago which could not look much farther ahead than the introduction of the 914, because that task was straining its every resource. In contrast, now it is an organization whose higher echelons are constantly nagged by consciousness of the need to have specific plans for 1968, 1969, 1970, 1971, 1972, 1973, 1974 and 1975. These men are worried that we do not yet have specific plans for new products and services to be introduced in 1972, let us say, and perhaps this is the most important part of the whole strategy. Just as it was important to make this whole organization dissatisfied with results in any year which projected a profit increase of less than 20% so it is important now to make it dissatisfied that we do not have a specific plan for the tenth year ahead (28, p. 529).

WHEN EACH TYPE OF PLANNING IS USED

Viewed over the long run, the organization and its subsystems may go through cycles of stability and change (20), using first one type of planning then the other. In large organizations it also seems likely that both types of planning may concurrently be in use by different subsystems. A research division, for example, may be using directional planning at the same time the production division is planning in terms of specific, measurable goals. The development of the matrix organization is one way that opportunities for both types of planning can be provided in one organization. For example, a task force can be brought together to explore fundamental direction and domain questions, while a project group can be charged with formulating and carrying out specific plans (12). However, the basic question is when and where to use each type. Mixups are painful, and it is costly to use a planning process that is inappropriate.

Since specifying goals is such a familiar and accepted part of the planning process, it may be helpful to list some situations in which this type of planning is *inappropriate* and which call for domain and direction planning instead.

1. When it is too early to set goals, that is, before an individual or organization has decided who it is or what it wants to do. For example, in the start-up stage in a new organization, the principals have to thrash it out to discover their domain and direction.

2. When the environment is unstable and uncertain. Well-defined and precisely

charted routes to a goal are undone when the character of the ground changes. There is little sense in planning to reach a highly specific goal when the context is being significantly altered under the direct impact of technological, social, economic, legal, and other changes.

3. When people cannot build enough trust or agreement to decide upon a common goal. These are situations in which the persons are pursuing such different courses that the only superordinate goals they can commit themselves to are so vague they are almost meaningless. In other words, the persons are a collection of individuals more than a purposeful system. It is significant that commentators have begun to notice trends to shape some organizations according to the growth needs of individual members (3, 4, 8). If these trends continue, the result may be less consensus on goals derived for the sake of the organization and greater use of a planning from thrust type of process.

Under some conditions planning toward goals is more likely to succeed, and domain and direction planning is wasteful if not distressing. To some extent, these situations represent the converse of the situations listed above.

1. When at a stage in the life of an organization the planners want to narrow their focus. In this case the principal actors in the organization are willing to forego other possibilities (at least for the time being) in order to concentrate on using resources very efficiently. As Abraham Kaplan points out in discussing the dangers of premature definition for theorists, one can define too early and miss interesting possibilities (11). But in the life of many organizations there comes a time to define more precisely the mission and goals of the organization. At that point planning toward goals is appropriate.

2. When the environment is relatively stable and certain. This means that the coding is straightforward, that categories are accepted, and that the organization has enough control over the environment or that the environment is predictable enough to warrant planning toward goals.

3. When there are severe time or resource limitations. March and Simon note that programmed activities drive out unprogrammed activities (18). Under the pressure of having to act, which unprogrammed activities does a manager need to protect in order to insure their getting done by programming and building them into his goals?

In addition to environmental conditions and the stage of an organization's growth, a further contingency influencing the choice of an appropriate planning process is the type of people involved (22). Personal differences in tolerance for ambiguity, cognitive complexity, and needs for adventure, variety, stimulation, and power play a role here. Some people work best and feel the most comfortable when working in the more settled and more defined conditions engendered by the planning with goals process. Other people are bored by this predictability and value more highly the chaos and involvement of a planning from thrust process. In addition, Machiavellians value the ambiguous setting for the opportunities to play power games—exploiting the confusion to maneuver, to broker, and to gain personal power. We need to learn more about the influence of personal differences and preferences in planning and other organization-environmental processes. Perhaps this area could be researched by comparing personality profiles on the above dimensions for graduates about to take jobs in more mature and stable industries in contrast to those taking jobs in newer and more unstable industries.

The two planning processes may well be associated with different organization forms (24). This also deserves to be researched. For example, domain and direction planning is dynamic, revisable, open to the environment, and has heavy information processing requirements. In emphasizing openness to the environment, an organic organization shares many of these characteristics, including the interactive quality and the heavy information processing requirements (19). Both take shape in response to environmental and organizational uncertainties.

On the other hand, planning toward goals seems more suited to a mechanistic organization form. This more traditional pyramidal organization or organizational unit builds strict boundaries to protect the organization's inner workings from the environment. Coding the environment is largely programmed; responsibilities and roles are well-defined (19). Planning with goals is also well defined and "narrowed," meaning relatively closed to the wider environment, and it has lower novel information requirements. Both the mechanistic organization form and the planning toward goals process need an environment that is relatively stable and certain.

Moving from direction and domain planning to planning toward goals is to move from less definition to greater definition of desired outcomes. In the former stage, creativity and innovation perhaps are more likely. There is also the excitement of creating something new, often seen in a small, dynamic organization or during the start-up of a new project. If the external environment (perhaps as a result of the organization's efforts) becomes stable enough to permit it, this stage often gives way to the "tightening up the ship" stage, when the emphasis and constraints shift to more efficient use of financial, facility, and human resources.

There is no need to be deterministic here. An organic organization can remain organic, and a planning from thrust process does not *necessarily* change over time to a planning toward goals process. However, the pressures mentioned above make the movement from directional planning to planning with goals a strong tendency in many organizations. It is also worth recalling that a longer view might show organizations and their subsystems cycling through both types of planning.

SUMMARY

Out of a continuum of planning processes, this paper describes two types of planning. Each type has strengths and weaknesses and is suited to certain conditions. Environmental, people, and organizational conditions determine the appropriateness of each type of planning. The principal contrasts between the two types of planning are shown in Table 1.

The first type is the familiar planning toward goals in which goals are chosen, means to those goals selected, measuring devices and deadlines agreed to. This type of planning is suited to a stable environment, mechanistic organization forms, and people who prefer a well-defined purpose and role. It has the advantages of giving a focus to work efforts and efficiently using energy. One consequence of focusing to attain specific goals is the tendency to revise rather than innovate. This type of planning process, therefore, is less apt to take advantage of unexpected opportunities, is less flexible, and can become routine.

A second type is planning from thrust in which the *domain* (the area in which the organization wishes to work), and the *direction* (tendencies or preferred styles of perceiving and doing on the part of organizational members) are identified. This type of planning process is suited to an unstable environment, organic organization forms, and people who prefer variety and stimulation. It has the advantages of being flexible and is more likely to make the most of unexpected opportunities. The disadvantages

Table 1   Contrast Between Planning with Goals and Directional Planning

Planning with Goals	Directional Planning
Characteristics	
teleological, directed toward external goals	directional, moving from internal preferences
goals are specific and measurable	domain is sometimes hard to define
rational, analytic	intuitive, use unquantifiable elements
focused, narrowed perception of task	broad perception of task
lower requirements to process novel information	greater need to process novel information
more efficient use of energy	possible redundancy, false leads
separate planning and acting phases	planning and acting not separate phases
Contingent Upon	
people who prefer well-defined tasks	people who prefer variety, change, and complexity
tasks and industries that are quantifiable and relatively stable	tasks and industries not amenable to quantification and which are rapidly changing
mechanistic organization forms, "closed" systems	organic organization forms, "open" systems
"tightening up the ship" phase of a project	"unfreezing" phase of a project

include a high stress cost, less efficient use of energy, and more ambiguity about basic purposes and identity.

The two planning processes are not mutually exclusive. Both planning processes involve the same basic steps of diagnosis, setting priorities, determining action steps, and developing a method of evaluation. At different stages in the life of a project, an individual or organization is likely to emphasize one type of planning more than the other. Over the long run an organization or individual goes through cycles of stability and change and uses first one and then the other type of planning. For example, directional planning may lay the foundation for, and be used at times to reconsider, planning toward specific goals. In addition, subsystems of the same organization may concurrently be using different planning processes. The manager of a subsystem should emphasize the planning process which best fits his people, the task environment they face, and the phase in the life of the project.

REFERENCES

1. Angyal, Andras. *Foundations for a Science of Personality* (New York: Viking Press, 1969).

2. Anthony, Robert B. *Planning and Control Systems* (Boston: Division of Research, Graduate School of Business Administration, Harvard University, 1965).

3. Argyris, Chris. "On Organizations of the Future" (Unpublished paper, Graduate Schools of Education and Business Administration, Harvard University, June, 1972).

4. Athos, Anthony G. "Is the Corporation the Next to Fall?" *Harvard Business Review,* Vol. 48, No. 1 (1970), pp. 49–61.

5. Baybrooke, David, and Charles E. Lindblom. *A Strategy of Decision* (New York: Free Press, 1963).

6. Burns, Tom, and G. M. Stalker. *The Management of Innovation* (London: Tavistock, 1961).

7. Cannon, J. Thomas. *Business Strategy and Policy* (New York: Harcourt, Brace and World, 1958).

8. Clark, James C., Charles Krone, and William H. McWhinney. *On Creating the Developmental Organization* (Unpublished paper, Graduate School of Management, UCLA, 1972).

9. Grundstein, Nathan D. "Planning Without Goals" (Unpublished paper, Case Western Reserve University, March, 1970).

10. Kahn, Robert L., Donald M. Wolfe, Robert P. Quinn, J. Diedrick Snoek, and Robert A. Rosenthal. *Organizational Stress: Studies in Role Conflict and Ambiguity* (New York: Wiley, 1964).

11. Kaplan, Abraham. *The Conduct of Inquiry* (San Francisco: Chandler, 1964).

12. Kingdon, Donald R. *Matrix Organization: Managing Information Technologies* (London: Tavistock, 1973).

13. Kolb, David, Irwin Rubin, and James McIntyre. *Organizational Psychology: An Experimental Approach* (Englewood Cliffs, N.J.: Prentice-Hall, 1971).

14. Kotter, John. "Managing the Joining-Up Process," *Personnel,* Vol. 49 (July–August, 1972), pp. 46–52.

15. Kotter, John, and Paul R. Lawrence. "The Mayor: An Interim Research Report" (Working Paper, Graduate School of Business Administration, Harvard University, 1972).

16. Lindblom, Charles E. *The Policy-Making Process* (Englewood Cliffs, N.J.: Prentice-Hall, 1968).

17. March, James G. "The Technology of Foolishness," *Stanford Alumni Almanac,* 11 (October, 1972), p. 6.

18. March, James G., and Herbert A. Simon. *Organizations* (New York: Wiley, 1958).

19. McCaskey, Michael B. "An Introduction to Organization Design" *California Management Review,* in press.

20. McKelvey, William W. "Toward a Holistic Morphology of Organizations" (Unpublished paper, Graduate School of Management, UCLA, July 1970).

21. McWhinney, William H. "Organizational Form, Decision Modalities and the Environment," *Human Relations* (August 1968), pp. 269–81.

22. Morse, John J., and Jay W. Lorsch. *Individuals/Organizations* (New York: Harper and Row, in press).

23. Sarason, Seymour B. *The Creation of Settings and the Future Societies* (San Francisco: Jossey-Bass, 1972).

24. Schlesinger, James R. "Organizational Structures and Planning" (Rand Corporation Report P-3316, February, 1966).

25. Schrage, Harry. "The R & D Entrepreneur: Profile of Success," *Harvard Business Review* (November–December 1965), pp. 56–69.

26. Simon, Herbert A. "The Corporation: Will It be Managed by Machines?" in M. L. Ashen and G. L. Bach (Eds.), *Management and Corporations 1985* (New York: McGraw-Hill, 1960).
27. Steiner, George A. *Top Management Planning* (New York: MacMillan, 1969).
28. "The Xerox Corporation Case," in E. P. Learned, C. R. Christensen, K. R. Andrews, and W. D. Guth, *Business Policy: Text and Cases*, rev. ed. (Homewood, Ill.: Irwin, 1969).
29. Thompson, J. D. *Organizations in Action* (New York: McGraw-Hill, 1967).

Management by Integration and Self-Control

Douglas McGregor

Let us consider in some detail a specific illustration of the operation of a managerial strategy based on Theory Y. The concept of "management by objectives" has received considerable attention in recent years, in part due to the writings of Peter Drucker. However, management by objectives has often been interpreted in a way which leads to no more than a new set of tactics within a strategy of management by direction and control.

The strategy to be illustrated in the following pages is an application of Theory Y. Its purpose is to encourage integration, to create a situation in which a subordinate can achieve his own goals *best* by directing his efforts toward the objectives of the enterprise. It is a deliberate attempt to link improvement in managerial competence with the satisfaction of higher-level ego and self-actualization needs. It is thus a special and not at all a typical case of the conventional conception of management by objectives.

This strategy includes four steps or phases:

1. The clarification of the broad requirements of the job.
2. The establishment of specific "targets" for a limited time period.
3. The management process during the target period.
4. Appraisal of the results.

Harry Evans is Vice President, Staff Services, for a manufacturing company with twenty plants throughout the Middle West and the South. The company is aggressively managed and financially successful; it is growing fairly rapidly through acquisition of smaller companies and the development of new markets for its products.

Evans was brought into the company three years ago by the President, who felt that the staff functions of the organization needed strengthening. One of the President's concerns was the personnel department, which had been something of a stepchild since it was established in the early forties. He felt that the management needed a lot of help and guidance in order to fulfill its responsibilities in this field.

Tom Harrison has been Director of Personnel Administration for a little less than a year. Evans selected him from among a number of candidates. Although he is not as well trained professionally as some of his colleagues, he appeared to have good promise as an administrator. He is in his young forties, intelligent, ambitious, personable, a hard worker with ten years of practical experience in personnel administration.

After Harrison had been on the job a few months, Evans had formed the following impressions about him:

1. He is overly anxious to make a good impression on top management, and this interferes with his performance. He watches too carefully to see which way the wind is blowing and trims his sails accordingly. He accepts even the most trivial assignments from any of the top management group, which makes a good impression but does little to strengthen the personnel function. He has done nothing to change the rather naïve top management expectation that personnel administration can be delegated to a staff department ("You take care of the personnel problems and we'll run the business.").

2. Harrison is a poor manager, somewhat to Evans's surprise, since he appeared to function well with more limited supervisory responsibilities. He uses his subordinates as errand boys rather than as resources, and he is much too ready to impose upon them his own practical and common-sense views of what should be done, brushing aside their specialized professional knowledge. He is anxious to reorganize the department, giving key responsibilities to men like himself who have practical experience but limited professional training.

These things added up, in Evans's eyes, to an inadequate conception of the nature of the personnel job and the proper role of the Department within the company. He recognized the value of management's acceptance of Harrison's practical orientation, but he felt that the real needs of the company would not be met unless management acquired a quite different point of view with respect to the function. He was not at all inclined to replace Harrison, since he believed he had the capacity to perform effectively, but he recognized that Harrison was not going to grow into the job without help. His strategy involved the four steps listed below.

STEP 1: DETERMINING THE MAJOR REQUIREMENTS OF THE JOB

Evans suggested to Harrison that he would like him to give some intensive thought to the nature of his job in the light of his experience so far. He asked him to list what he felt to be his major responsibilities, using the formal position description in his possession if he wished, but not limiting himself to it. He said, "I'd like to discuss with you at some length *your* view of your job after being on it for the past eight months."

The list of requirements which Harrison subsequently brought in for discussion with Evans was as follows:

1. Organization of the Department
2. Services to top management
   a. Awareness of company problems and provision of programs and policies for solving them
3. Productivity of the Department
   a. Efficient administration of personnel programs and services

b. Definite assignments of projects to staff with completion dates and follow-up
c. Periodic appraisals of the performance of department members, with appropriate action

4. Field relations
a. Providing the field units with advice, adequate programs, information
b. Periodic visits to assure the adequacy of field personnel units

Harrison and Evans had several lengthy discussions of this list of responsibilities. Evans began by saying, "Tom, I asked you to bring to this meeting a written statement of the major requirements of your job as you see them. Perhaps you expected me to define your job for you, to tell you what I want you to do. If I were to do so, it would not be your job. Of course, I don't expect that I will necessarily see eye to eye with you on everything you have written down. I do take it for granted that we have a common purpose: We both want yours to be the best damned personnel department anywhere.

"The difficulty we are likely to have in discussing your ideas is that if I disagree with you, you'll feel you have to accept what I say because I'm your boss. I want to help you end up with a list that we are both completely satisfied with, but I can't help if you simply defer to my ideas or if I don't express them for fear of dominating you. So try to think of me as a colleague whose experience and knowledge are at your disposal —not as your boss. I'm certain we can resolve any differences that may come up."

In the course of the discussion Evans did bring up his concerns, but he put major emphasis on encouraging Harrison to examine his own ideas critically. Evans talked quite frankly about the realities of the company situation as he saw them, and he discussed his conception of the proper role for a personnel department. He tried to persuade Harrison that his conception of the personnel function was too limited, and that his own subordinates, because of their training and experience, could help him arrive at a more adequate conception. Harrison held a couple of meetings with his own department staff to discuss this whole question, and after each of them he had further conversations with Evans.

The critically significant factor in these discussions was not their content, but the redefinition of roles which took place. Evans succeeded, by his manner more than by his specific words, in conveying to Harrison the essential point that he did not want to occupy the conventional role of boss, but rather, to the fullest extent possible, the role of a consultant who was putting all of his knowledge and experience at Harrison's disposal in the conviction that they had a genuine common interest in Harrison's doing an outstanding job.

As he began to sense this, and to believe it, Harrison's whole perception of his own role changed. Instead of seeking to find out, as would be natural under conventional circumstances, how Evans wanted him to define his job, what Evans wanted him to do, what Evans would approve or disapprove, Harrison began to think for himself. Moreover, with this greater sense of freedom about his own role (and with Evans's open encouragement) he began to perceive his own subordinates not as "hands," but as resources, and to use them thus.

The result, unrealistic as it may seem at first glance, was a dramatic change in Harrison's perception of himself and of his job. The true nature of the change that took place during these discussions with Evans and with his subordinates was revealed in his final statement of his responsibilities as he now perceived them:

1. Organization of the Department
2. Continuous assessment of both short- and long-run company needs through:

    a. Exploration in the field

    b. General awareness of management's problems

    c. Exploration of the views of members of the Department

    d. Knowledge of external trends

3. Professional help to all levels of management

    a. Problem solving

    b. Strategy planning

    c. Research studies

    d. Effective personnel programs and policies

    e. Efficient administration of services

4. Development of staff members

5. Personal development

This first step in Evans's managerial strategy with Harrison is thus consistent with his commitment to Theory Y. He believes that Harrison must take the major responsibility for his own development, but he believes he can help. He conceives of integration as an active process which inevitably involves differences of opinion and argument. He recognizes the likelihood that Harrison may accede too readily to his view without real conviction, and he does not want this to happen. Consequently he attempts to establish a relationship in which Harrison can perceive him as a genuine source of help rather than as a boss in the conventional sense. He knows that the establishment of this relationship will take time, but it is the long-term results which he considers important. Since he does not expect that Harrison will grow into his job overnight, he is prepared to accept a definition of Harrison's job which is considerably short of perfection. He is confident that it will be improved six months hence when they discuss it again.

If Harrison is going to learn and grow in competence, and if he is going to find opportunities to satisfy his higher-level needs in the process, it is essential that he find a genuine challenge in his job. This is unlikely if the job is defined for him by a formal position description or by a superior who simply tells him what he wants done. Thus, the principle of integration is important right at the start. It is not necessary in applying it to ignore the work of the organization planning staff. The necessity for a logical division of responsibilities within any organization is obvious. However, a position description is likely to become a straitjacket unless it is recognized to be a broad set of guidelines within which the individual literally makes his own job. The conception of an organization plan as a series of predetermined "slots" into which individuals are selectively placed denies the whole idea of integration.

The process involved at this step is similar, although more limited in scope, to the one so aptly described by Drucker as discovering "what business we are in." In the case of top management looking at the organization as a whole, this frequently is a highly instructive experience. The same thing can be true even in a limited setting such as this, especially if the superior can, by doing something like Evans is doing, encourage the subordinate to think creatively about his job.

STEP 2: SETTING TARGETS

When Evans and Harrison finished their discussion of the major requirements of Harrison's job, Evans suggested that Harrison think about some specific objectives or targets which he might set for himself and his department during the following six months. Evans suggested that he think both about improving the over-all performance of his unit and about his own personal goals. He asked him further to consider in broad terms what steps he proposed to take to achieve these targets. Evans said, "I don't want to tell you how to do your job, but I would like you to do some careful thinking about how you are going to proceed. Perhaps I can be helpful when we discuss your ideas." Finally, Evans asked Harrison to consider what information he would require, and how he might obtain it, in order to know at the end of the period how well he had succeeded in reaching his targets. He suggested that they get together to talk further when Harrison had completed his thinking and planning along these lines.

This is the planning phase, but again the process is one in which the subordinate is encouraged to take responsibility for his own performance. The conventional process is one in which objectives are conceived by higher levels and imposed on lower levels of the organization. The rationale is that only the higher levels have available the broader knowledge necessary for planning. To some extent this is true, but there is an important difference between the kind of planning in which a central group determines in detail what each division or department will do, and that in which the central group communicates what are believed to be the desirable over-all objectives and *asks* each unit to determine what it can contribute.

Even when general objectives are predetermined, they can usually be limited to certain aspects of performance such as production goals, costs, and profit margin. There are other aspects which are subject to local determination, as is, of course, the planning with respect to personal objectives.

The important theoretical consideration, derived from Theory Y, is that the acceptance of responsibility (for self-direction and self-control) is correlated with commitment to objectives. Genuine commitment is seldom achieved when objectives are externally imposed. Passive acceptance is the most that can be expected; indifference or resistance are the more likely consequences. Some degree of *mutual* involvement in the determination of objectives is a necessary aspect of managerial planning based on Theory Y. This is embodied in Evans's suggestions to Harrison.

In the discussion of targets, the superior again attempts a helping role rather than an authoritative one. His primary interest is in helping the subordinate plan his own job in such a fashion that both personal and organizational goals will be achieved. While the superior has a veto power by virtue of his position, he will exercise it only if it becomes absolutely necessary.

To be sure, subordinates will sometimes set unrealistic goals, particularly the first time they approach a task like this. Experience has indicated that the usual problem is that the goals are set too high, not too low. While the superior can, through judicious advice, help the subordinate adjust unrealistic goals, there may often be greater long-run advantages in permitting the subordinate to learn by experience than in simply telling him where his planning is unrealistic or inadequate.

The list of targets which Harrison brought for discussion with Evans was this:

1. Determination of major company needs, long and short range, by:
   a. Field visits and discussions with local management
   b. Intensive discussions with top management
   c. Exploration of the views of the personnel department staff
   A plan, with assignments of responsibility, and a time schedule will be worked out for this. I expect we can complete the study within six months, but a report and subsequent plans will probably not be completed by September.

2. Joint determination with department staff of current projects
   This will involve planning such as you and I are doing.
3. Development of departmental staff members
   Items 1 and 2 can be a vehicle for this. I need help in learning how to work better with my subordinates, and particularly on how to eliminate the friction between the old-timers and the college-trained youngsters.
4. Self-development
   a. I'd like to do some reading to improve my own thinking about personnel administration—or maybe take a university course. I'd like your advice.
   b. I guess I haven't gained as much skill as a manager as I need. I hear rumblings that some of my staff are not happy with me as a boss. I'd like to do something about this, but I'm not sure what is the best way to proceed.
5. Development of a good plan of organization for the department
   In working through some of the above projects, I think I'll get some good ideas about how we ought to be set up as a department.

Since the working relationship between the two men had been quite well established during their earlier discussions, there was a comfortable give and take at this stage. Evans saw the first target as a crucial one which could become the basis for an entirely new conception of the department's role. He felt also that it could be extremely educational for Harrison provided he tackled it with sensitivity and an open mind. Accordingly he spent several hours helping Harrison to think through his strategy for determining the needs of the company with respect to personnel administration. Harrison began to see that this project was a means by which he could work toward all the other targets on his list.

Evans had little difficulty after Harrison's earlier experiences in persuading him to involve his subordinates in developing plans for the project. He suggested that Harrison continue to meet with him to discuss and evaluate this process for a couple of months. He felt—and said—that this might be the best method for Harrison to begin improving his own managerial skills.

They agreed that Harrison would explore possible university programs during the next few months to see if some one of these might meet his needs a little later. Meanwhile, they worked out a reading list and a plan for an occasional session when Harrison could discuss his reading.

In view of the nature of the personnel function, and the particular problems facing Harrison, the targets did not lend themselves to quantitative measurement such as might have been possible in a production operation. Nevertheless, Harrison, under Evans's tutelage, worked out a fairly detailed plan with specific steps to be accomplished by the end of six months. Evans's interest was that Harrison would have a basis for evaluating his own accomplishments at the end of the period.

Evans brought into the discussion the question of their relationship during the ensuing period. He said, "I don't want to be in a position of checking up on you from week to week. These are your plans, and I have full confidence that you will make every effort to reach your targets. On the other hand, I want you to feel free to seek help if you want it. There are ways in which I believe my experience can be useful to you. Suppose we leave it that we'll get together on your initiative as often as you wish—not for you to report how you are doing, but to discuss any problems which you would like my help on, or any major revisions in your plans." Thus Evans helped Harrison still further to perceive the role that he wanted to occupy as a superior, and thus also to clarify his own responsibilities as a subordinate.

STEP 3: THE ENSUING PERIOD

Since this is a managerial strategy rather than a personnel technique, the period between the establishment of targets and the evaluation of accomplishment is just as important as the first two steps. What happens during this period will depend upon the unique circumstances. The aim is to further the growth of the subordinate: his increased competence, his full acceptance of responsibility (self-direction and self-control), his ability to achieve integration between organizational requirements and his own personal goals.

In this particular situation Evans's primary interests were two: (1) the emergence throughout the company of a more adequate conception of the personnel function, and (2) the development of a competent department which would provide leadership and professional help to all levels of management with respect to this function. He felt that, as a result of steps 1 and 2 of his strategy, Harrison too was committed to these objectives. Moreover, he was persuaded that Harrison's project for assessing company needs in the field of personnel administration—as now conceived—was a highly promising means to these ends. He warned himself that he must be careful on two counts. First he must not expect too much too fast. The company situation was in no sense critical and there was no need for a crash program. Harrison's project was certain to be a valuable learning experience for him and his staff.

Second, Evans recognized that if the best learning was to occur, he must curb his natural tendency to step in and guide the project. Harrison would make mistakes; at his present level of sophistication he would quite possibly fail to appreciate the full scope of the task. Nevertheless, Evans decided more would be gained if he limited his influence to those occasions when Harrison sought his help.

This is what he did. His confidence in Harrison proved to have been justified. He and his staff tackled the project with more ingenuity and sensitivity than Evans would have imagined possible and began rather quickly to understand the true dimensions of the problem. Harrison came in one day to tell him that they had decided to extend their explorations to include visits to several university centers in order to take advantage of the point of view of some top-flight academic people. Also, they planned to test some of their emerging ideas against the experience of several other companies.

After this discussion, and the evidence it provided concerning the expansion of Harrison's intellectual horizons and the use he was making of the resources represented by his subordinates, Evans stopped worrying. He would bail them out if they got into trouble, but he anticipated no such necessity.

STEP 4: SELF-APPRAISAL

At the end of August, Harrison reminded Evans (not vice versa!) that the six months was up. "When do you want a report?" was his question. Evans responded that a report was not what he wanted, but Harrison's own evaluation of what he had accomplished with respect to the targets he had set six months earlier. Said Evans, "This can give you a basis for planning for the next six months."

A week later Harrison brought the following notes to a discussion with Evans.

Appraisal, September 1

1. Determination of major company needs:
   a. The field work is completed.
   b. My staff and I are working on a proposal that will involve a new conception of personnel administration in this company. We will have a draft for discussion with you within thirty days, and we want you to take a full day to let us present our findings and proposals to you.
   c. The results of our work make it clear that we have an educational job to do with top management, and I want to include a plan along these lines in my next set of targets.
2. Joint determination with staff of current projects. I am now conducting a set of target-setting meetings with my department staff as a whole in which we are laying out plans for the next year. All major projects — individual or group — are being discussed out in detail there. These department meetings will be followed by individual planning sessions.
3. Development of department staff members:
   a. The major project we have been carrying out has changed my ideas about several of my subordinates. I'm learning how to work with them, and it's clear they are growing. Our presentation to you next month will show you what I mean.
   b. I've appreciated how much your target-setting approach has helped my development, and I'm attempting to use it with each of my subordinates. Also, I think the departmental planning mentioned under 2 above is a developmental tool. I've been talking with some people in the B——— Company who do this and I'm excited about its possibilities in our own company.
4. Self-development
   All I can say is I've learned more in the past six months than in the previous five years.
5. Departmental organization
   I haven't done a thing about it. It doesn't seem very important right now. We seem to be able to plan our work as a department pretty well without developing a new setup. Perhaps we'll need to come back to this during the next six months, but there are more important things to be done first.
6. General comment
   I would rate myself considerably lower than I would have six months ago in terms of how well I'm filling the responsibilities of my job. It's going to take me a couple of years to measure up to what you have a right to expect of the man in this spot, but I think I can do it.

The discussion of this self-appraisal went into considerable detail. Evans felt that Harrison had acquired quite a little insight into his own strengths and weaknesses, and they were able to discuss objectively where he needed to give thought to improving his competence further. Harrison, for example, opened up the whole problem of his "yes-man" attitude in dealing with top management and pointed out that his exploratory interviews with some of these men had resulted in increased self-confidence. He said, "I think maybe I can learn to stand up for my ideas better in the future. You have helped me to realize that I can think for myself, and that I can defend myself in an argument."

They agreed to postpone Harrison's discussion of plans for the next six months until after the one-day session at which Evans would meet with the whole department. "Then," said Harrison, "I want to talk over with you a new statement of my responsibilities which I'm working on."

Management of Objectives
Douglas S. Sherwin

It is now two decades since Peter Drucker wrote *The Practice of Management*,[1] and invented the phrase "management by objectives."

The usefulness of Drucker's observations seems totally obvious. The subject should have been almost wrung out by now. Yet the number of articles published since Drucker's book appeared, suggesting what to do and what to avoid in an MBO program, testifies that the results of many MBO programs have fallen short of the expectations that were originally entertained for them. I believe that if we consider "management by objectives" from the standpoint of organization, one or two additional insights can be developed that make MBO programs more successful.

"Organization," according to contemporary theory, is a strategy for achieving a specified purpose.[2] If one's specified purpose, then, is to achieve objectives, the strategy selected would surely possess the following two qualifications:

1. Recognizing that a single organization is probably not appropriate for every kind of objective, the strategy would distinguish among *kinds* of objectives.
2. The strategy would recognize that one person's effort cannot achieve most objectives — and certainly cannot achieve the most important ones — but that coordinating contributions from several people are required to do the job.

It is easy to distinguish at least two kinds of objectives in organizations. The first is maintaining predetermined standards of performance from the repetitive systems and functions of the business. The second is bringing about changes to improve the business. For convenience, let us call the first "functional performance objectives" or "performance maintenance objectives," and the second "change objectives" or "improvement objectives."

An example makes this distinction clear. To maintain accounts receivable at a planned level when the ability to achieve that level has already been demonstrated is a functional performance objective. To reduce accounts receivable to a level that has not yet been achieved is a change objective.

It should be evident that the strategy — and, therefore, the organization — for maintaining an accounts receivable performance objective will differ from the strategy and the organization required for improving it. Maintaining a functional performance objective requires perhaps only that those making contributions to it adhere carefully to their duties and procedures: restricting shipments within established credit limits, invoicing at the time of shipment, following up past due accounts, promptly resolving disputes with customers about count and documentation, and so on. Accounting, shipping, credit, and sales functions need to coordinate for this objective in a more or less routine fashion.

On the other hand, to achieve a new level of performance requires some distinct cognitive and creative effort, plus, probably, some change in policy, procedure, personnel, authority, or investment. So if the objective is to reduce accounts receivable to a lower level, a different set of contributions is needed, such as analyses of experience to determine which customers are chronically late; judgments to determine if the slow payers should be cut off, or whether higher credit limits should be set; or decisions to levy or increase penalties for slow payers.

Here, in addition to the routine performance functions, computing, sales management, financial management, and possibly general management may be involved in bringing the accounts receivable to a new level of performance. It is apparent, then, that a different organization, one which provides these contributions, is required to achieve change objectives.

One organizes differently, of course, not only for these two different kinds of objectives, but also for each and every objective itself. What is common to all the functional performance objectives is that the organization for each is more or less permanent, and that each is continually sought in a process of cooperation among functions. In contrast, what is common to all the change objectives is that the organizations which can bring them about are temporary until the new level has been achieved and demonstrated.

Performance objectives involve process; change objectives involve project.

The accounts receivable example illustrates that achieving an objective is seldom the result of a single person's contribution, but requires the cooperation of several functions. A moment's reflection about quality, production, maintenance, financial, development, sales, and safety objectives, and practically any other important objective, tells us the same requirement holds true for them. Organizing is, therefore, much more complex than simply parceling out objectives, one-on-one, to various members of the organization. But failing to recognize the multifunctional aspect of objectives may explain some of the problems with conventional MBO programs.

Now let's look at the traditional organization strategy for meeting both functional and change objectives. Then I want to propose a different strategy, which we are experimenting with at a couple of our plants, that distinguishes between the two kinds of objectives and provides for the combinations of functions necessary to achieve them.

THE TRADITIONAL FUNCTIONAL ORGANIZATION

The failure to recognize the limitations of the conventional functional organization as a strategy for achieving objectives, I believe, has contributed to the difficulties in achieving objectives. Briefly, let us see how the functional organization falls short of meeting the criteria of an adequate strategy for achieving objectives.

The functional organization is a strategy for operating the routine systems of the business—systems such as shipping, invoicing, receiving, accounting, selling, supplying technical service, inspecting, purchasing, warehousing, maintaining equipment, borrowing money, and operating machines. It is a strategy that not only does not distinguish between kinds of objectives, but also does not distinguish between tasks and duties, on the one hand, and objectives, on the other. It is in fact a counterstrategy because it fragments work and separates functions without then showing how they must be joined to achieve objectives.

The functional organization results from specializing the work—by dividing it into divisions, divisions into departments, departments into sections, and so on, each unit being a finer collection of tasks, activities, and functions, until at last every job is described. The whole effort is directed toward classifying, defining, and ranking jobs, duties, and functions. In short, the functional organization conceives the work of the business as consisting of a number of tasks and activities to be performed.

At the same time that it divides up the work, the functional organization divides up authority and territory. All authority is first vested in a board of directors. From there, portions are parceled in diminishing amounts to the officers and management and down through the organization, by division, department, section, and individual. When the processes of delegating authority and allocating domain are complete, all the increments of delegated authority add up exactly to what was originally vested in the directors, and the fragmented domains add up to the total activities of the business.

This total distribution of authority and domain handicaps the functional organization's strategy for achieving objectives in two ways. First, the fact that *all* the authority and domain are distributed, with nothing left over, implies that the functional organization is *the* organization; there is no other. The preeminence of this single organization diverts our attention from the many organizations, made up of combinations of functions, which achieve the total organization's objectives. Second, since everyone's authority and assigned domain come to him from his superiors in the line above, each person is oriented toward his or her section, department, and division.

The strategy for meeting objectives, however, requires that employees from different groups combine their functions. An employee's strong feeling of *belonging* to his functional group obscures his necessary membership in these other organizations.

TWO-DIMENSIONAL ORGANIZATION

The functional organization is by itself an incomplete—and, therefore, insufficient—strategy for achieving objectives.

The task before us, therefore, is to complete the strategy of the functional organization for the purpose of managing and achieving the objectives of the organization.

The simplest of ideas can help us here; it utilizes a grid as shown in *Exhibit I*. The horizontal rows of the grid each represent a position in an organization. The organization in this example would be typical of a small manufacturing business or profit center. The rows represent the entire functional organization. Indentations replace the pyramidal hierarchy. Each vertical column of the grid represents one of the objectives of the business. The blocks where the rows intersect the columns identify the jobs and employees whose contributions are needed to achieve each objective.

Functional Performance Objectives

Assume first that the objectives arrayed vertically in *Exhibit I* are functional performance objectives. There is nothing new, of course, in having functional performance

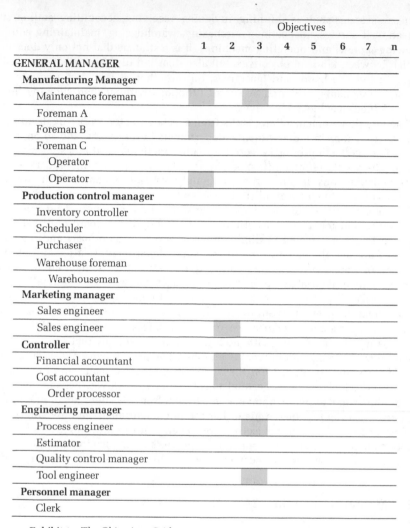

	Objectives							
	1	2	3	4	5	6	7	n
GENERAL MANAGER								
Manufacturing Manager								
Maintenance foreman	▨		▨					
Foreman A								
Foreman B	▨							
Foreman C								
Operator								
Operator	▨							
Production control manager								
Inventory controller								
Scheduler								
Purchaser								
Warehouse foreman								
Warehouseman								
Marketing manager								
Sales engineer								
Sales engineer		▨						
Controller								
Financial accountant		▨						
Cost accountant		▨	▨					
Order processor								
Engineering manager								
Process engineer			▨					
Estimator								
Quality control manager								
Tool engineer			▨					
Personnel manager								
Clerk								

Exhibit 1   The Objectives Grid

objectives, even if they are not called that. But in the usual MBO program, responsibility for meeting a given objective would probably be assigned to a particular individual and job. Maintaining a planned product standard would probably be assigned to the manufacturing manager; an objective for returns and allowances would be assigned to the quality control manager; keeping machine downtime at a certain level would be assigned to the maintenance supervisor, and so on.

The truth is, however, that maintaining a standard for rate of production requires that the maintenance, purchasing, and scheduling functions join efforts with manufacturing. Maintaining a returns and allowances performance standard requires that manufacturing, engineering, and maintenance join efforts with quality control. Meeting downtime standards requires that manufacturing, engineering, purchasing, and scheduling combine their efforts with maintenance.

The combinations of functions that maintain the functional performance objectives are more or less permanent organizations—exactly as permanent, in fact, as the functional organization itself. The grid connects the functions that must cooperate for each performance objective and, by making these functional relationships explicit, completes the functional organization for the purpose of achieving the performance objective. The grid shows who works with whom, and to what end. The functional organization by itself does neither of these things.

The ideal, then, is never to draw a functional organization chart without showing the performance objective coordinates of all functions in the chart. The composition of the teams accountable for the various functional performance objectives would then eventually become as well known to their members and others as the composition of the functional pyramid is now.

Change Objectives

The same grid that organizes the teams for functional performance objectives also serves for change objectives—only now, of course, the vertical columns in *Exhibit I* list the change objectives.

Every business is in tension between the need to get the routine operations of the day done and the need to bring about the changes that will improve the business for tomorrow. The functional organization is a strategy for getting the repetitive tasks done. It is an awkward strategy, however, for doing the usually nonrepetitive tasks that are required if the organization is to be changed and improved.

Management scientists and practitioners have employed two different organizational strategies to accomplish change within the functional organization. On the one hand, they have used the functional organization, but provided appendages to it, like product managers, project engineers, and market development groups, to help bring change about. On the other hand, they have created separate organizations, typically called project management teams, which exist outside the functional organization and live until the change project is completed.

The functional organization makes it difficult for either of these solutions, appended groups or project teams, to be effective.

Appended groups. The groups appended to bring about change face the problem of all staff groups: how to get their ideas accepted and implemented. The purpose of the appended structures is to change things. These structures exist only because without them the functional organization accomplishes less change than desired. That, in turn, is because the members of the operating groups, whose functional contributions are also essential to the change objective, perceive their prime mission as operating the systems of the business. If effecting change is perceived at all as a responsibility, it only takes second place. The result of these differing priorities is to compromise the effort needed for accomplishing the change objectives.

In addition to there being differing priorities as to mission, the authority, responsibility, and accountability for effecting change are skewed in the functional organization. Conventionally, someone in the appended structure is assigned responsibility for the change objective and is held accountable for its accomplishment. But his mode must be

Exhibit II Objective team concept for effecting change compared with appended structures and project management

Objective Teams	*Appended Structures*	*Project Groups*
1. Teams are temporary.	Functions are permanent.	Teams are temporary.
2. Mission to effect change is perceived with same priority by those contributing to change.	Mission to effect change is perceived with differing priorities by those contributing to change.	Mission to effect change is perceived with differing priorities by those contributing to change.
3. Concept integrates line and staff.	Concept separates line and staff.	Concept separates project team from functional organization.
4. Authority to implement change is explicit.	Authority to implement change is absent, reposing by convention in operating groups.	Authority to implement change is explicit but may be compromised by subsidiary relationship of project teams to line operations.
5. Competition between need for change and need for routine operations is recognized and is resolved by organizing for both.	Competition between need for change and need for routine operations is sharpened by adversary relationship between line and staff, and is resolved by power.	Competition between need for change and need for routine operations is sharpened by adversary relationship between project team and operating group; and is resolved by power.
6. All functions contributing to achieving an objective are necessary, therefore equal.	Appended functions are subordinate by convention to operating functions.	Project teams are subordinate by convention to operating functions.
7. Priorities are ordered between objectives that can be achieved with available resources and those that must be deferred, rather than between change objectives and performance objectives.	Priority is tacitly accorded to operating functions.	Priority is tacitly accorded to operating functions.
8. The team is charged with accountability for the change objective.	A *staff* person is charged with accountability for the change objective.	The team *leader* is charged with accountability for the change objective.
9. Each team member's chain of supervision is involved.	Only the staff member's chain of supervision is involved.	Only the team leader's chain of supervision is involved. Team members are borrowed and disconnected from their chain of supervision.
10. There is one organization, consisting of many teams, to achieve both change objectives and performance objectives.	No teams. There is one organization, with staff component subordinate to the line component.	There are essentially two separate organizations—one for operating the system, a second for effecting change.

persuasion—for staff proposes, line disposes. The staff must carry the proposal up the organization in order to get the enforcing approvals, and implementation may be resisted or even thwarted by the operating groups.

The objectives grid melds the appended groups and operating structures into one organization and, by identifying the functions and individuals whose contributions are needed to meet the objective, implies that once a change objective has been adopted by the organization, then all parties needed to bring it about are equally responsible. With the objectives grid, there are no primary and secondary *missions*, only a selection of objectives, according to determined priorities. Authority is not preempted by convention but, to the extent necessary, is spelled out ad hoc. *Exhibit II* summarizes the ways that the objectives grid differs from the use of appended groups to accomplish change.

Project teams.   The concept called "project management" has grown out of dissatisfaction with the ability of functional organization and its appendages to effect change. "Project management" effects change by forming separate teams with people borrowed from the functional organization. Members of the project organization may work on the project full time or part time.

The project team seems a good idea. Yet it is used sparingly, and its success is not outstanding. One major deterrent to its use is the burden of formalities that accompanies setting up the teams: appointing a project manager or leader; getting approval to borrow the services of the various team members; and justifying interruptions of the productive process. Establishing a project team is a project in itself.

The biggest problem I see with the project concept, however, is that it creates an organization separate from the functional one. That is indeed the very purpose of its methodology. But a separate organization is no match for the functional organization in the competition for time, power, or resources. In fact, as I mentioned earlier, the theory of the functional organization denies the possibility of another organization: it has already accounted for all the authority and all the domain.

Also, the theory undermines the position of team members. According to the theory, every person is part of and belongs to a certain section, department, and division of the organization. To participate in a project team, a person is borrowed from his place in the functional organization, and that disconnects him from the hierarchy of supervision. Connected now to the functional organization only through its leader, the project organization lies mainly outside the functional organization. The change it is working toward must hurdle this division between organizations if it is to be successfully introduced into, and accepted by, all parts of the functional organization.

The teams established by the objectives grid share two characteristics with project management teams. Each has a clear mission to effect change, and both types of organization are temporary, existing only until the change is completed. But the objectives grid recognizes that functional contributions from operating personnel are almost invariably required in bringing change about. The grid, therefore, makes it impossible for operating personnel to escape their responsibilities to contribute to a change objective by claiming a higher mission—namely, to operate. For once a change objective has been established for the organization, there are no preconceived primary or secondary missions, only a specified responsibility to contribute to the established objectives.

The objectives grid rejects the idea of separate organizations—one for change and one for operations—but creates a single organization with both missions—to operate the organization and to bring about changes that are established as organization objectives. *Exhibit II* also summarizes the various ways that the objectives grid differs from project management teams.

THE OBJECTIVES GRID AND MBO

The whole point of an MBO program, of course, must be the achieving of objectives. The objectives grid helps managers to do this in several ways.

In earlier and simpler times, the functional organization emerged as *the* organization because the proprietor was himself solely responsible for maintaining performance objectives and for bringing about the change objectives. The owner-manager knew everything that was going on; and the objectives, though probably not written, were firmly established in his head. He could personally coordinate the functions needed to maintain the performance objectives and appropriate the contributions required for change. There was no need for special organizations. But now, the complexity, size, competitiveness, and changing environment of modern business require a multiplicity of objectives that cannot be managed by one person, and that require multiple organizations to bring them about.

The business of an organization consists in meeting an array of functional and change objectives. Displaying the organization linearly, instead of as a pyramid, is little more than a trick. But it is a trick with benefits. Coupled with the array of objectives, the linear representation of the organization reveals dramatically that everyone in the organization contributes to the business of the organization. For when the objectives and the people are coordinated in a grid, it becomes a simple matter, checklisting against the entire organization, to identify the functions and people that must cooperate to achieve a given objective, thereby establishing the objectives team. By contrast, the conventional pyramid requires impenetrable geometry to show these connections.

Portraying the business of the organization as an array of objectives allows managers to observe priorities among objectives and, particularly, to maintain a realistic balance between the change and task needs of the organization. With the functional organization, the change needs, which can usually be postponed, are preempted as a class by the task needs, which recur daily. Employees' time, of course, is—and indeed should be—a scarce resource to be economized among competing and deserving ends. The grid helps managers order the priorities of objectives, keep the objectives within the capacity of the available manpower resources, and make sure that the necessary contributions are made to *all* established objectives.

In my experience, the greatest problem confronting change objectives is that when the manager first approves an objective, for example, near the beginning of the year, no one knows exactly how to reach it. The manager knows only what conditions he wants to prevail at some future time. If the means of achieving objectives were obvious, there would be no problem; it would be a matter of execution.

Conventionally, then, the manager designates someone to be responsible for achieving the objective, and holds that person accountable for the results. Unfortunately, that person also does not usually know how to reach the objective and is additionally handicapped by having less authority to enlist the needed contributions than the manager who assigned the objective to him. So, eventually, in many cases, the objective is simply reported as "not reached."

The way to accomplish an objective typically lies in fragments in several minds. Devising the means of reaching it involves the cooperation of minds and functions, but this process cannot take place until the people possessing the potential for the answer are brought together by organization. The objectives grid supplies that organization.

One of the greatest potentials of the objectives grid for completing objectives lies in its ability to extend the supervisory and administrative capacities of the organization. There are a tremendous number of things to do in even a small plant or business. If everything has to be overseen and managed by the relatively few supervisors and department heads, the number of transactions becomes physically unmanageable for them. The work of the business—the meeting of objectives—is then simply stretched out. Because the objectives grid gives team members a clearer idea of the ends they are trying to accomplish and assembles all the functions necessary for accomplishing them, team members can supervise their own work to a greater degree than in the functional organization.

SOME QUESTIONS AND IMPLICATIONS

A change in strategy for achieving objectives requires that managers take a new look at its effects on many issues. Five main questions come immediately to mind.

1 Who Sets the Objectives?

It is well to remember, while considering this question and the others, that the scheme offered in this discussion is not a departure from, nor an alternative to, "management by objectives," but is a facilitator of it. However and by whomever objectives are set in existing MBO plans, they would be set when the objectives grid is used. How this should be done is one of the most discussed aspects of MBO practices, and I don't intend to get into the question here except to the extent that using the objectives grid helps the process.[3]

Managers in our plants experimenting with the grid are finding that using it imposes some additional discipline on our thinking about objectives setting.

Current wisdom holds that objectives should originate at the lowest levels of management and move up the organization until they are accepted and approved at the top. We started with this assumption, but the grid revealed that in practice there are difficulties with it. While it is part of every manager's job to set objectives for his own area of responsibility, many of the organization's most important objectives lie outside the province and authority—and even the perspective—of any single manager and so need the involvement of peer and higher level managers at an early stage. As a result of this perception, we now discuss and agree upon objectives in interactive sessions involving a broad group of managers.

Consideration of priorities is an inseparable part of the objectives-setting process, and using the grid has informed our judgments on this. What is needed is not a complete ranking of objectives, but a discrimination between the objectives we most want to accomplish and can muster resources for and those we can forgo or defer. Thus the focus of attention is on ranking only at the margin between these two sets, rather than on complete ranking within each set.

Fortunately, therefore, we are not faced with asking ourselves whether, for example, a given performance objective may be more important than some goal of change, or vice versa. All the selected performance objectives must be met, and so must all the selected change objectives. Given that all these objectives must be met, we can array the performance objectives and change objectives on separate grids—enabling us to think separately about each set. Performance objectives are ongoing, and the teams to maintain them are permanent. So once the standards of performance have been defined and the teams organized and working, all that remains to be done is to monitor actual performance versus the standard and take corrective action as needed – only reviewing the adequacy of the performance standards from time to time. Change objectives, on the other hand, are temporary. When change objectives are achieved, they are dropped from the grid and new ones added in response to the requirements of the dynamic environment of business.

2 Who Selects the Teams?

In the standard MBO program, an objective is assigned to a particular individual. That individual later solicits the contributions needed from appropriate functions. On their own the contributors neither operate as a team nor perceive themselves as belonging to a team.

With the objectives grid, on the other hand, the team's membership is imposed by the requirements of the objective. That is, thinking about and observing what functions would actually operate together to meet an objective make the composition of the team obvious. The objectives grid merely connects the needed functions to the objective and makes the connections explicit.

In our experience so far, it seems that organizing teams for change objectives presents less of a problem than organizing teams for functional performance objectives. Change objectives are a familiar thing. Sometimes they are open-ended – for example, "Revise method of handling in-process inventory to conserve space." Here, the manager doesn't know how much space he wants to save – he has only an intuition that "better" is possible. Other change objectives are definite, and the team works toward a specific objective, such as "a certain rate of production from a given machine."

When designating the change objective teams, the manager delegates authority appropriate to the task and sets the team's reporting requirements. Each team, after assuring itself that the necessary functions are included, sets its own rules of procedure, such as regularity of meetings, and plans and carries out its work.

We are finding that organizing functional performance objective teams is, however, less straightforward. This was certainly an unexpected finding because, after all, such teams are only seeking the routine performance objectives of the organization. Nevertheless, the routine functions are *so* routine that managers many times do not bother to express the specific standards of performance they expect. Further, people are so absorbed in performing their own functions that they do not perceive that their job joins with others not just to get the work done, but also to do it to certain standards.

It seemed logical to us, therefore, to set functional performance objectives in the areas we wanted them, designate the teams, and let them go to work. Here we ran into an immediate snag. It was not too difficult to agree on the areas of operation in which we wanted to meet functional performance objectives. But we had to face the fact that we lacked numerical, or other specifications, for acceptable performance in many such areas. Some performance standards – like "shipping within x days of 'receipt of order'" – are simple to conceive. Others are complicated. For quality-cost performance, for example, are we interested in total costs, incremental costs, or in profits lost? And what assumptions do we make in calculating whichever criterion we choose? We were threatened with getting bogged down in conceptualizing the objectives and losing time in getting the teams into operation.

At this stage we decided, therefore, to bypass the difficulty of determining criteria of functional performance and to move directly to establishing the teams. We benefited immediately by enabling the team members to recognize and appreciate how their functional contributions joined with others in a given aspect of performance.

Now the team has the obligation to establish measures of performance, to select the performance standard, to arrange for regular feedback comparing actual performance with the performance objective, and to plan its own work. The plant controller (or whoever is responsible for the organization's information system) is an *ex officio* member of all teams and provides the information flow.

The important step is to get the teams functioning: where performance standards are easy to conceive, the team sets them; where they are complex, it sets interim standards while developing better ones.

3 Who is Accountable for Achieving the Objective?

This is a vital question: the credibility of the objectives team concept hinges, perhaps, on the answer.

In the usual MBO program, some one person is usually designated as the person responsible for the objective. He may be a peer of those from whom he solicits contributions, or, more usually, he may be someone higher in the organization so that the authority of position comes into play.

In assigning the objective to one person, a manager seeks accountability. Using the objectives grid, the manager has the possibility of doing the same thing: either by nominating one of the team members as leader, or by designating someone higher in the organization as the person responsible. But there is a trade-off when you assign responsibility to one person. You strengthen that person's commitment by making him important and by exposing him to fear of failure and to the opportunity to satisfy his need for achievement. But at the same time you weaken these same emotions and incentives in those on whom he will be dependent for the contributions necessary to achieve the objectives.

There is surely a net gain in this trade-off over assigning responsibility to no one. But the explicitness of the team's membership and the clarity of the team's purpose open an additional option. What about assigning responsibility to everyone? Would it not be better if we could find a way to make all the members of the team feel the same maximum accountability as the individual assigned sole responsibility?

Managers have been raised in their careers on the idea that not to assign responsibility to one person is to assign responsibility to no one. But there are precedents for organizing differently. In baseball, for example, when there is a man on first threatening to steal, the performance maintenance objective of the defensive team is to prevent him from doing so. The pitcher and first baseman must hold the base runner close to first. The pitcher must not kick too high or stride too long. He and the catcher know that the pitch should not be slow or to the catcher's left. The catcher must throw low to second base without wasted motion for the tag. The second baseman and the shortstop must have prearranged who will cover and who will back up the bag.

In this example, there is no leader of the defensive unit who is responsible for the result. All the players are accountable. If the defensive players all execute their assignments, it is impossible for the base runner to advance. But marginal execution on the part of any one of them may permit a successful steal, and expert baseball men, as well as members of the team, will know in that case where the execution was lacking.

Assigning accountability for an objective to all the members of an objectives team will, of course, in no way excuse their supervisors from accountability for ensuring that their subordinates are making the contributions essential to the objective. A supervisor's accountability for his subordinate's performance is of course the same whether one person on the team is assigned the objective or whether all are. But, as a practical matter, supervisors will feel their responsibility more keenly in the latter case. Because the grid exposes each team member's accountability, his supervisor's accountability becomes equally exposed. *Exhibit III* contrasts the chain of accountability of the ob-

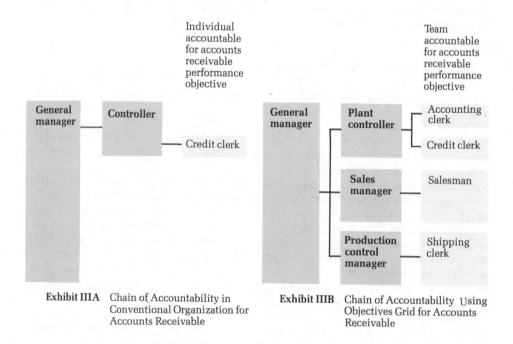

Exhibit IIIA Chain of Accountability in Conventional Organization for Accounts Receivable

Exhibit IIIB Chain of Accountability Using Objectives Grid for Accounts Receivable

jectives grid with that of the conventional organization for meeting (as an example) the accounts receivable performance standard. It shows how accountability is strengthened when all members of the team are made responsible and when shared accountabilities replace the single, tenuous line up the organization that pertains when an individual is made responsible.

Neither making all the members of the team responsible for meeting the objective, nor making one person responsible, excuses higher management from its own accountability for the objectives being met once they are set. Accountability, unlike authority, can, of course, not be delegated. Management control is the instrument for guarding this accountability. If the information system discloses that actual performance chronically deviates from the performance objective or that progress on a change objective persistently lags behind schedule, then management at the appropriate level must follow up to take corrective action. The objectives grid seeks to make everyone accountable for meeting the objectives, from the individuals on the teams to the highest manager in the program.

4 Will Teams Be Sufficiently Motivated to Accomplish the Objective?

All of a person's behavior, of course, is motivated. So this question seems to suggest that the behavior of team members would be less "properly" motivated than the behavior of employees when not organized into teams. Of course, that doesn't make any sense unless one assumes that the objectives teams would operate without the benefit of supervision, so would have to be internally better motivated if good results were to be achieved. This would, of course, be a Theory X assumption about human behavior.[4] But in any case, the objectives grid does not do away with supervision; rather it makes its responsibility more explicit.

The objectives grid also tends to change the character of supervision. We are beginning to find in our experiments with the objectives grid that supervision is becoming supportive rather than authoritarian when a team is made responsible for the objective. Each team member's exposure encourages him to seek the necessary support from his supervisor, since obscurity is no longer a choice for him, and the supervisor in turn is motivated to appeal higher for resources necessary for team success.

Although employees do not have to be better motivated to perform on objectives teams, they do seem to be. This is only to be expected. For if members of small teams were not better motivated toward good performance, then we would have an even more difficult problem with motivation and commitment than we have already recognized. In small groups, members grasp the mission of the group more easily and identify with it because they individually influence the result. Each employee feels the necessity for carrying his load, and peer respect and accountability become powerful factors for all, not just management employees. These are all strong social and psychological forces that engage the employee's emotional being and determine his motivation.

Without depreciating the importance of individuals' needs for achievement, there is a growing appreciation of the importance of group dynamics among both students and practitioners of the managing art. Alvin Zander has reported, for example, that people often work harder for small work teams than they do for themselves.[5]

This finding will not surprise practicing business managers, for they are very much aware, from direct experience, that group spirit and teamwork are indispensable to superior performance. But spirit and teamwork are most difficult to create. A big part of the problem in most organizations is that there are no teams. Managers call for teamwork from their people, but without identifying any team except the entire organization; and the entire organization is usually so large or complex that employees cannot identify with it. The whole organization can rarely be a team.

When managers ask for teamwork, they vaguely picture that the whole organization is made up of units that are good teams. Unfortunately, the units of a business organization, despite appearances lent by the functional organization, are not teams at all, but functional groups, the members of which actually work with members of other functional groups. Take the maintenance section as an example. The work of its members is not primarily with each other; it is with machine operators, shift foremen, tool crib personnel, procurement people, and so on. The objectives grid simply accepts the fact of these cross-functional combinations and gives them status according to their purposes. Because these combinations consist of people who actually work together, seeking teamwork from them is a justifiable and achievable aim of management.

5   What Are the Implications for Performance Appraisal?

There are many views as to the relationship between management by objectives and performance appraisal, two managerial tools that were born and raised together. To some managers, management by objectives is essentially a means to an end—namely, performance appraisals. There was a great uneasiness among management theorists and managers when employees were appraised, as they used to be, on such intangible characteristics as personality, potential, and ambition instead of on results. So theorists and practitioners alike fell enthusiastically upon "management by objectives" as the means of determining the results, or lack of them, by which performance could be appraised.

Although not everyone agrees with this view of the relationship, the assumed theory is that management by objectives and performance appraisals are inextricably bound together, that objectives will more often be achieved if the employee knows he will be evaluated on his success in achieving them, and that performance appraisals— for salary administration, promotion, and employee development—will be better and fairer if related to the employee's degree of success in achieving objectives.

The objectives grid poses a special dilemma for the relationship between performance appraisals and management by objectives. If it is true that many of the most important objectives of an organization's MBO program cannot be achieved by a single employee's effort, but require the contributions of several cooperating employees, then these objectives cannot be the ones that a single employee's performance can be measured against in performance appraisal programs. For the results of a multiperson objective cannot properly be used to measure a single person's performance.

So you either must sacrifice the important objectives of MBO programs in order to maintain a fair performance appraisal basis or keep the MBO program on important objectives and find another way to evaluate performance.

The dilemma, as I see it, has to be resolved in favor of "management by objectives." The purpose of any MBO program must be to reach the important objectives of the business. Performance appraisals are also indispensable, but they cannot logically be based upon the results of the MBO objectives. Instead, they should be based upon two other things:

1. Results of objectives that are within an employee's own scope.
2. The effectiveness of the employee in making his contribution to the multiperson objectives of the organization.

This circumscribed view of performance appraisal will be hard for many to swallow. And I would expect, because of the existing deep commitment to the connection between MBO and performance appraisal programs, that my conclusion will survive the reaction only if it is realistic. If it does survive, however, I think we have the opportunity to elevate performance appraisals to a much higher level of utility. Performance appraisals would become much more difficult to make, requiring a clear statement of the multifunctional objective, a clear measure and identification of the employee's required contribution to it, and a higher level of observation of employee performance. But responding to the challenges of these difficulties could yield appraisals that are more directly related to realistic expectations of performance and, hence, would be more useful and accurate for the important purposes of appraisal.

THE ORGANIZING OF OBJECTIVES

The basis of the objectives grid is a simple idea: organize directly for the objectives of the business. The functional organization perceives the total business as a number of tasks and functions; it is silent on the matter of objectives. The objectives grid, on the other hand, perceives the total business as an array of separate objectives to be pursued and it organizes directly to achieve these objectives. The emphasis of the objectives grid is on the combination of functions needed to bring the objectives about rather than on the authority and domain relationships. And teams of individuals are the basic units of organization, rather than individuals. The objectives grid assumes not "one person" per objective, but "one group" of persons per objective.

This shift in strategy — from organizing for functions to organizing for objectives — fits the purpose of MBO programs and offers an opportunity to make them more effective.

REFERENCES

1. P. Drucker, *The Practice of Management* (New York: Harper and Brothers), 1954.
2. See, for example, Alfred D. Chandler, Jr., *Strategy and Structure* (Cambridge: MIT Press), 1962.
3. See, for example, Harry Levinson, "Management by Whose Objectives?" *HBR*, July–August 1970, p. 125.
4. See Douglas McGregor, *The Human Side of Enterprise* (New York: McGraw-Hill), 1960.
5. Alvin F. Zander, "Team Spirit vs. the Individual Achiever," *Psychology Today*, November 1974, p. 65; see also Rensis Likert, *New Patterns of Management* (New York: McGraw-Hill), 1961.

Questions for Discussion

1. What arguments can be made for and against setting specific objectives?

2. Prepare and discuss a list of your own objectives for the next two years.

3. "What Harry Evans is trying to get Tom Harrison to do for the personnel department (in the McGregor reading) is actually what Philip Selznick is discussing in his reading." Explain this statement.

4. Under what conditions might the attempt to set specific goals rather than identify a direction be premature or otherwise undesirable? (See the McCaskey reading.)

5. Why does MBO seem to encounter so many difficulties in its application?

6. Now that you have seen some evidence of the effects of various characteristics of goals on performance, what recommendations can you make to managers?

7. MBO was created to shift emphasis away from the processes by which work was performed and stress the results of work as a basis for planning and appraisal. The emphasis on results may have been overdone, however, since MBO users sometimes complain that processes are now neglected. What is the answer to this problem?

Cases for Discussion

Games Planners Play

In 1974 Walcon Manufacturing Corporation adopted an approach to MBO that integrates objective-setting and budgeting. It includes the following steps which are designed to produce a complete set of objectives and budgets for the company by July 1st, the start of each fiscal year:

1. Each department submits its proposed objectives for the coming year to the executive committee, comprising the five top executives, by April 1st.
2. After review, discussion, negotiation, and perhaps modification, the executive committee approves a set of objectives.
3. After approval, each department submits the financial data for its objectives to the executive committee by May 1st.
   a. The Sales Department forecasts sales. Estimated new sales plus the backlog of inventory provide the basis for projecting total shipments for the coming year.
   b. The Manufacturing Department estimates production and provides an estimate of gross profit based on the estimated costs and revenues for each job.
   c. All so-called "overhead" departments, e.g., administrative departments such as Purchasing and Personnel, submit their own budgets. Special program expenses, such as research and development, are also prepared.
4. The planning staff then combines all these data and issues the new company plan by June 1st.

The trouble is that the Sales Department understates its objectives so that it will look good by surpassing them. Manufacturing does the same thing: It understates the anticipated gross profit for each job. This gives them a chance to exceed the objective. It also provides a reserve to meet unanticipated expenses.

The overhead departments always seem to ask for a larger budget and more employees than can possibly be supported by revenues projected by the sales forecast. The department heads are asked to make cuts. They never cut their budgets enough, so top management cuts them all across-the-board by, say, 10 percent.

What happens as a result of a low sales forecast is that we have too much work for the number of employees and the amount of money our budgets allowed. In an attempt to satisfy customers, however, top management authorizes overtime or subcontracting plus occasional special expenditures for air freight and other hurry-up efforts. These expenditures reduce gross profits.

As for the overhead departments, they are imposed upon by all this scrambling. Purchasing and Personnel, for example, are asked for special fast services. They usually try to help, but they often fail to meet their original objectives because of these added burdens. Sometimes they aren't very cooperative precisely because cooperation in coping with this annual emergency will interfere with their meeting their own objectives. In any event, they claim that the budget cuts caused any failures they do experience. They always inflate next year's estimates so that what is cut is more likely to be fat.

This happens every year.

Question

How would you advise Walcon to cope with these problems?

Performance and Cost Evaluation (PACE)

In early 1961 I was working for a large aerospace firm in California. Business and employment were at their peak, but costs were equally high. Because of the high costs, upper management decided to install a PACE program.

PACE was developed to assess performance and infer the management capability of an organization. It was started in 1958 by the manufacturing methods engineering department of another large aerospace corporation. Rather than measure the output of an organization as a basis for inferring management effectiveness, PACE was designed to measure certain selected inputs.

These inputs were actually losses in three factors related to the effective use of employees: (1) idleness, (2) out of area, and (3) group effort. Measures of these factors were combined into the PACE index. Then the index was used as a source of information to judge existing management control practices. PACE required a staff of people trained to observe the three inputs, using a random sampling technique.

Before PACE observers work in a firm, they are exposed to a period of indoctrination, during which they learn the group objectives, number of employees, assignments (who does what), and predicted activity. Before engaging in observation, PACE reps know what the group is supposed to be doing. The observers carry $5'' \times 7''$ black books as they go about their work. During their observations they record activities. After their walk and observation, they return to their office and chart their calculations. For each period of observation, they usually spend half as much time recording and charting.

The PACE observers and their management were brought into our firm for a period of indoctrination on the organization level. Then they were assigned to various areas and underwent further indoctrination at the group level. Measurements were to be taken at the working group level and combined to provide a program evaluation at the organizational level.

Of course, all of the measurements required some judgments. In measuring idleness, for example, the observer had to decide if an engineer sitting physically inactively at a desk was thinking about work or being idle. It was necessary for the observer to decide if people out of their own work areas were contributing to the task or were gone without contributing to the task.

Group effort was even more elusive to measure. For example, the PACE rep was supposed to determine if a secretary talking on the phone was chatting excessively or presenting facts in a business-like manner, or if an engineer was strolling through the factory at leisure or walking at a business-like pace. (During the job training period, the PACE rep was reportedly exposed to a mechanical walking machine which taught how to accurately measure walking speeds.) The total effort ratings of individuals provided a group effort rating.

At the end of each week, the PACE people met with group supervisors and called their attention to the charts and ratings. Each supervisor in turn called his or her group together in an effort to tighten their activities. This went on for several weeks in all areas in order to increase effectiveness.

My impression was that people reacted to PACE in some unanticipated and undesired ways. The PACE rep was an intruder and a villain in the eyes of almost every employee. Supervisors returned from PACE meetings to say that there was idleness and a lack of group effort. In reaction to that, people did things like vigorously shuffle through papers and jot down numbers—any numbers—whenever the PACE rep appeared. Machine operators performed unnecessary work to look busy. Such goings-on occurred frequently during the several months PACE was in operation.

The people felt as though they were under police observation. Tensions began to appear. Management made an attempt to convince the employees that the study was for the good of *their* company, but most of the people who were being observed found it difficult to associate the methods of evaluation with individual well-being. For instance, the workers didn't feel that the number of steps they took from one area to another was a significant measure of their ability to do a job. Since they felt that the measures were all wrong, employees just did not see how it was possible to get a fair rating of their performance.

One day the corporation president came to our plant and, after numerous meetings about PACE, dismissed the PACE people on the spot. Employees danced in the hallways and played darts in the chart room. From the workers' point of view, management had finally gathered their senses about them, after months of madness, and now everyone could quit playing games and get to work.

Questions

1. Based on the narrator's version of PACE, what objectives was it supposed to implement?

2. How was it used to develop objectives?

Controlling Organizational Behavior

Any dictionary will show that the word control has a number of different meanings. Control can mean directing, commanding, or exercising authority over someone. It can mean restraining or limiting someone's behavior. It can mean checking, measuring, and verifying. Control has also come to be used to describe the affirmative shaping of behavior patterns through the use of rewards and reinforcement. At one time or another managers and management theorists and researchers have used the term control to designate virtually every one of these alternatives (Giglioni and Bedeian, 1974).

For our purposes, however, control is the management process of attempting to ensure that objectives are implemented, that the efforts of managers and other employers will fulfill objectives. Control includes a number of activities:

1. Establishing policies and procedures.
2. Measuring and providing feedback on performance.
3. Administering rewards or reinforcement.

Each of these activities makes its distinctive contribution to control. Each can also cause a loss of control, plus various side-effects. Like the use of medication by a physician, the use of control by managers is best done with an awareness of the full range of possible consequences and an appreciation of the indications and contraindications of each approach.

Accordingly, we will explore the nature and use of the control process to help you appreciate both the power and the risk of various control techniques, and to identify the characteristics of situations in which advantages and disadvantages are likely to obtain.

CONTROL THROUGH POLICIES AND PROCEDURES

The first control activity or process, establishing policies and procedures, has its roots in the concept of control as direction. This approach emphasizes prescribing and regulating the activities of employees through the development of policies and procedures. It found voice long ago in Frederick W. Taylor (1906), who advocated ". . . taking the control of the machine shop out of the hands of the many workmen, and placing it completely in the hands of management, thus superseding 'rule of thumb' by scientific control" (p. 39). Taylor's idea was to place the burden upon management to learn the best procedures and methods of performing tasks, to express these best methods in written standard practices, and to teach well-selected employees how to perform the work according to these practices. This "scientific" approach would replace chancy reliance on the uneven talents and idiosyncrasies of assorted employees who had to figure out for themselves, by rule of thumb, what work methods seemed best. In short, it was the duty of managers (a duty they had not traditionally performed very well, as Taylor saw it), and not of employees, to prescribe and regulate objective-fulfilling work methods through policies and procedures.

What Are Policies and Procedures?

Policies and procedures, broadly conceived, include guidelines for making decisions, specified methods for carrying out tasks, and rules and regulations that prohibit or require certain conduct.

Policy refers to a guideline for decision. A policy for admission of students into a law school may, for example, direct those who decide who will be admitted to consider the motivation of applicants as well as their Law School Admission Test scores and undergraduate grade-point averages. The objective underlying the policy may be to admit an occasional student whose test score and grade-point average are comparatively low, but whose motivation impresses the decision-maker as a compensating virtue or indication of success. The policy helps the decision-maker know what to consider, but does not prescribe the outcomes of the decision process.

A procedure, on the other hand, prescribes the steps to take in accomplishing a piece of work. A cashier at the check-out counter of a supermarket, for example, may be required to take certain steps before cashing a check. The cashier might have to record the number of the customer's driver's license and the number from one of the customer's credit cards. If the check exceeds a specified amount, a rule might require the cashier to present the check to the assistant store manager for approval.

The distinctions between a policy, procedure, and rule are not always clear, however. Policies may prescribe steps, and procedures and rules may confer discretion on decision-makers. The policy of considering the motivation of law school applicants may imply a *procedure* whereby the admissions counselor records notes on indications of the applicant's motivation. The procedure requiring the cashier to obtain the assistant store manager's approval for checks in excess of specified amounts may be used so loosely that the cashier actually decides whether to notify the assistant manager or to ignore the procedure, depending on such factors as recognition of the customer or the length of the customer line at the checkout counter. In any event, precisely distinguishing between policy and procedure is not important as a practical matter. What is important is that managers devise policies and procedures that help employees act in ways that fulfill objectives.

Some Advantages

In its early days, a business may be quite successful by depending almost entirely on objectives, with few policies, procedures, or other controls. Eventually, however, controls are necessary, and they do develop. The Xerox Company (*Newsweek*, 1965) is an example.

Xerox has been one of the most impressive organizations in American business. Between 1954 and 1964 the old family-dominated Haloid Company, manufacturing specialized photographic products, transformed itself into the modern Xerox Company—and jumped from 30 to over 300 million dollars a year in sales. In 1959 the company was chaotic. Offices were located all over Rochester, N.Y., over delicatessens and in abandoned schools. Job descriptions were few, policies broad, procedures ignored, and controls weak. Yet the company was successful. And it was successful because of top management's ability to point out direction. Chairman Sol Linowitz and President Joseph Wilson saw their roles as the laying down of objectives—long-range, intermediate, and short-range. Wilson spent much of his time selling the Xerox Company to his own managers, describing the revolutionary and beneficial impact of its information technology on society—and also pointing out how each manager's own interest would be served if the company advanced. Given the fantastic expansion, he was aware that it would be impossible to control the entire company from the president's office. In order to take advantage of a divergent market and to exploit their technologically superior product, it was essential that managers at all levels be committed to manufacturing the product and getting it out to the market as quickly as possible. Premature policies, procedures, and controls would have interfered with the spontaneous cooperation and initiative demonstrated by Xerox management.

Eventually, however, policies and procedures did emerge at Xerox—and for good reason. First of all, why go on reinventing the wheel? Why must a company handle every problem as unique? Sam Jones wonders how Gail Smith has handled the problem of quality control on some gears. He asks about it. Gail's answer seems reasonable, and rather than search for new alternatives, Sam adopts Gail's procedure. Or Mike Stratton has had great success in handling rush orders within his production area. How does he do it? Some questioning will disclose his methods. Why not let everyone know about it? So an information memo is drafted and distributed. The basis for policies and procedures, then, rests upon an awareness of the usefulness of past experience. There is no reason why one should repeat the same mistakes over and over again without taking advantage of the accumulated knowledge of people in the organization. The famous words, in another context, of Oliver Wendell Holmes apply: "Three generations of idiots are enough!" The company decides to make some rules that trade upon experience and give guidance to people facing similar problems for the first time.

So in the beginning, procedures and policies are developed from the organization's own experience. After a while, however, management may feel that they should take advantage of experience outside the company as well. Experts can provide this knowledge, and so specialists, advisers, auditors, and controllers are hired. Once they are hired, there is a natural tendency for management to see that they are used, by giving them some authority to impose their experience on the rest of the organization.

At Xerox, the expansion of staff activities in the development of job descriptions, policies, and procedures was given impetus when management became concerned about internal efficiency. When their product is clearly superior and the market is fertile, management's main concern is getting the product made and out the door. Internal costs and efficiencies are of minor importance when production cost is a relatively small percentage of the selling or rental price. Xerox's main problem in the late fifties and early sixties was to get the jump on the competition and to put its machines into offices all over the world. Stiff competition has developed, however, and although the price factor is apparently not critical yet, there has been increased concern within Xerox about manufacturing costs. Such concern inevitably means rationalization of production operations: Rationalization means finding out what the best methods are, applying them throughout the organization, and seeing that people adhere to them—just as Taylor suggested many years ago.

A Xerox research and development engineer has indicated how such elaboration of procedures affected him. When he had an idea that required funds in 1959, he would walk into the office of the vice president with a scratch pad and pencil, sit down, and sketch out the idea. A decision would be made quickly, and the researcher would go to work. In 1967, however, the same researcher was required to complete, in multiple copies, a prescribed project form indicating potential equipment cost, material requirements, potential return, cash flow, etc. This is not simply red tape; multiple forms are not required just to complicate the lives of people in the organization. The decisions that have to be made about fund allocation are much more complex than they were in a simpler day. More and different projects are involved; they must be compared with one another on some consistent basis; and priority decisions have to be made about organizational objectives. Specific procedures for allocating capital funds facilitate comparison, prediction, and control—essential functions of management in any organization.

This development of job descriptions, policies, and procedures aids efficiency by promoting coordination and predictability. However fine the initiative of Xerox managers had been in the expansion stage, it was stressful and unstable. For a while, people will put up with instability, but order, regularity, and predictability become essential in the long run—especially if the rate of growth and promotional opportunities start to decline. Nor do managers necessarily dislike the development of policies and procedures. Order is brought out of chaos and predictability out of instability, and simple relief from making the same mistakes over and over again is achieved. Indeed, many managers perceive the development of control procedures as progress.

Some Disadvantages

However inevitable and necessary the development of policies and procedures is, equally inevitable is the development of problems with those policies and procedures. One of the so-called management principles of long repute has been the rule that delegated duties should be explicit and specific—with no gaps or overlaps. If this is true, and if procedures are inclusive, theoretically each manager need only follow directions. No initiative is required.

Of course, we have described an impossible condition. Such perfect planning, delegating, and controlling is impossible. Therefore, spontaneity is essential. To a greater or lesser degree, every manager must fill in the gaps, work out the conflicts resulting from overlaps, and exercise discretion in following policies and procedures. If they are followed blindly, the organization loses direction. There is an inversion of means and ends. To some people, following rules, plans, and controls becomes an end in itself, without a thought to whether or not they contribute to the organization's objectives. Indeed, in the eyes of many, such inversion of means and ends is almost synonymous with bureaucracy in an organization. Frequently, we assume such distortion characterizes governments and other public, nonprofit institutions. The comments of John Knowles, former Director of Massachusetts General Hospital, are illustrative: "In the teaching hospital, it has become set that the patient exists for the teaching programs, and not that the hospital exists for the patient" (De Hartog, 1966).

Such inversion of means and ends, however, also occurs in business. An advertisement in a prominent management journal once showed a hand holding a fancy notebook entitled "Policy Manual" over a wire-basket incinerator in which several similar notebooks were burning. Who was the advertiser? A management consulting firm. Its message? That one should not allow policies, procedures, and other controls to exist unchanged for too long, because they get out of date and hinder the organization instead of helping—better to burn them (and call in the consultant to write a new set).

Once established and accepted, policies and procedures tend to limit flexibility and initiative. In the beginning, at least, policies and procedures are usually good, and an organization gains in coordination and predictability what it may lose in initiative. Nonetheless, it is difficult to keep policies and procedures up-to-date: Some policies may no longer apply to new conditions, and those rational plans and controls which were developed to promote effectiveness may begin to interfere with the accomplishment of objectives. If managers blindly follow these rules, spontaneity is lost.

A Contingency View

As you can see, a basic problem for managers is to create policies and procedures that provide the right amount of direction. Excessive and inappropriate policies, procedures, or rules ensnare the employees in red tape and hinder performance. The result: inflexible and ineffectual bureaucracy.

On the other hand, insufficient policy guidelines can allow decision-makers *too much* discretion. Without policy guidance, one bank loan officer may decide to grant a loan, while another loan officer of the same bank facing a similar case may deny the loan. Without procedures and rules to govern employment decisions, one personnel interviewer might recommend hiring an applicant without checking past employment references, while another interviewer in the same company might check four references before recommending hiring in a similar case. In other words, just as Taylor warned, activities will reflect the idiosyncrasies, bad as well as good, of individual employees, rather than the careful analysis and design of work methods. The result: insufficient control and uneven performance.

Fortunately, a contingency approach to control through policy and procedure provides both a way of thinking about how to achieve the right amount of control and some research evidence that indicates roughly what the right amount is for different classes of situations. Fundamentally, a contingency view recognizes that control must be adapted to the task the organization is attempting to perform (Newman, 1975). This means that the pattern of policies and procedures will have to take into account such factors as technology and environment. It also means that control patterns will have to be consonant with certain predispositions or personality characteristics of the employees whose behavior management is attempting to regulate (Lorsch and Morse, 1974).

A substantial amount of research and theory suggests that the performance of relatively routine tasks, with relatively mechanistic technology, is facilitated by comprehensive policies and procedures that closely regulate work behavior, whereas the performance of nonroutine tasks, with less mechanistic technology, is aided by less comprehensive control through policy and procedure (Lawrence and Lorsch, 1967; Lorsch and Morse, 1974; Woodward, 1965; Woodward, 1970; Burns and Stalker, 1961; Perrow, 1970). Lorsch and Morse (1974), for example, compared the performance of a number of pairs of container manufacturing plants and a number of pairs of research laboratories. Each pair consisted of one effective and one ineffective organization. The container plants were characterized by routine tasks, mechanistic technology, and stable conditions, the research laboratories by opposite conditions. The effective container plants were found to have more abundant, elaborate, and comprehensive policies and procedures than their less effective counterparts. A supervisor in an effective container plant told the researchers, "We have rules and standards dealing with everything from how much powder to use in cleaning out toilet bowls to how to cart a dead body out of the plant. Everyone is subject to them . . . there are no exceptions" (pp. 69–70). In contrast, the effective research laboratories had fewer and less comprehensive policies and procedures than their less effective counterparts. As a male (and possibly chauvinist) scientist in an effective research laboratory joked: "We can't wear sandals because of safety regulations and we're not supposed to proposition secretaries on company time, but apart from that there's not much formality in the laboratory" (p. 92).

Lorsch and Morse (1974) went beyond the fairly well-established observation that the pattern of control must fit the nature of the task. They also measured four aspects of the personalities of managers within each of the organizations studied. The first of these was *integrative complexity*, a quality that refers to the ability of individuals ". . . to take in differentiated bits of information from the environment and then to integrate the differentiated bits" (p. 48). More of this ability is required to cope with complex and uncertain task situations. The second characteristic was *tolerance for ambiguity*; more of it is also required to function effectively in uncertain environments. The third quality identified *preferred ways of relating to authority*. Those persons who desired more autonomy and did not require strong relationships with authority figures and systems functioned better in uncertain environments. The fourth personality characteristic, *attitude toward individualism*, differentiated people according to whether they preferred working in groups or alone. Persons who preferred working alone functioned better in environments requiring little coordination with others.

What Lorsch and Morse found was that two different, effective combinations of tasks, people, and patterns of control through policies and procedures could be distinguished. One combination, found in the effective container manufacturing plants, brought together a structured, certain task; managers with comparatively low integrative complexity, low tolerance for ambiguity, a high propensity to accept authority, and a preference for working with others; and a pattern of comprehensive policies and procedures. The other combination, found in the effective research laboratories, brought together exactly the opposite pattern of task, personality, and administrative controls. Less effective container plants and less effective research laboratories showed greater deviation in one or another of these three variables from the pattern shown by their more effective counterparts.

Thus, control through policies and procedures must be attuned to the uncertainty of the task and to particular characteristics of the people who perform it. When the pattern of controls fits the task and the people, performance is facilitated. Effective performance under these conditions of "good fit" is also associated with enhanced feelings of competence for employees (Lorsch and Morse, 1974).

CONTROL THROUGH PERFORMANCE MEASUREMENT AND FEEDBACK

The second control process, measuring performance and providing feedback, has its roots in a concept of control not as direction but as verification — checking to see if activities conform to predetermined direction. "Control in this sense," observe Reeves and Woodward (1970), "is limited to monitoring the outcome of activities, reviewing feedback information about this outcome, and if necessary taking corrective action" (p. 38). This approach emphasizes developing and administering measures of key activities that will permit knowing if objectives are being fulfilled.

In general, systems of gathering information and using it for control purposes in organizations have the following characteristics (Lawler and Rhode, 1976):

1. They all collect, store, and transmit information in the form of abstract measures of reality. Usually, they deal with information about the condition of the organization in the form of measures that are quantitative (e.g., the cost and quantity of production) and that can be understood only by trained personnel.
2. The collected abstract information is stored and transmitted in a specific form and with a specific frequency. For example, a company makes quarterly profit reports based on a particular set of accounting practices regarding its method of treating inventory and depreciation.

3. The summarized information is distributed to a specific, usually predetermined, group of people. The group may or may not include all the members of the organization. Some information is given to only a few people in the organization while other information is more public (e.g., earnings reports for corporations) (pp. 5–6).*

Several issues arise in the design and use of control systems to collect and feed back performance data. These include determining what to measure, developing effective sensors or measures, considering costs and difficulties of alternative measurements, understanding the effects of feedback and deciding to whom it should be directed, and identifying and containing undesirable motivational and behavioral consequences associated with performance measurement and feedback. We will discuss these issues in the following sections.

The Choice of Measurements

What to measure is implied by the objectives established for the organization, the department, and the individuals involved. Retail stores, for example, have often set "productivity" objectives for store managers that specify sales per labor hour and sales per square foot. To develop information on how well these objectives are being met, it is necessary, of course, to measure sales. To do this, and to develop the most timely data possible, many retailers have installed computerized cash registers. J. C. Penney, for example, was thereby able to provide store managers with up-to-the-minute detailed data on sales volume, what was selling, and so on (*Business Week*, 1974). The sales figures could quickly be related to labor hours and square footage.

For other organizations, other objectives and therefore other measurements are important. Public utilities and regulated private industries such as airlines, for example, often have paramount service objectives that must be met if the organizations are to avoid inconveniencing and aggravating the public to the degree that government takeover becomes a serious possibility. To see how well their public contact employees serve customers, airlines and some utilities have devised various schemes for monitoring and developing quantitative measures of service.

One telephone company, for example, has for many years used what it calls the Business Office Contact Performance Measurement Plan. The Plan is a control designed to help implement the company's goal of providing customers with the best service possible in the shortest amount of time with the least inconvenience to the customer. The Plan contains a hundred or so pages of detailed specifications of different kinds of mistakes that Service Representatives might make in dealing with customers who telephone local Business Offices requesting service or information.

In order to check on the quality of the service to customers, a staff service-observing group monitors Service Representatives' contacts with customers.

---

* From *Information and Control in Organizations*, by E. E. Lawler III and John Grant Rhode, pp. 5–6. Copyright © 1976 by Goodyear Publishing Co. Reprinted by permission.

In a typical city, the service-observing group might be located in a separate office downtown. The office has special equipment which enables the service observers to dial into customer-Service Representative telephone conversations in the various business offices throughout the metropolitan area. The observer's line is silent, so the customer has no idea someone is listening to her or his conversation with the Service Representative. The service observer listens for the defects specified in the instruction manual and notes any that occur. The listening is done according to a systematic sampling method and the data are summarized and reported to each Business Office Manager. No individual Service Representatives are identified in these reports, but Business Office Managers receive data that show overall statistics on the type of defects in customer contacts for their office and for other business offices in their districts.

Ideally, the measurements required by the control system make it possible to see if objectives are being implemented. The measurements are logically derived from established objectives. How well the measurements are designed, however, makes a difference in how much they can help the organization reach its objectives.

Characteristics of the Measures

Lawler and Rhode (1976) identify three characteristics of the measures or sensors (such as sales or service defects) used by a control system: how complete or inclusive they are, how objective or impersonal they are, and how much they can be controlled or influenced by the members of an organization (p. 42). The telephone company's 100-page manual of contact performance defects, with detailed and exhaustive illustrations of each type, is an example of a relatively complete or inclusive system. J. C. Penney's measures of store square footage and sales volume illustrate relatively objective and impersonal measures. The degree to which the results measured by the telephone company and by J. C. Penney respond to the efforts of managers and employees to increase sales or avoid service-performance defects would reflect the extent to which the measures can be controlled or influenced by the members of those organizations.

Research on the effects upon motivation and behavior of differences in the three control-system characteristics leads to the conclusion that completeness, objectivity, and responsiveness to employee effort and performance are desirable qualities in virtually any control system (Lawler and Rhode, 1976, p. 179). They tend to enhance motivation because they highlight links between effort and performance. They tend to encourage appropriate behavior for several reasons. Complete measures help people concentrate on all aspects of the job instead of neglecting unmeasured tasks in favor of measured ones. Objective measures avoid the risks of bias and resentment inherent in personal and subjective assessments of performance. Measures that can be influenced or are responsive support the belief that effort and performance will lead to an improved showing in the control system.

It follows that control system design ought to reflect at least two fundamental qualities. The aspects of performance to be measured ought to reveal whether objectives are being met or not. And the measures or sensors themselves ought to be as complete, objective, and responsive as possible. As we shall see in the next section, however, these are not the only considerations in finding suitable ways to measure performance.

Cost and Difficulty of Measurement

The effort to design a good system of controls would be challenging enough if all that had to be considered was the relevance of measurements to objectives, and the completeness, objectivity, and responsiveness of the measures or sensors. But the job is made even more difficult by the different costs associated with alternative measurements and by the difficulty of measuring some kinds of performance.

Consider, for example, the telephone company's problems in measuring service. A basic objective may imply that service ought to be measured, but precisely what should be measured and how it should be measured to see if good service is being provided may not be obvious. The telephone company's service-observing system, for example, is an almost unbelievably elaborate control. It is also very expensive—so much so that managers in the telephone company sometimes argue that it is too costly and might better be replaced by a procedure of sending questionnaires to people who have recently had dealings with Service Representatives, simply asking them how they liked the service they received. There are also objections to the eavesdropping aspect of the system and arguments that this could be avoided with a questionnaire system. Our interest is not to judge the system as good or bad, but to suggest that there are often alternative measurements and methods of measuring to monitor performance relative to a single objective; that the alternatives can differ in costs; and that different controls may produce different emotional and behavioral responses in the people being measured. All of these considerations need to be weighed in choosing what to measure and when and how to measure it.

Another problem in performance measurement is posed by the difficulty of measuring some kinds of performance. Providing a high quality of customer service after sales may be an admirable intention for a wholesale industrial equipment manufacturer, but it may be difficult to select one or more measurable activities or results that will effectively reflect its achievement. Number of calls on customers may be both easy to measure and of some interest, but it also could be a trivial and misleading piece of evidence that has no direct or significant relationship to good service. It also may be difficult to measure the output of several interdependent contributors and attribute its strengths or weaknesses to any individuals or departments. Good service, as perceived by the customer, may result from a combination of courteous secretaries, well-trained technicians, knowledgeable field representatives, and a good product design to begin with. Seizing upon a measure of any one or two or three of these as the indication of how good service is may provide more of an illusion of a good control system than an accurate reflection of the diverse and inter-related contributions that produced the level of service experienced by customers.

In any event, once a performance measure is chosen, the issue arises as to what to do with the information it makes available.

The Importance of Feedback

Feedback is an integral part of control through the use of performance measurement. Without feedback on activities and results related to sales and service objectives, J. C. Penney's store managers and the telephone company's Business Office Managers would be managing without benefit of information on their progress toward goals. Feedback of performance measurements makes it possible to compare actual with intended results and to attempt adjustments where indicated. Store managers can use their up-to-the-minute sales data to decide if personnel changes are necessary or if slow-moving merchandise needs to be replaced with faster-moving items. Business Office Managers can use their reports to see if any patterns or defects in contacts with customers imply the need for more training for Service Representatives, changes in their leadership practice, or other changes.

A number of studies have also examined the relationship of feedback to motivation and performance. Older studies of learning demonstrated that feedback was necessary to enable people to improve their performance (Thorndike, 1927; Elwell and Grindley, 1938; and Bilodeau, Bilodeau, and Schumsky, 1959). Individuals who received no feedback simply didn't know how to modify their efforts, or even if they should modify them. Other studies showed that individuals worked longer and harder if they were given feedback (Orjos, 1920; Manzer, 1935; and Smode, 1958).

A number of more recent studies focus on the way performance feedback can affect motivation and effort through goal-setting (Locke, Cartledge, and Koeppel, 1968; Locke, Cartledge, and Knerr, 1970; and Cummings, Schwab, and Rosen, 1971). The Locke theory of goal-setting (which was discussed briefly in Chapter 8) holds that feedback or knowledge of results will affect motivation and performance only insofar as it affects goal-setting and goal-orientation. As Latham and Yukl (1975) point out, feedback might lead a person who did not have a specific goal to adopt one; it may lead to setting a higher goal after attaining a previous goal; or it may simply orient the person toward the existing goal by making it evident that more effort will be needed to reach it (p. 834). Generally, the evidence supports the proposition that feedback affects performance only if it leads to setting higher goals.

Cummings, Schwab, and Rosen (1971) have demonstrated that people do tend to set higher goals following attainment of past goals. However, when the effects of their previous performance levels were held constant, higher goals were set in proportion to the amount and accuracy of feedback. Inaccurate feedback, particularly incomplete feedback that leads to an unrealistically low impression of past performance, can result in poorer performance than that produced by providing no feedback at all.

But not every study confirms the earlier evidence and the popular belief that accurate feedback tends to lift performance. Neither Hackman and Lawler (1971) nor Steers (1973) could find any difference in the performance of public utility employees depending upon whether they received feedback or not. Steers (1973), however, found that feedback was associated with increased motivation and improved performance for employees who had high needs for achievement, affiliation, and independence. After reviewing the research on the effects of feedback on performance, Steers and Porter (1974) concluded that something more than a simple positive relationship exists, and that the outcome of providing feedback is likely to vary depending upon personality characteristics and the level of aspiration employees bring to their jobs (p. 440).

Finally, the effects of feedback can also vary depending upon who or what provides it. Feedback can come from the task or work equipment itself (e.g., from a machine that tabulates the parts its operator produces), from another person, such as a boss or staff specialist, or directly from a formal control system (Lawler and Rhode, 1976). Most individuals seem to find the task and themselves to be the preferred source (Greller and Herold, 1975). Resentment and other problems are more likely to occur if other persons intervene to relay the control data to the employee. "A sure way to create friction," observes one long-time student of control (Newman, 1975), "is to send control data to staff first so that they can call for remedial action before the operating people have an opportunity to respond on their own initiative" (pp. 21–22). Even supervisors often make a poor source of feedback. They commonly feel uncomfortable about giving it, give it at the wrong time, and add criticism to information (Porter, Lawler, and Hackman, 1975). The usual response to criticism is, of course, defensiveness; and it has been shown that critical feedback from supervisors in a performance appraisal system tends, indeed, to provide more stimulus to defensiveness than to improved performance (Meyer, Kay, and French, 1965).

In sum, feedback can be both valuable and risky. Its value would seem to be enhanced the more it is characterized by a neutral conveyance of data generated by complete, objective, and responsive sensors or measures of performance. The risk that it may stimulate conflict and defensiveness seems to be enhanced the more other persons, such as staff personnel or supervisors, figure in conveying the data to the person whose performance is being measured. They have difficulty in refraining from interpreting, judging, and criticizing activities, which can be detrimental.

Motivational and Behavioral Problems with Measurement and Feedback

We have already seen that measurement and feedback can affect motivation and behavior. But we also need to look more closely at *how* controls influence employees and why the results are sometimes disturbing. There is no doubt that controls do affect behavior. The problem is to predict and shape those effects; otherwise controls make little contribution to control. As the authors of one of this chapter's selected readings observe: "Organizations spend large amounts of money, time, and effort in designing and maintaining control systems. . . . Often, however, instead of increasing organizational control these systems reduce the amount of effective control that the organization exercises" (Cammann and Nadler, 1976, p. 65).

The first step in understanding how measurement and feedback can produce a loss rather than a gain of control is recognizing that the very act of measuring influences the behavior of the people being measured. When superiors measure subordinates' performance, they trigger a chain of perceptual, cognitive, and motivational processes. Subordinates tend to perceive the measurements as defining important aspects of the job. They assume that what is counted is what matters. As Harold Hook, the president of American General Insurance Co. puts it, "A company gets what it inspects, not what it expects" (*Business Week*, Dec. 15, 1975, p. 77).

How the apparently innocent and simple collection of information about certain aspects of employee performance can produce diverse and uncontrolled motivation and behavioral consequences in an organization is illustrated by Blau's study (1963) of a state employment office. The office's function was to administer unemployment compensation and assist clients in finding jobs.

The only measured aspect of the performance of the interviewers who worked in the office was the number of interviews held. This count alone seemed sufficient when jobs were abundantly available. But when jobs became scarce and more time and skill were necessary to match people and jobs, the bare count on interviews didn't reveal enough about interviewer performance. Even more serious were some unwanted effects on interviewer behavior.

In some instances, interviewers rushed applicants through the interview, thus securing a "point" quickly without carefully assessing either qualifications or openings, and without attending to the *unmeasured* tasks of referral and placement. Unless the supervisor directly observed these shortcomings, he or she faced the task of evaluating an interviewer's performance while being ignorant of these problems. Instead, he or she had only quantitative evidence of good performance. It would be like a dean evaluating a professor by the number of articles published, without reading those articles or seeing the more subtle effects of teaching neglect possibly brought on by taking time to write the articles.

When a new department head took over the state employment agency, she introduced a new set of statistical records of performance. What was counted now included:

1. The number of interviews held.
2. The number of clients referred to a job.
3. The number of placements (referred client was hired).
4. The proportion of interviews resulting in referrals.
5. The proportion of referrals resulting in placements.

Although the intent behind the use of the new measures was to obtain more information, and not to change behavior, the measures did indeed change behavior. More placements were made because interviewers concentrated less on producing a large number of interviews and more on carefully learning about applicants' qualifications and referring them to jobs that appeared to match their qualifications. Other results were less desirable, however. Some interviewers concealed information about job openings, or falsely recorded high experience requirements on the form describing the job, so that they alone could fill the job and obtain credit.

Examples of the same general phenomenon of making sure, by fair means or foul, that measurements will register at satisfactory levels abound in industry.

In a pioneering study, Argyris (1957) examined the impact of budget controls on those being controlled. He gave repeated examples of short-run compliance with control standards that in either the short-run or the long-run had adverse cost consequences to the organization. He reported instances of people who worked under fixed quotas of output with some opportunity to select items to be worked on, who chose easy, rapidly completed jobs as fillers toward the end of a period in order to meet the quota. Blau (1963) reports similar behavior among law enforcement officials who maintain an established case load and who pick easy or fast cases toward the end of each month if they anticipate falling short of their quotas. Jasinski (1956) describes a similar adaptation in assembly-line production of foremen "bleeding the line" by stuffing all work in progress through the measuring point (using augmented crews) in order to meet a quota, but losing efficiency in the succeeding period until the line is refilled with work in progress.

Deliberate evasion is also a response. Jasinski describes "making out with the pencil" as a means of giving the appearance on paper of meeting expected standards without actually doing so. Dalton (1955) reports a comparable instance of evasion where local plant officials, through blandishment of and subsequent conspiracy with the central office representative, were able to evade cost-control checks imposed by the central office.

Such managerial adaptation to controls is not culture-bound. Granick (1960) points out that monetary rewards and glory attend the Soviet plant manager who sets a new production record. There is pressure to set a record at the expense of operating repairs and preventive maintenance. The result is lower output in the subsequent period while the delayed maintenance is attended to—or its effects are felt in breakdowns. Meanwhile, the manager has received his payoff for the over-quota output of the earlier period. In addition, Berliner (1956) and Richman (1965) note the practice in Soviet industry of "storming" production to meet output standards toward the end of a quota period, again at the expense of maintenance and balanced output.

A selected reading at the end of this chapter by Lawler and Rhode discusses in more detail four types of behavioral problems associated with control systems.

We have considered the possibilities of controlling the behavior of people at work through policies and procedures and through performance measurement and feedback. In this and the next section we will consider yet another means of control—the design and administration of reward practices. "Here," as Peter Drucker (1974) puts it, "is the real control of the institution, that is, the ground of behavior and the cause of action. People act as they are being rewarded or punished" (p. 504). We will consider two distinctive approaches to control through rewards. The first, which we will discuss now, derives from motivation theory, and the second, which we will discuss in the next section, from behaviorism.

As Chapter 1 explained, motivation theory visualizes people as having needs and beliefs or expectancies about whether or not various ways of behaving will lead to satisfaction of those needs. Inner mental and emotional processes work to determine how people will behave. But these inner processes, which are called "motivation," can be influenced by how external conditions are arranged. In organizations, for example, managers can control behavior by deliberately arranging or attempting to affect two principal kinds of conditions: intrinsic and extrinsic rewards.

Intrinsic Rewards

Intrinsic rewards are those feelings of satisfaction that people obtain directly from their activities. People at work, for example, may satisfy their needs for achievement, for competence, and for self-actualization through solving problems that are built into their jobs. Job enrichment (Chapter 7) is based on the assumption that many people feel deprived of such satisfactions and that enriched jobs can make work instrumental to obtaining intrinsic rewards. Management-by-objectives reflects the same assumption. The anticipated benefits of both these practices are more involved, satisfied, and productive employees.

But intrinsic rewards have an important limitation. Managers can't give intrinsic rewards. Managers can only do things—enrich jobs, for example— which they hope might result in intrinsic rewards. Individuals define what is rewarding to themselves. They give or decline to give themselves their own intrinsic rewards, and only individuals with strong needs for achievement, competence, and self-actualization can be motivated by intrinsic rewards. Persons with weak higher-order needs show little intrinsic motivation, whether their jobs are enriched or not (Hackman and Lawler, 1971). Therefore, as Lawler and Rhode (1976) observe, ". . . no organization, unless it is populated by people who value intrinsic rewards, can depend on intrinsic motivation. Since it is unlikely that any organization will ever be populated entirely by such people, most organizations will probably have to rely to some extent on extrinsic motivation" (p. 68).

Extrinsic Rewards

Extrinsic rewards include tangible items, such as pay, promotion, fringe benefits, and status symbols (office furnishings, cars, and so on), which organizations may grant employees. It is not difficult to see how money can be instrumental to satisfying lower-level physiological and safety needs (Opsahl and Dunnette, 1966). Nor is it difficult to see how symbols of status and prestige, such as higher rank, fancier office furnishings, and cars, might contribute to feelings of esteem and power (Winter, 1972). But how financial rewards affect the need for achievement is a bit more subtle. As McClelland (1965) explains: "The person with high n Achievement works hard anyway, provided there is an opportunity of achieving something. He is interested in money rewards or profits primarily because of the feedback they give him as to how well he is doing. Money is not the incentive to effort but rather the measure of its success for the real entrepreneur" (p. 7).

Can Pay Motivate?

To some behavioral scientists, extrinsic rewards (money being the prime example) appear even less important then they do to McClelland. Specifically, money is viewed as contributing only to the satisfaction of lower-level needs and as having no important motivational effects through higher-level needs (McGregor, 1960; Herzberg, 1966). For Herzberg (1966), money, at best, can only stave off dissatisfaction temporarily. If workers are given an increase in pay it will cure their dissatisfaction momentarily. In time they will hunger for an increase again. Then they will be as dissatisfied as they were before. All the while, however, the increases will not motivate them to perform better. What appears to be the practical implication? "Forget about money as a motivator. Let someone else take care of it because it must be done." But the manager should ". . . dig in exclusively on improving the nature of the job" (Ford, 1969, p. 33).

True, there is evidence that pay influences the decision to accept and keep a job in a particular organization, and even to attend work regularly (Lawler, 1973). The accusation, however, is that pay and extrinsic rewards in general can't motivate people to perform their jobs well. Only intrinsic rewards, it is argued, can do that.

Money actually diminishes intrinsic motivation, according to three experiments conducted by Edward Deci (1972, 1973). He explored the effects that extrinsic rewards, specifically pay, have upon rewards intrinsic to the performance of work. Common to each experiment was the following sequence:

First, subjects were put in a situation where their activity could be observed and taken as evidence of their intrinsic level of motivation. For example, a college sophomore who had agreed to be a subject in an experiment in human problem solving showed up for the first session, was told about the experiment, and given a puzzle to be worked out as his part in the study. The experimenter said he had to leave to attend to some other matters. He said he would be back in 8 minutes and told the subject that he had 13 minutes to complete his puzzle assignment.

After the experimenter left to watch the subject through a one-way mirror, the subject observed that in addition to the puzzle, other items of interest were handy. There were the latest issues of *Playboy, Time, The New Yorker,* and other magazines. How long the subject worked on the puzzle rather than read magazines was measured and defined as his level of intrinsic motivation.

Next, the experimenter returned and started the second session. This time the subject was given a wage incentive, a dollar for each portion or configuration of the puzzle problem solved. The experimenter again said he had to leave. He went to the one-way mirror, took out his stop watch, and again measured how much time the subject worked on the puzzle.

The third period was the same as the first. No money.

Control groups also underwent the experiment. For them all three periods were without money.

The question was: What effects will the extrinsic reward in period two have upon intrinsic motivation in period three? Will it drop, rise, or remain about the same when compared to the first period and to the control group? The answer: Always, performance improved when pay was offered, but decreased when it was withdrawn.

Vroom (1971) comments upon Deci's research as follows: "The explanation of these findings is still problematical but let me give you mine. The introduction of pay for the performance of a task changes the meaning of a task for a person. Cognitively, it becomes something which he does for money, not because of its intrinsic enjoyment. This explanation is consistent with, if not derivable from, recent theories of cognitive dissonance" (p. 6). The point is that it becomes inconsistent in the third period to work hard for nothing. "It may mean, for example, that incentive compensation systems can increase performance but do so at the expense of intrinsic motivation that the person has for the performance of his job. Similarly, grading systems may be effective as motivators of students but may do so at the expense of student interest in learning for its own sake. The effects of these external control systems may be to change the person's perception of the locus of control over his behavior from himself to his environment" (p. 7).

On the other hand, Deci's results should not be taken as the final word. He did find that pay which was dependent upon performance weakened intrinsic motivation. But a subsequent study (Foster and Hamner, 1974) found that extrinsic rewards (pay) do not necessarily reduce intrinsic ones so long as the pay is not delayed. When not delayed, extrinsic rewards add to intrinsic ones. In other words, the supposed war between extrinsic and intrinsic rewards may be more apparent than real. The problem that Deci observed may be one of timing rather than any inherent conflict between the two kinds of rewards.

In any event, perhaps all the concern about the vices of monetary rewards and the virtues of intrinsic rewards has been necessary to correct an earlier naive view that money is the only factor that can motivate people at work. We have overcorrected, however, and neglected the capacity of pay to function as a reward. But fortunately, a minority of behavioral scientists, among the many who study organizations and management, have continued to concentrate on the relationships among money, motivation, and performance. Vroom (1964), Porter and Lawler (1968), and Lawler (1971), for example, have conducted research and developed practical recommendations, mainly within the framework of expectancy theory.

As we indicated in Chapter 1, the central idea of expectancy theory is that the likelihood that people will act in a particular way is a function of how strong their expectancy is that the act will be followed by a reward and what value that reward holds for them. Like grades or marks in school, pay in organizations can be a desired or valued reward. It can also come to be seen as only available or contingent upon performing particular acts. Therein lies its power to motivate.

According to Lawler (1971, pp. 91–92), assuming that necessary abilities and other enabling conditions are present, pay can motivate good performance if employees

1. value pay highly.
2. believe that good performance results in high pay.
3. believe that by exerting effort they can improve their performance.
4. reckon that the advantages of working hard, performing well, and obtaining high pay exceed the disadvantages and psychic opportunity costs.
5. see good performance as the most attractive of all possible behaviors in the situation.

Porter and Lawler (1968, pp. 173–182) recommend a series of steps that managers can take to see if these conditions exist. First, managers should question people in the organization to find out just what they believe about pay, effort, and performance in the organization: What rewards do they want? Is additional pay strongly desired? Do employees believe that good performance really brings high pay in this organization? Do they believe that if they put forth greater effort it will affect their performance? What disadvantages are there to good performance?

Next, managers can try to cement the connection between pay and performance. By making it come true, they can support the subjective perception that pay varies positively with performance. To make the connection really effective requires flexible compensation practices so that the rewards offered can be varied to some extent to provide what individuals want. For example, some employees may prefer a greater share of their total pay package in retirement benefits and insurance. Others may want more in straight salary. Why not meet these individual preferences where the cost to the firm is equal? On top of this willingness to tailor compensation to individual preferences, it remains important to give superior performers both more extrinsic rewards (pay and/or benefits) and more intrinsic rewards (interesting assignments and/or promotions).

Finally, managers can continue to survey perceptions and preferences concerning pay and promotion practices. They can also measure other job attitudes. The results, when related to performance measures, can tell if the most satisfied employees are the best performers. If they are not, then the pay system may be out of control, rewarding organizational membership and not performance.

To provide a better alignment of pay and performance, Lawler (1971) has recommended a specific pay plan which he believes to be appropriate for a wide variety of organizations. The essence of his plan is to divide each employee's pay into three components. The first of these would be for the job to which the person is assigned. It would be equal for everyone assigned to that type of job. The second would comprise cost-of-living and seniority pay, to be paid everyone and adjusted annually. The third would be individually determined, based upon measurements of each person's performance during the preceding period. Lawler explains the third part this way:

> The poor performer in the organization should find that this part of his or her pay package is minimal, while the good performer should find that this part of his or her pay is at least as great as the other two parts combined. This would not be a raise, however, since it could vary from year to year, depending on the individual's performance during the last performance period. Salary increases or raises would come only with changes in responsibility, cost of living, or seniority. The merit portion of the pay package would be highly variable, so that if a person's performance fell off, his or her pay would also be decreased by a cut in the size of the merit pay. The purpose of this kind of system is, of course, to make a large proportion of an individual's pay depend upon performance during the current period. Thus performance is chronologically closely tied to large changes in pay" (p. 167).

CONTROL THROUGH BEHAVIOR MODIFICATION

Behaviorism, as Chapter 1 explained, is an alternative theoretical approach to understanding and controlling behavior—an approach that does not rely on any concept of motivation. It does not consider needs, expectancies, preferences, perceived valences, or instrumentalities, or any of the inner mental processes that, according to motivation theory, explain why people do what they do. Instead, behaviorism simply looks at behavior and its consequences. According to behaviorism, the *consequences* of behavior, not any supposed inner mental or emotional goings-on, shape and determine particular ways of behaving.

Although there are differences between the theories and vocabularies of motivation and behaviorism, those differences may not be especially important to managers because both theories tend to imply similar management practices (Petrock and Gamboa, 1976). Thus, both theories may find merit in such practices as job enrichment and management-by-objectives—motivation theory because it finds in them intrinsic and extrinsic rewards that support expectancies and satisfy needs, behaviorism because it finds positive reinforcements in the same practices. Still, it makes sense to understand the behaviorist perspective because it offers a fresh and revealing way of thinking about the problem of influencing people to behave in ways that are helpful to the organization and to refrain from behaving in ways that are unhelpful. Therefore, we will examine the key ideas of behaviorism, and explore their application in controlling behavior at work.

Operant Conditioning

The consequences of behavior determine behavior by a process known as operant or instrumental conditioning. B. F. Skinner (1976) describes the process this way:

> Many things in the environment, such as food and water, sexual contact, and escape from harm, are crucial for the survival of the individual and the species, and any behavior which produces them therefore has survival value. Through the process of operant conditioning, behavior having this kind of consequence becomes more likely to occur. The behavior is said to be *strengthened* by its consequences, and for that reason the consequences themselves are called "reinforcers." Thus, when a hungry organism exhibits behavior that *produces* food, the behavior is reinforced by that consequence and is therefore more likely to recur. Behavior that *reduces* a potentially damaging condition, such as an extreme of temperature, is reinforced by that consequence and therefore tends to recur on similar occasions (p. 44).

Reinforcers, as Skinner implies, can be positive or negative. Some, such as food for a hungry organism, are positive reinforcers; *they are good, pleasant, or satisfying consequences of behavior.* Others, such as extreme cold for a freezing organism, are negative reinforcers; *they are bad, unpleasant, or unsatisfying conditions which are removed as a consequence of some behavior.*

In both positive and negative reinforcement, a consequence follows some behavior. A relationship is built between the behavior and the consequence. The consequence is *conditioned* upon the occurrence of the behavior; the behavior *operates* upon the environment, producing the consequence. Hence the term operant conditioning.

Several conditions combine to reinforce behavior. These include the circumstances under which an act occurs, the act itself, and the reinforcing consequences. The interrelationships among these factors are called the contingencies of reinforcement (Skinner, 1969). According to behaviorism, the key to controlling behavior, to establishing and maintaining it, is through arranging or managing these contingencies of reinforcement so that desired behavior will be reinforced, negatively or positively. In laboratory studies, experimental psychologists positively reinforce a pigeon who pecks a red disc by providing it with grain after it pecks at the red disc. Alternatively, they may negatively reinforce the pigeon by removing a noxious condition, e.g., an electric shock, after the pigeon pecks the red disc.

Suppose, however, that the problem is not to establish a pattern of behavior but to extinguish it. If the psychologists wish to extinguish the red disc pecking behavior, for example, they may provide no reinforcement, either positive or negative, after such pecking. This process is called omission (Rachlin, 1976). In omission, the peck no longer produces a grain or stops an electric shock. The former relationship between the behavior and the consequence is destroyed by this omission, and since the behavior no longer operates with any effect on the environment, it too fades and disappears.

Another way to extinguish behavior is by replacing a reinforcing consequence with a punishing one. Whereas the act of pecking the red disc formerly was followed, for example, by the positive reinforcement of grain, an electric shock may now be made to follow the same act. The result is that such behavior will become extinct.

To summarize then, there are four basic processes that can be used to influence behavior through operant conditioning:

1. Positive reinforcement
2. Negative reinforcement
3. Omission
4. Punishment

The same four processes, positive reinforcement, negative reinforcement, omission, and punishment, also determine human behavior. For example, an instructor may provide students with positive reinforcement in the form of high grades for writing good essay examinations. The examination system may provide students with negative reinforcement in the form of anxiety about examinations; the anxiety is removed by completing the examinations. The instructor may not reinforce (and thereby extinguish) class participation by omitting credit in any sense for it. The instructor may punish class participation by providing sarcastic and humiliating critiques of ideas voiced by participating students.

Two additional processes—generalization and discrimination—play important roles in operant conditioning. Both animals and people are capable of generalizing about and discriminating among the circumstances, acts, and consequences associated with reinforcement, omission or nonreinforcement, and punishment. Pigeons might peck at pink discs as they generalize a response developed originally by reinforcement for pecking at red discs. Students might refrain from voicing an idea in a management class whose instructor looks like an instructor in a mathematics class four years ago who ridiculed the ideas they expressed in class. But just as the ability to generalize broadens the range of situations in which a learned response might occur, so the ability to discriminate narrows that range. The pigeon schooled on red discs is less likely to peck at a yellow disc than a pink one because it looks so different. The student inhibited by the sarcasm of a short, pudgy, male mathematics instructor may be less inhibited by a tall, slender, female management instructor.

With an understanding of the elements of operant conditioning that we have just sketched, we can begin to consider how managers might use the processes to modify the behavior of people at work.

Modifying Work-Related Behavior

A recent text on behaviorism cautions those who seek to apply operant conditioning principles, developed by studying animals in laboratories, to human behavior (Rachlin, 1976). The author goes so far as to include in his book a conspicuous warning notice like those that appear on the labels of dangerous products (see Exhibit 9.1). We endorse that warning for the same reason that it was given. Indiscriminate and confused efforts to apply operant conditioning will prove difficult to correct. Trust and confidence in management, for example, can be damaged if unsuccessful behavior modification programs are installed in ways that resemble faddish attempts to apply sensitivity training, management-by-objectives, and job enrichment.

Exhibit 9.1 WARNING

In the physical sciences, trained engineers, familiar with both the physical sciences themselves and with machines and their operation, develop practical uses for the laws that scientists discover. In behavioral sciences we are all engineers in a sense. We are, ourselves, behaving organisms and we sometimes feel a pressing need for rules that will tell us how to behave. There is thus a strong temptation to draw analogies from pigeons to people—to attempt to apply laboratory data directly to our everyday lives. However, the behavior of an organism in response to the simple contingencies of an isolated laboratory environment may be quite different from the behavior of an organism exposed to the complex contingencies of a nonlaboratory environment. We hope to eventually apply what we have learned in the laboratory to the problems of everyday life. But such application must be undertaken with the utmost care.

Perhaps the greatest danger of premature application of the findings of behavioral science to the complex world outside the laboratory is that it gives us the illusion that we are acting scientifically when, in reality, our behavior is no more effective than it would be if it were guided simply by tradition. Since we know little of the complex effects of spanking on children, it is no more scientific to tell ourselves we are spanking a child "to reduce his maladaptive behavior" than to spank him "because we are mad at him." (It is for this reason that the examples that are drawn here from everyday life should not be regarded as direct guides to action.)

"Warning" from *Introduction to Modern Behaviorism*, 2nd ed., by Howard Rachlin. Copyright © 1976 by Howard Rachlin. Reprinted by permission of W. H. Freeman and Company, Publishers.

A major complication in applying behavior modification to people is that the contingencies of reinforcement normally cannot be controlled for free human beings as they can for animals confined in a laboratory. Experimental psychologists working with a pigeon may be able to deprive the bird of food so that it is hungry, provide grain immediately after the pigeon emits the desired behavior, and be certain the situation is free of extraneous influences that could account for changes in behavior. Managers must try to arrange contingencies of reinforcement, e.g., praise, pay, and so on, in situations where uncontrolled variables are always intruding. Managers may believe that by providing an employee with praise, for example, they are providing positive reinforcement for good work. They may be wrong for several reasons. It matters not at all whether the manager thinks the praise is reinforcing. It is only reinforcing if it actually strengthens the response—makes good work occur more often. The employee might be indifferent to praise from this manager or praise about this work. Praise from the boss might occur so long after the good work, that no connection is established between the two. In fact the praise might come a day after the good work and five minutes after the employee just prepared a padded expense account the manager hasn't seen yet. Which behavior has been reinforced? Or consider that praise from the boss might be followed by rejection from colleagues for making them look comparatively bad. Was the net effect more like reinforcement or punishment? These and an endless assortment of other complexities found in natural, as contrasted to laboratory, conditions have led a number of thoughtful students of organizational behavior to be dubious about the prospects of managerial control of the contingencies of reinforcement for work-related behavior (Argyris, 1970; Whyte, 1972; Fry, 1974).

On the other hand, there are reasons for optimism too. The research support for the basic principles of operant conditioning is impressive. So is the evidence of its use in controlling behavior in organizations such as mental hospitals and schools (Bandura, 1969). Therefore, even though, as Schneier notes (1974, pp. 542–43), "There is a dearth of empirical work conducted in the field which has been directly concerned with the testing of operant principles as they apply to work behavior," we should wring what lessons we can out of what evidence there is, keeping in mind that managerial use of operant conditioning is territory only partly explored.

A good way to begin our exploration is with the simplifying assumption that, as far as managers are concerned, there are two important kinds of employee behavior: desirable and undesirable. Assuming the managers' view reflects the objectives of the organization, desirable behavior is the sort that helps meet objectives. Undesirable behavior doesn't, and may even interfere with meeting objectives. The problem is to reinforce the desirable and extinguish the undesirable.

We have already seen that behaviorism offers two techniques to establish and maintain desirable behavior: positive and negative reinforcement. We have also seen that, to extinguish undesirable behavior, two other techniques are possible: omission and punishment. Exhibit 9.2 depicts all four of these techniques and the conditions that characterize each. It also designates two kinds of control strategies—affirmative and aversive. Positive reinforcement and omission are affirmative control strategies, the former because it adds a pleasant consequence, the latter if only because it does not impose a noxious one. Exhibit 9.2 designates punishment and negative reinforcement as aversive control strategies because punishment adds a noxious consequence and negative reinforcement uses noxious consequences as something to be escaped from by providing desirable behavior.

Exhibit 9.2 Control Strategies Using Operant Conditioning

	Consequences Presented	Consequences Removed	
Pleasant Consequences	Positive Reinforcement	Omission	Affirmative Control Strategies
Noxious Consequences	Punishment	Negative Reinforcement	Aversive Control Strategies

Source: Adapted from H. Rachlin, *Introduction to Modern Behaviorism*, 2nd ed.; Freeman, 1976, p. 77.

Aversive control is commonplace in organizations, through both negative reinforcement and punishment. Nagging supervisors are quieted; anxieties about making controversial decisions, meeting deadlines, and completing difficult tasks are relieved; irate customers are calmed; and so on, all by behaving in desired ways. The desired behavior terminates the noxious condition, and is thereby strengthened by negative reinforcement. Luthans and Kreitner (1975) note the near omnipresence of punishment: "The physical and social organizational environment is literally filled with potential and actual punishing consequences. Criticism, undesirable tasks, nagging, unsatisfactory performance evaluations, layoffs, pay docks, and terminations are common punishing consequences of organizational behavior" (p. 112).

Aversive control is common for several reasons. Some conditions for negative reinforcement arise "naturally" as part of many job situations. Schedules, quotas, and budgets must be met and knowing this makes the people who must meet them anxious. In turn, noxious anxiety is relieved by successful performance.

Luthans and Kreitner (1975) submit further that ". . . punishment appears to be a popular strategy because it is reinforcing to its user. More precisely, administrators of punishment are generally negatively reinforced. In most social situations one person's behavior is frequently another's consequence. People commonly fall back on the use of punishment to terminate the annoying behavior of others. If the punishing behavior has the immediate consequence of terminating the annoyance, it has been negatively reinforced" (pp. 116–117).

Despite the popularity or commonness of aversive control, it has serious drawbacks. Negative reinforcement and punishment rely upon noxious conditions. There are limits, however, to the degree of noxious conditions which people will tolerate on their jobs, especially if they are *contrived* by their employers. Moreover, the very prospect of contriving unpleasantness and inflicting it upon employees is repugnant to managers with wholesome personalities: It smacks of a parent-child relationship, with managers as parents and employees as children—a prospect that may also be repugnant to most employees.

Punishment also characteristically entails serious side effects. These include (Luthans and Kreitner, 1975, p. 118):

1. Temporary suppression of behavior rather than permanent change.
2. Dysfunctional emotional behavior.
3. Behavioral inflexibility; permanent damage to desirable behavior.
4. Conditioned fear of punishing agent.

People punished for goofing-off are likely to learn not to goof-off when the boss is around, rather than to foreswear goofing-off altogether. They also are quite apt to feel angry and resentful about being punished and to find various unproductive ways of acting out those feelings, by withholding cooperation and effort, for example. Punishment can also produce some unfortunate generalizations. Being criticized for volunteering an imperfect idea in a staff meeting, for example, can lead to an unwillingness to voice an excellent idea in a later meeting. Punishment can also produce fear and lead to efforts to escape and avoid the person who did the punishing, a result that may be detrimental to performance.

Because of the disadvantages of aversive control strategies, a strong case can be made for emphasizing affirmative control (Wiard, 1972; Beatty and Schneier, 1975). Omission can deny rewards for undesirable behavior without requiring managers to contrive noxious conditions and inflict them upon employees. Positive reinforcement, with its pleasant conditions contingent upon desirable behavior, is not only more appealing than aversive control but has a greater net effectiveness because it avoids the side effects of punishment and negative reinforcement.

Positive reinforcement can be applied according to a number of alternative schedules which have different effects upon how quickly behavior is learned and how resistant it will be to extinction (Ferster and Skinner, 1957; Aldis, 1961). A schedule of reinforcement refers to a specified arrangement for providing the designated reinforcement after the occurrence of the desired behavior. There are two basic schedules: continuous and intermittent (or partial). A continuous reinforcement schedule requires that the reinforcer be provided every time the behavior occurs. An intermittent schedule may vary either the number of times the behavior must occur before a reinforcer is provided or the amount of time that elapses before the reinforcer is provided. Exhibit 9.3 describes and indicates the effects of continuous and various intermittent reinforcement schedules.

Each schedule can be illustrated by familiar practices. Continuous reinforcement, for example, might occur when a worker is paid after each completed piece of work. The evidence on the effects of continuous reinforcement indicates that it helps speed up learning, but that the behavior learned by this schedule can be easily extinguished (Huebner and Johnson, 1974; Jablonsky and De Vries, 1974). In any event, the perfect consistency required for continuous reinforcement of on-the-job behavior would rarely be obtainable out-

Exhibit 9.3 Schedules of Reinforcement

Schedule	Description	Effects on Responding
Continuous (CRF)	Reinforcer follows every response.	(1) Steady high rate of performance as long as reinforcement continues to follow every response. (2) High frequency of reinforcement may lead to early satiation. (3) Behavior weakens rapidly (undergoes extinction) when reinforcers are withheld. (4) Appropriate for newly emitted, unstable, or low-frequency responses.
Intermittent	Reinforcer does not follow every response.	(1) Capable of producing high frequencies of responding. (2) Low frequency of reinforcement precludes early satiation. (3) Appropriate for stable or high-frequency responses.
Fixed ratio (FR)	A fixed number of responses must be emitted before reinforcement occurs.	(1) A fixed ratio of 1:1 (reinforcement occurs after every response) is the same as a continuous schedule. (2) Tends to produce a high rate of response which is vigorous and steady.
Variable ratio (VR)	A varying or random number of responses must be emitted before reinforcement occurs.	(1) Capable of producing a high rate of response which is vigorous, steady, and resistant to extinction.
Fixed interval (FI)	The first response after a specific period of time has elapsed is reinforced.	(1) Produces an uneven response pattern varying from a very slow, unenergetic response immediately following reinforcement to a very fast, vigorous response immediately preceding reinforcement.
Variable interval (VI)	The first response after varying or random periods of time have elapsed is reinforced.	(1) Tends to produce a high rate of response which is vigorous, steady, and resistant to extinction.

Source: Fred Luthans and Robert Kreitner, *Organizational Behavior Modification*. Scott, Foresman, 1975, p. 51. With permission.

side the laboratory. In the "real world," various intermittent schedules are far more commonplace.

There are four basic types of intermittent reinforcement schedules: fixed ratio, variable ratio, fixed interval, and variable interval. A good example of a fixed ratio schedule would be a piece-rate system which added a specified percent of a constant base pay rate, for each five units produced in excess of a quota. A variable ratio would operate under a commission system where, for example, the number of times the real estate agent must show a house or the number of times the sales person must demonstrate an appliance or automobile varies for each consummated sale. On one occasion it may take three showings or demonstrations to make a sale and obtain a commission. Next time it may take seventeen. A fixed interval schedule is illustrated by the weekly or monthly paycheck of the salaried employee. A variable interval schedule is less likely to be found in a pay plan, but occurs commonly in the irregular dispensing of promotions, compliments, and other nonmonetary rewards that may function as reinforcers.

Most operant conditioning in organizations is not the product of a conscious and explicit use of the concepts we have studied. Nonetheless, numerous illustrations of the effectiveness of positive reinforcement can be found. Nord, for example, describes two cases of the use of intermittent schedules to reinforce attendance and promptness in arriving at work (Nord, 1970). In both cases, the managers knew nothing about operant conditioning.

In one case a chain of hardware stores established a lottery. Employees at each store who had a perfect record of punctual attendance each month were eligible to participate in a drawing for an appliance worth about $25. This meant there was one prize for every 25 employees. At the end of six months, all employees having perfect attendance and punctuality were eligible to participate in a drawing for a major appliance, e.g., a color T.V. By the time the program was in its third six-month cycle, sick-leave payments were down 62 percent and absenteeism and tardiness were reduced by about 75 percent.

In another case, a school sought to reduce absenteeism among its teachers. Unlike the hardware store, whose lottery amounted to a variable ratio schedule, the school decided to pay $50 to every teacher who had completed a semester without absence. By providing every person who emitted the desired behavior with this reward, the school was using a schedule with both a fixed ratio and a fixed interval. The results: In its second and third year of operation, the program was associated with increases of approximately 15 to 20 percent in the number of teachers having perfect attendance records.

Managers in other organizations, with or without the aid of consultants, have consciously applied operant conditioning to modify work-related behavior. Exhibit 9.4 describes the scope, characteristics, and results of ten such applications. Generally, these programs of behavior modification through positive reinforcement follow a series of steps such as these:

1. Identify an area where behavior poses a problem, e.g., substandard performance.
2. Measure the behavior or performance.
3. Determine and state desired behavioral objectives. (Often this is done with employee participation.)
4. Design and apply the positive reinforcements.
5. Measure the behavior or performance at an appropriate later date to evaluate the effectiveness of the program.
6. Change the program as necessary.

Exhibit 9.4 Results of Positive Reinforcement and Similar Behavior Modification Programs in Organizations in 1976

Organization & Person Surveyed	Length of Program	Number of Employees Covered/Total Employees	Type of Employees	Specific Goals	Frequency of Feedback	Reinforcers Used	Results
Emery Air Freight John C. Emery, Jr., President Paul F. Hammond, Manager—Systems Performance	1969–1976	500/2800	Entire workforce	(a) Increase productivity (b) Improve quality of service	Immediate to monthly, depending on task	Previously only praise and recognition; others now being introduced	Cost savings can be directly attributed to the program
Michigan Bell— Operator Services E. D. Grady, General Manager— Operator Services	1972–1976	2000/5500	Employees at all levels in operator services	(a) Decrease turnover & absenteeism (b) Increase productivity (c) Improve union-management relations	(a) Lower level— weekly & daily (b) Higher level— monthly & quarterly	(a) Praise & recognition (b) Opportunity to see oneself become better	(a) Attendance performance has improved by 50% (b) Productivity and efficiency has continued to be above standard in areas where positive reinforcement (PR) is used
Michigan Bell— Maintenance Services Donald E. Burwell, Division Superintendent, Maintenance & Services Dr. W. Clay Hamner, Consultant	1974–1976	220/5500	Maintenance workers, mechanics, & first- & second-level supervisors	Improve (a) productivity (b) quality (c) safety (d) customer-employee relations	Daily, weekly, and quarterly	(a) Self-feedback (b) Supervisory feedback	(a) Cost efficiency increase (b) Safety improved (c) Service improved (d) No change in absenteeism (e) Satisfaction with superior & coworkers improved (f) Satisfaction with pay decreased
Connecticut General Life Insurance Co. Donald D. Illig, Director of Personnel Administration	1941–1976	3000/13,500	Clerical employees & first-line supervisors	(a) Decrease absenteeism (b) Decrease lateness	Immediate	(a) Self-feedback (b) System-feedback (c) Earned time off	(a) Chronic absenteeism & lateness has been drastically reduced (b) Some divisions refuse to use PR because it is "outdated"

Exhibit 9.4 (continued)

Organization & Person Surveyed	Length of Program	Number of Employees Covered/ Total Employees	Type of Employees	Specific Goals	Frequency of Feedback	Reinforcers Used	Results
GENERAL ELECTRIC[1] Melvin Sorcher, Ph.D., formerly Director of Personnel Research Now Director of Management Development, Richardson-Merrell, Inc.	1973–1976	1000	Employees at all levels	(a) Meet EEO objectives (b) Decrease absenteeism & turnover (c) Improve training (d) Increase productivity	Immediate—uses modeling & role playing as training tools to teach interpersonal exchanges & behavior requirements	Social reinforcers (praise, rewards, & constructive feedback)	(a) Cost savings can be directly attributed to the program (b) Productivity has increased (c) Worked extremely well in training minority groups and raising their self-esteem (d) Direct labor cost decreased
STANDARD OIL OF OHIO T. E. Standings, Ph.D. Manager of Psychological Services	1974	28	Supervisors	Increase supervisor competence	Weekly over 5 weeks (25-hour) training period	Feedback	(a) Improved supervisory ability to give feedback judiciously (b) Discontinued because of lack of overall success
WEYERHAEUSER COMPANY Gary P. Latham. Ph.D. Manager of Human Resource Research	1974–1976	500/40,000	Clerical, production (tree planters) & middle-level management & scientists	(a) To teach managers to minimize criticism & to maximize praise (b) To teach managers to make rewards contingent on specified performance levels & (c) To use optimal schedule to increase productivity	Immediate—daily & quarterly	(a) Pay (b) Praise & recognition	(a) Using money, obtained 33% increase in productivity with one group of workers, an 18% increase with a second group, and an 8% decrease in a third group (b) Currently experimenting with goal-setting & praise and/or money at various levels in organization (c) With a lottery-type bonus, the cultural & religious values of workers must be taken into account

Exhibit 9.4 (continued)

Organization & Person Surveyed	Length of Program	Number of Employees Covered/ Total Employees	Type of Employees	Specific Goals	Frequency of Feedback	Reinforcers Used	Results
City of Detroit Garbage Collectors[2]	1973–1975	1122/1930	Garbage collectors	(a) Reduction in paid man-hour per ton (b) Reduction on overtime (c) 90% of routes completed by standard (d) Effectiveness (quality)	Daily & quarterly based on formula negotiated by city & sanitation union	Bonus (profit sharing) & praise	(a) Citizen complaints declined significantly (b) City saved $1,654,000 first year after bonus paid (c) Worker bonus = $307,000 first year or $350 annually per man (d) Union somewhat dissatisfied with productivity measure and is pushing for more bonus to employee (e) 1975 results not yet available
B. F. Goodrich Chemical Co. Donald J. Barnicki, Production Manager	1972–1976	100/420	Manufacturing employees at all levels	(a) Better meeting of schedules (b) Increase productivity	Weekly	Praise & recognition; freedom to choose one's own activity	Production has increased over 300%
ACDC Electronics Division of Emerson Electronics Edward J. Feeney, Consultant	1974–1976	350/350	All levels	(a) 96% attendance (b) 90% engineering specifications met (c) Daily production objectives met 95% of time (d) Cost reduced by 10%	Daily & weekly feedback from foreman to company president	Positive feedback	(a) Profit up 25% over forecast (b) $550,000 cost reduction on $10 M sales (c) Return of 1900% on investment including consultant fees (d) Turnaround time on repairs went from 30 to 10 days (e) Attendance is now 98.2% (from 93.5%)

[1] Similar programs are now being implemented at Richardson-Merrell under the direction of Dr. Sorcher and at AT&T under the direction of Douglas W. Bray, Ph.D., director of management selection and development, along with several other smaller organizations (see A. P. Goldstein, Ph.D. & Melvin Sorcher, Ph.D. Changing Supervisor Behavior, Pergamon Press, 1974).

[2] From Improving Municipal Productivity: The Detroit Refuse Incentive Plan. The National Commission on Productivity. April, 1974.

Source: Hamner and Hamner, 1976.

One of the most widely publicized programs of behavior modification at work is the case of Emery Air Freight (*Business Week,* December 2, 1972, pp. 64–65; *Organizational Dynamics,* Winter 1973, pp. 41–50; *Training and Development Journal,* November 26, 1972, pp. 8–13). Emery has reported successful use of positive reinforcement in such areas as sales and sales training, Customer Service, and containerized shipments. In sales, a performance audit or measurement suggested that productivity — sales relative to customer contacts — was lower than that which sales representatives believed it should be. Sales representatives set an objective for themselves of obtaining a commitment from each customer to use Emery Air Freight in some way. Money was not used as a reinforcer but the company developed programmed instruction workbooks for managers to show them how to provide recognition, rewards, and feedback to reinforce successful performance. At the end of a year, sales had increased by 27.8 percent.

Teams of telephone receptionists in Customer Service set goals of answering incoming calls by the third ring and providing periodic assurances to customers who were placed on hold that they were not forgotten. Measurements showed that these goals were not being met. Hourly feedback to these teams on how well their goals were being met, however, served to reinforce the desired behavior and resulted in a 60 percent improvement in a single day. Another Customer Service objective was to respond to customer calls (with answers to problems) within 90 minutes of the initial call. A performance audit showed this goal was only met for 30 percent of the calls. A combination of feedback and praise in specific terms for particular cases increased this figure to over 90 percent, a rate maintained for three years.

In Container Operations a performance audit showed that containers were only used for 45 percent of Emery's shipments. Goals were set to increase this figure, and praise and feedback were provided to reinforce containerization. The rate of container use rose to 95 percent and was sustained for years. Savings for this program alone for one year were $650,000.

In all of its applications of positive reinforcement, Emery has used a changing mixture of what have been called "natural" and "contrived" reinforcers. Natural reinforcers are illustrated by the feedback provided by performance measurements. In Customer Service, for example, employees recorded how long they took to reply to each call. These figures were tabulated daily and compared with the 90-minute objective, thus providing daily feedback. Contrived reinforcers are illustrated by the praise given by supervisors for specific results. Feedback is provided at all stages, but is augmented with very frequent praise at early stages. But the frequency of praise or other contrived reinforcers diminishes over time and natural reinforcers become the major source of reinforcement.

Other reports of the effective use of positive reinforcement at work describe a similar use of supplemental verbal reinforcement as part of a technique called "shaping" (Huebner and Johnson, 1974; Beatty, 1971; and Beatty and Schneier, 1972). Shaping can be used in a program of positive reinforcement where the objective is to reinforce a complex pattern of behavior in persons who, at the outset, emit none or very little of the behavior. For example, the desired behavior may be the operation of a complicated machine. The problem is how to apply positive reinforcement to build the complex skill necessary.

Shaping involves breaking the complex behavior into elements that can be learned in a sequence. Positive reinforcement is provided for the first element, say setting the safety device in position and turning the machine on. Then as more elements are taught, positive reinforcement is omitted for the first element and provided only as subsequent elements are also performed. Reinforcement becomes contingent upon emitting an increasingly complex pattern. Finally, reinforcement is only provided when the total complex behavior is delivered.

A selected reading by Luthans and Kreitner following this chapter outlines a strategy for using shaping to develop and reinforce desired behavior.

SUMMARY

Control designates a number of different managerial activities whose common thread is their concern for monitoring and influencing the behavior of people at work so that their performance implements established organizational objectives. One control process consists of devising policies and procedures that help employees decide and act in conformance with objectives. But policies and procedures must be well-adapted to the task and the people who perform it. Insufficient or excessive control through policies and procedures can result in loss of direction or inflexible bureaucracy.

Another control process consists of measuring performance and providing feedback so that actual progress can be compared to plans and adjustments made where necessary. Measurements have the effect of defining important performance variables for employees; feedback permits them to monitor performance. Both measurement and feedback can improve performance, but both can also impair it through poorly selected measurements and inaccurate and critical feedback.

A final control process consists of administering rewards, guided by either the logic of motivation theory or the logic of behaviorism. The concepts of control through motivation or control through behavior modification imply the systematic administration of rewards or reinforcements to establish and maintain patterns of behavior at work that contribute to meeting organizational objectives. Though motivation theory and behaviorism use different terminology, they both tend to support similar practices, such as providing feedback and intrinsic rewards.

Aldis, O. "Of Pigeons and Men." *Harvard Business Review*, Vol. 39 (1961), pp. 59–63.

Argyris, C. "*Beyond Freedom and Dignity* by B. F. Skinner, A Review Essay." *Harvard Educational Review*, Vol. 41, No. 4 (1971), pp. 550–67.

———. *Personality and Organization*. Harper, 1957.

Arps, G. F. "Work with Knowledge of Results Versus Work Without Knowledge of Results." *Psychology Monographs*, Vol. 28, No. 3 (1920) (Whole no. 125).

"At Emery Air Freight: Positive Reinforcement Boosts Performance." *Organizational Dynamics*, Winter 1973, pp. 41–50.

Bandura, A. *Principles of Behavior Modification*. Holt, 1969.

Beatty, R. W. "First and Second Level Supervision and the Job Performance for the Hard-core Unemployed." *Proceedings of the 79th Annual Convention*, American Psychological Association, 1971.

———, and C. R. Schneier. "A Case for Positive Reinforcement." *Business Horizons*, Vol. 18 (April 1975), pp. 57–66.

———. "Training the Hard-core Unemployed Through Positive Reinforcement." *Human Resource Management*, Vol. II, No. 4 (1972), pp. 11–17.

Berliner, J. S. "A Problem in Soviet Business Administration." *Administrative Science Quarterly*, Vol. I (June 1965), pp. 87–101.

Bilodeau, E. A., I. M. Bilodeau, and D. A. Shumsky. "Some Effects of Introducing and Withdrawing Knowledge of Results Early and Late in Practice." *Journal of Experimental Psychology*, Vol. 58 (1959), pp. 142–44.

Blau, P. M. *The Dynamics of Bureaucracy*, rev. ed. University of Chicago Press, 1963.

Burns, T., and G. M. Stalker. *The Management of Innovation*. Tavistock, 1961.

Cammann, C., and D. A. Nadler. "Fit Control Systems to Your Managerial Style." *Harvard Business Review*, January–February 1976, pp. 65–72.

Cummings, L. L., D. P. Schwab, and M. Rosen. "Performance and Knowledge of Results as Determinants of Goal-Setting." *Journal of Applied Psychology*, Vol. 55 (1971), pp. 526–30.

Dalton, M. "Managing the Managers." *Human Organization*, Vol. 14 (Fall 1955), pp. 4–10.

Deci, E. L. "The Effects of Contingent and Non-Contingent Rewards and Controls on Intrinsic Motivation." *Organizational Behavior and Human Performance*, Vol. 8 (1972), pp. 217–29.

———. "Paying People Doesn't Always Work the Way You Expect It To." *Human Resource Management*, Vol. 12 (Summer 1973), pp. 28–32.

Drucker, P. *Management: Tasks, Responsibilities, Practices*. Harper & Row, 1974.

Elwell, J. L., and G. C. Grindley. "The Effect of Knowledge of Results on Learning and Performance 1: A Coordinated Movement of the Two Hands." *British Journal of Psychology*, Vol. 29 (1938), pp. 39–53.

Ferster, C. B., and B. F. Skinner. *Schedules of Reinforcement*. Appleton-Century-Crofts, 1957.

Fry, F. L. "Operant Conditioning in Organizational Settings: Of Mice or Men?" *Personnel*, Vol. 51 (July–August 1974), pp. 17–22.

Giglioni, G. B., and A. G. Bedeian. "A Conspectus of Management Control Theory: 1900–1972." *Academy of Management Journal*, Vol. 17, No. 2 (June 1974), pp. 292–305.

Granick, D. *The Red Executive*. Doubleday, 1960.

Greller, M. M., and D. M. Herold. "Sources of Feedback: A Preliminary Investigation." *Organizational Behavior and Human Performance*, Vol. 13 (1975), pp. 224–56.

Hackman, J. R., and E. E. Lawler, III. "Employee Reactions to Job Characteristics." *Journal of Applied Psychology*, Vol. 55 (1971), pp. 259–86.

Herzberg, F. *Work and the Nature of Man.* World, 1966.

Hamner, W. Clay, and Hamner, Ellen. "Behavior Modification on the Bottom Line." *Organizational Dynamics*, Spring 1976, pp. 3–21.

Huebner, H. J., and A. C. Johnson. "Behavior Modification: An Aid in Solving Personnel Problems." *The Personnel Administrator*, October 1974.

"J. C. Penney: Getting More From the Same Space." *Business Week*, December 4, 1974, pp. 72–78.

Jablonsky, S. F., and D. L. De Vries. "Operant Conditioning Principles Extrapolated to the Theory of Management." *Organizational Behavior and Human Performance*, Vol. 7 (1972), pp. 340–58.

Jasinski, F. "Use and Misuse of Efficiency Controls." *Harvard Business Review*, Vol. 34, No. 4 (July–August 1956), pp. 105–12.

Johnston, J. "Punishment of Human Behavior." *American Psychologist*, Vol. 27 (1972), pp. 1033–54.

Khandwalla, P. N. "Effect of Competition on the Structure of Top Management Control." *Academy of Management Journal*, Vol. 16, No. 2 (June 1973), pp. 285–95.

Latham, G. P., and G. A. Yukl. "A Review of Research on the Application of Goal Setting in Organizations." *Academy of Management Journal*, Vol. 18 (1975), pp. 824–45.

Lawler, E. E., III. *Motivation in Work Organizations.* Brooks/Cole, 1973.

——, and J. G. Rhode. *Information and Control in Organizations.* Goodyear, 1976.

Lawrence, P., and J. Lorsch. *Organization and Environment.* Graduate School of Business Administration, Harvard University, 1967.

Locke, E. A., N. Cartledge, and C. S. Knerr. "Studies of the Relationship Between Satisfaction, Goal-Setting and Performance." *Organizational Behavior and Human Performance.* Vol. 5 (1970), pp. 135–58.

Locke, E. A., N. Cartledge, and J. Koeppel. "Motivational Effects of Knowledge of Results: A Goal-Setting Phenomenon." *Psychological Bulletin*, Vol. 70 (1968), pp. 474–85.

Lorsch, J. W., and Morse, J. J. *Organizations and Their Members: A Contingency Approach.* Harper & Row, 1974.

Luthans, F., and R. Kreitner. *Organizational Behavior Modification.* Scott, Foresman, 1975.

McClelland, D. C. "Achievement Motivation Can Be Developed." *Harvard Business Review*, Vol. 43, No. 6 (November–December 1965), pp. 6–24, 178.

McGregor, D. *The Human Side of Enterprise.* McGraw-Hill, 1960.

Manzer, C. W. "The Effect of Knowledge of Output on Muscular Work." *Journal of Experimental Psychology*, Vol. 18 (1935), pp. 80–90.

Meyer, H. H., E. Kay, and J. R. P. French, Jr. "Split Roles in Performance Appraisal." *Harvard Business Review*, Vol. 43, No. 1 (January–February, 1965), pp. 123–29.

Newman, W. H. *Constructive Control: Design and Use of Control Systems.* Prentice-Hall, 1975.

Nord, W. "Beyond the Teaching Machine: The Neglected Area of Operant Conditioning in the Theory and Practice of Management." *Organizational Behavior and Human Performance*, Vol. 4 (November 1969), pp. 375–401.

——. "Improving Attendance Through Rewards." *Personnel Administration*, November–December 1970, pp. 37–41.

Opsahl, R. L., and M. D. Dunnette. "The Role of Financial Compensation in Industrial Motivation." *Psychological Bulletin*, Vol. 66, No. 2 (August 1966), pp. 94–118.

"Performance Audit, Feedback, and Positive Reinforcement." *Training and Development Journal*, Vol. 26 (November 1972), pp. 8–13.

Perrow, C. *Organizational Analysis: A Sociological View.* Wadsworth, 1970.

Petrock, F., and V. Gamboa. "Expectancy Theory and Operant Conditioning: A Conceptual Comparison," in *Concepts and Controversy in Organizational Behavior*, ed. by W. R. Nord. Goodyear, 1976.

Porter, Lyman W., Edward E. Lawler III, and J. Richard Hackman. *Behavior in Organizations.* McGraw-Hill, 1975.

Rachlin, H. *Introduction to Modern Behaviorism* (2nd ed.). Freeman, 1976.

Reeves, T. K., and J. Woodward. "The Study of Managerial Control" in J. Woodward (ed.), *Industrial Organization: Behaviour and Control.* Oxford University Press, 1970.

Richman, B. M. *Soviet Management.* Prentice-Hall, 1965.

Schneier, C. E. "Behavior Modification in Management: A Review and Critique." *Academy of Management Journal*, Vol. 17, No. 3 (1974), pp. 528–48.

Skinner, B. F. *About Behaviorism.* Vintage, 1976.

——. *Contingencies of Reinforcement.* Appleton-Century-Crofts, 1969.

——. *Science and Human Behavior.* The Free Press, 1953.

Smode, A. F. "Learning and Performance in a Tracking Task under Two Levels of Achievement Information Feedback." *Journal of Experimental Psychology*, Vol. 56 (1958), pp. 297–304.

Steers, R. M. *Task Goals, Individual Need Strengths, and Supervisory Performance.* Unpublished Doctoral Dissertation. Graduate School of Administration, University of California, Irvine, 1973.

——, and L. W. Porter. "The Role of Task-Goal Attributes in Employee Performance." *Psychological Bulletin*, Vol. 81 (1974), pp. 434–52.

Taylor, F. W. "On the Art of Cutting Metals." Paper No. 1119. *Transactions.* American Society of Mechanical Engineers, Vol. 27 (1906), pp. 31–350.

Thorndike, E. L. "The Law of Effect." *American Journal of Psychology*, Vol. 39 (1927), pp. 212–22.

"Where Skinner's Theories Work." *Business Week*, December 2, 1972, pp. 64–65.

Whyte, W. F. "Skinnerian Theory in Organizations." *Psychology Today*, Vol. 5, No. 11 (1972), pp. 66ff.

Wiard, H. "Why Manage Behavior? A Case for Positive Reinforcement." *Human Resource Management*, Summer 1972, pp. 15–20.

Winter, D. *The Power Motive.* The Free Press, 1972.

Woodward, J. *Industrial Organization: Theory and Practice.* Oxford University Press, 1965.

Woodward, J. *Industrial Organization: Behaviour and Control.* Oxford University Press, 1970.

Readings

Dysfunctional Effects of Control Systems
Edward E. Lawler III and John G. Rhode

There is no question that information and control systems often produce dysfunctional behavior. Numerous studies have documented the kinds of dysfunctional behavior that typically occur. Four types have received the most attention: rigid bureaucratic behavior, strategic behavior, the production of invalid information, and resistance. . . .

RIGID BUREAUCRATIC BEHAVIOR

Control systems can cause employees to behave in ways that look good in terms of the control system measures but that are dysfunctional as far as the generally agreed upon goals of the organization are concerned. This phenomenon, referred to as rigid bureaucratic behavior, has been described by a number of authors (see e.g., Merton, 1940; Selznick, 1949; and Gouldner, 1954). It comes about because certain conditions lead people to act in whatever ways will help them look good on the measures that are taken by control systems. In many cases this is a functional outcome, but in others it is not. In some cases it results in rigid, inflexible, dysfunctional behavior because that is what is "required" by the system. There are a number of examples of this phenomenon in the social science literature.

Blau (1955) analyzed the operation of a department in the public agency of a state government. The agency's "major responsibility is to serve workers seeking employment and employers seeking workers" (p. 19). The tasks performed by the department included interviewing clients, helping them to fill out application forms, counseling them, and referring them to jobs. The organization saw these activities as instrumental to the accomplishment of its objectives, and instituted a control system to be sure they were done. To evaluate the individual interviewers, managers kept statistical records of such things as how many interviews a particular interviewer conducted. The effect of this control system was to motivate the employees to perform those kinds of behavior that were measured by the system (e.g., interviewing). Unfortunately this did not always contribute to the organizational goal of placing workers in jobs. As Blau points out:

> An instrument intended to further the achievement of organizational objectives, statistical records constrained interviewers to think of maximizing the indices as their major goal, sometimes at the expense of these very objectives. They avoided

operations which would take up time without helping them to improve their record, such as interviewing clients for whom application forms had to be made out, and wasted their own and the public's time on activities intended only to raise the figures on their record. Their concentration upon this goal, since it was important for their ratings, made them unresponsive to requests from clients that would interfere with its attainment (p. 43).

Babchuk and Goode (1951) have provided an interesting case study that highlights how control systems, when combined with rewards, can cause employees to behave dysfunctionally. They studied a selling unit in a department store where a pay incentive plan was introduced to pay employees on the basis of sales volume. Total sales initially increased but the pay plan was not functional as far as the long term goals of the organization were concerned. There was considerable "sales grabbing" and "tying up the trade" as well as a general neglect of such unrewarded and unmeasured functions as stock work and arranging merchandise for displays.

It is possible to cite a number of other examples of situations where employees in large organizations respond to control systems with rigid control-system-oriented behavior that is dysfunctional from the point of view of the organization. In fact, the negative connotation that has become attached to the initially neutral term, bureaucracy, stems from just this kind of behavior. Each of us has probably had many experiences where people representing formal organizations have dealt with us in ways that all the parties acknowledged were dysfunctional for both the organization and ourselves. For example, one of the authors recently tried to rent a car from a large car rental company only to be told that it would be 30 to 60 minutes before one would be ready. Further questioning revealed that there were cars available but they had to be washed because "we never rent cars that aren't washed." The author then asked that an exception be made because he was in a hurry and needed the car immediately. The salesperson, however, stuck to the rule despite the fact that it lost the company business and goodwill and failed to serve the needs of a customer. The rule, of course, is basically a functional one since it probably does help business to rent clean cars.

The views of a number of sociologists about the bureaucratic behavior phenomenon have been summarized by March and Simon (1958). Merton's explanation for why it occurs is contained in Figure 1. It shows that rigidity stems from the emphasis on reliability; and from the need to defend individual actions. However, Merton does not explain why *all* individuals do not respond this way to the emphasis on reliability, nor does he say anything about the conditions that favor people responding this way. Clearly, everyone does not respond to control systems with rigid behavior all the time. People are often willing to break the rules to get things done. Frank (1959) in discussing Soviet management practices has noted that managers often violate some standards and even laws in order to keep their organizations functioning effectively. This occurs so much that it has become socially legitimate. It is also interesting that one form of labor bargaining is a work-to-rules action. What this means is that, unlike normal times, the employees follow the rules closely, observing the letter of the law, and as a result the organization functions much less effectively. It is also obvious that organizations differ widely in the degree to which the members rigidly respond to the rules and measures set up by the control system (Burns and Stalker, 1961). Part of the explanation for this difference rests in the nature of the control systems that are used in different organizations and part of it rests in the nature of the individuals that work in different organizations.

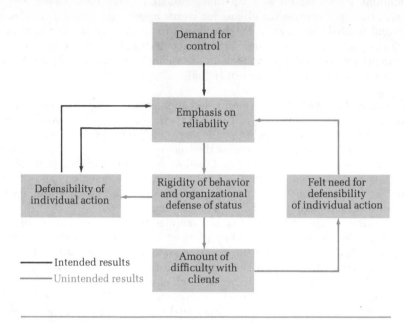

Figure 1   The Simplified Merton Model (adapted from March and
Simon, 1958.)

STRATEGIC BEHAVIOR

In addition to producing the kind of long-term rigid bureaucratic behavior that has
been described so far, information systems can cause employees to engage in what
Cammann (1974a, 1974b) has called strategic behavior. Strategic behavior involves
actions designed solely to influence information system results so that they will look
good or acceptable for a certain time period. This kind of behavior does not involve
feeding false data to the systems; rather, it usually involves altering behaviors for a
period of time to make the control system measures look acceptable. In this respect it
is like the kind of rigid bureaucratic behavior that has been discussed so far. Like
bureaucratic behavior it also is not always dysfunctional for the organization. However,
unlike bureaucratic behavior it only involves a short-term behavior change. For example,
if a manager needs to buy a piece of equipment and it's near the end of a budget period,
he or she may make a strategic choice. If money is left in the budget, he or she probably
will buy the equipment to use up the budget. On the other hand, if the budget has been
spent, the purchase probably will be deferred until the next budget period to keep from
overspending the budget. From the point of view of organizational effectiveness, it
probably won't make much difference if the equipment is bought at the beginning of one
period or the end of another and in either case valid data are being reported. Still, the
budget system is clearly influencing the behavior of the manager in the sense that he
or she is behaving in a strategic way in order to look good on the information system
measures.

On several occasions top management has been accused of a particular kind of
strategic behavior: smoothing out reported income over a period of years. Gordon,
Horowitz, and Meyers (1967) reported that the income of the U.S. Steel Corporation
appeared to be tempered through the judicious application of income smoothing accounting techniques. In a similar manner, Schiff (1966) indicated that the management

of the Chock Full O'Nuts Corporation appeared to even out reported income by deciding to either immediately expense or capitalize for expenses in future years the advertising costs of new products. This income alteration may result, as Lewin and Seidler (unpublished) propose, because the discretionary use of accounting methods is seemingly painless to apply and is, therefore, preferred by top management to the difficult alternative of correcting internal problems rationalized as temporary. No matter what the factors are that motivate financial decision makers to perform income smoothing, one thing is certain—it does occur.

Some strategic behavior can result in organizational ineffectiveness. An analysis of Soviet Union management practices has described what can happen when a certain kind of strategic behavior called storming occurs (Berliner, 1956).

In February 1941, G. M. Malenkov delivered to the Eighteenth Party Conference a report which, as it turned out, proved to be a summing up of the state of industry at the end of the prewar period. Among the many matters which he considered important enough to call to the attention of the assembled party leaders was the following:

Now, Comrades, matters stand thus—in most of our enterprises the output of finished production is carried out unevenly, in spurts, and is concentrated as a rule at the end of the month. Enterprises lack a firm, previously worked-out schedule of production. Here are some typical examples.

The Kolomensk Machinery Works in Moscow County worked this way in 1940: In the first ten days of every month it produced 5 to 7 percent of the month's output, in the second ten days, 10 to 15 percent, and in the third ten days, 75 to 80 percent.

The Karl Marx-Leningrad Plant, in December 1940, produced 2 percent of monthly output in the first ten days, 8 percent in the second ten days, and 90 percent in the third ten days.

In Moscow Pump and Compressor Plant, in December 1940, 3.4 percent of the month's output was produced in the first ten days, 27.5 percent in the second ten days, and 69.1 percent in the third ten days.

We must put an end to this lack of planning, to this uneven rate of production, to this storming in the work of enterprises. We must achieve a day-by-day fulfillment of the production program according to a previously worked-out schedule, by every factory, mill, mine, and railroad.

This practice of "storming" leads to a number of uneconomic consequences. States of emergency constantly arise; men and equipment are subject to periods of unnecessary idleness; during the days of storming the rate of spoilage increases, overtime pay mounts up, the machines suffer from speed-up, and customers' production schedules are interrupted. It is certainly a practice which the state would wish to eliminate if it could (Berliner, 1956, pp. 87–88).

An interesting example of managers engaging in strategic behavior to keep their facility open occurred in a gold mine. In this particular company, mines were shut down after the yield per ton of ore dropped below a certain level. One old marginal mine managed to stay open for several extra years because of the strategic behavior of its management. It happened that the mine contained one very rich pocket of ore. Instead of mining this all at once the management used it as its reserve. Everytime the yield of the ore it was mining fell below an acceptable level, it would mix in a little high grade ore so the mine would remain open. This was dysfunctional as far as the company was concerned since maximum cost effectiveness would have been achieved by mining all the high grade ore and then closing the mine.

There are numerous other examples of strategic behavior in the literature where employees develop JIC (just in case) and CYA (cover your ass) files in order to defend any decisions they have made. Jasinski (1956) and Hopwood (1972, 1973, 1974a, b) have written about how control systems have lead to dysfunctional maintenance and production schedules. Thus, the evidence is overwhelming that strategic behavior is fostered by information and control systems.

INVALID DATA REPORTING

All control systems need valid data about what is occurring in the organization to be effective, yet behavioral science research shows that often false data are obtained (see, e.g., Wilensky, 1967). As Argyris (1964, 1971) points out, control systems tend to be effective and to produce valid information only for the unimportant and programmed problems.

Evidence suggests that control systems produce two kinds of invalid data: invalid data about what can be done and invalid data about what has been done. The first kind of invalid data, of course, makes planning difficult, while the second makes the control of day-to-day activities difficult. The research on budgets and on piece rate payment systems provide a number of good examples of situations where organizations are given invalid data about what is possible. Much of the available research data is from case studies and thus it is difficult to establish how widespread the production of invalid data is. To understand how and why invalid data are reported it is worth reviewing a few of the case studies that have illustrated this phenomenon.

Whyte (1955) has provided some graphic case examples of how individuals distort the data that are fed into production measuring systems. Most of Whyte's examples are cases where individuals under pay incentive systems distort data about the kind of production possible on a given job. The following quote illustrates one worker's attitude toward the measurement system and the time-study men who run it.

"... you got to outwit that son-of-a-bitch! You got to use your noodle while you're working, and think your work out ahead as you go along! You got to add in movements you know you ain't going to make when you're running the job! remember, if you don't screw them, they're going to screw you! ... Every movement counts! ...

"Remember those bastards are paid to screw you," said Starkey. "And that's all they got to think about. They'll stay up half the night figuring out how to beat you out of a dime. They figure you're going to try to fool them, so they make allowances for that. They set the prices low enough to allow for what you do."

"Well, then, what the hell chance have I got?" asked Tennessee.

"It's up to you to figure out how to fool them more than they allow for," said Starkey.

"... when the time-study man came around, I set the speed at 180. I knew damn well he would ask me to push it up, so I started low enough. He finally pushed me up to 445, and I ran the job later at 610. If I'd started out at 445, they'd have timed it at 610. Then I got him on the reaming, too. I ran the reamer for him at 130 speed and .025 feed. He asked me if I couldn't run the reamer any faster than that, and I told him I had to run the reamer slow to keep the hole size. I showed him two pieces with oversize holes that the day man ran. I picked them out for the occasion! But later on I ran the reamer at 610 speed and .018 feed, same as the drill. So I didn't have to change gears — And then there was a burring operation on the job too. For the time-study man I burred each piece after I drilled and reamed, and I ran the burring tool by automatic feed. But afterwards, I let the burring go till I drill 25 pieces or so; and I just touched them up a little by holding them under the burring tool" (Whyte, 1955, pp. 15–18).*

Gardner (1945) has also pointed out that employees often give invalid data in industry and provides an example of how it can occur.

In one case, a group, who worked together in assembling a complicated and large sized steel framework, worked out a system to be used only when the rate setter was present. They found that by tightening certain bolts first, the frame would be slightly sprung and all the other bolts would bind and be very difficult to tighten. When the rate setter was not present, they followed a different sequence and the work went much faster (pp. 164–165).

Argyris (1951, 1964), Hofstede (1967), Hopwood (1973), and others have pointed out that employees also often provide misleading data when they are asked to give budgetary estimates. Not surprisingly, they tend to ask for much larger amounts than they need. On the other hand, in instances where a low budget estimate is needed in order to get a budget or project approved (e.g., under some Program Planning and Budgeting systems, Lyden and Miller, 1968), a low estimate is submitted. Managers submit high budget requests because they realize that their budget request will be cut and to play the game they must come in with a high initial budget figure. The bargaining process they go through is not too dissimilar from the one that goes on between the time-study man and the blue collar employee. Both the time-study man and the manager try to get valid data about what is possible in the future and the employees who are subject to the control system often give invalid data and try to get as favorable a standard, or budget, as they can. Budget setting sessions can degenerate into a game of seeing how much slack can be placed in the budget by the subordinate and how little slack is allowed by the superior. As Schiff and Lewin (1970) have cogently stated, slack in budgets, the process of underestimating revenues and overstating costs, exists because many managers prefer to operate in a slack environment. It makes sense for managers to opt for slack since the negative sanctions for missing a tight budget are likely to have more impact than the rewards for making a tight budget (Onsi, 1973).

How frequently do employees consciously provide invalid data when standards and budgets are being set? It is impossible to come up with any hard figures but the research on standard setting suggests that it happens much of the time (Lawler, 1971). There is less evidence on how often it occurs in budget setting but what data there are suggest it happens much of the time there too. In this situation as in the standard setting situation there is usually low trust, and, as a study by Mellinger (1956) shows, when there is low trust people are likely to conceal data or to communicate invalid data (see also Rosen and Tesser, 1970).

There are also a number of examples in the behavioral science literature of cases where employees have fed invalid information about what has happened into a control system. Again it is difficult from the literature to determine just how often this overt falsification occurs, but it seems likely that it is not as common as the practice of making

* From pp. 15–18 in *Money and Motivation* by William Foote Whyte. Copyright © 1955 by Harper & Row Publishers, Inc. Reprinted by permission of the publisher.

consciously invalid estimates of what is possible. Undoubtedly one of the reasons for this is that it is easier to catch and punish an employee who has misreported what has happened than it is to punish one who has consciously given an erroneous estimate of what can happen.

Roethlisberger and Dickson (1939) in their classic study of the Bank Wiring Room point out how employees can manage the kind of production reports that go outside their work group. In the Bank Wiring Room the employees were on a pay incentive plan and they wanted to show a consistent daily production figure. They did this by not reporting what they produced on some days and on other days reporting things as having been produced that were never produced. Similar examples have been cited by others who have looked at the way employees react to financial incentive systems (e.g., Whyte, 1955; Lawler, 1971).

There are also data that suggest employees will consciously feed invalid information into management information systems (e.g., Argyris, 1971; Mumford and Banks, 1967; Pettigrew, 1970, 1972, 1973). One reason for such falsification seems to be to cover up errors or poor performance. Employees also feed invalid data to the management information systems to make the system look bad and to discourage people from using it. Invalid data are also sometimes fed into a control system simply because control systems occasionally demand data that simply are not and cannot be collected. Faced with this situation an employee may choose to estimate the data rather than admit that it does not exist or give up on the system. This would seem to be a particular problem where computer-based management information systems are being installed. They often call for historical cost, production, and other data that simply are not available (Argyris, 1971).

RESISTANCE

Every discussion of the behavioral problems associated with control systems points out that they often meet strong resistance from the people who are subject to them. Rarely, however, do these discussions show, as we have in the preceding chapters, that control systems can also fulfill some important needs people have because they provide feedback and structure and that for this reason many people want a control system. Virtually every author who discusses control systems tends to explain the resistance to them in terms of their being perceived as a threat to the need satisfaction of employees (e.g., Argyris, 1971; Caplan, 1971; Mumford and Banks, 1967; Pettigrew, 1970; and Whisler, 1970a, 1970b). They then go on to emphasize how control systems can threaten the satisfaction of a number of different needs. Lawler (1971) and Whyte (1955) have shown how the imposition of a pay incentive, performance measurement system can threaten the satisfaction of social, esteem, and security needs. Argyris (1951) and others have shown how budgets can do the same thing. Along similar lines, Argyris (1971), Gibson and Nolan (1974), Mumford and Banks (1967), and Whisler (1970b) have pointed out how computer-based management information systems can threaten the satisfaction of social, security, esteem, autonomy, and self-realization needs. Pettigrew (1970, 1972) has pointed out that control systems also often significantly change the power and status relationships in an organization.

The questions that remain concern why control systems are generally seen as such significant threats to the satisfaction of so many needs and why they significantly change the power relationships in organizations. There are a number of reasons, the most significant of which will be discussed next.

Control systems can automate expertise. Control systems can automate or computerize jobs that presently are considered to require expertise (Carroll, 1967; Pettigrew, 1970, 1973; and Gibson and Nolan, 1974). The effect of this can be to make superfluous a skill that a person has developed and has been respected for having. This phenomenon seems to occur most frequently when management information systems (MIS) are installed. Such systems can have a tremendous impact on the nature of middle- and lower-level management jobs. For example, they can make costing, purchasing, and production decisions that previously were the essence of many management jobs. Because of this, Leavitt and Whisler (1958) have pointed out that the potential is present for the elimination of many management jobs. This has not happened, and it may not ever happen, but there is still the potential for automating or computerizing many jobs. Even if systems don't lead to the elimination of managerial jobs, they may make managerial jobs less desirable because they lead to a "rationalization" and "depersonalization" of managerial work (Carroll, 1967).

The elimination and depersonalization of jobs certainly is not restricted to managerial jobs. Pettigrew (1973) has provided an example of how stock order clerks saw computerization as potentially making unnecessary the skills they had developed to do their jobs. It didn't turn out that way, but the point is they feared it would happen. A study on the impact of computerization on white collar jobs in a bank also found that computerization was seen as making useless the expertise that was required to do some jobs (Mumford and Banks, 1967). A crucial factor in understanding the impact of computerized information systems seems to be the stage of their development. Gibson and Nolan (1974) have suggested that there are four stages. During the first stage (installation) computers have a tendency to produce strong job displacement anxieties. This problem is particularly likely to occur at the lower levels of organizations. It is only when the systems reach stage four (maturity) that they are likely to be in a position to displace middle-level managers. At this point they are devoted to applications touching on critical business operations and the head of the system is a member of top management.

To the extent that control systems can automate, standardize, and rigidify work, people will see them as threatening their need satisfaction in a number of areas. Particularly relevant would appear to be satisfaction in the status, autonomy, and security need areas. Security because the person may feel more expendable, status because what the person is respected for can become valueless, and autonomy because the new system may seriously restrict the person's freedom to perform the job (Argyris, 1971).

Control systems can create new experts and give them power. Pettigrew (1970, 1973) gives an excellent example of how the installation of a computerized MIS created a new power elite in one organization. There was considerable jockeying for position within the organization and some groups' power and status were reduced. The individuals who ended up in control of the system, however, gained in power; they not only didn't resist the system, they pushed for its expansion and development into a stage four system. In another paper, Pettigrew (1972) stresses how information can be a source of power in an organization and how the individuals who run MIS can find themselves in the sometimes powerful and satisfying role of gatekeeper even though they are in staff positions. This is particularly likely to occur as the systems approach stage four.

It is probably safe to assume that no matter what control system is involved, there is some group that will gain as a result of its installation and another that will lose. In the case of budgets the winners typically are the accountants that run them, in the case of incentive systems it is the time-study experts, and in the case of MIS it is the computer experts and staff people who run them. These people favor installation of the system because the system helps them. However, there are usually others who lose power to these people. They typically see their power, status, and job security threatened as a result of the new control system and resist it.

Control systems have the potential to measure individual performance more accurately and completely. Certain kinds of control systems can increase the validity of performance measurement in an organization by improving both the accuracy of the performance data collected and its inclusivity. For example, moving from a simple superior's rating of performance to a performance evaluation system based on both quantitative responsibility accounting data and production data can increase the accuracy of the available performance data. Some employees welcome this since it reflects positively on their performance and increases their own position in the organization. Others feel that such objective data will put them in a less favorable light than they are in presently. In fact, they might see the installation of such an objective evaluation system as threatening their job security, their status, and their power in the organization. Thus, while one group will favor better measurement, another group is likely to resist it.

Argyris (1971) has talked about how an MIS can lead to leadership based more on competence than on power. In many ways this point is similar to the one being made here. Both are pointing out that with better performance data the highest level of need satisfaction is more likely to go to the more competent. This is a positive outcome for some but it may be resisted by those who doubt their own competence but have achieved reasonably satisfactory positions in organizations.

Control systems can change the social structure of an organization. Changes in a control system can produce major changes in the social relationships in an organization (Mumford and Banks, 1967). They can break up social groups, pit one friend against another, create new social groups, and, as was pointed out earlier, by creating new experts they can change the status and power of organization members. This is dramatically illustrated in studies where pay incentive plans, work measurement systems, and computerized MIS have been installed or altered. Changes in these control systems almost always have a strong impact on the social relations in the organization. Some people have less opportunity to form friendships after the changes have been made, others have more. Some people end up pitted in a competitive way against people with whom they formerly had cooperative relationships. Because of the potential impact of control systems on social need satisfaction, it is not surprising that some employees see control systems as threats to their social need satisfaction and for that reason resist the installation of such systems.

Control systems can reduce opportunities for intrinsic need satisfaction. Information systems can help provide feedback about performance, thus they can help create opportunities for psychological success and intrinsic satisfaction. However, they can also reduce the opportunities available for experiencing psychological success if, as often happens, they reduce the amount of autonomy employees have by specifying in considerable detail how jobs have to be done. This has already happened in many jobs where incentive pay and budget systems are in effect and it appears to be about to happen in many jobs because of the installation of automated information systems. If, as Carroll (1967) says, real time decisions will soon be made by centralized management information systems, then it certainly appears that many lower level jobs in organizations will lose their autonomy.

The fact that control systems can provide feedback may not compensate for the fact that they may decrease autonomy since this often is enough to prevent people from experiencing intrinsic satisfaction from task accomplishment. Naturally when people see that the control system will reduce their autonomy and thereby their opportunities for experiencing psychological success and intrinsic satisfaction, they will resist the system if they value these feelings.

REFERENCES

Argyris, Chris, *The Impact of Budgets on People*. New York: Controllership Foundation, 1951.

———, *Integrating the Individual and the Organization*. New York: Wiley, 1964.

———, "Management Information Systems: the Challenge to Rationality and Emotionality," *Management Science*, 17 (1971), 275–92.

Babchuk, N., and W. J. Goode, "Work Incentives in a Self-Determined Group," *American Social Review*, 16 (1951), 679–87.

Berliner, Joseph S., "A Problem in Soviet Business Administration," *Administrative Science Quarterly*, 1 (1956), 86–101.

Blau, P. M., *The Dynamics of Bureaucracy*. Chicago: University of Chicago Press, 1955.

Burns, Thomas J., and G. M. Stalker, *The Management of Innovation*. London: Tavistock, 1961.

Cammann, C., "Can Accounting Systems Produce Change?" Presented at the APA Convention, 1974a.

Caplan, Edwin H., *Management Accounting and Behavioral Sciences*. Reading, Mass.: Addison-Wesley, 1971.

Carroll, D. C., "Implications of On-Line, Real-Time Systems for Managerial Decision-Making," in C. A. Meyers, ed., *The Impact of Computers on Management*. Cambridge: MIT Press, 1967, 140–66.

Frank, A. G., "Goal Ambiguity and Conflicting Standards: An Approach to the Study of Organization," *Human Organization*, 17 (1959), 8–13.

Gardner, B. B., *Human Relations in Industry*. Chicago: Irwin, 1945.

Ghiselli, E. E., *The Validity of Occupational Attitude Tests*. New York: Wiley, 1966.

Gibson, C. F., and R. L. Nolan, "Managing the Four Stages of EDP Growth," *Harvard Business Review*, 74 (1974), 76–88.

Gordon, M. J., B. Horwitz, and P. Meyers, *Empirical Research in Accounting: Selected Studies*. Evanston, Ill.: American Accounting Association, 1967, 164–80.

Gouldner, A. W., *Patterns of Industrial Bureaucracy*. Glencoe, Ill.: Free Press, 1954.

Hofstede, G. H., *The Game of Budget Control*. Assen, Netherlands: Van Gorcum, 1967.

Hopwood, A. G., "An Empirical Study of the Role of Accounting Data in Performance Evaluation," *Empirical Research in Accounting: Selected Studies, 1972*. Supplement to Vol. 10, *Journal of Accounting Research*.

———, *An Accounting System and Managerial Behavior*. Lexington, Mass.: Lexington Books, 1973.

———, "Leadership Climate and the Use of Accounting Data in Performance Evaluation," *The Accounting Review*, 49 (1974a), 485–95.

———, *Accounting and Human Behavior*. London: Haymarket Publishing, 1974b.

Jasinski, F. J., "Use and Misuse of Efficiency Controls," *Harvard Business Review*, 34 (1956), 105–12.

Lawler, E. E., *Pay and Organizational Effectiveness: A Psychological View*. New York: McGraw-Hill, 1971.

Leavitt, H. J., and T. C. Whisler, "Management in the 1980's," *Harvard Business Review*, 36 (1958), 41–48.

Lyden, F. J., and E. G. Miller, eds., *Planning, Programming and Budgeting: A Systems Approach to Management*. Chicago: Markham, 1968.

March, J. G., and H. A. Simon, *Organizations*. New York: Wiley, 1958.

Mellinger, G. D., "Interpersonal Trust as a Factor in Communication," *Journal of Abnormal and Social Psychology*, 52 (1956), 304–9.

Merton, R. K., "Bureaucratic Structure and Personality," *Social Forces*, 18 (1940), 560–8.

Mumford, E., and O. Banks, *The Computer and the Clerk*. London: Routledge and Kegan Paul, 1967.

Onsi, M., "Behavioral Variables Affecting Budgetary Slack," *The Accounting Review*, 48 (1973), 535–48.

Pettigrew, A., *A Behavioral Analysis of an Innovative Decision*. Published Ph.D. dissertation, University of Manchester, 1970.

———, "Information Control as a Power Resource," *Sociology*, 6 (1972), 187–204.

———, *The Politics of Organization Decision-Making*. London: Tavistock, 1973.

Roethlisberger, F. J., and W. J. Dickson, *Management and the Worker*. Cambridge Harvard University Press, 1939.

Rosen, S., and A. Tesser, "On Reluctance to Communicate Undesirable Information: The Mum Affect," *Sociometry*, 33 (1970), 253–63.

Schiff, M., "Accounting Tactics and the Theory of the Firm," *Journal of Accounting Research*, 4 (August 1966), 62–67.

Schiff, M., and A. Y. Lewin, "The Impact of People on Budgets," *The Accounting Review*, 45 (1970), 259–68.

Selznick, P., *TVA and the Grass Roots*. Berkeley: University of California Press, 1949.

Whisler, T. L., *The Impact of Computers on Organizations*. New York: Praeger, 1970a.

———, *Information Technology and Organizational Change*. Belmont, Calif.: Wadsworth, 1970b.

Whyte, W. F., ed., *Money and Motivation: An Analysis of Incentives in Industry*. New York: Harper, 1955.

Wilensky, H. L., *Organizational Intelligence*. New York: Basic Books, 1967.

Fit Control Systems to Your Managerial Style

Cortlandt Cammann and David A. Nadler

Not long ago, the Boy Scouts of America revealed that membership figures coming in from the field had been falsified. In response to the pressures of a national membership drive, people within the organization had vastly overstated the number of new Boy Scouts. To their chagrin, the leaders found something that other managers have also discovered: organizational control systems often produce unintended consequences.

The drive to increase membership had motivated people to increase the number of new members reported, but it had not motivated them to increase the number of Boy Scouts actually enrolled.

The case of the Boy Scouts is a clear example of a widespread problem. Organizations spend large amounts of money, time, and effort in designing and maintaining control systems. These systems are intended to enhance an organization's ability to coordinate the actions of its members and to identify problems as they arise. Often, however, instead of increasing organizational control these systems reduce the amount of effective control that the organization exercises.

Why does this happen? Our research and the research of others indicate that the problem often lies with the ways that managers use control systems.[1] Most control systems, including budgetary, management information, and financial accounting systems, are essentially measurements. They regularly collect information about specific aspects of organizational performance.

The systems themselves are not capable of directly controlling organizational performance. Rather, they provide information to the managers who are in a position to exercise control. If managers use the information well, the control system works. If they use it poorly, the system may produce unintended effects.

Significantly, organizations seldom invest much effort in training managers to use control systems. Instead, most spend a lot of time designing, constructing, refining, and improving the technical aspects of their systems. The result is that while organizational control systems continually become more precise, accurate, and technologically sophisticated, two questions are often overlooked:

1. How effective is the system (and the way it is used) in doing what it is supposed to do?
2. How could the system be better used?

Recent research in a number of organizations has provided some answers to these questions.[2] First, control systems influence the way organization members direct their energies on the job; the members are more likely to put time and effort into those areas covered by the systems. Second, how members respond to control systems depends largely on the way managers use the systems. Third, different managers develop different strategies for using control systems. Finally, each strategy has certain drawbacks and benefits.

Only when managers understand (a) how these systems influence the behavior of their subordinates and (b) what trade-offs occur in each control strategy can they learn to use organizational control systems effectively.

In the balance of this article we shall discuss what managers should consider when they choose a control style. We shall examine the various ways in which control systems influence managerial behavior. Then, we shall discuss two major strategies for using control systems, the various issues that ought to be considered when choosing a particular control style, and the implications of the final decision.

INFLUENCE ON SUBORDINATES

When an area is covered by a control system, organization members concentrate on improving their performance in the measured area. There are three reasons for this direction of energy:

1. Measurement of an area of activity indicates that top management feels the area is important and bears watching.
2. Managers generally use control system measures when they evaluate subordinate performance. Since the subordinate usually feels that the manager's evaluation influences his or her rewards, the subordinate tends to put energy into the measured areas.
3. It is easy for an organization member to see changes in performance measures that are part of the control system. If his performance is improving, this can be a source of personal satisfaction.

Exhibit I provides an example of how performance measurement directs subordinate energy. In two different organizations — one a northeastern public utility, the other a midwestern bank — employees were asked to indicate to what degree different areas of activity were measured. At another point, they were asked how much time and effort they put into each area. As shown in the exhibit, the general pattern is that the more people perceive that an area is measured, the more time and effort they put into it.

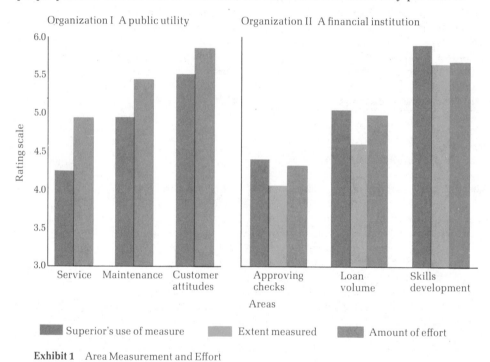

Exhibit 1 Area Measurement and Effort
in Two Organizations

Effects of Control Systems

It appears that control systems direct how much energy subordinates put into an area, but how is this energy used? On one hand, subordinates may be motivated to increase their levels of performance, producing larger quantities or higher quality work.

On the other hand, measurement may produce the results we saw in the Boy Scouts' example. Subordinates direct their efforts into "game playing" to "beat the system." Rather than performing well, employees often set low goals that can be easily met, manipulate measures to come out with the desired results, and actually sabotage the system's information base.

For example, a large government organization required each person to fill out a form accounting for the way he spent his time in 20-minute blocks. The intent was to motivate the employees to manage their time and to generate valid information about how much time they were allocating to different tasks. The result, however, was vastly different. The employees saw the system as an attempt to regiment their lives and activities.

Thus, instead of being a useful tool, the time sheets became a recreational activity. On Friday afternoons at the work break, employees got together to fill out their time sheets, each competing to see who could come up with the most preposterous record of activities. Needless to say, these records had no relation to actual work done. The system did not motivate people to increase performance; it motivated them to play games with the system.

Exhibit II summarizes the effects of control systems. The existence of measures in an area has an effect on subordinate behavior, but measurement is not the only factor. The measures have to be perceived by the employees as being reasonably accurate, and they have to be used skillfully by the managers.

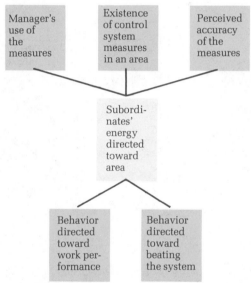

Exhibit II   How Control Systems and Their Use
Affect Behavior

STRATEGIES OF CONTROL

A manager must give serious thought to his use of control system measures in any one area. He must consider the consequences of his actions in terms of the kinds of behavior that he motivates in his subordinates. Although there is a range of strategies for control, two major approaches—external control and internal motivation—seem to prove most useful for many managers. *Exhibit III* shows that each of these strategies requires different behavior on the part of the manager; each can have either desirable or undesirable effects on subordinate behavior.

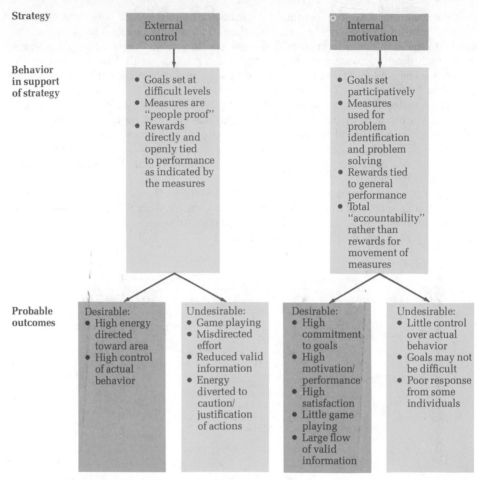

Exhibit III   Two Different Strategies of Control

External Control

This strategy is based on the assumption that subordinates in the particular situation are motivated primarily by external rewards and need to be controlled by their supervisors. To use the control system effectively in this way requires three steps.

First, the goals and standards associated with the system need to be made relatively difficult in order to "stretch" subordinates and leave little room for slack.

Second, the area measures need to be constructed so that they are "people proof," to prevent individuals from being able to manipulate the measures.

Third, rewards need to be directly and openly tied to performance, as indicated by the measures in the control system, to ensure that the subordinates have an incentive to work hard.

An example of the external control approach would be to evaluate a manager solely on the performance of his profit center, with relatively high levels of profit being budgeted and with his compensation tied primarily and directly to the number of dollars of profit.

This external control strategy can have different effects. On one hand, subordinates may channel a great deal of energy into measured areas and may try hard to make their measures move, since they can gain rewards by doing so. Where the system is very tightly structured, the result will be a high degree of control of subordinate behavior. On the other hand, several undesirable results may occur.

First, such a strategy may motivate organization members to improve their performance measures but not create any commitment to their doing a better job. The subordinates will begin to develop an attitude toward performance in which "doing well" means doing well on the performance measures, not necessarily performing their jobs more effectively. As a result, if they can increase their "performance" by manipulating the measures, providing false information, intentionally setting low goals and standards, or sabotaging the system, the organization members can be expected to do so.

Second, such a strategy may result in misdirected effort. Subordinates may put all of their energies into the particular behavior that is measured, while forgetting other behavior that, although not measured, is also vital. For example, if all efforts are directed toward increasing sales volume, the amount of effort devoted to ongoing customer service may be decreased. In this case, the result is short-term maximization in the measured area with possible negative long-term effects on unmeasured areas.

Third, such a strategy may tend to reduce the flow of valid information, particularly negative information. If people are directly rewarded for positive movement of measures, they may become motivated to withhold information that would negate the meaning of those measures and to withhold negative information from higher-level managers who need it for decision making.

Finally, such a strategy may bring about excessive caution, directing energy toward justification of all actions. Subordinates may be motivated to ensure that the measures either continue to look good (by not taking any risks), or to assemble "just in case" files filled with information justifying a decrease in measured performance. In either case, energy is directed toward coping with the system, rather than toward the larger goal of making the organization more effective.

Internal Motivation

In this strategy, management assumes that subordinates can be motivated by building their commitments to organizational goals and by their being involved in the necessary tasks. They assume that employees will be motivated by the feelings of accomplishment, achievement, recognition, and self-esteem that come from having performed a job well. The strategy of internal motivation is implemented by using the control system in a very different manner than in the external control strategy.

First, although goals are set, the most important feature of this approach is not the difficulty in achieving the goals but the fact that they are set participatively. Those people who are responsible for achieving goals are given some influence over the nature of those goals.

Second, the measures are used for joint problem identification and solution rather than for punishment or blame. When a performance begins to move in an undesired direction, it is not the time for heads to roll. It is the time for managers and subordinates to meet together (a) to determine the reasons for the change, and (b) to develop solutions to the problems that have come up. Thus the system takes on an "early warning" function of surfacing problems, beginning the resolution process before those problems reach the crisis state.

Finally, although rewards are tied to performance, they are not tied to one or two specific measures. Rather, the reward structure emphasizes accountability for the entire job performance, only part of which may be represented by the measures. In general, the control system becomes problem-based and future-oriented. The system helps the manager exercise control of subordinate behavior by directing future efforts, rather than by punishing each person's past actions.

This internal motivation strategy may have different effects. It may generate high commitment to goals because the organization member participates in setting them and feels responsible for seeing that they are achieved. This may lead to greater energy directed toward task performance. As performance increases and as the individual monitors his progress through the measures of the control system, the strategy may also enhance the employee's satisfaction in performing his job well.

Thus the open nature of the control system and its general, rather than specific, accountability mean that there is little incentive for subordinates to play games or to behave dysfunctionally. More important, it encourages and rewards the flow of valid information, particularly negative information.

At the same time, such a strategy may have some undesirable effects. The comparatively loose nature of this approach means that the manager will have less control over the behavior of his subordinates. Because the manager gives up total control over the specific goals, subordinates may establish less ambitious goals.

In addition, since the information provided by the control system is for problem solving and not for evaluation, it becomes difficult to use it as a basis for giving rewards. Thus the manager has to sacrifice some of the value that is inherent in the external control approach in order to build internal motivation on the part of subordinates.

Finally, some individuals may not respond to the participative process because of differences in working style or personality. These people, therefore, will not be motivated to perform well within this strategy framework.

CHOICE STRATEGIES

Neither of the two strategies just discussed is necessarily the "right" strategy to use in all cases. Since each has certain drawbacks and benefits, a manager must consciously and carefully choose the approach that suits his particular situation. In making that choice, he needs to consider the following four issues:

1. *Consistency between strategy choice and managerial style.*
In choosing a control strategy, a manager may have to modify either his style or the strategy so that his total approach to managing is consistent. For instance, if a manager generally makes all important decisions without involving subordinates, it would be a mistake for him to use an internal motivation approach. The subordinates would be accustomed to following the manager's lead. They may not be capable of setting realistic goals on their own; or worse, they may use their influence to set easy objectives that

1. In general, what kind of managerial style do I have?

Participative	*Directive*
I frequently consult my subordinates on decisions, encourage them to disagree with my opinion, share information with them, and let them make decisions whenever possible.	I usually take most of the responsibility for and make most of the major decisions, pass on only the most relevant job information, and provide detailed and close direction for my subordinates.

2. In general, what kind of climate, structure, and reward system does my organization have?

Participative	*Nonparticipative*
Employees at all levels of the organization are urged to participate in decisions and influence the course of events. Managers are clearly rewarded for developing employee skills and decision-making capacities.	Most important decisions are made by a few people at the top of the organization. Managers are not rewarded for developing employee competence or for encouraging employees to participate in decision making.

3. How accurate and reliable are the measures of key areas of subordinate performance?

Accurate	*Inaccurate*
All major aspects of performance can be adequately measured; changes in measures accurately reflect changes in performance; and measures cannot be easily sabotaged or faked by subordinates.	Not all critical aspects of performance can be measured; measures often do not pick up on important changes in performance; good performance cannot be adequately defined in measurement terms; and measures can be easily sabotaged.

4. Do my subordinates desire to participate and respond well to opportunities to take responsibility for decision making and performance?

High desire to participate	*Low desire to participate*
Employees are eager to participate in decisions, are involved in the work itself, can make a contribution to decision making, and want to take more responsibility.	Employees do not want to be involved in many decisions, do not want additional responsibility, have little to contribute to decisions being made, and are not very involved in the work itself.

they know they can achieve. It is only in the context of a generally participative manager-subordinate relationship that an internal motivation approach to organizational control is likely to be effective.

2. Organizational climate, structure, and reward system.
A control strategy, to be most effective, should be consistent with other factors in the organization that determine employee behavior. For example, a tight control system in an organization that normally provides a great deal of discretion and freedom for employees would soon run into problems.

3. Reliability of job performance measures.
In some cases, control system measures accurately reflect job performance. In others, the measures do not adequately indicate how well the job is being done. When the

control system is an unreliable indicator of performance, it is hard to implement a tight external control strategy since the use of inaccurate or unreliable measures as a basis for evaluation and reward could have disastrous consequences. Under such conditions, a looser and more internally oriented organizational control strategy is required.

4. *Individual differences among subordinates.*
Because people are motivated by different needs, they may respond differently to the same organizational structure. The choice of control strategy assumes that the manager knows something about the nature of the people who work for him. Individuals who are committed to the work itself (e.g., in many professional occupations) are likely to be less responsive to an external control strategy than those individuals whose primary motivation is financial reward or promotion.

A manager must also consider how much employees desire to participate in decision making. Some people may respond well to the opportunity for participation, while others may not want to become more involved or assume the responsibility. Thus the types of people who work for the manager should be a factor influencing his choice of a control strategy.

An Informed Choice

At first glance, it may appear that a manager has too many factors to juggle to enable him to make an effective choice. One way around this problem is for the manager to lay out the key decisions and choice points sequentially.

First, the manager needs to ask himself a number of questions (see Exhibit IV). What kind of managerial style does he generally use? What kind of organization is he in? How accurate and reliable are his important performance measures? Finally, how much do his subordinates desire to participate in decision making?

Second, the manager must systematically evaluate his answers to determine which strategy is most appropriate. One way of doing this is by using a decision-tree approach (see *Exhibit V*). As indicated by the exhibit, different combinations of answers to the key questions lead the manager to different recommended strategies with different issues concerning their implementation.

In addition to the decision steps outlined in *Exhibit V*, the manager also needs to consider the trade-offs between the different strategies that may apply to his particular situation. Obviously, he must weigh the desirable or undesirable effects (as listed in *Exhibit III*) that a control system may have on his particular group of subordinates.

For example, if the opportunities for game playing are few and the costs to the company of game playing are low, the external control strategy may be more feasible. In most organizations, however, the potential costs of game playing are high. Therefore, managers should give serious consideration to the internal motivation strategy, especially if the basic decision-making process indicates that subordinate participation is feasible.

A control system and the way that it is used constitutes a potentially powerful tool for influencing the behavior of individuals in organizations. Just as the manager needs to make a careful and informed choice among control strategies, the organization needs to be conscious of the alternative approaches to designing and using control systems. Becoming aware of the potential effects of control systems and of the great importance of the process of control—as opposed to the technology of control—is central to making an organization and its people more productive and effective.

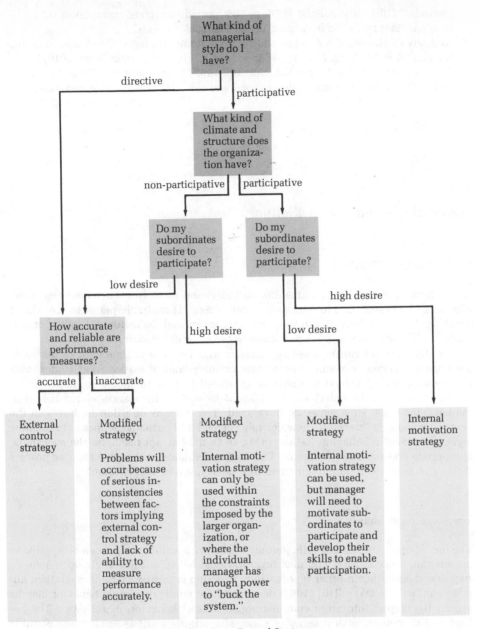

Exhibit V A Decision Tree for Choosing a Control Strategy

NOTES AND REFERENCES

1. Studies such as Chris Argyris's *The Impact of Budgets on People* (Ithaca, N.Y.: Cornell University, 1952) and Frank J. Jasinsky's "Use and Misuse of Efficiency

Controls," *HBR*, July–August 1956, p. 105, provide concrete examples of the problems that can arise from poor use of feedback systems.

2. Anthony G. Hopwood's *An Accounting System and Managerial Behavior* (London: Haymarket Publishing, Ltd., 1974) and Geert H. Hofstede's *The Game of Budget Control* (Assen, Netherlands: Van Gorsum, 1967) look systematically at the ways in which accounting information is used and the impact these uses can have.

Shaping
Fred Luthans and Robert Kreitner

THE SHAPING PROCESS

At the time of joining an organization, an individual possesses a behavior repertoire which can be classified into four general categories: (1) desirable performance-related behavior; (2) potentially disruptive performance-related behavior; (3) behavior unrelated to performance; and (4) performance behavior deficiencies.

Positive control can be used to maintain and increase the strength of desirable performance-related behavior. Appropriate negative control may weaken undesirable performance-related behavior. Behavior unrelated to performance can simply be ignored. However, if an individual is deficient in some performance-related behavior, the behavior must, in a sense, be developed. The obvious question is, how can the practicing manager "develop" new desirable behavior? The manager does not somehow mystically develop behavior. Rather, using an O. B. Mod. approach, he/she may *shape* appropriate organizational behavior. This section explains how such a shaping process works and how it can be implemented in human resource management.

The Meaning of Shaping

The old adage, "A thousand-mile journey begins with a single step," can be applied to the shaping process. Most complex organizational behavior must begin with a single step and then build. In other words, if the first step is positively reinforced, then another step will be taken. Hill (1963) described how relatively simple behavior may be eventually shaped into more complex organizational behavior, as follows: "The behavior is shaped through a series of successive approximations, each made possible by selectively reinforcing certain responses and not others. Thus behavior is gradually brought closer and closer to the desired pattern" (p. 71).

The shaping of organizational behavior involves the careful use of a combination extinction/positive reinforcement intervention strategy. Successively closer approximations to a target organizational behavior are first positively reinforced and then put on extinction as closer approximations are reinforced. The earlier illustration of how on-the-job behavior of hard-core unemployables was systematically shaped to a level consistent with gainful employment demonstrates the practical utility that the shaping process has for human resource management. Most training programs, whether deliberate or not, depend largely on the shaping process. Of even more importance is the role shaping can and does play in organizational behavior in general.

Organizational Socialization Through Shaping

The process whereby organizational participants learn to play performance roles leading to organizational goal attainment, can be called, for lack of a better term, organizational socialization. McGinnies (1970) has noted the following about such a process: "It seems likely that much of what we call socialization is achieved by various methods of *behavior shaping*, that is, selective reinforcement of performances that approach some socially acceptable standard" (p. 97).

Socialization begins early in life. A person growing up is influenced by family, church, school, and peers. More important from an O. B. Mod. perspective, however, socialization also occurs in a person's adult life. Since adults spend about half of their waking life in the organization that employs them, the organization is an important component of the socialization process. Although the consequence sources of an adult operating in a complex, modern organization differ from those in childhood, the shaping process is omnipresent.

Even Chester Barnard (1938), the pioneering management theorist, noted the presence of the shaping process as an aspect of organizational socialization when he observed: ". . . the process of decision is one of successive approximations — constant refinement of purpose, closer and closer discrimination of fact — in which the march of time is essential" (p. 206). In other words, Barnard depicted decision making as a shaping process. Just as a quarterback is shaped into passing accuracy by the reinforcement of completions, the busy executive is shaped into making effective decisions by desirable outcomes. Greater profit, a lower cost of capital, an adequate supply of scarce raw material, a greater return on investment, or a greater share of the market are all desirable organizational outcomes that serve to differentially reinforce or shape effective managerial decision making. Organizational socialization consists of things like following rules, working on tasks, solving problems and making decisions. In general, the successful achievement of organizational objectives can be thought of as a shaping process in which closer and closer approximations of established objectives are positively reinforced.

The shaping process will take place regardless of managerial action or intent. Since shaping plays such an important role in organizational socialization, it is crucial to O. B. Mod. that it be properly controlled. The choice is between the haphazard shaping of random behavior, some productive and some counterproductive, or the careful systematic shaping of key performance-related behavior. Consequently, the challenge for

O. B. Mod. is to create a work environment in which positive reinforcement is made systematically contingent on steadily improving performance. Systematic shaping should play an important role in vestibule training, on-the-job training, management development, and, most importantly for organizational socialization, the management of everyday performance.

Odiorne (1970, p. 316), in discussing the manager as a teacher, identified three types: (1) the manager who does his subordinates' work for them; (2) the manager who does his own job competently by intuition; and (3) the manager who does his own work well and teaches others. It is the last type who is capable of incorporating the shaping process into everyday human resource management, resulting in effective organizational socialization.

A Shaping Strategy for Human Resource Management

To implement an effective shaping strategy, several specific steps should be followed. For example, an O. B. Mod. approach to shaping would involve the following:

1) Precisely define the goal or target behavior. This target behavior should always be related to performance.
2) If the target behavior is a complex chain of behavior, reduce it to a discrete, observable, and thus measurable sequence of behavioral events or steps.
3) Make sure the individual is capable of meeting the technical skill or ability requirements for each step.
4) Select potentially effective positive reinforcers on the basis of the individual's history of reinforcement.
5) Structure the contingent environment so that appropriate antecedent conditions will increase the probability of the desired behavior.
6) Make all positive reinforcement contingent upon successively closer approximations to the target behavior. The behavioral chain must be built link by link.
7) Once achieved, maintain and strengthen the target behavior, first with continuous reinforcement and later with an intermittent schedule of reinforcement.

To obtain a better understanding of the shaping process, it would be helpful to expand the steps listed above.

Define the target behavior.　What must the employee do to effectively accomplish organizational objectives? This is a fundamental question in O. B. Mod. Answers such as "greater initiative," "more independence," "better performance," "improved attitude," and "increased responsibility" are too general to be appropriate target behavior for a shaping strategy. Specific behavior is the key. According to Mathis et al. (1970): "Unless terminal objectives can be specified as behaviors, it is impossible to determine the reinforcement contingencies needed to accomplish those terminal objectives" (p. 127). Examples of more appropriate target behavior would include: "Punch in at 8:00 A.M. every workday"; "Eliminate temper tantrums as soon as possible when dealing with subordinates"; "Take action on customers' complaints within two days"; and "Reduce work-order errors to 3 percent by the end of the month."

Notice how each of these examples directly expresses or at least implies a definite time dimension. The net result is a clear definition of the desired state of the target behavior (or of the effect of that behavior in terms of performance) by a specified time. Even the example of the elimination of temper tantrums has a time dimension (i.e., as soon as the systematic shaping of incompatible responses with positive consequences will permit).

This first step in the shaping process is closely related to Management By Objectives (MBO). MBO was developed by Peter Drucker (1954) and is currently a widely used and accepted method of management. It can be simply defined as setting objectives and appraising performance results. It can be both a total philosophy of management and a specific technique of planning and control. In addition, MBO can be thought of as an effective blend of both the plan, organize, and control requirements and the necessary behavioral requirements for effective modern management.

One thing that all MBO experts tend to agree upon is the need for specific, quantifiable objectives. This, of course, is directly comparable to the shaping process in O. B. Mod. For example, one MBO expert (Murray, 1973) listed three important elements of effective management objectives. They include: (1) a statement of specific results in behavioral terms; (2) a statement of a specific time frame; and (3) a statement of specific criteria. The close parallel between such objectives and target behavior descriptions in the shaping process is obvious. However, there are differences.

For example, the O. B. Mod. shaping process gives closer attention to specific performance-related behavioral events. MBO relies heavily on self-control with the commitment to and accomplishment of mutually determined objectives. Shaping entails a more precise and systematic program of positive consequences for improvement than the typical MBO approach. However, the self-control concept found in MBO can be incorporated into O. B. Mod.

As indicated a few years ago (Luthans and White, 1971), there is a very close relationship between O. B. Mod. and MBO. (Interestingly, the initials for O. B. Mod. put in reverse order are MBO.) One of the eventual goals of O. B. Mod., as will be discussed in the last chapter, is to bring MBO and O. B. Mod. even closer together in actual practice. Both approaches can learn from each other and improve each other's effectiveness.

Once the target behavior has been precisely defined in the shaping process, the subsequent steps fall into place. But overgeneralization or imprecision during this first step will negate the subsequent steps and permanently cripple any attempts to successfully shape organizational behavior. Precise definitions of target behavior not only help the controller of the consequences in a shaping strategy, but also help the behaver know what is expected of him/her. As emphasized before, knowledge of self-improvement can be a very potent positive reinforcer.

Break behavior down into sequential steps. A natural followup to the first step of the shaping process is to break down complex behavior chains into sequences of observable behavioral events. As you will recall from the discussion of behavior chaining in Chapter 3,* the consequence in one contingency is often the antecedent in another contingency. If positive reinforcement is to be made contingent on successive approximations to the precisely defined target behavior, then those successive approximations also must be precisely defined.

---

* See Chapter 3 of *Organizational Behavior Modification*, Luthans and Kreitner (Scott, Foresman, 1975).

Consider, for example, the common case of the overly dependent subordinate — the one who asks for answers to daily problems rather than attempting to solve the problems himself/herself. Generally, the appropriate strategy should involve removing the supporting consequences of the dependent behavior and implementing a program of positive consequences for the weaker, incompatible problem-solving behavior. The former could be achieved with an extinction strategy while the latter could be systematically shaped. Shaping is simply a systematic way of administering positive reinforcement.

More specifically, some approximations of the target behavior that would be reinforced in this example include: (1) paying any attention at all to a problem; (2) giving more extensive attention to a problem — five minutes, ten minutes, fifteen minutes, and so on; (3) carefully studying and analyzing all facets of a problem; (4) making early attempts at actually solving a problem; (5) making successively closer approximations to a workable solution to a problem; and (6) developing final workable solution(s) to problems. By reducing a rather complex behavior such as problem solving down to a sequence of observable and thus reinforceable steps, the practitioner using O. B. Mod. can effectively shape a desirable organizational behavior.

Meet skill requirements. This third step emphasizes that the manager using a shaping strategy must consider all technical skill requirements which, if not mastered by the individual, could block the attainment of the target behavior. As examples, a touch-typing skill and the ability to insert the drum card in a keypunch machine are key determinants of success in rapidly and efficiently typing letters and punching data cards. In describing a two-step clerical training program for the hard-core unemployed using a token economy, Brief and Filley (1974) explain how the problem of technical skills may be overcome: "Each trainee works independently on various learning tasks such as typing or record keeping. The learning tasks are broken down into modules allowing each trainee to learn at her own pace and to allow [the manager] to frequently evaluate each trainee's performance." This suggests that each requisite technical skill can be shaped to a level of desired proficiency before it can become a reinforceable step in a larger shaping strategy for organizational socialization.

Select positive reinforcers. Just as the target behavior and its component parts must be identified, the appropriate positive reinforcers must be identified as well. Any one of the methods for identifying potential positive reinforcers (analyzing histories of reinforcement, self-report instruments, or trial and error) may be used. The important point is to make sure that the most potentially powerful positive consequences are made part of the shaping process. Rewarding successive approximations with consequences which turn out not to be positive reinforcers will postpone the ultimate successful achievement of the target behavior in the shaping process.

Favorably structure the antecedent environment. An O. B. Mod. approach involves not only the systematic programming of contingent consequences, but attention to antecedent conditions. In terms of the A→B→C contingency, the antecedent conditions (A) set the occasion for behavior (B) to be emitted by the individual. Once emitted, a program of positive consequences (C) ensures the reoccurrence of the behavior. When organizational behavior is being shaped, the practicing manager cannot rely on consequences alone. Coaching techniques, directions, instructions or rules, or simulated exercises (role playing or experiential games) may provide the appropriate antecedent conditions for cueing or prompting the successive approximations of desired behavior.

Returning to the example of the overly dependent subordinate, the manager using a shaping strategy may increase the probability of an early approximation of the target behavior (such as simply studying a problem) by presenting a relatively simple but highly interesting (for the individual) problem. In the O. B. Mod. terms, the presentation of a simple but highly interesting problem is the antecedent condition (A) which sets the occasion for the response of studying the problem (B) which, in turn, is positively reinforced (C) by the manager. As closer and closer approximations are required for contingent reinforcement, other antecedent conditions may be used.

Apply contingent reinforcers to approximations.   Complex chains of responses leading to target behavior must be built link by link. This is accomplished through a carefully managed program of positive consequences. As mentioned earlier, shaping most effectively results from a combination extinction/positive reinforcement strategy. Each link in the behavioral chain is first positively reinforced and later put on extinction as the reinforcement criterion is stretched to require the successful performance of an additional link. Because self-reinforcement is a part of goal achievement, this reinforcement stretching effect should always be completely aboveboard in terms of the employee's knowledge of what is happening and what the manager expects.

Maintain and strengthen target behavior.   Once the desired target response is emitted, it must be continually monitored and managed. Continuous or at least high-frequency fixed or variable ratio schedules of reinforcement must be employed initially to ensure the steady emission of the shaped behavior. Once established in the individual's behavior repertoire, the desirable behavior can be maintained and strengthened through an appropriate program of antecedent conditions, intermittent positive reinforcement, and eventually self-reinforcement.

The foregoing seven-step shaping strategy . . . permits the practicing manager to systematically reduce behavioral performance deficits in an employee's behavior repertoire. In a sense, shaping permits the development of desirable (from the viewpoint of goal attainment) organizational behavior. Practicing human resource managers can benefit from a working knowledge and systematic strategy of shaping organizational behavior.

REFERENCES

Barnard, C. *The Functions of the Executive.* Harvard, 1938.

Brief, A., and A. C. Filley. "Contingency Management, Poor People, and the Firm." *MSU Business Topics*, Vol. 22 (Spring 1974), pp. 45–52.

Drucker, P. *The Practice of Management.* Harper and Row, 1954.

Hill, W. F. *Learning: A Survey of Psychological Interpretations.* Chandler Publishing Company, 1963.

Luthans, F., and D. White. "Behavior Modification: Application to Manpower Management." *Personnel Administration*, Vol. 34 (July–August 1971), pp. 41–47.

McGinnies, E. *Social Behavior: A Functional Analysis.* Houghton Mifflin, 1970.

Mathis, B., J. Cotton, and L. Sechrest. *Psychological Foundations of Education.*
Academic Press, 1970.
Murray, R. "Behavioral Management Objectives." *Personnel Journal,* Vol. 52 (April
1973), pp. 304–306.
Odiorne, G. *Training by Objectives: An Economic Approach to Management Train-
ing.* Macmillan, 1970.

Questions for Discussion

1.   A sales manager desires to improve the quality of after-the-sales customer relations and service provided by her sales force. She can exhort sales representatives to pay more attention to this part of their job. Or she can change the commission system. But what might be done through performance measurement and feedback to achieve the desired result?

2.   Think of any policies or procedures that had an important effect on the way you carried out any job you have held. What advantages and disadvantages can you identify in the policies or procedures?

3.   In a large Eastern state, high-school teachers were once evaluated and rewarded by school administrators on the basis of their students' scores on statewide Regents' examinations. Discuss the advantages and disadvantages of such a measure.

4.   Edward Lawler has argued that secrecy in compensation administration is undesirable because it fosters guessing about pay rates, and such guessing is often inaccurate. Thus, secrecy can lead to perceived inequity where none exists. Also, since subordinates often underestimate the pay of their superiors, secrecy can in effect undermine subordinates' motivation to work hard for promotion. Others say that where pay is not, in fact, related to performance (and often it is not), it might be a good idea to keep pay rates secret. Discuss the advantages and disavantages of pay secrecy.

5.   What dysfunctional behaviors can you identify which are associated with the measurement practices used to evaluate the performance of students?

6.   If an affirmative control strategy (omission and positive reinforcement) is superior to an aversive control strategy (negative reinforcement and punishment) why does aversive control continue to be so prevalent?

7.   Since the effectiveness of what motivation theory calls *rewards* and behaviorism calls *reinforcement* depends upon the receiver and not the provider, how can managers be certain their efforts at control through administering rewards or reinforcements are correct?

8.   Critics of the use of behavior modification as a management tool say it won't work and shouldn't be used because it treats people like pigeons, it is manipulative, and it is simplistic. Discuss these criticisms.

Cases for Discussion

Hell Week

The Navy has a jet pilot training station at Kingsville, Texas. About one half of the Navy's fighter and attack pilots must complete their training there before receiving their Navy wings. These symbols of completion of flight training are earned after approximately 350 hours of training in the air and countless hours of ground school and military training.

The other half of the Navy's fighter and attack pilots complete their formal training at nearby Beeville, Texas. Other types of training, such as antisubmarine warfare training, take place at Naval Air Stations in Corpus Christi and New Iberia, Louisiana. The headquarters for advanced training is located on the Naval Air Station at Corpus Christi.

One Tuesday morning each month, the commanding officers from the eleven advanced training squadrons are invited (command performance) to attend the admiral's conference. This conference covers general subjects of interest to the groups and progress reports on the status of each squadron in the production of naval aviators, with heavy emphasis placed on the previous week's statistical figures, shown in graphic and chart format. Various formulas are used—some complicated and confusing—to depict the amount of training performed in relation to several factors, such as the type of flying weather, aircraft availability, student and instructor availability, the number of students who completed flight training during the period, and use of flight simulators, and other things. Running totals are depicted, as are comparisons with the same periods of previous years.

Searching and detailed questions are asked the commanding officers of the squadrons whose charts show discrepancies and shortcomings which are not self-explanatory. Questions on any phase of the squadron's operation are asked. Those which cannot be answered by the commanding officer cause him great embarrassment and discomfort in front of the admiral, who must sign his personal evaluation report. Very few questions are asked concerning squadron training of those squadrons which have high production figures for the week preceding the meeting. Therefore, it becomes important to have high figures for at least this one week of the month, and so avoid questions.

Since the formula by which the graphs and charts are made is known to the squadrons, steps can be taken to beat the system. The graphs having the most variables are the easiest to manipulate. Even the figures for the weather can be controlled, since this is a variable used to reflect the differences in squadron training—i.e., 100% good flying weather for an instrument training phase might only be 20% good flying weather for a fighter tactics flight. The weather percentage is turned in by each squadron training officer, based on his own best judgment.

The number of flying days per week, when weather is not a factor, can be adjusted by subtracting time taken to perform military drills or inspections. Since the official work week is a five-day period, weekend flying does not add flying days to the figures, although it does add flight hours. Thus, problems during the week can be remedied by working six or seven-day weeks. For example, a squadron having flown only 300 hours during the official five-day week might add 200 hours to the total by flying Saturday and Sunday, thus getting credit for 500 hours for the five days.

The number of aircraft available for flight is an easy one to adjust. Aircraft which are out of commission awaiting parts at the beginning of the period and not counted as available can be put into commission by exchanging parts from other grounded aircraft. Extra aircraft above the normal squadron allowance are also assigned as a pool of replacements, and these have to be flown periodically. Instructors can combine instruction flights with minor test flights. All of these methods make aircraft available which are not chargeable against the squadron's use figures, but which improve the reported figures.

Other measures used in determining the squadron's standing on the graphs and charts can also be manipulated, and are not illegal, unsafe, or unrecognized by the admiral's staff. In fact, some of the maneuvers are condoned and recommended. The loophole provided by the Saturday and Sunday flying, for example, was intentional. It provides an incentive to work overtime to get the job done.

The week preceding the monthly conference attended by the commanding officers is appropriately called "hell week" by some instructors. No matter how bad the weather is or what the aircraft and personnel situation might be, this week is usually a six or seven-day work week. The flight day starts before sunrise and ends late at night, and all sorts of finagling takes place to improve the statistical figures. Since none of the personnel wants to work Saturdays and Sundays when it can be avoided, all of them contribute their part in boosting the figures which have to be reported. The mechanics work harder with fewer breaks for personal business; aircraft availability seems automatically to be higher. The line personnel refuel the aircraft and make minor adjustments and repairs more quickly, and more flights are flown. Fewer flights are cancelled for any reason. Instructor and student availability are improved with less illness, and more of the "can do" spirit prevails. More students are graduated during this particular week. The weather is always less than 100%.

The statistics used to produce the charts and graphs assume great importance. Squadron personnel tend to concentrate on those items which are reported and pay less attention to unreported ones. It becomes more important in some minds to have aircraft reported up and flyable than to be certain that aircraft meet rigid quality control inspections. Since the quality control people work for the men responsible for high aircraft availability, a relaxation of quality standards sometimes results. Some of the best qualified inspectors are transferred to head production units, with less qualified inspectors assigned to quality control units.

Students are often held over from the previous week so that student completions during "hell week" will be higher. Scheduling is arranged so that students who could have been completed the previous Friday are actually completed early in the following week. This sometimes fouls up their travel arrangements and lengthens their time in the squadron. Other students will be rushed to completion at an unnecessarily fatiguing pace.

Questions

1. Why does finagling with the numbers occur?

2. What are the advantages and disadvantages of the system of measurement and evaluation described in this case?

Universal Office Supply Company

The Universal Office Supply Company has its offices and major retail store in Los Angeles. Its commercial sales force consisted of eleven men, who called on business firms in western states. Six of the salesmen operated out of the Los Angeles headquarters and worked the Southern California territory.

The company had acquired a large supply of file folders purchased at an exceptionally low price from a bankrupt competitor. Universal's president and sales manager decided to develop a special month-long sales promotion to unload them. Along with the normal quota commission system, he added during the month of May a five-percent override on folders sold, and also staged a contest. First, second, and third prizes were $100.00, $75.00, and $50.00.

Normally, all of the eleven men worked on commission, amounting to 10 percent of the total dollar value of sales. Each salesman had his own monthly quota, based on a combination of his past sales record for that month in each of the past three years and a projected increase reflecting long-term trends. Normally, the salesmen met their quotas, each earning approximately $1000 per month.

After the contest ended, one salesman examined the daily sales and commission records for the month of May for the six salesmen working out of the Los Angeles office. He plotted the sales of folders per day for the three salesmen who finished highest, and the three who finished lowest in the file folder sales contest. Exhibit 1 shows what happened.

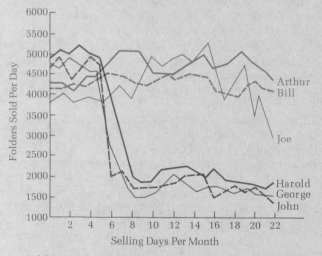

Exhibit 1   File Folder Sales Per Day: Contest Winners and Losers

The salesman reported: "John, Harold, and I (George) get together every Friday afternoon for a drink after work. At the end of the first week I mentioned to the others that I thought my total sales were down. Harold said he was not pushing the special any more because it took too much time to sell and his other products would suffer. All three of us decided to stop pushing the folder special and return to our normal sales method and program, which put greater emphasis on more expensive items during customer contacts."

Indeed, as Exhibit 2 shows, those salesmen most responsive to the contest had lower sales, brought less revenue to the company, and less commission to themselves.

As management, through its promotional contest, pushed the sale of file folders, time and sales effort were focused on a comparatively unprofitable line. Sales of the other merchandise (including many higher-priced items) were neglected, and this neglect brought down the total sales and commissions. In fact, the only real success came from ignoring the contest.

Exhibit 2   Percentage of Monthly Sales Quota: Contest Winners and Losers

Top Three in Special Sale	Percent of Monthly Sales Quota	Bottom Three in Special Sale	Percent of Monthly Sales Quota
Arthur	82	Harold	114
Bill	80	George	107
Joe	78	John	106

Question

Discuss the operation of control in this case.

Part Three

Managerial Behavior

LEADERSHIP

CONFLICT AND CONFLICT MANAGEMENT

ORGANIZATION DEVELOPMENT

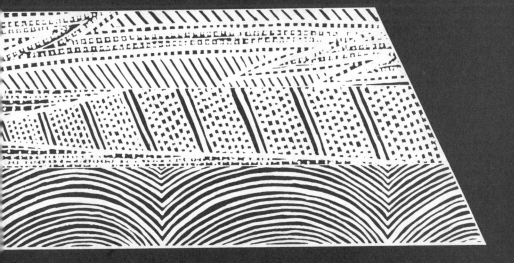

Leadership

The purpose of this chapter is to review five approaches which have been developed in the social sciences to answer a question which has intrigued both managers and social scientists for many years. That question is: What makes a good leader?

Looking back some years, the first answer to that question was given by what is now called the "trait approach" to leadership. It held that leaders possess certain personality characteristics that enable them to assume positions of leadership. This seemed valid for a time. But it soon became recognized that leaders could always be found who did not have those characteristics. The next group to approach the question therefore, said, "Let's stop searching for traits of a leader and concentrate on the *behavior* of a leader, actions that can be seen and tested, rather than speculated about." The behavioral school proceeded to formulate some useful notions about what leaders do, as contrasted with what leaders are. But again the answer proved elusive. Many instances were found where a given leader simply did not behave in the standard way postulated in the research.

About this time, the pendulum swung to an opposite notion: It is not what a leader is, or how a leader behaves, which determines effectiveness. Rather, it is the *situation* a leader is in that determines what leaders are and how they behave. This "situational" or "contingency" school has much to offer in understanding the leadership phenomena. Three approaches which follow this philosophy stand out in the literature. The first was formulated by Fiedler. It emphasizes two kinds of leader behavior, each of which is appropriate under certain conditions. The second, path-goal theory, focuses on the way subordinates' minds interpret the actions of a leader. It builds on the expectancy theory of motivation discussed in Chapter 1. The third approach, which we call "more complex models of leadership," analyzes a wide variety of forces at work in a given department or organization, showing how those forces ultimately determine which form of leadership is best in a particular situation.

This chapter and its accompanying readings will explain each of these approaches in some detail. Though some are older and some are new, and though they vary in the way they "see" a leader's behavior, all have some use to the practicing manager. In addition, one can see how one school of thought often builds upon another, retaining some of its features and discarding others.

LEADERSHIP TRAITS AND LEADERSHIP BEHAVIORS

In the two sections which follow, we will review two schools of thought about what determines who is a leader (what a leader is like), and what kinds of actions (behavior) a leader might engage in that distinguish him or her from other individuals.

The first of these questions has been addressed by researchers who pursue a *trait approach to leadership.* They assume that leaders are different from other people in the population, and that there must be some deeper personality traits which cause some people to become leaders in the first place and to be successful enough to continue in leadership positions.

The second question focuses not on personality traits, but on the kinds of actions or behaviors that leaders engage in. We might term this the *behavioral approach to leadership*. Like the trait approach, the behavioral approach holds that because leaders carry out certain kinds of actions, they are distinguishable from other individuals in the population. Each of these schools of thought will be examined separately.

Do Leaders Have Certain Traits?

The question of why some people become leaders and remain leaders has been the subject of considerable research. Many people have believed that certain individuals must have specific qualifications which enable them to "rise above the population," to assume responsibilities not everyone can execute, and therefore become leaders. This philosophy dominated the behavioral sciences until about 1947, during which time many sociologists and psychologists searched for the traits that differentiate leaders from other people.

In a massive review of the literature on leadership, Stogdill (1974) studied 124 research projects carried out between 1904 and 1947, and another 163 projects carried out between 1948 and 1970. Exhibit 10.1 shows certain personality traits which these studies stress as important for success in leadership. In more formal terms, the researchers measured the existence of a given trait among a group of people in leadership positions and among another group of people not in leadership positions. There was a positive correlation between those in leadership positions and the traits listed. The figures to the right in Exhibit 10.1 show the number of research studies which found such a positive correlation.

One must exercise some care in interpreting this data. In the first place, the list is not complete. Stogdill grouped many characteristics postulated by different researchers into a list of 34 characteristics. This table presents only those for which there is most evidence (the greatest number of studies which seem to prove that the characteristic is a leadership trait). Second, the number of studies in the right column represents not "which trait is most important for a leader" but which ones were most often investigated by psychologists. Therefore, the hypotheses of the researchers, representing their own interests, would influence the number of "proofs."

A third limitation of this research is that researchers since 1948 have pointed out that leaders who are successful in one situation, say, a railroad labor crew, may not be successful in another situation, a branch bank or an air force squadron. This school of thought, the situation school (which will be treated in more detail later), often makes statements that seem to say that the trait approach is virtually worthless. What it takes to be a leader is determined by the situation surrounding the leader, not found within the leader.

The final limitation to this research is that it is sometimes contradictory. One researcher will find a trait which is predicted to be found in all leaders, while another researcher, using the same methodology, will find that certain

	Number of Studies
Fluency of speech	28
Ascendance, dominance	42
Knowledge	23
Emotional balance, control	25
Originality, creativity	20
Self confidence	45
Achievement drive, desire to excel	28
Drive for responsibility	29
Task orientation (interest in work)	19
Sociability, interpersonal skills	49
Participation in social exchange	29

leaders do not possess the specific characteristic. For example, leaders in 42 studies were found to possess traits of ascendance or dominance. In six other studies, the leader did *not* possess this characteristic. Though leaders in 25 studies showed high measures of emotional balance and control, leaders in 8 studies did *not* seem to differ from other people on this dimension.

For those interested in applying knowledge about leadership to practical managerial affairs, it is nevertheless worthwhile to review the trait approach. Researchers, like almost every other group of people, go through stages in which they are interested in one subject. When that subject is exhausted, it tends to become "old hat." It is no longer the "in" thing to carry out research on universal leader traits. We shall see that the critics of the trait approach do indeed have some valid criticisms. But the complete denial of any traits could be an overcorrection. A more realistic attitude for the practicing executive might well be that suggested by Stogdill (1974, pp. 81–82), one of the most distinguished scholars in the field of leadership:

> The leader is characterized by a strong drive for responsibility and task completion, vigor and persistence in pursuit of goals, venturesomeness and originality in problem solving, drive to exercise initiative in social situations, self-confidence and sense of personal identity, willingness to accept consequences of decision and action, readiness to absorb interpersonal stress, willingness to tolerate frustration and delay, ability to influence other persons' behavior, and capacity to structure social interaction systems to the purpose at hand.

It can be concluded that the clusters of characteristics listed above differentiate (1) leaders from followers, (2) effective from ineffective leaders, and (3) higher echelon from lower echelon leaders. In other words, different strata of leaders and followers can be described in terms of the extent to which they exhibit some of the characteristics. . . .

The characteristics, considered singly, hold little diagnostic or predictive significance. In combination, it would appear that they interact to generate personality dynamics advantageous to the person seeking the responsibilities of leadership. The conclusion that personality is a factor in leadership differentiation does not represent a return to the trait approach. It does represent a sensible modification of the extreme situationist point of view. The *trait approach* tended to treat personality variables in an atomistic fashion, suggesting that each trait acted singly to determine leadership effects. The *situationist approach*, on the other hand, denied the influences of individual differences, attributing all variance between persons to fortuitous demands of the environment.

The element of chance would appear to play a part in the rise of individual leaders. A given leader may be able to rise to the top of the hierarchy in competition with one group of peers, whereas he might be unable to do so in another group of peers. Assuming potentiality for leadership, an individual's upward mobility would seem to depend to a considerable degree upon his being at the right place at the right time.

Finally, it should be noted that to a very large extent our conceptions of characteristics of leadership are culturally determined. According to Frankfort et al. (1949), the ancient Egyptians attributed three qualities of divinity to their king. They said of him, "Authoritative utterance is in thy mouth, perception is in thy heart, and thy tongue is the shrine of justice." The form of this statement would suggest that the Egyptians were demanding of their leader the qualities of authority, discrimination, and just behavior. Sarachek (1968) made an analysis of Greek concepts of leadership, as exemplified by different leaders in Homer's *Iliad*. Four aspects were identified: (1) justice and judgment—Agamemnon; (2) wisdom and counsel—Nestor; (3) shrewdness and cunning—Odysseus; and (4) valor and action—Achilles. All these qualities were admired by the Greeks. Shrewdness and cunning are not as highly regarded in our contemporary society as they once were. Thus, the patterns of behavior regarded as acceptable in leaders differ from time to time and from one culture to another.*

Do Leaders Act or Behave in Certain Ways? The Ohio State Studies

Because of the difficulties encountered by the personality trait approach to leadership, social scientists in the early 1950s began to concentrate on leader behavior—what a leader *does*—rather than on leader personalities—what a leader *is*. We shall see that this emphasis on behavior rather than traits has carried through many subschools of thought right up to the present. At this point, there are two reasons for stopping to look at one of the earlier theories of leader behavior, that developed by a group of researchers at The Ohio State University and popularly known as the Ohio State Studies.

One reason for studying this model of leader behavior is that it figures prominently in one of the later leadership explanations, the path-goal theory.

The other is that this was the first description of leader behavior that made a clear distinction between the *technical* actions of a leader and the *human actions* of a leader. Put in loose terms, part of a leader's activities have to do with *things* and another set of activities have to do with *people*. This distinction, too, has carried through to many later theories of leadership, which use terms like "task-oriented" behavior versus "people-oriented" behavior.

Like the earlier trait theorists, the Ohio State group hypothesized that if you observe a group of leaders, and compare them to another observed group of nonleaders, the former would differ from the latter; but the observations and measurements would be of leader *behavior* rather than leader *traits*. Perhaps the greatest contribution of the Ohio State work was to bring some order and simplicity out of a great deal of confusion among those engaged in describing leader behavior. Different researchers had generated a list of literally hundreds of different actions. If anyone asked, "How does a leader behave?" he or she would be confronted with many overlapping, but similar actions. By using a statistical technique called factor analysis, the researchers were able to sift through the many terms and come up with a much shorter list. The most widely accepted classification turned out to be a simple distinction between two kinds of leadership actions. One was called *initiation of structure* and the other *consideration* (Fleishman, Harris, and Burtt, 1955; Stogdill and Coons, 1957).

By initiation of structure they meant a variety of actions taken by the leader to "get the work out." Leaders make plans or formulate procedures, for example. They may set standards, such as the expectation that a typist will type four pages of error-free manuscript per hour (notice the quantity, time and quality standards). They communicate to subordinates various messages about the work to be done: "The customers are waiting in line to have savings deposits entered into their passbooks," or, "We are behind schedule in getting the advertising copy mailed to the newspaper this week." They watch how production is going and compare actual production with the standard, making certain control decisions: "I know the labor cost in the electrical department is above standard this month." These kinds of actions, whether planning work, directing work, or controlling work, are all, according to the Ohio State classification, actions of initiating structure.

By consideration is meant any action which the leader takes to perceive the human needs of subordinates and to support subordinates in their own attempts to satisfy their needs. It may be a matter of adjusting work schedules to accommodate one group of employees, or of helping a person obtain necessary money or materials from other departments. It may mean understanding and empathizing with an employee who has a problem at home, away from work. In either case, this means an honest and concerned attempt to be considerate. It does not mean, as one writer put it, simply a friendly pat on the back. Further, it always means a degree of open communication. Without this, it would be impossible for the leader to think realistically about what other people want and need.

One of the main uses to be made of these definitions by the practicing manager is to connect them with effective leadership. Stated bluntly, if a leader hopes to increase the productivity of a group of subordinates, or if one hopes to increase the morale, loyalty, and satisfaction of subordinates, what does social science research tell him or her to do—act in an initiating style or a considerate style? Which style is more likely to prove better if judged by the two dimensions of effectiveness: productivity, and satisfaction of subordinates?

Research to date suggests that productivity of individuals and work groups is higher when the leader initiates structure than if the leader is lacking in this kind of behavior. In other words, the leader who devotes time to planning, clarifying jobs to be done, and emphasizing the need to get work out, is more effective in actually getting work out than the one who for some reason neglects these kinds of actions. This is not too surprising. If you have ever taken a course with a teacher who fails to clarify what class assignments are, or who is unclear about how the grading system works, you can see that it would be difficult for the class to perform meaningful work.

Whether or not considerate behavior increases or decreases productivity is unclear, at least so far as existing research is concerned. The evidence is contradictory. A number of studies have found that productivity increases with such leadership behavior. On the other hand, an equally impressive number of studies have found either no effect of this leadership style on productivity, or a negative effect. Evidence presented in Chapter 6 strongly suggests that subordinates' reactions depend to a great degree on the kind of task, or job to be done. If there is a well known and stable job, and if the rules of the game (the "structure") are clearly spelled out, employees might well resent a lot of added communications or directions ("initiations") passed down by the leader. They do, however, expect direction on changes in production schedules, orders, and the like.

Turning next to the satisfaction, loyalty, and feelings of subordinates, the evidence shows that initiation of structure is received differently by different people working in different situations. For example, a number of studies have shown that structure initiating actions are often viewed negatively by unskilled or semiskilled workers (Filley, House, and Kerr, 1976). According to one authority, "Employees in large groups have been found either to prefer a leader who initiates structure over a leader who shows no interest in getting work out, or at least to dislike the directive leadership less than employees in small groups" (House, 1971). This indicates that the larger the organization becomes, the more human beings employed in it feel a need for some sort of stability, order, and direction.

The research evidence showing how considerate behavior by the leader affects employee satisfaction is much clearer than in the case of how this behavior affects productivity. All of the studies which have been done show that considerate behavior almost always produces a more satisfied group of employees. This, too, is not surprising.

Where does this leave us with regard to the most effective kind of leader behavior? In summary, initiating structure seems to result in productivity, while consideration seems to result in more satisfied employees. In some happy situations (e.g., large organizations as opposed to small groups, and organizations with a stable technology) the leader may be able to have cake and eat it too—initiation of structure may be effective in both respects.

The reader may well ask whether the leader should not simply strive to do both, to be a good planner and director at the same time he or she takes a lot of considerate actions in day-to-day operations. For some reason, the Ohio State group assumed that these were two different kinds of behavior, and that leaders did not often excel at both. Perhaps they, like the early researchers at the University of Michigan, reasoned that the type of human relationships involved in initiating directions was not the same as the kind involved in identifying with employees as persons, and that a given leader tends to behave more in one direction than the other. The Michigan group labeled these two the "autocratic" leader and the "participative" leader, terms which hardly advanced the understanding of leadership because they raised such emotive, as contrasted with objective or realistic, images. We shall see that a later theory, Fiedler's contingency model, also assumes that a given leader tends to be either "task-motivated" or "relationship-oriented."

It remained for two other schools of thought—contingency theory and path-goal theory—to explain that *neither* type of leader is *more* effective. These viewpoints hold that the type of leadership style that will be effective for productivity and employee satisfaction is dependent not on a simplistic blending of initiation and consideration, but on a more complex analysis of the particular situation surrounding the work organization (both leader and followers).

In addition, the path-goal model helps considerably to show how initiating structure is related to consideration for needs of members, rather than that these are two somewhat discrete or separate acts.

LEADERS AND SITUATIONS

In this and the following sections we will review several recent approaches to the study of leadership, which hold that the leadership style used by a given individual is to a large extent dependent upon the kind of situation the leader finds himself or herself in. These are the contingency model, developed by Fiedler and his associates (see Fiedler, 1965, 1967, 1974, and 1976; and Fiedler and Chemers, 1974); the path-goal model, which uses the expectancy theory of motivation as its starting point (see Evans, 1968, 1970(a), 1970(b), and 1974; Georgopoulos, Mahoney, and Jones, 1957; House, 1971, and House and Mitchell, 1974); and two decision-making models, developed by Tannenbaum and Schmidt and by Vroom and his associates (see Tannenbaum and Schmidt, 1973; Vroom, 1957, 1973, 1974, 1976; Vroom and Jago, 1974; and Vroom and Yetton, 1973).

Fiedler's Contingency Model

Fiedler's theory of leadership can be traced to experiments and field studies which began at the University of Illinois in 1951. Since then, a large number of research projects have uncovered the performance and leadership of high school basketball teams, air force combat crews, chemical research departments, supermarkets, hospital wards, public health teams, cadets at West Point on maneuvers, and consumer cooperatives. Over 800 studies were completed from 1951 to 1963. Other studies have continued during the 1960s and 1970s.

One characteristic of all of these studies which should be of interest to practicing managers is the criteria used to measure leader effectiveness. A number of approaches have assumed that satisfied, contented subordinates will be more productive; they treat leadership behavior as an independent variable which in turn causes satisfaction. Satisfaction is then an intervening variable which causes productivity. These studies therefore measured only the human satisfaction generated by the leader, and simply assumed that productivity would follow. Fiedler, by contrast, has always measured productivity directly. Basketball teams were measured in number of games won in league competition, air force bomber crews were measured in the accuracy of bombing, tank crews were measured on the time-in-seconds to hit a target, and consumer retail companies were measured on their profit on investment.

Types of leadership styles.   Given these criteria of effective leadership, Fiedler adopted a notion of different kinds of leader behavior similar to that advanced earlier by the Ohio State group. Some leaders are *task-motivated:* They "tell people what to do and how to do it" (1965). This person's major goal is "the accomplishment of some tangible evidence of his or her worth." Satisfaction comes "from the task itself and from knowing that he or she has done well" (1974). This does not mean that the task-motivated leader has no regard whatsoever for other human beings, or for subordinates. Though this leader's primary goal is accomplishment, Fiedler postulates a secondary goal for this type of person, that of concern for subordinates' feelings and satisfactions. Just as Maslow saw a hierarchy of needs (Chapter 1), Fiedler believes that the task-motivated leader also has a hierarchy. "When he or she has considerable control and influence and knows, therefore, the task will get done, he or she will relax and be concerned for the satisfactions and feelings of subordinates" (1974, p. 66).

The second type of leader is the *relationship-motivated* individual. This leader is inclined to "share leadership responsibilities with group members and involve them in the planning and execution of the task" (1965). In other words, this person "primarily seeks to maintain good interpersonal relationships with co-workers. These basic goals become very apparent in uncertain and anxiety provoking situations. . . . Under these conditions this individual will seek out others and solicit their support. However, under conditions in which he or she feels quite secure and relaxed — because this individual has achieved the major goals of having close relations with subordinates — he or she will seek the esteem and admiration of others. In a leadership situation where task performance results in esteem and admiration from superiors, this leader will tend to concentrate on behaving in a task-relevant manner." The relationship-motivated leader, too, has primary and secondary goals. In Maslow's terms, the need for prestige and status (esteem of others) comes into play only when one has satisfied the need for close personal relationships.

The way one measures each person's style, by the "LPC Score," is explained in the reading by Fiedler at the end of this chapter.

Favorable and unfavorable situations.   While leader personality is one factor that determines effectiveness, the other factor is the situation in the particular department, hospital, or military unit. "Situation" is a vague and ambiguous term. Some way must be found to describe it more concretely. Fiedler does this by visualizing eight types of work group situations, varying in degree as to how favorable each is to the leader when he or she attempts to have influence on the group. More simply, in some situations it is easier for leaders to exercise influence, to control behavior of others, and to know (predict) what they can or cannot do, than in others. These eight situations are seen by counting the different squares across the bottom of Exhibit 10.2.

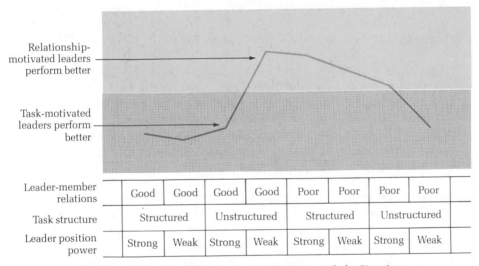

Leader-member relations	Good	Good	Good	Good	Poor	Poor	Poor	Poor	
Task structure	Structured		Unstructured		Structured		Unstructured		
Leader position power	Strong	Weak	Strong	Weak	Strong	Weak	Strong	Weak	

Exhibit 10.2   How the Style of Effective Leadership Varies with the Situation.

Source: Modified from Fiedler, 1965, with the permission of the *Harvard Business Review*.

How do we recognize favorable, unfavorable, or moderately unfavorable situations? By looking at three things:

1. Leader-member relations. Do members and leader have good relations of mutual respect? If so, the situation is favorable; if not, it is unfavorable.
2. Task structure. Is the job to be done one that is known, routine, and standard, or is it some new job that has never been done before? If known and standard, the situation is favorable because the leader can make judgments about how it should be done. If it is totally novel, it would be difficult for the leader to make judgments any better than anyone else.
3. Leader position power. Is the leader in a clear position of power and author-

ity, with either the backing of higher authority or the legitimate deference from those below, or both? If so, the situation is favorable for influencing the group. If not, the situation is unfavorable.

To illustrate how these affect the favorableness of the situation, take a case where the leader is, for whatever reason, well liked. The job to be done is clearly laid out, and the leader has recognized authority to give directions. This is the case at the extreme left of Fiedler's eight types of situations (Exhibit 10.2). An example might be the pilot of an airplane. "We neither expect nor want the trusted air-line pilot to turn to his crew and ask, 'What do you think we ought to check before takeoff?'" (1965).

At the other extreme, think of a group of volunteer citizens which is organized to advise the mayor what to do about crime increases in the city. Though the mayor appoints the chairperson, he or she has no authority to decide what should be done. Nor is there a clear idea of who does what in the committee (the task is nebulous, ambiguous, or "new" to the group and to the leader). If the leader also happens not to be liked by the group, we have an extremely unfavorable situation (the eighth square to the right on Fiedler's chart).

This same leadership situation can be transformed to one that is moderately favorable for the leader (fourth square from the left) if the same task and the same authority position of the leader are maintained, but for some reason or another the leader and followers have good relations, i.e., they like each other. It will be even more favorable if the mayor assigns to some official the authority to recommend to the mayor a policy of crime prevention, even if the task is still ambiguous (third square from the left).

When do task-motivated leaders perform best? We are now ready to understand the most important findings from this research. From all studies done to date, Fiedler and his followers have found that groups that are led by task-motivated leaders outperform those who are relationship-motivated, *under two types of conditions:* when the situation is very favorable for the leader to exert influence, and when it is very unfavorable for the leader to exert influence. The captain of a professional football team whose teammates know clearly their movements on a play (have a structured task), who is expected to have legitimate authority to call the play (has authority and power), and who has good relations with his teammates, is in a very favorable situation. We can predict that the team will win more games if the capitain is task-motivated than if we replace him with a well-liked relationship-motivated captain.

At the other extreme, imagine a group of high school seniors gathered together at a summer camp to play an afternoon of football. The task is unstructured, since none are specialists, they do not know the same standard plays, and they have their own ideas of what to do. The captain of the team is chosen because he played varsity football, but he has no official authority. Nor, as the game progresses, is he particularly well liked. The Fiedler model would predict that in this situation (with poor leader-member relations, an unstructured task, and no formal authority), this task-oriented leader's team would win over an identical opponent if it were headed by a relationship-motivated leader!

When do relationship-motivated leaders perform best? Referring again to Exhibit 10.2, groups headed by relationship-oriented leaders perform best when the situation is either moderately favorable or moderately unfavorable. They do not perform best under conditions that are extreme on either end of the continuum. Here is an example of the moderately unfavorable situation (square five, counting from the left). Imagine a professional football team with clear and structured tasks. Each player, tackle and guard alike, knows the rules, his own job, and the various plays that govern how the team operates as a unit. The leader's position has authority because coaches and owners have appointed him and supported his decisions. But relations between captain and players are not particularly good. Can you predict whether this team, led by a task-oriented leader, will win against another team which is exactly like it except that it has a relationship-oriented leader?

Implications for managerial action. It is Fiedler's belief that when it comes to basic personality tendencies such as those described by "task-motivated" or "relationship-motivated," individuals do not change very easily. "We will be better served by training our leaders in how to change their leadership situations than in how to change their personalities" (1976, p. 16). "The leadership situation is an arena in which a leader must satisfy his or her own needs as well as the needs of the organization. Where a leader's and an organization's needs are incompatible, the leader's needs are apt to take precedence" (1976, p. 8).

There seem to be three things which managers might do to improve productivity by increasing the "fit" between a leader's own personality and the type of leader called for in a given situation. The most obvious way is by selection of leaders to fill certain situations. Higher management might use this model as a tool to try to predict what kind of person to hire as Chicago Sales Manager, Milwaukee Plant Manager, or New York Advertising Manager.

There is one difficulty with this. Fiedler believes that he has found evidence that the most important of the three situational variables is leader-member relations, the next important is the structure of the task, and the least important is formal authority. In other words, relations carry more weight than authority in determining the total favorableness of a situation. "It is, for instance, quite possible for a person of low rank to lead a group of higher ranking persons in a structured task—as is done when junior officers conduct some standard parts of the training program for medical officers who enter the army. But it is not so easy for a disrespected manager to lead a creative, policy-formulating session well, even if he or she is the senior executive present" (1965).

Because it is difficult to predict *scientifically* whether a given leader will be liked by subordinates, and vice versa, Fiedler can hardly advocate selection of leaders as a managerial tool. The model may well aid in selecting people for certain positions, however, if the executive making this decision can predict from first hand *judgment* the kind of person who would be liked in the situation.

Fiedler's other reason for not advocating use of this analysis for selecting and hiring is because of the cost involved. The supply of leadership talent is limited, and companies should concentrate on some way of applying the model which takes advantage of the talents of all people, rather than rejecting some people because they don't fit a particular position (1965).

For these two reasons, Fiedler sees two quite different applications which offer more promise. First, higher managers might look at the situations that face subordinate middle-level managers and try to adjust the *situation to the person* rather than hire a *person to fit the situation.* Management can vary the amount of formal authority delegated to a given leadership position. Or, the degree of structure in a position of Chicago Sales Manager can be varied if higher management itself spells out very broad goals (little structure) versus more detailed goals and specifications of "how to do it" (1965).

A final application is through leader training. But we must recognize that this is a special type of training. It is not the kind described in Chapter 12, which attempts, through such means as sensitivity training and confrontation meetings, to change leaders' perceptions about themselves or other people. Rather, it is training to analyze the *situation* in the leaders' departments, using the model described above, in the hope that the leaders themselves can adjust the situation around them to fit their own behavioral tendencies (1974).

PATH-GOAL THEORIES OF LEADERSHIP

The behavioral approach to leadership concentrated on the effects of two kinds of behavior on *productivity* and on the *feelings of satisfaction* this behavior produces in subordinates. About 1957, however, certain psychologists (Evans, 1968; Georgopoulos, Mahoney, and Jones, 1957; Vroom, 1959) began to look at the cognitive or reasoning processes subordinates might go through in response to the behavior of leaders. This school of thought holds that individuals act to a large extent on a rational (to them) basis, that they *pursue* or *devote effort to* certain goals in preference to others because these "pay off" ultimately in certain things highly valued by the individual.

A Brief Review of Expectancy Theory

Before studying the path-goal theory of leadership, it would be a good idea to have firmly in mind the expectancy theory of motivation on which the path-goal theories are based. Expectancy theory, as you remember, was examined in Chapter 1; if time permits, one would do well to go back to that chapter and review its central arguments. Here, we can only summarize it in briefest terms:

1. Human beings are reasonable—at least from their point of view. A person is motivated to perform a certain action because he or she predicts (expects) that the action will lead to pleasant payoffs or avoid painful payoffs.
2. In Chapter 1, we noted that there are two kinds of payoffs. *Basic payoffs* satisfy some basic need—physiological, security, social needs and friendship, self-esteem, esteem of others, and self-actualization. *Instrumental payoffs* may be viewed as rewards (such as money, transfer to a more satisfying job, a promotion, etc.) which lead to (are instrumental for) attainment of basic payoffs. In path-goal theories of leadership, these instrumental payoffs, and the way they relate to basic payoffs, are the *paths* to the *goal* of need-fulfillment.
3. All payoffs have different weights or values in a person's mind. Security may be more valued than friendship. Friendship may be more valued than the esteem of large numbers of people. Expectancy theorists have borrowed the term "valences" from atomic physicists to use in place of "weights," indicating that they are dynamic and active in the individual's mind.
4. Human beings make rough, subjective estimates of the payoffs, the valences attached to each payoff, and the probability that payoffs will follow some action or effort. They will then decide upon an action or make the effort which will yield the greatest expected payoff.

We shall now see that this kind of behavior has an important bearing on how leaders should behave. In briefest terms, leaders should help set instrumental payoffs in the form of incentives (incentives become rewards if they actually happen) *and* help subordinates see the paths they might take to attain their basic goals (and, not incidentally, the goals of the organization).

Path-Goal Leadership Theory: Evans' Model

The crucial reason for studying expectancy theory first, and then asking how it affects leadership behavior, is that the former tells us the *key mental processes* in the minds of subordinates which must be influenced *if managers are to influence the motivation of their subordinates.* Vroom (1959) suggested this in his original work: "In order for participative leadership to affect motivation for effective performance, it would not only have to be a source of satisfaction, but would also have to affect the probability that an individual would be able to attain further satisfaction from performing well in his job. In other words, the participative process would have to involve not only goal attainment, but also goal setting." Thus, participation would have to help people know the payoffs available *and* the probabilities that a given effort would actually produce these payoffs.

Evans (1968, 1970a) picked up this theme in developing his path-goal theory of leadership. The two leader behaviors conceptualized earlier in the Ohio State studies were taken to be the two principal ways leaders "lead"— by initiating structure and by acting considerately for the needs and welfare of subordinates. Evans measured the performance ratings of subordinate groups and found that three kinds of leader actions, if they are all present, will increase the productivity of a work group. *If* the leader acts in a supportive (considerate) way, *and* provides initiation of structure in a way that clarifies the paths people can use to achieve their goals (the instrumental payoffs and the basic need payoffs), *and* at the same time clearly lets people know that these payoffs are contingent on their performing in a certain way—then motivation and productivity will *both* increase. Notice that the first of these "ifs" may be *both* a direct (basic) payoff and a path (instrumental) to other basic payoffs. The second clarifies what the payoffs are. The third takes care of the expectancies and instrumentalities: They let a person know that the probability is very high that the rewards in the path-goal map will in fact materialize (1970a) (see Exhibit 10.3).

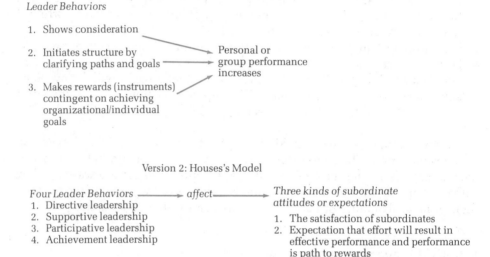

Version 1: Evans' Model

Leader Behaviors

1. Shows consideration

2. Initiates structure by clarifying paths and goals ⟶ Personal or group performance increases

3. Makes rewards (instruments) contingent on achieving organizational/individual goals

Version 2: Houses's Model

Four Leader Behaviors ⟶ *affect* ⟶ Three kinds of subordinate attitudes or expectations
1. Directive leadership
2. Supportive leadership
3. Participative leadership
4. Achievement leadership

1. The satisfaction of subordinates
2. Expectation that effort will result in effective performance and performance is path to rewards
3. Subordinates' acceptance of the leader

Exhibit 10.3   Two Versions of Path-Goal Leadership Theory

Other authors have stressed that many times managers do not tie rewards to performance, or attainment, of intermediate, instrumental goals. For example, in a department where there are no clear standards of output, path-goal theory suggests that expectations and probabilities cannot be calculated accurately by subordinates. It also suggests that if instrumental rewards like pay are given out regardless of performance, subordinates can calculate the probabilities involved and pay will not be a motivating factor. Leaders should make the probabilities clear, and then be consistent in rewarding people.

Path-Goal Leadership: House's Model

House (1971) extended this theory to include four types of leader behavior, rather than the two types proposed by Evans. These are explained more fully in the attached reading by House and Mitchell (1974). According to this version, leadership is not a simple matter of initiating structure (paths, rewards) and engaging in considerate acts toward subordinates. Rather, there are four distinct types of leadership (1974, p. 83). The *directive* leader "lets subordinates know what is expected of them, gives specific guidance as to what should be done and how it should be done, makes his or her part in the group understood, schedules work to be done, maintains definite standards of performance and asks that group members follow standard rules and regulations." A *supportive* leader "shows concern for the status, well-being and needs of subordinates. Such a leader does little things to make the work more pleasant, treats members as equals and is friendly and approachable." A *participative* leader "consults with subordinates, solicits their suggestions and takes these suggestions seriously into consideration before making a decision." Finally, an *achievement-oriented* leader "sets challenging goals, expects subordinates to perform at their highest level, continuously seeks improvement in performance and shows a high degree of confidence that the subordinates will assume responsibility, put forth effort and accomplish challenging goals. This kind of leader constantly emphasizes excellence in performance and simultaneously displays confidence that subordinates will meet high standards of excellence." We can see that the achievement-oriented leader is performing in a way that might well arouse the achievement motive in subordinates, as explained in Chapter 1.

What are the most important effects of these different types of leadership styles? According to this view, there are three (see Exhibit 10.3). Depending on whether the leader acts in a directive, supportive, participative, or achievement-oriented style will determine whether or not subordinates feel satisfaction with their work; whether they can "see" and "predict" that their efforts will in fact lead to instrumental performance goals; and whether these performance goals will in fact lead to satisfying the basic needs which each human being is pursuing.

At this point the path-goal model implies (though the authors are not always too clear on this point) that instrumental goals are the work standards, procedures, policies, and job descriptions of the organization. In our example in Chapter 1, it was a certain productivity on the examination (a correct answer) with a payoff of an A or a B. In a manufacturing plant, this may be a certain number of parts produced per day, a certain standard of daily attendance without being absent, and the like.

Some Contingencies for Using the Path-Goal Models

Social scientists have been confronted with one difficulty in trying to use the methods of physical science (physics, chemistry) in real life situations. The (physical) scientific method dictates that an investigator must study the relationship between two variables, one of which (the independent variable) *causes* the other (the dependent variable). Cast in these terms, leadership researchers would be able to make a "law" of leadership which says that if one kind of leader behavior (for example, participative two-way decision-making) is used, it will cause subordinates to accept the leader, to feel satisfied with his or her behavior, and to produce more. This was precisely what the early University of Michigan studies tried to prove. But it never did get proved, because no two situations were alike. One researcher would find that participative supervision caused high morale and high productivity, but another might duplicate the experiment and find either neutral effects or contradictory effects.

To get out of this type of bind, some social scientists have developed what they call "contingency factors."

One of the first to call attention to these factors was Vroom (1959), who found that the *personality of the subordinate,* in the form of one person's high need for independence as contrasted with another person's low need for independence, "moderated" the effects of participative management. Thus, some people would feel satisfied with participative leaders while others would feel dissatisfied.

In their version of path-goal theory, House and Mitchell focus on two characteristics of the situation which may interfere with any real predictive laws about how a leader should behave in all situations. Some people are "internals," whose life-experiences have taught them that much of what happens to them occurs because of their own active control. They believe that people and things around them are always responding to their influence. These people respond well to participative management. They accept the leader who acts this way. They feel personally satisfied when he or she acts this way. They put high probabilities (expectancies, instrumentalities) on what will happen if they get motivated and exert effort, because they believe they can influence events. For other subordinates, who are "externals"—whose life-experiences have taught them that many events occur through luck or chance (or perhaps through playing politics instead of honest path- and goal-setting)—the participatory aspects of path-goal theory will not work. Therefore, when leaders try to use path-goal behavior as a motivating style, they should be well aware that it depends on *whom* they are facing as subordinates as to whether the predictions of the theorists will actually come true in a given situation.

Ability is another contingency. It will do no good for a leader to try to use path-goal behavior with people who feel that their own ability to carry out the instrumental performances is not adequate. A football coach at Michigan State University would find that path-goal actions may not be received well by a person who believes that his own skills, physique, and abilities are suited to a small high school but not a Big Ten university. Conversely, if a person's abilities are thought to be very high relative to the task required, that person might resent (rather than respond favorably to) direction and guidance behavior. The conductor of the Boston Symphony, if invited to conduct the London Philharmonic, would resent extensive clarification of paths to goals in conducting Tchaikovsky's Second Piano Concerto!

These two contingency factors have to do with the characteristics of subordinates—their personalities. Other contingencies have to do with the nature of the task, the nature of the formal authority system, and the nature of the primary work group. Each may have some moderating effect on whether path-goal leadership styles are workable in a given situation. They are discussed in the attached readings.

The comments already made about the use of contingency factors cue the reader as to how difficult it is to develop a realistic theory or model of effective leadership. The social scientist is caught in a dilemma between trying to abstract from the world of reality (by keeping the number of variables small) yet trying also to include the many rich forces in the world of reality that are influencing the satisfaction and productivity of a work group. These many forces are a "can of worms" which theorists try to untangle by looking at only a few "worms" at a time. Using the methods of physical science, they cannot include the whole situation.

And yet, if theories are going to get closer to reality, some way must be found to take into account more and more things going on around a leader, things *in addition to* the leader's behavior which *also* affect morale and productivity.

Notice that the original Ohio State approach narrowed leadership alternatives to two: consideration and structure initiation. Fiedler also followed with two: task-motivated style and relationship-oriented style. House expanded this to include four styles: directive, participative, supportive, and achievement-oriented. The literature is full of writers who choose two, four, or six styles (Bowers and Seashore, 1966; Stogdill, 1974).

These leadership styles are, of course, supposed to be independent variables. They "cause" certain other things (the dependent variables) which the researcher "sees" in the world. The Ohio State group saw two dependent variables: satisfaction and productivity. Fiedler saw principally one dependent variable: performance or productivity. House saw three: acceptance of the leader, satisfaction with his or her behavior, and expectancies in the mind of the subordinate.

In this section we will examine two theories of leadership which in effect say that there are many more contingencies, and many more causes and effects, which must be considered if one is really to understand the leadership styles that will be effective.

The first of these, the Tannenbaum/Schmidt model (1973), was originally published almost 20 years ago. It is still one of the most realistic and understandable explanations available. The second, the Vroom/Yetton model, is much more recent. This model probably has the advantage of moving much closer to reality than other path-goal approaches, but it is so complex that it would be difficult for a leader to use it in any but the most crucial decisions.

How to Choose a Leadership Pattern: Tannenbaum and Schmidt

The reading by Tannenbaum and Schmidt (1973) which follows this chapter has the advantage of being readily understandable to the manager, without a great deal of definitions, cause-and-effect relationships and precise scientific analysis. At the time the article was written, the academic literature on leadership, mostly coming out of the University of Michigan, seemed to infer that what was called "democratic leadership" produced both better human satisfaction and better productivity. Research since then has failed to substantiate these early claims, which turned out to be in part normative arguments rather than scientific truth.

The Tannenbaum/Schmidt article was a reaction to this literature. To get closer to the real world of action, these authors have posited seven different leadership styles, ranging on a continuum from what they call "boss-centered leadership" to "subordinate-centered leadership." Its theme is that a wide range of factors determine whether or not directive leadership, participative leadership, or something in between, is "best." These factors fall into three groups: forces in the manager himself (four characteristics), forces in the subordinate (seven characteristics), and forces in the situation (four characteristics). Though this large number of variables (fifteen factors which influence choice among seven leadership styles) seems formidable to understand, the article makes such understanding easy reading. The factors are intended to be a kind of checklist which a manager can use to diagnose a situation (manager, subordinates, and work situation) in order to judge which style of leadership will work best. For example, one of the forces in the manager is his or her confidence in the knowledge and competence of subordinates to do the job involved, and their competence to participate in management. One might imagine, for example, a large public beach on which there is a chief lifeguard and sixteen others, spread along different beach areas. The confidence the chief lifeguard has in allowing the others to manage the operation over the summer might well hinge on his or her beliefs about their experience level and skills.

One of the forces in the situation that determines style of leadership is the amount of time available for the decision. In times of crisis, one form of leadership is appropriate; in times of stability, another style is appropriate. The nature of the problem also has an effect. "It is possible to do subordinates a real disservice by assigning a problem that their experience does not equip them to solve" (1973).

How to Choose a Leadership Pattern: Vroom and Yetton

A second way to choose a leadership pattern, by analyzing the large number of factors involved, is known as the "Vroom-Yetton Model." It was first put forth in a book by these authors (1973). An abbreviated version of this theory of leadership is included with this chapter (Vroom, 1976).

While it takes some time to understand and think through the implications of this model, it is probably one of the most valid and sophisticated approaches to leadership developed to date. It involves a clear statement of what leadership is supposed to accomplish: (1) quality decisions (which are accurate in terms of organizational productivity and performance), and (2) acceptance by those subordinates who must carry out the decisions. Though one can see some resemblance between these two criteria and the older task-oriented leader behavior and relationship-oriented leader behavior, the two ultimate aims are quite different. In fact, the whole model is aimed at how to get *decisions* made and implemented, rather than how to achieve productivity and satisfied feelings.

Types of decisions which must be made.   Since problems and decisions are the phenomena being studied, it is not surprising that the whole analysis starts with determining what kind of problem must be solved. Seven different characteristics are described (A through G at the top of Figure 2 in the reading). The reason these are phrased as though the leader is asking himself a question is that managers may use the characteristics as a checklist to diagnose the problem type. For example: (a) does the problem possess a quality require-ment, or (b) do I have sufficient information to make a high quality decision? By answering this set of questions, the leader will know the situational forces that "ought to influence him or her in the *amount of opportunity he or she gives to subordinates to participate in the making of a decision.*"

Types of leadership styles.   These authors pose five types of leadership styles available to the manager:

Autocratic Processes

AI   "the manager solves the problem by himself using whatever information is available to him at that time"

AII "the manager obtains any necessary information of a specific nature from subordinates before making the decision himself"

Consultative Processes

CI   "the manager shares the problem with relevant subordinates individually, getting their ideas and suggestions before making the decision"

CII similar to above "but the consultation takes place within the context of a group meeting"

Group Processes

GI   "corresponds with Norman Maier's concept of group decision in which the manager's role is that of chairperson of a group meeting aimed at reaching consensus on the action to be taken"

Narrowing the possible choices.   Selecting a decision method is not an easy thing, especially if one hopes to reach the Holy Grail of complete integration of the best technology of the organization on the one hand and the best reaction of subordinate human beings on the other. Like other writers on leadership, these two authors are searching for the magic formula that will let the leader have his or her cake (organizational efficiency through high quality decisions) and eat it too (human satisfaction as an insurance that quality decisions will be implemented). In this pursuit many have tried and many have failed. There is not a single example in all of management and social science literature that comes as convincingly close as this decision method. But there is a price to be paid. A complex analytical logic must be obeyed. There are two steps in this logic. First, one must eliminate from the list of five leadership styles those that are clearly unacceptable, either because the particular style violates the first criterion of leadership (the need for quality decisions) or because it violates the second criterion of leadership (the need to have decisions carried out by subordinates, either because they accept the decision or because they carry it out for other reasons).

The way unacceptable leader styles are ruled out is by obeying certain rules of logic. These rules are spelled out in a means-end logic chain (see their Figure 1), which operates by starting at the left of the chain and then answering *in sequence* the seven questions that tell the leader what kind of problem he or she is dealing with. Each question has a yes/no answer. Depending on whether the answer is yes or no, the logic chain shows which question to address next, and whether to skip some questions. At the end of each path down the chain, there is a list of acceptable styles. Some paths end with only one acceptable style (such as the two at the very bottom of the diagram). Others end with the entire list of five styles being acceptable (the very top path indicates that any style, from the manager alone making the decision to group consensus, will work). At this point, the leader knows what will work and what will not, but not which one is best (except when the logic path shows only one after all others are eliminated).

The final choice.   Some way must be found to choose the style that is best, from those remaining. Here, the authors pose two criteria on which to judge:

If time is important, it is a well-known fact that participation is very costly. The experience many city governments have had with citizen participation groups attests to this. In one seacoast city which attempted to get citizen inputs into a decision about how to protect the environment of the coastline, 23 months of meetings elapsed and still there was not any clarity or consensus as to what regulations should be written. Therefore, the authors reason that any logic path which ends with several alternatives should be chosen toward the autocratic end of the list, *if* time becomes more and more important. In time of crisis, they advocate that the most autocratic of the workable alternatives be selected.

However, *if long-term development* of the skills and competences of the subordinates is the most important criteria, the choice process is reversed. That is, as this factor becomes more important, the authors recommend choosing the most participative of the workable alternatives.

Is this process really usable by practicing managers? Or is it too complex? The authors clearly believe that it is usable, especially after training managers with practical case problems which have been written to illustrate the various paths of logic. Their training methods are explained in the reading.

CONCLUSION

In this chapter we have looked at five approaches to the questions of what makes a good leader and how effective leaders behave. Two of these approaches, the trait approach and the behavioral approach, essentially held that leaders are leaders. Their personalities or behavior are similar in almost all kinds of organizations, departments, or societies. Though these approaches have been superseded in the academic literature by the situational approaches, the practicing manager should not be misled into believing that there is no truth in them. Rather, a more balanced view is that probably *both* the characteristics of the leader *and* the characteristics of a given situation interact to determine what is and what is not effective leadership.

The three situational approaches we have looked at add much to our present understanding of leadership. Fiedler's contingency model pointed out that there are favorable and unfavorable situations for a leader, and that certain kinds of leaders do better in favorable situations while other kinds of leaders do better in unfavorable situations. The path-goal approach revived the notion that subordinates attempt to be reasonable-minded people, and that the leader who can help them in this process will succeed. Finally, the Tannenbaum/Schmidt and Vroom/Yetton approaches show how really complex the forces can be which play on a leader in attempting to fit his or her behavior to the situation.

REFERENCES

Bowers, David G. and Stanley E. Seashore. "Predicting Organization Effectiveness with a Four Factor Theory of Leadership." *Administrative Science Quarterly*, Vol. 11, No. 2 (1966), pp. 238–63.

Evans, M. G. *The Effects of Supervisory Behavior Upon Worker Perception of Their Path-Goal Relationships.* Yale University, Doctoral Dissertation, 1968.

———. "The Effects of Supervisory Behavior on the Path-Goal Relationship." *Organizational Behavior and Human Performance*, Vol. 55 (1970a), pp. 277–98.

———. "Leadership and Motivation: A Core Concept." *Academy of Management Journal*, Vol. 13, No. 1 (March 1970b), pp. 91–102.

———. "Extensions of a Path Goal Theory of Motivation." *Journal of Applied Psychology*, Vol. 59 (1974), pp. 172–78.

Fiedler, Fred E. "Engineer the Job to Fit the Manager." *Harvard Business Review*, Vol. 43, No. 5 (September–October 1965), pp. 115–22.

———. *A Theory of Leadership Effectiveness.* McGraw-Hill Book Company, 1967.

———. "The Contingency Model – New Directions for Leadership Utilization." *Journal of Contemporary Business*, Vol. 3, No. 4 (1974), pp. 65–79.

———. "The Leadership Game: Matching the Man to the Situation." *Organizational Dynamics*, Vol. 4, No. 3 (Winter 1976), pp. 6–16.

———, and Martin Chemers. *Leadership and Effective Management.* Scott, Foresman and Company, 1974.

Georgopoulous, B. S., G. M. Mahoney, and N. W. Jones. "A Path Goal Approach to Productivity." *Journal of Applied Psychology*, Vol. 41 (1957), pp. 345–53.

Filley, A. C., R. J. House, and S. Kerr. *Managerial Process and Organizational Behavior.* Scott, Foresman and Company, 1976.

Fleishman, E. A., E. F. Harris, and H. E. Burtt. "Leadership and Supervision in Industry." Ohio State University, 1955.

Frankfort, H., H. A. Frankfort, J. A. Wilson, and T. Jacobsen. *Before Philosophy.* Penguin Books, 1949.

House, R. J. "A Path Goal Theory of Leadership Effectiveness." *Administrative Science Quarterly,* Vol. 16, No. 3 (September 1971), pp. 321–38.

———, and T. R. Mitchell. "Path-Goal Theory of Leadership." *Journal of Contemporary Business,* Vol. 3, No. 4 (Autumn 1974), pp. 81–97.

Sarachek, B. "Greek Concepts of Leadership." *Academy of Management Journal,* Vol. 11 (1968), pp. 39–48.

Stogdill, R. M. *Handbook of Leadership.* Macmillan/Free Press, 1974.

———, and A. E. Coons. "Leader Behavior: Its Description and Measurement." Research Monograph No. 88, Ohio State University, 1957.

Tannenbaum, R., and W. H. Schmidt. "How to Choose a Leadership Pattern." *Harvard Business Review,* May–June 1973.

Vroom, V. H. *Some Personality Determinants of the Effects of Participation.* University of Michigan, Doctoral Dissertation, 1959.

———. "A New Look at Managerial Decision Making." *Organizational Dynamics,* Vol. 2, No. 1 (Spring 1973).

———. "Leadership." *Handbook of Industrial and Organizational Psychology.* Ed. by M. Dunnette. Rand McNally, 1974.

———. "Can Leaders Learn to Lead?" *Organizational Dynamics,* Vol. 4, No. 3 (Winter 1976).

———, and P. W. Yetton. *Leadership and Decision-Making.* University of Pittsburgh Press, 1973.

———, and A. Jago. "Decision Making as a Social Process: Normative and Descriptive Models of Leader Behavior." *Decision Sciences,* Vol. 5, No. 5 (December 1974).

Readings

Leadership and Effective Management
Fred E. Fiedler and Martin Chemers

SITUATIONAL FACTORS AND LEADERSHIP THEORY

We have presented several attributes of the situation and we have undoubtedly left out many others, such as employee attributes, motivation, and abilities, which are just as likely to affect the behavior of the leader and of his group members. There is little doubt that the situation plays an important role in leadership performance, but we need to ask what specific features of the situation affect the leader.

We have long cherished Kurt Lewin's famous formula, $B = f(P,E)$, that behavior is a function of personality and the environment. But what particular aspects of the environment interact with personality in affecting behavior? In order to make sense of the many situational variables which might be crucial to our understanding of leadership effectiveness, we need to go back to a few fundamentals. We know that different types of leaders perform well in different types of situations. But what are the critical differences in the situations which will help us predict leadership effectiveness?

If leadership is indeed a relationship based on power and influence, then it seems reasonable to classify situations on the basis of the power and influence which they give the leader. The liked chairman of a volunteer committee has considerably more power than one who is disliked and rejected. The captain of a ship has more power than the director of a church choir. When the captain gives an order to one of his subordinates, he can be fairly certain that it will be carried out. The committee chairman faces considerably more uncertainty: will his group support him? Will his instructions lead to the solution of the problem? If he expresses his wish to move in one direction rather than another, will the group members agree or resign?

Underlying these questions are two related dimensions of the situation. The first one is the degree to which the situation provides the leader with control and influence, that is, the extent to which the leader is, or feels, able to obtain the outcomes he desires. Closely related to this is the question of predictability. To what extent can the leader predict what will happen when he gives an order, when he opts for one method of attacking the job as against another, when he rewards or disciplines one of his subordinates?

Note that the aspects of the situation with which we are here concerned are quite similar to those which Campbell and his associates (1970) saw as common to organizational climate factors. They spoke of consideration, warmth, and support, of orientation toward rewards and punishments, and of the degree to which the job and the task were structured. How, then, do we measure the control and influence which the situation provides the leader? The success of measuring or classifying the situation must be judged by how well this method enables us to predict leadership performance. A wide variety of methods have been developed to characterize leadership situations. At this point we plan to present the method basic to understanding the leadership effectiveness theory on which this book is based. It involves three components which are described below.

Leader-Member Relations

From a theoretical as well as an intuitive point of view, the interpersonal relationship between the leader and his group members is likely to be the most important single variable which determines his power and influence. This assumption is also supported by several empirical studies (e.g., Fishbein et al., 1969). The leader's authority depends upon his acceptance by his members. If others are willing to follow him because of his pleasant personality, his trustworthiness, or his charisma, the leader has little need for the organizational support provided by task structure and position power. If the leader is distrusted, his situation will necessarily be less favorable even when organizational support is at his disposal. Very few tasks can be so structured that they cannot be sabotaged or delayed by a disaffected subordinate. Very few supervisors have enough power to coerce a recalcitrant worker or to fire him as long as he performs on a minimally acceptable level.

While the leader's personality undoubtedly affects his relationship with his group members, it is not by any means completely determined by them. The personality of group members plays a part (e.g., Haythorne et al., 1956) which has sometimes been neglected. A person who is replacing a highly successful and admired leader is likely to obtain considerably less support from his group than is one who replaces a despised martinet. Moreover, someone promoted to management from the ranks might or might not have good rapport with his new subordinates. They may consider him one of their own and support him, or they may be jealous of his success.

The leader-member relations dimension has been measured in two ways. One method involves asking the members of the group to indicate on a sociometric preference scale whether they accept or endorse their leader. These questions are rather difficult to ask, and the answers must be regarded with considerable caution. A man who says that he does not regard his supervisor very highly is really laying his career on the line.

Questions of this type have to be carefully formulated so that they will allow subordinates to choose or not to choose their own supervisor without directly compromising themselves. Thus, one might ask, "With which three employees and managers whom you know in this company would you most prefer to work?" or "Suppose you were to be transferred to a new office. Which three people in this company would you most prefer to have with you?" A respondent may thus indicate his lack of enthusiasm for his boss by naming either others from his own group or managers from outside his group.

In our own research, the groups were usually divided into those above and below the median of choices for the leader. Half of the groups were therefore considered to have good leader-member relations, while half were considered to have poor relations. Where sufficient groups were available, we divided the groups into an upper, a middle, and a lower third, in order to obtain a better differentiation between groups with good and poor leader-member relations.

An alternative method for identifying leader-member relations is the short "Group Atmosphere" (GA) scale. This measure consists of ten eight-point bipolar items which can be answered in the space of two or three minutes. The leader is simply asked to describe his work group on this scale. Two sample items are shown here:

Pleasant _____:_____:_____:_____:_____:_____:_____:_____ Unpleasant
           8   7   6   5   4   3   2   1

Friendly _____:_____:_____:_____:_____:_____:_____:_____ Unfriendly
        8   7   6   5   4   3   2   1

The other items are Bad—Good; Worthless—Valuable; Distant—Close; Cold—Warm; Quarrelsome—Harmonious; Self-assured—Hesitant; Efficient—Inefficient; and Gloomy —Cheerful.

The item scores are summed and they may be averaged. An analysis by Posthuma (1970) of 2415 subjects shows the median GA score for a ten-item scale for real-life groups to be 64.9 and for laboratory groups 67.0. McNamara (1968) found that the leader's GA score indicates the degree to which the group is loyal and supportive of the leader, even when the group members do not feel that the leader is very efficient. Chemers and Skrzypek (1972) also found a substantial relationship between sociometric preferences expressed by group members and the leader's GA score. However, in some studies the leader's group atmosphere score has been unrelated to the group members' preference ratings. This has been especially true in short-term laboratory studies in which the leader has practically no chance to become well acquainted with his coworkers and in which sociometric preference ratings are unlikely to be meaningful since the leader may be unable to estimate the group members' feelings toward him. In most cases, the group atmosphere score seems to provide a very quick and valid measure of the leader's *feeling* of being accepted which may, of course, affect his behavior much more than the degree of *actual* acceptance by his group.

Task Structure

The second most important measure of situational favorableness is the task-structure dimension. The degree to which the task requirements are spelled out determines in large part the leader's authority to give instructions and to evaluate performance. We generally do not think of the task as providing the leader with power and influence. Yet it is clear upon brief reflection that the supervisor who has a manual of operating procedures in his hand, or who follows in step-by-step fashion the organization's requirements for performing a particular task, enjoys the complete backing of the organization. It would be very difficult for an employee to challenge the leader's right to tell him what to do when the leader can point to the manual's detailed operating instructions.

At the other extreme is the task which is completely unstructured and vague. Here the leader usually has no more knowledge than his members, and he therefore enjoys no advantage over them. His own preferences for proceeding with the task are perhaps no more justified than would be those of any other member of the group. If the task consists, for instance, of developing a new policy statement, it is highly unlikely that the leader will have much advantage in expertise. It is even more unlikely that his method of proceeding is on its face more meritorious than that proposed by any other group member as an alternative. The members are therefore quite justified in questioning the leader's approach, even where his formal position power is quite high. As a result, an unstructured task implies correspondingly lower control and influence.

Shaw's (1963, 1971) dimensions of task characteristics, mentioned above, provide a useful means of evaluating the structure of the task. Of the several features of his *solution multiplicity* factor which can be measured, four have been used in our own studies. These are:

1) *Goal clarity.* This is the degree to which the requirements of a job (the tasks and duties which typically make up the job) are clearly stated or known to people performing the job. It would be quite low for such jobs as director of a railroad switching yard or private detective, but quite high for an axle assembler in an auto plant who secures front and rear assemblies to chassis springs.

2) *Goal-path multiplicity.* This is the degree to which the problems encountered in the job can be solved by a variety of procedures (number of different alternatives in performing the job, number of different ways the problems typically encountered in the job can be solved). A job with very low goal-path multiplicity, and hence with high structure, would be that of a date puller, who "cuts open dates, removes the stones, and cuts the dates into pieces for use in making candy." High in this category would be the job of research engineer who "conducts engineering research concerned with processing a particular kind of commodity with a view to improving present products and discovering new products. . . . Plans and executes experimental work to check theories advanced. . . ."

3) *Decision verifiability.* This is the degree to which the "correctness" of the solutions or decisions typically encountered in a job can be demonstrated by appeal to authority or authoritative source (e.g., the census of 1960), by logical procedures (e.g., mathematical demonstration), or by feedback (e.g., examination of the consequences of the decision, as in action tasks). A social welfare research worker's job, which involves "research to facilitate investigation and alleviation of social problems . . ." would be very low on this scale. A nut and bolt sorter who ". . . sorts nuts and bolts by hand according to size, length, and diameter . . ." would be very high.

4) *Decision specificity.* This is the degree to which there is generally more than one "correct solution" involved in tasks which typically make up a job. Some tasks, like arithmetic problems, are high on this dimension since they have only one solution that is acceptable; others have an almost infinite number of possible solutions, all of which may be equally good. Examples might be human relations problems or problems about which managers must make decisions. Low on this scale, and hence low in task structure, would again be a social welfare research worker's job. Very high would be the job of a barrel drainer who "empties water from barrel that has been inspected or weighed by rolling barrel onto a stand and pulling bung from hole by hand."

In our research, we have generally had each of the four dimensions scored by judges on a scale from 1 (low structure) to 8 (high structure). Groups above the median (a score of 5.0) are generally considered to have high task structure and those below the median to have low structure. Hunt (1967) has developed a more extensive scaling procedure, which is particularly useful for studies of ongoing organizations.

Position Power

As we have discussed before, the most obvious way in which we vest power in the leader (though not the most important) is by giving him the right to direct, evaluate, and reward and punish those he is asked to supervise, though these legitimate aspects of his job can be exercised only within rather strictly defined boundaries. In most situations, the subordinates have a very clear idea of the leader's legitimate authority, and only rarely is this authority seriously challenged.

The scale which we have found useful in determining leader position power in business organizations is a simple check list also devised by Hunt (1967). Each of the items can be answered yes or no.

1) Can the supervisor recommend subordinate rewards and punishments to his boss?

2) Can the supervisor punish or reward subordinates on his own?

3) Can the supervisor recommend promotion or demotion of subordinates?

4) Does the supervisor's special knowledge allow him to decide how subordinates are to proceed on their jobs?

5) Can the supervisor promote or demote subordinates on his own?

6) Can the supervisor specifically instruct subordinates concerning what they are to do?

7) Is it an important part of the supervisor's job to motivate his subordinates?

8) Is it an important part of the supervisor's job to evaluate subordinate performance?

9) Does the supervisor have a great deal of knowledge about the jobs under him but require his subordinates to do them?

10) Can the supervisor supervise and evaluate subordinate jobs?

11) Does the supervisor know both his own and his subordinates' jobs so that he could finish subordinate work himself if it were necessary and he had enough time?

12) Has the supervisor been given an official title by the company which differentiates him from subordinates?

While these checklists are quite helpful in operationally defining high or low position power, it is in fact only rarely necessary to rate leadership positions in work contexts. Practically all managers, supervisors, foremen, and superintendents in business and industry have high position power. Practically all committee chairmen and leaders of groups of colleagues tend to have low position power. The scales are needed mostly for those cases in which there is an unusual leadership situation.

SITUATIONAL FAVORABLENESS

The three aspects of the situation which appear to be of most importance in determining the leader's control and influence appear to be (1) whether the leader's group atmosphere score, or the sociometric preference for the leader, is high or low; (2) whether the task is relatively structured or unstructured; and (3) whether the position power is relatively high or low. A particular group may be classified by first ordering it on leader-member relations, then on task structure, and finally on position power. A group may then be placed in one of eight conceptual cells, ranging from the most favorable one, in which leader-member relations, task structure, and position power are all high, to the least favorable, in which all three values are low. The resulting classification is shown in Figure 1.

Figure 1. The Situational Favorableness Dimension.

	I	II	III	IV	V	VI	VII	VIII
Leader-member Relations	Good				Poor			
Task Structure	High		Low		High		Low	
Position Power	Strong	Weak	Strong	Weak	Strong	Weak	Strong	Weak

This definition of situational favorableness is not without its problems or its critics. It is at best a rough index, which, we hope, will eventually become more precise. We must develop new methods for measuring favorableness in absolute rather than relative terms, that is, for determining not only whether one situation is higher or lower in task structure, but also by how much it is higher or lower. We must also find ways of taking into account the possibility that position power in some organizations, such as a marine recruit unit, may be much more important than the leader's relationship with his members, or that task structure in a highly programmed operation like a countdown procedure may be the single most important aspect of that situation.

There is also evidence that other aspects of the situation might play an important part. These include the motivation, intelligence, training, and experience of leaders and group members, as well as such extra-organizational factors as the community's economic situation. Which of these will have to be included in future studies of more complex leadership problems is a question for further research.

Having said all this, it is nevertheless true that the situational favorableness dimension is a very useful empirical and theoretical tool which has contributed a great deal to our understanding of leadership performance and leadership behavior. . . .

WHAT MAKES GROUPS EFFECTIVE?

As we have seen, no single personality trait, trait pattern, or particular style of leader behavior assures good organizational performance in all leadership situations. A person may be a very effective leader in one situation but very ineffective in another. A number of recent theories of leadership have therefore investigated the particular conditions under which one or another type of leadership behavior or leader personality is most effective.

The best articulated theory of this kind is the *Contingency Model* of leadership effectiveness, according to which the performance of a group is *contingent* upon both the motivational system of the leader and the degree to which the leader has control and influence in a particular situation, the "situational favorableness."

This theory represents a departure from previous thinking. It views the leadership situation as an arena in which the leader seeks to satisfy his own as well as the organization's goals. The degree to which he will be able to do so will, of course, depend upon the control and influence at his disposal.

The personality measure which is the key variable in the contingency theory is the so-called Least Preferred Coworker (LPC) score. It is obtained by asking the individual to think of everybody with whom he has ever worked and to describe the person with whom he could work least well, his "least preferred coworker." Each item of this simple bipolar scale is scored from one to eight, with eight as the most favorable point on the scale, and the LPC score is the sum of the item scores. In most of our work we have used a scale of sixteen items, reproduced in Figure 2.

Figure 2. Think of the Person with Whom You Can Work Least Well. He May Be Someone You Work with Now, or He May Be Someone You Knew in the Past. He Does Not Have to Be the Person You Like Least Well, But Should Be the Person with Whom You Had the Most Difficulty in Getting a Job Done. Describe This Person as He Appears to You.

Left	8/1	7/2	6/3	5/4	4/5	3/6	2/7	1/8	Right
Pleasant	8	7	6	5	4	3	2	1	Unpleasant
Friendly	8	7	6	5	4	3	2	1	Unfriendly
Rejecting	1	2	3	4	5	6	7	8	Accepting
Helpful	8	7	6	5	4	3	2	1	Frustrating
Unenthusiastic	1	2	3	4	5	6	7	8	Enthusiastic
Tense	1	2	3	4	5	6	7	8	Relaxed
Distant	1	2	3	4	5	6	7	8	Close
Cold	1	2	3	4	5	6	7	8	Warm
Cooperative	8	7	6	5	4	3	2	1	Uncooperative
Supportive	8	7	6	5	4	3	2	1	Hostile
Boring	1	2	3	4	5	6	7	8	Interesting
Quarrelsome	1	2	3	4	5	6	7	8	Harmonious
Self-assured	8	7	6	5	4	3	2	1	Hesitant
Efficient	8	7	6	5	4	3	2	1	Inefficient
Gloomy	1	2	3	4	5	6	7	8	Cheerful
Open	8	7	6	5	4	3	2	1	Guarded

It takes only two or three minutes to complete the scale, and the score is fairly reliable. That is, most people will fill it out consistently on successive tests. They may produce a very negative description (low LPC) or a relatively more positive description (middle or high LPC) of their least preferred coworker, but the LPC scale seems to be about as stable over time as many other personality measures. . . . A low score indicates the degree to which an individual is ready to reject completely those with whom he cannot work, an attitude which is reflected by describing them in negative terms on attributes which are not directly related to their work. A highly rejecting description indicates a very strong emotional reaction and not merely the calm and reasoned judgment of a detached observer. A more positive score indicates a willingness to perceive even the worst coworker as having some reasonably positive attributes and again reflects more than a simple objective judgment. The high LPC person who sees both good and bad points in his least preferred coworker takes a much more analytical point of view which suggests a greater concern with knowing even those with whom he cannot work.

WHAT DOES THE LPC SCORE MEASURE?

Despite the simplicity of the LPC score and the way we obtain it, the road to understanding LPC has been a maddening and frustrating odyssey. For nearly 20 years, we have been attempting to correlate it with every conceivable personality trait and every conceivable behavior observation score. By and large these analyses have been uniformly fruitless. In fact, for many years we despaired of finding any relationship at all between LPC and personality test scores. At the same time, it was quite obvious that this score must measure a very important personality variable since the correlations between LPC and group performance were quite high and significant. We knew that we were on to something, but not until quite recently were we able to specify more exactly what this might be.

It now appears that LPC is an index of a motivational hierarchy, or of behavioral preferences, implying that some goals are more important to the individual than others. That such hierarchies exist is a well-known fact of everyday life: If I give each of ten people $100, it is a safe bet that they will spend this money differently. Some will buy food rather than clothes; some will put it into a savings account rather than take a vacation. Likewise, if I tell them that they will have a free day next week, some may decide to sleep, others may want to spend it with their families, and still others may plan to go fishing or sailing. These choice behaviors reflect the hierarchical arrangement of their goals.

Let us assume then that each individual has a hierarchy of goals, that is, that individual A's first priority might be getting through school and his second priority, having a good time. In contrast, individual B's first priority might be having a good time and his second, getting through school. It is now highly probable that the preferred behaviors of A and B will differ. If the time is limited, A will study and forgo dates and parties, while B will go on dates and parties instead of studying. If, on the other hand, there is no time pressure, and A has already done his studying, or feels that it will surely get done, he will go out to have a good time. B, on the other hand, might feel that he will not lose out on having a good time, and he will therefore spend some of his time on his studies. As Maslow (1954) has pointed out, satisfied needs no longer motivate. If I have satisfied my hunger, I will no longer be motivated by more food, and I will then seek to satisfy my less basic goals, the "luxuries" of life.

Let us now return to the leadership situation and the part which LPC plays. Recent research strongly suggests that the high LPC person, who perceives his least preferred coworker in a more favorable, more differentiated manner, has as his basic goal the desire to be "related." That is, he seeks to have strong emotional and affective ties with others in the work situation (and probably in other situations as well).[1] If this basic goal is achieved, if he feels that he has achieved such an affective relationship, he will also seek, as his secondary goals, status and esteem. He will want to be admired and to be recognized (Fiedler, 1972).

The low LPC person has a different hierarchy of goals. His basic goal is to accomplish the task. His self-esteem is derived from achievement. However, as long as accomplishing the task presents no problems, why not also have friendly, pleasant relations with the members of the work group? In other words, as long as the low LPC leader knows that the task accomplishment is in the bag, he can afford to be friendly and concerned with the feelings of his coworkers. It is only when task accomplishment is threatened that good interpersonal relations must take second place.

The person who sees even his least preferred coworker in a relatively positive manner (high LPC) tends, somewhat like McGregor's (1967) Theory Y person, to be more optimistic about human nature and more ready to allow others greater freedom (Nebeker and Hansson, 1973).[2]

LPC AND LEADERSHIP PERFORMANCE

Let us now ask how it will affect a leader's performance if he is primarily motivated to seek close interpersonal relations, or, alternatively, effective task performance. Most books on leadership tacitly assume that the leader will as a matter of course seek to accomplish the organization's goals. Hence, the more power and influence the organization is able to give him, the better he will be able to ensure that the organizational goals will be obtained.

This rather simplistic concept of leadership does not take sufficient account of the fact that human beings have strong needs. While all foremen in a plant are likely to tell us that they want high productivity, they will differ in how this productivity should be achieved, and they will differ in the price they are willing to pay for high productivity. And above all, they will view the job in terms of the particular way it will satisfy their needs.

As we have stressed before, leadership is a relationship based on control and influence. It is obvious that the person with complete control and influence over his own fate and that of others can ensure that all his goals are achieved. Under these favorable conditions he will be able to pursue his secondary goals. Hence, the high LPC leader will concern himself with such status-enhancing activities as ordering people around, assigning tasks, and assuming responsibility. The low LPC leader, given this high degree of control, will be relaxed, friendly, and considerate, in the knowledge that the task presents no problem.

---

[1] It should be pointed out, by the way, that being related need not necessarily mean that the relationship is positive. Many people prefer even a negative or hostile relationship to not being related. Consider, for example, the married couples who continually fight with each other, or the work relations which are characterized by friendly sarcasm and an undertone of hostility.

[2] Mitchell (1970) and Foa, Mitchell, and Fiedler (1971) have shown that the high LPC person tends to be cognitively more complex and that he differentiates more in his perception and evaluation of his interpersonal environment. This is quite compatible with the interpretation of LPC as an index of a motivational hierarchy. A person who values relationships more is likely to pay more attention to others and to trust them more than someone who is indifferent about his interpersonal relations.

In the unfavorable situation in which the leader's control is low, where he cannot be sure of his group's support, has little power to coerce his subordinates, and cannot be certain of the way the task should be done, the high LPC leader will seek first of all the anxiety-reducing comfort of the close relationship with his group members. The low LPC leader will try to get the task done even if he has to step on toes and ruffle feathers.

LPC AND GROUP PERFORMANCE

Obviously, the favorableness of the leadership situation makes a big difference in the behavior and performance of the group. In the preceding chapter we discussed a method of classifying situations which was based on three aspects of the situation—acceptance, structure, and power. Each of these three dimensions was divided in half so that any group can be classified high or low on each dimension, yielding an eight-celled classification system.

Let us now see what happens when we classify various types of groups in this way. For each set of groups which falls into one of the eight cells or octants, we can compute a correlation coefficient which tells us the degree to which the leader's LPC score is correlated with the group's performance. If we find that leaders with high LPC scores are more successful, that they have better group performance than do leaders with low LPC scores, the correlation will be positive. If the task-motivated leaders with low LPC scores are more successful than high LPC leaders, the correlation will be negative.

DEVELOPMENT OF THE CONTINGENCY MODEL

The data for the original analyses of LPC and situational variables came from a program of leadership research which was begun in 1951 at the University of Illinois. All studies involved interacting groups—groups in which the members had to interact and coordinate their efforts to achieve a common goal—rather than coacting groups. In essence, we have an interacting group when it is impossible to arrive at a group product by simply adding the performance scores of each group member (e.g., a basketball team or a policy-making group). Examples of coacting groups are departments in which employees perform on a piece-work basis or classroom situations in which each student receives an individual grade.

Wherever possible, we used "hard" or objective performance criteria which reflected the major assigned goal of the group. Thus, in a study of high school basketball teams, the criterion of performance consisted of the win/loss ratio of games played in league competition. In a second study of land surveying parties, the criterion was the accuracy of measuring various sections of land, as rated by class instructors. Other studies in the program dealt with B-29 air force combat crews where performance was measured by means of circular error bombing accuracy, tank crews where performance was based on time-in-seconds to hit a target, antiaircraft artillery crews where effectiveness ratings were available, and management and boards of directors of 32 consumer cooperative companies where various profit indices were assessed. Also included were a wide variety of experimentally assembled groups consisting of ROTC students, executives participating in leadership training workshops, and students who had to take part in research as one of the requirements for a course. Well over 800 groups were studied between 1951 and 1963, and the theory was based on the findings of these various studies.

The averaged results of the various analyses are plotted in Figure 3. The horizontal axis of this graph indicates the favorableness of the situation with the most favorable cell or octant shown on the far left and the least favorable cell on the far right. The vertical axis indicates the degree to which the leader's LPC score and his group's performance are correlated in various sets of groups within a cell. A point on the graph above the midline shows a positive correlation between LPC and group performance, that is, it shows that the high LPC leaders performed better than did the low LPC leaders. A point below the midline shows that the low LPC leaders performed better than did the high LPC leaders, that the correlation was negative. The heavy line connects the median correlation coefficients and indicates the most likely value of the correlation coefficient in each of the eight cells – in other words, the best prediction for the correlations.

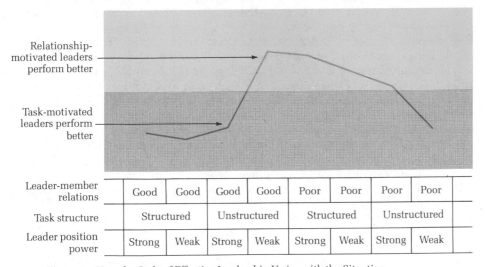

Leader-member relations	Good	Good	Good	Good	Poor	Poor	Poor	Poor	
Task structure	Structured		Unstructured		Structured		Unstructured		
Leader position power	Strong	Weak	Strong	Weak	Strong	Weak	Strong	Weak	

Figure 3   How the Style of Effective Leadership Varies with the Situation.

Source: Modified from Fiedler, 1965, with the permission of the *Harvard Business Review*.

As Figure 3 shows, the task-motivated (low LPC) leaders performed most effectively in the very favorable situations of octants I, II, and III, and in the relatively unfavorable situations, such as octant VIII. Hence, we obtain negative correlations between LPC and group performance scores. Relationship-motivated (high LPC) leaders obtain optimal group performance under situations of moderate or intermediate favorableness (octants IV and V). These are situations in which (A) the task is structured but the leader is disliked and must, presumably, be diplomatic and concerned with the feeling of his men, or (B) the liked leader has an unstructured task and must therefore depend upon the creativity and willing participation of his members.

The Contingency Model leads to the major hypothesis that leadership effectiveness depends upon the leader's style of interacting with his group members and the favorableness of the group-task situation. Specifically, low LPC leaders who are primarily task-motivated perform best under conditions that are very favorable or very unfavorable for them. Relationship-motivated leaders perform best under conditions that are of moderate favorableness.

REFERENCES

Campbell, J. P., M. D. Dunnette, E. E. Lawler III, and K. E. Weick. *Managerial Behavior, Performance, and Effectiveness.* McGraw-Hill, 1970.

Chemers, M. M., and G. J. Skrzypek. "An Experimental Test of the Contingency Model of Leadership Effectiveness." *Journal of Personality and Social Psychology,* 24 (1972), pp. 172–77.

Fiedler, F. E. *A Theory of Leadership Effectiveness.* McGraw-Hill, 1967.

———. "Change the Job to Fit the Manager." *Harvard Business Review,* 43 (1965), pp. 115–22.

———. "Predicting the Effects of Leadership Training and Experience from the Contingency Model." *Journal of Applied Psychology,* 56 (1972), pp. 114–19.

Fishbein, M., E. Landy, and G. Hatch. "Consideration of Two Assumptions Underlying Fiedler's Contingency Model for the Prediction of Leadership Effectiveness." *American Journal of Psychology,* 4 (1969), pp. 457–73.

Foa, U. G., T. R. Mitchell, and F. E. Fiedler. "Differentiation Matching." *Behavioral Science,* 16 (1971), pp. 130–42.

Haythorne, W., A. Couch, D. Haefner, P. Langhan, and L. Carter. "The Effects of Varying Combinations of Authoritarian and Equalitarian Leaders and Followers." *Journal of Abnormal and Social Psychology,* 53 (1956), pp. 210–19.

Hunt, J. G. "Fiedler's Leadership Contingency Model: An Empirical Test in Three Organizations." *Organizational Behavior and Human Performance,* 2 (1967), pp. 290–308.

McGregor, D. *The Professional Manager.* McGraw-Hill, 1967.

McNamara, V. D. "Leadership, Staff, and School Effectiveness." Unpublished doctoral dissertation, University of Alberta, 1968.

Maslow, A. H. *Motivation and Personality.* Harper and Row, 1954.

Mitchell, T. R. "Cognitive Complexity and Leadership Style." *Journal of Personality and Social Psychology,* 16 (1970), pp. 166–73.

Nebeker, D. M., and R. O. Hansson. "Confidence in Human Nature and Leader Style." Paper presented at the Western Psychological Association Meetings, April 11–14, 1973.

Posthuma, A. B. "Normative Data on the Least Preferred Co-worker Scale (LPC) and the Group Atmosphere Questionnaire (GA)." Organizational Research, University of Washington, 1970.

Shaw, M. E. "Scaling Group Tasks: A Method for Dimensional Analysis." Technical Report No. 1, University of Florida, 1963.

———. *Group Dynamics: The Psychology of Group Behavior.* McGraw-Hill, 1971.

Path-Goal Theory of Leadership

Robert J. House and Terence R. Mitchell

An integrated body of conjecture by students of leadership, referred to as the "Path-Goal Theory of Leadership," is currently emerging. According to this theory, leaders are effective because of their impact on subordinates' motivation, ability to perform effectively and satisfactions. The theory is called Path-Goal because its major concern is how the leader influences the subordinates' perceptions of their work goals, personal goals and paths to goal attainment. The theory suggests that a leader's behavior is motivating or satisfying to the degree that the behavior increases subordinate goal attainment and clarifies the paths to these goals.

HISTORICAL FOUNDATIONS

The path-goal approach has its roots in a more general motivational theory called expectancy theory.[1] Briefly, expectancy theory states that an individual's attitudes (e.g., satisfaction with supervision or job satisfaction) or behavior (e.g., leader behavior or job effort) can be predicted from: (1) the degree to which the job, or behavior, is seen as leading to various outcomes (expectancy) and (2) the evaluation of these outcomes (valences). Thus, people are satisfied with their job if they think it leads to things that are highly valued, and they work hard if they believe that effort leads to things that are highly valued. This type of theoretical rationale can be used to predict a variety of phenomena related to leadership, such as why leaders behave the way they do, or how leader behavior influences subordinate motivation.[2]

This latter approach is the primary concern of this article. The implication for leadership is that subordinates are motivated by leader behavior to the extent that this behavior influences expectancies, e.g., goal paths and valences, e.g., goal attractiveness.

Several writers have advanced specific hypotheses concerning how the leader affects the paths and the goals of subordinates.[3] These writers focused on two issues: (1) how the leader affects subordinates' expectations that effort will lead to effective performance and valued rewards, and (2) how this expectation affects motivation to work hard and perform well.

While the state of theorizing about leadership in terms of subordinates' paths and goals is in its infancy, we believe it is promising for two reasons. First, it suggests effects of leader behavior that have not yet been investigated but which appear to be fruitful areas of inquiry. And, second, it suggests with some precision the situational factors on which the effects of leader behavior are contingent.

The initial theoretical work by Evans asserts that leaders will be effective by making rewards available to subordinates and by making these rewards contingent on the subordinate's accomplishment of specific goals.[4] Evans argued that one of the strategic functions of the leader is to clarify for subordinates the kind of behavior that leads to goal accomplishment and valued rewards. This function might be referred to as path clarification. Evans also argued that the leader increases the rewards available to subordinates by being supportive toward subordinates, i.e., by being concerned about their status, welfare and comfort. Leader supportiveness is in itself a reward that the leader has at his or her disposal, and the judicious use of this reward increases the motivation of subordinates.

Evans studied the relationship between the behavior of leaders and the subordinates' expectations that effort leads to rewards and also studied the resulting impact on ratings of the subordinates' performance. He found that when subordinates viewed leaders as being supportive (considerate of their needs) and when these superiors provided directions and guidance to the subordinates, there was a positive relationship between leader behavior and subordinates' performance ratings.

However, leader behavior was only related to subordinates' performance when the leader's behavior also was related to the subordinates' expectations that their effort would result in desired rewards. Thus, Evans' findings suggest that the major impact of a leader on the performance of subordinates is clarifying the path to desired rewards and making such rewards contingent on effective performance.

Stimulated by this line of reasoning, House, and House and Dessler advanced a more complex theory of the effects of leader behavior on the motivation of subordinates.[5] The theory intends to explain the effects of four specific kinds of leader behavior on the following three subordinate attitudes or expectations: (1) the satisfaction of subordinates, (2) the subordinates' acceptance of the leader and (3) the expectations of subordinates that effort will result in effective performance and that effective performance is the path to rewards. The four kinds of leader behavior included in the theory are: (1) directive leadership, (2) supportive leadership, (3) participative leadership and (4) achievement-oriented leadership. Directive leadership is characterized by a leader who lets subordinates know what is expected of them, gives specific guidance as to what should be done and how it should be done, makes his or her part in the group understood, schedules work to be done, maintains definite standards of performance and asks that group members follow standard rules and regulations. Supportive leadership is characterized by a friendly and approachable leader who shows concern for the status, well-being and needs of subordinates. Such a leader does little things to make the work more pleasant, treats members as equals and is friendly and approachable. Participative leadership is characterized by a leader who consults with subordinates, solicits their suggestions and takes these suggestions seriously into consideration before making a decision. An achievement-oriented leader sets challenging goals, expects subordinates to perform at their highest level, continuously seeks improvement in performance *and* shows a high degree of confidence that the subordinates will assume responsibility, put forth effort and accomplish challenging goals. This kind of leader constantly emphasizes excellence in performance and simultaneously displays confidence that subordinates will meet high standards of excellence.

A number of studies suggest that these different leadership styles can be shown by the same leader in various situations.[6] For example, a leader may show directiveness toward subordinates in some instances and be participative or supportive in other instances.[7] Thus, the traditional method of characterizing a leader as either highly participative and supportive or highly directive is invalid; rather, it can be concluded that leaders vary in the particular fashion employed for supervising their subordinates. Also, the theory, in its present stage, is a tentative explanation of the effects of leader behavior—it is incomplete because it does not explain other kinds of leader behavior and does not explain the effects of the leader on factors other than subordinate acceptance, satisfaction and expectations. However, the theory is stated so that additional variables may be included in it as new knowledge is made available.

PATH-GOAL THEORY

General Propositions

The first proposition of path-goal theory is that leader behavior is acceptable and satisfying to subordinates to the extent that the subordinates see such behavior as either an immediate source of satisfaction or as instrumental to future satisfaction.

The second proposition of this theory is that the leader's behavior will be motivational, i.e., increase effort, to the extent that (1) such behavior makes satisfaction of subordinate's needs contingent on effective performance and (2) such behavior complements the environment of subordinates by providing the coaching, guidance, support and rewards necessary for effective performance.

These two propositions suggest that the leader's strategic functions are to enhance subordinates' motivation to perform, satisfaction with the job and acceptance of the leader. From previous research on expectancy theory of motivation, it can be inferred that the strategic functions of the leader consist of: (1) recognizing and/or arousing subordinates' needs for outcomes over which the leader has some control, (2) increasing personal payoffs to subordinates for work-goal attainment, (3) making the path to those payoffs easier to travel by coaching and direction, (4) helping subordinates clarify expectancies, (5) reducing frustrating barriers and (6) increasing the opportunities for personal satisfaction contingent on effective performance.

Stated less formally, the motivational functions of the leader consist of increasing the number and kinds of personal payoffs to subordinates for work-goal attainment and making paths to these payoffs easier to travel by clarifying the paths, reducing road blocks and pitfalls and increasing the opportunities for personal satisfaction en route.

Contingency Factors

Two classes of situational variables are asserted to be contingency factors. A contingency factor is a variable which moderates the relationship between two other variables such as leader behavior and subordinate satisfaction. For example, we might suggest that the degree of structure in the task moderates the relationship between leaders' directive behavior and subordinates' job satisfaction. Figure I shows how such a relationship might look. Thus, subordinates are satisfied with directive behavior in an unstructured task and are satisfied with nondirective behavior in a structured task. Therefore, we say that the relationship between leader directiveness and subordinate satisfaction is contingent upon the structure of the task.

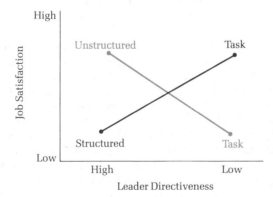

Figure I Hypothetical Relationship Between Directive Leadership and Subordinate Satisfaction with Task Structure as a Contingency Factor

The two contingency variables are (a) personal characteristics of the subordinates and (b) the environmental pressures and demands with which subordinates must cope in order to accomplish the work goals and to satisfy their needs. While other situational factors also may operate to determine the effects of leader behavior, they are not presently known.

With respect to the first class of contingency factors, the characteristics of subordinates, path-goal theory asserts that leader behavior will be acceptable to subordinates to the extent that the subordinates see such behavior as either an immediate source of satisfaction or as instrumental to future satisfaction. Subordinates' characteristics are hypothesized to partially determine this perception. For example, Runyon[8] and Mitchell[9] show that the subordinate's score on a measure called Locus of Control moderates the relationship between participative leadership style and subordinate satisfaction. The Locus-of-Control measure reflects the degree to which an individual sees the environment as systematically responding to his or her behavior. People who believe that what happens to them occurs because of their behavior are called internals; people who believe that what happens to them occurs because of luck or chance are called externals. Mitchell's findings suggest that internals are more satisfied with a participative leadership style and externals are more satisfied with a directive style.

A second characteristic of subordinates on which the effects of leader behavior are contingent is subordinates' perception of their own ability with respect to their assigned tasks. The higher the degree of perceived ability relative to task demands, the less the subordinate will view leader directiveness and coaching behavior as acceptable. Where the subordinate's perceived ability is high, such behavior is likely to have little positive effect on the motivation of the subordinate and to be perceived as excessively close control. Thus, the acceptability of the leader's behavior is determined in part by the characteristics of the subordinates.

The second aspect of the situation, the environment of the subordinate, consists of those factors that are not within the control of the subordinate but which are important to need satisfaction or to ability to perform effectively. The theory asserts that effects of the leader's behavior on the psychological states of subordinates are contingent on other parts of the subordinates' environment that are relevant to subordinate motivation. Three broad classifications of contingency factors in the environment are:

- The subordinates' tasks
- The formal authority system of the organization
- The primary work group

Assessment of the environmental conditions makes it possible to predict the kind and amount of influence that specific leader behaviors will have on the motivation of subordinates. Any of the three environmental factors could act upon the subordinate in any of three ways: first, to serve as stimuli that motivate and direct the subordinate to perform necessary task operations; second, to constrain variability in behavior. Constraints may help the subordinate by clarifying expectancies that effort leads to rewards or by preventing the subordinate from experiencing conflict and confusion. Constraints also may be counterproductive to the extent that they restrict initiative or prevent increases in effort from being associated positively with rewards. Third, environmental factors may serve as rewards for achieving desired performance, e.g., it is possible for the subordinate to receive the necessary cues to do the job and the needed rewards for satisfaction from sources other than the leader, e.g., coworkers in the primary work group. Thus, the effect of the leader on subordinates' motivation will be a function of how deficient the environment is with respect to motivational stimuli, constraints or rewards.

With respect to the environment, path-goal theory asserts that when goals and paths to desired goals are apparent because of the routine nature of the task, clear group norms or objective controls of the formal authority systems, attempts by the leader to clarify paths and goals will be both redundant and seen by subordinates as imposing unnecessary, close control. Although such control may increase performance by preventing soldiering or malingering, it also will result in decreased satisfaction (see Figure 1). Also with respect to the work environment, the theory asserts that the more dissatisfying the task, the more the subordinates will resent leader behavior directed at increasing productivity or enforcing compliance to organizational rules and procedures.

Finally, with respect to environmental variables the theory states that leader behavior will be motivational to the extent that it helps subordinates cope with environmental uncertainties, threats from others or sources of frustration. Such leader behavior is predicted to increase subordinates' satisfaction with the job context and to be motivational to the extent that it increases the subordinates' expectations that their effort will lead to valued rewards.

These propositions and specification of situational contingencies provide a heuristic framework on which to base future research. Hopefully, this will lead to a more fully developed, explicitly formal theory of leadership:

Figure II presents a summary of the theory. It is hoped that these propositions, while admittedly tentative, will provide managers with some insights concerning the effects of their own leader behavior and that of others.

Leader Behavior and	Contingency Factors		Cause	Subordinate Attitudes and Behavior
1 Directive	1 Subordinate characteristics authoritarianism locus of control	Influence →	Personal perceptions	1 Job satisfaction Job — rewards
2 Supportive	ability			2 Acceptance of leader Leader — rewards
3 Achievement-Oriented	2 Environmental factors The task Formal authority system	Influence →	Motivational stimuli constraints	3 Motivational behavior Effort — performance Performance — rewards
4 Participative	Primary work group		rewards	

Figure 2 Summary of Path-Goal Relationships

EMPIRICAL SUPPORT

The theory has been tested in a limited number of studies which have generated considerable empirical support for our ideas and also suggest areas in which the theory requires revision. A brief review of these studies follows.

Leader Directiveness

Leader directiveness has a positive correlation with satisfaction and expectancies of subordinates who are engaged in ambiguous tasks and has a negative correlation with satisfaction and expectancies of subordinates engaged in clear tasks. These findings were predicted by the theory and have been replicated in seven organizations. They suggest that when task demands are ambiguous or when the organization procedures, rules and policies are not clear, a leader behaving in a directive manner complements the tasks and the organization by providing the necessary guidance and psychological structure for subordinates.[10] However, when task demands are clear to subordinates, leader directiveness is seen more as a hindrance.

However, other studies have failed to confirm these findings.[11] A study by Dessler[12] suggests a resolution to these conflicting findings—he found that for subordinates at the lower organizational levels of a manufacturing firm who were doing routine, repetitive, unambiguous tasks, directive leadership was preferred by closed-minded, dogmatic, authoritarian subordinates and nondirective leadership was preferred by nonauthoritarian, open-minded subordinates. However, for subordinates at higher organizational levels doing nonroutine, ambiguous tasks, directive leadership was preferred for both authoritarian and nonauthoritarian subordinates. Thus, Dessler found that two contingency factors appear to operate simultaneously: subordinate task ambiguity and degree of subordinate authoritarianism. When measured in combination, the findings are as predicted by the theory; however, when the subordinate's personality is not taken into account, task ambiguity does not always operate as a contingency variable as predicted by the theory. House, Burill and Dessler recently found a similar interaction between subordinate authoritarianism and task ambiguity in a second manufacturing firm, thus adding confidence in Dessler's original findings.[13]

Supportive Leadership

The theory hypothesizes that supportive leadership will have its most positive effect on subordinate satisfaction for subordinates who work on stressful, frustrating or dissatisfying tasks. This hypothesis has been tested in 10 samples of employees,[14] and in only one of these studies was the hypothesis disconfirmed.[15] Despite some inconsistency in research on supportive leadership, the evidence is sufficiently positive to suggest that managers should be alert to the critical need for supportive leadership under conditions where tasks are dissatisfying, frustrating or stressful to subordinates.

Achievement-Oriented Leadership

The theory hypothesizes that achievement-oriented leadership will cause subordinates to strive for higher standards of performance and to have more confidence in the ability to meet challenging goals. A recent study by House, Valency and Van der Krabben provides a partial test of this hypothesis among white collar employees in service organizations.[16] For subordinates performing ambiguous, nonrepetitive tasks, they found a positive relationship between the amount of achievement orientation of the leader and subordinates' expectancy that their effort would result in effective performance. Stated less technically, for subordinates performing ambiguous, nonrepetitive tasks, the higher the achievement orientation of the leader, the more the subordinates were confident that their efforts would pay off in effective performance. For subordinates performing moderately unambiguous, repetitive tasks, there was no significant relationship between achievement-oriented leadership and subordinate expectancies that their effort would lead to effective performance. This finding held in four separate organizations.

Two plausible interpretations may be used to explain these data. First, people who select ambiguous, nonrepetitive tasks may be different in personality from those who select a repetitive job and may, therefore, be more responsive to an achievement-oriented leader. A second explanation is that achievement orientation only affects expectancies in ambiguous situations because there is more flexibility and autonomy in such tasks. Therefore, subordinates in such tasks are more likely to be able to change in response to such leadership style. Neither of the above interpretations have been tested to date; however, additional research is currently under way to investigate these relationships.

In theorizing about the effects of participative leadership it is necessary to ask about the specific characteristics of both the subordinates and their situation that would cause participative leadership to be viewed as satisfying and instrumental to effective performance.

Mitchell recently described at least four ways in which a participative leadership style would impact on subordinate attitudes and behavior as predicted by expectancy theory.[17] First, a participative climate should increase the clarity of organizational contingencies. Through participation in decision making, subordinates should learn what leads to what. From a path-goal viewpoint participation would lead to greater clarity of the paths to various goals. A second impact of participation would be that subordinates, hopefully, should select goals they highly value. If one participates in decisions about various goals, it makes sense that this individual would select goals he or she wants. Thus, participation would increase the correspondence between organization and subordinate goals. Third, we can see how participation would increase the control the individual has over what happens on the job. If our motivation is higher (based on the preceding two points), then having greater autonomy and ability to carry out our intentions should lead to increased effort and performance. Finally, under a participative system, pressure towards high performance should come from sources other than the leader or the organization. More specifically, when people participate in the decision process they become more ego-involved; the decisions made are in some part their own. Also, their peers know what is expected and the social pressure has a greater impact. Thus, motivation to perform well stems from internal and social factors as well as formal external ones.

A number of investigations prior to the above formulation supported the idea that participation appears to be helpful,[18] and Mitchell presents a number of recent studies that support the above four points.[19] However, it is also true that we would expect the relationship between a participative style and subordinate behavior to be moderated by both the personality characteristics of the subordinate and the situational demands. Studies by Tannenbaum and Alport and Vroom have shown that subordinates who prefer autonomy and self-control respond more positively to participative leadership in terms of both satisfaction and performance than subordinates who do not have such preferences.[20] Also, the studies mentioned by Runyon[21] and Mitchell[22] showed that subordinates who were external in orientation were less satisfied with a participative style of leadership than were internal subordinates.

House also has reviewed these studies in an attempt to explain the ways in which the situation or environment moderates the relationship between participation and subordinate attitudes and behavior.[23] His analysis suggests that where participative leadership is positively related to satisfaction, regardless of the predispositions of subordinates, the tasks of the subjects appear to be ambiguous and ego-involving. In the studies in which the subjects' personalities or predispositions moderate the effect of participative leadership, the tasks of the subjects are inferred to be highly routine and/or nonego-involving.

House reasoned from this analysis that the task may have an overriding effect on the relationship between leader participation and subordinate responses, and that individual predispositions or personality characteristics of subordinates may have an effect only under some tasks. It was assumed that when task demands are ambiguous, subordinates will have a need to reduce the ambiguity. Further, it was assumed that when task demands are ambiguous, participative problem solving between the leader and the subordinate will result in more effective decisions than when the task demands are unambiguous. Finally, it was assumed that when the subordinates are ego-involved in their tasks they are more likely to want to have a say in the decisions that affect them. Given these assumptions, the following hypotheses were formulated to account for the conflicting findings reviewed above:

- When subjects are highly ego-involved in a decision or a task and the decision or task demands are ambiguous, participative leadership will have a positive effect on the satisfaction and motivation of the subordinate, *regardless* of the subordinate's predisposition toward self-control, authoritarianism or need for independence.
- When subordinates are not ego-involved in their tasks and when task demands are clear, subordinates who are not authoritarian and who have high needs for independence and self-control will respond favorably to leader participation and their opposite personality types will respond less favorably.

These hypotheses were derived on the basis of path-goal theorizing; i.e., the rationale guiding the analysis of prior studies was that both task characteristics and characteristics of subordinates interact to determine the effect of a specific kind of leader behavior on the satisfaction, expectancies and performance of subordinates. To date, one major investigation has supported some of these predictions[24] in which personality variables, amount of participative leadership, task ambiguity and job satisfaction were assessed for 324 employees of an industrial manufacturing organization. As expected, in nonrepetitive, ego-involving tasks, employees (regardless of their personality) were more satisfied under a participative style than a nonparticipative style. However, in repetitive tasks which were less ego-involving the amount of authoritarianism of subordinates moderated the relationship between leadership style and satisfaction. Specifically, low authoritarian subordinates were *more satisfied* under a participative style. These findings are exactly as the theory would predict; thus, it has promise in reconciling a set of confusing and contradictory findings with respect to participative leadership.

SUMMARY AND CONCLUSIONS

We have attempted to describe what we believe is a useful theoretical framework for understanding the effect of leadership behavior on subordinate satisfaction and motivation. Most theorists today have moved away from the simplistic notions that all effective leaders have a certain set of personality traits or that the situation completely determines performance. Some researchers have presented rather complex attempts at matching certain types of leaders with certain types of situations, e.g., the articles written by Vroom and Fiedler in this issue. But, we believe that a path-goal approach goes one step further. It not only suggests what type of style may be most effective in a given situation—it also attempts to explain *why* it is most effective.

We are optimistic about the future outlook of leadership research. With the guidance of path-goal theorizing, future research is expected to unravel many confusing puzzles about the reasons for and effects of leader behavior that have, heretofore, not been solved. However, we add a word of caution: the theory, and the research on it, are relatively new to the literature of organizational behavior. Consequently, path-goal theory is offered more as a tool for directing research and stimulating insight than as a proven guide for managerial action.

[This article is also to be reprinted in *Readings in Organizational and Industrial Psychology* by G. A. Yukl and K. N. Wexley, 2nd edition (1975). The research by House and his associates was partially supported by a grant from the Shell Oil Company of Canada. The research by Mitchell and his associates was partially supported by the Office of Naval Research Contract NR 170–761, N00014–67–A–0103–0032 (Terence R. Mitchell, Principal Investigator).]

1. T. R. Mitchell, "Expectancy Model of Job Satisfaction, Occupational Preference and Effort: A Theoretical, Methodological and Empirical Appraisal," *Psychological Bulletin* (1974, in press).

2. D. M. Nebeker and T. R. Mitchell, "Leader Behavior: An Expectancy Theory Approach," *Organization Behavior and Human Performance*, 11 (1974), pp. 355–367.

3. M. G. Evans, "The Effects of Supervisory Behavior on the Path-Goal Relationship," *Organization Behavior and Human Performance*, 55 (1970), pp. 277–298; T. H. Hammer and H. T. Dachler, "The Process of Supervision in the Context of Motivation Theory," Research Report No. 3 (University of Maryland, 1973); F. Dansereau, Jr., J. Cashman and G. Graen, "Instrumentality Theory and Equity Theory As Complementary Approaches in Predicting the Relationship of Leadership and Turnover Among Managers," *Organization Behavior and Human Performance*, 10 (1973), pp. 184–200; R. J. House, "A Path-Goal Theory of Leader Effectiveness," *Administrative Science Quarterly*, 16, 3 (September 1971), pp. 321–338; T. R. Mitchell, "Motivation and Participation: An Integration," *Academy of Management Journal*, 16, 4 (1973), pp. 160–179; G. Graen, F. Dansereau, Jr. and T. Minami, "Dysfunctional Leadership Styles," *Organization Behavior and Human Performance*, 7 (1972), pp. 216–236; ———, "An Empirical Test of the Man-in-the-Middle Hypothesis Among Executives in a Hierarchical Organization Employing a Unit Analysis," *Organization Behavior and Human Performance*, 8 (1972), pp. 262–285; R. J. House and G. Dessler, "The Path-Goal Theory of Leadership: Some Post Hoc and A Priori Tests," to appear in J. G. Hunt, ed., *Contingency Approaches to Leadership* (Carbondale, Ill.: Southern Illinois University Press, 1974).

4. M. G. Evans, "Effects of Supervisory Behavior"; ———, "Extensions of a Path-Goal Theory of Motivation," *Journal of Applied Psychology*, 59 (1974), pp. 172–178.

5. R. J. House, "A Path-Goal Theory"; R. J. House and G. Dessler, "Path-Goal Theory of Leadership."

6. R. J. House and G. Dessler, "Path-Goal Theory of Leadership"; R. M. Stogdill, *Managers, Employees, Organization* (Ohio State University, Bureau of Business Research, 1965); R. J. House, A. Valency and R. Van der Krabben, "Some Tests and Extensions of the Path-Goal Theory of Leadership" (in preparation).

7. W. A. Hill and D. Hughes, "Variations in Leader Behavior As a Function of Task Type," *Organization Behavior and Human Performance* (1974, in press).

8. K. E. Runyon, "Some Interactions Between Personality Variables and Management Styles," *Journal of Applied Psychology*, 57, 3 (1973), pp. 288–294; T. R. Mitchell, C. R. Smyser and S. E. Weed, "Locus of Control: Supervision and Work Satisfaction," *Academy of Management Journal* (in press).

9. T. R. Mitchell, "Locus of Control."

10. R. J. House, "A Path-Goal Theory"; ——— and G. Dessler, "Path-Goal Theory of Leadership"; A. D. Szalagyi and H. P. Sims, "An Exploration of the Path-Goal Theory of Leadership in a Health Care Environment," *Academy of Management*

Journal (in press); J. D. Dermer, "Supervisory Behavior and Budget Motivation" (Cambridge, Mass.: unpublished, MIT, Sloan School of Management, 1974); R. W. Smetana, "The Relationship Between Managerial Behavior and Subordinate Attitudes and Motivation: A Contribution to a Behavioral Theory of Leadership" (Ph.D. diss, Wayne State University, 1974).

11. S. E. Weed, T. R. Mitchell and C. R. Smyser, "A Test of House's Path-Goal Theory of Leadership in an Organizational Setting" (paper presented at Western Psychological Assoc., 1974); J. D. Dermer and J. P. Siegel, "A Test of Path-Goal Theory: Disconfirming Evidence and a Critique" (unpublished, University of Toronto, Faculty of Management Studies, 1973); R. S. Schuler, "A Path-Goal Theory of Leadership: An Empirical Investigation" (Ph.D. diss, Michigan State University, 1973); H. K. Downey, J. E. Sheridan and J. W. Slocum, Jr., "Analysis of Relationships Among Leader Behavior, Subordinate Job Performance and Satisfaction: A Path-Goal Approach" (unpublished mimeograph, 1974); J. E. Stinson and T. W. Johnson, "The Path-Goal Theory of Leadership: A Partial Test and Suggested Refinement," *Proceedings* (Kent, Ohio: 7th Annual Conference of the Midwest Academy of Management, April 1974), pp. 18–36.

12. G. Dessler, "An Investigation of the Path-Goal Theory of Leadership" (Ph.D. diss, City University of New York, Bernard M. Baruch College, 1973).

13. R. J. House, D. Burrill and G. Dessler, "Tests and Extensions of Path-Goal Theory of Leadership, I" (unpublished, in process).

14. R. J. House, "A Path-Goal Theory"; ——— and G. Dessler, "Path-Goal Theory of Leadership"; A. D. Szalagyi and H. P. Sims, "Exploration of Path-Goal"; J. E. Stinson and T. W. Johnson, *Proceedings*; R. S. Schuler, "Path-Goal: Investigation"; H. K. Downey, J. E. Sheridan and J. W. Slocum, Jr., "Analysis of Relationships"; S. E. Weed, T. R. Mitchell and C. R. Smyser, "Test of House's Path-Goal."

15. A. D. Szalagyi and H. P. Sims, "Exploration of Path-Goal."

16. R. J. House, A. Valency and R. Van der Krabben, "Tests and Extensions of Path-Goal Theory of Leadership, II" (unpublished, in process).

17. T. R. Mitchell, "Motivation and Participation."

18. H. Tosi, "A Reexamination of Personality As a Determinant of the Effects of Participation," *Personnel Psychology*, 23 (1970), pp. 91–99; J. Sadler, "Leadership Style, Confidence in Management and Job Satisfaction," *Journal of Applied Behavior Sciences*, 6 (1970), pp. 3–19; K. N. Wexley, J. P. Singh and J. A. Yukl, "Subordinate Personality As a Moderator of the Effects of Participation in Three Types of Appraisal Interviews," *Journal of Applied Psychology*, 83 1 (1973), pp. 54–59.

19. T. R. Mitchell, "Motivation and Participation."

20. A. S. Tannenbaum and F. H. Allport, "Personality Structure and Group Structure: An Interpretive Study of Their Relationship Through an Event-Structure Hypothesis," *Journal of Abnormal and Social Psychology*, 53 (1956), pp. 272–280; V. H. Vroom, "Some Personality Determinants of the Effects of Participation," *Journal of Abnormal and Social Psychology*, 59 (1959), pp. 322–327.

21. K. E. Runyon, "Some Interactions Between Personality Variables and Management Styles," *Journal of Applied Psychology*, 57, 3 (1973), pp. 288–294.

22. T. R. Mitchell, C. R. Smyser and S. E. Weed, "Locus of Control."

23. R. J. House, "Notes on the Path-Goal Theory of Leadership" (University of Toronto, Faculty of Management Studies, May 1974).

24. R. S. Schuler, "Leader Participation, Task Structure and Subordinate Authoritarianism" (unpublished mimeograph, Cleveland State University, 1974).

Can Leaders Learn to Lead?

Victor H. Vroom

Like my fellow authors, I start with certain preconceptions. These preconceptions — some may call them biases — influence the way in which I view issues of leadership, particularly leadership training. I have tried to depict these preconceptions in Figure 1.

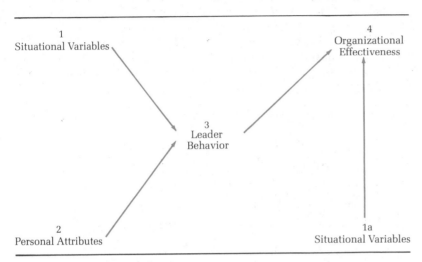

Figure 1 Schematic Representation of Variables Used in Leadership Research.

The central variable in this figure is the behavior of the leader, which I believe is determined by two classes of variables, attributes of the leader himself and attributes of the situation he encounters. Furthermore, I assume that many of the differences in the behavior of leaders can be explained only by examining their joint effects, including interactions between these two classes of variables.

The left-hand portion of the diagram is the descriptive side of the leader behavior equation. Much of my research has focused on these relationships in an attempt to understand the ways in which managers actually respond to situations that vary in a number of dimensions. If you examine the right-hand side of Figure 1, however, you encounter issues that are potentially normative or prescriptive in character. They deal with the consequences of leader behavior for the organization and here I share with Fiedler (and probably disagree with Argyris) a conviction that a contingency model is required. I do not see any form of leader behavior as optimal for all situations. The

This article is based on a paper delivered at the 1975 annual meeting of the American Psychological Association.

contribution of a leader's actions to the effectiveness of his organization cannot be determined without considering the nature of the situation in which that behavior is displayed.

WORKING WITH THE CONTINGENCY MODEL

I am going to assume that most of you are familiar with the model that Phil Yetton and I developed and have described in detail in our recent book. As a normative model, it deals with the right-hand side of Figure 1, but it is a limited model because it deals with only one facet of leadership behavior — the extent to which the leader shares his decision-making power with his subordinates.

Figure 2 shows the latest version of our model. For purposes of simplicity, the presentation here is restricted to the model for group problems, that is, problems or decisions that affect all or a substantial portion of the manager's subordinates. At the

A. Does the problem possess a quality requirement?
B. Do I have sufficient information to make a high-quality decision?
C. Is the problem structured?
D. Is acceptance of the decision by subordinates important for effective implementation?
E. If I were to make the decision by myself, am I reasonably certain that it would be accepted by my subordinates?
F. Do subordinates share the organizational goals to be attained in solving this problem?
G. Is conflict among subordinates likely in preferred solutions?

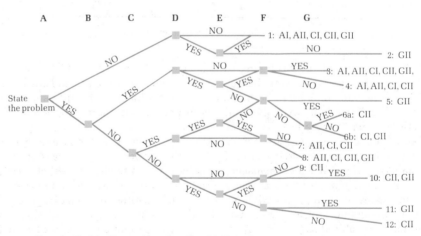

Figure 2　Decision Process Flowchart (Feasible Set)

top of the figure are problem attributes — that is, situational variables that ought to influence the decision process used by the leader — specifically, the amount of opportunity that the leader gives his subordinates to participate in the making of a decision. To use the model, one first selects an organization problem to be solved or decision to be made. Starting at the left-hand side of the diagram, one asks oneself the question pertaining to each attribute that is encountered, follows the path developed, and finally determines the problem type (numbered 1 through 12). This problem type specifies one or more decision processes that are deemed appropriate to that problem. These decision processes are called the "feasible set" and represent the methods that remain after a set of seven rules has been applied. The first three of these rules eliminate methods that threaten the quality of the decisions, while the last four rules eliminate methods that are likely to jeopardize acceptance of the decision by subordinates.

For those who are unfamiliar with the Vroom-Yetton model, let me point out that the decision processes are described here in a kind of code. AI and AII are variants of an autocratic process. In AI the manager solves the problem by himself using whatever information is available to him at that time; in AII he obtains any necessary information of a specific nature from his subordinates before making the decision himself. CI and CII are variants of a consultative process. In CI he shares the problem with relevant subordinates individually, getting their ideas and suggestions before making the decision; CII is similar, but the consultation takes place within the context of a group meeting. Finally, GII corresponds with Norman Maier's concept of group decision in which the manager's role is that of chairperson of a group meeting aimed at reaching consensus on the action to be taken.

The part of the model described so far specifies how decisions should *not* be made, not how they should be made. For most problem types, there exist more than one decision process consistent with the rules and therefore contained in the feasible set. We have also been concerned with the consequences of various ways of choosing from these alternatives. There is considerable evidence that the time required to make the decision (defined either as the elapsed time or the number of man-hours needed to make the decision) increases with the intensity of involvement or participation of subordinates. Thus a time-efficient model (which we term Model A) would select the most autocratic alternative within the feasible set, a choice that would be clearly indicated in crisis or emergency situations and in situations in which one seeks to minimize the number of man-hours that enter into making the decision.

Of course, time is not the only dimension to include in deciding the degree to which the leader should encourage the participation of his subordinates in decision making. In addition to the possibilities that participation may increase decision quality or its acceptance (considerations that are incorporated into the rules referred to previously), there are also grounds for believing that participation contributes to individual and team development and is likely to result in more informed and responsible behavior by subordinates in the future. Hence Model B, which could be thought of as a time-investment or developmental model, dictates the choice of the most participative process within the feasible set. It is important to note that Models A and B are consistent with the same rules (to protect decision quality and acceptance) but represent extremely different ways of operating within these rules. Model A maximizes a short-run value—time; Model B maximizes a long-run value—development.

What is the image of the effective leader portrayed by this normative model? He is neither universally autocratic nor universally participative but utilizes either approach in response to the demands of a situation *as he perceives them.* Above all, he is a flexible leader who has thought through his values and who has a repertoire of skills necessary to execute effectively each of the decision processes.

VALIDATING THE MODEL

When Philip Yetton and I wrote our book, we had no evidence validating the model other than the consistency of our rules with existing empirical evidence concerning the consequences of alternative approaches. During the past six months, Art Jago and I have been working to remedy this deficiency. We have asked managers, all of whom were unfamiliar with the model, to select two decisions that they had made — one that proved to be successful and one that proved to be unsuccessful. Each manager wrote up each decision situation as a case and specified the decision process he used in solving the problem. Later these managers were trained in the problem attributes and went back over each of these two cases, coding each in a manner that would permit the researcher to determine the problem type and the feasible set of methods for that problem type.

The data for this study are still coming in. To date, we have written accounts of 46 successful decisions and 42 unsuccessful ones. (It seems that some managers have difficulty in recalling the decisions they made that did not turn out too well!) Figure 3 shows the results available so far. These results clearly support the validity of the model. If the manager's method of dealing with the case corresponded with the model, the probability of the decision's being deemed successful was 65 percent; if the method disagreed with the model, the probability of its being deemed successful was only 29 percent.

It is important to note, however, that behavior that corresponds with the model is no guarantee that the decision will ultimately turn out to be successful — nor is behavior outside the feasible set inevitably associated with an unsuccessful decision.

To create a model of decision processes that completely predicts decision outcomes (that is, which generates 100 percent observations in upper left and lower right cells) is an impossibility. Any fantasies that we may have entertained about having created a model of process that would completely determine decision outcomes have been permanently dashed against the rocks of reality! Insofar as organizations are open systems and decisions within them are made under conditions of risk and uncertainty, it will be impossible to generate complete predictability for a model such as ours. To be sure, we may be able to use the data from the study I have described to improve the "batting average" of the model, but the limit of success must be less than perfection.

Figure 3   Relationship Between Model Agreement and Decision Outcome

	Percent Successful	Percent Unsuccessful	Total
Method used agrees with feasible set	65	35	100%
Method used disagrees with feasible set	29	71	100%

IMPLICATIONS FOR TRAINING

I would now like to turn to the central issue of this symposium, the use of the model in leadership training. Over the past few years, several thousand managers have received training in the concepts underlying the model. The workshops have ranged from two to over five days in length, and the participants have included admirals, corporation presidents, school superintendents, and senior government officials. I have been personally involved in enough of this training to have learned some important things about what to do and what not to do. And because I believe that there are substantial but understandable misconceptions about how training based on the Vroom and Yetton model works, I would like to describe the things I have learned.

It would have been possible to build a training program around the model that was completely cognitive and mechanistic. Participants would be sold on the model and then trained in its use through intensive practice—first on standardized cases and later on real problems drawn from their own experiences. Such an approach would represent a new domain for Taylorism and could even be accomplished through Skinnerian programmed learning. I believe that, at best, this behavioral approach would influence what Argyris calls espoused theories and would not have any long-lasting behavioral effects.

Our methods have been much more influenced by Carl Rogers than by B. F. Skinner. We have assumed that behavioral changes require a process of self-discovery and insight by each individual manager.

One method of stimulating this process is to provide the participant with a picture of his own leadership style. This picture includes a comparison of his style with that of others, the situational factors that influence his willingness to share his power with others, and similarities and differences between his own "model" and the normative models.

In advance of the training program, each participant sits down with a set of cases, each of which depicts a leader confronted with an actual organizational problem. We call these cases "problem sets," and the number of cases in different problem sets ranges from 30 to 54. The common feature in each of the eight or nine problem sets that have been developed is that the cases vary along each of the situational dimensions used in the construction of the normative model. The set is designed so that the variation is systematic and that the effects of each situational attribute on a given manager's choice of decision process can be readily determined. This feature permits the assessment of each of the problem attributes in the decision processes used by a given manager.

The manager's task is to select the decision process that comes closest to depicting what he would do in each situation. His responses are recorded on a standardized form and processed by computer along with other participants' responses in the same program.

Instead of writing about information contained on a printout, I thought that it might be more efficient to let you see what it looks like. The next figure reproduces three of the seven pages of feedback that a manager recently received. Examine the first page of the printout shown in Figure 4. Consider A first in that figure. The first row opposite "your frequency" shows the proportion of cases in which the manager indicated he would use each of the five decision processes. The next row (opposite "peer frequency") shows the average use of these processes by the 41 managers constituting his training group. A comparison of these two rows indicates the methods he used more and less frequently than average.

The third row shows the distribution of decision processes that would be used by a manager using Model A, the time-efficient model in the 30 cases. The final row shows a distribution for Model B, the developmental or time-investment model.

To obtain an overall picture of how participative this manager's responses are in relation to other members of his training group and to Models A and B, it is necessary to assign scale values to each of the five decision processes. The actual numbers used for this purpose are based on research on the relative amounts of participation perceived to result from each process. AI is given a value of 0; AII a value of 1; CI a value of 5; CII a value of 8; and GII a value of 10.

With the aid of these scale values a mean score can be computed for the manager,

Leadership Style Analysis

NAME OR I.D. -- JOHN DOE

A-- PROPORTION OF CASES IN WHICH
EACH DECISION PROCESS IS USED

	AI	AII	CI	CII	GII
YOUR FREQUENCY	43%	3%	23%	30%	0%
PEER FREQUENCY	25%	14%	19%	27%	15%
MODEL A (MINIMIZE PARTICIPATION)	40%	13%	3%	23%	20%
MODEL B (MAXIMIZE PARTICIPATION)	0%	0%	0%	40%	60%

B--SCALED PARTICIPATION SCORES

	MEAN	SD
YOUR RESPONSE	3.60	3.48
PEER AVERAGE	4.73	3.66
MODEL A	4.17	4.31
MODEL B	9.20	0.98

* - YOUR SCORE IN FIGURE L

C--FREQUENCY DISTRIBUTION OF SCALE SCORES
(MEAN LEVELS OF PARTICIPATION)

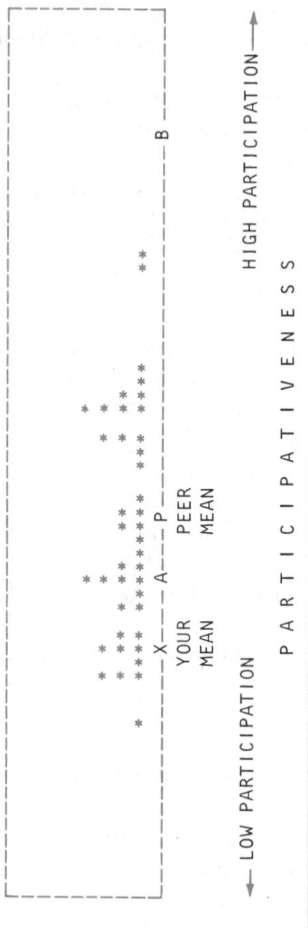

←LOW PARTICIPATION   HIGH PARTICIPATION→

PARTICIPATIVENESS

X--- YOUR MEAN   A---P PEER MEAN   B

Figure 4. Page 1 of Printout

his peers, and both models. These are obtained by multiplying the percentage of times each process is used by its scale value and dividing by 100. These mean scores are shown in B along with the standard deviation (SD), a measure of dispersion around the mean—that is, an indicator of how much behavior is varied over situations.

These mean scores are shown graphically in the figure at the bottom. Each asterisk is the mean score of one of the group members. The symbol X is printed underneath this manager's mean score, the symbol P under the group average, and the symbols A and B show the location on the scale of Models A and B respectively.

D through F in Figure 4 are on the second page of the printout. As we previously

Leadership Style Analysis

D ----BEHAVIOR BY PROBLEM TYPE

PROBLEM TYPE	PROBLEM NUMBERS	MODEL "A"	MODEL "B"	FEASIBLE SET	YOUR BEHAVIOR			
1	14,15,17,28	AL	GII	AI,AII,CI,CII,GII	AI	AI	AI	AI
2	3,5,	GII	GII	CII	CII	CII	CII	
3	2,22,27,30	AI	GII	AI,AII,CI,CII,GII	AI	AI	AI	CII
4	12,25,26,29	AI	GII	AI,AII,CI,CII	AI	CI	CI	AI
5	7,8,20	GII	CII	AI, GII	CII	CII	CII	
6A	1,10	CII	CII	CII	CII	CII		
6B	11	CII	CII	CI,CII	CI			
7	21,24	AII	CII	AII,CI,CII	CII	AII		
8	19,23	AII	GII	AII,CI,CII,GII	CII	AII		
9	4,16	CII	CII	CII	AI	CI		
10	6,9	CII	GII	CII,GII	AI	CI		
11	13	GII	GII	GII	CII			
12	18	CII	CII	CII	CII			

E --- FREQUENCY OF AGREEMENT WITH THE NORMATIVE MODEL

	YOUR MEAN	PEER AVERAGE
AGREEMENT WITH FEASIBLE SET	17 (57%)	20.8 (69%)
AGREEMENT MODEL A (MINIMUM PARTICIPATION)	12 (40%)	12.1 (40%)
AGREEMENT WITH MODEL B (MAXIMUM PARTICIPATION)	4 (13%)	6.3 (21%)

F---FREQUENCY OF RULE VIOLATIONS

RULE	RESPONSES IN VIOLATION	YOUR FREQUENCY	PEER AVERAGE	PROBLEM NUMBERS
1 LEADER INFORMATION RULE	AI	3.0 (25%)	0.7 (6%)	6 19 24
2 GOAL CONGRUENCE RULE	GII	0.0 (0%)	1.3 (10%)	0 9 16
3 UNSTRUCTURED PROBLEM RULE	AI,AII,CI	3.0 (50%)	2.8 (47%)	6 9 16
4 ACCEPTANCE RULE	AI,AII	1.0 (10%)	1.3 (13%)	5 10
5 CONFLICT RULE	AI,AII,CI	3.0 (60%)	1.9 (39%)	1 5 10
6 FAIRNESS RULE	AI,AII,CI,CII	2.0 (100%)	1.3 (63%)	3 5
7 ACCEPTANCE PRIORITY RULE	AI,AII,CI,CII	40 (100%)	2.9 (72%)	7 8 13 20

*---PROBABILITY OF RULE VIOLATION (THAT IS, FREQUENCY OF VIOLATION EXPRESSED AS A PERCENTAGE OF RULE APPLICABILITY)

Figure 4. Page 2 of Printout

mentioned, the normative model identifies 12 problem types corresponding to the terminal nodes of the decision tree shown in Figure 2. There is at least one case within the set of 30 problems that has been designated by the authors and most managers as representative of each type. The problem types and corresponding problem numbers are shown in the two left-hand columns of D. In the third and fourth columns, the prescriptions of Models A and B are given, and the fifth column shows the feasible set for that problem type. The last column, marked "your behavior," indicates the manager's responses to each of the cases of the indicated problem type. If there is more than one case of that type, the methods used are shown in the same order as the problem numbers at the left-hand side.

Leadership Style Analysis

G---MAIN EFFECTS OF PROBLEM ATTRIBUTES

YOUR MEAN = X MODEL A MEAN = A
PEER MEAN = P MODEL B MEAN = B

PROBLEM ATTRIBUTES		PARTICIPATIVENESS ON PROBLEMS WITH ATTRIBUTE < LOW PARTICIPATION — HIGH PARTICIPATION >	PROBLEMS WITH ATTRIBUTE
IMPORTANCE OF THE QUALITY OF THE FINAL SOLUTION (ATTRIBUTE A)	HIGH X=4.17 P=4.97 A=4.38	XA — P — B	(1,2,4,6,7,8,9,10,11,12,13 16,18,19,20,21,22,23,24,25 26,27,29,30)
	LOW x=1.33 P=3.75 A=3.33	X — A — P — B	(3,5,14,15,17,28)
ADEQUACY OF MANAGER'S INFORMATION AND EXPERTISE (ATTRIBUTE B)	HIGH x=3.67 P=4.24 A=2.75	A — X — P — B	(1,2,8,11,12,20,22,25,26 27,23,30)
	LOW x=4.67 P=5.71 A=6.00	X — P-A — B	(7,10,19,21,23,24)
DEGREE OF STRUCTURE IN PROBLEM (ATTRIBUTE C)	HIGH x=3.67 P=4.97 A=3.67	X — P — B	(7,10,19,21,23,24)
	LOW x=5.67 P=6.46 A=8.33	X — P — A — B	(4,6,9,13,16,18)
IMPORTANCE OF SUBORDINATE ACCEPTANCE (ATTRIBUTE D)	HIGH x=3.20 P=5.30 A-5.35	X — P — B	(1,3,5,6,7,8,10,11,12,13,14 15,16,18,19,20,22,24,29,30)
	LOW X=3.20 P=3.59 A=1.80	A — X—P P — B	(2,4,9,17,21,23,25,26,27,28)
PROBABILITY OF LEADER'S SELLING HIS OWN SOLUTION (ATTRIBUTE E)	HIGH X=1.30 P=3.68 A-1.80	X — A — P — B	(6,12,14,15,16,19,22,24,29,30)
	LOW X=6.30 P=6.91 A=8.90	X — P — A-B	(1,3,5,7,8,10,11,13,18,20_
DEGREE TO WHICH SUBORDINATES SHARE GOALS (ATTRIBUTE F)	HIGH X=3.58 P=5.45 A=4.83	X — A — P — B	(2,6,7,8,9,13,19,20,22,23,27, 30)
	LOW X=4.75 P=4.49 A=3.92	A — P — X — B	(1,4,10,11,12,16,18,21,24, 25,26,29)
PROBABILITY OF CONFLICT AMONG SUBORDINATES (ATTRIBUTE G)	HIGH 3.27 P=3.99 A=4.27	X — P — A — B	(1,2,5,8,9,10,13,15,16,19 2021,22,26,28,29)
	LOW X=3.93 P=5.47 A=4.07	X — P — B	(3,4,6,7,11,12,14,17,18 2020,23,24,25,27,30)

****** NOTE: THE THREE ATTRIBUTES WITH THE GREATEST EFFECT ON YOUR RESPONSES ARE A, C, AND E. *******

Figure 4. Page 3 of Printout

E reports the frequency with which the manager's behavior agreed with the feasible set, with Model A, and with Model B. For comparison purposes, the average rates of agreement for members of the manager's training group are also presented.

Each time our manager chose a decision process that was outside the feasible set, he violated at least one of the seven rules underlying the model. F in Figure 4 reports the frequencies with which each rule was violated both by this manager and by his peer group. The right-hand column shows the specific cases in which the rule violations occurred. It should be noted that each manager understands the seven rules by the time he receives the feedback, and it is possible for him to reexamine the problems with the appropriate rule in mind.

We have previously noted that the cases included in a problem set are selected in accordance with a multifactorial experimental design. Each of the problem attributes is varied in a manner that will permit the manager to examine its role in his leadership style. Figure 4 (page 3 of printout) depicts these results. Consider problem attribute A — the importance of the quality of the final solution. The problem set contains cases that have a high quality requirement and those without a quality requirement (the identifying numbers of these cases are shown at the right-hand side of this table).

The mean scores for the manager's behavior on these two sets of cases are specified at the left-hand side of each row and are designated by the symbol X. They are also designated by the symbol X on each of the scales, and the slope of the line made by connecting the two letters (X) provides a visual representation of that difference.

If the score opposite "high" is greater (that is, more toward the right-hand side of the scale), it means that the manager encourages more participation from his subordinates on important decisions than on so-called "trivial" ones. However, if the score opposite "high" is lower, it means that the manager is willing to use more participative methods on problems for which the course of action adopted makes little difference and is more autocratic on "important" decisions.

The letter P shown on both scales designates the average effects of this attribute on the manager's peer group, and the letters A and B designate the effects on Models A and B respectively.

A similar logic can be used in interpreting the effects of each of the other attributes in the model. At the bottom of the page, the computer prints out the three attributes that have the greatest effect on the manager's behavior — magnitude of effect referring to the amount of difference the attribute makes in his willingness to share his decision-making power with subordinates.

The results shown in Figure 4 pertain to only one manager and to his peer group. Similar data have been obtained from several thousand managers, a sufficient number to provide the basis for some tentative generalizations about leadership patterns. One of our conclusions is that differences among managers in what might be termed a general trait of participativeness or authoritarianism are small in comparison with differences within managers. On the standardized cases in the problem sets, no manager has indicated that he would use the same decision process on all problems or decisions — and most use all methods under some circumstances.

It is clear that no one score computed for a manager and displayed on his printout adequately represents his leadership style. To begin to understand his style, the entire printout must be considered. For example, two managers may appear to be equally participative or autocratic on the surface, but a close look at the third page of the printout (Figure 4) may reveal crucial differences. One manager may limit participation by his subordinates to decisions where the quality element is unimportant, such as the time and place of the company picnic, while the other manager may limit participation by his subordinates to those decisions with a demonstrable impact on important organizational goals.

In about two-thirds of the cases we have examined — both those used in the problem sets and those reported to us by managers from their experiences — the manager's behavior was consistent with the feasible set of methods given by the model. Rules that helped ensure the acceptance of or commitment to a decision tend to be violated much more frequently than rules that protect the quality of the decision. Our findings suggest strongly that decisions made by typical managers are more likely to prove ineffective because subordinates don't fully accept decisions than because decision quality is deficient.

Let me now turn to another thing that we have learned in the design of this training—the usefulness of the small, informal group as a vehicle in the change process. The first four or five hours in the training process are spent in creating six- to eight-person teams operating under conditions of openness and trust. Each participant spends more than 50 percent of the training time with his small group before receiving feedback. Group activities include discussing cases in the problem set and trying to reach agreement on their mode of resolution, practicing participative leadership styles within their own groups, analyzing videotapes of group problem-solving activities; then group members give one another feedback on the basis of predictions of one another's leadership styles.

After feedback, group members compare results with one another and with their prior predictions and share with one another what they have learned as well as their plans to change. The use of small, autonomous groups greatly decreases the dependence of participants on the instructor for their learning and increases the number of people who can undergo the training at the same time. I have personally worked with as many as 140 managers at the same time (22 groups), and 40 to 50 is commonplace.

One criticism that has been correctly leveled at the Vroom and Yetton work stems from the fact that the data on which the feedback is based are, at best, reports of intended actions rather than observations of actual behavior. While we have evidence that most managers honestly try to portray what they think they would do in a particular situation rather than what they think they should do, I am persuaded by Argyris's evidence that many people are unaware of discrepancies between their espoused theories and their actions. Small groups can be helpful in pointing out these discrepancies. I have seen managers who were universally predicted by other group members to have a highly autocratic style, who were provided with very specific evidence of the ground for this assumption by other group members, but who later received a printout reflecting a much more participative style. I am less concerned about the relative validity of these discrepant pieces of data than I am about the fact that they are frequently confronted and discussed in the course of the training experience.

In fact, we have begun using a different source of potential inconsistencies, and it is logical to assume that this source will have more information about a manager's behavior than do the other members of his small group. I am referring to the manager's subordinates.

In a recent variant of the training program, subordinates were asked to predict their managers' behavior on each of the cases in the problem set. These predictions were made individually and processed by computer, which generated for each manager a detailed comparison of his perceptions of his leadership style with the mean perception of his subordinates. Not surprisingly, these two sources of information are not always in perfect agreement. Most managers, as seen by their subordinates, are substantially more autocratic (about one point on the 10-point scale) and in substantially less agreement with the model. Once again, I am less concerned with which is the correct description of the leader's behavior than I am with the fact that discrepancies generate a dialogue between the manager and his subordinates that can be the source of mutual learning.

We are still experimenting with methods of using the Vroom-Yetton model in leadership training and, I believe, still learning from the results of this experimentation. How effective is the training in its present form? Does it produce long-lasting behavioral changes? I must confess that I do not know. Art Jago and I are in the first stages of designing an extensive follow-up study of almost 200 managers in 20 different countries who have been through a four- or five-day version of the training within the past two and one-half years. If we can solve the incredible logistical and methodological problems in a study of this kind, we should have results within a year.

On the basis of the evidence, I am optimistic on two counts: first, as to the leader's potential to vary his style to meet the requirements of a situation; second, as to the leader's ability, through training and development, to enlarge the repertoire of his styles. In short, like Argyris and unlike Fiedler, I believe that managers can learn to become more effective leaders. But like Fiedler (and unlike Argyris), I believe that such effectiveness requires a matching of one's leadership style to the demands of the situation. I also am confident that 50 years from now both contingency models will be found wanting in detail if not in substance. If we are remembered at that time, it will be for the kinds of questions we posed rather than the specific answers we provided.

SELECTED BIBLIOGRAPHY

Victor Vroom and Philip Yetton's *Leadership and Decision Making* (University of Pittsburgh Press, 1973) presents a comprehensive description of their normative model, its research underpinnings, and its use in leadership training. Vroom's "A New Look at Managerial Decision Making" (*Organizational Dynamics*, Spring 1973) gives a brief description of the model and a summary of early research results. Victor Vroom and Arthur Jago's "Decision Making as a Social Process: Normative and Descriptive Models of Leader Behavior" (*Decision Sciences*, Vol. 5, 1974) extends the model to individual problems (affecting only a single subordinate) and incorporates delegation as a process. It compares and contrasts behavior on group and individual problems.

Norman Maier's *Problem Solving Discussions and Conferences* (McGraw-Hill, 1963) contains the most useful account of the conference leadership skills necessary to execute a participative approach to decision making.

Robert Tannenbaum and Warren Schmidt's "How to Choose a Leadership Pattern" (*Harvard Business Review*, March–April 1958) presents another perspective on the normative issues surrounding participation in decision making.

Any reader interested in further exploring the approach to leadership training described in this article should write to Kepner-Tregoe, Inc.; P.O. Box 704; Research Road; Princeton, New Jersey 08540.

How to Choose a Leadership Pattern
Robert Tannenbaum and Warren H. Schmidt

"I put most problems into my group's hands and leave it to them to carry the ball from there. I serve merely as a catalyst, mirroring back the people's thoughts and feelings so that they can better understand them. . . ."

"How to Choose a Leadership Pattern" by Robert Tannenbaum and Warren Schmidt in *Harvard Business Review*, May–June 1973, pp. 162–180. © 1973 by the President and Fellows of Harvard College; all rights reserved.

"It's foolish to make decisions oneself on matters that affect people. I always talk things over with my subordinates, but I make it clear to them that I'm the one who has to have the final say. . . ."

"Once I have decided on a course of action, I do my best to sell my ideas to my employees. . . ."

"I'm being paid to lead. If I let a lot of other people make the decisions I should be making, then I'm not worth my salt. . . ."

"I believe in getting things done. I can't waste time calling meetings. Someone has to call the shots around here, and I think it should be me. . . ."

Each of these statements represents a point of view about "good leadership." Considerable experience, factual data, and theoretical principles could be cited to support each statement, even though they seem to be inconsistent when placed together. Such contradictions point up the dilemma in which the modern manager frequently finds himself.

NEW PROBLEM

The problem of how the modern manager can be "democratic" in his relations with subordinates and at the same time maintain the necessary authority and control in the organization for which he is responsible has come into focus increasingly in recent years.

Earlier in the century this problem was not so acutely felt. The successful executive was generally pictured as possessing intelligence, imagination, initiative, the capacity to make rapid (and generally wise) decisions, and the ability to inspire subordinates. People tended to think of the world as being divided into "leaders" and "followers."

New Focus

Gradually, however, from the social sciences emerged the concept of "group dynamics" with its focus on *members* of the group rather than solely on the leader. Research efforts of social scientists underscored the importance of employee involvement and participation in decision-making. Evidence began to challenge the efficiency of highly directive leadership, and increasing attention was paid to problems of motivation and human relations.

Through training laboratories in group development that sprang up across the country, many of the newer notions of leadership began to exert an impact. These training laboratories were carefully designed to give people a first-hand experience in full participation and decision-making. The designated "leaders" deliberately attempted to reduce their own power and to make group members as responsible as possible for setting their own goals and methods within the laboratory experience.

It was perhaps inevitable that some of the people who attended the training laboratories regarded this kind of leadership as being truly "democratic" and went home with the determination to build fully participative decision-making into their own organizations. Whenever their bosses made a decision without convening a staff meeting, they tended to perceive this as authoritarian behavior. The true symbol of democratic leadership to some was the meeting — and the less directed from the top, the more democratic it was.

Some of the more enthusiastic alumni of these training laboratories began to get the habit of categorizing leader behavior as "democratic" or "authoritarian." The boss who made too many decisions himself was thought of as an authoritarian, and his directive behavior was often attributed solely to his personality.

New Need

The net result of the research findings and of the human relations training based upon them has been to call into question the stereotype of an effective leader. Consequently, the modern manager often finds himself in an uncomfortable state of mind.

Often he is not quite sure how to behave; there are times when he is torn between exerting "strong" leadership and "permissive" leadership. Sometimes new knowledge pushes him in one direction ("I should really get the group to help make this decision"), but at the same time his experience pushes him in another direction ("I really understand the problem better than the group and therefore I should make the decision"). He is not sure when a group decision is really appropriate or when holding a staff meeting serves merely as a device for avoiding his own decision-making responsibility.

The purpose of our article is to suggest a framework which managers may find useful in grappling with this dilemma. First, we shall look at the different patterns of leadership behavior that the manager can choose from in relating himself to his subordinates. Then, we shall turn to some of the questions suggested by this range of patterns. For instance, how important is it for a manager's subordinates to know what type of leadership he is using in a situation? What factors should he consider in deciding on a leadership pattern? What difference do his long-run objectives make as compared to his immediate objectives?

Range of Behavior

Figure 1 presents the continuum or range of possible leadership behavior available to a manager. Each type of action is related to the degree of authority used by the boss and to the amount of freedom available to his subordinates in reaching decisions. The actions seen on the extreme left characterize the manager who maintains a high degree of control while those seen on the extreme right characterize the manager who releases a high degree of control. Neither extreme is absolute; authority and freedom are never without their limitations.

Now let us look more closely at each of the behavior points occurring along this continuum.

The manager makes the decision and announces it.   In this case the boss identifies a problem, considers alternative solutions, chooses one of them, and then reports this decision to his subordinates for implementation. He may or may not give consideration to what he believes his subordinates will think or feel about his decision; in any case, he provides no opportunity for them to participate directly in the decision-making process. Coercion may or may not be used or implied.

The manager "sells" his decision.   Here the manager, as before, takes responsibility for identifying the problem and arriving at a decision. However, rather than simply announcing it, he takes the additional step of persuading his subordinates to accept it. In doing so, he recognizes the possibility of some resistance among those who will be faced with the decision, and seeks to reduce this resistance by indicating, for example, what the employees have to gain from his decision.

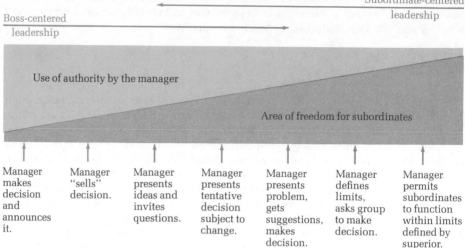

Figure 1   Continuum of Leadership Behavior

The manager presents his ideas, invites questions.   Here the boss who has arrived at a decision and who seeks acceptance of his ideas provides an opportunity for his subordinates to get a fuller explanation of his thinking and his intentions. After presenting the ideas, he invites questions so that his associates can better understand what he is trying to accomplish. This "give and take" also enables the manager and the subordinates to explore more fully the implications of the decision.

The manager presents a tentative decision subject to change.   This kind of behavior permits the subordinates to exert some influence on the decision. The initiative for identifying and diagnosing the problem remains with the boss. Before meeting with his staff, he has thought the problem through and arrived at a decision—but only a tentative one. Before finalizing it, he presents his proposed solution for the reaction of those who will be affected by it. He says in effect, "I'd like to hear what you have to say about this plan that I have developed. I'll appreciate your frank reactions, but will reserve for myself the final decision."

The manager presents the problem, gets suggestions, and then makes his decision.   Up to this point the boss has come before the group with a solution of his own. Not so in this case. The subordinates now get the first chance to suggest solutions. The manager's initial role involves identifying the problem. He might, for example, say something of this sort: "We are faced with a number of complaints from newspapers and the general public on our service policy. What is wrong here? What ideas do you have for coming to grips with this problem?"

The function of the group becomes one of increasing the manager's repertory of possible solutions to the problem. The purpose is to capitalize on the knowledge and experience of those who are on the "firing line." From the expanded list of alternatives developed by the manager and his subordinates, the manager then selects the solution that he regards as most promising.[1]

The manager defines the limits and requests the group to make a decision.   At this point the manager passes to the group (possibly including himself as a member) the right to make decisions. Before doing so, however, he defines the problem to be solved and the boundaries within which the decision must be made.

An example might be the handling of a parking problem at a plant. The boss decides that this is something that should be worked on by the people involved, so he calls them together and points up the existence of the problem. Then he tells them:

"There is the open field just north of the main plant which has been designated for additional employee parking. We can build underground or surface multilevel facilities as long as the cost does not exceed $100,000. Within these limits we are free to work out whatever solution makes sense to us. After we decide on a specific plan, the company will spend the available money in whatever way we indicate."

The manager permits the group to make decisions within prescribed limits. This represents an extreme degree of group freedom only occasionally encountered in formal organizations, as, for instance, in many research groups. Here the team of managers or engineers undertakes the identification and diagnosis of the problem, develops alternative procedures for solving it, and decides on one or more of these alternative solutions. The only limits directly imposed on the group by the organization are those specified by the superior of the team's boss. If the boss participates in the decision-making process, he attempts to do so with no more authority than any other member of the group. He commits himself in advance to assist in implementing whatever decision the group makes.

KEY QUESTIONS

As the continuum in Figure 1 demonstrates, there are a number of alternative ways in which a manager can relate himself to the group or individuals he is supervising. At the extreme left of the range, the emphasis is on the manager—on what *he* is interested in, how *he* sees things, how *he* feels about them. As we move toward the subordinate-centered end of the continuum, however, the focus is increasingly on the subordinates—on what *they* are interested in, how *they* look at things, how *they* feel about them.

When business leadership is regarded in this way, a number of questions arise. Let us take four of especial importance:

Can a boss ever relinquish his responsibility by delegating it to someone else? Our view is that the manager must expect to be held responsible by his superior for the quality of the decisions made, even though operationally these decisions may have been made on a group basis. He should, therefore, be ready to accept whatever risk is involved whenever he delegates decision-making power to his subordinates. Delegation is not a way of "passing the buck." Also, it should be emphasized that the amount of freedom the boss gives to his subordinates cannot be greater than the freedom which he himself has been given by his own superior.

Should the manager participate with his subordinates once he has delegated responsibility to them? The manager should carefully think over this question and decide on his role prior to involving the subordinate group. He should ask if his presence will inhibit or facilitate the problem-solving process. There may be some instances when he should leave the group to let it solve the problem for itself. Typically, however, the boss has useful ideas to contribute, and should function as an additional member of the group. In the latter instance, it is important that he indicate clearly to the group that he sees himself in a *member* role rather than in an authority role.

How important is it for the group to recognize what kind of leadership behavior the boss is using? It makes a great deal of difference. Many relationship problems between boss and subordinate occur because the boss fails to make clear how he plans to use his authority. If, for example, he actually intends to make a certain decision himself, but the subordinate group gets the impression that he has delegated this authority, considerable confusion and resentment are likely to follow. Problems may also occur when the boss uses a "democratic" facade to conceal the fact that he has already made a decision which he hopes the group will accept as its own. The attempt to "make them think it was their idea in the first place" is a risky one. We believe that it is highly important for the manager to be honest and clear in describing what authority he is keeping and what role he is asking his subordinates to assume in solving a particular problem.

Can you tell how "democratic" a manager is by the number of decisions his subordinates make? The sheer *number* of decisions is not an accurate index of the amount of freedom that a subordinate group enjoys. More important is the *significance* of the decisions which the boss entrusts to his subordinates. Obviously a decision on how to arrange desks is of an entirely different order from a decision involving the introduction of new electronic data-processing equipment. Even though the widest possible limits are given in dealing with the first issue, the group will sense no particular degree of responsibility. For a boss to permit the group to decide equipment policy, even within rather narrow limits, would reflect a greater degree of confidence in them on his part.

DECIDING HOW TO LEAD

Now let us turn from the types of leadership which are possible in a company situation to the question of what types are *practical* and *desirable.* What factors or forces should a manager consider in deciding how to manage? Three are of particular importance:

Forces in the manager;
Forces in the subordinates;
Forces in the situation.

We should like briefly to describe these elements and indicate how they might influence a manager's action in a decision-making situation.[2] The strength of each of them will, of course, vary from instance to instance, but the manager who is sensitive to them can better assess the problems which face him and determine which mode of leadership behavior is most appropriate for him.

Forces in the Manager

The manager's behavior in any given instance will be influenced greatly by the many forces operating within his own personality. He will, of course, perceive his leadership problems in a unique way on the basis of his background, knowledge, and experience. Among the important internal forces affecting him will be the following:

1. *His value system.* How strongly does he feel that individuals should have a share in making the decisions which affect them? Or, how convinced is he that the official who is paid to assume responsibility should personally carry the burden of decision-making? The strength of his convictions on questions like those will tend to move

the manager to one end or the other of the continuum shown in Figure 1. His behavior will also be influenced by the relative importance that he attaches to organizational efficiency, personal growth of subordinates, and company profits.[3]

2. *His confidence in his subordinates.* Managers differ greatly in the amount of trust they have in other people generally, and this carries over to the particular employees they supervise at a given time. In viewing his particular group of subordinates, the manager is likely to consider their knowledge and competence with respect to the problem. A central question he might ask himself is: "Who is best qualified to deal with this problem?" Often he may, justifiably or not, have more confidence in his own capabilities than in those of subordinates.

3. *His own leadership inclinations.* There are some managers who seem to function more confortably and naturally as highly directive leaders. Resolving problems and issuing orders come easily to them. Other managers seem to operate more comfortably in a team role, where they are continually sharing many of their functions with their subordinates.

4. *His feelings of security in an uncertain situation.* The manager who releases control over the decision-making process thereby reduces the predictability of the outcome. Some managers have a greater need than others for predictability and stability in their environment. This "tolerance for ambiguity" is being viewed increasingly by psychologists as a key variable in a person's manner of dealing with problems.

The manager brings these and other highly personal variables to each situation he faces. If he can see them as forces which, consciously or unconsciously, influence his behavior, he can better understand what makes him prefer to act in a given way. And understanding this, he can often make himself more effective.

Forces in the Subordinate

Before deciding how to lead a certain group, the manager will also want to consider a number of forces affecting his subordinates' behavior. He will want to remember that each employee, like himself, is influenced by many personality variables. In addition, each subordinate has a set of expectations about how the boss should act in relation to him (the phrase "expected behavior" is one we hear more and more often these days at discussions of leadership and teaching). The better the manager understands these factors, the more accurately he can determine what kind of behavior on his part will enable his subordinates to act most effectively.

Generally speaking, the manager can permit his subordinates greater freedom if the following essential conditions exist:

If the subordinates have relatively high needs for independence. (As we all know, people differ greatly in the amount of direction that they desire.)

If the subordinates have a readiness to assume responsibility for decision-making. (Some see additional responsibility as a tribute to their ability; others see it as "passing the buck.")

If they have a relatively high tolerance for ambiguity. (Some employees prefer to have clear-cut directives given to them; others prefer a wider area of freedom.)

If they are interested in the problem and feel that it is important.

If they understand and identify with the goals of the organization.

If they have the necessary knowledge and experience to deal with the problem.

If they have learned to expect to share in decision-making. (Persons who have come to expect strong leadership and are then suddenly confronted with the request to share more fully in decision-making are often upset by this new experience. On the other hand, persons who have enjoyed a considerable amount of freedom resent the boss who begins to make all the decisions himself.)

The manager will probably tend to make fuller use of his own authority if the above conditions do *not* exist; at times there may be no realistic alternative to running a "one-man show."

The restrictive effect of many of the forces will, of course, be greatly modified by the general feeling of confidence which subordinates have in the boss. Where they have learned to respect and trust him, he is free to vary his behavior. He will feel certain that he will not be perceived as an authoritarian boss on those occasions when he makes decisions by himself. Similarly, he will not be seen as using staff meetings to avoid his decision-making responsibility. In a climate of mutual confidence and respect, people tend to feel less threatened by deviations from normal practice, which in turn makes possible a higher degree of flexibility in the whole relationship.

Forces in the Situation

In addition to the forces which exist in the manager himself and in his subordinates, certain characteristics of the general situation will also affect the manager's behavior. Among the more critical environmental pressures that surround him are those which stem from the organization, the work group, the nature of the problem, and the pressures of time. Let us look briefly at each of these:

Type of organization. Like individuals, organizations have values and traditions which inevitably influence the behavior of the people who work in them. The manager who is a new-comer to a company quickly discovers that certain kinds of behavior are approved while others are not. He also discovers that to deviate radically from what is generally accepted is likely to create problems for him.

These values and traditions are communicated in numerous ways—through job descriptions, policy pronouncements, and public statements by top executives. Some organizations, for example, hold to the notion that the desirable executive is one who is dynamic, imaginative, decisive, and persuasive. Other organizations put more emphasis upon the importance of the executive's ability to work effectively with people—his human relations skills. The fact that his superiors have a defined concept of what the good executive should be will very likely push the manager toward one end or the other of the behavioral range.

In addition to the above, the amount of employee participation is influenced by such variables as the size of the working units, their geographical distribution, and degree of inter- and intra-organizational security required to attain company goals. For example, the wide geographical dispersion of an organization may preclude a practical system of participative decision-making, even though this would otherwise be desirable. Similarly, the size of the working units or the need for keeping plans confidential may make it necessary for the boss to exercise more control than would otherwise be the case. Factors like these may limit considerably the manager's ability to function flexibly on the continuum.

Group effectiveness.   Before turning decision-making responsibility over to a subordinate group, the boss should consider how effectively its members work together as a unit.

One of the relevant factors here is the experience the group has had in working together. It can generally be expected that a group which has functioned for some time will have developed habits of cooperation and thus be able to tackle a problem more effectively than a new group. It can also be expected that a group of people with similar backgrounds and interests will work more quickly and easily than people with dissimilar backgrounds, because the communication problems are likely to be less complex.

The degree of confidence that the members have in their ability to solve problems as a group is also a key consideration. Finally, such group variables as cohesiveness, permissiveness, mutual acceptance, and commonality of purpose will exert subtle but powerful influence on the group's functioning.

The problem itself.   The nature of the problem may determine what degree of authority should be delegated by the manager to his subordinates. Obviously he will ask himself whether they have the kind of knowledge which is needed. It is possible to do them a real disservice by assigning a problem that their experience does not equip them to handle.

Since the problems faced in large or growing industries increasingly require knowledge of specialists from many different fields, it might be inferred that the more complex a problem, the more anxious a manager will be to get some assistance in solving it. However, this is not always the case. There will be times when the very complexity of the problem calls for one person to work it out. For example, if the manager has most of the background and factual data relevant to a given issue, it may be easier for him to think it through himself than to take the time to fill in his staff on all the pertinent background information.

The key question to ask, of course, is: "Have I heard the ideas of everyone who has the necessary knowledge to make a significant contribution to the solution of this problem?"

The pressure of time.   This is perhaps the most clearly felt pressure on the manager (in spite of the fact that it may sometimes be imagined). The more that he feels the need for an immediate decision, the more difficult it is to involve other people. In organizations which are in a constant state of "crisis" and "crash programming" one is likely to find managers personally using a high degree of authority with relatively little delegation to subordinates. When the time pressure is less intense, however, it becomes much more possible to bring subordinates in on the decision-making process.

These, then, are the principal forces that impinge on the manager in any given instance and that tend to determine his tactical behavior in relation to his subordinates. In each case his behavior ideally will be that which makes possible the most effective attainment of his immediate goal within the limits facing him.

LONG-RUN STRATEGY

As the manager works with his organization on the problems that come up day by day, his choice of a leadership pattern is usually limited. He must take account of the forces just described and, within the restrictions they impose on him, do the best that he can. But as he looks ahead months or even years, he can shift his thinking from tactics to large-scale strategy. No longer need he be fettered by all of the forces mentioned, for he can view many of them as variables over which he has some control. He can, for example, gain new insights or skills for himself, supply training for individual subordinates, and provide participative experiences for his employee group.

In trying to bring about a change in these variables, however, he is faced with a challenging question: At which point along the continuum *should* he act?

Attaining Objectives

The answer depends largely on what he wants to accomplish. Let us suppose that he is interested in the same objectives that most modern managers seek to attain when they can shift their attention from the pressure of immediate assignments:

1. To raise the level of employee motivation;
2. To increase the readiness of subordinates to accept change;
3. To improve the quality of all managerial decisions;
4. To develop teamwork and morale;
5. To further the individual development of employees.

In recent years the manager has been deluged with a flow of advice on how best to achieve these longer-run objectives. It is little wonder that he is often both bewildered and annoyed. However, there are some guidelines which he can usefully follow in making a decision.

Most research and much of the experience of recent years give a strong factual basis to the theory that a fairly high degree of subordinate-centered behavior is associated with the accomplishment of the five purposes mentioned.[4] This does not mean that a manager should always leave all decisions to his assistants. To provide the individual or the group with greater freedom than they are ready for at any given time may very well tend to generate anxieties and therefore inhibit rather than facilitate the attainment of desired objectives. But this should not keep the manager from making a continuing effort to confront his subordinates with the challenge of freedom.

CONCLUSION

In summary, there are two implications in the basic thesis that we have been developing. The first is that the successful leader is one who is keenly aware of those forces which are most relevant to his behavior at any given time. He accurately understands himself, the individuals and groups he is dealing with, and the company and broader social environment in which he operates. And certainly he is able to assess the present readiness for growth of his subordinates.

But this sensitivity or understanding is not enough, which brings us to the second implication. The successful leader is one who is able to behave appropriately in the light of these perceptions. If direction is in order, he is able to direct; if considerable participative freedom is called for, he is able to provide such freedom.

Thus, the successful manager of men can be primarily characterized neither as a strong leader nor as a permissive one. Rather, he is one who maintains a high batting average in accurately assessing the forces that determine what his most appropriate behavior at any given time should be and in actually being able to behave accordingly.

Being both insightful and flexible, he is less likely to see the problems of leadership as a dilemma.

RETROSPECTIVE COMMENTARY

Since this HBR Classic was first published in 1958, there have been many changes in organizations and in the world that have affected leadership patterns. While the article's continued popularity attests to its essential validity, we believe it can be reconsidered and updated to reflect subsequent societal changes and new management concepts.

The reasons for the article's continued relevance can be summarized briefly:

The article contains insights and perspectives which mesh well with, and help clarify, the experiences of managers, other leaders, and students of leadership. Thus it is useful to individuals in a wide variety of organizations – industrial, governmental, educational, religious, and community.

The concept of leadership the article defines is reflected in a continuum of leadership behavior (see Figure 1 in original article). Rather than offering a choice between two styles of leadership, democratic or authoritarian, it sanctions a range of behavior.

The concept does not dictate to managers but helps them to analyze their own behavior. The continuum permits them to review their behavior within a context of other alternatives, without any style being labeled right or wrong.

(We have sometimes wondered if we have, perhaps, made it too easy for anyone to justify his or her style of leadership. It may be a small step between being nonjudgmental and giving the impression that all behavior is equally valid and useful. The latter was not our intention. Indeed, the thrust of our endorsement was for the manager who is insightful in assessing relevant forces within himself, others, and the situation, and who can be flexible in responding to these forces.)

In recognizing that our article can be updated, we are acknowledging that organizations do not exist in a vacuum but are affected by changes that occur in society. Consider, for example, the implications for organizations of these recent social developments:

The youth revolution that expresses distrust and even contempt for organizations identified with the establishment.

The civil rights movement that demands all minority groups be given a greater opportunity for participation and influence in the organizational processes.

The ecology and consumer movements that challenge the right of managers to make decisions without considering the interest of people outside the organization.

The increasing national concern with the quality of working life and its relationship to worker productivity, participation, and satisfaction.

These and other societal changes make effective leadership in this decade a more challenging task, requiring even greater sensitivity and flexibility than was needed in the 1950s. Today's manager is more likely to deal with employees who resent being treated as subordinates, who may be highly critical of any organizational system, who expect to be consulted and to exert influence, and who often stand on the edge of alienation from the institution that needs their loyalty and commitment. In addition, he is frequently confronted by a highly turbulent, unpredictable environment.

In response to these social pressures, new concepts of management have emerged in organizations. Open-system theory, with its emphasis on subsystems' interdependency *and* on the interaction of an organization with its environment, has made a powerful impact on managers' approach to problems. Organization development has emerged as a new behavioral science approach to the improvement of individual, group, organizational, and interorganizational performance. New research has added to our understanding of motivation in the work situation. More and more executives have become concerned with social responsibility and have explored the feasibility of social audits. And a growing number of organizations, in Europe and in the United States, have conducted experiments in industrial democracy.

In light of these developments, we submit the following thoughts on how we would rewrite certain points in our original article.

The article described forces in the manager, subordinates, and the situation as givens, with the leadership pattern a resultant of these forces. We would now give more attention to the *interdependency* of these forces. For example, such interdependency occurs in: (a) the interplay between the manager's confidence in his subordinates, their readiness to assume responsibility, and the level of group effectiveness; and (b) the impact of the behavior of the manager on that of his subordinates, and vice versa.

In discussing the forces in the situation, we primarily identified organizational phenomena. We would now include forces lying outside the organization, and would explore the relevant interdependencies between the organization and its environment.

In the original article we presented the size of the rectangle in Figure 1 as a given, with its boundaries already determined by external forces—in effect, a closed system. We would now recognize the possibility of the manager and/or his subordinates taking the initiative to change those boundaries through interaction with relevant external forces—both within their own organization and in the larger society.

The article portrayed the manager as the principal and almost unilateral actor. He initiated and determined group functions, assumed responsibility, and exercised control. Subordinates made inputs and assumed power only at the will of the manager. Although the manager might have taken into account forces outside himself, it was *he* who decided where to operate on the continuum—that is, whether to announce a decision instead of trying to sell his idea to his subordinates, whether to invite questions, to let subordinates decide an issue, and so on. While the manager has retained this clear prerogative in many organizations, it has been challenged in others. Even in situations where he has retained it, however, the balance in the relationship between manager and subordinates at any given time is arrived at by interaction—direct or indirect—between the two parties.

Although power and its use by the manager played a role in our article, we now realize that our concern with cooperation and collaboration, common goals, commitment, trust, and mutual caring limited our vision with respect to the realities of power. We did not attempt to deal with unions, other forms of joint worker action, or with individual workers' expressions of resistance. Today, we would recognize much more clearly the power available to *all* parties, and the factors that underlie the interrelated decisions on whether to use it.

In the original article, we used the terms "manager" and "subordinate." We are now uncomfortable with "subordinate" because of its demeaning, dependency-laden connotations and prefer "nonmanager." The titles "manager" and "nonmanager" make the terminological difference functional rather than hierarchical.

We assumed fairly traditional organizational structures in our original article. Now we would alter our formulation to reflect newer organizational modes which are slowly emerging, such as industrial democracy, intentional communities, and "phenomenarchy."[5] These new modes are based on observations such as the following:

Both manager and nonmanagers may be governing forces in their group's environment, contributing to the definition of the total area of freedom.

A group can function without a manager, with managerial functions being shared by group members.

A group, as a unit, can be delegated authority and can assume responsibility within a larger organizational context.

Our thoughts on the question of leadership have prompted us to design a new behavior continuum (see Figure 2) in which the total area of freedom shared by manager and nonmanagers is constantly redefined by interactions between them and the forces in the environment.

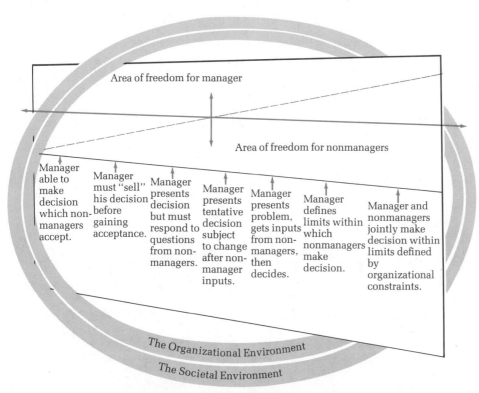

Figure 2   Continuum of Manager–Nonmanager Behavior

The arrows in the exhibit indicate the continual flow of interdependent influence among systems and people. The points on the continuum designate the types of manager and nonmanager behavior that become possible with any given amount of freedom available to each. The new continuum is both more complex and more dynamic than the 1958 version, reflecting the organizational and societal realities of the 1970s.

NOTES AND REFERENCES

1. For a fuller explanation of this approach see Leo Moore, "Too Much Management, Too Little Change," *Harvard Business Review*, 41 (January–February 1956).
2. See also Robert Tannenbaum and Fred Massarik, "Participation by Subordinates

in the Managerial Decision-making Process," *Canadian Journal of Economics and Political Science,* 1950 (August), p. 413.

3. See Chris Argyris, "Top Management Dilemma: Company Needs v. Individual Development," *Personnel,* 1955 (September), pp. 123–24.

4. For example, see Warren H. Schmidt and Paul C. Buchanan, *Techniques That Produce Teamwork* (New London: Arthur C. Croft Publications, Inc., 1954); and Morris S. Viteles, *Motivation and Morale in Industry* (New York: W. W. Norton, 1953).

5. For a description of phenomenarchy, see Will McWhinney, "Phenomenarchy: A Suggestion for Social Redesign," *Journal of Applied Behavioral Science,* May 1973.

Questions for Discussion

1. Do you believe that self confidence is a characteristic which helps a person to become a leader and remain a leader? Give your reasoning or any evidence for your answer. Give also any doubts or qualifications you have.

2. If you were a practicing manager in charge of a large supermarket how would you view the "truthfulness" or "usefulness" of the trait approach to leadership?

3. Suppose we have a leader whose style is to devote a great deal of time to planning work of the department, and who further gives directions to subordinates based on these plans. According to the Ohio State findings, is this good for productivity or not? Having answered this, what reservations do you have about the "truth" of your answer?

4. Some theories of leadership argue that most human beings in leadership positions tend either to be task oriented *or* people oriented. Other writers do not look at what leaders *are*, but what they *should* be. These writers tend to say that a good leader should be both at once—task oriented and people oriented. What is Fiedler's position on this question?

5. We all can recognize by intuition that "we neither expect nor want the trusted airline pilot to turn to his crew and ask, 'what do you think we ought to check before takeoff?'." In this case, subordinates (passengers, crew) want a leader that makes decisions and gives orders. Using Fiedler's model, why is it easy to be a leader of an airplane crew (i.e., why is the situation favorable for leadership actions)?

6. Fiedler believes that it is very difficult to change people from task oriented behavior to people oriented behavior—indeed that it is very difficult to change people's personalities *at all*. If this be true, what use can a real manager make of Fiedler's theory? If Fiedler were to recommend a training program for managers, what could it possibly look like, since he would not be trying to tamper with the participants' leadership styles?

7. There is a paradox when a manager uses performance rules or objectives to delegate work to subordinates. On one hand, such objectives (if set at "headquarters") take away from the freedom and autonomy of subordinates. From another viewpoint, however, rules and objectives are *absolutely necessary* to, and add to, a subordinate's freedom. Explain the latter argument, using expectancy theory of motivation. Give an example using the students' relationship with their professor.

8. There is an old saying that "people are different." If one takes this seriously, then it is not wise for a leader to assume that subordinates *in general* are motivated by *any* basic needs, whether those needs be security, social friendship, achievement, or self esteem. In light of this reasoning, how might House's theory of leadership be more useful than some others?

9. Answer Question 5 using Tannenbaum and Schmidt's checklist to diagnose the leadership situation (rather than Fiedler's model as called for in Question 5).

Cases for Discussion

Norman Manufacturing Company

The Norman Manufacturing Company produces a variety of industrial machinery and equipment, including electrical switches and relay boxes; the small items of coal-mining equipment; and chains, hoists, conveyers and other materials-handling products. In addition to these lines, the company has expanded, through acquisition in the past ten years, into two lines less closely connected with its original product line: the manufacture of sporting goods and of furnishings (hardware, plumbing, furniture) for pleasure yachts. At the present time, the company employs 1,650 people, and its annual sales have averaged $40 million for the past three years.

Regarding the objectives of the Company, L. D. Norman, Jr., the President, states:

> Since my father's death 13 years ago, we have endeavored to stress even more strongly the objective of growth over the years. The public now owns 63 percent of our stock, but they, as well as our family and our management, have certain principal accomplishments in mind: to have this company grow in assets, market coverage, profitability, and prestige over the years; and to have it gain a national reputation for quality and service to our customers. This is the reason why we have taken on two new divisions that are not connected with our past experience. We feel that the company has a future in many product lines. Technology and consumer tastes mean you can't stand still with your same traditional products and ways of doing things.

The Lange Division

Seven years ago, the Norman Company purchased the Lange Sporting Goods Company and established it as the Lange Division of NMC. The research bulletin of a New York investment firm, at that time, carried the following statement:

> The Lange Company, with a good stable line of products, has suffered in recent years from a lack of vitality in keeping its products, production methods, and advertising up to the zip displayed by its competitors. We believe that Norman's record of capable and aggressive management should enable this company to show good growth over the intermediate term future.

The management of Lange had been in the hands of four members of the Lange family, all of whom retired at the time of the merger. L. D. Norman, Jr., immediately replaced them with Fred K. Gibbs as general manager of the Lange Division.

Fred Gibbs, 42, had been executive vice president of a competing sporting goods manufacturing company. After graduation from Stanford University, he held positions as production-scheduling trainee, salesman, sales manager, and marketing vice president for that company. Reference checks at the time of his employment with Norman

Manufacturing Company indicated that he was well liked by his fellow executives.

L. Donald Norman, Jr., has been president of the Norman Manufacturing Company for 13 years. At age 50, he has worked for the Company 26 years, first in the plants, then as a salesman, and for 10 years as a staff man to his father, designing and supervising procedures to coordinate production, sales, shipping, and inventories. As president he has spent most of his time planning new customer strategy and sales incentive programs, and projecting financial statements to plan increases in plant investment. Together with T. M. Farish, executive vice president, and C. A. Langford, treasurer, he sits on the executive committee. This committee meets three times a week to discuss all important matters in sales, production, and finance.

Mr. Norman, the minutes also show, gave the committee a summary of the study he had been making of decentralization. He pointed out that such companies as General Motors and du Pont were able to grow by creating independent divisions, selecting capable men to run them, and retaining only very broad measures of performance. In this way, he said, the Norman Company could delegate virtually the entire management task to Fred Gibbs and his team. We do not have to know much about the details of the division, so long as we establish broad controls.

In the five months after the acquisition, the three top Norman officials drew up the following control points. They were careful to make clear, Norman says, that Gibbs' own performance would be measured only in terms of these controls. "Everything else—all of the details of running the division—would be left to Fred."

Rate of return on investment: Lange was earning an average of 14% (before taxes) on book value, and it was agreed to raise the target to 19% within five years.

Sales as a percentage of industry sales: Norman judged that the Lange Company had been performing as indicated below, and new targets were set for Lange's three principal products:

Product	Present	Five Year Target
Tennis equipment	11%	15%
Golf bags	8	12
Gym clothing	10	25

Of the total dollar sales volume of Lange, averaged over the five-year period prior to acquisition, tennis equipment accounted for 40%, gym clothing for 45%, and golf bags for 15%.

In setting these figures, all three executives agreed that there was no accurate way to be scientific about what percentages could be reached. All recognized that the Lange Company had been, in the words of Norman, "conservative, lacking in morale, and complacent. It therefore seemed reasonable that with a hard-hitting management and some new ideas, the targets are neither over- nor understated—they are realistic."

Gibbs at first expressed the idea that the gym clothing sales target was too high. But Langford and Norman showed him the results of their study of profits in this line compared to others. The profitability of selling gym clothing, particularly to institutions, was much higher than the other items. Gibbs, too, agreed that his target was a wise one.

Operating Results: First Six Years of Operation

At the time this case is written, Lange Division has been in operation for six fiscal years. Rates of return on investment and percentages of industry sales appear in Exhibits 1 and 2, respectively.

During the first four years, the executive committee of the Norman Company had a verbal agreement, of which they frequently reminded themselves, that none of Norman's management should initiate inquiries about *specific* operations in Lange. Langford reports, for instance, that when he noticed on the expense statements furnished for the first year, that telephone and telegraph expenses of Lange were, in his opinion, far out of line with the rest of the company, he felt that he should not use these statements as detailed controls.

The committee also agreed that Norman should make fairly frequent (perhaps bimonthly) visits to Lange headquarters in Providence for the purpose of inquiring about overall sales improvement. He should also encourage Gibbs to come to New York whenever "he feels the need to discuss any matter, broad, detailed, or otherwise."

As a matter of practice, Norman, Gibbs, and Langford did meet about three times a month, at which times (a) they discussed overall sales results for 10 to 20 minutes, and (b) they discussed and approved lump-sum amounts of money requested by Gibbs to be budgeted for both capital expenditures and current expenses.

At the end of the fourth year, Langford, who had been raising questions with Norman all along about the wisdom of Gibbs' expenditures, suggested that investment return and sales targets were far less than satisfactory. We have been holding off telling him how to manage various phases of his budget too long. There is little doubt but that he has gone too fast and too far in increasing expenditures for advertising, salesmen's bonuses, and salesmen's expense accounts. Furthermore, his expenditures for employee-recreation facilities and increases in factory salaries have been unwise when we are trying to increase return on investment. The former increased the investment side of the ratio, and the latter decreased the income side.

Langford, incidentally, received expense summaries regularly — as he says, "not as control reports, but for the purpose of consolidating the figures with the rest of the company divisions for the profit and loss statement." These summaries contained 35 account captions (for excerpts of five captions, see Exhibit 3).

After reviewing Langford's cost statements, the executive committee agreed that "Gibbs needs some helpful guidance." Since Langford knew more about the details of expense and capital budgets, they also agreed that he should visit Gibbs once a month to go over the 35 expense accounts and see how each progresses during the year.

Gibbs recalls that early in his fifth year at Lange, when Langford first came to Providence and told him what the executive committee had decided,

> I was surprised. I guess it scared me a little right off the bat, since I had no idea they were thinking like that. The targets weren't being met, but I thought that surely they must know that things were going quite well, considering all of the things which must be done to put this division on a solid footing for the future. After my initial anxiousness and surprise, I got downright mad for a few days.

Gibbs also states that

> early in the fifth year, I began to cut back on some of the spending inaugurated in the beginning. I got the salesmen together on four occasions and gave them a talk about the necessity of cutting their expense-account expenditures, and the fact that we would have to stop making some of the purely promotional calls, and

concentrate on those customers that looked more like immediate prospects. I also cut the number of direct-mail promotional brochures from 12 mailings a year to six, and decided to let one man go whom we had hired as a merchandising man. He had helped, in the four years he had been with us, in designing the products for eye appeal, in creating point-of-sale displays, and in improving the eye appeal of our packages. I did not cut down on the number of salesmen employed, however.

The Question of Advertising and Research Costs

As early as February of the second year, Gibbs objected—in his words, "mildly"—to Norman "because of the way Langford entered on certain financial statements the money spent for advertising, the market research department, and the product research department." When the first year statement of return was prepared by Lange's own controller, Gibbs and he felt that the total of $340,000 represented an investment rather than a current operating expense. They reasoned that the increase in new products and the increase in good will or consumer acceptance would not begin to pay off for two or three years. Since return on investment is the ratio of income to investment, charging these three items to investment showed a higher performance (14% in the first year) than the same statement prepared by Langford (12% in the same year). It seemed to Gibbs that by subtracting the $340,000 from profits "was a real injustice— Tom Farish and Norman family stockholders have pretty much stayed out of my end of the business, but I don't want them to get the wrong impression. They will, from that kind of misleading figure."

Gibbs and Langford both feel that, in spite of this disagreement, the relationship of the Norman management group to Gibbs is "a pretty good one." Gibbs states that as of now,

I pretty much go along with their guidance, though it one time looked like interference. The only thing I'm still darn mad about is this way of figuring return. Norman overruled me when Langford and I had it out in front of him one time, but it's still such a hot subject that Langford and I won't bring it up any more. Why, just look at the figures for the whole period that the division has been in existence! (See Exhibit 1.)

Exhibit 1 Ratio of Profit (Before Tax) to Investment in the Lange Division

Year	Method 1*	Method 2**
First	14%	12%
Second	14	11
Third	15	13
Fourth	15	13
Fifth	17	16
Sixth	17	16
Present***	17	16

* Used by Lange Division controller, charging advertising and research to capital investment, the lower half of the ratio.

** Used by Norman Company management, charging advertising and research to current expense, thus decreasing the top of the ratio.

*** First quarter adjusted.

Exhibit 2 Sales as a Percentage of Total Industry Sales

Year	Tennis Equipment	Golf Bags	Gym Clothing
First	11%	9%	10%
Second	12	10	15
Third	12	9	21
Fourth	13	11	22
Fifth	12	10	23
Sixth	12	10	22
Present (1st quarter)	12	10	21

Exhibit 3 Selected Expense Captions and Amounts from Lange Division Expense Tabulation

Expense Caption	Fourth Year	Year Prior to Merger
Advertising	$280,000	$ 47,000
Salesmen Bonuses	210,000	23,000
Salesmen Expense	145,000	68,000
Factory Salaries	665,000	550,000*
Employee Service	80,000	2,010

* Average salary per employee in the year prior to merger was $6,540. If this is adjusted for cost-of-living increase from that time to the fourth year, it comes out to an equivalent of $7,185. Average actual salary paid by Lange in the fourth year was $7,540.

Question

Using the path-goal theory of leadership, (1) diagnose the leadership problem from the point of view of L. D. Norman as chief executive of the company; and (2) if you were Norman, what actions would you take to make your leadership of the company more effective?

Mississippi Valley Equipment Corporation

Mississippi Valley Equipment Corporation, with headquarters in St. Louis, is a whole-sale hardware company distributing a line of 17,400 items in its product line. The Company acts as manufacturer's agent for 11,400 items and purchases for its own account 6,000 items. Products range in value fron nuts and bolts that sell for a few cents to large gas compressors which sell for $15,000 each. Storage and sale of equipment is carried out through six branches: two in St. Louis, and one each in Houston, New Orleans, Kansas City and Cincinnati. At each branch the Company maintains a large warehouse facility and employs a resident sales force to sell to retail hardware stores and large manufacturing plants. James D. Skinner was employed as President by the St. Louis board of directors three years ago. At that time the board issued a statement which said,

> MVEC is now growing beyond the size and scope of a small wholesaler. It is employing the latest technologies in accounting, inventory control, materials handling and personnel management. Only by giving attention to these matters can a complex company like ours offer the best products and the lowest price to our customers. The headquarters staff has been instructed by the board to institute the very latest methods in order to maintain low cost products for customers. It is with pleasure that we announce the employment of Mr. Skinner as President of our company. He has extensive training in large operations such as ours and we expect that he will help develop MVEC into one of the most up-to-date organizations in our industry.

In the three years since assuming the presidency, Skinner has developed the expertise of the headquarters staff in order that the staff might train branch managers in various specialties. He established the position of Inventory and Purchasing Manager, and filled it with a graduate of Carnegie-Mellon University, specializing in operations research and applied mathematics. In personnel management, MVEC has employed two executives to plan policies and practices for the whole company. It is felt that this will give MVEC a significant lead over its competitors through greater cooperation of employees, less employee turnover, and less damage to stock in the receiving and storing departments at each branch.

Immediately after he was employed as Manager of Personnel, Oliver Cooper obtained Skinner's agreement on a list of objectives for the Personnel Department at headquarters. Two of these objectives were:

• to draw up policies and procedures which will increase the efficiency of employees at all branches.
• to draw up policies that will increase the morale of employees in the branches, thus creating a more loyal work force and making MVEC a better place to work.

Cooper then traveled to all branches, spending one week asking branch managers what kinds of personnel problems they faced. He also did further research in publications of the National Industrial Conference Board on how the better companies solve personnel problems, and drew on his training in labor relations at Cornell University.

In the resulting policy manual, approved by Skinner, were contained two policies which, Cooper later discovered, are not being followed in the Kansas City Branch:

> It is the policy of Mississippi Valley Equipment Corporation that:
> • all branch managers should hold a meeting of foremen and supervisors once a week, for the purpose of training, informing them on problems, and developing open lines of communications.

• the branch manager should hold a meeting of all employees once each three months to explain any changes in employee benefits being paid for by the Company.

Since Jack Duncan, Manager in Kansas City, was scheduled to be in St. Louis on a routine trip, Cooper asked him if he would come by the latter's office for a discussion of how things were going in Kansas City. On the appointed morning the following conversation took place.

Cooper: "Jack, we have a problem in getting our personnel policies into operation. I'm not criticizing you personally, it's just that you and I and all managers have so many urgent things on our minds that we don't have time to give attention to things that seem of less immediate importance."

Duncan: "I surely know what you mean by that, Oliver. We've got our hands full meeting competition and generating sales. I work very hard with the sales force, continuously do market research, and plan new customer strategies."

Cooper: "You have a good reputation in headquarters here as a sales minded executive. Skinner is always praising you for that. But I'm concerned that those two employee communications policies aren't being carried out in Kansas City. Personnel is important, too."

Duncan: "I agree it is important. Close relations between management and employees is vital. Out there in Kansas City I spend a lot of time talking with foremen and employees. That kind of spontaneous talk is better than holding meetings, I think."

Cooper: "We just believe that such things as employee benefits will over the long haul get ignored in the pressure of other activities. An orderly way of making time for these kinds of communications is vital to the success of this company. Of course, as you know, I am only a consultant to branch managers. I neither have nor want authority over the branches. Everyone knows branch managers are responsible to the President. What I'm really doing is proposing something that will pay off for you and the employees. Your own sales and cost record will show improvement in the long run.

Duncan: "Oliver, I appreciate your position. And I will think about what you have said. I do hope, though, that you appreciate my position, too. Skinner holds us responsible for total dollar sales volume per year, for number of new customers gained during the year, and for the number of customers lost during the year, and for cost of warehouse operations. These are the things he looks at when he gives salary raises to the branch managers. I will do what I can in the area of personnel, but it takes a lot of my time to plan sales and work enthusiastically with salesmen. Maybe I will try your meetings, though, and see if they really help."

Eight months later, Cooper met Duncan at the annual meeting of headquarters and field managers. He asked Duncan again about the meetings. Duncan said, "I'm still with you, Oliver, on the importance of good communications. But I just honestly have not had the time away from other pressing operations to hold this kind of meeting."

Use your knowledge of leadership gained in the chapter to analyze what is going on between Cooper and Duncan. If you were Cooper, and believed that you had objective evidence that employees in Kansas City actually do not understand what the company is doing for them in terms of extra benefits, what would you do?

Conflict Management

A dramatic development in the literature on organizations and management has been a reexamination of internal conflict. Conflict is increasingly perceived as inevitable, often legitimate, and perhaps even desirable. Whenever there is interdependence between parties, their relationships must be worked out across boundaries—between individuals and among groups in organizations (Walton et al., 1969; Aldrich, 1971). The process is, in the words of Walton and McKersie (1965), "The deliberate interaction of two or more complex social units which are attempting to define or redefine the terms of their interdependence" (p. 3). Such interaction is not infrequently accompanied by stress and conflict. Indeed, as Barnard (1950) suggested, the social patterns of stress, conflict, and bargaining are inevitable, because they seem "inherent in the conception of free will in a changing environment" (p. 36).

Thus, conflict does not necessarily indicate a breakdown of the organization or failure of management, as implied by classical management theory and human relations philosophy. Indeed, classical management says little about conflict among managers. One reason for this lack of comment might be the assumption that managers are basically rational. This view implies that, because of their rationality, managers can clearly see the objectives of their organization and can plan logically. It further implies that management rationality is sufficient to bring about the required cooperation. Reality, however, proves the assumption to be an illusion.

In an introduction to a study on conflict in research organizations, Evan (1965, p. 37) advanced three assumptions which characterize recent attitudes about conflict:

> An underlying assumption of this study is that conflicts are endemic in organizations because of a lack of consensus as to the expectations and prescriptions for various organizational positions or because of a lack of uniform commitment to organizational objectives.
>
> A second assumption is that some types of conflicts are detrimental and others are beneficial from the point of view of both organizational and individual goals.
>
> Thirdly, the principle of minimizing conflict subscribed to by some managers and social scientists may have some validity for crisis organizations, such as armies, or for so-called routine organizations, such as some manufacturing organizations. However, this principle may not be valid for knowledge- and technology-producing organizations, such as those engaged in research and development.

Bennis (1970) argues that formulating objectives for handling conflict and promoting collaboration is one of the eight major organizational objectives. And Kelly (1970) suggests that conflict and tension are beneficial (within certain limits) if they reflect commitment which promotes challenge, heightened attention, and effort. The emerging thesis is that too little manifestation of conflict is stagnancy, but uncontrolled conflict threatens chaos. Since individuals and organizations have differing abilities to withstand stress, an appropriate level is necessary. In short, it is not conflict itself that is alarming, but rather its mismanagement (Coser, 1956).

Nonetheless, many managers still emphasize organizational harmony and personal rationality. Zaleznik writes (1970): "There are few business activities more prone to a credibility gap than the way in which executives approach organizational life. A sense of disbelief occurs when managers purport to make decisions in rationalistic terms while most observers and participants know that personalities and politics play a significant if not overriding role" (p. 47).

Whether openness to conflict and rational response is more or less characteristic of real organizations today is impossible to determine, but it appears so. Managers report that they now spend 20 percent of their time dealing with conflict and that their ability to manage conflict has become more important over the past ten years (Thomas and Schmidt, 1976). The "organization man" complaint seems much less common (among managers if not among youth) than it used to be (Porter, 1963). Matrix organizations have been designed which intentionally foster controlled conflict along with mechanisms for conflict resolution. Lawrence and Lorsch (1962) have found empirical evidence that some managers pursue open confrontation, and that such a style is more effective than forcing conformity or denying differences. Indeed, many recent books and articles about various aspects of American life have proposed more open recognition and rational treatment of conflict. The goal of much marriage counseling (for example, in a volume entitled *The Intimate Enemy — How to Fight Fair in Marriage*), sensitivity training, psychoanalytic therapy, and so on, is not to eliminate conflict, but to manage it.

In this chapter we shall discuss the common sources of conflict in organizations, conditions that increase its probability, and psychological factors that perpetuate its existence. Then we shall consider various approaches to managing conflict, including flight, dominance, hierarchical appeals, system restructuring, and bargaining.

SOURCES OF CONFLICT

The study of conflict and bargaining goes by many titles in the literature — conflict, social resolution, social negotiations, collective bargaining, and so on. Underlying all of these approaches however, is a commonality. The inaugural editorial in the *Journal of Conflict Resolution* (March 1957) stated:

> Many of the patterns and processes which characterize conflict in one area may also characterize it in others. Negotiations and mediation go on in labor disputes as well as international relations. Price wars and domestic quarrels have much the pattern of an arms race. Frustration breeds aggression both in the individual and the state. The jurisdictional problems of labor unions and the territorial disputes of states are not dissimilar. It is not too much to claim that out of the contributions of many fields a general theory of conflict is emerging (p. 2).

Berelson and Steiner (1964) define social conflict as "the pursuit of incompatible, or at least seemingly incompatible, goals, such that gains to one side come about at the expense of the other" (p. 588), although perhaps it is not necessary that one side "lose" in the absolute sense. A general, if abstract, definition of conflict is where two or more entities try to occupy simultaneously the same state or space, but only one can do so.

Conflict Potential

Exhibit 11.1 illustrates that the potential for conflict depends on how incompatible the goals of the entities are, the extent to which required resources are scarce and shared, and the degree of interdependence of task activities (Schmidt and Kochan, 1972). Thus, the chances of conflict are small between people who have their own resources and perform entirely different tasks directed toward completely separate goals. There is seldom any conflict between physics professors and cosmetics salespeople, for example, because their worlds are generally separate. The potential for conflict is much greater between professors and deans, or between salespeople and company credit managers. These pairs draw on common resources, their tasks are interdependent, and they may pursue incompatible objectives (new experimental equipment versus control of university expenditures, or expanded cosmetic sales versus losses from customers' nonpayment).

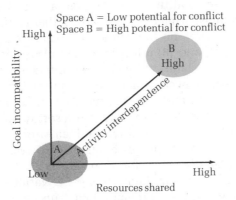

Exhibit 11.1   Potential for Conflict

Forms of Conflict

Individual versus individual.   There are numerous examples of individual conflict: two individuals fighting over territory, two managers competing for the same promotion, two men vying for the same woman, two executives arguing for a larger share of corporate capital, and so on. In each case, the individuals are competing for a scarce "resource" by actually or symbolically eliminating the rival. The desired scarce resource may be a material object or a nonmaterial state (status, prestige, fame, power, etc.).

For some people, conflict may even be pleasurable in itself; it may be ritualistic and intrinsically rewarding. Adler's analysis of the power motive implies certain love for conflict (see Ansbacher and Ansbacher, 1956). On a more popular level, Berne (1964) described several interpersonal games in his bestselling *Games People Play*. In Berne's analysis, interpersonal conflict becomes satisfying in itself, and is not just a response to the inability to satisfy other needs.

Individual versus group. Conflict sometimes occurs when an individual wishes to satisfy security, affiliative, or esteem needs in a group situation, but the group demands excessive conformity or stressful behavior. Such conflict may also arise from an individual's efforts to promote his or her own interests, such as making more money by breaking the group's norms on permissible production. Such transgression of the emergent rules will often result in collective retaliation on the unfortunate offender.

Group versus group. Down (1968) suggests a "law of interorganizational conflict—every organization is in partial conflict with every other social agent it deals with." Perhaps this is an exaggeration, but interdepartmental conflicts over authority, jurisdiction, and work flow are exceedingly common, as are conflicts between labor and management, competition between corporations, and international warfare. One reason for the frequency of intergroup conflict is that conditions necessary for intergroup cooperation are rare. As summarized by Dalton (1963), these conditions are (1) internal social stability within each unit; (2) external value-sharing between parties (that is, they are aware of their interdependence and agree on the values and objectives of the larger unit of which they are a part); and (3) a legitimate authority hierarchy (both parties agree as to their relative status, authority, and interaction flow).

The difficulty experienced in maintaining internal social stability may reflect how difficult it is to reconcile the need for differentiation and the need for integration. To deal with complexity, we resort to specialization and specialists—people with diverse cognitive and emotional orientations—in the various functional areas. Such people frequently experience difficulty in communicating and cooperating. Yet, for an organization to act as a unity, there must be integration or collaboration among the various departments. Thus, management frequently faces a problem: Long-run performance requires substantial integration, but efforts to generate collaboration often produce short-run conflict. It is often easier simply to allow differentiation to dominate over integration.

Instances of inadequate sharing of values and of competing goals are numerous. Individual self-actualization versus collective will is one value conflict that has been and will be fought on many battlefields. At a business level, salespeople value company responsiveness to the customer, while production personnel value equilibrium and predictability; engineers value ingenuity and quality, while finance values the profit margin; marketing emphasizes gross income, while the credit department values minimum credit loss, and so on.

Also numerous are disagreements about relative status and authority, often manifest in conflict over the pattern of work and of interactions between the parties—who initiates to whom, who responds. Production people sometimes feel that they are just as important, competent, and high in status as engineers. Therefore, they resent having to accept all of the engineers' initiations and changes. Or field personnel may be angry that the home office changes procedures so frequently that control is gradually (and illegitimately, in the eyes of the field) centralized (Lourenco and Glidewell, 1975).

Competition. Conflict and competition are similar, but there is one essential difference. In both cases there is perceived incompatibility between goals; both can't win the war or the race; the success of one party has to come at the expense of the other. In conflict, however, at least one side perceives an opportunity to interfere with the other's ability to obtain resources, perform activities, or achieve goals (Kochan et al., 1975). Competitors, in contrast, see their activities as being quite independent, with no opportunity to interfere with each other (Aubert, 1963; Dutton and Walton, 1966). Thus, football is definitely a conflict situation, while a high jump, where each competitor performs alone, is competition. A track race is somewhere in between—but it is closer to competition than conflict because most runners adhere to rules that limit interference.

Conflict Reinforcement

Once conflict and hostility exist, we tend to develop supporting stereotypes that maintain the conflict. Thus each side exaggerates the differences that exist—and once the perception is established, only small actual differences are necessary to maintain the stereotype. This is facilitated by a decrease in intergroup communication that accompanies conflict. If forced to interact, each side listens only to its own representatives. Indeed, in the absence of any shared goals, communication tends to reinforce stereotypes and relations deteriorate further. From their laboratory research on intergroup conflict, Blake and Mouton (1961b) observed "two findings stemming from trends toward uniformities in membership behavior associated with protection of group interests which have unusual significance in determining barriers to the resolution of conflict between groups. They suggest that under competitive conditions members of one group perceive that they understand the other's proposal when in fact they do *not*. Inadequate understanding makes it all the more difficult for competing groups to view each other's proposals realistically. Areas they share in common are likely to go unrecognized and in fact be seen as characteristic of one's own group only. Under conditions of competition, areas of true agreement will go undiscovered" (p. 252).

Perpetual distortion thus exaggerates the differences between groups, so that actual overlap is underestimated. For example, even given their unreliability, cultural bias, and questionable validity, intelligence tests in the past have suggested that the mean intelligence for whites slightly exceeded that for blacks (probably because of the greater prevalence of poor schooling and deprived childhoods in black communities). Nonetheless, the differences were so narrow that perhaps one-third of all blacks were superior to the average white on even the traditional IQ tests. It is doubtful that the "average white" would grant this. Similarly, there may be differences in sexual mores and behavior between middle-aged adults and today's youth, but they are probably less than perceived and there is great variation on each side and substantial overlap. A sizable number of older people demonstrate more promiscuity than exists among average youth. Nonetheless, peering across the gap, many people exaggerate the differences instead of looking for the commonalities.

Stereotyping also occurs within groups. During conflict with other groups, group solidarity and cooperation increase and members tend to accept each other as honest, rational, and peace-loving. Most even think that their group is better than others. In Blake and Mouton's research (1961a), *all* groups rated themselves as better than average. A "superiority complex" seems to exist; regardless of what the group is really like, a member can say "poor though it may be, my group is at least above average!" We do not recognize the selective and self-protective distortion present.

Thus conflict heightens positive identification with the group. Its members close ranks and become more single-minded. Now they have a clear goal — to win. Even after objective measurement of their performance, Blake and Mouton's groups tended toward more favorable subjective evaluations of their own performance and a downgrading of other groups.

In general, then, we tend to homogenize differences within the boundaries of our groups, and exaggerate the differences across boundaries. We also tend to reverse cause and effect. We say that the terrible characteristics of the other group justify our hostility and cause the conflict (e.g., Vietnamese "gooks" are treacherous, hence we should either kill them or get out; welfare "chiselers" are shiftless and promiscuous, therefore they deserve no help). The social scientist sees the opposite causal direction: conflict leads to distorted perceptions in the interest of justifying hostility. Note that any differences may serve for stimulating hostility; the other side may be too dumb or too smart, too flexible (unprincipled) or too fixed (stubborn). It is difference that counts.

Intergroup conflict occurs even between the most reasonable and secure people, but it can be exacerbated by personal attributes (Thompson, 1960). Differences in background, education, age, and culture lower the probability of collaboration because of their adverse impact on values, knowledge, and communication. This is even more likely if one party is clearly superior in position, pay, or seniority.

Some people seem more predisposed toward conflict. Just *who* is unclear, and the whole question is distorted by old wives' tales and equally old prejudices. Hard evidence is rare. Nonetheless, it appears that certain personality attributes increase conflict behavior (Walton and McKersie, 1965). These include low self-esteem, high dogmatism, and authoritarianism. People who think little of themselves and who fear ambiguity in status, beliefs, or authority seem more likely to seek supremacy and clarity by vanquishing their real or imaginary enemies. In addition, some evidence suggests that trusting people are more likely to be belligerent toward those perceived as violating their trust (Cummings et al., 1971). In comparison with managers in several other nations, Americans exhibit the most trust towards those who appear friendly, but are the most belligerent toward provocative others. More suspicious and cynical Greek and Spanish managers don't expect as much from others, but tend to be more conciliatory toward unfriendly, quarrelsome, and hostile others.

Even within the United States, differences seem to exist between managers in different functions: engineering and production seem more trusting and more belligerent; finance, accounting, marketing, and sales less trusting and less belligerent.

All of this suggests that greater behavioral flexibility is likely to decrease conflict while narrow values and rigid beliefs increase it. Locked in their inappropriate styles, less flexible people are unable to compromise or collaborate. Total victory or complete withdrawal become the only permissible alternatives.

APPROACHES TO MANAGING CONFLICT

Some of the most common methods for responding to conflict do not so much attempt to resolve it as to "handle" it in any way that will eliminate or obscure the problem. For example, avoidance or flight are probably most common (Fromm, 1973). Such actions are usually accompanied by psychological stress, arising from conflict among the needs for safety, social esteem, and self-respect, so various rationalizations are developed to relieve it. We may simply reexamine our "real" desires and "rationally" conclude that overt conflict is not worth whatever we thought we wanted. Or we may convince ourselves that postponing conflict is desirable in order to allow time to prepare, frequently deluding ourselves that our objectives are so noble and important that we had better not run the risk of losing by premature conflict. Finally, we may feel that conflict avoidance is more mature and reasonable than "childish" argument. Knowing whether these judgments are valid or merely self-serving rationalizations is extremely difficult (Tedeschi et al., 1971).

Assuming that flight is not possible or desirable, what other general mechanisms for handling conflict exist? Four stand out: dominance, hierarchical appeal, system restructuring, and bargaining (Pondy, 1967; Walton and Dutton, 1969; Deutsch, 1973).

Dominance

Some definitions of conflict presuppose that dominance is the method of handling it. Thus, conflict is "a struggle over values or claims to status, power, and scarce resources, in which the claims of the conflicting parties are not only to gain the desired values, but also to neutralize, injure, or eliminate their rivals" (Coser, quoted in Turner, 1969). Elimination of the antagonist seems to take on an autonomous existence almost independent of the matters in conflict. Dominance may develop through individuals, coalitions, or majorities.

Individual dominance. Many creatures settle conflict by individual dominance, based on fighting ability or physical strength. Conflict over territory or a prospective mate results in the strongest or most aggressive individuals obtaining their desires, while simultaneously promoting the survival of the species. Under such circumstances, "the strategy of conflict centers about injuring the other party without simultaneously injuring the self, while inhibiting and defending against retaliatory injury from the opponent'' (Turner, 1969). As Lorenz (1966) has pointed out, the process is not as bloody as we might expect. Most animals, including humans, replace actual injury or death with symbolic injury. Aggression is checked when both agree who is the loser. The loser follows the rules and withdraws from the conflict, usually going elsewhere to compete with less formidable foes. Among some group animals the loser may remain, but will never again strive for leadership. In addition, the loser must demonstrate obeisance to the victor through symbolic acts of subservience.

In organizations, the loser is sometimes fired; more often, he or she resigns voluntarily or under pressure. One comparison of business and academia (Bensman, 1967) observes that conflict losers are more likely to leave the former, but remain in the latter. Because of tenure, schools are likely to have more ''walking wounded.'' However, all organizations have individuals who have symbolically withdrawn from conflict. In the United States these tend to be people who have resolved their job-home conflict in favor of the latter, putting in minimal time and energy at work. Or they are apathetic older managers performing meaningless duties or working below their capacity. In short, we are not too effective in utilizing such losers. In Japan, such people are effectively utilized as parent-figures to younger people in the organization to lend guidance and advice (Yoshino, 1968).

By virtue of their formal authority, managers can sometimes exercise dominance and dismiss one or more of the conflicting parties. This is a tempting step because it seems simple and complete. Richardson (1961) reports a managerial tendency to deal with production problems by replacing supervisors: ''Of the twelve changes introduced by upper plant management during the ten-month period, eight were attempts to deal with situations diagnosed largely as problems of supervision. Of these eight, seven involved changes in supervisory personnel'' (p. 10). To take another example: In a small steel mill the work and work-process were modified. Interaction patterns were upset, stress resulted, and productivity suffered. The general manager was infuriated by the lag in output and by the fact that the welders had refused to work overtime for a few weeks, even though they would be handsomely paid. ''Replace them all,'' he told the plant foreman. But to regard all problems as personnel problems is too limited — many problems are simply not solved by ''getting a new worker.'' Furthermore, personnel shifts may aggravate stress. Excessive transfers are both an indication of and a cause of stress. Personnel transfers cannot correct faulty work-flow design.

Coalition dominance. The Bolsheviks' faith in ultimate success before the Russian Revolution rested less on Marxian inevitability than in their belief that a minority coalition could prevail if it were willing to work harder, longer, and more intelligently than the majority. Coalitions of two or more people are common because they can generate support out of proportion to their numbers. The presence of just one other supporter lends substantial strength to an individual's position (Asch, 1951).

In the reading ''Power and Politics in Organizational Life,'' Zaleznik (1970) suggests that no organization can function without a coalition that consolidates power around a central figure. The failure to establish a coalition within the executive structure of an organization can result in severe problems such as paralysis in the form of inability to make decisions and to evaluate performance, and infighting and overt rivalry within the executive group" (p. 51). This is illustrated by Zaleznik's discussion of the difficulty Semon Knudsen experienced at Ford Motor Company in the late 1960s. Knudsen had lost the contest for the presidency of General Motors. He could have remained at GM, but he left when Henry Ford II offered him the presidency at Ford. Knudsen lasted less than a year, however, apparently because he could not establish personal dominance and was unable to develop a strong coalition with Ford's vice-presidents, who seemingly opposed him. Their coalition won.

Examination of business career paths (Jennings, 1967) suggests that sponsor-protege coalitions characterize the most upwardly mobile people. Mobile young managers are sensitive to superiors who have promotion potential, and are effective in attaching themselves to them.

To promote short-run cooperation and to buy time for more fundamental conflict resolution, managers may assume the burden of conflict onto themselves and off of their subordinates by forming a coalition with them. Thus, they may tell competing subordinates that resolution does not rest on their level; that they will represent their interests upward in order to obtain more resources or a different distribution. Meanwhile, the subordinates should drop their fight and get on with the job.

Such an approach looks dangerously like buck-passing, but if leaders succeed, they reinforce their influence with their subordinates. If they fail, however, their leadership may be seriously undermined. Nonetheless, managers should be able to serve as a conflict sponge from time to time by encouraging subordinates to redirect their antagonism from among themselves onto them. President Truman's observation of being able to stand the heat in the kitchen applies if you want to be a manager. The most effective managers may be able to do this yet still maintain a calm composure of grace under pressure. Such an example can carry a potent message of competence and attractiveness.

Majority dominance. A manager may endeavor to develop such a majority consensus that the nonconforming minority possesses so little power that they can safely be ignored. The minority is expected to withdraw or remain quiet. Historically, introducing a transcendent objective has been the most common device of great leaders. Ideally, it renders existing conflict irrelevant by introducing a new superordinate objective that unites the conflicting parties. In William Golding's novel *Lord of the Flies*, the marooned boys were able to transcend their differences as long as they accepted the superordinate objective of keeping the signal fire lighted. When they gave up hope of rescue, the fire lost meaning as a common goal and the group decomposed into warring factions.

Sherif (1958) described superordinate goals as "compelling and highly appealing to members of two or more groups in conflict but which cannot be attained by the resources and energies of the groups separately." He concludes:

"When individuals interact in a series of situations toward goals which appeal to all and which require that they coordinate their activities, group structures arise having hierarchical status arrangements and a set of norms regulating behavior in matters of consequence to the objectives of the group" (p. 355).

The creative conflict resolver looks for common, not divergent elements. For example, political leaders have long united squabbling followers by pointing out a common enemy who would destroy them all unless they fight together (think of George Washington and Europe, Castro and the United States, Mao and the Soviet Union). Or the leader articulates the serious internal problems facing everyone, problems of such gravity that chaos will result unless petty dissension is dropped and cooperative behavior evidenced (think of Franklin Roosevelt and the Depression, Lyndon Johnson and civil rights). At a more mundane level, a manager can alter the reward system so that contending parties are rewarded for cooperative performance rather than for individual behavior. For example, rather than rewarding production department managers for performance on their departmental budgets, a plant-wide total cost index could be tied to a plant-wide bonus. The intent is to create an objective to which all parties are committed and which requires cooperative behavior to achieve. Schermerhorn (1976) indicates that openness to superordinate objectives and willingness to cooperate depends more on positive motivation than on negative. Fear and distress is less motivating to cooperation than high performance and hoped-for even better results.

Unfortunately, there is a limit to such expansion of objectives. Where the transcendent objective becomes too large, encompassing a large number of individuals and groups, it tends to lose its motivating force. Each individual feels too small to really affect the whole; achievement of the objective would not significantly reflect individual efforts. Hence the individual may give up. The individual worker or even a whole production department simply may not see a direct relation between performance and the plant bonus. Nonetheless, the fact that the technique of offering a transcendent and unifying objective is used by demagogues and dictators, as well as saints and democrats, testifies to its potency as a mechanism for managing conflict.

Dominance in action. Research with student problem-solving groups under time pressure (Webber, 1972) suggests a preference for dominance techniques. A typical scenario runs as follows: First, there is an attempt to find consensus or unanimity through informal polling. The students seem to hope that there is no conflict. Even at this stage there is some majority dominance, in that some individuals do not express their disagreement when the majority seems against them.

Second, if there is no consensus, the group tends to respond to the dominant individual or the small coalition. The source of dominance may be perceived external status, but more frequently it is the degree of certainty demonstrated by an individual or pair. Where time is limited, certainty dominates uncertainty.

Third, where status or certainty is absent, formal voting occurs. The majority dominates.

Finally, if no majority results, the group tends to accept plurality coalition dominance without certainty, or gives up the conflict, does not solve the problem, and moves on to the next one.

The most rational steps toward problem-solving are found during phase three. When no one is certain and before a vote is taken, some discussion of individual thoughts and experiences in relation to the problem will occur. Substantive questions are raised: "What do the words mean?" "Has anyone ever been in this situation?" "Didn't some famous novelist talk about this?" Out of this discussion, a dominant position sometimes emerges.

Appeal to Hierarchy

One of humanity's great innovations was the transfer of conflict management from dominance to hierarchical appeal. For some scholars, it marks the beginning of civilization (Piggott, 1961).

Appeal to God or chance. Initially, this shift was more philosophical than physical. The battle went on, but it was assumed that God's might was on the side of the right, that the human combat was just the vehicle for God's will. The desirability of looking for the deity's wishes in less contentious ways was recognized some time ago, however. The stars, animal entrails, and tea leaves all served as communication media. Rationalists consider such appeals superstitious, but this is beside the point. Appeal to even a fictitious god made a major contribution to human advancement through more efficient conflict management.

Appeal to chance also serves the same purpose, even if it is less philosophically and religiously satisfying. An external event not under the control of the contending parties is used to indicate which will dominate. The loser is expected to withdraw actually or symbolically.

Appeal to positional authority. The difficulty with simple appeal to God or Lady Luck is that tremendous faith is necessary to believe that justice has been dispensed. Being of relatively little faith, civilized people began to look for justice in conflict management through more rational ways. Thus was born the idea of a judge or hierarchical superior who would resolve conflicts. A person in a recognized superior position is to listen to the parties in conflict, then decide who is correct.

If the principles of chain of command and unity of command are followed in a society and its organizations, any two parties in conflict can find the common superior who links them and who can deal with the conflict. Thus in Exhibit 11.2, if N and P are in disagreement, their common superior G can act as conflict resolver. If H and K are in conflict, their common superior is A. A common superior can act as a judge, rendering a just decision while possessing the authority to enforce it.

The judicial mechanism of courts, attorneys, judges, and juries is an elaboration of the basic system to provide added protection to the defendant and

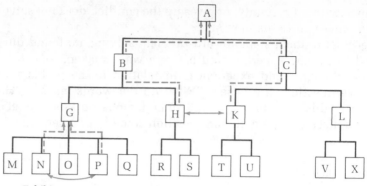

Exhibit 11.2 Appeal to Positional Authority

to promote wisdom and justice, but the central feature is the same—the provision for conflict management through a judicial/bureaucratic, hierarchical structure. People in certain positions are defined as having the authority and responsibility to make difficult and sometimes unpopular decisions. With all the attacks today on hierarchical authority systems, we do well to remember this central fact: This system was an enormous step forward in conflict management. This is perhaps the greatest contribution of hierarchy.

The hierarchical decision-maker still has an important role. Nonetheless, it is shrinking. Optimal performance of the mechanism depends on a happy congruence of authority, knowledge, wisdom, and subordinate respect. When the decision-makers cannot understand the issues, or the conflicting parties do not believe they do, or don't respect their authority, their ability to resolve conflict is sharply curtailed. People will not accept the superior's judgment. They will attempt to fight it out without the judge; they will try to eliminate each other like gang leaders contending over turf in an urban ghetto. Of course, a hierarchical superior can resort to dominance to force acceptance, but this sharply undermines the efficiency of the system.

The American court system faces this crisis. Simple overload introduces delays before the conflict mechanism acts. And justice long-delayed is not justice. In addition, substantial segments of society do not recognize the nation's laws as *their* laws, and neither respect nor recognize the judge or jury's decisions. Most organizational managers do not yet face problems of such great magnitude, but their ability to resolve conflict by hierarchical decisions is similarly eroding because of declining effectiveness of traditional authority.

An additional problem for hierarchical conflict management is that the neat departmental boxes and lines are breaking down in and between organizations. Boundaries are becoming indistinct. Systems are expanding so that more people who are in conflict do not have a definite common superior to whom they can appeal. Who is the common superior of college alumni and administrators? Of government regulatory agencies and business executives? Of Ralph Nader's "raiders" and company management? Or, indeed, of a corporate president and dissenting vice-presidents, when the Board of Directors is mainly an inside board?

A dramatic increase in unofficial advocacy groups has characterized our society in recent years. Concern for the poor, for minorities, and for the environment has expressed itself in autonomous groups making demands on older, more formal organizations. Such confrontations are increasing and they, too, are ill-suited to the traditional judicial/bureaucratic mode of conflict management.

Appeal to higher authority. Hierarchical decisions are only as good as the managers are wise and just—and have the time to judge. Unfortunately, these conditions don't always prevail, so appeal mechanisms have been developed to supplement the hierarchical process (Evan, 1961; Scott, 1965).

If organizational members feel that a problem has not been handled fairly or properly by an immediate superior, they may have the right to appeal to a higher manager, that is, have an "open door" to their boss's boss. In Exhibit 11.3, E could appeal to A, who would make a decision binding on B and E. The assumption is that A will make a better judgment because he or she has fewer operational pressures, possesses more time, and is less emotionally involved than B.

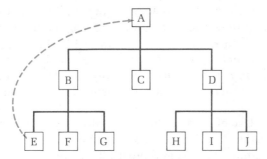

Exhibit 11.3 Appeal to Higher Authority

This right of appeal is a fine supplement to hierarchical decisions, but problems exist. The higher superior A may be too busy to devote time to E's complaint. Or, even though A may be angry with B for not handling the problem satisfactorily, A may still affirm B's influence downward because if A were to override B too frequently, everyone would bypass B. Finally, B may hold a grudge against "trouble-maker" E for bypassing B. For all of these reasons, E may conclude that he or she runs a grave risk in appealing to A.

Appeal to arbitration. To provide greater impartiality and protection, an independent arbitrator may be engaged to listen to E's appeal, gather information, and render a judgment binding on A, B, E, and the organization (see Exhibit 11.4). Such a judge could be a trained specialist who has a professional reputation of making appropriate nonbiased decisions.

The use of arbitrators is best known in labor-management relations to handle grievances in a manner that avoids the breakdown of the relationship in a strike. Under such arrangements, the arbitrator is hired in advance under mutual agreement of the two parties. But, arbitrators don't enjoy tenure; if

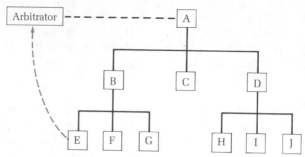

Exhibit 11.4   Appeal to Arbitration

they render judgments that distress either party, they are unlikely to be retained for another contract period. Thus, there is no way for an arbitrator to be totally independent. Still, most arbitrators feel that the only proper way to judge cases is to call them as they see them—without regard to personal consequences.

There have been widespread calls for expanding the use of arbitration in conflict disputes. We see it used in professional sports to an increasing degree, for example. Nonetheless, most managements rightly fear loss of control of their organizations if they allow arbitration to become the predominant mode of conflict resolution. It could extend to areas like investment and product policies, which are generally felt to be management's central concern. And arbitrators tend to emphasize short-run equity and legality in their decisions rather than long-run functionality for the institution or society.

The ombudsman.   Use of ombudsmen is not directly a mechanism for conflict resolution, but because the position stands outside the hierarchical structure, it can facilitate communications and ensure that lower levels in the hierarchy can bring their problems up to the top. In Exhibit 11.5, for example, if H feels that proper treatment has not been received from C, H can go directly to the Ombudsman O, who will investigate the issue and approach C or even the top executive A to achieve a solution. Unlike an arbitrator or appeals committee, however, ombudsmen have no authority to make a decision. They can merely recommend. Yet the right to ask questions can lead to substantial informal authority for the ombudsman.

The greatest contribution of the ombudsman is helping people get informa-

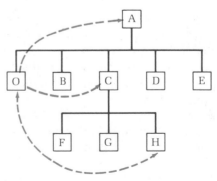

Exhibit 11.5   The Ombudsman

tion and overcoming misunderstanding. They may help people to feel less alienated by expressing individual interest. They are not likely, however, to contribute to resolution of major conflicts. Since they receive their salaries from the organization and possess no formal power, they are unlikely to be allowed to deal with big issues that affect many people. The reading "The Roles of the Ombudsman" considers these matters in greater detail.

System Restructuring

Any organization involves the simultaneous coordination of people who must pass paper, materials, or ideas among themselves in some controlled sequence: giving orders, soliciting suggestions, responding to technological breakdowns, planning, etc. All of these activities and functions must be carried out through interactions with others. Thus, organizational structure is most fundamentally a design of human relationships and patterns of interaction.

In order to minimize the adverse impact of conflict on organizational effectiveness, managers must design and modify organizational structure to prevent upsetting work patterns (Chapple and Sayles, 1961; Thompson and Van Houten, 1970).

Rotating personnel.   To counter narrow loyalties and misunderstanding due to perceptual distortions, management may periodically rotate people among interdependent groups. In the short-run, the newcomers are unlikely to be accepted because of mistrust. Already existing conflict will probably not be reduced. In the long-run, however, exchanging people may create a favorable background for future prevention of intergroup conflict (Blake and Mouton, 1961a).

Decoupling with a buffer.   Since much conflict derives from interdependence, managers can attempt to reduce this by "decoupling" the conflicting parties. They can attempt to reduce dependence on common resources, or provide iron-clad, impersonal rules for allocation. Giving each entity control of their own resources or introducing large buffer inventories can be expensive, but they do reduce interdependence. Thus State I in Exhibit 11.6 may be converted into State II.

An example of this technique is where Department A sends its semifinished products into a buffer inventory that may simply be a big bin. Department B takes goods to be finished from this inventory. Under this system, if Department A has problems and falls behind, Department B wouldn't be affected because it has the inventory to draw on.

Buffering with a linking role.   Another form of buffering can be introduced through a "linking" position, coordinator, or integrator (Lawrence and Lorsch, 1967). As State III in Exhibit 11.6 suggests, this role facilitates communication and coordination between interdependent and potentially conflicting depart-

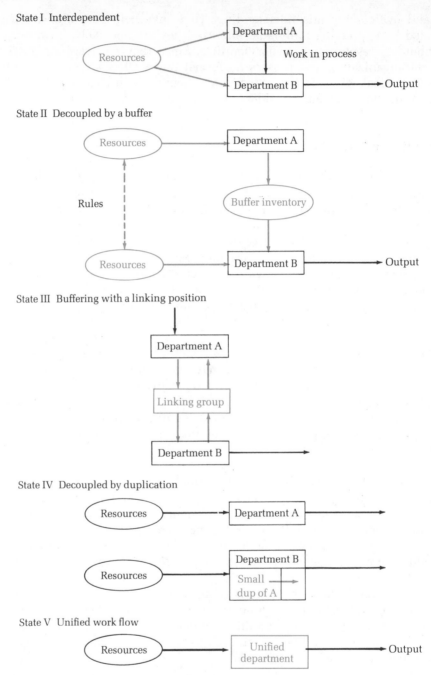

State I Interdependent

State II Decoupled by a buffer

State III Buffering with a linking position

State IV Decoupled by duplication

State V Unified work flow

Exhibit 11.6 Reducing Conflict by System Restructuring

ments. It carries no substantial authority (other than right of access), but is supposed to detect and manage differences. In the past, this role has usually been filled by fairly passive and low status individuals such as older employees whose expertise was outdated—who, in fact, were "expendable" (Dalton, 1963). They were not personally threatening to any group, who could vent their antagonisms on them without fear of retaliation. It appears, however, that stronger and more promotable people, who will confront differences rather than paper them over, may be desirable. Examples of linking groups include: field engineers, between customers and sales representatives and design engineers; development engineers, between research scientists and production managers; order fillers, between chefs and waiters; public relations/press representatives, between political leaders and the press/media/public; and directors of student activities, between students and academic administrators.

To play such a role can be extremely stressful. Many go-betweens are caught in war's crossfire. The person must be able to absorb substantial flack and withstand great pressure — or perhaps not feel the heat because of insensitivity, guaranteed security, or independent satisfactions.

Decoupling by duplication. Decoupling sometimes takes the form of duplicating the facilities of one department upon which another is dependent. Thus, research may develop a small production unit under its control for pilot runs. Or a production department may recruit some engineers on its own to reduce its dependence on central engineering. Interdependent State I may be converted to decoupled State IV, as in Exhibit 11.6.

It is tempting and common for managers to reduce interdependence by introducing duplicate facilities and excess resources, or "organizational slack," at various stages. Extra employees, money, and machines can make life easier, but such sub-optimization may harm the whole organization.

Unifying the work flow. Much stress and conflict stems from violation of the old organizational principle: "Authority should equal responsibility." Managers may not control everything that is needed to perform a mission. Controlling "everything" is probably impossible, but the system might be restructured into more logical complete work units which bring more control under one hierarchical position, thus decreasing ambiguity. This does increase unit size, of course, and additional costs for internal coordination are necessary, but benefits of defining a hierarchical judge may outweigh the costs. Thus State I may be converted into State V in Exhibit 11.6.

The difference between decoupling through duplication, as in State IV, and unifying the work flow, as in State V, is sometimes a matter of judgment and perception. Thus, production may feel that developing its own small research or engineering capacity is logically unifying the task, while these other groups consider it wasteful slack and illegitimate empire building. The difference is subtle, but as a rule State IV evolves informally while State V is a formal organizational change. In fact, most unified work groups may just be legitimization of previously existing duplication.

Matrix organization. Perhaps the most persistent theme in recent literature on conflict management is confrontation. Limited research suggests that more effective managers facilitate conflict recognition and conciliation, rather than "smoothing" conflict over by denying its reality or "forcing" solutions by superior power (Lawrence and Lorsch, 1967). Such managers recognize that conflict is inevitable if they create a climate where people express independent ideas rather than just conforming to the prevailing view. What is desired is that this conflict be expressed by following certain rules of confrontation.

Within organizations, a matrix structure offers one means for facilitating such confrontation. The most common matrix is shown in Exhibit 11.7. Such a structure is intended to promote the flexible use of specialized staff on interdisciplinary programs (e.g., a sophisticated product team drawing on various scientists and engineers in electronics, hydraulics, operations research, metallurgy, etc.). Just as important, however, is that the matrix defines a battlefield and its participants. It recognizes the competing interests of program and specialist departments, such as short-run program completion versus long-run career development. It provides separate managers to stand up for those interests. The overall executive's major role is to facilitate communication and bargaining, stepping in to be a judicial/bureaucratic decision-maker only when absolutely necessary.

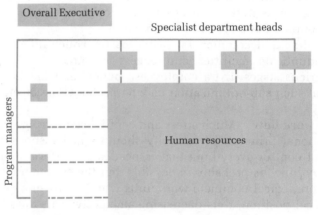

Exhibit 11.7   Matrix Organization

Based on survey data in research laboratories, Evan (1965) concluded that interpersonal conflict (i.e., personality conflict) is negatively associated with performance, while technical conflict (i.e., differences of opinion on design, technology, methods, etc.) is positively associated with performance. The matrix approach encourages technical conflict, while bringing interpersonal conflict out into the open where it can be seen and dealt with.

Bargaining

"Bargaining power," as Chamberlain tells us, "refers to another person's inducement to agree on your terms. Or, to put it in another way, your bargaining power is my cost of disagreeing on your terms relative to my cost of agreeing on your terms. This ratio measures the extent of my inducement to accept what you propose. Similarly, my bargaining power is your cost of disagreeing on my terms relative to your cost of agreeing on my terms" (1955, p. 227). The power may have been bestowed by an external party—such as the power over working conditions given to the manager by corporate directors, or the power to negotiate agreements delegated to elected union officers by the union membership. Or the power may grow out of the relationship between the two parties—such as the power that management gives, perhaps inadvertently, to any workers when it hires them and thus becomes dependent upon them.

Bargaining can be explicit or implicit. In the explicit situation, the two parties are aware that each is trying to influence the other and that agreement is a function of the power they bring to the situation and their skill as bargainers. Where bargaining is implicit, at least one party does not consciously recognize the situation as one of bargaining. Leavitt (1972) describes this as a manipulative process: The manipulator attempts to develop a relationship of value to the other party and then to trade on that relationship by threatening to terminate or change it. Such implicit bargaining is frequently associated with two individuals who have no formal power over one another, such as the production-line supervisor and the maintenance manager. Nonetheless, an individual may attempt to bargain implicitly with a large number of people. A paternalistic manager who gives turkeys and bonuses at Christmas or builds an employee recreation park is often, consciously or unconsciously, attempting to manipulate subordinates into giving the firm greater loyalty.

The presence of a union is not essential for explicit bargaining, although employees do tend to create formal structures for dealing with management. As Zaleznik and Moment (1964) explain: "Where this problem (conflict) occurs *within* an interacting group, some communication channels exist or are possible for increasing the mutual understanding of real differences in task requisites, as well as the amount and kind of social differences required for group maintenance. When this problem occurs *between* socially isolated groups, such as managers and workers, the tendency is to resort to institutionalized means for resolving intergroup conflict in lieu of primary systems of communication" (p. 346). Nonetheless, conflict and bargaining do take place between management and employee groups, whether formal unions are involved or not.

Explicit bargaining may be difficult to distinguish from simple dominance. Employers once strove to physically eliminate unions by firing their leaders and coercing members (some still try this, of course). The crucial difference between dominance and bargaining, however, is interdependence: in dominance, the dominator doesn't need the loser any longer; in bargaining, both sides recognize their mutual dependence and that they must work together after the conflict (Slusher et al., 1974). The two parties are aware that each is trying to influence the other, and that agreement is a function of the power they bring to the situation and their skill as bargainers.

What we are dealing with is a continuum of attitudes: from open hostility to closer cooperation. Two perspectives along this continuum are distributive bargaining and integrative bargaining.

Distributive bargaining. Distributive bargaining is somewhat like dominance, but with the recognition that the other party can hurt you and will remain after the round of conflict. In the short-run, the relationship is viewed as a zero-sum game; what either side gains is at the expense of the other (Zechmeister and Druckman, 1963; Rapoport, 1966). Hence, it is bargaining over the pieces to be cut from the pie. The method of resolution is to find the size of slice for each that reflects each side's power and ability to harm the other, without totally disrupting the relationship.

Each side attempts to inflate its projected power and willingness to endure injury, while endeavoring to discover the other's true minimum position. Confusion, obfuscation, and deception are inherent and necessary. When meaningful and substantive communication occurs, it is mainly on specifics of how much each side is willing to reduce its stated demands. Most labor-management bargaining falls in this category.

Integrative bargaining. Integrative bargaining is a rare phenomenon. It is not a rejection of conflict, because the parties still must look out for their own interests; rather, it is a transcendence of conflict, the conversion from bargaining to problem-solving. The focus shifts from reducing demands toward expanding the pool of resources; from how the small pie is to be sliced toward how to bake a larger pie so that both sides can increase their welfare. Ideally, the new satisfactions are bigger than the original demands, so that whatever concessions the parties must make are perceived not as surrenders, but, in Kissinger's words (1972), as "sacrifices to the common cause."

This philosophy was actually the intent of Taylor's scientific management (1911). He hoped to eliminate harmful "soldiering" and destructive conflict through new industrial engineering techniques which were to be used to determine the "best way" to perform each task. Since the work measurement techniques were "scientific," labor and management would accept them, thus eliminating this argument. Bargaining could then be directed toward expanding production and income so that both sides could gain.

Taylor's denial of inevitable class conflict and his philosophy of cooperation were typically American, stirring, and idealistic. For the most part, however, the techniques caught on while the philosophy was rejected. Perhaps it is just too naive to expect rational agreement on distributing any limited resources, regardless of how large they are absolutely. Nonetheless, it may not be too much to expect collaborative efforts to improve the pool of resources upon which both sides must draw. Then the basis could shift to distributive bargaining. Thus integrative and distributive bargaining might alternate.

The problem, of course, is that keeping the two approaches separate is very difficult; the attitudes of distributive bargaining tend to poison the climate for integrative bargaining. In addition, entering a bargaining situation with an integrative perspective can be very dangerous if the other side views it from the distributive perspective. Integrative bargaining depends on candid disclosure, which reduces the possibility of bluffing and therefore handicaps distributive bargaining by exposing one party to the other's exploitation. In laboratory experiments in black-white relations, whites were most cooperative when blacks were described beforehand as being "very competitive" (Baxter, 1973). The white was *less* cooperative with a black described as "cooperative." A tough reputation and stance seems to help relations.

In a conflict bargaining situation, the party who doesn't fight tends to elicit exploitative behavior from the other party. People tend to walk over "fools" who leave themselves vulnerable. Since strong retaliation tends to escalate the conflict, the most cooperation arises when the response is mild retaliation (Miller, 1967; Meeker and Shure, 1969; Gruder and Duslak, 1973). Bargainers seem to concede more when the other party makes only small initial concessions than when initial concessions are large. Large concessions increase the opponent's expectations (Yukl, 1974; Lindskold et al., 1976). In general, "cautious trust," indicating a willingness to cooperate but also a firmness which prevents partners from exploiting their cooperativeness, seems to characterize people who work out cooperative arrangements in competitive games (Santa-Barbara and Epstein, 1974). Finally, effective bargaining requires a certain cool rationality rather than emotional game-playing (Acuff and Villere, 1976). Of course, anger may be used as a calculative device.

Mediation. Not all conflict management depends exclusively on managers' hierarchical positions. Managers may allow and encourage conflicting subordinates to bargain directly. As we indicated earlier, Chamberlain (1955) suggests that virtually all organizational decisions are made on the basis of the relative bargaining powers of those whose views and interests clash. Because of the complexity of these internal bargaining processes and their potential danger to organizational effectiveness, management must guide and control them: "Because of the number of individuals and groups involved, because of the number of issues concerned of which each has his preferences, because of the requirement that with respect to any issue only one resolution can be made, applying to all affected, and because of the further requirement that the decision on any issue must be consistent; and compatible with the decisions on all other issues—because of all these conditions it is necessary that there be a coordinator of the bargaining" (p. 228). This task—the coordination of the bargains of all those who comprise the organization—is a unique function of management.

Mediation or conciliation is a way of fulfilling this function. The purpose of a mediator is not to decide who is right or what is just (an arbitrator or judge does that). Rather, mediators attempt to stop the spiral of conflict by eliminating surrender as a demand and by encouraging each party to acknowledge that they have injured the other (in effect, to grant some justification for the other's hostility to them); they attempt to promote more authentic communication; and, if requested, they suggest possible solutions.

Since "the key to all conflict resolution is the repair of previous injury and protection against future injury, conciliation is any act whose aim is to avert or discontinue conflict without either side asking or offering surrender" (Turner, 1969). By discovering and communicating the true positions of the parties, mediators assist them in confronting their real differences and in discovering their common problems. As we have seen, the major tragedy in conflict is that efforts to injure the other party dominate the issues dividing the two. Hence, conflict shifts from item to item, philosophy to philosophy, and the original substantive matters may be forgotten. The mediating manager's great contribution can be to return the conflict to the real issues. He or she can articulate the potential damage to all parties if conflict continues.

In the reading "Third Party Roles in Interdepartmental Conflict," Walton (1967) offers the following advice to managers for setting a proper example for handling conflict:

Confront, invite differences.
Listen with understanding, rather than evaluation.
Clarify the nature of the issue.
Recognize and accept feelings.
Suggest a procedure for resolving differences.
Cope with threats to reasonable agreement.

He also points out that mediators need synchronization in confrontation. That is, they must make a judgment that the parties are both ready to confront each other and are potentially willing to communicate. Premature confrontation may only promote escalation (a phenomenon long known to astute national leaders who delay "summit" conferences until agreement potential is high). Rejection of one party's overture to talk is viewed as particularly demeaning, which "justifies" strong attack from the rejected party (an event which has characterized many recent conflicts—Israel and Egypt, United States and North Vietnam, Pakistan and India).

The essence of successful mediation lies in making the warring parties realize they are dependent on each other, and in finding an area of common agreement (Henderson, 1971). Such an approach assumes that the issues to be resolved are objective and substantive, not merely reflections of irrational behavior by the contending parties. An objective definition of the problem, agreed upon by both sides, may be the single most important step in resolution (Blake and Mouton, 1961b). Upon this common definition can sometimes be built a transcendent objective.

Substantial laboratory research under conditions where two parties apparently want to maximize their individual incomes indicates that many choices (almost 50 percent) are made *not* to maximize personal income, but to decrease the competitor's income. Relative standing seems more important than absolute benefits (Scodel et al., 1959). If the mediator can stretch the minds of quarreling individuals or groups so they can see how their parochial viewpoints fit into a larger system, a higher understanding may be developed that integrates seemingly diverse goals. A sense of shared goals is critical.

Internal organizational bargaining. Managers increasingly must face the anxiety of presiding over conflicts below them as well as participating in bargaining themselves. Some will see bargaining as an improvement over dominance: Autonomous people can look out for their own interests and manage their own affairs; they are less dependent on a superior to resolve their difficulties. However, people new to bargaining attempt to dominate the other parties, so that coordination breaks down and the effects of conflict spread. The emphasis tends to be on distributive rather than integrative bargaining. This is the current state of affairs in many institutions where parties have begun to deal with each other directly: students and administrators, players and coaches, professionals and government bureaucrats, and even enlisted personnel and officers. All of this is similar to the early days of labor-management negotiation, before some unions and employers came to recognize the commonality of their problems.

In the words of the eminent labor economist and mediator George Taylor (1966), it is imperative that we come to see bargaining not as a game to be won or lost, but as a problem-solving process; that we need a new "philosophy of losing" — a philosophy that sees exchange in bargaining not as a defeat, but as a continuous process of conflict resolution.

However exasperating collective negotiations are, they represent one of the most important mechanisms of social conflict management. At its best, such bargaining signifies recognition and acceptance by the conflicting parties of each other's competing claims on resources within an orderly framework of law and custom. It appears that this mechanism will be expanded to many areas beyond labor and management relations. For interorganizational conflicts, for example, there might be permanent panels of highly trained citizens to serve as "community mediation boards," appointed as quasi-public bodies and available at all times for any dispute that would otherwise fester, clutter court calendars, or be resolved by power plays (Henderson, 1971). The activities of most informal advocacy groups have been initially disruptive because they bring submerged issues to the surface, where they inevitably clash with established institutions and contrary public opinion. For this reason, they often trigger opposition and repression. But as they gain legitimacy and develop support, they will represent another means of resolving conflict between minority interests and the dominant culture.

CONCLUSION

Organizations appear to be moving toward more open and rational handling of conflict. Conflict between two or more entities endeavoring to occupy the same space or state comes in various forms: interpersonal, intergroup, and interorganizational. The potential for such conflict depends upon the degree of shared resources, goal incompatibility, and activity interdependence. Once existing, conflict tends to be maintained through stereotyped and distorted perceptions that exaggerate the differences between conflicting parties.

Humans have always been tempted to resort to simple dominance to handle conflict. Violence and war are not necessarily more common today than in the past, but we can less afford them because the complexity and interdependence of modern life mean that such solutions are not restricted to the people directly involved. Others are drawn in. In the sparsely populated and independent American frontier, two men "reconciling" their problems via the ubiquitous gun was sad, but affected few people. Such behavior today threatens chaos.

Accordingly, it is of ever-increasing importance that we make alternative conflict management systems work. We have considered various social mechanisms that have been developed for managing conflict in addition to dominance: appeal to chance; hierarchical decisions and appeal procedures; system restructuring by rotating personnel, decoupling, buffering, duplicating, or unifying; and distributive and integrative bargaining and mediation. Unfortunately, there are problems associated with each.

Managers can play several roles in managing conflict. They might be judicial-bureaucratic decision-makers (although this aspect may be declining in importance). They might restructure the system to decrease interdependence or to introduce linking roles. They might introduce superordinate objectives that transcend the conflict or shift it to a higher level, thus unifying the parties. They might even facilitate bargaining by designing an appropriate matrix structure and acting as mediator.

We desperately need more effective conflict management. All of our mechanisms face difficulty because of changing patterns of authority and respect, because of emerging groups promoting change, and simply because of the large volume of conflicts to be managed. We need to utilize existing methods more effectively and to develop novel systems. In few arenas is human ingenuity more critical. In few areas is existing theory less helpful to developing effective operational techniques (Deutsch, 1973).

We do not mean to add to the currently popular view of businesses and large organizations as areas for political infighting and polite backstabbing. All organizational activity engenders some conflict—and business is no worse than other areas in this respect. Human beings, simply, are political creatures; this springs from our social nature (Tiger and Fox, 1971). However, when competition and conflict do appear, managers must deal with them. Only by understanding the process can managers use conflict constructively, to "make conflict *do* something for us," as Follett (1940) suggested years ago.

REFERENCES

Acuff, F. L., and M. Villere. "Games Negotiators Play." *Business Horizons*, Vol. 19, No. 1 (February 1976), pp. 70–76.

Aldrich, H. "Organizational Boundaries and Interorganizational Conflict." *Human Relations*, Vol. 24 (August 1971), pp. 279–93.

Ansbacher, H. L., and R. R. Ansbacher (eds). *The Individual Psychology of Alfred Adler*. Basic Books, 1956.

Asch, S. E. "Effects of Group Pressure Upon the Modification and Distortion of Judgments." In H. Guetzkow (ed), *Groups, Leadership and Men*. Carnegie Press, 1951.

Aubert, V. "Competition and Dissensus: Two Types of Conflict." *Journal of Conflict Resolution*, Vol. 7, No. 1 (1963), pp. 26–42.

Barnard, C. *The Functions of the Executive*. Harvard University Press, 1938.

Baxter, G. W., Jr. "Prejudiced Liberals? Race and Information Effects in a Two-Person Game." *Journal of Conflict Resolution*, Vol. 17, No. 1 (1973), p. 131.

Bennis, W. G. *Organizational Development*. Addison-Wesley, 1970.

Bensman, J. *Dollars and Sense*. Macmillan, 1967.

Berelson, B., and G. A. Steiner. *Human Behavior: An Inventory of Scientific Findings.* Harcourt Brace Jovanovich, 1964.

Berne, E. *Games People Play.* Grove Press, 1964.

Blake, R. R., and J. S. Mouton. "Loyalty of Representatives to Group Position During Intergroup Competition." *Sociometry*, Vol. 24 (1961a), pp. 177–83.

———, and ———. "Reactions to Intergroup Competition Under Win-Lose Conditions." *Management Science*, Vol. 4, No. 4 (July 1961b).

Chamberlain, N. A. *General Theory of Economic Process.* Harper and Row, 1955.

Chapple, E., and L. R. Sayles. *The Measure of Management.* Macmillan, 1961.

Coser, L. A. *The Functions of Social Conflict.* Free Press, 1956.

Cummings, L. L., D. L. Harnett, and O. J. Stevens. "Risk, Fate, Conciliation and Trust: An International Study of Attitudinal Differences Among Executives." *Academy of Management Journal*, Vol. 14, No. 3 (September 1971), pp. 285–304.

Dalton, G. W. "Diagnosing Interdepartmental Conflict." *Harvard Business Review*, September–October 1963.

Deutsch, M. *The Resolution of Conflict.* Yale University Press, 1973.

Down, A. *Inside Bureaucracy.* Little, Brown, 1968.

Dutton, J. M., and R. E. Walton. "Interdepartmental Conflict and Cooperation: Two Contrasting Studies." *Human Organization*, Vol. 25 (1966), pp. 207–20.

Evan, W. M. "Conflict and Performance in R&D Organizations." *Industrial Management Review*, Vol. 7, No. 2 (Fall, 1965), pp. 37–46.

———. "Organization Man and Due Process of Law." *American Sociological Review*, August 1961, pp. 540–47.

Follett, M. P. *Dynamic Administration.* Harper and Row, 1940.

Fromm, E. *The Anatomy of Human Destructiveness.* Holt, Rinehart, and Winston, 1973.

Gruder, C. L., and R. L. Duslak. "Elicitation of Cooperation by Retaliatory and Nonretaliatory Strategies in a Mixed-Motive Game." *Journal of Conflict Resolution*, Vol. 17, No. 1 (1973), pp. 162–74.

Henderson, H. "Toward Managing Social Conflict." *Harvard Business Review*, May–June 1971, pp. 82–90.

Jennings, E. E. *The Mobile Manager.* Bureau of Industrial Relations, University of Michigan, 1967.

Kelly, J. "Make Conflict Work for You." *Harvard Business Review*, July–August 1970, pp. 103–14.

Kissinger, H. Quoted in *The New York Times* (July 28, 1972).

Kochan, T. A., G. P. Huber, and L. L. Cummings. "Determinants of Interorganizational Conflict in Collective Bargaining in the Public Sector." *Administrative Science Quarterly*, Vol. 20, No. 1 (March 1975).

Lawrence, P. R., and J. W. Lorsch. "New Management Job: The Integrator." *Harvard Business Review*, Vol. 45, No. 6 (November–December 1967), pp. 142–51.

———. *Organization and Environment.* Division of Research, Harvard Graduate School of Business, 1962.

Leavitt, H. *Managerial Psychology*, 3rd ed. University of Chicago Press, 1972.

Lindskold, S., R. Bennett, and M. Wayner. "Retaliation Level as a Foundation for Subsequent Conciliation." *Behavioral Science*, Vol. 21 (January 1976), pp. 13–20.

Lorenz, K. *On Aggression.* Harcourt Brace Jovanovich, 1966.

Lourenco, S. V., and J. C. Glidewell. "A Dialectical Analysis of Organizational Conflict." *Administrative Science Quarterly*, December 1975, pp. 489–508.

Meeker, R. J., and G. H. Shure. "Pacifist Bargaining Tactics: Some 'Outsider' Influences." *Journal of Conflict Resolution,* Vol. 15 (1969), pp. 261–69.

Miller, R. "No Play: A Means of Conflict Resolution." *Journal of Personality and Social Psychology,* Vol. 6, No. 2 (1967), pp. 150–56.

Piggott, S. (ed). *The Dawn of Civilization.* McGraw-Hill, 1961.

Pondy, L. R. "Organization Conflict: Concepts and Models." *Administrative Science Quarterly,* Vol. 12, No. 2 (September 1967).

Porter, L. "Where is the Organization Man?" *Harvard Business Review,* November–December 1963, pp. 53–61.

Rapoport, A. *Two-Person Game Theory: The Essential Ideas.* University of Michigan, 1966.

Richardson, F. L. W. *Talk, Work, and Action.* Monograph No. 3, The Society for Applied Anthropology, 1961.

Santa-Barbara, J., and N. B. Epstein. "Conflict Behavior in Clinical Families: Preasymptotic Interactions and Stable Outcomes." *Behavioral Science,* Vol. 19 (1974), pp. 100–110.

Schermerhorn, J. R., Jr. "Openness to Interorganizational Cooperation." *Academy of Management Journal,* Vol. 19, No. 2 (June 1976), pp. 225–36.

Schmidt, S. M., and T. A. Kochan. "Conflict: Toward Conceptual Clarity." *Administrative Science Quarterly,* Vol. 17, No. 3 (September 1972), pp. 359–370.

Scodel, A., J. S. Minas, P. Ratoosh, and M. Lipetz. "Some Descriptive Aspects of Two-Person, Non-Zero Sum Games." *Journal of Conflict Resolution,* Vol. 3 (1959), pp. 114–19.

Scott, W. G. "Appeal Systems in Organizations." In *The Management of Conflict.* Irwin-Dorsey, 1965, pp. 114–26.

Sherif, M. "Superordinate Goals in the Reduction of Intergroup Conflict." *American Journal of Sociology,* Vol. 63, No. 4 (January 1958).

Silver, I. "The Corporate Ombudsman." *Harvard Business Review,* May–June 1967, p. 77.

Slusher, E. A., K. J. Roering, and G. L. Rose. "The Effects of Commitment to Future Interaction in Single Plays of Three Games." *Behavioral Science,* Vol. 19 (1974), pp. 119–32.

Taylor, F. W. *The Principles of Scientific Management.* Harper and Row, 1911.

Taylor, G. W. "Ideas for Social Change." World Academy of Art and Science, Junk, The Hague, 1966.

Tedeschi, J. T., B. R. Schlenker, and T. V. Bonoma. "Cognitive Dissonance: Private Ratiocination or Public Spectacles?" *American Psychologist,* Vol. 26 (1971), pp. 685–95.

Thomas, K. W., and W. H. Schmidt. "A Survey of Managerial Interests with Respect to Conflict." *Academy of Management Journal,* Vol. 19, No. 2 (June 1976), pp. 315–18.

Thompson, J. D. "Organizational Management of Conflict." *Administrative Science Quarterly,* Vol. 4 (1960), pp. 389–409.

———, and D. R. Van Houten. *The Behavioral Sciences: An Interpretation.* Addison-Wesley, 1970.

Tiger, L., and R. Fox. *The Imperial Animal.* Holt, Rinehart, and Winston, 1971.

Turner, R. "The Public Perception of Protest." *American Sociological Review,* Vol. 34 (1969), pp. 815–31.

Walton, R. E. "Third-Party Roles in Interdepartmental Conflict." *Industrial Relations,* Vol. 7, No. 1 (October 1967), p. 29.

————, and J. M. Dutton. "The Management of Interdepartmental Conflict: A Model and Review." *Administrative Science Quarterly*, Vol. 14, No. 1 (March 1969), pp. 73–84.

————, ————, and T. P. Cafferty. "Organizational Context and Interdepartmental Conflict." *Administrative Science Quarterly*, Vol. 14 (December 1969), pp. 538–55.

————, and R. B. McKersie. *A Behavioral Theory of Labor Negotiations — An Analysis of a Social Interaction System*. McGraw-Hill, 1965.

————, and ————. "Behavioral Dilemmas in Mixed-Motive Decision Making." *Behavioral Science*, Vol. 11 (1966), pp. 370–84.

Webber, R. A. *Time and Management*. Van Nostrand Reinhold, 1972.

Yoshino, M. *Japan's Management System*. The MIT Press, 1968.

Yukl, G. A. "Effects of Situational Variables and Opponent Concessions on a Bargainer's Perception, Aspirations and Concessions." *Journal of Personality and Social Psychology*, Vol. 29, No. 2 (1974), pp. 227–36.

Zaleznik, A. "Power and Politics in Organizational Life." *Harvard Business Review*, May–June 1970, pp. 47–60.

————, and D. Moment. *The Dynamics of Interpersonal Behavior*. Wiley, 1964.

Zechmeister, K., and D. Druckman. "Determinants of Resolving a Conflict of Interest." *Journal of Conflict Resolution*, Vol. 17, No. 1 (1963), pp. 63–88.

Readings

An Analysis of Intergroup Conflict and Conflict Management

J. David Hunger

This selection reviews the literature on intergroup conflict and conflict management techniques. It is concluded that (1) frustration is a significant cause of conflict; (2) a group's goal attempts can be frustrating in various ways; (3) frustration, although a sufficient condition for conflict, is not a necessary condition—some conflict occurs even in the absence of frustration. Methods of conflict reduction are then categorized, including: (1) changing the parameters, (2) dividing available resources, (3) isolating the groups, (4) reducing ethnocentrism, and (5) reducing aggressive behavior.

INTRODUCTION

A considerable amount of research over the years has been concerned with group dynamics. Most of it, however, has involved intragroup processes. Nevertheless, the investigation of intergroup relations in the laboratory as well as in the field has greatly accelerated in recent years. Research efforts have dealt with stereotype formation (6) and ethnocentrism (40), international relations (17, 23), lateral relations within organizations (24, 45), race and ethnic prejudice (18, 46), game theory (30, 42), frustration and aggression (3, 13), labor negotiations, (44), and bargaining (35), in addition to work in social conflict (8, 25), conflict resolution or reduction (5, 10, 34), and recent attempts to find an optimum level of functional conflict via conflict management (31). Definitions of terms and approaches vary widely, but scholars in the area would probably agree that the end goal of the research is to find methods of keeping relations between groups from becoming harmful or dysfunctional to themselves and/or to their organization. Thus most research has been engaged in developing a theory of social conflict or in finding ways to reduce conflict.

Conflict may be defined as an opponent-centered episode or series of episodes based upon incompatibility of goals, aims, or values. It involves direct and personal interaction in which the opposing party is perceived as controlling the desired goal. This is basically an extension of Stern's (36) definition and generally agrees with the approach taken by Pondy (28) and Thomas (43) that conflict may be viewed as a process. Such a model of conflict identifies various events within a conflict episode and traces the effects of each event upon succeeding events. Thomas' process model depicts five main events within an episode from the viewpoint of one of the parties: frustration, conceptualization, behavior, other's reactions, outcome. The conflict episode is produced by the party's experiencing frustration, present or anticipated, to the realization

"An Analysis of Intergroup Conflict and Conflict Management" by J. David Hunger, from *Proceedings of the Eastern Academy of Management*, 13th Annual Meeting, 1976, edited by L. K. Bragaw and E. K. Winslow. Reprinted by permission of J. David Hunger and the Eastern Academy of Management.

of one of his goals. Frustration here is considered to be a blocking action. The party then conceptualizes the situation as being one of conflict. This is a cognitive state similar to that referred to by Pondy as "perceived conflict" in which the party is objectively aware of being in a conflict situation. The conceptualization event also appears to be composed of an effective state referred to by Pondy as "felt conflict" in which conflict is personalized by opponent-centered attitudes. Based largely upon his conceptualization of the situation, the party engages in behavior with the other party to cope with the situation. Behavior could be considered to include aggression toward the other party as well as other actions resulting from a displacement of hostility. The other party then reacts to this behavior creating a feedback effect upon the first party's conceptualization. When the interaction on a given issue ceases, some sort of outcome occurs. This outcome, depending upon the preceding behaviors, may take various forms such as joint agreement, domination by one party, joint avoidance of the issue, or unresolved disagreements. This outcome sets the stage for subsequent episodes.

This process model of social conflict by Thomas is in contrast to narrower definitions, such as by Schmidt and Kochan (32) which view conflict only as "overt behavior." This difference in viewpoint has important implications for research in intergroup conflict and social conflict in general. When conflict is defined only as "opponent-centered behavior," attention is directed only at aggression. If, however, conflict is defined more broadly to include "antecedent conditions" (28) as well as attitudes, it is more likely that conflict management mechanisms can be devised and tested. Conflict is thus seen to be a dynamic process arising from certain causes and resulting in certain effects. Seen in this more inclusive view, intergroup conflict can be better understood and more easily manipulated.

THE DYNAMICS OF INTERGROUP CONFLICT

Research in the area of intergroup conflict has been primarily concerned with conflict arising between two equally powerful groups. An analysis of research done in this area suggests the following conclusions:

1. *Frustration, that is, a blocking of a group's goal attempts, is a significant cause of conflict.* Experiments by Sherif and Sherif (34), Sussman and Weil (41), Blake and Mouton (4), Avigdor (1), Rabbie and Horwitz (29), Wilson and Kayatani (47), Stern, Sternthal, and Craig (37, 38, 39), and Hunger (20, 21) indicate that the frustration of a group's goal attempts by another group results in definite in-group/out-group biasing. Where behavioral measures were used, this frustration also led to verbal, and in some cases, to physical aggression. These findings support Thomas' process model of conflict.

2. *A group's goal attempts can be frustrated in various ways.*
a. Competition in a zero-sum sense (A zero-sum is defined as a game in which the outcomes of the players sum to zero, so that on any given play one player gains precisely the amount that has been lost by his opponent) causes a win-lose syndrome in which both groups realize that their goal attempts are being frustrated or at least threatened. Sherif and Sherif (34), Blake and Mouton (4), and Sussman and Weil (41), used competition between two groups to generate conflict. Two-party competition appears to be a very unstable phenomenon—dissolving often into opponent-centered

conflict. The difference between beating an opponent and winning a game is very tenuous in a two-party zero-sum situation.

b. Rewarding one group and not the other (a zero-sum reward system minus the competition) frustrates the nonrewarded group. This method of developing conflict is well-known to child psychologists and parents everywhere. The experiment by Rabbie and Horwitz (29), in which a toss of a coin dictated which group received portable radios, is an example. Sherif et al. (33), used the same tactic in the instance when only enough ice cream in good containers was available to feed the members of one group. The other group had to settle for ice cream in damaged containers. Avigdor (1), used this technique in the form of circus tickets given to one group and not to the other groups.

c. Making a non-zero-sum reward to two groups depend upon an agreement which, unknown to them, is very difficult to reach can frustrate the goal achievement of both groups. Stern, Sternthal, and Craig (37, 38, 39) and Hunger (20, 21) utilized this tactic in a bargaining situation in which two groups were led to perceive each other as frustrating their goal attempts.

3. *Frustration, although a sufficient condition for conflict, is not a necessary condition.* Manheim (26) showed that behavioral conflict can be induced merely by manipulating a group's perception of its social distance with another group. Although Manheim did not measure for bias effects, it could be suggested that telling a group that another group is very different from it in characteristics important to the task is a method of directly inducing an in-group/out-group bias which, in turn, leads to the behavioral indications of conflict measured by Manheim. Stern, Sternthal, and Craig (37, 38, 39) and Hunger (20, 21) also told high conflict groups that they were different. Their bias results, nevertheless, were confounded with the matrix and aspiration inductions. Manheim's results, however, suggest that it is possible to induce intergroup conflict without a frustration episode by directly manipulating a group's cognitions of the situation.

Other researchers, such as Druckman (15) and Deutsch (9) have found conflict can be manipulated via what Druckman calls the "instructional set." Through variations in the instructional set, Deutsch aroused different attributions of the other's intent, as well as attributions of values to the payoffs. The type of set, contained in the instructions, was shown to affect the players' motivation as well as their game behavior. Druckman (14) created prenegotiation conditions, in a simulation of collective bargaining, that were shown to arouse definitions of the situation as either a win-lose contest or a collaborative problem-solving session. These findings suggest that a group's cognitive definition of the same situation is a determinant of game behavior. This would explain Manheim's findings of behavioral conflict in the absence of frustration. Thus, the structure of the conflict situation must be considered as a major factor in any experiment dealing with intergroup conflict.

4. *Evaluating the in-group higher than an out-group may not, in itself, reflect conflict.* Bass and Dunteman (2) found that groups tend to evaluate themselves higher than other comparable groups even when the groups are merely participating in sensitivity training sessions. Merely being in the presence of *potentially rival* groups may be enough to develop an initial in-group/out-group bias favoring the in-group. Studies by Hunger (20, 21), Harvey (19), Doise (12), Rabbie and Horwitz (29), and Kahn

and Ryen (22) appear to support this possibility. This phenomenon may simply reflect a desire for a person to see himself and *his* group in the most favorable light. Thus a person may tend to notice mainly the good points of his group while he continues to see the bad as well as good points of an out-group. Size of the group may effect this phenomenon (16). A high evaluation of one's own group may also reflect a group's cohesiveness. If so, a positive relationship would be expected between cohesiveness and in-group evaluation. There is some evidence to suggest this relationship (11). Thus, evaluating the in-group higher than an out-group may not, in itself, indicate the presence of conflict.

Studies by Sherif and Sherif (34), Blake and Mouton (4), Hunger (20, 21), and Bass and Dunteman (2) among others, do indicate that the presence of conflict between two groups does act to increase the amount of in-group/out-group bias between them. Sherif and Sherif and Blake and Mouton found that intergroup conflict tends to be accompanied by an increase in the evaluation of one's own group and a decrease in the evaluation (derogation) of the out-group. Bass and Dunteman and Hunger did not find such an increase in in-group evaluation. These studies reported merely a slight drop in in-group evaluation as the contest got underway. The competitive out-group, however, dropped significantly in evaluation. This evidence suggests that just as conflict cannot be inferred merely by the existence of an in-group/out-group bias, it cannot be inferred merely by an increase in in-group evaluation. It appears that an increasing derogation of the out-group must be present for conflict to be present.

The studies mentioned above appear to fit into Thomas' process model of conflict. Intergroup competition has been used by Sherif and Sherif and by Blake and Mouton, among others, to generate a mutually frustrating situation. A group's goal attempts have also been secretly frustrated by the researchers themselves (1, 20, 21, 37, 38, 39). Such frustrations have normally led to a win-lose conceptualization of the situation. It is at this point that the groups develop opponent-centered attitudes which derogate the out-group (opponent) and often glorify the in-group. If circumstances are right (as they were in the Sherif et al. studies), these attitudes lead to aggressive behavior. This behavior acts to instigate reactions from the other group, thus reinforcing an opponent-centered orientation and generating a "self-fulfilling prophecy" (27) effect.

THE MANAGEMENT OF INTERGROUP CONFLICT

Since it is now recognized that conflict can be functional as well as dysfunctional (8), research emphasis has shifted from resolution to management. Conflict management in the literature still seems to be concerned mainly with reducing conflict to a functional level. The inverse, that is developing conflict where none exists, has just begun to be investigated (31) and could be a future research area of some significance.

Methods of conflict reduction may be categorized on the basis of *how* they work. In any conflict of interest situation based upon an incompatibility of goals, aims, or values, there appear to be five basic approaches to the resolution of intergroup conflict.

1. *Change the parameters* of the conflict, such as increasing the supply of a product which is in great demand, so that both groups will be able to achieve their goals. This method aims to resolve the conflict by getting at the underlying source of the problem. Unfortunately, this approach is not always practical in a world of limited resources.

2. *Divide available resources* so that each group is able to partially attain its goal. This is the classic solution of the economist. It includes the techniques of bargaining, mediation, and arbitration which are in great use in today's world.

3. *Isolate the groups* via structural or legal devices so that each group is more independent of the other, and thus less likely to have its goals frustrated by the other. The groups can be isolated structurally in two ways.

a. A buffer can be placed between the conflicting groups. The buffer then has the responsibility of making sure each group attains its goal. If a group does not, the buffer is blamed. Thus hostility is successfully displaced from the out-group to the buffer.

b. The environment of the conflicting groups is modified so that each group is able to achieve its goal independently of the other. Examples of this technique are decentralization and local options.

4. *Reduce ethnocentrism* (in-group/out-group bias) between the groups so that each can perceive each other objectively. The implicit assumption of this approach is that the group will then be able to better resolve the underlying conflict of interest problem. Empirical evidence has shown that in-group/out-group bias can be reduced via superordinate goals and conciliation techniques, such as Blake and Mouton's intergroup "therapy." Research by Stern, Sternthal, and Craig (37) has produced some evidence that an exchange of persons also acts to resolve intergroup conflict by reducing in-group/out-group bias.

5. *Reduce aggressive behavior* between the groups so that actions of each group will no longer serve to "fan the flame." This approach aims to stop the effect epitomised by the terms "self-fulfilling prophecy" (27) and "Gresham's Law of Conflict" (7). Examples of this approach are cooling-off periods, withdrawal, smoothing attempts, and, of course, surrender. There is little empirical evidence that any of these aggression-reducing methods work to reduce serious intergroup conflict, at least where conflict of interest is concerned. These methods, however, are probably very helpful in reducing aggressive behavior erupting from "nonrealistic" conflict (8) sources such as insanity, drunkenness, or displaced anger (for example, husband yells at wife after boss yells at husband).

Thomas' model suggests that conflict is a process which feeds itself. Thus the model implies that the way to reduce or manage conflict is to break the circle at some point. One could aim at the source of the episode by reducing the cause of the frustration. This would involve any of the first three approaches: changing the parameters, dividing available resources, or isolating the groups (by modifying the environment). One could also aim at the conceptualization aspect of the episode, via the fourth approach, by reducing the in-group/out-group bias between groups. One could also attempt to reduce aggressive behavior by methods mentioned under the fifth approach. To the extent that buffers would serve a displacement of hostility function, isolating the groups may serve to reduce aggressive behavior. (The groups may not act as aggressively toward a buffer as they would toward each other.)

Given (1) that an intergroup conflict situation erupts out of frustration caused by a conflict of interest, (2) that these frustrations cause ethnocentric attitudes (in-group/out-group bias favoring the in-group), (3) that these attitudes set the cognitive stage for some sort of conflict behavior on both sides, (4) that this behavior generates a feedback effect, and (5) that this feedback tends to reinforce ethnocentric attitudes in both groups, the following key questions arise:

1. *Will reducing the frustrations, by itself, reduce intergroup conflict?* If the conflict has been going on for a long time, it has probably developed aspects of a nonrealistic conflict complete with ethnocentrism and aggression. These could probably keep "fanning the flame" even after the original conflict of interest has been resolved. Generally speaking, however, one probably can assume that reducing a conflict-causing frustration will eventually reduce conceptual and behavioral aspects of conflict.

2. *Will reducing ethnocentrism, by itself, reduce intergroup conflict?* If in-group/out-group biasing results from the frustration of goal attempts, the continued presence of the same frustration should serve to rekindle the conflict. Sherif and Sherif (34) and Blake, Shepard, and Mouton (5) suggest this in their comments concerning the temporary value of the "common enemy" approach. Would not the same criticism pertain to superordinate goals and conciliation attempts if the conflict of interest problem could not be resolved? The Sherifs' many experiments did not resolve this question because they removed the frustration aspects of the situation (competitive episodes and experimenter-induced frustrations) at the same time as they began inserting superordinate goals. A study by Hunger (20, 21) attempted to resolve this question by comparing groups which received an achievable superordinate goal with groups which did not. The frustrating antecedent condition (conflict of interest) was kept constant. Results indicated that the superordinate goal in this situation acted to *retard* the development of felt conflict, rather than to reduce it.

3. *Will reducing aggressive behavior, by itself, reduce intergroup conflict?* A consensus of theory and research findings indicate that reducing aggression will not, by itself, reduce realistic conflict. It is possible, however, that any conflict situation contains a certain amount of nonrealistic conflict generated by the feedback effect. This could be reduced by stopping aggressive behavior.

CONCLUSION

On the basis of this survey of the literature, the process model of conflict appears to be most helpful in explaining the development and management of intergroup conflict. It has been shown that just as conflict can be induced experimentally, it can also be reduced experimentally. The process model suggests various approaches for the management of intergroup conflict. Stern, Sternthal, and Craig (37) are presently engaged in comparing the effectiveness of various conflict reduction techniques. Others such as Robbins (31), are concerned with various techniques to induce conflict. It is suggested that a contingency approach be taken regarding intergroup conflict. A level of conflict which is clearly dysfunctional for one set of groups may be functional for others. A conflict reduction technique may be feasible and effective in one situation, but not in another. Much research is needed before a normative theory of conflict management can be fully developed. The conflict process needs to be more fully defined and quantified to allow the development of better measurement techniques. Research is needed to better pinpoint when conflict is considered dysfunctional. As Robbins suggests, intergroup conflict may be dysfunctional for the people involved but functional for the organization as a whole. For those many situations where conflict is judged dysfunctional, it is important not only to compare the effectiveness of conflict reduction techniques, but also to search for key variables in conflict situations which may determine the appropriateness of these techniques.

REFERENCES

1. Avigdor, R. "The Development of Stereotypes as a Result of Group Interaction." Unpublished Ph.D. dissertation, New York University, 1952. Summarized in

Groups in Harmony and Tension by Muzafer and Carolyn Sherif (New York: Harper, 1953).

2. Bass, B. M., and Dunteman, G. "Biases In the Evaluation of One's Own Group, Its Allies and Opponents." *Journal of Conflict Resolution,* 7 (1963), pp. 16–20.

3. Berkowitz, L., ed. *Roots of Aggression.* (New York: Atherton Press, 1969).

4. Blake, R. R., and Mouton, J. "Reactions to Intergroup Competition Under Win-Lose Conditions." *Management Science,* 7 (1961), pp. 420–435.

5. Blake, R. R.: Shepard, H. A.; and Mouton, J. S. *Managing Intergroup Conflict In Industry.* (Houston: Texas: Gulf Publishing Co., 1964).

6. Campbell, D. T. "Stereotypes and the Perception of Group Differences." *American Psychologist,* 22 (1967), pp. 817–829.

7. Coleman, J. S. *Community Conflict.* (New York: The Free Press, 1957).

8. Coser, L. *The Functions of Social Conflict.* (New York: The Free Press, 1956).

9. Deutsch, M. "The Effect of Motivational Orientation Upon Trust and Suspicion." *Human Relations,* 13 (1960), pp. 123–140.

10. Deutsch, M. *The Resolution of Conflict.* (New Haven: Yale University Press, 1973).

11. Dion, K. "Cohesiveness as a Determinant of Ingroup Outgroup Bias." *Journal of Personality and Social Psychology,* 28 (1973), pp. 163–171.

12. Doise, W. "Intergroup Relations and Polarization of Individual and Collective Judgments." *Journal of Personality and Social Psychology,* 12, (1969), pp. 136–143.

13. Dollard, J., Doob, N., Miller, N., Mowrer, O., and Sears, R. *Frustration and Aggression.* (New Haven: Yale University Press, 1939).

14. Druckman, D. "Prenegotiation Experience and Dyadic Conflict Resolution in a Bargaining Situation." *Journal of Experimental Social Psychology,* 4 (1968), pp. 367–383.

15. Druckman, D. "The Influence of the Situation in Inter-Party Conflict." *Journal of Conflict Resolution,* 15 (1971), pp. 523–554.

16. Gerard, H. B. and Hoyt, M. F. "Distinctiveness of Social Categorization and Attitudes Toward Ingroup Members." *Journal of Personality and Social Psychology,* 29 (1974), pp. 836–842.

17. Guetzkow, H., ed. *Simulation in Social Science: Readings* (Englewood Cliffs: Prentice-Hall, 1962).

18. Harding, J.; Proshansky, H.; Kutner, B.; and Chein, I. "Prejudice and Ethnic Relations," in *The Handbook of Social Psychology,* Vol. V. Edited by Gardner Lindzey and Elliot Aronson (Reading, Massachusetts: Addison-Wesley, 1969).

19. Harvey, O. J. "An Experimental Investigation of Negative and Positive Relations Between Small Groups through Judgmental Indices." *Sociometry,* 19 (1956), pp. 201–209.

20. Hunger, J. D. *An Empirical Test of the Superordinate Goal as a Means of Reducing Intergroup Conflict in a Bargaining Situation.* Unpublished Ph.D. dissertation. (The Ohio State University, 1973).

21. Hunger, J. D. and Stern, L. W. "An Assessment of the Functionality of Super-ordinate Goal in Reducing Conflict." *Academy of Management Journal,* 19 (December 1976), pp. 591–605.

22. Kahn, A. and Ryen, A. H. "Factors Influencing the Bias Towards One's Own Group." *International Journal of Group Tensions,* 2 (1972), pp. 33–50.

23. Kelman, H. C. *International Behavior: A Social Psychological Analysis* (New York: Holt, Rinehart, and Winston, 1965).

24. Landsberger, H. A. "The Horizontal Dimension in Bureaucracy." *Administrative Science Quarterly,* 6 (1961), pp. 299–332.

25. Mack, R. W., and Snyder, R. C. "The Analysis of Social Conflict—Toward an Overview and Synthesis." *Journal of Conflict Resolution*, 1 (1957), pp. 212–248.

26. Manheim, H. L. "Intergroup Interaction as Related to Status and Leadership Differences Between Groups." *Sociometry*, 23 (1960), pp. 415–427.

27. Merton, R. K. *Social Theory and Social Structure* (Glencoe, Ill.: Free Press, 1957).

28. Pondy, L. R. "Organizational Conflict: Concepts and Models." *Administrative Science Quarterly*, 12 (1967), pp. 296–320.

29. Rabbie, J. M. and Horwitz, M. "Arousal of Ingroup-Outgroup Bias by a Chance Win or Loss." *Journal of Personality and Social Psychology*, 13 (1969), pp. 269–277.

30. Rapoport, A. *Fights, Games and Debates* (Ann Arbor, Michigan: University of Michigan Press, 1960).

31. Robbins, S. P. *Managing Organizational Conflict* (Englewood Cliffs: Prentice Hall, 1974).

32. Schmidt, S. M. and Kochan, T. A. "Conflict: Toward Conceptual Clarity." *Administrative Science Quarterly*, 17 (1972), pp. 359–369.

33. Sherif, M.; Harvey, O. J.; White, B. J.; Hood, W. R.; and Sherif, C. W. *Intergroup Conflict and Cooperation: The Robbers' Cave Experiment* (Norman, Oklahoma: The University Book Exchange, 1961).

34. Sherif, M., and Sherif, C. W., *Social Psychology* (New York: Harper and Row, 1969).

35. Siegel, S., and Fouraker, L. E. *Bargaining and Group Decision Making.* (New York: McGraw-Hill, 1960).

36. Stern, L. W. "Potential Conflict Management Mechanisms in Distribution Channels: An Interorganizational Analysis." *Contractual Marketing Systems.* Ed. by Donald N. Thompson (Boston: Heath-Lexington Books, 1971).

37. Stern, L. W.; Sternthal, B.; and Craig, C. S. "Managing Conflict in Distribution Channels: A Laboratory Study." *Journal of Marketing Research*, 10, (1973), pp. 169–179.

38. Stern, L. W.; Sternthal, B.; and Craig, C. S., "A Parasimulation of Interorganizational Conflict," *International Journal of Group Tensions*, 3 (1973), pp. 68–90.

39. Stern, L. W., Sternthal, B., and Craig, C. S., "Strategies for Managing Interorganizational Conflict: A Laboratory Paradigm." *Journal of Applied Psychology*, 60 (1975), pp. 472–482.

40. Sumner, W. G. *Folkways* (Boston: Ginn, 1906).

41. Sussman, M. B., and Weil, W. B. "An Experimental Study on the Effects of Group Interaction Upon the Behavior of Diabetic Children." *International Journal of Social Psychiatry*, 6 (1960), pp. 120–125.

42. Swingle, P., Ed. *The Structure of Conflict* (New York: Academic Press, 1970).

43. Thomas, K. W. "Conflict and Conflict Management." *Handbook of Industrial and Organizational Psychology.* Edited by Marvin D. Dunnette (Chicago: Rand McNally, 1976).

44. Walton, R. E., and McKersie, R. B. *A Behavioral Theory of Labor Negotiations* (New York: McGraw-Hill, 1965).

45. Walton, R. E., and Dutton, J. M. "The Management of Interdepartmental Conflict: A Model and Review." *Administrative Science Quarterly*, 14 (1969), pp. 73–84.

46. Williams, R. M. *The Reduction of Intergroup Tensions* (New York: Social Science Research Council, 1947).

47. Wilson, W., and Kayatani, M. "Intergroup Attitudes and Strategies in Games Between Opponents of the Same or of a Different Race." *Journal of Personality and Social Psychology*, 9 (1968), pp. 24–30.

Power and Politics in Organizational Life

Abraham Zaleznik

Most literature on management exaggerates the element of rationality and minimizes the emotional content in organizational life. This selection examines why this is so and what personality phenomena contribute to conflict in organizations. The author's contention is not that conflict reflects management failure, but that it does reflect human nature. Therefore, effective managers must recognize the inevitability of conflict and be wise in developing coalitions and problem-solving approaches that curtail the adverse impact of conflict.

There are few business activities more prone to a credibility gap than the way in which executives approach organizational life. A sense of disbelief occurs when managers purport to make decisions in rationalistic terms while most observers and participants know that personalities and politics play a significant if not an overriding role. Where does the error lie? In the theory which insists that decisions should be rationalistic and nonpersonal? Or in the practice which treats business organizations as political structures?

Whatever else organizations may be (problem-solving instruments, sociotechnical systems, reward systems, and so on), they are political structures. This means that organizations operate by distributing authority and setting a stage for the exercise of power. It is no wonder, therefore, that individuals who are highly motivated to secure and use power find a familiar and hospitable environment in business.

At the same time, executives are reluctant to acknowledge the place of power both in individual motivation and in organizational relationships. Somehow, power and politics are dirty words. And in linking these words to the play of personalities in organizations, some managers withdraw into the safety of organizational logics.

As I shall suggest in this article, frank recognition of the importance of personality factors and a sensitive use of the strengths and limitations of people in decisions on power distributions can improve the quality of organizational life.

POLITICAL PYRAMID

Organizations provide a power base for individuals. From a purely economic standpoint, organizations exist to create a surplus of income over costs by meeting needs in the marketplace. But organizations also are political structures which provide opportunities for people to develop careers and therefore provide platforms for the expression of individual interests and motives. The development of careers, particularly at high managerial and professional levels, depends on accumulation of power as the vehicle for transforming individual interests into activities which influence other people.

Scarcity and Competition

A political pyramid exists when people compete for power in an economy of scarcity. In other words, people cannot get the power they want just for the asking. Instead, they have to enter into the decisions on how to distribute authority in a particular formal organization structure. Scarcity of power arises under two sets of conditions:

1. Where individuals gain power in absolute terms at someone else's expense.
2. Where there is a gain comparatively—not literally at someone else's expense—resulting in a relative shift in the distribution of power.

In either case, the psychology of scarcity and comparison takes over. The human being tends to make comparisons as a basis for his sense of self-esteem. He may compare himself with other people and decide that his absolute loss or the shift in proportional shares of authority reflects an attrition in his power base. He may also compare his position relative to others against a personal standard and feel a sense of loss. This tendency to compare is deeply ingrained in people, especially since they experience early in life the effects of comparisons in the family where—in an absolute sense—time and attention, if not love and affection, go to the most dependent member.

Corporate acquisitions and mergers illustrate the effects of both types of comparisons. In the case of one merger, the president of the acquired company resigned rather than accept the relative displacement in rank which occurred when he no longer could act as a chief executive officer. Two vice presidents vied for the position of executive vice president. Because of their conflicting ambitions, the expedient of making them equals drove the competition underground, but not for long. The vice president with the weaker power base soon resigned in the face of his inability to consolidate a workable definition of his responsibilities. His departure resulted in increased power for the remaining vice president and the gradual elimination of "rival camps" which had been covertly identified with the main contenders for power.

The fact that organizations are pyramids produces a scarcity of positions the higher one moves in the hierarchy. This scarcity, coupled with inequalities, certainly needs to be recognized. While it may be humane and socially desirable to say that people are different rather than unequal in their potential, nevertheless executive talent is in short supply. The end result should be to move the more able people into the top positions and to accord them the pay, responsibility, and authority to match their potential.

On the other side, the strong desires of equally able people for the few top positions available means that someone will either have to face the realization of unfulfilled ambition or have to shift his interest to another organization.[1]

Constituents and Clients

Besides the conditions of scarcity and competition, politics in organizations grows out of the existence of constituencies. A superior may be content himself with shifts in the allocation of resources and consequently power, but he represents subordinates who, for their own reasons, may be unhappy with the changes. These subordinates affirm and support their boss. They can also withdraw affirmation and support, and consequently isolate the superior with all the painful consequences this entails.

While appointments to positions come from above, affirmation of position comes from below. The only difference between party and organizational politics is in the subtlety of the voting procedure. Consider:

In a large consumer products corporation, one division received almost no capital funds for expansion while another division, which had developed a new marketing approach for products common to both, expanded dramatically. The head of the static division found his power diminished considerably, as reflected in how seriously his subordinates took his efforts at influence (e.g., in programs to increase the profit return from existing volume).

He initiated one program after another with little support from subordinates because he could not make a claim for capital funds. The flow of capital funds in this corporation provided a measure of power gains and losses in both an absolute and a relative sense.

Power and Action

Still another factor which heightens the competition for power that is characteristic of all political structures is the incessant need to use whatever power one possesses. Corporations have an implicit "banking" system in power transactions. The initial "capitalization" which makes up an individual's power base consists of three elements:

1. The quantity of formal authority vested in his position relative to other positions.
2. The authority vested in his expertise and reputation for competence (a factor weighted by how important the expertise is for the growth areas of the corporation as against the historically stable areas of its business).
3. The attractiveness of his personality to others (a combination of respect for him as well as liking, although these two sources of attraction are often in conflict).

This capitalization of power reflects the total esteem with which others regard the individual. By a process which is still not too clear, the individual internalizes all of the sources of power capital in a manner parallel to the way he develops a sense of self-esteem. The individual knows he has power, assesses it realistically, and is willing to risk his personal esteem to influence others.

A critical element here is the risk in the uses of power. The individual must perform *and* get results. If he fails to do either, an attrition occurs in his power base in direct proportion to the doubts other people entertained in their earlier appraisals of him.

What occurs here is an erosion of confidence which ultimately leads the individual to doubt himself and undermines the psychological work which led him in the first place to internalize authority as a prelude to action. (While, as I have suggested, the psychological work that an individual goes through to consolidate his esteem capital is a crucial aspect of power relations, I shall have to reserve careful examination of this problem until a later date. The objective now is to examine from a political framework the problems of organizational life.)

What distinguishes alterations in the authority structure from other types of organizational change is their direct confrontation with the political character of corporate life. Such confrontations are real manipulations of power as compared with the indirect approaches which play on ideologies and attitudes. In the first case, the potency and reality of shifts in authority have an instantaneous effect on what people do, how they interact, and how they think about themselves. In the second case, the shifts in attitude are often based on the willingness of people to respond the way authority figures want them to; ordinarily, however, these shifts in attitude are but temporary expressions of compliance.

One of the most common errors executives make is to confuse compliance with commitment. Compliance is an attitude of acceptance when a directive from an authority figure asks for a change in an individual's position, activities, or ideas. The individual complies or "goes along" usually because he is indifferent to the scope of the directive and the changes it proposes. If compliance occurs out of indifference, then one can predict little difficulty in translating the intent of directives into actual implementation.[2]

Commitment, on the other hand, represents a strong motivation on the part of an individual to adopt or resist the intent of a directive. If the individual commits himself to a change, then he will use his ingenuity to interpret and implement the change in such a way as to assure its success. If he decides to fight or block the change, the individual may act as if he complies but reserve other times and places to negate the effects of directives. For example:

In one large company, the top management met regularly for purposes of organizational planning. The executives responsible for implementing planning decisions could usually be counted on to carry them out when they had fought hard and openly in the course of reaching such decisions. When they seemed to accept a decision, giving all signs of compliance, the decision usually ended up as a notation in the minutes. Surface compliance occurred most frequently when problems involved loyalties to subordinates.

In one instance, a division head agreed to accept a highly regarded executive from another division to meet a serious manpower shortage in his organization. When the time came to effect the transfer, however, this division general manager refused, with some justification, on the grounds that bringing someone in from outside would demoralize his staff. He used compliance initially to respond to the problem of "family" loyalties to which he felt committed. Needless to say, the existence of these loyalties was the major problem to be faced in carrying out organizational planning.

Compliance as a tactic to avoid changes and commitment as an expression of strong motivation in dealing with organizational problems are in turn related to how individuals define their interests. In the power relations among executives, the so-called areas of common interest are usually reserved for the banalities of human relationships. The more significant areas of attention usually force conflicts of interest, especially competition for power, to the surface.

INTEREST CONFLICTS

Organizations demand, on the one hand, cooperative endeavor and commitment to common purposes. The realities of experience in organizations, on the other hand, show that conflicts of interest exist among people who ultimately share a common fate and are supposed to work together. What makes business more political and less ideological and rationalistic is the overriding importance of conflicts of interest.

If an individual (or group) is told that his job scope is reduced in either absolute or proportional terms for *the good of the corporation,* he faces a conflict. Should he acquiesce for the idea of common good or fight in the service of his self-interest? Any rational man will fight (how constructively depends on the absence of neurotic conflicts and on ego strength). His willingness to fight increases as he comes to realize the intangible nature of what people think is good for the organization. And, in point of fact, his willingness may serve the interests of corporate purpose by highlighting issues and stimulating careful thinking before the reaching of final decisions.

SECONDARY EFFECTS

Conflicts of interest in the competition for resources are easily recognized, as for example, in capital budgeting or in allocating money for research and development. But these conflicts can be subjected to bargaining procedures which all parties to the competition validate by their participation.

The secondary effects of bargaining do involve organizational and power issues. However, the fact that these power issues *follow* debate on economic problems rather than *lead* it creates a manifest content which can be objectified much more readily than in areas where the primary considerations are the distributions of authority.

In such cases, which include developing a new formal organization structure, management succession, promotions, corporate mergers, and entry of new executives, the conflicts of interest are severe and direct simply because there are no objective measures of right or wrong courses of action. The critical question which has to be answered in specific actions is: Who gets power and position? This involves particular people with their strengths and weaknesses and a specific historical context in which actions are understood in symbolic as well as rational terms. To illustrate:

A large corporation, General Motors in fact, inadvertently confirmed what every seasoned executive knows: that coalitions of power to overcome feelings of rivalry and the play of personal ambitions are fragile solutions. The appointment of Edward Cole to the presidency followed by Semon Knudsen's resignation shattered the illusion that the rational processes in business stand apart or even dominate the human emotions and ties that bind men to one another. If any corporation prides itself on rationality, General Motors is it. To have to experience so publicly the inference that major corporate life, particularly at the executive levels, is not so rational after all, can be damaging to the sense of security people get from belief in an idea as it is embodied in a corporate image.

The fact that Knudsen subsequently was discharged from the presidency of Ford (an event I shall discuss later in this article) suggests that personalities and the politics of corporations are less aberrations and more conditions of life in large organizations.

But just as General Motors wants to maintain an image, many executives prefer to ignore what this illustration suggests: that organizations are political structures which feed on the psychology of comparison. To know something about the psychology of comparison takes us into the theory of self-esteem in both its conscious manifestations and its unconscious origins. Besides possibly enlightening us in general and giving a more realistic picture of people and organizations, there are some practical benefits in such knowledge. These benefits include:

Increased freedom to act more directly; instead of trying to "get around" a problem, one can meet it.

Greater objectivity about people's strengths and limitations, and, therefore, the ability to use them more honestly as well as effectively.

More effective planning in organizational design and in distribution of authority;

instead of searching for the "one best solution" in organization structure, one accepts a range of alternatives and then gives priority to the personal or emotional concerns that inhibit action.

POWER RELATIONS

Organizational life within a political frame is a series of contradictions. It is an exercise in rationality, but its energy comes from the ideas in the minds of power figures the content of which, as well as their origins, are only dimly perceived. It deals with sources of authority and their distribution; yet it depends in the first place on the existence of a balance of power in the hands of an individual who initiates actions and gets results. It has many rituals associated with it, such as participation, democratization, and the sharing of power; yet the real outcome is the consolidation of power around a central figure to whom other individuals make emotional attachments.

Faulty Coalitions

The formal organization structure implements a coalition among key executives. The forms differ, and the psychological significance of various coalitions also differs. But no organization can function without a consolidation of power in the relationship of a central figure with his select group. The coalition need not exist between the chief executive and his immediate subordinates or staff. It may indeed bypass the second level as in the case of Presidents of the United States who do not build confident relationships within their cabinets, but instead rely on members of the executive staff or on selected individuals outside the formal apparatus.

The failure to establish a coalition within the executive structure of an organization can result in severe problems, such as paralysis in the form of inability to make decisions and to evaluate performance, and in-fighting and overt rivalry within the executive group.

When a coalition fails to develop, the first place to look for causes is the chief executive and his problems in creating confident relationships. The causes are many and complex, but they usually hinge around the nature of the chief executive's defenses and what he needs to avoid as a means of alleviating stress. For example:

The "palace revolt," which led to Semon Knudsen's departure from Ford Motor Company, is an illustration of the failure in the formation of a coalition. While it is true that Henry Ford II named Knudsen president of the company, Knudsen's ultimate power as a newcomer to an established power structure depended on forming an alliance. The particular individual with whom an alliance seemed crucial was Lee Iacocca. For some reason, Knudsen and Iacocca competed for power and influence instead of using cooperatively a power base to which both contributed as is the case with most workable coalitions. In the absence of a coalition, the alternate postures of rivalry and battle for control erupted. Ford ultimately responded by weighing his power with one side over the other.

As I have indicated, it is not at all clear why in Knudsen's case the coalition failed to develop. But in any failure the place to look is in the personalities of the main actors and in the nature of their defenses which make certain coalitions improbable no matter how strongly other realities indicate their necessity.

But defensiveness on the part of a chief executive can also result in building an unrealistic and unworkable coalition, with the self-enforced isolation which is its consequence. One of the most frequently encountered defensive maneuvers which leads to the formation of unrealistic coalitions or to the isolation of the chief executive is the fear of rivalry.

A realistic coalition matches formal authority and competence with the emotional commitments necessary to establish and maintain the coalition. The fear of rivals on the part of chief executives, or the jealousy on the part of subordinates of the chief executive's power, can at the extreme result in paranoid distortions. People become suspicious of one another, and through selective perceptions and projections of their own fantasies create a world of plots and counterplots.

The displacement of personal concerns onto substantive material in decision making is potentially the most dangerous form of defensiveness. The need for defenses arises because people become anxious about the significance of evaluations within existing power coalitions. But perhaps even more basic is the fear and the rivalry to which all coalitions are susceptible given the nature of investments people make in power relations. While it is easy to dismiss emotional reactions like these as neurotic distortions, their prevalence and impact deserve careful attention in all phases of organizational life.

Unconscious Collusions

All individuals and consequently groups experience areas of stress which mobilize defenses. The fact that coalitions embody defensive maneuvers on those occasions where stress goes beyond the usual level of tolerance is not surprising. An even more serious problem, however, occurs when the main force that binds men in a structure is the need to defend against or to act out the conflicts which individuals cannot tolerate alone.

Where coalitions represent the aggregation of power with conscious intention of using the abilities of members for constructive purposes, collusions represent predominance of unconscious conflict and defensive behavior. In organizational life, the presence of collusions and their causes often becomes the knot which has to be unraveled before any changes can be implemented.

The collusion of latent interests among executives can become the central theme and sustaining force of an organization structure of top management. For a collusion to take hold, the conflicts of the "power figure" have to be communicated and sensed by others as an overriding need which seeks active expression in the form of a theme. The themes vary just as do the structures which make a collusion. Thus one common theme is the need to control; another is the need to be admired and idealized; and still another is the need to find a scapegoat to attack in response to frustrations in solving problems.

If people could hold on to and keep within themselves areas of personal conflict, there would be far fewer collusions in organizational life. But it is part of the human condition for conflicts and needs to take over life situations. As a result, we find numerous instances of collusions controlling the behavior of executives. To illustrate:

A multidivisional corporation found itself with a revolution on its hands. The president was sensitive to the opinions of a few outside board members representing important stockholder interests. He was so concerned that he would be criticized by these board members, he demanded from vice presidents full information on their activities and complete loyalty to him. Over a period of years, he moved divisional chief executives to corporate headquarters so he could assure himself of their loyalty. Other executives joined in to gratify the president's need for control and loyalty.

The result of this collusion, however, was to create a schism between headquarters and field operations. Some of the staff members in the field managed to inform the board members of the lack of attention to and understanding of field problems. Discontent grew to such an extent that the board placed the president on early retirement.

Subsequently, the new president, with the support of the board, decentralized authority and appointed new division heads who were to make their offices in divisional headquarters with full authority to manage their respective organizations. One of the lingering problems of the new president was to dissolve the collusion at headquarters without wholesale firing of vice presidents.

Just as power distributions are central to the tasks of organizational planning, so the conservation of power is often the underlying function of collusions. Thus:

A manufacturing vice president of a medium-sized company witnessed over a period of 15 years a procession of changes in top management and ownership. He had managed to retain his job because he made himself indispensable in the management of the factory.

To each new top management, he stressed the importance of "home rule" as a means of assuring loyalty and performance in the plant. He also tacitly encouraged each supervisor to go along with whatever cliques happened to form and dominate the shop floor.

However, over time a gradual loss of competitive position, coupled with open conflict among cliques in the form of union disputes, led to the dismissal of the vice president. None of his successors could reassert control over the shop, and the company eventually moved or liquidated many of the operations in this plant.

'LIFE DRAMAS'

Faulty coalitions and unconscious collusions, as I have illustrated, can result from the defensive needs of a chief executive. These needs, which often appear as a demand on others to bolster the self-esteem of the chief executive, are tolerated to a remarkable degree and persist for a long time before harmful effects become apparent to outside stockholders, bankers, or boards of directors which ultimately control the distributions of power in organizations. Occasionally, corporations undergo critical conflicts in organizational politics which cannot be ignored in the conscious deliberations which affect how power gets distributed or used.

Intertwined with the various expressions of power conflicts in organizations are three underlying "life dramas" deserving careful attention:

The *first* portrays stripping the powers of a *parental figure*.

The *second* portrays the predominance of *paranoid thinking*, where distortions of reality result from the surfacing of conflicts which formerly had been contained in collusions.

The *third* portrays a *ritualistic ceremonial* in which real power issues are submerged or isolated in compulsive behavior but at the cost of real problem solving and work.

Parental Figure

The chief executive in a business, along with the heads of states, religious bodies, and social movements, becomes an object for other people. The term "object" should be understood, in a psychological sense, as a person who is the recipient of strong emotional attachments from others. It is obvious that a chief executive is the *object* because he controls so many of the levers which ultimately direct the flow of rewards and punishments. But there is something to say beyond this obvious calculation of rewards and punishments as the basis for the emotional attachments between leader and led as *object* and *subject*.

Where a leader displays unusual attributes in his intuitive gifts, cultivated abilities, or deeper personal qualities, his fate as the *object* is governed by powerful emotions. I hesitate to use the word "charismatic" to describe such a leader, partially because it suggests a mystique but also because, in its reference to the "great" man as charismatic leader, it expands to superhuman proportions what really belongs to the psychology of everyday life.

What makes for strong emotional attachments is as much in the need of the *subject* as in the qualities of the *object*. In other words, the personalities of leaders take on proportions which meet what subordinates need and even demand. If leaders in fact respond with the special charisma that is often invested in them at the outset, then they are parties to a self-fulfilling prophecy. Of course, the qualities demanded have to be present in some nascent form ready to emerge as soon as the emotional currents become real in authority relationships.

The emotional attachments I am referring to usually contain mixtures of positive and negative feelings. If the current were only of one kind, such as either admiration or hostility, then the authority relationship would be simpler to describe as well as to manage. All too often, the way positive feelings blend into the negative sets off secondary currents of emotion which intensify the relationships.

On the one side, subordinates cannot help but have fantasies of what they would do if they held the No. 1 position. Such fantasies, besides providing fleeting pleasures and helping one to regulate his ambitions, also provide channels for imaginative and constructive approaches to solving problems. It is only a short step from imagining what one would do as chief executive to explaining to the real chief executive the ideas which have been distilled from this flight into fantasy. If the chief executive senses envy in back of the thoughts, he may become frightened and choke off ideas which can be used quite constructively.

Critical Episode

But suppose a situation arises where not one but several subordinates enjoy the same fantasy of being No. 1? Suppose also that subordinates feel deprived in their relationship with the chief executive? Suppose finally that facing the organization there are substantive problems which are more or less out of control. With these three conditions, and depending on the severity of the real problems besetting the enterprise, the stage is set for a collusion which, when acted out, becomes a critical episode of displacing the parental figure. To demonstrate:

In November 1967, the directors of the Interpublic Group, a $700 million complex in advertising and public relations, moved for the resignation of the leader and chief executive officer, Marion Harper, Jr. Briefly, Harper had managed over a period of 18 years to build the world's largest conglomerate in market services, advertising, and information on the base of a personally successful agency career. In expanding from this base, Harper made acquisitions, started new companies, and widened his orbit into international branches and companies.

As often happens, the innovator and creative person is careless in controlling what he has built so that financial problems become evident. In Harper's case, he appeared either unwilling or unable to recognize the seriousness of his financial problems and, in particular, the significance of allowing cash balances to go below the minimum required in agreements with lending institutions.

Harper seemed careless in another, even more telling, way. Instead of developing a strong coalition among his executive group, he relied on individual ties to him in which he clearly dominated the relationship. If any of the executives "crossed" him, Harper would exile the offender to one of the "remote" branches or place him on partial retirement.

When the financial problems became critical, the aggrieved executives who had once been dependent on Harper and then cast out, formed their own coalition, and managed to garner the votes necessary to, in effect, fire the head man. Although little information is available on the aftermath of this palace revolution, the new coalition had its own problems—which, one would reasonably judge, included contentions for power.

A cynic viewing this illustration of the demise of a parental figure could conclude that if one seeks to maintain power by dominance, then one had best go all the way. This means that to take some but not all of the power away from rebellious sons sets the stage for a cabal among the deprived. With a score to settle, they await only the right circumstances to move in and depose the aggressor.

While this cynical view has its own appeal, it ignores the deeper issues of why otherwise brilliant men fail to recognize the realistic needs for coalitions in the relationships of superior and subordinates. To answer this question, we would need to understand how powerful people operate with massive blind spots which limit vision and the ability to maneuver in the face of realistic problems.

The one purpose that coalitions serve is to guard against the effects of blind spots, since it is seldom the case that two people have identical limitations in their vision and ability to respond. The need to control and dominate in a personalistic sense is perhaps the most serious of all possible blind spots which can affect a chief executive, because he makes it difficult for people to help him, while creating grievances which sooner or later lead to attacks on him.

The unseating of a chief executive by a coalition of subordinates seldom reduces the emotional charge built up in the uncertain attachments to the ousted leader. A new head man has to emerge and establish a confident coalition. Until the contentions for power subside and the guilt reactions attached to deposing the leader dissolve, individuals remain vulnerable to their own blind spots and unconscious reactions to striving for power.

The references to a parental figure in the preceding discussion may appear to exaggerate the meaning of power conflicts. In whatever ways it exaggerates, it also condenses a variety of truths about coalitions among executives. The chief executive is the central *object* in a coalition because he occupies a position analogous to parents in the family. He is at the nucleus of a political structure whose prototype is the family in which jealousy, envy, love, and hate find original impetus and expression.

It would be a gross error to assume that in making an analogy between the family and formal organizations the parental role is strictly paternal. There are also characteristics of the mother figure in certain types of chief executives and combinations of mother-father in the formation of executive coalitions.

Chief executives can also suffer from depersonalization in their roles and as a result become emotionally cold and detached. The causes of depersonalization are complex but, in brief, have some connections to the narrow definitions of rationality which exclude the importance of emotions in guiding communication as well as thought.

For the purpose of interpreting how defensive styles affect the behavior of leaders, there is some truth to the suggestion that the neutrality and lack of warmth characteristic of some leaders is a result of an ingrained fear of becoming the *object* for other people — for to become the *object* arouses fears that subordinates will become envious and compete for power.

Paranoid Thinking

This is a form of distortion in ideas and perception to which all human beings are susceptible from time to time. For those individuals who are concerned in their work with the consolidation and uses of power, the experience with suspiciousness, the attribution of bad motives to others, jealousy, and anxiety (characteristics of paranoid thinking), may be more than a passing state of mind.

In fact, such ideas and fantasies may indeed be communicated to others and may even be the main force which binds men into collusions. Organizational life is particularly vulnerable to the effects of paranoid thinking because it stimulates comparisons while it evokes anticipations of added power or fears of diminished power.

To complicate matters even more and to suggest just how ambiguous organizational decisions become, there may be some truth and substance in back of the suspicions, distrust, and jealousies which enflame thinking. Personality conflicts do affect decisions in allocating authority and responsibility, and an individual may not be distorting at all to sense that he had been excluded or denied an ambition based on some undercurrents in his relationships with others. To call these sensitivities paranoid thinking may itself be a gross distortion. But no matter how real the events, the paranoid potential is still high as a fallout of organizational life.

Paranoid thinking goes beyond suspiciousness, distrust, and jealousy. It may take the form of grandiose ideas and overestimation of one's power and control. This form of distortion leads to swings in mood from elation to despair, from a sense of omnipotence to helplessness. Again, when acted out, the search for complete control produces the tragedies which the initial distortions attempt to overcome. The tragedy of Jimmy Hoffa is a good case in point. Consider:

> From all indications, Hoffa performed brilliantly as president of the teamsters' union. He was a superb organizer and bargainer, and in many ways a highly moral and even prudish man. There is little evidence to support allegations that he used his office to enrich himself.
>
> Hoffa's troubles stemmed from his angry reactions when he could not get his way in managing the union's pension fund and from his relations with the government. In overestimating his power, Hoffa fell victim to the illusion that no controls outside himself could channel his actions. At this writing, Hoffa is serving a sentence in Lewisburg Penitentiary, having been found guilty of tampering with a jury.
>
> It is interesting to note that Hoffa's successor delegated considerable authority to

regional officers, a step that removed him from direct comparisons with Hoffa and served to cement a coalition of top officers in the teamsters.

Executives, too, can be victims of their successes just as much as of their failures. If past successes lead to the false sense of omnipotence which goes unchecked in, say, the executive's control of the board of directors, then he and his organization become the victims of changing times and competitive pressures along with the weakening in perception and reasoning which often accompanies aging.

One could speculate with some reason that paranoid distortions are the direct result of senility and the inability to accept the fact of death. While intellectually aware of the inevitability of death, gifted executives can sometimes not accept emotionally the ultimate in the limitations of power. The disintegration of personality in the conflict between the head and the heart is what we come to recognize as the paranoid potential in all forms of our collective relations.

Ritualistic Ceremonial

Any collective experience, such as organizational life with its capacity for charging the atmosphere in the imagery of power conflicts, can fall victim to rigidities. The rigidities I have in mind consist mainly of the formation and elaboration of structures, procedures, and other ceremonials which create the illusion of solving problems but in reality only give people something to act on to discharge valuable energies.

The best example of a ritualistic approach to real problems is the ever-ready solution of bringing people together in a committee on the naive grounds that the exchange of ideas is bound to produce a solution. There are even fads and fashions to ritualism as in the sudden appearance of favorite words like "brain-storming" or "synergism."

It is not that bringing people together to discuss problems is bad. Instead, it is the naive faith which accompanies such proposals, ultimately deflecting attention from where it properly belongs. Thus:

In one research organization, professionals faced severe problems arising from personal jealousies as well as differences of opinion on the correct goals and content for the research program. Someone would periodically suggest that the problems could not be solved unless people came together, preferably for a weekend away from the job, to share ideas and really get down to the "nitty-gritty" of the problem. (It is interesting to note that no one ever defines the "nitty-gritty.") The group would indeed follow such suggestions and typically end the weekend with a feeling of euphoria brought on by considerable drinking and a sumptuous meal.

The most concrete proposal for action was in the idea that the basic problem stemmed from the organization's increased size so that people no longer knew one another and their work. The solution which appeared, only shortly to disappear, was to publish a laboratory newsletter that would keep people abreast of their colleagues' newest ideas.

In a more general vein, ritualism can be invoked to deal with any real or fancied danger, with uncertainty, ambivalent attitudes, or a sense of personal helplessness. Rituals are used even in the attempt to manipulate people. That power relations in organizations should become a fertile field for ritualism should not surprise anyone.

As I have tried to indicate, the problems of organizational life involve the dangers associated with losses of power; the uncertainties are legion especially in the recognition that there is no one best way to organize and distribute power, and yet any individual must make a commitment to some form of organization.

Ambivalent attitudes, such as the simultaneous experience of love and hate, are also associated with authority relationships, particularly in how superior-subordinate become the subject and object for the expression of dependency reactions. In addition, the sense of helplessness is particularly sensitized in the events which project gains and losses in power and status.

Finally, superior and subordinate in any power structure are constantly tempted to manipulate each other as a way of gaining control over one's environment, and the more so when there is a lack of confidence and credibility in the organization's efforts to solve problems in realistic ways.

The negative effects of ritualism are precisely in the expenditure of energy to carry out the rituals and also in the childlike expectation that the magic formulas of organizational life substitute for diagnosing and solving real problems. When the heads of organizations are unsure of the bases for the exercise of power and become defensive, the easy solution is to play for time by invoking rituals which may temporarily relieve anxiety.

Similarly, when executives fail to understand the structure and potential of the power coalitions they establish (either consciously or unconsciously), they increasingly rely on rituals to deflect attention away from their responsibilities. And, when leaders are timid men incapable of initiating or responding, the spontaneous reaction is to use people to act out rituals. Usually, the content and symbolism in the rituals provide important clues about the underlying defensiveness of the executive.

Obsessional leaders.   The gravitational pull to ceremonials and magic is irresistible. In positions of power, obsessional leaders use in their public performances the mechanisms of defense which originate in their private conflicts. These defenses include hyper-rationality, the isolation of thought and feeling, reactive behavior in turning anger into moral righteousness, and passive control of other people as well as their own thought processes.

Very frequently, particularly in this day and age of psychologizing conflict, obsessive leaders "get religion" and try to convert others into some new state of mind. The use of sensitivity training with its attachment to "openness" and "leveling" in power relations seems to be the current favorite.

What these leaders do not readily understand is the fallacy of imposing a total solution for the problem of power relations where reality dictates at best the possibility of only partial and transient solutions. To force openness through the use of group pressure in T-groups and to expect to sustain this pressure in everyday life is to be supremely ritualistic. People intelligently resist saying everything they think to other people because they somehow have a deep recognition that this route leads to becoming overextended emotionally and, ultimately, to sadistic relationships.

Intelligent uses of power.   The choice fortunately is not between ritualistic civility and naive openness in human relationships, particularly where power is concerned. In between is the choice of defining those partial problems which can be solved and through which bright people can learn something about the intelligent uses of power.

We should not lose sight of the basic lesson that people in positions of power differ from "ordinary" human beings mainly in their capacity to impose their personal defenses onto the stage of corporate life. Fortunately, the relationships are susceptible to intelligent management, and it is to the nature of this intelligence that I wish to address the conclusion of this article.

COMING FULL CIRCLE

The main job of organizational life, whether it concerns developing a new political pyramid, making new appointments to executive positions, or undergoing management succession at top levels, is to bring talented individuals into location for the legitimate uses of power. This is bound to be a highly charged event in corporate relationships because of the real changes in power distributions and the emotional reactions people experience along with the incremental gains and losses of power.

The demand, on the one hand, is for objectivity in assessing people and needs (as opposed to pseudorationality and rationalizing). This objectivity, on the other hand, has to be salvaged from the impact of psychological stresses which impel people to act out fantasies associated with power conflicts. The stresses of change in power relations tend to increase defensiveness to which counterreactions of rationalizing and of mythmaking serve no enduring purpose except perhaps to drive underground the concerns which make people react defensively in the first place.

Stylistic Biases

Thought and action in the politics of organizational life are subject to the two kinds of errors commonly found in practical life: the errors of omission and those of commission. It is both what people do and what they neglect to do that result in the negative effects of action outweighing the positive. But besides the specific errors of omission and commission (the tactical aspects of action), there are also the more strategic aspects which have to be evaluated. The strategic aspects deal both with the corporate aims and objectives and with the style of the leaders who initiate change.

In general, leaders approach change with certain stylistic biases over which they may not have too much control. There is a preferred approach to power problems which derives from the personality of the leader and his defenses as well as from the realities of the situation. Of particular importance as stylistic biases are the preferences for partial, as contrasted with total, approaches and the preferences for substance over form.

Partial vs. total. The partial approaches attempt to define and segregate problems which become amenable to solution by directive, negotiation, consensus, and compromise.

The total approaches usually escalate the issues in power relations so that implicitly people act as though it were necessary to undergo major conversions. The conversions can be directed toward personality structure, ideals, and beliefs, or toward values which are themselves connected to important aspects of personal experience.

When conversions become the end products of change, then one usually finds the sensitization of concerns over such matters as who dominates and who submits, who controls and who is being controlled, who is accepted and who is rejected. The aftermath of these concerns is the heightening of fantasy and defense at the expense of reality.

It may come as something of a disappointment to readers who are favorably disposed to psychology to consider the possibility that while organizations do have an impact on the attitudes of their constituent members, they cannot change personality structures or carry out therapeutic procedures. People may become more effective while working in certain kinds of organizations, but only when effectiveness is not dependent on the solution of neurotic conflict.

The advocates of total approaches seem to miss this point in their eagerness to convert people and organizations from one set of ideals to another. It becomes a good deal wiser, if these propositions are true, to scale down and make concrete the objectives that one is seeking to achieve.

A good illustration is in the attention given to decentralization of authority. Decentralization can be viewed in the image of conversion to certain ideals about who should have power and how this power should be used responsibly, or through an analytical approach to decide selectively where power is ill-placed and ill-used and to work on change at these locations. In other words, the theory of the partial approach to organizations asserts priorities and depends on good diagnostic observation and thought.

Substance vs. form. Leaders can also present a stylistic bias in their preference for substance or form. Substance, in the language of organizations, is the detail of goals and performance—that is, who has to do what with whom to meet specific objectives. Form directs attention to the relationship of "who to whom" and attempts to achieve goals by specifying how the people should act in relation to each other.

There is no way in which matters of form can be divorced from substance. But students of organization should at least be clear that attention to form *ahead of* substance threatens a person's sense of what is reasonable in undertaking actions. Attention to form may also present an implicit attack on one's conception of his independence and freedom from constraint.

Making form secondary to substance has another virtue: it can secure agreement on priorities without the need of predetermining who will have to give way in the ultimate give-and-take of the negotiations that must precede decisions on organization structure.

The two dimensions of bias, shown in the Exhibit 1 matrix, along with the four

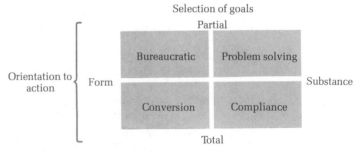

Exhibit 1   Cognitive Management Styles in Organizational Life

cells which result, clarify different executive approaches to power. The two dimensions define the executive's cognitive biases in: (1) selection of goals (partial vs. total), and (2) orientation toward action (form vs. substance).

In the *bureaucratic* approach — that is, partial goals and attachment to form as a mode of acting — the emphasis is on procedure and the establishment of precedent and rule to control the uses of power.

The appeal of this approach is its promise of certainty in corporate relationships and in the depersonalization of power. The weaknesses of the bureaucratic approach are too familiar to need detailing here. Its major defect, however, is its inability to separate the vital from the trivial. It more easily commands energy over irrelevant issues because the latent function of the bureaucratic approach is to bypass conflict.

My contention here is that few important problems can be attended to without conflict of ideas and interests. Eventually organizations become stagnant because the bureaucratic approaches seldom bring together power and the vital issues which together make organizations dynamic.

The *conversion* approach (total-form) is notable through the human relations and sensitivity training movements as well as ideological programs, such as the Scanlon Plan and other forms of participative management. The popularity of "management by objectives" bears some scrutiny as a conversion movement directed toward power figures.

Another "total" approach which differs from conversion in its emphasis on substance is *compliance* with the directives of the powerful leader. This is the arena of the authoritarian personality (in both the leader, who has the power, and in the led, who seek submission), for whom personal power gets expressed in some higher goal that makes it possible for ends to justify means. The ideals may, for example, be race, as with dictator Adolf Hitler, or religion, as with Father Charles Coughlin, a dictator-type of the depression. In business, the illustrations are of a technological variety as with Frederick Winslow Taylor's "scientific management" and Henry Ford's automobile and assembly line.

Almost any technology can assume the proportions of the total approach if it is advanced by a charismatic leader and has deep emotional appeal. This explains the popularity of "management information systems," "value analysis," and "program planning and budgeting" which lead to a belief that the system itself is based on order, rationality, and control; therefore, the belief in turn helps to counteract the fears of chaos and lack of control which make people willing to demand total dependence and compliance in power relations. The effects of this fear on how people seek to arrange power relations in business, government, and the community cannot be overestimated.

Problem-Solving Approach

It should be perfectly obvious by now that my favored approach to organizational life combines the biases in Exhibit 1 of the partial substantive quadrant which I have designated "problem solving." From observation of competent business executives, we know it is precisely their ability to define problems worthy of thought and action and to use their organization to evolve solutions which characterize their style.

The contrary notion that executives are primarily caretakers, mediators, and seekers of consensus is more a myth than an accurate portrayal of how the competent ones attach themselves to power. To have power and not direct it to some substantive end that can be attained in the real world is to waste energy. The difficulties with the problem-solving approach are in risking power in favor of a substantive goal.

While there are no absolute right answers in problem solving, there are ways of evaluating the correctness of a program and plan. With a favorable average, the executive finds his power base enhanced and his ability to take risks increased.

The problem-solving approach to organization structure operates according to certain premises:

1. That organization structure is an instrument rather than an end. This means that a structure should be established or modified quickly instead of stringing out deliberations as though there actually exists a best and single solution for the problem of allocating power.
2. That organization structure can be changed but should not be tinkered with. This means that members of an executive organization can rely on a structure and can implement it without the uncertainty which comes from the constant modification of the organization chart.
3. That organization structure expresses the working coalition attached to the chief executive. In other words, the coalition has to be established de facto for the structure to mean anything. If the structure is out of line with the coalition, there will be an erosion of power and effectiveness. If no coalition exists in the minds of participants, putting it on paper in the form of an organization chart is nothing more than an academic exercise and a confusing one at that.
4. That organization structure represents a blend of people and job definitions, but the priority is in describing the structure to accommodate competent people. The reason for this priority lies in the fact that competent executives are hard to find. Therefore, as an action principle, one should ensure the effective uses of the scarcest resources rather than conform to some ideal version of power relations.
5. That organization structure is a product of negotiation and compromise among executives who hold semiautonomous power bases. The more the power base of an executive is his demonstrated competence, the greater his autonomy of power and therefore capacity to determine the outcome in the allocations of power. The basic criticism of the problem-solving approach is in the danger of defining issues narrowly and ultimately undermining the moral-ethical basis of leadership. This criticism is valid, but as with so many problems in practical affairs, it can be overcome only by leaders who can see beyond the limits of immediate contingencies. In fact, I have tried to show throughout this article how the limitations of leaders, in both their cognitive and their emotional capacities, become the causes of power problems.

We have therefore come full circle in this analysis: because power problems are the effects of personality on structure, the solutions demand thinking which is free from the disabilities of emotional conflicts. This insight is often the margin between enduring with what exists or taking those modest steps which align competence with institutional authority in the service of human needs.

REFERENCES

1. See my article, "The Management of Disappointment," *HBR* November–December 1967, p. 59.
2. See Chester Barnard, *The Functions of the Executive* (Cambridge, Harvard University Press, 1938), p. 167.

Third Party Roles in Interdepartmental Conflict

Richard E. Walton

One of the critical skills needed in modern life is the ability to play a mediating role in reducing conflict. The following selection analyzes third party roles and interventions which are designed to assist in the resolution or control of interunit conflict. It also reviews organizational studies which have implications for such analysis. The principal role relationships between third parties and conflicting persons/units that are reviewed include: organizational superior, organizational peer, separate coordinating unit, and organizational consultant.

Almost inherent in specialization of skills and differentiation of functions performed by organizational units is the development of interunit differences. Reward systems, communication obstacles, status incongruity, and other factors often make it harder to achieve coordination and integration. Manifest or potential lateral conflict is a fact of organizational life. The growing literature on the subject has focused primarily on the determinants and dynamics of the conflict and has given relatively less attention to how this conflict is managed in the interest of organizational effectiveness.

The following article analyzes third party roles and interventions which are designed to assist in the resolution or control of interunit conflict; the paper reviews organizational studies which have implications for such an analysis.[1]

"Lateral conflict" refers to conflict between peer units, that is, where there are no superior-subordinate relations. The conflict may involve entire groups or merely unit representatives. It may have its foundation in stereotypes and emotional reactions or in organizational roles and forces. It may reflect differences over factors, methods, or goals.

"Third party" refers to any nonparticipant in the conflict who may facilitate the resolution or control of conflict between primary departments. In terms of organizational positions, potential third parties include: a higher organizational executive, a third peer department not directly involved in the interunit conflict, a separate unit formally assigned to coordinate the activities of two primary units, or an internal or outside organizational consultant. These various types of role relationships are depicted in Figure 1.

A focus on third party control and resolution of conflict assumes a diagnosis that the particular conflict involved has more dysfunctional than functional consequences. For example, the conflict may be more debilitating than energizing for the participants. Or it may tend to obscure rather than clarify alternatives available to the organization. The purpose in controlling conflict is to decrease or eliminate some of the more negative consequences.

"Third Party Roles in Interdepartmental Conflict," by Richard E. Walton from *Industrial Relations*, Vol. 7, No. 1 (October 1967). Reprinted by permission of the author and the Institute of Industrial Relations.

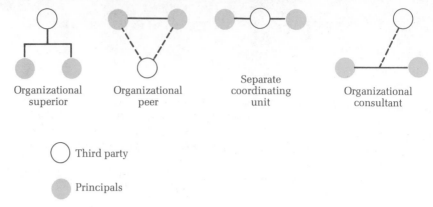

Figure 1   Role Relationships Between Third Parties and Principals

The discussion takes up four types of intervention: (1) to reduce or eliminate the conflict potential in a situation; (2) to resolve directly a substantive issue in dispute; (3) to facilitate the parties' efforts to manage a particular conflict, and (4) to help the parties change their conflict-prone relationship. A section follows which summarizes how and why each of these types of interventions is differentially available to superiors, peers, coordinative units, and consultants.

REDUCING CONFLICT POTENTIAL

A great many factors can contribute to interunit conflict. Frequently the conflict potential is inherent in the technology, organizational environment, or some essential administrative apparatus. In other cases, however, higher executives have latitude to modify the organizational structure or personnel assignment. For example:

1. Organizational superiors may adjust the allocation of rewards, status symbols, and other resources in order to ameliorate some of the sharper sources of conflict;[2] and they may decrease the specificity of those individual unit performance measures which lead to a suboptimizing orientation.[3]
2. They may reduce task load or increase capacity of units where an overload condition or task difficulty is creating bargaining or frustration among subordinate units.[4]
3. Higher executives may take steps to stabilize organizational jurisdictions for a period of time in order to decrease the ambiguity surrounding departmental status which sometimes underlies competitive interunit maneuvering. Similarly, they may make explicit rules to assign final authority for decisions on interunit matters in order to depersonalize irritating lateral influence patterns, or they may develop rules to cover an increasing proportion of interunit transactions, confining interunit decision-making to exceptional situations.[5]
4. Organizational designers may utilize mechanisms of segregation, including stricter role separation, between those organizational functions requiring affect and human relations and those requiring more impersonal social relations — because of the contradictory nature of these forms of relationship.[6]
5. Superiors may recruit, select, and assign personnel in ways that minimize the diversity of backgrounds which tends to create conflict among subordinate units[7] and that reduce the incompatibility of personalities or personal styles of unit representatives.

While the above list is not exhaustive, it includes the more important factors which   **727**
both create conflict potential and are subject to the control of organizational architects   *Walton: Third Party*
or superiors.   *Roles in Conflict*

RESOLVING SUBSTANTIVE ISSUES

Higher Executives

Brown emphasizes the frequency with which interunit conflict signals the need for superiors to become involved and to contribute to the substance of the decision. Often a disputed point between managers indicates that finely balanced judgments are involved. Only a manager with broader understanding and responsibility should make the judgments. Therefore, in Brown's experience, "rapid exposure of the disagreement at the cross-over point" is necessary. The cross-over point is the first executive to whom both departments report. As an extension of the superior's own power and judgment, he may bring in an outside technical expert to evaluate the merits of the positions of the contending parties.[8]

By taking an active role on substantive issues, executives offset the tendency for subordinates either to persist in or to compromise disagreements when the final decision should be made at a higher level. This pattern also satisfies a higher manager's need to be informed.[9]

According to Brown, higher managers are more likely to play this type of third party role in a timely and appropriate way if they avoid communicating that they regard subordinate conflict as personal failure, and, rather, communicate that they see the interunit conflict as reflecting inherent executive dilemmas or poor organizational policies, or both.[10]

Taking a somewhat different position, Blake, Shepard, and Mouton argue that third party judgments in win-lose struggles simply relieve the parties from the struggle itself, but not from the problems of defeat. They find that losers tend to feel an imposed decision was unfair, to suspect the third party, and to doubt his competence or understanding of the problem. These authors also mention third party use of fate mechanisms, such as the flip of a coin, to decide interunit conflicts regarded as inevitable. Even a superior's appeal to the disputants to accept his judgment in a "good sportsman-like way" is a subtle use of a fate mechanism.[11]

Separate Coordinating Units

Where basic departments which are interdependent in work-flow sequence are highly differentiated from each other, there is a tendency to use a permanent separate unit to help achieve coordination between them. In a study by Lawrence and Lorsch, such third party units used their own substantive analysis to influence decisions.[12] The authors differentiated three principal units—research, sales, and production—on four dimensions: (1) degree of structure, i.e., tightness of rules, narrowness of span of supervisory control, and frequency and specificity of performance review; (2) members' orientation toward time, i.e., length of time perspective; (3) members' orientation toward others, i.e., openness and permissiveness of interpersonal relationships; and (4) members' orientation toward different subgoals and segments of the organizational environment, i.e., new scientific knowledge versus customer problems and opportunities versus raw materials and processing costs. Thus, for example, a sales unit compared with the production unit may tend to be less structured, to have a longer time perspective, to be more permissive in interpersonal orientation, and to be more oriented toward the market environment.

Measurements of the degree of differentiation among the three departments were applied to firms in the plastics, food, and container industries. In plastics, the research, sales, and production departments were most differentiated; all six firms used a separate coordinating unit. In the food and container industries, only one of the two firms studied used a separate unit.

What factors influenced the effectiveness of these separate third party units? If a coordinating unit had an intermediate or balanced orientation to those factors which differentiated the basic departments, it was better able to facilitate interdepartmental decision-making. The managers of the basic departments apparently believed it was especially important for the third parties to have balanced time perspective and subgoal orientation.

Technical expertise is also important if third parties are to settle substantive disputes. The coordinating units in all six plastics firms studied by Lawrence and Lorsch had considerable power relative to their counterparts in the basic departments. However, in the two plastics firms where there was great respect for the technical competence of the third party personnel, there was also a higher level of integration. The experience of the food company's integrative unit was slightly different. At first its power was perceived by the basic departments as being based on its proximity to the president; however, as the basic departments gained respect for its expertise, the integrative unit made an increasingly positive contribution to conflict resolution.

What is the relative effectiveness of using a separate coordinating unit as opposed to relying on the crossover executive to resolve differences? Lawrence and Lorsch compared the way two container firms achieved interunit integration in the areas of scheduling and customer service, both frequently the subject of disagreement. One firm utilized a formal third party unit to facilitate coordination. The other firm relied on the crossover executive alone. The second arrangement was more effective in resolving conflict and more acceptable to the basic departments. Why? Although both arrangements provided a third party with a balanced orientation, the coordinating unit lacked the power and relevant information that the crossover executive had in the second firm (see Table 1).

Participation of a Peer Department

Still another potential source of third party influence on the substance of an interunit issue is a peer department which is not essentially involved.

Zald studied the pattern of interunit conflict among teachers, social service workers, and cottage parents in five delinquency institutions. The relative influence of the three types of units varied from institution to institution. The two lower influence departments tended to be more in conflict with the high influence department than with each other. Zald suggested that these conflict patterns reflected a tendency to balance off the high power of one department.[13] Presumably the entry of a third party into an issue primarily between two units reduced unilateral decision-making and allowed the third party to exercise some substantive influence.

Dalton described the use of third party peer departments to force resolution of decisions which might otherwise represent an impasse.[14] Whether or not this represents third party intervention in the sense of this paper depends on whether the third unit

Table 1 Relative Effectiveness of Coordinating Unit and Crossover Executive in Dispute Resolution, Two Firms

	Attributes		
Third Parties	Balanced Orientation	Power	Relevant Information[a]
Coordinating unit	High	Low	Moderate
Crossover executive	High	High	High

[a] About plant capacity and customer requirements.

is interested primarily in helping to resolve the conflict or in entering into a coalition for the purpose of exchanging favors and influence.

MANAGING MANIFEST CONFLICT

The type of third party intervention described immediately above is concerned with the substance of the issues in dispute. In contrast, the interventions to help manage manifest conflict act on the *processes* of conflict and conflict management.

Influencing Gross Patterns of Contact

It is often possible to improve conflict management processes by affecting the gross pattern of interunit contact and coordination efforts. Some of these control techniques are available to the parties through their own initiative as well as at the initiative of a third party.

Sometimes control involves constraining interunit contact. In one production-sales relationship studied by Walton, Dutton, and Fitch, certain restrictions were designed to preserve a tenuously improving relationship. Interunit business transactions were channeled through the chief liaison personnel representing each department in order to reduce the likelihood of accidents or other provocative acts. For example, salesmen were not allowed to go onto the shipping dock or directly contact the shipping clerk.[15]

Direct contact between principals is sometimes reduced by using a low status, "expendable-linker" in interface activities.[16] This person elicits less hostility and absorbs the inevitable punishment more easily as he has less emotional energy invested in the relationship. In a similar vein, buffer inventories can be used to reduce the tightness of dependency and resulting need for frequent close coordination.[17]

In other instances, collaboration can be improved between departments by promoting interunit contacts. An obvious and basic way is to increase physical proximity. As an example, the ambassador of a large overseas mission reorganized office space and dispersed many sections of the AID mission in order to bring together physically the following and other combinations: assistant director of AID, economic counselor of the State Department, and the Treasury attaché; the AID capital development office and the Commerce attaché; etc. These changes facilitated functional coordination.[18]

Brown prescribes several roles for superiors who are aware of conflict between subordinates, including (1) ensuring that they confront their conflict, with a view toward resolving it; and (2) discussing with subordinates those lateral conflicts they fail to resolve on their own. Thus, the supervisor simply adds his own pressure for continued work on the conflict to that already inherent in the issues.[19] According to the "linking pin" concept of Likert, supervisors also can play an even more positive, social-emotional role in facilitating the resolution of conflict among subordinate units.[20]

In the overseas mission referred to above, the ambassador and his staff assistant had leadership patterns which combined to promote increased interunit contact and coordination. The ambassador let it be known that he had firm expectations that the separate agencies in the mission would find ways to coordinate their affairs and collaborate where appropriate. He asked for information about friction and was willing to exercise the force at his command to bring reluctant agencies into interagency contact. His staff assistant complemented the ambassador's harsh approach by encouraging, arranging, facilitating, and reinforcing interagency contacts and instances of coordination. He did use the influence of the ambassador, but subtly enough that his interpersonal and organizational skills at facilitation were the more apparent part of his approach. Thus, the moderately high power third party who punished instances of noncooperation was complemented by the low power, socially skillful third party who could facilitate the necessary interunit contacts. Both were more effective because their third party roles were combined and coordinated.

In other cases it is unclear whether the use of process intermediaries increases or decreases the gross rate of interunit interaction. Blake, Shepard, and Mouton cite a company in which a man was employed full time at the corporate level "for the sole purpose of trying to bring competing components of the organization into some reasonable alignment."[21] Burns and Stalker refer to "liaison specialists — whose job was to move across the linguistic and functional frontiers and to act as intermediaries between the people getting on with the job."[22] The use of such intermediaries was apparently a symptom of less effective organizations in the firms they studied.

Influencing the Approach to Issues in Dispute

A variety of distinctions have been made in how parties handle their differences. Schmidt and Tannenbaum cite avoidance, repression, sharpening into conflict, and transformation into problem-solving.[23] Blake, Shepard, and Mouton contrast a "win-lose" approach and problem-solving.[24] Walton elaborates two joint decision-making models, bargaining and problem-solving; these engagement approaches both contrast with a withdrawal posture.[25] Lawrence and Lorsch identify problem-solving, smoothing, and forcing.[26]

Common to all of these studies is problem-solving, where both parties strive toward: defining the problem in terms of underlying needs, exploring a wide range of alternatives, portraying accurately the strength of one's needs and preferences, and selecting alternatives that create the most joint gain. The outcomes of problem-solving are often integrative solutions rather than compromises. All authors appear to advocate strongly more frequent use of problem-solving, though they also acknowledge that under some conditions another approach makes sense. This general predeliction for confrontation and problem-solving appears to be justified in terms of the results of the Lawrence and Lorsch studies. The better performing firms tended to handle conflict by confronting it, rather than by smoothing it over or forcing outcomes.

Schmidt and Tannenbaum spelled out some of the third party interventions which facilitate problem-solving. The interventions are presumably available to superiors, consultants, and perhaps organizational peers.[27]

1. The third party can invite differences and stress their value in increasing the range of alternatives for the organization. To the extent that the parties perceive value to the confrontation process, each is less likely to define success in terms of attaining the particular outcome which he preferred initially.
2. The third party can listen with understanding rather than evaluation. The conflicting parties themselves usually don't listen to one another. Each is too busy trying to be understood. By listening and understanding, the third party can contribute to the parties' understanding of each other's position. Also, the third party's listening example is frequently followed by the participants themselves.
3. The third party can clarify the nature of the issue, e.g., whether it revolves around different perceptions of facts, methods, values, or goals. Disputants themselves often depart from the original issue by chasing a tangential point or by transposing the issue. The more detached third party can perform a welcome function by helping the disputants develop a common understanding of the issue and by repeatedly bringing them back to it.
4. The third party can recognize and accept the feelings of the individuals involved. Interunit disagreements are often compounded by the irrational feelings they generate, such as fear, jealousy, anger, or anxiety. When a third party communicates to a person that he can understand and accept these feelings he assists both participants to accept these feelings and to analyze their impact on the outstanding disagreement. The risk associated with identifying these "negative" feelings is that the person who is identified with them will feel criticized and become more defensive.
5. The third party can suggest procedures for resolving differences—the particular techniques depending on whether facts, methods, goals, or values are at issue. Walton and McKersie also suggest a variety of techniques to promote problem-solving when the mixed motive nature of the issue also requires some bargaining: differentiating the two types of interunit decision processes by fractionating the issue, by interunit representatives, by time, by ground rules, etc.[28]
6. Blake, Shepard, and Mouton, who approach interdepartmental and union-management conflict in similar ways, emphasize intergroup dynamics. The third party can help the groups cope with what the authors call the "traitor threat," which involves loss of status and rejection of any representative who concedes points to the other group. The third party can influence the composition of the intergroup meeting or help regulate meeting caucuses and recesses in order to allow more continuous interchange between representatives and other members of their respective units.[29]

FACILITATING CHANGING THE RELATIONSHIP

Now, rather than analyzing interventions which act either on the substance or process of conflict, we treat third party interventions which enable two units to perceive and move toward a new equilibrium—a relationship in which there is less emotional conflict and a generally improved capacity to solve differences.

In a Task Leadership Context: Interagency Relations in Washington and Overseas

Many different departments and agencies of the U.S. government play a role in the conduct of foreign affairs: State, Defense, Agriculture, AID, Peace Corps, Commerce, CIA, to mention merely the more important ones. The agencies are coordinated in the field missions by the ambassador and his country team. Also, interdepartmental groups, comprised of several of these departments and chaired by an assistant secretary of state, have been created in Washington to coordinate foreign affairs on a regional basis. However, with very few exceptions, no such mechanism in Washington exists for coordinating these agencies' interest pertaining to an individual country. Generally the separate efforts are not well integrated, considerable mutual suspicion and low regard exists among agencies, and no well developed problem-solving mechanisms exist for resolving interagency differences.

Walton studied the innovative efforts of one country director (i.e., the ambassador's counterpart in the Washington, D.C., organization of the State Department) who has tried to increase interdepartmental integration and coordination at his level.[30] Beginning in May 1966, he scheduled meetings on a monthly basis, inviting representatives from about a dozen agencies—those persons directly concerned with the affairs of the same foreign country.

The country director, who did not have the power to compel membership or attendance, relied on his own skill in managing the sessions to make discussions productive and valuable to individual members. Many meetings featured informal presentations by persons with unique knowledge about the country, followed by round-table discussions of the issues raised. His method of handling meetings included relating himself to members directly and personally; urging continuity in the personnel representing an agency, differentiating one-time observers from regular members; encouraging, accepting, and helping develop views which differed from his own; and not keeping minutes on the meetings.

By the way he managed the sessions he gradually achieved certain states that in turn improved the problem-solving and conflict resolution capacity of this interagency network. Common exposure of the agency representatives to experts and to each other, and their own mutual education and information exchange activities, decreased the likelihood of future interagency conflict based on differences in perceived facts and tended to break down many negative intergroup stereotypes that exist about Peace Corps, Military, CIA, and State, etc. The development of personal relationships among agency representatives increased their tendency to check with each other for specific advice, information, and to coordinate activities generally. Encouragement of dissent and challenge in the absence of compelling policy or action decisions was effective in setting a group norm of sharpening, accepting, and exploring differences—a norm which could carry over into solving specific problems. A corollary group norm was one of identifying the additional information which the group would need if it were to choose between the alternative views. The agency representatives not only achieved a better understanding from State Department officials of overall goals for U.S. relations with the country in question but also became more committed to them by virtue of a sense of identification with the interagency group. This enhanced sense of membership in the group and commitment to superordinate goals increased a member's personal discomfort whenever his agency's actions ignored the interests of other agencies.

Interagency matters pertaining to a given country are somewhat better coordinated in the field than in Washington.[31] For example, the country team, comprised of the top officials of the important agencies and headed by the ambassador, is an established concept and usually provides some integration. Nevertheless, the amount of coordination is limited by many pervasive factors: (1) interagency stereotypes; resentments about incongruities among formal status, actual influence, and privileges (such as automobile allowances and invitations to diplomatic parties); (2) an agency's fears that its programs' identities will be blurred, its personnel misused, and its program activities oversupervised.

In the overseas mission studied, the ambassador and his staff had been relatively effective in encouraging interagency contacts. The third party roles they normally played are described above. An additional important experimental device for achieving a higher and more creative level of integration of the many strands of foreign affairs activities was referred to as the "Think Tank." It was an informal weekly meeting of a group drawn from many agencies to think imaginatively about problems of concern to the foreign affairs community as a whole. The ambassador's staff assistant had played a key role in initiating the idea. The group also included a second staff assistant to the ambassador, the deputy director of AID, an assistant director of AID, two military men, and a second level official from USIS. A ground rule for members was that they were to address the problems rather than represent their respective agencies' viewpoints.[32] Generally this group included bright young men below the country team level. Apparently group meetings not only weakened stereotypes but also increased members' confidence in their similar goals and the complementary competencies of their respective agencies. At the time of the study, they had identified some new potential areas of collaboration which they intended to recommend pursuing.

The examples of the country director in Washington and the staff assistant in the overseas mission both illustrate a third party whose relationship to the other person involved slightly greater organizational power, somewhat higher status, and higher access to information. Their interventions centered on task activities which did not require immediate action outside the group, but were nevertheless immediately gratifying to members. Their critical intervention strategy was to build a social system and their process tactics ensured that the system had norms and other attributes which facilitated the productive use of differences.

In a Behavioral Science Consulting Context: An Intergroup Laboratory

Modifying the barriers to interunit collaboration is part of the more general problem of planned organizational change.[33] Blake, Shepard, and Mouton have utilized sensitivity training laboratory methods to improve intergroup relations in industry. Illustrative of their change strategy is the following account of their efforts which focused on the relations between headquarters and a field unit of a diversified and moderately decentralized industrial firm. This particular interunit relationship had attributes of both vertical and lateral relationships. The headquarters unit of Tennex Corporation performed staff as well as supervisory functions for the large Scofield unit.

The behavioral science consultants called in to help improve relationships first acquainted themselves with key management in both locations and the patterns of interactions, frustrations, and stereotypes in a generally deteriorating relationship.

> Headquarters personnel felt the division managers were 'secretive' and 'unresponsive.' The division was looked upon as unwilling to provide information that headquarters felt it needed. In turn, Scofield division management saw the headquarters management as 'prying' and 'arbitrary.' For example, headquarters was critical of the labor relations practices of the division. The division management resented the criticism, regarding it as prejudiced and ill-informed. Again, headquarters felt that Scofield managers had been 'dragging their feet' in implementing corporate marketing policies. Scofield felt that headquarters' demands in this area were unrealistic and that the corporate marketing group was behaving 'unilaterally,' and so on.[34]

The first of two basic types of intervention was training in group and intergroup dynamics. Separate three-day conferences with each group were designed to provide members with laboratory experiences which were in many respects analogous to those they face in their organizational roles. In this somewhat protected context, the consultants could identify the social dynamics while they were occurring, increase managers' awareness about how they were coping with them, and provide theory which generalized the experience and made credible its application to other situations.

> ... First, managers were able to see the headquarters-field problem in sufficient perspective to analyze the destructive consequences of the win-lose trap which had been dictating their actions. Second, an intergroup experiment and its analysis created a degree of openness within each group of managers that enabled them to review their own intragroup relationships and to develop greater mutual understanding and acceptance. This teamwork training is an important prelude to intergroup confrontation, because friction, 'politics,' or inability to level within each team clouds and confuses intergroup communication when the two groups are brought together.[35]

The second basic intervention was a three-day conference in which the two groups met together. This intervention involved the following phased activities:

Phase I: meeting together the groups listed and assigned priorities to those issues they felt required joint problem-solving.

Phase II: meeting separately each group prepared a description of itself as viewed by its members, constructed a verbal image of the other group, and finally built a description of their mutual relationships. These images supplemented the previously developed list of substantive issues, by providing an inventory of existing perceptions and feelings which needed to be examined, understood, and overcome.

Phase III: each group in turn exposed its own image of itself and in turn listened to the image as perceived by the other group. By their previous interventions, the consultants had created among participants a spirit of inquiry and a desire to listen for understanding rather than evaluation. As a result, the present activity of bringing these images into the open increased the general feelings of being understood and accepted. Then the participants again reviewed the substantive issues between the units.

Phase IV: several subgroups were formed of headquarters and field personnel with corresponding functional responsibilities. They first explored interpersonal issues and then tabled the functional problems they shared.

Phase V: a review was made of the progress in subgroups and between the units as a whole, and an analysis followed of the kinds of changes required in order to bring about actual improvements. One of the results of Phases IV and V was that headquarters personnel saw more clearly the alternative of conceiving themselves as "consultants" to the field rather than as persons who "control" field operations. They also better perceived the advantages of more mutual influence on policy-making and more continuous feedback about implementation. The groups agreed to reconvene for review and evaluation after a period of implementation.

By the end of Phase V the groups had increased their mutual trust, respect, and understanding. In addition, they had made a number of commitments to new ways of either preventing or handling interunit differences.

Walton has described and analyzed the functions performed by a behavioral science consulting intervention which facilitated the confrontation of differences between the officials of two interdependent units in a government agency.[36]

The confrontation occurred between two program officers, whom we shall refer to as Bill and Lloyd. Bill's unit had overall project responsibility for designing an organizational system. Lloyd's unit provided many of the professional personnel engaged in the design work of the project. Lloyd himself had only recently assumed responsibility for supervising his unit's activities on the systems project. Friction had developed immediately between them. Bill decided to arrange a meeting with Lloyd specifically to review the working relationship between them and their respective units. He invited the consultant to participate as a third party. Lloyd agreed to the arrangement.

When the three of them met, Lloyd's initial statement of their difficulty stressed several intergroup issues. He asserted that his unit's personnel were being used below their capabilities and should be used more strategically. He felt that his unit had too little decision influence. He also believed that his own leadership position within his group was undermined by Bill's operating style. For his part, Bill was annoyed and harassed by what he regarded as dominating patterns of behavior by Lloyd in a combined group meeting. He objected to a similar pattern in their current interaction.

With the help of the third party they identified and discussed the issues which separated them, testing whether the differences were real or only apparent. Interestingly, as Lloyd realized that he was being listened to and understood and that the initially stated intergroup issues were being taken seriously, he began to identify more personal concerns about his own role and identity. For example, he did not feel sufficiently "connected" with the total project; moreover, he believed his own relevant experience and competence were not being recognized by Bill. It became apparent that these interpersonal concerns were an underlying part of the intergroup issues stated initially.

The confrontation was regarded by both participants and the consultant as successful. Some differences were resolved, and although other differences persisted, both principals believed they had established a basis for continuing to work on the issues. Further reports confirmed that the confrontation had been a significant factor in the improvement which occurred in their relationship and indicated that the consultant had played an important role in the confrontation.

Analysis of the confrontation suggests the functions performed by the third party. First, the consultant's presence facilitated openness in the confrontation, which enabled the parties to get the issues out and to redefine intergroup issues as interpersonal problems where appropriate. Both previously had participated in separate one-week sensitivity training workshops where high openness is normative. The consultant who was identified with sensitivity training emphasized the relevance of that prior sensitivity experience and made other attempts to invoke the norm of openness.

Second, the consultant was a synchronizing element. Arranging for the consultant's presence for a specific meeting served to create and confirm mutual expectations that they would confront their outstanding differences. Different expectations and different degrees of readiness often result in one person feeling "caught off guard" by another's attempt to raise the issues. The person who isn't prepared or doesn't recognize the other's attempt at confrontation certainly won't respond satisfactorily. Then the person whose attempt to confront is not reciprocated subsequently may well feel he overexposed himself and react by himself avoiding discussion of their issues in the future. Once Bill and Lloyd were into an exploration of their differences, the limited time availability of the consultant added further pressure to somewhat offset a natural tendency for the participants to smooth over their differences.

Third, the participants perceived the consultant as possessing behavioral skills and techniques which they could call upon if necessary. They believed that they ran less risk that the confrontation would bog down, get repetitive, and result in more frustration and bitterness. As a result, they entered into the meeting with more readiness.

Finally, the consultant both helped diagnose the underlying issues and provided an ingredient of emotional support for the participants. The third party listened to each discuss his views and feelings and sharpened what he understood to be an issue; the participants then responded in ways which tended to confirm or disconfirm that this was the underlying issue. An effort was made to state the issues in ways which made each person's position understandable, legitimate, and acceptable. One apparent effect of this was to encourage Lloyd to go on to identify the more personal concerns he had about not being involved and not being recognized as a competent person with experience relevant to the project.

ROLE ATTRIBUTES AND INTERVENTIONS: A SUMMARY

A third party may be related to the principals as an organizational superior, consultant, separate coordinating unit, or peer. These four role relationships differ in many respects, including the magnitude and types of power available to the third party, the degree of impartiality likely to be attributed to the third party, and the degree of relevant knowledge possessed by the third party. We can summarize how these and other aspects of the role relationships of a third party govern which of the four types of interventions are available to him.

Superiors

Superiors are the only third parties likely to have the organizational power to reduce conflict potential by restructuring the organization or reassigning personnel. Also, assuming that a superior's responsibility embraces both units, his view would be balanced enough to play this third party role. The main difficulty is that superiors often do not have an adequate information base or diagnostic framework by which to assess the dysfunctional consequences of conflict and the basic underlying causes. Moreover, elimination of the factors which induced the dysfunctional conflict in the first instance may not significantly reduce the conflict because of the number of self-reinforcing and regenerating processes involved in the relationship pattern.[37] Hence, structural interventions to reduce conflict potential need to be accompanied by process or clinical interventions to facilitate the change in lateral relationships.

Organization superiors can be too little or too much involved in the substance of a dispute. If deciding the issue requires unique judgment, he should be involved. He is more likely to be brought into the conflict if he tends to view interunit differences as based on task realities rather than arising from the emotional interreactions of line subordinates. However, substantive intervention by superiors runs the risk of creating "win-lose" reactions on the part of subordinates, especially if his action on the issue is intended merely to avoid further effects of the conflict process rather than to contribute unique knowledge.

Superiors sometimes facilitate the process of confronting and solving differences. To do this, a superior needs certain behavioral skills rather than unique knowledge about the issue in dispute. High organizational power is a mixed blessing to him in promoting problem-solving. On the one hand, he can require subordinates to change their gross pattern of interunit contact. On the other hand, his high power may inhibit

the participants and discourage them from taking the personal risks associated with
sharpening the issues in dispute. Similarly, high organizational power complicates a
third party's attempts to create a nonevaluative social-emotional climate conducive
to identifying and working through negative interunit attitudes.

737
*Walton: Third Party
Roles in Conflict*

Organizational Consultants

The organizational consultant lacks the superior's power to modify directly the conflict potential factors or to decide the substantive issues in dispute. However, he is
usually in a relatively better position to influence the interaction processes. This is
true to the extent that the consultant is perceived to have little or no preference regarding the outcome of a dispute, to have both objectivity and expertise which make him a
fruitful source of diagnostic insight, to be nonevaluative, to be a source of emotional
support, and to have high skills in facilitating interaction processes. The consultant
can be used first to help the subordinate departments identify the organizational factors
contributing to the conflict. Then, in association with organizational changes designed
to reduce conflict potential, the consultant third party can facilitate the change in actual
relationships.

Although we have not treated the problem here in any detail, it should be noted
that the interpersonal styles and institutional props which create the appropriate role
identity for consultant third parties are often as important as his active interventions.

Coordinating Units

Given the need for interdepartmental coordination, the more differentiated are the
basic department's orientations, the more likely it is that a continuous, specialized
third party can contribute to the resolution of inter-unit conflicts. If organizational differentiation is not great the interventions of a third party can reduce rather than enhance coordination.

The separate coordinative units studied were all intended to manage interdepartmental differences via substantive contributions to decision-making. The requisite
role attributes for this type of intervention are balanced (or intermediate) orientation,
high substantive knowledge, and moderately high organizational power (relative to
the basic departments).

Peer Units

There is very little evidence of peer organizational units performing neutral third party
roles. Perhaps there is little reward and high risk associated with informally taking on
third party functions. A peer organizational unit may have certain inherent disadvantages. First, it would not have the high power of a superior. Second, it would not
have the substantive expertise of a coordinative unit. Third, typically, it would have an
even more difficult time than a superior or a separate coordinative group in convincing
the disputants that it had a balanced orientation. Fourth, it probably would not possess
the process skills of the organizational consultant.

Ambiguous Organizational Role Relationships

The State Department's relationship to the other foreign affairs agencies is an ambiguous mixture of the various types treated here. It is primarily a peer unit, but with legitimacy for certain supervisory and coordinative functions. State lacks authority to modify the basic structure within which the agencies deal with each other. Nevertheless, State personnel have an opportunity to design certain joint task activities and provide task leadership.

The studies reported on here focused on officials who had relatively high behavioral skill which they used to improve interagency relationships. In particular, they took advantage of slightly higher organizational power and status and higher task information in order to design and lead collaborative task activities, which in turn created group membership and norms more favorable to the constructive management of interagency differences.

CONCLUSION

The present treatment is tentative and less than comprehensive in treating the range of issues involved in third party analysis. Under what conditions is it useful to intervene? What are the optimum third party role attributes for resolving types of conflicts? How are these role attributes established? By individual? Or by organization? When should an intervention be specific to a dispute? When should it treat the relationship? When should it focus on the conflict potential in the organizational context? These questions are important enough to warrant much additional research.

NOTES AND REFERENCES

1. This research was supported by AF 49(638)–1751, ARPA contract for "The Role of Third Parties in Conflict Resolution and Control."
2. James D. Thompson, "Organizational Management of Conflict," *Administrative Science Quarterly*, IV (1960), pp. 389–409.
3. Richard E. Walton, "Theory of Conflict in Lateral Organizational Relationships," in J. R. Lawrence, editor, *Operational Research and the Social Sciences* (London: Tavistock, 1966), pp. 409–28.
4. *Ibid.*
5. Wilfred Brown, *Explorations in Management* (London: Tavistock, 1960); Henry A. Landsberger, "The Horizontal Dimension in a Bureaucracy," *Administrative Science Quarterly*, VI (1961), pp. 298–333.
6. Eugene Litwak, "Models of Bureaucracy Which Permit Conflict," *American Journal of Sociology*, LXVII (1961), pp. 177–84.
7. Thompson, *op. cit.*
8. Brown, *op cit.*, p. 69.
9. George Strauss, "Work-Flow Frictions, Interfunctional Rivalry, and Professionalism: A Case Study of Purchasing Agents," *Human Organization*, XXIII (1964), pp. 137–49.
10. Brown, *op. cit.*
11. Robert R. Blake, Herbert A. Shepard, and Jane S. Mouton, *Intergroup Conflict in Organizations* (Ann Arbor, Mich.: Foundation for Research on Human Behavior, 1964).

12. Paul R. Lawrence and Jay W. Lorsch, *New Directions for Organizations* (Boston: Graduate School of Business Administration, Harvard University, 1967).

13. Myer N. Zald, "Power Balance and Staff Conflict in Correctional Institutions," *Administrative Science Quarterly*, VII (1962), pp. 22–49.

14. Melville Dalton, *Men Who Manage* (New York: Wiley, 1959).

15. Richard E. Walton, John M. Dutton, and H. G. Fitch, "A Study of Conflict in the Process, Structure, and Attitudes of Lateral Relationships," in Albert Rubenstein and Chadwick Haberstroh, editors, *Some Theories of Organization* (Rev. ed.: Homewood, Ill.: Irwin, 1966), pp. 444–65.

16. John A. Seiler, "Diagnosing Interdepartmental Conflict," *Harvard Business Review*, XLI (September–October, 1963), pp. 121–32.

17. Louis R. Pondy, *Organizational Conflict: Concepts and Models* (mimeographed, Graduate School of Business, University of Pittsburgh, 1965).

18. Richard E. Walton, *Interagency Coordination in the Overseas Mission* (mimeographed, 1966).

19. Brown, *op. cit.*

20. Rensis Likert, *New Patterns of Management* (New York: McGraw-Hill, 1961).

21. Blake, Shepard, and Mouton, *op. cit.*, p. 109.

22. Tom Burns and G. M. Stalker, *The Management of Innovation* (London: Tavistock, 1961).

23. Warren Schmidt and Robert Tannenbaum, "The Management of Differences," *Harvard Business Review*, XXXVIII (November–December, 1960), pp. 107–15.

24. Blake, Shepard, and Mouton, *op. cit.*

25. "Theory of Conflict . . ."

26. Lawrence and Lorsch, *op. cit.*

27. Schmidt and Tannenbaum, *op. cit.*

28. Richard E. Walton and Robert B. McKersie, "Behavioral Dilemmas in Mixed Motive Decision Making," *Behavioral Science*, XI (1966), pp. 370–84.

29. Blake, Shepard, and Mouton, *op. cit.*

30. Richard E. Walton, *A Centripetal Force in Foreign Affairs* (mimeographed, 1967).

31. Walton, *Interagency Coordination.* . . .

32. The "Think Tank" is very similar to an informal problem-solving and strategic-thinking group at Case Institute of Technology, which referred to itself as the "Hats Group" because each person was expected to leave his departmental hat at the door.

33. Chris Argyris, *Interpersonal Competence and Organizational Effectiveness* (Homewood, Ill.: Dorsey, 1962); Edgar H. Schein and Warren G. Bennis, *Personal and Organizational Change Through Group Methods: The Laboratory Approach* (New York: Wiley, 1965).

34. Blake, Shepard, and Mouton, *op. cit.*, p. 116.

35. *Ibid.*, p. 117.

36. Richard E. Walton, "Interpersonal Confrontation and Basic Third Party Roles: A Case Study," *Journal of Applied Behavioral Science* (1967).

37. John M. Dutton and Richard E. Walton, "Interdepartmental Conflict and Cooperation: Two Contrasting Studies," *Human Organization*, XXV (1966), pp. 207–20.

The Corporate Ombudsman
Isidore Silver

One of the most publicized and intriguing conflict management techniques in recent years has been the ombudsman. It is a device adapted from Scandinavian govern-ment practice to give lower level personnel an equitable hearing before higher authorities. The following selections, one by Silver and one from Business Week, examine the position and how it is used in different institutions.

"The modern corporation is no longer merely a unit of economic production; it is a dispenser of justice." Although this quote is mythical, it does not differ significantly from a statement by Frank Abrams, retired chairman of the board of Standard Oil:

> "The job of professional management is to conduct the affairs of the enterprise in its charge in such a way as to maintain an equitable and workable balance among the claims of the various interested groups – stockholders, employees, customers, and the public at large."[1]

A management text points out, "No one can exercise power effectively these days without conveying the conviction that he does so responsibly, that is, with justice."[2] Thus some concept of justice is certainly close to, if not encompassed within, the heart of corporate awareness of its social responsibilities.

Yet corporate justice, especially to the company's nonunion employees – as envisaged by Abrams – is incomplete unless some mechanism to review management decisions is established by top management itself. The function of such a mechanism would be to assure an impartial outlet for an employee's dissatisfaction with decisions adverse to him. If the corporation is to provide fair and equal treatment to employees, it should ideally combine the virtue of fair-mindedness with the necessities of thrift and efficiency. Such an impartial grievance outlet exists in the political world and, I would argue, could readily be adapted to the corporate realm. It is the institution of the ombudsman.

The ombudsman has come to America's startled attention as a kind of Scandinavian fairy tale. A superficial reading of the press (which, these days, is filled with intriguing speculation on the subject) could lead one to believe that this strangely named fellow is a knight-errant, armed with great investigative and punitive powers, who will save us all from overweening bureaucracy. Accordingly, he is conceived of as the representa-tive of an aggrieved citizenry, cutting through red tape and bureaucratic boondoggling, reversing unfair decisions, and righting numerous (if not continuous) official wrongs. Unfortunately, but inevitably, such a simplistic view describes a Don Quixote rather than a harried Scandinavian public servant.

If the ombudsman is not Douglas Fairbanks, then who is he? What does he do? And why does he set the hearts of all "little men" aflame? The ombudsman is, quite simply, a person of some eminence, learned in the law, who is appointed by a legislative body to inquire into complaints against administrative officials and to make periodic reports about his findings. He is responsible only to the appointing authority.

The ombudsmen who now operate in Sweden (where the system started in 1809), and in Denmark, Norway, Finland, and New Zealand (much more recently) have varying powers. In Sweden, for instance, the ombudsman is empowered to commence prosecutions against officials who have violated the law in particular administrative situations. In Denmark, he can comment on the quality of administration and suggest better administrative methods. In all countries, he is empowered to investigate the basis of any decision, whether or not there has been a complaint, and to make his findings public. The system has been favorably commented on by those Americans who have studied it, and it is the subject of much serious discussion in respectable political circles.

Manifold Advantages

Although he has no power to change any decisions, the mere possibility of criticism by the ombudsman encourages administrators to find sufficient reasons for their decisions. Some countries publicize the ombudsman's findings, and this imposes yet another constraint. Observations seem to confirm that administrative decisions are often made more thoughtfully now than in pre-ombudsman days.

The ombudsman has the great virtue of being "visible." Persons aggrieved by administrative decisions know that there is someone they can turn to for impartial investigation. They may not know where else they can go in the bureaucratic maze, but the ombudsman is there. Generally, even when the political ombudsman dismisses a particular claim as being insubstantial, he satisfies the claimant's desire for a full and fair investigation, although the investigation itself may only consist of an appraisal in an office and a courteous letter denying the claim. Thus the raw edges of conflict are rubbed smooth, and in human affairs this is no inconsiderable achievement.

The ombudsman also serves to vindicate administrative decision making where such decision is just. Interestingly, most administrative decisions, even the contested ones, are reasonable. The Danish ombudsman, for example, censures officials in only 5% of the cases before him. Indeed, he takes only 15% of the complaints submitted. Extant information clearly demonstrates that administrators now regard the ombudsman system as a protective device—rather than a hindrance at worst, or a nuisance at best. Since most of the investigated administrative decisions have proved to be just, the initial bureaucratic antipathy toward the ombudsman has become transformed into wholehearted acceptance. Walter Gellhorn, the leading authority on the subject, concludes, "The ombudsman's work has indubitably had a tonic effect upon public administration."[3]

Prescribed Limitations

Much of this acceptance of the ombudsman is engendered by certain prescribed limitations on his authority. He can only investigate and recommend; he cannot reverse particular decisions. He cannot attack an exercise of discretion (except in Norway, where he may find that a particular decision is "unjust," and in New Zealand, where he may think it is "wrong"). He cannot make policy decisions, although he is empowered to make recommendations for policy changes on the basis of his investigative findings. The available evidence indicates that the policy recommendation aspect of his function is the weakest; thus, his primary role is to act in limited defense of the "little man" against the arbitrary "bureaucrat" and not to reform basic procedures.

WHY JUSTICE IS NEEDED

Lest anyone doubt the necessity of providing justice to employees, let us pause a moment. There are two primary reasons for this need:

(1) Management itself genuinely believes the corporation has evolved so that it is now a socially responsible institution. Understandably, however, there is some confusion about the precise meaning of justice in the corporate context.
(2) It is clearly in the long-range interest of the corporation to seek mechanisms to effect employee justice. If justice is a dominant value of American life, there can be no question that corporate employees bring this value into the office in the morning and leave with it at night. Employees expect justice in their lives and cannot arbitrarily divorce their existence into "work" and "leisure" components. People do not create such simple categories, in either their conscious or their psychological lives. An employee who feels that his legitimate grievances are being justly dealt with cannot help but be a better employee, and more importantly, a better citizen.

Existence of Conflict

Another reason why justice is needed is related to what might be called the "communications gap," which often creates organizational conflict. Indeed, one of the great problems of corporate life, and a cause for frequent grievance, is not the unfairness of management actions, but the inexplicability. It is ironic that in our overcommunicative society, communications breakdowns frequently occur. Even in corporations—where internal communications networks are the lifeblood of their activity—decisions are sometimes made without adequate explanation. Often, such decisions appear to be arbitrary when in fact they are not. Equally often, work discontent is caused by a lack of understanding as to the reasons for such apparently unfavorable decisions. Even what at first blush appears to be "insubordination" may well be nothing more than a communications gap. One arbitrator observes:

> Authority is exercised by people. Insubordination is always man against man. It involves tempers, personalities, problems of communication, and differing points of view. Did the employee understand the order? Did he realize beyond all question that he was violating it? . . . Did he try to make amends . . . ?[4]

The failure is by no means one-way. "Clearing the air" is frequently more efficacious to everyone involved than "changing the decision."

Management should not, and generally does not, deceive itself about the existence of conflict within organizations. The wise corporate manager recognizes the existence of conflict (what the employee's superiors in the organization want him to do and what others who influence him want him to do) and job ambiguity (what he is supposed to do). These forms of conflict result in stress (not only job stress), and recent studies confirm this: "Conflict and ambiguity are among the major characteristics of our society, and . . . are among the unintended consequences of . . . the growth of large-scale organizations."[5]

The existence of conflict does not end there. The modern corporation finds itself greatly in need of ever more skilled and, indeed, professional employees. A modern enterprise simply cannot maximize its economic and technological goals without an educated, intellectually equipped cadre. Educated people come to the corporation with great expectations; they want more intellectual comforts — in the form of autonomy and responsibility — than their predecessors desired. They want to do "meaningful" work and to have their work respected by their superiors. These desires are not unreasonable, and they must be recognized if the corporation is to retain a fair proportion of these educated employees.

Further, professional people such as lawyers, accountants, and scientists are imbued with professional goals which include peer esteem, job integrity, and opportunity for research. But these goals often conflict with corporate goals based on other considerations (the need to meet competition or the need to control the innovative process). Neither of these sets of goals — professional and corporate — is good or bad per se; both are worthy, and their reconciliation is a legitimate concern of corporate management. Astute management should reasonably move to meet the expectations of professional employees, despite those inherent conflicts with corporate goals. Often, of course, this does not happen, and the professional turnover rate mounts.

Even beyond the issue of conflicting employee-company goals, contemporary managers of economically powerful modern corporations are currently pondering the problem of deciding to what primary ethic the company feels itself bound. Is its duty to the shareholder? If so, how can management justify charitable contributions which result in a lessened dividend? Is there a duty to the community in which the company operates? If so, can management ever move a plant from a town dependent on it? If the community is in the South, should management adhere to local mores and not hire Negroes, for instance?

Perhaps one answer to the problem is to recognize a duty to these and other groups, but to argue that the primary duty is to the enterprise itself — to ensure future growth and continued functioning as a profit-making supplier of goods and services.

Of course, management perceives other goals which take precedence over profit. The corporation pays taxes because what is good for society is good for the corporation. It contributes to charity both because it is "right" to do so and to enhance its image and sense of participation in the community. It pays dividends to retain favor among present shareholders and to make itself attractive to potential shareholders. It curbs its own initiatives to avoid costly economic and legal battles with others (and also because it recognizes its substantial economic power).

Surely, there is as great an interest in satisfying employees, and that interest should properly be countervailing to any interest in short-term profits. Indeed, an interest in long-term profits may be more directly enhanced by recognizing the claims of its employee-citizens than by acknowledging some of the previously mentioned demands.

CURRENT PROCEDURES

Given the need for corporate justice, is an ombudsman necessary? Does the corporate community presently have the mechanisms for dispensing equity? Are other grievance institutions available? There is little hard information on hand, since grievance procedures, if any, are kept flexible and informal. Apparently, particular grievances are resolved by (a) "grinning" (or grudging) and "bearing" them, (b) resigning from the corporate community, or (c) using available "political" means within the corporate hierarchy to compel a reversal of the adverse decision.

None of these existing grievance mechanisms are desirable, from either the corporation's or the employee's point of view, since the likely results are impaired efficiency, in (a) and (c); costly retraining, in (b); or fellow employee or immediate superior resentment, in (c). Clearly, the ends of corporate justice are not satisfied by these unpleasant alternatives; in addition, economic costs are increased.

Formal Systems

Some corporations, including IBM, utilize the famous "open-door" policy, whereby aggrieved employees are encouraged to step in and see some executive (or perhaps even a member of the board of directors).

The significant question here is whether the procedure is effective; and, lacking hard evidence, the pragmatic answer would seem to be *no*. An employee who feels he has a legitimate grievance may not necessarily know where to go. He may accost a harried executive who, in effect, shrugs him off. He may be confronted by a superior who may not wish to "weaken" a position taken by another manager. If a particular factual dispute exists, an executive may not have the time to investigate the facts. Also, an executive approached at a particular moment by a particular employee may lack the information to determine how other employees similarly situated have been treated. Moreover, however great his goodwill and sincerity of interest, the average executive may simply be unequipped to deal with the ramifications of an apparently innocuous complaint.

On the other hand, the inclination not to waste an executive's time with a trivial complaint may result in an employee's acquiescence to the adverse decision—and increased personal tensions.

Beyond these factors, there is always the imponderable middle-management ethic that a gentleman does not resort to these procedures, even if they are available. If a subordinate finds himself unable to work out a decent relationship with a superior, he may quit (or at least seek a transfer) before overtly challenging management authority. Certainly, an outstanding characteristic of all management appeal systems, including those discussed in this article, is the failure to utilize them, often in situations fully appropriate for such use. Here, both the corporation and the employee suffer in the name of a dubious ethic. Also, there may be a belief that future promotion may depend on *not* using the available system.

While some corporations have institutionalized other forms of appeal, such as a one- or two-step review of initial management action, the effectiveness of these procedures is always questionable. Such systems tend to be rigid and time-consuming for all involved, and the harassed judge, rather than take the time necessary to review the case thoroughly, often makes the all too human choice to substantiate a lower-level decision. Moreover, a lower-level decision tends to place a strong burden of proof on the aggrieved—as one political ombudsman observes:

> The first decision, even if made at a relatively low official level, tends to generate its own defenses. . . . The official bias is toward maintenance of the original decision, and accordingly an objection must generally bear the onus of demonstrating manifest error. . . .[6]

Even more lamentable, there is no fact-finding mechanism to resolve the more serious disputes; indeed, it is often difficult to ascertain what the first supervisor regarded as a "fact."

Informal Appeals

Corporations frequently operate according to informal, rather than formal, procedures. It is conceivable that personnel departments might play crucial roles, especially where the ultimate management sanction—dismissal—is contemplated. Some corporations might require a countersignature of the vice president in charge of industrial or personnel relations under these circumstances, and a "strong" vice president might well "fight for" someone he believes to be a victim of caprice.

Yet the few studies on the subject, and my own personal observations, indicate that the personnel department generally regards itself as a service adjunct to the other divisions of the corporation. Rarely does it seriously question a decision from the "line" —and justifiably so, since it has no independent role within the corporation. In fact, many of the corporations which have attempted to institute an appeals policy do not even use the personnel department as a primary feature of their system.

In sum, corporate appeals procedures—where they exist—are ineffective. As one scholar of the subject puts it:

> In recent years, a few firms have introduced a form of appeals procedure which permits nonunion employees to question management decisions, but the number of these firms is small and the handicaps great.[7]

Clearly, then, corporate justice is not being achieved. This is not because of existing arbitrariness or maliciousness, but because of a lack of knowledge—both of facts and of defined standards by which human conduct is to be judged.

It must be emphasized that corporate injustice is not the primary reason for having an ombudsman. In New Zealand, "The ombudsman was created not to clean up a mess, but, rather, simply to provide insurance against further messes."[8] Preventive medicine is often more vital than harsh cures. Corporations can, and should, regard the ombudsman proposal as a valuable device to prevent future injustice.

WHERE HE FITS IN

How would the ombudsman operate in the corporate context? To whom would he be responsible? What are the limits of his functions? If corporate justice means that an aggrieved employee must be provided with a fair and effective means of stating "his case" to an impartial person who has investigative powers, then it is clear that the ombudsman must be understood to be just such a person. Hence, he must be "of" rather than "in" the corporation. If the ombudsman is thought of as just another management functionary, then his most important attribute—that of perceived impartiality —is destroyed.

Chancellor's Role

In addition, the ombudsman must be thought of as something more than a mere "stage" in a dispute-resolution process. He must be deemed to represent the ultimate decision-making authority in the corporation, and he can only do this if he is a member of the president's personal staff. The president of the corporation is recognized (in both corporate and political society) as the embodiment of the corporation. He is the ultimate authority within the corporation and stands in much the same position as did the medieval king to his society.

The prerogative of the medieval king extended to the rendering of "justice," to the granting of clemency even where justice had been achieved, and to the exercise of the "conscience" of the state. The same is true of the corporate president; by virtue of his position and authority, he is perceived to be the conscience of the corporation. Just as the king exercised his powers to dispense justice through a chancellor, so the president needs someone with the time and facilities to conduct investigations, and to render advice. In effect, the ombudsman would stand in the role of chancellor to the president.

The role of the president itself must be more than formalistic. While political society provides the means to review administrative decisions which substantially affect the lives and liberties of individuals, such safeguards do not exist on the corporate level. Whereas political decisions often affect only a portion of a person's total interests, a corporate decision may affect his continued presence in the organization or even his future chances for gainful employment. Since most corporations do not provide any formal means of appeal and reconsideration of particular decisions, and indeed are seldom geared to do so, the role of the president becomes crucial.

The corporate ombudsman must be a member of the president's personal staff to ensure prestige. He must have an independence similar to that enjoyed by his political counterpart. In corporate terms, he must have a long-term contract at substantial pay. In a fundamental sense, he should function as the "eyes" and "ears" of the president and should acquaint higher management with the problems he perceives at lower levels. A wisely used ombudsman would serve as a source of information about personnel problems. (This is often true of the role of the arbitrator in union-management disputes.) In addition, of course, the ombudsman would be management's conscience.

Broad Authority

The ombudsman's powers should — within their proper sphere — be broad. Therefore, he should have the authority to investigate *any* written complaint by *any* aggrieved employee (with certain exceptions to be discussed later). And he should also have the authority to dismiss any complaint, with or without a hearing, subject to the duty of stating reasons for such a dismissal in writing.

The value of detailed, complete, and informative answers to a complaint cannot be overlooked. Management literature is replete with statements to the effect that "no one ever actually told me what they expect of me." As one analysis concludes:

> Much as he would like to 'do right' by the organization, [an employee] does not know what doing right means. Moreover, he learns only indirectly that he has failed; his job is taken away without explanation, or at least one that he can understand and accept. It is perhaps understandable that his feelings of helplessness and futility are expressed with a touch of bitterness.[9]

Where two "languages" are spoken, the ombudsman's most vital role may well be that of interpreter.

Why this virtually unlimited power to entertain complaints? As we shall see, his function requires that certain types of complaints be dismissed. But this is far different from arguing that he should not have the power to entertain them, and to make the initial determination of whether they fall within his competence. As an arbitrator has said, "Whether a man has a grievance or not is primarily his own feeling about the matter. Generally speaking, if a man thinks he has a grievance, he has a grievance."[10]

This power to assume jurisdiction is vital; it assures every employee (within certain categories) that the complaint will be looked at and will not merely be dismissed out of hand, with no explanation or a feeble statement relating to jurisdiction. It assures even the employee whose complaint is dismissed that his particular case at least has been looked at. Most importantly, having broad powers frees the ombudsman from getting embroiled in arguments about his jurisdiction and the inevitable discords and irritants which follow jurisdictional determinations.

HOW HE FUNCTIONS

Once he assumes jurisdiction and decides that a complaint is meritorious *on its face*, his power to act should parallel that of his political counterpart. Thus he may call for the employee file if the question raised can be answered by an examination of that record. He should have the power to obtain that information.

If a factual dispute is involved, the ombudsman should be able to call in company witnesses for informal conferences in a *nonadversary* setting. (If the problem involves technical considerations—such as measurement of the quality of work—the ombudsman should be able to call in any technical expert from within or, if necessary, from outside the corporation for his opinion.) On the other hand, if the facts remain in dispute, an *adversary* confrontation might be called for, and the ombudsman might act as "devil's advocate" for both sides. At any stage of the process, the ombudsman should have the sole discretionary power to dismiss the complaint.

Policy Interpreter

After a complaint is filed, the ombudsman must ascertain and interpret corporate policy on the matter at issue. For example, perhaps the practice of the corporation has traditionally been to permit a certain form of conduct which technically breaks a rule. If the rule is now to be invoked against a particular individual, there should be a reason for such deviation from the traditional practice. If the corporation decides, as a matter of policy, to enforce the regulation, then the employees should be forewarned about it. Since corporate "law" consists of what is knowingly tolerated as well as what is formally forbidden, fairness demands that prior warning of potential violation be afforded. Thus the legal principle of *nulla poena sine lege* ("no punishment without law") should be honored.

If a particular manager is attempting to enforce what he conceives to be corporate policy when, in fact, such policy either is nonexistent or is not adhered to, then the ombudsman has the duty to point this out. Indeed, to quote Gellhorn again, his "greatest effectiveness appears in cases that involve departures from accepted norms, and not in cases where he must deal with clashes of values."[11] In short, the ombudsman should function to clarify true, as distinct from formal, corporate policy, and to acquaint the unknowing with that policy.

Decision Recommender

Once the ombudsman makes a ruling in a given case, he should write it down and submit it both to the complainant and to the manager involved before the president ever sees it. It should be remembered that the ombudsman's ruling is cast in the form of a recommendation, and its only value is persuasive. The reason for initial submission to the disputing parties is obvious: they may well concede that the "decision" is reasonable and voluntarily agree to adhere to it. Sometimes, and this has occurred, his recommendation contains additional facts to justify an ultimate reversal of the original management decision.

Agreement is likely, since most disputes are the result of (a) misunderstanding about the nature of the initial action taken by management, (b) lack of knowledge of the factual basis for the initial decision, or (c) a misunderstood corporate policy which constitutes the basis for that decision. There can be little doubt that the primary function of the ombudsman here, as in political life, is simply to clarify the basis for a particular and generally correct decision.

If the manager disagrees with the ombudsman's finding, he may wish to hold a conference for the purpose of presenting more facts or to argue that there is an error in the ombudsman's reasoning. This is perfectly compatible with the ombudsman's functions and should be encouraged. The ombudsman, in turn, should reconsider any of his recommendations, on the request either of the manager or of the aggrieved—and he may find that he should change the recommendation in the light of a new perspective.

Of course, this procedural flexibility should never be thought of as a convenient means of placating an irate manager. The intrinsic value of the system is severely undermined if the ombudsman quakes in the face of a managerial storm. On the other hand, the ombudsman must often be a politician—in the legitimate sense of the word—and if he can achieve a particular goal indirectly, he should do so. After all, a respected politician is called a statesman.

In cases where the manager contests the recommendation, the ombudsman may refer the entire matter to the president. At that point the ombudsman's function ceases, and the final outcome lies within the president's discretion. Of course, the president may call on the ombudsman (a) to explain or to amplify the reasoning underlying the recommendation, or (b) to consider possible revisions or novel factors that might change the recommendation. And the ombudsman may choose to do so, just as the president may choose to follow or to reject the advice which he is offered. The two functions, recommending and deciding, remain completely separate, and no power in the world should force one on the other.

Complaint Denier

If the ombudsman decides to deny the complaint, then the matter is ended. Although in some ideal sense it might be desirable to permit the employee to "appeal" over the ombudsman's head, this would be valueless to the corporation. It would diminish the importance of the ombudsman; he would come to be regarded as only the first step in the corporation's appeals procedure, rather than as the focus of that procedure. Since most complaints are insubstantial, any institutionalized form of appeal would serve to duplicate unnecessary work and would, in effect, constitute a return to an inadequate open-door policy.

Perhaps a fastidious president, concerned with the problem of who serves as the "conscience" of the "conscience," would request the ombudsman to submit copies of all denials of complaints to him. Thus an occasional unconscionable decision (and ombudsmen are doubtlessly capable of making them) might be overruled by this informal method.

SPECIFIC BOUNDARIES

Certain formal limitations should be imposed on the ombudsman's authority. For instance, two classes of employees automatically excluded from the system would be unionized personnel and top management.

Exempt Personnel

Top management—a term including corporate officers and divisional vice presidents, and somewhat ambiguously including others beyond them—simply functions too intimately with the president to come under the ombudsman's jurisdiction. At the top management level, the relationships are too personal, the conflicts too broad, and the standards for questioning judgments simply too ill-defined for an ombudsman. To turn to a political analogy, the president of a corporation is to his top executives as the President of the United States is to his Cabinet. The subordinates in each case are the president's "men" and serve only at his pleasure (although the corporate board of directors may have an additional role here).

Jurisdictional coverage at the top level by an ombudsman would embroil him in the kind of fundamental battles that are beyond the scope of his position. After all, he functions to carry out corporate policy (or to define it in narrow situations) and not to participate in its creation. Just as the U.S. Supreme Court never enjoins a war, so the ombudsman never interferes with the fundamental decision-making rights of top management.

For equally compelling reasons, employees subject to labor union contracts that contain grievance procedures are also exempt. They already have a system which affords a considerable degree of protection. In addition, union-management relations, always difficult at best, would be strained further by a procedure which excludes union influence on the dispute-resolution process.

Policy Issues

The ombudsman likewise exercises no jurisdiction where the contest involves clear company policy of general application. As Gellhorn points out, "The broad contours of ... administration ... are primarily questions for political determination."[12] For example, a mandatory policy of retirement at age 65, operating equally (or unequally) but rationally, should preclude claims by the production manager who wants to stay on after 65. Policy questions such as this are simply beyond the reasonable scope of any powers conferred on an ombudsman.

Yet there may be an area where the company has a general policy which works a particular hardship either on an individual or on a limited group of individuals. Here the ombudsman need not necessarily dismiss a complaint. For instance, in a company which has a mandatory policy of job relocation as new plants or offices in different cities open up, all staff employees are subject to relocation. But if a particular employee has a strong reason for contesting such an assignment (e.g., if he has already moved twice in the past four years, or he has a sick relative and someone else in his department can more readily be moved), any grievance on that issue falls within the jurisdiction of the ombudsman.

Note that the essential differences between the two situations just discussed involve a general corporate policy applicable to all (mandatory age 65 retirement) and a policy applicable to only a limited group (those who are actually asked to move). In the first case, the policy is defeated by granting a particular claim; in the second, it is not.

But policy issues are of little significance in the corporate context, since most problems arise because of the exercise of management discretion. Policy is often stated broadly, but its implementation is generally discretionary. Thus employees are urged to act in the "best interests" of the company. But what does this mean? Who defines it? What standards are being used? These questions of discretion constitute the vast majority of present personnel problems, and they would certainly constitute the focus of a corporate ombudsman's concerns.

CORPORATE FEARS

There are, of course, legitimate objections to a corporate ombudsman system. Clearly, a manager who must submit a particular decision to someone else's scrutiny (and perhaps have to defend it personally) is bound to be somewhat restrained in making that decision. Yet the restraint often can be a beneficial one, since it allows him to weigh, in advance, the utility of the action against the potential harm to an individual. He may even see possible (and perhaps better) alternatives before he takes an action that may create conflict. It may even help managers at all levels to understand what is happening and to require subordinates to exercise discretion reasonably.

Would some managers "freeze" into immobility and refuse to act? Perhaps. But the manager who believes his action is correct should not freeze; if he believes that his action cannot be rationally justified, why should he take it in the first place? There are few emergency situations which compel completely unpremeditated action. When an emergency arises, the dynamic manager "acts," and the last concern on his mind is that of accountability to someone else. If the situation is less urgent, perhaps precipitous action is unwarranted, and accountability is then a consideration in the manager's mind.

'Flood of Litigation'

Possibly, the very existence of an ombudsman would encourage filing of numerous frivolous complaints; managers would spend all of their time answering baseless accusations, and corporate efficiency would be impaired. In law, this is called the "flood of litigation" argument. However, such fears usually prove to be unfounded. Rarely does the trickle of complaints become a flood. Arbitration was questioned on these very grounds initially, but statistics show that there was little cause to worry. To cite one example:

> During an $8\frac{1}{2}$-year period, Bethlehem Steel experienced 17,000 initial protests against management decisions. Of these, 30% were bargained out prior to arbitration, 58% were dropped altogether, 12% went to arbitration, and only 5% were actually settled by the arbitrator.[13]

Since the ombudsman would enjoy the prerogative of dismissing complaints, he would doubtlessly weed out most of the frivolous ones at their inception. As we have seen, the Danish ombudsman regularly dismisses without any investigation about 85% of all complaints.

Usurpation of Rights

While it is clear that the ombudsman system would tend to weaken the prerogatives of management, the danger that its exercise may be abused is minimal when appropriate institutional safeguards have been provided. Perhaps the best argument against this understandable reservation can be gleaned from political experience. The political ombudsman has served to protect administrators from *their* superiors more often than he has invoked the citizen's interest against the "bureaucrat." Initial bureaucratic animosity toward the ombudsman, evident in every country when the system was originally instituted, rapidly became enthusiastic approval, for that precise reason. Today, a manager may feel his prerogatives are being undermined; tomorrow, he may wish that his superior's "arbitrariness" toward him could be curbed. It is often a matter of whose prerogatives are being gored.

Of course, the ultimate question is really whether the ombudsman system keeps fundamental decision making in the hands of management. If the answer is *yes* — as it is here — then abstract shibboleths should not be invoked to defeat an otherwise reasonable proposal. After all, our society suffers enormously by furnishing criminals with a highly sophisticated system of justice, but most of us agree that we prefer this to living in a society which does otherwise.

Disruptive Intrusion

Another real fear centers about the possible snooper's role of an ombudsman. Would he constantly wander through executive offices, rummage through files, startle secretaries, peer over trembling shoulders to read what someone is writing, and in general play Sherlock Holmes? Such conduct would admittedly disrupt management functioning and create serious problems. The question, while entirely legitimate, fails to take into account the ombudsman's truly limited role.

As I view the corporate ombudsman in this proposal, he generally sits in an office and receives complaints — when and if filed. He conducts an appropriate investigation, often one involving written communications or requests for files. If more information is needed, he calls in the manager involved and requests a conference at a mutually convenient time. Very few cases go further, although it is conceivable that a visit to a particular place might be necessary. Certainly, this can be arranged tactfully and with little disruption. As Gellhorn, in reference to a New Zealand ombudsman, observes:

> Without exception the interviewed public agencies maintained that the ombudsman's access to informal staff notes and other working papers had not had the feared effects.[14]

If a complaint, or a sequence of them, indicates substantial irregularity, then the ombudsman might well become a snooper. But, then, there might well be a substantial problem worth investigating. Most likely, any general problem raised by several complaints would not involve a disruptive investigation; it would merely be the subject of a report to the president. Remember, the ombudsman exists to serve the corporation, not to destroy it. A reasonable sense of tact on his part would preclude any "bull in the china shop" attitude; and unless the corporation is totally mismanaged, there would be no necessity for substantial intrusion into daily operations. If the corporation is totally mismanaged, it is highly unlikely that its management would even consider having an ombudsman.

Are we giving the ombudsman too much power? He has the power only to advise and to dismiss unjustified complaints. He gets no more money or prestige for finding management "guilty." He is not paid by the number of cases he adjudicates. He has no vested interest—such as his own job—to defend. He competes with no one in the organization for power or for limited resources. In short, he is just there. His role is to be objective. His only concern is for the maintenance of corporate integrity toward employees and for the incidence of arbitrary action at almost any level of decision making.

STANDARDS & SOURCES

But how can we be sure that this "saint" will not be governed by whim and caprice, that he will act on a case-to-case basis, or in accordance with some "eternal" principle? If the ombudsman is to be something more than an "uncontrolled" (and erratic) conscience, he must act within a framework provided by the recognized concepts of "due process" of law and the industrial concepts of "just cause" for discipline. If discipline is the issue, for example, due process requires:

- That the policy be known (or at least published) prior to the act.
- That the standard allegedly violated be fairly specific.
- That the charge be stated.
- That some sort of proof in support be adduced at an impartial hearing (if a factual dispute exists).
- That the punishment be appropriate to both the "crime" and the "criminal," which automatically means a curb on the punishment of dismissal.

Body of Precedent

The ombudsman should create, and reasonably follow, a body of precedent. If incompetence is the issue, then the ombudsman should ascertain whether reasonable job requirements for the position existed and were known to the aggrieved employee. If a new job requirement is necessary because the nature of the job has changed, perhaps some advance notice of this—as well as an opportunity to acquire the new skills—should have been afforded. "Insufficient supervision" may well be a defense to disciplinary action, for management has a reasonable retraining obligation. For instance, an ombudsman might well be upset if a production manager who had suddenly been required to write formal reports was discharged because he could not do so at first.

The significant aspect of the ombudsman's role is that he brings sophisticated concepts to an institution whose function is narrow but whose importance is great. A reasonable ombudsman might decide that the right to counsel is unnecessary, since the proceeding is investigative, but that prior warning or inadequate job performance is a prerequisite to disciplinary action.

Then, if there is a hearing, the ombudsman should neither feel bound to strict legal rules of evidence nor permit the introduction of illegally obtained evidence. To use illegal evidence is to encourage antisocial practices; and this is acknowledged by both courts and arbitrators. In particular, damaging evidence *unrelated* to the charge should not be introduced (unless a "second offense" situation is involved), while, on the other hand, some consideration should be given to a previous good employment record.

Thus, within the constraints imposed by corporate life, operative principles of adjusting disputes can be formulated.

Background Possibilities

The ombudsman might be drawn from any one of several sources. He could be a lawyer familiar with corporate operations; it is obviously most desirable to have someone familiar with both environments. Accordingly, an experienced member of the corporate legal division might well serve this function.

Another possibility might be an arbitrator, or ex-arbitrator, who has served in a particular industry and is familiar with its problems. Because such a person has been conditioned by an environment of "industrial jurisprudence," he is likely to have a "feel" for both human relations and corporate necessity, as well as an appreciation of the process of dispute resolution.

A former top executive who has retired or who is interested in human relations problems might also be an effective ombudsman. Although such a man is not likely to be thoroughly familiar with legal principles, he may benefit from numerous educational opportunities in large communities. A night college or even law school course and some intensive reading could provide him with the requisite background. Since due process in this context is often little more than applied wisdom, the basic resources should be present within the individual himself.

It is even conceivable that management might designate a certain official to act as ombudsman and educate him to the role. However, this should not be done as a matter of grace, and it will appear to be just that if he either serves on a part-time basis or is thought of as merely a "management man." If this modus operandi is adopted, he should clearly demonstrate his independence in accordance with the recommendations previously discussed (long-term contract, salary, and so forth).

CONCLUSION

The concept of the corporate ombudsman should not be regarded as an expedient or a temporary device—or worse, as a gimmick. If the institution is to mean something, and not merely be a waste of time, money, and hope, then top management must be prepared to live with it.

The role of the ombudsman is to serve as an embodiment of the corporate conscience. The system proposed in this article is inexpensive. It does not unduly hamper corporate functioning. It should ultimately, if not initially, create a better corporate climate, even if rarely used. As one observer notes:

> An ombudsman's achievement cannot be measured solely by the frequency with which he criticizes administrators. He serves especially well when he dampens hostile suspicions and helps create the public confidence upon which democratic government must be based.[15]

If in the above we substitute the terms "employee" for "public," "corporate" for "democratic," and "should" for "must," we have succinctly stated the ombudsman's true value. Indeed, the corporations that are most likely to adopt this system are probably those *least* in need of it—as is true of their political counterparts. The operative word here is "least," for all human enterprises need an ombudsman. All enterprises involve stress and conflict of one sort or another, and no one can legitimately claim that "his" organization is a haven for his associates. As fallible beings, we may conclude, as does one group of organizational observers:

> The issue, then, is not the elimination of conflict . . . from organizational life; it is the containment of this condition at levels and in forms which are at least human, tolerable, and low in costs, and which might at best be positive in contribution to individual and organization.[16]

A better definition of the need and the role of the ombudsman cannot be found.

The experience of the political ombudsman has demonstrated that he is a most useful tool to society. Nobody, including his initial detractors, wants to give him up. Yet society must be willing to accept him as a check on its accidental and intentional excesses. He can only be successful in his limited role if he is allowed to be; all the power in the world without support is of no consequence.

Ultimate justice obviously cannot be achieved on earth. The ombudsman is not the great panacea for social ill implied by much of the folklore. He has always been, and will continue to be, most effective in cases of petty dimension. Yet political society has found him to be truly indispensable. In all enterprise, justice *felt* is often justice *achieved*. The corporation, in our time, is a "dispenser of justice"—both actual and perceived.

NOTES AND REFERENCES

1. Quoted in "Have Corporations a Higher Duty than Profits?" *Fortune*, August 1960, p. 108.
2. Benjamin M. Selekman, *A Moral Philosophy for Management* (New York, McGraw-Hill Book Company, Inc., paperback edition, 1959), p. 75.
3. *Ombudsmen and Others* (Cambridge, Harvard University Press, 1966), p. 36.
4. Orme W. Phelps, *Discipline and Discharge in the Unionized Firm* (Berkeley, University of California Press, 1959), pp. 98–99.
5. Robert L. Kahn et al., *Organizational Stress* (New York, John Wiley & Sons, Inc., 1964), p. 3.
6. "The New Zealand Ombudsman," as quoted in Gellhorn, op. cit., p. 146.
7. Phelps, op. cit., p. 5.
8. Gellhorn, op. cit., p. 103.
9. Kahn, op. cit., p. 81.
10. Quoted in Frank Elkouri, *How Arbitration Works* (Washington, Bureau of National Affairs Press, 1952), p. 65.
11. Op. cit., p. 44.
12. Op. cit., p. 47.
13. Phelps, op. cit., p. 15.
14. Op. cit., p. 126.
15. Gellhorn, op. cit., p. 142.
16. Kahn, op. cit., p. 387.

Where Ombudsmen Work Out

Business Week

Five years ago the concept of the corporate ombudsman to represent the interests of employees seemed ready to spread through U.S. industry. But the idea has not caught on even though results appear good where it has been tried — as scores of both managers and employees can attest.

Ombudsmen in one form or another had been around for 150 years — usually picked to curb abuses by government against individuals. Corporate use began in 1972 when Xerox Corp. named an ombudsman for its largest division, and General Electric Co. and the Boeing Vertol Co. division of Boeing Co. were quick to follow.

Xerox has expanded the role of its ombudsman so that he now represents most of the company's U.S. employees. GE has two ombudsmen in its Aircraft Engine Group. Boeing Vertol abolished the post a year ago, while retaining the "essence" of the program, says an executive, in an expanded industrial relations section.

One problem is that incorporating an ombudsman into the corporate structure has turned out to be a very tricky business. "Some managers felt very threatened at first by the fact that their subordinates came to me," says Frederica Dunn, who recently moved out of an ombudsman post at GE to another position in the company. "It seemed a reflection on them. Later a fair number of managers recommended that individuals under them come to me. Then many of the managers themselves began coming."

All the ombudsmen agree they must demonstrate that the job is more than window-dressing, and that requires support at the top. At GE the ombudsmen report to the manager of group organization, who reports directly to Gerhard Neumann, vice-president and group executive for the Aircraft Engine Group. "The office draws its power from Neumann," says Lois Campbell, Dunn's replacement at GE. It was Neumann who appointed the first GE ombudsmen in 1973, to give employees "an objective review of their complaints and appeals by a competent third party."

CONFIDENTIAL

Where there is an ombudsman, the most frequent complaints are over salary, job performance appraisal, efforts to find a better job within the company, layoffs, and the scale of employee benefits. Some problems can be solved in just a few hours; others take weeks, and the GE ombudsmen say they each handle about 150 cases a year.

The ombudsman goes to an employee's manager to discuss a grievance only if the employee agrees. If the employee, the manager, and the ombudsman cannot work out a settlement that the ombudsman thinks is fair, the GE ombudsman can go to the manager's manager, all the way to Neumann. But the ombudsmen have no power themselves to overrule managers' decisions.

Confidentiality is important. At Boeing Vertol, ombudsman Eldon Christopher's office was "well back" on the first floor of a wing of the main complex — secluded but near rest rooms, pay telephones, and vending machines. "We put it where it would not seem unusual for anybody to be there," says Christopher. "If anybody became apprehensive about being seen, they could use the toilet or buy a candy bar."

TAKING IT HIGHER

Ombudsmen do not always favor the employee, but they have to be independent enough not to mind ruffling feathers of higher-ups, even when it might damage their own careers. "It certainly should be a career opportunity, but it's not the kind of job that should be sold that way," says Robert H. Gudger, Xerox's first ombudsman, who left the post for a higher-level job just two months ago. "If that word gets around, people start to say, 'You rise in the corporation on our backs.'" Gudger says that about 40% of his decisions favored the employee, 30% were compromises, and 30% went against the employee.

"There was a very low percentage of cases—perhaps 10%—you could do nothing about," says GE's Dunn. In many cases involving promotions, where it was sometimes too late to reverse decisions, and in cases involving performance appraisals, she says, the employee often was not entirely satisfied with what the ombudsman could do. "But in cases where a manager was not responding and the complaint against him was justified, I never had any fear of going the next level up," says Dunn.

Dunn had expected that some employees who had used the ombudsman would be back with complaints that they had experienced retribution for going to her in the first place. It never happened. But Christopher says that employees who felt they had legitimate beefs often feared retaliation. "I simply had to overcome that fear," he says.

One aspect of the ombudsman's job is to recommend fundamental changes in the system where it is producing a multitude of complaints. All three companies, for example, adopted job-posting programs, giving all employees a chance to apply for vacant positions, at least partly as a result of complaints about the way jobs were filled. The Boeing office was also instrumental in introducing flexible work hours for the engineering and office staff. But an ombudsman cannot cure everything. Despite all the complaints about performance appraisals at GE, they are still not always timely and complete.

Still, the ombudsman is one way that management can run a check on itself. "One thing a position like this does is let you recognize how effective some management policies are," says Christopher at Boeing Vertol. "It's a window management can look through for a reaction to its style."

Questions for Discussion

1. Why have hierarchical organizations in the past (and still, to a large extent) tended to deny the presence of internal conflict? How have views on conflict changed in recent years?

2. Upon what three elements does the potential for conflict depend?

3. What is a state of high potential for conflict? What is a state of low potential?

4. What organizational conditions contribute to and reinforce conflict? What organizational conditions promote cooperation?

5. What is similar about conflict and competition? What is different?

6. How do parties in conflict tend to misperceive each other? How do they misperceive themselves?

7. What general conflict management techniques are there?

8. President Harry Truman once complained that he could seldom solve any conflict by ordering people to do something. He could only "persuade" them. The President of the United States is supposed to be the most powerful person in the world. Why can't the President just solve conflicts by individual dominance or judicial decision?

9. How do transcendant objectives reduce conflict? Describe a person or situation of which you have knowledge where this technique was used.

10. Sit in a local eating establishment. Observe and plot the flow of work and interactions, indicating the points of stress and conflict. What are their causes? Redesign the work flow to reduce conflict.

11. Plot the flows of work and interactions during college registration. Where are the points of stress for students? For faculty and secretaries? For administrators? Recommend changes to reduce stress and conflict.

12. What are the central objectives and techniques of the mediator? Have you ever mediated a conflict (between family members, school friends, teammates, etc.)? What did you do? Did it work?

13. Describe and analyze a conflict situation in which you were involved. How was the conflict resolved?

Cases for Discussion

Grover Lestin

Grover Lestin is a 34-year-old black banker with an amazing background of experiences and jobs. Work has taken on several meanings for him as he has moved from a Southern farm to Assistant Vice-President in a Northeastern bank.

Grover's parents were poor but independent farmers owning a small piece of Virginia. It was a life of hard work, but with much love and joy. His mother was a vivacious woman who was a perfectionist in everything she did: cooking, sewing, and attending church. She continually told her five children that they could do better, that they shouldn't just settle for "getting by." Grover's father was a giant of a man whose physical strength and psychological stability conveyed to his young son a fundamental sense of security and an abiding optimism that you could fight the world on even terms. In those early years, the family was never starving and enjoyed substantial status in the local black community. Mr. Lestin would frequently say to his son that the world was changing and that Grover would be able to do things seldom dreamed of by Negroes in the past.

Young Grover was not really lazy, but he didn't relish working out in the hot fields. Sometimes he proposed labor-saving devices to his father and he enjoyed formulating these ideas while lying under a shady tree. His father would merely kick him in the seat of his well-worn dungarees and say that they couldn't afford a tractor or anything else. So Grover would work because he had to if he wanted to eat.

Mr. Lestin died when Grover was fourteen. His mother had to give up the farm and become a housekeeper for a wealthy white family in town. Grover became the all-purpose "step-n-fetch-it" for the household. Although he loved being in town, he hated being treated as if he were stupid. Grover did attend school more regularly, but the work was so boring that his grades were poor. The teachers seemed to expect him to make trouble so he obliged them. No one was interested in his ideas.

Grover especially disliked confronting the fact that he was black for the first time. Out in the country he had rarely met any whites, but in town they were all around telling him that he was different. For a time he dreamed of somehow changing his skin so that everyone would see how ambitious and smart he was.

At seventeen Grover left home and joined the Army where he spent almost three years mainly in a variety of European posts. While in the service he completed his high school equivalency and even a couple of college correspondent courses. He liked the military and was nominated for staff sergeant shortly before he was discharged.

Upon leaving the Army Grover attended Tidewater State College, a predominately black college, where he majored in business administration. He worked hard, performed well, and graduated in the top 5 percent of his class. Unfortunately, the job opportunities weren't very good and Grover decided to apply for an Army commission. He was subsequently commissioned a Second Lieutenant and embarked on a successful military career of eight years leading to promotions up to Captain and including a Bronze Star and Purple Heart for action in Vietnam.

Four years ago, Grover decided to leave the military and try the civilian world again.

He enjoyed the Army but felt that job opportunities for educated blacks had significantly improved in recent years. Besides, he had three young children to support and he wanted to earn more money.

Grover resigned his commission and accepted a position with the Reliable Trust Company in Northeastern City. He was the first black professional ever hired by this medium-sized bank and he was to initiate a new bank activity—loans to minority enterprises who in the past had not been eligible for loans through the regular procedures.

After a two month training program, Grover was appointed an Assistant Treasurer (AT) and given the title of Manager of Minority Enterprise Credit. He was assigned a modest office and a secretary whom he shared with a regular loan officer. Grover was a little older than the others at his level, but his salary seemed fair at $16,000 and he was enthusiastic.

Grover's immediate superior, Frank Swain, Assistant Vice-President of Credit, was not enthusiastic about lower credit standards for minority applicants, but President Alfred Robbins put his weight behind the effort and Grover was given substantial autonomy in making loans below $25,000. Indeed, the bank's advertising emphasized its awareness of its social responsibility and featured Grover on many television commercials.

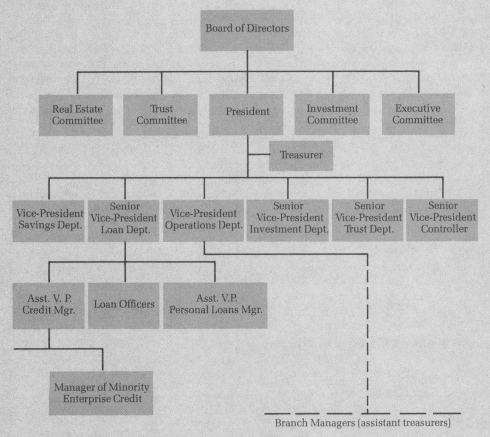

Exhibit 1   Partial Organization Chart of Reliable Trust Company

During the past four years, Grover has enjoyed good relations with the bank's president. Many times, Robbins has directly called him about specific problems with minority enterprises and even solicited advice on personnel policies toward clerical employees. Several times, Grover was invited to accompany the president on speaking engagements. In total, Grover has probably spent more time with the president than anyone except the Senior Vice-Presidents. And last year, his title was upgraded to Assistant Vice-President, with a salary of $25,000.

All of this has been heavy stuff to Grover and he feels a great sense of satisfaction (and some anxiety) when he considers how far he has come from the Virginia farm. He and his family live in a predominantly white suburb where his kids walk to school and his wife drives to the supermarket.

Nonetheless, Grover has become increasingly unhappy with his situation. He enjoys his job and autonomy, but feels that his limited responsibility curtails his ability to contribute. Last year when his title was upgraded, he requested an increase in his loan authorization authority to a level more equal to that of equally experienced regular loan officers. Frank Swain said he would look into it, but then he transferred to the Trust department. His replacement, Andrew Widder, has put off Grover's request because "changes are necessary in this operation—we're losing too much money."

Grover is beginning to feel that he has spent enough time in minority loans. He would like to transfer into the regular loan department or into trust or investments where he can learn more about the banking business and prepare himself for future promotions. Grover has been especially upset by the fact that he has not been invited to the weekly informal training conferences conducted by the Senior Vice-President of Loans, where large and interesting loans are discussed. Grover has requested a transfer through Widder, but so far nothing has happened. Recently, Grover has been experiencing severe headaches, which his physician feels are psychosomatic.

Questions

1. Describe and analyze the conflicts that Lestin confronts.

2. What alternatives does he have? What are the potential advantages and dangers of each?

3. What would you recommend to Lestin? Why?

4. What would you recommend to the bank's president? Why?

City Community College

City Community College is a two-year, publicly supported urban institution of higher education. According to its statement of philosophy and purpose, its programs are designed to accommodate the diverse educational needs and aspirations of recent high school graduates and adults. The college believes that the key ingredient in a satisfactory experience for its students is excellence of classroom instruction. For this reason the college requires a commitment to college teaching as a fundamental qualification for its faculty. According to a recent statement of policy, each faculty member, in addition to holding professional credentials, must manifest a sincere interest in the instruction and counseling of students. The establishment of selection criteria and the actual hiring of staff is left to individual departments.

The college has no formal organization chart. Instead the Dean of Instruction stated in a memo to department heads, "The college will arrive at its full divisional structuring via departmental paths and not by the filling in of a master organization chart." There are currently fifteen department heads of which all report directly to the Dean of Instruction who in turn reports to the President of the College. Also reporting to the President is a Dean of Students and a business manager.

The Department of Nursing provides a good illustration of the type of situation that characterizes many departments at City. The Department of Nursing consists of the following eight people:

Associate Professors:

| Gail Mauldin | 28 years old | 1st year faculty |
| Bill Gunner | 38 years old | Chairman of the Department (Teaches both 1st & 2nd Yr.) |

Assistant Professors:

| Yvette Sturm | 40 years old | 1st year faculty |
| Jill Purdy | 27 years old | 2nd year faculty |

Instructors:

Pam Lowy	25 years old	2nd year faculty
Ardella Prince	33 years old	1st year faculty
Delores Rosenberg	30 years old	2nd year faculty
Francis MacDonald	62 years old	1st year faculty

The method of teaching used in the department has been described by the chairperson (Bill Gunner) simply as group teaching. The faculty has been made to understand that no one is excused from any class unless the department chairperson approves. In general, group teaching means that several faculty members are present in most classes.

The faculty members teaching first-year students and those teaching second-year students meet once each week to discuss issues common to both. Each group seems to regard the other with suspicion, or at best cool tolerance. At a recent joint meeting, the first-year faculty accused the second-year faculty of failing to establish "critical elements" (those elements considered critical to proper nursing performance). The second-year faculty retorted that the problem lay in the poor preparation the students received in their first year. Most of the exchange took place between Mauldin and Purdy, who by virtue of their academic rank seem to have assumed the role of senior staff. Mauldin admitted that the nursing students enter "a different world" during their second year. She stated, "It's probably because we don't get together to share exactly what we all teach."

During the past two months a crisis has developed in the first-year faculty. Apparently there had been dissension between Ardella Prince and the other first-year faculty almost from the time Prince joined the faculty six months earlier (in Septem-

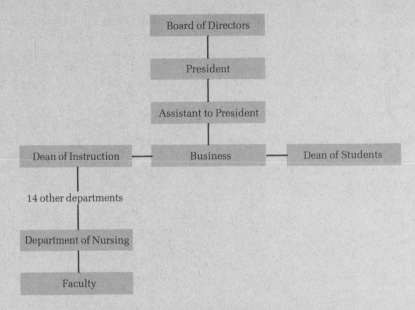

EXHIBIT 1 Apparent Organization Chart of the City Community College

ber). Prince is an R.N. and has a Master's degree in Nursing Administration, and confided that she had been unable to secure a position in the field because she is black. The faculty had been particularly anxious to hire a black instructor as they felt it would be beneficial for their many black students (approximately 40 percent). Prince had been more closely associated with Gail Mauldin during the first semester than any of the other faculty, and Mauldin had complained to Gunner on several occasions that Prince was not competent.

The situation worsened at the beginning of the second semester when Yvette Sturm became the lead teacher for a unit on psychiatric nursing. (Faculty members are the "lead" teachers when their area of specialization is taught.) She and Prince sharply disagreed on many issues and were constantly waging verbal battles—at first in faculty meetings and later in student-faculty conferences. MacDonald, otherwise a quiet person, frequently found herself acting as the mediator in these disputes. Although MacDonald's efforts usually resulted in a temporary accord, disagreement would surely flare again. Sturm found herself increasingly in the position of giving directives to Prince. The disagreements between the two became sharper and more polarized. Prince always thought of nursing service (at a local hospital where the students gain clinical experience working), while Sturm insisted that the students were in the school for education, not service.

Students frequently complained that Prince praised them and told them they were "doing fine" while Sturm told them they *weren't* doing so fine. Sturm insisted on correcting the tests and papers of Prince's students after Prince had already done so. Sturm often marked the students' papers as much as twenty points lower. Prince then would tell the students that she had no idea why they had been awarded such a grade. In sum, the students received "double messages" almost constantly.

In late February some first-year students presented a letter to the faculty deploring the treatment of Prince. Among other complaints the students listed inattention to her points of view, failure to solicit her ideas, and rude treatment of her by other faculty members in the classroom. The faculty members denied these charges and tried to reason with the students. Privately Prince stated, "The students see how shabbily I am being treated." Meanwhile other faculty members pointed out that Prince's strong identification with nursing administration often made her view completely incompatible with their own. Her comments in class appeared to embarrass and even stun them at times so that they did not always reply to her when she spoke.

Gunner talked with the Dean of Instruction and the President about the students' letter and about the worsening situation within the faculty. In describing his actions Gunner said, "The Dean isn't too strong a figure, so I usually end up going directly to the President. In fact, the President often issues directives right around the Dean. Frequently I find myself writing a note to him explaining some action I'm taking or policy I'm implementing." In mid-March Gunner recommended that Prince not be retained for the following school year. This proved to be somewhat of a problem since notice of non-reappointment should have been given (according to policy) no later than March 1.

When the contracts went out on the first of April, Prince did not receive one. The following day all but a handful of the first-year students failed to report for classes.

Exhibit 2   Guidelines for Initial Appointments and Promotions in Academic Rank

---

(a) *Instructor*   Minimum Qualifications—Master's degree or equivalent. Skilled technical, scientific or artisan qualifications or extensive academic or professional experience may be substituted for degree requirement based on President's recommendations and approval of the Board of Trustees.

(b) *Assistant Professor*   Minimum Qualifications—In addition to Instructor qualifications, an Assistant Professor should have a minimum of three years successful collegiate or professional experience in a field related to his college teaching position. Holders of the doctor's degree may achieve this rank in less than three years.

(c) *Associate Professor*   Minimum Qualifications—In addition to Instructor qualifications, an Associate Professor should have a minimum of six years successful collegiate or professional experience in a field related to his college teaching position. Holders of the doctor's degree may achieve this rank in less than six years.

(d) *Professor*   Minimum Qualifications—Doctor's degree or equivalent. Appointments will very rarely be made.

Questions

1.   What are the various forms of conflict at City Community College? What are the causes of each?

2.   What recommendations do you have for managing each of the forms of conflict? Who should do what when?

3.   Should anyone speak to the students? Who? What should they be told? Are there any dangers in this?

4.   Should anyone speak to Ardella Prince? Who? What should she be told?

5.   What recommendations do you have for the President?

Organization Development

We come now to a way of managing individual and group processes in an organization which has been called variously "planned change" or "organization development." The target of OD management is to change the beliefs and attitudes of people. Most OD practitioners hold that only people who have previously learned to trust, help, and cooperate with one another can then keep their minds on technical and structural problems, and devote their full intellectual and creative abilities to running the business. As Blake and Mouton (1967) put it, "Organization Development deliberately shifts the emphasis away from the organization's structure, from technical skill, from wherewithal and results *per se*, as it diagnoses the organization's ills. Focusing on organization purpose, the human interaction process, and organization culture, it accepts these as the areas in which problems are preventing the fullest possible integration within the organization" (p. 11).

A simplified way of viewing the OD approach would be to draw an arrow from a question in the first column of Exhibit 12.1 to the related question in the second column.

Exhibit 12.1

Personal and Interpersonal (Cultural) Questions	*Structural Questions*
1. Does an advertising manager see salespeople as valuable people in the organization, or does he see himself as being more important? Do salespeople see the advertising manager as helpful, or as a "hard-nosed" headquarters checker? Does the advertising manager see the salespeople as helpful?	1. What is the job of the advertising manager in introducing a new product? What is the job of the salespeople in selling a new product when it is introduced?
2. Does a sales manager see the controller (financial planner) as helpful? Does the controller believe the sales manager to be a valuable person?	2. What is the cost of selling? How many salespeople can we afford? How much television advertising can we afford?
3. How does a head nurse in a hospital see herself in relation to the nurses? How does she *think* the nurses see her? How do the nurses *really* see her (in terms of her ability to communicate, her ability to evoke trust on the part of others, etc.)?	3. What is the authority of the head nurse? On what kinds of actions are nurses supposed to obey her? Who works out the daily shift schedule in the ward?

The arrow would be one of causation. Thus, in question 2, we would say that if the sales manager sees the controller as a useful person, if he views the controller as helpful (instead of a policeman), and if the controller believes the sales manager to be a worthy person, then they would more likely be able to view selling the company product as a joint or team goal. The probability is much greater that they can then answer questions such as those in the second column: What is the cost of selling? How many salespeople can we afford? How much television advertising can we afford?

To summarize, we might say that organization development reverses the typical sequence of "what changes who." It is the change in personal values in the system, coupled with the change in ways in which people treat one another, which comes first. Only then is a group capable of tackling the operating problems of maximizing organizational effectiveness.

Viewed in this way, the general model for most organization development efforts is as follows:

1. Plan the change processes (done primarily by trained consultants [behavioral scientists] advising the client [top management] who approves the program).
2. Change the attitudes and habits of individuals (the ways people treat one another).
3. Change group climate or culture (the collective attitudes and habits of individuals).
4. Work out new structures, such as (a) subgoals (products, types of patient care, allocation of budget money); (b) who does what (a new specialization pattern); and (c) who has final authority over whom.
5. Solve day-to-day problems, involving (a) new demands from outside the organization, and (b) new discoveries or demands from inside the organization.

For those interested in theories and models, OD not only reverses the practical steps in applying the change process to the real world, it also reverses the dependent and independent variables. Operating procedures, costs, job descriptions, production schedules—the whole rational side of the firm—become dependent on how a group of people feel about themselves as people and about others as people. One must not expect, for example, that operations research experts can really increase organizational effectiveness by figuring out a production schedule which is then conveyed in a memo to foremen on the assembly line; nor can market research managers at headquarters (however much they may have studied statistics and consumer psychology) really increase company sales to the maximum by determining what customers or geographic market segment the company should concentrate upon, especially if the resulting policy is passed on in directives to district sales managers. Rather, it is the production expert learning how to relate to the foremen (and vice versa), or the market researcher learning how to relate to the district sales managers (and vice versa) which is the key causal event in maximizing organizational effectiveness.

It should be pointed out that, as the training proceeds, OD practitioners vary greatly in the relative "mix" they seek in discussing operating problems versus discussing human and interpersonal problems. In some OD efforts, the change agent begins, for example, by discussing the technical or operational reasons why the sale of a new product did not go well, and moves rather quickly into discussing the behavioral reasons why the new product did not go well (whether the people involved have been cooperative and helpful, or uncooperative and nonhelpful). Other OD consultants may devote considerably more time to discussing operational problems, assuming that the group will get the message on interpersonal problems without explicitly confronting each other in this respect. Nevertheless, all OD efforts carry out the philosophy suggested in the above model, of placing human and cultural factors first, as the most important targets of change.

Douglas McGregor (1967) clearly sets out the philosophy of the team as a principal determinant of organizational effectiveness. It is a team of people who analyze the various role pressures on all personnel. The team perhaps discovers that the advertising manager is indeed under pressure from the field sales force, and that the field sales managers are indeed dependent on the advertising manager. It is the team who then draws implications from these pressures and dependencies — implications for what the organization expects of each person in terms of such structural matters as job duties or responsibilities.

McGregor's instrument for directing the team's attention to its attitudes and beliefs also shows what he believes a team should work on first. He wants it to "discuss in depth each variable," such as:

In our day-to-day work

- do we trust each other? or do we suspect each other?
- do we have genuine concern for each other, or is it everyone for themselves?
- do we communicate openly our true feelings and thoughts, or are we guarded and cautious?
- do we listen to others or do we act on our own?
- do we accept conflicts and work them through, or do we deny, avoid, or suppress conflicts?
- does the team utilize the abilities, knowledge, and experience of each member, or does the team ignore the capabilities of some?
- does everyone understand and feel committed to work objectives, or do some fail to understand them or feel negative toward them?

NEED FOR ORGANIZATION DEVELOPMENT

Environmental Complexity and Work Specialization

Managers today are faced with a much more turbulent technical world in the external environment. The time when customers, competitive products, distributive channels, production methods, and labor costs or skills were stable and orderly has changed to a time when product life cycles are short, new products must be developed to meet changing population patterns and tastes, and a host of other adjustments must be made. The same is true of other institutions in our society. We have changed from hospitals that met one set of needs in society to those which must cope with new and different classes of patients, new methods of medical diagnosis and treatment, and a much larger number of patients. We have changed from a U.S. Office of Education that operated under one set of social conditions to a full-fledged Department of Health, Education, and Welfare which must cope with new numbers and classes of students in schools, new curriculum content, and new physical facilities on a scale not before imagined.

All of this has meant an increase in the size and complexity of organizations—of the number of specialists required, and the ability of these specialists to collectively guide the operations of the organization. No longer can a single sales vice president or regional sales manager be sufficiently acquainted in a specialized way with market research, inventory control techniques, financial cost techniques, advertising methods, or scientific product research to make wise decisions. Nor can the specialist in any one of these areas *alone* make decisions that are wise. No longer can the hospital director, the chief of internal medicine, the chief of anesthesiology, the financial controller, the head nurse or the director of the emergency ward *alone* make decisions. It is a price we pay for modern large-scale organizations that everything depends on everything else—what the emergency ward does affects the finances of the hospital, the way anesthesiologists deaden pain, and the hours doctors work in internal medicine.

This complexity and interdependence has been clearly explained by Burns and Stalker (1961) in a selection following Chapter 6. They found that organizations in the Scottish electronics industry which were *organic,* in that they had more open and fluid work relationships among people holding different internal functional positions, were the ones that were most successful in changing their production and marketing to meet the rapid developments in British and world markets.

Some writers on OD focus on the *systems* concept to explain the need for this form of management (e.g., Alderfer, 1971). They are in effect saying that all of the changes taking place in a turbulent environment do (and must) reach directly the relevant specialists inside the organization (e.g., customer information to marketing specialist, new discovery in hydrocarbon chemistry to the research department, etc.). They cannot reach only the president—it would cause an overload in his or her decision-making, nor would the president be able to comprehend the detailed *meaning* as would a specialist. The only answer is *teamwork,* with the president or general manager the one who sets up the process and procedures for *group* decision-making. In most of the OD literature showing how companies go about this kind of management, it is stressed that some general manager initially sees the need for this kind of approach and at some point becomes committed to it. The general manager is the one who, with the change agent, schedules the various meetings, attends them, and otherwise lends official authority and procedure to its being carried out.

Another development in the environment is a rapid change in *human* culture, as contrasted with rapid technological changes. The top executives, middle managers, and employees of any organization are, after all, people who hold the beliefs, values, needs, and demands of their times, culture, and society. Warren Bennis (1969), one of the leading developers of the OD form of management, has this to say about this kind of environmental change:

"The environment now is busy, clogged and dense with opportunities and threats; it is turbulent, uncertain, and dynamic. The people who work for organizations are more complicated than ever before. They have needs, motives, anxieties, and to make matters even more complicated, they bring higher expectations than ever before to our institutions. The institutions themselves are changing, through the press of environmental challenges and the internal demands of its people" (p. 81).

Exchanging Commitment and Loyalty for Satisfaction of Needs

At this point we can pull together two ideas already learned from the chapter on individual motivation and the chapter on influence. In those two chapters it was pointed out that one important kind of influence exists when an organization satisfies the human needs of another person. If a doctor in a hospital finds that many of the things he or she wants in life are gained by working in this particular hospital, the doctor is more likely to develop positive attitudes toward it and to carry out the duties and responsibilities necessary for the success of the hospital as an institution. In this sense, OD teamwork provides this doctor with much more opportunity for problem solving, for determining his or her own destiny through having a voice in the way the hospital operates, and for greater accomplishment than could be hoped for in private practice. It might, by increasing the doctor's social function in society, provide more self-esteem as well as more freedom and autonomy.

Thus, if one sees the logic of a person's relationship to an employing institution as a "psychological contract," involving the exchange by the employee of work and commitment for an offer by the institution of all of these other things, one can also see that OD might well be a key to the elusive problem of commitment and loyalty. Economists, while stressing that "economic man" works for wages and money, have always recognized that people in certain jobs also work for what they called "psychic benefits." The good court judge works for less money than many private lawyers on Wall Street, the good professor of engineering works for less money than he or she could get with IBM or General Motors.

Overcoming Maladaptive Attitudes from the Past

A second basic force recognized by many who advocate organization development is one which is brought into the organization as part of the personality of participants when they join it—whether they be top managers, middle managers, or employees. In the process of maturation and development, certain basic attitudes derived during one's growth are deep seated, quite stable, and tend to affect one's present relations with other people. Of particular importance in organizational life are attitudes toward authority and attitudes toward intimacy (Bennis and Shepard, 1965). An overly *dependent* person — who has a pronounced feeling of comfort in having others be leaders, or in having rules and procedures to guide his or her life — may be in for some trouble. Since the world really is not one where a benevolent leader and rule system attends to every need of an active person, the dependent person may feel underneath a strong sense of hostility and resentment toward the organization. Or he or she may feel a sense of personal failure. Finally, an overly dependent person may vacillate between submissiveness and rebelliousness.

Conversely, overly *counterdependent* people — with pronounced feelings of discomfort toward people in authority, or toward rules and regulations — may also be in for some trouble. As they move through life, running upon some "good" and some "bad" organizations (both *do* exist in the real world), they do not always act realistically. In their attempts to get through life, they too may vacillate between wanting more direction (submissiveness) and hating all direction (rebelliousness), always trying to make sense out of the world but feeling underneath that all organization is "bad."

Another interpersonal attitude is the one toward intimacy. Some people may have learned to be overly *personal* — they cannot rest until they have stabilized a relatively high degree of intimacy with others. Others have learned to be overly *counterpersonal* — they tend to avoid any intimacy or personal talk at any cost. They are only comfortable talking about the work to be done, or the costs, or the output. But the world is not really like either stereotypical view. If either kind of person clings to one or the other extreme, he or she may find himself vacillating between both.

Although organization development practitioners may differ in their terminology, and in how strongly they aim their efforts at changing basic attitudes, all OD efforts try to get people to see the world as it is, here-and-now, and to see themselves and others as they are, not as some stereotype.

Another effort made is to get people to learn how to learn. This is an elusive objective. Those who practice OD assume that it takes skill to see one's self, other team members, and the job to be done in realistic terms. Such skill must be learned. It is as if every day, in each specific problem that arises in a company, one has a new learning experience. One learns what *is* rather than spending one's life confirming previous attitudes and beliefs. Anderson (1970) shows how feedback not only can help another person to learn, but that one must *learn* how to give feedback which is constructive, rather than destructive.

John Dewey, the famous philosopher who developed important insights about how the human mind solves problems, coined the phrase "trained incapacity" to denote how specialization has tended to block a person's ability to understand another person's job and point of view. In a company, the sales force thinks only about sales, while the finance department thinks only about costs or investments. In a hospital, the surgeons spend their lives operating, while the controller deals with patients who pay bills or vendors who sell beds and pharmaceuticals. Dewey meant that the very training of controllers, salespeople, or surgeons (including their day-to-day experiences) builds into them a predisposition to see the whole corporation or the whole hospital from their own viewpoint, and an *incapacity* to see the needs of the organization as a whole.

Sociologists who study bureaucracy have pointed out that if a person lives in the same organization for a long time, with the same policy rules and the same job descriptions, his or her mind is likely to play strange tricks, to "displace" the original goal of serving the customer (or another part of the organization) with a different goal: abiding by the rule book. One of us recently appeared at Kennedy airport 15 minutes before takeoff time. At the gate, both he and the passenger agent could see that the airplane had not yet left. "I'm sorry," he was told, "closing time for the aircraft was a few minutes ago; you'll have to get the next flight to Chicago." After much heated exchange, another passenger agent, overhearing the conversation, said, "Let him on. They're delayed because of food delivery to the airplane." The first agent was not problem solving or thinking about the airline's main goal of transporting passengers. He was thinking about the rule book.

Another explanation of why large organizations might become more interested in maintaining status, prestige, and office than in solving up-to-date problems is given by Thompson in a selection following Chapter 6. According to this view, general managers have the traditional *right* to decide policies and changes in the organization, yet the *ability* to decide drifts more and more into the hands of specialists. As a result, managers engage in activity designed to maintain their perquisites and prestige, rather than in solving real operating problems.

A further explanation of the need for breaking down rigid bureaucratic practices is found in the study by Burns and Stalker (also following Chapter 6). In the Scottish electronic companies, the authors found that the companies most successful in changing to meet the times (bringing out new products, developing new ways of selling, resisting the decay of producing out-of-date government products) seemed to be *organic* types of organizations, characterized by:

- loose boundaries between departments—everyone seemed concerned with everyone else's business.
- flexible job assignments—a person's role might change from time to time, depending on the kind of problem the company was trying to solve.
- commitment toward company goals, not toward departments.
- a great deal of discussion, committee meetings, and task forces which cut across divisions and jobs.

On the other hand, the companies less successful in adapting to change in the British marketplace were those "mechanistic" companies which stuck to clear and precise departmental and job descriptions, and in which the managers by their own words and behavior seemed to spend more time demonstrating loyalty and commitment to their immediate superiors than they did to thinking about and solving problems.

While various OD practitioners differ somewhat on how much stress they place on this point, there is little doubt that all such efforts attempt to decrease significantly the degree to which structural rules exist, the degree to which they actually influence human behavior, and the amount of power held by the "legal" hierarchy. This move toward sharing of power, rather than concentration of status and power, takes place in a pronounced way during the actual training or "planned change" period. And it is intended to be a more or less permanent result if the OD effort is successful. With respect to the transformation period, the selection by Greiner accompanying this chapter takes perhaps the clearest position. He states that one of the central or key goals of OD is to achieve shared power.

Management of Conflict

A final reason often cited as to why organization development is needed in modern organizations is that it is an effective way to *manage* conflict, rather than let conflict become persistent and destructive. According to this view, maladaptive interpersonal attitudes from the past, or departmental conflicts of interest, or both, tend to cause conflicts between various parties in the organization—managers versus subordinates, specialists versus specialists, one department versus another. In our society, so this reasoning goes, and especially in many work organizations, there is a built-in belief that people should not bring such conflict into the open. A sales manager who shows some hostility toward the production department when orders are late, and who says in a committee meeting, "You people always seem uncooperative to me," is not playing by the rules. It is o.k. to *feel* hostile, or to make jokes behind the engineers' backs: "Those slide-rule boys are really not as important to this company as the sales managers, who earn the engineers' salaries." But to *say* that production is not very important to company success is to violate good manners and create disruption. Someone in the meeting is very likely to change the subject by starting to talk "business," technical matters of production scheduling, or other "objective" matters.

According to this view, such minor hostilities, if constantly swept under the rug, can build up to polarized positions, wherein each side is in a "win-lose" frame of mind. Instead of searching for creative solutions to the problems of selling and producing, or working to get each of these specialities to help one another, the parties spend much time in what appears on the surface to be politely using technical reasoning, statistical facts, or business arguments. Underneath, in reality, this kind of behavior is often directed at proving that the other side is wrong (cutting them down) while "we are the real brains around here" (building us up).

Lawrence and Lorsch (1967) place the management of conflict as a key concept in their argument on how to promote *integration* among many specialized technical processes in an organization, and among the many specialists whose interests might conflict. They have in mind a set of events that look like this:

a conflict resolution process characterized by directly confronting conflicts instead of smoothing them over and achieved by organization members *learning* how to be open and frank $\rightarrow$ greater integration of teams and among people in diverse departments $\rightarrow$ firms successful in adapting to a changing environment

We should be careful to distinguish between the *management* of conflict and the *elimination* of feelings of conflict. While it is true that some OD consultants (and some unrealistic managers) attempt to eliminate conflict, it is also true that most OD practitioners view overt conflict in moderate amounts not only as a fact of life, but as a source of creativity and innovation.

METHODS OF ORGANIZATION DEVELOPMENT

There are many approaches to organization development. All of them involve (1) gathering data about the state of operations in the organization, the state of interpersonal attitudes and behavior, or both; (2) feedback of data to the various parties involved, who then analyze it to see how the human attitude and behavior system is affecting solution of the organization's operating problems; and (3) team planning of new solutions to operating problems or new structures of duties, procedures, policies, and rules for the organization's operations.

Beyond this general similarity, there are almost as many methods of organization development as there are consultants engaging in this kind of work. While some may say that this proliferation of methods is due to the newness of this kind of management development, it is probably equally due to the fact that human behavior is a very rich and variable phenomena. It is so subject to diverse viewpoints and interpretations that we shall probably always have considerable variation among OD methods.

The first two stages above can be conveniently classed as the *diagnosis* or *unfreezing* stage of planned organization change. This is the stage in which participants in the organization look deeply at the present state of affairs in the organization—its operations, its successes and failures, and particularly the way human attitudes and relationships either foster or hinder the solving of operating problems. A number of applied behavioral scientists have used the term "unfreezing" to denote the diagnosis phase of OD. This term implies what has already been said in other parts of the book: that people in organizations have a way of becoming "frozen" into out-of-date *operating* policies, customs, and job descriptions; or "frozen" into *interpersonal attitudes* of formality (rather than reality), of competition, of ritual, or of distrust. Still other practicing OD consultants have taken the term "action research" from Kurt Lewin, a founder of this type of change philosophy, implying that OD is similar to any type of applied research except that "the relationship of researcher and subject may reverse—the subjects becoming the researchers" (Bennis, 1965). Viewed in this way, the participants on OD teams within an organization literally become researchers to discover how rigid operating practices, or rigid interpersonal attitudes, or both, are hampering organizational effectiveness. The OD consultant, on the other hand, becomes an educator, training teams in how to do research on these two types of problems.

The third stage, *action planning* or *refreezing*, is the stage when the same participants, having faced up to and eliminated some of the structural and human blocks to effective problem solving, proceed to devise *new* ways of operating—they solve patient care problems or advertising problems, and they invent new organization structures such as new job descriptions, new procedures for the flow of work, or new policies for patient care or advertising.

DIAGNOSIS OF ORGANIZATIONAL PROBLEMS

Questionnaire Feedback Methods

One of the earlier organization development efforts was that carried out by Floyd Mann (1957) and his colleagues at the University of Michigan. They were bothered by the fact that companies were trying to improve effectiveness and change by training individual managers. The "manager development" approach did not seem to be working. According to Mann, it assumes that managers attend training sessions, that their own attitudes and beliefs change, and that when they return to the job their behavior will change. This change will in turn be seen by their subordinates, who will then become more effective in their jobs, and begin to contribute new and effective ways for operating the company. Yet even in training programs designed and conducted by supposedly competent people, Mann found no evidence that the attitudes and beliefs of managers changed, or that they behaved any differently when they got back on the job. In fact, his assessment of these programs pointed to the fact that certain factors *other* than attending a training program were more powerful in determining how managers act on the job, and how their departments perform.

As a result of this recognition, the Michigan group endeavored to find a way "for changing attitudes, perceptions, and relationships among individuals in complex hierarchies without changing the personnel of the units"—in other words, a way to report findings from human relations research to organizations so that they could understand what the research meant and how to use it in day-to-day operations.

A company-wide study was made by questionnaire of employee and management attitudes. Over a period of the next two years, three different sets of data were fed back to members of the company organization: (1) information on the attitudes of 8000 workers toward their work, their managers, and fellow employees; (2) information on the feelings of first and second-line managers plus their beliefs about how to manage; and (3) attitudes and beliefs of top and intermediate managers about their own philosophies of how to manage, their role in decision-making, and their problems of organizational integration.

The process which seemed to maximize the usefulness of the survey findings was an interlocking chain of conferences—a report to the president and senior officers, and then reports to successively lower hierarchical levels until the foremen and their employees were discussing the data. In these meetings, the line executive met with the group of people in a particular department to discuss the data pertaining to that department, and to all subunits for which members of the department were responsible. Members of each group were asked to help interpret the data and then decide what further meaning could be derived from it in order to formulate plans for constructive future action. Behavioral researchers attended these meetings as resource people, to help interpret the data and its meaning.

Since this effort at organization development, many innovations have been made. Nevertheless, this early effort attempted to get "families" within the organizations together for team diagnosis. And the presence of outside researchers undoubtedly had some of the effects, to be discussed later, of interrupting the "old" organization.

In a more recent effort, which also involved interviews and direct feedback as well as questionnaires, the Boise Cascade Corporation (1970) engaged in a comprehensive organization renewal project. More than 2000 managers in this billion-dollar company completed a questionnaire for later summarization and feedback. A team of outside and inside consultants on organization development assisted in the project. Following are examples of the type of information gathered:

One part of the questionnaire dealt with what the manager thinks the present aims of the company *are*. This part also sought to find out what managers thought the broad goals of the company *should be*. Specific questions covered such items as "growing as rapidly as possible," "becoming a significant multinational company," "long-term security for employees," "gaining a reputation as a socially concerned corporation," "achieving above-average profit in this industry," and "creating an environment that employees find stimulating and challenging."

A second part of the questionnaire dealt with how managers view the organizational climate. Managers were asked whether jobs are clearly defined and logically structured for good operations, whether a friendly atmosphere prevails, whether it is unclear as to who has authority to make a decision, whether people in the organization trust each other, whether there seems to be personal loyalty to the organization, whether subordinates' ideas are sought and used, whether upward communication is accurate and whether cooperation or competitiveness more nearly describe how people act toward each other.

A third part of the questionnaire sought to find out how managers feel or believe about themselves. They were asked to rate themselves on a seven-point scale under each of 29 characteristics—whether the particular characteristic was "very characteristic," "somewhat characteristic," or "not at all charac-teristic." Examples of these characteristics are:

Enthusiastic about what I do, getting excited about my work.

Have many strong opinions and feelings which are important to me.

Having many friends, giving affection and receiving it from others.

Getting and using suggestions from others.

Being a leader; having other people look up to me for direction; taking over when things are confused.

A fourth part sought information on the way strategic decisions at Boise are made, and the way capital is allocated. Managers marked a five-point scale—from strongly agree to strongly disagree—on the following kinds of statements:

I think the annual strategy process is a good thing.

Strategies are prepared more for the benefit of top management than for my part of the organization.

I have been greatly involved in this kind of decision making.

Whether the results of such a questionaire actually influence real changes depends on what is done with the information. In this and other companies, teams of people are expected to get down to diagnosing fundamental causes of what is going on. If people in one department feel that there is not much personal loyalty to the company, the reasons for this might be explored in a nonthreatening way so as to bring about a greater degree of commitment.

Some behavioral scientists (e.g., Schein, 1969) do not believe that ques-tionnaires are as effective as face-to-face giving of information. They feel that the categories in a questionnaire are not rich enough in content, powerful enough in force, or personal enough in impact to have a real and meaningful effect on attitudes and perceptions.

T-Groups and Sensitivity Training

Perhaps no other method in organization development has received so much attention, and been the subject of so much controversy, as T-Group or sensi-tivity training. The method is difficult to describe to one who has not been through it so that he or she can understand or have any real feeling for what goes on and what is accomplished. Furthermore, it has numerous variations, each depending on the personality and *modus operandi* of the trainer. Never-theless, no book on organizational behavior today would be complete without some attempt to explain this method of training. The selection by Schein and Bennis (1967) following this chapter is such an attempt.

One characteristic of all such efforts is that the individual is placed in an *unstructured* situation with other people. In purest form (perhaps few trainers stick to the "purest"), this means that there is no agenda, no subject to be dis-cussed, no rules or traditions for operating, and no leader or authority figure. The trainer serves principally to remind the group (when asked or when de-manded), "We are here to observe our own behavior and the behavior of others, and to learn from it." Often the presence of the trainer (and therefore the hope that "something must come of this," or the belief "this can't be sheer nonsense, though it looks like it to me") serves to keep people in the room for specified periods before the group has existed long enough for the people in it to recognize the experience as useful.

A second characteristic of most T-Group efforts is that they concentrate on "here-and-now" experiences. They do not analyze the external factors in some story a member might tell about "what it's like back in my company" or "the latest Russian-American incident." Sooner or later it is the intent of the trainer that, if such talk arises to pass the time (or to evade what is going on in the room), these subjects will be converted to such questions as, "What is John Jones doing in this room when he tells us about the personnel problems back in his company?" Or "What is Joan Smith doing here in this room when she raises the subject of Russian-American relations?" Some trainers may remind the group of the "here-and-now" rule, or others may simply let the group discover it for themselves. Sooner or later, if Joan Smith keeps talking about Russian relations, the national football league, or her recent readings in Buddhism, someone will question what she is doing.

We can imagine how such a deliberately contrived "vacuum" might reveal behavioral insights never seen before. With no family, no parent, no prescribed duties or agenda, no boss, no organization, no rules, no customs, no policies, people are forced to rely only on the inner attitudes and beliefs they bring to the group. There are many theories of what happens in such a group over a period of time. Some of the goals of such training most frequently mentioned by professionals in the field are increased insight into one's own interpersonal attitudes, beliefs, or habits of behavior (including how competent and successful one is), insights into those attitudes and habits on the part of other people (including how competent and successful they are), and insights about the various processes of conflict, harmony, leadership, or followership which occur in a structureless group over time.

T-Groups are used for other reasons than organization development—and some OD efforts do not use T-Groups. However, the T-Group method, or some method which has some of its characteristics, is often used as *part* of the total OD program. One way is by having a large number of individual managers from one organization attend "stranger" labs (no one from the same company or work group) offered by the National Training Laboratories. It is thought that if many people in the same organization have developed greater interpersonal awareness and competence by attending stranger group training, two results will follow: each manager is more likely to be able to solve operating problems effectively; and the work in a stranger lab will make each manager better at going through other steps in organization development, such as confrontation meetings, chains of interlocking conferences, or action planning sessions. Participants would already have had some experience, and would be better able to "unfreeze" in their own organizations. However, stranger labs are more often used by companies for *manager* development than for *organization* development.

The most direct application of T-Groups to OD, however, is what has been called cousin, brother, and family labs (Beckhard, 1965). Cousins are people taken from "a diagonal slice of the organization, cutting through two or three vertical hierarchical levels but without a boss and subordinate being in the same group." Brother labs include people who occupy similar horizontal roles in an organization (again without bosses and subordinates in the same group). For example, a group of branch managers from the same bank, a group of nurses who are heads of wards in a hospital, or a group of territory managers in the Bureau of Indian Affairs would be brothers. Finally, family labs are made up of a whole department: the line executive and the people who report to him or her. The chief nurse in a hospital meeting with the head nurses in charge of various wards, or the chief of branch bank operations meeting with the branch managers, is a family T-Group.

The advantage of such familial T-Groups is that people get to know themselves in relation to the individuals in their own organizations, and vice versa. When the time comes to go back to work, it is thought by some trainers, these people will be better able to solve operating problems together than will people who have attended stranger laboratories. The disadvantages of familial labs compared to stranger labs include the fact that it is more difficult to get people who know each other historically to concentrate on "here and now," and the danger that unstructured experiences might generate some animosities which would jeopardize, rather than help, future work relations.

Another controversy over the use of T-Group training centers on the possibility of permanently damaging an unstable personality, and on the ethics involved in subjecting or otherwise influencing a person to expose his or her private attitudes in a "no agenda" situation. Beckhard (1965) would avoid such criticisms by specifying that T-Groups are inappropriate "if the goal of training is primarily to deal with a 'sick' person or one who cannot be handled in the organization, to convert a person to a new way of life, to institute rapid change in personality and/or behavior, or to produce a maverick—one with 'new ideas' —in a hostile back-home culture. . . . [but] T-Group training for teams and units within an organization tends to be appropriate where the primary goals are establishment of new norms, establishment of new values, or establishment of new ways of work—such as consensual decision-making."

T-Groups have in fact been successfully used in a wide variety of organization development efforts. Anderson (1970) shows, for example, that Procter & Gamble utilized T-Groups with beneficial results; their dangers did not materialize, at least in the opinion of the company and the trainers. The drawbacks and dangers of such training will be minimized by more rigorous certification procedures for competent trainers, and more effective ways of determining admission to such programs, based on who can benefit (or who may be harmed) by such training. The most serious problem seems to be how to maintain for people in organizations a truly voluntary choice of such training. If, as we have said, it is almost impossible for one to have a true understanding of what goes on in a T-Group unless one has been through it, how do we "educate" a person to the point where he or she can make the choice? Or, if the "company" or the "boss" decides on an OD effort, how does one refuse on grounds of privacy without incurring the boss' displeasure or some form of social penalty in the form of suspicion by fellow employees?

No discussion of T-Group training would be complete without reference to the study done by Dunnette and Campbell (1968). They set out to find evidence that such training actually accomplishes the goals claimed by those who advocate it. They concluded (1) that no researcher has yet demonstrated that T-Groups have any marked effect on scores on objective attitude tests, (2) that T-Groups may result in increased self-awareness and interpersonal sensitivity, (3) that the associates of most persons who have received T-Group training report observable changes in their behavior back on the job (e.g., more openness in communication, better leadership styles), but (4) that no hard evidence exists to show that organizations have increased in productivity, output, or other organizational results.

Focused Exercises and Confrontation Meetings

Focused exercises are in one sense a halfway house between unfettered behavior in a structureless group and the more circumscribed behavior we all engage in in the real world. On the one hand, these exercises are like T-Groups. They provide experiential learning (rather than reading about or hearing about someone else's experience), and they set up a situation in which people are removed from *part* of the real world of agendas, time limits, leaders, hierarchies, quality controls, competition, scarce resources, technology, and so on. But in another way they differ from T-Groups. By creating situations which include *certain* of these things but not others, the trainer is able to design an experience which allows a group of participants to "see" things they might not otherwise see: how these constraints affect human behavior, and vice versa.

Such exercises have existed for years in the military form of "war games." These have been played by officers in training who use toy soldiers and weapons on elaborate terrain boards (some boards from the eighteenth and nineteenth centuries can be bought in European antique shops). And as all infantry trainees for World War II, Korea, and Vietnam know well, they may be played on bivouacs with "enemies" firing overhead while troops crawl on the ground, send out night patrols, or evade air attack. The fire drills in buildings, the lifeboat drills on ships, and the forced landing procedures in pilot training are all forms of "experiences" or "games" designed to let people know how it "feels" to be in a given situation. Perhaps the most elaborate simulations of real experience we have today are the ground trainers which enable airline pilots to experience everything from sudden crosswinds to loss of engine power to vertigo (loss of inner ear balance) by climbing into a cockpit on the ground, "flying" the trainer, but never leaving the earth.

A wide variety of simulated experiences have been devised which generate some specific behavior, such as competition, trust and openness, conflict, shared problem solving, hierarchical problem solving, division of scarce resources, and one-way versus two-way communication. In a selection following this chapter, Schein and Bennis discuss two such exercises. The classic computer games, devised originally to demonstrate certain economic phenomena, are played at some schools with emphasis on how team members behave in relation to each other during the decision-making process. These and other games have also been used to show *intergroup* relations—how one group might distrust another, how the two groups compete, and how a winning group has high cohesiveness. Conversely, a losing group often experiences an *intragroup* divisiveness, and a lack of loyalty to the leader who led the group in competition.

These experiences differ from T-Groups in a second important way. Not only is there an "agenda," but the "agenda" is imposed from the outside world. Remembering that human beings are motivated partly by what they bring to an organization and partly by what is in the organization around them, it is easy to see the importance of the externally imposed agenda. A stranger T-Group would emphasize what is within the individual, while the focused experience would enable participants to analyze both. The design imposed by the trainer can be arranged to highlight the organizational environment, enabling participants to "see" how agendas affect behavior, and vice versa.

One variation of the focused experience is the confrontation meeting. Beckhard (1967) describes the conditions under which he believes that such a technique is applicable and the steps involved in such a confrontation. In confrontation meetings, it is the *operating* problems of an organization—hotel reservation procedures, the way financial information is funneled to subunits, and the like—which occupy most of the group's time. At the beginning, however, the consultant focuses on such human processes as problems of communication in a large organization, the need for mutual understanding, and the need for shared responsibility for future successful operations.

A quite different type of confrontation meeting focuses exclusively on the difficulties among people as they work in a complex organization. One study describes a five-day confrontation meeting between the headquarters sales executives and the field sales executives—regional managers plus division managers—in a large company (Golembiewski and Blumberg, 1967).

This company had had problems because the field sales managers often complained that sales promotion display or advertising materials were not of the quality that actually "sold" the products, or were not the kind that the field salesmen could get customers actually to display, or did not appear physically, or in newspapers, at the most advantageous *time* to help salesmen sell the products. The management recognized that these "today's irritations" could well become "tomorrow's tangled problems," so they engaged consultants in OD to institute a development effort.

The consultants had already conducted cognitive training (reading, lectures, theories) about rigidity and change in large organizations, leadership styles, and the effectiveness of counseling (rather than authority and "ordering") as a managerial style. After the confrontations, the operating problems identified during confrontation were to be followed up by core-issue task forces in a full-scale OD program.

There were 29 division sales managers who met in three groups, one with each regional manager. There was one group from the headquarters promotion department, and one group of sales department staff executives—the head of hospital sales, the head of sales personnel and training, the controller of the sales division, etc. Thus, there were five learning groups.

The first exercise involved each of these groups choosing *who* outside their group was a *relevant other.* Consultants defined "relevant other" as any position or organization unit with whom effective relations are necessary if the choosing party is to do a good job. A group of division sales managers, for example, could (and did) list the headquarters promotion group as a relevant other. After the relevant others were chosen, the consultants received the reports of the five groups. They drew a 5 × 5 grid and checked off for each party who the relevant others were. They left plenty of space for listing "free" relevant others—specific persons, positions, or parts of other groups. These checkmarks were entered "in an atmosphere of tense horseplay." As the choosing proceeded, the division managers erupted. "That proves it," one shouted. "All of the regional groups chose *them* [the promotion group] but promotion didn't think we were relevant for *them.* As usual, they look only upward [to the vice president and headquarters]. They chose our regional bosses and the director of sales. But *we* aren't relevant for them." At this point, the consultants suggested that while the other groups work on the intense feelings aroused, the promotion department retire separately and evaluate its position. This evaluation was done by the "3-D Image" technique.

The 3-D technique requires that a group construct a three dimensional image of its position *vis-a-vis* another group:

1. *Describe how we see ourselves in relation to some relevant other.* The promotion department saw itself "as a united group which provides sales strategy and sales promotion materials to the division managers, designed to enhance their selling abilities," "as a vital factor in success of the division managers' selling efforts," "as cooperative allies with the division managers in achieving common selling goals," and "as dependent on division managers for important field intelligence from customers."
2. *Describe how we feel the relevant other sees us.* The promotion group saw the division managers "as not fully understanding the role and responsibility of product managers at headquarters in our marketing philosophy," "as the most important factor in any promotion effort we provide," and "as feeling frustration as a result of their not having more say in developing promotion materials."
3. *Describe how we see the relevant other.* The promotion group never got around to describing this. However, Exhibit 12.2 summarizes the third dimension for a *reverse* relationship: how field sales division managers saw the three dimensions, including the promotion department.

If we study carefully both the three-dimensional pattern for one group, and the pattern of the other group, we can see the richness of data and information that might be discussed in diagnosis sessions, such as the one that occurred when consultants suggested that groups "work on the intense feelings aroused." They scheduled 12 confrontation periods of up to 90 minutes each for relevant others to confront each other in such discussions.

Exhibit 12.2 A Sample 3-D Image by One Regional Aggregate with Promotion as the Relevant Other

A. *How Members of Regional Aggregate 1 See Themselves in Relation to Promotion Department*

1. Circumvented
2. Manipulated
3. Receiving benefits of their efforts
4. Nonparticipating (relatively)
5. Defensive

6. Used
7. Productive
8. Instrument of their success
9. Have never taken us into their confidence in admitting that a promotion "bombed"
10. The field would like to help, but must be a two-way street

B. *How Members of Regional Aggregate 1 Feel Promotion Department Sees Them*

1. Insensitive to corporate needs
2. Noncommunicative upwards, as holding back ideas and suggestions
3. Productive in field saleswork
4. Naïf about the promotion side of business
5. Unappreciative of promotion efforts

6. As lacking understanding about their sales objectives
7. Belligerent
8. Overly independent operators
9. Not qualified to evaluate the promotions sent to us
10. Honest in opinions

C. *How Members of Regional Aggregate 1 Characterize Promotion Department*

1. Autocratic
2. Productive
3. Unappreciative of field efforts
4. Competent with "things" but not "people"
5. Industrious
6. Inflexible

7. Unrealistic
8. Naïf
9. Progressive in promotion philosophy and programs
10. Overly competitive within own department
11. Plagiarists who take field ideas but do not always give credit

Source: Golembiewski and Blumberg, 1967.

Later in the confrontation, an additional technique was used — the identification of "core issues." In a general meeting of all participants, the whole group, with the help of the consultants, developed a list of important issues to be worked on in action planning sessions. These issues were listed on large newsprint sheets. Anyone could sign up to work on this or that issue. The names on these lists became "core groups." They met to decide when and where to meet again to begin work on the issue.

Interview Methods

So far, we have seen two ways in which information (research data) is made available to participants in an organization: by questionnaire and by direct feedback (T-Groups and focused exercises) from one part of the organization to another. A third method, that of interview by an outside consultant and feedback by him to the teams, is today the principal method used by most OD consultants. In this method, the consultant interviews various people in the organization and feeds back to others, and to the whole group, certain selected or summarized information on a wide range of subjects. While some of this information pertains to operating matters ("the branch managers seem to believe that the company is charging too little for the product"), consultants are especially valuable in the feeding back of information on *human* processes in the team ("they say you won't let them have a voice in decisions such as pricing, which affect them"). Presumably, the consultant has the skill to state such feedback in a nonthreatening way, and as an outsider, can state touchy matters in a way less likely to cause the recipient immediately to blame the other party. For both reasons, OD theory suggests, people receiving such feedback are more likely to *think*, rather than react in an aggressive way without thinking. They are more likely to concentrate on the problem, regardless of whether it is their "fault," someone else's "fault," or both.

Another reason for using the interview method is that the human problems in an organization, which cannot readily be "seen" by untrained perceivers, or by people who have lived in a particularly structured organization, can be highlighted and emphasized. This may be accomplished by directive questioning in the interviews: "When the company charges prices so low that it keeps pressure on your plant to lower costs, doesn't that make you wonder who is doing the pricing?" Or, "That must make you feel pretty bad when you get the price list each quarter." Such emphasis can also be accomplished by selecting from interview data which information is to be reported back in feedback sessions: "One of the things we found is that most plant managers resent not being consulted on company pricing decisions."

OD consultants differ in the degree to which they stress direction or selection by the outside consultant in the OD process. Some consider them very important functions. A few deny that they seek to "filter" or "highlight" information, since their function is objective research—to discover and feed back, without bias or selectivity, all information reported to them in interviews. Regardless of this disagreement, it is highly likely that all consultants, given their training and interest in human affairs, do in fact select out, filter, or otherwise reinterpret data. It is also safe to say that, if OD is a worthy effort conducted by competent practitioners, reinterpretation is a vital part of the whole process. In fact, even in questionnaire and most direct group dynamics methods, the consultant's interpretations are an integral part of diagnosis.

Sequence of Experience and Explanation

It is perhaps a central thesis of all OD logic that people learn by *experience*, rather than by listening to lectures, reading books, or otherwise listening to the results of other people's experiences summarized in the form of theories or research principles. Few full-scale OD efforts leave out these cognitive inputs altogether, but most consultants stress the fact that they should come *after* an experience-type exercise, not before. For example, a focused exercise might be devised which places members of the team in competition with one another. Only after the group has acted out the exercise does the consultant give a lecture on how people act toward one another and feel toward one another when they are in competition. As another example, Zand et al. (1971) created temporary systems or problem-solving teams of managers and foremen in a manufacturing plant. After some problem-solving sessions, and throughout the program, the consultants scheduled a lecture on styles of supervision, an interpreted exercise on giving and receiving help, a lecture on organization theory, a film on problem solving under conflict, and an interpreted exercise showing what happens when a manager's upward influence is reduced.

There are exceptions to this principle of experience first, theory later. The first session of Beckhard's confrontations (1967) include lectures on the problem of communication, the need for understanding, or the concept of shared responsibility for the future of the organization. This reverse in procedure is apparently thought desirable when very limited time is available for the activity, top management wishes to improve the conditions quickly, and when there is a major and rapid change in the organization (merger, change in organization structure, change in leadership) which causes confusion and expenditure of dysfunctional energy that negatively affects both productivity and morale.

A COMPLETE ORGANIZATION DEVELOPMENT PROGRAM

In theory, at least, all OD consultants intend that organization development programs will, after the diagnosis stage, evolve into an action planning stage. After all, productive organizations do not exist only to improve human understanding, sensitivity, and diagnostic skills. The goals of productive organizations are to produce goods and services for society. And this means curing patients (a hospital), offering education (a school system), producing antibiotics (a drug company), or improving a standard of living (a government poverty bureau).

The action phase of organization development involves solving operating problems. But there is actually relatively little in the literature of OD which treats action planning in any detail. Perhaps this is because many OD consultants feel that, once the group or team becomes proficient in the human skills of joint problem solving, the planning of specific operations and procedures is "their business." On the other hand, certain OD specialists have recognized the danger of spending all efforts on diagnosis and research, and giving little attention to action planning. Such a procedure may be criticized for "all talk and no action," or be compared to the well-known criticism of "all we do is appoint another committee."

We have already referred to the interlocking chain of conferences, committees, and task forces which were set up by one consultant to deal with operating problems, and to the core-issue groups set up at the end of a confrontation meeting. The selection by Beckhard following this chapter is one of the most comprehensive descriptions of a total program available, including both diagnosis and action phases. In an effort to change the operating practices, financial operations, policies, procedures, and job duties in a chain of 26 hotels operating internationally, the consultants set up an elaborate program. They utilized top executive conferences for the hotel chain headquarters, key executive conferences of hotel managers, problem-solving conferences within each hotel, annual goal-setting processes for each hotel and between top management and the group of hotels, management schools, technical seminars, new-hotel-management team programs (one for operating teams, one for staff teams), overhead cost-reduction teams, and a variety of other action-oriented task forces. The elaborate nature of this effort shows the amount of time and planning required if the OD logic is to be applied thoroughly to an entire organization. In studying this selection, you should be cognizant of both the type of operating subjects discussed, and the kinds of behavior the consultant sought while problem solving took place.

Another point of importance in such a full-scale action program is the fact that the hierarchical management, working with the consultant, set up a strong *structural* element in organization development. To the extent that the existing hierarchy of headquarters management and subsidiary management of individual hotels is partly dictated by technology and geography (every hotel must have a management team), the OD effort must utilize the structural approach especially in the action stages. However, the consultant in the hotel project sought to build *new* connective structures, based on what it takes to get the job done, and to integrate them with the technologically determined hierarchy.

CRUCIAL ROLE OF THE CONSULTANT

One of the hallmarks of organization development, and a characteristic which separates it from older management methods, is the assumption of part of the management task by an outside consultant, trained in the behavioral sciences. Some studies refer to this individual as a "change agent," a "practitioner," or an "interventionist." Whatever the consultants are called, the literature on OD strongly suggests that OD management cannot be carried out without them.

Who are consultants or change agents, and what functions do they perform? Authorities in the field differ as to how they describe them and their functions — perhaps both their characteristics and functions in management can be looked at in different ways:

Consultants have certain knowledge. The chief certification agency for the profession is the National Training Laboratories, though there are undoubtedly many managers and consultants doing OD-type work who are either intuitively trained or unaware that this approach now has a name. Certification procedures at this stage are not too clear, but evidence of advanced work in the behavioral sciences, plus recommendation by some existing practitioner under whom the candidate has worked, are necessary. Within NTL, the organization development network affords the opportunity for those who do this work to meet and exchange knowledge and experience, and NTL operates a training institute in Colorado offering a month of more formal training.

Consultants also have certain emotional characteristics — interests, attitudes, values, beliefs, and assumptions. These assumptions, attitudes, and interests relate to human behavior in organizations, both as it *is* and as it *ought* to be. Normative values are strong enough in the makeup of typical OD consultants that they separate them from behavioral scientists. While the latter usually confine themselves to the descriptive or analytical *study* organizations, OD consultants want to *act*, to make the organization operate as they think it ought to operate. The orientation of consultants can be characterized as having a strong "humanistic" quality (see for example, Raia, 1970, and Davis and Tannenbaum, 1969). According to one authority, many OD strategies "are based upon the assumptions that man is rational and reasonable; that he can be influenced by logic and knowledge; that he is responsible and will respond to the truth; and that he is loving, caring, and trusting of others" (Raia, 1970). Another puts this even more strongly: "Organization Development practitioners rely exclusively on two sources of influence, truth and love" (Bennis, 1969).

A third way of describing consultants is in terms of skill. For example, they have worked in practical affairs enough that they are able to translate practical events into terms of human interaction theory (and vice versa), to give feedback in a way that is helpful instead of destructive, and to recognize when "the truth hurts too much."

Given these characteristics of typical OD consultants, what functions do they perform that cannot be performed by a member of the operating team itself, or by one of the hierarchical managers? First, there is the consultants' knowledge of behavioral sciences and particularly of change methods. Second, it is thought that, because they are exempt from the intellectual and emotional biases of the organization, and partially exempt from the power (punishment) biases of an operating manager, they can bring freshness of perspective and a degree of stimulation not possible were they operating members of the organization (Alderfer, 1971). Third, with their skill in constructive feedback, they not only can protect individuals when "too much truth hurts," they can also help demonstrate openness and truth in a way that is constructive instead of destructive. Fourth, in the diagnosis stage, they can set up a system that will actually undermine certain value systems (e.g., overemphasis on formal authority) in order to build a new value system based on open and honest communication (Greiner, 1967a, p. 83). Fifth, they can meet some of the dependency needs of a team in the early stages when the usual hierarchical bosses are not "bossing," and even be useful models with whom team members might identify and thus learn from by imitation (Zand, 1971, p. 21).

Finally, overriding many of these other functions, consultants serve an important function of promoting *power equalization.* They often moderate or act as discussion leaders for team meetings rather than the formal managers who do have sanctions. In fact, many consultants stress that this structural approval of higher management, in the form of permission to start an OD effort and in the form of turning the meeting over to the consultant, serves both to give *structural* support to a change effort (as opposed to the unstructured aspect), and to equalize the power among team members (Greiner, 1967b). Without such power equalization, it would be difficult for team members to "open up" and engage in the kind of exchanges that otherwise might seem threatening to higher authority (and dangerous to lower participants).

Though most OD writers stress the necessity of an outside consultant (either from outside the parent organization or as a top staff member within the organization who is not part of the operations being changed), one of the most respected earlier members of the profession did not think consultants were mandatory. Douglas McGregor first made the point that *any* trial-and-error learning of complex human interactions can be dangerous without a profes-sional — it is dangerous for people to try to be their own doctor or lawyer. But management of any kind (OD or otherwise) is a professional action field, and McGregor (1967) thought he had evidence that managers in the real world can produce real physical and mental dangers for people working in the organiza-tion. Therefore, he thought, self development of management teams, involving a "do-it-yourself" diagnosis of interpersonal relations using a rating scale, probably involves "no greater danger than is inherent in many widely accepted managerial policies and practices such as budgeting, cost control, promotion, or performance appraisal. . . . I believe a managerial group *can* successfully undertake its own self development, with or without the help of a behavioral scientist consultant" (p. 170).

LIMITATIONS TO AND CONDITIONS FOR
ORGANIZATION DEVELOPMENT

There is no doubt that organization development is one of the most significant *practical* techniques which depart from traditional management based on division of labor and formal authority. For years, behavioral scientists have referred to participative management and structural job enlargement as the main alternatives to traditional management. But until the advent of OD nobody made them *operational*. It is as easy to preach participation as it is to preach motherhood and democracy, but for the same reasons that preaching has never eliminated sin, it would be difficult to bring about participation in a bureaucratic organization by advocacy alone.

But OD has its limitations. Analysis, clarity, reality, openness, and facing up to the truth may be an alternative to closed-system stereotypical thinking, but there is no guarantee that it will work in all organizations. The view-point which the modern manager must take, therefore, is that this method of management has both powerful benefits and powerful limitations. The key is to try to understand when and under what circumstances such a technique will succeed.

The first set of conditions to watch for in deciding when to use OD are summarized by Greiner (1967b) (treated more fully in Greiner, 1967a). The organizations where OD has been successful were under considerable ex-ternal and internal pressure to change the organization radically, long before OD consultants entered the picture. This suggests that, like drinkers who choose on their own to go to Alcoholics Anonymous rather than have someone sell them on it, the organization itself must be searching for new ways of managing, must want help, and must call on the consultant — not vice versa.

Second, the hierarchical managers must be willing to experiment with OD and become deeply involved, devoting their time and energies to the change process. It is possible to share power *too much* by relying on group dynamics alone, without including structural aspects. In the organizations which did not succeed with OD, Greiner found that some made the mistake of too much unilateral "forcing" or "selling" of OD procedures, while others went overboard in the other direction—they utilized T-Groups with virtual abdiction of power, with no active participation of formal authority figures, or with data discussions that did not get to an action stage based on a combination of consensus and legitimate authority.

A second set of conditions which the wise manager should attend to concern the hiring of a consultant—whether a total outsider, or an internal staff person at headquarters who is an "outsider" to operating departments. Even some OD specialists themselves (e.g., Bennis, 1969) recognize that consultants often are ignorant, unskilled, or uninterested in that part of the world which does not fit their model of open communication and trust. Power and authority, as well as technical operations and output, are not only facts of life in most organizations but very important facts at that. Unless consultants also possess interest in the organization's purpose, procedures, and technical operations, they are likely either to let these take distinctly second place behind its human processes, or to let them become lost in the maze of human process techniques. OD is not an end in itself, at least to a society that wants hospital care, police protection, air transportation, and pharmaceuticals, as well as trust and harmony. The very logic of OD makes it clear that solving the organization's problems is the end value desired.

A further limitation of OD has to do with *time*. It is a process which aims at long-term changes in organizational productivity and success. If events in the environment warrant a quick and coordinated response of the entire organization, the method is probably inferior to management by structure and authority. If a Nazi bombing squadron had been detected by radar headed toward Westminster Abbey during the Battle of Britain, one would not have expected a British fighter squadron commander to call a meeting and ask his pilots, "Who do you think are your relevant others?" Nor would General Motors spend two years on developing interlocking chains of committees in response to the sudden introduction of prohibitive tariffs against U.S. automobiles around the world.

A final limitation has to do with the possibility that OD consultants might themselves become susceptible to advocating stereotyped answers to problems. One authority in the field notices that some OD consultants, having discovered a method appropriate under *certain conditions,* tend to apply the same method to any and all organizations, without regard to whether the specific organization is suitable for this kind of management. Frederick Taylor had his time and motion study, his separation of planning from operations, and his industrial engineers as the ultimate planners. Today's OD specialists have their open communications, their involvement of a team in both operations and planning, and their expert behavioral scientist in charge of the change process.

There is probably value in OD. But it should not be applied in the same way to all organizations. This chapter has sought to give the practicing manager

enough understanding of organization development to know that it is one
alternative for managing a complex organization and that it is useful under
certain conditions.

SUMMARY

Organization development is a philosophy and method of management which
focuses on the *informal culture* of the organization, rather than on the formal
structure of jobs, authority, technical procedures, and financial procedures.
It attacks the prevailing attitudes, mores, and beliefs of the people in the organization as a group. Particularly, it seeks to develop such attitudes and beliefs
as "other people are valuable in themselves," "other people are valuable as
co-workers in getting the job done," "trust and openness are productive for me
and for them," and "only if we can communicate with trust and frankness can
we then solve financial problems, marketing problems, or other technical,
operating, and work problems." This philosophy of management also attempts
to develop certain *skills* in the organization's culture, particularly skill in
giving and receiving honest feedback.

According to the OD philosophy of management, such cultural attitudes,
mores, and skills are necessary *before* the members of the firm can move on to
solve successfully the technical side of the business: job descriptions, the structure of authority (who can or should make certain decisions), questions of
technology (what is our product line and our method of selling), or economic-
financial matters (what are our income statement figures and what do they
mean?).

The OD philosophy of management has arisen because of several problems which develop as organizations grow and mature. The organization's
goals must change to meet the changing tastes and demands of society, yet such
organizations sometimes have a tendency to train participants to be more
interested in maintaining their own position in the status hierarchy. People
become so specialized that they cannot deal with one another with any degree
of real understanding without becoming impatient. The further one goes
down the line in the hierarchy, the more starvation one finds — for *involvement*
in the wider world, as opposed to the smaller world of performing in a specialized corner of the organization. The ever more complex patterns of specialization seem to defeat this desire. Both the organization and the people
need some way to settle the many interpersonal and interdepartmental conflicts that arise as a result of specialization.

A number of different methods have been developed to implement OD
management: questionnaire feedback, T-Groups or sensitivity training, focused
exercises and confrontation meetings, interviews, and cognitive "lectures" to
help people logically interpret what they have learned from the more emotional
experiential methods. Finally, a complete OD program, integrating a number
of these methods, culminates in team management projects in which newly

trained participants proceed to plan the authority structure, economic aspects, and technical operations of a business.

There are three essential steps involved in all of these methods, regardless of which are selected for an individual OD project: gathering data, feedback of data, and planning of new solutions.

Most authorities on OD today believe that a full-time executive, of the traditional line or staff type, cannot carry out the role of the change agent or OD practitioner. Members of the organization are likely to be unwilling or unable to practice skills or examine attitudes as required, particularly if the "manager" of the process holds a position of formal power (or has a stake in the existing status and operating structures).

Authorities differ as to whether this "outsider" must be a total stranger, not employed in the organization (a consultant), or can be a "semi-outsider," a staff specialist in OD. Even Douglas McGregor, who believed that people could engage in a kind of do-it-yourself organization development, without the active presence of a consultant, nevertheless assumed that (1) the group initiates and maintains the process, not a "boss," and (2) the consultant's expert knowledge, reflected in the instrument or questionnaire the team uses, is a necessary adjunct.

OD is not to be construed, as some advocates unfortunately seem to imply, as a long-awaited ideal management method. It has its problems. Among these is that it is one thing to preach a philosophy and yet another to act it out in practice. Not all organizations are rigid bureaucracies in dire need of change. People in the organization must feel the need for improvement *before* an outsider attempts to impose an "ideal." Furthermore, the ad hoc and unstructured relationships required to carry out such a program exact a high price in terms of human energy, anxiety, and effort, and a high price in terms of time commitment. They also tend to go against another human need: the need for structure, stability, and familiarity. Too much uncertainty over time, with little or no familiar routine, will tax the abilities of people to work effectively. Finally, the OD effort which ignores the technical side may eventually result in the method being labeled as theoretical, unreal, or even mystical by those who work in organizations and those who manage them. The economic production of goods for outsiders in society, as well as human satisfaction inside the organization, are equally important.

These are the kinds of situations which may limit the effectiveness of the method and which any manager must consider in determining when it is appropriately used.

REFERENCES

Alderfer, C. P. "Change Processes in Organizations." In *Handbook of Industrial and Organizational Psychology*, ed. M. D. Dunnette. Rand McNally, 1976.

Anderson, J. "Giving and Receiving Feedback." In *Organizational Change and Development*, ed. G. W. Dalton, P. R. Lawrence, and L. E. Greiner. Irwin-Dorsey, 1970.

Beckhard, R. "The Appropriate Use of T-Groups in Organizations." A.T.N.
Occasional Papers, No. 2, in *T-Group Training: Group Dynamics in Management
Education*, ed. B. Blackwell. Oxford, 1965.

———. "The Confrontation Meeting." *Harvard Business Review*, March–April 1967.

Bennis, W., and H. Shepard. "A Theory of Group Development." *Human Relations*,
Vol. 9, No. 4, 1965.

———. "Unsolved Problems Facing Organization Development." *The Business
Quarterly*, Winter 1969.

Blake, R. R., and J. S. Mouton. "Grid Organization Development." *Personnel
Administration*, January–February 1967.

Boise Cascade Corporation. *Organization Renewal Questionnaire.* Human Resources
Committee, Boise, Idaho, 1970.

Davis, S., and R. Tannenbaum. "Values, Man and Organizations." *Industrial
Management Review*, Winter 1969.

Dunnette, M. D., and J. P. Campbell. "Laboratory Education: Impact on People and
Organizations." *Industrial Relations*, October 1968.

Golembiewski, R. T., and A. Blumberg. "Confrontation as a Training Design in
Complex Organizations." *Journal of Applied Behavioral Science*, Vol. 3, No. 4,
1967.

Greiner, L. E. "Antecedents of Planned Organization Change." *Journal of Applied
Behavioral Science*, Vol. 3, No. 1, 1967a.

———. "Patterns of Organization Change." *Harvard Business Review*, Vol. 45, May–
June 1967b.

Lawrence, P. R., and J. W. Lorsch. *Organization and Environment.* Cambridge,
Harvard University, Graduate School of Business Administration, 1967.

McGregor, D. "Team Development." In *The Professional Manager.* McGraw-Hill,
1967.

Mann, F. C. "Studying and Creating Change: A Means to Understanding Social
Organization." *Research in Industrial Human Relations*, ed. C. Arensberg,
S. Barkin, W. E. Chalmers, H. Willensky, J. Worthy, and B. Dennis. Harper &
Row, 1957.

Raia, A. P. *Organizational Development: Some Issues and Challenges.* Unpubl. ms,
November 1970.

Schein, E. H., and W. G. Bennis. *Personal and Organizational Change Through
Group Methods.* Wiley, 1967.

Schein, E. H. *Process Consultation, Its Role in Organization Development.* Addison-
Wesley, 1969.

Zand, D. E., M. B. Miles, and W. O. Lytle. "Development of a Collateral Problem-
Solving Organization Through Use of a Temporary System." In *Proceedings of
the Academy of Management*, August 1971.

Readings

Team Development

Douglas McGregor

The skills involved in social interaction are often compared to those involved in sports like golf and tennis. Since the concern here is with team skills, the analogy to baseball or football teams might appear to be appropriate. However, these analogies are too oversimplified for our purposes. The common aspect is the necessity for practice, for experience-based learning. One cannot acquire the skills of golf without playing golf, nor can one acquire the skills of team operation without being a team member.

Let us say that a manager wishes to undertake a process of team development involving himself and all his immediate subordinates, both staff and line. In my view this is perfectly appropriate and practical. He is concerned with changing certain characteristics of this sociotechnical system. He cannot impose these conditions on the group, as we have seen. Nothing can be gained by any kind of secret manipulation of the system. The process must be public and transactional. He would begin, therefore, with an open discussion in a meeting of the whole group. He would discuss his reasons for suggesting such a process. If he were tentative, perhaps even doubtful (which would be natural), he would say so. He would encourage a discussion about its feasibility. He would ask his subordinates to express their own feelings openly, because there would be little point in the process in the face of strong reservations. If negative reactions were expressed, however tentatively, he would be careful not to override them or even try to persuade. Instead he would encourage the group to understand them fully.

He would need to be prepared with some ideas (not firm convictions) to answer questions like: "How would we go about it?" One way would be to discuss the primary task of the group with the purpose of clarifying and coming to mutual agreement about it.

If this process is to be transactional, it will involve much more than a cursory examination of the organization chart and the position description of the members' jobs. It will involve a critical, deep analysis by the whole team of the role pressures to which they are subjected and of the implications of these for what the organization expects of this unit formally and informally.

From this analysis will follow an attempt to formulate the primary task that encompasses all these expectations. If, as often happens, this proves impossible, the discussion will proceed to determine what *is* possible, from the point of view of both the team and the larger organization.

The outcome may be a conception of the team's primary task that resembles neither the formal organization chart and position descriptions nor the role expectations of the organization as experienced by the team. If the analysis conducted by the group and the manager has been thorough, they will have a persuasive rationale for seeking change in one direction or the other. The manager would normally be the person to attempt this.

If the group's conception of its primary task is acceptable, there remains the organization of work within the team. Members should be given considerable freedom in working this out themselves. The ideal would be a structure of responsibilities that is flexible enough to permit adjustment to changing situational requirements whether these arise within the team or in the wider organizational system or in the external environment of society (which of course includes the market).

The overall value of a process like this is not only the classification that results, but the growth of identification with the team and its responsibilities, and the sense of a degree of control by the group over its environment. There will have been compromises and adjustments, but the active involvement of the whole team and the sense of achievement when the task is completed provide important intrinsic rewards to all the members.

A second step — or possibly an alternative first step — would be to analyze together the current state of the group, to attempt to agree on those characteristics which require improvement.

I have seen groups make effective use of a simple rating scale like the accompanying exhibit for purposes of analysis. After a little discussion of the meaning of each of the variables, each member fills out the form anonymously, rating his personal view of the current state of the group. The ratings are then pooled and a chart prepared by a couple of members showing the mean of the ratings and the high and low "score" for each variable. On the basis of these data, the group discusses what aspects of its group operation need work.

Analyze your team (the group here in this room) by rating it on a scale (Exhibit 1) from 1 to 7 (7 being what you consider to be ideal) with respect to each of these variables. Then (with the rest of the team) discuss in depth the situation with respect to each variable, paying particular attention to those for which the average rating is below 5 or for which the range of individual ratings is particularly wide. Formulate some ideas about *why* these perceptions exist. The "ways" are likely to be quite different for different variables.

In using an approach like this, it is important to agree in advance on a ground rule that there will be no attempt to ferret out the "author" of any individual rating, although any member may *volunteer* comment about his own rating. If the group leader feels comfortable about it, his ratings might also be used. However, in most circumstances it would be advisable to wait until a fairly high degree of mutual trust and open communication is revealed by the data before attempting to analyze the leader's behavior separately.

The ratings of most groups tend to be unrealistically high on the first attempt to use an instrument like this. After some initial discussion it is usually fruitful to wait a week or two and then use it again, applying it the second time to a regular group meeting concerned with normal operating problems. A few minutes before the close of the meeting can be set aside for the purpose.

The problems that provide the agenda for meetings of the team, whatever they may be, are grist for the mill with respect to group development. The way to use them for this purpose is first to provide time for looking back directly after the group has dealt with a problem in order to examine together "how we operated." The experience is fresh; the data for examination are the behavior of the group members (including the leader) as they carried on the normal activities of the group. The process involves

Exhibit 1 Analyzing Team Effectiveness

1. *Degree of mutual trust:*
   High suspicion _____ High trust
   (1)   (7)

2. *Degree of mutual support:*

   Every man for himself _____ Genuine concern for
   (1)   each other
                                                  (7)

3. *Communications:*
   Guarded, cautious_____ Open, authentic
   (1)   (7)

   We don't listen to _____ We listen; we understand
   each other   and are understood
   (1)   (7)

4. *Team objectives*

   Not understood by team _____ Clearly understood by
   (1)   team
                                                   (7)

   Team is negative _____ Team is committed
   toward objectives   to objectives
   (1)   (7)

5. *Handling conflicts within team:*
   We deny, avoid, or _____ We accept conflicts and
   suppress conflicts   "work them through"
   (1)   (7)

6. *Utilization of member resources:*
   Our abilities, knowledge,   Our abilities, knowledge,
   and experience aren't   and experience are fully
   utilized by the team _____ utilized by the team
   (1)   (7)

7. *Control methods:*
   Control is imposed on us_____ We control ourselves
   (1)   (7)

8. *Organizational environment:*
   Restrictive; pressure   Free; supportive; respect
   toward conformity _____ for individual differences
   (1)   (7)

comments by individual members, if they feel free to express themselves, on how they felt when this or that happened and on their reaction to the whole process.

The group will gain most from such a feedback process if they give consideration to the consequences of different kinds of feedback. One of the purposes is to help each member of the group to recognize the impact of his behavior on others. Under ordinary circumstances individuals rarely acquire this information, *particularly* with respect to an immediate and specific situation when all the details are "here and now." More often than not, an individual discovers that the reactions of others to his own words or actions are not the same as he perceived them to be. Thus the feedback provides him an opportunity to test his perceptions against reality and to modify his future behavior *if he chooses to do so.*

If this is a purpose of feedback, it is quite unlikely to be helpful if it takes the form of a critical attack that simply puts the person on the defensive and makes it unlikely that he will either understand or accept the feedback. Nor is there any help in feedback that attempts to probe the motives behind his behavior. To turn feedback into a "two-bit analysis" defeats the purpose and may be highly disturbing to the recipient.

The guiding notion is that feedback tells the other individual: "This is how your behavior affected me." The information should be authentic. If his behavior made me angry or suspicious, or if it led me to become his ally or to feel especially positive about him, or if it led me to agree or disagree with him—*I should try to help him to understand my reactions, my feelings.* If others provide him with feedback on the same basis, he may discover that my reactions were like those of others in the group or that they were quite different. (In the latter case *I* may learn something, too!) The same considerations would apply to feedback by an individual member to the rest of the group.

Honest, sincere feedback between all the members of a team (including the leader) is one of the foundations on which mutual trust is built. It is in this sense that open communications and trust are reciprocal. It may seem inconsistent to think that one can be supportive and at the same time tell another person: "Your behavior angers me." However, there is a tremendous difference between responding with anger (attacking) and feeding back information about one's feelings in the hope of correcting a situation that is interfering with group accomplishment. The same is true of a reaction of mistrust or indifference or rejection. Genuine feedback of this kind (information) *identifies a problem that can be explored* and probably solved.

I argued earlier that *absolute* open communication may be dysfunctional. In the context of the immediate situation one must always make judgments about how far to go. The problem in the ordinary situation is that feedback (if it occurs at all) is so limited and cautious that it seldom provides much help. My experience with groups that are deliberately trying to create mutual trust, support, and open communications is that most people are quite skillful in sensing intuitively when they are at the limit in a given situation. Subtle cues from the other person—gestures, flushing, particular verbal responses, and the like—are noted. In a group setting particularly, it is remarkable how often some member will respond to these cues, even if the individual giving the feedback does not, and will find ways to divert the discussion. This is fortunate because there are no simple rules for setting the limits. Human beings differ widely in the amount and kind of feedback they can accept. On the other hand, the limits are not fixed. They usually become extended substantially as mutual trust and support increase.

Of course, these skills and sensitivities are not immediately present when a group begins to use this method. Discussion of the reasons for using feedback and examination of what the reactions are as the process goes along can pretty well prevent any lasting damaging consequences.

The process of using feedback to explore and examine a just-ended group session can gradually be extended so that many difficulties arising in group operation are corrected as a matter of course almost as they happen rather than being postponed to a post mortem. Part of the skill acquired is in recognizing when it is important to interrupt an ongoing activity in order to save time and trouble later and when to refrain from doing so because it is recognized that the effects on group performance are relatively unimportant. During the initial phases of acquiring skill along these lines, groups often become unduly preoccupied and overly sensitive about the needs for feedback on minor matters. This is, however, a natural and useful part of the process of acquiring skill.

Intellectual, cognitive learning is also an integral part of effective team development. This can occur in two different ways, and both are important. I have stressed continuously throughout this volume the many ways in which beliefs, assumptions, perceptions of reality, and theories about the nature of man and organized human effort affect managerial strategy.

Thus, effective use of feedback *for purposes of team development* requires another step: generalization. The value for the group in undertaking an analysis of their behavior is not in the analysis itself, but in what can be learned from it that can be used to improve the future performance of this and any other groups with which these members may be associated. For purposes of group development it is not enough that a particular problem may have been solved. The particular problem may never appear again in exactly the same form. However, it may well appear again under other circumstances and in other guises. Will the analysis of this single experience help the group to recognize the problem in other forms and deal with it? The probability is "no," unless the group has answered for itself the question: What have we learned from this experience? The learning may pertain to the meeting that was analyzed or the process that was used for analysis, or both. The generalizations may be quite tentative, subject to modification as a result of future experience. Nevertheless, the group's conscious generalizations concerning its own learning are the rungs of the ladder it is seeking to climb.

Every time the group faces a business problem that cannot be solved easily and quickly on the basis of habit, past experience, or existing policy, there is an opportunity for team development. Blake and Mouton refer to this as the "dilemma-invention-feedback-generalization" process, and it is in many ways a model for all kinds of learning.[1] A dilemma or problem confronts the group (or the individual). If it is solved by conventional, known formulas, there is no learning. If, however, it can be solved only by some form of ingenuity or inventiveness (or if that ingenuity is used to find a new and better solution to an old problem), there is an opportunity for learning by analyzing how the solution was arrived at and generalizing on the analysis.

That is why feedback, whether simple, brief, and essentially intellectual (as it will be sometimes) or complex, time-consuming, and emotion-laden, is crucial for team development. This is what is implied by "experience-based" learning.

What Is Laboratory Training?

Edgar Schein and Warren Bennis

Many attempts have been made to characterize the nature of laboratory training, but most of them have not been successful for several reasons: (1) laboratories *vary tremendously* in goals, training design, delegate population, length, and setting, making it difficult to describe this experience in general; (2) laboratories attempt to provide a *total* and *integrated* learning experience for the participants, making it difficult to

---

[1] R. R. Blake, *Tenth Proceedings of the Action Research Training Laboratory*, West Point, New York, 1960.

communicate in written words the interdependence of the many separate aspects of the laboratory training design; (3) laboratories intend to provide a learning experience which is, in part, *emotional*, and to provide the opportunity for the participants to explore the interdependence of emotional and intellectual learning. It is difficult without observing the process first-hand to describe and understand the nature of this emotional learning and its meaning to the learner.

In spite of these difficulties, it is important to attempt to communicate some of the flavor of the typical laboratory training experience. By giving a bird's-eye view of laboratory training, we hope to highlight and exemplify the differences in assumptions and methods between the laboratory approach and more traditional educational activities. For our case, we will use a typical *two-week residential* laboratory for a group such as middle level managers in industry. By residential, we mean that all the participants live at the conference center and spend their entire time in training activities. There are many other types of laboratories. We have chosen the two-week residential one as our example because it represents the most typical kind of laboratory. The primary focus of the laboratory is the *personal* learning of the individual delegate.

ARRIVAL AT THE "CULTURAL ISLAND"

Most laboratories are held somewhere away from the pressures of day-to-day urban living, generally in an isolated comfortable hotel or conference center. The preliminary information sent to the delegate makes it clear that the atmosphere of the laboratory is informal and that the delegate will be expected to live in, in the sense of having minimal contacts with job or family during the course of the laboratory.

When he arrives at the conference center, the delegate is assigned to a room with one or more other delegates—a situation which may be of considerable emotional significance if he has been used to staying alone when traveling or attending conventions. He is given a notebook which contains general information, schedules, and group assignments. He is also given a name tag which has only his name on it, making it clear at the outset that he is at the laboratory as a *person*, not as a representative of the organization.

Initial conversations among the delegates, perhaps while unpacking, often involve attempts to discover what the laboratory is all about and how expert others are about it. The range of responses is likely to be from complete ignorance and confusion among some, to tales of "emotional bloodbaths" among others who have undergone experiences that they believe to have been similar or who have read about T-groups in popularized articles. The uncertainty about what lies ahead is preoccupying and provokes tension.

This newness, the uncertainty, and the apprehension all work toward a situation in which the delegate arrives at his first orientation session unable to comprehend what is being said. He is too busy trying to get acclimatized and to get control of his own feelings of tension and uncertainty. Some delegates have read portions of their notebook, but these are not informative either, at this stage of the game.

FIRST SESSION

The orientation session for the entire group of from 50 to 75 delegates is generally held in the early afternoon of the first day. It deals with matters of housekeeping (dining room hours, recreation facilities, how to get laundry done, and so forth), provides an opportunity to introduce the staff of the laboratory, and states in brief form the goals of the laboratory and the kinds of learning activities which hopefully will enable the delegates to achieve these goals.

For example, in a typical introduction, the "dean" of the laboratory or some other staff member points out that the *goals* of the laboratory are to create opportunities for the delegates *to learn* about the following kinds of things:

1. *Self.* The delegates' own behavior in groups and the impact which their behavior has on other members.
2. *Others.* The behavior of others in a group and the impact which their behavior has on them.
3. *Groups.* How groups work; what makes them function.
4. *Larger systems.* How organizations and larger social systems work.
5. *The learning process.* How to learn from their own experience ("learning how to learn").

These are deceptively simple goals and are in general only vaguely understood when first outlined. In discussing the *method* by which we learn in a laboratory setting, the speaker indicates that the basic difference between the laboratory and the traditional learning experience is that in the former we attempt to learn *from an analysis of our own experiences in groups* rather than from what some expert tells us. Thus, the term laboratory implies that the delegate has an opportunity to become a researcher and a student of his own and others' group behavior; he becomes both the subject and the experimenter-observer. The speaker points out that it is easier to explain this method after the delegates have had some experience in the laboratory. He then turns to an explanation of the daily schedule (see Table 1), after which he sends the delegates to their groups for the first training group (T-group) session.

Table 1 Typical Schedule for the Week

	Sun.	Mon.	Tues.	Wed.	Thurs.	Fri.
9:00–11:00		T-group	T-group	T-group	T-group	T-group
11:00–11:30		Coffee break	Coffee break	Coffee break	Coffee break	Coffee break
11:30–12:30		General session	General session	General session	General session	General session
12:30–1:30		Lunch	Lunch	Lunch	Lunch	Lunch
1:30–3:30		T-group	T-group	Exercise	Exercise	Exercise
3:30–6:00	Opening session	Free time	Free time	Free time	Free time	Free time
6:00–7:30		Dinner	Dinner	Dinner	Dinner	Dinner
7:30–9:30	T-group	T-group	Tape listening exercise	Free	Exercise or training film	Free

The schedule which is given to the delegate will indicate the major training activities of the laboratory:

1. *T-groups.* These are basic learning groups which continue to meet throughout the course of the laboratory. They usually contain 10 to 15 members with one or two staff members or "trainers." T-groups are generally "unstructured," in the sense that the staff provides a minimum of agenda and formal leadership. [The T in T-group stands for training. Such groups have also been called D-groups (development) and study groups.]
2. *Information or theory sessions.* These are general sessions during which a staff member lectures and/or gives a demonstration to impart some concepts or ideas or research findings about an area relevant to the laboratory goals.
3. *Focused exercises.* These are activities which may involve small or large groups. They are usually introduced by a staff member who describes the learning goals and the specific activities, such as role-playing or group observation, which are to be engaged in by the delegates.
4. *Other activities.* Most laboratories involve seminars, two-man interview groups (dyads), informal bull sessions, and other activities which may be introduced during its course. Some of these will be described below in our chronicle. They are usually not included on the delegate's regular schedule because of their informal or optional status.

Scheduled activities generally take place from 9 to 12 in the morning, 1 to 3 in the afternoon, and 8 to 10 in the evening. What the schedule can only half-successfully impart, but which is crucial is the degree to which the training design is an attempt to integrate the scheduled activities, and the degree to which informal unscheduled activities form an integral part of the total training. Furthermore, the schedule itself overstates the rigidity of the laboratory. Actually, the staff communicates to delegates that they, as well as the staff, have the power to change the schedule if training needs dictate such changes.

THE T-GROUP

The T-group is, for most delegates, the major emotional focus of their laboratory experience. From their notebooks, they discover which group they are in. Also in the notebook is a roster of all delegates including their job title and organization. Finding out who the other members of their group are, including the staff member, becomes one of the first anchors around which the delegates organize their experience. This anchor takes on additional importance as the delegate discovers the unstructured nature of the T-group.

The group meets in a room around a large table. Each person is given a name card which is placed in front of him. There is usually a tape-recorder on or near the table. When the group has settled down, the staff member gives a short introduction, usually lasting less than five minutes, in which he restates some of the learning goals. He points out that the T-group's primary task is to create learning opportunities for its members, and that it has no formal leader, preset agenda, or rules by which it must operate. It is up to the whole group, including the staff member, to decide what to do and how best to learn from its experience.

Whether he emphasizes it in the introduction or later, the trainer makes it clear that it is legitimate and likely to be profitable for the group to try to learn from its *own* experienced behavior—the "here-and-now" situation—rather than to discuss problems outside the group, from the world they left, the "there-and-then" world. The tape-recorder, which will be running at all times unless the group decides to turn it off, is available as a learning aid to enable the group to recapitulate and study some of its earlier experiences. The tapes are the property of the group and are erased at the end of the laboratory. If the staff member comments on his own role at all, he is likely to state that he does not perceive himself to be the chairman or leader of the group, but rather a person who will help the learning process in whatever way he can. [We have had to qualify so often this description of what the staff member does because of the huge variation among trainers in how they open the T-group and the kind of role they make for themselves. For a more complete discussion of the role of the trainer, the reader is referred to Chapter 16 of Schein and Bennis (1965) and to the volume on training by Bradford, Gibb, and Benne (1964).]

When the trainer finishes his introduction, the group is suddenly left to its own resources. It is difficult to describe the full emotional impact of the beginning minutes of a T-group because the members are struggling with so many emotional issues at once. They are confronted with a violation of many expectations they have taken for granted in educational settings, most of all that the trainer will define an agenda, some ground rules and some goals which are meaningful for the group. Instead, each member confronts some major problems — "what do we do and what are our goals"; "who am I to be in this unstructured situation and what kind of role should I play"; "how can I keep sufficient control over the group to prevent it from doing things which will make me too uncomfortable?"

In coping with these problems, different members use different strategies. Some ask further questions of the trainer; some try to get him to be more of a leader or guide; some lapse into an anxious watchful silence; some get angry; and some attempt to organize the group with various tasks like "introducing ourselves." As the members fill the vacuum with their behavior, they begin to generate the raw data from which they will have the opportunity to learn about themselves, their impact on others, others' reactions to them, and how groups work.

How the T-group goes about its business of creating learning opportunities during the first and subsequent sessions is hard to characterize because each group has its own unique history. It has its own particular combination of people; its own particular trainer with his own theory of learning and style of intervention; its unforeseen incidents, dilemmas, and crises. It creates, for each member, a unique set of emotional and intellectual experiences.

T-groups do have in common the kinds of issues or dilemmas which have to be resolved in the process of building a group and learning from this procedure — what to do, how to spend the time, how to distribute power, control and influence, how to develop group standards and a climate which permits maximum learning, how to develop group goals and a sense of group progress, how to keep the group process within bounds. It is the particular solutions to such dilemmas which make each group unique.

A DIGRESSION: THE LEARNING PROCESS IN THE T-GROUP

What does the delegate begin to learn from the unstructured group experience? In what manner does he first discover for himself the meaning of the laboratory method of learning? For some delegates, learning begins immediately with the opportunity to study their own reactions to this novel experience, and to compare their reactions with those of others. For other delegates, the learning process does not begin until they become involved in some incident in the life of the T-group in which they are confronted with unexpected feelings on the part of others, either in reaction to their own behavior or to the behavior of others. Both kinds of delegates gain an *increased awareness of their own feelings and the feelings of others.* What is this increased awareness about?

For many delegates, the learning process first focuses around the problem of *communication.* While most delegates admit at the outset that they are not as good listeners as it might be hoped, rarely do they realize how little listening they or anyone else in the group does during the early sessions. The discovery that they missed many things altogether and that various group members heard the same speaker say entirely different things is shocking and thought provoking. *They become more aware of the complexity of the communication process.*

For some delegates, the problem of communication is not as salient as the problem of structure and organization in the group. Those who wish to get the group organized often find themselves confronted by others who are comfortable in an unstructured setting and vice versa. An important first learning step for this group is the *awareness and acceptance of genuine differences in member needs, goals, and ways of approaching problems.*

Another kind of learning which occurs results from a group member getting reactions from others in areas about which he is relatively blind. The person who leaps into the early power vacuum of the group with the sincere motive of getting the group moving may discover that a number of other members perceived him as attempting to dominate and control the group. The silent member may discover that he communicates more of his feelings through his silence than he realizes, and that for many members his behavior is a subtle but powerful way of controlling the group. The person who tries to help by giving reactions to others whenever the impulse moves him may discover that others do not find his "feedback" helpful, either because it is too evaluative, too ill-timed, or too hostile in undertone. The person who hides his own feelings by being constantly analytical about what the group is doing may discover that several members view his behavior as a real barrier to group progress instead of an aid. For all of these delegates, the crucial learning process is *increased awareness of their own impact on others* which enables them to check the assumptions they have made about themselves.

Some delegates focus their learning effort on the level of group processes. They discover that group decisions are tricky things to observe and to manage intelligently. Sometimes a minority pushes the group into action because each of the silent members erroneously assumes that the silence of the others means consent. Sometimes the group votes and then acts on majority rule only to discover that the minority is effectively able to block the action. The group may elect or appoint a chairman only to discover that he is unable to control the vicissitudes of the meeting because the same members who were willing to have him be chairman discover that they are unwilling to have him exercise any kind of control. Sometimes the group sets up an agenda only to discover that the agenda tyrannizes the group and prevents it from doing what it really wants to do. Yet, no one knows how to undo the group decision, particularly if it was hard won in the first place. *Increased awareness of how groups function and the consequences of certain kinds of group action* are the learning result.

Usually these discoveries result from an emotionally taxing reconstruction of some of the earlier events in the group's life. In the process of making such a reconstruction, members learn how to be better observers of group action, learn what sorts of observation other members have made, and learn what sorts of reaction have been aroused by various incidents in the group's history. Almost in spite of themselves group members become more observant, more analytical, and more cautious in making assumptions about group behavior. They are, in this sense, *learning how to learn* from their own experience.

Out of increased awareness in all these areas comes the possibility of changed attitudes. The delegate develops new attitudes toward the learning process, toward himself, toward others, and toward groups. Out of such attitude changes will come new behavior and greater competence in dealing with others. The major learning outcomes, therefore, will be *increased awareness, changed attitudes,* and *greater interpersonal competence.*

THEORY SESSIONS

It is a basic assumption of laboratory training that experience must precede the introduction of a theoretical concept. Equally important is the assumption that raw experience without some degree of intellectual understanding is insufficient to produce learning which is useful and can be generalized. The delegate must be able to fit his experience into a framework of concepts and ideas which will allow him to relate to situations and persons other than in the laboratory.

In order to optimize learning, delegates attend daily information or theory sessions. The content of these sessions is designed to help them understand the experiences they are having in the T-group by focusing on topics such as the following: what to observe in a group, emotional problems of becoming a member of a new group, decision making and problem solving in groups, the communication process, styles of emotional expression and presentation of self to others.

For example, after the first T-group session, the entire delegate group usually goes to a general session during which the speaker discusses in greater detail the set of assumptions which underlie the laboratory method, in particular why the T-group is so unstructured. He points out that the removal of structure, agenda, and ground rules facilitates a *maximum exposure* of the reactions of the group members to the group situation. There is no place to hide, no agenda or set of rules behind which to obscure feelings. He also points out that merely creating a situation in which members expose some of their typical reactions does not, by itself, lead to learning. In addition, there must develop a *frank sharing of reactions and feelings* and a *climate of support and encouragement* which facilitates further exposure; there must develop a *willingness to engage in genuine mutual exploration* of group phenomena and a group atmosphere in which *experimentation* and *exploration* are viewed as positive sources of learning; there must develop a set of ground rules and a climate which permits *behavior to be viewed objectively* as data for analysis, rather than as something to be evaluated, rewarded, or punished. Finally, for the learning experience to be fully useful to the person, there must develop some degree of *intellectual understanding* of what is happening at the emotional level.

The speaker generally attempts to draw his illustrations from his own T-group experience and to show that the seemingly unique events in the groups do fit some theoretical framework and can be generalized, to some extent, to other groups in other settings. When such lectures are well done, the delegates have a genuine sense of integration with the realization that *neither the T-group nor the lectures would make complete sense without the other.* Together, they can make a potent learning experience.

In designing the content of theory sessions, the staff draws on its general knowledge of what issues the T-groups are likely to be facing at any given time and how these relate to other laboratory and back-home realities. In many instances, however, they will introduce new topics on short notice if it appears that several groups are facing some new issue which was not going to be dealt with. This requires close coordination among staff members and a sharing of what they perceive to be happening in their T-groups from day to day.

During the second week, the emphasis in theory sessions usually shifts somewhat from T-group issues to issues which arise in social systems, organizations, and communities. More attention is given to the occupational role which the delegate plays, to problems of authority and delegation, theories of management and organization, the consequences of collaboration or competition, and the like. As we will see below, an attempt is made to integrate this material with experiences generated in focused exercises.

FOCUSED EXERCISES

The purpose of focused exercises is to generate some specific behavior so that a particular area can be studied (e.g., the communication process), or to practice some skill which is important for further learning (e.g., how to observe group action). An example of the former is an experiment highlighting the differences between one- and two-way communication. A delegate is asked to give some complex instructions to a group under two kinds of conditions: *one-way communication*, defined by the ground rule that the group is not allowed to ask any questions during the instructions, and *two-way communication*, defined by the ground rule that the group may say anything during the instructions. The one-way and two-way conditions can then be compared in terms of accuracy of communication, length of time taken, feelings of the sender and the receivers, and so forth.

An example of the latter, practicing a skill, is an exercise on skills of observation. One half of the T-group is asked to engage in a short role-playing sequence while the other half of the group observes the interaction in terms of categories decided on prior to the exercise. If observation is the sole focus, the different observers then take time to compare their observation and discuss the possible sources of difference in them. If, in addition, the exercise is designed to practice the skill of giving feedback to make the participant group more effective, a period is set aside for the observers to report on their findings to the participants. The participants are then interviewed to obtain their reactions to the feedback, or are allowed to engage in further interaction to determine what difference, if any, the feedback has made. A final portion of the exercise is a joint discussion or a reversal of roles among the groups between that of actor and that of observer.

An exercise such as any of these involves practice in several kinds of activities: actually observing others while remaining silent, analyzing observations and reconciling differences between observers, deciding what observations to report back to the group in order to be helpful, and the actual process of giving the feedback in such a way as to maximize learning opportunities. The behavior to be watched may be left entirely to the observers or may be structured into the exercise through instructions and observational forms. Such forms deal with communication patterns, the kinds of membership roles which different people play, patterns of influence and leadership, methods of group decision, style of expressing emotions, and so forth.

Toward the end of the first week or beginning of the second week, a more complicated and extensive exercise may be introduced. One frequently used exercise is on intergroup competition. Two or three T-groups are each given instructions to produce some product—a one or two page paper on some relevant topic—which is evaluated by a panel of judges consisting of members drawn from the competing groups. For example, the instructions may be to produce a 200-word statement outlining a plan for the conversion of a highly autocratic organization into one which practices participative management techniques, or a plan for the movement of a plant from one city to another with minimum negative consequences. One product is judged the winner. The purpose of the exercise is to give the groups a chance to work on some concrete task and to explore the dynamics of intergroup competition. By the time this exercise is introduced, the groups are usually more ready to begin a concrete task and to test themselves against other groups, a situation which produces high levels of motivation for the exercise.

The group first selects one or two of its members to join the judging panel, after which it works on its product for two hours or so. In the meantime, the judges meet to develop criteria by which the product will be judged. When each group has finished, the paper is turned over to the laboratory secretary for duplication and distribution to the competing groups. In the free time after the work period, one typically sees the groups clustered in separate parts of the conference center reviewing how they worked, expressing confidence in their own product, and generally derogating (though in a joking manner) the other groups. Questionnaire data on how the groups perceive their own effectiveness and that of the other groups are gathered by the staff before the groups begin working on the product and again after they have finished.

The following morning, the groups meet to look at their own product and that of the other groups. They are told that a general session is scheduled at which time they will have a chance to argue for their product through a spokesman who will engage in a debate with spokesmen from the other competing groups. The groups spend some time electing this spokesman and developing a strategy for him to follow in the debate. During the general session, each group sits behind its spokesman and is allowed to pass notes to him but not to communicate with him in any other way. At various points during the morning, data are gathered on each group's opinion of which is the best product, and whether it feels the judges will be influenced primarily by the merit of the product or by loyalty to their group.

After the debate, the judges deliberate in front of all the groups and reach a decision. At this point, feelings run very high, particularly in the losing group or groups. Each group is sent back to its own room for 30 minutes or so to consider how it feels about the decision. In the meantime, the data gathered at various points are being tabulated in preparation for a total feedback and analysis session. After the half hour of separate group meetings, the groups are brought back into general session to be interviewed by a staff member—do they feel the decision was fair, do they feel the judges were swayed by loyalty, and so forth?

In line with the general assumption that for maximum learning the experiences which the groups have had must be analyzed and put into a framework, the final portion of the exercise is devoted to an hour or more of systematic recapitulation supported by the results of the questionnaires which had been administered at various points during the total exercise.[1] One effective way to conduct the general session is to have a staff member make some predictions about group reactions to (1) having a concrete

---

[1] This particular intergroup competition exercise was adapted from a previously employed and systematically conducted experiment, thus permitting some predictions to be made about the outcome. The exercise was developed by Blake and Shepard and is based on experiments conducted by Muzafer Sherif.

task to perform under time pressure, (2) being in a competitive situation, and (3) actually winning or losing. He may also point out some of the strains of being a judge or being a group spokesman. The delegates are then invited to comment on the predictions—did they observe the phenomenon predicted or not, and if not, why do they feel it did not occur in their group. Finally, the questionnaire data, which also bear on the predictions, are presented. These usually support the predictions in a clear fashion and create a dramatic finale to the exercise.

In this type of exercise, an attempt is made to simulate the realities of organizations and social systems. The exercise highlights for delegates the positive and negative consequences of intergroup competition, what it feels like to be a winner or a loser, a judge or a group representative. The exercise also begins to refocus the delegate on his back-home situation. Where the T-group is oriented to the here-and-now, the intergroup exercise begins to bridge the gap to the job situation with all of its intergroup conflict problems. Delegates usually have little difficulty generalizing some of their observations to labor-management negotiations, staff-line conflicts, interdepartmental rivalries, and majority-minority conflicts in committee meetings and other instances of intergroup discord.

One important learning outcome of the exercise is the discovery by most delegates that the losing group rarely changes its mind about which product was the best; rather, it rationalizes in a variety of ways reasons for its loss. Once a group becomes committed to its product, it has difficulty seeing the merit in another group's product. Even if the delegate already knows that this phenomenon tends to occur, his knowledge takes on a new and more significant meaning when he relates it to his own intense and often irrational feelings of loyalty to his T-group, and when he studies the nature of his own feelings and shares them with other members who have similar feelings.

THE SECOND WEEK

The main task of the first week is entry into the laboratory culture. Re-entry into the back-home world is the primary task of the second week. During this week, the increasing attention on back-home problems is manifested in a variety of ways. Sometimes groups are brought together with the task of discussing how they might apply some of their new knowledge to the back-home situation. Or, meetings of groups are held at which members take turns discussing some particular back-home problem they have, while the other members attempt, through interviewing and careful diagnosis, to give help to each other on the problem. The real benefit of this kind of activity is to give the helpers practice in the art of giving help. If the problem presenter gains new insight into his back-home situation, this is a secondary gain. In some laboratory designs, a new set of groups is started with the purpose of giving every member the experience of making a transition from one group to another. The problems of re-entry into the back-home groups can then be assessed in the light of the transitional experience within the laboratory.

To support the theoretical material on problems of organizations and change, additional exercises are sometimes used. For example, to deepen understanding of the forces which make for or restrain change, the T-groups may be asked to diagnose the forces which have led to greater openness of communication in the group and those forces which have tended to prevent it. To obtain increased insight into organizational phenomena, groups may be given the task of simulating a company to market an actual product, while observers study the procedures used by the groups to establish their organization and to handle the kinds of problems that develop.

INFORMAL CONTACTS

One other type of activity which takes on increasing importance as the laboratory proceeds is the informal contact made with the staff in individual or seminar sessions. Sometimes seminars are scheduled around topics which are of particular interest to staff members. In some laboratories, the delegates survey their own needs and ask that certain seminar topics be covered by any staff member (or other delegate) who is willing to act as seminar leader. Topics, such as the role of values in business, reconciliation of problems of family and career, the place of religion in modern life, the possibility of a similarity between laboratory training and brainwashing, may be proposed. Even if no one is found to be an expert resource person in the area, the group is encouraged to meet and discuss the issue.

In addition to seminars, a variety of informal contacts with staff develop in which either small groups or individuals get together with a staff member, often the trainer of their own T-group, to discuss anything ranging from the possible applications of the laboratory method to back-home problems to more general issues like the nature of organization theory. The staff member may be asked to elaborate on a lecture he gave or discuss what is new in a given area of research. Or, he may be sought out for guidance relating to a delegate's personal problem. If the staff member feels that the pursuit of such an area would create a problem (because of the special relationship which this would imply between himself and a single member of the T-group or because he might not feel qualified to enter such a counseling relationship), he can suggest that the delegate take the problem to a particular staff member, usually a psychiatrist hired for this purpose, who holds himself more available for individual help.

Informal contacts among *delegates* are also of great importance in furthering the learning process. To facilitate such contacts, meal times, coffee breaks, cocktail hours, and periods of recreation are kept as informal as possible and are scheduled to be as long as possible. Delegates are encouraged to review and work through what is going on in their groups and what they have heard in lectures; to work out in subgroups those problems which the total T-group could not solve; to explore in greater depth issues which have arisen in the group; to get other members to elaborate on feedback which was given initially in the group; to explore with others, who have similar jobs or come from similar organizations, the relevance of things learned to the job situation.

The focus during T-group meetings is on here-and-now group events; informal times provide an opportunity to talk about there-and-then back-home problems or more general issues. Informal contacts also provide important supports. The skeptic can seek out other skeptics and share his doubts about the value of the laboratory method; the enthusiast can seek out other enthusiasts; the person who is troubled by something said to him in the group can talk it over with someone whom he perceives as being supportive. Incidentally, in those laboratories where the physical facilities require delegates to share rooms, it is found that the late evening bull sessions among roommates are one of the most meaningful of these informal contacts.

OUTCOMES OF THE LABORATORY

As the laboratory draws to a close, a variety of reactions among the delegates is noticed. There are those for whom the opportunity to concentrate on themselves and their own problems has been so meaningful and so releasing that they are genuinely reluctant to see the experience end. They feel they have become better acquainted with themselves. They may not be sure how this will affect them on the job or at home, but they are sure that the experience has been very worth while.

There are others who feel they have had a revelation as to what makes other people and groups work. They have had the opportunity, for the first time perhaps, to study the reactions of others and to observe how a group must struggle with the diversity of its human resources. Sometimes such insights lead to sharply changed attitudes toward groups and group action. Outright hostility toward any form of committee often changes into a more sensitive understanding of groups, and into recognition that groups can only be effective if allowed to mature and work through their initial problems.

There are some delegates for whom the most meaningful experience has been that they have been accepted and liked by the other group members. They go back home with a renewed sense of confidence in themselves. There are others for whom the experience has been primarily disturbing because they may have discovered that they were not as persuasive, clever, or powerful as they had assumed. They will go home with more questions about themselves than they had brought, and many of these questions will remain unanswered for some time after the laboratory.

Still others will see in the laboratory some gimmicks and devices for use in back-home groups, and will attempt to utilize these in spite of entreaties from staff not to take the laboratory method as a model of how to run a work group or a business. For some of these "alumni," the gimmicks will fail; they may then turn against the laboratory method feeling it to be a fraud, without recognizing their own misuse of the method.

Some delegates will cherish the fact that the laboratory provided a two-week period during which they could leave behind their work and family and ruminate about basic issues of life. For them, it offered a retreat and an opportunity to revitalize themselves. Some delegates will find that among their fellow T-group members, roommates, or other contacts, they can now count several close friends with whom they will maintain a relationship in the future. Some of these friendships may be more intimate than any they have in their back-home situation.

Some delegates will suffer intensely during the entire laboratory period because, from their point of view, very little was actually accomplished; they will go home puzzled, confused, and still skeptical.

All delegates, whether they are aware of it or not, go home with greater skills as group observers and diagnosticians, and with greater sensitivity to the complexity of interpersonal relationships. Whether they *utilize* this increased sensitivity constructively or not depends upon them, but there is little doubt that they have acquired it. All delegates become familiar with a new approach to learning—utilizing their own experience and learning from it. All delegates finally understand why it was so difficult for others to tell them what the laboratory would be about. As they think back over their own experiences, they realize how personal and unique these have been and how difficult it will be to tell others what has transpired.

REFERENCES

Bradford, L. P., J. R. Gibb, and K. D. Benne. *T-Group Theory and Laboratory Method*. Wiley, 1964.

Schein, E. H., and W. G. Bennis. *Personal and Organization Change Through Group Methods*. Wiley, 1965.

Patterns of Organization Change

Larry E. Greiner

Today many top managers are attempting to introduce sweeping and basic changes in the behavior and practices of the supervisors and the subordinates throughout their organizations. Whereas only a few years ago the target of organization change was limited to a small work group or a single department, especially at lower levels, the focus is now converging on the organization as a whole, reaching out to include many divisions and levels at once, and even the top managers themselves. There is a critical need at this time to understand better this complex process, especially in terms of which approaches lead to successful changes and which actions fail to achieve the desired results.

REVOLUTIONARY PROCESS

The shifting emphasis from small- to large-scale organization change represents a significant departure from past managerial thinking. For many years, change was regarded more as an evolutionary than a revolutionary process. The evolutionary assumption reflected the view that change is a product of one minor adjustment after another, fueled by time and subtle environmental forces largely outside the direct control of management. This relatively passive philosophy of managing change is typically expressed in words like these:

"Our company is continuing to benefit from a dynamically expanding market. While our share of the market has remained the same, our sales have increased 15% over the past year. In order to handle this increased business, we have added a new marketing vice president and may have to double our sales force in the next two years."

Such an optimistic statement frequently belies an unbounding faith in a beneficent environment. Perhaps this philosophy was adequate in less competitive times, when small patchwork changes, such as replacing a manager here and there, were sufficient to maintain profitability. But now the environments around organizations are changing rapidly and are challenging managements to become far more alert and inventive than they ever were before.

Management Awakening

In recent years more and more top managements have begun to realize that fragmented changes are seldom effective in stemming the underlying tides of stagnation and complacency that can subtly creep into a profitable and growing organization. While rigid and uncreative attitudes are slow to develop, they are also slow to disappear, even in the face of frequent personnel changes. Most often these signs of decay can be recognized in managerial behavior that (a) is oriented more to the past than to the future, (b) recognizes the obligations of ritual more than the challenges of current problems, and (c) owes allegiance more to department goals than to overall company objectives.

Management's recent awakening to these danger signs has been stimulated largely by the rapidly changing tempo and quality of its environment. Consider:

- Computer technology has narrowed the decision time span.
- Mass communication has heightened public awareness of consumer products.
- New management knowledge and techniques have come into being.
- Technological discoveries have multiplied.
- New world markets have opened up.
- Social drives for equality have intensified.
- Governmental demands and regulations have increased.

As a result, many organizations are currently being challenged to shift, or even reverse, gears in order to survive, let alone prosper.

A number of top managements have come around to adopting a revolutionary attitude toward change, in order to bridge the gap between a dynamic environment and a stagnant organization. They feel that they can no longer sit back and condone organizational self-indulgence, waiting for time to heal all wounds. So, through a number of means, revolutionary attempts are now being made to transform their organizations rapidly by altering the behavior and attitudes of their line and staff personnel at all levels of management. While each organization obviously varies in its approach, the overarching goal seems to be the same: to get everyone psychologically redirected toward solving the problems and challenges of today's business environment. Here, for example, is how one company president describes his current goal for change:

"I've got to get this organization moving, and soon. Many of our managers act as if we were still selling the products that used to be our bread and butter. We're in a different business now, and I'm not sure that they realize it. Somehow we've got to start recognizing our problems, and then become more competent in solving them. This applies to everyone here, including me and the janitor. I'm starting with a massive reorganization which I hope will get us pulling together instead of in fifty separate directions."

Striking Similarities

Although there still are not many studies of organization change, the number is growing; and a survey of them shows that it is already possible to detect some striking similarities running throughout their findings. I shall report some of these similarities, under two headings:

1. *Common approaches* being used to initiate organization change.
2. *Reported results*—what happened in a number of cases of actual organization change.

I shall begin with the approaches, and then attempt to place them within the perspective of what has happened when these approaches were applied. As we shall see, only a few of the approaches used tend to facilitate successful change, but even here we find that each is aided by unplanned forces preceding and following its use.

Finally, I shall conclude with some tentative interpretations as to what I think is actually taking place when an organization change occurs.

COMMON APPROACHES

In looking at the various major approaches being used to *introduce* organization change, one is immediately struck by their position along a "power distribution" continuum. At one extreme are those which rely on *unilateral* authority. More toward the middle of the continuum are the *shared* approaches. Finally, at the opposite extreme are the *delegated* approaches.

As we shall see later, the *shared* approaches tend to be emphasized in the more successful organization changes. Just why this is so is an important question we will consider in the concluding section. For now, though, let us gain a clearer picture of the various approaches as they appear most frequently in the literature of organization change.

Unilateral Action

At this extreme on the power distribution continuum, the organization change is implemented through an emphasis on the authority of a man's hierarchical position in the company. Here, the definition and solution to the problem at hand tend to be specified by the upper echelons and directed downward through formal and impersonal control mechanisms. The use of unilateral authority to introduce organization change appears in three forms.

By decree. This is probably the most commonly used approach, having its roots in centuries of practice within military and government bureaucracies and taking its authority from the formal position of the person introducing the change. It is essentially a "one-way" announcement that is directed downward to the lower levels in the organization. The spirit of the communication reads something like "today we are this way — tomorrow we must be that way."

In its concrete form it may appear as a memorandum, lecture, policy statement, or verbal command. The general nature of the decree approach is impersonal, formal, and task-oriented. It assumes that people are highly rational and best motivated by authoritative directions. Its expectation is that people will comply in their outward behavior and that this compliance will lead to more effective results.

By replacement. Often restored to when the decree approach fails, this involves the replacement of key persons. It is based on the assumption that organization problems tend to reside in a few strategically located individuals, and that replacing these people will bring about sweeping and basic changes. As in the decree form, this change is usually initiated at the top and directed downward by a high authority figure. At the same time, however, it tends to be somewhat more personal, since particular individuals are singled out for replacement. Nevertheless, it retains much of the formality and explicit concern for task accomplishment that is common to the decree approach. Similarly, it holds no false optimism about the ability of individuals to change their own behavior without clear outside direction.

By structure. This old and familiar change approach is currently receiving much reevaluation by behavioral scientists. In its earlier form, it involved a highly rational approach to the design of formal organization and to the layout of technology. The basic assumption here was that people behaved in close agreement with the structure and technology governing them. However, it tended to have serious drawbacks, since what seemed logical on paper was not necessarily logical for human goals.

Recently attempts have been made to alter the organizational structure in line with what is becoming known about both the logics and nonlogics of human behavior, such as engineering the job to fit the man, on the one hand, or adjusting formal authority to match informal authority, on the other hand. These attempts, however, still rely heavily on mechanisms for change that tend to be relatively formal, impersonal, and located outside the individual. At the same time, however, because of greater concern for the effects of structure on people, they can probably be characterized as more personal, subtle, and less directive than either the decree or replacement approaches.

Sharing of Power

More toward the middle of the power distribution continuum, as noted earlier, are the shared approaches, where authority is still present and used, yet there is also interaction and sharing of power. This approach to change is utilized in two forms.

By group decision making. Here the problems still tend to be defined unilaterally from above, but lower-level groups are usually left free to develop alternative solutions and to choose among them. The main assumption tends to be that individuals develop more commitment to action when they have a voice in the decisions that affect them. The net result is that power is shared between bosses and subordinates, though there is a division of labor between those who define the problems and those who develop the solutions.

By group problem solving. This form emphasizes both the definition and the solution of problems within the context of group discussion. Here power is shared throughout the decision process, but, unlike group decision making, there is an added opportunity for lower-level subordinates to define the problem. The assumption underlying this approach is not only that people gain greater commitment from being exposed to a wider decision-making role, but also that they have significant knowledge to contribute to the definition of the problem.

Delegated Authority

At the other extreme from unilateral authority are found the delegated approaches, where almost complete responsibility for defining and acting on problems is turned over to the subordinates. These also appear in two forms.

By case discussion. This method focuses more on the acquisition of knowledge and skills than on the solution of specific problems at hand. An authority figure, usually a teacher or boss, uses his power only to guide a general discussion of information describing a problem situation, such as a case or a report of research results. The "teacher" refrains from imposing his own analysis or solutions on the group. Instead, he encourages individual members to arrive at their own insights, and they are left to use them as they see fit. The implicit assumption here is that individuals, through the medium of discussion about concrete situations, will develop general problem-solving skills to aid them in carrying out subsequent individual and organization changes.

By T-group sessions. These sessions, once conducted mainly in outside courses for representatives of many different organizations, are increasingly being used inside individual companies for effecting change. Usually, they are confined to top management, with the hope that beneficial "spill-over" will result for the rest of the organization. The primary emphasis of the T-group tends to be on increasing an individual's self-awareness and sensitivity to group social processes. Compared to the previously discussed approaches, the T-group places much less emphasis on the discussion and solution of task-related problems. Instead, the data for discussion are typically the interpersonal actions of individuals in the group; no specific task is assigned to the group.

The basic assumption underlying this approach is that exposure to a structureless situation will release unconscious emotional energies within individuals, which, in turn, will lead to self-analysis, insight, and behavioral change. The authority figure in the group, usually a professional trainer, avoids asserting his own authority in structuring the group. Instead, he often attempts to become an accepted and influential member of the group. Thus, in comparison to the other approaches, much more authority is turned over to the group, from which position it is expected to chart its own course of change in an atmosphere of great informality and highly personal exchanges.

REPORTED RESULTS

As we have seen, each of the major approaches, as well as the various forms within them, rests on certain assumptions about what *should* happen when it is applied to initiate change. Now let us step back and consider what actually *does* happen — before, during, and after a particular approach is introduced.

To discover whether there are certain dimensions of organization change that might stand out against the background of characteristics unique to one company, we conducted a survey of 18 studies of organization change. Specifically, we were looking for the existence of dominant patterns of similarity and/or difference running across all of these studies. As we went along, relevant information was written down and compared with the other studies in regard to (a) the conditions leading up to an attempted change, (b) the manner in which the change was introduced, (c) the critical blocks and/or facilitators encountered during implementation, and (d) the more lasting results which appeared over a period of time.

The survey findings show some intriguing similarities and differences between those studies reporting "successful" change patterns and those disclosing "less successful" changes — i.e., failure to achieve the desired results. The successful changes generally appear as those which:

• Spread throughout the organization to include and affect many people.
• Produce positive changes in line and staff attitudes.
• Prompt people to behave more effectively in solving problems and in relating to others.
• Result in improved organization performance.

Significantly, the less successful changes fall short on all of these dimensions.

Using the category breakdown just cited as the baseline for "success," the survey reveals some very distinct patterns in the evolution of change. In all, eight major patterns are identifiable in five studies reporting successful change, and six other success studies show quite similar characteristics, although the information contained in each is somewhat less complete. (See the Appendix for studies included in the survey.) Consider:

1. The organization, and especially top management, is under considerable external and internal pressure for improvement long before an explicit organization change is contemplated. Performance and/or morale are low. Top management seems to be groping for a solution to its problems.
2. A new man, known for his ability to introduce improvements, enters the organization, either as the official head of the organization, or as a consultant who deals directly with the head of the organization.
3. An initial act of the new man is to encourage a reexamination of past practices and current problems within the organization.
4. The head of the organization and his immediate subordinates assume a direct and highly involved role in conducting this reexamination.
5. The new man, with top management support, engages several levels of the organization in collaborative, fact-finding, problem-solving discussions to identify and diagnose current organization problems.
6. The new man provides others with new ideas and methods for developing solutions to problems, again at many levels of the organization.
7. The solutions and decisions are developed, tested, and found creditable for solving problems on a small scale before an attempt is made to widen the scope of change to larger problems and the entire organization.
8. The change effort spreads with each success experience, and as management support grows, it is gradually absorbed permanently into the organization's way of life.

The likely significance of these similarities becomes more apparent when we consider the patterns found in the less successful organization changes. Let us briefly make this contrast before speculating further about why the successful changes seem to unfold as they do.

'Failure' Forms

Apart from their common "failure" to achieve the desired results, the most striking overall characteristic of seven less successful change studies is a singular lack of consistency—not just between studies, but within studies. Where each of the successful changes follows a similar and highly consistent route of one step building on another, the less successful changes are much less orderly (see Appendix for a list of these studies).

There are three interesting patterns of inconsistency:

1. The less successful changes begin from a variety of starting points. This is in contrast to the successful changes, which begin from a common point—i.e., strong pressure both externally and internally. Only one less successful change, for example, began with outside pressure on the organization; another originated with the hiring of a consultant; and a third started with the presence of internal pressure, but without outside pressure.

2. Another pattern of inconsistency is found in the sequence of change steps. In the successful change patterns, we observe some degree of logical consistency between steps, as each seems to make possible the next. But in the less successful changes, there are wide and seemingly illogical gaps in sequence. One study, for instance, described a big jump from the reaction to outside pressure to the installation of an unskilled newcomer who immediately attempted large-scale changes. In another case, the company lacked the presence of a newcomer to provide new methods and ideas to the organization. A third failed to achieve the cooperation and involvement of top management. And a fourth missed the step of obtaining early successes while experimenting with new change methods.

3. A final pattern of inconsistency is evident in the major approaches used to introduce change. In the successful cases, it seems fairly clear that *shared* approaches are used—i.e., authority figures seek the participation of subordinates in joint decision making. In the less successful attempts, however, the approaches used lie closer to the extreme ends of the power distribution continuum. Thus, in five less successful change studies, a *unilateral* approach (decree, replacement, structural) was used, while in two other studies a *delegated* approach (data discussion, T-group) was applied. None of the less successful change studies reported the use of a *shared* approach.

How can we use this lack of consistency in the sequence of change steps and this absence of shared power to explain the less successful change attempts? In the next section, I shall examine in greater depth the successful changes, which, unlike the less successful ones, are marked by a high degree of consistency and the use of shared power. My intent here will be not only to develop a tentative explanation of the more successful changes, but in so doing to explain the less successful attempts within the same framework.

POWER REDISTRIBUTION

Keeping in mind that the survey evidence on which both the successful and the less successful patterns are based is quite limited, I would like to propose a tentative explanatory scheme for viewing the change process as a whole, and also for considering specific managerial action steps within this overall process. The framework for this scheme hinges on two key notions:

1. Successful change depends basically on a *redistribution of power* within the structure of an organization. (By *power*, I mean the locus of formal authority and influence which typically is top management. By *redistribution*, I mean a significant alteration in the traditional practices that the power structure uses in making decisions. I propose that this redistribution move toward the greater use of *shared* power.)

2. Power redistribution occurs through a *developmental process of change*. (This implies that organization change is not a black to white affair occurring overnight through a single causal mechanism. Rather, as we shall see, it involves a number of phases, each containing specific elements and multiple causes that provoke a needed *reaction* from the power structure, which, in turn, sets the stage for the next phase in the process.)

Using the survey evidence from the successful patterns, I have divided the change process into six phases, each of them broken down into the particular stimulus and reaction which appear critical for moving the power structure from one phase to another. Exhibit 1 represents an abstract view of these two key notions in operation.

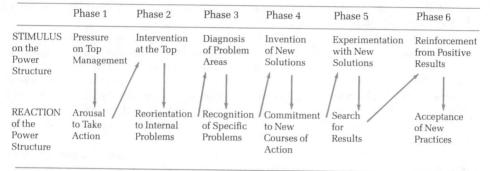

	Phase 1	Phase 2	Phase 3	Phase 4	Phase 5	Phase 6
STIMULUS on the Power Structure	Pressure on Top Management	Intervention at the Top	Diagnosis of Problem Areas	Invention of New Solutions	Experimentation with New Solutions	Reinforcement from Positive Results
REACTION of the Power Structure	Arousal to Take Action	Reorientation to Internal Problems	Recognition of Specific Problems	Commitment to New Courses of Action	Search for Results	Acceptance of New Practices

Exhibit 1 Dynamics of Successful Organization Change

Let us now consider how each of these phases and their specific elements make themselves evident in the patterns of successful change, as well as how their absence contributes to the less successful changes.

I. Pressure and Arousal

This initial stage indicates a need to shake the power structure at its very foundation. Until the ground under the top managers begins to shift, it seems unlikely that they will be sufficiently aroused to see the need for change, both in themselves and in the rest of the organization.

The success patterns suggest that strong pressures in areas of top management responsibility are likely to provoke the greatest concern for organization change. These pressures seem to come from two broad sources: (1) serious environmental factors, such as lower sales, stockholder discontent, or competitor breakthroughs; and (2) internal events, such as a union strike, low productivity, high costs, or interdepartmental conflict. These pressures fall into responsibility areas that top managers can readily see as reflecting on their own capability. An excerpt from one successful change study shows how this pressure and arousal process began:

" 'Pressure' was the common expression used at all levels. Urgent telephone calls, telegrams, letters and memoranda were being received by the plant from central headquarters. . . . Faced with an increase in directives from above and cognizant of Plant Y's low performance position, the manager knew that he was, as he put it, 'on the spot.' "[1]

As this example points out, it is probably significant when both environmental and internal pressures exist simultaneously. When only one is present, or when the two are offsetting (e.g., high profits despite low morale), it is easier for top management to excuse the pressure as only temporary or inconsequential. However, when both are present at once, it is easier to see that the organization is not performing effectively.

The presence of severe pressure is not so clearly evident in the less successful changes. In one case, there was internal pressure for more effective working relations between top management and lower levels; yet the company was doing reasonably well from a profit standpoint. In another case, there was environmental pressure for a centralized purchasing system, but little pressure from within for such a change.

II. Intervention and Reorientation

While strong pressure may arouse the power structure, this does not provide automatic assurance that top management will see its problems or take the correct action to solve them. Quite likely, top management, when under severe pressure, may be inclined to rationalize its problems by blaming them on a group other than itself, such as "that lousy union" or "that meddling government."

As a result, we find a second stage in the successful change patterns — namely, intervention by an outsider. Important here seems to be the combination of the fact that the newcomer enters at the top of the organization and the fact that he is respected for his skills at improving organization practices. Being a newcomer probably allows him to make a relatively objective appraisal of the organization; entering at the top gives him ready access to those people who make decisions affecting the entire organization; and his being respected is likely to give added weight to his initial comments about the organization.

Thus we find the newcomer in an ideal position to reorient the power structure to its own internal problems. This occurs in the successful changes as the newcomer encourages the top managers to reexamine their past practices and current problems. The effect appears to be one of causing the power structure to suspend, at least temporarily, its traditional habit of presuming beforehand where the "real" problems reside. Otherwise, we would not find top management undertaking the third stage — identifying and diagnosing organization problems. We can see how an outsider was accomplishing this reorientation in the following comment by the plant manager in one successful change study:

"I didn't like what the consultant told me about our problems being inside the organization instead of outside. But he was an outsider, supposedly an expert at this sort of thing. So maybe he could see our problems better than we could. I asked him what we ought to do, and he said that we should begin to identify our specific problems."[2]

Three of the less successful changes missed this step. Two of the three attempted large-scale changes without the assistance of an outsider, while the third relied on an outsider who lacked the necessary expertise for reorienting top management.

III. Diagnosis and Recognition

Here, we find the power structure, from top to bottom, as well as the newcomer, joining in to assemble information and collaborate in seeking the location and causes of problems. This process begins at the top, then moves gradually down through the organizational hierarchy. Most often, this occurs in meetings attended by people from various organization levels.

A *shared* approach to power and change makes itself evident during this stage. Through consulting with subordinates on the nature of problems, the top managers are seen as indicating a willingness to involve others in the decision-making process. Discussion topics, which formerly may have been regarded as taboo, are now treated as legitimate areas for further inquiry. We see the diagnosis and recognition process taking place in this example from one successful change study:

"The manager's role in the first few months, as he saw it, was to ask questions and to find out what ideas for improvement would emerge from the group as a whole. The process of information gathering took several forms, the principal one being face-to-face conversations between the manager and his subordinates, supervisors on the lower levels, hourly workers, and union representatives. Ideas were then listed for the agenda of weekly planning sessions."[3]

The significance of this step seems to go beyond the possible intellectual benefits derived from a thorough diagnosis of organization problems. This is due to the fact that in front of every subordinate there is evidence that (a) top management is willing to change, (b) important problems are being acknowledged and faced up to, and (c) ideas from lower levels are being valued by upper levels.

The less successful changes all seem to avoid this step. For example, on the one hand, those top managements that took a *unilateral* approach seemed to presume ahead of time that they knew what the real problems were and how to fix them. On the other hand, those that took a *delegated* approach tended to abdicate responsibility by turning over authority to lower levels in such a nondirective way that subordinates seemed to question the sincerity and real interest of top management.

IV. Invention and Commitment

Once problems are recognized, it is another matter to develop effective solutions and to obtain full commitment for implementing them. Traditional practices and solutions within an organization often maintain a hold that is difficult to shed. The temptation is always there, especially for the power structure, to apply old solutions to new problems. Thus, a fourth phase—the invention of new and unique solutions which have high commitment from the power structure—seems to be necessary.

The successful changes disclose widespread and intensive searches for creative solutions, with the newcomer again playing an active role. In each instance the newcomer involves the entire management in learning and practicing new forms of behavior which seek to tap and release the creative resources of many people. Again, as in the previous phase, the method for obtaining solutions is based on a *shared* power concept. Here the emphasis is placed on the use of collaboration and participation in developing group solutions to the problems identified in Phase III.

The potency of this model for obtaining both quality decisions and high commitment to action has been demonstrated repeatedly in research. In three successful changes, the model was introduced as a part of the Phase III diagnosis sessions, with the newcomer either presenting it through his informal comments or subtly conveying it through his own guiding actions as the attention of the group turned to the search for a solution. In two other studies, formal training programs were used to introduce and to help implement the model. For all successful changes, the outcome is essentially the same—a large number of people collaborate to invent solutions that are of their own making and which have their own endorsement.

It is significant that none of the less successful changes reach this fourth stage. Instead, the seeds of failure, sown in the previous phases, grow into instances of serious resistance to change. As a result, top management in such cases falls back, gives up, or regroups for another effort. Because these studies conclude their reports at this stage, we are not able to determine the final outcome of the less successful change attempts.

V. Experimentation and Search

Each of the successful change studies reports a fifth stage—that of "reality testing" before large-scale changes are introduced. In this phase not only the validity of specific decisions made in Phase IV, but also the underlying model for making these decisions (*shared* power), falls under careful organization scrutiny. Instead of making only big decisions at the top, a number of small decisions are implemented at *all* levels of the organization. Further, these decisions tend to be regarded more as experiments than as final, irreversible decisions. People at all organization levels seem to be searching for supporting evidence in their environment—e.g., dollar savings or higher motivation—before judging the relative merits of their actions. This concern is reflected in the comment of a consultant involved in one successful change:

"As might be expected, there was something less than a smooth, unresisted, uncomplicated transition to a new pattern of leadership and organizational activity. Events as they unfolded presented a mixture of successes and failures, frustrations and satisfactions. . . . With considerable apprehension, the supervisors agreed to go along with any feasible solution the employees might propose."[4]

This atmosphere of tentativeness is understandable when we think of a power structure undergoing change. On the one hand, lower-level managers are undoubtedly concerned with whether top management will support their decisions. If lower-level managers make decisions that fail, or are subsequently reversed by top levels, then their own future careers may be in jeopardy. Or, on the other hand, if higher-level managers, who are held responsible for the survival of the firm, do not see tangible improvements, then they may revert to the status quo or seek other approaches to change.

Thus, with these experimental attempts at change and the accompanying search for signs of payoff, there begins a final stage where people receive the results and react to them.

VI. Reinforcement and Acceptance

Each of the studies of successful change reports improvements in organization performance. Furthermore, there are relatively clear indications of strong support for change from all organization levels. Obviously, positive results have a strong reinforcing effect—that is, people are rewarded and encouraged to continue and even to expand the changes they are making. We see this expansion effect occurring as more and more problems are identified and a greater number of people participate in the solution of them. Consider this comment by a foreman in one study:

"I've noticed a real difference in the hourly workers. They seem a lot more willing to work, and I can't explain just why it is, but something has happened all right. I suppose it's being treated better. My boss treats me better because he gets treated better. People above me listen to me, and I hope, at least, that I listen to my people below me."[5]

The most significant effect of this phase is probably a greater and more permanent acceptance at all levels of the underlying methods used to bring about the change. In each of the successful changes, the use of *shared* power is more of an institutionalized and continuing practice than just a "one shot" method used to introduce change. With such a reorientation in the decision-making practices of the power structure, it hardly appears likely that these organizations will "slip back" to their previous behavior.

LOOKING AHEAD

What is needed in future changes in organization is less intuition and more consideration of the evidence that is now emerging from studies in this area. While it would be unwise to take too literally each of the major patterns identified in this article (future research will undoubtedly dispel, modify, or elaborate on them), their overall import suggests that it is time to put to bed some of the common myths about organization change. As I see it, there are four positive actions called for.

1. *We must revise our egocentric notions that organization change is heavily dependent on a master blueprint designed and executed in one fell swoop by an omniscient consultant or top manager.*

The patterns identified here clearly indicate that change is the outgrowth of several actions, some planned and some unplanned, each related to the other and occurring over time. The successful changes begin with pressure, which is unplanned from the organization's point of view. Then the more planned stages come into focus as top management initiates a series of events designed to involve lower-level people in the problem-solving process. But, even here, there are usually unplanned events as subordinates begin to "talk back" and raise issues that top management probably does not anticipate. Moreover, there are the concluding stages of experiencing success, partly affected by conscious design but just as often due to forces outside the control of the planners.

2. *We too often assume that organization change is for "those people downstairs," who are somehow perceived as less intelligent and less productive than "those upstairs."*

Contrary to this assumption, the success patterns point to the importance of top management seeing itself as part of the organization's problems and becoming actively involved in finding solutions to them. Without the involvment and commitment of top management, it is doubtful that lower levels can see the need for change or, if they do, be willing to take the risks that such change entails.

3. *We need to reduce our fond attachment for both unilateral and delegated approaches to change.*

The *unilateral* approach, although tempting because its procedures are readily accessible to top management, generally serves only to perpetuate the myths and disadvantages of omniscience and downward thinking. On the other hand, the *delegated* approach, while appealing because of its "democratic" connotations, may remove the power structure from direct involvement in a process that calls for its strong guidance and active support.

The findings discussed in this article highlight the use of the more difficult, but perhaps more fruitful, *shared* power approach. As top managers join in to open up their power structures and their organizations to an exchange of influence between upper and lower levels, they may be unleashing new surges of energy and creativity not previously imagined.

4. *There is a need for managers, consultants, skeptics, and researchers to become less parochial in their viewpoints.*

For too long, each of us has acted as if cross-fertilization is unproductive. Much more constructive dialogue and joint effort are needed if we are to understand better and act wisely in terms of the complexities and stakes inherent in the difficult problems of introducing organization change.

APPENDIX: SURVEY OF STUDIES

Those reporting "successful" organization changes include:

Robert R. Blake, Jane S. Mouton, Louis B. Barnes, and Larry E. Greiner, "Break-through in Organization Development," HBR November–December 1964, p. 133.

Robert H. Guest, *Organization Change: The Effect of Successful Leadership* (Homewood, Illinois, The Dorsey Press, Inc., 1962).

Elliott Jaques, *The Changing Culture of a Factory* (New York, The Dryden Press, Inc., 1952).

A. K. Rice, *Productivity and Social Organization: The Ahmedabad Experiment* (London, Tavistock Publications, Ltd., 1958).

S. E. Seashore and D. G. Bowers, *Changing the Structure and Functioning of an Organization* (Ann Arbor, Survey Research Center, The University of Michigan, Monograph No. 33, 1963).

Those showing similar "success" patterns, but containing somewhat less complete information:

Gene W. Dalton, Louis B. Barnes, and Abraham Zaleznik, *The Authority Structure as a Change Variable* (Paper presented at the 57th meeting of the American Sociological Association, August 1962, Washington, D.C.).

Paul R. Lawrence, *The Changing of Organization Behavior Patterns: A Case Study of Decentralization* (Boston, Division of Research, Harvard Business School, 1958).

Paul R. Lawrence et al, "Battleship Y," *Organizational Behavior and Administration* (Homewood, Illinois, The Dorsey Press, Inc.), p. 328 (1965 edition).

Floyd C. Mann, "Studying and Creating Change: A Means to Understanding Social Organization," *Research in Industrial Human Relations*, edited by C. M. Arensberg et al (New York, Harper and Brothers, 1957).

C. Sofer, *The Organziation from Within* (London, Tavistock Publications, Ltd., 1961).

William F. Whyte, *Pattern for Industrial Peace* (New York, Harper and Brothers, 1951).

Included here are studies which reveal "less successful" change patterns:

Chris Argyris, *Interpersonal Competence and Organizational Effectiveness* (Homewood, Illinois, The Dorsey Press, Inc., 1962), especially pp. 254–257.

A. Gouldner, *Patterns of Industrial Bureaucracy* (Glencoe, Illinois, The Free Press, 1964).

Paul R. Lawrence et al, "The Dashman Company" and "Flint Electric," *Organizational Behavior and Administration* (Homewood, Illinois, The Dorsey Press, Inc.), p. 16 (1965 edition) and p. 600 (1961 edition).

George Strauss, "The Set-Up Man: A Case Study of Organizational Change," *Human Organization*, Vol. 13, 1954, p. 17.

A. J. M. Sykes, "The Effects of a Supervisory Training Course in Changing Supervisors' Perceptions and Expectations of the Role of Management," *Human Relations*, Vol. 15, 1962, p. 227.

William F. Whyte, *Money and Motivation* (New York, Harper and Brothers, 1955).

REFERENCES

1. Robert H. Guest, *Organization Change: The Effect of Successful Leadership* (Homewood, Illinois, The Dorsey Press, Inc., 1962), p. 18.
2. From my unpublished doctoral dissertation, *Organization and Development* (Harvard Business School, June 1965).
3. Robert H. Guest, op. cit., p. 50.
4. S. E. Seashore and D. G. Bowers, *Changing the Structure and Functioning of an Organization* (Ann Arbor, Survey Research Center, The University of Michigan, Monograph No. 33, 1963), p. 29.
5. Robert H. Guest, op. cit., p. 64.

Improvement in a Decentralized Organization

Richard Beckhard

In the past few years, some "giant steps" have been taken in the application of behavioral science knowledge to the problems of organization improvement and growth. It is becoming increasingly possible for organization managers to scientifically diagnose the conditions in their organization both in terms of practices, procedures, and ways of producing integrated effort and in terms of motivation, attitudes, and values of the people who make up the organization. It is also possible, from such diagnosis, to make a realistic assessment of the state of an organization's health and from this assessment to plan systematic steps for improving its health and effectiveness.

SOME ASSUMPTIONS ABOUT ORGANIZATION CHANGE

Organization Diagnosis

In introducing change into a system, it is assumed that the following phases of initial diagnosis would apply:

Defining the change problem;
Determining the appropriate client systems within the total organization system;
Determining each system's readiness and capacity to change;
Determining appropriate change objectives;
Assessing the change agent's own resources.

It is also assumed that for change to take place, the current status or set of conditions must be unfrozen, new inputs made available, and the system refrozen in a new set of conditions. For this to occur effectively in an organization, the education or change program needs to be organic; that is, it should grow out of itself and out of the needs identified as relevant to the organization's purposes. Specifically:

Reproduced by special permission from *The Journal of Applied Behavioral Science*, "An Organization Improvement Program in a Decentralized Organization," by Richard Beckhard. Vol. 2, No. 1, pp. 3–25. © 1966 NTL Institute for Applied Behavioral Science.

The program must be *goal-related*, that is, clearly related to organization purposes;
The program must be seen as *relevant* to *individual purposes* as well as to organization
    purposes by the people participating in it;
The program should have maximum *spread potential* throughout the organization.

Induction of Change

The change strategy should ensure that the organization can continue to learn from its own experience. This implies activities and tactics that provide for operating units to look at their own operations, test them against alternatives, and plan future improvement. It also implies a process of systematic information collecting, feedback, and action planning based on the information. For such purposes the organization should be divided into learning groups such as work families, peer groups, or project groups.

Change goals need to be clearly defined in terms of the *types* of changes desired. One type is change in *organizational climate* (as evidenced in the organization's practices, its communications, its ways of handling conflict). A second type is change in *attitudes* and *values* of the people in the organization (for example, treating conflict as an appropriate and necessary condition of organization life or recognizing that frank and open communication is a desirable value). A third type is a change in *skills* (e.g., in problem solving or interpersonal relationships).

Although all of these types of change goals are existent in any organization change effort, it is important that relatively explicit priorities be established.

In the management of change it is necessary to find appropriate educational methods to achieve any of these change goals. The function of the educational consultant is to help the organization provide conditions in which it can introduce appropriate educational methods, collect more systematic data on its own organizational functioning, increase its ability to use such data in improvement planning, and build a training and educational orientation into its line management so that organization improvement becomes a way of life.

THE ORGANIZATION

Let us look at this particular organization, its purposes, and general structure.

The company is a medium-sized concern which operates 26 hotel properties in the United States, Canada, the Caribbean, and Great Britain. At the time the improvement program started, the company managed five hotels with about 2,000 employees. Today, its activities include hotels, motor hotels, and motor lodges, with about 7,000 employees. The period covered by this report, 1958 to 1963, was one of rapid growth resulting from the building and establishment of new hotels. The requirements for staffing, financing, and operating each new property made extreme demands on management personnel as well as on the finances of the company. Also, during this period conditions in the hotel industry changed. A rapid increase in the number of hotel and motor hotel units led to increased competition in rates and special services. These outside influences, plus rapid expansion and major investment in new properties, made the company's profit position precarious. At the time of this writing, however, a major upturn is being reported.

The organization improvement program with which we are concerned begins in the spring of 1958 and deals with the hotel division of the company. The president of the hotel division had reporting to him at central headquarters a staff consisting of the directors of five departments: operations, sales and advertising, purchasing and food, personnel employment, and controller. The general managers of each of the hotels also reported directly to the president. (See Figure 1.) The company had moved to an administratively decentralized operating policy. Each general manager was quite autonomous in terms of decision making, with the exception of a central accounting and control system and certain corporate policies relative to centralized purchasing. Large capital expenditures were approved centrally. General managers did not have actual profit targets, but profit estimates were a standard procedure. Each of the hotel properties was a unique unit with very few of the characteristics of a "chain" operation.

During the period of the change effort with which this paper is concerned, the company moved into the motor hotel field, developed a motor hotel division, and later, a motor lodge division.

Figure 1 1958 Organization Chart

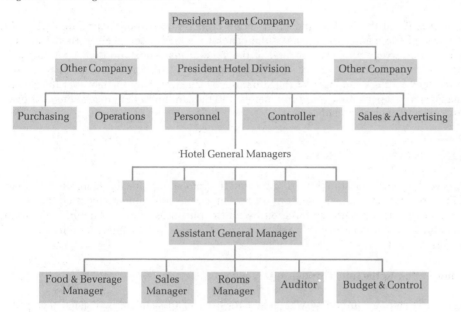

IDENTIFICATION OF THE NEED FOR IMPROVEMENT

The president initiated the change program. In the spring of 1958 he attended a workshop at which the consultant was a trainer. In discussing his organization, the president identified as a serious managerial problem the communication difficulties between corporate or central staff and line top managers. He felt that, although he had brought these two elements of the organization together regularly at quarterly management meetings, there still existed a lack of trust, openness, and clarity in terms of decision-making authority. The causes for these difficulties were perceived to be both organizational and interpersonal. The president also felt that the communication from the top group to second-level line managers in the hotels was not so effective as it should be. He was looking for help.

In describing his concern, the president pointed to various evidences of the problem:

Central staff reported considerable difficulty in trying to initiate new ideas or improvement efforts into the hotels. They felt there were too many debates with general managers as to what could or could not be done in an improvement effort. In some cases staff were required to communicate *only* through general managers rather than through counterpart department heads.

On the other hand, general managers complained to the president about the confusion caused by the central staff's coming into hotels and making recommendations and suggestions. Some general managers saw this as an intrusion by people who lacked the experience and know-how of the hotel business. In a few cases general managers had barred central staff from their hotels, unless specifically requested by the general manager.

Although attempts had been made during the quarterly meetings to work through these problems, there seemed to be a lack of willingness to deal openly with them.

Because of the background of the hotel industry, essentially entrepreneurial, and because of the managerial styles of the general managers, relatively little direct communication existed between several of the general managers and their operating subordinates except on necessary operational matters. Furthermore, social distance was reinforced by the economics of the situation, as illustrated by the fact that the general manager's compensation is approximately 100 percent more than that of the next nearest subordinate staff member.

FIRST PHASES OF THE PROGRAM

Proceeding on the assumption that information collecting, feedback, and action planning are three essential steps in initiating change, the consultants suggested that a program be developed with the top group with the purposes of further defining the problem, broadening its base of information, and setting some conditions for joint planning to deal with it.

Information Collection Through Interviews

As a first step, an interview was held with each of the general managers, each of the central staff department heads, with a sample of the subordinates of the general managers, and a sample of the subordinates of the central staff heads. In each of these interviews, the respondents were told why the interview was being held, what use would be made of the data, that there would be a meeting of the general managers and central staff heads to work on improving communications and operations, and that they as individual respondents could contribute to the effectiveness of this meeting by sharing their information about the causes of difficulties and by giving their suggestions as to ways for improving communications.

In each case these interviews lasted from one to two hours, were nondirected, and ranged over a wide variety of topics. The interviewer recorded information, and at the close of the interview reported back to the respondent what he had heard. He also cleared with the respondent the information to be reported out, with the assurance that the identity of the respondent would be held confidential.

The material from all these interviews was organized into a series of management process headings such as—

1. communications between president and line (or staff)
2. line-staff communications
3. location of decision making
4. role clarification or confusion
5. communications procedures.

The interview results were then listed under these categories and color-coded to identify the category of respondent (i.e., general manager, staff head, staff assistant, and so on).

Feedback of Information from Interviews and Initiation of Planning

A three-day meeting was convened at an off-site area. This meeting was attended by the president, the general managers, the central staff heads, and two consultants. On the first half-day of the meeting the findings from the interviews were presented. During this presentation, the members of the group could check for clarification, but no discussion of the information was allowed.

In the second phase of the meeting the group as a whole went through the list and determined the priority items. As the group analyzed the findings and the sources of information, it became clear that solutions to most of the problems listed could be achieved only through the joint efforts of those present. The type of information could not be dealt with by legislation from the top but required problem solving by all those affected. Sample items were—

From staff heads: The president expects us to introduce changes and maintain and upgrade quality but the general managers won't let us into the hotels to do it.

From general managers: The advertising policy of the corporation is ridiculous. We talk decentralization and yet we have no voice in setting our own advertising policy.

From subordinates of general managers: Where are we going in this organization? We have no feeling of belonging to a corporation but only to a hotel.

There were over 90 individual items representing issues on which the group would need to work. The process of selecting priority issues for discussion took the better part of the first day. On reconvening the first night, as a change of pace, and with the purpose of giving a framework for looking at the difficulties the group would be facing as it worked on the issues in subsequent days, the consultants introduced some theory about communications in organizations.

The second and third days were spent in digging into some of the central issues, bringing up the conflicts that existed among the various groups, and looking for areas of agreement and ways of working through the problems. This process involved identification of the causes of an issue in terms of past backgrounds of the staff and the managers, the behavior of the president, the problems of structure, and the nature of the business. The group explored possible changes in practices, procedures, and attitudes that would be required for correcting some of the problems that had been identified.

During the discussions, the consultants' contributions pinpointed how the group was functioning, guidelines for working on a problem, bringing conflict to the surface where it could be worked on, and systematic diagnosis of the causes of some of the problems that were identified.

The three days were active, volatile, and tiring. But by the end of this period, the group felt that it had made only a start and that it needed to continue. A meeting was therefore scheduled for one month later.

The second meeting was held in a hotel and was less exciting than the first. The members of the group came with the expectation of picking up where they had been, that is, with the climate of openness and problem solving that had existed at the end of the first session. They were surprised to discover that in the intervening time there had been considerable regression. In order for discussions to continue profitably, it was necessary to spend a few hours in re-establishing the earlier climate of trust.

A significant outcome of this second meeting was the top management's recognition of, and attention to, concerns of subordinates about the state of affairs. Some of the concerns that had been reported were that subordinate managers did not feel they could influence the corporate management in any significant way; that they considered their primary rewards and punishments as coming from the general manager of their hotel, that therefore their primary and almost exclusive loyalty lay there; and that they thought no one at corporate headquarters was much concerned with their needs, career plans, or current performance. Related to this, they felt little identification with the corporation's future objectives and plans, but saw their career planning in terms either of their own unit or of the total industry.

Most felt a lack of communication with counterparts in other of the organization's hotels. For example, sales managers had never had a meeting together, nor had other functional counterparts. In a number of cases, due to the entrepreneurial management style, subordinates did not see themselves as part of a management team but rather as individuals reporting to "the boss."

The management group decided that it would be desirable to set up a series of meetings, modeled after the ones they themselves were having, for the subordinate manager group. They set up two sets of meetings: one with sales, food, and rooms managers (customer-contact departments) and another with assistant general managers, auditors, and budget and control directors (administrative departments). Second-level central staff counterparts were assigned to meet with the relevant groups.

It was agreed that for these meetings there would again be a need for collecting information from those attending and for providing a method to feed this information back and make it available for group work. In creating these sets of conferences, the management group recognized that it would be necessary to ensure some follow-up from the output of the conferences if any real organization improvement were to occur. During discussion on this point, the consultants suggested that, to deal with the feelings of lack of connection with the corporation that were repeatedly expressed by their subordinates, it might be desirable to include some face-to-face contact with the president of the division during these meetings. This was programmed into the meetings. It was also suggested that the meetings should try to deal simultaneously with a variety of stated needs, including: need for communication between counterparts, need for improved problem solving between staff and line at the same level, need for strengthening of hotel teams, and need for establishing communication between the hotel teams and the system.

The hotel managers agreed that they would report and present the plan to their teams and that they would build in follow-up meetings in the hotels so that the outputs of the conferences could be built back into the hotel organizations. To establish some identifying label, the series of meetings were called "Key Executive Conferences."

Key Executive Conferences

827

*Beckhard:
Improvement
in a Decentralized
Organization*

The methodology of these conferences was similar to that of the top management conference. Consultants interviewed the participants, organized the material by categories, and scheduled problem-solving meetings.

The first phase of each of these meetings was concerned with the feedback of information. The second phase differed slightly from the top management meetings in that the groups were asked by the consultant to go through the agenda and rate each item as —

1. An item we want to recommend to top management
2. An item we want to discuss and work through
3. An item that no longer seems relevant.

The items that were seen as ready for immediate recommendation were accumulated throughout the conference on a separate list. The items identified as needing discussion by the group became the group's major agenda during the three-day period. As each of these items was discussed, it was either attached to the list of recommendations or identified as completed and therefore eliminated from the agenda.

The cumulative list of recommendations to the corporation was presented to the president in a confrontation meeting held on the last half-day of the conference. He discussed each item and noted some action. That is, he made a decision, yes or no, or referred a question to a task force or to some other part of the organization. A specific issue will serve to illustrate this process.

One question of central concern to a number of people was: "How can we reorganize advertising policy to allow hotels to have more voice in planning their own advertising programs?"

After discussion of this issue, the group sent a delegation to the president to discuss it with him in detail. At this confrontation he announced that with the information he now had from the field (previously screened from him) he was hereby appointing a field-oriented man (a member of the group attending) as sales and advertising director to provide the needed liaison between the field and central office. This was a major policy change from highly centralized advertising direction by a corporate vice-president with little or no field consultation. It also demonstrated dramatically a successful and useful influence effort on the part of second-level management on top management.

These key executive conferences were scheduled twice a year. On the third round the groups reviewed the status of the conferences, their original purposes, and their current relevance. It was felt that the need for across-the-board problem-solving meetings had diminished as intrahotel communications improved and channels to the top were clearly opened. However, the need for technical counterpart meetings was stronger than ever.

It was decided, and agreed to by top management, that the key executive conferences would be terminated and that technical meetings on a periodically scheduled basis would be instituted.

Problem-Solving Conferences in Hotels

Emerging from these conferences was a general improvement in the communications and working effectiveness of the top team in each hotel. Some of the managers suggested that similar conferences within hotels would be profitable, and such programs were set up.

The format of these hotel "self-survey, action-planning meetings" was essentially similar to that of the meetings already described. After interviews with all middle- and first-line supervision, the information was categorized and fed back to the respondents who met in working groups composed of representatives of all departments. These groups worked through the agenda and made recommendations to top (hotel) management. The recommendations were then fed back to the top team and a confrontation meeting similar to those described above was held, but with the general manager conducting the meeting and setting the action plans.

These meetings have proved to be continuously effective and are held today on a semiannual or annual basis in all of the hotels. They have become a "way of life" for identifying current concerns, organizing work to deal with them, and planning action. The consultants' role has become that of "sponge" (collecting their data), "water faucet" (giving the information back to them), and "catalyst" (bringing all elements of management together).

A REDEFINITION OF THE CHANGE GOALS

This initial improvement effort was designed to deal with the effects of decentralization, the needs for improvement of interunit and interpersonal communications skills, and with techniques for better problem solving. The same set of goals guided the activities with the key executives and the initial efforts within the hotels.

Concurrently with the development of this program, the nature of the mission of the organization changed as the corporation went into the motor hotel business. This expansion necessitated a structural reorganization. From it emerged an organization in which two group vice-presidents reported to the president, one for motor hotels and one for hotels. (Later a motor lodge group was added.) Reporting to the group vice-president for hotels were the general managers of all the hotels and a small staff of specialists. Reporting to the group vice-president for motor hotels were the general managers of the motor hotels. Reporting to the president at a staff level were directors of corporate service: planning (for new hotels), purchasing, personnel, and sales and advertising.

During the period previously described, the president had attended a National Training Laboratories human relations laboratory and had subsequently encouraged his key executives to attend. The two group vice-presidents, several of the hotel general managers, and two or three of the staff directors had done so. As a result of these and other activities, the president became quite explicit in his desire to move the entire organization toward a management-by-objectives or Theory-Y orientation.

The president convened a two-day planning conference with the central staff directors and group vice-presidents to explore how far the organization had progressed in this direction and what would be needed to move the total culture toward a Theory-Y or management-by-objectives orientation. (See Figure 2.) At this conference the group reviewed the relationships between the president and staff and line management. These were seen to be quite improved although there were still difficulties between line management and some central office departments, and between the president and his staff. It was agreed that a periodic series of organization improvement meetings should be held with this group, with the minimum of one annual off-site conference and a series of on-site, shorter meetings.

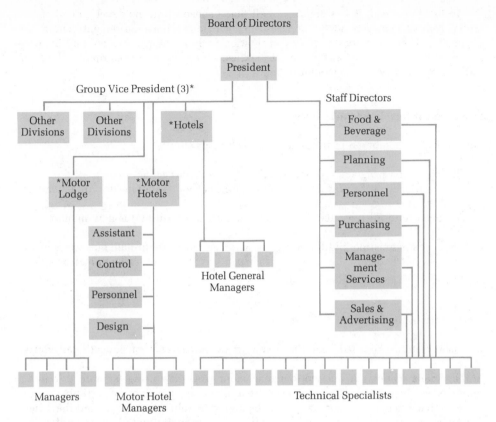

Figure 2 1964 Organization Chart

The group recognized that a systematic target-setting[1] or goal-setting program was a necessary tool of any management-by-objectives operation. It was agreed that a unit-by-unit goal-setting process would be instituted during the coming year and that an individual performance-improvement target-setting process would be developed within the top management and corporate staff group.

A need was also felt for a program with the motor hotel management group working toward the development of a concept of team management. Another area identified was building a team for a new hotel; another was building intergroup relationships between the planning division (the corporate representatives in building and preparing a new hotel) and the general manager and his team (who take over its operation when it opens).

[1] Target setting, a management practice, reverses the traditional method of performance appraisal in which the supervisor writes the job description and evaluates the subordinate's performance against his, or the organization's, criteria for effective performance. In target setting, the subordinate develops his own position description and discusses this with his supervisor, with joint agreement on the position description. The incumbent then sets performance-improvement targets for a short period, such as six months. These improvement targets are discussed with the supervisor and become the joint goals of the supervisor and subordinate for the subordinate's performance improvement. At the end of the period, the incumbent analyzes his results in terms of goals achieved or not achieved and this analysis provides a basis for joint discussion with the supervisor and for the joint replanning and setting of new goals for the next period. The process requires that the supervisor function as a consultant and at the same time represent organization requirements. It may produce some strain on the subordinate who must now commit himself to improvement targets rather than work toward targets set for him by either the supervisor or the organization.

In looking ahead, it was obvious to all that a speed-up in the development of potential general management talent was a major organization requirement. The rapid expansion of the industry, the policy of rotation within the organization, and the proposed additional expansion for the late sixties, all combined to require acceleration in the preparation of management talent.

Management Development Training

Several factors combined to influence the next major effort:

1. The expansion program and organization policy discussed above
2. The experience of the president and most of the corporate staff heads with laboratory training
3. The need for additional technical development and training for new management trainees
4. The needs of existing middle managers who had come up through one phase of the business but had little training in either management or other technical phases of the business.

Organization Improvement Activities

It was therefore proposed that there should be three types of educational efforts.

Management school. A one-week management workshop using laboratory training methods was scheduled. The purposes were to increase the insights of participants into the effectiveness of their own managerial behavior; to help them understand the different types of managerial styles and their effects on productivity; to help them develop some concepts of organizational effectiveness; to help make them aware of the corporate philosophy of *management by objectives* and its application to the units in which they performed; to broaden their concept of team effectiveness and team development.

These workshops were staffed by a faculty of behavioral scientists. They were scheduled for a group of 24 middle management executives selected by a task force composed of the president, the two group vice-presidents, and the personnel department head.

The first of these workshops was held in 1962 and additional workshops have since been held twice a year. The entire middle management group from the hotel and motor hotel operations and from the central staff have participated.

Technical seminars. To deal with the broadening of technical skills, a series of technical meetings on food and beverage, budget and control, and auditing have been established. Participants from a variety of settings within the organization have attended these sessions.

Counterpart meetings. The regularly scheduled technical counterpart meetings mentioned earlier have broadened their agenda to include some training and development work on problem solving, communications, and management. A series of special workshops on interviewing and consulting have been given to large numbers of managers.

In addition to the above specific educational efforts, the personnel office provides a central clearing house for offsite educational activities both in hotel operations and management.

Target and Goal Setting

As reported earlier, one of the major areas identified at the planning conference as needing attention was the process of goal setting in hotel units, in the field, and in individual performance improvement.

A program was established by which, on a semiannual basis, the top management of each hotel meet with the group vice-president of their division, the president of the corporation, and the key central staff, to review unit goals and jointly determine what is necessary to implement the goals for the coming year or months. This process requires the active participation of the management team within the unit. This has had the effect of building in much more involvement throughout the organization and a feeling of "ownership" in the unit and organization goals.

Personal performance improvement via systematic goal setting was established initially by the president and the group vice-presidents. This included the preparation of position descriptions by subordinates; the setting of improvement targets; the sharing of perceptions between the president and his subordinates about the reality and achievability of these various targets; their priority; and the periodic, joint review of progress toward targets. By constant evaluation of the process as well as by the refinement of the techniques employed, this has become a useful method of continuous information collecting and planning for the top group. Several of the general managers felt the method would be a helpful management tool in their hotels, and two of them introduced it within their organizations. In one case, the program included a series of training meetings for the entire management group in which they were given lectures on the process, opportunities to develop position descriptions, practice in interviews, and so forth. The process received substantial favorable lip service. However, because of pressure from the general manager to "do" the program, it met with considerable resistance in practice. As soon as the pressure abated, the program fell apart. This was one of the more dramatic failure incidents in this total effort and serves to reinforce the fact that an externally imposed program, without real involvement and participation on the part of those responsible for its implementation, is probably doomed from the start.

On the other hand, the unit goal setting which is organic to the corporate requirements has been seen as relevant by all concerned and has become an increasingly effective instrument for planning and communication among the several field units and the central office.

Team Training—Intergroup Staff and Line in New Hotels

One of the innovations in the organization improvement program has been the training of new management teams. The hotel industry is constantly developing new management teams as new properties open. It also sets up temporary systems which are established for a limited time only, such as the team that comes into existence to design and supervise the building and furnishing of a new hotel. This team goes out of existence when the hotel opens.

There were two specific sets of groups that were identified by the staff and the group vice-presidents as needing help in improving their communications and teamwork. One was the technical team responsible for the planning and construction supervision of a new hotel. The other was the general manager and his top team who would operate the hotel. A specific area of concern was the interface between these two groups (the planning team and the operating team) during the period of the final phases of construction and the preopening activities.

A series of conferences was held with the technical staff to analyze the problems of multiple authority, change-over from staff to line operation, problems of the preopening period, selection of personnel for the new hotel (previously handled by central staff), and training of staff (by central specialists or line heads). A result of these joint meetings was a series of revised procedures whereby the general manager was brought into the picture at a much earlier date, had a more active role in the selection of his own staff, and had more influence on the final design of the facility.

Training Operating Teams

The training of new hotel management operating teams was established as a high priority need. In order to understand the significance of this training, one needs a picture of previous practice.

The selection of people to serve as department heads in new hotels had been based on their proved technical competence in their own fields, such as housekeeping, engineering, food preparation, and so on. Each of the members making up a new management team came from a background of experience in which he had learned to operate *with* a particular managerial style and *under* a particular managerial style. The general manager, in each case an experienced man, had his own managerial style and ways of work which he intended to employ in his future operations. When the team came together on the job, the demands of the work required their fullest effort in the technical area. No time was spent on discussion of ways of work, relationships, communications procedures. For the first few months after the hotel opened, all the problems of a new property created similar demands and pressures. Matters of relationship, communication, and so forth usually did not get much attention by the team until well along in the first year. Consequently, considerable inefficiency might well have been avoided had better communication been established earlier among the several key members of the management team.

It was hypothesized that the effective building of a new team could be accomplished more efficiently if, as a part of their earliest experiences as a team, they could spend some time concentrating on the building of a culture. This would include explicit discussion of norms and procedures to be followed in terms of communication, decision making, and job responsibilities.

Experiments were set up with three hotels which were due to open within a year or two. In each case, the first activity of the top management team (general manager and key department heads) was to attend a two- or three-day off-site conference with the purpose clearly to begin building the management team.

The format of these conferences was as follows: After an opening statement by the head of the team (general manager), the group built an agenda of relevant concerns and problems to be tackled in the area of team effectiveness, work relationships, communications, training, and the like. Explicit attention was paid to the establishment of an open communications climate through such devices as asking each member to share with the group his reasons for taking the job, what his career aspirations were, and so on. Another mechanism was for each member to describe for the group how he saw his responsibilities and authority in the new unit. The general manager then reacted to this statement, as did the colleagues, and a consensus was arrived at relative to each job.

Other agenda items included plans for communication (staff meetings, among others); training programs for staff coordination and use of resources; clarification of practices—for example, what things needed approval; relationships to the technical planning staff; and special problems of the "opening week."

In each of these three experiments, follow-up meetings were held approximately six to eight months after the opening to check on results and to review the various commitments made at the earlier meeting. Respondents reported considerable progress toward more openness and improved communication; but, in each case, there were some regressions which were reviewed and worked through again.

As reported by the president, the corporate staff, the board of directors, the general managers involved, and the teams themselves, the openings of these three hotels were the smoothest in the corporation's history. Teams were able to deal with a much larger number of complex problems; turnover was reduced dramatically as compared with experience at previous openings in similar hotels; and, contrary to the trend for new hotels, there was virtually no turnover in the middle management groups within the first year. These activities were seen by the participants and the corporate leadership as highly useful in terms of developing the health of the organization.

Operations Improvement Committees

With the continually increased need to improve its competitive position, an operations improvement program was introduced into the organization. Profit improvement or operations improvement committees were developed in most units with rank-and-file and management participation. The mission of these committees was to develop innovations, service improvements, and more efficiency in the quality and handling of food, lodging, and service.

These activities have produced a high degree of involvement on a fairly broad base and have resulted in a considerable number of improvements in performance, in increased service and reduced costs. Management reports much more concern for profit and costs on the part of rank-and-file employees. This shows up in such ways as reduced breakage in the kitchens, less waste in handling laundry, and so on.

Overhead Cost Reduction Program

With the tightening economic conditions, due to overexpansion in the industry, there was the need for an appreciable cut in overhead costs at the central staff level.

The president brought together the heads of staff departments and told them of the amounts of cuts that would probably be required, using two figures: a minimum and a maximum. He asked each staff head, in consultation with two or three of his colleagues from other departments, to form task forces to think through what he and his department would do if the minimum cut or the maximum cut were required and also to think through what the consequences would be to the corporation this year, and for several years ahead. Staff heads were asked to include some colleagues with points of view different from their own.

A historian for this project was selected early in the program to keep a record of the processes operating throughout the program. Some bases for selection of task forces were recorded as follows:

Knowledge of the activity of the other department
Use of the services of the other department
Involvement in effects of reduction
Range of ideas and viewpoints
Challenge to certain items
Individual bias in favor of the particular department's services
Need to be involved in the decision making
Special skills
Decision-making power and importance of approval.

Following the series of task force meetings, a general meeting was held during which each staff head explained his present budget, his recommendations for reducing his budget, and the consequences on both a long- and short-term basis of these reductions.

The final results as indicated in the report were as follows: Individual department reductions range from zero to $50,000. The total effect of this program, provided all recommendations are put into effect, results in reducing the central office budget by approximately $225,000 and in reducing the number of persons employed in central office by 12.

Significant aspects of this effect, in addition to the obvious savings in dollars, are the high degree of shared commitment to the solution of the problem and the ability to cope with layoffs and belt-tightening without any loss to the viability of the organization.

PROGRAM EFFECTS

Dramatic profit improvement was recorded in 1964, with highest earnings in the company's ten-year history. This profit was against an industry trend of stabilized profits. It is impossible to correlate this profit improvement fully with the educational effort; but it is clear that the program has made a significant contribution through developing attitudes of commitment to company objectives, a shared value of concern for costs, and a measurable increase in operating efficiency of almost all units.

Specific evidence of changes in organization climate include very low turnover in a highly mobile industry, an increase in rotation of management personnel, the promotion into higher positions of more than a hundred management people, an increase of performance effectiveness in most units in terms of costs as related to sales, more efficient staffing, and reduction of costs with no appreciable decrease of service.

There are clear indications that the organization is able to handle crises in much more effective ways. The organization has recently withstood a reorganization at the corporate level, major modifications in proposed expansion plans, major relocations of numbers of management personnel into new assignments, yet has shown an increase in performance return.

Increasingly, the units of the organization are learning from their own experience, are able to function more effectively with less dependence on outside help, and, at the same time, are making more creative use of a variety of resources within the organization.

SUMMARY

835
Beckhard:
Improvement
in a Decentralized
Organization

The change effort started with the president's recognition of the need for improving problem-solving skills, interpersonal communication skills, and intergroup communication as a function of the decentralization policy. The key line management and the corporate staff management, together with the president, were seen as an initial learning group; first efforts were with them, to help identify and work through the problems of the organization as they perceived them.

The next major effort was with the subordinates of the above-mentioned key line and staff executives. Here the primary concerns (in addition to improving skills and individual effectiveness) were to change the influence pattern between middle management and the top management of the organization, to build the effectiveness of the team within each operating unit, and to establish communication links between counterparts in various segments of the system.

Building team effectiveness, improving communications, and problem solving in the several individual units made up the next major phase, with emphasis on improved linkage between the corporate headquarters and the middle line management through top management of each unit, intergroup and interpersonal communication within a unit, and vertical communication between the general manager and the rest of his team. Increased operating effectiveness in terms of better procedures and more generally shared concern for costs, controls, and efficiency were the organization goals of this phase.

The major goal shifted to moving the entire organization toward a management-by-objectives or "Theory-Y" orientation. Changing external conditions and increasing requirements for management talent also meant speeding up the preparation of existing management personnel to enable them to handle greater responsibilities.

To meet these goals, new learning groups were created. Groups of peers from across the system were brought together in one-week management laboratories for intensive exploration of their own managerial styles and of organization behavior. Technical sessions dealing with food and beverage preparation, budget and controls, auditing procedures, and so on, were held for specialists in these fields and for others in management who wished to broaden their repertoire of skills.

Goal-setting programs were introduced for all operating units on a systematic basis; and performance-improvement, target-setting sessions were instituted at the central staff level and in some of the operating units. The training of new hotel teams received major emphasis.

When economic conditions required tightening of the belt, improved efficiency throughout the organization, and reduction in overhead costs, the *total resources* of the organization were mobilized. Operations improvement committees consisting of rank-and-file management personnel in all units were set up in each hotel, and a series of task forces was developed to achieve a rather drastic cut in central staff overhead costs.

Questions for Discussion

1. What are the advantages and disadvantages of "in-house" laboratory training as compared to "stranger" laboratories?

2. What are the principal functions performed by an organization development consultant? Why is it unlikely that a line manager employed in the company could perform the same functions?

3. In deciding whether to use OD as a method of managing, the line management in a company must consider its limitations, and the conditions under which it may be applicable. What are these limitations and conditions?

4. Some writers on management believe that in spite of the limitations of OD (Question 3), this technique of management is becoming *in general* more applicable in *all* organizations. What is their reasoning?

5. Organization development philosophy differs in a very important way from *structural* philosophy—OD has to do with a vision of how the organization should function, how people should behave and act, and what *causes* organizations (and people) to change. Explain this difference, and give the OD argument for why structuralist philosophy "puts the cart before the horse."

6. In what way is a nondirective T-Group a scientifically designed, closed-system experiment? In order for a feather and a lead ball to obey the laws of physics (gravity) and fall at the same speed through space, the scientist must close the system and exclude the friction of air, wind, or other forces. This is done by enclosing the falling objects in a vacuum chamber. The T-Group excludes all but certain things. What is excluded and what is included?

7. T-Groups are often criticized because a person returning to work finds the real working environment not like the atmosphere created in the laboratory "vacuum." Is this a valid criticism? Is it an invalid criticism? Is it both? Use the example from Question 6: Everyone knows that a feather and a lead ball do not fall at exactly the same rate—except in a vacuum.

8. Study Greiner's emphasis on *power redistribution* as part of the OD process. In what sense would this aspect of OD overcome some of Thompson's (Chapter 6) concept of conflict between line officers ("with the right to decide but not the ability") and staff officers ("with the ability to decide but not the right")?

Cases for Discussion

University Student Union

The snack bar in the university student union employs three students on the day shift: Jim, Jack, and Bill. Jack has concluded that Jim is hard to get along with. Jim is very intelligent, almost brilliant. Every time a problem comes up, such as rearranging the shelves or scheduling holiday shifts, he has a quick answer, and usually the best one. But he does not seem to care at all about the feelings and views of Jack and Bill. He comes out with a quick answer, tells them what it is, and then goes on to other things. Jack thinks Jim expects the other two to admire his intelligence.

Finally, Jack decided he was going to "stop playing Jim's game." Jim figured out a different way to stack the post cards sold at the snack bar counter. Jack ignored the idea, and so did Bill. In fact, they deliberately continued to put the post cards up in the same way they always had. Jack could tell by Jim's manner that he was angry, but Jim did not say anything.

Later, Jim suggested a way they might improve the candy display. Candy was stored in shelves behind the cash register. According to Jim, there were problems because the three workers bumped into each other frequently in getting at the candy, and people bunched up around the cash register, not knowing what kind of candy they wanted, "shopping" the display, and then pointing at their choice. In making his suggestion, Jim said, "You guys just don't know how to operate efficiently. Put the damn candy in two identical bunches, one at each end of the counter in front of the cash register." To Jack, he seemed deliberately sarcastic.

Jack and Bill felt that it was more important to put post cards, cigarettes, and notions such as shaving cream and chapsticks on the counter. They argued that cigarettes would cause even more of a jam-up at the cash register if put behind it on shelves, because they were higher volume sellers. So they ignored Jim's second suggestion.

Questions

1. If you were Jack, what rating would you give Jim on item 2 in Douglas McGregor's team rating scale (in the article, "Team Development")?

2. McGregor stresses a certain kind of feedback as a means of building a team. If you were Jack, and attempting to give such feedback, what would you say to Jim in the above episode?

3. If you were Bill, what rating would you give Jack on item 2 in McGregor's rating scale at the time of the episode?

(Note: The above answers may be written. If they are, try to capture in your writing style the way you would talk.)

4. For additional insight into the answers to Questions 1–3, the instructor may ask for volunteers to play the roles of Jim, Jack, and Bill. The remainder of the class will

have responsibility for listening to *specific* things that are said during the role play. One third of the class can rate Jack on McGregor's item 2 on the rating scale, and one third can rate each of the other two characters. After the role play, each class group will report their ratings (and reasons for them) to the rest of the class.

5. · In the role play in Question 4, the characters undoubtedly mentioned the rearranging of shelves behind the counter, the way post cards are stored, and the way candy is displayed. These are *technological* aspects, as opposed to *human* aspects. The *organization* of the snack bar, if it is to be *developed*, must include both. Did you see any progress in the development of candy-display technology which would help the snack bar in its goal of supplying students with candy? That is, how did the characters perform in (a) the initial phase of diagnosing and solving *human* problems, and (b) in the second phase of working as a team to operate the technical aspects of the snack bar?

6. As a test of the second phase of Question 5, the same three students who role played will be asked to continue. This time, see if the three make progress on settling the best arrangements to accomplish the team goal (optimizing the service of the concession to the student public).

Century National Bank

Four months ago, the president of Century National Bank decided that the bank had grown large enough that people in various departments were losing touch with each other. This resulted in bureaucratic red tape, some mixups where a customer was told one thing by one department of the bank and a contradictory thing by another department, and a feeling among employees that "everything has to be done by the book."

In dealing with this problem, the president, aided by the vice president for personnel, sent a questionnaire to 48 key managers in the bank. One section of this questionnaire was for the purpose of finding out how managers viewed themselves and their own jobs. They were asked to check, for each of the two following characteristics, whether it was "very characteristic," "somewhat characteristic," or "not at all characteristic."

	Very	Somewhat	Not at all
a) Enthusiastic about what I do; get excited about my work.	33	10	5
b) Being a leader; having other people look up to me for direction; taking over when things are confused.	19	20	9

Question

The tabulation above was made after the 48 managers returned their questionnaires. What would you, as president, conclude from this tabulation about whether you should proceed with an organization development program? Why?

Name Index

Subject Index